Financial
Accounting

Ninth Edition

Belverd E. Needles, Jr., Ph.D., C.P.A., C.M.A.
DePaul University

Marian Powers, Ph.D.
Northwestern University

Houghton Mifflin Company   Boston   New York

To Annabelle and Abigail Needles
In memory of Mr. and Mrs. Belverd E. Needles, Sr., and
    Mr. and Mrs. Benjamin E. Needles
To Mr. and Mrs. Thomas R. Powers

Publisher: George Hoffman
Senior Sponsoring Editor: Ann West
Senior Development Editor: Chere Bemelmans
Editorial Assistants: James R. Dimock, Alison McGonagle
Project Editor: Margaret M. Kearney
Editorial Assistant: Brett Pasinella
Art and Design Manager: Gary Crespo
Senior Photo Editor: Jennifer Meyer Dare
Composition Buyer: Chuck Dutton
Senior Manufacturing Buyer: Renee Ostrowski
Marketing Manager: Mike Schenk
Marketing Associate: Kathleen Mellon

Cover engine image © Svenja-Foto/zefa/Corbis
Cover county fair image (The Erie County Fair, Hamburg, Eric County, New York)
© Panoramic Images/James Schwabel

CVS Annual Report reprinted courtesy of CVS.
Portions of Southwest Airlines Annual Report courtesy of Southwest Airlines Co.

COMPANY LOGO CREDITS: page 7, By permission of CVS; page 107, BOEING trademark
used with permission; page 158, By permission of Yahoo!; page 228, Courtesy of Dell Inc.;
page 283, By permission of Costco Wholesale; page 418, Amazon, Amazon.com, and the
Amazon.com logo are registered trademarks of Amazon.com, Inc. or its affiliates; page 615,
Motorola, Inc.; page 660, By permission of Marriott International, Inc.; page 756, eBay and
the eBay logo are trademarks of eBay Inc.

PHOTO CREDITS: page 3, Getty Images; page 9, AP/Wide World Photos; page 17, © Jim
West/The Image Works; page 21, By permission of CVS; page 21, © Frank Trapper/Corbis;
page 105, AFP/Getty Images; page 110, © Reuters/Corbis; page 126, Getty Images; (*continued
on page* 850)

Printed in the U.S.A.

Library of Congress Control Number: 2005935736

Student Text
    ISBN 13: 978-0-618-62676-2
    ISBN 10: 0-618-62676-X
Instructor's Examination Copy
    ISBN 13: 978-0-618-72187-0
    ISBN 10: 0-618-72187-8

56789-DJM-10 09 08

LIQUIDITY RATIOS

Ratio	Formula	Description	Reference
Current ratio	$\dfrac{\text{Current Assets}}{\text{Current Liabilities}}$	Measures short-term debt-paying ability	Chapter 4, LO5
Quick ratio	$\dfrac{\text{Cash + Marketable Securities + Receivables}}{\text{Current Liabilities}}$	Measures short-term debt-paying ability	Chapter 14, LO3
Receivable turnover	$\dfrac{\text{Net Sales}}{\text{Average Accounts Receivable}}$	Average number of times receivables are turned into cash during an accounting period	Chapter 7, LO1
Days' sales uncollected	$\dfrac{\text{Days in Year}}{\text{Receivable Turnover}}$	Average number of days a company must wait to receive payment for credit sales or to collect accounts receivable	Chapter 7, LO 1
Inventory turnover	$\dfrac{\text{Costs of Goods Sold}}{\text{Average Inventory}}$	Number of times a company's average inventory is sold during an accounting period	Chapter 6, LO1
Days' inventory on hand	$\dfrac{\text{Days in Year}}{\text{Inventory Turnover}}$	Average number of days taken to sell inventory on hand	Chapter 6, LO1
Payables turnover	$\dfrac{\text{Costs of Goods Sold +/- Change in Inventory}}{\text{Average Accounts Payable}}$	Average number of times a company pays its accounts payable in an accounting period	Chapter 8, LO1
Days' payable	$\dfrac{\text{Days in Year}}{\text{Payables Turnover}}$	Average number of days a company takes to pay accounts payable	Chapter 8, LO1

PROFITABILITY RATIOS

Ratio	Formula	Description	Reference
Profit margin	$\dfrac{\text{Net Income}}{\text{Net Sales}}$	Percentage of each sales dollar that contributes to net income	Chapter 4, LO5
Asset turnover	$\dfrac{\text{Net Sales}}{\text{Average Total Assets}}$	How efficiently assets are used to produce sales	Chapter 4, LO5
Return on assets	$\dfrac{\text{Net Income}}{\text{Average Total Assets}}$	How efficiently a company uses its assets to produce income, or the amount earned on each dollar of assets invested	Chapter 4, LO5
Return on equity	$\dfrac{\text{Net Income}}{\text{Average Stockholders' Equity}}$	Relates the amount earned by a business to each dollar stockholders invested in the business	Chapter 4, LO5

LONG-TERM SOLVENCY RATIOS

Ratio	Formula	Description	Reference
Debt to equity ratio	$\dfrac{\text{Total Liabilities}}{\text{Stockholders' Equity}}$	Proportion of a company's assets financed by creditors and the proportion financed by stockholders	Chapter 4, LO5
Interest coverage ratio	$\dfrac{\text{Income Before Income Taxes + Interest Expense}}{\text{Interest Expense}}$	Degree of protection a company has from default on interest payments	Chapter 10, LO1

CASH FLOW ADEQUACY RATIOS

Ratio	Formula	Description	Reference
Cash flow yield	$\dfrac{\text{Net Cash Flows from Operating Activities}}{\text{Net Income}}$	Measures a company's ability to generate operating cash flows in relation to net income	Chapter 13, LO2
Cash flows to sales	$\dfrac{\text{Net Cash Flows from Operating Activities}}{\text{Net Sales}}$	Ratio of net cash flows from operating activities to sales	Chapter 13, LO2
Cash flows to assets	$\dfrac{\text{Net Cash Flows from Operating Activities}}{\text{Average Total Assets}}$	Measures the ability of assets to generate operating cash flows	Chapter 13, LO2
Free cash flow	Net Cash Flows from Operating Activities – Dividends – (Purchases of Plant Assets – Sales of Plant Assets)	Measures the amount of cash that remains after deducting the funds a company must commit to continue operating at its planned level	Chapter 9, LO1

MARKET STRENGTH RATIOS

Ratio	Formula	Description	Reference
Price/ earnings ratio	$\dfrac{\text{Market Price per Share}}{\text{Earnings per Share}}$	Measures investors' confidence in a company's future; a means of comparing stock values	Chapter 11, LO1
Dividends yield	$\dfrac{\text{Dividends per Share}}{\text{Market Price per Share}}$	Measures a stock's current return to an investor or stockholder	Chapter 11, LO1

Brief Contents

1   Uses of Accounting Information and the Financial Statements   2

SUPPLEMENT TO CHAPTER **1**   How to Read an Annual Report   55

2   Analyzing Business Transactions   104

3   Measuring Business Income   156

SUPPLEMENT TO CHAPTER **3**   Closing Entries and the Work Sheet   209

4   Financial Reporting and Analysis   224

SUPPLEMENT TO CHAPTER **4**   The Annual Report Project   277

5   The Operating Cycle and Merchandising Operations   280

6   Inventories   332

7   Cash and Receivables   374

8   Current Liabilities and the Time Value of Money   416

9   Long-Term Assets   462

10   Long-Term Liabilities   512

11   Contributed Capital   566

12   The Corporate Income Statement and the Statement of Stockholders' Equity   610

13   The Statement of Cash Flows   656

14   Financial Performance Measurement   704

15   Investments   754

APPENDIX **A**   Accounting for Unincorporated Businesses   798

APPENDIX **B**   Future Value and Present Value Tables   808

Contents

Preface   xiii

User's Guide to *Financial Accounting*   xix

Check Figures   xxvii

About the Authors   xxix

CHAPTER 1 — Uses of Accounting Information and the Financial Statements   2

■ **DECISION POINT: A USER'S FOCUS   CVS CORPORATION**   3

Accounting as an Information System   4

Business Goals, Activities, and Performance Measures   5

■ **FOCUS ON BUSINESS PRACTICE: What Does CVS Have to Say About Itself?**   6

■ **FOCUS ON BUSINESS PRACTICE: Cash Bonuses Depend on Accounting Numbers!**   6

Financial and Management Accounting   7

Processing Accounting Information   7

■ **FOCUS ON BUSINESS PRACTICE: How Did Accounting Develop?**   8

Ethical Financial Reporting   8

Decision Makers: The Users of Accounting Information   10

Management   10

■ **FOCUS ON BUSINESS PRACTICE: What Do CFOs Do?**   11

Users with a Direct Financial Interest   12

Users with an Indirect Financial Interest   12

Governmental and Not-for-Profit Organizations   13

Accounting Measurement   13

Business Transactions   14

Money Measure   14

Separate Entity   15

The Corporate Form of Business   15

Characteristics of Corporations, Sole Proprietorships, and Partnerships   16

■ **FOCUS ON BUSINESS PRACTICE: Are Most Corporations Big or Small Businesses?**   16

Formation of a Corporation   17

Organization of a Corporation   17

Corporate Governance   19

Financial Position and the Accounting Equation   19

Assets   20

Liabilities   20

Stockholders' Equity   20

Financial Statements   23

Income Statement   23

Statement of Retained Earnings   23

The Balance Sheet   24

Statement of Cash Flows   24

Relationships Among the Financial Statements   25

Generally Accepted Accounting Principles   27

GAAP and the Independent CPA's Report   28

Organizations That Influence GAAP   29

Professional Ethics   30

■ **A LOOK BACK AT CVS CORPORATION**   31

CHAPTER REVIEW   33

CHAPTER ASSIGNMENTS   39

SUPPLEMENT TO CHAPTER 1 — How to Read an Annual Report   55

The Components of an Annual Report   55

Letter to the Stockholders   55

Financial Highlights   56

Description of the Company   56

Management's Discussion and Analysis   56

Financial Statements   56

Notes to the Financial Statements   61

Reports of Management's Responsibilities   62

Reports of Certified Public Accountants   63

CVS Corporation 2004 Annual Report   65

Financial Statements of Southwest Airlines Co.   95

CHAPTER 2 Analyzing Business Transactions   104

- ■ DECISION POINT: A USER'S FOCUS SINGAPORE AIRLINES AND THE BOEING CO.   105
- ▤ Measurement Issues   106
- Recognition   106
  - ■ FOCUS ON BUSINESS PRACTICE: Accounting Policies: Where Do You Find Them? 106
  - ■ FOCUS ON BUSINESS PRACTICE: Is It Always Cost?   108
- Valuation   108
  - ■ FOCUS ON BUSINESS PRACTICE: No Dollar Amount: How Can That Be?   108
- Classification   109
- Ethics and Measurement Issues   109
- ▤ Double-Entry System   110
- Accounts   111
- The T Account   111
- The T Account Illustrated   111
- Rules of Double-Entry Accounting   112
- Normal Balance   113
- Stockholders' Equity Accounts   113
- ▤ Business Transaction Analysis   115
- Owners' Investment in the Business   116
- Economic Event That Is Not a Business Transaction   116
- Prepayment of Expenses in Cash   116
- Purchase of an Asset on Credit   117
- Purchase of an Asset Partly in Cash and Partly on Credit   117

- Payment of a Liability   118
- Revenue in Cash   118
- Revenue on Credit   119
- Revenue Received in Advance   119
- Collection on Account   119
- Expense Paid in Cash   120
- Expense to Be Paid Later   120
- Dividends   121
- Summary of Transactions   121
- ▤ The Trial Balance   123
- Preparation and Use of a Trial Balance   123
  - ■ FOCUS ON BUSINESS PRACTICE: Are All Trial Balances Created Equal?   124
- Finding Trial Balance Errors   124
  - ■ FOCUS ON BUSINESS PRACTICE: Should Earnings Be Aligned with Cash Flows?   125
- ▤ Cash Flows and the Timing of Transactions   125
- ▤ Recording and Posting Transactions   127
- Chart of Accounts   127
- General Journal   128
- General Ledger   130
- Some Notes on Presentation   132
  - ■ A LOOK BACK AT SINGAPORE AIRLINES AND THE BOEING COMPANY   133
- CHAPTER REVIEW   135
- CHAPTER ASSIGNMENTS   139

CHAPTER 3 Measuring Business Income   156

- ■ DECISION POINT: A USER'S FOCUS YAHOO! INC.   157
- ▤ Profitability Measurement: Issues and Ethics   158
- Net Income   158
- Income Measurement Assumptions   158
  - ■ FOCUS ON BUSINESS PRACTICE: Fiscal Years Vary   159
- Ethics and the Matching Rule   160
  - ■ FOCUS ON BUSINESS PRACTICE: Are Misstatements of Earnings Always Overstatements?   161
- ▤ Accrual Accounting   162
- Recognizing Revenues   162
- Recognizing Expenses   162
- Adjusting the Accounts   162
- Adjustments and Ethics   163
- ▤ The Adjustment Process   164
- Type 1 Adjustment: Allocating Recorded Costs (Deferred Expenses)   165
- Type 2 Adjustment: Recognizing Unrecorded Expenses (Accrued Expenses)   169

- Type 3 Adjustment: Allocating Recorded, Unearned Revenues (Deferred Revenues)   171
- Type 4 Adjustment: Recognizing Unrecorded, Earned Revenues (Accrued Revenues)   172
  - ■ FOCUS ON BUSINESS PRACTICE: Ecommerce: What's Its Impact?   174
- A Note About Journal Entries   174
- ▤ Using the Adjusted Trial Balance to Prepare Financial Statements   175
- ▤ The Accounting Cycle   177
- Closing Entries   177
- The Post-Closing Trial Balance   179
  - ■ FOCUS ON BUSINESS PRACTICE: Entering Adjustments with the Touch of a Button   180
- ▤ Cash Flows from Accrual-Based Information   181
  - ■ A LOOK BACK AT YAHOO! INC.   183
- CHAPTER REVIEW   184
- CHAPTER ASSIGNMENTS   191

SUPPLEMENT TO CHAPTER 3 — Closing Entries and the Work Sheet — 209

Preparing Closing Entries 209
Step 1: Closing the Credit Balances 209
Step 2: Closing the Debit Balances 209
Step 3: Closing the Income Summary Account Balance 212
Step 4: Closing the Dividends Account Balance 212

The Accounts After Closing 212
The Work Sheet: An Accountant's Tool 213
Preparing the Work Sheet 213
Using the Work Sheet 216
SUPPLEMENT ASSIGNMENTS 217

CHAPTER 4 — Financial Reporting and Analysis — 224

■ DECISION POINT: A USER'S FOCUS **DELL COMPUTER CORPORATION** 225
Foundations of Financial Reporting 226
Objectives of Financial Reporting 226
Qualitative Characteristics of Accounting Information 226
Management's Certification of the Financial Statements 228
Accounting Conventions 229
Comparability and Consistency 229
Materiality 230
■ FOCUS ON BUSINESS PRACTICE: **Are Yahoo! and Google Comparable? Can an Internet Company Be Conservative?** 230
■ FOCUS ON BUSINESS PRACTICE: **How Much Is Material? It's Not Only a Matter of Numbers** 231
Conservatism 231
Full Disclosure 231
Cost-Benefit 232
■ FOCUS ON BUSINESS PRACTICE: **When Is "Full Disclosure" Too Much? It's a Matter of Cost and Benefits** 232
Classified Balance Sheet 233
Assets 234

■ FOCUS ON BUSINESS PRACTICE: **There's More Than One Way to Balance a Balance Sheet** 234
Liabilities 237
Stockholders' Equity 237
Owner's Equity and Partners' Equity 237
Dell's Balance Sheets 239
Forms of the Income Statement 240
Multistep Income Statement 240
Dell's Income Statements 245
Single-Step Income Statement 245
Using Classified Financial Statements 247
Evaluation of Liquidity 247
Evaluation of Profitability 248
■ FOCUS ON BUSINESS PRACTICE: **Who Is Right: The Credit-Worthiness Analyst or the Profitability Analyst?** 249
■ FOCUS ON BUSINESS PRACTICE: **To What Level of Profitability Should a Company Aspire?** 252
■ A LOOK BACK AT **DELL COMPUTER CORPORATION** 254
CHAPTER REVIEW 257
CHAPTER ASSIGNMENTS 261

SUPPLEMENT TO CHAPTER 4 — The Annual Report Project — 277

CHAPTER 5 — The Operating Cycle and Merchandising Operations — 280

■ DECISION POINT: A USER'S FOCUS **COSTCO WHOLESALE CORPORATION** 281
Managing Merchandising Businesses 282
Operating Cycle 282
Choice of Inventory System 283
■ FOCUS ON BUSINESS PRACTICE: **How Have Bar Codes Influenced the Choice of Inventory Systems?** 284
Foreign Business Transactions 285
The Need for Internal Controls 285
Management's Responsibility for Internal Control 287

■ FOCUS ON BUSINESS PRACTICE: **How Hard Is Financial Fraud to Detect When Its Effects Are Not Material?** 287
Terms of Sale 288
Sales and Purchases Discounts 288
Transportation Costs 289
Terms of Debit and Credit Card Sales 290
■ FOCUS ON BUSINESS PRACTICE: **How Are Buying Habits Changing?** 290
Perpetual Inventory System 291
Purchases of Merchandise 291

■ FOCUS ON BUSINESS PRACTICE: **Are Purchase Allowances Revenues?** 292

Sales of Merchandise 293

■ FOCUS ON BUSINESS PRACTICE: **How Are Web Sales Doing?** 294

Periodic Inventory System 295

Purchases of Merchandise 297

Sales of Merchandise 298

■ FOCUS ON BUSINESS PRACTICE: **Are Sales Returns Worth Accounting For?** 299

Internal Control: Components, Activities, and Limitations 300

■ FOCUS ON BUSINESS PRACTICE: **Which Frauds Are Most Common?** 301

Components of Internal Control 301

Control Activities 301

Limitations on Internal Control 303

Internal Control over Merchandising Transactions 303

Internal Control and Management Goals 304

■ FOCUS ON BUSINESS PRACTICE: **How Do Computers Promote Internal Control?** 305

Control of Cash Sales Receipts 305

Control of Purchases and Cash Disbursements 306

■ A LOOK BACK AT COSTCO WHOLESALE CORPORATION 311

CHAPTER REVIEW 312

CHAPTER ASSIGNMENTS 316

CHAPTER 6 Inventories 332

■ DECISION POINT: A USER'S FOCUS CISCO SYSTEMS, INC. 333

Managing Inventories 334

Inventory Decisions 334

Evaluating the Level of Inventory 335

■ FOCUS ON BUSINESS PRACTICE: **A Whirlwind Inventory Turnover-How Does Dell Do It?** 335

Effects of Inventory Misstatements on Income Measurement 337

■ FOCUS ON BUSINESS PRACTICE: **What Do You Do to Cure a Bottleneck Headache?** 338

Inventory Cost and Valuation 340

Goods Flow and Cost Flows 341

Lower-of-Cost-or-Market (LCM) Rule 342

Disclosure of Inventory Methods 342

Inventory Cost Under the Periodic Inventory System 344

Specific Identification Method 344

Average-Cost Method 345

First-In, First-Out (FIFO) Method 345

Last-In, First-Out (LIFO) Method 346

■ FOCUS ON BUSINESS PRACTICE: **What's a "Category Killer"?** 346

Impact of Inventory Decisions 347

Effects on the Financial Statements 348

Effects on Income Taxes 349

■ FOCUS ON BUSINESS PRACTICE: **Does a Company's Inventory Costing Method Affect Its Operating Decisions?** 350

Effects on Cash Flows 350

Inventory Cost Under the Perpetual Inventory System 351

■ FOCUS ON BUSINESS PRACTICE: **More Companies Enjoy LIFO!** 352

Valuing Inventory by Estimation 353

Retail Method 353

Gross Profit Method 354

■ A LOOK BACK AT CISCO SYSTEMS, INC. 355

CHAPTER REVIEW 357

CHAPTER ASSIGNMENTS 361

CHAPTER 7 Cash and Receivables 374

■ DECISION POINT: A USER'S FOCUS NIKE, INC. 375

Management Issues Related to Cash and Receivables 376

Cash Needs 376

■ FOCUS ON BUSINESS PRACTICE: **How Do Good Companies Deal with Bad Times?** 376

Accounts Receivables and Credit Policies 377

Evaluating the Level of Accounts Receivable 379

■ FOCUS ON BUSINESS PRACTICE: **How Do Powerful Buyers Cause Problems for Small Suppliers?** 379

Financing Receivables 380

Ethics and Estimates in Accounting for Receivables 382

Cash Equivalents and Cash Control 384

Cash Equivalents 384

Cash Control Methods 384

Bank Reconciliations 385

Uncollectible Accounts 388

The Allowance Method 388

Disclosure of Uncollectible Accounts 389

Estimating Uncollectible Accounts Expense 389

■ **FOCUS ON BUSINESS PRACTICE: Why Are Estimates Difficult to Make?** 390

Writing Off Uncollectible Accounts 394

Notes Receivable 396

Maturity Date 396

Duration of a Note 397

Interest and Interest Rate 398

Maturity Value 398

Accrued Interest 398

Dishonored Note 399

■ **A LOOK BACK AT NIKE, INC.** 400

CHAPTER REVIEW 401

CHAPTER ASSIGNMENTS 403

CHAPTER 8   Current Liabilities and the Time Value of Money   416

■ **DECISION POINT: A USER'S FOCUS AMAZON.COM, INC.** 417

Management Issues Related to Current Liabilities 418

Managing Liquidity and Cash Flows 418

Evaluating Accounts Payable 418

■ **FOCUS ON BUSINESS PRACTICE: Debt Problems Can Plague Even Well-Known Companies** 419

Reporting Liabilities 420

Common Types of Current Liabilities 422

Definitely Determinable Liabilities 422

■ **FOCUS ON BUSINESS PRACTICE: Small Businesses Offer Benefits, Too** 425

Estimated Liabilities 429

■ **FOCUS ON BUSINESS PRACTICE: Those Little Coupons Can Add Up** 430

■ **FOCUS ON BUSINESS PRACTICE: What Is the Cost of Frequent Flyer Miles?** 431

Contingent Liabilities and Commitments 433

The Time Value of Money 434

Future Value 435

Present Value 437

Applications of the Time Value of Money 440

Valuing an Asset 440

Deferred Payment 441

Investment of Idle Cash 442

Accumulation of a Fund for Loan Repayment 442

Other Applications 443

■ **A LOOK BACK AT AMAZON.COM, INC.** 444

CHAPTER REVIEW 445

CHAPTER ASSIGNMENTS 448

CHAPTER 9   Long-Term Assets   462

■ **DECISION POINT: A USER'S FOCUS APPLE COMPUTER, INC.** 463

Management Issues Related to Long-Term Assets 464

Acquiring Long-Term Assets 466

Financing Long-Term Assets 467

Applying the Matching Rule 468

Acquisition Cost of Property, Plant, and Equipment 469

General Approach to Acquisition Costs 470

Specific Applications 471

Depreciation 474

■ **FOCUS ON BUSINESS PRACTICE: How Long Is the Useful Life of an Airplane?** 475

Factors in Computing Depreciation 475

Methods of Computing Depreciation 475

■ **FOCUS ON BUSINESS PRACTICE: Accelerated Methods Save Money!** 478

Special Issues in Depreciation 479

Disposal of Depreciable Assets 481

Discarded Plant Assets 481

Plant Assets Sold for Cash 482

Exchanges of Plant Assets 483

Natural Resources 483

Depletion 484

Depreciation of Related Plant Assets 485

Development and Exploration Costs in the Oil and Gas Industry 485

■ **FOCUS ON BUSINESS PRACTICE: How Do You Measure What's Underground? With a Good Guess** 485

Intangible Assets 486

■ **FOCUS ON BUSINESS PRACTICE: Who's Number One in Brands?** 488

■ **FOCUS ON BUSINESS PRACTICE: What Is the Useful Life of a Customer List?** 489

Research and Development Costs 489

Computer Software Costs 490

Goodwill 490

■ FOCUS ON BUSINESS PRACTICE: Wake Up, Goodwill Is Growing! 490

■ A LOOK BACK AT APPLE COMPUTER, INC. 491

CHAPTER REVIEW 493

CHAPTER ASSIGNMENTS 497

CHAPTER 10 Long-Term Liabilities — 512

■ DECISION POINT: A USER'S FOCUS McDONALD'S CORPORATION 513

Management Issues Related to Issuing Long-Term Debt 514

Deciding to Issue Long-Term Debt 514

Evaluating Long-Term Debt 515

■ FOCUS ON BUSINESS PRACTICE: How Does Debt Affect a Company's Ability to Borrow? 516

Types of Long-Term Debt 517

The Nature of Bonds 522

■ FOCUS ON BUSINESS PRACTICE: Check Out Those Bond Prices! 523

Bond Issue: Prices and Interest Rates 523

Characteristics of Bonds 524

■ FOCUS ON BUSINESS: Some Companies Are Saying "Yes-Yes" to "No-Nos" 525

Accounting for the Issuance of Bonds 526

Bonds Issued at Face Value 526

Bonds Issued at a Discount 527

■ FOCUS ON BUSINESS PRACTICE: 100-Year Bonds Are Not for Everyone 527

Bonds Issued at a Premium 528

Bond Issue Costs 528

Using Present Value to Value a Bond 529

Case 1: Market Rate Above Face Rate 529

Case 2: Market Rate Below Face Rate 530

Amortization of Bond Discounts and Premiums 531

Amortizing a Bond Discount 531

Amortizing a Bond Premium 535

■ FOCUS ON BUSINESS: Speed Up the Calculations! 537

Retirement of Bonds 540

Calling Bonds 540

Covering Bonds 541

Other Bonds Payable Issues 541

Sale of Bonds Between Interest Dates 541

Year-End Accrual of Bond Interest Expense 543

■ A LOOK BACK AT McDONALD'S CORPORATION 544

CHAPTER REVIEW 546

CHAPTER ASSIGNMENTS 550

CHAPTER 11 Contributed Capital — 566

■ DECISION POINT: A USER'S FOCUS GOOGLE, INC. 567

Management Issues Related to Contributed Capital 568

The Corporate Form of Business 568

Equity Financing 570

Dividend Policies 572

Using Return on Equity to Measure Performance 574

Stock Options as Compensation 575

■ FOCUS ON BUSINESS PRACTICE: How Did Accounting for Stock Options Become Political? 576

Components of Stockholders' Equity 576

■ FOCUS ON BUSINESS PRACTICE: Are You a First-Class or Second-Class Stockholder? 577

Preferred Stock 580

Preference as to Dividends 580

Preference as to Assets 581

■ FOCUS ON BUSINESS PRACTICE: How Does a Stock Become a Debt? 582

Convertible Preferred Stock 582

Callable Preferred Stock 583

Issuance of Common Stock 584

Par Value Stock 584

No-Par Stock 585

Issuance of Stock for Noncash Assets 586

Accounting for Treasury Stock 587

Purchase of Treasury Stock 587

■ FOCUS ON BUSINESS PRACTICE: When Are Share Buybacks a Bad Idea? 588

Sale of Treasury Stock 588

Retirement of Treasury Stock 590

■ A LOOK BACK AT GOOGLE, INC. 591

CHAPTER REVIEW 592

CHAPTER ASSIGNMENTS 596

CHAPTER 12 The Corporate Income Statement and the Statement of Stockholders' Equity 610

■ DECISION POINT: A USER'S FOCUS MOTOROLA, INC. 611

Performance Measurement: Quality of Earnings Issues 612

- ■ FOCUS ON BUSINESS PRACTICE: Why Do Investors Study Quality of Earnings? 612

The Effect of Accounting Estimates and Methods 613

- ■ FOCUS ON BUSINESS PRACTICE: Were Preussag's Year-End Results Really "Remarkable"? 615

Gains and Losses 615

Write-downs and Restructurings 615

- ■ FOCUS ON BUSINESS PRACTICE: Can You Believe "Pro-Forma" Earnings? 616

Nonoperating Items 616

Quality of Earnings and Cash Flows 616

Income Taxes 618

Deferred Income Taxes 619

Net of Taxes 620

Nonoperating Items 622

Discontinued Operations 622

Extraordinary Items 622

Earnings per Share 623

Basic Earnings per Share 623

Diluted Earnings Per Share 625

Comprehensive Income and the Statement of Stockholders' Equity 626

Comprehensive Income 626

The Statement of Stockholders' Equity 626

Retained Earnings 628

Stock Dividends and Stock Splits 629

Stock Dividends 629

Stock Splits 631

- ■ FOCUS ON BUSINESS PRACTICE: Do Stock Splits Help Increase a Company's Market Price? 632

Book Value 634

- ■ A LOOK BACK AT MOTOROLA, INC. 635

CHAPTER REVIEW 636

CHAPTER ASSIGNMENTS 640

CHAPTER 13 The Statement of Cash Flows 656

■ DECISION POINT: A USER'S FOCUS MARRIOTT INTERNATIONAL, INC. 657

Overview of the Statement of Cash Flows 658

Purposes of the Statement of Cash Flows 658

Uses of the Statement of Cash Flows 658

Classification of Cash Flows 659

Noncash Investing and Financing Transactions 660

Format of the Statement of Cash Flows 660

- ■ FOCUS ON BUSINESS PRACTICE: How Universal Is the Statement of Cash Flows? 662

Ethical Considerations and the Statement of Cash Flows 662

Analyzing Cash Flows 663

Cash-Generating Efficiency 663

Free Cash Flow 664

- ■ FOCUS ON BUSINESS PRACTICE: Cash Flows Tell All 664

- ■ FOCUS ON BUSINESS PRACTICE: What Do You Mean, "Free Cash Flow"? 665

Operating Activities 666

Depreciation 668

Gains and Losses 669

Changes in Current Assets 670

Changes in Current Liabilities 670

- ■ FOCUS ON BUSINESS PRACTICE: What Is EBITA, and Is It Any Good? 671

Schedule of Cash Flows from Operating Activities 671

Investing Activities 673

Investments 673

Plant Assets 674

Financing Activities 676

Bonds Payable 677

Common Stock 677

- ■ FOCUS ON BUSINESS PRACTICE: How Much Cash Does a Company Need? 678

Retained Earnings 678

Treasury Stock 679

- ■ A LOOK BACK AT MARRIOTT INTERNATIONAL, INC. 681

CHAPTER REVIEW 682

CHAPTER ASSIGNMENTS 686

CHAPTER 14   Financial Performance Measurement   704

■ DECISION POINT: A USER'S FOCUS   STARBUCKS CORPORATION   705

Foundations of Financial Performance Measurement   706

Financial Performance Measurement: Management's Objectives   706

Financial Performance Measurement: Creditors' and Investors' Objectives   706

Standards of Comparison   707

■ FOCUS ON BUSINESS PRACTICE: Take the Numbers with a Grain of Salt   708

Sources of Information   710

Executive Compensation   711

Tools and Techniques of Financial Analysis   714

Horizontal Analysis   714

Trend Analysis   717

Vertical Analysis   718

Ratio Analysis   721

Comprehensive Illustration of Ratio Analysis   721

Evaluating Liquidity   722

■ FOCUS ON BUSINESS PRACTICE: There's More Than One Way to Measure Performance   724

Evaluating Profitability   724

Evaluating Long-term Solvency   725

Evaluating the Adequacy of Cash Flows   726

Evaluating Market Strength   728

■ A LOOK BACK AT STARBUCKS CORPORATION   730

CHAPTER REVIEW   731

CHAPTER ASSIGNMENTS   737

CHAPTER 15   Investments   754

■ DECISION POINT: A USER'S FOCUS   eBAY, INC.   755

The Management Issues Related to Investments   756

Recognition   756

Valuation   756

Classification   756

Disclosure   758

Ethics of Investing   758

■ FOCUS ON BUSINESS PRACTICE: What Are Special-Purpose Entities?   758

Short-Term Investments in Equity Securities   760

Trading Securities   760

■ FOCUS ON BUSINESS PRACTICE: How Can Even a Big Company Make an Accounting Mistake?   761

Available-for-Sale Securities   763

Long-Term Investments in Equity Securities   763

Noninfluential and Noncontrolling Investment   763

Influential but Noncontrolling Investment   766

■ FOCUS ON BUSINESS PRACTICE: Accounting for International Joint Ventures   767

Consolidated Financial Statements   768

Consolidated Balance Sheet   769

Consolidated Income Statement   774

Restatement of Foreign Subsidiary Financial Statements   775

Investments in Debt Securities   776

Held-to-Maturity Securities   777

Long-Term Investments in Bonds   777

■ A LOOK BACK AT eBAY, INC.   778

CHAPTER REVIEW   780

CHAPTER ASSIGNMENTS   783

Appendix A   Accounting for Unincorporated Businesses   798

Appendix B   Future Value and Present Value Tables   808

Answers to Stop, Review, and Apply Questions   815

Endnotes   833

Company Name Index   837

Subject Index   839

Preface

This revision of *Financial Accounting* is the most significant in the book's long history. The substantial changes we have made are geared to meeting the needs of today's students, who not only face a business world increasingly complicated by ethical issues, globalization, and technology, but who also have more demands on their time. To help them meet these challenges, we have placed a heavy emphasis on developing their decision-making and critical-thinking skills and on providing information that is easy to understand and process.

We invite you to read the User's Guide that follows this preface to get a sense of how this book was written to help students master financial accounting. Here, we elaborate on exactly what we set out to achieve in this ninth edition.

Streamlined Coverage and Redesign of Text

While maintaining a solid foundation in double-entry accounting, we have reduced complexity by eliminating 30 percent of in-text journal entries and all nonessential procedural coverage and by condensing learning objectives. Through extensive editing, we have reduced excessive detail, shortened headings, simplified explanations, and increased readability.

We have also made the text more accessible to students by using small, diverse companies to illustrate concepts and techniques and well-known public companies to relate the concepts and techniques to the real world.

To make the text as readable, visually appealing, and pedagogically useful as possible, we have broken it into "user friendly" blocks by using more bulleted and numbered lists and by interspersing the text with new art, photographs, end-of-section review material, and Focus on Business boxes.

▶ We have included more line art to clarify concepts, which will appeal to students who are visual learners.

▶ We have added photographs to increase visual interest and accompanied them with captions that underscore the points made in the text.

▶ We have introduced a new feature called "Stop•Review•Apply" that presents review questions at the end of each main section; the answers to the questions follow the appendixes. Many of these features also present short exercises together with their solutions.

▶ As in previous editions, learning objectives are clearly presented throughout the text and in the end-of-chapter assignments.

▶ To reduce distractions, we have used the margins of the text only for key ratio and cash flow icons, which highlight discussions of profitability and liquidity; accounting equations; and Study Notes that alert students to common misunderstandings of concepts and techniques.

Use of Accounting Information in Successful Decision Making

We have increased our emphasis on how businesses use accounting information in making decisions, and we have provided a framework for developing decision-making skills.

▶ To emphasize how important financial statements are in decision making, the first page of each chapter now includes a graphic model of the income statement, balance sheet, and statement of cash flows and a brief description of how these statements relate to the chapter's topic.

▶ Each chapter opening also includes a new Decision Point that shows how a well-known company—one that students will immediately recognize—uses financial information to make decisions. The Decision Point poses questions that challenge students to think about the relationship between financial information and the decisions management makes. The company discussed in the Decision Point is highlighted throughout the chapter and is revisited in "A Look Back At," a new feature that shows how the questions posed in the Decision Point can now be answered.

▶ We have emphasized how ratios are used in evaluating a company's profitability and liquidity and, as noted, we have highlighted those discussions with key ratio and cash flow icons.

▶ To relate accounting concepts to real-world decision making, we have referred to more than 200 actual companies and have used some of those companies' recent financial statements as illustrations.

▶ The assignment material in every chapter includes a case that compares CVS with Southwest Airlines or Walgreens and that refers to both companies' financial statements. Among other things, the comparison cases require students to compute ratios, make assumptions, report on the effect of seasonal sales, and describe each company's inventory management system. CVS's complete annual report and Southwest Airlines' financial statements and Note 1 to the statements appear in the Supplement to Chapter 1.

▶ Using annual reports as the focus of term projects in the financial accounting course has become increasingly popular. In the Supplement to Chapter 4, we provide an annual report project that we have used in our own classes for several years.

▶ We have used the latest available data in updating tables, figures, and exhibits and have incorporated the most recent FASB pronouncements into the text. We have illustrated current practices in financial reporting by referring to data from the AICPA's *Accounting Trends and Techniques* and have integrated international topics wherever appropriate.

Ethical Financial Reporting

We believe students need to know more about what constitutes ethical financial reporting and good corporate governance, and we have revised the text to address this need.

▶ The preview at the start of each chapter points out ethical and governance issues related to the chapter topic. We discuss these issues in the first section of each chapter.

▶ We cover the provisions of the Sarbanes-Oxley Act of 2002 and stress its importance in Chapter 1 and at appropriate points throughout the text.

▶ In the end-of-chapter material, we continue to provide short cases, based on real companies, that require students to address an ethical dilemma directly related to the chapter content.

Reorganized Assignment Material

This text has always provided a rich assortment of assignments that address instructors' needs. While keeping the range and depth of assignments from previous editions, we have tried to simplify their organization for easier use.

▶ The end-of-chapter assignments are organized into two main sections: Building Your Basic Knowledge and Skills—which consists of Short Exercises, Exercises, Problems, and Alternate Problems—and Enhancing Your Knowledge, Skills, and Critical Thinking—which consists of cases. The cases are grouped under headings that allow instructors to focus on the skills most important to them and their students (e.g., Conceptual Understanding Cases, Interpreting Financial Reports, Decision Analysis Using Excel, Ethical Dilemma Case). Each chapter also has an Annual Report Case that focuses on CVS's annual report and, as noted earlier, a Comparison Case.

▶ The first two exercises in each chapter present questions useful in generating class discussion about the decision-making aspects of the chapter topics.

▶ Almost every problem includes at least one "User Insight" question, which challenges students to think about the numbers and how they are used in decision making.

▶ Problems have been carefully scrutinized to reduce the number of transactions involved and the time it takes to work the problems.

New Instructional Technologies for Today's Business Environment

New technologies are a driving force behind business growth and accounting education today. We have developed for the ninth edition an integrated text and technology program dedicated to helping instructors take advantage of the opportunities created by new instructional technologies. Whether an instructor takes a more user or more procedural approach to teaching, wants to incorporate new instructional strategies, wants to develop students' core skills and competencies, or desires to integrate technology into the classroom, the ninth edition of *Financial Accounting* provides a total solution. (See the inside back cover of the textbook for a complete listing of supplements.)

Course Management Systems

We know that homework and practice are an integral part of financial accounting courses, and grading homework and tests can present a challenge to instructors. The Eduspace® online learning tool pairs the widely recognized resources of Blackboard with quality, text-specific content from Houghton Mifflin. Auto-graded homework exercises, algorithmic practice exercises, SMARTHINKING online tutoring, MP3 files of chapter summaries, and other resources come ready to use. Premium Blackboard course cartridges and WebCT ePacks are also available.

HMClassPrep with HMTesting

Available on the HMClassPrep CD, HMTesting—now powered by Diploma®—contains the computerized version of the Test Bank. HMTesting provides instructors with all the tools they need to create, customize, and deliver multiple types of tests. Instructors can add their own questions or edit existing algorithmic questions all within Diploma's powerful electronic platform. Instructors can select, edit, and add questions, or generate randomly selected questions to produce a test master for easy duplication. HMTesting also contains test questions with algorithms. Online Testing and Gradebook functions allow instructors to administer tests via their local area network or the Internet, set up classes, record grades from tests or assignments, analyze grades, and compile class and individual statistics. HMTesting can be used on both PCs and Mac computers.

The Test Bank is also available in print. The printed Test Bank provides the same questions found in HMTesting—more than 3,000 true-false, multiple choice, short essay, and critical-thinking questions, as well as exercises and problems, all of which test students' ability to recall, comprehend, apply, and analyze information. Two achievement tests are provided for each chapter.

HMClassPrep also includes the complete Course Manual, the Electronic Solutions (fully functioning Excel spreadsheets for all exercises, problems, and cases in the text; also available in print); completely revised PowerPoint slides with audio, video, and original content; Video Cases; check figures for end-of-chapter problems; and web links to the Needles Accounting Online Teaching/Online Study Centers.

Instructor and Student Websites

The Online Teaching and Online Study Centers provide instructors and students with text-specific resources that reinforce key concepts in the *Financial Accounting* program. For instructors, the Online Teaching Center includes password-protected course materials, such as completely revised PowerPoint slides with audio, video, and original content; Classroom Response System content; sample syllabi; accounting news updates; and Electronic Solutions, which are fully functioning Excel spreadsheets for all exercises, problems, and cases in the text. The Online Study Center links students to ACE practice tests, Flashcards and Crossword Puzzles to reinforce vocabulary, websites for companies featured in the text, chapter summaries in MP3 format, *Annual Report Activities*, and other resources.

See the User's Guide on p. xix for a complete listing of all the student supplements available.

The Bottom Line

Although we have done more in this revision than in any previous one to make accounting concepts accessible to students, there is one thing we have not changed: we still teach students that financial statements tell a company's story. For investors and creditors, they reveal a company's financial health, prosperity, and future. For management, they are a means of guiding a company's progress and profitability. Our goal is to improve students' understanding of the "story" revealed in a company's financial statements, and never has that goal been as critical as in current times, with business events underscoring this fact: accounting really matters.

To read financial statements and follow the "story," students have to learn how to think. *Financial Accounting* teaches students to think about what they are reading, how they might make a financial decision, and what roles they might play as future users of financial statements. Students also have to learn how to analyze and interpret the numbers in the financial statements—where did the numbers come from? What is the meaning behind the numbers? What do the numbers say about a company's financial health? Today, financial accounting students need to learn more than how to prepare financial statements; they also must learn how to find meaningful information in them. *Financial Accounting, Ninth Edition*, focuses on teaching students to do just that.

Acknowledgments

A successful textbook is a collaborative effort. We are grateful to the many professors, other professional colleagues, and students who have taught and studied from our book, and we thank all of them for their constructive comments. In the space available, we cannot possibly mention everyone who has been helpful, but we do want to recognize those who made special contributions to our efforts in preparing the ninth edition of *Financial Accounting*.

We wish to express our deep appreciation to colleagues at DePaul University, who have been extremely supportive and encouraging.

The thoughtful and meticulous work of Edward H. Julius (California Lutheran University) is reflected not only in the Study Guide, but also in our Test Bank and Eduspace course as well. We would also like to thank Jeri Condit for creating the PowerPoint slides, Sue Garr and Linda Burkell for HMAccounting Tutor, and Cathy Larson for her accuracy review of the text and solutions. Sarah Evans deserves special recognition for her thoroughness and clarity in editing and laying out the ninth edition.

Also very important to the quality of this book is the supportive collaboration of our senior sponsoring editor, Ann West; senior development editor, Chere Bemelmans; editorial assistants, Jim Dimock and Alison McGonagle; and project editor, Margaret Kearney—to whom we give special thanks.

Others who have had a major impact on this book through their reviews, suggestions, and participation in surveys, interviews, and focus groups are listed below. We cannot begin to say how grateful we are for the feedback from the many instructors who have generously shared their responses and teaching experiences with us.

Glenn Owen Alan, *Hancock College*
Gregory D. Barnes, *Clarion University*
Mohamed E. Bayou, *University of Michigan—Dearborn*
LuAnn Bean, *University of Arkansas*
Charles M. Betts, *Delaware Technical and Community College*
Eric Blazer, *Millersville University*
Michael C. Blue, *Bloomsburg University*
Cindy E. Bolt, *The Citadel*
Gary R. Bower, *Community College of Rhode Island*
Beth Brooks Patel, *University of California—Berkeley*
Chuck Bunn, *Wake Technical College*
Mike Campbell, *Montana State University—Billings*
Lee Cannell, *El Paso Community College*
Nancy Cassidy, *Texas A&M University*
James Cieslak, *Cuyahoga Community College*
Michael Cornick, *University of North Carolina, Charlotte*
John D. Cunha, *University of California—Berkeley*
Mark W. Dawson, *Duquesne University*
Patricia A. Doherty, *Boston University*
Cathy Duffy, *Carthage College*
Lizabeth England, *American Language Academy*
Van Feller, *Wilbur Wright Community College*
David Fetyko, *Kent State University*
Micah Frankel, *California State University, Hayward*
Sue Garr, *Wayne State University*
John Gillett, *Bradley University*

Roxanne Gooch, *Cameron University*
Rita Grant, *Gand Valley State University*
Christine Uber Grosse, *The American Graduate School of International Management*
Dennis A. Gutting, *Orange County Community College*
John Hancock, *University of California—Davis Graduate School of Management*
George Heyman, *Oakton Community College*
Ann Hicks, *Northpark University*
Marianne James, *California State University, Los Angeles*
Edward H. Juilus, *California Lutheran University*
Howard A. Kanter, *DePaul University*
Stacy Kovar, *Kansas State University*
Cathy X. Larson, *Middlesex Community College*
Elliott S. Levy, *Bentley College*
Dawn W. Massey, *Fairfield University*
Kevin McClure, *ESL Language Center*
George McGowan
Gail A. Mestas
Melanie Middlemist, *Colorado State University*
Jenine Moscove
Michael F. Monahan
Mark Myring, *Ball State University*
Maureen O'Brien, *Illinois State University*
Janet Papiernik, *Indiana University*
Betty Pilchard, *Heartland Community College*
LaVonda Ramey, *Schoolcraft College*
Roberta Rettner, *American Ways*
James B. Rosa, *Queensborough Community College*
Yehia Salama, *University of Illinois—Chicago*
Marguerite Savage, *Elgin Community College*
Donald Shannon, *DePaul Univeristy*
S. Murray Simons, *Northeastern University*
Marion Taube, *University of Pittsburgh*
Kathleen Villani, *Queensborough Community College*
John Weber, *DeVry Institute*
Kay Westerfield, *University of Oregon*
Bill Wootton, *Eastern Illinois*
W.T. Wrege, *Ball State University*
Carol Yacht
Glenn Allen Young, *Tulsa Junior College*
Marilyn J. Young, *Tulsa Junior College*
Mary Zenner, *College of Lake County*

B.N. *and* M.P.

User's Guide to *Financial Accounting*

We have designed *Financial Accounting* with you—the student—in mind. Becoming familiar with this textbook will help you succeed in this course: you will study more effectively and improve your grades on tests and assignments. The following User's Guide will introduce you to your *Financial Accounting* textbook.

Preview the Chapter

Use these features to preview the chapter. First, become familiar with the **Learning Objectives** (they appear throughout the chapter), and then read how a leading business uses accounting information. Review **Making a Statement**; this feature tells you which financial statements are important in this chapter.

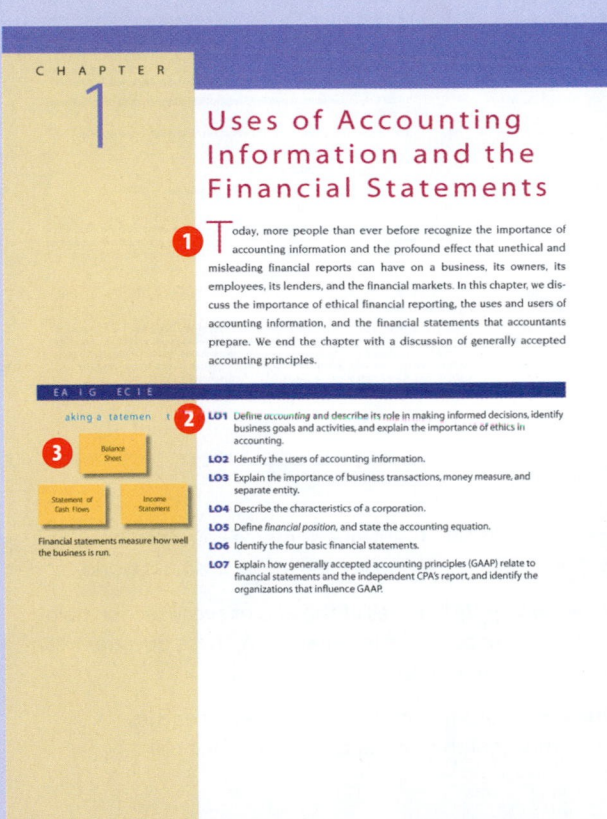

1 The **Chapter Preview** focuses on management and ethical issues. As you read this section, consider the following: Why are the concepts in this chapter important to managers? What are the ethical issues?

2 The **Learning Objectives (LOs)** help guide you toward mastery of the material. These brief statements summarize what you should know after reading the chapter. You will see many references to *LOs* throughout each chapter.

3 **Making a Statement** reinforces the connection between the financial statements and the chapter's topics. It indicates which financial statements are important in each chapter.

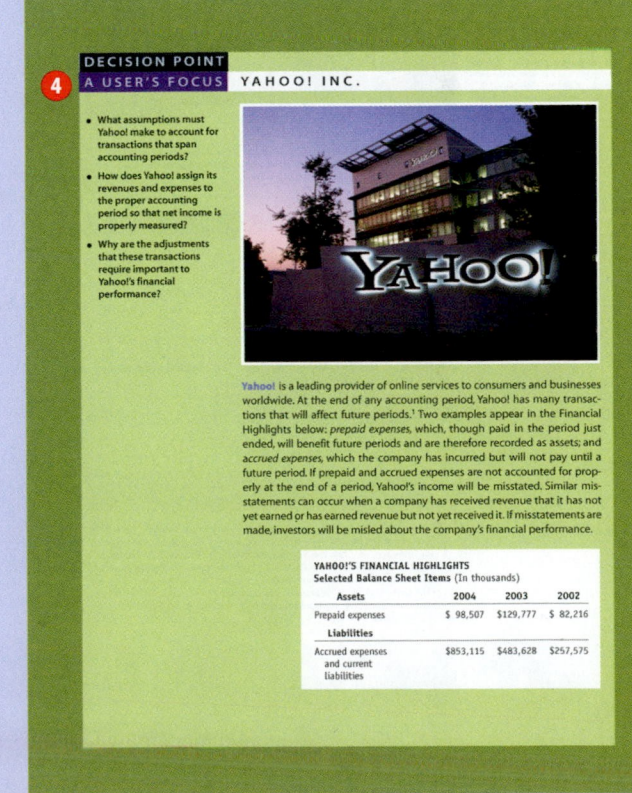

4 Use the **Decision Point** feature to see how real companies depend on accounting information in decision making. Look for references to the **Decision Point** company throughout the chapter. Many of the companies profiled are among the most successful in the world.

Reinforce What You Read

As you read each chapter, use the features described below to reinforce the concepts. Look for the LO before every each main section, and note boldface words: they are terms and definitions you should know. Use the *Stop, Review, and Apply* questions at the end of each main section to assess your understanding of the material.

5 *Learning Objectives* introduce the key points of each section and are integrated throughout the text.

6 **Boldface** terms call out important concepts and their definitions. These words also appear in a glossary at the end of the chapter.

7 *Study Notes* highlight important information and provide useful tips on ways to avoid common mistakes.

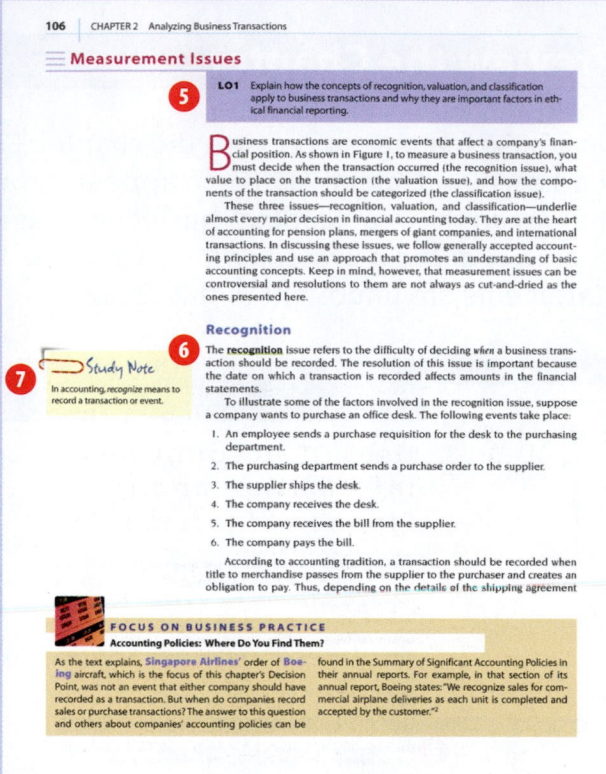

106 CHAPTER 2 Analyzing Business Transactions

Measurement Issues

5 **LO1** Explain how the concepts of recognition, valuation, and classification apply to business transactions and why they are important factors in ethical financial reporting.

Business transactions are economic events that affect a company's financial position. As shown in Figure 1, to measure a business transaction, you must decide when the transaction occurred (the recognition issue), what value to place on the transaction (the valuation issue), and how the components of the transaction should be categorized (the classification issue).

These three issues—recognition, valuation, and classification—underlie almost every major decision in financial accounting today. They are at the heart of accounting for pension plans, mergers of giant companies, and international transactions. In discussing these issues, we follow generally accepted accounting principles and use an approach that promotes an understanding of basic accounting concepts. Keep in mind, however, that measurement issues can be controversial and resolutions to them are not always as cut-and-dried as the ones presented here.

Recognition

6 The **recognition** issue refers to the difficulty of deciding *when* a business transaction should be recorded. The resolution of this issue is important because the date on which a transaction is recorded affects amounts in the financial statements.

7 *Study Note*
In accounting, recognize means to record a transaction or event.

To illustrate some of the factors involved in the recognition issue, suppose a company wants to purchase an office desk. The following events take place:

1. An employee sends a purchase requisition for the desk to the purchasing department.
2. The purchasing department sends a purchase order to the supplier.
3. The supplier ships the desk.
4. The company receives the desk.
5. The company receives the bill from the supplier.
6. The company pays the bill.

According to accounting tradition, a transaction should be recorded when title to merchandise passes from the supplier to the purchaser and creates an obligation to pay. Thus, depending on the details of the shipping agreement

FOCUS ON BUSINESS PRACTICE
Accounting Policies: Where Do You Find Them?

As the text explains, Singapore Airlines' order of Boeing aircraft, which is the focus of this chapter's Decision Point, was not an event that either company should have recorded as a transaction. But when do companies record sales or purchase transactions? The answer to this question and others about companies' accounting policies can be found in the Summary of Significant Accounting Policies in their annual reports. For example, in that section of its annual report, Boeing states: "We recognize sales for commercial airplane deliveries as each unit is completed and accepted by the customer."[2]

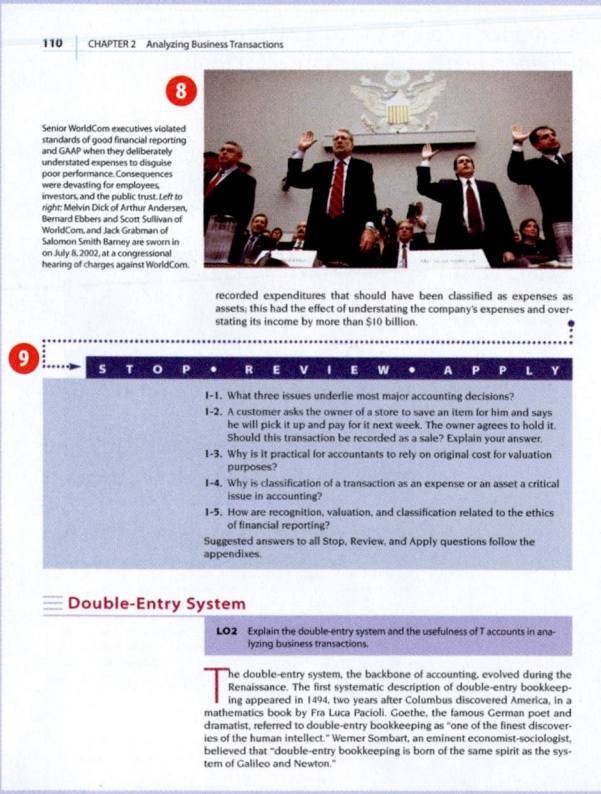

110 CHAPTER 2 Analyzing Business Transactions

Senior WorldCom executives violated standards of good financial reporting and GAAP when they deliberately understated expenses to disguise poor performance. Consequences were devastating for employees, investors, and the public trust. *Left to right:* Melvin Dick of Arthur Andersen, Bernard Ebbers and Scott Sullivan of WorldCom, and Jack Grabman of Salomon Smith Barney are sworn in on July 8, 2002, at a congressional hearing of charges against WorldCom.

recorded expenditures that should have been classified as expenses as assets; this had the effect of understating the company's expenses and overstating its income by more than $10 billion.

9 **S T O P • R E V I E W • A P P L Y**

1-1. What three issues underlie most major accounting decisions?

1-2. A customer asks the owner of a store to save an item for him and says he will pick it up and pay for it next week. The owner agrees to hold it. Should this transaction be recorded as a sale? Explain your answer.

1-3. Why is it practical for accountants to rely on original cost for valuation purposes?

1-4. Why is classification of a transaction as an expense or an asset a critical issue in accounting?

1-5. How are recognition, valuation, and classification related to the ethics of financial reporting?

Suggested answers to all Stop, Review, and Apply questions follow the appendixes.

Double-Entry System

LO2 Explain the double-entry system and the usefulness of T accounts in analyzing business transactions.

The double-entry system, the backbone of accounting, evolved during the Renaissance. The first systematic description of double-entry bookkeeping appeared in 1494, two years after Columbus discovered America, in a mathematics book by Fra Luca Pacioli. Goethe, the famous German poet and dramatist, referred to double-entry bookkeeping as "one of the finest discoveries of the human intellect." Werner Sombart, an eminent economist-sociologist, believed that "double-entry bookkeeping is born of the same spirit as the system of Galileo and Newton."

8 **Photographs** with detailed captions reinforce concepts in the textbook and show how accounting is used in the business world.

9 *Stop, Review, and Apply* features at the end of every section help you review important concepts in the section. These questions can also be used for discussion in class.

10 **Accounting equations** next to important journal entries reinforce the impact of the transaction on the financial statements.

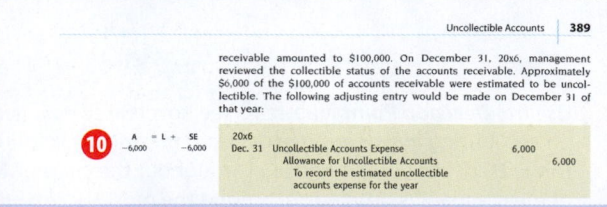

Uncollectible Accounts | **389**

receivable amounted to $100,000. On December 31, 20x6, management reviewed the collectible status of the accounts receivable. Approximately $6,000 of the $100,000 of accounts receivable were estimated to be uncollectible. The following adjusting entry would be made on December 31 of that year:

10
A = L + SE
−6,000   −6,000

20x6			
Dec. 31	Uncollectible Accounts Expense	6,000	
	Allowance for Uncollectible Accounts		6,000
	To record the estimated uncollectible accounts expense for the year		

Reinforce Concepts Visually

These features visually reinforce the concepts in your textbook. Line art helps explain concepts, exhibits show financial statements and other information, and tables include material to support topics covered in the chapter. Also look for icons throughout the text; they are visual guides to key features.

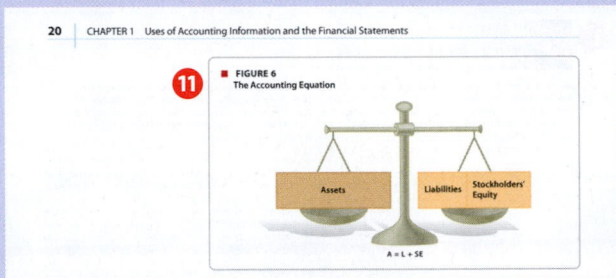

11 An abundance of **line art** illustrates the relationships between concepts and processes.

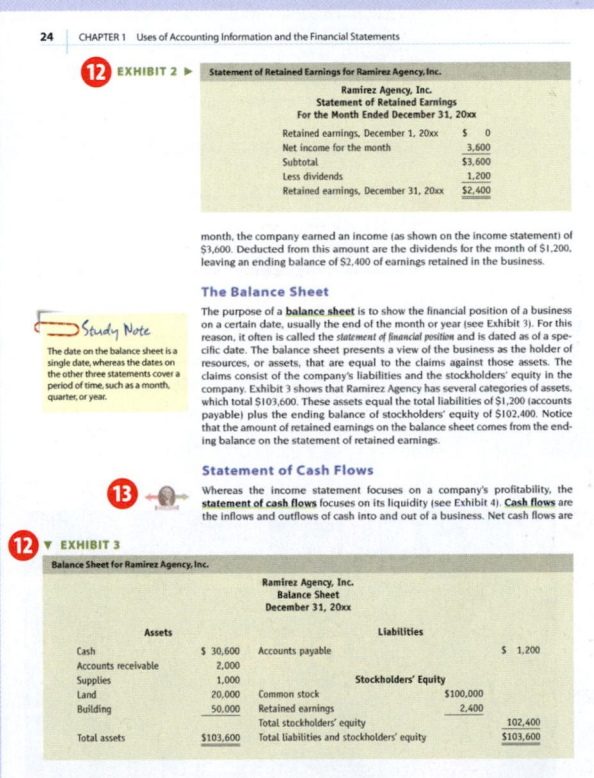

12 **Exhibits** throughout the text show financial information.

13 The **cash flow icon** highlights discussion of cash as a measure of liquidity. Measurement of cash flows serves as an indicator of a company's success; hence the emphasis on cash flows in this book.

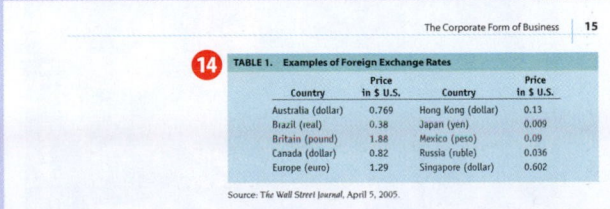

14 **Tables** present factual information referred to in the text.

Learn Why Accounting Is Relevant

These features demonstrate how and why accounting is relevant. *Focus on Business Practice* boxes introduce you to real companies and real issues. The Supplement to Chapter 1 helps you learn how to read—and understand—real financial statements and interpret what management says about them.

15 *Focus on Business Practice* boxes highlight the relevance of accounting to business today.

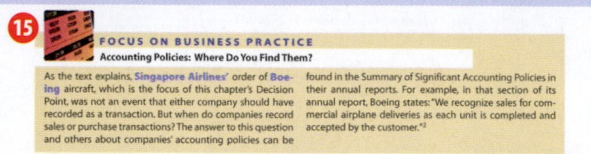

16 The textbook refers to over 200 public, private, and not-for-profit companies. The **Needles Online Study Center** website (**http://college.hmco.com/pic/needlesfa9e**) provides a direct link to the websites of these companies. The book also has a company name index.

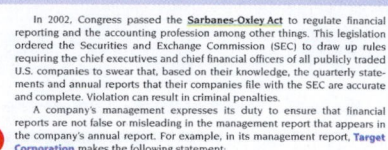

17 **Graphs** and **tables** illustrate how actual business practices relate to chapter topics. Data for these illustrations come from *Accounting Trends & Techniques* and from Dun & Bradstreet, key sources of business information.

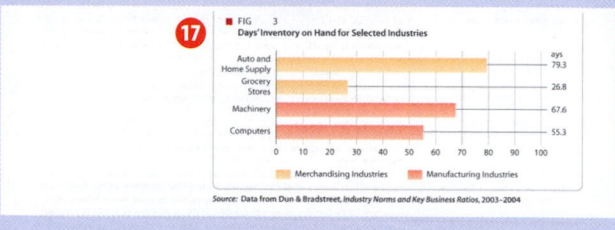

18 **Ratios** are used to measure a company's performance. The key ratio icon appears in the margin to highlight discussions of important ratios.

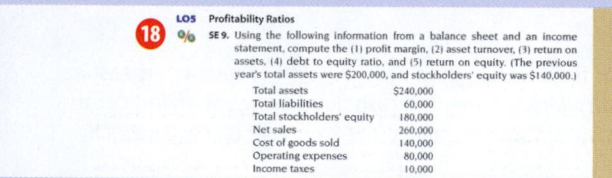

19 The complete **annual report** for CVS and the **financial statements** of Southwest Airlines are in the supplement to Chapter 1. CVS's financial statements with annotations also appear in the Supplement to Chapter 1.

Summarize and Review

The end-of-chapter features provide summary, review, and assignments for practice. *A Look Back At* relates the chapter's concepts to the company you read about in the *Decision Point* at the beginning of the chapter. Review sections include a *Review of Learning Objectives* and a *Review of Concepts and Terminology*.

20 *A Look Back At* shows how the concepts learned in the chapter can be used to evaluate a company's performance.

21 The **Chapter Review** restates each learning objective and its main ideas.

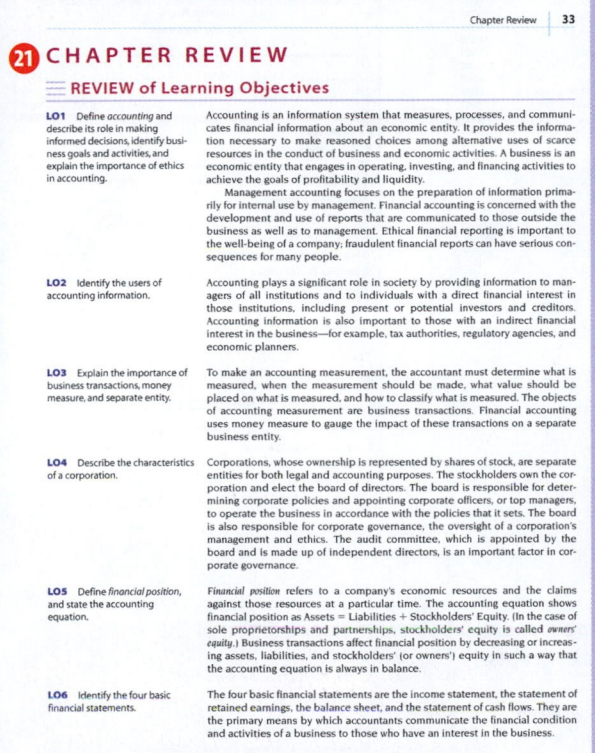

22 Each chapter includes a glossary of the key concepts and terms defined in the chapter. The *LO* next to each term indicates the section in which it is discussed.

Want more study aids and review exercises? The **Study Guide** for this book provides a thorough review of each learning objective, a detailed outline, true/false and multiple-choice questions, and exercises. Answers are included. Ask for it at your bookstore.

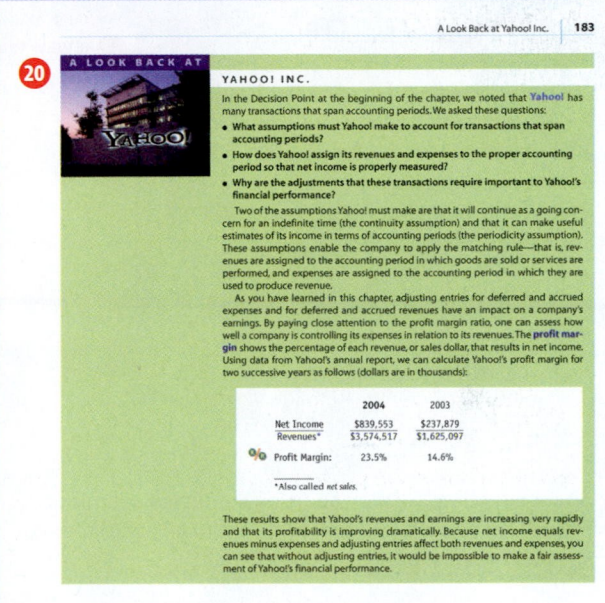

Review and Practice

Continue your review of the chapter with the *Review Problem*, which reflects computations or analyses covered in the chapter. For practice at different levels of difficulty, *Chapter Assignments*—from *Short Exercises* to *Cases*—let you develop skills learned in the chapter. All assignments are identified by *Learning Objective* so you can easily review the concepts presented in the text.

23 Not sure if you understand the techniques and calculations? Want to find out if you're ready for a test? The *Review Problem* models main computations or analyses presented in the chapter and end-of-chapter assignments. The answer, usually shown in Excel, is provided for immediate feedback.

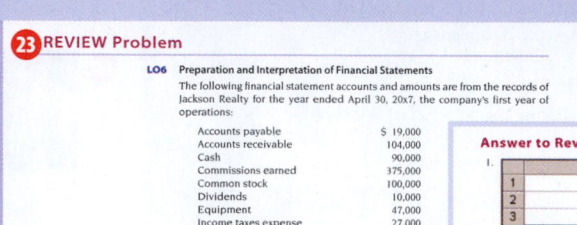

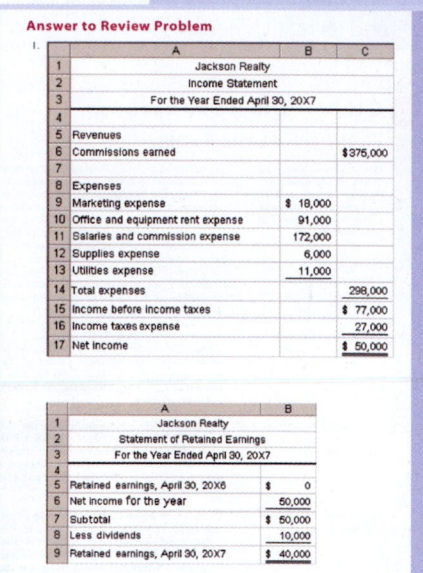

24 **Short exercises** provide additional practice. Learning Objectives appear in the margin next to all assignments so you can refer to the text for help.

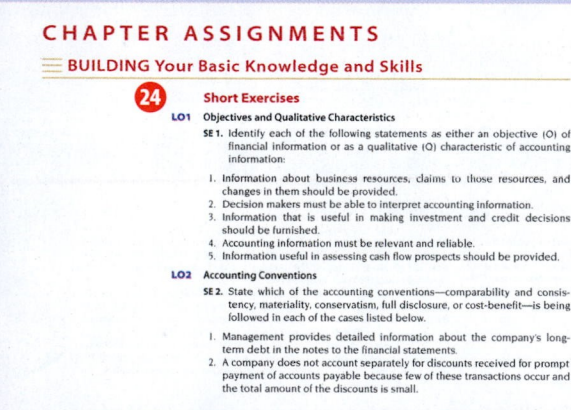

25 **Single-topic exercises** stress the application of the chapter's concepts.

Develop Important Skills

Use these end-of-chapter features to develop important skills. Five problems and three alternate problems per chapter allow extensive application of chapter topics, often covering more than one *Learning Objective*. *Cases* provide opportunities for group assignments, Internet research, analysis with Excel, and critical thinking.

26 Most problems include at least one *User Insight* question. These questions challenge you to think about how financial information is used for business decision making.

27 Problems with this icon can be solved by using **General Ledger Software**, which is available on your student CD. Problems often contain financial data and cover more than one *Learning Objective*.

28 *Cases* at the end of each chapter have been organized to highlight important skills, such as conceptual understanding, interpretation of financial statements, Excel analysis, decision making, Internet research, and business communication.

≡ ENHANCING Your Knowledge, Skills, and Critical Thinking

Conceptual Understanding Cases

28 **LO2** Consistency and Full Disclosure

C 1. Cuyahoga Parking, which operates a seven-story parking building in downtown Cleveland, has a calendar year end. It serves daily and hourly parkers, as well as monthly parkers who pay a fixed monthly rate in advance. The company traditionally has recorded all cash receipts as revenues when received. Most monthly parkers pay in full during the month prior to that in which they have the right to park. The company's auditors have said that beginning in 20x6, the company should consider recording the cash receipts from monthly parking on an accrual basis, crediting Unearned Revenues. Total cash receipts for 20x6 were $1,250,000, and the cash receipts received in 20x6 and applicable to January 20x7 were $62,500. Discuss the relevance of the accounting conventions of consistency and full disclosure to the decision to record the monthly parking revenues on an accrual basis.

Annual Report Case: CVS Corporation

LO3, LO4, LO5 Classified Balance Sheet and Multistep Income Statement

C 6. Refer to **CVS Corporation's** annual report in the Supplement to Chapter 1 to answer the following questions. (Note that 2004 refers to the year ended January 1, 2005, and 2003 refers to the year ended January 3, 2004.)

1. Consolidated balance sheets: (a) Did the amount of working capital increase or decrease from 2003 to 2004? By how much? (b) Did the current ratio improve from 2003 to 2004? (c) Does the company have long-term investments or intangible assets? (d) Did the debt to equity ratio of CVS change from 2003 to 2004? (e) What is the contributed capital for 2004? How does contributed capital compare with retained earnings?
2. Consolidated statements of operations: (a) Does CVS use a multistep or single-step income statement? (b) Is it a comparative statement? (c) What is the trend of net earnings? (d) How significant are income taxes for CVS?

Decision Analysis Using Excel

LO5 Financial Analysis for Loan Decision

C 5. Esteban Almada was recently promoted to loan officer at First Federal Bank. He has authority to issue loans up to $75,000 without approval from a higher bank official. This week two small companies, Dubrovnik Supplies, Inc., and Shimano Fashions, Inc., have each submitted a proposal for a six-month, $75,000 loan. To prepare financial analyses of the two companies, Almada has obtained the information summarized below.

Dubrovnik Supplies, Inc., is a local lumber and home improvement company. Because sales have increased so much during the past two years, Dubrovnik Supplies has had to raise additional working capital, especially as represented by receivables and inventory. The $75,000 loan is needed to assure the company of enough working capital for the next year. Dubrovnik Supplies began the year with total assets of $1,110,000 and stockholders' equity of $390,000. During the past year, the company had a net income of $60,000 on net sales of $1,140,000. Dubrovnik Supplies' unclassified balance sheet as of the current date appears as follows:

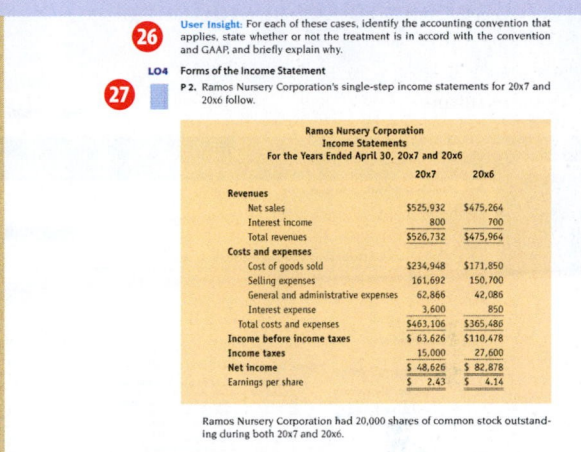

26 **User Insight:** For each of these cases, identify the accounting convention that applies, state whether or not the treatment is in accord with the convention and GAAP, and briefly explain why.

LO4 Forms of the Income Statement

27 **P 2.** Ramos Nursery Corporation's single-step income statements for 20x7 and 20x6 follow.

Ramos Nursery Corporation
Income Statements
For the Years Ended April 30, 20x7 and 20x6

	20x7	20x6
Revenues		
Net sales	$525,932	$475,264
Interest income	800	700
Total revenues	$526,732	$475,964
Costs and expenses		
Cost of goods sold	$234,948	$171,850
Selling expenses	161,692	150,700
General and administrative expenses	62,866	42,086
Interest expense	3,600	850
Total costs and expenses	$463,106	$365,486
Income before income taxes	$ 63,626	$110,478
Income taxes	15,000	27,600
Net income	$ 48,626	$ 82,878
Earnings per share	$ 2.43	$ 4.14

Ramos Nursery Corporation had 20,000 shares of common stock outstanding during both 20x7 and 20x6.

Student Resources and Study Aids

Financial Accounting offers a variety of print and multimedia tools to complement the way you learn. From study guides to downloadable MP3 audio review files, the Needles *Financial Accounting* program keeps you engaged and on track for success. The following student resources may come packaged with your new copy of *Financial Accounting*, or can be purchased separately at your local college bookstore or directly from Houghton Mifflin's virtual bookstore at **http://college.hmco.com/students**.

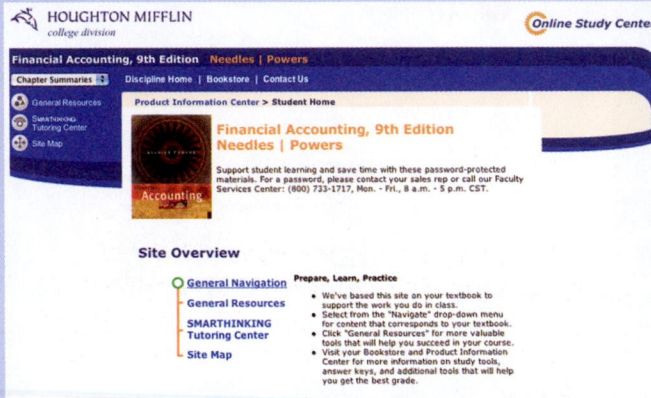

The *Financial Accounting* **Online Study Center** contains a variety of resources intended to help you improve your performance, including ACE Practice Tests, Company Links, Crossword Puzzles, Glossary, HMAccounting Tutor, Learning Objectives, *To the Student*, and business readings from leading periodicals on current business issues and careers.

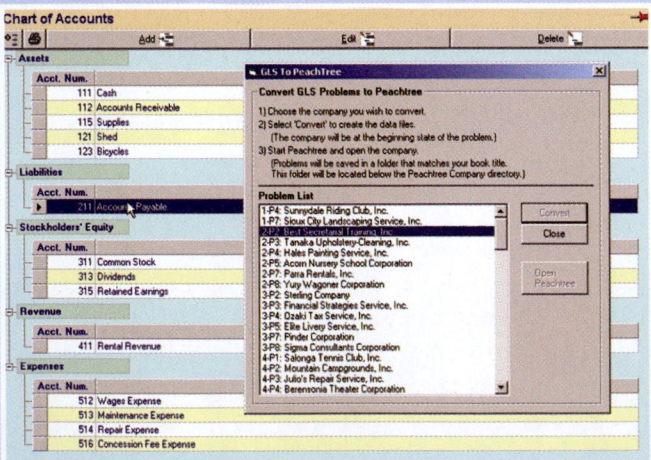

The **HMAccounting Tutor and General Ledger Software CD** (0-618-62684-0) reinforces students' understanding of both accounting concepts and financial accounting procedures with numerous tutorials and demonstration problems that relate to the text's learning objectives. Nearly all of the problems in *Financial Accounting* can be solved with General Ledger Software (GLS) and are clearly identified with icons throughout the textbook. Our updated GLS also includes *Export to Peachtree* functionality.

The *Financial Accounting* **Electronic Working Papers CD** (0-618-62682-4) is an alternative to printed working papers. These Excel-based files contain templates that allow you to work the exercises, problems, and cases in the text; a new interface makes it easy to navigate among working paper assignments. With the Electronic Working Papers CD, you master both accounting concepts and the basic skills required for spreadsheet applications.

Also available are print **Working Papers** (0-618-62678-6), which provide the appropriate accounting forms for solving the computational exercises, problems, and cases from the text.

The **SMARTHINKING**™ online tutoring center provides real-time access to experienced "e-structors" (online tutors). In addition to live, one-on-one interaction, you can submit questions, assignments, and spreadsheets and receive personalized feedback—usually within 24 hours.

The *Financial Accounting* print **Student Study Guide** (0-618-62677-8) is designed to help you improve your performance in the course. This resource consists of five parts: "Reviewing the Chapter," "Self-Test," "Testing Students' Knowledge," "Applying Your Knowledge," and "Answers."

To help you become familiar with computerized accounting systems used in practice, the **Peachtree Accounting CD** (0-618-62683-2) features the educational version of this leading software program. The experience you gain from working with actual software makes you more desirable as a potential employee.

The Houghton Mifflin Accounting **Bridge Tutorial CD** (0-618-31876-3) emphasizes accounting transactions, presents a review of the debit/credit mechanism, and provides a foundation for the preparation of financial statements. This CD features pre- and post-test activities on accounting concepts, designed to test your basic understanding of the accounting cycle. Key concept tutorials provide reinforcement and practice. Interactive Review and Reinforce questions with rejoinders provide feedback on right and wrong answers. Tutorials also include demonstration problems with voice-over narrations and a built-in glossary with pop-up definitions.

Check Figures

Chapter 1
P 1. No check figure
P 2. Total assets, Set C: $580; Total liabilities and stockholders' equity, Set A: $6,600; Total liabilities and stockholders' equity, Set B: $31,000
P 3. Total assets: $125,650
P 4. Total assets: $20,900
P 5. No check figure
P 6. Total assets, Set A: $2,700; Total liabilities and stockholders' equity, Set B: $26,000; Total liabilities and stockholders' equity, Set C: $1,900
P 7. Total assets: $130,850
P 8. Total assets: $27,300

Chapter 2
P 1. Total assets: $28,540
P 2. No check figure
P 3. Trial balance: $16,200
P 4. Trial balance: $14,800
P 5. Trial balance: $23,805
P 6. Total assets: $67,790
P 7. Trial balance: $10,540
P 8. Trial balance: $30,710

Chapter 3
P 1. No check figure
P 2. No check figure
P 3. Adjusted trial balance: $125,792
P 4. Adjusted trial balance: $31,578
P 5. Adjusted trial balance: $654,209
P 6. No check figure
P 7. No check figure
P 8. Adjusted trial balance: $109,167

Supplement to Chapter 3
P 1. Total assets: $627,800
P 2. Adjusted trial balance, May 31: $10,338
     Adjusted trial balance, June 30: $10,908
P 3. Net income: $78,622
P 4. Net income: $25,196

Chapter 4
P 1. No check figure
P 2. Income from operations: 20x7: $66,426; 20x6: $110,628
P 3. Total assets: $595,600
P 4. No check figure
P 5. Net income: $72,260; Total assets: $1,083,800
P 6. No check figure

P 7. Income from operations: 20x8: $34,320; 20x7: $84,748
P 8. No check figure

Chapter 5
P 1. Net income: $13,435
P 2. No check figure
P 3. Net income: $18,941
P 4. No check figure
P 5. No check figure
P 6. Net income: $5,522
P 7. No check figure
P 8. Net income: $2,435
P 9. No check figure

Chapter 6
P 1. 1. Cost of goods available for sale: $157,980
P 2. 2. Cost of goods sold: March, $4,500; April, $10,540
P 3. 1. Cost of goods sold: March, $4,579; April, $10,518
P 4. 3. Estimated inventory shortage: At cost, $6,052; At retail, $8,900
P 5. 1. Estimated loss of inventory in fire: $653,027
P 6. 1. Cost of goods available for sale: $10,560,000
P 7. 1. Cost of goods sold: April, $9,660; May, $22,119
P 8. 2. Cost of goods sold: April, $9,500; May, $21,880

Chapter 7
P 1. 1. Adjusted book balance: $149,473.28
P 2. 2. Uncollectible accounts expense: percentage of net sales method, $17,952; accounts receivable aging method, $15,700
P 3. 4. Amount of uncollectible accounts expense: $9,109
P 4. 2. Total accrued interest income as of June 30: $1,928.22
P 5. 1. Adjusted book balance: $54,485.60
P 6. 2. Uncollectible accounts expense: percentage of net sales method, $24,965; accounts receivable aging method, $27,100
P 7. 4. Amount of uncollectible accounts expense: $73,413

Chapter 8
P 1. No check figure
P 2. June 30 Interest Expense: $552.33
P 3. 1.b. Estimated Product Warranty Liability: $10,800
P 4. Total current liabilities: $36,988.20
P 5. Fund balance: $58,300; Initial deposit: $110,250; Purchase price: $399,300; Annual payments: $136,355.89

P 6. December 31 Interest Expense: $426.08
P 7. 1.b. Estimated Product Warranty Liability: $20,160
P 8. Fund balance: $3,310,000; Annual payment: $327,600; Cost of buyout: $317,000; Fund balance: $798,600

Chapter 9
P 1. No check figure
P 2. Totals: Land: $426,212; Land Improvements: $166,560; Buildings: $833,940; Machinery: $1,262,640; Expense: $18,120
P 3. 1. Depreciation, Year 3: a. $5,000; b. $8,000; c. $2,813
P 4. 1. Depreciation, Year 3: a. $54,250; b. $81,375; c. $53,407
P 5. 2. Depletion expense: $288,000
P 6. Totals: Land: $723,900; Land Improvements: $142,000; Building: $1,383,600; Equipment: $210,800
P 7. 1. Depreciation, Year 3: a. $165,000; b. $132,000; c. $90,000
P 8. 2. Depletion expense: $243,000

Chapter 10
P 1. No check figure
P 2. 1.d. Interest expense: $510,000, 2.d. Interest expense: $540,000
P 3. 1. Feb. 28, Bond Interest Expense: $377,071; 2. Feb. 28, Bond Interest Expense: $382,308
P 4. 1. June 30, Bond Interest Expense: $289,332; Sept. 1, Bond Interest Expense: $186,580
P 5. 2. Loss on early retirement: $2,261,504
P 6. 1.d. Interest expense: $374,400; 2. d. Interest Expense: $385,600
P 7. 1. Nov. 30, Bond Interest Expense: $1,040,300; 2. Nov. 30, Bond Interest Expense: $1,057,300
P 8. 1. June 30, Bond Interest Expense: $93,195; Sept. 1, Bond Interest Expense: $191,900

Chapter 11
P 1. 2. Total stockholders' equity: $1,342,000
P 2. 1. 20x7 Total dividends: Preferred, $280,000; Common, $820,000
P 3. No check figure
P 4. 2. Total stockholders' equity: $1,765,900
P 5. 1. Ending balance, Treasury Stock, Common: 0
P 6. 2. Total stockholders' equity: $302,400
P 7. 1. 20x9 Total dividends: Preferred, $80,000; Common, $180,000
P 8. 2. Total stockholders' equity: $473,040

Chapter 12
P 1. 2. Difference in net income: $97,600
P 2. 1. Income before extraordinary items: $216,000

P 3. 1. Income from continuing operations, December 31, 20x7: $157,500
P 4. 2. Total stockholders' equity: $2,964,000
P 5. 2. Retained earnings: $250,000; Total stockholders' equity: $2,350,000
P 6. 2. Retained earnings: $148,800; Total stockholders' equity: $2,802,800
P 7. 1. Income before extraordinary items: $410,000
P 8. 2. Retained earnings: $211,600; Total stockholders' equity: $524,500

Chapter 13
P 1. No check figure
P 2. 1. Net cash flows from: operating activities, $46,800; investing activities, ($14,400); financing activities, $102,000
P 3. 1. Net cash flows from: operating activities, ($106,000); investing activities, $34,000; financing activities, $24,000
P 4. 1. Net cash flows from: operating activities, $548,000; investing activities, $6,000; financing activities, ($260,000)
P 5. No check figure
P 6. 1. Net cash flows from: operating activities, $63,300; investing activities, ($12,900); financing activities, $7,000

Chapter 14
P 1. No check figure
P 2. Increase: a, b, e, f, l, m
P 3. 1.c. Receivable turnover, 20x8: 14.1 times; 20x7: 14.4 times; 1.e. Inventory turnover, 20x8: 3.6 times; 20x7: 3.5 times
P 4. 1.b. Quick ratio, Lewis: 1.5 times; Ramsey: 1.2 times; 2.d. Return on equity, Lewis: 8.8%; Ramsey: 4.9%
P 5. Increase: d, h, i
P 6. 1.a. Current ratio, 20x8: 1.5 times; 20x7: 1.5 times; 2.c. Return on assets, 20x8: 5.0%; 20x7: 10.7%

Chapter 15
P 1. No check figure
P 2. 1. Investment in Waters Corporation, Ending Balance: $734,000
P 3. 1. Consolidated Balance Sheet, Total assets: $1,280,000
P 4. 1. Consolidated Balance Sheet, Total assets: $4,488,000
P 5. No check figure
P 6. No check figure
P 7. 1. Consolidated Balance Sheet, Total assets: $4,790,000
P 8. No check figure

About the Authors

Central to the success of any accounting text is the expertise of its author team. This team brings a wealth of classroom teaching experience, relevant business insight, and pedagogical expertise, as well as first-hand knowledge of today's students.

Belverd E. Needles, Jr., Ph.D., C.P.A., C.M.A.
DePaul University

During his more than thirty years of teaching beginning accounting students, Belverd Needles has been an acknowledged innovator in accounting education. He has won teaching and education awards from DePaul University, the American Accounting Association, the Illinois CPA Society, the American Institute of CPAs, and the national honorary society, Beta Alpha Psi. The Conference on Accounting Education, started by Dr. Needles and sponsored by Houghton Mifflin, is in its twenty-second year; it has helped more than 2,000 accounting instructors improve their teaching. Dr. Needles is editor of the *Accounting Instructors' Report*, in its nineteenth year, a newsletter that thousands of accounting teachers rely on for new ideas in accounting education.

Marian Powers, Ph.D.
Northwestern University

With more than twenty-five years of teaching experience, Marian Powers has taught beginning accounting at every level, from large lecture halls of 250 students to small classes of graduate students. She is a dynamic teacher who incorporates a variety of instructional strategies designed to broaden students' skills and experiences in critical thinking, group interaction, and communication. Consistently, Dr. Powers receives the highest ratings from students. She also brings practical experience to her students, including examples of how managers in all levels of business use and evaluate financial information. In recent years, Dr. Powers has concentrated on executive education. She has taught thousands of executives from leading companies around the world how to read and analyze the financial statements of their own companies and those of their competitors.

Financial
Accounting

Uses of Accounting Information and the Financial Statements

Today, more people than ever before recognize the importance of accounting information and the profound effect that unethical and misleading financial reports can have on a business, its owners, its employees, its lenders, and the financial markets. In this chapter, we discuss the importance of ethical financial reporting, the uses and users of accounting information, and the financial statements that accountants prepare. We end the chapter with a discussion of generally accepted accounting principles.

LEARNING OBJECTIVES

Making a Statement

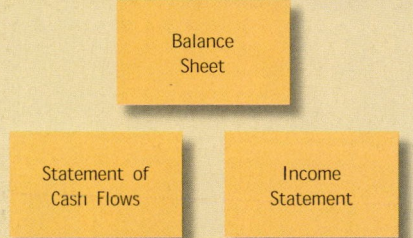

Financial statements measure how well the business is run.

LO1 Define *accounting* and describe its role in making informed decisions, identify business goals and activities, and explain the importance of ethics in accounting.

LO2 Identify the users of accounting information.

LO3 Explain the importance of business transactions, money measure, and separate entity.

LO4 Describe the characteristics of a corporation.

LO5 Define *financial position,* and state the accounting equation.

LO6 Identify the four basic financial statements.

LO7 Explain how generally accepted accounting principles (GAAP) relate to financial statements and the independent CPA's report, and identify the organizations that influence GAAP.

- Is CVS meeting its goal of profitability?

- As a manager at CVS, what financial knowledge would you need to measure progress toward the company's goals?

- As a potential investor or creditor, what financial knowledge would you need to evaluate CVS's financial performance?

CVS operates a nationwide chain of more than 5,000 drugstores. Having opened 1,300 new stores in the last five years, the company has increased sales and profits by more than 50 percent. This performance places it among the fastest-growing retail companies.

Why is CVS considered successful? Customers give the company high marks because of the quality of the products that it sells and the large selection and good service that its stores offer. Investment firms and others with a stake in CVS evaluate the company's success in financial terms.

Whether a company is large or small, the same financial measures are used to evaluate its management and to compare it with other companies. In this chapter, as you learn more about accounting and the business environment, you will become familiar with these financial measures.

Accounting as an Information System

LO1 Define *accounting* and describe its role in making informed decisions, identify business goals and activities, and explain the importance of ethics in accounting.

Accounting is an information system that measures, processes, and communicates financial information about an economic entity.[1] An economic entity is a unit that exists independently, such as a business, a hospital, or a governmental body. Although the central focus of this book is on business entities, we include other economic units at appropriate points in the text and end-of-chapter assignments.

Accountants focus on the needs of decision makers who use financial information, whether those decision makers are inside or outside a business or other economic entity. Accountants provide a vital service by supplying the information decision makers need to make "reasoned choices among alternative uses of scarce resources in the conduct of business and economic activities."[2] As shown in Figure 1, accounting is a link between business activities and decision makers.

1. Accounting measures business activities by recording data about them for future use.

2. The data are stored until needed and then processed to become useful information.

3. The information is communicated through reports to decision makers.

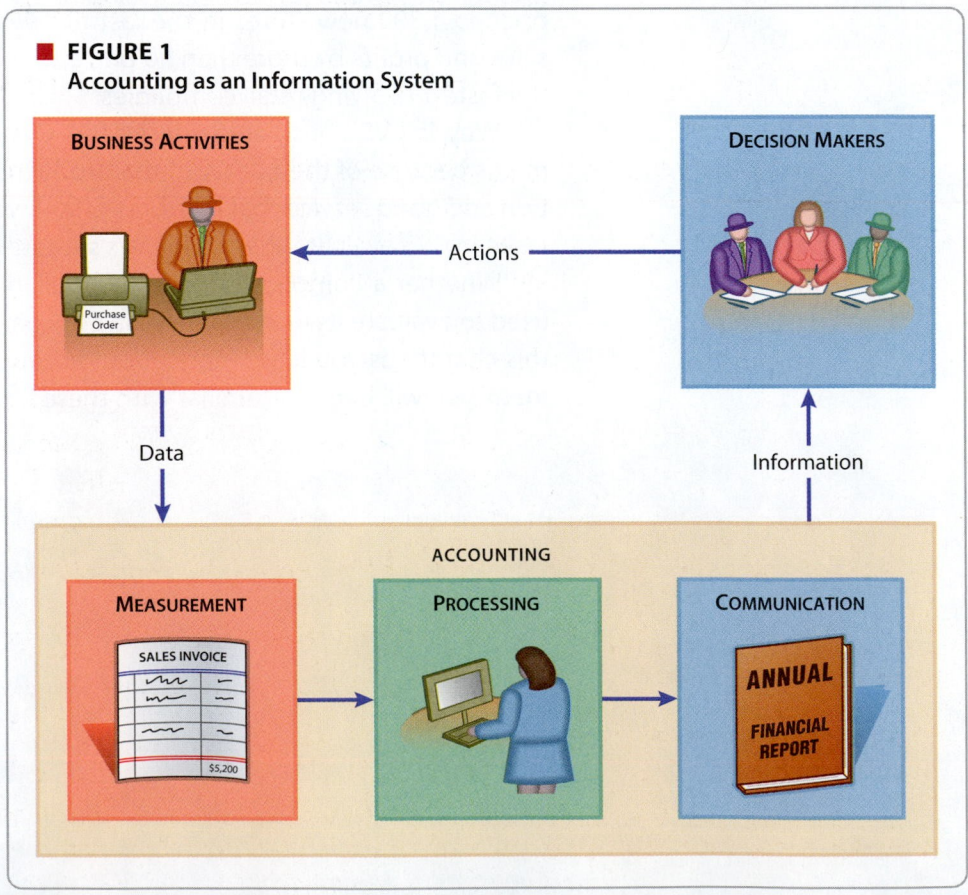

■ FIGURE 1
Accounting as an Information System

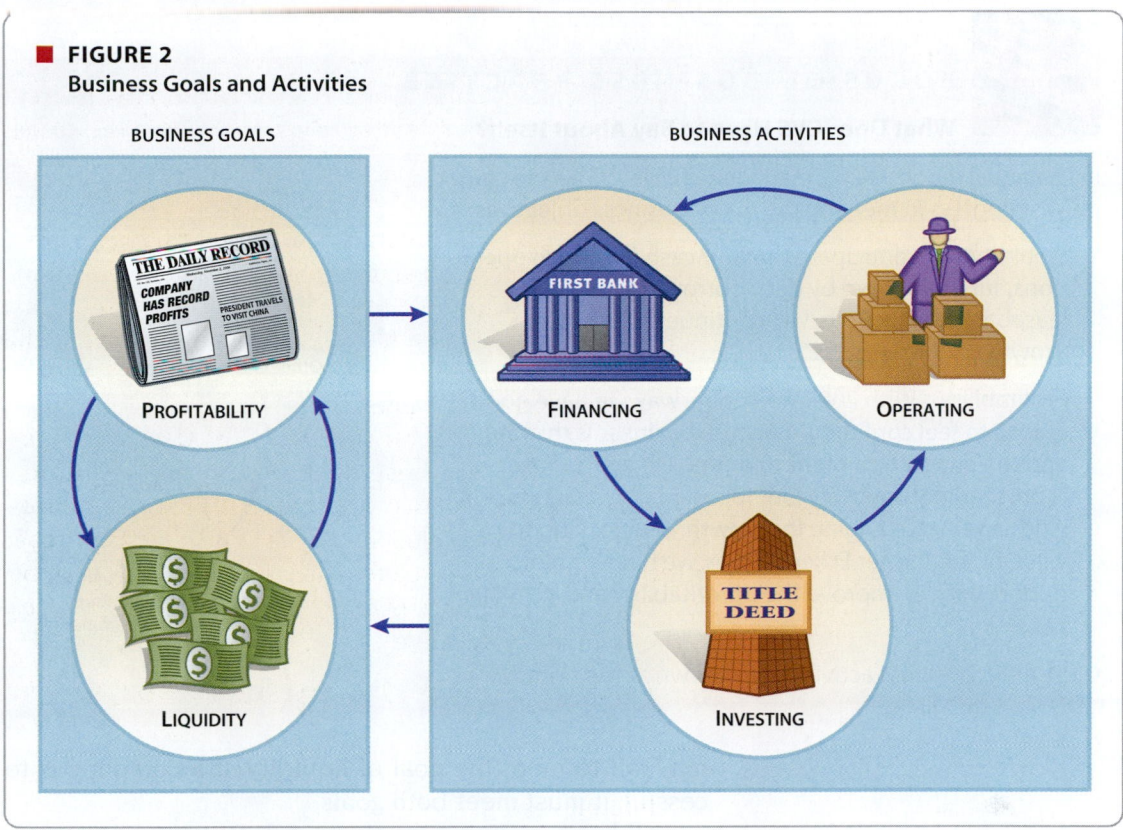

■ **FIGURE 2**
Business Goals and Activities

In other words, data about business activities are the input to the accounting system, and useful information for decision makers is the output.

Business Goals, Activities, and Performance Measures

A **business** is an economic unit that aims to sell goods and services to customers at prices that will provide an adequate return to its owners. The list that follows contains the names of some well-known businesses and the principal goods or services that they sell.

Wal-Mart Corp.	Comprehensive discount store
Reebok International Ltd.	Athletic footwear and clothing
Best Buy Co.	Consumer electronics, personal computers
Wendy's International Inc.	Food service
Starbucks Corp.	Coffee
Southwest Airlines Co.	Passenger airline

Despite their differences, these businesses have similar goals and engage in similar activities, as shown in Figure 2.

The two major goals of all businesses are profitability and liquidity.

▸ **Profitability** is the ability to earn enough income to attract and hold investment capital.

▸ **Liquidity** is the ability to have enough cash to pay debts when they are due.

For example, **Toyota** may meet the goal of profitability by selling many cars at a price that earns a profit, but if its customers do not pay for their cars quickly enough to enable Toyota to pay its suppliers and employees, the company

Study Note

Multiple financial goals, namely profitability and liquidity, signal that more than one measure of performance is of interest to users of accounting information. For example, lenders are concerned primarily with cash flow, and owners are concerned with earnings and dividends.

What Does CVS Have to Say About Itself?

In its annual report, **CVS's** management describes the company's progress in meeting the major business objectives:

> Liquidity: "We anticipate that our cash flow from operations, supplemented by debt borrowings and sale-leaseback transactions, will continue to fund the growth of our business."

> Profitability: "With 2005 well underway, we have good reason to feel confident. Our core business is thriving and the integration of the acquired Eckerd businesses is proceeding smoothly. Our focus on new markets provides a valuable engine for growth. In unlocking the value of the former Eckerd stores, we have a great opportunity to improve their profitability and gain market share."[3]

CVS's main business activities are shown at the right.

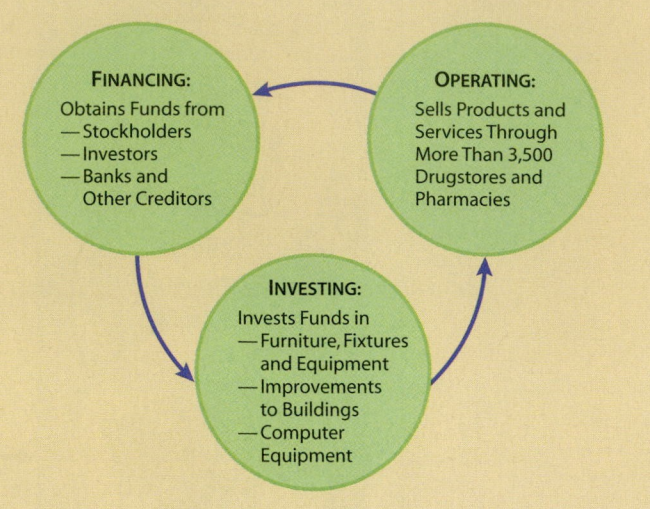

may fail to meet the goal of liquidity. If a company is to survive and be successful, it must meet both goals.

All businesses pursue their goals by engaging in operating, investing, and financing activities.

- **Operating activities** include selling goods and services to customers, employing managers and workers, buying and producing goods and services, and paying taxes.

- **Investing activities** involve spending the capital a company receives in productive ways that will help it achieve its objectives. These activities include buying land, buildings, equipment, and other resources that are needed to operate the business and selling them when they are no longer needed.

- **Financing activities** involve obtaining adequate funds, or capital, to begin operations and to continue operating. These activities include obtaining capital from creditors, such as banks and suppliers, and from owners. They also include repaying creditors and paying a return to the owners.

An important function of accounting is to provide **performance measures**, which indicate whether managers are achieving their business goals and whether the business activities are well managed. These performance measures must align with the goals of the business. For example, **CVS**, like all other companies, considers earned income to be a measure of profitability and cash flow to be a measure of liquidity.

Cash Bonuses Depend on Accounting Numbers!

Nearly all businesses use the amounts reported in their financial statements as a basis for rewarding management. Because managers act to achieve these accounting measures, selecting measures that are not easily manipulated is important. Equally important is maintaining a balance of measures that reflect the goals of profitability and liquidity.[4]

Ratios of accounting measures are also used as performance measures. For instance, a performance measure for operating activities might be the ratio of expenses to the revenue of the business. A performance measure for financing activities might be the ratio of money owed by the company to the total resources that it controls. Because managers are usually evaluated on whether targeted levels of specific performance measures are achieved, they must have a knowledge of accounting to understand how they are evaluated and how they can improve their performance. In addition, because managers will act to achieve targeted performance measures, these measures must be crafted in a way that motivates them to act in the best interests of the owners of the business.

Financial and Management Accounting

Accounting's role of assisting decision makers by measuring, processing, and communicating financial information is usually divided into the categories of management accounting and financial accounting. Although the functions of management accounting and financial accounting overlap, the two can be distinguished by the principal users of the information that they provide.

Management accounting provides *internal* decision makers who are charged with achieving the goals of profitability and liquidity with information about financing, investing, and operating activities. Managers and employees who conduct the activities of the business need information that tells them how they have done in the past and what they can expect in the future. For example, **The Gap**, a retail clothing business, needs an operating report on each outlet that tells how much was sold at that outlet and what costs were incurred, and it needs a budget for each outlet that projects the sales and costs for the next year.

Financial accounting generates reports and communicates them to *external* decision makers so they can evaluate how well the business has achieved its goals. These reports are called **financial statements**. **CVS**, whose stock is traded on the New York Stock Exchange, sends its financial statements to its owners (called *stockholders*), its banks and other creditors, and government regulators. Financial statements report directly on the goals of profitability and liquidity and are used extensively both inside and outside a business to evaluate the business's success. It is important for every person involved with a business to understand financial statements. They are a central feature of accounting and a primary focus of this book.

Processing Accounting Information

It is important to distinguish accounting from the ways in which accounting information is processed by bookkeeping, computers, and management information systems.

Accounting includes the design of an information system that meets users' needs, and its major goals are the analysis, interpretation, and use of information. **Bookkeeping**, on the other hand, is mechanical and repetitive; it is the process of recording financial transactions and keeping financial records. It is a small—but important—part of accounting.

A **computer** is an electronic tool used to collect, organize, and communicate vast amounts of information with great speed. Computers can perform both routine bookkeeping chores and complex calculations. Accountants were

> **Study Note**
>
> Computerized accounting information is only as reliable and useful as the data that go into the system. The accountant must have a thorough understanding of the concepts that underlie accounting to ensure the data's reliability and usefulness.

among the earliest and most enthusiastic users of computers, and today they use computers in all aspects of their work.

Computers make it possible to create a management information system to organize a business's many information needs. A **management information system (MIS)** consists of the interconnected subsystems that provide the information needed to run a business. The accounting information system is the most important subsystem because it plays the key role of managing the flow of economic data to all parts of a business and to interested parties outside the business.

Ethical Financial Reporting

Ethics is a code of conduct that applies to everyday life. It addresses the question of whether actions are right or wrong. Actions—whether ethical or unethical, right or wrong—are the product of individual decisions. Thus, when an organization acts unethically by using false advertising, cheating customers, polluting the environment, or treating employees unfairly, it is not the organization that is responsible—it is the members of management and other employees who have made a conscious decision to act in this manner.

Ethics is especially important in preparing financial reports because users of these reports must depend on the good faith of the people involved in their preparation. Users have no other assurance that the reports are accurate and fully disclose all relevant facts.

The intentional preparation of misleading financial statements is called **fraudulent financial reporting**.[5] It can result from the distortion of records (e.g., the manipulation of inventory records), falsified transactions (e.g., fictitious sales), or the misapplication of various accounting principles. There are a number of motives for fraudulent reporting—for instance, to cover up financial weakness in order to obtain a higher price when a company is sold, to meet the expectations of stockholders and financial analysts, or to obtain a loan. The incentive can also be personal gain, such as additional compensation, promotion, or avoidance of penalties for poor performance.

Whatever the motive for fraudulent financial reporting, it can have dire consequences, as the accounting scandals that erupted at **Enron Corporation** and **WorldCom** in 2001 and 2002 attest. Unethical financial reporting and accounting practices at those two major corporations caused thousands of people to lose their jobs, their investment incomes, and their pensions. They also resulted in prison sentences and fines for the corporate executives who were involved.

In the wake of one of the largest accounting scandals in history, current and former members of Enron's board of directors John Duncan *(left)*, Herbert Winokur *(center)*, and Norman Blake listen to opening remarks at a hearing of the Senate Permanent Subcommittee on Investigations, May 7, 2002. Unethical accounting practices at Enron led to the collapse of the company and the loss of thousands of jobs and pensions.

In 2002, Congress passed the **Sarbanes-Oxley Act** to regulate financial reporting and the accounting profession among other things. This legislation ordered the Securities and Exchange Commission (SEC) to draw up rules requiring the chief executives and chief financial officers of all publicly traded U.S. companies to swear that, based on their knowledge, the quarterly statements and annual reports that their companies file with the SEC are accurate and complete. Violation can result in criminal penalties.

A company's management expresses its duty to ensure that financial reports are not false or misleading in the management report that appears in the company's annual report. For example, in its management report, **Target Corporation** makes the following statement:

> Management is responsible for the consistency, integrity and presentation of the information in the Annual Report.[6]

However, it is accountants, not management, who physically prepare and audit financial reports. To meet the high ethical standards of the accounting profession, they must apply accounting concepts in such a way as to present a fair view of a company's operations and financial position and to avoid misleading readers of their reports. Like the conduct of a company, the ethical conduct of a profession is a collection of individual actions. As a member of a profession, each accountant has a responsibility—not only to the profession, but also to employers, clients, and society as a whole—to ensure that any report he or she prepares or audits provides accurate, reliable information.

The high regard that the public has historically had for the accounting profession is evidence that an overwhelming number of accountants have upheld the ethics of the profession. Even as the Enron and WorldCom scandals were making headlines, a Gallup Poll showed an increase of 14 percent in the accounting profession's reputation between 2001 and 2002—larger than the increase for any other profession and one that placed it among the most highly rated.[7]

Accountants and top managers are, of course, not the only people responsible for ethical financial reporting. Managers and employees at all levels must be conscious of their responsibility for providing accurate financial information to the people who rely on it.

S T O P • R E V I E W • A P P L Y

1-1. Why is accounting considered an information system?

1-2. What is the role of accounting in the decision-making process, and what broad business goals and activities does it help management achieve and manage?

1-3. Distinguish between management accounting and financial accounting.

1-4. Distinguish among these terms: *accounting*, *bookkeeping*, and *management information systems*.

1-5. What is the difference between misstated financial statements and fraudulent financial reporting?

Suggested answers to all Stop, Review, and Apply questions follow the appendixes.

Decision Makers: The Users of Accounting Information

LO2 Identify the users of accounting information.

As shown in Figure 3, the people who use accounting information to make decisions fall into three categories:

1. Those who manage a business

2. Those outside a business enterprise who have a direct financial interest in the business

3. Those who have an indirect financial interest in a business

These categories apply to governmental and not-for-profit organizations as well as to profit-oriented ventures.

Management

Management refers to the people who are responsible for operating a business and meeting its goals of profitability and liquidity. In a small business, management may consist solely of the owners. In a large business, management usually consists of people who have been hired to do the job. Managers must decide what to do, how to do it, and whether the results match their original plans. Successful managers consistently make the right decisions based on timely and valid information. To make good decisions, managers at **CVS** and other companies need answers to such questions as:

▸ What were the company's earnings during the past quarter?

▸ Is the rate of return to the owners adequate?

▸ Does the company have enough cash?

▸ Which products or services are most profitable?

▸ What is the cost of manufacturing each product or providing each service?

Study Note

Managers are internal users of accounting information.

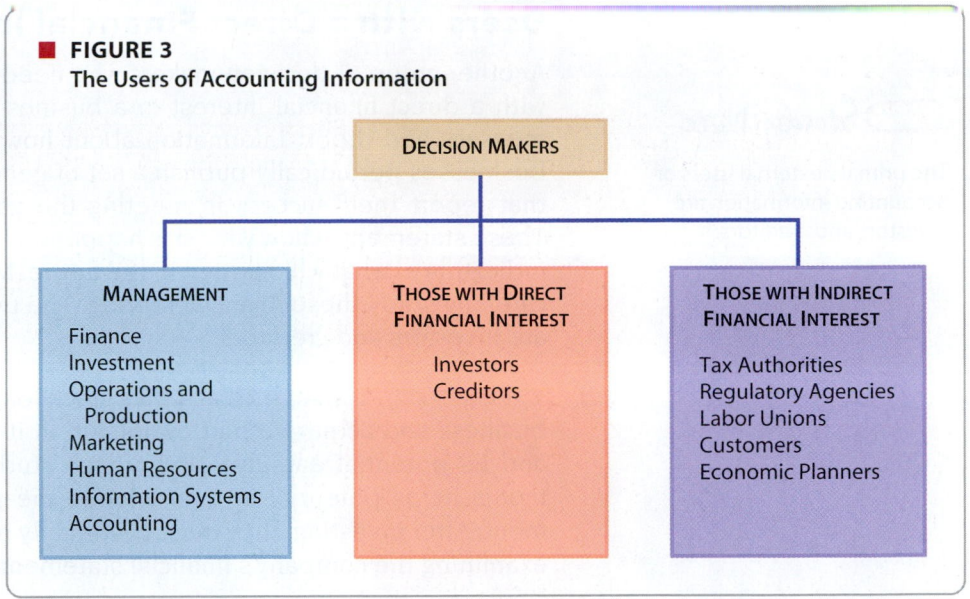

■ **FIGURE 3**
The Users of Accounting Information

Because so many key decisions are based on accounting data, management is one of the most important users of accounting information.

In its decision-making process, management performs functions that are essential to the operation of a business. Although large businesses have more elaborate operations than small ones, the same basic functions must be performed, and each requires accounting information on which to base decisions. The basic management functions are:

Financing the business—obtaining funds so that a company can begin and continue operating

Investing resources—investing assets in productive ways that support a company's goals

Producing goods and services—managing the production of goods and services

Marketing goods and services—overseeing how goods or services are advertised, sold, and distributed

Managing employees—overseeing the hiring, evaluation, and compensation of employees

Providing information to decision makers—gathering data about all aspects of a company's operations, organizing the data into usable information, and providing reports to managers and appropriate outside parties. Accounting plays a key role in this function.

FOCUS ON BUSINESS PRACTICE

What Do CFOs Do?

According to a recent survey, the chief financial officer (CFO) is the "new business partner of the chief executive officer" (CEO). CFOs are increasingly required to take on responsibilities for strategic planning, mergers and acquisitions, and tasks involving international operations, and many of them are becoming CEOs of their companies. Those who do become CEOs are finding that "a financial background is invaluable when they're saddled with the responsibility of making big calls."[8]

Study Note

The primary external users of accounting information are investors and creditors.

Users with a Direct Financial Interest

Another group of decision makers who need accounting information are those with a direct financial interest in a business. They depend on accounting to measure and report information about how a business has performed. Most businesses periodically publish a set of general-purpose financial statements that report their success in meeting the goals of profitability and liquidity. These statements show what has happened in the past, and they are important indicators of what will happen in the future. Many people outside the company carefully study these financial reports. The two most important outside groups are investors and creditors.

Investors Those, such as **CVS's** stockholders, who invest or may invest in a business and acquire a part ownership in it are interested in its past success and its potential earnings. A thorough study of a company's financial statements helps potential investors judge the prospects for a profitable investment. After investing, they must continually review their commitment, again by examining the company's financial statements.

Creditors Most companies, including **CVS**, borrow money for both long- and short-term operating needs. Creditors, those who lend money or deliver goods and services before being paid, are interested mainly in whether a company will have the cash to pay interest charges and to repay the debt at the appropriate time. They study a company's liquidity and cash flow as well as its profitability. Banks, finance companies, mortgage companies, securities firms, insurance firms, suppliers, and other lenders must analyze a company's financial position before they make a loan.

Users with an Indirect Financial Interest

In recent years, society as a whole, through governmental and public groups, has become one of the largest and most important users of accounting information. Users who need accounting information to make decisions on public issues include tax authorities, regulatory agencies, and various other groups.

Tax Authorities Government at every level is financed through the collection of taxes. Companies and individuals pay many kinds of taxes, including federal, state, and city income taxes; social security and other payroll taxes; excise taxes; and sales taxes. Each tax requires special tax returns and often a complex set of records as well. Proper reporting is generally a matter of law and can be very complicated. The Internal Revenue Code, for instance, contains thousands of rules governing the preparation of the accounting information used in computing federal income taxes.

Regulatory Agencies Most companies must report periodically to one or more regulatory agencies at the federal, state, and local levels. For example, all publicly traded corporations must report periodically to the **Securities and Exchange Commission (SEC)**. This body, set up by Congress to protect the public, regulates the issuing, buying, and selling of stocks in the United States. Companies listed on a stock exchange also must meet the special reporting requirements of their exchange.

Other Groups Labor unions study the financial statements of corporations as part of preparing for contract negotiations; a company's income and costs often play an important role in these negotiations. Those who advise investors and creditors—financial analysts, brokers, underwriters, lawyers, economists, and the financial press—also have an indirect interest in the financial performance and prospects of a business. Consumer groups, customers, and the general public have become more concerned about the financing and earnings of corporations as well as the effects that corporations have on inflation, the environment, social issues, and the quality of life. And economic planners, among them the President's Council of Economic Advisers and the Federal Reserve Board, use aggregated accounting information to set and evaluate economic policies and programs.

Governmental and Not-for-Profit Organizations

More than 30 percent of the U.S. economy is generated by governmental and not-for-profit organizations (hospitals, universities, professional organizations, and charities). The managers of these diverse entities perform the same functions as managers of businesses, and they therefore have the same need for accounting information and a knowledge of how to use it. Their functions include raising funds from investors, creditors, taxpayers, and donors, and deploying scarce resources. They must also plan how to pay for operations and to repay creditors on a timely basis. In addition, they have an obligation to report their financial performance to legislators, boards, and donors, as well as to deal with tax authorities, regulators, and labor unions. Although most of the examples in this text focus on business enterprises, the same basic principles apply to governmental and not-for-profit organizations.

S T O P • R E V I E W • A P P L Y

2-1. Who are the decision makers that use accounting information?

2-2. A business is an economic unit whose goal is to sell goods or services at prices that will provide an adequate return to its owners. What functions must management perform to achieve this goal?

2-3. Why are investors and creditors interested in reviewing a company's financial statements?

2-4. Among the users of accounting information are people and organizations with an indirect interest in business entities. Briefly identify these people and organizations.

2-5. Why has society as a whole become one of the largest users of accounting information?

Accounting Measurement

LO3 Explain the importance of business transactions, money measure, and separate entity.

I n this section, we begin the study of the measurement aspects of accounting—that is, what accounting actually measures. To make an accounting measurement, the accountant must answer four basic questions:

1. What is measured?

2. When should the measurement be made?

3. What value should be placed on what is measured?

4. How should what is measured be classified?

Accountants in industry, professional associations, public accounting, government, and academic circles debate the answers to these questions constantly, and the answers change as new knowledge and practice require. But the basis of today's accounting practice rests on a number of widely accepted concepts and conventions, which are described in this book. We begin by focusing on the first question: What is measured? We discuss the other three questions (recognition, valuation, and classification) in the next chapter.

Every system must define what it measures, and accounting is no exception. Basically, financial accounting uses money to gauge the impact of business transactions on separate business entities.

Business Transactions

Business transactions are economic events that affect a business's financial position. Businesses can have hundreds or even thousands of transactions every day. These transactions are the raw material of accounting reports.

A transaction can be an exchange of value (a purchase, sale, payment, collection, or loan) between two or more parties. A transaction also can be an economic event that has the same effect as an exchange transaction but that does not involve an exchange. Some examples of "nonexchange" transactions are losses from fire, flood, explosion, and theft; physical wear and tear on machinery and equipment; and the day-by-day accumulation of interest.

To be recorded, a transaction must relate directly to a business entity. Suppose a customer buys toothpaste from **CVS** but has to buy shampoo from a competing store because CVS is out of shampoo. The transaction in which the toothpaste was sold is entered in CVS's records. However, the purchase of the shampoo from the competitor is not entered in CVS's records because even though it indirectly affects CVS economically, it does not involve a direct exchange of value between CVS and the customer.

Money Measure

Study Note

The common unit of measurement used in the United States for financial reporting purposes is the dollar.

All business transactions are recorded in terms of money. This concept is called **money measure**. Of course, nonfinancial information may also be recorded, but it is through the recording of monetary amounts that a business's transactions and activities are measured. Money is the only factor common to all business transactions, and thus it is the only unit of measure capable of producing financial data that can be compared.

The monetary unit a business uses depends on the country in which the business resides. For example, in the United States, the basic unit of money is the dollar. In Japan, it is the yen; in Europe, the euro; and in the United Kingdom, the pound. In international transactions, exchange rates must be used to translate from one currency to another. An **exchange rate** is the value of one currency in terms of another. For example, a British person purchasing goods from a U.S. company like **CVS** and paying in U.S. dollars must exchange British pounds for U.S. dollars before making payment. In effect, currencies are goods that can be bought and sold.

Table 1 illustrates the exchange rates for several currencies in dollars. It shows the exchange rate for British pounds as $1.88 per pound on a particular

TABLE 1. Examples of Foreign Exchange Rates

Country	Price in $ U.S.	Country	Price in $ U.S.
Australia (dollar)	0.769	Hong Kong (dollar)	0.13
Brazil (real)	0.38	Japan (yen)	0.009
Britain (pound)	1.88	Mexico (peso)	0.09
Canada (dollar)	0.82	Russia (ruble)	0.036
Europe (euro)	1.29	Singapore (dollar)	0.602

Source: *The Wall Street Journal*, April 5, 2005.

date. Like the prices of many goods, currency prices change daily according to supply and demand. For example, a year earlier, the exchange rate for British pounds was $1.85. Although our discussion in this book focuses on dollars, some examples and assignments involve foreign currencies.

Separate Entity

For accounting purposes, a business is a **separate entity**, distinct not only from its creditors and customers but also from its owners. It should have its own set of financial records, and its records and reports should refer only to its own affairs.

For example, Just Because Flowers Company should have a bank account separate from the account of Holly Sapp, the owner. Holly Sapp may own a home, a car, and other property, and she may have personal debts, but these are not the resources or debts of Just Because Flowers. Holly Sapp may own another business, say a stationery shop. If she does, she should have a completely separate set of records for each business.

Study Note

For accounting purposes, a business is *always* separate and distinct from its owners, creditors, and customers. Note, however, that there is a difference between separate economic entity and separate legal entity.

S T O P • R E V I E W • A P P L Y

3-1. Use the terms *business transactions*, *money measure*, and *separate entity* in a single sentence that demonstrates their relevance to financial accounting.

3-2. Suppose you buy a disposable camera from **CVS**. From CVS's perspective, how would the terms *business transactions*, *money measure*, and *separate entity* relate to your purchase?

The Corporate Form of Business

LO4 Describe the characteristics of a corporation.

The three basic forms of business enterprise are the sole proprietorship, the partnership, and the corporation. The characteristics of corporations make them very efficient in amassing capital, which enables them to grow extremely large. As Figure 4 shows, even though corporations are fewer in number than sole proprietorships and partnerships, they contribute much more to

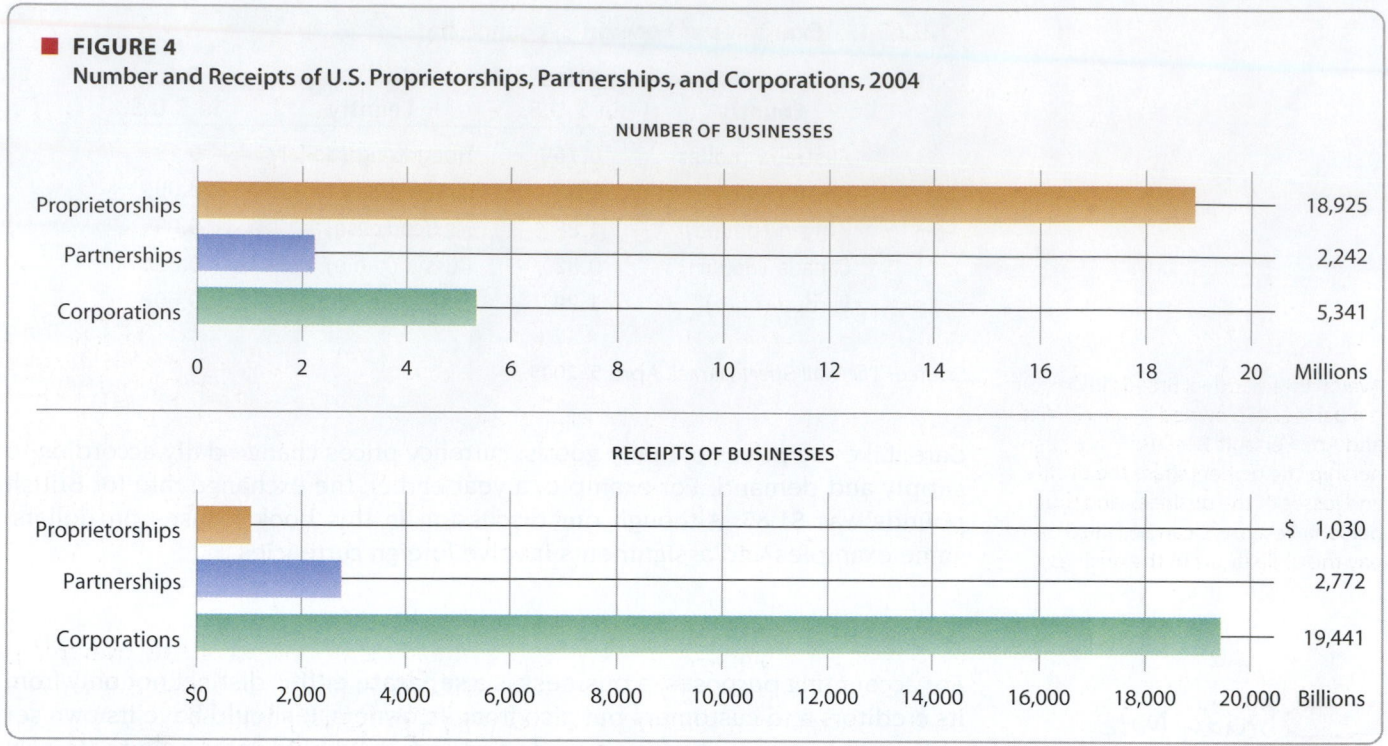

■ **FIGURE 4**
Number and Receipts of U.S. Proprietorships, Partnerships, and Corporations, 2004

Source: U.S. Treasury Department, Internal Revenue Service, *Statistics of Income Bulletin,* Fall 2004.

the U.S. economy in monetary terms. For example, in 2004, **Exxon Mobil** generated more revenues than all but 30 of the world's countries. Because of the economic significance of corporations, this book emphasizes accounting for the corporate form of business.

Characteristics of Corporations, Sole Proprietorships, and Partnerships

A **sole proprietorship** is a business owned by one person. The owner takes all the profits or losses of the business and is liable for all its obligations. Sole proprietorships represent the largest number of businesses in the United States, but typically they are the smallest in size.

A **partnership** is like a sole proprietorship in most ways, but it has two or more owners. The partners share the profits and losses of the business according to a prearranged formula. Generally, any partner can obligate the business to another party, and the personal resources of each partner can be called on

FOCUS ON BUSINESS PRACTICE

Are Most Corporations Big or Small Businesses?

Most people think of corporations as large national or global companies whose shares of stock are held by thousands of people and institutions. Indeed, corporations can be huge and have many stockholders. However, of the approximately 4 million corporations in the United States, only about 15,000 have stock that is publicly bought and sold. The vast majority of corporations are small businesses privately held by a few stockholders. Illinois alone has more than 250,000 corporations. Thus, the study of corporations is just as relevant to small businesses as it is to large ones.

Avalon International Breads in Detroit is a partnership owned by Jackie Victor and Ann Perrault. Because it is a partnership, the owners share the profits and losses of the business, and their personal resources can be called on to pay the obligations of the business.

 Study Note

A key disadvantage of a partnership is the unlimited liability of its owners. Unlimited liability can be avoided by organizing the business as a corporation or, in some states, by forming what is known as a limited liability partnership.

to pay the obligations. A partnership must be dissolved if the ownership changes, as when a partner leaves or dies. If the business is to continue as a partnership after this occurs, a new partnership must be formed.

Both the sole proprietorship and the partnership are convenient ways of separating the owners' commercial activities from their personal activities. Legally, however, there is no economic separation between the owners and the businesses.

A **corporation**, on the other hand, is a business unit chartered by the state and legally separate from its owners (the *stockholders*). The stockholders, whose ownership is represented by shares of stock, do not directly control the corporation's operations. Instead, they elect a board of directors to run the corporation for their benefit. In exchange for their limited involvement in the corporation's operations, stockholders enjoy limited liability; that is, their risk of loss is limited to the amount they paid for their shares. Thus, stockholders are often willing to invest in risky, but potentially profitable, activities. Also, because stockholders can sell their shares without dissolving the corporation, the life of a corporation is unlimited and not subject to the whims or health of a proprietor or a partner.

Formation of a Corporation

To form a corporation, most states require individuals, called incorporators, to sign an application and file it with the proper state official. This application contains the **articles of incorporation**. If approved by the state, these articles, which form the company charter, become a contract between the state and the incorporators. The company is then authorized to do business as a corporation.

Organization of a Corporation

The authority to manage a corporation is delegated by its stockholders to a board of directors and by the board of directors to the corporation's officers (see Figure 5). That is, the stockholders elect a board of directors, which sets corporate policies and chooses the corporation's officers, who in turn carry out the corporate policies in their management of the business.

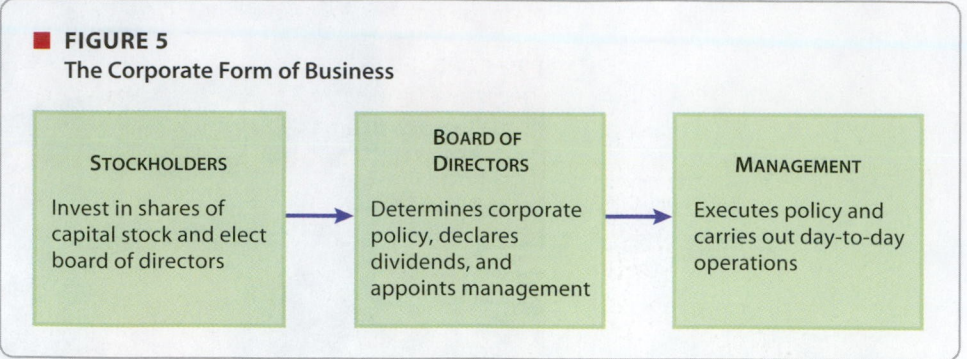

■ **FIGURE 5**
The Corporate Form of Business

Stockholders

A unit of ownership in a corporation is called a **share of stock**. The articles of incorporation state the maximum number of shares that a corporation is authorized to issue. The number of shares held by stockholders is the outstanding stock; this may be less than the number authorized in the articles of incorporation. To invest in a corporation, a stockholder transfers cash or other resources to the corporation. In return, the stockholder receives shares of stock representing a proportionate share of ownership in the corporation. Afterward, the stockholder may transfer the shares at will. Corporations may have more than one kind of stock, but in the first part of this book, we refer only to **common stock**—the most universal form of stock.

Board of Directors

As noted, a corporation's board of directors decides on major business policies. Among the board's specific duties are authorizing contracts, setting executive salaries, and arranging major loans with banks. The declaration of dividends is also an important function of the board of directors. **Dividends** are distributions of resources, generally in the form of cash, to stockholders, and only the board of directors has the authority to declare them. Paying dividends is one way of rewarding stockholders for their investment when the corporation has been successful in earning a profit. (The other way is through a rise in the market value of the stock.) Although there is usually a delay of two or three weeks between the time the board declares a dividend and the date of the actual payment, we assume in the early chapters of this book that declaration and payment are made on the same day.

The composition of the board of directors varies from company to company, but generally it includes several officers of the corporation and several outsiders. The outsiders are called *independent directors* because they do not directly participate in managing the business.

Management

Management, appointed by the board of directors to carry out corporate policies and run day-to-day operations, consists of the operating officers—generally the president, or chief executive officer; vice presidents; chief financial officer; and chief operating officer. Besides being responsible for running the business, management has the duty of reporting the financial results of its administration to the board of directors and the stockholders. Though management must, at a minimum, make a comprehensive annual report, it generally reports more often. The annual reports of large public corporations are available to the public. Excerpts from many of them appear throughout this book.

Corporate Governance

The financial scandals at **Enron, WorldCom**, and other companies highlighted the importance of **corporate governance**, which is the oversight of a corporation's management and ethics by its board of directors. Corporate governance is growing and is clearly in the best interests of a business. A recent survey of 124 corporations in 22 countries found that 78 percent of boards of directors had established ethical standards, a fourfold increase over a 10-year period. In addition, research has shown that, over time, companies with codes of ethics tend to have higher stock prices than those that have not adopted such codes.[9]

To strengthen corporate governance, a provision of the Sarbanes-Oxley Act required boards of directors to establish an **audit committee** made up of independent directors who have financial expertise. This provision was aimed at ensuring that boards of directors would be objective in evaluating management's performance. The audit committee is also responsible for engaging the corporation's independent auditors and reviewing their work. Another of the committee's functions is to ensure that adequate systems exist to safeguard the corporation's resources and that accounting records are reliable. In short, the audit committee is the front line of defense against fraudulent financial reporting.

S T O P • R E V I E W • A P P L Y

4-1. How do sole proprietorships, partnerships, and corporations differ?

4-2. What are the functions of a corporation's stockholders, board of directors, and management?

4-3. What is the role of a corporation's audit committee of the board of directors?

Financial Position and the Accounting Equation

LO5 Define *financial position,* and state the accounting equation.

Financial position refers to a company's economic resources, such as cash, inventory, and buildings, and the claims against those resources at a particular time. Another term for claims is *equities.*

Every corporation has two types of equities: creditors' equities, such as bank loans, and stockholders' equity. (In the case of sole proprietorships and partnerships, which do not have stockholders, stockholders' equity is called *owners' equity.*) The sum of these equities equals a corporation's resources:

Economic Resources = Creditors' Equities + Stockholders' Equity

In accounting terminology, economic resources are called *assets* and creditors' equities are called *liabilities.* So the equation can be written like this:

Assets = Liabilities + Stockholders' Equity

This equation is known as the **accounting equation**. The two sides of the equation must always be equal, or "in balance," as shown in Figure 6. To evaluate

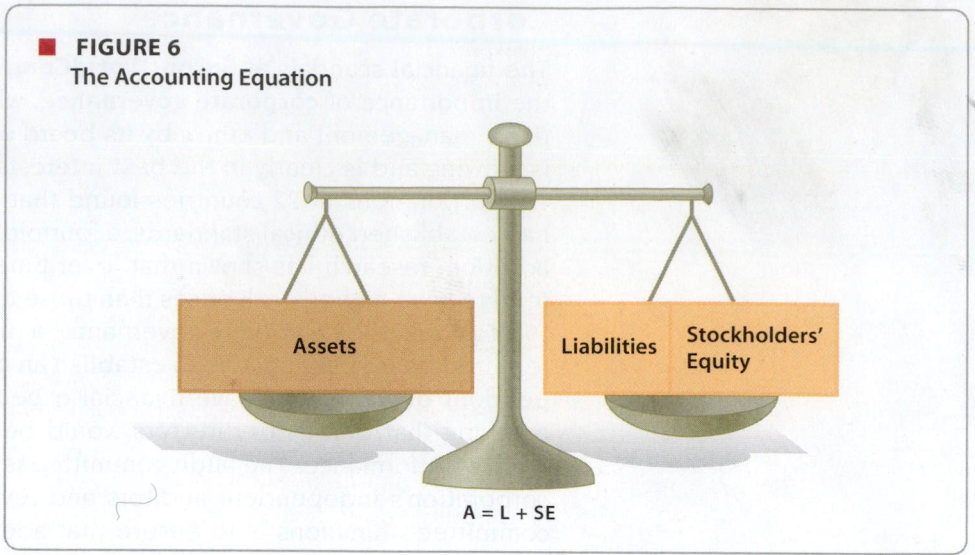

FIGURE 6
The Accounting Equation

Assets

Liabilities | Stockholders' Equity

A = L + SE

the financial effects of business activities, it is important to understand their effects on this equation.

Assets

Assets are the economic resources of a company that are expected to benefit the company's future operations. Certain kinds of assets—for example, cash and money that customers owe to the company (called *accounts receivable*)—are monetary items. Other assets—inventories (goods held for sale), land, buildings, and equipment—are nonmonetary, physical items. Still other assets—the rights granted by patents, trademarks, and copyrights—are nonphysical.

Liabilities

Liabilities are a business's present obligations to pay cash, transfer assets, or provide services to other entities in the future. Among these obligations are amounts owed to suppliers for goods or services bought on credit (called *accounts payable*), borrowed money (e.g., money owed on bank loans), salaries and wages owed to employees, taxes owed to the government, and services to be performed.

As debts, liabilities are claims recognized by law. That is, the law gives creditors the right to force the sale of a company's assets if the company fails to pay its debts. Creditors have rights over stockholders and must be paid in full before the stockholders receive anything, even if payment of the debt uses up all the assets of the business.

Stockholders' Equity

Stockholders' equity (also called *shareholders' equity*) represents the claims of the owners of a corporation (the shareholders) to the assets of the business. Theoretically, it is what would be left over if all liabilities were paid, and it is sometimes said to equal **net assets**. By rearranging the accounting equation, we can define stockholders' equity this way:

$$\text{Stockholders' Equity} = \text{Assets} - \text{Liabilities}$$

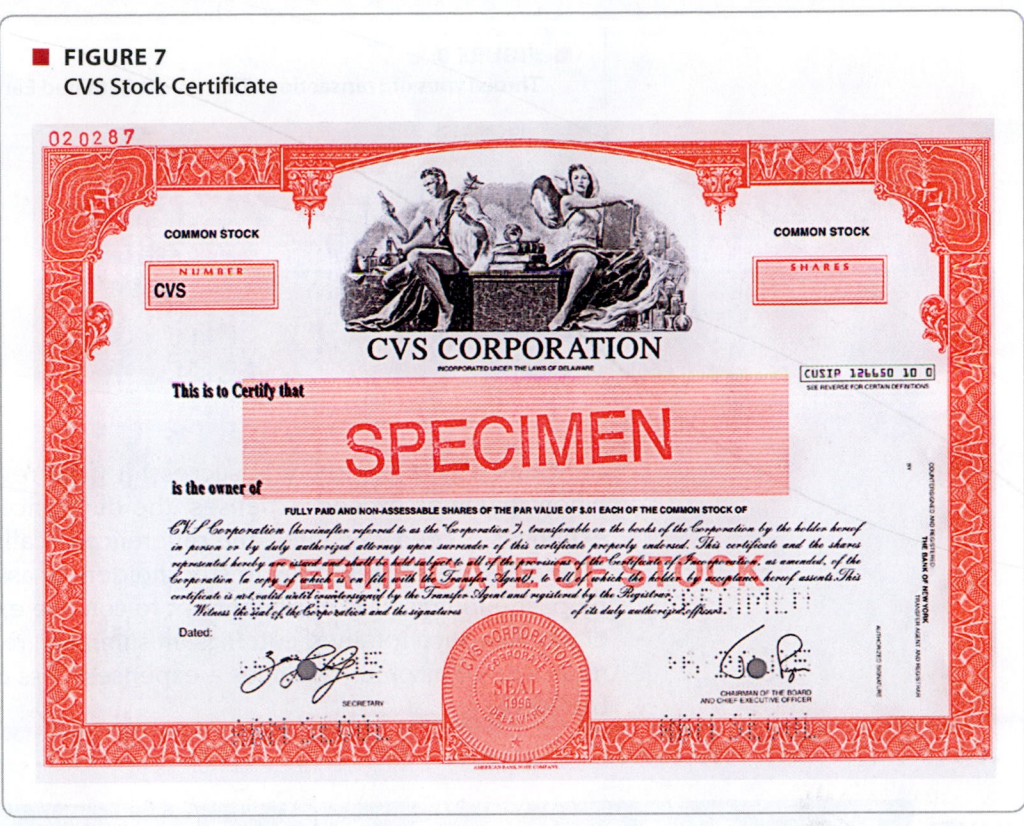

■ **FIGURE 7**
CVS Stock Certificate

Stockholders' equity has two parts, contributed capital and retained earnings:

Stockholders' Equity = Contributed Capital + Retained Earnings

Contributed capital is the amount that stockholders invest in the business. As noted earlier, their ownership in the business is represented by shares of capital stock. Figure 7 is a **CVS** stock certificate, which represents such ownership.

Typically, contributed capital is divided between par value and additional paid-in capital. **Par value** is an amount per share that when multiplied by the number of common shares becomes the corporation's common stock amount; it is the minimum amount that can be reported as contributed capital. When the value received is greater than par value, the amount over par value is called **additional paid-in capital**.*

Retained earnings represent stockholders' equity that has been generated by the business' income-producing activities and kept for use in the business. As you can see in Figure 8, retained earnings are affected by three kinds of transactions: revenues, expenses, and dividends.

Simply stated, **revenues** and **expenses** are the increases and decreases in stockholders' equity that result from operating a business. For example, the amount a customer pays (or agrees to pay in the future) to **CVS** in return for a product or service is a revenue to CVS. CVS's assets (cash or accounts receivable) increase, as does its stockholders' equity in those assets. On the other hand, the amount CVS must pay out (or agree to pay out) so that it can provide a product or service is an expense. In this case, the assets (cash) decrease or the liabilities (accounts payable) increase, and the stockholders' equity decreases.

---

*We assume in the early chapters of this book that common stock is listed at par value.

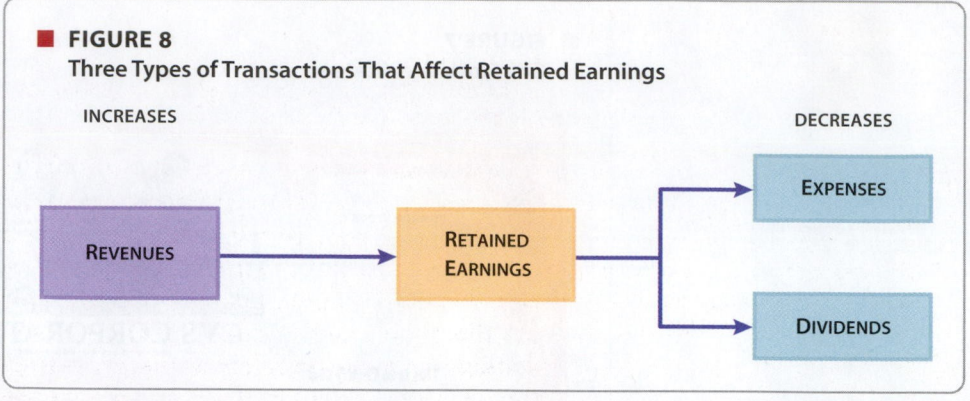

■ **FIGURE 8**
Three Types of Transactions That Affect Retained Earnings

Generally, a company is successful if its revenues exceed its expenses. When revenues exceed expenses, the difference is called **net income**. When expenses exceed revenues, the difference is called **net loss**. As noted earlier, dividends are distributions to stockholders of assets (usually cash) generated by past earnings. It is important not to confuse expenses and dividends, both of which reduce retained earnings. In summary, retained earnings are the accumulated net income (revenues – expenses) less dividends over the life of the business.

S T O P • R E V I E W • A P P L Y

5-1. What are assets?

5-2. How are liabilities and stockholders' equity similar, and how do they differ?

5-3. What three elements affect retained earnings, and what is the effect of each?

5-4. Give an example of a single transaction that causes both an increase and decrease in assets.

The Accounting Equation and Net Income   Johnson Company had assets of $140,000 and liabilities of $60,000 at the beginning of the year, and assets of $200,000 and liabilities of $70,000 at the end of the year. During the year, $20,000 was invested in the business, and dividends of $24,000 were paid. What amount of net income did the company earn during the year?

Beginning of the year

Assets	=	Liabilities	+	Stockholders' Equity
$140,000	=	$60,000	+	$ 80,000

During year

	Investment	+	20,000
	Dividends	–	24,000
	Net income		?

End of year

$200,000	=	$70,000	+	$130,000

SOLUTION

Net income = $54,000

Start by finding the stockholders' equity at the beginning of the year. (Check: $140,000 – $60,000 = $80,000)

Then find the stockholders' equity at the end of the year. (Check: $200,000 – $70,000 = $130,000)

Then determine net income by calculating how the transactions during the year led to the stockholders' equity amount at the end of the year. (Check: $80,000 + $20,000 – $24,000 + $54,000 = $130,000)

Financial Statements

LO6 Identify the four basic financial statements.

> **Study Note**
>
> Businesses use four basic financial statements to communicate financial information to decision makers.

Financial statements are the primary means of communicating important accounting information about a business to those who have an interest in the business. These statements are models of the business enterprise in that they show the business in financial terms. As is true of all models, however, financial statements are not perfect pictures of the real thing. Rather, they are the accountant's best effort to represent what is real. Four major financial statements are used to communicate accounting information about a business: the income statement, the statement of retained earnings, the balance sheet, and the statement of cash flows.

Income Statement

The **income statement** summarizes the revenues earned and expenses incurred by a business over an accounting period (see Exhibit 1). Many people consider it the most important financial report because it shows whether a business achieved its profitability goal—that is, whether it earned an acceptable income. Exhibit 1 shows that Ramirez Agency, Inc., had revenues in the form of commissions earned of $7,000. From this amount, total expenses of $2,800 were deducted (equipment rental expense of $1,400, wages expense of $800, and utilities expense of $600) to arrive at income before income taxes of $4,200. Income taxes of $600 were deducted to arrive at net income of $3,600. To show the period to which the statement applies, it is dated "For the Month Ended December 31, 20xx."

Statement of Retained Earnings

The **statement of retained earnings** shows the changes in retained earnings over an accounting period. In Exhibit 2, beginning retained earnings are zero because Ramirez began operations in this accounting period. During the

EXHIBIT 1 ▶ **Income Statement for Ramirez Agency, Inc.**

Ramirez Agency, Inc.
Income Statement
For the Month Ended December 31, 20xx

Revenues		
Commissions earned		$7,000
Expenses		
Equipment rental expense	$1,400	
Wages expense	800	
Utilities expense	600	
Total expenses		2,800
Income before income taxes		$4,200
Income taxes expense		600
Net income		$3,600

EXHIBIT 2 ▶

Statement of Retained Earnings for Ramirez Agency, Inc.

Ramirez Agency, Inc.
Statement of Retained Earnings
For the Month Ended December 31, 20xx

Retained earnings, December 1, 20xx	$ 0
Net income for the month	3,600
Subtotal	$3,600
Less dividends	1,200
Retained earnings, December 31, 20xx	$2,400

month, the company earned an income (as shown on the income statement) of $3,600. Deducted from this amount are the dividends for the month of $1,200, leaving an ending balance of $2,400 of earnings retained in the business.

The Balance Sheet

Study Note

The date on the balance sheet is a single date, whereas the dates on the other three statements cover a period of time, such as a month, quarter, or year.

The purpose of a **balance sheet** is to show the financial position of a business on a certain date, usually the end of the month or year (see Exhibit 3). For this reason, it often is called the *statement of financial position* and is dated as of a specific date. The balance sheet presents a view of the business as the holder of resources, or assets, that are equal to the claims against those assets. The claims consist of the company's liabilities and the stockholders' equity in the company. Exhibit 3 shows that Ramirez Agency has several categories of assets, which total $103,600. These assets equal the total liabilities of $1,200 (accounts payable) plus the ending balance of stockholders' equity of $102,400. Notice that the amount of retained earnings on the balance sheet comes from the ending balance on the statement of retained earnings.

Statement of Cash Flows

Whereas the income statement focuses on a company's profitability, the **statement of cash flows** focuses on its liquidity (see Exhibit 4). **Cash flows** are the inflows and outflows of cash into and out of a business. Net cash flows are

▼ EXHIBIT 3

Balance Sheet for Ramirez Agency, Inc.

Ramirez Agency, Inc.
Balance Sheet
December 31, 20xx

Assets		Liabilities		
Cash	$ 30,600	Accounts payable		$ 1,200
Accounts receivable	2,000			
Supplies	1,000	**Stockholders' Equity**		
Land	20,000	Common stock	$100,000	
Building	50,000	Retained earnings	2,400	
		Total stockholders' equity		102,400
Total assets	$103,600	Total liabilities and stockholders' equity		$103,600

▼ **EXHIBIT 1**

Statement of Cash Flows for Ramirez Agency, Inc.

Ramirez Agency, Inc.
Statement of Cash Flows
For the Month Ended December 31, 20xx

Cash flows from operating activities

Net income		$ 3,600
Adjustments to reconcile net income to net cash flows from operating activities		
Increase in accounts receivable	($ 2,000)	
Increase in supplies	(1,000)	
Increase in accounts payable	1,200	(1,800)
Net cash flows from operating activities		$ 1,800
Cash flows from investing activities		
Purchase of land	($ 20,000)	
Purchase of building	(50,000)	
Net cash flows from investing activities		(70,000)
Cash flows from financing activities		
Investments by stockholders	$100,000	
Dividends	(1,200)	
Net cash flows from financing activities		98,800
Net increase (decrease) in cash		$30,600
Cash at beginning of month		0
Cash at end of month		$30,600

Note: Parentheses indicate a negative amount.

Study Note

The purpose of the statement of cash flows is to explain the change in cash in terms of operating, investing, and financing activities over an accounting period. It provides valuable information that cannot be determined in an examination of the other financial statements.

the difference between the inflows and outflows. The statement of cash flows shows the cash produced by business operations during an accounting period as well as important investing and financing transactions that took place during the period. Notice that the statement of cash flows in Exhibit 4 explains how Ramirez Agency's cash balance changed during the period. Cash increased by $30,600. Operating activities produced net cash flows of $1,800, and financing activities produced net cash flows of $98,800. Investing activities used cash flows of $70,000.

The statement of cash flows is related directly to the other three financial statements. Notice that net income comes from the income statement and that dividends come from the statement of retained earnings. The other items in the statement represent changes in the balance sheet accounts: accounts receivable, supplies, accounts payable, land, building, and common stock. Here we focus on the importance and overall structure of the statement. Its construction and use are discussed in a later chapter.

Relationships Among the Financial Statements

Exhibit 5 illustrates the relationships among the four financial statements by showing how they would appear for Ramirez Agency. The period covered is the month of December 20xx. Notice the similarity of the headings at the top of each statement. Each identifies the company and the kind of statement. The income statement, the statement of retained earnings, and the statement of

▼ **EXHIBIT 5**

Income Statement, Statement of Retained Earnings, Balance Sheet, and Statement of Cash Flows for Ramirez Agency, Inc.

Ramirez Agency, Inc.
Income Statement
For the Month Ended December 31, 20xx

Revenues		
Commissions earned		$7,000
Expenses		
Equipment rental expense	$1,400	
Wages expense	800	
Utilities expense	600	
Total expenses		2,800
Income before income taxes		$4,200
Income taxes expense		600
Net income		$3,600

Ramirez Agency, Inc.
Statement of Retained Earnings
For the Month Ended December 31, 20xx

Retained earnings, December 1, 20xx	$ 0
Net income for the month	3,600
Subtotal	$3,600
Less dividends	1,200
Retained earnings, December 31, 20xx	$2,400

Ramirez Agency, Inc.
Statement of Cash Flows
For the Month Ended December 31, 20xx

Cash flows from operating activities		
Net income		$ 3,600
Adjustments to reconcile net income to net cash flows from operating activities		
Increase in accounts receivable	($ 2,000)	
Increase in supplies	(1,000)	
Increase in accounts payable	1,200	(1,800)
Net cash flows from operating activities		$ 1,800
Cash flows from investing activities		
Purchase of land	($ 20,000)	
Purchase of building	(50,000)	
Net cash flows from investing activities		(70,000)
Cash flows from financing activities		
Investments by stockholders	$100,000	
Dividends	(1,200)	
Net cash flows from financing activities		98,800
Net increase (decrease) in cash		$30,600
Cash at beginning of month		0
Cash at end of month		$30,600

Ramirez Agency, Inc.
Balance Sheet
December 31, 20xx

Assets		Liabilities	
Cash	$ 30,600	Accounts payable	$ 1,200
Accounts receivable	2,000		
Supplies	1,000	**Stockholders' Equity**	
Land	20,000	Common stock	$100,000
Building	50,000	Retained earnings	2,400
		Total stockholders' equity	$102,400
		Total liabilities and	
Total assets	$103,600	stockholders' equity	$103,600

Study Note

Notice the sequence in which these financial statements must be prepared. The statement of retained earnings is a link between the income statement and the balance sheet, and the statement of cash flows is prepared last.

cash flows indicate the period to which they apply; the balance sheet gives the specific date to which it applies. Much of this book deals with developing, using, and interpreting more complete versions of these statements.

S T O P • R E V I E W • A P P L Y

6-1. What is the purpose of the statement of retained earnings?

6-2. Why is the balance sheet sometimes called the statement of financial position?

6-3. Contrast the purposes of the balance sheet and the income statement.

6-4. A statement for an accounting period that ends in June can be headed "June 30, 20xx" or "For the month ended June 30, 20xx." Which heading is appropriate for (a) a balance sheet and (b) an income statement?

6-5. How do the income statement and the statement of cash flows differ?

Interrelationship of the Financial Statements Complete the following financial statements by determining the amounts that correspond to the letters. (Assume no new investments by stockholders.)

Income Statement	
Revenues	$2,775
Expenses	(a)
Net income	$ (b)

Statement of Retained Earnings	
Beginning balance	$7,250
Net income	(c)
Less dividends	500
Ending balance	$7,500

Balance Sheet	
Total assets	$ (d)
Liabilities	$4,000
Stockholders' equity	
Common stock	5,000
Retained earnings	(e)
Total liabilities and stockholders' equity	$ (f)

SOLUTION

Net income links the income statement and the statement of retained earnings. The ending balance of retained earnings links the statement of retained earnings and the balance sheet.

Thus, start with (c), which must equal $750 (check: $7,250 + $750 − $500 = $7,500). Then, (b) equals (c), or $750. Thus, (a) must equal $2,025 (check: $2,775 − $2,025 = $750). Because (e) equals $7,500 (ending balance from the statement of retained earnings), (f) must equal $16,500 (check: $4,000 + $5,000 + $7,500 = $16,500). Now, (d) equals (f), or $16,500.

Generally Accepted Accounting Principles

LO7 Explain how generally accepted accounting principles (GAAP) relate to financial statements and the independent CPA's report, and identify the organizations that influence GAAP.

To ensure that financial statements are understandable to their users, a set of practices, called **generally accepted accounting principles (GAAP)**, has been developed to provide guidelines for financial accounting.

TABLE 2. Large International Certified Public Accounting Firms		
Firm	**Home Office**	**Some Major Clients**
Deloitte & Touche	New York	General Motors, Procter & Gamble
Ernst & Young	New York	Coca-Cola, McDonald's
KPMG	New York	General Electric, Xerox
PricewaterhouseCoopers	New York	Exxon Mobil, IBM, Ford

Although the term has several meanings in the literature of accounting, perhaps this is the best definition: "Generally accepted accounting principles encompass the conventions, rules, and procedures necessary to define accepted accounting practice at a particular time."[10] In other words, GAAP arise from wide agreement on the theory and practice of accounting at a particular time. These "principles" are not like the unchangeable laws of nature in chemistry or physics. They evolve to meet the needs of decision makers, and they change as circumstances change or as better methods are developed.

In this book, we present accounting practice, or GAAP, as it is today,* and we try to explain the reasons or theory on which the practice is based. Both theory and practice are important to the study of accounting. However, accounting is a discipline that is always growing, changing, and improving. Just as years of research are necessary before a new surgical method or lifesaving drug can be introduced, it may take years for new accounting discoveries to be implemented. As a result, you may encounter practices that seem contradictory. In some cases, we point out new directions in accounting. Your instructor also may mention certain weaknesses in current theory or practice.

GAAP and the Independent CPA's Report

Because financial statements are prepared by management and could be falsified for personal gain, all companies that sell shares of their stock to the public and many companies that apply for sizable loans have their financial statements audited by an independent **certified public accountant (CPA)**. *Independent* means that the CPA is not an employee of the company being audited and has no financial or other compromising ties with it. CPAs are licensed by all states for the same reason that lawyers and doctors are—to protect the public by ensuring the quality of professional service. The firms listed in Table 2 employ about 25 percent of all CPAs.

An **audit** is an examination of a company's financial statements and the accounting systems, controls, and records that produced them. The purpose of the audit is to ascertain that the financial statements have been prepared in accordance with generally accepted accounting principles. If the independent CPA is satisfied that this standard has been met, his or her report contains the following language:

> In our opinion, the financial statements . . . present fairly, in all material respects . . . in conformity with generally accepted accounting principles . . .

This wording emphasizes that accounting and auditing are not exact sciences. Because the framework of GAAP provides room for interpretation and the appli-

Study Note

The purpose of an audit is to lend credibility to a set of financial statements. The auditor does *not* attest to the absolute accuracy of the published information or to the value of the company as an investment. All he or she renders is an opinion, based on appropriate testing, about the fairness of the presentation of the financial information.

---

*In May 2005, the AICPA passed a resolution to start working with the FASB to develop GAAP for privately held, for-profit companies, which would result in recognition, measurement, and disclosure differences, where appropriate, from current GAAP for public companies. If and when this resolution is acted upon, two sets of GAAP will exist: one for private companies and one for public companies.

Accountants from Ernst & Young arrive at the 55th Annual Emmy Awards at the Shrine Auditorium, Los Angeles, September 2003. The independent accounting firm receives and tallies the votes. *Independent* means that the firm has no financial or other compromising ties with the Academy of Television Arts & Sciences, the organization that presents the Emmy Awards.

cation of GAAP necessitates the making of estimates, the auditor can render only an opinion about whether the financial statements *present fairly* or conform *in all material respects* to GAAP. The auditor's report does not preclude minor or immaterial errors in the financial statements. However, a favorable report from the auditor does imply that on the whole, investors and creditors can rely on the financial statements.

Historically, auditors have enjoyed a strong reputation for competence and independence. As a result, banks, investors, and creditors are willing to rely on an auditor's opinion when deciding to invest in a company or to make loans to it. The independent audit has been an important factor in the worldwide growth of financial markets.

Organizations That Influence GAAP

Many organizations directly or indirectly influence GAAP and so influence much of what is in this book.

The **Public Company Accounting Oversight Board (PCAOB)**, a governmental body created by the Sarbanes-Oxley Act, regulates the accounting profession and has wide powers to determine the standards that auditors must follow and to discipline them if they do not.

The **Financial Accounting Standards Board (FASB)** is the most important body for developing rules on accounting practice. This independent body has been designated by the Securities and Exchange Commission (SEC) to issue the *Statements of Financial Accounting Standards*.

The **American Institute of Certified Public Accountants (AICPA)**, the professional association of certified public accountants, influences accounting practice through the activities of its senior technical committees.

The **Securities and Exchange Commission (SEC)** is an agency of the federal government that has the legal power to set and enforce accounting practices for companies whose securities are offered for sale to the general public. As such, it has enormous influence on accounting practice.

The **Governmental Accounting Standards Board (GASB)**, which was established in 1984 under the same governing body as the FASB, is responsible for issuing accounting standards for state and local governments.

Study Note

The FASB is the primary source of GAAP.

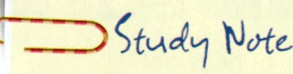

Study Note

The AICPA is the primary professional organization of certified public accountants.

With the growth of financial markets throughout the world, global cooperation in the development of accounting principles has become a priority. The **International Accounting Standards Board (IASB)** has approved more than 40 international standards.

U.S. tax laws that govern the assessment and collection of revenue for operating the federal government also influence accounting practice. Because a major source of the government's revenue is the income tax, the tax laws specify the rules for determining taxable income. The **Internal Revenue Service (IRS)** interprets and enforces these rules. In some cases, the rules conflict with good accounting practice, but they are nonetheless an important influence on practice. Cases in which the tax laws affect accounting practice are noted throughout this book.

Professional Ethics

Professional ethics are key to the accountant's reputation for independence and competence. The code of professional ethics of the American Institute of Certified Public Accountants (and adopted, with variations, by each state) governs the conduct of CPAs. Fundamental to this code is responsibility to clients, creditors, investors, and anyone else who relies on the work of a CPA. The code requires CPAs to act with integrity, objectivity, and independence.

▶ **Integrity** means the accountant is honest and candid and subordinates personal gain to service and the public trust.

▶ **Objectivity** means the accountant is impartial and intellectually honest.

▶ **Independence** means the accountant avoids all relationships that impair or even appear to impair his or her objectivity.

The accountant must also exercise **due care** in all activities, carrying out professional responsibilities with competence and diligence. For example, an accountant must not accept a job for which he or she is not qualified, even at the risk of losing a client to another firm, and careless work is unacceptable. These broad principles are supported by more specific rules that public accountants must follow; for instance, with certain exceptions, client information must be kept strictly confidential. Accountants who violate the rules can be disciplined or even suspended from practice.

The **Institute of Management Accountants (IMA)** also has a code of professional conduct. It emphasizes that management accountants have a responsibility to be competent in their jobs, to keep information confidential except when authorized or legally required to disclose it, to maintain integrity and avoid conflicts of interest, and to communicate information objectively and without bias.[11]

 *Study Note*

The IMA is the primary professional associate of management accountants.

S T O P • R E V I E W • A P P L Y

7-1. What are GAAP? Why are they important to readers of financial statements?

7-2. As used in an auditor's report, what does *in all material respects* mean?

7-3. What is the PCAOB, and why is it important?

7-4. What organization has the most influence on GAAP?

7-5. Why are codes of ethics important in the accounting profession?

CVS CORPORATION

The Decision Point at the beginning of this chapter focused on **CVS**, a successful nationwide chain of more than 5,000 drugstores. It posed these questions:

- **Is CVS meeting its goal of profitability?**
- **As a manager at CVS, what financial knowledge would you need to measure progress toward the company's goals?**
- **As a potential investor or creditor, what financial knowledge would you need to evaluate CVS's financial performance?**

As you've learned in this chapter, managers and others with an interest in a business measure its profitability in financial terms, such as net sales, net income, total assets, and stockholders' equity. Managers report on the progress they have made toward their financial goals in their company's financial statements.

As you can see in the highlights from CVS's financial statements, the company's net sales, net earnings (net income), total assets, and stockholders' equity have increased over the years.[12] But how do we use these data to determine if CVS is meeting its goal of profitability?

> **Study Note**
>
> Most companies list the most recent year of information in the first column, as shown here.

CVS'S FINANCIAL HIGHLIGHTS
(In millions)

	2004	2003	2002
Net sales	**$30,594.3**	$26,588.0	$24,181.5
Net earnings	**918.8**	847.3	716.6
Total assets	**14,546.8**	10,543.1	9,645.3
Stockholders' equity	**6,987.2**	6,021.8	5,197.0

As mentioned earlier in the chapter, one way to measure financial performance is through ratios. Ratios are used to compare a company's financial performance from one year to the next and to make comparisons among companies. The ratio that tells us if CVS is meeting its goal of profitability is the **return on assets** ratio. This ratio shows how efficiently a company is using its assets to produce income.

We use two values to calculate return on assets: net income, which is what is left over after expenses are subtracted from revenues (see the income statement in Exhibit 1), and average total assets. Average total assets are the total of this year's assets plus last year's assets divided by two (see the balance sheet in Exhibit 3).

The return on assets ratio for CVS is calculated as follows (amounts are in millions):

	2004	2003
$\dfrac{\text{Net Income}}{\text{Average Total Assets}}$	$\dfrac{\$918.8}{(\$14,546.8 + \$10,543.1) \div 2}$	$\dfrac{\$847.3}{(\$10,543.1 + \$9,645.3) \div 2}$
	$\dfrac{\$918.8}{\$12,545.0}$	$\dfrac{\$847.3}{\$10,094.2}$
Return on Assets:	.073 × 100 = 7.3%	.084 × 100 = 8.4%

We can draw several conclusions from this ratio. First, CVS earned 7.3 to 8.4 cents on each dollar it invested in assets. Second, from 2003 to 2004, its profitability declined from 8.4 to 7.3 percent. Third, CVS is a growing company as demonstrated by the increases in its net sales, net earnings, total assets, and stockholders' equity in every year of the three-year period. These amounts indicate that CVS is a profitable and successful company but faces challenges in maintaining its profitability. You will learn much more about ratios in the chapters that follow.

If you aspire to be a manager of a business, an accountant, an investor, a business owner, or just a good employee, you will need to be familiar with measures like the return on assets ratio. You will also need to master other accounting concepts and terminology and know how financial information is produced, interpreted, and analyzed. The purpose of this book is to help you acquire that knowledge.

CHAPTER REVIEW

REVIEW of Learning Objectives

LO1 Define *accounting* and describe its role in making informed decisions, identify business goals and activities, and explain the importance of ethics in accounting.

Accounting is an information system that measures, processes, and communicates financial information about an economic entity. It provides the information necessary to make reasoned choices among alternative uses of scarce resources in the conduct of business and economic activities. A business is an economic entity that engages in operating, investing, and financing activities to achieve the goals of profitability and liquidity.

Management accounting focuses on the preparation of information primarily for internal use by management. Financial accounting is concerned with the development and use of reports that are communicated to those outside the business as well as to management. Ethical financial reporting is important to the well-being of a company; fraudulent financial reports can have serious consequences for many people.

LO2 Identify the users of accounting information.

Accounting plays a significant role in society by providing information to managers of all institutions and to individuals with a direct financial interest in those institutions, including present or potential investors and creditors. Accounting information is also important to those with an indirect financial interest in the business—for example, tax authorities, regulatory agencies, and economic planners.

LO3 Explain the importance of business transactions, money measure, and separate entity.

To make an accounting measurement, the accountant must determine what is measured, when the measurement should be made, what value should be placed on what is measured, and how to classify what is measured. The objects of accounting measurement are business transactions. Financial accounting uses money measure to gauge the impact of these transactions on a separate business entity.

LO4 Describe the characteristics of a corporation.

Corporations, whose ownership is represented by shares of stock, are separate entities for both legal and accounting purposes. The stockholders own the corporation and elect the board of directors. The board is responsible for determining corporate policies and appointing corporate officers, or top managers, to operate the business in accordance with the policies that it sets. The board is also responsible for corporate governance, the oversight of a corporation's management and ethics. The audit committee, which is appointed by the board and is made up of independent directors, is an important factor in corporate governance.

LO5 Define *financial position,* and state the accounting equation.

Financial position refers to a company's economic resources and the claims against those resources at a particular time. The accounting equation shows financial position as Assets = Liabilities + Stockholders' Equity. (In the case of sole proprietorships and partnerships, stockholders' equity is called *owners' equity*.) Business transactions affect financial position by decreasing or increasing assets, liabilities, and stockholders' (or owners') equity in such a way that the accounting equation is always in balance.

LO6 Identify the four basic financial statements.

The four basic financial statements are the income statement, the statement of retained earnings, the balance sheet, and the statement of cash flows. They are the primary means by which accountants communicate the financial condition and activities of a business to those who have an interest in the business.

LO7 Explain how generally accepted accounting principles (GAAP) relate to financial statements and the independent CPA's report, and identify the organizations that influence GAAP.

Acceptable accounting practice consists of the conventions, rules, and procedures that make up generally accepted accounting principles at a particular time. GAAP are essential to the preparation and interpretation of financial statements and the independent CPA's report.

Among the organizations that influence the formulation of GAAP are the Public Company Accounting Oversight Board, the Financial Accounting Standards Board, the American Institute of Certified Public Accountants, the Securities and Exchange Commission, and the Internal Revenue Service.

All accountants must follow a code of professional ethics, which is based on responsibility to the public. Accountants must act with integrity, objectivity, and independence, and they must exercise due care in all their activities.

REVIEW of Concepts and Terminology

The following concepts and terms were introduced in this chapter:

Accounting: An information system that measures, processes, and communicates financial information about an economic entity. **(LO1)**

Accounting equation: Assets = Liabilities + Stockholders' (or Owners') Equity. **(LO5)**

Additional paid-in capital: The amount over par value in a corporation's contributed capital. **(LO5)**

American Institute of Certified Public Accountants (AICPA): The professional association of certified public accountants. **(LO7)**

Articles of incorporation: An official document filed with and approved by a state that authorizes the incorporators to do business as a corporation. **(LO4)**

Assets: The economic resources of a company that are expected to benefit future operations. **(LO5)**

Audit: An examination of a company's financial statements in order to render an independent professional opinion about whether they have been presented fairly, in all material respects, in conformity with generally accepted accounting principles. **(LO7)**

Audit committee: A subgroup of a corporation's board of directors that is charged with ensuring that the board will be objective in reviewing management's performance; it engages the company's independent auditors and reviews their work. **(LO4)**

Balance sheet: The financial statement that shows a business's assets, liabilities, and stockholders' equity as of a specific date. Also called the *statement of financial position*. **(LO6)**

Bookkeeping: The process of recording financial transactions and keeping financial records. **(LO1)**

Business: An economic unit that aims to sell goods and services to customers at prices that will provide an adequate return to its owners. **(LO1)**

Business transactions: Economic events that affect a business's financial position. **(LO3)**

Cash flows: The inflows and outflows of cash into and out of a business. **(LO6)**

Certified public accountant (CPA): A public accountant who has met stringent state licensing requirements. **(LO7)**

Common stock: The most common form of stock. **(LO4)**

Computer: An electronic tool for the rapid collection, organization, and communication of large amounts of information. **(LO1)**

Contributed capital: The part of stockholders' equity that represents the amount invested in the business by the owners (stockholders). **(LO5)**

Corporate governance: The oversight of a corporation's management and ethics by the board of directors. **(LO4)**

Corporation: A business unit granted a state charter recognizing it as a separate legal entity having its own rights, privileges, and liabilities distinct from those of its owners. **(LO4)**

Dividends: Distributions to stockholders of assets (usually cash) generated by past earnings. **(LO4)**

Due care: Competence and diligence in carrying out professional responsibilities. **(LO7)**

Ethics: A code of conduct that addresses whether actions are right or wrong. **(LO1)**

Exchange rate: The value of one currency in terms of another. **(LO3)**

Expenses: Decreases in stockholders' equity that result from operating a business. **(LO5)**

Financial accounting: The process of generating and communicating accounting information in the form of financial statements to those outside the organization. **(LO1)**

Financial Accounting Standards Board (FASB): The most important body for developing rules on accounting practice; it issues *Statements of Financial Accounting Standards*. **(LO7)**

Financial position: The economic resources that belong to a company and the claims (equities) against those resources at a particular time. **(LO5)**

Financial statements: The primary means of communicating important accounting information to users. They include the income statement, statement of retained earnings, balance sheet, and statement of cash flows. **(LO1)**

Financing activities: Activities undertaken by management to obtain adequate funds to begin and to continue operating a business. **(LO1)**

Fraudulent financial reporting: The intentional preparation of misleading financial statements. **(LO1)**

Generally accepted accounting principles (GAAP): The conventions, rules, and procedures that define accepted accounting practice at a particular time. **(LO7)**

Governmental Accounting Standards Board (GASB): The board responsible for issuing accounting standards for state and local governments. **(LO7)**

Income statement: A financial statement that summarizes the revenues earned and expenses incurred by a business over an accounting period. **(LO6)**

Independence: The avoidance of all relationships that impair or appear to impair an accountant's objectivity. **(LO7)**

Institute of Management Accountants (IMA): A professional organization made up primarily of management accountants. **(LO7)**

Integrity: Honesty, candidness, and the subordination of personal gain to service and the public trust. **(LO7)**

Internal Revenue Service (IRS): The agency that interprets and enforces the tax laws governing the assessment and collection of revenue for operating the federal government. **(LO7)**

International Accounting Standards Board (IASB): An organization that encourages worldwide cooperation in the development of accounting principles; it has approved more than 40 international standards of accounting. **(LO7)**

Investing activities: Activities undertaken by management to spend capital in productive ways that will help a business achieve its objectives. **(LO1)**

Liabilities: A business's present obligations to pay cash, transfer assets, or provide services to other entities in the future. **(LO5)**

Liquidity: Having enough cash available to pay debts when they are due. **(LO1)**

Management: The people who have overall responsibility for operating a business and meeting its goals. **(LO2)**

Management accounting: The process of producing accounting information for internal use by managers. **(LO1)**

Management information system (MIS): The interconnected subsystems that provide the information needed to run a business. **(LO1)**

Money measure: The recording of all business transactions in terms of money. **(LO3)**

Net assets: Assets minus liabilities; stockholders' equity or owners' equity. **(LO5)**

Net income: The difference between revenues and expenses when revenues exceed expenses. **(LO5)**

Net loss: The difference between expenses and revenues when expenses exceed revenues. **(LO5)**

Objectivity: Impartiality and intellectual honesty. **(LO7)**

Operating activities: Activities undertaken by management in the course of running a business. **(LO1)**

Partnership: A business that is owned by two or more people and that is not incorporated. **(LO4)**

Par value: An amount per share that is entered in the corporation's capital stock account; it is the minimum amount that can be reported as contributed capital. **(LO5)**

Performance measures: Indicators of whether managers are achieving business goals and whether business activities are well managed. **(LO1)**

Professional ethics: A code of conduct that applies to the practice of a profession. **(LO7)**

Profitability: The ability to earn enough income to attract and hold investment capital. **(LO1)**

Public Company Accounting Oversight Board (PCAOB): A governmental body created by the Sarbanes-Oxley Act to regulate the accounting profession. **(LO7)**

Retained earnings: Stockholders' equity that has been generated by business operations and kept for use in the business. **(LO5)**

Revenues: Increases in stockholders' equity that result from operating a business. **(LO5)**

Sarbanes-Oxley Act: An act of Congress that regulates financial reporting in public corporations. **(LO1)**

Securities and Exchange Commission (SEC): A governmental agency that regulates the issuing, buying, and selling of stocks. It has the legal power to set and enforce accounting practices for firms whose securities are sold to the general public. **(LO2)**

Separate entity: A business that is treated as distinct from its creditors, customers, and owners. **(LO3)**

Share of stock: A unit of ownership in a corporation. **(LO4)**

Sole proprietorship: A business that is owned by one person and that is not incorporated. **(LO4)**

Statement of cash flows: A financial statement that shows the inflows and outflows of cash from operating activities, investing activities, and financing activities over an accounting period. **(LO6)**

Statement of retained earnings: A financial statement that shows the changes in retained earnings over an accounting period. **(LO6)**

Stockholders' equity: The claims of the owners of a corporation to the assets of the business; Contributed Capital + Retained Earnings. Also called *shareholders' equity* and *owners' equity*. **(LO5)**

Key Ratio

Return on assets: A ratio that shows how efficiently a company is using its assets to produce income; Net Income ÷ Average Total Assets.

REVIEW Problem

LO6 **Preparation and Interpretation of Financial Statements**

The following financial statement accounts and amounts are from the records of Jackson Realty for the year ended April 30, 20x7, the company's first year of operations:

Accounts payable	$ 19,000
Accounts receivable	104,000
Cash	90,000
Commissions earned	375,000
Common stock	100,000
Dividends	10,000
Equipment	47,000
Income taxes expense	27,000
Income taxes payable	6,000
Marketing expense	18,000
Office and equipment rent expense	91,000
Salaries and commission expense	172,000
Salaries payable	78,000
Supplies	2,000
Supplies expense	6,000
Utilities expense	11,000

Required

1. Prepare an income statement, statement of retained earnings, balance sheet, and statement of cash flows for Jackson Realty. For examples, refer to Exhibit 5.

2. From the statement of cash flows, does it appear that Jackson Realty will need to borrow money to continue operations? Why or why not?

Answer to Review Problem

1.

	A	B	C
1	Jackson Realty		
2	Income Statement		
3	For the Year Ended April 30, 20X7		
4			
5	Revenues		
6	Commissions earned		$375,000
7			
8	Expenses		
9	Marketing expense	$ 18,000	
10	Office and equipment rent expense	91,000	
11	Salaries and commission expense	172,000	
12	Supplies expense	6,000	
13	Utilities expense	11,000	
14	Total expenses		298,000
15	Income before income taxes		$ 77,000
16	Income taxes expense		27,000
17	Net income		$ 50,000

	A	B
1	Jackson Realty	
2	Statement of Retained Earnings	
3	For the Year Ended April 30, 20X7	
4		
5	Retained earnings, April 30, 20X6	$ 0
6	Net income for the year	50,000
7	Subtotal	$ 50,000
8	Less dividends	10,000
9	Retained earnings, April 30, 20X7	$ 40,000

	A	B	C	D	E	F
1				Jackson Realty		
2				Balance Sheet		
3				April 30, 20X7		
4						
5	Assets			Liabilities		
6	Cash	$ 90,000		Accounts payable	$ 19,000	
7	Accounts receivable	104,000		Salaries payable	78,000	
8	Supplies	2,000		Income taxes payable	6,000	
9	Equipment	47,000		Total liabilities		$103,000
10						
11				Stockholders' Equity		
12				Common stock	$100,000	
13				Retained earnings	40,000	
14				Total stockholders' equity		140,000
15	Total assets	$243,000		Total liabilities and stockholders' equity		$ 243,000

	A	B	C
1	Jackson Realty		
2	Statement of Cash Flows		
3	For the Year Ended April 30, 20X7		
4			
5	Cash flows from operating activities		
6	Net Income		$ 50,000
7	Adjustments		
8	Increase in accounts receivable	$ (104,000)	
9	Increase in supplies	(2,000)	
10	Increase in accounts payable	19,000	
11	Increase in salaries payable	78,000	
12	Increase in income taxes payable	6,000	(3,000)
13	Net cash flows from operating activities		$ 47,000
14			
15	Cash flows from investing activities		
16	Purchase of equipment	$ (47,000)	
17	Net cash flows from investing activities		(47,000)
18			
19	Cash flows from financing activities		
20	Investments by stockholders	$ 100,000	
21	Dividends paid	(10,000)	
22	Net cash flows from financing activities		90,000
23	Net increase (decrease) in cash		$ 90,000
24	Cash at beginning of year		0
25	Cash at end of year		$ 90,000

2. It does not appear that Jackson Realty will need to borrow money to continue in business next year. Total cash increased $90,000. In the current year, cash flows from operating activities are sufficient to cover 100 percent of the investing activities.

CHAPTER ASSIGNMENTS

≡ BUILDING Your Basic Knowledge and Skills

Short Exercises

LO1 **Accounting and Business Enterprises**

SE 1. Match the terms on the left with the definitions on the right:

_____ 1. Accounting	a. The process of producing accounting information for the internal use of a company's management
_____ 2. Profitability	
_____ 3. Liquidity	
_____ 4. Financing activities	b. Having enough cash available to pay debts when they are due
_____ 5. Investing activities	c. Activities management engages in to obtain adequate funds for beginning and continuing to operate a business
_____ 6. Operating activities	
_____ 7. Financial accounting	d. The process of generating and communicating accounting information in the form of financial statements to decision makers outside the organization
_____ 8. Management accounting	
_____ 9. Ethics	e. Activities management engages in to spend capital in ways that are productive and will help a business achieve its objectives
_____ 10. Fraudulent financial reporting	
	f. The ability to earn enough income to attract and hold investment capital
	g. An information system that measures, processes, and communicates financial information about an identifiable economic entity
	h. The intentional preparation of misleading financial statements
	i. Activities management engages in to operate the business
	j. A code of conduct that applies to everyday life

LO3 **Accounting Concepts**

SE 2. Indicate whether each of the following words or phrases relates most closely to (a) a business transaction, (b) a separate entity, or (c) a money measure:

1. Partnership
2. U.S. dollar
3. Payment of an expense
4. Corporation
5. Sale of an asset

LO4 **Forms of Business Enterprises**

SE 3. Match the descriptions on the left with the forms of business enterprise on the right:

____ 1. Most numerous	a. Sole proprietorship
____ 2. Commands most revenues	b. Partnership
____ 3. Two or more co-owners	c. Corporation
____ 4. Has stockholders	
____ 5. Owned by only one person	
____ 6. Has a board of directors	

LO5 **The Accounting Equation**

SE 4. Determine the amount missing from each accounting equation below.

	Assets	=	Liabilities	+	Stockholders' Equity
1.	?		$50,000		$70,000
2.	$156,000		$84,000		?
3.	$292,000		?		$192,000

LO5 **The Accounting Equation**

SE 5. Use the accounting equation to answer each question below.

1. The assets of Tiller Company are $240,000, and the liabilities are $180,000. What is the amount of the stockholders' equity?
2. The liabilities of Cochran Company equal one-fifth of the total assets. The stockholders' equity is $40,000. What is the amount of the liabilities?

LO5 **The Accounting Equation**

SE 6. Use the accounting equation to answer each question below.

1. At the beginning of the year, Salinas Company's assets were $90,000, and its stockholders' equity was $50,000. During the year, assets increased by $30,000 and liabilities increased by $5,000. What was the stockholders' equity at the end of the year?
2. At the beginning of the year, Alejandro Company had liabilities of $100,000 and stockholders' equity of $96,000. If assets increased by $40,000 and liabilities decreased by $30,000, what was the stockholders' equity at the end of the year?

LO5 **The Accounting Equation and Net Income**

SE 7. Carlton Company had assets of $280,000 and liabilities of $120,000 at the beginning of the year, and assets of $400,000 and liabilities of $140,000 at the end of the year. During the year, there was an investment of $40,000 in the business, and the company paid dividends of $48,000. What amount of net income did the company earn during the year?

LO6 **Preparation and Completion of a Balance Sheet**

SE 8. Use the following accounts and balances to prepare a balance sheet with the accounts in proper order for Anatole Company at June 30, 20x6, using Exhibit 3 as a model:

Accounts Receivable	$ 1,600
Wages Payable	500
Retained Earnings	3,500
Common Stock	24,000
Building	20,000
Cash	?

LO6 **Preparation of Financial Statements**

SE 9. Tarech Corporation engaged in activities during the first year of its operations that resulted in the following: service revenue, $4,800; total expenses, $2,450; and dividends, $410. In addition, the year-end balances of selected accounts were as follows: Cash, $1,890; Other Assets, $1,000; Accounts Payable, $450; and Common Stock, $500. In proper format, prepare the income statement, statement of retained earnings, and balance sheet for Tarech Corporation (assume the year ends on December 31, 20x6). (**Hint:** You must solve for the beginning and ending balances of retained earnings for 20x6.)

Return on Assets

SE 10. Jason Company had net income of $15,000 in 20x7. Total assets were $100,000 at the beginning of the year and $140,000 at the end of the year. Calculate return on assets.

Exercises

LO1, LO2, LO3, LO4 **Discussion Questions**

E 1. Develop a brief answer to each of the following questions.

1. What makes accounting a valuable discipline?
2. Why do managers in governmental and not-for-profit organizations need to understand financial information as much as managers in profit-seeking businesses?
3. Are all economic events business transactions?
4. Sole proprietorships, partnerships, and corporations differ legally; how and why does accounting treat them alike?

LO5, LO6, LO7 **Discussion Questions**

E 2. Develop a brief answer to each of the following questions.

1. How are expenses and dividends similar, and how are they different?
2. In what ways are **CVS** and **Southwest Airlines** comparable? Not comparable?
3. How do generally accepted accounting principles (GAAP) differ from the laws of science?
4. What are some unethical ways in which a business may do its accounting or prepare its financial statements?

LO1, LO2, LO7 **The Nature of Accounting**

E 3. Match the terms below with the descriptions in the list that follows:

____ 1. Bookkeeping	____ 8. Securities and
____ 2. Creditors	Exchange Commission
____ 3. Money measure	(SEC)
____ 4. Financial Accounting	____ 9. Investors
Standards Board (FASB)	____ 10. Sarbanes-Oxley Act
____ 5. Business transactions	____ 11. Management
____ 6. Computer	____ 12. Management
____ 7. Communication	information system

a. The recording of all business transactions in terms of money
b. A process by which information is exchanged between individuals through a common system of symbols, signs, or behavior

   c. The process of identifying and assigning values to business transactions

   d. Legislation ordering CEOs and CFOs to swear that any reports they file with the SEC are accurate and complete

   e. An electronic tool for the rapid collection, organization, and communication of large amounts of information

   f. Collectively, the people who have overall responsibility for operating a business and meeting its goals

   g. People who commit money to earn a financial return

   h. The interconnected subsystems that provide the information needed to run a business

   i. The most important body for developing and issuing rules on accounting practice, called *Statements of Financial Accounting Standards*

   j. An agency set up by Congress to protect the public by regulating the issuing, buying, and selling of stocks

   k. Economic events that affect a business's financial position

   l. People to whom money is due

LO2, LO4   **Users of Accounting Information and Forms of Business Enterprise**

E 4. Siglo Pharmaceuticals has recently been formed to develop a new type of drug treatment for cancer. Previously a partnership, Siglo has now become a corporation. Describe the various groups that will have an interest in the financial statements of Siglo. What is the difference between a partnership and a corporation? What advantages does the corporate form have over the partnership form of business organization?

LO3   **Business Transactions**

E 5. Max owns and operates a minimart. Which of Max's actions described below are business transactions? Explain why any other actions are not considered transactions.

1. Max reduces the price of a gallon of milk in order to match the price offered by a competitor.
2. Max pays a high school student cash for cleaning up the driveway behind the market.
3. Max fills his son's car with gasoline in payment for his son's restocking the vending machines and the snack food shelves.
4. Max pays interest to himself on a loan he made to the business three years ago.

LO3, LO4   **Accounting Concepts**

E 6. Financial accounting uses money measures to gauge the impact of business transactions on a separate business entity. Tell whether each of the following words or phrases relates most closely to (a) a business transaction, (b) a separate entity, or (c) a money measure:

1. Corporation
2. Euro
3. Sales of products
4. Receipt of cash
5. Sole proprietorship
6. U.S. dollar
7. Partnership
8. Stockholders' investments
9. Japanese yen
10. Purchase of supplies

LO3   **Money Measure**

E 7. You have been asked to compare the sales and assets of four companies that make computer chips to determine which company is the largest in each category. You have gathered the following data, but they cannot be used for direct comparison because each company's sales and assets are in its own currency:

Company (Currency)	Sales	Assets
DigiChip (U.S. dollar)	2,000,000	1,300,000
Nanhai (Hong Kong dollar)	5,000,000	2,400,000
Tosa (Japanese yen)	350,000,000	250,000,000
Holstein (Euro)	3,000,000	3,900,000

Assuming that the exchange rates in Table 1 are current and appropriate, convert all the figures to U.S. dollars and determine which company is the largest in sales and which is the largest in assets.

LO5   **The Accounting Equation**

E 8. Use the accounting equation to answer each question that follows. Show any calculations you make.

1. The assets of Dusan Corporation are $400,000, and the stockholders' equity is $155,000. What is the amount of the liabilities?
2. The liabilities and stockholders' equity of Highbeam Corporation are $72,000 and $79,500, respectively. What is the amount of the assets?
3. The liabilities of Acosta Corporation equal one-third of the total assets, and stockholders' equity is $160,000. What is the amount of the liabilities?
4. At the beginning of the year, Leary Corporation's assets were $275,000, and its stockholders' equity was $150,000. During the year, assets increased $75,000 and liabilities decreased $22,500. What is the stockholders' equity at the end of the year?

LO5, LO6 · Identification of Accounts

E 9.   1. Indicate whether each of the following accounts is an asset (A), a liability (L), or a part of stockholders' equity (SE):
   a. Cash   e. Land
   b. Salaries Payable   f. Accounts Payable
   c. Accounts Receivable   g. Supplies
   d. Common Stock
2. Indicate whether each account below would be shown on the income statement (IS), the statement of retained earnings (RE), or the balance sheet (BS).
   a. Repair Revenue   e. Rent Expense
   b. Automobile   f. Accounts Payable
   c. Fuel Expense   g. Dividends
   d. Cash

LO6   **Preparation of a Balance Sheet**

E 10. Listed in random order are some of the account balances for the Rojas Company as of December 31, 20xx.

Accounts Payable	$ 50,000	Accounts Receivable	$62,500
Building	112,500	Cash	25,000
Common Stock	125,000	Equipment	50,000
Supplies	12,500	Retained Earnings	87,500

Place the balances in proper order and prepare a balance sheet similar to the one in Exhibit 3.

LO6 **Preparation and Integration of Financial Statements**

E 11. Kaisha Corporation engaged in the following activities during the year: Service Revenue, $13,200; Rent Expense, $1,200; Wages Expense, $8,340; Advertising Expense, $1,350; Utilities Expense, $900; Income Taxes Expense, $200; and Dividends, $700. In addition, the year-end balances of selected accounts were as follows: Cash, $1,550; Accounts Receivable, $750; Supplies, $100; Land, $1,000; Accounts Payable, $450; and Common Stock, $1,000.

In proper format, prepare the income statement, statement of retained earnings, and balance sheet for Kaisha Corporation (assume the year ends on December 31, 20x6). (**Hint:** You must solve for the beginning and ending balances of retained earnings for 20x6.)

LO5 **Stockholders' Equity and the Accounting Equation**

E 12. The total assets and liabilities at the beginning and end of the year for Luther Company are listed below.

	Assets	Liabilities
Beginning of the year	$175,000	$ 68,750
End of the year	275,000	162,500

Determine Luther Company's net income or loss for the year under each of the following alternatives:

1. The stockholders made no investments in the business, and no dividends were paid during the year.
2. The stockholders made no investments in the business, but dividends of $27,500 were paid during the year.
3. The stockholders invested $16,250 in the business, but no dividends were paid during the year.
4. The stockholders invested $12,500 in the business, and dividends of $27,500 were paid during the year.

LO6 **Statement of Cash Flows**

E 13. Primorsk Corporation began the year 20x6 with cash of $55,900. In addition to earning a net income of $32,500 and paying a cash dividend of $19,500, Primorsk borrowed $78,000 from the bank and purchased equipment with $117,000 of cash. Also, Accounts Receivable increased by $7,800, and Accounts Payable increased by $11,700.

Determine the amount of cash on hand at December 31, 20x6, by preparing a statement of cash flows similar to the one in Exhibit 4.

LO4, LO5, LO6 **Statement of Retained Earnings**

E 14. Below is information from the statement of retained earnings of Mrs. Bell's Cookies, Inc. for a recent year.

Dividends	0
Net income	?
Retained earnings, January 31, 20x5	$159,490
Retained earnings, January 31, 20x4	$102,403

Prepare the statement of retained earnings for Mrs. Bell's Cookies in good form. You will need to solve for the amount of net income. What are retained earnings? Why would the company's board of directors decide not to pay any dividends to its owners?

LO7 **Accounting Abbreviations**

E 15. Identify the accounting meaning of each of the following abbreviations: AICPA, SEC, PCAOB, GAAP, FASB, IRS, GASB, IASB, IMA, and CPA.

Return on Assets

E 16. Saxon wants to know if its profitability performance has increased from 20x6 to 20x7. The company had net income of $24,000 in 20x6 and $25,000 in 20x7. Total assets were $200,000 at the end of 20x5, $240,000 at the end of 20x6, and $280,000 at the end of 20x7. Calculate return on assets for 20x6 and 20x7 and comment on the results.

Problems

LO6 **Preparation and Interpretation of the Financial Statements**

P 1. Below is a list of financial statement items.

___ Utilities expense	___ Accounts payable
___ Building	___ Rent expense
___ Common stock	___ Dividends
___ Net income	___ Income taxes expense
___ Land	___ Fees earned
___ Equipment	___ Cash
___ Revenues	___ Supplies
___ Accounts receivable	___ Wages expense

Required

1. Indicate whether each item is found on the income statement (IS), statement of retained earnings (RE), and/or balance sheet (BS).
2. **User insight:** Which statement is most closely associated with the goal of profitability?

LO6 **Integration of Financial Statements**

P 2. Below are three independent sets of financial statements with several amounts missing.

Income Statement	Set A	Set B	Set C
Revenues	$1,100	$ g	$240
Expenses	a	5,200	m
Net income	$ b	$ h	$ 80
Statement of Retained Earnings			
Beginning balance	$2,900	$15,400	$200
Net income	c	1,600	n
Less dividends	200	i	o
Ending balance	$3,000	$ j	$ p
Balance Sheet			
Total assets	$ d	$31,000	$ q
Liabilities	$1,600	$ 5,000	$ r
Stockholders' equity			
Common stock	2,000	10,000	100
Retained earnings	e	k	280
Total liabilities and stockholders' equity	$ f	$ l	$580

Required

1. Complete each set of financial statements by determining the amounts that correspond to the letters.
2. **User insight:** In what order is it necessary to prepare the financial statements and why?

LO1, LO6   **Preparation and Interpretation of the Income Statement, Statement of Retained Earnings, and Balance Sheet**

P 3. Below are the financial accounts of Landscape Design, Inc. The company has just completed its third year of operations ended November 30, 20x8.

Accounts Receivable	$ 9,100
Accounts Payable	7,400
Cash	115,750
Common Stock	15,000
Dividends	40,000
Income Taxes Expense	38,850
Income Taxes Payable	13,000
Marketing Expense	19,700
Design Service Revenue	248,000
Office Rent Expense	18,200
Retained Earnings, November 30, 20x7	55,400
Salaries Expense	96,000
Salaries Payable	2,700
Supplies	800
Supplies Expense	3,100

Required

1. Prepare the income statement, statement of retained earnings, and balance sheet for Landscape Design, Inc.
2. **User insight:** Evaluate the company's ability to meet its bills when they come due.

LO4, LO6   **Preparation and Interpretation of Financial Statements**

P 4. Below are the accounts of Collegiate Painters, Inc. The company has just completed its first year of operations ended September 30, 20x7.

Accounts Receivable	$13,200
Accounts Payable	10,500
Cash	2,600
Common Stock	2,000
Dividends	1,000
Equipment	4,700
Equipment Rental Expense	1,300
Income Taxes Expense	3,000
Income Taxes Payable	3,000
Marketing Expense	1,500
Painting Service Revenue	78,800
Salaries Expense	56,000
Salaries Payable	700
Supplies	400
Supplies Expense	4,100
Truck Rent Expense	7,200

Required

1. Prepare the income statement, statement of retained earnings, and balance sheet for Collegiate Painters, Inc.
2. **User insight:** Why would the owners of Collegiate Painters set their business up as a corporation and not a partnership?

LO1, LO6, LO7   **Use and Interpretation of Financial Statements**

P 5. The financial statements for the Wichita Riding Club follow.

Wichita Riding Club, Inc.
Income Statement
For the Month Ended November 30, 20xx

Revenues		
Riding lesson revenue	$4,650	
Locker rental revenue	1,275	
Total revenues		$5,925
Expenses		
Salaries expense	$1,125	
Feed expense	750	
Utilities expense	450	
Total expenses		2,325
Income before income taxes		$3,600
Income taxes expense		600
Net income		$3,000

Wichita Riding Club, Inc.
Statement of Retained Earnings
For the Month Ended November 30, 20xx

Retained earnings, October 31, 20xx	$5,475
Net income for the month	3,000
Subtotal	$8,475
Less dividends	2,400
Retained earnings, November 30, 20xx	$6,075

Wichita Riding Club, Inc.
Balance Sheet
November 30, 20xx

Assets		Liabilities	
Cash	$ 6,525	Accounts payable	$13,350
Accounts receivable	900		
Supplies	750	**Stockholders' Equity**	
Land	15,750	Common stock	$34,500
Building	22,500	Retained earnings	6,075
Horses	7,500	Total stockholders' equity	40,575
		Total liabilities and	
Total assets	$53,925	stockholders' equity	$53,925

Wichita Riding Club, Inc.
Statement of Cash Flows
For the Month Ended November 30, 20xx

Cash flows from operating activities

Net income		$3,000
Adjustments to reconcile net income to net cash flows from operating activities		
Increase in accounts receivable	(400)	
Increase in supplies	(550)	
Increase in accounts payable	400	(550)
Net cash flows from operating activities		$2,450
Cash flows from investing activities		
Purchase of horses	$2,000	
Sale of horses	(1,000)	
Net cash flows from financing activities		1,000
Cash flows from financing activities		
Issue of common stock	$5,000	
Cash dividends	(2,400)	
Net cash flows from financing activities		2,600
Net increase in cash		$6,050
Cash at beginning of month		475
Cash at end of month		$6,525

Required

1. **User insight:** Explain how the four statements for Wichita Riding Club, Inc. are related to each other.
2. **User insight:** Which statements are most closely associated with the goals of liquidity and profitability? Why?
3. **User insight:** If you were the owner of this business, how would you evaluate the company's performance? Give specific examples.
4. **User insight:** If you were a banker considering Wichita Riding Club for a loan, why might you want the company to get an audit by an independent CPA? What would the audit tell you?

Alternate Problems

LO6 **Integration of Financial Statements**

P 6. The following three independent sets of financial statements have several amounts missing:

Income Statement	Set A	Set B	Set C
Revenues	$5,320	$ 9,000	$ m
Expenses	a	g	1,900
Net income	$ 490	$ h	$ n
Statement of Retained Earnings			
Beginning balance	$1,800	$15,400	$ 200
Net income	b	i	450
Less dividends	c	1,000	o
Ending balance	$ d	$16,000	$ p

Balance Sheet

Total assets	$ e	$ j	$1,900
Liabilities	$ f	$ 2,000	$1,300
Stockholders' equity			
Common stock	200	8,000	50
Retained earnings	2,100	k	q
Total liabilities and stockholders' equity	$2,700	$ l	$ r

Required

1. Complete each set of financial statements by determining the amounts that correspond to the letters.
2. **User insight:** Why is it necessary to prepare the income statement prior to the balance sheet?

LO1, LO6 **Preparation and Interpretation of the Income Statement, Statement of Retained Earnings, and Balance Sheet**

P 7. Below are the financial accounts of Dodge Realty, Inc. The company has just completed its 10th year of operations ended December 31, 20x8.

Accounts Receivable	$ 4,500
Accounts Payable	3,600
Cash	65,750
Commissions Expense	225,000
Commissions Payable	22,700
Commission Sales Revenue	450,000
Common Stock	15,000
Dividends	40,000
Equipment	59,900
Income Taxes Expense	38,850
Income Taxes Payable	13,000
Marketing Expense	29,200
Office Rent Expense	36,000
Retained Earnings, December 31, 20x7	35,300
Supplies	700
Supplies Expense	2,600
Telephone and Computer Expenses	5,100
Wages Expense	32,000

Required

1. Prepare the income statement, statement of retained earnings, and balance sheet for Dodge Realty, Inc.
2. **User insight:** The owners are considering expansion. What other statement would be useful to the owners in assessing whether the company's operations are generating sufficient funds to support the expenses? Why would it be useful?

LO1, LO6 **Preparation and Interpretation of Financial Statements**

P 8. The following are the accounts of Creative Advertising, Inc., an agency that develops marketing materials for print, radio, and television. The agency's first year of operations ended on January 31, 20x7.

Accounts Receivable	$ 24,600
Accounts Payable	19,400
Cash	1,800
Common Stock	5,000
Dividends	0

Equipment Rental Expense	$ 37,200
Income Taxes Expense	560
Income Taxes Payable	560
Marketing Expense	4,500
Advertising Service Revenue	159,200
Salaries Expense	86,000
Salaries Payable	1,300
Supplies	900
Supplies Expense	19,100
Office Rent Expense	10,800

Required

1. Prepare the income statement, statement of retained earnings, and balance sheet for Creative Advertising, Inc.

2. **User insight:** Review the financial statements and comment on the financial challenges Creative Advertising faces.

≡ ENHANCING Your Knowledge, Skills, and Critical Thinking

Conceptual Understanding Cases

LO1, LO2 **Business Activities and Management Functions**

C 1. Costco Wholesale Corporation is America's largest membership retail company. According to its letter to stockholders:

> Our mission is to bring quality goods and services to our members at the lowest possible price in every market where we do business . . . A hallmark of Costco warehouses has been the extraordinary sales volume we achieve.[13]

To achieve its strategy, Costco must organize its management by functions that relate to the principal activities of a business. Discuss the three basic activities Costco will engage in to achieve its goals, and suggest some examples of each. What is the role of Costco's management? What functions must its management perform to carry out these activities?

LO3 **Concept of an Asset**

C 2. Southwest Airlines Co. is one of the most successful airlines in the United States. Its annual report contains this statement: "We are a company of People, not Planes. That is what distinguishes us from other airlines and other companies. At Southwest Airlines, People are our most important asset."[14] Are employees considered assets in the financial statements? Why or why not? Discuss in what sense Southwest considers its employees to be assets.

LO7 **Generally Accepted Accounting Principles**

C 3. Fidelity Investments Company is a well-known mutual fund investment company. It makes investments worth billions of dollars in companies listed on the New York Stock Exchange and other stock markets. Generally accepted accounting principles (GAAP) are very important for Fidelity's investment analysts. What are generally accepted accounting principles? Why are financial statements that have been prepared in accordance with GAAP and audited by an independent CPA useful for Fidelity's investment analysts? What organizations influence GAAP? Explain how they do so.

LO1 **Operating Cash**

C 4. In May 2001, unable to get credit from enough of its lenders, housewares retailer **Lechters, Inc.,** filed for Chapter 11 bankruptcy. It then secured new bank financing in the amount of $86 million. Suppliers, however, remained concerned about Lechters' ability to meet future obligations. Therefore, many suppliers took back their terms of sale specifying the number of days the company had to pay for its merchandise and instead asked for cash in advance or on delivery. Smaller home-furnishing retailers like Lechters struggle against big rivals, such as **Bed Bath & Beyond,** which are more valuable to suppliers and thus can demand better terms and pricing. In spite of these problems and an annual net loss of $101.8 million on sales of $405 million, management believed the company could eventually succeed with its strategy under the bankruptcy.[15] Which is more critical to the short-term survival of a company faced with Lechters' problems: liquidity or profitability? Which is more important in the long term? Explain your answers.

Interpreting Financial Reports

LO6 **Nature of Cash, Assets, and Net Income**

C 5. **H&R Block, Inc.** is a well-known income tax services firm. Information for 2004 and 2003 from the company's annual report is presented below.[16] (All numbers are in thousands.) Three students who were looking at H&R Block's annual report were overheard to make the following comments:

Student A: What a great year H&R Block had in 2004! The company earned income of $612,718,000 because total assets increased from $4,767,308,000 to $5,380,026,000.

Student B: But the company didn't do that well because the change in total assets isn't the same as net income! The company had a net income of only $196,303,000 because its cash increased from $875,373,000 to $1,071,676,000.

Student C: I see from the annual report that H&R Block paid cash dividends of $138,397,000 in 2004. Don't you have to take that into consideration when analyzing the company's performance?

H&R Block, Inc.
Condensed Balance Sheets
December 31, 2004 and 2003
(In thousands)

	2004	2003
Assets		
Cash	$ 1,071,676	$ 875,373
Other assets	4,308,350	3,891,935
Total assets	$ 5,380,026	$ 4,767,308
Liabilities		
Total liabilities	$ 3,483,017	$ 3,103,599
Stockholders' Equity		
Common stock	$ (884,359)*	$ (558,159)*
Retained earnings	2,781,368	2,221,868
Total liabilities and stockholders' equity	$ 5,380,026	$ 4,767,308

*Net of treasury stock.

1. Comment on the interpretations of Students A and B, and then answer Student C's question.
2. Calculate H&R Block's net income for 2004. (**Hint:** Reconstruct the statement of retained earnings.)

Decision Analysis Using Excel

LO5, LO6 **Effect of Transactions on the Balance Sheet**

C 6. The summer after finishing her junior year in college, Beth Murphy started a lawn service business in her neighborhood. On June 1, she deposited $2,700 in a new bank account in the name of her corporation. The $2,700 consisted of a $1,000 loan from her father and $1,700 of her own money. In return for her investment, Murphy issued 1,700 shares of $1 par value common stock to herself.

Using the money in this checking account, Murphy rented lawn equipment, purchased supplies, and hired local high school students to mow and trim the lawns of neighbors who had agreed to pay her for the service. At the end of each month, she mailed bills to her customers.

On August 31, Murphy was ready to dissolve her business and go back to school for the fall term. Because she had been so busy, she had not kept any records other than her checkbook and a list of amounts owed by customers.

Her checkbook had a balance of $3,520, and her customers owed her $875. She expected these customers to pay her during September. She planned to return unused supplies to the Lawn Care Center for a full credit of $50. When she brought back the rented lawn equipment, the Lawn Care Center also would return a deposit of $200 she had made in June. She owed the Lawn Care Center $525 for equipment rentals and supplies. In addition, she owed the students who had worked for her $100, and she still owed her father $700. Although Murphy feels she did quite well, she is not sure just how successful she was. You have agreed to help her find out.

1. Prepare one balance sheet dated June 1 and another dated August 31 for Murphy Lawn Services, Inc.
2. Using information that can be inferred from comparing the balance sheets, write a memorandum to Murphy commenting on her company's performance in achieving profitability and liquidity. (Assume that she used none of the company's assets for personal purposes.) Also, mention the other two financial statements that would be helpful to her in evaluating these business goals.

Annual Report Case: CVS Corporation

LO6 **Analysis of Four Basic Financial Statements**

C 7. Refer to the **CVS** annual report in the Supplement to Chapter 1 to answer the questions below. Keep in mind that every company, while following basic principles, adapts financial statements and terminology to its own special needs. Therefore, the complexity of CVS's financial statements and the terminology in them will differ somewhat from the financial statements in the text.

1. What names does CVS give to its four basic financial statements? (Note that the word *consolidated* in the names of the financial statements means that these statements combine those of several companies owned by CVS.)
2. Prove that the accounting equation works for CVS on January 1, 2005, by finding the amounts for the following equation: Assets = Liabilities + Stockholders' Equity.

3. What were the total revenues of CVS for the year ended January 1, 2005?
4. Was CVS profitable in the year ended January 1, 2005? How much was net income (loss) in that year, and did it increase or decrease from the year ended January 3, 2004?
5. Did the company's cash and cash equivalents increase from January 3, 2004 (fiscal 2003), to January 1, 2005 (fiscal 2004)? If so, by how much? In what two places in the statements can this number be found or computed?
6. Did cash flows from operating activities, cash flows from investing activities, and cash flows from financing activities increase or decrease from fiscal years 2003 to 2004?
7. Who is the auditor for the company? Why is the auditor's report that accompanies the financial statements important?

Comparison Case: CVS Versus Southwest

LO1, LO5, LO7   **Performance Measures and Financial Statements**

C 8. Refer to the **CVS** annual report and the financial statements of **Southwest Airlines Co.** in the Supplement to Chapter 1 to answer these questions:

1. Which company is larger in terms of assets and in terms of revenues? What do you think is the best way to measure the size of a company?
2. Which company is more profitable in terms of net income? What is the trend of profitability over the past three years for both companies?
3. Compute the return on assets for each company for fiscal 2004. By this measure, which company is more profitable? Is this a better measure than simply comparing the net income of the two companies? Explain your answer.
4. Which company has more cash? Which increased its cash the most in the last year? Which has more liquidity as measured by cash flows from operating activities?

Ethical Dilemma Case

Professional Ethics

LO7   **C 9.** Discuss the ethical choices in the situations below. In each instance, describe the ethical dilemma, determine the alternative courses of action, and tell what you would do.

1. You are the payroll accountant for a small business. A friend asks you how much another employee is paid per hour.
2. As an accountant for the branch office of a wholesale supplier, you discover that several of the receipts the branch manager has submitted for reimbursement as selling expenses actually stem from nights out with his spouse.
3. You are an accountant in the purchasing department of a construction company. When you arrive home from work on December 22, you find a large ham in a box marked "Happy Holidays—It's a pleasure to work with you." The gift is from a supplier who has bid on a contract your employer plans to award next week.
4. As an auditor with one year's experience at a local CPA firm, you are expected to complete a certain part of an audit in 20 hours. Because of your lack of experience, you know you cannot finish the job within that time. Rather than admit this, you are thinking about working late to finish the job and not telling anyone.

5. You are a tax accountant at a local CPA firm. You help your neighbor fill out her tax return, and she pays you $200 in cash. Because there is no record of this transaction, you are considering not reporting it on your tax return.

6. The accounting firm for which you work as a CPA has just won a new client, a firm in which you own 200 shares of stock that you received as an inheritance from your grandmother. Because it is only a small number of shares and you think the company will be very successful, you are considering not disclosing the investment.

Internet Case

LO1, LO5 **Financial Performance Comparison of Two High-Tech Companies**

C 10. **Microsoft** and **Intel** are two very successful high-tech corporations. Access their websites by going to the Needles/Powers Online Study Center at http://college.hmco.com/pic/needlesfa9e for a link to their websites. Access each company's annual report and locate the consolidated balance sheet and consolidated statement of income. Find the amount of total assets, revenues, and net income for the most recent year shown. Then compute net income to revenues and net income to total assets for both companies. Which company is larger? Which is more profitable?

Group Activity Case

LO2, LO7 **Users of Accounting Information**

C 11. Public companies report quarterly and annually on their success or failure in making a net income. The following item appeared in *The Wall Street Journal*: **"Coca-Cola Co.'s** fourth-quarter net income plunged 27%, a dismal end to a disappointing year, as economic weakness in several overseas markets hurt sales of soft drinks."[17]

Your instructor will divide the class into groups representing the following users. Discuss why the user your group is representing needs accounting information. Be prepared to discuss in class.

1. The management of Coca-Cola
2. The stockholders of Coca-Cola
3. The creditors of Coca-Cola
4. Potential stockholders of Coca-Cola
5. The Internal Revenue Service
6. The Securities and Exchange Commission
7. The Teamsters' union
8. A consumers' group called Public Cause
9. An economic adviser to the president of the United States

Business Communication Case

LO1, LO6 **Business Goals, Financial Performance, Financial Statements**

C 12. Assume you are working part-time for a small business that does not make any use of financial statements. Based on your knowledge after studying Chapter 1, write the owner a brief business memo in good form that identifies the two major goals of a business. In the memo, explain how financial statements can help the owner achieve these goals. Be sure to tell which statements relate to each of the goals.

How to Read an Annual Report

More than 4 million corporations are chartered in the United States. Most of them are small, family-owned businesses. They are called *private* or *closely held corporations* because their common stock is held by only a few people and is not for sale to the public. Larger companies usually find it desirable to raise investment funds from many investors by issuing common stock to the public. These companies are called *public companies*. Although they are fewer in number than private companies, their total economic impact is much greater.

Public companies must register their common stock with the Securities and Exchange Commission (SEC), which regulates the issuance and subsequent trading of the stock of public companies. The SEC requires the management of public companies to report each year to stockholders on their companies' financial performance. This report, called an *annual report*, contains the company's annual financial statements and other pertinent data. Annual reports are a primary source of financial information about public companies and are distributed to all of a company's stockholders. They must also be filed with the SEC on a Form 10-K.

The general public may obtain an annual report by calling or writing the company or accessing the report online at the company's website. If a company has filed its 10-K electronically with the SEC, it can be accessed at http://www.sec.gov/edgar.shtml. Many libraries also maintain files of annual reports or have them available on electronic media, such as *Compact Disclosure*.

This supplement describes the major components of the typical annual report. We have included most of these components in the annual report of **CVS Corporation**, one of the country's most successful retailers. Case assignments in each chapter refer to this annual report. For purposes of comparison, the supplement also includes the financial statements and summary of significant accounting policies of **Southwest Airlines Co.**, one of the largest and most successful airlines in the United States.

The Components of an Annual Report

In addition to listing the corporation's directors and officers, an annual report usually contains a letter to the stockholders (also called *shareholders*), a multi-year summary of financial highlights, a description of the company, management's discussion and analysis of the company's operating results and financial condition, the financial statements, notes to the financial statements, a statement about management's responsibilities, and the auditors' report.

Letter to the Stockholders

Traditionally, an annual report begins with a letter in which the top officers of the corporation tell stockholders about the company's performance and prospects. In CVS's 2004 annual report, the chairman and chief executive officer wrote to the stockholders about the highlights of the past year, the key priorities for the new year, and other aspects of the business. He reported as follows:

> This past year has been a rewarding one at CVS. While continuing to build on our solid core business, we made a significant purchase that positions us for even stronger performance in the years ahead. Our acquisition of 1,268 Eckerd stores gives us a substantial presence in the high-growth

Florida and Texas markets. . . . We know what it takes to implement "CVS easy," improve customer satisfaction, open new stores, and drive productivity, and we aim to excel at doing all of them virtually every hour of every day in every store.

Financial Highlights

The financial highlights section of an annual report presents key statistics for at least a five-year period but often for a ten-year period. It is often accompanied by graphs. CVS's annual report, for example, gives key figures for sales, operating profits, and other key measures. Note that the financial highlights section often includes nonfinancial data and graphs, such as the number of stores in CVS's case.

Description of the Company

An annual report contains a detailed description of the company's products and divisions. Some analysts tend to scoff at this section of the annual report because it often contains glossy photographs and other image-building material, but it should not be overlooked because it may provide useful information about past results and future plans.

Management's Discussion and Analysis

In this section, management describes the company's financial condition and results of operations and explains the difference in results from one year to the next. For example, CVS's management explains the effects of its strategy to relocate some of its stores:

> Total net sales continued to benefit from our ongoing relocation program, which moves existing in-line shopping center stores to larger, more convenient, freestanding locations. Historically, we have achieved significant improvements in customer count and net sales when we do this. Our relocation strategy remains an important component of our overall growth strategy, as only 55% of our existing stores were freestanding as of January 1, 2005.

CVS's management also describes the decrease in cash flows from operating activities:

> The decrease in net cash provided by operations during 2004 primarily resulted from increased inventory payments as a result of higher inventory levels, and higher operating costs associated with the Acquired Businesses and investments in extending store hours. The elevated inventory levels are primarily the result of inventory purchased to reset the acquired stores with the CVS/pharmacy product mix. Offsetting this was additional cash receipts resulting from increased sales and decreased accounts receivables.

Financial Statements

All companies present the same four basic financial statements in their annual reports, but the names they use may vary. As you can see in Exhibits S-1 to S-4, CVS presents statements of operations (income statements), balance sheets, statements of shareholders' equity (includes retained earnings), and statements of cash flows. (Note that the numbers given in the statements are in millions, but the last six digits are omitted. For example, $1,454,700,000 is shown as $1,454.7.)

▼ EXHIBIT S-1

CVS's Income Statements

Consolidated means that data from all companies owned by CVS are combined. ➤

CVS Corporation
Consolidated Statements of Operations

CVS's fiscal year ends on the Saturday closest to December 31.

Fiscal Year Ended

(In millions, except per share amounts)	Jan. 1, 2005 (52 WEEKS)	Jan. 3, 2004 (53 WEEKS)	Dec. 28, 2002 (52 WEEKS)
Net sales	$30,594.3	$26,588.0	$24,181.5
Cost of goods sold, buying and warehousing costs	22,563.1	19,725.0	18,112.7
Gross margin	8,031.2	6,863.0	6,068.8
Selling, general and administrative expenses	6,079.7	5,097.7	4,552.3
Depreciation and amortization	496.8	341.7	310.3
Total operating expenses	6,576.5	5,439.4	4,862.6
Operating profit[1]	1,454.7	1,423.6	1,206.2
Interest expense, net[2]	58.3	48.1	50.4
Earnings before income tax provision	1,396.4	1,375.5	1,155.8
Income tax provision	477.6	528.2	439.2
Net earnings[3]	918.8	847.3	716.6
Preference dividends, net of income tax benefit[4]	14.2	14.6	14.8
Net earnings available to common shareholders	$ 904.6	$ 832.7	$ 701.8
BASIC EARNINGS PER COMMON SHARE:[5]			
Net earnings	$ 2.27	$ 2.11	$ 1.79
Weighted average common shares outstanding	398.6	394.4	392.3
DILUTED EARNINGS PER COMMON SHARE:			
Net earnings	$ 2.20	$ 2.06	$ 1.75
Weighted average common shares outstanding	415.4	407.7	405.3
DIVIDENDS DECLARED PER COMMON SHARE	$ 0.265	$ 0.230	$ 0.230

1. This section shows earnings from ongoing operations.
2. CVS shows interest expense and income taxes separately. Income taxes appear under income tax provision.
3. The net earnings figure moves to the statements of shareholders' equity.
4. CVS shows the dividends distributed to preferred shareholders. This distribution is not an expense.
5. CVS discloses various breakdowns of earnings per share.

The headings of CVS's financial statements are preceded by the word *consolidated*. A corporation issues *consolidated* financial statements when it consists of more than one company and has combined the companies' data for reporting purposes.

CVS provides several years of data for each financial statement: two years for the balance sheet and three years for the others. Financial statements presented in this fashion are called *comparative financial statements*. Such statements are in accordance with generally accepted accounting principles and help readers assess the company's performance over several years.

CVS's fiscal year ends on the Saturday nearest the end of December (January 1, 2005 in the latest year). Retailers commonly end their fiscal years during a slow period, usually the end of January, which is in contrast to CVS's choosing the end of December.

▼ **EXHIBIT S-2**

CVS's Balance Sheets

CVS Corporation
Consolidated Balance Sheets

(In millions, except shares and per share amounts)	Jan. 1, 2005	Jan. 3, 2004
ASSETS:		
Cash and cash equivalents	$ 392.3	$ 843.2
Accounts receivable, net	1,764.2	1,349.6
Inventories	5,453.9	4,016.5
Deferred income taxes	243.1	252.1
Other current assets	66.0	35.1
Total current assets	7,919.5	6,496.5
Property and equipment, net	3,505.9	2,542.1
Goodwill	1,898.5	889.0
Intangible assets, net	867.9	403.7
Deferred income taxes	137.6	—
Other assets	217.4	211.8
Total assets	$14,546.8	$10,543.1
LIABILITIES:		
Accounts payable	$ 2,275.9	$ 1,666.4
Accrued expenses	1,666.7	1,499.6
Short-term debt	885.6	—
Current portion of long-term debt	30.6	323.2
Total current liabilities	4,858.8	3,489.2
Long-term debt	1,925.9	753.1
Deferred income taxes	—	41.6
Other long-term liabilities	774.9	237.4
Commitments and contingencies (Note 9)		
SHAREHOLDERS' EQUITY:		
Preferred stock, $0.01 par value: authorized 120,619 shares; no shares issued or outstanding	—	—
Preference stock, series one ESOP convertible, par value $1.00: authorized 50,000,000 shares; issued and outstanding 4,273,000 shares at January 1, 2005 and 4,541,000 shares at January 3, 2004	228.4	242.7
Common stock, par value $0.01: authorized 1,000,000,000 shares; issued 414,276,000 shares at January 1, 2005 and 410,187,000 shares at January 3, 2004	4.2	4.1
Treasury stock, at cost: 13,317,000 shares at January 1, 2005 and 14,803,000 shares at January 3, 2004	(385.9)	(428.6)
Guaranteed ESOP obligation	(140.9)	(163.2)
Capital surplus	1,691.4	1,557.2
Retained earnings	5,645.5	4,846.5
Accumulated other comprehensive loss	(55.5)	(36.9)
Total shareholders' equity	6,987.2	6,021.8
Total liabilities and shareholders' equity	$14,546.8	$10,543.1

CVS categorizes certain assets as current assets.

These are noncurrent or long-term assets.

CVS categorizes certain liabilities as current liabilities.

These are noncurrent or long-term liabilities.

Balances in the shareholders' (stockholders') section are from the statements of shareholders' equity.

▼ **EXHIBIT S-3**

CVS's Statements of Stockholders' Equity

CVS Corporation
Consolidated Statements of Shareholders' Equity

(In millions)	Shares Jan. 1, 2005	Shares Jan. 3, 2004	Shares Dec. 28, 2002	Dollars Jan. 1, 2005	Dollars Jan. 3, 2004	Dollars Dec. 28, 2002
PREFERENCE STOCK:						
Beginning of year	4.5	4.7	4.9	$ 242.7	$ 250.4	$ 261.2
Conversion to common stock	(0.2)	(0.2)	(0.2)	(14.3)	(7.7)	(10.8)
End of year	4.3	4.5	4.7	228.4	242.7	250.4
COMMON STOCK:						
Beginning of year	410.2	409.3	408.5	4.1	4.1	4.1
Stock options exercised and awards	4.1	0.9	0.8	0.1	—	—
End of year	414.3	410.2	409.3	4.2	4.1	4.1
TREASURY STOCK:						
Beginning of year	(14.8)	(16.2)	(17.6)	(428.6)	(469.5)	(510.8)
Purchase of treasury shares	—	—	—	(0.8)	(0.5)	—
Conversion of preference stock	0.6	0.3	0.5	17.9	9.6	13.5
Employee stock purchase plan issuance	0.9	1.1	0.9	25.6	31.8	27.8
End of year	(13.3)	(14.8)	(16.2)	(385.9)	(428.6)	(469.5)
GUARANTEED ESOP OBLIGATION:						
Beginning of year				(163.2)	(194.4)	(219.9)
Reduction of guaranteed ESOP obligation				22.3	31.2	25.5
End of year				(140.9)	(163.2)	(194.4)
CAPITAL SURPLUS:						
Beginning of year				1,557.2	1,546.6	1,539.6
Conversion of preference stock				(3.6)	(1.9)	(2.7)
Stock option activity and awards				119.4	9.2	6.7
Tax benefit on stock options and awards				18.4	3.3	3.0
End of year				1,691.4	1,557.2	1,546.6
ACCUMULATED OTHER COMPREHENSIVE LOSS:						
Beginning of year				(36.9)	(44.6)	—
Unrealized loss on derivatives				(19.8)	—	—
Minimum pension liability adjustment				1.2	7.7	(44.6)
End of year				(55.5)	(36.9)	(44.6)
RETAINED EARNINGS:						
Beginning of year				4,846.5	4,104.4	3,492.7
Net earnings				918.8	847.3	716.6
Preference stock dividends				(16.6)	(17.7)	(18.3)
Tax benefit on preference stock dividends				2.4	3.1	3.5
Common stock dividends				(105.6)	(90.6)	(90.1)
End of year				5,645.5	4,846.5	4,104.4
TOTAL SHAREHOLDERS' EQUITY				$6,987.2	$6,021.8	$5,197.0
COMPREHENSIVE INCOME:						
Net earnings				$ 918.8	$ 847.3	$ 716.6
Unrealized loss on derivatives				(19.8)	—	—
Minimum pension liability, net of income tax				1.2	7.7	(44.6)
COMPREHENSIVE INCOME				$ 900.2	$ 855.0	$ 672.0

Each component of stockholders' equity is explained.

Net earnings are from the income statement.

▼ EXHIBIT S-4

CVS's Statements of Cash Flows

CVS Corporation
Consolidated Statements of Cash Flows

Cash flows are shown for operating activities, investing activities, and financing activities.

(In millions)	Fiscal Year Ended		
	Jan. 1, 2005 (52 weeks)	Jan. 3, 2004 (53 weeks)	Dec. 28, 2002 (52 weeks)
CASH FLOWS FROM OPERATING ACTIVITIES:			
Cash receipts from sales	$30,545.8	$26,276.9	$24,128.4
Cash paid for inventory	(22,469.2)	(19,262.9)	(17,715.1)
Cash paid to other suppliers and employees	(6,528.5)	(5,475.5)	(4,832.5)
Interest and dividends received	5.7	5.7	4.1
Interest paid	(70.4)	(64.9)	(60.6)
Income taxes paid	(569.2)	(510.4)	(319.5)
NET CASH PROVIDED BY OPERATING ACTIVITIES	914.2	968.9	1,204.8
CASH FLOWS FROM INVESTING ACTIVITIES:			
Additions to property and equipment	(1,347.7)	(1,121.7)	(1,108.8)
Proceeds from sale-leaseback transactions	496.6	487.8	448.8
Acquisitions, net of cash and investments	(2,293.7)	(133.1)	(93.5)
Cash outflow from hedging activities	(32.8)	—	—
Proceeds from sale or disposal of assets	14.3	13.4	17.7
NET CASH USED IN INVESTING ACTIVITIES	(3,163.3)	(753.6)	(735.8)
CASH FLOWS FROM FINANCING ACTIVITIES:			
Reductions in long-term debt	(301.5)	(0.8)	(3.1)
Additions to long-term debt	1,204.1	—	300.0
Proceeds from exercise of stock options	129.8	38.3	34.0
Dividends paid	(119.8)	(105.2)	(104.9)
Purchase of treasury shares	—	—	—
Additions to/(reductions in) short-term debt	885.6	(4.8)	(230.9)
NET CASH PROVIDED BY (USED IN) FINANCING ACTIVITIES	1,798.2	(72.5)	(4.9)
Net (decrease) increase in cash and cash equivalents	(450.9)	142.8	464.1
Cash and cash equivalents at beginning of year	843.2	700.4	236.3
CASH AND CASH EQUIVALENTS AT END OF YEAR	$ 392.3	$ 843.2	$ 700.4
RECONCILIATION OF NET EARNINGS TO NET CASH PROVIDED BY OPERATING ACTIVITIES			
Net earnings	$ 918.8	$ 847.3	$ 716.6
Adjustments required to reconcile net earnings to net cash provided by operating activities:			
Depreciation and amortization	496.8	341.7	310.3
Deferred income taxes and other non-cash items	(23.6)	41.1	71.8
Change in operating assets and liabilities providing/ (requiring) cash, net of effects from acquisitions:			
Accounts receivable, net	(48.4)	(311.1)	(53.1)
Inventories	(509.8)	2.1	(95.3)
Other current assets	35.7	(3.0)	12.5
Other assets	8.5	(0.4)	(35.3)
Accounts payable	109.4	(41.5)	172.0
Accrued expenses	(144.2)	116.5	105.0
Other long-term liabilities	71.0	(23.8)	0.3
NET CASH SPROVIDED BY OPERATING ACTIVITIES	$ 914.2	$ 968.9	$ 1,204.8

Cash and cash equivalents move to balance sheets.

Income Statements   CVS uses a multistep form of the income statement in that results are shown in several steps (in contrast to the single-step form illustrated in the chapter). The steps are gross margin, operating profit, earnings before income tax provision, and net earnings (see Exhibit S-1). The company also shows net earnings available to common shareholders, and it discloses the basic earnings per share and diluted earnings per share. Basic earnings per share is used for most analysis. Diluted earnings per share assumes that all rights that could be exchanged for common shares, such as stock options, are in fact exchanged. The weighted average number of shares of common stock, used in calculating the per share figures, are shown at the bottom of the income statement.

Balance Sheets   CVS has a typical balance sheet for a retail company (see Exhibit S-2). In the assets and liabilities sections, the company separates out the current assets and the current liabilities. Current assets will become available as cash or will be used up in the next year; current liabilities will have to be paid or satisfied in the next year. These groupings are useful in assessing a company's liquidity.

Several items in the shareholders' equity section of the balance sheet may need explanation. Common stock represents the number of shares outstanding at par value. Capital surplus (additional paid-in capital) represents amounts invested by stockholders in excess of the par value of the common stock. Preferred stock is capital stock that has certain features that distinguish it from common stock. Treasury stock represents shares of common stock the company repurchased.

Statements of Shareholders' Equity   Instead of a simple statement of retained earnings, CVS presents consolidated statements of shareholders' equity (see Exhibit S-3). These statements explain the changes in components of stockholders' equity, including retained earnings.

Statements of Cash Flows   Whereas the income statement reflects CVS's profitability, the statement of cash flows reflects its liquidity (see Exhibit S-4). This statement provides information about a company's cash receipts, cash payments, and investing and financing activities during an accounting period.

The first major section of CVS's consolidated statements of cash flows shows cash flows from operating activities. It shows the cash received and paid for various items related to the company's operations. The second major section is cash flows from investing activities. Except for the acquisition in 2004, the largest outflow in this category is additions for property and equipment. This figure demonstrates that CVS is a growing company. The third major section is cash flows from financing activities. You can see here that CVS's largest cash inflows are for borrowing of long-term and short-term debt.

At the bottom of the statements of cash flows, you can see a reconciliation of net earnings to net cash provided by operating activities. This disclosure is important to the user because it relates the goal of profitability (net earnings) to liquidity (net cash provided). Most companies substitute this disclosure for the operating activities at the beginning of their statement of cash flows as illustrated in Chapter 1.

Notes to the Financial Statements

To meet the requirements of full disclosure, a company must add notes to the financial statements to help users interpret some of the more complex items. The notes are considered an integral part of the financial statements. In recent years, the need for explanation and further details has become so great that the notes often take more space than the statements themselves. The notes to the financial statements include a summary of significant accounting policies and explanatory notes.

Summary of Significant Accounting Policies   Generally accepted accounting principles require that the financial statements include a *Summary of Significant Accounting Policies*. In most cases, this summary is presented in the first note to the financial statements or as a separate section just before the notes. In this summary, the company tells which generally accepted accounting principles it has followed in preparing the statements. For example, in CVS's report, the company states the principles followed for revenue recognition:

> The Company recognizes revenue from the sale of merchandise at the time the merchandise is sold. Service revenue from the Company's pharmacy benefit management segment, which is recognized using the net method.

Explanatory Notes   Other notes explain some of the items in the financial statements. For example, CVS describes its commitments for future lease payments as follows:

Following is a summary of the future minimum lease payments under capital and operating leases as of January 1, 2005:

(In millions)	Capital Leases	Operating Leases
2005	$0.2	$ 1,181.3
2006	0.2	1,120.8
2007	0.2	1,060.0
2008	0.2	1,008.1
2009	0.1	972.8
Thereafter	0.2	9,997.1
	$1.1	$15,340.1

Information like this is very useful in determining the full scope of a company's liabilities and other commitments.

Supplementary Information Notes   In recent years, the FASB and the SEC have ruled that certain supplemental information must be presented with financial statements. Examples are the quarterly reports that most companies present to their stockholders and to the SEC. These quarterly reports, called *interim financial statements*, are in most cases reviewed but not audited by a company's independent CPA firm. In its annual report, CVS presents unaudited quarterly financial data from its 2004 quarterly statements. The quarterly data also includes the high and low price for the company's common stock during each quarter.

Reports of Management's Responsibilities

Separate statements of management's responsibility for the financial statements and for internal control structure accompany the financial statements as required by the Sarbanes-Oxley Act of 2002. In its reports, CVS's management acknowledges its responsibility for the consistency, integrity, and presentation of the financial information and for the system of internal controls.

■ **FIGURE 9**
Auditor's Report for CVS Corporation

Report of Independent Registered Public Accounting Firm KPMG
The Board of Directors and Shareholders
CVS Corporation

(1) We have audited the accompanying consolidated balance sheets of CVS Corporation and subsidiaries as of January 1, 2005 and January 3, 2004, and the related consolidated statements of operations, shareholders' equity and cash flows for the fifty-two week period ended January 1, 2005, the fifty-three week period ended January 3, 2004 and the fifty-two week period ended December 28, 2002. These consolidated financial statements are the responsibility of the Company's management. Our responsibility is to express an opinion on these consolidated financial statements based on our audits.

(2) We conducted our audits in accordance with the standards of the Public Company Accounting Oversight Board (United States). Those standards require that we plan and perform the audit to obtain reasonable assurance about whether the financial statements are free of material misstatement. An audit includes examining, on a test basis, evidence supporting the amounts and disclosures in the financial statements. An audit also includes assessing the accounting principles used and significant estimates made by management, as well as evaluating the overall financial statement presentation. We believe that our audits provide a reasonable basis for our opinion.

(3) In our opinion, the consolidated financial statements referred to above present fairly, in all material respects, the financial position of CVS Corporation and subsidiaries as of January 1, 2005 and January 3, 2004, and the results of their operations and their cash flows for the fifty-two week period ended January 1, 2005, the fifty-three week period ended January 3, 2004 and the fifty-two week period ended December 28, 2002, in conformity with accounting principles generally accepted in the United States of America.

(4) We also have audited, in accordance with the Public Company Accounting Oversight Board (United States), the effectiveness of CVS Corporation's internal control over financial reporting as of January 1, 2005, based on criteria established in Internal Control—Integrated Framework issued by the Committee of Sponsoring Organizations of the Treadway Commission (COSO), and our report dated March 8, 2005 expressed an unqualified opinion on management's assessment of, and the effective operation of, internal control over financial reporting.

KPMG LLP

KPMG LLP
Providence, Rhode Island

March 8, 2005

Reports of Certified Public Accountants

The *registered independent auditors' report* deals with the credibility of the financial statements. This report, prepared by independent certified public accountants, gives the accountants' opinion about how fairly the statements have been presented. Because management is responsible for preparing the financial statements, issuing statements that have not been independently audited would be like having a judge hear a case in which he or she was personally involved. The certified public accountants, acting independently, add the necessary credibility to management's figures for interested third parties. They report to the board of directors and the stockholders rather than to the company's management.

In form and language, most auditors' reports are like the one shown in Figure 9. Usually, such a report is short, but its language is very important. It normally has four parts, but it can have a fifth part if an explanation is needed.

1. The first paragraph identifies the financial statements that have been audited. It also identifies responsibilities. The company's management is responsible for the financial statements, and the auditor is responsible for expressing an opinion on the financial statements based on the audit.

2. The second paragraph, or *scope section*, states that the examination was made in accordance with standards of the Public Company Accounting Oversight Board (PCAOB). This paragraph also contains a brief description of the objectives and nature of the audit.

3. The third paragraph, or *opinion section*, states the results of the auditors' examination. The use of the word *opinion* is very important because the auditor does not certify or guarantee that the statements are absolutely correct. To do so would go beyond the truth, because many items, such as depreciation, are based on estimates. Instead, the auditors simply give an opinion about whether, overall, the financial statements "present fairly," in all material respects, the company's financial position, results of operations, and cash flows. This means that the statements are prepared in accordance with generally accepted accounting principles. If, in the auditors' opinion, the statements do not meet accepted standards, the auditors must explain why and to what extent.

4. The fourth paragraph says the company's internal controls are effective.

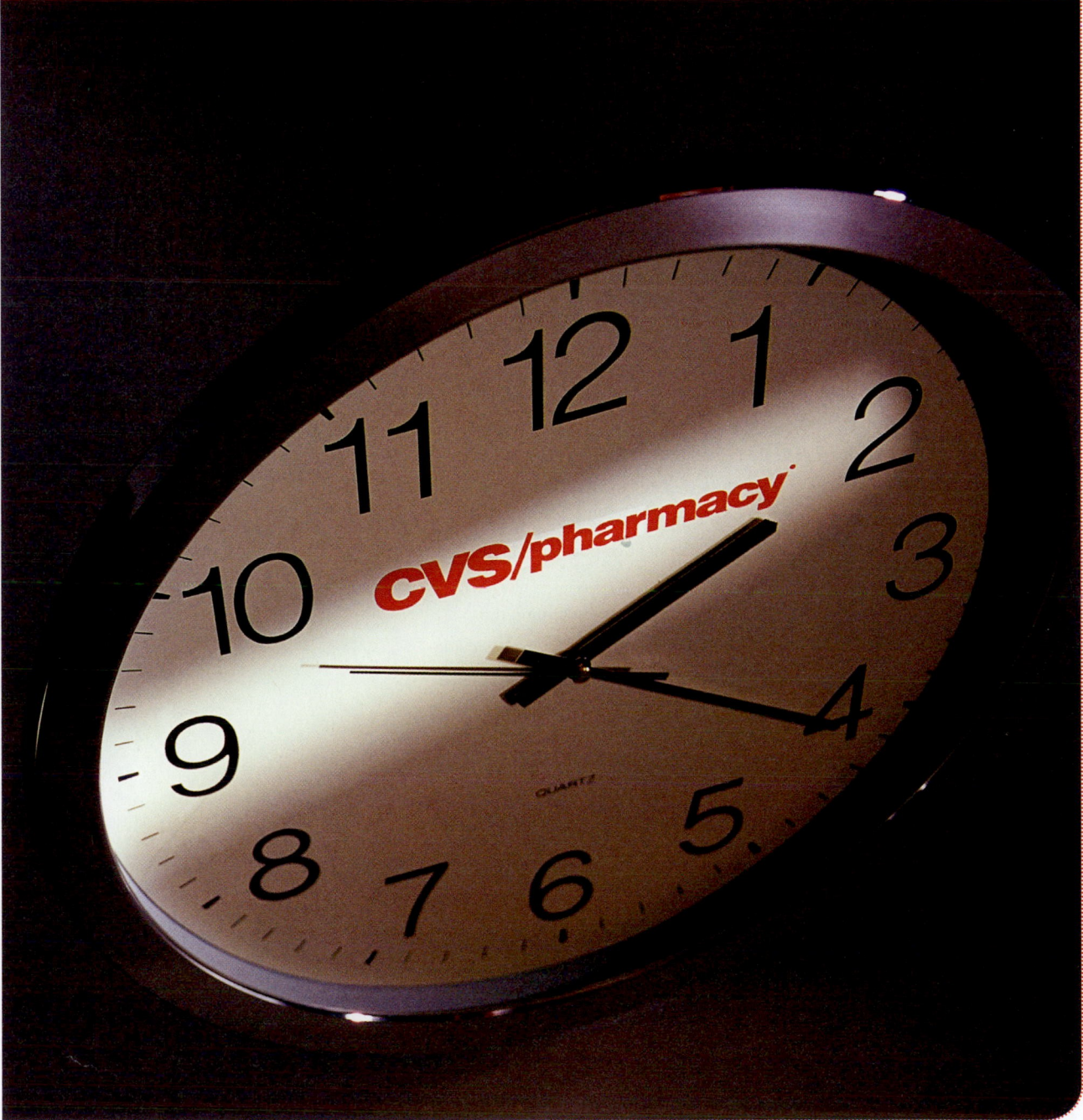

At CVS, it's all in a day's work...

CVS Corporation 2004 Annual Report

Financial Highlights

In millions, except per share	2004 52 weeks	2003 53 weeks	% Change
Sales	$30,594.3	$26,588.0	15.1
Operating profit	1,454.7	1,423.6	2.2
Net earnings	918.8	847.3	8.4
Diluted earnings per common share	2.20	2.06	6.8
Stock price at calendar year end	45.07	36.12	24.8
Market capitalization at calendar year end	18,071	14,281	26.5

To Our Shareholders:

The past year has been a rewarding one at CVS. While continuing to build on our solid core business, we made a significant purchase that positions us for even stronger performance in the years ahead. Our acquisition of 1,268 Eckerd stores gives us a substantial presence in the high-growth Florida and Texas markets. Moreover, the addition of Eckerd Health Services (EHS) to our PharmaCare subsidiary makes us the fourth-largest full-service pharmacy benefits manager (PBM) in the United States, significantly broadening the diversity of our client base and enhancing our competitive position.

We knew that executing our organic growth strategy while integrating the Eckerd acquisition would seem to be an ambitious undertaking to many outside CVS. However, as the opening pages of this report reveal, challenges like these are really all in a day's work for our experienced management team and CVS colleagues across the country. We know what it takes to implement "CVS easy," improve customer satisfaction, open new stores, and drive productivity, and we aim to excel at doing all of them virtually every hour of every day in every store.

Enjoying strong sales and earnings growth

Before discussing our activities in more detail, let me review the good news regarding our 2004 results. Driven by the strength of our existing business and the addition of the former Eckerd assets, sales rose 15.1 percent to a record $30.59 billion. Diluted earnings per share were $2.20, including a one-time, non-cash tax benefit of 14.5 cents as well as a one-time, non-cash negative adjustment of 10 cents relating to a change in accounting practices for leases. The acquisition diluted per-share earnings by 16 cents, and we also had one less week included in our 2004 results compared to 2003.

Chairman, President, and CEO Tom Ryan

Investors have responded enthusiastically to our ongoing success and to our prospects following the acquisition. CVS stock produced a 25.5 percent total return to shareholders in 2004. That number far exceeded the returns of the S&P 500 Index, the S&P Retail Index, and the chain drug industry. Our balance sheet remains among the strongest in the industry, as evidenced by our A– debt rating from Standard & Poor's and our A3 rating from Moody's Investor Services. Our continued financial strength allowed us to announce a 9 percent dividend increase in the first quarter of 2005.

Same-store sales grew 5.5 percent, excluding the acquired stores, with pharmacy same-store sales up 7.0 percent. Our pharmacy business continues to gain share and now has 13.5 percent of the U.S. retail pharmacy market. Meanwhile, front-end same-store sales climbed 2.3 percent. We gained significant retail share in all our key front-end categories, especially photo, cosmetics, skin care, candy, and healthcare. With CVS proprietary products such as Nuprin healthcare products, the first disposable digital camera with color preview, and other new CVS private label and exclusive brands, we continued to differentiate our offerings.

Rapidly integrating our new businesses; expanding in high-growth markets
I'm happy to report that the Eckerd integration is proceeding faster than any large-scale integration in our industry's history. Thanks to the talents of our management team, their experience with prior acquisitions, and our state-of-the-art technology, we've already put the greatest risks associated with the integration behind us. We completed the migration of all financial and store systems by Thanksgiving, less than four months after closing the deal and ahead of our end-of-year target.

We had to close only 160 former Eckerd stores in 2004, fewer than anticipated, and our infrastructure is now supporting the remaining 1,100-plus stores. We have re-merchandised every location to the CVS product mix and planogram and have significantly lowered everyday prices on over 5,000 items. More than 300 locations now look like CVS stores inside and out. We have ramped up our remodeling effort and expect to complete the entire conversion by July 2005. As we complete remodeling by market, we will hold special events to re-introduce the stores to customers. Once completed, we should be well positioned to reap the benefits of a sales turnaround. Furthermore, we see tremendous opportunities for margin improvement as we bring our operating capabilities and technology to bear. In fact, we expect the acquisition to add 15–20 cents to earnings per share in 2005 based largely on productivity gains.

The addition of EHS was also a key factor in the acquisition. It gives us the unmatched combination of a PBM covering 30 million lives, the industry's leading retail presence, and a specialty pharmacy offering. As a result, we are strategically positioned to provide all payors—patients, insurers, managed care companies, and employers alike—with a complete and flexible pharmacy solution. Our core PharmaCare business is growing, with the EHS integration progressing well as we focus on retaining clients and gaining new ones. (Read more about our PharmaCare opportunity on page 6.)

Even as we were busy integrating Eckerd assets, CVS maintained a brisk pace of new store openings in 2004. We opened 225, with net unit growth of 88 stores factoring in relocations and closings. As a result, square footage grew 3.4 percent. With the acquired stores, retail square footage increased 33 percent. Virtually all our net growth took place in newer CVS markets such as Texas, Florida, Phoenix, Las Vegas, and Chicago. We opened our first stores in Los Angeles and Orange County, California, as well as Minneapolis. All these markets boast faster-than-average growth among the 55 and over population, a demographic that uses three times as many prescription drugs as people under 55.

Leveraging our "CVS easy" efforts

As with any CVS location, the success of the converted Eckerd stores will be driven in part by our ability to make the customer shopping experience "CVS easy." Former Eckerd customers are providing us with very positive feedback on this front. They appreciate the ease with which they get into and out of our stores, the extended hours we've added at 80 percent of the acquired stores, and the addition of 180 24-hour locations. As for location, the overwhelming majority of the acquired Eckerd properties were already well situated.

We've completed our ExtraCare® rollout at the acquired stores. With more than 50 million cardholders, ExtraCare is the largest and most successful retail loyalty

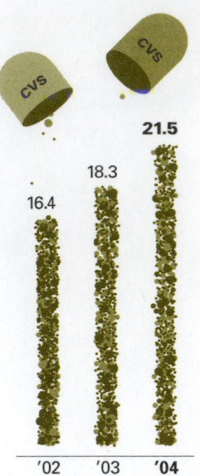

Pharmacy Sales
In billions of dollars

16.4 '02
18.3 '03
21.5 '04

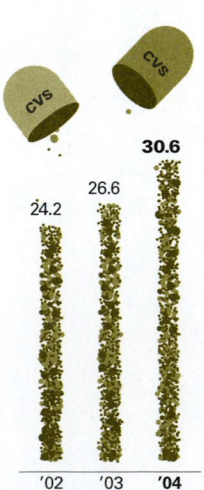

Total Sales
In billions of dollars

24.2 '02
26.6 '03
30.6 '04

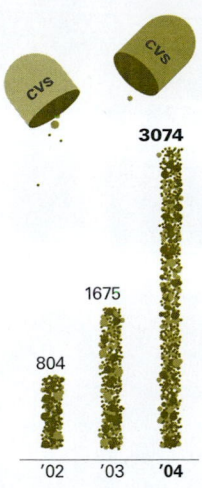

3074

1675

804

'02 '03 '04

**24- and Extended-
Hour Stores**

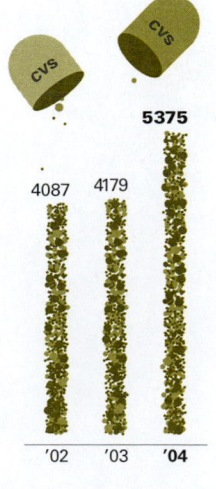

5375

4087 4179

'02 '03 '04

Store Count

program in the U.S. Now former Eckerd customers in the South are enjoying advertised discounts without the hassle of clipping coupons. They are also reaping the benefits of the ExtraBucks™ cash rewards that come with their sales receipts each quarter. These are just a few examples of "CVS easy" in action, and we continue to look for ways to further improve our customer experience.

Robust pipeline and new generics to help drive future growth

We are seeing a temporary slowdown in industry prescription growth, which is due to a number of factors. They include the slow pace of new drug approvals, higher co-pays and growing co-insurance arrangements, Rx to over-the-counter switches, and the growth in mandatory mail order plans. However, ours is still a growth industry. Pharmaceutical and biotech companies are hard at work discovering new drugs, and $40–$50 billion worth of branded drug sales will come off patent by 2008. Generic equivalents will make these medications less expensive and more accessible to a larger population. Furthermore, prescription drugs often remain the most cost-effective form of healthcare delivery, reducing the need for hospitalization and surgery and getting people back to work sooner.

The Medicare Prescription Drug, Improvement and Modernization Act of 2003 will go into effect in January 2006, and we expect to be significant participants in delivering this new benefit through our retail stores as well as our PBM. Although we expect it to put some pressure on margins, this program should prove to be a net positive for CVS. By making prescription drugs more affordable to millions of senior citizens, this new benefit should increase their utilization.

Before signing off, I want to thank the more than 145,000 colleagues who focus on our "CVS easy" mission every day they come to work. Some have been with CVS for many years. Others—like the experienced and valued former Eckerd employees—are relatively new to our company. Together their efforts made this company stronger in 2004. I also want to acknowledge the work of our talented and engaged board of directors, in particular the late Terry Lautenbach. Everyone at CVS held Terry in high regard for his keen intellect. I valued the wise counsel he gave our company and me personally during his tenure on our board, and his sudden death has been a great loss. On a happier note, Hasbro President and CEO Alfred Verrecchia joined our board in September, and we've quickly put the financial and operational skills of this seasoned executive to work on your behalf.

With 2005 well underway, we have good reason to feel confident. Our core business is thriving and the integration of the acquired Eckerd businesses is proceeding smoothly. Our focus on new markets provides a valuable engine for growth. In unlocking the value of the former Eckerd stores, we have a great opportunity to improve their profitability and gain market share. Our retail and PBM strengths also leave us uniquely positioned in our industry. Although we don't have a silver bullet to address all of today's healthcare challenges, our ability to offer flexible solutions for payors can help lead the way to improving pharmaceutical healthcare in this country. Moreover, I believe that we can help payors control costs without compromising patient care.

On behalf of the entire management team, you can trust that we will continue to work hard around the clock, putting your capital to its best possible use. Thank you for investing in CVS.

Thomas M. Ryan
Chairman of the Board, President, and Chief Executive Officer

March 8, 2005

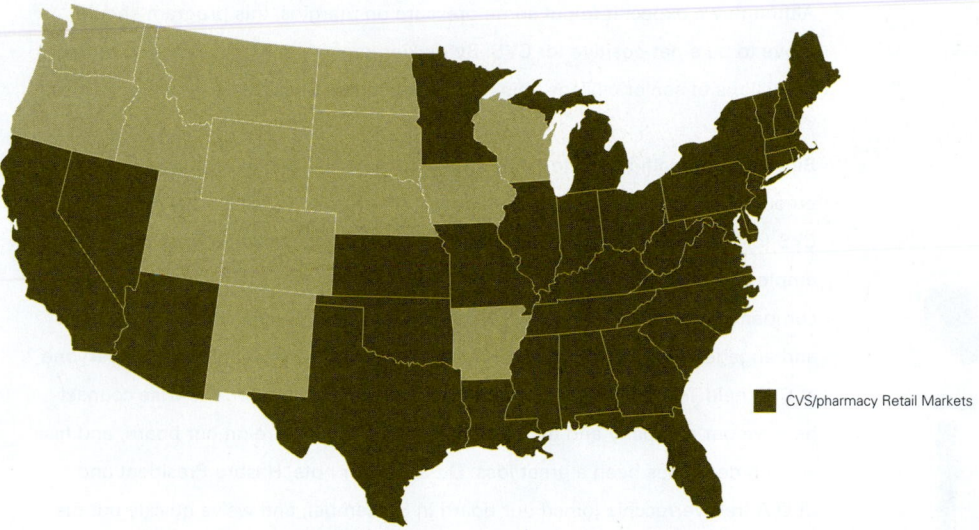

■ CVS/pharmacy Retail Markets

Expanding Our Reach

Five years ago, CVS/pharmacy stores filled prescriptions in 4,098 stores in 26 states and the District of Columbia. Today, we fill prescriptions in 5,375 stores across 36 states and Washington, D.C. More than 1,300 stores—25 percent of our current store base—were built or acquired in new territories over the past five years. They have given us a substantial presence in some of America's fastest growing markets.

2004 Financial Report

Management's Discussion and Analysis of
Financial Condition and Results of Operation — **18**

Management's Report on Internal Control
Over Financial Reporting — **26**

Report of Independent Registered Public Accounting Firm — **27**

Consolidated Statements of Operations — **28**

Consolidated Balance Sheets — **29**

Consolidated Statements of Shareholders' Equity — **30**

Consolidated Statements of Cash Flows — **31**

Notes to Consolidated Financial Statements — **32**

Five-Year Financial Summary — **46**

Report of Independent Registered Public Accounting Firm — **47**

Management's Report on Internal Control Over Financial Reporting

We are responsible for establishing and maintaining effective internal control over financial reporting. Our Company's internal control over financial reporting includes those policies and procedures that pertain to the Company's ability to record, process, summarize and report a system of internal accounting controls and procedures to provide reasonable assurance, at an appropriate cost/benefit relationship, that the unauthorized acquisition, use or disposition of assets are prevented or timely detected and that transactions are authorized, recorded and reported properly to permit the preparation of financial statements in accordance with GAAP and receipt and expenditures are duly authorized. In order to ensure the Company's internal control over financial reporting is effective, management regularly assesses such controls and did so most recently for its financial reporting as of January 1, 2005.

We conduct an evaluation of the effectiveness of our internal controls over financial reporting based on the framework in *Internal Control—Integrated Framework* issued by the Committee of Sponsoring Organizations of the Treadway Commission. This evaluation included review of the documentation, evaluation of the design effectiveness and testing of the operating effectiveness of controls. Our system of internal control over financial reporting is enhanced by periodic reviews by our internal auditors and independent registered public accounting firm, written policies and procedures and a written Code of Conduct adopted by our Company's Board of Directors, applicable to all employees of our Company. In addition, we have an internal Disclosure Committee, comprised of management from each functional area within the Company, which performs a separate review of our disclosure control and procedures. There are inherent limitations in the effectiveness of any system of internal controls over financial reporting.

Based on our evaluation, we conclude our Company's internal control over financial reporting is effective and provide reasonable assurance that assets are safeguarded and that the financial records are reliable for preparing financial statements as of January 1, 2005.

KPMG LLP, independent registered public accounting firm, is appointed by the Board of Directors and ratified by our Company's shareholders. They were engaged to render an opinion regarding the fair presentation of our consolidated financial statements as well as conducting a review of the system of internal accounting controls. Their accompanying report is based upon an audit conducted in accordance with the Public Company Accounting Oversight Board (United States) and includes an attestation on management's assessment of internal controls over financial reporting.

March 8, 2005

Report of Independent Registered Public Accounting Firm

THE BOARD OF DIRECTORS AND SHAREHOLDERS
CVS CORPORATION

We have audited management's assessment, included in the accompanying Management's Report on Internal Control Over Financial Reporting, that CVS Corporation and subsidiaries maintained effective internal control over financial reporting as of January 1, 2005, based on criteria established in Internal Control–Integrated Framework issued by the Committee of Sponsoring Organizations of the Treadway Commission (COSO). The Company's management is responsible for maintaining effective internal control over financial reporting and for its assessment of the effectiveness of internal control over financial reporting. Our responsibility is to express an opinion on management's assessment and an opinion on the effectiveness of the Company's internal control over financial reporting based on our audit.

We conducted our audit in accordance with the standards of the Public Company Accounting Oversight Board (United States). Those standards require that we plan and perform the audit to obtain reasonable assurance about whether effective internal control over financial reporting was maintained in all material respects. Our audit included obtaining an understanding of internal control over financial reporting, evaluating management's assessment, testing and evaluating the design and operating effectiveness of internal control, and performing such other procedures as we considered necessary in the circumstances. We believe that our audit provides a reasonable basis for our opinion.

A company's internal control over financial reporting is a process designed to provide reasonable assurance regarding the reliability of financial reporting and the preparation of financial statements for external purposes in accordance with generally accepted accounting principles. A company's internal control over financial reporting includes those policies and procedures that (1) pertain to the maintenance of records that, in reasonable detail, accurately and fairly reflect the transactions and dispositions of the assets of the company; (2) provide reasonable assurance that transactions are recorded as necessary to permit preparation of financial statements in accordance with generally accepted accounting principles, and that receipts and expenditures of the company are being made only in accordance with authorizations of management and directors of the company; and (3) provide reasonable assurance regarding prevention or timely detection of unauthorized acquisition, use or disposition of the company's assets that could have a material effect on the financial statements.

Because of its inherent limitations, internal control over financial reporting may not prevent or detect misstatements. Also, projections of any evaluation of effectiveness to future periods are subject to the risk that controls may become inadequate because of changes in conditions, or that the degree of compliance with the policies or procedures may deteriorate.

In our opinion, management's assessment that CVS Corporation and subsidiaries maintained effective internal control over financial reporting as of January 1, 2005, is fairly stated, in all material respects, based on criteria established in Internal Control–Integrated Framework issued by COSO. Also, in our opinion, CVS Corporation and subsidiaries maintained, in all material respects, effective internal control over financial reporting as of January 1, 2005, based on criteria established in Internal Control–Integrated Framework issued by COSO.

We also have audited, in accordance with the standards of the Public Company Accounting Oversight Board (United States), the consolidated balance sheets of CVS Corporation and subsidiaries as of January 1, 2005 and January 3, 2004, and the related consolidated statements of operations, shareholders' equity, and cash flows for the fifty-two week period ended January 1, 2005, the fifty-three week period ended January 3, 2004 and the fifty-two week period ended December 28, 2002, and our report, dated March 8, 2005, expressed an unqualified opinion on those consolidated financial statements.

KPMG LLP
Providence, Rhode Island

March 8, 2005

Consolidated Statements of Operations

	fiscal year ended		
In millions, except per share amounts	JAN. 1, 2005 (52 WEEKS)	JAN. 3, 2004 (53 WEEKS)	DEC. 28, 2002 (52 WEEKS)
Net sales	$ 30,594.3	$ 26,588.0	$ 24,181.5
Cost of goods sold, buying and warehousing costs	22,563.1	19,725.0	18,112.7
Gross margin	8,031.2	6,863.0	6,068.8
Selling, general and administrative expenses	6,079.7	5,097.7	4,552.3
Depreciation and amortization	496.8	341.7	310.3
Total operating expenses	6,576.5	5,439.4	4,862.6
Operating profit	1,454.7	1,423.6	1,206.2
Interest expense, net	58.3	48.1	50.4
Earnings before income tax provision	1,396.4	1,375.5	1,155.8
Income tax provision	477.6	528.2	439.2
Net earnings	918.8	847.3	716.6
Preference dividends, net of income tax benefit	14.2	14.6	14.8
Net earnings available to common shareholders	$ 904.6	$ 832.7	$ 701.8
BASIC EARNINGS PER COMMON SHARE:			
Net earnings	$ 2.27	$ 2.11	$ 1.79
Weighted average common shares outstanding	398.6	394.4	392.3
DILUTED EARNINGS PER COMMON SHARE:			
Net earnings	$ 2.20	$ 2.06	$ 1.75
Weighted average common shares outstanding	415.4	407.7	405.3
DIVIDENDS DECLARED PER COMMON SHARE	$ 0.265	$ 0.230	$ 0.230

See accompanying notes to consolidated financial statements.

Consolidated Balance Sheets

In millions, except shares and per share amounts	JAN. 1, 2005	JAN. 3, 2004
ASSETS:		
Cash and cash equivalents	$ 392.3	$ 843.2
Accounts receivable, net	1,764.2	1,349.6
Inventories	5,453.9	4,016.5
Deferred income taxes	243.1	252.1
Other current assets	66.0	35.1
Total current assets	7,919.5	6,496.5
Property and equipment, net	3,505.9	2,542.1
Goodwill	1,898.5	889.0
Intangible assets, net	867.9	403.7
Deferred income taxes	137.6	—
Other assets	217.4	211.8
Total assets	$ 14,546.8	$ 10,543.1
LIABILITIES:		
Accounts payable	$ 2,275.9	$ 1,666.4
Accrued expenses	1,666.7	1,499.6
Short-term debt	885.6	—
Current portion of long-term debt	30.6	323.2
Total current liabilities	4,858.8	3,489.2
Long-term debt	1,925.9	753.1
Deferred income taxes	—	41.6
Other long-term liabilities	774.9	237.4
Commitments and contingencies (Note 9)		
SHAREHOLDERS' EQUITY:		
Preferred stock, $0.01 par value: authorized 120,619 shares;		
no shares issued or outstanding	—	—
Preference stock, series one ESOP convertible, par value $1.00: authorized		
50,000,000 shares; issued and outstanding 4,273,000 shares at January 1, 2005		
and 4,541,000 shares at January 3, 2004	228.4	242.7
Common stock, par value $0.01: authorized 1,000,000,000 shares; issued		
414,276,000 shares at January 1, 2005 and 410,187,000 shares at January 3, 2004	4.2	4.1
Treasury stock, at cost: 13,317,000 shares at January 1, 2005 and		
14,803,000 shares at January 3, 2004	(385.9)	(428.6)
Guaranteed ESOP obligation	(140.9)	(163.2)
Capital surplus	1,691.4	1,557.2
Retained earnings	5,645.5	4,846.5
Accumulated other comprehensive loss	(55.5)	(36.9)
Total shareholders' equity	6,987.2	6,021.8
Total liabilities and shareholders' equity	$ 14,546.8	$ 10,543.1

See accompanying notes to consolidated financial statements.

Consolidated Statements of Shareholders' Equity

In millions	shares			dollars		
	JAN. 1, 2005	JAN. 3, 2004	DEC. 28, 2002	JAN. 1, 2005	JAN. 3, 2004	DEC. 28, 2002
PREFERENCE STOCK:						
Beginning of year	4.5	4.7	4.9	$ 242.7	$ 250.4	$ 261.2
Conversion to common stock	(0.2)	(0.2)	(0.2)	(14.3)	(7.7)	(10.8)
End of year	4.3	4.5	4.7	228.4	242.7	250.4
COMMON STOCK:						
Beginning of year	410.2	409.3	408.5	4.1	4.1	4.1
Stock options exercised and awards	4.1	0.9	0.8	0.1	—	—
End of year	414.3	410.2	409.3	4.2	4.1	4.1
TREASURY STOCK:						
Beginning of year	(14.8)	(16.2)	(17.6)	(428.6)	(469.5)	(510.8)
Purchase of treasury shares	—	—	—	(0.8)	(0.5)	—
Conversion of preference stock	0.6	0.3	0.5	17.9	9.6	13.5
Employee stock purchase plan issuance	0.9	1.1	0.9	25.6	31.8	27.8
End of year	(13.3)	(14.8)	(16.2)	(385.9)	(428.6)	(469.5)
GUARANTEED ESOP OBLIGATION:						
Beginning of year				(163.2)	(194.4)	(219.9)
Reduction of guaranteed ESOP obligation				22.3	31.2	25.5
End of year				(140.9)	(163.2)	(194.4)
CAPITAL SURPLUS:						
Beginning of year				1,557.2	1,546.6	1,539.6
Conversion of preference stock				(3.6)	(1.9)	(2.7)
Stock option activity and awards				119.4	9.2	6.7
Tax benefit on stock options and awards				18.4	3.3	3.0
End of year				1,691.4	1,557.2	1,546.6
ACCUMULATED OTHER COMPREHENSIVE LOSS:						
Beginning of year				(36.9)	(44.6)	—
Unrealized loss on derivatives				(19.8)	—	—
Minimum pension liability adjustment				1.2	7.7	(44.6)
End of year				(55.5)	(36.9)	(44.6)
RETAINED EARNINGS:						
Beginning of year				4,846.5	4,104.4	3,492.7
Net earnings				918.8	847.3	716.6
Preference stock dividends				(16.6)	(17.7)	(18.3)
Tax benefit on preference stock dividends				2.4	3.1	3.5
Common stock dividends				(105.6)	(90.6)	(90.1)
End of year				5,645.5	4,846.5	4,104.4
TOTAL SHAREHOLDERS' EQUITY				$ 6,987.2	$ 6,021.8	$ 5,197.0
COMPREHENSIVE INCOME:						
Net earnings				$ 918.8	$ 847.3	$ 716.6
Unrealized loss on derivatives				(19.8)	—	—
Minimum pension liability, net of income tax				1.2	7.7	(44.6)
COMPREHENSIVE INCOME				$ 900.2	$ 855.0	$ 672.0

See accompanying notes to consolidated financial statements.

Consolidated Statements of Cash Flows

	fiscal year ended		
In millions	**JAN. 1, 2005** (52 WEEKS)	**JAN. 3, 2004** (53 WEEKS)	**DEC. 28, 2002** (52 WEEKS)
CASH FLOWS FROM OPERATING ACTIVITIES:			
Cash receipts from sales	$ 30,545.8	$ 26,276.9	$ 24,128.4
Cash paid for inventory	(22,469.2)	(19,262.9)	(17,715.1)
Cash paid to other suppliers and employees	(6,528.5)	(5,475.5)	(4,832.5)
Interest and dividends received	5.7	5.7	4.1
Interest paid	(70.4)	(64.9)	(60.6)
Income taxes paid	(569.2)	(510.4)	(319.5)
NET CASH PROVIDED BY OPERATING ACTIVITIES	914.2	968.9	1,204.8
CASH FLOWS FROM INVESTING ACTIVITIES:			
Additions to property and equipment	(1,347.7)	(1,121.7)	(1,108.8)
Proceeds from sale-leaseback transactions	496.6	487.8	448.8
Acquisitions, net of cash and investments	(2,293.7)	(133.1)	(93.5)
Cash outflow from hedging activities	(32.8)	—	—
Proceeds from sale or disposal of assets	14.3	13.4	17.7
NET CASH USED IN INVESTING ACTIVITIES	(3,163.3)	(753.6)	(735.8)
CASH FLOWS FROM FINANCING ACTIVITIES:			
Reductions in long-term debt	(301.5)	(0.8)	(3.1)
Additions to long-term debt	1,204.1	—	300.0
Proceeds from exercise of stock options	129.8	38.3	34.0
Dividends paid	(119.8)	(105.2)	(104.9)
Purchase of treasury shares	—	—	—
Additions to/(reductions in) short-term debt	885.6	(4.8)	(230.9)
NET CASH PROVIDED BY (USED IN) FINANCING ACTIVITIES	1,798.2	(72.5)	(4.9)
Net (decrease) increase in cash and cash equivalents	(450.9)	142.8	464.1
Cash and cash equivalents at beginning of year	843.2	700.4	236.3
CASH AND CASH EQUIVALENTS AT END OF YEAR	$ 392.3	$ 843.2	$ 700.4
RECONCILIATION OF NET EARNINGS TO NET CASH PROVIDED BY OPERATING ACTIVITIES:			
Net earnings	$ 918.8	$ 847.3	$ 716.6
Adjustments required to reconcile net earnings to net cash provided by operating activities:			
Depreciation and amortization	496.8	341.7	310.3
Deferred income taxes and other non-cash items	(23.6)	41.1	71.8
Change in operating assets and liabilities providing/(requiring) cash, net of effects from acquisitions:			
Accounts receivable, net	(48.4)	(311.1)	(53.1)
Inventories	(509.8)	2.1	(95.3)
Other current assets	35.7	(3.0)	12.5
Other assets	8.5	(0.4)	(35.3)
Accounts payable	109.4	(41.5)	172.0
Accrued expenses	(144.2)	116.5	105.0
Other long-term liabilities	71.0	(23.8)	0.3
NET CASH PROVIDED BY OPERATING ACTIVITIES	$ 914.2	$ 968.9	$ 1,204.8

See accompanying notes to consolidated financial statements.

Notes to Consolidated Financial Statements

1 ◆ Significant accounting policies

Description of business–CVS Corporation (the "Company") is a leader in the retail drugstore industry in the United States. The Company sells prescription drugs and a wide assortment of general merchandise, including over-the-counter drugs, beauty products and cosmetics, film and photofinishing services, seasonal merchandise, greeting cards and convenience foods, through its CVS/pharmacy® retail stores and online through CVS.com.® The Company also provides pharmacy benefit management, mail order services and specialty pharmacy services through PharmaCare Management Services and PharmaCare Pharmacy® stores. As of January 1, 2005, the Company operated 5,375 retail and specialty pharmacy stores in 36 states and the District of Columbia.

Basis of presentation–The consolidated financial statements include the accounts of the Company and its wholly-owned subsidiaries. All material intercompany balances and transactions have been eliminated.

Fiscal year–The Company's fiscal year is a 52 or 53 week period ending on the Saturday nearest to December 31. Fiscal 2004, which ended on January 1, 2005, and fiscal 2002, which ended on December 28, 2002, each included 52 weeks. Fiscal 2003, which ended on January 3, 2004, included 53 weeks. Unless otherwise noted, all references to years relate to these fiscal years.

Reclassifications–Certain reclassifications have been made to the consolidated financial statements of prior years to conform to the current year presentation. Most significantly, the presentation of reporting cash flows was modified from the indirect to the direct method of presentation, the preferred presentation under Statement of Financial Accounting Standards ("SFAS") No. 95, "Statement of Cash Flows."

Use of estimates–The preparation of financial statements in conformity with generally accepted accounting principles requires management to make estimates and assumptions that affect the reported amounts in the consolidated financial statements and accompanying notes. Actual results could differ from those estimates.

Cash and cash equivalents–Cash and cash equivalents consist of cash and temporary investments with maturities of three months or less when purchased.

Accounts receivable–Accounts receivable are stated net of an allowance for uncollectible accounts of $57.3 million and $58.4 million as of January 1, 2005 and January 3, 2004, respectively. The balance primarily includes amounts due from third party providers (e.g., pharmacy benefit managers, insurance companies and governmental agencies) and vendors.

Fair value of financial instruments–As of January 1, 2005, the Company's financial instruments include cash and cash equivalents, accounts receivable, accounts payable and short-term debt. Due to the short-term nature of these instruments, the Company's carrying value approximates fair value. The carrying amount of long-term debt was $1.9 billion and $1.1 billion, and the estimated fair value was $1.9 billion and $1.1 billion as of January 1, 2005 and January 3, 2004, respectively. The fair value of long-term debt was estimated based on rates currently offered to the Company for debt with similar maturities. The Company had outstanding letters of credit, which guaranteed foreign trade purchases, with a fair value of $7.8 million as of January 1, 2005, and $65 million as of January 3, 2004. The Company also had outstanding letters of credit associated with insurance programs with a fair value of $124.7 million as of January 1, 2005 and $655 million as of January 3, 2004. There were no outstanding investments in derivative financial instruments as of January 1, 2005 or January 3, 2004.

Inventories–Inventory is stated at the lower of cost or market on a first-in, first-out basis using the retail method of accounting to determine cost of sales and inventory in our stores and the cost method of accounting to determine inventory in our distribution centers. Independent physical inventory counts are taken on a regular basis in each store and distribution center location to ensure that the amounts reflected in the accompanying consolidated financial statements are properly stated. During the interim period between physical inventory counts, the Company accrues for anticipated physical inventory losses on a location-by-location basis based on historical results and current trends.

Property and equipment–Property, equipment and improvements to leased premises are depreciated using the straight-line method over the estimated useful lives of the assets, or when applicable, the term of the lease, whichever is shorter. Estimated useful lives generally range from 10 to 40 years for buildings, building improvements and leasehold improvements and 5 to 10 years for fixtures and equipment. Repair and maintenance costs are charged directly to expense as incurred. Major renewals or replacements that substantially extend the useful life of an asset are capitalized and depreciated.

Following are the components of property and equipment included in the consolidated balance sheets as of the respective balance sheet dates:

In millions	JAN. 1, 2005	JAN. 3, 2004
Land	$ 262.6	$ 180.7
Building and improvements	612.6	492.8
Fixtures and equipment	2,943.8	2,123.3
Leasehold improvements	1,286.5	1,012.8
Capitalized software	168.2	149.5
Capital leases	1.3	1.3
	5,275.0	3,960.4
Accumulated depreciation and amortization	(1,769.1)	(1,418.3)
	$ 3,505.9	$ 2,542.1

In accordance with Statement of Position No. 98-1, "Accounting for the Costs of Computer Software Developed or Obtained for Internal Use," the Company capitalizes application stage development costs for significant internally developed software projects. These costs are amortized over a five-year period. Unamortized costs were $78.6 million as of January 1, 2005 and $90.6 million as of January 3, 2004.

Impairment of long-lived assets–The Company groups and evaluates fixed and intangible assets excluding goodwill, for impairment at the individual store level, which is the lowest level at which individual cash flows can be identified. When evaluating assets for potential impairment, the Company first compares the carrying amount of the asset to the asset's estimated future cash flows (undiscounted and without interest charges). If the estimated future cash flows used in this analysis are less than the carrying amount of the asset, an impairment loss calculation is prepared. The impairment loss calculation compares the carrying amount of the asset to the asset's estimated future cash flows (discounted and with interest charges). If the carrying amount exceeds the asset's estimated future cash flows (discounted and with interest charges), the loss is allocated to the long-lived assets of the group on a pro rata basis using the relative carrying amounts of those assets.

Goodwill–The Company accounts for goodwill and intangibles under SFAS No. 142, "Goodwill and Other Intangible Assets." As such, goodwill and other indefinite-lived assets are not amortized, but are subject to annual impairment reviews. See Note 3 for further information on goodwill.

Intangible assets–Purchased customer lists are amortized on a straight-line basis over their estimated useful lives of up to 10 years. Purchased leases are amortized on a straight-line basis over the remaining life of the lease. See Note 3 for further information on intangible assets.

Revenue recognition–The Company recognizes revenue from the sale of merchandise at the time the merchandise is sold. Service revenue from the Company's pharmacy benefit management segment, which is recognized using the net method under Emerging Issues Task Force ("EITF") No. 99-19, "Reporting Revenue Gross as a Principal Versus Net as an Agent," is recognized at the time the service is provided. Service revenue totaled $129.3 million in 2004, $96.0 million in 2003 and $84.9 million in 2002. The Company offers sales incentives that entitle customers to receive a reduction in the price of a product or service. For sales incentives in which the Company is the obligor, the reduction in revenue is recognized at the time the product or service is sold. Customer returns are immaterial.

Vendor allowances–The Company accounts for vendor allowances under the guidance provided by EITF Issue No. 02-16, "Accounting by a Reseller for Cash Consideration Received from a Vendor" and EITF Issue No. 03-10, "Application of EITF Issue No. 02-16, 'Accounting by a Customer (Including a Reseller) for Certain Consideration Received from a Vendor,' by Resellers to Sales Incentives Offered to Consumers by Manufacturers." Vendor allowances reduce the carrying cost of inventory unless they are specifically identified as a reimbursement for promotional programs and/or other services provided. Funds that are directly linked to advertising commitments are recognized as a reduction of advertising expense in the selling, general and administrative expenses line when the related advertising commitment is satisfied. Any such allowances received in excess of the actual cost incurred also reduce the carrying cost of inventory. The total value of any upfront payments received from vendors that are linked to purchase commitments is initially deferred. The deferred amounts are then amortized to reduce cost of goods sold over the life of the contract based upon purchase volume. The total value of any upfront payments received from vendors that are not linked to purchase commitments is also initially deferred. The deferred amounts are then amortized to reduce cost of goods sold on a straight-line basis over the life of the related contract. The total amortization of these upfront payments was not material to the accompanying consolidated financial statements.

Store opening and closing costs–New store opening costs, other than capital expenditures, are charged directly to expense when incurred. When the Company closes a store, the present value of estimated unrecoverable costs, including the remaining lease obligation less estimated sublease income and the book value of abandoned property and equipment, are charged to expense.

Insurance–The Company is self-insured for certain losses related to general liability, workers' compensation and automobile liability. The Company obtains third party insurance coverage to limit exposure from these claims. The Company's self-insurance accruals, which include reported claims and claims incurred but not reported, are calculated using standard insurance industry actuarial assumptions and the Company's historical claims experience.

Stock-based compensation–The Company accounts for its stock-based compensation plans under the recognition and measurement principles of Accounting Principles Board ("APB") Opinion No. 25, "Accounting for Stock Issued to Employees,"

and related interpretations. As such, no stock-based employee compensation cost is reflected in net earnings for options granted under those plans since they had an exercise price equal to the market value of the underlying common stock on the date of grant. See Note 8 for further information on stock-based compensation.

The following table summarizes the effect on net earnings and earnings per common share if the company had applied the fair value recognition provisions of SFAS No. 123, "Accounting for Stock-Based Compensation," to stock-based employee compensation for the respective years:

In millions, except per share amounts		2004	2003	2002
Net earnings, as reported		$ 918.8	$ 847.3	$ 716.6
Add: Stock-based employee compensation expense included in reported net earnings, net of related tax effects[1]		1.5	2.2	2.7
Deduct: Total stock-based employee compensation expense determined under fair value based method for all awards, net of related tax effects		40.2	52.4	56.8
Pro forma net earnings		$ 880.1	$ 797.1	$ 662.5
Basic EPS:	As reported	$ 2.27	$ 2.11	$ 1.79
	Pro forma	2.17	1.98	1.65
Diluted EPS:	As reported	$ 2.20	$ 2.06	$ 1.75
	Pro forma	2.11	1.95	1.62

(1) Amounts represent the after-tax compensation costs for restricted stock grants.

Advertising costs–Advertising costs are expensed when the related advertising takes place. Advertising costs, net of vendor funding, which is included in selling, general and administrative expenses, were $205.7 million in 2004, $178.2 million in 2003 and $152.2 million in 2002.

Interest expense, net–Interest expense was $64.0 million, $53.9 million and $54.5 million and interest income was $5.7 million, $5.8 million and $4.1 million in 2004, 2003 and 2002, respectively. Capitalized interest totaled $10.4 million in 2004, $11.0 million in 2003 and $6.1 million in 2002.

Income taxes–The Company provides for federal and state income taxes currently payable, as well as for those deferred because of timing differences between reporting income and expenses for financial statement purposes versus tax purposes. Federal and state incentive tax credits are recorded as a reduction of income taxes. Deferred tax assets and liabilities are recognized for the future tax consequences attributable to differences between the carrying amount of assets and liabilities for financial reporting purposes and the amounts used for income tax purposes. Deferred tax assets and liabilities are measured using the enacted tax rates expected to apply to taxable income in the years in which those temporary differences are expected to be recoverable or settled. The effect of a change in tax rates is recognized as income or expense in the period of the change.

Accumulated other comprehensive loss–Accumulated other comprehensive loss consists of a minimum pension liability and unrealized losses on derivatives. The minimum pension liability totaled $57.7 million pre-tax ($35.7 million after-tax) as of January 1, 2005. The unrealized loss on derivatives totaled $31.2 million pre-tax ($19.8 million after-tax) as of January 1, 2005. The minimum pension liabilities totaled $59.4 million pre-tax ($36.9 million after-tax) and $71.9 million pre-tax ($44.6 million after-tax) as of January 3, 2004 and December 28, 2002, respectively.

Earnings per common share–Basic earnings per common share is computed by dividing: (i) net earnings, after deducting the after-tax Employee Stock Ownership Plan ("ESOP") preference dividends, by (ii) the weighted average number of common shares outstanding during the year (the "Basic Shares").

When computing diluted earnings per common share, the Company assumes that the ESOP preference stock is converted into common stock and all dilutive stock options are exercised. After the assumed ESOP preference stock conversion, the ESOP Trust would hold common stock rather than ESOP preference stock and would receive common stock dividends ($0.265 per share in 2004 and $0.230 per share in 2003 and 2002) rather than ESOP preference stock dividends (currently $3.90 per share). Since the ESOP Trust uses the dividends it receives to service its debt, the Company would have to increase its contribution to the ESOP Trust to compensate it for the lower dividends. This additional contribution would reduce the Company's net earnings, which in turn, would reduce the amounts that would be accrued under the Company's incentive compensation plans.

Diluted earnings per common share is computed by dividing: (i) net earnings, after accounting for the difference between the dividends on the ESOP preference stock and common stock and after making adjustments for the incentive compensation plans by (ii) Basic Shares plus the additional shares that would be issued assuming that all dilutive stock options are exercised and the ESOP preference stock is converted into common stock. Options to purchase 4.7 million and 18.5 million shares of common stock were outstanding as of January 1, 2005 and January 3, 2004, respectively, but were not included in the calculation of diluted earnings per share because the options' exercise prices were greater than the average market price of the common shares and, therefore, the effect would be antidilutive.

New accounting pronouncements–The Company adopted EITF Issue No. 03-10, "Application of EITF Issue No. 02-16, 'Accounting by a Customer (Including a Reseller) for Certain Consideration Received from a Vendor,' by Resellers to Sales Incentives Offered to Consumers by Manufacturers," effective January 4, 2004. The adoption of this pronouncement did not have an impact on the Company's consolidated results of operations or financial position.

The Company adopted Financial Accounting Standard Board's Staff Position No. FAS 106-2, "Accounting and Disclosure Requirements Related to the Medicare Prescription Drug, Improvement and Modernization Act of 2003," effective June 15, 2004. This statement requires disclosure of the effects of the Medicare Prescription Drug, Improvement and Modernization Act and an assessment of the impact of the federal subsidy on the accumulated postretirement benefit obligation and net periodic postretirement benefit cost. The adoption of this Statement did not have a material impact on the Company's consolidated results of operations or financial position.

In December 2004, SFAS No. 123R, "Share-Based Payment" was issued. This statement establishes standards for the accounting for transactions in which an entity exchanges its equity instruments for goods or services. The statement focuses primarily on accounting for transactions in which an entity obtains employee services in share-based payment transactions. The provisions of this statement are required to be adopted for interim or annual periods beginning after June 15, 2005. The Company is currently evaluating the effect of adopting this statement.

2 ✧ Acquisition

On July 31, 2004, the Company acquired certain assets and assumed certain liabilities from J.C. Penney Company, Inc. and certain of its subsidiaries, including Eckerd Corporation ("Eckerd"). The acquisition included 1,268 Eckerd retail drugstores and Eckerd Health Services, which includes Eckerd's mail order and pharmacy benefit management businesses (collectively, the "Acquired Businesses"). The Company believes that the acquisition of the Acquired Businesses is consistent with its long-term strategy of expanding its retail drugstore business in high-growth markets and increasing the size and product offerings of its pharmacy benefits management business. The results of operations of the Acquired Businesses from August 1, 2004 through January 1, 2005, have been included in the Company's consolidated statements of operations for the 52-week period ended January 1, 2005.

The purchase price under the Asset Purchase Agreement is $2.15 billion, which was adjusted for estimated working capital at closing. The final purchase price is subject to adjustment based on the final working capital of the Acquired Businesses as of the closing date. The Company anticipates that the adjustment to the purchase price will be finalized during fiscal 2005. The Company obtained funding for the acquisition through a combination of cash and commercial paper and subsequently repaid a portion of the commercial paper used to fund the acquisition with the proceeds received from the issuance of $650 million of 4.0% unsecured senior notes due September 15, 2009 and $550 million of 4.875% unsecured senior notes due September 15, 2014.

Following is a summary of the estimated assets acquired and liabilities assumed, which includes estimated transaction costs, as of July 31, 2004. This estimate is preliminary and based on information that was available to management at the time the financial statements were prepared. Accordingly, the allocation will change and the impact of such changes could be material.

estimated assets acquired and liabilities assumed as of July 31, 2004	
In millions	
Cash and cash equivalents	$ 3.0
Accounts receivable	366.1
Inventories	927.8
Other current assets	67.1
Total current assets	1,364.0
Property and equipment	455.1
Goodwill	1,011.9
Intangible assets	501.0
Other assets	133.2
Total assets acquired	3,465.2
Accounts payable	500.1
Accrued expenses	275.9
Total current liabilities	776.0
Other long-term liabilities	469.7
Total liabilities	1,245.7
Net assets acquired	2,219.5

The following pro forma combined results of operations have been provided for illustrative purposes only and do not purport to be indicative of the actual results that would have been achieved by the combined companies for the periods presented or that will be achieved by the combined companies in the future:

In millions, except per share amounts	2004	2003
Pro forma:[1][2]		
Net Sales	$ 34,564.3	$ 33,830.0
Net Earnings	907.0	865.5
Basic earnings per share	$ 2.24	$ 2.16
Diluted earnings per share	2.17	2.14

(1) The pro forma combined results of operations assume that the acquisition of the Acquired Businesses occurred at the beginning of each period presented. Such results have been prepared by adjusting the historical results of the Company to include the historical results of the Acquired Businesses, the incremental interest expense and the impact of the preliminary purchase price allocation discussed above.

(2) The pro forma combined results of operations do not include any cost savings that may result from the combination of the Company and the Acquired Businesses or any costs that will be incurred by the Company to integrate the Acquired Businesses.

3 ✧ Goodwill and other intangibles

Goodwill represents the excess of the purchase price over the fair value of net assets acquired. The Company accounts for goodwill and intangibles under SFAS No. 142, "Goodwill and Other Intangible Assets." As such, goodwill and other indefinite-lived assets are not amortized, but are subject to annual impairment reviews, or more frequent reviews if events or circumstances indicate there may be an impairment. When evaluating goodwill for potential impairment, the Company first compares the fair value of the reporting unit, based on estimated future discounted cash flows, with its carrying amount. If the estimated fair value of the reporting unit is less than its carrying amount, an impairment loss calculation is prepared. The impairment loss calculation compares the implied fair value of reporting unit goodwill with the carrying amount of that goodwill. If the carrying amount of reporting unit goodwill exceeds the implied fair value of that goodwill, an impairment loss is recognized in an amount equal to that excess. During the third quarter of 2004, the Company performed its required annual goodwill impairment test, which concluded there was no impairment of goodwill.

The carrying amount of goodwill was $1,898.5 million and $889.0 million as of January 1, 2005 and January 3, 2004, respectively. During 2004, gross goodwill increased $1,009.5 million, primarily due to the acquisition of the Acquired Businesses. There was no impairment of goodwill during 2004.

Intangible assets other than goodwill are required to be separated into two categories: finite-lived and indefinite-lived. Intangible assets with finite useful lives are amortized over their estimated useful life, while intangible assets with indefinite useful lives are not amortized. The Company currently has no intangible assets with indefinite lives.

Following is a summary of the Company's amortizable intangible assets as of the respective balance sheet dates:

	Jan. 1, 2005		Jan. 3, 2004	
In millions	GROSS CARRYING AMOUNT	ACCUMULATED AMORTIZATION	GROSS CARRYING AMOUNT	ACCUMULATED AMORTIZATION
Customer lists and Covenants not to compete[1]	$ 1,102.8	$ (321.8)	$ 571.3	$ (241.4)
Favorable leases and Other[1]	173.8	(86.9)	152.3	(78.5)
	$ 1,276.6	$ (408.7)	$ 723.6	$ (319.9)

(1) The increase in the gross carrying amount during 2004 was primarily due to the acquisition of the Acquired Businesses.

The amortization expense for these intangible assets totaled $95.9 million in 2004, $63.2 million in 2003 and $53.3 million in 2002. The anticipated annual amortization expense for these intangible assets is $124.7 million in 2005, $118.8 million in 2006, $113.3 million in 2007, $104.7 million in 2008 and $96.2 million in 2009.

4 ✧ Borrowing and credit agreements

Following is a summary of the Company's borrowings as of the respective balance sheet dates:

In millions	JAN. 1, 2005	JAN. 3, 2004
Commercial paper	$ 885.6	$ —
5.5% senior notes due 2004	—	300.0
5.625% senior notes due 2006	300.0	300.0
3.875 % senior notes due 2007	300.0	300.0
4.0% senior notes due 2009	650.0	
4.875% senior notes due 2014	550.0	
8.52% ESOP notes due 2008[1]	140.9	163.2
Mortgage notes payable	14.8	12.2
Capital lease obligations	0.8	0.9
	2,842.1	1,076.3
Less:		
Short-term debt	(885.6)	—
Current portion of long-term debt	(30.6)	(323.2)
	$ 1,925.9	$ 753.1

(1) See Note 6 for further information about the Company's ESOP Plan.

In connection with our commercial paper program, the Company maintains a $650 million, five-year unsecured back-up credit facility, which expires on May 21, 2006, and a $675 million, 364-day unsecured back-up credit facility, which expires on June 10, 2005. In addition, the Company maintains a $675 million, five-year unsecured backup credit facility, which expires on June 11, 2009. The credit facilities allow for borrowings at various rates depending on the Company's public debt ratings and require the Company to pay a quarterly facility fee of 0.8%, regardless of usage. As of January 1, 2005, the Company had no outstanding borrowings against the credit facilities. The weighted average interest rate for short-term debt was 1.8% as of January 1, 2005 and there were no outstanding short-term borrowings as of January 3, 2004.

In September 2004, the Company issued $650 million of 4.0% unsecured senior notes due September 15, 2009 and $550 million of 4.875% unsecured senior notes due September 15, 2014 (collectively the "Notes"). The Notes pay interest semi-annually and may be redeemed at any time, in whole or in part at a defined redemption price plus accrued interest.

Net proceeds from the Notes were used to repay a portion of the outstanding commercial paper issued to finance the acquisition of the Acquired Businesses.

To manage a portion of the risk associated with potential changes in market interest rates, the Company entered into Treasury-Lock Contracts (the "Contracts") with total notional amounts of $600 million. The Company settled these Contracts during the third quarter of 2004 in conjunction with the placement of the long-term financing at a loss of $32.8 million. The Company accounts for derivatives in accordance with SFAS No. 133, "Accounting for Derivative Instruments and Hedging Activities" as modified by SFAS No. 138, "Accounting for Derivative Instruments and Certain Hedging Activities," which requires the resulting loss to be recorded in shareholders' equity as a component of accumulated other comprehensive loss. This unrealized loss will be amortized as a component of interest expense, over the life of the related long-term financing.

As of January 1, 2005, the Company had no freestanding derivatives in place.

The Credit Facilities and unsecured senior notes contain customary restrictive financial and operating covenants. The covenants do not materially affect the Company's financial or operating flexibility.

The aggregate maturities of long-term debt for each of the five years subsequent to January 1, 2005 are $30.6 million in 2005, $335.0 million in 2006, $341.7 million in 2007, $45.6 million in 2008 and $651.3 million in 2009.

5 ✧ Leases

The Company leases most of its retail locations and eight of its distribution centers under non-cancelable operating leases, whose initial terms typically range from 15 to 25 years, along with options that permit renewals for additional periods. The Company also leases certain equipment and other assets under non-cancelable operating leases, whose initial terms typically range from 3 to 10 years. The Company recently conformed its accounting for operating leases and leasehold improvements to the views expressed by the Office of the Chief Accountant of the Securities and Exchange Commission to the American Institute of Certified Public Accountants on February 7, 2005. As a result, the Company recorded a $65.9 million non-cash pre-tax ($40.5 million after-tax) adjustment to total operating expenses, which represents the cumulative effect of the adjustment for a period of approximately 20 years (the "Lease Adjustment"). Since the effect of the Lease Adjustment was not material to any previously reported fiscal year, the cumulative effect was recorded in the fourth quarter of 2004. Minimum rent is expensed on a straight-line basis over the term of the lease. In addition to minimum rental payments, certain leases require additional payments based on sales volume, as well as reimbursements for real estate taxes, maintenance and insurance.

Following is a summary of the Company's net rental expense for operating leases for the respective years:

In millions	2004	2003	2002
Minimum rentals	$ 1,020.6	$ 838.4	$ 790.4
Contingent rentals	61.7	62.0	65.6
	1,082.3	900.4	856.0
Less: sublease income	(14.0)	(10.1)	(9.3)
	$ 1,068.3	$ 890.3	$ 846.7

Following is a summary of the future minimum lease payments under capital and operating leases as of January 1, 2005:

In millions	CAPITAL LEASES	OPERATING LEASES
2005	$ 0.2	$ 1,181.3
2006	0.2	1,120.8
2007	0.2	1,060.0
2008	0.2	1,008.1
2009	0.1	972.8
Thereafter	0.2	9,997.1
	1.1	$ 15,340.1
Less: imputed interest	(0.3)	
Present value of capital lease obligations	$ 0.8	

The Company finances a portion of its store development program through sale-leaseback transactions. The properties are sold at net book value and the resulting leases qualify and are accounted for as operating leases. The Company does not have any retained or contingent interests in the stores nor does the Company provide any guarantees, other than a corporate level guarantee of lease payments, in connection with the sale-leasebacks. Proceeds from sale-leaseback transactions totaled $496.6 million in 2004, $487.8 million in 2003 and $448.8 million in 2002. The operating leases that resulted from these transactions are included in the above table.

6 ✧ Employee stock ownership plan

The Company sponsors a defined contribution Employee Stock Ownership Plan (the "ESOP") that covers full-time employees with at least one year of service.

In 1989, the ESOP Trust issued and sold $357.5 million of 20-year, 8.52% notes due December 31, 2008 (the "ESOP Notes"). The proceeds from the ESOP Notes were used to purchase 6.7 million shares of Series One ESOP Convertible Preference Stock (the "ESOP Preference Stock") from the Company. Since the ESOP Notes are guaranteed by the Company, the outstanding

balance is reflected as long-term debt and a corresponding guaranteed ESOP obligation is reflected in shareholders' equity in the accompanying consolidated balance sheets.

Each share of ESOP Preference Stock has a guaranteed minimum liquidation value of $53.45, is convertible into 2.314 shares of common stock and is entitled to receive an annual dividend of $3.90 per share. The ESOP Trust uses the dividends received and contributions from the Company to repay the ESOP Notes. As the ESOP Notes are repaid, ESOP Preference Stock is allocated to participants based on (i) the ratio of each year's debt service payment to total current and future debt service payments multiplied by (ii) the number of unallocated shares of ESOP Preference Stock in the plan.

As of January 1, 2005, 4.3 million shares of ESOP Preference Stock were outstanding, of which 2.8 million shares were allocated to participants and the remaining 1.5 million shares were held in the ESOP Trust for future allocations.

Annual ESOP expense recognized is equal to (i) the interest incurred on the ESOP Notes plus (ii) the higher of (a) the principal repayments or (b) the cost of the shares allocated, less (iii) the dividends paid. Similarly, the guaranteed ESOP obligation is reduced by the higher of (i) the principal payments or (ii) the cost of shares allocated.

Following is a summary of the ESOP activity for the respective years:

In millions	2004	2003	2002
ESOP expense recognized	$ 19.5	$ 30.1	$ 26.0
Dividends paid	16.6	17.7	18.3
Cash contributions	19.5	30.1	26.0
Interest payments	13.9	16.6	18.7
ESOP shares allocated	0.3	0.4	0.4

7 ✧ Pension plans and other postretirement benefits

Defined contribution plans

The Company sponsors a voluntary 401(k) Savings Plan that covers substantially all employees who meet plan eligibility requirements. The Company makes matching contributions consistent with the provisions of the plan. At the participant's option, account balances, including the Company's matching contribution, can be moved without restriction among various investment options, including the Company's common stock. The Company also maintains a nonqualified, unfunded Deferred Compensation Plan for certain key employees. This plan provides participants the opportunity to defer portions of their compensation and receive matching contributions that they would have otherwise received under the 401(k) Savings Plan if not for certain restrictions and limitations under the Internal

Revenue Code. The Company's contributions under the above defined contribution plans totaled $52.1 million in 2004, $46.9 million in 2003 and $29.1 million in 2002. The Company also sponsors an Employee Stock Ownership Plan. See Note 6 for further information about this plan.

Other postretirement benefits

The Company provides postretirement healthcare and life insurance benefits to certain retirees who meet eligibility requirements. The Company's funding policy is generally to pay covered expenses as they are incurred. For retiree medical plan accounting, the Company reviews external data and its own historical trends for healthcare costs to determine the healthcare cost trend rates.

For measurement purposes, future healthcare costs are assumed to increase at an annual rate of 10.0%, decreasing to an annual growth rate of 5.0% in 2009 and thereafter. A one percent change in the assumed healthcare cost trend rate would change the accumulated postretirement benefit obligation by $0.8 million and the total service and interest costs by $0.1 million.

During 2004, the Company adopted the Financial Accounting Standards Board Staff Position No. FAS 106-2, "Accounting and Disclosure Requirements Related to the Medicare Prescription Drug, Improvement and Modernization Act of 2003." This statement requires disclosure of the effects of the Medicare Prescription Drug, Improvement and Modernization Act and an assessment of the impact of the federal subsidy on the accumulated postretirement benefit obligation and net periodic postretirement benefit cost. The adoption of this statement did not have a material impact on the Company's consolidated results of operations, financial position or related disclosures.

Pension plans

The Company sponsors a non-contributory defined benefit pension plan that covers certain full-time employees of Revco, D.S., Inc. who were not covered by collective bargaining agreements. On September 20, 1997, the Company suspended future benefit accruals under this plan. Benefits paid to retirees are based upon age at retirement, years of credited service and average compensation during the five-year period ending September 20, 1997. The plan is funded based on actuarial calculations and applicable federal regulations.

Pursuant to various labor agreements, the Company is also required to make contributions to certain union-administered pension and health and welfare plans that totaled $15.0 million in 2004, $13.2 million in 2003 and $12.1 million in 2002. The Company also has nonqualified supplemental executive retirement plans in place for certain key employees for whom it has purchased cost recovery variable life insurance.

The Company uses an investment strategy which emphasizes equities in order to produce higher expected returns, and in the long run, lower expense and cash contribution requirements. The pension plan assets allocation targets 70% equity and 30% fixed income.

Following is the pension plan assets allocation by major category for the respective years:

	2004	2003
Equity	70%	72%
Fixed Income	29%	27%
Other	1%	1%
	100%	100%

The equity investments primarily consist of large cap value and international value equity funds. The fixed income investments primarily consist of intermediate-term bond funds. The other category consists of cash and cash equivalents held for benefit payments.

The Company utilized a measurement date of December 31 to determine pension and other postretirement benefit measurements. Following is a summary of the net periodic pension cost for the defined benefit and other postretirement benefit plans for the respective years:

In millions	defined benefit plans			other postretirement benefits		
	2004	2003	2002	2004	2003	2002
Service cost	$ 0.9	$ 0.8	$ 0.8	$ —	$ —	$ —
Interest cost on benefit obligation	20.5	20.5	20.4	0.7	0.8	0.9
Expected return on plan assets	(18.6)	(18.4)	(19.3)	—	—	—
Amortization of net loss (gain)	3.3	1.5	0.1	—	(0.1)	(0.2)
Amortization of prior service cost	0.1	0.1	0.1	(0.1)	(0.1)	(0.1)
Settlement gain	—	—	—	—	—	—
Net periodic pension cost	$ 6.2	$ 4.5	$ 2.1	$ 0.6	$ 0.6	$ 0.6
ACTUARIAL ASSUMPTIONS:						
Discount rate	6.00%	6.25%	6.50%	6.00%	6.25%	6.50%
Expected return on plan assets[1]	8.50%	8.50%	8.75%	—	—	—
Rate of compensation increase	4.00%	4.00%	4.00%	—	—	—

(1) The expected long-term rate of return is determined by using the target allocation and historical returns for each asset class.

Following is a reconciliation of the benefit obligation, fair value of plan assets and funded status of the Company's defined benefit and other postretirement benefit plans as of the respective balance sheet dates:

In millions	defined benefit plans		other postretirement benefits	
	JAN. 1, 2005	JAN. 3, 2004	JAN. 1, 2005	JAN. 3, 2004
CHANGE IN BENEFIT OBLIGATION:				
Benefit obligation at beginning of year	$ 339.1	$ 322.8	$ 13.3	$ 13.8
Service cost	0.8	0.8	—	—
Interest cost	20.5	20.5	0.7	0.8
Actuarial loss (gain)	10.1	11.0	(0.5)	(0.3)
Benefits paid	(17.6)	(16.0)	(1.4)	(1.0)
Benefit obligation at end of year	$ 352.9	$ 339.1	$ 12.1	$ 13.3
CHANGE IN PLAN ASSETS:				
Fair value at beginning of year	$ 226.6	$ 186.8	$ —	$ —
Actual return on plan assets	25.8	38.4	—	—
Company contributions	20.4	17.4	1.4	1.0
Benefits paid	(17.6)	(16.0)	(1.4)	(1.0)
Fair value at end of year	$ 255.2	$ 226.6	$ —	$ —
FUNDED STATUS:				
Funded status	$ (97.7)	$ (112.5)	$ (12.1)	$ (13.3)
Unrecognized prior service cost	0.5	0.6	(0.4)	(0.5)
Unrecognized loss	63.8	64.2	0.3	0.7
Net liability recognized	$ (33.4)	$ (47.7)	$ (12.2)	$ (13.1)
AMOUNTS RECOGNIZED IN THE CONSOLIDATED BALANCE SHEET:				
Accrued benefit liability	$ (91.1)	$ (107.1)	$ (12.2)	$ (13.1)
Minimum pension liability	57.7	59.4	—	—
Net liability recognized	$ (33.4)	$ (47.7)	$ (12.2)	$ (13.1)

$17.1 million of the accrued benefit liability was included in accrued expenses, while the remaining amount was recorded in other long-term liabilities, as of January 1, 2005 and January 3, 2004. The accumulated benefit obligation for the defined benefit pension plans was $345.9 million and $333.5 million at January 1, 2005 and January 3, 2004, respectively. The Company estimates it will make cash contributions to the plan during the next fiscal year of approximately $17.1 million. Estimated future benefit payments for the defined benefit plans and other postretirement benefit plans, respectively, are $16.7 million and $1.3 million in 2005, $17.3 million and $1.3 million in 2006, $18.0 million and $1.3 million in 2007, $19.1 million and $1.2 million in 2008, $20.0 million and $1.2 million in 2009 and $120.3 million and $5.0 million in aggregate for the following five years. The Company recorded a minimum pension liability of $57.7 million as of January 1, 2005, and $59.4 million as of January 3, 2004, as required by SFAS No. 87. A minimum pension liability is required when the accumulated benefit obligation exceeds the combined fair value of the underlying plan assets and accrued pension costs. The minimum pension liability adjustment is reflected in other long-term liabilities, long-term deferred income taxes and accumulated other comprehensive loss, included in shareholders' equity, in the consolidated balance sheet.

8 ✧ Stock incentive plans

The 1996 Directors Stock Plan (the "Directors Plan") provides for the granting of up to 346,000 shares of common stock to the Company's non-employee directors. In anticipation of the Directors Plan not having sufficient shares to meet the Company's needs for anticipated awards to non-employee directors, an amendment to the Company's 1997 Incentive Compensation Plan (the "ICP") was approved by shareholders in 2004, allowing non-employee directors to receive awards under the ICP. Upon approval of this amendment to the ICP, all authority to make future grants under the Directors Plan was terminated, although previously granted awards remain outstanding in accordance with their terms and the terms of the Directors Plan.

The ICP provides for the granting of up to 42.9 million shares of common stock in the form of stock options and other awards to selected officers and employees of the Company. All grants under the ICP are awarded at fair market value on the date of grant. Options granted prior to 2004 generally become exercisable over a four-year period from the grant date and expire ten years after the date of grant. Options granted during fiscal 2004 generally become exercisable over a three-year period from the grant date and expire seven years after the date of grant. As of January 1, 2005, there were 14.1 million shares available for future grants under the ICP.

The ICP allows for up to 3.6 million restricted shares to be issued. The Company granted 412,000, 213,000 and 26,000 shares of restricted stock with a weighted average per share grant date fair value of $36.81, $25.26 and $31.20, in 2004, 2003 and 2002, respectively. The fair value of the restricted shares is expensed over the period during which the restrictions lapse. Compensation costs for restricted shares totaled $2.4 million in 2004, $3.6 million in 2003 and $4.3 million in 2002.

Following is a summary of the stock option activity for the respective years:

Shares in thousands	2004		2003		2002	
	SHARES	WEIGHTED AVERAGE EXERCISE PRICE	SHARES	WEIGHTED AVERAGE EXERCISE PRICE	SHARES	WEIGHTED AVERAGE EXERCISE PRICE
Outstanding at beginning of year	27,079	$ 34.22	23,390	$ 36.42	17,627	$ 39.48
Granted	2,932	35.50	6,401	25.21	8,022	29.89
Exercised	(3,782)	27.75	(707)	20.26	(517)	18.31
Canceled	(1,315)	38.17	(2,005)	35.84	(1,742)	41.66
Outstanding at end of year	24,914	35.16	27,079	34.22	23,390	36.42
Exercisable at end of year	12,549	$ 38.97	14,870	$ 35.53	8,048	$ 30.21

Following is a summary of the stock options outstanding and exercisable as of January 1, 2005:

Shares in thousands	options outstanding			options exercisable	
RANGE OF EXERCISE PRICES	NUMBER OUTSTANDING	WEIGHTED AVERAGE REMAINING LIFE	WEIGHTED AVERAGE EXERCISE PRICE	NUMBER EXERCISABLE	WEIGHTED AVERAGE EXERCISE PRICE
$ 1.81 to $ 15.00	129	1.2	$ 13.81	129	$ 13.81
15.01 to 25.00	1,362	1.7	20.28	1,323	20.15
25.01 to 30.00	10,993	7.5	27.53	2,520	29.85
30.01 to 35.00	2,248	5.3	31.89	2,148	31.91
35.01 to 50.00	6,529	4.8	38.51	3,661	40.86
50.01 to 61.23	3,654	6.0	60.44	2,768	60.42
Total	24,914	6.0	$ 35.16	12,549	$ 38.97

The Company applies APB Opinion No. 25 to account for its stock incentive plans. Accordingly, no compensation cost has been recognized for stock options granted. Had compensation cost been recognized based on the fair value of stock options granted consistent with SFAS No. 123, net earnings and net earnings per common share ("EPS") would approximate the pro forma amounts shown below:

In millions, except per share amounts	2004	2003	2002
Net earnings:			
As reported	$ 918.8	$ 847.3	$ 716.6
Pro forma	880.1	797.1	662.5
Basic EPS:			
As reported	$ 2.27	$ 2.11	$ 1.79
Pro forma	2.17	1.98	1.65
Diluted EPS:			
As reported	$ 2.20	$ 2.06	$ 1.75
Pro forma	2.11	1.95	1.62

The per share weighted average fair value of stock options granted during 2004, 2003 and 2002 was $12.93, $9.01 and $10.46, respectively.

The fair value of each stock option grant was estimated using the Black-Scholes Option Pricing Model with the following assumptions:

	2004	2003	2002
Dividend yield	0.65%	0.85%	0.96%
Expected volatility	30.50%	29.63%	29.50%
Risk-free interest rate	3.9%	3.5%	4.0%
Expected life	6.6	7.0	7.0

The 1999 Employee Stock Purchase Plan provides for the purchase of up to 7.4 million shares of common stock. Under the plan, eligible employees may purchase common stock at the end of each six-month offering period, at a purchase price equal to 85% of the lower of the fair market value on the first day or the last day of the offering period. During 2004, 0.9 million shares of common stock were purchased at an average price of $26.89 per share. As of January 1, 2005, 4.2 million shares of common stock have been issued since inception of the plan.

9 ✧ Commitments & contingencies

Between 1991 and 1997, the Company sold or spun off a number of subsidiaries, including Bob's Stores, Linens 'n Things, Marshalls, Kay-Bee Toys, Wilsons, This End Up and Footstar. In many cases, when a former subsidiary leased a store, the Company provided a corporate level guarantee of the store's lease obligations. When the subsidiaries were disposed of, the Company's guarantees remained in place, although each purchaser indemnified the Company for any lease obligations the Company was required to satisfy. If any of the purchasers were to become insolvent and failed to make the required payments under a store lease, the Company could be required to satisfy these obligations. As of January 1, 2005, the Company guaranteed approximately 525 such store leases, with terms extending as long as 2018. Assuming that each respective purchaser became insolvent, and the Company was required to assume all of these lease obligations, management estimates that the Company could settle the obligations for approximately $517 million as of January 1, 2005.

Management believes the ultimate disposition of any of the corporate level guarantees will not have a material adverse effect on the Company's consolidated financial condition, results of operations or future cash flows.

As of January 1, 2005, the Company had outstanding commitments to purchase $116 million of merchandise inventory for use in the normal course of business. The Company currently expects to satisfy these purchase commitments by 2008.

Beginning in August 2001, a total of nine actions were filed against the Company in the United States District Court for the District of Massachusetts asserting claims under the federal securities laws. The actions were subsequently consolidated under the caption *In re CVS Corporation Securities Litigation*, No. 01-CV-11464 (JLT) (D. Mass.) and a consolidated and amended complaint was filed on April 8, 2002 (the "Securities Action"). The consolidated amended complaint names as defendants the Company, its chief executive officer and its chief financial officer and asserts claims for alleged securities fraud under sections 10(b) and 20(a) of the Securities Exchange Act of 1934 and

Rule 10b-5 thereunder on behalf of a purported class of persons who purchased shares of the Company's common stock between February 6, 2001 and October 30, 2001. The discovery phase is now complete, a motion for summary judgment has been denied and a trial date has been set for May 9, 2005. The Company believes the Securities Action is without merit and intends to defend against it vigorously.

On October 29, 2004, a class action lawsuit asserting claims under the Employee Retirement Income Security Act was filed under the caption *Fescina v. CVS Corp., et. al.*, No. 04-CV-12309 (JLT) (D. Mass.) (the "ERISA Action"). The purported class includes persons who were participants in or beneficiaries of the CVS 401(k) plan between December 1, 2000 and October 30, 2001. The suit was filed in the United States District Court for the District of Massachusetts and designated as related to the Securities Action. The complaint names as defendants the Company, its chief executive officer, certain members of the CVS Board of Directors and certain unnamed fiduciaries. The Company believes the ERISA Action is entirely without merit and intends to defend the action vigorously.

On December 17, 2004, Richard Krantz filed a shareholder derivative suit under the caption *Krantz v. Ryan, et. al.*, No. 04-CV-12650 (REK) (D. Mass), based upon essentially the same allegations that underlie the Securities Action and the ERISA Action. The suit was filed in the United States District Court for the District of Massachusetts. The complaint names as defendants the Company (as nominal defendant), its chief executive officer, its chief financial officer and certain members of its Board of Directors. The Company believes this action is entirely without merit and intends to defend the action vigorously.

The Company is also a party to other litigation arising in the normal course of its business, none of which is expected to be material to the Company.

10 ◇ Income taxes

The provision for income taxes consisted of the following for the respective years:

In millions	2004	2003	2002
Current:			
Federal	$ 397.7	$ 421.5	$ 347.1
State	62.6	77.3	57.0
	460.3	498.8	404.1
Deferred:			
Federal	22.5	31.0	32.0
State	(5.2)	(1.6)	3.1
	17.3	29.4	35.1
Total	$ 477.6	$ 528.2	$ 439.2

Following is a reconciliation of the statutory income tax rate to the Company's effective tax rate for the respective years:

	2004	2003	2002
Statutory income tax rate	35.0%	35.0%	35.0%
State income taxes, net of federal tax benefit	3.8	3.6	3.4
Other	(0.3)	(0.2)	(0.4)
Federal and net State reserve release	(4.3)	—	—
Effective tax rate	34.2%	38.4 %	38.0%

Following is a summary of the significant components of the Company's deferred tax assets and liabilities as of the respective balance sheet dates:

In millions	JAN. 1, 2005	JAN. 3, 2004
Deferred tax assets:		
Lease and rents	$ 298.7	$ 127.6
Inventory	111.3	93.4
Employee benefits	51.8	57.2
Accumulated other comprehensive items	33.4	22.6
Retirement benefits	15.0	22.3
Allowance for bad debt	20.8	25.2
Amortization method	19.9	20.4
Other	61.3	35.8
Total deferred tax assets	612.2	404.5
Deferred tax liabilities:		
Accelerated depreciation	(231.5)	(194.0)
Total deferred tax liabilities	(231.5)	(194.0)
Net deferred tax assets	$ 380.7	$ 210.5

During the fourth quarter of 2004, the Company's assessment of its tax reserves resulted in a reduction that was principally based on finalizing certain tax return years and on a recent court decision relevant to the industry. As a result, the Company reversed $60.0 million of previously recorded tax reserves through the income tax provision. The Company believes it is more likely than not that the deferred tax assets included in the above table will be realized during future periods in which the Company generates taxable earnings.

11 ◇ Business segments

The Company currently operates two business segments, Retail Pharmacy and Pharmacy Benefit Management ("PBM").

The operating segments are segments of the Company for which separate financial information is available and for which operating results are evaluated regularly by executive management in deciding how to allocate resources and in assessing performance.

As of January 1, 2005, the Retail Pharmacy segment included 5,328 retail drugstores and the Company's online retail website, CVS.com.® The retail drugstores are located in 34 states and the District of Columbia and operate under the CVS® or CVS/pharmacy® name. The Retail Pharmacy segment is the Company's only reportable segment.

The PBM segment provides a full range of prescription benefit management services to managed care providers and other organizations. These services include mail order pharmacy services, specialty pharmacy services, plan design and administration, formulary management and claims processing. The specialty pharmacy business focuses on supporting individuals that require complex and expensive drug therapies. The PBM segment operates under the PharmaCare Management Services and PharmaCare Pharmacy® names and includes

47 retail pharmacies, located in 19 states and the District of Columbia.

The Company evaluates segment performance based on operating profit before the effect of non-recurring charges and gains and certain intersegment activities and charges. The accounting policies of the segments are substantially the same as those described in Note 1.

Following is a reconciliation of the significant components of the Company's net sales for the respective years:

	2004	2003	2002
Pharmacy	70.0%	68.8%	67.6%
Front store	30.0	31.2	32.4
	100.0%	100.0%	100.0%

Following is a reconciliation of the Company's business segments to the consolidated financial statements:

In millions	RETAIL PHARMACY SEGMENT	PBM SEGMENT	CONSOLIDATED TOTALS
2004:			
Net sales	$ 28,728.7	$ 1,865.6	$ 30,594.3
Operating profit	1,320.8	133.9	1,454.7
Depreciation and amortization	471.1	25.7	496.8
Total assets	13,118.5	1,428.3	14,546.8
Goodwill	1,257.4	641.1	1,898.5
Additions to property and equipment	1,341.5	6.2	1,347.7
2003:			
Net sales	$ 25,280.7	$ 1,307.3	$ 26,588.0
Operating profit	1,323.1	100.5	1,423.6
Depreciation and amortization	326.5	15.2	341.7
Total assets	9,975.0	568.1	10,543.1
Goodwill	690.4	198.6	889.0
Additions to property and equipment	1,114.2	7.5	1,121.7
2002:			
Net sales	$ 23,060.2	$ 1,121.3	$ 24,181.5
Operating profit	1,134.6	71.6	1,206.2
Depreciation and amortization	297.6	12.7	310.3
Total assets	9,132.1	513.2	9,645.3
Goodwill	690.4	188.5	878.9
Additions to property and equipment	1,104.5	4.3	1,108.8

12 ✦ Reconciliation of earnings per common share

Following is a reconciliation of basic and diluted earnings per common share for the respective years:

In millions, except per share amounts	2004	2003	2002
NUMERATOR FOR EARNINGS PER COMMON SHARE CALCULATION:			
Net earnings	$ 918.8	$ 847.3	$ 716.6
Preference dividends, net of income tax benefit	(14.2)	(14.6)	(14.8)
Net earnings available to common shareholders, basic	$ 904.6	$ 832.7	$ 701.8
Net earnings	$ 918.8	$ 847.3	$ 716.6
Dilutive earnings adjustment	(5.2)	(6.3)	(6.7)
Net earnings available to common shareholders, diluted	$ 913.6	$ 841.0	$ 709.9
DENOMINATOR FOR EARNINGS PER COMMON SHARE CALCULATION:			
Weighted average common shares, basic	398.6	394.4	392.3
Effect of dilutive securities:			
Preference stock	10.2	10.6	10.7
Stock options	6.6	2.7	2.3
Weighted average common shares, diluted	415.4	407.7	405.3
BASIC EARNINGS PER COMMON SHARE:			
Net earnings	$ 2.27	$ 2.11	$ 1.79
DILUTED EARNINGS PER COMMON SHARE:			
Net earnings	$ 2.20	$ 2.06	$ 1.75

13 ✦ Quarterly financial information (unaudited)

Dollars in millions, except per share amounts	FIRST QUARTER	SECOND QUARTER	THIRD QUARTER	FOURTH QUARTER	FISCAL YEAR
2004:					
Net sales	$ 6,818.6	$ 6,943.1	$ 7,909.4	$ 8,923.2	$ 30,594.3
Gross margin	1,771.7	1,826.5	2,070.8	2,362.2	8,031.2
Operating profit[1]	405.6	387.2	316.0	345.9	1,454.7
Net earnings[2]	244.6	234.5	184.6	255.1	918.8
Net earnings per common share, basic[2]	0.61	0.58	0.45	0.63	2.27
Net earnings per common share, diluted[2]	0.59	0.56	0.44	0.61	2.20
Dividends per common share	0.06625	0.06625	0.06625	0.06625	0.2650
Stock price: (New York Stock Exchange)					
High	38.23	42.64	43.63	46.90	46.90
Low	34.21	36.46	39.06	42.28	34.21
Registered shareholders at year-end					11,720
2003:					
Net sales	$ 6,312.8	$ 6,444.9	$ 6,378.1	$ 7,452.2	$ 26,588.0
Gross margin	1,605.5	1,633.8	1,658.6	1,965.1	6,863.0
Operating profit	331.3	337.0	316.7	438.6	1,423.6
Net earnings	196.3	199.8	187.8	263.4	847.3
Net earnings per common share, basic	0.49	0.50	0.47	0.66	2.11
Net earnings per common share, diluted	0.48	0.49	0.46	0.64	2.06
Dividends per common share	0.0575	0.0575	0.0575	0.0575	0.2300
Stock price: (New York Stock Exchange)					
High	26.67	28.50	32.60	37.46	37.46
Low	21.99	23.08	27.43	31.06	21.99

(1) Operating profit for the fourth quarter and fiscal year 2004, includes the pre-tax effect of a $65.9 million Lease Adjustment. Please see Note 5 for additional information regarding the Lease Adjustment.

(2) Net earnings and net earnings per common share for the fourth quarter and fiscal year 2004, include the after-tax effect of the Lease Adjustment discussed in (1) above, and the reversal of $60.0 million of previously recorded tax reserves as discussed in Note 10 above.

Five-Year Financial Summary

In millions, except per share amounts	2004 (52 WEEKS)	2003 (53 WEEKS)	2002 (52 WEEKS)	2001 (52 WEEKS)	2000 (52 WEEKS)
STATEMENT OF OPERATIONS DATA:					
Net sales	$ 30,594.3	$ 26,588.0	$ 24,181.5	$ 22,241.4	$ 20,087.5
Gross margin[1]	8,031.2	6,863.0	6,068.8	5,691.0	5,361.7
Selling, general and administrative expenses[2]	6,079.7	5,097.7	4,552.3	4,256.3	3,761.6
Depreciation and amortization[2][3]	496.8	341.7	310.3	320.8	296.6
Merger, restructuring and other non-recurring charges and (gains)	—	—	—	343.3	(19.2)
Total operating expenses	6,576.5	5,439.4	4,862.6	4,920.4	4,039.0
Operating profit[4]	1,454.7	1,423.6	1,206.2	770.6	1,322.7
Interest expense, net	58.3	48.1	50.4	61.0	79.3
Income tax provision[5]	477.6	528.2	439.2	296.4	497.4
Net earnings[6]	$ 918.8	$ 847.3	$ 716.6	$ 413.2	$ 746.0
PER COMMON SHARE DATA:					
Net earnings:[6]					
Basic	$ 2.27	$ 2.11	$ 1.79	$ 1.02	$ 1.87
Diluted	2.20	2.06	1.75	1.00	1.83
Cash dividends per common share	0.265	0.230	0.230	0.230	0.230
BALANCE SHEET AND OTHER DATA:					
Total assets	$ 14,546.8	$ 10,543.1	$ 9,645.3	$ 8,636.3	$ 7,949.5
Long-term debt	1,925.9	753.1	1,076.3	810.4	536.8
Total shareholders' equity	6,987.2	6,021.8	5,197.0	4,566.9	4,304.6
Number of stores (at end of period)	5,375	4,179	4,087	4,191	4,133

(1) Gross margin includes the pre-tax effect of a $5.7 million ($3.6 million after-tax) non-recurring charge in 2001 related to the markdown of certain inventory contained in stores closed as part of a strategic restructuring program.

(2) In 2004, the Company conformed its accounting for operating leases and leasehold improvements to the views expressed by the Office of the Chief Accountant of the Securities and Exchange Commission to the American Institute of Certified Public Accountants on February 7, 2005. As a result, the Company recorded a non-cash pre-tax adjustment of $9.0 million ($5.4 million after-tax) to selling, general and administrative expenses and $56.9 million ($35.1 after tax) to depreciation and amortization, which represents the cumulative effect of the adjustment for a period of approximately 20 years. Since the effect of this non-cash adjustment was not material to any previously reported fiscal year, the cumulative effect was recorded in the fourth quarter of 2004.

(3) As a result of adopting SFAS No. 142, "Goodwill and Other Intangible Assets" at the beginning of 2002, the Company no longer amortizes goodwill and other indefinite-lived intangible assets. Goodwill amortization totaled $31.4 million pre-tax ($28.2 million after-tax) in 2001 and $33.7 million pre-tax ($31.9 million after-tax) in 2000.

(4) Operating profit includes the pre-tax effect of the charges discussed in Note (1) above and the following merger, restructuring and other non-recurring charges and gains: (i) in 2004, $65.9 million ($40.5 million after-tax) relating to conforming the Company's accounting for operating leases and leasehold improvements, (ii) in 2001, $346.8 million ($226.9 million after-tax) related to restructuring and asset impairment costs associated with the strategic restructuring and the $3.5 million ($2.1 million after-tax) net non-recurring gain resulting from the net effect of the $50.3 million of settlement proceeds received from various lawsuits against certain manufacturers of brand name prescription drugs and the Company's contribution of $46.8 million of these settlement proceeds to the CVS/pharmacy Charitable Trust, Inc. to fund future charitable giving, and (iii) in 2000, $19.2 million ($11.5 million after-tax) non-recurring gain representing partial payment of the Company's share of the settlement proceeds from a class action lawsuit against certain manufacturers of brand-name prescription drugs.

(5) In 2004, the Company's assessment of tax reserves resulted in a reduction that was principally based on finalizing certain tax return years and on a recent court decision relevant to the industry. As a result, the Company reversed $60.0 million of previously recorded tax reserves through the income tax provision.

(6) Net earnings and net earnings per common share include the after-tax effect of the charges and gains discussed in Notes (1), (2), (3), (4) and (5) above.

Report of Independent Registered Public Accounting Firm

THE BOARD OF DIRECTORS AND SHAREHOLDERS
CVS CORPORATION

We have audited the accompanying consolidated balance sheets of CVS Corporation and subsidiaries as of January 1, 2005 and January 3, 2004, and the related consolidated statements of operations, shareholders' equity and cash flows for the fifty-two week period ended January 1, 2005, the fifty-three week period ended January 3, 2004 and the fifty-two week period ended December 28, 2002. These consolidated financial statements are the responsibility of the Company's management. Our responsibility is to express an opinion on these consolidated financial statements based on our audits.

We conducted our audits in accordance with the standards of the Public Company Accounting Oversight Board (United States). Those standards require that we plan and perform the audit to obtain reasonable assurance about whether the financial statements are free of material misstatement. An audit includes examining, on a test basis, evidence supporting the amounts and disclosures in the financial statements. An audit also includes assessing the accounting principles used and significant estimates made by management, as well as evaluating the overall financial statement presentation. We believe that our audits provide a reasonable basis for our opinion.

In our opinion, the consolidated financial statements referred to above present fairly, in all material respects, the financial position of CVS Corporation and subsidiaries as of January 1, 2005 and January 3, 2004, and the results of their operations and their cash flows for the fifty-two week period ended January 1, 2005, the fifty-three week period ended January 3, 2004 and the fifty-two week period ended December 28, 2002, in conformity with accounting principles generally accepted in the United States of America.

We also have audited, in accordance with the Public Company Accounting Oversight Board (United States), the effectiveness of CVS Corporation's internal control over financial reporting as of January 1, 2005, based on criteria established in Internal Control – Integrated Framework issued by the Committee of Sponsoring Organizations of the Treadway Commission (COSO), and our report dated March 8, 2005 expressed an unqualified opinion on management's assessment of, and the effective operation of, internal control over financial reporting.

KPMG LLP
Providence, Rhode Island

March 8, 2005

YOU ARE NOW FREE TO MOVE ABOUT THE COUNTRY.

SOUTHWEST.COM®

2004 ANNUAL REPORT

Item 8. *Financial Statements and Supplementary Data*

SOUTHWEST AIRLINES CO.

CONSOLIDATED BALANCE SHEET

	December 31,	
	2004	2003
	(In millions, except share data)	

ASSETS

Current assets:		
Cash and cash equivalents	$ 1,305	$1,865
Accounts and other receivables	248	132
Inventories of parts and supplies, at cost	137	93
Fuel hedge contracts	428	164
Prepaid expenses and other current assets	54	59
Total current assets	2,172	2,313
Property and equipment, at cost:		
Flight equipment	10,037	8,646
Ground property and equipment	1,202	1,117
Deposits on flight equipment purchase contracts	682	787
	11,921	10,550
Less allowance for depreciation and amortization	3,198	3,107
	8,723	7,443
Other assets	442	122
	$11,337	$9,878

LIABILITIES AND STOCKHOLDERS' EQUITY

Current liabilities:		
Accounts payable	$ 420	$ 405
Accrued liabilities	1,047	650
Air traffic liability	529	462
Current maturities of long-term debt	146	206
Total current liabilities	2,142	1,723
Long-term debt less current maturities	1,700	1,332
Deferred income taxes	1,610	1,420
Deferred gains from sale and leaseback of aircraft	152	168
Other deferred liabilities	209	183
Commitments and contingencies		
Stockholders' equity:		
Common stock, $1.00 par value: 2,000,000,000 shares authorized; 790,181,982 and 789,390,678 shares issued in 2004 and 2003, respectively	790	789
Capital in excess of par value	299	258
Retained earnings	4,089	3,883
Accumulated other comprehensive income	417	122
Treasury stock, at cost: 5,199,192 shares in 2004	(71)	—
Total stockholders' equity	5,524	5,052
	$11,337	$9,878

See accompanying notes

SOUTHWEST AIRLINES CO.

CONSOLIDATED STATEMENT OF INCOME

	Years Ended December 31,		
	2004	2003	2002
	(In millions, except per share amounts)		
OPERATING REVENUES:			
Passenger	$6,280	$5,741	$5,341
Freight	117	94	85
Other	133	102	96
Total operating revenues	6,530	5,937	5,522
OPERATING EXPENSES:			
Salaries, wages, and benefits	2,443	2,224	1,993
Fuel and oil	1,000	830	762
Maintenance materials and repairs	458	430	390
Agency commissions	2	48	55
Aircraft rentals	179	183	187
Landing fees and other rentals	408	372	345
Depreciation and amortization	431	384	356
Other operating expenses	1,055	983	1,017
Total operating expenses	5,976	5,454	5,105
OPERATING INCOME	554	483	417
OTHER EXPENSES (INCOME):			
Interest expense	88	91	106
Capitalized interest	(39)	(33)	(17)
Interest income	(21)	(24)	(37)
Other (gains) losses, net	37	(259)	(28)
Total other expenses (income)	65	(225)	24
INCOME BEFORE INCOME TAXES	489	708	393
PROVISION FOR INCOME TAXES	176	266	152
NET INCOME	$ 313	$ 442	$ 241
NET INCOME PER SHARE, BASIC	$ .40	$ .56	$ .31
NET INCOME PER SHARE, DILUTED	$ .38	$ .54	$ .30

See accompanying notes.

SOUTHWEST AIRLINES CO.

CONSOLIDATED STATEMENT OF STOCKHOLDERS' EQUITY

Years Ended December 31, 2004, 2003, and 2002

	Common Stock	Capital in Excess of Par Value	Retained Earnings	Accumulated Other Comprehensive Income (Loss)	Treasury Stock	Total
			(In millions, except per share amounts)			
Balance at December 31, 2001	$767	$ 51	$3,228	$(32)	$ —	$4,014
Issuance of common stock pursuant to Employee stock plans	10	47	—	—	—	57
Tax benefit of options exercised	—	38	—	—	—	38
Cash dividends, $.018 per share	—	—	(14)	—	—	(14)
Comprehensive income (loss)						
Net income	—	—	241	—	—	241
Unrealized gain on derivative instruments	—	—	—	88	—	88
Other	—	—	—	(2)	—	(2)
Total comprehensive income						327
Balance at December 31, 2002	777	136	3,455	54	—	4,422
Issuance of common stock pursuant to Employee stock plans	12	81	—	—	—	93
Tax benefit of options exercised	—	41	—	—	—	41
Cash dividends, $.018 per share	—	—	(14)	—	—	(14)
Comprehensive income (loss)						
Net income	—	—	442	—	—	442
Unrealized gain on derivative instruments	—	—	—	66	—	66
Other	—	—	—	2	—	2
Total comprehensive income						510
Balance at December 31, 2003	789	258	3,883	122	—	5,052
Purchase of shares of treasury stock . . .	—	—	—	—	(246)	(246)
Issuance of common and treasury stock pursuant to Employee stock plans . . .	1	6	(93)	—	175	89
Tax benefit of options exercised	—	35	—	—	—	35
Cash dividends, $.018 per share	—	—	(14)	—	—	(14)
Comprehensive income (loss)						
Net income	—	—	313	—	—	313
Unrealized gain on derivative instruments	—	—	—	293	—	293
Other	—	—	—	2	—	2
Total comprehensive income						608
Balance at December 31, 2004	$790	$299	$4,089	$417	$ (71)	$5,524

See accompanying notes.

SOUTHWEST AIRLINES CO.

CONSOLIDATED STATEMENT OF CASH FLOWS

	Years Ended December 31,		
	2004	2003	2002
	(In millions)		
CASH FLOWS FROM OPERATING ACTIVITIES:			
Net income	$ 313	$ 442	$ 241
Adjustments to reconcile net income to net cash provided by operating activities:			
Depreciation and amortization	431	384	356
Deferred income taxes	184	183	170
Amortization of deferred gains on sale and leaseback of aircraft	(16)	(16)	(15)
Amortization of scheduled airframe inspections and repairs	52	49	46
Income tax benefit from Employee stock option exercises	35	41	38
Changes in certain assets and liabilities:			
Accounts and other receivables	(75)	43	(103)
Other current assets	(44)	(19)	(10)
Accounts payable and accrued liabilities	231	129	(149)
Air traffic liability	68	50	(38)
Other	(22)	50	(16)
Net cash provided by operating activities	1,157	1,336	520
CASH FLOWS FROM INVESTING ACTIVITIES:			
Purchases of property and equipment, net	(1,775)	(1,238)	(603)
Initial payment for assets of ATA Airlines, Inc.	(34)	—	—
Debtor in possession loan to ATA Airlines, Inc.	(40)	—	—
Other	(1)	—	—
Net cash used in investing activities	(1,850)	(1,238)	(603)
CASH FLOWS FROM FINANCING ACTIVITIES:			
Issuance of long-term debt	520	—	385
Proceeds from trust arrangement	—	—	119
Proceeds from Employee stock plans	88	93	57
Payments of long-term debt and capital lease obligations	(207)	(130)	(65)
Payments of trust arrangement	—	—	(385)
Payment of revolving credit facility	—	—	(475)
Payments of cash dividends	(14)	(14)	(14)
Repurchase of common stock	(246)	—	—
Other, net	(8)	3	(4)
Net cash provided by (used in) financing activities	133	(48)	(382)
NET INCREASE (DECREASE) IN CASH AND CASH EQUIVALENTS	(560)	50	(465)
CASH AND CASH EQUIVALENTS AT BEGINNING OF PERIOD	1,865	1,815	2,280
CASH AND CASH EQUIVALENTS AT END OF PERIOD	$ 1,305	$ 1,865	$1,815
CASH PAYMENTS FOR:			
Interest, net of amount capitalized	$ 38	$ 62	$ 80
Income taxes	$ 2	$ 51	$ 3

See accompanying notes.

31

SOUTHWEST AIRLINES CO.

NOTES TO CONSOLIDATED FINANCIAL STATEMENTS
December 31, 2004

1. Summary of Significant Accounting Policies

Basis Of Presentation. Southwest Airlines Co. (Southwest) is a major domestic airline that provides point-to-point, low-fare service. The Consolidated Financial Statements include the accounts of Southwest and its wholly owned subsidiaries (the Company). All significant intercompany balances and transactions have been eliminated. The preparation of financial statements in conformity with accounting principles generally accepted in the United States (GAAP) requires management to make estimates and assumptions that affect the amounts reported in the financial statements and accompanying notes. Actual results could differ from these estimates.

Cash And Cash Equivalents. Cash in excess of that necessary for operating requirements is invested in short-term, highly liquid, income-producing investments. Investments with maturities of three months or less are classified as cash and cash equivalents, which primarily consist of certificates of deposit, money market funds, and investment grade commercial paper issued by major corporations and financial institutions. Cash and cash equivalents are stated at cost, which approximates market value.

Inventories. Inventories of flight equipment expendable parts, materials, and supplies are carried at average cost. These items are generally charged to expense when issued for use.

Property And Equipment. Depreciation is provided by the straight-line method to estimated residual values over periods generally ranging from 20 to 25 years for flight equipment and 5 to 30 years for ground property and equipment once the asset is placed in service. Residual values estimated for aircraft are 15 percent, except for 737-200 aircraft, which were retired from the Company's fleet in January 2005. The estimated residual value for these aircraft is two percent, based on current market values. Residual value percentages for ground property and equipment range from zero to 10 percent. Property under capital leases and related obligations are recorded at an amount equal to the present value of future minimum lease payments computed on the basis of the Company's incremental borrowing rate or, when known, the interest rate implicit in the lease. Amortization of property under capital leases is on a straight-line basis over the lease term and is included in depreciation expense.

In estimating the lives and expected residual values of its aircraft, the Company primarily has relied upon actual experience with the same or similar aircraft types and recommendations from Boeing, the manufacturer of the Company's aircraft. Subsequent revisions to these estimates, which can be significant, could be caused by changes to the Company's maintenance program, changes in utilization of the aircraft (actual flight hours or cycles during a given period of time), governmental regulations on aging aircraft, changing market prices of new and used aircraft of the same or similar types, etc. The Company evaluates its estimates and assumptions each reporting period and, when warranted, adjusts these estimates and assumptions. Generally, these adjustments are accounted for on a prospective basis through depreciation and amortization expense, as required by GAAP.

When appropriate, the Company evaluates its long-lived assets used in operations for impairment. Impairment losses would be recorded when events and circumstances indicate that an asset might be impaired and the undiscounted cash flows to be generated by that asset are less than the carrying amounts of the asset. Factors that would indicate potential impairment include, but are not limited to, significant decreases in the market value of the long-lived asset(s), a significant change in the long-lived asset's physical condition, operating or cash flow losses associated with the use of the long-lived asset, etc. While the airline industry as a whole has experienced many of these indicators, Southwest has continued to operate all of its aircraft and continues to experience positive cash flow.

Aircraft And Engine Maintenance. The cost of scheduled engine inspections and repairs and routine maintenance costs for all aircraft and engines are charged to maintenance expense as incurred. For the Company's 737-200, 737-300, and 737-500 aircraft fleet types, scheduled airframe inspections and repairs, known as D checks, are generally performed every ten years. Costs related to D checks are capitalized and amortized over the estimated period benefited, presently the least of ten years, the time until the next D check, or the remaining life of the aircraft. Modifications that significantly enhance the operating performance or ex-

SOUTHWEST AIRLINES CO.

NOTES TO CONSOLIDATED FINANCIAL STATEMENTS — (Continued)

tend the useful lives of aircraft or engines are capitalized and amortized over the remaining life of the asset.

The Company's newest aircraft fleet type, the 737-700, is maintained under a different, more efficient "next-generation" maintenance program. This program bundles tasks based on data gathered relative to fleet performance. Scheduled maintenance is still performed at recommended intervals; however, this program does not contain a D check. The costs of scheduled airframe inspections and repairs under this maintenance program are expensed as incurred, as those expenses more readily approximate the underlying scheduled maintenance tasks.

Intangible Assets. Intangible assets primarily consist of rights to airport owned gates acquired by the Company. These assets are amortized on a straight-line basis over the expected useful life of the lease.

Revenue Recognition. Tickets sold are initially deferred as "Air traffic liability". Passenger revenue is recognized when transportation is provided. "Air traffic liability" primarily represents tickets sold for future travel dates and estimated refunds and exchanges of tickets sold for past travel dates. The majority of the Company's tickets sold are nonrefundable. Tickets that are sold but not flown on the travel date can be reused for another flight, up to a year from the date of sale, or refunded (if the ticket is refundable). A small percentage of tickets (or partial tickets) expire unused. The Company estimates the amount of future refunds and exchanges, net of forfeitures, for all unused tickets once the flight date has passed. These estimates are based on historical experience over many years. The Company and members of the airline industry have consistently applied this accounting method to estimate revenue from forfeited tickets at the date travel is provided. Estimated future refunds and exchanges included in the air traffic liability account are constantly evaluated based on subsequent refund and exchange activity to validate the accuracy of the Company's revenue recognition method with respect to forfeited tickets.

Events and circumstances outside of historical fare sale activity or historical Customer travel patterns can result in actual refunds, exchanges or forfeited tickets differing significantly from estimates; however, these differences have historically not been material. Additional factors that may affect estimated refunds, exchanges, and forfeitures include, but may not be limited to, the Company's refund and exchange policy, the mix of refundable and nonrefundable fares, and fare sale activity. The Company's estimation techniques have been consistently applied from year to year; however, as with any estimates, actual refund and exchange activity may vary from estimated amounts.

Subsequent to third quarter 2001 and through second quarter 2002, the Company experienced a higher than historical mix of discount, nonrefundable ticket sales. The Company also experienced changes in Customer travel patterns resulting from various factors, including new airport security measures, concerns about further terrorist attacks, and an uncertain economy. Consequently, the Company recorded $36 million in additional passenger revenue in second quarter 2002 as Customers required fewer refunds and exchanges, resulting in more forfeited tickets. During 2003 and 2004, refund, exchange, and forfeiture activity returned to more historic, pre-September 11, 2001, patterns.

Frequent Flyer Program. The Company accrues the estimated incremental cost of providing free travel for awards earned under its Rapid Rewards frequent flyer program. The Company also sells frequent flyer credits and related services to companies participating in its Rapid Rewards frequent flyer program. Funds received from the sale of flight segment credits and associated with future travel are deferred and recognized as "Passenger revenue" when the ultimate free travel awards are flown or the credits expire unused.

Advertising. The Company expenses the costs of advertising as incurred. Advertising expense for the years ended December 31, 2004, 2003, and 2002 was $158 million, $155 million, and $156 million, respectively.

Stock-based Employee Compensation. The Company has stock-based compensation plans covering the majority of its Employee groups, including a plan covering the Company's Board of Directors and plans related to employment contracts with certain Executive Officers of the Company. The Company accounts for stock-based compensation utilizing the intrinsic value method in accordance with the provisions of Accounting Principles Board Opinion No. 25 (APB 25), "Accounting for Stock Issued to Employees" and related Interpretations. Accordingly, no compensation expense is recognized for fixed option plans because the exercise prices of Employee stock options equal or exceed the

SOUTHWEST AIRLINES CO.

NOTES TO CONSOLIDATED FINANCIAL STATEMENTS — (Continued)

market prices of the underlying stock on the dates of grant. Compensation expense for other stock options is not material.

The following table represents the effect on net income and earnings per share if the Company had applied the fair value based method and recognition provisions of Statement of Financial Accounting Standards (SFAS) No. 123, "Accounting for Stock-Based Compensation", to stock-based Employee compensation:

	2004	2003	2002
	(In millions, except per share amounts)		
Net income, as reported	$313	$442	$241
Add: Stock-based Employee compensation expense included in reported income, net of related tax effects	—	—	—
Deduct: Stock-based Employee compensation expense determined under fair value based methods for all awards, net of related tax effects	(74)	(57)	(53)
Pro forma net income	$239	$385	$188
Net income per share Basic, as reported	$ .40	$ .56	$ .31
Basic, pro forma	$ .31	$ .49	$ .24
Diluted, as reported	$ .38	$ .54	$ .30
Diluted, pro forma	$ .30	$ .48	$ .23

As required, the pro forma disclosures above include options granted since January 1, 1995. For purposes of pro forma disclosures, the estimated fair value of stock-based compensation plans and other options is amortized to expense primarily over the vesting period. See Note 13 for further discussion of the Company's stock-based Employee compensation.

In December 2004, the FASB issued SFAS No. 123R, "Share-Based Payment". SFAS No. 123R is a revision of SFAS No. 123, "Accounting for Stock Based Compensation", and supersedes APB 25. Among other items, SFAS 123R eliminates the use of APB 25 and the intrinsic value method of accounting, and requires companies to recognize the cost of employee services received in exchange for awards of equity instruments, based on the grant date fair value of those awards, in the financial statements. The effective date of SFAS 123R is the first reporting period beginning after June 15, 2005, which is third quarter 2005 for calendar year companies, although early adoption is allowed. SFAS 123R permits companies to adopt its requirements using either a "modified prospective" method, or a "modified retrospective" method. Under the "modified prospective" method, compensation cost is recognized in the financial statements beginning with the effective date, based on the requirements of SFAS 123R for all share-based

payments granted after that date, and based on the requirements of SFAS 123 for all unvested awards granted prior to the effective date of SFAS 123R. Under the "modified retrospective" method, the requirements are the same as under the "modified prospective" method, but also permits entities to restate financial statements of previous periods based on proforma disclosures made in accordance with SFAS 123.

The Company currently utilizes a standard option pricing model (i.e., Black-Scholes) to measure the fair value of stock options granted to Employees. While SFAS 123R permits entities to continue to use such a model, the standard also permits the use of a "lattice" model. The Company has not yet determined which model it will use to measure the fair value of employee stock options upon the adoption of SFAS 123R. See Note 13 for further information.

SFAS 123R also requires that the benefits associated with the tax deductions in excess of recognized compensation cost be reported as a financing cash flow, rather than as an operating cash flow as required under current literature. This requirement will reduce net operating cash flows and increase net financing cash flows in periods after the effective date. These future amounts cannot be estimated, because they depend on, among other things, when employees exercise stock

NOTES TO CONSOLIDATED FINANCIAL STATEMENTS — (Continued)

options. However, the amount of operating cash flows recognized in prior periods for such excess tax deductions, as shown in the Company's Consolidated Statement of Cash Flows, were $35 million, $41 million, and $38 million, respectively, for 2004, 2003, and 2002.

The Company currently expects to adopt SFAS 123R effective July 1, 2005; however, the Company has not yet determined which of the aforementioned adoption methods it will use. Subject to a complete review of the requirements of SFAS 123R, based on stock options granted to Employees through December 31, 2004, and stock options expected to be granted during 2005, the Company expects that the adoption of SFAS 123R on July 1, 2005, would reduce both third quarter 2005 and fourth quarter 2005 net earnings by approximately $10 million ($.01 per share, diluted) each. See Note 13 for further information on the Company's stock-based compensation plans.

Financial Derivative Instruments. The Company accounts for financial derivative instruments utilizing Statement of Financial Accounting Standards No. 133 (SFAS 133), "Accounting for Derivative Instruments and Hedging Activities", as amended. The Company utilizes various derivative instruments, including both crude oil and heating oil-based derivatives, to hedge a portion of its exposure to jet fuel price increases. These instruments primarily consist of purchased call options, collar structures, and fixed-price swap agreements, and are accounted for as cash-flow hedges, as defined by SFAS 133. The Company has also entered into interest rate swap agreements to convert a portion of its fixed-rate debt to floating rates. These interest rate hedges are accounted for as fair value hedges, as defined by SFAS 133.

Since the majority of the Company's financial derivative instruments are not traded on a market exchange, the Company estimates their fair values. Depending on the type of instrument, the values are determined by the use of present value methods or standard option value models with assumptions about commodity prices based on those observed in underlying markets. Also, since there is not a reliable forward market for jet fuel, the Company must estimate the future prices of jet fuel in order to measure the effectiveness of the hedging instruments in offsetting changes to those prices, as required by SFAS 133. Forward jet fuel prices are estimated through the observation of similar commodity futures prices (such as crude oil, heating oil,

and unleaded gasoline) and adjusted based on historical variations to those like commodities. See Note 10 for further information on SFAS 133 and financial derivative instruments.

Income Taxes. The Company accounts for deferred income taxes utilizing Statement of Financial Accounting Standards No. 109 (SFAS 109), "Accounting for Income Taxes", as amended. SFAS 109 requires an asset and liability method, whereby deferred tax assets and liabilities are recognized based on the tax effects of temporary differences between the financial statements and the tax bases of assets and liabilities, as measured by current enacted tax rates. When appropriate, in accordance with SFAS 109, the Company evaluates the need for a valuation allowance to reduce deferred tax assets.

2

Analyzing Business Transactions

Most accounting frauds and mistakes violate basic accounting concepts. They may involve recording a transaction at the wrong time, placing the wrong value on it, or calling it by the wrong name. What you learn in this chapter will help you avoid making such mistakes. It will also help you recognize correct accounting practices.

LEARNING OBJECTIVES

LO1 Explain how the concepts of recognition, valuation, and classification apply to business transactions and why they are important factors in ethical financial reporting.

LO2 Explain the double-entry system and the usefulness of T accounts in analyzing business transactions.

LO3 Demonstrate how the double-entry system is applied to common business transactions.

LO4 Prepare a trial balance, and describe its value and limitations.

LO5 Show how the timing of transactions affects cash flows and liquidity.

SUPPLEMENTAL OBJECTIVE

SO6 Define the *chart of accounts,* record transactions in the general journal, and post transactions to the ledger.

Making a Statement

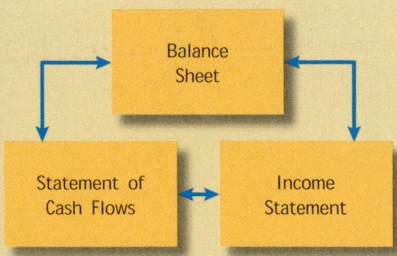

Business transactions can affect all the financial statements.

- An order for airplanes is obviously an important economic event to both the purchaser and the seller. Is there a difference between an economic event and a business transaction that should be recorded in the accounting records?

- Should Singapore and Boeing record the order in their accounting records?

- How important are liquidity and cash flows to Boeing?

In August 2004, **Singapore Airlines** announced that it had ordered 18 long-range Boeing 777-300ERs to replace its aging Boeing 747s. The order, valued at about $4 billion, was an important endorsement of **The Boeing Company's** newest long-range aircraft. It enabled Boeing to continue developing the plane, which is to carry 365 passengers more than 9,000 miles nonstop. Delivery of the planes was scheduled to begin in about four years.[1]

☰ Measurement Issues

Business transactions are economic events that affect a company's financial position. As shown in Figure 1, to measure a business transaction, you must decide when the transaction occurred (the recognition issue), what value to place on the transaction (the valuation issue), and how the components of the transaction should be categorized (the classification issue).

These three issues—recognition, valuation, and classification—underlie almost every major decision in financial accounting today. They are at the heart of accounting for pension plans, mergers of giant companies, and international transactions. In discussing these issues, we follow generally accepted accounting principles and use an approach that promotes an understanding of basic accounting concepts. Keep in mind, however, that measurement issues can be controversial and resolutions to them are not always as cut-and-dried as the ones presented here.

Recognition

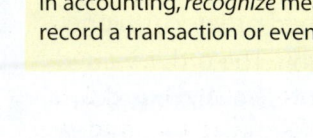

Study Note

In accounting, *recognize* means to record a transaction or event.

The **recognition** issue refers to the difficulty of deciding *when* a business transaction should be recorded. The resolution of this issue is important because the date on which a transaction is recorded affects amounts in the financial statements.

To illustrate some of the factors involved in the recognition issue, suppose a company wants to purchase an office desk. The following events take place:

1. An employee sends a purchase requisition for the desk to the purchasing department.

2. The purchasing department sends a purchase order to the supplier.

3. The supplier ships the desk.

4. The company receives the desk.

5. The company receives the bill from the supplier.

6. The company pays the bill.

According to accounting tradition, a transaction should be recorded when title to merchandise passes from the supplier to the purchaser and creates an obligation to pay. Thus, depending on the details of the shipping agreement

FOCUS ON BUSINESS PRACTICE

Accounting Policies: Where Do You Find Them?

As the text explains, **Singapore Airlines'** order of **Boeing** aircraft, which is the focus of this chapter's Decision Point, was not an event that either company should have recorded as a transaction. But when do companies record sales or purchase transactions? The answer to this question and others about companies' accounting policies can be found in the Summary of Significant Accounting Policies in their annual reports. For example, in that section of its annual report, Boeing states: "We recognize sales for commercial airplane deliveries as each unit is completed and accepted by the customer."[2]

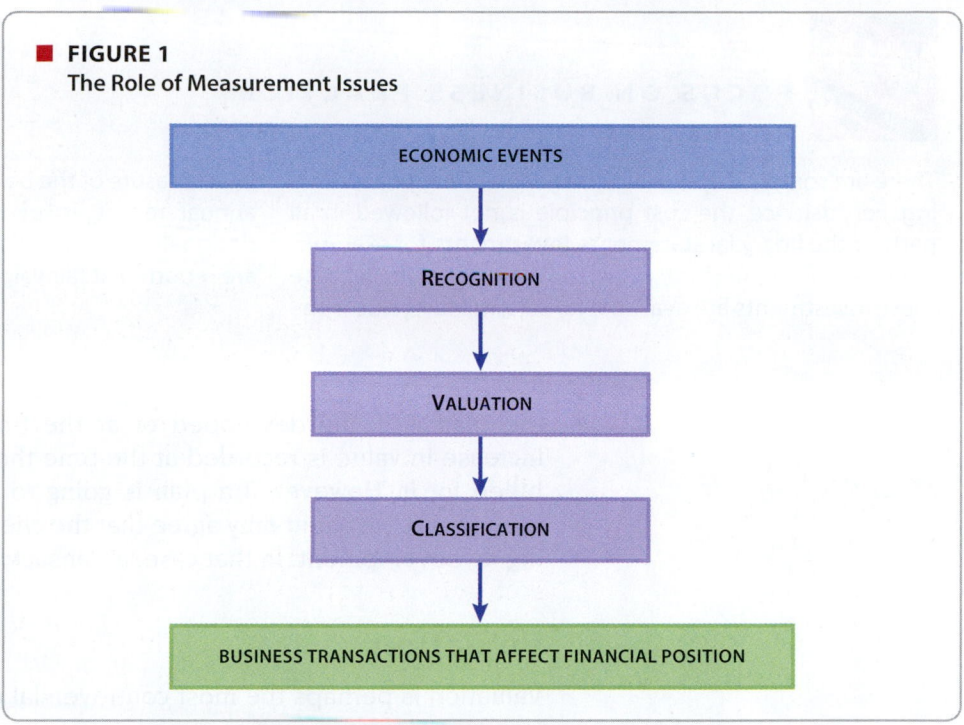

■ FIGURE 1
The Role of Measurement Issues

ECONOMIC EVENTS

RECOGNITION

VALUATION

CLASSIFICATION

BUSINESS TRANSACTIONS THAT AFFECT FINANCIAL POSITION

> *Study Note*
>
> A purchase should usually not be recognized (recorded) before title is transferred because until that point, the vendor has not fulfilled its contractual obligation and the buyer has no liability.

for the desk, the transaction should be recognized (recorded) at the time of either event **3** or **4**. This is the guideline we generally use in this book. However, many small businesses that have simple accounting systems do not record a transaction until they receive a bill (event **5**) or pay it (event **6**) because these are the implied points of title transfer. The predetermined time at which a transaction should be recorded is the **recognition point**.

Although purchase requisitions and purchase orders (events **1** and **2**) are economic events, they do not affect a company's financial position, and they are not recognized in the accounting records. Even the most important economic events may not be recognized in the accounting records. For example, the order of 18 long-range planes described in the Decision Point was a very important economic event for both **Singapore Airlines** and **Boeing**, but the recognition point for the transaction for both companies is several years in the future—that is, when the planes are delivered and title to them transfers from Boeing to Singapore Airlines.

Here are some more examples of economic events that should and should not be recorded as business transactions:

Events That Are Not Recorded as Transactions	Events That Are Recorded as Transactions
A customer inquires about the availability of a service.	A customer buys a service.
A company hires a new employee.	A company pays an employee for work performed.
A company signs a contract to provide a service in the future.	The company performs the service.

The recognition issue can be difficult to resolve. Consider an advertising agency that is planning a major advertising campaign for a client. Employees may work on the plan several hours a day for a number of weeks. They add value to the plan as they develop it. Should this added value be recognized as

FOCUS ON BUSINESS PRACTICE

Is It Always Cost?

There are some exceptions to the general rules of accounting. For instance, the cost principle is not followed in all parts of the financial statements. Investments, for example, are often accounted for at fair, or market, value. Because these investments are available for sale, the fair value is the best measure of the potential benefit to the company. In its annual report, **Intel Corporation** states: "Investments designated as available-for-sale on the balance sheet date are reported at fair value."[3]

the plan is being developed or at the time it is completed? Usually, the increase in value is recorded at the time the plan is finished and the client is billed for it. However, if a plan is going to take a long time to develop, the agency and the client may agree that the client will be billed at key points during its development. In that case, a transaction is recorded at each billing.

Valuation

Valuation is perhaps the most controversial issue in accounting. The **valuation** issue focuses on assigning a monetary value to a business transaction. Generally accepted accounting principles state that the original cost (often called *historical cost*) is the appropriate value to assign to all business transactions—and therefore to all assets, liabilities, and components of stockholders' equity, including revenues and expenses. **Cost** is defined as the *exchange price* associated with a business transaction at the time the transaction is recorded.

According to GAAP, the purpose of valuation is not to account for value in terms of worth, which can change after a transaction occurs, but to account for value in terms of cost at the time of the transaction. Thus, the cost of an asset is recorded when the asset is acquired. The value is held at that level until the asset is sold, expires, or is consumed. In this context, *value* means the cost at the time of the transaction. The practice of recording transactions at cost is called the **cost principle**.

The cost principle is used because the cost, or exchange price, is verifiable. The **exchange price** results from an agreement between the buyer and seller that can be verified by evidence created at the time of the transaction. It is this price at which the transaction is recorded. For example, when the order referred to in the Decision Point is finally complete and **Boeing** delivers the

Study Note

The value of a transaction usually is based on a business document—a canceled check or an invoice. Appraisals or other subjective amounts are generally not recorded.

FOCUS ON BUSINESS PRACTICE

No Dollar Amount: How Can That Be?

Determining the value of a sale or purchase transaction isn't difficult when the value equals the amount of cash that changes hands. However, barter transactions, in which exchanges are made but no cash changes hands, can make valuation more complicated. Barter transactions are quite common in business today. Here are some examples:

- A consulting company provides its services to an auto dealer in exchange for the loan of a car for a year.

- An office supply company provides a year's supply of computer paper to a local weekly newspaper in exchange for an advertisement in 52 issues of the paper.

- Two Internet companies each provide an advertisement and link to the other's website on their own websites.

Determining the value of these transactions is a matter of determining the fair value of the items being traded.

planes to **Singapore Airplanes,** the two companies will record the transaction at the price they have agreed on.

To illustrate further, suppose a person offers a building for sale at $120,000. It may be valued for real estate taxes at $75,000, and it may be insured for $90,000. One prospective buyer may offer $100,000 for the building, and another may offer $105,000. At this point, several different, unverifiable opinions of value have been expressed. Finally, suppose the seller and a buyer settle on a price and complete the sale for $110,000. All these figures are values of one kind or another, but only the last is sufficiently reliable to be used in the accounting records. The market value of the building may vary over the years, but the building will remain on the new buyer's records at $110,000 until it is sold again. At that point, the accountant will record the new transaction at the new exchange price, and a profit or loss will be recognized.

Classification

The **classification** issue has to do with assigning all the transactions in which a business engages to appropriate categories, or accounts. Classification of debts can affect a company's ability to borrow money, and classification of purchases can affect its income. For example, purchases of tools may be considered repair expenses (a component of stockholders' equity) or equipment (asset).

As noted in the Decision Point, it will take **Boeing** several years to manufacture the 18 planes that **Singapore Airlines** ordered. Over those years, many classification issues will arise. One of the most important is how to classify the numerous costs that Boeing will incur in building the planes. As you will see, generally accepted accounting principles require that these costs be classified as assets until the sale is recorded at the time the planes are delivered. At that time, they will be reclassified as expenses. In this way, the costs will offset the revenues from the sale. It will then be possible to tell whether Boeing made a profit or loss on the transaction.

As we explain later in the chapter, proper classification depends not only on correctly analyzing the effect of each transaction on a business, but also on maintaining a system of accounts that reflects that effect.

Ethics and Measurement Issues

Recognition, valuation, and classification are important factors in ethical financial reporting, and generally accepted accounting principles provide direction about their treatment. These guidelines are intended to help managers meet their obligation to their company's owners and to the public. Many of the most egregious financial reporting frauds over the past several years have resulted from violations of these guidelines.

‣ **Xerox Corporation** violated the guidelines for recognition when it overstated its revenues by recording revenue from lease agreements at the time the leases were signed rather than over the lease term.

‣ Among its many other transgressions, **Enron Corporation** violated the guidelines for valuation when it valued assets that it transferred to related companies at far more than their actual value.

‣ By a simple violation of the guidelines for classification, **WorldCom** (now **MCI**) perpetrated the largest financial fraud in history, which resulted in the largest bankruptcy in history. Over a period of several years, the company

Study Note

If CVS buys paper towels to resell to customers, the cost would be recorded as an asset in the Inventory account. If the paper towels are used for cleaning in the store, the cost is an expense.

Senior WorldCom executives violated standards of good financial reporting and GAAP when they deliberately understated expenses to disguise poor performance. Consequences were devasting for employees, investors, and the public trust. *Left to right:* Melvin Dick of Arthur Andersen, Bernard Ebbers and Scott Sullivan of WorldCom, and Jack Grabman of Salomon Smith Barney are sworn in on July 8, 2002, at a congressional hearing of charges against WorldCom.

recorded expenditures that should have been classified as expenses as assets; this had the effect of understating the company's expenses and overstating its income by more than $10 billion.

STOP • REVIEW • APPLY

1-1. What three issues underlie most major accounting decisions?

1-2. A customer asks the owner of a store to save an item for him and says he will pick it up and pay for it next week. The owner agrees to hold it. Should this transaction be recorded as a sale? Explain your answer.

1-3. Why is it practical for accountants to rely on original cost for valuation purposes?

1-4. Why is classification of a transaction as an expense or an asset a critical issue in accounting?

1-5. How are recognition, valuation, and classification related to the ethics of financial reporting?

Suggested answers to all Stop, Review, and Apply questions follow the appendixes.

Double-Entry System

LO2 Explain the double-entry system and the usefulness of T accounts in analyzing business transactions.

The double-entry system, the backbone of accounting, evolved during the Renaissance. The first systematic description of double-entry bookkeeping appeared in 1494, two years after Columbus discovered America, in a mathematics book by Fra Luca Pacioli. Goethe, the famous German poet and dramatist, referred to double-entry bookkeeping as "one of the finest discoveries of the human intellect." Werner Sombart, an eminent economist-sociologist, believed that "double-entry bookkeeping is born of the same spirit as the system of Galileo and Newton."

What is the significance of the double-entry system? The system is based on the *principle of duality*, which means that every economic event has two aspects—effort and reward, sacrifice and benefit, source and use—that offset, or balance, each other. In the **double-entry system**, each transaction must be recorded with at least one debit and one credit, and the total amount of the debits must equal the total amount of the credits. Because of the way it is designed, the whole system is always in balance. All accounting systems, no matter how sophisticated, are based on the principle of duality.

Study Note

Each transaction must include at least one debit and one credit, and the debit totals must equal the credit totals.

Accounts

Accounts are the basic storage units for accounting data and are used to accumulate amounts from similar transactions. An accounting system has a separate account for each asset, each liability, and each component of stockholders' equity, including revenues and expenses. Whether a company keeps records by hand or by computer, managers must be able to refer to accounts so that they can study their company's financial history and plan for the future. A very small company may need only a few dozen accounts; a multinational corporation may need thousands.

An account title should describe what is recorded in the account. However, account titles can be rather confusing. For example, *Fixed Assets*, *Plant and Equipment*, *Capital Assets*, and *Long-Lived Assets* are all titles for long-term assets. Moreover, many account titles change over time as preferences and practices change.

When you come across an account title that you don't recognize, examine the context of the name—whether it is classified in the financial statements as an asset, liability, or component of stockholders' equity—and look for the kind of transaction that gave rise to the account.

The T Account

The **T account** is a good place to begin the study of the double-entry system. Such an account has three parts: a title, which identifies the asset, liability, or stockholders' equity account; a left side, which is called the **debit** side; and a right side, which is called the **credit** side. The T account, so called because it resembles the letter T, is used to analyze transactions. It looks like this:

Study Note

Many students have preconceived ideas about what *debit* and *credit* mean. They think *debit* means "decrease" (or implies something bad) and *credit* means "increase" (or implies something good). It is important to realize that *debit* simply means "left side" and *credit* simply means "right side."

TITLE OF ACCOUNT	
Debit	Credit
(left) side	(right) side

Any entry made on the left side of the account is a debit, and any entry made on the right side is a credit. The terms *debit* (abbreviated Dr., from the Latin *debere*) and *credit* (abbreviated Cr., from the Latin *credere*) are simply the accountant's words for "left" and "right" (*not* for "increase" or "decrease"). We present a more formal version of the T account, the ledger account form, later in this chapter.

The T Account Illustrated

Suppose a company had several transactions that involved the receipt or payment of cash. These transactions can be summarized in the Cash account by recording receipts on the left (debit) side of a T account and payments on the right (credit) side.

CASH		
100,000	70,000	
3,000	400	
	1,200	
103,000	**71,600**	
Bal. **31,400**		

The cash receipts on the left total $103,000. (The total is written in bold figures so that it cannot be confused with an actual debit entry.) The cash payments on the right side total $71,600. These totals are simply working totals, or **footings**. Footings, which are calculated at the end of each month, are an easy way to determine cash on hand. The difference in dollars between the total debit footing and the total credit footing is called the **balance**, or *account balance*. If the balance is a debit, it is written on the left side. If it is a credit, it is written on the right side. Notice that the Cash account has a debit balance of $31,400 ($103,000 − $71,600). This is the amount of cash the business has on hand at the end of the month.

Rules of Double-Entry Accounting

The two rules of the double-entry system are that every transaction affects at least two accounts and that total debits must equal total credits. In other words, for every transaction, one or more accounts must be debited, or entered on the left side of the T account, and one or more accounts must be credited, or entered on the right side of the T account, and the total dollar amount of the debits must equal the total dollar amount of the credits.

Look again at the accounting equation:

$$\text{Assets} = \text{Liabilities} + \text{Stockholders' Equity}$$

You can see that if a debit increases assets, then a credit must be used to increase liabilities or stockholders' equity because they are on opposite sides of the equal sign. Likewise, if a credit decreases assets, then a debit must be used to decrease liabilities or stockholders' equity. These rules can be shown as follows:

ASSETS		=	LIABILITIES		+	STOCKHOLDERS' EQUITY	
Debit for increases (+)	Credit for decreases (−)		Debit for decreases (−)	Credit for increases (+)		Debit for decreases (−)	Credit for increases (+)

1. Debit increases in assets to asset accounts. Credit decreases in assets to asset accounts.

2. Credit increases in liabilities and stockholders' equity to liability and stockholders' equity accounts. Debit decreases in liabilities and stockholders' equity to liability and stockholders' equity accounts.

One of the more difficult points to understand is the application of double-entry rules to the components of stockholders' equity. The key is to remember that dividends and expenses are deductions from stockholders' equity. Thus, transactions that *increase* dividends or expenses *decrease* stockholders' equity. Consider this expanded version of the accounting equation.

Stockholders' Equity

| Assets | = | Liabilities | + | Common Stock | + | Retained Earnings | − | Dividends | + | Revenues | − | Expenses |

ASSETS		LIABILITIES		COMMON STOCK		RETAINED EARNINGS		DIVIDENDS		REVENUES		EXPENSES	
+	−	−	+	−	+	−	+	+	−	−	+	+	−
(Dr.)	(Cr.)	(Dr.)	(Cr.)	(Dr.)	(Cr.)	(Dr.)	(Cr.)	(Dr.)	(Cr.)	(Dr.)	(Cr.)	(Dr.)	(Cr.)

Normal Balance

The **normal balance** of an account is its usual balance and is the side (debit or credit) that increases the account. Table 1 summarizes the normal account balances of the major account categories. If you have difficulty remembering the normal balances and the rules of debit and credit, try using the acronym ADE: Asset accounts, Dividends, and Expenses are always increased by debits. All other accounts are increased by credits.

TABLE 1. Normal Account Balances of Major Account Categories

Account Category	Increases Recorded by		Normal Balance	
	Debit	Credit	Debit	Credit
Assets	x		x	
Liabilities		x		x
Stockholders' equity:				
Common stock		x		x
Retained earnings		x		x
Dividends	x		x	
Revenues		x		x
Expenses	x		x	

Stockholders' Equity Accounts

Figure 2 illustrates how stockholders' equity accounts relate to each other and to the financial statements. The distinctions among these accounts are important for both legal purposes and financial reporting.

▶ Stockholders' equity accounts represent the legal claims of stockholders to the assets of a corporation. The Common Stock account represents stockholders' claims arising from their investments in the business, and the Retained Earnings account represents stockholders' claims arising from profitable operations. Both are claims against the general assets of the company, not against specific assets. Dividends are deducted from the stockholders' claims on retained earnings and are shown on the statement of retained earnings.

Study Note

Although dividends are a component of stockholders' equity, they normally appear only in the statement of retained earnings. They do not appear in the stockholders' equity section of the balance sheet or as an expense on the income statement.

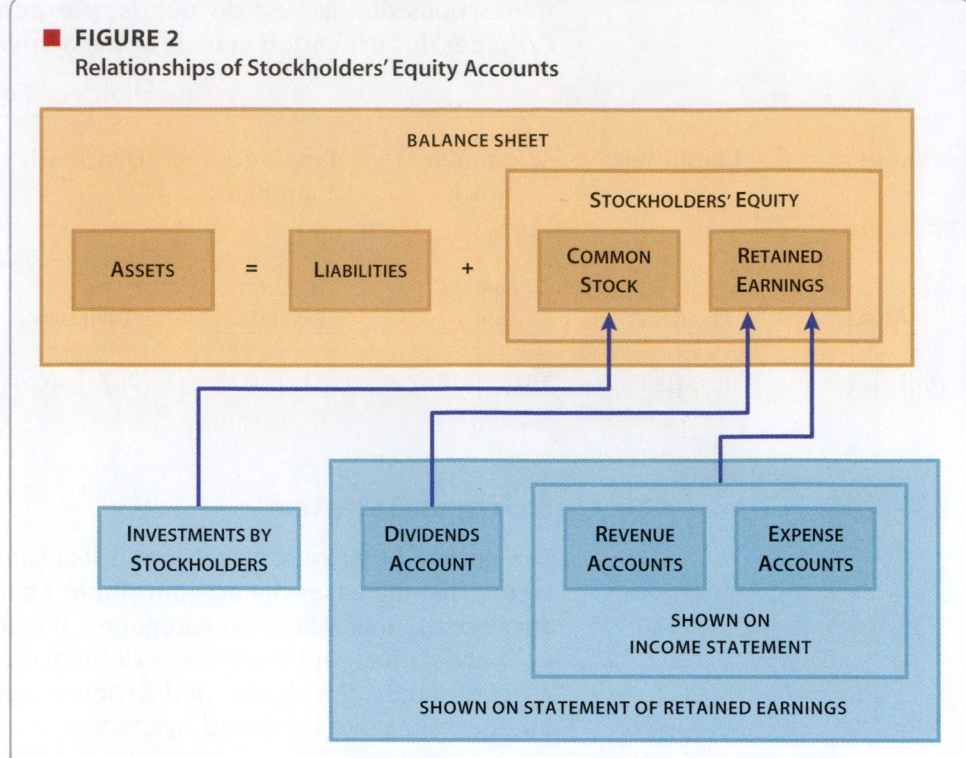

FIGURE 2
Relationships of Stockholders' Equity Accounts

Study Note

Although revenues and expenses are components of stockholders' equity, they appear on the income statement, not in the stockholders' equity section of the balance sheet. Figure 2 illustrates this point.

▶ By law, investments by stockholders and dividends must be separated from revenues and expenses for both income tax purposes and financial reporting purposes.

▶ Managers need a detailed breakdown of revenues and expenses for budgeting and operating purposes. From the Revenue and Expense accounts on the income statement, they can identify the sources of all revenues and the nature of all expenses. In this way, accounting gives managers information about whether they have achieved a primary business goal—that is, whether they have enabled their company to earn a net income.

STOP • REVIEW • APPLY

2-1. Why is the system of recording entries called the double-entry system? What is significant about this system?

2-2. Is the statement "Debits are bad; credits are good" true? Explain your answer.

2-3. What is an account, and what is its normal balance?

2-4. What are T accounts, and why are they useful?

2-5. What are the rules of double entry for (a) assets, (b) liabilities, and (c) stockholders' equity?

2-6. In the stockholders' equity accounts, why do accountants maintain separate accounts for revenues and expenses rather than using the Retained Earnings account?

T Accounts, Normal Balance, and the Accounting Equation You are given the following list of accounts with dollar amounts:

Dividends	$ 75	Common Stock	$300
Accounts Payable	200	Fees Revenue	250
Wages Expense	150	Retained Earnings	100
Cash	625		

Insert the account title at the top of its corresponding T account and enter the dollar amount as a normal balance in the account. Then show that the accounting equation is in balance.

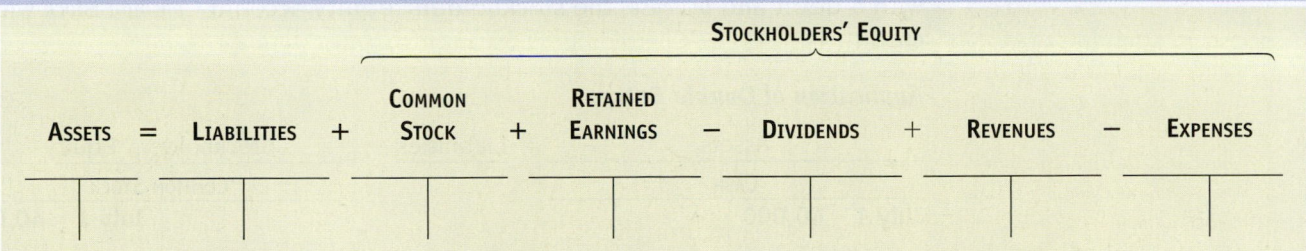

SOLUTION

CASH	ACCOUNTS PAYABLE	COMMON STOCK	RETAINED EARNINGS	DIVIDENDS	FEES REVENUE	WAGES EXPENSE
625	200	300	100	75	250	150

Assets = Liabilities + Stockholders' Equity
$625 = $200 + ($300 + $100 − $75 + $250 − $150)
$625 = $200 + $425
$625 = $625

Business Transaction Analysis

LO3 Demonstrate how the double-entry system is applied to common business transactions.

In the next few pages, we show how to apply the double-entry system to some common business transactions. **Source documents**—invoices, receipts, checks, or contracts—usually support the details of a transaction. We focus on the transactions of a small firm, Treadle Website Design, Inc. For each transaction, we follow these steps:

1. State the transaction.

2. Analyze the transaction to determine which accounts are affected.

3. Apply the rules of double-entry accounting by using T accounts to show how the transaction affects the accounting equation.

4. Show the transaction in **journal form**. The journal form is a way of recording a transaction with the date, debit account, and debit amount shown on one line, and the credit account (indented) and credit amount on the next line.

The amounts are shown in their respective debit and credit columns. (We discuss journals later in this chapter.)

5. Provide a comment that will help you apply the rules of double entry.

Owner's Investment in the Business

July 1: To begin the business, Priscilla Treadle files articles of incorporation with the state to receive her charter and invests $40,000 in Treadle Website Design, Inc., in exchange for 40,000 shares of $1 par value common stock.

Analysis: An owner's investment in the business *increases* the asset account *Cash* with a debit and *increases* the stockholders' equity account *Common Stock* with a credit.

Application of Double Entry:

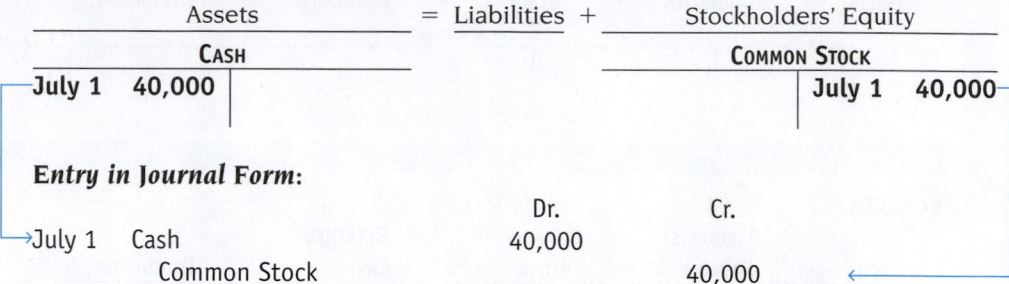

Assets	= Liabilities +	Stockholders' Equity
CASH		**COMMON STOCK**
July 1 40,000		July 1 40,000

Entry in Journal Form:

	Dr.	Cr.
July 1 Cash	40,000	
Common Stock		40,000

Comment: If Priscilla Treadle had invested assets other than cash in the business, the appropriate asset accounts would be increased with a debit.

Economic Event That Is Not a Business Transaction

July 2: Orders office supplies, $5,200.

Comment: When an economic event does not constitute a business transaction, no entry is made. In this case, there is no confirmation that the supplies have been shipped or that title has passed.

Prepayment of Expenses in Cash

July 3: Rents an office; pays two months rent in advance, $3,200.

Analysis: The prepayment of office rent in cash *increases* the asset account *Prepaid Rent* with a debit and *decreases* the asset account *Cash* with a credit.

Application of Double Entry:

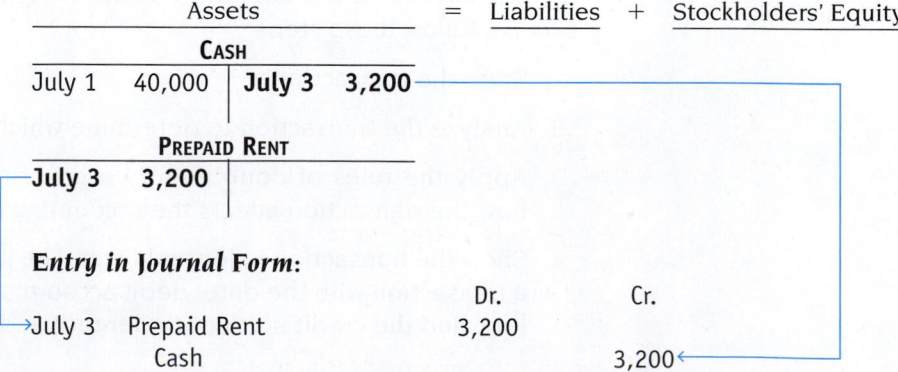

Assets	= Liabilities +	Stockholders' Equity
CASH		
July 1 40,000	July 3 3,200	
PREPAID RENT		
July 3 3,200		

Entry in Journal Form:

	Dr.	Cr.
July 3 Prepaid Rent	3,200	
Cash		3,200

Comment: A prepaid expense is an asset because the expenditure will benefit future operations. This transaction does not affect the totals of assets or liabilities and stockholders' equity because it simply trades one asset for another asset. If the company had paid only July's rent, the stockholders' equity account *Rent Expense* would be debited because the total benefit of the expenditure would be used up in the current month.

Purchase of an Asset on Credit

July 5: Receives office supplies ordered on July 2 and an invoice for $5,200.

Analysis: The purchase of office supplies on credit *increases* the asset account *Office Supplies* with a debit and *increases* the liability account *Accounts Payable* with a credit.

Application of Double Entry:

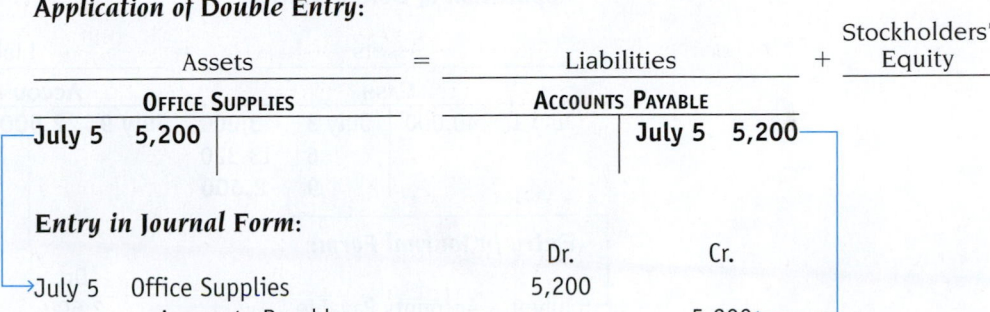

	Assets	=	Liabilities	+	Stockholders' Equity

OFFICE SUPPLIES		ACCOUNTS PAYABLE	
July 5 5,200			July 5 5,200

Entry in Journal Form:

		Dr.	Cr.
July 5	Office Supplies	5,200	
	Accounts Payable		5,200

Comment: Office supplies are considered an asset (prepaid expense) because they will not be used up in the current month and thus will benefit future periods. Accounts Payable is used when there is a delay between the time of the purchase and the time of payment.

Purchase of an Asset Partly in Cash and Partly on Credit

July 6: Purchases office equipment, $16,320; pays $13,320 in cash and agrees to pay the rest next month.

Analysis: The purchase of office equipment in cash and on credit *increases* the asset account *Office Equipment* with a debit, *decreases* the asset account *Cash* with a credit, and *increases* the liability account *Accounts Payable* with a credit.

Application of Double Entry:

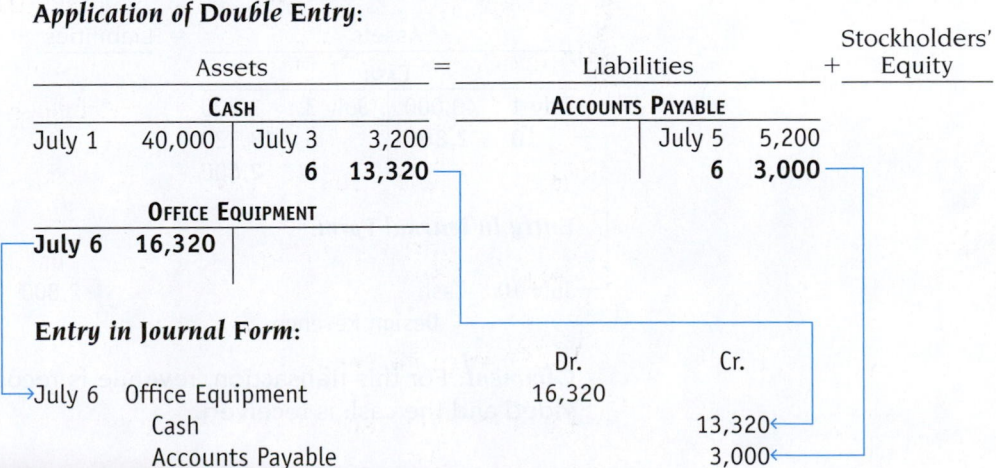

	Assets	=	Liabilities	+	Stockholders' Equity

CASH			ACCOUNTS PAYABLE	
July 1 40,000	July 3 3,200			July 5 5,200
	6 13,320			6 3,000

OFFICE EQUIPMENT	
July 6 16,320	

Entry in Journal Form:

		Dr.	Cr.
July 6	Office Equipment	16,320	
	Cash		13,320
	Accounts Payable		3,000

Comment: As this transaction illustrates, assets may be paid for partly in cash and partly on credit. When more than two accounts are involved in a journal entry, as they are in this one, it is called a **compound entry**.

Payment of a Liability

July 9: Makes a partial payment of the amount owed for the office supplies received on July 5, $2,600.

Analysis: A payment of a liability *decreases* the liability account *Accounts Payable* with a debit and *decreases* the asset account *Cash* with a credit.

Application of Double Entry:

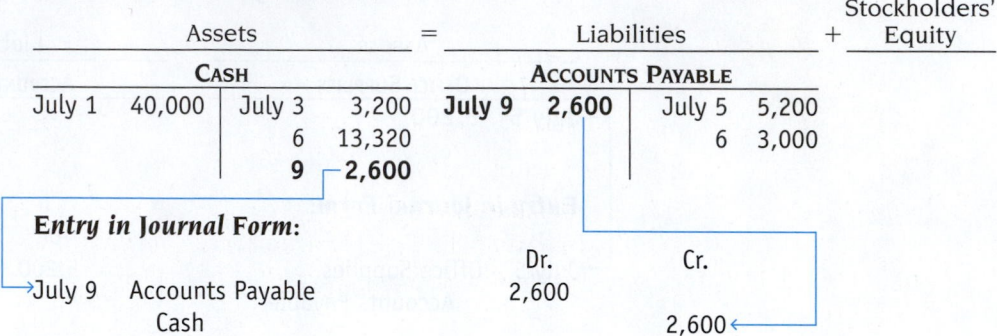

| | Assets | = | | Liabilities | + | Stockholders' Equity |

CASH

July 1	40,000	July 3	3,200
		6	13,320
		9	2,600

ACCOUNTS PAYABLE

| July 9 | 2,600 | July 5 | 5,200 |
| | | 6 | 3,000 |

Entry in Journal Form:

		Dr.	Cr.
July 9	Accounts Payable	2,600	
	Cash		2,600

Comment: Note that the office supplies were recorded when they were purchased on July 5.

Revenue in Cash

July 10: Performs a service for an automobile dealer by designing a website and collects a fee in cash, $2,800.

Analysis: A revenue received in cash *increases* the asset account *Cash* with a debit and *increases* the stockholders' equity account *Design Revenue* with a credit.

Application of Double Entry:

| | Assets | = Liabilities + | Stockholders' Equity |

CASH

July 1	40,000	July 3	3,200
10	2,800	6	13,320
		9	2,600

DESIGN REVENUE

| | | July 10 | 2,800 |

Entry in Journal Form:

		Dr.	Cr.
July 10	Cash	2,800	
	Design Revenue		2,800

Comment: For this transaction, revenue is recognized when the service is provided and the cash is received.

Revenue on Credit

July 15: Performs a service for a department store by designing a website; bills for the fee now but will be paid later, $9,600.

Analysis: A revenue billed to a customer *increases* the asset account *Accounts Receivable* with a debit and *increases* the stockholders' equity account *Design Revenue* with a credit. Accounts Receivable is used to indicate the customer's obligation until it is paid.

Application of Double Entry:

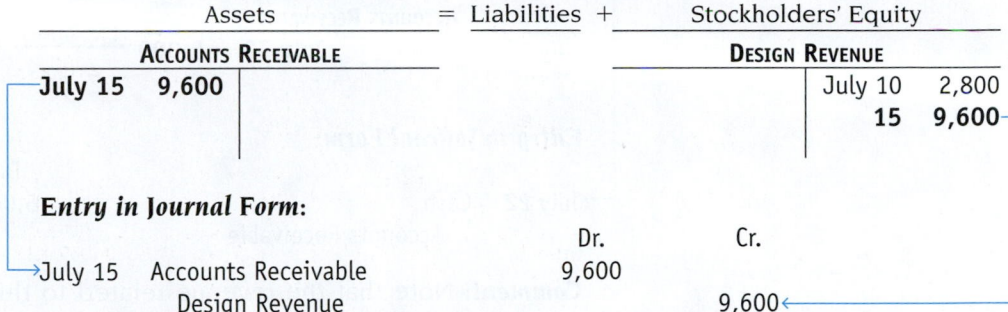

Assets	= Liabilities +	Stockholders' Equity
ACCOUNTS RECEIVABLE		**DESIGN REVENUE**
July 15 9,600		July 10 2,800
		15 9,600

Entry in Journal Form:

	Dr.	Cr.
July 15 Accounts Receivable	9,600	
Design Revenue		9,600

Comment: In this case, there is a delay between the time revenue is earned and the time the cash is received. Revenues are recorded at the time they are earned and billed regardless of when cash is received.

Revenue Received in Advance

July 19: Accepts an advance fee as a deposit on a website to be designed, $1,400.

Analysis: A revenue received in advance *increases* the asset account *Cash* with a debit and *increases* the liability account *Unearned Design Revenue* with a credit.

Application of Double Entry:

Assets	=	Liabilities	+	Stockholders' Equity
CASH		**UNEARNED DESIGN REVENUE**		
July 1 40,000 | July 3 3,200		July 19 1,400		
10 2,800 | 6 13,320				
19 1,400 | 9 2,600				

Entry in Journal Form:

	Dr.	Cr.
July 19 Cash	1,400	
Unearned Design Revenue		1,400

Comment: In this case, payment is received before the fees are earned. Unearned Design Revenue is a liability because the firm must provide the service or return the deposit.

Collection on Account

July 22: Receives partial payment from customer billed on July 15, $5,000.

Analysis: Collection of an account receivable from a customer previously billed *increases* the asset account *Cash* with a debit and *decreases* the asset account *Accounts Receivable* with a credit.

Application of Double Entry:

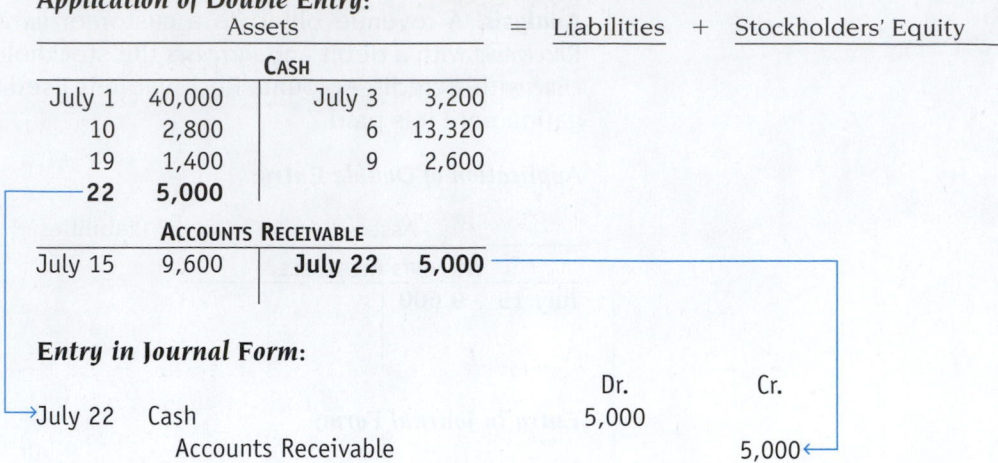

Comment: Note that the revenue related to this transaction was recorded on July 15. Thus, no revenue is recorded at this time.

Expense Paid in Cash

July 26: Pays employees four weeks' wages, $4,800.

Analysis: This cash expense *increases* the stockholders' equity account *Wages Expense* with a debit and *decreases* the asset account *Cash* with a credit.

Application of Double Entry:

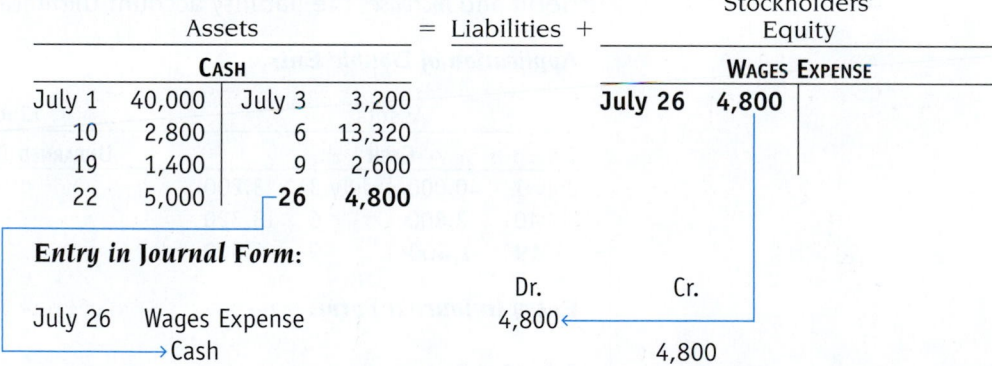

Comment: Note that the increase in Wages Expense will *decrease* stockholders' equity.

Expense to Be Paid Later

July 30: Receives, but does not pay, the utility bill which is due next month, $680.

Analysis: This cash expense *increases* the stockholders' equity account *Utilities Expense* with a debit and *increases* the liability account *Accounts Payable* with a credit.

Application of Double Entry:

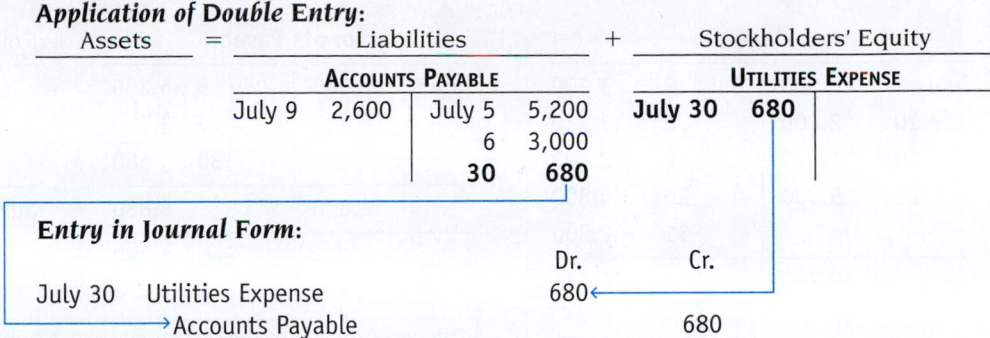

Assets	=	Liabilities	+	Stockholders' Equity

		ACCOUNTS PAYABLE		**UTILITIES EXPENSE**
	July 9 2,600	July 5 5,200	**July 30 680**	
		6 3,000		
		30 680		

Entry in Journal Form:

		Dr.	Cr.
July 30	Utilities Expense	680	
	Accounts Payable		680

Comment: The expense is recorded if the benefit has been received and the amount is owed, even if the cash is not to be paid until later. Note that the increase in Utility Expense will *decrease* stockholders' equity.

Dividends

July 31: Declares and pays a dividend, $2,800.

Analysis: Payment of a cash dividend *increases* the stockholders' equity account *Dividends* with a debit and *decreases* the asset account *Cash* with a credit.

Application of Double Entry:

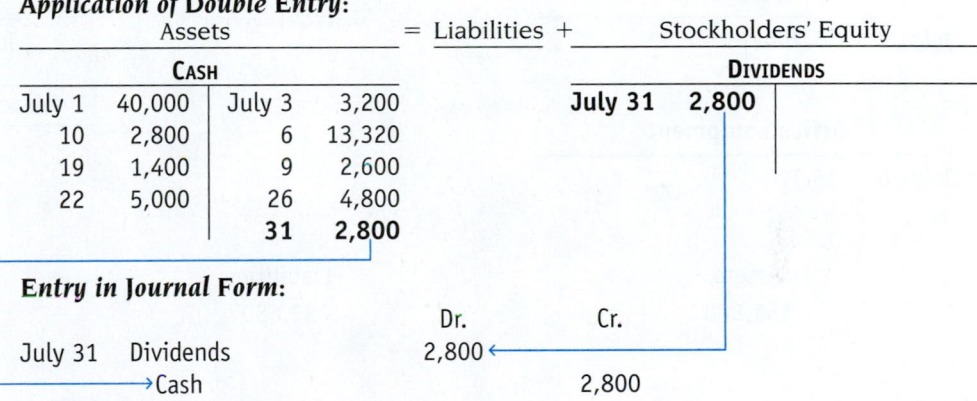

	Assets		= Liabilities +		Stockholders' Equity

	CASH				**DIVIDENDS**
July 1	40,000	July 3	3,200	**July 31 2,800**	
10	2,800	6	13,320		
19	1,400	9	2,600		
22	5,000	26	4,800		
		31	**2,800**		

Entry in Journal Form:

		Dr.	Cr.
July 31	Dividends	2,800	
	Cash		2,800

Comment: Note that the increase in Dividends will *decrease* stockholders' equity.

Summary of Transactions

Exhibit 1 uses the accounting equation to summarize the transactions of Treadle Website Design, Inc. Note that the income statement accounts appear under stockholders' equity and that the transactions in the Cash account will be reflected on the statement of cash flows. No Retained Earnings account appears under stockholders' equity because this is the company's first month of operation.

▼ EXHIBIT 1

Summary of Transactions of Treadle Website Design, Inc.

| Assets | = | Liabilities | + | Stockholders' Equity |

Cash

July	1	40,000	July	3	3,200
	10	2,800		6	13,320
	19	1,400		9	2,600
	22	5,000		26	4,800
				31	2,800
		49,200			26,720
Bal.		22,480			

Accounts Payable

July 9	2,600	July	5	5,200
			6	3,000
			30	680
	2,600			8,880
		Bal.		6,280

> This account links to the statement of cash flows.

Common Stock

		July	1	40,000

Dividends

July 31	2,800	

Accounts Receivable

July 15	9,600	July 22	5,000
Bal.	4,600		

Unearned Design Revenue

	July 19	1,400

Design Revenue

	July 10	2,800
	15	9,600
	Bal.	12,400

Office Supplies

July 5	5,200	

Wages Expense

July 26	4,800	

Prepaid Rent

July 3	3,200	

Utilities Expense

July 30	680	

> These accounts link to the income statement.

Office Equipment

July 6	16,320	

Assets	=	Liabilities	+	Stockholders' Equity
$51,800	=	$7,680	+	$44,120

S T O P • R E V I E W • A P P L Y

3-1. Explain the meaning of this statement: "The Cash account has a debit balance of $500."

3-2. Explain why debits, which decrease stockholders' equity, increase expenses, which are a component of stockholders' equity.

3-3. What steps are followed in analyzing a business transaction?

3-4. What is the normal balance of Accounts Payable? Under what conditions could Accounts Payable have a debit balance?

The Trial Balance

LO4 Prepare a trial balance, and describe its value and limitations.

For every amount debited, an equal amount must be credited. This means that the total of debits and credits in the T accounts must be equal. To test this, the accountant periodically prepares a **trial balance**. Exhibit 2 shows a trial balance for Treadle Website Design, Inc. It was prepared from the accounts in Exhibit 1.

Preparation and Use of a Trial Balance

Although a trial balance may be prepared at any time, it is usually prepared on the last day of the accounting period. These are the steps involved in preparing a trial balance:

1. List each account that has a balance, with debit balances in the left column and credit balances in the right column. Accounts are listed in the order in which they appear on the financial statements.

2. Add each column.

3. Compare the totals of the columns.

Once in a while, a transaction leaves an account with a balance that isn't "normal." For example, when a company overdraws its bank account, its Cash account (an asset) will show a credit balance instead of a debit balance. The "abnormal" balance should be copied into the trial balance columns as it stands, as a debit or a credit.

The trial balance proves whether the ledger is in balance. *In balance* means that the total of all debits recorded equals the total of all credits recorded. But the trial balance does not prove that the transactions were analyzed correctly or recorded in the proper accounts. For example, there is no way of determining

> **Study Note**
>
> A trial balance is usually prepared at the end of an accounting period. It is an initial check that the accounts are in balance.

EXHIBIT 2 ▶ Trial Balance

Treadle Website Design, Inc.
Trial Balance
July 31, 20xx

	Debit	Credit
Cash	$22,480	
Accounts Receivable	4,600	
Office Supplies	5,200	
Prepaid Rent	3,200	
Office Equipment	16,320	
Accounts Payable		$ 6,280
Unearned Design Revenue		1,400
Common Stock		40,000
Dividends	2,800	
Design Revenue		12,400
Wages Expense	4,800	
Utilities Expense	680	
	$60,080	$60,080

from the trial balance that a debit should have been made in the Office Supplies account rather than in the Office Equipment account. And the trial balance does not detect whether transactions have been omitted, because equal debits and credits will have been omitted. Also, if an error of the same amount is made in both a debit and a credit, it will not be evident in the trial balance. The trial balance proves only that the debits and credits in the accounts are in balance.

Finding Trial Balance Errors

If the debit and credit balances in a trial balance are not equal, look for one or more of the following errors:

1. A debit was entered in an account as a credit, or vice versa.

2. The balance of an account was computed incorrectly.

3. An error was made in carrying the account balance to the trial balance.

4. The trial balance was summed incorrectly.

Other than simply adding the columns incorrectly, the two most common mistakes in preparing a trial balance are

1. Recording an account as a credit when it usually carries a debit balance, or vice versa. This mistake causes the trial balance to be out of balance by an amount divisible by 2.

2. Transposing two digits when transferring an amount to the trial balance (for example, entering $23,459 as $23,549). This error causes the trial balance to be out of balance by a number divisible by 9.

So, if a trial balance is out of balance and the addition of the columns is correct, determine the amount by which the trial balance is out of balance and divide it first by 2 and then by 9. If the amount is divisible by 2, look in the trial balance for an amount that is equal to the quotient. If you find such an amount, chances are it's in the wrong column. If the amount is divisible by 9, trace each amount back to the T account balance, checking carefully for a transposition error. If neither of these techniques is successful in identifying the error, first recompute the balance of each T account. Then, if you still have not found the error, retrace each posting from the journal to the T account.

S T O P • R E V I E W • A P P L Y

4-1. What is a trial balance, and why is it useful?

4-2. Is it possible for errors to be present in a trial balance whose debit and credit balances are equal? Explain your answer.

Cash Flows and the Timing of Transactions

LO5   Show how the timing of transactions affects cash flows and liquidity.

> **Study Note**
>
> Recording revenues and expenses when they occur will provide a clearer picture of a company's profitability on the income statement. The change in cash flows will provide a clearer picture of the company's liquidity on the statement of cash flows.

To avoid financial distress, a company must be able to pay its bills on time. Because the timing of cash flows is critical to maintaining adequate liquidity to pay bills, managers and other users of financial information must understand the difference between transactions that generate immediate cash and those that do not. Consider the transactions of Treadle Website Design, Inc., shown in Figure 3. Most of them involve either an inflow or outflow of cash.

As you can see in Figure 3, Treadle's Cash account has more transactions than any of its other accounts. Look at the transactions of July 10, 15, and 22. On July 10, Treadle received a cash payment of $2,800. On July 15, the firm billed a customer $9,600 for a service it had already performed. On July 22, it received a partial payment of $5,000 from the customer, but it had not received the remaining $4,600 by the end of the month. Because Treadle incurred expenses in providing this service, it must pay careful attention to its cash flows and liquidity.

One way Treadle can manage its expenditures is to rely on its creditors to give it time to pay. Compare the transactions of July 3, 5, and 9 in Figure 3. On July 3, Treadle prepaid rent of $3,200. That immediate cash outlay may have caused a strain on the business. On July 5, the company received an invoice for

---

■ **FIGURE 3**
Transactions of Treadle Website Design, Inc.

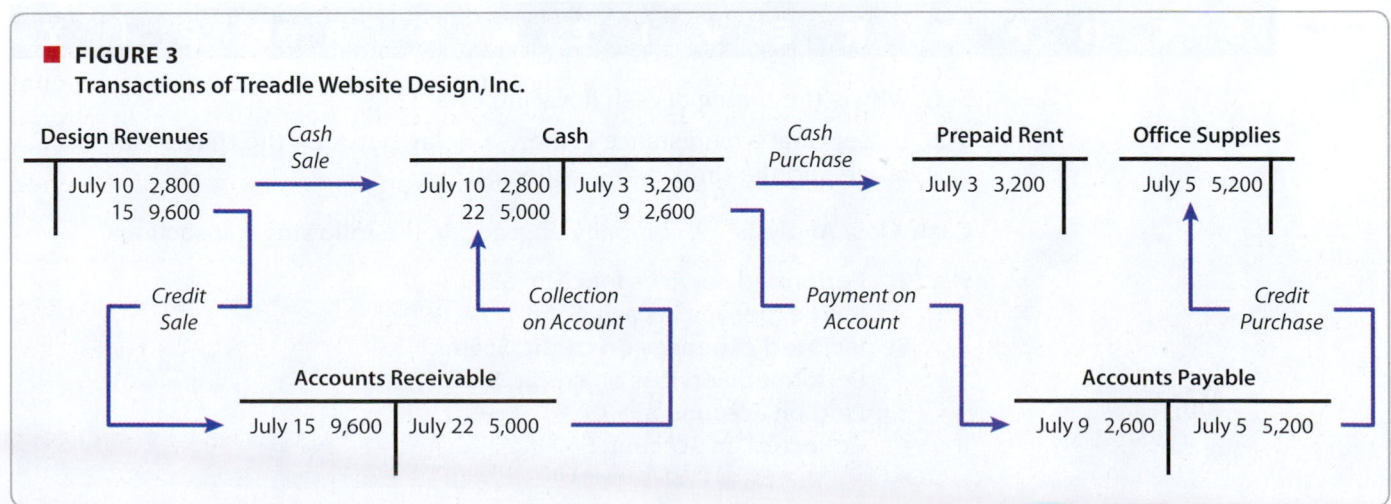

Because Boeing takes years to plan and make the airplanes that customers have ordered, Boeing's management must carefully plan the company's needs for cash. The timing of cash flows is critical to maintaining adequate liquidity.

office supplies in the amount of $5,200. In this case, it took advantage of the opportunity to defer payment. It paid $2,600 on July 9, but it had not paid the remaining $2,600 by the end of the month.

Of course, Treadle expects to receive the rest of the cash from the customer that it billed on July 15, and it must eventually pay the rest of what it owes on the office supplies. In the meantime, the firm must perform a delicate balancing act with its cash flows to ensure that it achieves the goal of liquidity so that it can grow and be profitable.

Large companies face the same challenge, but often on a much greater scale. Recall from the Decision Point that **Boeing** takes years to plan and make the aircraft that **Singapore Airlines** and other customers order. At the end of 2003, Boeing had orders for 6,349 airplanes totaling $63.9 billion, or about $10 million per plane.[5] Think of the cash outlays Boeing must make before it delivers the planes and collects payment for them. To maintain liquidity so that Boeing can eventually reap the rewards of delivering the planes, Boeing's management must carefully plan the company's needs for cash.

S T O P • R E V I E W • A P P L Y

5-1. Why is the timing of cash flows important?

5-2. Under what circumstance is there a delay between the time a sale is made and the time cash is collected?

Cash Flow Analysis   A company engaged in the following transactions:

Oct. 1   Performed services for cash, $750.
      2   Paid expenses in cash, $550.
      3   Incurred expenses on credit, $650.
      4   Performed services on credit, $900.
      5   Paid on account, $350.
      6   Collected on account, $600.

Enter the correct titles in the following T accounts, and enter the above transactions in the accounts. Determine the cash balance after these transactions, the amount still to be received, and the amount still to be paid.

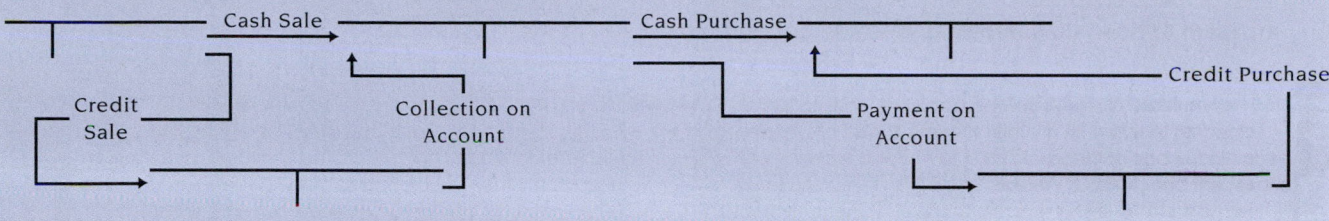

SOLUTION

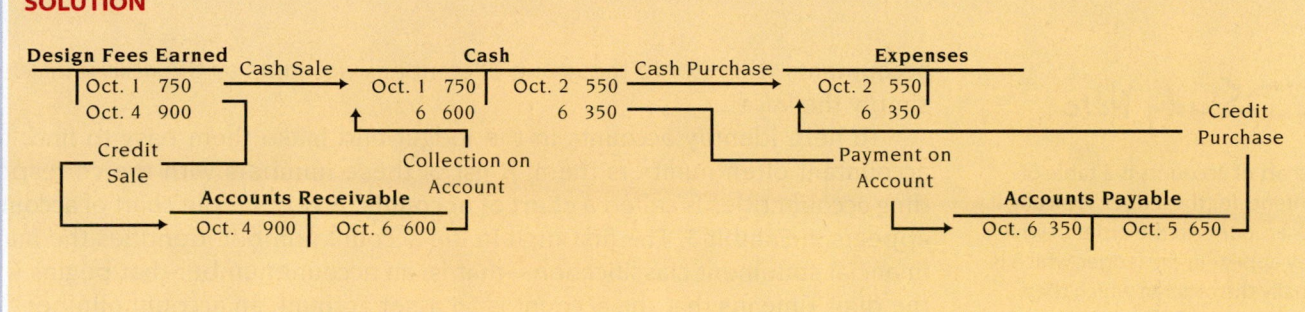

Cash balance after transactions: $750 + $600 − $550 − $350 = $450
Amount still to be received: $900 − $600 = $300
Amount still to be paid: $650 − $350 = $300

Recording and Posting Transactions

SO6 Define the *chart of accounts*, record transactions in the general journal, and post transactions to the ledger.

Earlier in the chapter, we described how transactions are analyzed according to the rules of double entry and how a trial balance is prepared. As Figure 4 shows, transaction analysis and preparation of a trial balance are the first and last steps in a four-step process. The two intermediate steps are recording the entry in the general journal and posting the entry to the ledger. In this section, we demonstrate how these steps are accomplished in a manual accounting system.

Chart of Accounts

In a manual accounting system, each account is kept on a separate page or card. These pages or cards are placed together in a book or file called the **general ledger**. In the computerized systems that most companies have today, accounts are maintained electronically. However, as a matter of convenience,

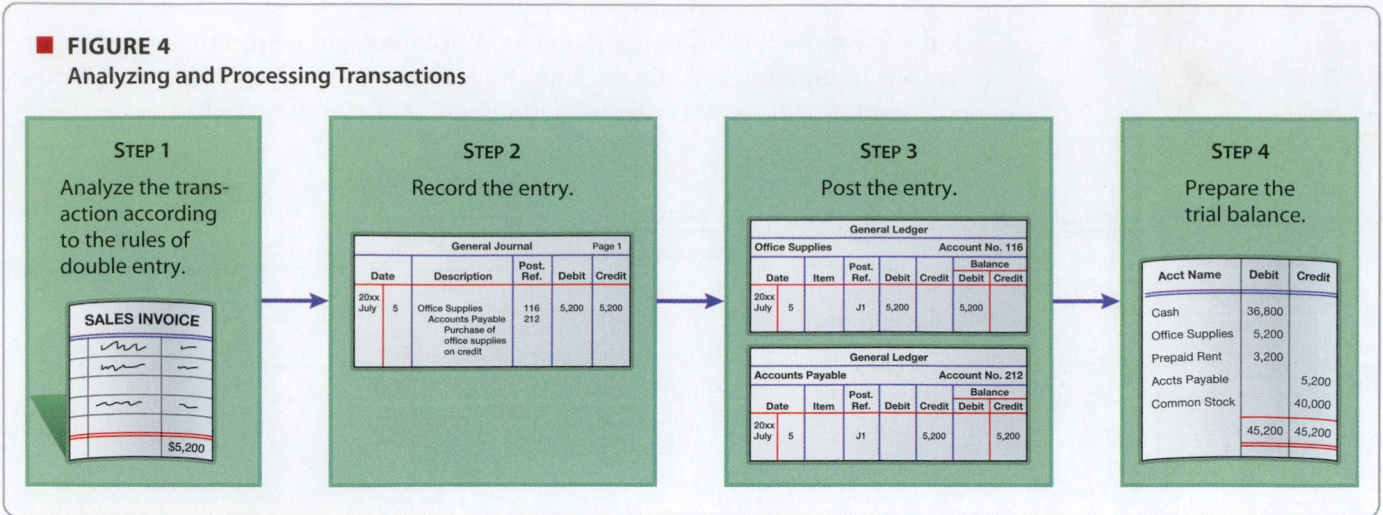

■ FIGURE 4
Analyzing and Processing Transactions

Study Note

A chart of accounts is a table of contents for the ledger. Typically, it lists accounts in the order in which they appear in the ledger, which is usually the order in which they appear on the financial statements. The numbering scheme allows for some flexibility.

accountants still refer to the group of company accounts as the *general ledger*, or simply the *ledger*.

To help identify accounts in the ledger and make them easy to find, the accountant often numbers them. A list of these numbers with the corresponding account titles is called a **chart of accounts**. A very simple chart of accounts appears in Exhibit 3. The first digit in the account number identifies the major financial statement classification—that is, an account number that begins with the digit 1 means that the account is an asset account, an account number that begins with a 2 means that the account is a liability account, and so forth. The second and third digits identify individual accounts. The gaps in the sequence of numbers allow the accountant to expand the number of accounts.

General Journal

Although transactions can be entered directly into the ledger accounts, this method makes identifying individual transactions or finding errors very difficult because the debit is recorded in one account and the credit in another. The solution is to record all transactions chronologically in a **journal**. The journal is sometimes called the *book of original entry* because it is where transactions first enter the accounting records. Later, the debit and credit portions of each transaction are transferred to the appropriate accounts in the ledger. A separate **journal entry** is used to record each transaction; the process of recording transactions is called **journalizing**.

Most businesses have more than one kind of journal. The simplest and most flexible kind is the **general journal**, the one we focus on here. Businesses will also have several special-purpose journals, each for recording a common transaction, such as credit sales, credit purchases, cash receipts, and cash disbursements. At this point, we cover only the general journal. Exhibit 4, which displays two of the transactions of Treadle Website Design that we discussed earlier, shows the format for recording entries in a general journal.

As you can see in Exhibit 4, the entries in a general journal include the following information about each transaction:

1. The date. The year appears on the first line of the first column, the month on the next line of the first column, and the day in the second column opposite the month. For subsequent entries on the same page for the same month and year, the month and year can be omitted.

Study Note

The journal is a chronological record of events.

▼ EXHIBIT 3

Chart of Accounts for a Small Business

Account Number	Account Name	Description
		Assets
111	Cash	Money and any medium of exchange (coins, currency, checks, money orders, and money on deposit in a bank)
112	Notes Receivable	Promissory notes (written promises to pay definite sums of money at fixed future dates) due from others
113	Accounts Receivable	Amounts due from others for revenues or sales on credit (sales on account)
116	Office Supplies	Prepaid expense; office supplies purchased and not used
117	Prepaid Rent	Prepaid expense; rent paid in advance and not used
118	Prepaid Insurance	Prepaid expense; insurance purchased and not expired
141	Land	Property owned for use in the business
142	Buildings	Structures owned for use in the business
143	Accumulated Depreciation, Buildings	Periodic allocation of the cost of buildings to expense
146	Office Equipment	Office equipment owned for use in the business
147	Accumulated Depreciation, Office Equipment	Periodic allocation of the cost of office equipment to expense
		Liabilities
211	Notes Payable	Promissory notes due to others
212	Accounts Payable	Amounts due to others for purchases on credit
213	Unearned Design Revenue	Unearned revenue; advance deposits for website design to be provided in the future
214	Wages Payable	Amounts due to employees for wages earned and not paid
215	Income Taxes Payable	Amounts due to government for income taxes owed and not paid
		Stockholders' Equity
311	Common Stock	Stockholders' investments in a corporation for which they receive shares of stock
312	Retained Earnings	Stockholders' claims against company assets derived from profitable operations
313	Dividends	Distributions of assets (usually cash) that reduce retained earnings
314	Income Summary	Temporary account used at the end of the accounting period to summarize the revenues and expenses for the period
		Revenues
411	Design Revenue	Revenues derived from website design services
		Expenses
511	Wages Expense	Amounts earned by employees
512	Utilities Expense	Amounts for utilities, such as water, electricity, and gas, used
513	Telephone Expense	Amounts of telephone services used
514	Rent Expense	Amounts of rent on property and buildings used
515	Insurance Expense	Amounts for insurance expired
517	Office Supplies Expense	Amounts for office supplies used
518	Depreciation Expense, Buildings	Amount of buildings' cost allocated to expense
520	Depreciation Expense, Office Equipment	Amount of office equipment cost allocated to expense
521	Income Taxes Expense	Amount of tax on income

EXHIBIT 4 ▶ **The General Journal**

			General Journal	Post. Ref.	Debit	Page 1 Credit
	Date		Description			
	20xx					
	July	3	Prepaid Rent		3,200	
			Cash			3,200
			Paid two months' rent in advance			
		5	Office Supplies		5,200	
			Accounts Payable			5,200
			Purchase of office supplies on credit			

A = L + SE
+ 3,200
− 3,200

A = L + SE
+ 5,200   + 5,200

2. The names of the accounts debited and credited, which appear in the Description column. The names of the accounts that are debited are placed next to the left margin opposite the dates; on the line below, the names of the accounts credited are indented.

3. The debit amounts, which appear in the Debit column opposite the accounts that are debited, and the credit amounts, which appear in the Credit column opposite the accounts credited.

4. An explanation of each transaction, which appears in the Description column below the account names. An explanation should be brief but sufficient to explain and identify the transaction.

5. The account numbers in the Post. Ref. column, if they apply.

At the time the transactions are recorded, nothing is placed in the Post. Ref. (posting reference) column. (This column is sometimes called LP or *Folio*.) Later, if the company uses account numbers to identify accounts in the ledger, the account numbers are filled in. They provide a convenient cross-reference from the general journal to the ledger and indicate that the entry has been posted to the ledger. If the accounts are not numbered, the accountant uses a checkmark (✓) to signify that the entry has been posted.

General Ledger

The general journal is used to record the details of each transaction. The general ledger is used to update each account.

The Ledger Account Form
The T account is a simple, direct means of recording transactions. In practice, a somewhat more complicated form of the account is needed to record more information. The **ledger account form**, which contains four columns for dollar amounts, is illustrated in Exhibit 5.

The account title and number appear at the top of the account form. As in the journal, the transaction date appears in the first two columns. The Item column is rarely used to identify transactions because explanations already appear in the journal. The Post. Ref. column is used to note the journal page on which the original entry for the transaction can be found. The dollar amount is entered in the appropriate Debit or Credit column, and a new account balance is computed in the last two columns opposite each entry. The advantage of this account form over the T account is that the current balance of the account is readily available.

> **Study Note**
>
> A T account is a means of quickly analyzing a set of transactions. It is simply an abbreviated version of a ledger account. Ledger accounts, which provide more information, are used in the accounting records.

EXHIBIT 5 ▶

Accounts Payable in the General Ledger

General Ledger

Accounts Payable   **Account No. 212**

Date		Item	Post. Ref.	Debit	Credit	Balance Debit	Balance Credit
20xx							
July	5		J1		5,200		5,200
	6		J1		3,000		8,200
	9		J1	2,600			5,600
	30		J2		680		6,280

Posting   After transactions have been entered in the journal, they must be transferred to the ledger. The process of transferring journal entry information from the journal to the ledger is called **posting**. Posting is usually done after several entries have been made—for example, at the end of each day or less frequently, depending on the number of transactions. As Exhibit 6 shows, in

EXHIBIT 6 ▶

Posting from the General Journal to the Ledger

$A = L + SE$
$+ 680 - 680$

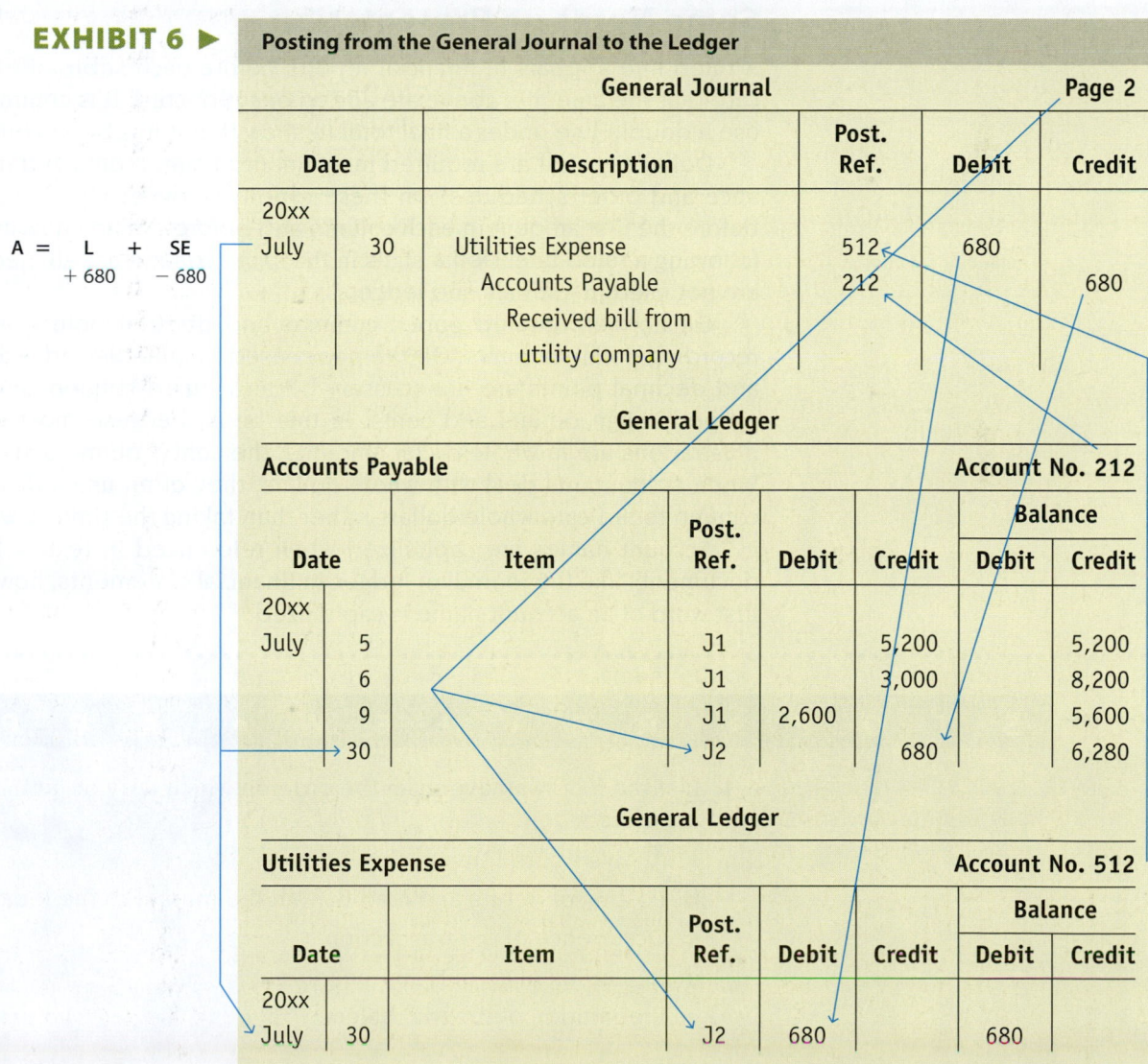

posting, each amount in the Debit column of the journal is transferred to the Debit column of the appropriate account in the ledger, and each amount in the Credit column of the journal is transferred to the Credit column of the appropriate account in the ledger. The steps in the posting process are as follows:

1. In the ledger, locate the debit account named in the journal entry.

2. Enter the date of the transaction in the ledger and, in the Post. Ref. column, the journal page number from which the entry comes.

3. In the Debit column of the ledger account, enter the amount of the debit as it appears in the journal.

4. Calculate the account balance and enter it in the appropriate Balance column.

5. Enter in the Post. Ref. column of the journal the account number to which the amount has been posted.

6. Repeat the same five steps for the credit side of the journal entry.

Notice that step **5** is the last step in the posting process for each debit and credit. As noted earlier, in addition to serving as an easy reference between the journal entry and the ledger account, this entry in the Post. Ref. column of the journal indicates that the entry has been posted to the ledger.

Some Notes on Presentation

A ruled line appears in financial reports before each subtotal or total to indicate that the amounts above are added or subtracted. It is common practice to use a double line under a final total to show that it has been verified.

Dollar signs ($) are required in all financial statements and in the trial balance and other schedules. On these reports, a dollar sign should be placed before the first amount in each column and before the first amount in a column following a ruled line. Dollar signs in the same column are aligned. Dollar signs are not used in journals and ledgers.

On normal, unruled paper, commas and decimal points are used when recording dollar amounts. On the paper used in journals and ledgers, commas and decimal points are unnecessary because ruled columns are provided to properly align dollars and cents. In this book, because most problems and illustrations are in whole dollar amounts, the cents column usually is omitted. When accountants deal with whole dollars, they often use a dash in the cents column to indicate whole dollars rather than taking the time to write zeros.

Account names are capitalized when referenced in text or listed in work documents like the journal or ledger. In financial statements, however, only the first word of an account name is capitalized.

STOP • REVIEW • APPLY

6-1. List the following events in the order in which they occur in an accounting system:

a. Analysis of the transaction

b. Posting of debits and credits from the journal to the ledger

c. Occurrence of the transaction

d. Recording of an entry in the journal

e. Preparation of the trial balance

6-2. In recording entries in a journal, which is written first, the debit or the credit? How is indentation used in the journal?

6-3. What is the relationship between the journal and the ledger?

6-4. Indicate whether each of the following is more closely related to the journal, the ledger, or both:

a. Chart of accounts	**d.** Journalizing
b. Book of original entry	**e.** Posting
c. Post. Ref. column	**f.** Footings

A LOOK BACK AT

SINGAPORE AIRLINES AND THE BOEING COMPANY

The Decision Point at the beginning of the chapter described the order for 18 planes that **Singapore Airlines** placed with **Boeing**. It posed the following questions:

- **The order was obviously an important economic event for both companies, but is there a difference between an economic event and a business transaction that should be recorded in the accounting records?**
- **Should Singapore and Boeing record the order in their accounting records?**
- **How important are liquidity and cash flows to Boeing?**

Despite its importance, the order did not constitute a business transaction, and neither company should have recognized it in its accounting records. At the time Singapore Airlines placed the order, Boeing had not yet built the planes, and it would not deliver the first of them for several years. Until Boeing does delivers the planes and title to them shifts to Singapore Airplanes, it cannot record any revenue, and until that time, the planes are not assets that Singapore Airlines needs to account for.

Even for "firm" orders like the one from Singapore Airlines, Boeing cautions that "an economic downturn could result in airline equipment requirements less than currently anticipated resulting in requests to negotiate the rescheduling or possible cancellation of firm orders."[6] In fact, in the period following the 9/11 attacks on the World Trade Center and the war in Iraq, many airlines cancelled or renegotiated orders they had placed with Boeing.

Because it takes almost two years to manufacture an airplane, Boeing must pay close attention to its liquidity and cash flows. One measure of liquidity is the **cash return on assets** ratio, which shows how productive assets are in generating cash flows from operations. In other words, it shows how much cash is generated by each dollar of assets invested in operations. This ratio is different from the return on assets ratio, a profitability measure, introduced in Chapter 1. Using amounts (in millions) from Boeing's balance sheet and statement of cash flows in its annual report, we can calculate the company's cash return on assets as follows:[7]

		2004	2003
Cash Return on Assets	= $\dfrac{\text{Net Cash Flows from Operating Activities}}{\text{Average Total Assets}}$	$\dfrac{\$3,458}{(\$53,963 + \$52,986) \div 2}$	$\dfrac{\$2,709}{(\$52,986 + \$52,342) \div 2}$
		$\dfrac{\$3,458}{\$53,474.5}$	$\dfrac{\$2,709}{\$52,664}$
		.065 (6.5%)	.051 (5.1%)

What do these results tell us? First, in 2004, each dollar of assets that Boeing invested in operations generated about 6.5¢, but that was better than the 5.1¢ generated a year earlier. Second, cash flows from operations increased from $2,709 million to $3,458 million, while average total assets increased slightly. This trend is favorable. It indicates a stronger cash-generating ability and Boeing may have improved operations after the bad effects of 9/11 and subsequent events.

CHAPTER REVIEW

REVIEW of Learning Objectives

LO1 Explain how the concepts of recognition, valuation, and classification apply to business transactions and why they are important factors in ethical financial reporting.

To measure a business transaction, you must determine when the transaction occurred (the recognition issue), what value to place on the transaction (the valuation issue), and how the components of the transaction should be categorized (the classification issue). In general, recognition should occur when title passes, and a transaction should be valued at the exchange price—the cost at the time the transaction is recognized. Classification refers to assigning transactions to the appropriate accounts. Generally accepted accounting principles provide guidance about the treatment of these three basic measurement issues. Failure to follow these guidelines is a major reason some companies issue unethical financial statements.

LO2 Explain the double-entry system and the usefulness of T accounts in analyzing business transactions.

In the double-entry system, each transaction must be recorded with at least one debit and one credit, and the total amount of the debits must equal the total amount of the credits. Each asset, liability, and component of stockholders' equity, including revenues and expenses, has a separate account, which is a device for storing transaction data. The T account is a useful tool for quickly analyzing the effects of transactions. It shows how increases and decreases in assets, liabilities, and stockholders' equity are debited and credited to the appropriate accounts.

LO3 Demonstrate how the double-entry system is applied to common business transactions.

The double-entry system is applied by analyzing transactions to determine which accounts are affected and by using T accounts to show how the transactions affect the accounting equation. The transactions may be recorded in journal form with the date, debit account, and debit amount shown on one line, and the credit account (indented) and credit amount on the next line. The amounts are shown in their respective debit and credit columns.

LO4 Prepare a trial balance, and describe its value and limitations.

A trial balance is used to check that the debit and credit balances are equal. It is prepared by listing each account balance in the appropriate Debit or Credit column. The two columns are then added, and the totals are compared. The major limitation of a trial balance is that even when it shows that debit and credit balances are equal, it does not guarantee that the transactions were analyzed correctly or recorded in the proper accounts.

LO5 Show how the timing of transactions affects cash flows and liquidity.

Some transactions generate immediate cash. For those that do not, there is a holding period in either Accounts Receivable or Accounts Payable before the cash is received or paid. The timing of cash flows is critical to a company's ability to maintain adequate liquidity so that it can pay its bills on time.

Supplemental Objective

SO6 Define the *chart of accounts,* record transactions in the general journal, and post transactions to the ledger.

The chart of accounts is a list of account numbers and titles; it serves as a table of contents for the ledger. The general journal is a chronological record of all transactions; it contains the date of each transaction, the titles of the accounts involved, the amounts debited and credited, and an explanation of each entry. After transactions have been entered in the general journal, they are posted to the ledger. Posting is done by transferring the amounts in the Debit and Credit columns of the general journal to the Debit and Credit columns of the corresponding account in the ledger. After each entry is posted, a new balance is entered in the appropriate Balance column.

REVIEW of Concepts and Terminology

The following concepts and terms were introduced in this chapter:

Accounts: Basic units for accumulating and storing accounting data from similar transactions. **(LO2)**

Balance: The difference in dollars between the total debit footing and the total credit footing of an account. Also called *account balance*. **(LO2)**

Chart of accounts: A list of account numbers and titles that facilitates finding accounts in the ledger. **(SO6)**

Classification: The process of assigning transactions to the appropriate accounts. **(LO1)**

Compound entry: An entry that has more than one debit or credit entry. **(LO3)**

Cost: The exchange price associated with a business transaction at the point of recognition. **(LO1)**

Cost principle: The practice of recording transactions at cost. **(LO1)**

Credit: The right side of an account. **(LO2)**

Debit: The left side of an account. **(LO2)**

Double-entry system: The accounting system in which each transaction is recorded with at least one debit and one credit, so that the total amount of debits equals the total amount of credits. **(LO2)**

Exchange price: The price resulting from an agreement between the buyer and seller that can be verified by evidence created at the time of the transaction; the price at which a transaction is recorded. **(LO1)**

Footings: Working totals of columns of numbers. To *foot* means to total a column of numbers. **(LO2)**

General journal: The simplest and most flexible type of journal. **(SO6)**

General ledger: A book or file that contains all of a company's accounts arranged in the order of the chart of accounts. Also called the *ledger*. **(SO6)**

Journal: A chronological record of all transactions; the place where transactions first enter the accounting records. Also called *book of original entry*. **(SO6)**

Journal entry: A journal notation that records a single transaction. **(SO6)**

Journal form: A way of recording a transaction in which the date, debit account, and debit amount appear on one line and the credit account and credit amount appear on the next line. **(LO3)**

Journalizing: The process of recording transactions in a journal. **(SO6)**

Ledger account form: An account form that has four dollar amount columns: one column for debit entries, one column for credit entries, and two columns (debit and credit) for showing the balance of the account. **(SO6)**

Normal balance: The usual balance of an account; the side (debit or credit) that increases the account. **(LO2)**

Posting: The process of transferring journal entry information from the journal to the ledger. **(SO6)**

Recognition: The determination of when a business transaction should be recorded. **(LO1)**

Recognition point: The predetermined time at which a transaction should be recorded; usually, the point at which title passes to the buyer. **(LO1)**

Source documents: Invoices, checks, receipts, or other documents that support a transaction. **(LO3)**

T account: The simplest form of account, which is used to analyze transactions. **(LO2)**

Trial balance: A comparison of the total of debit and credit balances in the accounts to check that they are equal. **(LO4)**

Valuation: The process of assigning a monetary value to a business transaction. **(LO1)**

Key Ratio

Cash return on assets: A ratio that shows how much cash is generated by each dollar of assets; Net Cash Flows from Operating Activities ÷ Average Total Assets.

REVIEW Problem

Transaction Analysis, T Accounts, Journalizing, and the Trial Balance

LO1, LO3, LO4, SO6 After graduating from veterinary school, Laura Cox started a private practice. The transactions of her company in May are as follows:

20xx

May 1 Laura Cox invested $2,000 in 2,000 shares of $1 par value common stock of her newly chartered company, Pet Clinic, Inc.

3 Paid $300 in advance for two months' rent of an office.

9 Purchased medical supplies for $200 in cash.

12 Purchased $400 of equipment on credit; made a 25 percent down payment.

15 Delivered a calf for a fee of $35 on credit.

18 Made a payment of $50 on the equipment purchased on May 12.

27 Paid a utility bill of $40.

Required

1. Record the company's transactions in journal form.
2. Post the transactions to the following T accounts: Cash, Accounts Receivable, Medical Supplies, Prepaid Rent, Equipment, Accounts Payable, Common Stock; Veterinary Fees Earned, and Utilities Expense.
3. Prepare a trial balance for the month of May.
4. How does the transaction of May 15 relate to recognition and cash flows? How do the transactions of May 9 and May 27 relate to classification?

Answer to Review Problem

1. Transactions recorded in journal form:

	A	B	C	D	E	F
1	May	1		Cash	2,000	
2				Common Stock		2,000
3				Issued 2,000 shares of $1 par value common stock		
4		3		Prepaid Rent	300	
5				Cash		300
6				Paid two months' rent in advance for an office		
7		9		Medical Supplies	200	
8				Cash		200
9				Purchased medical supplies for cash		
10		12		Equipment	400	
11				Accounts Payable		300
12				Cash		100
13				Purchased equipment on credit, paying 25 percent down		
14		15		Accounts Receivable	35	
15				Veterinary Fees Earned		35
16				Fee on credit for delivery of a calf		
17		18		Accounts Payable	50	
18				Cash		50
19				Partial payment for equipment purchased May 12		
20		27		Utilities Expense	40	
21				Cash		40
22				Paid utility bill		

2. Transactions posted to T accounts:

	A	B	C	D	E	F	G	H	I	J	K	L	M
1			Cash							Accounts Payable			
2	May	1	2,000	May	3	300		May	18	50	May	12	300
3					9	200					Bal.		250
4					12	100							
5					18	50				Common Stock			
6					27	40					May	1	2,000
7			2,000			690							
8	Bal.		1,310							Veterinary Fees Earned			
9											May	15	35
10			Accounts Receivable										
11	May	15	35							Utilities Expense			
12								May	27	40			
13			Medical Supplies										
14	May	9	200										
15													
16			Prepaid Rent										
17	May	3	300										
18													
19			Equipment										
20	May	12	400										

3. Trial balance:

	A	B	C
1	Pet Clinic, Inc.		
2	Trial Balance		
3	May 31, 20xx		
4			
5	Cash	$1,310	
6	Accounts Receivable	35	
7	Medical Supplies	200	
8	Prepaid Rent	300	
9	Equipment	400	
10	Accounts Payable		$ 250
11	Common Stock		2,000
12	Veterinary Fees Earned		35
13	Utilities Expense	40	
14		$2,285	$2,285

4. The transaction of May 15 is recorded, or recognized, on that date even though the company received no cash. The company earned the revenue

by providing the service, and the customer accepted the service and now has an obligation to pay for it. The transaction is recorded as an account receivable because the company allowed the customer to pay for the service later. The transaction of May 9 is classified as an asset, Medical Supplies, because these supplies will benefit the company in the future. The transaction of May 27 is classified as an expense, Utilities Expense, because the utilities have already been used and will not benefit the company in the future.

CHAPTER ASSIGNMENTS

BUILDING Your Basic Knowledge and Skills

Short Exercises

LO1 **Recognition**

SE 1. Which of the following events would be recognized and entered in the accounting records of Tanaka Corporation? Why?

Jan. 10 Tanaka Corporation places an order for office supplies.
Feb. 15 Tanaka Corporation receives the office supplies and a bill for them.
Mar. 1 Tanaka Corporation pays for the office supplies.

LO1, LO3 **Recognition, Valuation, and Classification**

SE 2. Tell how the concepts of recognition, valuation, and classification apply to this transaction:

Cash		Supplies	
June 1 500		June 1 500	

LO1 **Classification of Accounts**

SE 3. Tell whether each of the following accounts is an asset, a liability, a revenue, an expense, or none of these:

a. Accounts Payable
b. Supplies
c. Dividends
d. Fees Earned
e. Supplies Expense
f. Accounts Receivable
g. Unearned Revenue
h. Equipment

LO2 **Normal Balances**

SE 4. Tell whether the normal balance of each account in **SE 3** is a debit or a credit.

LO3 **Transaction Analysis**

SE 5. For each transaction that follows, indicate which account is debited and which account is credited.

May 2 Leon Stoker started a computer programming business, Stoker's Programming Service, Inc., by investing $10,000 in exchange for common stock.

5 Purchased a computer for $5,000 in cash.

7 Purchased supplies on credit for $600.

19 Received cash for programming services performed, $1,000.

22 Received cash for programming services to be performed, $1,200.

25 Paid the rent for May, $1,300.

31 Billed a customer for programming services performed, $500.

LO3 **Recording Transactions in T Accounts**

SE 6. Set up T accounts and record each transaction in **SE 5**. Determine the balance of each account.

LO4 **Preparing a Trial Balance**

SE 7. From the T accounts created in **SE 6**, prepare a trial balance dated May 31, 20x7.

LO5 **Timing and Cash Flows**

SE 8. Use the T account for Cash below to record the portion of each of the following transactions, if any, that affect cash. How do these transactions affect the company's liquidity?

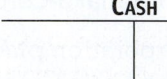

CASH

Jan. 2 Provided services for cash, $1,200

4 Paid expenses in cash, $700

8 Provided services on credit, $1,100

9 Incurred expenses on credit, $800

SO6 **Recording Transactions in the General Journal**

SE 9. Prepare a general journal form like the one in Exhibit 4 and label it Page 4. Record the following transactions in the journal:

Sept. 6 Billed a customer for services performed, $3,800.

16 Received partial payment from the customer billed on Sept. 6, $1,800.

SO6 **Posting to the Ledger Accounts**

SE 10. Prepare ledger account forms like the ones in Exhibit 5 for the following accounts: Cash (111), Accounts Receivable (113), and Service Revenue (411). Post the transactions that are recorded in **SE 9** to the ledger accounts, at the same time making the proper posting references.

Cash Return on Assets

SE 11. Calculate cash return on assets for 20x7 using the following data: A company has net cash flows from operating activities of $3,000 in 20x7, beginning total assets of $26,000, and ending total assets of $28,000.

Exercises

LO1, LO2, LO3 **Discussion Questions**

E 1. Develop a brief answer to each of the following questions.

1. Which is the most important issue in recording a transaction: recognition, valuation, or classification?

2. What is an example of how a company could make false financial statements through a violation of the recognition concept?
3. How are assets and expenses related, and why are the debit and credit effects for assets and expenses the same?
4. In what way are unearned revenues the opposite of prepaid expenses?

LO4, LO5, SO6 **Discussion Questions**

E 2. Develop a brief answer to each of the following questions.

1. Which account would be most likely to have an account balance that is not normal?
2. A company incurs a cost for a part that is needed to repair a piece of equipment. Is the cost an asset or an expense? Explain.
3. If a company's cash flows for expenses temporarily exceed its cash flows from revenues, how might it make up the difference so that it can maintain liquidity?
4. How would the asset accounts in the chart of accounts for Treadle Website Design, Inc., differ if it were a retail company that sold advertising products instead of a service company?

LO1 **Recognition**

E 3. Which of the following events would be recognized and recorded in the accounting records of Villa Corporation on the date indicated?

Jan. 15   Villa Corporation offers to purchase a tract of land for $140,000. There is a high likelihood that the offer will be accepted.
Feb.   2   Villa Corporation receives notice that its rent will increase from $500 to $600 per month effective March 1.
Mar. 29   Villa Corporation receives its utility bill for the month of March. The bill is not due until April 9.
June 10   Villa Corporation places an order for new office equipment costing $21,000.
July   6   The office equipment Villa Corporation ordered on June 10 arrives. Payment is not due until August 1.

LO1 **Application of Recognition Point**

E 4. Davis Parts Shop, Inc., uses a large amount of supplies in its business. The following table summarizes selected transaction data for supplies that Davis Parts Shop purchased:

Order	Date Shipped	Date Received	Amount
a	June 26	July 5	$300
b	July 10	15	750
c	16	22	400
d	23	30	600
e	27	Aug. 1	750
f	Aug. 3	7	500

Determine the total purchases of supplies for July alone under each of the following assumptions:

1. Davis Parts Shop, Inc., recognizes purchases when orders are shipped.
2. Davis Parts Shop, Inc., recognizes purchases when orders are received.

LO2 **T Accounts, Normal Balance, and the Accounting Equation**

E 5. You are given the following list of accounts with dollar amounts:

Rent Expense $ 450
Cash   1,725

Service Revenue	$ 750
Retained Earnings	300
Dividends	375
Accounts Payable	600
Common Stock	900

Insert each account name at the top of its corresponding T account and enter the dollar amount as a normal balance in the account. Then show that the accounting equation is in balance.

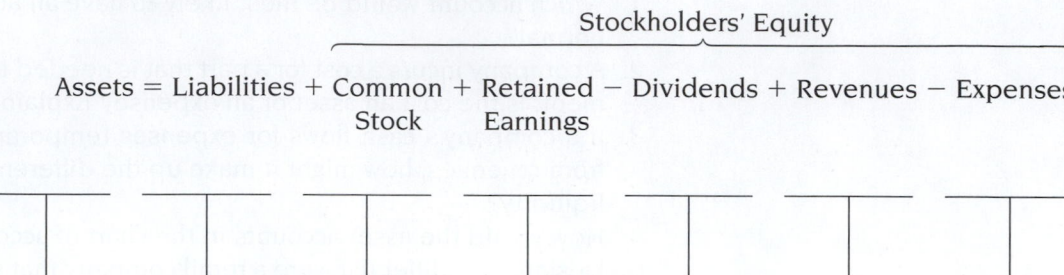

$$\text{Assets} = \text{Liabilities} + \underset{\text{Stock}}{\text{Common}} + \underset{\text{Earnings}}{\text{Retained}} - \text{Dividends} + \text{Revenues} - \text{Expenses}$$

LO2 Classification of Accounts

E 6. The following ledger accounts are for the Tuner Service Corporation:

a. Cash
b. Wages Expense
c. Accounts Receivable
d. Common Stock
e. Service Revenue
f. Prepaid Rent
g. Accounts Payable
h. Investments in Securities
i. Income Taxes Payable
j. Income Taxes Expense
k. Land
l. Supplies Expense
m. Prepaid Insurance

n. Utilities Expense
o. Fees Earned
p. Dividends
q. Wages Payable
r. Unearned Revenue
s. Office Equipment
t. Rent Payable
u. Notes Receivable
v. Interest Expense
w. Notes Payable
x. Supplies
y. Interest Receivable
z. Rent Expense

Complete the following table, using X's to indicate each account's classification and normal balance (whether a debit or a credit increases the account).

			Type of Account						
					Stockholders' Equity			**Normal Balance**	
						Retained Earnings		**(increases balance)**	
			Common						
Item	Asset	Liability	Stock	Dividends	Revenue	Expense		Debit	Credit
a.	X							X	

LO3 Transaction Analysis

E 7. Analyze transactions **a–g**, using the example that follows.

a. Sarah Linton established Kitty-Kat Beauty Parlor, Inc., by incorporating and investing $2,400 in exchange for 240 shares of $10 par value common stock.
b. Paid two months' rent in advance, $1,680.
c. Purchased supplies on credit, $120.
d. Received cash for barbering services, $600.
e. Paid for supplies purchased in **c**.
f. Paid utility bill, $72.
g. Declared and paid a dividend of $100.

Example:

a. The asset account Cash was increased. Increases in assets are recorded by debits. Debit Cash $2,400. A component of stockholders' equity, Common Stock, was increased. Increases in stockholders' equity are recorded by credits. Credit Common Stock $2,400.

LO3 Transaction Analysis

E 8. The following accounts are applicable to Dale's Lawn Service, Inc., a company that maintains condominium grounds:

1. Cash
2. Accounts Receivable
3. Supplies
4. Equipment
5. Accounts Payable
6. Lawn Services Revenue
7. Wages Expense
8. Rent Expense

Dale's Lawn Service, Inc., completed the following transactions:

	Debit	Credit
a. Paid for supplies purchased on credit last month.	5	1
b. Received cash from customers billed last month.	___	___
c. Made a payment on accounts payable.	___	___
d. Purchased supplies on credit.	___	___
e. Billed a client for lawn services.	___	___
f. Made a rent payment for the current month.	___	___
g. Received cash from customers for lawn services.	___	___
h. Paid employee wages.	___	___
i. Ordered equipment.	___	___
j. Received and paid for the equipment ordered in **i**.	___	___

Analyze each transaction and show the accounts affected by entering the corresponding numbers in the appropriate debit or credit columns as shown in transaction **a**. Indicate no entry, if appropriate.

LO3 Recording Transactions in T Accounts

E 9. Open the following T accounts: Cash; Repair Supplies; Repair Equipment; Accounts Payable; Common Stock; Dividends; Repair Fees Earned; Salaries Expense; and Rent Expense. Record the following transactions for the month of June directly in the T accounts; use the letters to identify the transactions in your T accounts. Determine the balance in each account.

a. Michael Change opened Ceramics Repair Service, Inc., by investing $8,600 in cash and $3,200 in repair equipment in return for 11,800 shares of the company's $1 par value common stock.
b. Paid $800 for the current month's rent.
c. Purchased repair supplies on credit, $1,000.
d. Purchased additional repair equipment for cash, $600.
e. Paid salary to a helper, $900.
f. Paid $400 of amount purchased on credit in **c**.
g. Accepted cash for repairs completed, $3,720.
h. Declared and paid a dividend of $1,200.

LO4 Trial Balance

E 10. After recording the transactions in **E 9**, prepare a trial balance in proper sequence for Ceramics Repair Service, Inc., as of June 30, 20xx.

LO3   Analysis of Transactions

E 11. Explain each transaction (**a–h**) entered in the following T accounts:

CASH				ACCOUNTS RECEIVABLE				EQUIPMENT			
a.	30,000	b.	7,500	c.	3,000	g.	750	b.	7,500	h.	450
g.	750	e.	1,500					d.	4,500		
h.	450	f.	2,250								

ACCOUNTS PAYABLE				COMMON STOCK				SERVICE REVENUE			
f.	2,250	d.	4,500			a.	30,000			c.	3,000

WAGES EXPENSE			
e.	1,500		

LO4   Preparing a Trial Balance

E 12. The list that follows presents the accounts (in alphabetical order) of the Chapala Metal Corporation as of March 31, 20xx. The list does not include the amount of Accounts Payable.

Accounts Payable	?
Accounts Receivable	$ 1,800
Building	20,400
Cash	5,400
Common Stock	12,000
Equipment	7,200
Land	3,120
Notes Payable	12,000
Prepaid Insurance	660
Retained Earnings	6,870

Prepare a trial balance with the proper heading (see Exhibit 2) and with the accounts listed in the chart of accounts sequence (see Exhibit 3). Compute the balance of Accounts Payable.

LO4   Effects of Errors on a Trial Balance

E 13. Which of the following errors would cause a trial balance to have unequal totals? Explain your answers.

a. A payment to a creditor was recorded as a debit to Accounts Payable for $129 and as a credit to Cash for $102.
b. A payment of $150 to a creditor for an account payable was debited to Accounts Receivable and credited to Cash.
c. A purchase of office supplies of $420 was recorded as a debit to Office Supplies for $42 and as a credit to Cash for $42.
d. A purchase of equipment for $450 was recorded as a debit to Supplies for $450 and as a credit to Cash for $450.

LO4   Correcting Errors in a Trial Balance

E 14. The trial balance for Kilda Services, Inc., at the end of July appears at the top of the opposite page. It does not balance because of a number of errors. Kilda's accountant compared the amounts in the trial balance with the ledger, recomputed the account balances, and compared the postings. He found the following errors:

a. The balance of Cash was understated by $400.
b. A cash payment of $420 was credited to Cash for $240.
c. A debit of $120 to Accounts Receivable was not posted.
d. Supplies purchased for $60 were posted as a credit to Supplies.
e. A debit of $180 to Prepaid Insurance was not posted.

Kilda Services, Inc.
Trial Balance
July 31, 20xx

Cash	$ 3,840	
Accounts Receivable	5,660	
Supplies	120	
Prepaid Insurance	180	
Equipment	8,400	
Accounts Payable		$ 4,540
Common Stock		4,000
Retained Earnings		7,560
Dividends		700
Revenues		5,920
Salaries Expense	2,600	
Rent Expense	600	
Advertising Expense	340	
Utilities Expense	26	
	$21,766	$22,720

f. The Accounts Payable account had debits of $5,320 and credits of $9,180.

g. The Notes Payable account, with a credit balance of $2,400, was not included on the trial balance.

h. The debit balance of Dividends was listed in the trial balance as a credit.

i. A $200 debit to Dividends was posted as a credit.

j. The actual balance of Utilities Expense, $260, was listed as $26 in the trial balance.

Prepare a corrected trial balance.

LO5   **Cash Flow Analysis**

E 15. A company engaged in the following transactions:

Dec.	1	Performed services for cash, $1,500
	1	Paid expenses in cash, $1,100
	2	Performed services on credit, $1,800
	3	Collected on account, $1,200
	4	Incurred expenses on credit, $1,300
	5	Paid on account, $700

Enter the correct titles on the following T accounts and enter the above transactions in the accounts. Determine the cash balance after these transactions, the amount still to be received, and the amount still to be paid.

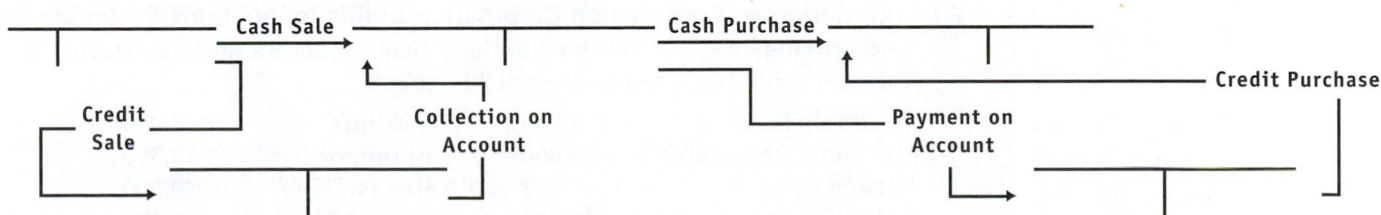

LO3, SO6 **Analysis of Unfamiliar Transactions**

E 16. Managers and accountants often encounter transactions with which they are unfamiliar. Use your analytical skills to analyze and record in journal form the following transactions, which have not yet been discussed in the text.

May 1 Purchased merchandise inventory on account, $1,200.
2 Purchased marketable securities for cash, $2,800.
3 Returned part of merchandise inventory purchased for full credit, $250.
4 Sold merchandise inventory on account, $800 (record sale only).
5 Purchased land and a building for $300,000. Payment is $60,000 cash, and there is a 30-year mortgage for the remainder. The purchase price is allocated as follows: $100,000 to the land and $200,000 to the building.
6 Received an order for $12,000 in services to be provided. With the order was a deposit of $4,000.

SO6 **Recording Transactions in the General Journal and Posting to the Ledger Accounts**

E 17. Open a general journal form like the one in Exhibit 4, and label it Page 10. After opening the form, record the following transactions in the journal:

Dec. 14 Purchased equipment for $12,000, paying $4,000 as a cash down payment.
28 Paid $6,000 of the amount owed on the equipment.

Prepare three ledger account forms like the one shown in Exhibit 5. Use the following account numbers: Cash, 111; Equipment, 144; and Accounts Payable, 212. Then post the two transactions from the general journal to the ledger accounts, being sure to make proper posting references. Assume that the Cash account has a debit balance of $16,000 on the day prior to the first transaction.

Cash Return on Assets

E 18. Julio Company wants to know if its liquidity performance has improved. Calculate cash return on assets for 20x6 and 20x7 using the following data:

Net cash flows from operating activities, 20x6	$ 4,300
Net cash flows from operating activities, 20x7	5,000
Total assets, 20x5	36,000
Total assets, 20x6	40,000
Total assets, 20x7	46,000

By this measure has liquidity improved? Why is it important to use average total assets in the calculation?

Problems

LO2 **T Accounts, Normal Balance, and the Accounting Equation**

P 1. The Anderson Construction Corporation builds foundations for buildings and parking lots. The following alphabetical list shows Anderson Construction's account balances as of April 30, 20xx:

Accounts Payable	$ 1,950	Dividends	$ 3,900
Accounts Receivable	5,060	Equipment	13,350
Cash	?	Notes Payable	10,000
Common Stock	15,000	Retained Earnings	5,000

Revenue Earned	$ 8,700	Utilities Expense	$ 210
Supplies	3,250	Wages Expense	4,400
Supplies Expense	3,600		

Required

Insert the account at the top of its corresponding T account and enter the dollar amount as a normal balance in the account. Determine the balance of cash and then show that the accounting equation is in balance.

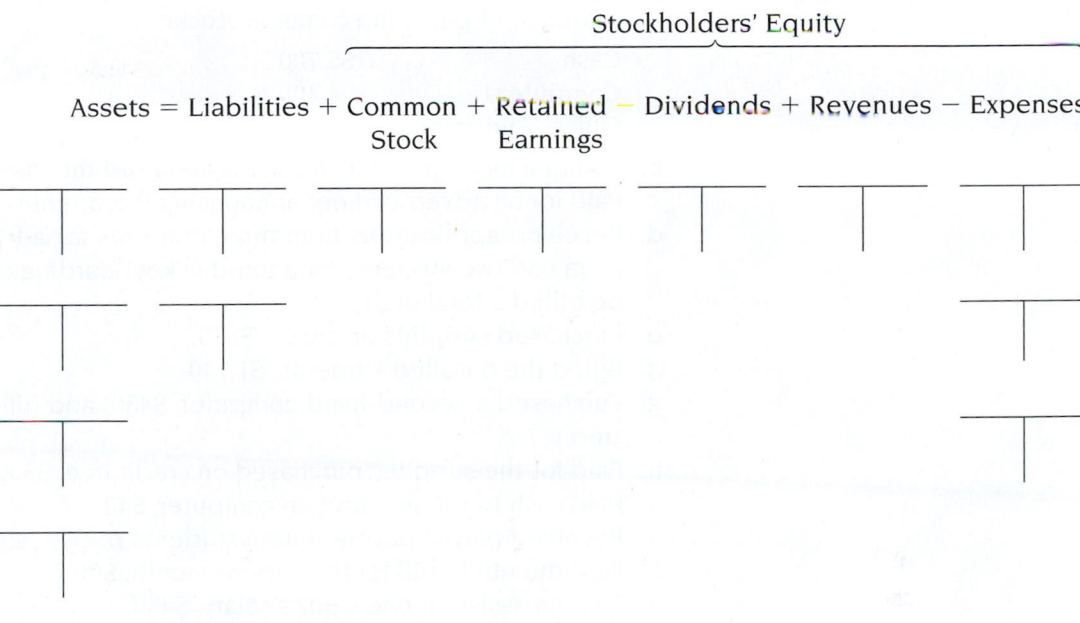

Stockholders' Equity

Assets = Liabilities + Common + Retained − Dividends + Revenues − Expenses
Stock   Earnings

LO3   **Transaction Analysis**

P 2. The following accounts are applicable to Walter's Chimney Sweeps, Inc.:

1.	Cash	8.	Common Stock
2.	Accounts Receivable	9.	Retained Earnings
3.	Supplies	10.	Dividends
4.	Prepaid Insurance	11.	Service Revenue
5.	Equipment	12.	Rent Expense
6.	Notes Payable	13.	Repair Expense
7.	Accounts Payable		

Walter's Chimney Sweeps, Inc., completed the following transactions:

		Debit	Credit
a.	Paid for supplies purchased on credit last month.	7	1
b.	Billed customers for services performed.		
c.	Paid the current month's rent.		
d.	Purchased supplies on credit.		
e.	Received cash from customers for services performed but not yet billed.		
f.	Purchased equipment on account.		
g.	Received a bill for repairs.		
h.	Returned part of the equipment purchased in **f** for a credit.		
i.	Received payments from customers previously billed.		
j.	Paid the bill received in **g**.		
k.	Received an order for services to be performed.		
l.	Paid for repairs with cash.		
m.	Made a payment to reduce the principal of the note payable.		
n.	Declared and paid a dividend.		

Required

Analyze each transaction and show the accounts affected by entering the corresponding numbers in the appropriate debit or credit column as shown in transaction **a**. Indicate no entry, if appropriate.

LO3, LO4, LO5

Transaction Analysis, T Accounts, and Trial Balance

P 3. Bob Lutz opened a secretarial school called Best Secretarial Training, Inc.

a. Lutz contributed the following assets to the business in exchange for 13,600 shares of $1 par value common stock:

Cash	$5,700
Computers	4,300
Office Equipment	3,600

b. Found a location for his business and paid the first month's rent, $260.
c. Paid for an advertisement announcing the opening of the school, $190.
d. Received applications from three students for a four-week secretarial program and two students for a ten-day keyboarding course. The students will be billed a total of $1,300.
e. Purchased supplies on credit, $330.
f. Billed the enrolled students, $1,740.
g. Purchased a second-hand computer, $480, and office equipment, $380, on credit.
h. Paid for the supplies purchased on credit in **e**, $330.
i. Paid cash to repair a broken computer, $40.
j. Received partial payment from students previously billed, $1,080.
k. Paid the utility bill for the current month, $90.
l. Paid an assistant one week's salary, $440.
m. Declared and paid a dividend of $300.

Required

1. Set up the following T accounts: Cash; Accounts Receivable; Supplies; Computers; Office Equipment; Accounts Payable; Common Stock; Dividends; Tuition Revenue; Salaries Expense; Utilities Expense; Rent Expense; Repair Expense; and Advertising Expense.
2. Record the transactions directly in the T accounts, using the transaction letter to identify each debit and credit.
3. Prepare a trial balance using today's date.
4. **User insight**: Examine transactions **f** and **j**. What were the revenues and how much cash was received from the revenues? What business issues might you see arising from the differences in these numbers?

LO1, LO3, LO4

Transaction Analysis, T Accounts, and Trial Balances

P 4. Hiroshi Mori began an upholstery cleaning business on October 1 and engaged in the following transactions during the month:

Oct. 1 Began business by depositing $12,000 in a bank account in the name of the corporation in exchange for 12,000 shares of $1 par value common stock.

2 Ordered cleaning supplies, $1,000.

3 Purchased cleaning equipment for cash, $2,800.

4 Made two months' van lease payment in advance, $1,200.

7 Received the cleaning supplies ordered on October 2 and agreed to pay half the amount in 10 days and the rest in 30 days.

9 Paid for repairs on the van with cash, $80.

12 Received cash for cleaning upholstery, $960.

Oct 17 Paid half the amount owed on supplies purchased on October 7, $500.
21 Billed customers for cleaning upholstery, $1,340.
24 Paid cash for additional repairs on the van, $80.
27 Received $600 from the customers billed on October 21.
31 Declared and paid a dividend of $700.

Required

1. Set up the following T accounts: Cash; Accounts Receivable; Cleaning Supplies; Prepaid Lease; Cleaning Equipment; Accounts Payable; Common Stock; Dividends; Cleaning Revenue; and Repair Expense.
2. Record transactions directly in the T accounts. Identify each entry by date.
3. Prepare a trial balance for Mori Upholstery Cleaning, Inc., as of October 31, 20xx.
4. **User insight:** Compare and contrast how the issues of recognition, valuation, and classification are settled in the transactions of October 7 and 9.

LO3, LO4, LO5, SO6 **Transaction Analysis, General Journal, Ledger Accounts, and Trial Balance**

P 5. The Acorn Nursery School Corporation provides baby-sitting and child-care programs. On January 31, 20xx, the company had the following trial balance:

Acorn Nursery School Corporation Trial Balance January 31, 20xx		
Cash (111)	$ 1,870	
Accounts Receivable (113)	1,700	
Equipment (141)	1,040	
Buses (143)	17,400	
Notes Payable (211)		$15,000
Accounts Payable (212)		1,640
Common Stock (311)		4,000
Retained Earnings (312)		1,370
	$22,010	$22,010

During the month of February, the company completed the following transactions:

Feb. 2 Paid this month's rent, $270.
3 Received fees for this month's services, $650.
4 Purchased supplies on account, $85.
5 Reimbursed the bus driver for gas expenses, $40.
6 Ordered playground equipment, $1,000.
8 Made a payment on account, $170.
9 Received payments from customers on account, $1,200.
10 Billed customers who had not yet paid for this month's services, $700.
11 Paid for the supplies purchased on February 4.
13 Received and purchased playground equipment ordered on February 6 for cash, $1,000.
17 Purchased equipment on account, $290.
19 Paid this month's utility bill, $145.

Feb. 22 Received payment for one month's services from customers previously billed, $500.
  26 Paid part-time assistants for services, $460.
  27 Purchased gas and oil for the bus on account, $325.
  28 Declared and paid a dividend of $110.

Required

1. Open accounts in the ledger for the accounts in the trial balance plus the following ones: Supplies (115); Dividends (313); Service Revenue (411); Rent Expense (511); Gas and Oil Expense (512); Wages Expense (513); and Utilities Expense (514).
2. Enter the January 31, 20xx, account balances from the trial balance.
3. Enter the above transactions in the general journal (Pages 17 and 18).
4. Post the entries to the ledger accounts. Be sure to make the appropriate posting references in the journal and ledger as you post.
5. Prepare a trial balance as of February 28, 20xx.
6. **User insight:** Examine the transactions for February 3, 9, 10, and 22. What were the revenues and how much cash was received from the revenues? What business issue might you see arising from the differences in these numbers?

Alternate Problems

LO2 T Accounts, Normal Balance, and The Accounting Equation

 P 6. The Buy-It Design Corporation creates radio and television advertising for local businesses in the twin cities. The following alphabetical list shows Buy-It Design's account balances as of January 31, 20xx:

Accounts Payable	$ 3,210	Loans Payable	$ 5,000
Accounts Receivable	36,000	Retained Earnings	22,000
Cash	7,200	Rent Expense	5,940
Common Stock	10,000	Telephone Expense	480
Design Revenue	105,000	Unearned Revenue	9,000
Dividends	18,000	Wages Expense	62,000
Equipment	?		

Required

Insert the account title at the top of its corresponding T account and enter the dollar amount as a normal balance in the account. Determine the balance of Equipment and then show that the accounting equation is in balance.

Stockholders' Equity

Assets = Liabilities + Common + Retained − Dividends + Revenues − Expenses
                          Stock   Earnings

LO1, LO3, LO4   **Transaction Analysis, Journal Form, T Accounts, and Trial Balance**

P 7. Nomar Parra bid for and won a concession to rent bicycles in the local park during the summer. During the month of June, Parra completed the following transactions for his bicycle rental business:

June 2 Began business by placing $7,200 in a business checking account in the name of the corporation in exchange for 7,200 shares of $1 par value common stock.
       3 Purchased supplies on account for $150.
       4 Purchased 10 bicycles for $2,500, paying $1,200 down and agreeing to pay the rest in 30 days.
       5 Paid $2,900 in cash for a small shed to store the bicycles and to use for other operations.
       8 Paid $400 in cash for shipping and installation costs (considered an addition to the cost of the shed) to place the shed at the park entrance.
       9 Hired a part-time assistant to help out on weekends at $7 per hour.
      10 Paid a maintenance person $75 to clean the grounds.
      13 Received $970 in cash for rentals.
      17 Paid $150 for the supplies purchased on June 3.
      18 Paid a $55 repair bill on bicycles.
      23 Billed a company $110 for bicycle rentals for an employee outing.
      25 Paid the $100 fee for June to the Park District for the right to operate the bicycle concession.
      27 Received $960 in cash for rentals.
      29 Paid the assistant $240.
      30 Declared and paid a dividend of $500.

Required

1. Prepare entries to record these transactions in journal form.
2. Set up the following T accounts and post all the journal entries: Cash; Accounts Receivable; Supplies; Shed; Bicycles; Accounts Payable; Common Stock; Dividends; Rental Revenue; Wages Expense; Maintenance Expense; Repair Expense; and Concession Fee Expense.
3. Prepare a trial balance for Parra Rentals, Inc., as of June 30, 20xx.
4. **User Insight:** Compare and contrast how the issues of recognition, valuation, and classification are settled in the transactions of June 3 and 10.

LO3, LO4, LO5, SO6   **Transaction Analysis, General Journal, Ledger Accounts, and Trial Balance**

P 8. Yury Wagoner Corporation is a marketing firm. The company's trial balance on July 31, 20xx, appears at the top of the next page. During the month of August, the company completed the following transactions:

Aug. 2 Paid rent for August, $650.
       3 Received cash from customers on account, $2,300.
       7 Ordered supplies, $380.
      10 Billed customers for services provided, $2,800.
      12 Made a payment on accounts payable, $1,100.
      14 Received the supplies ordered on August 7 and agreed to pay for them in 30 days, $380.
      17 Discovered some of the supplies were not as ordered and returned them for full credit, $80.
      19 Received cash from a customer for services provided, $4,800.

Yury Wagoner Corporation
Trial Balance
July 31, 20xx

Cash (111)	$10,200	
Accounts Receivable (113)	5,500	
Supplies (115)	610	
Office Equipment (141)	4,200	
Accounts Payable (212)		$ 2,600
Common Stock (311)		12,000
Retained Earnings (312)		5,910
	$20,510	$20,510

Aug. 24 Paid the utility bill for August, $280.

26 Received a bill, to be paid in September, for advertisements placed in the local newspaper during the month of August to promote Yury Wagoner Corporation, $700.

29 Billed a customer for services provided, $2,700.

30 Paid salaries for August, $3,800.

31 Declared and paid a dividend of $1,200.

Required

1. Open accounts in the ledger for the accounts in the trial balance plus the following accounts: Dividends (313); Marketing Fees (411); Salaries Expense (511); Rent Expense (512); Utilities Expense (513); and Advertising Expense (515).

2. Enter the July 31, 20xx, account balances from the trial balance.

3. Enter the above transactions in the general journal (Pages 22 and 23).

4. Post the journal entries to the ledger accounts. Be sure to make the appropriate posting references in the journal and ledger as you post.

5. Prepare a trial balance as of August 31, 20xx.

6. **User Insight:** Examine the transactions for August 3, 10, 19, and 29. How much were revenues and how much cash was received from the revenues? What business issues might you see arising from the differences in these numbers?

ENHANCING Your Knowledge, Skills, and Critical Thinking

Conceptual Understanding Cases

LO1 **Valuation Issue**

C 1. Nike, Inc. manufactures athletic shoes and related products. In one of its annual reports, Nike made this statement: "Property, plant, and equipment are recorded at cost."[8] Given that the property, plant, and equipment undoubtedly were purchased over several years and that the current value of those assets is likely to be very different from their original cost, what authoritative basis is there for carrying the assets at cost? Does accounting generally recognize changes in value after the purchase of property, plant, and equipment? Assume you are an accountant for Nike. Write a memo to management explaining the rationale underlying Nike's approach.

LO3   Recording of Rebates

C 2. Is it revenue or a reduction of an expense? That is the question companies that receive manufacturer's rebates for purchasing a large quantity of product must answer. Food companies like **Sara Lee, Kraft Foods,** and **Nestlé** give supermarkets special manufacturer's rebates of up to 45 percent, depending on the quantities purchased. Some firms were recording these rebates as revenue, whereas others were recording them as a reduction of the cost until the SEC said that only one way is correct. What, then, is the correct way for supermarkets to record these rebates? Would your answer change net income?

Interpreting Financial Reports

LO2, LO3   Interpreting a Bank's Financial Statements

C 3. **Mellon Bank** is a large bank holding company. Selected accounts from the company's 2004 annual report are as follows (in millions):[9]

Cash and Due from Banks	$2,775	Securities Available for Sale	$13,376
Loans to Customers	6,754	Deposits by Customers	23,591

1. Indicate whether each of the accounts just listed is an asset, a liability, or a component of stockholders' equity on Mellon Bank's balance sheet.
2. Assume that you are in a position to do business with this large company. Show how Mellon Bank's accountants would prepare the entry in T account form to record each of the following transactions:

 a. You sell securities in the amount of $2,000 to the bank.
 b. You deposit in the bank the $2,000 received from selling the securities.
 c. You borrow $5,000 from the bank.

LO5   Cash Flows

C 4. You have been promoted recently and now have access to the firm's monthly financial statements. Business is good. Revenues are increasing rapidly, and income is at an all-time high. The balance sheet shows growth in receivables, and accounts payable have declined. However, the chief financial officer is concerned about the firm's cash flows from operating activities because they are decreasing. What are some reasons why a company with a positive net income may fall short of cash from its operating activities? What could be done to improve this situation?

Decision Analysis Using Excel

LO2, LO3, LO4   Transaction Analysis and Evaluation of a Trial Balance

C 5. Demetrius Carver hired an attorney to help him start Carver Repair Service Corporation. On March 1, Carver deposited $14,375 cash in a bank account in the name of the corporation in exchange for 575 shares of $25 par value common stock. When he paid the attorney's bill of $875, the attorney advised him to hire an accountant to keep his records. Carver was so busy that it was March 31 before he hired you to straighten out his records. Your first task is to develop a trial balance based on the March transactions, which are described in the next two paragraphs.

After investing in his business and paying his attorney, Carver borrowed $6,250 from the bank. He later paid $325, including interest of $75, on this loan. He also purchased a used pickup truck in the company's name, paying $3,125 down and financing $9,250. The first payment on the truck is due April 15. Carver then rented an office and paid three months' rent, $1,125, in advance.

Credit purchases of office equipment of $1,000 and repair tools of $625 must be paid by April 10.

In March, Carver Repair Service completed repairs of $1,625, of which $500 were cash transactions. Of the credit transactions, $375 were collected during March, and $750 remained to be collected at the end of March. The company paid wages of $562 to its employees. On March 31, the company received a $93 bill for the March utilities expense and a $62 check from a customer for work to be completed in April. A customer requested a repair on March 31 to be done the following week and agreed to pay $250 for it. Carver is considering recording this agreement as revenue in March to make the business look better.

1. Record all of the transactions for March in journal form. Label each of the entries alphabetically.
2. Set up T accounts. Then post the entries to the T accounts. Identify each posting with the letter corresponding to the transaction.
3. Determine the balance of each account.
4. Prepare a trial balance for Carver Repair Service Corporation as of March 31.
5. Demetrius Carver is unsure how to evaluate the trial balance. The Cash account balance is $15,550, which exceeds the original investment of $14,375 by $1,175. Did the company make a profit of $1,175? Explain why the Cash account is not an indicator of business earnings. Cite specific examples to show why it is difficult to determine net income by looking solely at figures in the trial balance.
6. What are the ethical implications of recording the repair order received on March 31 as revenue in March?

Annual Report Case: CVS Corporation

LO1 **Recognition, Valuation, and Classification**

C 6. Refer to the Summary of Significant Accounting Policies in the notes to the financial statements in **CVS Corporation's** annual report in the Supplement to Chapter 1 to answer these questions:

1. How does the concept of recognition apply to advertising costs?
2. How does the concept of valuation apply to inventories?
3. How does the concept of classification apply to cash and cash equivalents?

Comparison Analysis: CVS Versus Southwest

Cash Return on Assets

C 7. Refer to the financial statements of **CVS** and **Southwest Airlines Co.** in the Supplement to Chapter 1. Compute cash return on assets for the past two years for both companies and comment on the results. Total assets in fiscal 2002 were $9,645.3 million for CVS and $8,954 million for Southwest.

Ethical Dilemma Case

LO1 **Recognition Point and Ethical Considerations**

C 8. Jerry Hasbrow, a sales representative for Penn Office Supplies Corporation, is compensated on a commission basis and received a substantial bonus for meeting his annual sales goal. The company's recognition point for sales is the day of shipment. On December 31, Hasbrow realizes he needs sales of $2,000 to reach his sales goal and receive the bonus. He calls a purchaser for a local insurance company, whom he knows well, and asks him to buy $2,000 worth of copier paper today. The purchaser says, "But Jerry, that's more than a year's supply for us." Hasbrow says, "Buy it today. If you decide it's too much, you can return however much you want for full credit next month." The purchaser says, "Okay, ship it." The paper is shipped on December 31 and recorded as a sale. On January 15, the purchaser returns $1,750 worth of paper for full credit (approved by Hasbrow) against the bill. Should the shipment on December 31 be recorded as a sale? Discuss the ethics of Hasbrow's action.

Internet Case

LO1   **Financial Misstatements**

C 9. WorldCom changed its name to **MCI.** Go to www.CFO.com and enter the words "extreme makeover" into the search box. From a review of the article, identify the major steps the new CFO carried out to fix WorldCom's financial statements. Also, find out what eventually happened to MCI. Be prepared to discuss your findings in class.

Group Activity Case

LO1, LO3   **Valuation and Classification Issues for Dot.Coms**

C 10. The dot.com business has raised many issues about accounting practices, some of which are of great concern to both the SEC and the FASB. Important ones relate to the valuation and classification of revenue transactions. Many dot-com companies seek to report as much revenue as possible because revenue growth is seen as a key performance measure for these companies. **Amazon.com** is a good example. Consider the following situations:

a. An Amazon.com customer orders and pays $28 for an electronic Gameboy on the Internet. Amazon sends an email to the company that makes the product, which sends the Gameboy to the customer. Amazon collects $28 from the customer and pays $24 to the other company. Amazon never owns the Gameboy.

b. Amazon agrees to place a banner advertisement on its website for another dot-com company. Instead of paying cash for the advertisement, the other company agrees to let Amazon advertise on its website.

c. Assume the same facts as in situation **b** except that Amazon agrees to accept the other company's common stock in this barter transaction. Over the next six months, the price of that stock declines.

Divide the class into three groups. Assign each group one of the above situations. Each group should discuss the valuation and classification issues that arise in the assigned situation, including how Amazon should account for each transaction.

Business Communication Case

LO1, LO3   **Valuation and Classification of Business Transactions**

C11. Hibbard Garden Center has purchased two pre-owned trucks for delivery of plants and flowers to its customers. The trucks were purchased at a cash-only auction for 15 percent below current market value. The owners have asked you to record these trucks in the financial records at current market value. You don't think that is correct. In response to the owners, write a brief business memorandum in good form based on your knowledge of Chapter 2. Explain how the purchase of the pre-owned trucks will affect the balance sheet, include the entry to record the transaction, and explain why the amount must be at the price paid for the trucks.

Measuring Business Income

Income, or earnings, is the most important measure of a company's success or failure. Thus, the incentive to manage, or misstate, earnings by manipulating the numbers can be powerful, and because earnings are based on estimates, manipulation can be easy. For these reasons, ethical behavior is extremely important when measuring business income.

LEARNING OBJECTIVES

Making a Statement

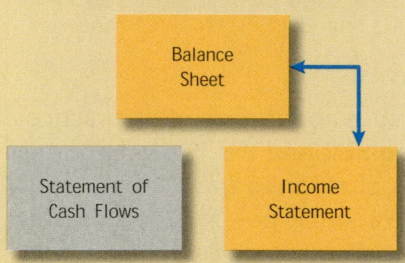

Adjusting entries affect the balance sheet and income statement but not the statement of cash flows.

LO1 Define *net income,* and explain the assumptions underlying income measurement and their ethical application.

LO2 Define *accrual accounting,* and explain how it is accomplished.

LO3 Identify four situations that require adjusting entries, and illustrate typical adjusting entries.

LO4 Prepare financial statements from an adjusted trial balance.

LO5 Describe the accounting cycle, and explain the purposes of closing entries.

LO6 Use accrual-based information to analyze cash flows.

- What assumptions must Yahoo! make to account for transactions that span accounting periods?

- How does Yahoo! assign its revenues and expenses to the proper accounting period so that net income is properly measured?

- Why are the adjustments that these transactions require important to Yahoo!'s financial performance?

Yahoo! is a leading provider of online services to consumers and businesses worldwide. At the end of any accounting period, Yahoo! has many transactions that will affect future periods.[1] Two examples appear in the Financial Highlights below: *prepaid expenses,* which, though paid in the period just ended, will benefit future periods and are therefore recorded as assets; and *accrued expenses,* which the company has incurred but will not pay until a future period. If prepaid and accrued expenses are not accounted for properly at the end of a period, Yahoo!'s income will be misstated. Similar misstatements can occur when a company has received revenue that it has not yet earned or has earned revenue but not yet received it. If misstatements are made, investors will be misled about the company's financial performance.

YAHOO!'S FINANCIAL HIGHLIGHTS
Selected Balance Sheet Items (In thousands)

Assets	2004	2003	2002
Prepaid expenses	$ 98,507	$129,777	$ 82,216
Liabilities			
Accrued expenses and current liabilities	$853,115	$483,628	$257,575

Profitability Measurement: Issues and Ethics

LO1 Define *net income,* and explain the assumptions underlying income measurement and their ethical application.

As you know, profitability and liquidity are the two major goals of a business. For a business to succeed, or even to survive, it must earn a profit. **Profit**, however, means different things to different people. Accountants prefer to use the term **net income** because it can be precisely defined from an accounting point of view as the *net increase in stockholders' equity that results from a company's operations.*

Net income is reported on the income statement, and management, stockholders, and others use it to measure a company's progress in meeting the goal of profitability. Readers of income statements need to understand what net income means and be aware of its strengths and weaknesses as a measure of a company's performance.

Net Income

Net income is accumulated in the Retained Earnings account. In its simplest form, it is measured as the difference between revenues and expenses when revenues exceed expenses:

$$\text{Net Income} = \text{Revenues} - \text{Expenses}$$

When expenses exceed revenues, a **net loss** occurs.

Revenues are increases in stockholders' equity resulting from selling goods, rendering services, or performing other business activities. When a business delivers a product or provides a service to a customer, it usually receives cash or a promise to pay cash in the near future. The promise to pay is recorded in either Accounts Receivable or Notes Receivable. The total of these accounts and the total cash received from customers in an accounting period are the company's revenues for that period.

Expenses are decreases in stockholders' equity resulting from the cost of selling goods or rendering services and the cost of the activities necessary to carry on a business, such as attracting and serving customers. In other words, expenses are the cost of the goods and services used in the course of earning revenues. Examples include salaries expense, rent expense, advertising expense, utilities expense, and depreciation (allocation of cost) of a building or office equipment. These expenses are often called the *cost of doing business* or *expired costs.*

Not all increases in stockholders' equity arise from revenues, nor do all decreases in stockholders' equity arise from expenses. Stockholders' investments increase stockholders' equity but are not revenues, and dividends decrease stockholders' equity but are not expenses.

Income Measurement Assumptions

Users of financial reports should be aware that assumptions play a major role in the measurement of net income and other key indicators of performance. **Yahoo!'s** management acknowledges this in its annual report, as follows:

> The preparation of . . . financial statements in conformity with generally accepted accounting principles requires management to make assumptions that affect the reported amounts of assets and liabilities . . . and the reported amounts of revenue and expense.[2]

Study Note

The essence of revenue is that something has been *earned* through the sale of goods or services. That is why cash received through a loan does not constitute revenue.

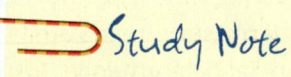
Study Note

The primary purpose of an expense is to generate revenue.

The major assumptions made in measuring business income have to do with continuity, periodicity, and matching.

Continuity Measuring business income requires that certain expense and revenue transactions be allocated over several accounting periods. Choosing the number of accounting periods raises the issue of **continuity**. What is the expected life of the business? Many businesses last less than five years, and in any given year, thousands of businesses go bankrupt. The majority of companies present annual financial statements on the assumption that the business will continue to operate indefinitely—that is, that the company is a **going concern**. The continuity assumption is as follows:

> Unless there is evidence to the contrary, the accountant assumes that the business will continue to operate indefinitely.

Justification for all the techniques of income measurement rests on the assumption of continuity. Consider, for example, the value of assets on the balance sheet. The continuity assumption allows the cost of certain assets to be held on the balance sheet until a future accounting period, when the cost will become an expense on the income statement.

When a firm is facing bankruptcy, the accountant may set aside the assumption of continuity and prepare financial statements based on the assumption that the firm will go out of business and sell all of its assets at liquidation value—that is, for what they will bring in cash.

Periodicity Measuring business income requires assigning revenues and expenses to a specific accounting period. However, not all transactions can be easily assigned to specific periods. For example, when a company purchases a building, it must estimate the number of years the building will be in use. The portion of the cost of the building that is assigned to each period depends on this estimate and requires an assumption about **periodicity**. The assumption is as follows:

> Although the lifetime of a business is uncertain, it is nonetheless useful to estimate the business's net income in terms of accounting periods.

Financial statements may be prepared for any time period, but generally, to make comparisons easier, the periods are of equal length. A 12-month accounting period is called a **fiscal year**; accounting periods of less than a year are called **interim periods**. The fiscal year of many organizations is the calendar

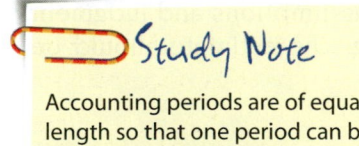

Study Note

Accounting periods are of equal length so that one period can be compared with the next.

FOCUS ON BUSINESS PRACTICE

Fiscal Years Vary.

The fiscal years of many schools and governmental agencies end on June 30 or September 30. The table at the right shows the last month of the fiscal year of some well-known companies.

Company	Last Month of Fiscal Year
Caesars World	July
The Walt Disney Company	September
Fleetwood Enterprises	April
H.J. Heinz	March
Kelly Services	December
MGM-UA Communications	August
Toys "R" Us	January

year, January 1 to December 31. However, retailers often end their fiscal years during a slack season, and in this case, the fiscal year corresponds to the yearly cycle of business activity.

Matching

The **cash basis of accounting** is the practice of accounting for revenues in the period in which cash is received and for expenses in the period in which cash is paid. Some individuals and businesses use this method to account for income taxes. With this method, taxable income is calculated as the difference between cash receipts from revenues and cash payments for expenses.

Although the cash basis of accounting works well for some small businesses and many individuals, it does not meet the needs of most businesses. To measure net income adequately, revenues and expenses must be assigned to the accounting period in which they occur, regardless of when cash is received or paid. This is an application of the **matching rule**:

> Revenues must be assigned to the accounting period in which the goods are sold or the services performed, and expenses must be assigned to the accounting period in which they are used to produce revenue.

In other words, expenses should be recognized in the same accounting period as the revenues to which they are related. However, a direct cause-and-effect relationship between expenses and revenues is often difficult to identify. When there is no direct means of connecting expenses and revenues, costs are allocated in a systematic way among the accounting periods that benefit from the costs. For example, a building's cost is expensed over the building's expected useful life.

Ethics and the Matching Rule

As shown in Figure 1, applying the matching rule involves making assumptions. It also involves exercising judgment. Consider the assumptions and judgment involved in estimating the useful life of a building. The estimate should be

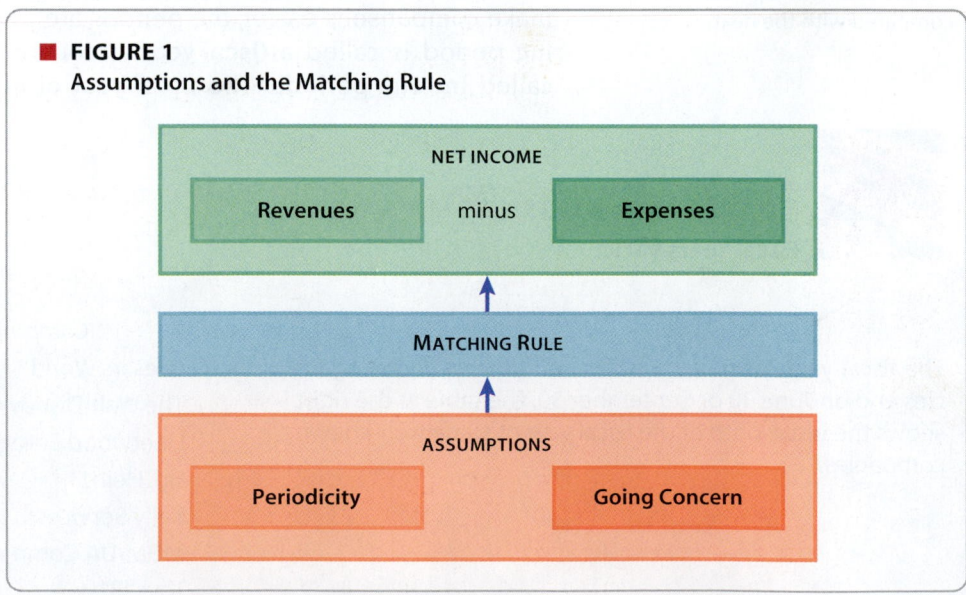

■ **FIGURE 1**
Assumptions and the Matching Rule

FOCUS ON BUSINESS PRACTICE
Are Misstatements of Earnings Always Overstatements?

Not all misstatements of earnings are overstatements. For instance, privately held companies, which do not have to be concerned about the effect of their earnings announcements on stockholders or investors, may understate income to reduce or avoid income taxes. In an unusual case involving a public company, the SEC cited and fined **Microsoft** for understating its income. Microsoft, a very successful company, accomplished this by overstating its unearned revenue on the balance sheet. The company's motive in trying to appear less successful than it actually was may have been that it was facing government charges of being a monopoly.[3]

based on realistic assumptions, but management has latitude in making that estimate, and its judgment will affect the final net income that is reported.

The manipulation of revenues and expenses to achieve a specific outcome is called **earnings management**. Research has shown that companies that manage their earnings are much more likely to exceed projected earnings targets by a little than to fall short by a little. Why would management want to manage earnings to keep them from falling short? It may want to

▶ Meet a previously announced goal and thus meet the expectations of the market.

▶ Keep the company's stock price from dropping.

▶ Meet a goal that will enable it to earn bonuses.

▶ Avoid embarrassment.

Earnings management, though not the best practice, is not illegal. However, when the estimates involved in earnings management begin moving outside a reasonable range, the financial statements become misleading. For instance, net income is misleading when revenue is overstated or expenses are understated by significant amounts. As noted earlier in the text, the preparation of financial statements that are intentionally misleading constitutes fraudulent financial reporting.

Most of the enforcement actions that the Securities and Exchange Commission has brought against companies in recent years involve misapplications of the matching rule resulting from improper accrual accounting. In the rest of this chapter, we focus on accrual accounting and its proper application.

STOP • REVIEW • APPLY

1-1. Why do accountants refer to *profit* as *net income*?

1-2. How does the need to assign revenues and expenses to a specific accounting period create problems?

1-3. What is the significance of the continuity assumption?

1-4. "The matching rule is the most significant concept in accounting." Do you agree with this statement? Explain your answer.

Suggested answers to all Stop, Review, and Apply questions follow the appendixes.

Accrual Accounting

LO2 Define *accrual accounting,* and explain how it is accomplished.

Accrual accounting encompasses all the techniques accountants use to apply the matching rule. In accrual accounting, revenues and expenses are recorded in the periods in which they occur rather than in the periods in which they are received or paid.

Accrual accounting is accomplished in the following ways:

1. Recording revenues when they are earned.

2. Recording expenses when they are incurred.

3. Adjusting the accounts.

Recognizing Revenues

As you may recall, the process of determining when revenue should be recorded is called **revenue recognition**. The Securities and Exchange Commission requires that all the following conditions be met before revenue is recognized:[4]

▶ Persuasive evidence of an arrangement exists.

▶ A product or service has been delivered.

▶ The seller's price to the buyer is fixed or determinable.

▶ Collectibility is reasonably assured.

For example, suppose Treadle Website Design, Inc., has created a website for a customer and that the transaction meets the SEC's four criteria: Treadle and the customer agree that the customer owes for the service, the service has been rendered, both parties understand the price, and there is a reasonable expectation that the customer will pay the bill. When Treadle bills the customer, it records the transaction as revenue by debiting Accounts Receivable and crediting Design Revenue. Note that revenue can be recorded even though cash has not been collected; all that is required is a reasonable expectation that cash will be paid.

Recognizing Expenses

Expenses are recorded when there is an agreement to purchase goods or services, the goods have been delivered or the services rendered, a price has been established or can be determined, and the goods or services have been used to produce revenue. For example, when Treadle Website Design receives its utility bill, it recognizes the expense as having been incurred and as having helped produce revenue. Treadle records this transaction by debiting Utilities Expense and crediting Accounts Payable. Until the bill is paid, Accounts Payable serves as a holding account. Note that recognition of the expense does not depend on the payment of cash.

Adjusting the Accounts

Accrual accounting also involves adjusting the accounts. Adjustments are necessary because the accounting period, by definition, ends on a particular day. The balance sheet must list all assets and liabilities as of the end of that day, and the income statement must contain all revenues and expenses applicable

Study Note

The accountant waits until the end of an accounting period to update certain revenues and expenses even though the revenues and expenses theoretically change during the period. There usually is no need to adjust them until the end of the period, when the financial statements are prepared.

EXHIBIT 1 ▶   **Trial Balance**

Treadle Website Design, Inc.
Trial Balance
July 31, 20xx

Cash	$22,480	
Accounts Receivable	4,600	
Office Supplies	5,200	
Prepaid Rent	3,200	
Office Equipment	16,320	
Accounts Payable		$ 6,280
Unearned Design Revenue		1,400
Common Stock		40,000
Dividends	2,800	
Design Revenue		12,400
Wages Expense	4,800	
Utilities Expense	680	
	$60,080	$60,080

to the period ending on that day. Although operating a business is a continuous process, there must be a cutoff point for the periodic reports. Some transactions invariably span the cutoff point, and some accounts therefore need adjustment.

As you can see in Exhibit 1, some of the accounts in Treadle Website Design's trial balance as of July 31 do not show the correct balances for preparing the financial statements. The trial balance lists prepaid rent of $3,200. At $1,600 per month, this represents rent for the months of July and August. So, on July 31, one-half of the $3,200 represents rent expense for July, and the remaining $1,600 represents an asset that will be used in August. An adjustment is needed to reflect the $1,600 balance in the Prepaid Rent account on the balance sheet and the $1,600 rent expense on the income statement.

As you will see, several other accounts in Treadle Website Design's trial balance do not reflect their correct balances. Like the Prepaid Rent account, they need to be adjusted.

Adjustments and Ethics

Accrual accounting can be difficult to understand. The account adjustments take time to calculate and enter in the records. Also, adjusting entries do not affect cash flows in the current period because they never involve the Cash account. You might ask, "Why go to all the trouble of making them? Why worry about them?" For one thing, the SEC has identified issues related to accrual accounting and adjustments as an area of utmost importance because of the potential for abuse and misrepresentation.[5]

All adjustments are important because of their effect on performance measures of profitability and liquidity. Adjusting entries affect net income on the income statement, and they affect profitability comparisons from one accounting period to the next. They also affect assets and liabilities on the balance sheet and thus provide information about a company's *future* cash inflows and outflows. This information is needed to assess management's performance in achieving sufficient liquidity to meet the need for cash to pay ongoing obligations. The potential for abuse arises because considerable judgment underlies the application of adjusting entries. When this judgment is misused, performance measures can be misleading.

STOP • REVIEW • APPLY

2-1. What are the conditions for recognizing revenue?

2-2. What is the difference between the cash basis and the accrual basis of accounting?

2-3. In what three ways is accrual accounting accomplished?

2-4. Why are adjusting entries necessary?

2-5. "Why worry about adjustments? Doesn't it all come out in the wash?" Describe how you would answer these questions.

The Adjustment Process

LO3 Identify four situations that require adjusting entries, and illustrate typical adjusting entries.

When transactions span more than one accounting period, accrual accounting requires the use of **adjusting entries**. Figure 2 shows the four situations in which adjusting entries must be made. Each adjusting entry affects one balance sheet account and one income statement account. As we have already noted, adjusting entries never affect the Cash account.

The four types of adjusting entries are as follows:

Type 1. Allocating recorded costs between two or more accounting periods.
Examples of these costs are prepayments of rent, insurance, and sup-

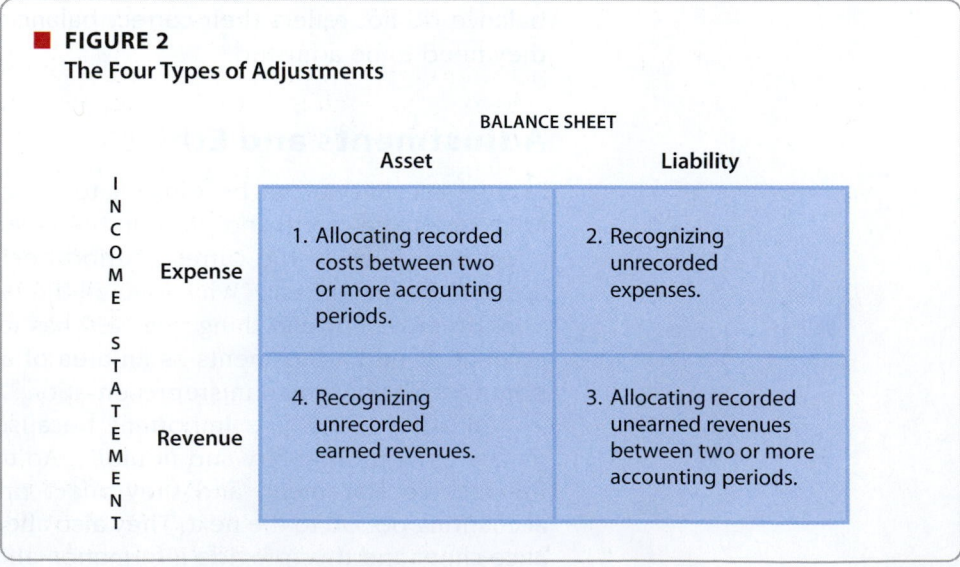

■ **FIGURE 2**
The Four Types of Adjustments

		BALANCE SHEET	
		Asset	**Liability**
INCOME STATEMENT	**Expense**	1. Allocating recorded costs between two or more accounting periods.	2. Recognizing unrecorded expenses.
	Revenue	4. Recognizing unrecorded earned revenues.	3. Allocating recorded unearned revenues between two or more accounting periods.

When transactions span more than one accounting period, an adjusting entry is necessary. Depreciation of plant and equipment, such as that found in this book warehouse area of Amazon.com's shipping and receiving facility in Fernley, Nevada, is a type of transaction that requires an adjusting entry. In this case, the adjusting entry involves an asset account and an expense account.

plies, and the depreciation of plant and equipment. The adjusting entry in this case involves an asset account and an expense account.

Type 2. Recognizing unrecorded expenses. Examples of these expenses are wages, interest, and income taxes that accrue but are not recorded during an accounting period. The adjusting entry involves an expense account and a liability account.

Type 3. Allocating recorded, unearned revenues between two or more accounting periods. Examples include payments received in advance and deposits made on goods or services. The adjusting entry involves a liability account and a revenue account.

Type 4. Recognizing unrecorded, earned revenues. An example is revenue that a company has earned for providing a service but for which it has not billed or been paid by the end of the accounting period. The adjusting entry involves an asset account and a revenue account.

Adjusting entries are either deferrals or accruals.

▶ A **deferral** is the postponement of the recognition of an expense already paid (Type 1 adjustment) or of revenue received in advance (Type 3 adjustment). The cash receipt or payment is recorded before the adjusting entry is made.

▶ An **accrual** is the recognition of a revenue (Type 4 adjustment) or expense (Type 2 adjustment) that has arisen but not been recorded during the accounting period. The cash receipt or payment occurs in a future accounting period, after the adjusting entry has been made.

Type 1 Adjustment: Allocating Recorded Costs (Deferred Expenses)

Companies often make expenditures that benefit more than one period. These costs are debited to an asset account. At the end of an accounting period, the amount of the asset that has been used is transferred from the asset account to

■ **FIGURE 3**
Adjustment for Prepaid (Deferred) Expenses

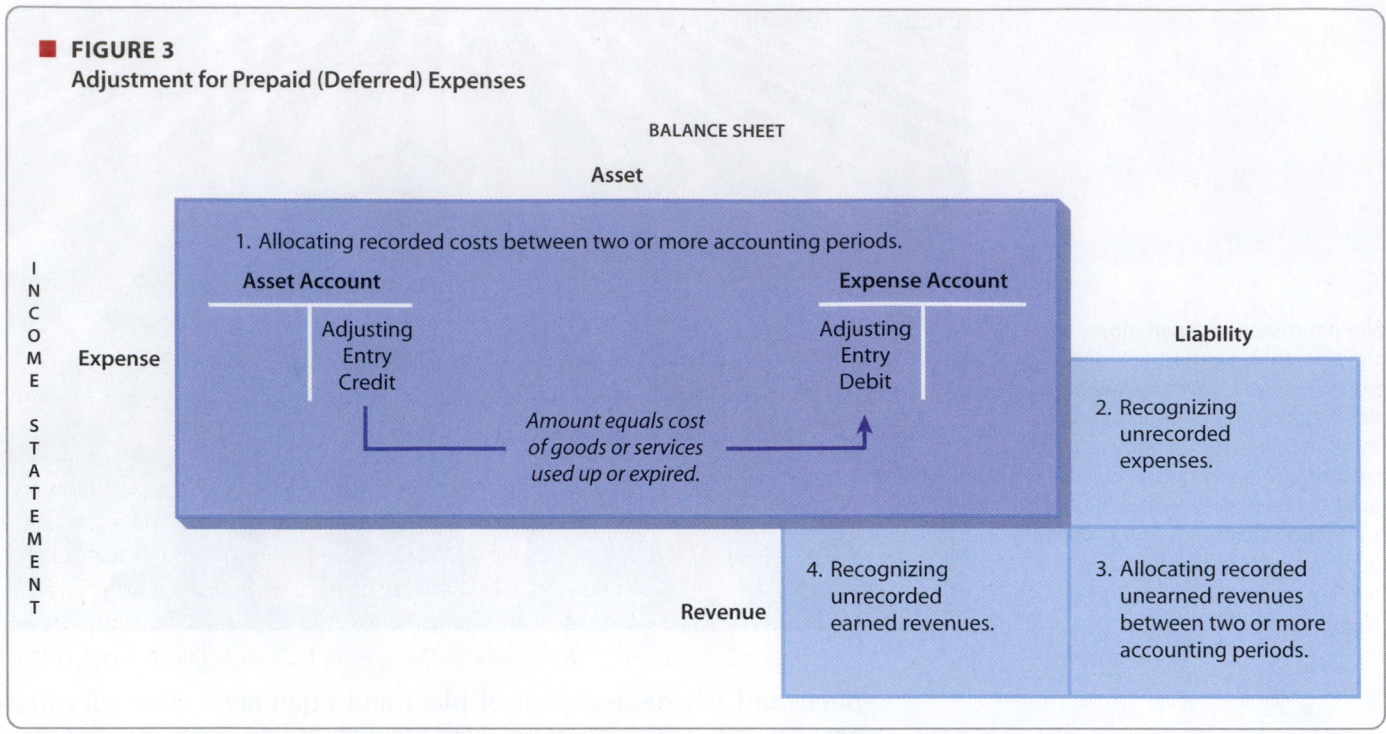

an expense account. Two important adjustments of this type are for prepaid expenses and the depreciation of plant and equipment.

Prepaid Expenses   Companies customarily pay some expenses, including those for rent, supplies, and insurance, in advance. These costs are called **prepaid expenses**. By the end of an accounting period, a portion or all of prepaid services or goods will have been used or have expired. The required adjusting entry reduces the asset and increases the expense, as shown in Figure 3. The amount of the adjustment equals the cost of the goods or services used or expired.

If adjusting entries for prepaid expenses are not made at the end of an accounting period, both the balance sheet and the income statement will present incorrect information. The company's assets will be overstated, and its expenses will be understated. Thus, stockholders' equity on the balance sheet and net income on the income statement will be overstated.

To illustrate this type of adjusting entry and the others discussed below, we refer again to the transactions of Treadle Website Design, Inc.

At the beginning of July, Treadle Website Design paid two months' rent in advance. The advance payment resulted in an asset consisting of the right to occupy the office for two months. As each day in the month passed, part of the asset's cost expired and became an expense. By July 31, one-half of the asset's cost had expired and had to be treated as an expense. The adjustment is as follows:

Adjustment for Prepaid Rent
July 31: Expiration of one month's rent, $1,600

Analysis: Expiration of prepaid rent *decreases* the asset account *Prepaid Rent* with a credit and *increases* the expense account *Rent Expense* with a debit.

> *Study Note*
>
> The expired portion of a prepayment is converted to an expense; the unexpired portion remains an asset.

Application of Double Entry:

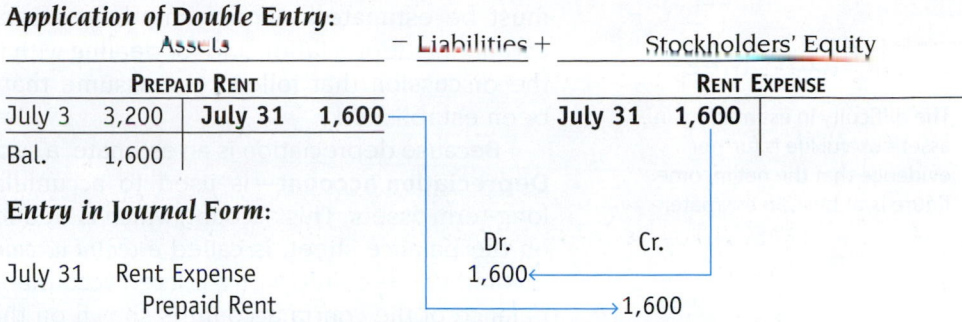

Assets			− Liabilities +	Stockholders' Equity	
PREPAID RENT				**RENT EXPENSE**	
July 3	3,200	July 31 1,600		July 31	1,600
Bal.	1,600				

Entry in Journal Form:

		Dr.	Cr.
July 31	Rent Expense	1,600	
	Prepaid Rent		1,600

Comment: The Prepaid Rent account now has a balance of $1,600, which represents one month's rent that will be expensed during August. The logic in this analysis applies to all prepaid expenses.

Treadle purchased $5,200 of office supplies in early July. A careful inventory of the supplies is made at the end of the month. It records the number and cost of supplies that have not yet been consumed and are thus still assets of the company. Suppose the inventory shows that office supplies costing $3,660 are still on hand. This means that of the $5,200 of supplies originally purchased, $1,540 worth were used (became an expense) in July. The adjustment is as follows:

Adjustment for Supplies
July 31: Consumption of supplies, $1,540

Analysis: Consumption of office supplies *decreases* the asset account *Office Supplies* with a credit and *increases* the expense account *Office Supplies Expense* with a debit.

Application of Double Entry:

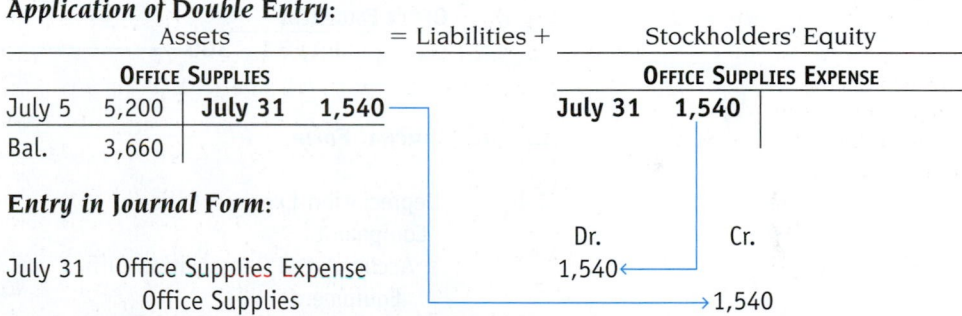

Assets			= Liabilities +	Stockholders' Equity	
OFFICE SUPPLIES				**OFFICE SUPPLIES EXPENSE**	
July 5	5,200	July 31 1,540		July 31	1,540
Bal.	3,660				

Entry in Journal Form:

		Dr.	Cr.
July 31	Office Supplies Expense	1,540	
	Office Supplies		1,540

Comment: The asset account Office Supplies now reflects the correct balance of $3,660 of supplies yet to be consumed. The logic in this example applies to all kinds of supplies.

Depreciation of Plant and Equipment

When a company buys a long-term asset—such as a building, truck, computer, or store fixture—it is, in effect, prepaying for the usefulness of that asset for as long as it benefits the company. Because a long-term asset is a deferral of an expense, the accountant must allocate the cost of the asset over its estimated useful life. The amount allocated to any one accounting period is called **depreciation**, or *depreciation expense*. Depreciation, like other expenses, is incurred during an accounting period to produce revenue.

It is often impossible to tell exactly how long an asset will last or how much of the asset has been used in any one period. For this reason, depreciation

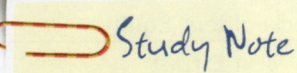

must be estimated. Accountants have developed a number of methods for estimating depreciation and for dealing with the related complex problems. (In the discussion that follows, we assume that the amount of depreciation has been established.)

Because depreciation is an estimate, a separate account—the **Accumulated Depreciation account**—is used to accumulate the depreciation on specific long-term assets. This account, which is deducted from its related asset account on the balance sheet, is called a *contra account*. A **contra account** is a separate account that is paired with a related account—in this case, an asset account. The balance of the contra account is shown on the financial statement as a deduction from its related account. The net amount is called the **carrying value**, or *book value*, of the asset. As the months pass, the amount of the accumulated depreciation grows, and the carrying value shown as an asset declines.

Adjustment for *Plant and Equipment*

July 31: Depreciation of office equipment, $300

Analysis: Depreciation *decreases* the asset account *Office Equipment* by *increasing* the contra account *Accumulated Depreciation–Office Equipment* with a credit and *increasing* the expense account *Depreciation Expense–Office Equipment* with a debit, as shown below.

Application of Double Entry:

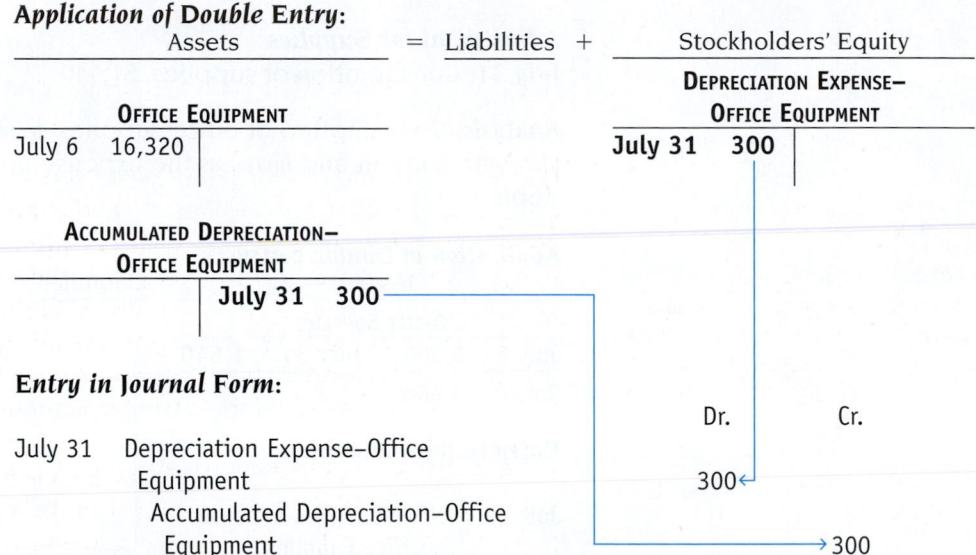

Comment: The carrying value of Office Equipment is $16,020 ($16,320 − $300) and is presented on the balance sheet as follows:

PROPERTY, PLANT, AND EQUIPMENT

Office equipment	$16,320	
Less accumulated depreciation	300	$16,020

Application to Yahoo! Inc.

Yahoo! has prepaid expenses and property and equipment similar to those in the examples we have presented. Among Yahoo!'s prepaid expenses are fixed payments that it makes to other Internet companies in an effort to increase the number of visitors to its site. These fixed payments are debited to prepaid expense when the payments are made and are expensed through adjusting entries "pro-rata over the term the fixed payment covers."[6]

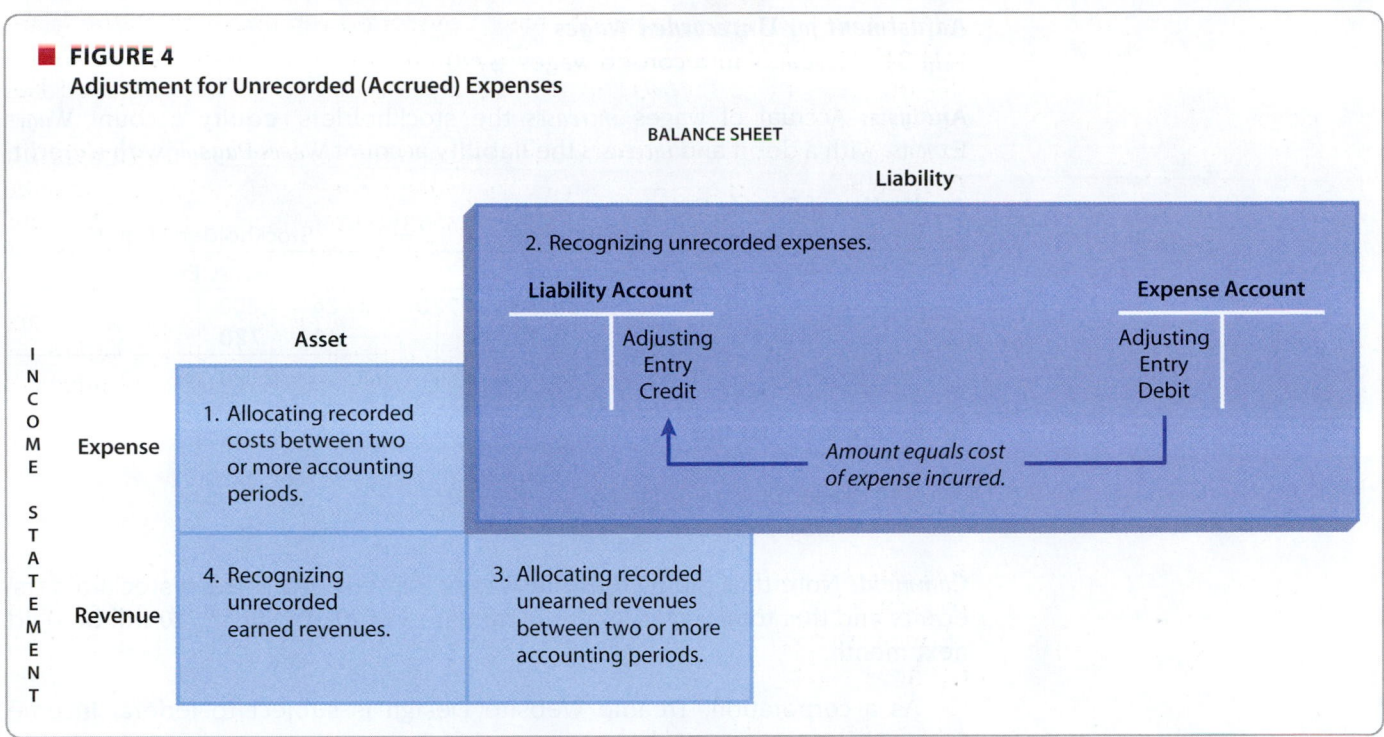

■ **FIGURE 4**
Adjustment for Unrecorded (Accrued) Expenses

Type 2 Adjustment: Recognizing Unrecorded Expenses (Accrued Expenses)

> *Study Note*
>
> Remember that in accrual accounting, an expense must be recorded in the period in which it is incurred, regardless of when payment is made.

Usually, at the end of an accounting period, some expenses incurred during the period have not been recorded in the accounts. These expenses require adjusting entries. One such expense is interest on borrowed money. Each day, interest accumulates on the debt. As shown in Figure 4, at the end of the accounting period, an adjusting entry is made to record the accumulated interest, which is an expense of the period, and the corresponding liability to pay the interest. Other common unrecorded expenses are wages, taxes, and utilities. As the expense and the corresponding liability accumulate, they are said to *accrue*—hence, the term **accrued expenses**.

To illustrate how an adjustment is made for unrecorded wages, suppose Treadle Website Design has two pay periods a month rather than one. In July, its pay periods end on the 12th and the 26th, as indicated in this calendar:

July

Su	M	T	W	Th	F	Sa
	1	2	3	4	5	6
7	8	9	10	11	12	13
14	15	16	17	18	19	20
21	22	23	24	25	26	27
28	29	30	31			

By the end of business on July 31, Treadle's secretary will have worked three days (Monday, Tuesday, and Wednesday) beyond the last pay period. The employee has earned the wages for those days but will not be paid until the first payday in August. The wages for these three days are rightfully an expense for July, and the liabilities should reflect that the company owes the secretary for those days. Because the secretary's wage rate is $2,400 every two weeks, or $240 per day ($2,400 ÷ 10 working days), the expense is $720 ($240 × 3 days).

Adjustment for Unrecorded Wages
July 31: Accrual of unrecorded wages, $720

Analysis: Accrual of wages *increases* the stockholders' equity account *Wages Expense* with a debit and *increases* the liability account *Wages Payable* with a credit.

Application of Double Entry:

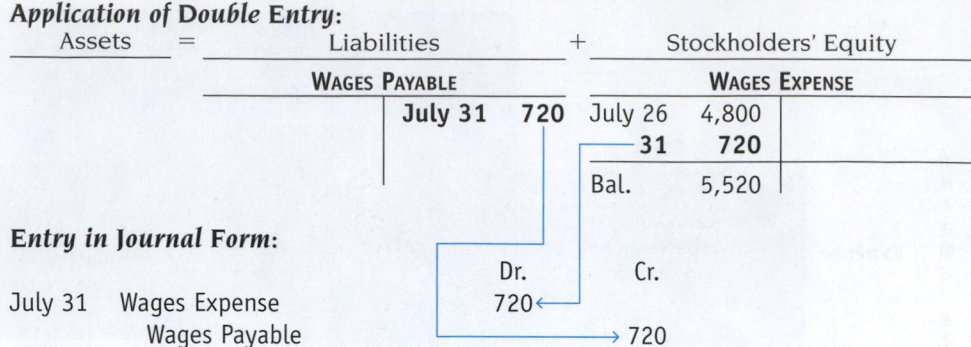

Entry in Journal Form:

		Dr.	Cr.
July 31	Wages Expense	720	
	Wages Payable		720

Comment: Note that the increase in Wages Expense will *decrease* stockholders' equity and that total wages for the month are $5,520, of which $720 will be paid next month.

As a corporation, Treadle Website Design is subject to federal income taxes. Although the actual amount owed for taxes cannot be determined until after net income is computed at the end of the fiscal year, each month should bear its part of the total year's expense, in accordance with the matching rule. Therefore, the amount of income taxes expense for the current month must be estimated. Assume that after analyzing the firm's operations in its first month of business and conferring with her CPA, Priscilla Treadle estimates July's share of income taxes for the year to be $800.

Adjustment for Estimated Income Taxes
July 31: Accrual of estimated income taxes, $800

Analysis: Accrual of income taxes *increases* the stockholders' equity account *Income Taxes Expense* with a debit and *increases* the liability account *Income Taxes Payable* with a credit.

Application of Double Entry:

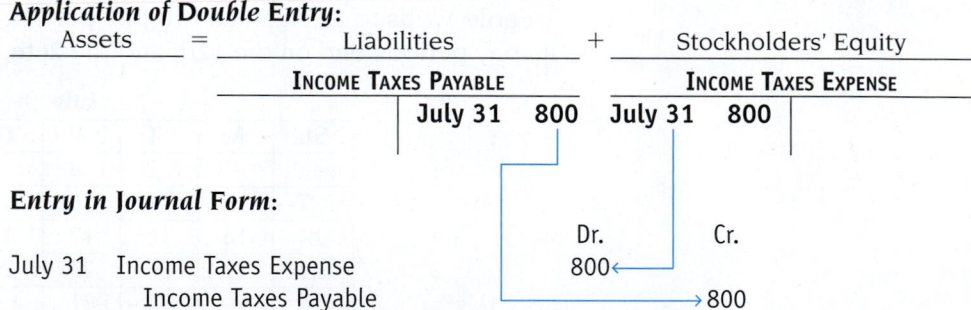

Entry in Journal Form:

		Dr.	Cr.
July 31	Income Taxes Expense	800	
	Income Taxes Payable		800

Comment: Note that the increase in Income Taxes Expense will *decrease* stockholders' equity. There are many types of accrued expenses, and the adjustments made for all of them follow the same procedure as the one used for accrued wages and accrued income taxes.

Application to Yahoo! Inc.
In 2004, **Yahoo!** had accrued expenses and current liabilities of $853,115.[7] If the expenses were not accrued, Yahoo!'s debt

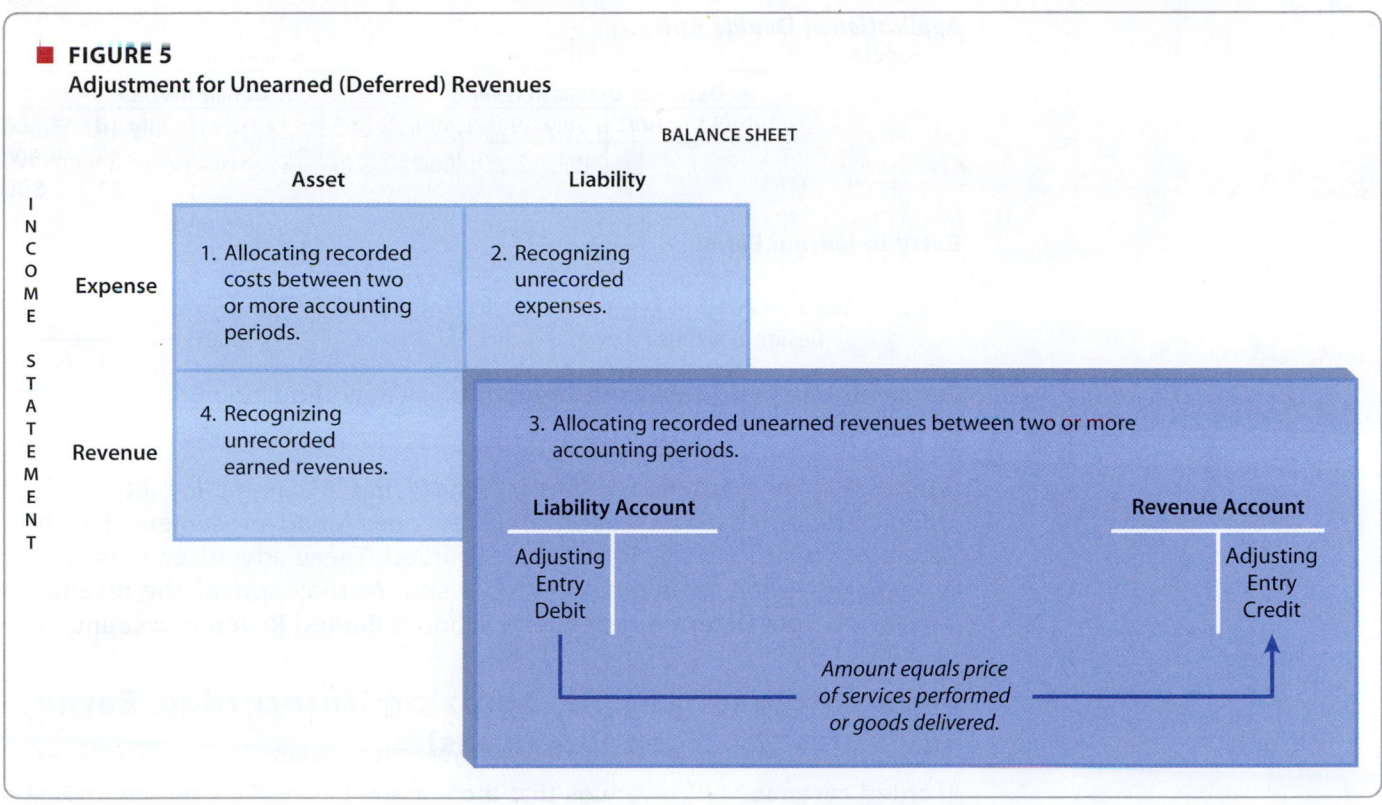

■ **FIGURE 5**
Adjustment for Unearned (Deferred) Revenues

would be significantly understated, as would the corresponding expenses on its income statement. The result would be an overstatement of the company's earnings.

Type 3 Adjustment: Allocating Recorded, Unearned Revenues (Deferred Revenues)

Just as expenses can be paid before they are used, revenues can be received before they are earned. When a company receives revenues in advance, it has an obligation to deliver goods or perform services. **Unearned revenues** are therefore shown in a liability account.

For example, publishing companies usually receive payment in advance for magazine subscriptions. These receipts are recorded in a liability account, Unearned Subscriptions. If the company fails to deliver the magazines, subscribers are entitled to their money back. As the company delivers each issue of the magazine, it earns a part of the advance payments. This earned portion must be transferred from the Unearned Subscriptions account to the Subscription Revenue account, as shown in Figure 5.

During July, Treadle Website Design received $1,400 from another firm as advance payment for a website design. By the end of the month, it had completed $800 of work on the design, and the other firm had accepted the work.

Adjustment for Unearned Revenue
July 31: Performance of services paid for in advance, $800

Analysis: Payment received in advance for services to be performed in the future *increases* the stockholders' equity account *Design Revenue* with a credit and *decreases* the liability account *Unearned Design Revenue* with a debit.

Study Note

Unearned revenue is a liability because there is an obligation to deliver goods or perform a service, or to return the payment. Once the goods have been delivered or the service performed, the liability is converted to revenue.

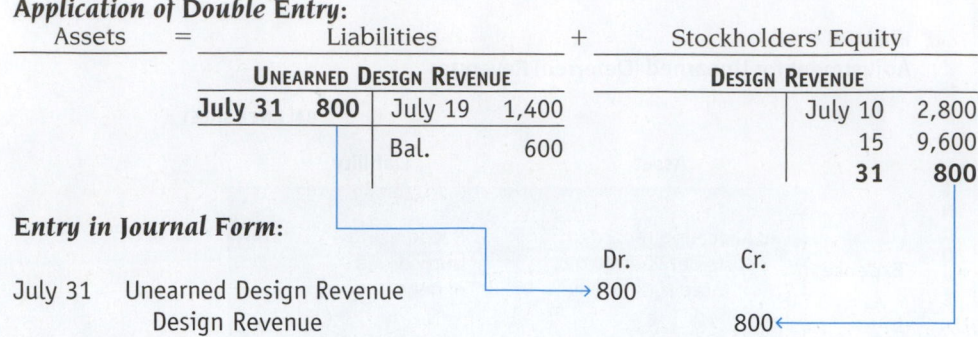

Application of Double Entry:

| Assets | = | Liabilities | + | Stockholders' Equity |

UNEARNED DESIGN REVENUE

| July 31 | 800 | July 19 | 1,400 |
| | | Bal. | 600 |

DESIGN REVENUE

July 10	2,800
15	9,600
31	800

Entry in Journal Form:

		Dr.	Cr.
July 31	Unearned Design Revenue	800	
	Design Revenue		800

Comment: Unearned Design Revenue now reflects the amount of work still to be performed, $600.

Application to Yahoo! Inc.   **Yahoo!** has a current liability account called Deferred Revenue. It represents revenues for advertisements for which Yahoo! has billed but that it has not yet earned. These advertisements appear as "banners" when users access Yahoo!'s site. As they appear, the revenue is transferred from Deferred Revenue to Yahoo!'s Earned Revenue account.

Type 4 Adjustment: Recognizing Unrecorded, Earned Revenues (Accrued Revenues)

Accrued revenues are revenues that a company has earned by performing a service or delivering goods but for which no entry has been made in the accounting records. Any revenues earned but not recorded during an accounting period require an adjusting entry that debits an asset account and credits a revenue account, as shown in Figure 6. For example, the interest on a note

■ **FIGURE 6**
Adjustment for Unrecorded (Accrued) Revenues

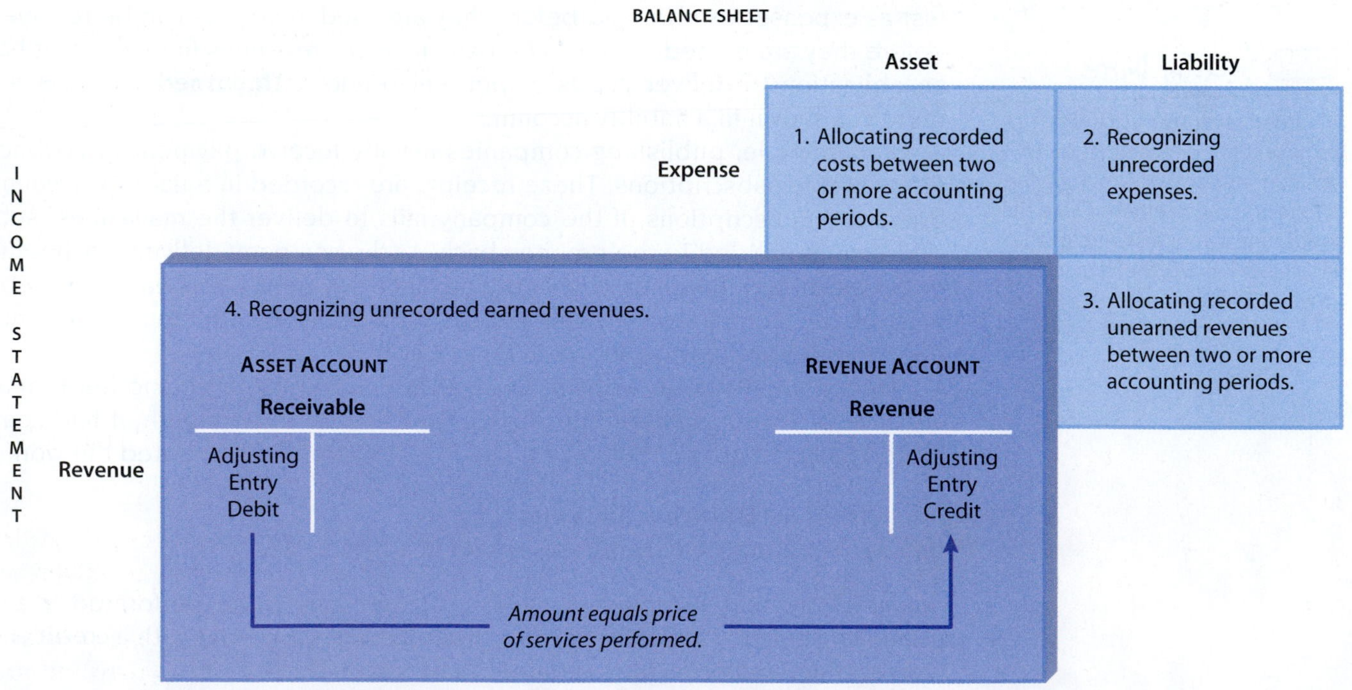

BALANCE SHEET

| | | Asset | Liability |
| **Expense** | | 1. Allocating recorded costs between two or more accounting periods. | 2. Recognizing unrecorded expenses. |

4. Recognizing unrecorded earned revenues.

ASSET ACCOUNT		**REVENUE ACCOUNT**
Receivable		Revenue
Adjusting Entry Debit		Adjusting Entry Credit

Revenue

3. Allocating recorded unearned revenues between two or more accounting periods.

Amount equals price of services performed.

INCOME STATEMENT

When a company earns revenue by performing a service—such as designing a website or developing marketing plans—but will not receive the revenue for the service until a future accounting period, it must make an adjusting entry. This type of adjusting entry involves an asset account and a revenue account.

receivable is earned day by day but may not be received until another accounting period. Interest Receivable should be debited and Interest Income should be credited for the interest accrued at the end of the current period.

During July, Treadle Website Design agreed to design a website for Marsh Tire Company. It also agreed to have the first section of the site operational by July 31. By the end of the month, Treadle had earned $400 for completing the first section but had not billed Marsh Tire Company or recorded the fee.

Adjustment for Design Revenue

July 31: Accrual of unrecorded revenue, $400

Analysis: Accrual of unrecorded revenue *increases* the stockholders' equity account *Design Revenue* with a credit and *increases* the asset account *Accounts Receivable* with a debit.

Application of Double Entry:

Assets		= Liabilities +	Stockholders' Equity

ACCOUNTS RECEIVABLE

July 15	9,600	July 22	5,000
31	**400**		
Bal.	5,000		

DESIGN REVENUE

		July 10	2,800
		15	9,600
		31	800
		31	**400**
		Bal.	13,600

Entry in Journal Form:

		Dr.	Cr.
July 31	Accounts Receivable	400	
	Design Revenue		400

Comment: Design Revenue now reflects the total revenue earned during July, $13,600.

Application to Yahoo! Inc.

Yahoo! recognizes revenue from text-link and hypertext link advertisements, including pay-for-performance advertisements of search results, in the period in which "click-throughs" occur. "Click-throughs" are the number of times users click on an advertisement or search result. They are the performance measure that enables Yahoo! to accrue revenue and establish a receivable.

A Note About Journal Entries

Thus far, we have presented a full analysis of each journal entry. The analyses showed you the thought process behind each entry. By now, you should be fully aware of the effects of transactions on the accounting equation and the rules of debit and credit. For this reason, in the rest of the book, we present journal entries without full analysis.

STOP • REVIEW • APPLY

3-1. What are the four situations that require adjusting entries? Give an example of each.

3-2. "Some assets are expenses that have not expired." Explain this statement.

3-3. What do plant and equipment, office supplies, and prepaid insurance have in common?

3-4. How do accumulated depreciation and depreciation expense differ?

3-5. What is a contra account? Give an example.

3-6. Why are contra accounts used to record depreciation?

3-7. How does unearned revenue arise? Give an example.

3-8. Where does unearned revenue appear in the financial statements?

3-9. Under what circumstances does a company have accrued revenues? Give an example. What asset arises when an adjustment for accrued revenues is made?

3-10. What is an accrued expense? Give two examples.

Identification of Adjusting Entries

The four types of adjusting entries are as follows:

Type 1. Allocating recorded costs between two or more accounting periods

Type 2. Recognizing unrecorded expenses

Type 3. Allocating recorded, unearned revenue between two or more accounting periods

Type 4. Recognizing revenues earned but not yet recorded

For each of the following items, identify the type of adjusting entry required:

___ a. Revenues earned but not yet collected or billed to customers

___ b. Interest incurred but not yet recorded

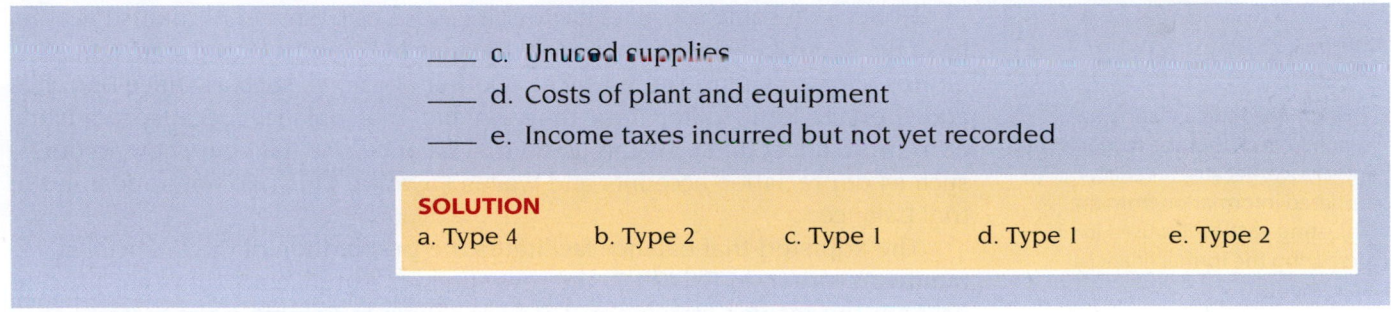

c. Unused supplies

_____ d. Costs of plant and equipment

_____ e. Income taxes incurred but not yet recorded

SOLUTION

a. Type 4   b. Type 2   c. Type 1   d. Type 1   e. Type 2

Using the Adjusted Trial Balance to Prepare Financial Statements

LO4 Prepare financial statements from an adjusted trial balance.

After adjusting entries have been recorded and posted, an **adjusted trial balance** is prepared by listing all accounts and their balances. If the adjusting entries have been posted to the accounts correctly, the adjusted trial balance will have equal debit and credit totals. The adjusted trial balance for Treadle Website Design is shown in Exhibit 2.

▼ EXHIBIT 2

Relationship of the Adjusted Trial Balance to the Income Statement

Treadle Website Design, Inc.
Adjusted Trial Balance
July 31, 20xx

Cash	$22,480	
Accounts Receivable	5,000	
Office Supplies	3,660	
Prepaid Rent	1,600	
Office Equipment	16,320	
Accumulated Depreciation–		
Office Equipment		$ 300
Accounts Payable		6,280
Unearned Design Revenue		600
Wages Payable		720
Income Taxes Payable		800
Common Stock		40,000
Dividends	2,800	
Design Revenue		13,600
Wages Expense	5,520	
Utilities Expense	680	
Rent Expense	1,600	
Office Supplies Expense	1,540	
Depreciation Expense–Office		
Equipment	300	
Income Taxes Expense	800	
	$62,300	$62,300

Treadle Website Design, Inc.
Income Statement
For the Month Ended July 31, 20xx

Revenues		
Design revenue		$13,600
Expenses		
Wages expense	$5,520	
Utilities expense	680	
Rent expense	1,600	
Office supplies expense	1,540	
Depreciation expense–office		
equipment	300	
Income taxes expense	800	
Total expenses		10,440
Net income		$ 3,160

> **Study Note**
>
> The net income figure from the income statement is needed to prepare the statement of retained earnings, and the bottom-line figure of that statement is needed to prepare the balance sheet. This dictates the order in which the statements are prepared.

Notice that some accounts in Exhibit 2, such as Cash and Accounts Payable, have the same balances as in the trial balance in Exhibit 1 because no adjusting entries affected them. The balances of other accounts, such as Office Supplies and Prepaid Rent, differ from those in the trial balance because adjusting entries did affect them. The adjusted trial balance also has some new accounts, such as depreciation accounts and Wages Payable, which do not appear in the trial balance.

The adjusted trial balance facilitates the preparation of the financial statements. As shown in Exhibit 2, the revenue and expense accounts are used to prepare the income statement. Then, as shown in Exhibit 3, the statement of retained earnings and the balance sheet are prepared. Notice that the net

▼ EXHIBIT 3

Relationship of the Adjusted Trial Balance to the Balance Sheet and Statement of Retained Earnings

Treadle Website Design, Inc.
Adjusted Trial Balance
July 31, 20xx

Cash	$22,480	
Accounts Receivable	5,000	
Office Supplies	3,660	
Prepaid Rent	1,600	
Office Equipment	16,320	
Accumulated Depreciation–		
Office Equipment		$ 300
Accounts Payable		6,280
Unearned Design Revenue		600
Wages Payable		720
Income Taxes Payable		800
Common Stock		40,000
Dividends	2,800	
Design Revenue		13,600
Wages Expense	5,520	
Utilities Expense	680	
Rent Expense	1,600	
Office Supplies Expense	1,540	
Depreciation Expense–Office		
Equipment	300	
Income Taxes Expense	800	
	$62,300	$62,300

Treadle Website Design, Inc.
Balance Sheet
July 31, 20xx

Assets

Cash		$ 22,480
Accounts receivable		5,000
Office supplies		3,660
Prepaid rent		1,600
Office equipment	$16,320	
Less accumulated depreciation	300	16,020
Total assets		$48,760

Liabilities

Accounts payable	$ 6,280
Unearned design revenue	600
Wages payable	720
Income taxes payable	800
Total liabilities	$ 8,400

Stockholders' Equity

Common stock	$40,000	
Retained earnings	360	
Total stockholders' equity		40,360
Total liabilities and stockholders' equity		$48,760

Treadle Website Design, Inc.
Statement of Retained Earnings
For the Month Ended July 31, 20xx

Retained earnings, July 1, 20xx	—
Net income	$3,160
Subtotal	$3,160
Less dividends	2,800
Retained earnings, July 31, 20xx	$ 360

income from the income statement is combined with dividends on the statement of retained earnings to give the net change in Treadle Website Design's Retained Earnings account. The resulting balance of Retained Earnings at July 31 is used in preparing the balance sheet, as are the asset and liability account balances in the adjusted trial balance.

S T O P • R E V I E W • A P P L Y

4-1. Why is the income statement usually the first statement prepared from the adjusted trial balance?

4-2. Why does the ending balance for Retained Earnings not appear on the adjusted trial balance?

The Accounting Cycle

LO5 Describe the accounting cycle, and explain the purposes of closing entries.

As Figure 7 shows, the **accounting cycle** is a series of steps whose ultimate purpose is to provide useful information to decision makers. These steps are as follows:

1. *Analyze* business transactions from source documents.

2. *Record* the transactions by entering them in the general journal.

3. *Post* the journal entries to the ledger, and prepare a trial balance.

4. *Adjust* the accounts, and prepare an adjusted trial balance.

5. *Prepare* financial statements.

6. *Close* the accounts, and prepare a post-closing trial balance.

Note that steps 3, 4, and 6 entail the preparation of trial balances to ensure that the accounts are in balance.

You are already familiar with steps 1 through 5. In this section, we describe step 6, which may be performed before or after step 5.

Closing Entries

Balance sheet accounts, such as Cash and Accounts Payable, are considered **permanent accounts**, or *real accounts*, because they carry their end-of-period balances into the next accounting period. In contrast, revenue and expense accounts, such as Revenues Earned and Wages Expense, are considered **temporary accounts**, or *nominal accounts*, because they begin each accounting period with a zero balance, accumulate a balance during the period, and are then cleared by means of closing entries.

Closing entries are journal entries made at the end of an accounting period. They have two purposes:

1. Closing entries set the stage for the next accounting period by clearing revenue and expense accounts and the Dividends account of their balances. Recall that the income statement reports net income (or loss) for a single accounting period and shows revenues and expenses for that period only.

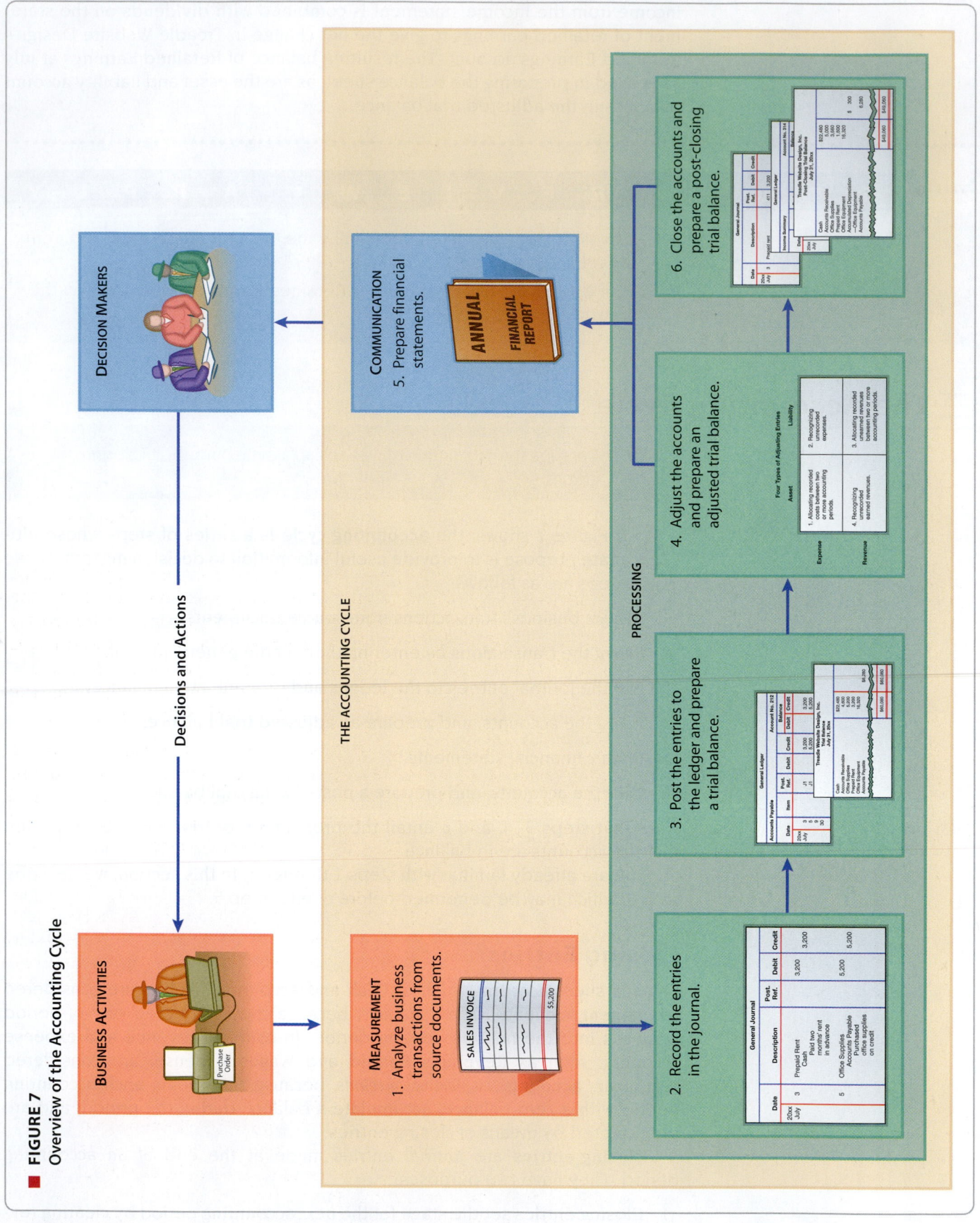

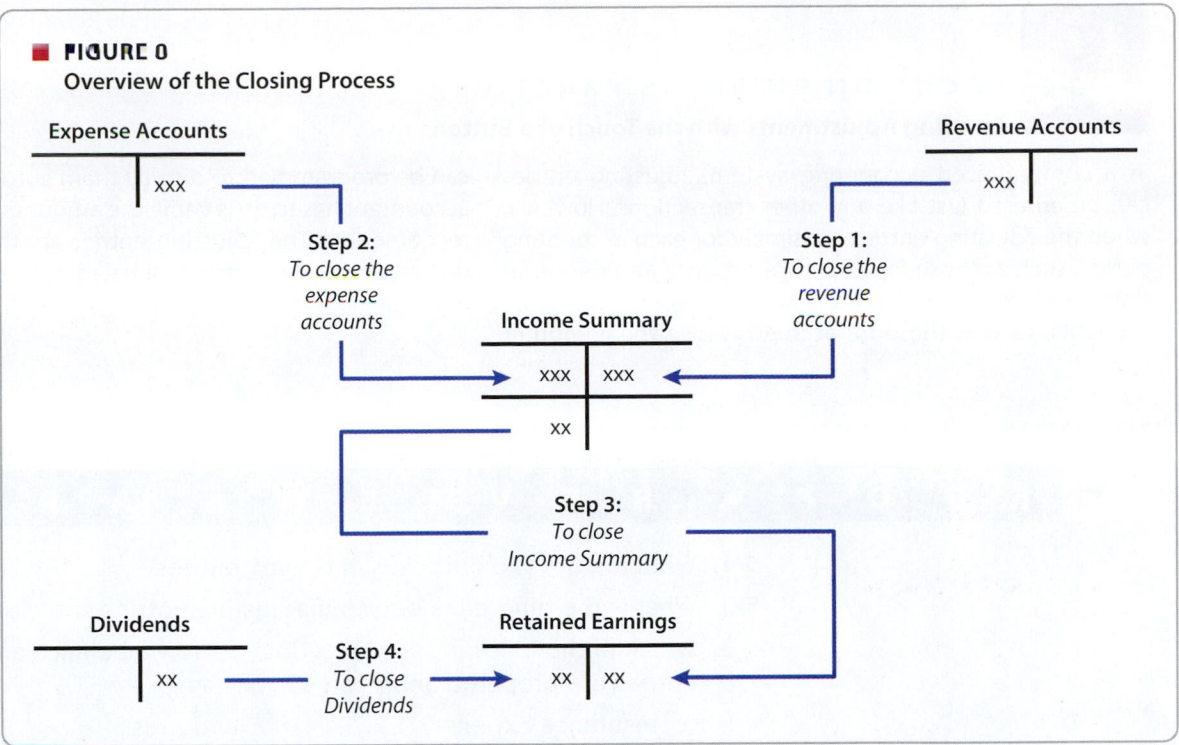

FIGURE 8
Overview of the Closing Process

2. Closing entries summarize a period's revenues and expenses. This is done by transferring the balances of revenue and expense accounts to the Income Summary account. The **Income Summary account** is a temporary account that summarizes all revenues and expenses for the period. It is used only in the closing process—never in the financial statements. Its balance equals the net income or loss reported on the income statement. The net income or loss is then transferred to the Retained Earnings account.

The net income or loss is transferred from the Income Summary account to Retained Earnings because even though revenues and expenses are recorded in revenue and expense accounts, they actually represent increases and decreases in stockholders' equity. Closing entries transfer the net effect of increases (revenues) and decreases (expenses) to stockholders' equity. Figure 8 shows an overview of the closing process.

Closing entries are required at the end of any period for which financial statements are prepared. **Yahoo!** prepares financial statements each quarter, and when it does, it must close its books. Such interim information is helpful to investors and creditors in assessing a company's ongoing financial performance. Many companies close their books monthly to give management a more timely view of ongoing operations.

The Post-Closing Trial Balance

Because errors can be made in posting closing entries to the ledger accounts, it is necessary to prepare a **post-closing trial balance** to determine that all temporary accounts have zero balances and to double-check that total debits equal total credits. This final trial balance contains only balance sheet accounts because the income statement accounts and the Dividends account have all been closed and now have zero balances. We discuss closing entries and the post-closing trial balance further in the Supplement to Chapter 3.

FOCUS ON BUSINESS PRACTICE

Entering Adjustments with the Touch of a Button

In a computerized accounting system, adjusting entries can be entered just like any other transactions. However, when the adjusting entries are similar for each accounting period, such as those for insurance expense and depreciation expense, or when they always involve the same accounts, such as those for accrued wages, the computer can be programmed to display them automatically. All the accountant has to do is verify the amounts or enter the correct amounts. The adjusting entries are then entered and posted, and the adjusted trial balance is prepared with the touch of a button.

STOP • REVIEW • APPLY

5-1. What are the two purposes of closing entries?

5-2. What is the difference between adjusting entries and closing entries?

5-3. Which of the following accounts do not show a balance after the closing entries are prepared and posted?

a. Insurance Expense   e. Dividends

b. Accounts Receivable   f. Supplies

c. Commission Revenue   g. Supplies Expense

d. Prepaid Insurance   h. Retained Earnings

5-4. What is the significance of the post-closing trial balance?

Preparation of Closing Entries   Prepare the necessary closing entries from the following partial adjusted trial balance for Westwood Movers, Inc. (except for Retained Earnings, balance sheet accounts have been omitted), and compute the ending balance of retained earnings.

Westwood Movers, Inc. Partial Adjusted Trial Balance June 30, 20xx		
Retained Earnings		24,740
Dividends	18,000	
Moving Services Revenue		185,400
Driver Wages Expense	88,900	
Fuel Expense	19,000	
Wages Expense	14,400	
Packing Supplies Expense	6,200	
Office Equipment Rental Expense	3,000	
Utilities Expense	4,450	
Insurance Expense	4,200	
Interest Expense	5,100	
Depreciation Expense	10,040	
Income Taxes Expense	9,000	
	$417,190	$417,190

SOLUTION

Closing entries prepared:

June 30	Moving Services Revenue		185,400	
	Income Summary			185,400
	To close the revenue account			
30	Income Summary		164,290	
	Driver Wages Expense			88,900
	Fuel Expense			19,000
	Wages Expense			14,400
	Packing Supplies Expense			6,200
	Office Equipment Rental Expense			3,000
	Utilities Expense			4,450
	Insurance Expense			4,200
	Interest Expense			5,100
	Depreciation Expense			10,040
	Income Taxes Expense			9,000
	To close the expense accounts			
30	Income Summary		21,110	
	Retained Earnings			21,110
	To close the Income Summary account $185,400 − $164,290 = $21,110			
30	Retained Earnings		18,000	
	Dividends			18,000
	To close the Dividends account			

Ending balance of retained earnings computed:

RETAINED EARNINGS

June 30	18,000	Beg. Bal.	24,740
		June 30	21,110
		End. Bal.	27,850

Cash Flows from Accrual-Based Information

LO6 Use accrual-based information to analyze cash flows.

Management has the short-range goal of ensuring that its company has sufficient cash to pay ongoing obligations—in other words, management must ensure the company's liquidity. To plan payments to creditors and assess the need for short-term borrowing, managers must know how to use accrual-based information to analyze cash flows.

Almost every revenue or expense account on the income statement has one or more related accounts on the balance sheet. For instance, Supplies Expense is related to Supplies, Wages Expense is related to Wages Payable, and Design Revenue is related to Unearned Design Revenue. As we have shown, these accounts are related by making adjusting entries, the purpose of which is to apply the matching rule to the measurement of net income.

The cash inflows that a company's operations generate and the cash outflows that they require can also be determined by analyzing these relationships. For example, suppose that after receiving the financial statements in Exhibits 2 and 3, management wants to know how much cash was expended for office supplies. On the income statement, Office Supplies Expense is $1,540, and on the balance sheet, Office Supplies is $3,660. Because July was the company's first month of operation, there was no prior balance of office supplies, so the amount of cash expended for office supplies during the month was $5,200 ($1,540 + $3,660 = $5,200).

Thus, the cash flow used in purchasing office supplies—$5,200—was much greater than the amount expensed in determining income—$1,540. In planning for August, management can anticipate that the cash needed may be less than the amount expensed because, given the large inventory of office supplies, the company will probably not have to buy office supplies in the coming month. Understanding these cash flow effects enables management to better predict the business's need for cash in August.

The general rule for determining the cash flow received from any revenue or paid for any expense (except depreciation, which is a special case not covered here) is to determine the potential cash payments or cash receipts and deduct the amount not paid or received. As shown below, the application of the general rule varies with the type of asset or liability account:

Type of Account	Potential Payment or Receipt Not Paid or Received	Result
Prepaid Expense	Ending Balance + Expense for the Period − Beginning Balance =	Cash Payments for Expenses
Unearned Revenue	Ending Balance + Revenue for the Period − Beginning Balance =	Cash Receipts from Revenues
Accrued Payable	Beginning Balance + Expense for the Period − Ending Balance	= Cash Payments for Expenses
Accrued Receivable	Beginning Balance + Revenue for the Period − Ending Balance	= Cash Receipts from Revenues

For instance, suppose that on May 31, a company had a balance of $480 in Prepaid Insurance and that on June 30, the balance was $670. If the insurance expense during June was $120, the amount of cash expended on insurance during June can be computed as follows:

Prepaid Insurance at June 30	$670
Insurance Expense during June	120
Potential cash payments for insurance	$790
Less Prepaid Insurance at May 31	480
Cash payments for insurance during June	$310

The beginning balance is deducted because it was paid in a prior accounting period. Note that the cash payments equal the expense plus the increase in the balance of the Prepaid Insurance account [$120 + ($670 − $480) = $310]. In this case, the cash paid was almost three times the amount of insurance expense. In future months, cash payments are likely to be less than the expense.

STOP • REVIEW • APPLY

6-1. Explain the effect that adjusting entries have on a company's cash flows.

6-2. Why does the cash paid for expenses in an accounting period often differ from the amount of expenses on the income statement?

6-3. Why does the cash received for services in an accounting period often differ from the amount of revenue on the income statement?

A LOOK BACK AT

YAHOO! INC.

In the Decision Point at the beginning of the chapter, we noted that **Yahoo!** has many transactions that span accounting periods. We asked these questions:

- **What assumptions must Yahoo! make to account for transactions that span accounting periods?**
- **How does Yahoo! assign its revenues and expenses to the proper accounting period so that net income is properly measured?**
- **Why are the adjustments that these transactions require important to Yahoo!'s financial performance?**

Two of the assumptions Yahoo! must make are that it will continue as a going concern for an indefinite time (the continuity assumption) and that it can make useful estimates of its income in terms of accounting periods (the periodicity assumption). These assumptions enable the company to apply the matching rule—that is, revenues are assigned to the accounting period in which goods are sold or services are performed, and expenses are assigned to the accounting period in which they are used to produce revenue.

As you have learned in this chapter, adjusting entries for deferred and accrued expenses and for deferred and accrued revenues have an impact on a company's earnings. By paying close attention to the profit margin ratio, one can assess how well a company is controlling its expenses in relation to its revenues. The **profit margin** shows the percentage of each revenue, or sales dollar, that results in net income. Using data from Yahoo!'s annual report, we can calculate Yahoo!'s profit margin for two successive years as follows (dollars are in thousands):

	2004	2003
Net Income	$839,553	$237,879
Revenues*	$3,574,517	$1,625,097
Profit Margin:	23.5%	14.6%

*Also called *net sales*.

These results show that Yahoo!'s revenues and earnings are increasing very rapidly and that its profitability is improving dramatically. Because net income equals revenues minus expenses and adjusting entries affect both revenues and expenses, you can see that without adjusting entries, it would be impossible to make a fair assessment of Yahoo!'s financial performance.

CHAPTER REVIEW

REVIEW of Learning Objectives

LO1 Define *net income,* and explain the assumptions underlying income measurement and their ethical application.

Net income is the net increase in stockholders' equity that results from a company's operations. Net income equals revenues minus expenses; when expenses exceed revenues, a net loss results. Revenues equal the price of goods sold or services rendered during a specific period. Expenses are the costs of goods and services used in the process of producing revenues.

The continuity assumption recognizes that even though businesses face an uncertain future, without evidence to the contrary, accountants must assume that a business will continue to operate indefinitely. The periodicity assumption recognizes that although the lifetime of a business is uncertain, it is nonetheless useful to estimate the business's net income in terms of accounting periods. The matching rule holds that revenues must be assigned to the accounting period in which the goods are sold or the services performed, and expenses must be assigned to the accounting period in which they are used to produce revenue.

Because applying the matching rule involves making assumptions and exercising judgment, it can lead to earnings management, which is the manipulation of revenues and expenses to achieve a specific outcome. When the estimates involved in earnings management move outside a reasonable range, financial statements become misleading. Financial statements that are intentionally misleading constitute fraudulent financial reporting.

LO2 Define *accrual accounting,* and explain how it is accomplished.

Accrual accounting consists of all the techniques accountants use to apply the matching rule. It is accomplished by recognizing revenues when they are earned, by recognizing expenses when they are incurred, and by adjusting the accounts.

LO3 Identify four situations that require adjusting entries, and illustrate typical adjusting entries.

Adjusting entries are required when (1) recorded costs must be allocated between two or more accounting periods, (2) unrecorded expenses exist, (3) recorded, unearned revenues must be allocated between two or more accounting periods, and (4) unrecorded, earned revenues exist. The preparation of adjusting entries is summarized as follows:

Type of Adjusting Entry	Type of Account		Examples of Balance Sheet Accounts
	Debited	Credited	
1. Allocating recorded costs (previously paid, expired)	Expense	Asset (or contra-asset)	Prepaid rent Prepaid insurance Office supplies Accumulated depreciation–office equipment
2. Accrued expenses (incurred, not paid)	Expense	Liability	Wages payable Income taxes payable
3. Allocating recorded, unearned revenues (previously received, earned)	Liability	Revenue	Unearned design revenue
4. Accrued revenues (earned, not received)	Asset	Revenue	Accounts receivable Interest receivable

LO4 Prepare financial statements from an adjusted trial balance.

An adjusted trial balance is prepared after adjusting entries have been posted to the accounts. Its purpose is to test whether the adjusting entries have been posted correctly before the financial statements are prepared. The balances in the revenue and expense accounts in the adjusted trial balance are used to prepare the income statement. The balances in the asset and liability accounts in the adjusted trial balance and in the statement of retained earnings are used to prepare the balance sheet.

LO5 Describe the accounting cycle, and explain the purposes of closing entries.

The accounting cycle has six steps: (1) analyzing business transactions from source documents; (2) recording the transactions by entering them in the journal; (3) posting the entries to the ledger, and preparing a trial balance; (4) adjusting the accounts, and preparing an adjusted trial balance; (5) preparing the financial statements; and (6) closing the accounts, and preparing a post-closing trial balance.

Closing entries have two purposes: (1) they clear the balances of all temporary accounts (revenue, expense, and Dividends accounts) so that they have zero balances at the beginning of the next accounting period, and (2) they summarize a period's revenues and expenses in the Income Summary account so that the net income or loss for the period can be transferred as a total to Retained Earnings. As a final check on the balance of the ledger and to ensure that all temporary accounts have been closed, a post-closing trial balance is prepared after the closing entries have been posted to the ledger accounts.

LO6 Use accrual-based information to analyze cash flows.

To ensure a company's liquidity, managers must know how to use accrual-based information to analyze cash flows. The general rule for determining the cash flow received from any revenue or paid for any expense (except depreciation) is to determine the potential cash payments or cash receipts and deduct the amount not paid or received.

≡ REVIEW of Concepts and Terminology

The following concepts and terms were introduced in this chapter:

Accounting cycle: A series of six steps whose ultimate purpose is to provide useful information to decision makers. **(LO5)**

Accrual: The recognition of an expense or revenue that has arisen but has not yet been recorded. **(LO3)**

Accrual accounting: Recording transactions in the periods in which they occur, rather than in the periods in which cash is received or paid; all the techniques that accountants use to apply the matching rule. **(LO2)**

Accrued expenses: Expenses incurred but not recognized in the accounts; unrecorded expenses. **(LO3)**

Accrued revenues: Revenues for which a service has been performed or goods delivered but for which no entry has been made; unrecorded revenues. **(LO3)**

Accumulated Depreciation account: A contra-asset account used to accumulate depreciation on specific long-term assets. **(LO3)**

Adjusted trial balance: A trial balance prepared after all adjusting entries have been recorded and posted to the accounts. **(LO4)**

Adjusting entries: Entries made to apply accrual accounting to transactions that span accounting periods. **(LO3)**

Carrying value: The unexpired portion of the cost of an asset. Also called *book value*. **(LO3)**

Cash basis of accounting: Accounting for revenues and expenses on a cash-received and cash-paid basis. **(LO1)**

Closing entries: Journal entries made at the end of a period that set the stage for the next period by clearing the temporary accounts of their balances and transferring them to Retained Earnings; they summarize a period's revenues and expenses. **(LO5)**

Continuity: The difficulty associated with not knowing how long a business will survive. **(LO1)**

Contra account: An account whose balance is subtracted from an associated account in the financial statements. **(LO3)**

Deferral: The postponement of the recognition of an expense already paid or of a revenue received in advance. **(LO3)**

Depreciation: The portion of the cost of a long-term asset allocated to any one accounting period. Also called *depreciation expense*. **(LO3)**

Earnings management: The manipulation of revenues and expenses to achieve a specific outcome. **(LO1)**

Expenses: Decreases in stockholders' equity resulting from the costs of goods and services used in the course of earning revenues. Also called *cost of doing business* or *expired costs*. **(LO1)**

Fiscal year: Any 12-month accounting period. **(LO1)**

Going concern: The assumption that unless there is evidence to the contrary, a business will continue to operate indefinitely. **(LO1)**

Income Summary account: A temporary account used during the closing process that holds a summary of all revenues and expenses before the net income or loss is transferred to the Retained Earnings account. **(LO5)**

Interim periods: Accounting periods of less than one year. **(LO1)**

Matching rule: The principle that revenues must be assigned to the accounting period in which the goods are sold or the services performed, and expenses must be assigned to the accounting period in which they are used to produce revenue. **(LO1)**

Net income: The net increase in stockholders' equity that results from business operations and is accumulated in the Retained Earnings account; revenues less expenses when revenues exceed expenses. **(LO1)**

Net loss: The net decrease in stockholders' equity when expenses exceed revenues. **(LO1)**

Periodicity: The assumption that although the lifetime of a business is uncertain, it is still useful to estimate its net income in terms of accounting periods. **(LO1)**

Permanent accounts: Balance sheet accounts whose balances extend into the next accounting period. Also called *real accounts*. **(LO5)**

Post-closing trial balance: A trial balance prepared at the end of an accounting period after all adjusting and closing entries have been posted; a final check on the balance of the ledger to ensure that all temporary accounts have zero balances and that total debits equal total credits. **(LO5)**

Prepaid expenses: Expenses paid in advance that have not yet expired; an asset account. **(LO3)**

Profit: The increase in stockholders' equity that results from business operations. **(LO1)**

Revenue recognition: The process of determining when revenue is earned. **(LO2)**

Revenues: Increases in stockholders' equity resulting from selling goods, rendering services, or performing other business activities. **(LO1)**

Temporary accounts: Accounts that show the accumulation of revenues and expenses over an accounting period and that at the end of the period are transferred to stockholders' equity. Also called *nominal accounts*. **(LO5)**

Unearned revenues: Revenues received in advance for which the goods have not yet been delivered or the services performed; a liability account. **(LO3)**

Key Ratio

Profit margin: A ratio that shows the percentage of each sales dollar that results in net income; Net Income ÷ Net Revenues.

≡ REVIEW Problem

LO3, LO4 **Posting to T Accounts, Determining Adjusting Entries, and Using an Adjusted Trial Balance to Prepare Financial Statements**

The following is the unadjusted trial balance for Certified Answering Service, Inc., on December 31, 20x7:

	A	B	C
1	**Certified Answering Service, Inc.**		
2	**Trial Balance**		
3	**December 31, 20x7**		
4			
5	Cash	$2,160	
6	Accounts Receivable	1,250	
7	Office Supplies	180	
8	Prepaid Insurance	240	
9	Office Equipment	3,400	
10	Accumulated Depreciation–Office Equipment		$ 600
11	Accounts Payable		700
12	Unearned Revenue		460
13	Common Stock		2,000
14	Retained Earnings		2,870
15	Dividends	400	
16	Answering Service Revenue		2,900
17	Wages Expense	1,500	
18	Rent Expense	400	
19		$9,530	$9,530

The following information is also available:

a. Insurance that expired during December amounted to $40.
b. Office supplies on hand on December 31 totaled $75.
c. Depreciation for December totaled $100.
d. Accrued wages on December 31 totaled $120.
e. Revenues earned for services performed in December but not billed by the end of the month totaled $300.
f. Revenues received in December in advance of services yet to be performed totaled $160.
g. Income taxes for December are estimated to be $250.

Required

1. Prepare T accounts for the accounts in the trial balance, and enter the balances.
2. Determine the required adjusting entries, and record them directly in the T accounts. Open new T accounts as needed.
3. Prepare an adjusted trial balance.
4. Prepare an income statement and a statement of retained earnings for the month ended December 31, 20x7, as well as a balance sheet at December 31, 20x7.

Answer to Review Problem

1. T accounts set up and amounts from trial balance entered
2. Adjusting entries recorded

	A	B	C	D	E	F	G	H	I	J	K	L	M	N
1		Cash					Accounts Receivable							
2	Bal.	2,160				Bal.	1,250							
3						(e)	300							
4						Bal.	1,550							
5														
6		Office Supplies					Prepaid Insurance					Office Equipment		
7	Bal.	180	(b)	105		Bal.	240	(a)	40		Bal.	3,400		
8	Bal.	75				Bal.	200							
9														
10	Accumulated Depreciation– Office Equipment						Accounts Payable					Unearned Revenue		
11			Bal.	600				Bal.	700		(f)	160	Bal.	460
12			(c)	100									Bal.	300
13			Bal.	700										
14														
15		Wages Payable					Income Taxes Payable					Common Stock		
16			(d)	120				(g)	250				Bal.	2,000
17														
18		Retained Earnings					Dividends					Answering Service Revenue		
19			Bal.	2,870		Bal.	400						Bal.	2,900
20													(e)	300
21													(f)	160
22													Bal.	3,360
23														
24		Wages Expense					Rent Expense					Insurance Expense		
25	Bal.	1,500				Bal.	400				(a)	40		
26	(d)	120												
27	Bal.	1,620												
28														
29		Office Supplies Expense				Depreciation Expense– Office Equipment						Income Taxes Expense		
30	(b)	105				(c)	100				(g)	250		

3. Adjusted trial balance prepared

	A	B	C
1	Certified Answering Service, Inc.		
2	Adjusted Trial Balance		
3	December 31, 20X7		
4			
5	Cash	$ 2,160	
6	Accounts Receivable	1,550	
7	Office Supplies	75	
8	Prepaid Insurance	200	
9	Office Equipment	3,400	
10	Accumulated Depreciation—Office Equipment		$ 700
11	Accounts Payable		700
12	Unearned Revenue		300
13	Wages Payable		120
14	Income Taxes Payable		250
15	Common Stock		2,000
16	Retained Earnings		2,870
17	Dividends	400	
18	Answering Service Revenue		3,360
19	Wages Expense	1,620	
20	Rent Expense	400	
21	Insurance Expense	40	
22	Office Supplies Expense	105	
23	Depreciation Expense—Office Equipment	100	
24	Income Taxes Expense	250	
25		$10,300	$10,300

4. Financial statements prepared

	A	B	C
1	Certified Answering Service, Inc.		
2	Income Statement		
3	For the Month Ended December 31, 20X7		
4			
5	**Revenues**		
6	Answering service revenue		$3,360
7			
8	**Expenses**		
9	Wages expense	$1,620	
10	Rent expense	400	
11	Insurance expense	40	
12	Office supplies expense	105	
13	Depreciation expense–office equipment	100	
14	Income taxes expense	250	
15	Total expenses		2,515
16	**Net income**		$ 845

	A	B
1	Certified Answering Service, Inc.	
2	Statement of Retained Earnings	
3	For the Month Ended December 31, 20X7	
4		
5	Retained earnings, November 30, 20X7	$2,870
6	Net income	845
7	Subtotal	$3,715
8	Less dividends	400
9	Retained earnings, December 31, 20X7	$3,315

	A	B	C
1	Certified Answering Service, Inc.		
2	Balance Sheet		
3	December 31, 20X7		
4			
5	**Assets**		
6	Cash		$2,160
7	Accounts receivable		1,550
8	Office supplies		75
9	Prepaid insurance		200
10	Office equipment	$3,400	
11	Less accumulated depreciation	700	2,700
12	Total assets		$6,685
13			
14	**Liabilities**		
15	Accounts payable		$ 700
16	Unearned revenue		300
17	Wages payable		120
18	Income taxes payable		250
19	Total liabilities		$1,370
20			
21	**Stockholders' Equity**		
22	Common stock	$2,000	
23	Retained earnings	3,315	
24	Total stockholders' equity		5,315
25	Total liabilities and stockholders' equity		$6,685

CHAPTER ASSIGNMENTS

BUILDING Your Basic Knowledge and Skills

Short Exercises

LO1, LO2 **Accrual Accounting Concepts**

SE 1. Match the concepts of accrual accounting on the right with the assumptions or actions on the left:

1. Assumes expenses should be assigned to the accounting period in which they are used to produce revenues
2. Assumes a business will last indefinitely
3. Assumes revenues are earned at a point in time
4. Assumes net income that is measured for a short period of time, such as one quarter, is a useful measure

   a. Periodicity
   b. Going concern
   c. Matching rule
   d. Revenue recognition

LO3   **Adjustment for Prepaid Insurance**

SE 2. The Prepaid Insurance account began the year with a balance of $460. During the year, insurance in the amount of $1,040 was purchased. At the end of the year (December 31), the amount of insurance still unexpired was $700. Prepare the year-end entry in journal form to record the adjustment for insurance expense for the year.

LO3   **Adjustment for Supplies**

SE 3. The Supplies account began the year with a balance of $380. During the year, supplies in the amount of $980 were purchased. At the end of the year (December 31), the inventory of supplies on hand was $440. Prepare the year-end entry in journal form to record the adjustment for supplies expense for the year.

LO3   **Adjustment for Depreciation**

SE 4. The depreciation expense on office equipment for the month of March is $100. This is the third month that the office equipment, which cost $1,900, has been owned. Prepare the adjusting entry in journal form to record depreciation for March and show the balance sheet presentation for office equipment and related accounts after the March 31 adjustment.

LO3   **Adjustment for Accrued Wages**

SE 5. Wages are paid each Saturday for a six-day workweek. Wages are currently running $1,380 per week. Prepare the adjusting entry required on June 30, assuming July 1 falls on a Tuesday.

LO3   **Adjustment for Unearned Revenue**

SE 6. During the month of August, deposits in the amount of $1,100 were received for services to be performed. By the end of the month, services in the amount of $760 had been performed. Prepare the necessary adjustment for Service Revenue at the end of the month.

LO4   **Preparation of an Income Statement and Statement of Retained Earnings from an Adjusted Trial Balance**

SE 7. The adjusted trial balance for Shimura Company on December 31, 20x6, contains the following accounts and balances: Retained Earnings, $4,300; Dividends, $175; Service Revenue, $1,300; Rent Expense, $200; Wages Expense, $450; Utilities Expense, $100; Telephone Expense, $25; and Income Taxes Expense, $175. Prepare an income statement and statement of retained earnings in proper form for the month of December.

LO5   **Preparation of Closing Entries**

SE 8. Using the data in **SE 7**, prepare required closing entries for Shimura Company.

LO6   **Determination of Cash Flows**

SE 9. Unearned Revenue had a balance of $650 at the end of November and $450 at the end of December. Service Revenue was $2,550 for the month of December. How much cash was received for services provided during December?

Profit Margin

   SE 10. Calculate profit margin for 20x7 using the following data: A company has net income of $7,000 and net sales of $82,000 in 20x7.

Exercises

LO1, LO2, LO3 | **Discussion Questions**

E 1. Develop a brief answer to each of the following questions.

1. When a company has net income, what happens to its assets and/or to its liabilities?
2. Why must a company that gives a guaranty or warranty with its product or service show an expense in the year of sale rather than in a later year when a repair or replacement is made?
3. Is accrual accounting more closely related to a company's goal of profitability or liquidity?
4. Will the carrying value of a long-term asset normally equal its market value?

LO4 | **Discussion Questions**

E 2. Develop a brief answer to each of the following questions.

1. Why is Retained Earnings not listed on the trial balance for Treadle Website Design, Inc., in Exhibits 1 and 2?
2. If, at the end of the accounting period, you were looking at the T account for a prepaid expense like supplies, would you look for the amounts expended in cash on the debit or credit side? On which side would you find the amount expensed during the period?
3. Would you expect profit margin to be a good measure of a company's liquidity? Why or why not?

LO1, LO2, LO3 | **Applications of Accounting Concepts Related to Accrual Accounting**

E 3. The accountant for Villegas Company makes the assumptions or performs the activities listed below. Tell which of the following concepts of accrual accounting most directly relates to each assumption or action: (a) periodicity, (b) going concern, (c) matching rule, (d) revenue recognition, (e) deferral, and (f) accrual.

1. In estimating the life of a building, assumes that the business will last indefinitely
2. Records a sale when the customer is billed
3. Postpones the recognition of a one-year insurance policy as an expense by initially recording the expenditure as an asset
4. Recognizes the usefulness of financial statements prepared on a monthly basis even though they are based on estimates
5. Recognizes, by making an adjusting entry, wages expense that has been incurred but not yet recorded
6. Prepares an income statement that shows the revenues earned and the expenses incurred during the accounting period

LO2 | **Application of Conditions for Revenue Recognition**

E 4. Four conditions must be met before revenue should be recognized. In each of the following cases, tell which condition has *not* been met.

a. Company A accepts a contract to perform services in the future for $2,000.
b. Company B ships products worth $3,000 to another company without an order from the other company but tells the company it can return the products if it does not sell them.
c. Company C performs services for $10,000 for a company that is in financial difficulty.

d. Company D agrees to work out a price later for services that it performs for another company.

LO3 **Adjusting Entry for Unearned Revenue**

E 5. City-Alive Company of Fargo, North Dakota, publishes a monthly magazine featuring local restaurant reviews and upcoming social, cultural, and sporting events. Subscribers pay for subscriptions either one year or two years in advance. Cash received from subscribers is credited to an account called Magazine Subscriptions Received in Advance. On December 31, 20x6, the end of the company's fiscal year, the balance of this account is $750,000. Expiration of subscriptions revenue is as follows:

During 20x6	$150,000
During 20x7	375,000
During 20x8	225,000

Prepare the adjusting entry in journal form for December 31, 20x6.

LO3 **Adjusting Entries for Prepaid Insurance**

E 6. An examination of the Prepaid Insurance account shows a balance of $10,280 at the end of an accounting period, before adjustment. Prepare entries in journal form to record the insurance expense for the period under the following independent assumptions:

1. An examination of the insurance policies shows unexpired insurance that cost $4,935 at the end of the period.
2. An examination of the insurance policies shows insurance that cost $1,735 has expired during the period.

LO3 **Adjusting Entries for Supplies: Missing Data**

E 7. Each of the following columns represents a Supplies account:

	a	b	c	d
Supplies on hand at July 1	$264	$217	$196	$?
Supplies purchased during the month	52	?	174	1,928
Supplies consumed during the month	194	972	?	1,632
Supplies on hand at July 31	?	436	56	1,118

1. Determine the amounts indicated by the question marks.
2. Make the adjusting entry for column **a**, assuming supplies purchased are debited to an asset account.

LO3 **Adjusting Entry for Accrued Salaries**

E 8. Basil Incorporated has a five-day workweek and pays salaries of $70,000 each Friday.

1. Prepare the adjusting entry required on May 31, assuming that June 1 falls on a Wednesday.
2. Prepare the entry to pay the salaries on June 3, including the amount of salaries payable from requirement 1.

LO3 **Revenue and Expense Recognition**

E 9. Schuss Company produces computer software that Dushan Comp, Inc. sells. Schuss receives a royalty of 15 percent of sales. Dushan Comp pays royalties to Schuss Company semiannually—on May 1 for sales made in July through December of the previous year and on November 1 for sales made in January through June of the current year. Royalty expense for

Dushan Comp and royalty income for Schuss Company in the amount of $6,000 were accrued on December 31, 20x5. Cash in the amounts of $6,000 and $10,000 was paid and received on May 1 and November 1, 20x6, respectively. Software sales during the July to December 20x6 period totaled $150,000.

1. Calculate the amount of royalty expense for Dushan Comp and royalty income for Schuss during 20x6.
2. Record the adjusting entry that each company made on December 31, 20x6.

LO4 **Preparation of Financial Statements**

E 10. Prepare the monthly income statement, statement of retained earnings, and balance sheet for Fish Bowl Cleaning Company, Inc., from the data provided in the following adjusted trial balance:

Fish Bowl Cleaning Company, Inc.
Adjusted Trial Balance
August 31, 20xx

Cash	$ 4,590	
Accounts Receivable	2,592	
Prepaid Insurance	380	
Prepaid Rent	200	
Cleaning Supplies	152	
Cleaning Equipment	3,200	
Accumulated Depreciation–Cleaning Equipment		$ 320
Truck	7,200	
Accumulated Depreciation–Truck		720
Accounts Payable		420
Wages Payable		80
Unearned Janitorial Revenue		920
Income Taxes Payable		800
Common Stock		4,000
Retained Earnings		11,034
Dividends	2,000	
Janitorial Revenue		14,620
Wages Expense	5,680	
Rent Expense	1,200	
Gas, Oil, and Other Truck Expenses	580	
Insurance Expense	380	
Supplies Expense	2,920	
Depreciation Expense–Cleaning Equipment	320	
Depreciation Expense–Truck	720	
Income Taxes Expense	800	
	$32,914	$32,914

LO5 **Preparation of Closing Entries**

E 11. From the adjusted trial balance in **E 10**, prepare the required closing entries for Fish Bowl Cleaning Company, Inc.

LO3   Adjusting Entries

E 12. Prepare year-end adjusting entries for each of the following:

1. Office Supplies has a balance of $168 on January 1. Purchases debited to Office Supplies during the year amount to $830. A year-end inventory reveals supplies of $570 on hand.
2. Depreciation of office equipment is estimated to be $4,260 for the year.
3. Property taxes for six months, estimated at $1,750, have accrued but have not been recorded.
4. Unrecorded interest receivable on U.S. government bonds is $1,700.
5. Unearned Revenue has a balance of $1,800. Services for $600 received in advance have now been performed.
6. Services totaling $400 have been performed; the customer has not yet been billed.

LO3   Accounting for Revenue Received in Advanced

E 13. Waldemar Gott, a lawyer, was paid $72,000 on October 1 to represent a client in real estate negotiations over the next 12 months.

1. Record the entries required in Gott's records on October 1 and at the end of the fiscal year, December 31.
2. How would this transaction be reflected on the income statement and balance sheet on December 31?

LO5   Preparation of Closing Entries

E 14. The adjusted trial balance for Phoenix Consultant Corporation at the end of its fiscal year is shown below. Prepare the required closing entries.

Phoenix Consultant Corporation
Trial Balance
December 31, 20xx

Cash	$ 7,275	
Accounts Receivable	2,325	
Prepaid Insurance	585	
Office Supplies	440	
Office Equipment	6,300	
Accumulated Depreciation–Office Equipment		$ 765
Automobile	6,750	
Accumulated Depreciation–Automobile		750
Accounts Payable		1,700
Unearned Consulting Fees		1,500
Income Taxes Payable		3,000
Common Stock		10,000
Retained Earnings		4,535
Dividends	7,000	
Consulting Fees Earned		31,700
Office Salaries Expense	13,500	
Advertising Expense	2,525	
Rent Expense	2,650	
Telephone Expense	1,600	
Income Taxes Expense	3,000	
	$53,950	$53,950

LO4, LO5 **Preparation of a Statement of Retained Earnings**

E 15. The Retained Earnings, Dividends, and Income Summary accounts for Lou's Hair Salon, Inc., are shown in T account form below. The closing entries have been recorded for the year ended December 31, 20x6. Prepare a statement of retained earnings for Lou's Hair Salon, Inc.

RETAINED EARNINGS					INCOME SUMMARY			
12/31/x6	9,000	12/31/x5	26,000		12/31/x6	43,000	12/31/x6	62,000
		12/31/x6	19,000		12/31/x6	19,000		
		Bal.	36,000		Bal.	—		

DIVIDENDS			
4/1/x6	3,000	12/31/x6	9,000
7/1/x6	3,000		
10/1/x6	3,000		
Bal.	—		

LO6 **Determination of Cash Flows**

E 16. After adjusting entries had been made, the balance sheets of Matuska Company showed the following asset and liability amounts at the end of 20x6 and 20x7:

	20x7	20x6
Prepaid insurance	$1,200	$1,450
Wages payable	600	1,100
Unearned fees	2,100	950

The following amounts were taken from the 20x7 income statement:

Insurance expense	$1,900
Wages expense	9,750
Fees earned	4,450

Calculate the amount of cash paid for insurance and wages and the amount of cash received for fees during 20x7.

LO6 **Relationship of Expenses to Cash Paid**

E 17. The income statement for Leon Company included the following expenses for 20xx:

Rent expense	$ 78,000
Interest expense	11,700
Salaries expense	124,500

Listed below are the related balance sheet account balances at year end for last year and this year.

	Last Year	This Year
Prepaid rent	—	$ 1,350
Interest payable	$1,800	—
Salaries payable	7,500	114,000

1. Compute the cash paid for rent during the year.
2. Compute the cash paid for interest during the year.
3. Compute the cash paid for salaries during the year.

Profit Margin

E 18. Julio Company wants to know if its profitability has improved. Calculate its profit margin for 20x6 and 20x7 using the following data:

Net Income, 20x6	$ 4,300
Net Income, 20x7	5,000

Net Sales, 20x6 $80,000
Net Sales, 20x7   96,000

By this measure has profitability improved?

Problems

LO3 **Determining Adjustments**

P 1. At the end of its fiscal year, the trial balance for Roosevelt Cleaners, Inc., appears as follows:

Roosevelt Cleaners, Inc.
Trial Balance
September 30, 20x7

Cash	$ 11,788	
Accounts Receivable	26,494	
Prepaid Insurance	3,400	
Cleaning Supplies	7,374	
Land	18,000	
Building	185,000	
Accumulated Depreciation–Building		$ 45,600
Accounts Payable		20,400
Unearned Cleaning Revenue		1,600
Mortgage Payable		110,000
Common Stock		40,000
Retained Earnings		16,560
Dividends	10,000	
Cleaning Revenue		157,634
Wages Expense	101,330	
Cleaning Equipment Rental Expense	6,000	
Delivery Truck Expense	4,374	
Interest Expense	11,000	
Other Expenses	7,034	
	$391,794	$391,794

The following information is also available:

a. A study of the company's insurance policies shows that $680 is unexpired at the end of the year.
b. An inventory of cleaning supplies shows $1,244 on hand.
c. Estimated depreciation on the building for the year is $12,800.
d. Accrued interest on the mortgage payable is $1,000.
e. On September 1, the company signed a contract, effective immediately, with Kings County Hospital to dry clean, for a fixed monthly charge of $400, the uniforms used by doctors in surgery. The hospital paid for four months' service in advance.
f. Sales and delivery wages are paid on Saturday. The weekly payroll is $2,520. September 30 falls on a Thursday and the company has a six-day pay week.
g. Estimated federal income taxes for the period are $2,000.

Required

All adjustments affect one balance sheet account and one income statement account. For each of the above situations, show the accounts affected, the amount of the adjustment (using a + or − to indicate an increase or decrease), and the balance of the account after the adjustment in the following format:

Balance Sheet Account	Amount of Adjustment (+ or −)	Balance after Adjustment	Income Statement Account	Amount of Adjustment (+ or −)	Balance after Adjustment

LO2, LO3 **Preparing Adjusting Entries**

P 2. On June 30, the end of the current fiscal year, the following information is available to Sterling Company's accountants for making adjusting entries:

a. Among the liabilities of the company is a mortgage payable in the amount of $240,000. On June 30, the accrued interest on this mortgage amounted to $12,000.

b. On Friday, July 2, the company, which is on a five-day workweek and pays employees weekly, will pay its regular salaried employees $19,200.

c. On June 29, the company completed negotiations and signed a contract to provide services to a new client at an annual rate of $3,600.

d. The Supplies account shows a beginning balance of $1,615 and purchases during the year of $3,766. The end-of-year inventory reveals supplies on hand of $1,186.

e. The Prepaid Insurance account shows the following entries on June 30:

Beginning Balance	$1,530
January 1	2,900
May 1	3,366

The beginning balance represents the unexpired portion of a one-year policy purchased the previous year. The January 1 entry represents a new one-year policy, and the May 1 entry represents the additional coverage of a three-year policy.

f. The following table contains the cost and annual depreciation for buildings and equipment, all of which were purchased before the current year:

Account	Cost	Annual Depreciation
Buildings	$185,000	$ 7,300
Equipment	218,000	21,800

g. On June 1, the company completed negotiations with another client and accepted a payment of $21,000, representing one year's services paid in advance. The $21,000 was credited to Services Collected in Advance.

h. The company calculates that as of June 30 it had earned $3,500 on a $7,500 contract that will be completed and billed in August.

i. Federal income taxes for the year are estimated to be $7,500.

Required

1. Prepare adjusting entries for each item listed above.

2. **User insight:** Explain how the conditions for revenue recognition are applied to transactions **c** and **h**.

LO3 **Determining Adjusting Entries, Posting to T Accounts, and Preparing an Adjusted Trial Balance**

P 3. The trial balance for Financial Strategies Service, Inc., on December 31 is presented on the following page.

Financial Strategies Service, Inc.
Trial Balance
December 31, 20xx

Cash	$ 16,500	
Accounts Receivable	8,250	
Office Supplies	2,662	
Prepaid Rent	1,320	
Office Equipment	9,240	
Accumulated Depreciation–Office Equipment		$ 1,540
Accounts Payable		5,940
Notes Payable		11,000
Unearned Service Revenue		2,970
Common Stock		10,000
Retained Earnings		14,002
Dividends	22,000	
Service Revenue		72,600
Salaries Expense	49,400	
Rent Expense	4,400	
Utilities Expense	4,280	
	$118,052	$118,052

The following information is also available:

a. Ending inventory of office supplies, $264.
b. Prepaid rent expired, $440.
c. Depreciation of office equipment for the period, $660.
d. Accrued interest expense at the end of the period, $550.
e. Accrued salaries at the end of the period, $330.
f. Service revenue still unearned at the end of the period, $1,166.
g. Service revenue earned but unrecorded, $2,200.
h. Estimated income taxes for the period, $4,000.

Required

1. Open T accounts for the accounts in the trial balance plus the following: Interest Payable; Salaries Payable; Income Taxes Payable; Office Supplies Expense; Depreciation Expense–Office Equipment; Interest Expense; and Income Taxes Expense. Enter the balances shown on the trial balance.
2. Determine the adjusting entries and post them directly to the T accounts.
3. Prepare an adjusted trial balance.
4. **User insight:** What financial statements do each of the above adjustments affect? What financial statement is *not* affected by the adjustments?

LO3, LO4   **Determining Adjusting Entries and Tracing Their Effects to Financial Statements**

P 4. Joyce Ozaki opened a small tax-preparation service. At the end of its second year of operation, Ozaki Tax Service, Inc., had the trial balance shown at the top of the next page. The following information is also available:

a. Office supplies on hand, December 31, 20x7, $227.
b. Insurance still unexpired, $120.
c. Estimated depreciation of office equipment, $770.
d. Telephone expense for December, $19; the bill was received but not recorded.

Ozaki Tax Service, Inc.
Trial Balance
December 31, 20x7

Cash	$ 2,268	
Accounts Receivable	1,031	
Prepaid Insurance	240	
Office Supplies	782	
Office Equipment	7,100	
Accumulated Depreciation–Office Equipment		$ 770
Accounts Payable		635
Unearned Tax Fees		219
Common Stock		2,000
Retained Earnings		3,439
Dividends	6,000	
Tax Fees Revenue		21,926
Office Salaries Expense	8,300	
Advertising Expense	650	
Rent Expense	2,400	
Telephone Expense	218	
	$28,989	$28,989

e. The services for all unearned tax fees had been performed by the end of the year.

f. Estimated federal income taxes for the year, $1,800.

Required

1. Open T accounts for the accounts in the trial balance plus the following: Income Taxes Payable; Insurance Expense; Office Supplies Expense; Depreciation Expense–Office Equipment; and Income Taxes Expense. Record the balances shown in the trial balance.

2. Determine the adjusting entries and post them directly to the T accounts.

3. Prepare an adjusted trial balance, an income statement, a statement of retained earnings, and a balance sheet.

4. **User insight:** Why is it not necessary to show the effects of the above transactions on the statement of cash flows?

LO3, LO4 **Determining Adjusting Entries and Tracing Their Effects to Financial Statements**

P 5. The Elite Livery Service, Inc., was organized to provide limousine service between the airport and various suburban locations. It has just completed its second year of business. Its trial balance appears at the top of the next page. The following information is also available:

a. To obtain space at the airport, Elite paid two years' rent in advance when it began the business.

b. An examination of insurance policies reveals that $2,800 expired during the year.

c. To provide regular maintenance for the vehicles, Elite deposited $12,000 with a local garage. An examination of maintenance invoices reveals charges of $10,944 against the deposit.

d. An inventory of spare parts shows $1,902 on hand.

e. Elite depreciates all of its limousines at the rate of 12.5 percent per year. No limousines were purchased during the year.

Elite Livery Service, Inc.
Trial Balance
June 30, 20x7

Cash (111)	$ 9,812	
Accounts Receivable (112)	14,227	
Prepaid Rent (117)	12,000	
Prepaid Insurance (118)	4,900	
Prepaid Maintenance (119)	12,000	
Spare Parts (141)	11,310	
Limousines (142)	200,000	
Accumulated Depreciation–Limousines (143)		$ 25,000
Notes Payable (211)		45,000
Unearned Passenger Service Revenue (212)		30,000
Common Stock (311)		30,000
Retained Earnings (312)		48,211
Dividends (313)	20,000	
Passenger Service Revenue (411)		428,498
Gas and Oil Expense (511)	89,300	
Salaries Expense (512)	206,360	
Advertising Expense (513)	26,800	
	$606,709	$606,709

f. A payment of $10,500 for one full year's interest on notes payable is now due.

g. Unearned Passenger Service Revenue on June 30 includes $17,815 for tickets that employers purchased for use by their executives but which have not yet been redeemed.

h. Federal income taxes for the year are estimated to be $12,000.

Required

1. Determine adjusting entries and enter them in the general journal (Page 14).

2. Open ledger accounts for the accounts in the trial balance plus the following: Interest Payable (213); Income Taxes Payable (214); Rent Expense (514); Insurance Expense (515); Spare Parts Expense (516); Depreciation Expense–Limousines (517); Maintenance Expense (518); Interest Expense (519); and Income Taxes Expense (520). Record the balances shown in the trial balance.

3. Post the adjusting entries from the general journal to the ledger accounts, showing proper references.

4. Prepare an adjusted trial balance, an income statement, a statement of retained earnings, and a balance sheet.

5. **User insight:** Do adjustments affect the profit margin? After the adjustments, is the profit margin for the year more or less than it would have been if the adjustments had not been made?

Alternate Problems

LO3 Determining Adjustments

P 6. At the end of the first three months of operation, the trial balance of Metropolitan Answering Service, Inc., appears as shown on the opposite page.

Oscar Rienzo, the owner of Metropolitan, has hired an accountant to prepare financial statements to determine how well the company is doing after three months. Upon examining the accounting records, the accountant finds the following items of interest:

a. An inventory of office supplies reveals supplies on hand of $133.
b. The Prepaid Rent account includes the rent for the first three months plus a deposit for April's rent.
c. Depreciation on the equipment for the first three months is $208.
d. The balance of the Unearned Answering Service Revenue account represents a 12-month service contract paid in advance on February 1.
e. On March 31, accrued wages total $80.
f. Federal income taxes for the three months are estimated to be $1,500.

Metropolitan Answering Service, Inc.
Trial Balance
March 31, 20x5

Cash	$ 3,482	
Accounts Receivable	4,236	
Office Supplies	903	
Prepaid Rent	800	
Equipment	4,700	
Accounts Payable		$ 2,673
Unearned Answering Service Revenue		888
Common Stock		5,933
Dividends	2,130	
Answering Service Revenue		9,002
Wages Expense	1,900	
Office Cleaning Expense	345	
	$18,496	$18,496

Required

All adjustments affect one balance sheet account and one income statement account. For each of the above situations, show the accounts affected, the amount of the adjustment (using a + or − to indicate an increase or decrease), and the balance of the account after the adjustment in the following format:

Balance Sheet Account	Amount of Adjustment (+ or −)	Balance after Adjustment	Income Statement Account	Amount of Adjustment (+ or −)	Balance after Adjustment

LO2, LO3 **Preparing Adjusting Entries**

P 7. On November 30, the end of the current fiscal year, the following information is available to assist Pinder Corporation's accountants in making adjusting entries:

a. Pinder Corporation's Supplies account shows a beginning balance of $2,174. Purchases during the year were $4,526. The end-of-year inventory reveals supplies on hand of $1,397.
b. The Prepaid Insurance account shows the following on November 30:

Beginning balance	$3,580
July 1	4,200
October 1	7,272

The beginning balance represents the unexpired portion of a one-year policy purchased the previous year. The July 1 entry represents a new one-year policy, and the October 1 entry represents additional coverage in the form of a three-year policy.

c. The following table contains the cost and annual depreciation for buildings and equipment, all of which Pinder Corporation purchased before the current year:

Account	Cost	Annual Depreciation
Buildings	$286,000	$14,500
Equipment	374,000	35,400

d. On September 1, the company completed negotiations with a client and accepted an advance payment of $16,800 for services to be performed in the next year. The $16,800 was credited to Unearned Services Revenue.

e. The company calculated that as of November 30, it had earned $4,000 on an $11,000 contract that would be completed and billed in January.

f. Among the liabilities of the company is a note payable in the amount of $300,000. On November 30, the accrued interest on this note amounted to $15,000.

g. On Saturday, December 2, the company, which is on a six-day workweek, will pay its regular salaried employees $12,300.

h. On November 29, the company completed negotiations and signed a contract to provide services to a new client at an annual rate of $17,500.

i. Management estimates income taxes for the year to be $25,000.

Required

1. Prepare adjusting entries for each item listed above.
2. **User insight:** Explain how the conditions for revenue recognition are applied to transactions **e** and **h**.

LO3, LO4   **Determining Adjusting Entries, Posting to T Accounts, and Preparing and Adjusted Trial Balance**

P 8. The schedule at the top of the opposite page presents the trial balance for Sigma Consultants Corporation on December 31, 20x7. The following information is also available:

a. Ending inventory of office supplies, $86.
b. Prepaid rent expired, $700.
c. Depreciation of office equipment for the period, $600.
d. Interest accrued on the note payable, $600.
e. Salaries accrued at the end of the period, $200.
f. Service revenue still unearned at the end of the period, $1,410.
g. Service revenue earned but not billed, $600.
h. Estimated federal income taxes for the period, $3,000.

Required

1. Open T accounts for the accounts in the trial balance plus the following: Interest Payable; Salaries Payable; Income Taxes Payable; Office Supplies Expense; Depreciation Expense–Office Equipment; Interest Expense; and Income Taxes Expense. Enter the account balances.
2. Determine the adjusting entries and post them directly to the T accounts.
3. Prepare an adjusted trial balance.
4. **User insight:** What financial statements do each of the above adjustments affect? What financial statement is *not* affected by the adjustments?

Sigma Consultants Corporation
Trial Balance
December 31, 20x7

Cash	$ 12,786	
Accounts Receivable	24,840	
Office Supplies	991	
Prepaid Rent	1,400	
Office Equipment	6,700	
Accumulated Depreciation–Office Equipment		$ 1,600
Accounts Payable		1,820
Notes Payable		10,000
Unearned Service Revenue		2,860
Common Stock		10,000
Retained Earnings		19,387
Dividends	15,000	
Service Revenue		58,500
Salaries Expense	33,000	
Utilities Expense	1,750	
Rent Expense	7,700	
	$104,167	$104,167

ENHANCING Your Knowledge, Skills, and Critical Thinking

Conceptual Understanding Cases

LO1, LO2, LO3 — Importance of Adjustments

C 1. Never Flake Company, which operated in the northeastern part of the United States, provided a rust-prevention coating for the underside of new automobiles. The company advertised widely and offered its services through new car dealers. When a dealer sold a new car, the salesperson attempted to sell the rust-prevention coating as an option. The protective coating was supposed to make cars last longer in the severe northeastern winters. A key selling point was Never Flake's warranty, which stated that it would repair any damage due to rust at no charge for as long as the buyer owned the car.

For several years, Never Flake had been very successful in generating enough cash to continue operations. But in 2005, the company suddenly declared bankruptcy. Company officials said that the firm had only $5.5 million in assets against liabilities of $32.9 million. Most of the liabilities represented potential claims under the company's lifetime warranty. It seemed that owners were keeping their cars longer now than previously. Therefore, more damage was being attributed to rust. Discuss what accounting decisions could have helped Never Flake to survive under these circumstances.

LO1 — Earnings Management and Fraudulent Financial Reporting

C 2. In recent years, the Securities and Exchange Commission (SEC) has been waging a public campaign against corporate accounting practices that manage or manipulate earnings to meet the expectations of Wall Street analysts. Corporations engage in such practices in the hope of avoiding shortfalls that might cause serious declines in their stock price. For each of the following cases that the SEC challenged, tell why each is a violation of the matching rule and how it should be accounted for:

a. **Lucent Technologies** sold telecommunications equipment to companies from which there was no reasonable expectation of payment because of the companies' poor financial condition.
b. **America Online (AOL)** recorded advertising as an asset rather than as an expense.
c. **Eclipsys** recorded software contracts as revenue even though it had not yet rendered the services.
d. **KnowledgeWare** recorded revenue from sales of software even though it told customers they did not have to pay until they had the software.

Interpreting Financial Reports

LO2, LO3 **Application of Accrual Accounting**

C 3. The **Lyric Opera of Chicago** is one of the largest and best-managed opera companies in the United States. Managing opera productions requires advance planning, including the development of scenery, costumes, and stage properties and the sale of tickets. To measure how well the company is operating in any given year, management must apply accrual accounting to these and other transactions. At year end, April 30, 2004, Lyric Opera's balance sheet showed deferred production costs of $2,289,573 and deferred ticket revenue of $18,984,555.[9] Be prepared to discuss what accounting policies and adjusting entries are applicable to these accounts. Why are they important to Lyric Opera's management?

LO2, LO3 **Analysis of an Asset Account**

C 4. **The Walt Disney Company** is engaged in the financing, production, and distribution of motion pictures and television programming. In Disney's 2004 annual report, the balance sheet contains an asset called "film and television costs." Film and television costs, which consist of the costs associated with producing films and television programs less the amount expensed, were $5,938,000,000. The notes reveal that the amount of film and television costs expensed (amortized) during the year was $2,364,000,000. The amount spent for new film productions was $2,824,000,000.[10]

1. What are film and television costs, and why would they be classified as an asset?
2. Prepare an entry in T account form to record the amount the company spent on new film and television production during the year (assume all expenditures are paid for in cash).
3. Prepare an adjusting entry in T account form to record the expense for film and television productions.
4. Suggest a method by which The Walt Disney Company might have determined the amount of the expense in **3** in accordance with the matching rule.

Decision Analysis Using Excel

LO1, LO3 **Adjusting Entries, Divided Performance Evaluation, and Dividend Policy**

C 5. Maurice Turner, the owner of a newsletter for managers of hotels and restaurants, has prepared the following condensed amounts from his company's financial statements for 20x6:

Revenues	$432,500
Expenses	352,500
Net income	$ 80,000
Total assets	$215,000
Liabilities	$ 60,000
Stockholders' equity	155,000
Total liabilities and stockholders' equity	$215,000

Given these figures, Turner is planning a cash dividend of $62,500. However, Turner's accountant has found that the following items were overlooked:

a. Although the balance of the Printing Supplies account is $40,000, only $17,500 in supplies is on hand at the end of the year.

b. Depreciation of $25,000 on equipment has not been recorded.

c. Wages of $11,750 have been earned by Turner's employees but not recognized in the accounts.

d. No provision has been made for estimated income taxes payable of $13,500.

e. A liability account called Unearned Subscriptions has a balance of $20,250, although it has been determined that one-third of these subscriptions have been mailed to subscribers.

1. Prepare the necessary adjusting entries.
2. Recast the condensed financial statement figures after you have made the necessary adjustments.
3. Discuss the performance of Turner's business after the adjustments have been made. (**Hint:** Compare net income to revenues and total assets before and after the adjustments.) Do you think that paying the dividend is advisable? Why or why not?

Annual Report Case: CVS Corporpation

LO3 **Analysis of Balance Sheet and Adjusting Entries**

C 6. In **CVS Corporation's** annual report in the Supplement to Chapter 1, refer to the balance sheet and the Summary of Significant Accounting Policies in the notes to the financial statements.

1. Examine the accounts in the current assets, property and equipment, and current liabilities sections of CVS's balance sheet. Which are most likely to have had year-end adjusting entries? Describe the nature of the adjusting entries. For more information about the property and equipment section, refer to the notes to the financial statements.

2. Where is depreciation (and amortization) expense disclosed in CVS's financial statements?

3. CVS has a statement on the "Use of Estimates" in its Summary of Significant Accounting Policies. Read this statement and tell how important estimates are to the determination of depreciation expense. What assumptions do accountants make that allow these estimates to be made?

Comparison Analysis: CVS Versus Southwest

Profit Margin

C 7. The profit margin is an important measure of profitability. Use data from **CVS's** income statement and the financial statements of **Southwest Airlines Co.** in the Supplement to Chapter 1 to calculate each company's profit margin for the past two years. By this measure, which company is more profitable?

Ethical Dilemma Case

LO1, LO2, LO3 **Importance of Adjustments**

C 8. Central Appliance Service Co., Inc., has achieved fast growth in the St. Louis area by selling service contracts on large appliances, such as washers, dryers, and refrigerators. For a fee, Central Appliance agrees to provide all parts and labor on an appliance after the regular warranty runs out. For example, by paying a fee of $200, a person who buys a dishwasher can add two years (years 2 and 3) to the regular one-year (year 1) warranty on the appliance. In 2006, the company sold service contracts in the amount of $1.8 million, all of which applied to future years. Management wanted all the sales recorded as revenues in 2006, contending that the amount of the contracts could be determined and the cash had been received. Discuss whether you agree with this logic. How would you record the cash receipts? What assumptions do you think Central Appliance should make? Would you consider it unethical to follow management's recommendation? Who might be hurt or helped by this action?

Internet Case

LO3 **Comparison of Accrued Expenses**

C 9. How important are accrued expenses? Randomly choose four different companies. Go to each company's website and find their annual reports. For each company, find the section of the balance sheet labeled "Current Liabilities" and identify the current liabilities that are accrued expenses (sometimes called accrued liabilities). More than one account may be involved. On a pad, write the information you find in four columns: name of company, total current liabilities, total accrued liabilities, and total accrued liabilities as a percentage of total current liabilities. Write a brief statement listing the companies you chose, telling how you obtained their reports, reporting the data you have gathered in the form of a table, and stating a conclusion, with reasons, as to the importance of accrued expenses to the companies you studied.

Group Activity Case

LO3 **Types of Adjusting Entries**

C 10. In this chapter, we discussed adjusting entries for deferred revenue, deferred expense, accrued revenue, and accrued expense. In informal groups in class, discuss how each type of adjusting entry applies to **Yahoo!**. Be prepared to present your group's findings to the class.

Business Communication Case

LO3 **Real-World Observation of Business Activities**

C 11. Visit a company with which you are familiar and observe its operations. (The company can be where you work, where you eat, or where you buy things.) Identify at least two sources of revenue for the company and six types of expenses. For each type of revenue and each type of expense, determine whether it is probable that an adjusting entry is required at the end of the accounting period. Then specify the adjusting entry as a deferred revenue, deferred expense, accrued revenue, or accrued expense. Design a table with columns and rows that summarize your results in an easy-to-understand format.

Closing Entries and the Work Sheet

Preparing Closing Entries

As you know, closing entries have two purposes: (1) they clear the balances of all temporary accounts (revenue, expense, and Dividends accounts) so that they have zero balances at the beginning of the next accounting period, and (2) they summarize a period's revenues and expenses in the Income Summary account so that the net income or loss for the period can be transferred as a total to Retained Earnings.

The steps involved in making closing entries are as follows:

Step 1. Close the credit balances on the income statement accounts to the Income Summary account.

Step 2. Close the debit balances on the income statement accounts to the Income Summary account.

Step 3. Close the Income Summary account balance to the Retained Earnings account.

Step 4. Close the Dividends account balance to the Retained Earnings account.

As you will learn in later chapters, not all revenue accounts have credit balances, and not all expense accounts have debit balances. For that reason, when referring to closing entries, we often use the term *credit balances* instead of *revenue accounts* and the term *debit balances* instead of *expense accounts*.

An adjusted trial balance provides all the data needed to record the closing entries. Exhibit S-1 shows the relationships of the four kinds of closing entries to Treadle Website Design's adjusted trial balance.

Study Note

Although it is not absolutely necessary to use the Income Summary account when preparing closing entries, it does simplify the procedure.

Step 1: Closing the Credit Balances

On the credit side of the adjusted trial balance in Exhibit S-1, Design Revenue shows a balance of $13,600. To close this account, a journal entry must be made debiting the account in the amount of its balance and crediting it to the Income Summary account. Exhibit S-2 shows how the entry is posted. Notice that the entry sets the balance of the revenue account to zero and transfers the total revenues to the credit side of the Income Summary account.

Study Note

The Income Summary account now reflects the account balance of the revenue account before it was closed.

Step 2: Closing the Debit Balances

Several expense accounts show balances on the debit side of the adjusted trial balance in Exhibit S-1. A compound entry is needed to credit each of these expense accounts for its balance and to debit the Income Summary account for the total. Exhibit S-3 shows the effect of posting the closing entry. Notice how the entry reduces the expense account balances to zero and transfers the total of the account balances to the debit side of the Income Summary account.

▼ **EXHIBIT S-1**

Preparing Closing Entries from the Adjusted Trial Balance

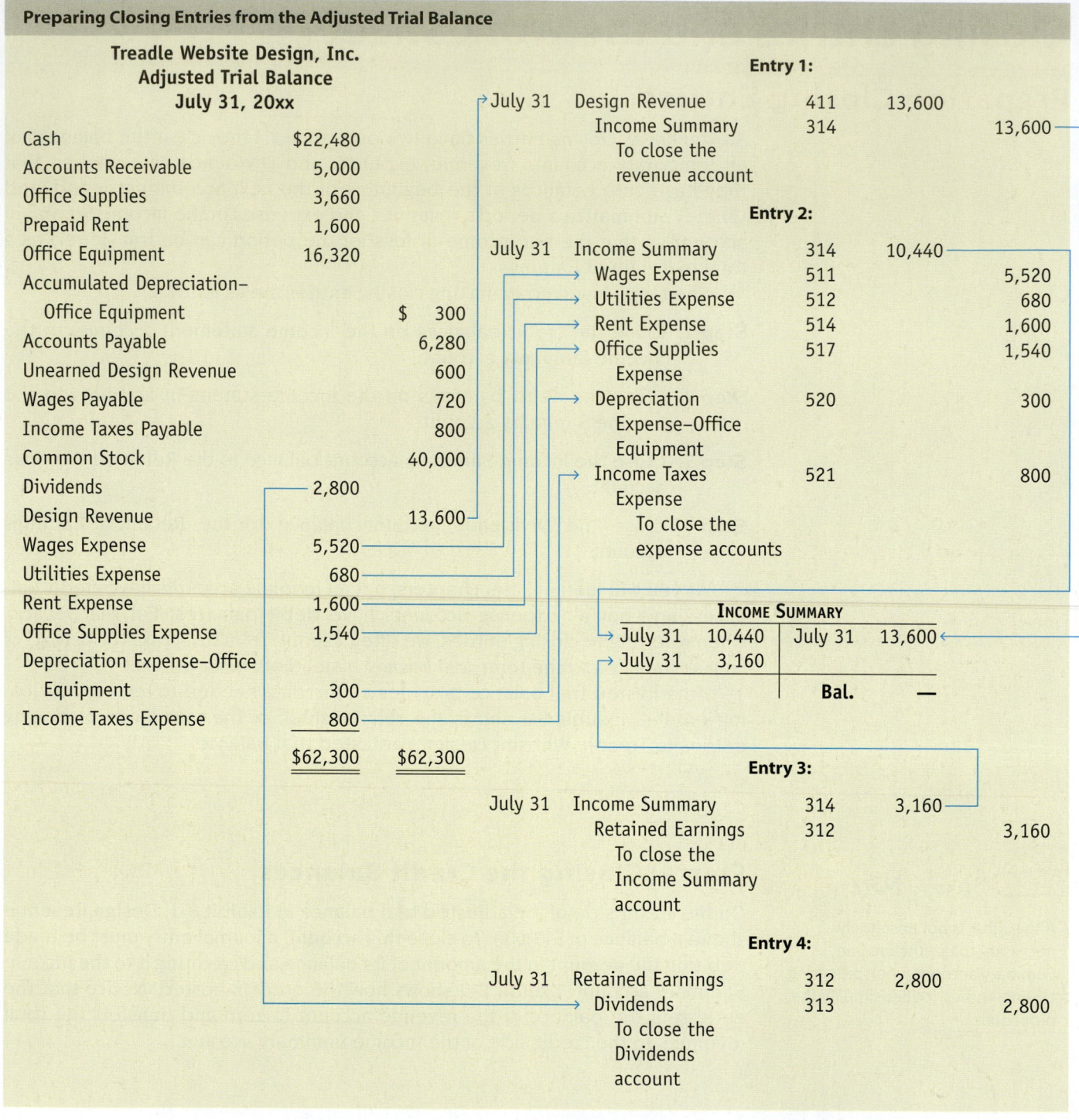

EXHIBIT S-2 ▶ **Posting the Closing Entry of a Credit Balance to the Income Summary Account**

Design Revenue — Account No. 411

Date	Item	Post. Ref.	Debit	Credit	Balance Debit	Balance Credit
July 10		J2		2,800		2,800
15		J2		9,600		12,400
31		J3		800		13,200
31		J3		400		13,600
31	Closing	J4	13,600			—

Income Summary — Account No. 314

Date	Item	Post. Ref.	Debit	Credit	Balance Debit	Balance Credit
July 31	Closing	J4		13,600		13,600

▼ **EXHIBIT S-3**

Posting the Closing Entry of Debit Balances to the Income Summary Account

Income Summary — Account No. 314

Date	Item	Post. Ref.	Debit	Credit	Balance Debit	Balance Credit
July 31	Closing	J4		13,600		13,600
31	Closing	J4	10,440			3,160

Office Supplies Expense — Account No. 517

Date	Item	Post. Ref.	Debit	Credit	Balance Debit	Balance Credit
July 31		J3	1,540		1,540	
31	Closing	J4		1,540	—	

Wages Expense — Account No. 511

Date	Item	Post. Ref.	Debit	Credit	Balance Debit	Balance Credit
July 26		J2	4,800		4,800	
31		J3	720		5,520	
31	Closing	J4		5,520	—	

Depreciation Expense—Office Equipment — Account No. 520

Date	Item	Post. Ref.	Debit	Credit	Balance Debit	Balance Credit
July 31		J3	300		300	
31	Closing	J4		300	—	

Utilities Expense — Account No. 512

Date	Item	Post. Ref.	Debit	Credit	Balance Debit	Balance Credit
July 30		J2	680		680	
31	Closing	J4		680	—	

Income Taxes Expense — Account No. 521

Date	Item	Post. Ref.	Debit	Credit	Balance Debit	Balance Credit
July 31		J3	800		800	
31	Closing	J4		800	—	

Rent Expense — Account No. 514

Date	Item	Post. Ref.	Debit	Credit	Balance Debit	Balance Credit
July 31		J3	1,600		1,600	
31	Closing	J4		1,600	—	

▼ EXHIBIT S-4

Posting the Closing Entry of the Income Summary Account Balance to the Retained Earnings Account

Income Summary						Account No. 314	Retained Earnings						Account No. 312
Date	Item	Post. Ref.	Debit	Credit	Balance Debit	Balance Credit	Date	Item	Post. Ref.	Debit	Credit	Balance Debit	Balance Credit
July 31	Closing	J4		13,600		13,600	July 31	Closing	J4		3,160		3,160
31	Closing	J4	10,440			3,160							
31	Closing	J4	3,160			—							

Study Note

The credit balance of the Income Summary account at this point ($3,160) represents net income—the key measure of performance. When a net loss occurs, you debit the Retained Earnings account (to reduce it) and credit the Income Summary account (to close it).

Step 3: Closing the Income Summary Account Balance

After the entries closing the revenue and expense accounts have been posted, the balance of the Income Summary account equals the net income or loss for the period. A credit balance in the Income Summary account represents a net income (revenues exceed expenses), and a debit balance represents a net loss (expenses exceed revenues).

At this point, the balance of the Income Summary account, whatever its nature, is closed to the Retained Earnings account, as shown in Exhibit S-1. Exhibit S-4 shows how the closing entry is posted when a company has a net income. Notice the dual effect of closing the Income Summary account and transferring the balance to Retained Earnings.

Step 4: Closing the Dividends Account Balance

Study Note

Notice that the Dividends account is closed to the Retained Earnings account, not to the Income Summary account.

The Dividends account shows the amount by which cash dividends reduce retained earnings during an accounting period. The debit balance of the Dividends account is closed to the Retained Earnings account, as illustrated in Exhibit S-1. Exhibit S-5 shows the posting of the closing entry and the transfer of the balance of the Dividends account to the Retained Earnings account.

The Accounts After Closing

After all the steps in the closing process have been completed and all closing entries have been posted, everything is ready for the next accounting period. The revenue, expense, and Dividends accounts (temporary accounts) have zero balances. The Retained Earnings account has been increased or decreased to reflect net income or net loss (net income in our example) and has been decreased for dividends. The balance sheet accounts (permanent

▼ EXHIBIT S-5

Posting the Closing Entry of the Dividends Account Balance to the Retained Earnings Account

Dividends						Account No. 313	Retained Earnings						Account No. 312
Date	Item	Post. Ref.	Debit	Credit	Balance Debit	Balance Credit	Date	Item	Post. Ref.	Debit	Credit	Balance Debit	Balance Credit
July 31		J2	2,800		2,800		July 31	Closing	J4		3,160		3,160
31	Closing	J4		2,800		—	31	Closing	J4	2,800			360

EXHIBIT S-6 ▶

Post-Closing Trial Balance

Treadle Website Design, Inc.
Post-Closing Trial Balance
July 31, 20xx

Cash	$22,480	
Accounts Receivable	5,000	
Office Supplies	3,660	
Prepaid Rent	1,600	
Office Equipment	16,320	
Accumulated Depreciation–Office Equipment		$ 300
Accounts Payable		6,280
Unearned Design Revenue		600
Wages Payable		720
Income Taxes Payable		800
Common Stock		40,000
Retained Earnings		360
	$49,060	$49,060

accounts) show the correct balances, which are carried forward to the next period, as shown in the post-closing trial balance in Exhibit S-6.

The Work Sheet: An Accountant's Tool

Accountants must collect relevant data to determine what should be included in financial reports. For example, they must examine insurance policies to calculate how much prepaid insurance has expired, examine plant and equipment records to determine depreciation, and compute the amount of accrued wages. To organize such data and avoid omitting important information that might affect the financial statements, accountants use *working papers*. Because working papers provide evidence of past work, they also enable accountants to retrace their steps when they need to verify information in the financial statements.

The *work sheet* is a special kind of working paper. It is often used as a preliminary step in preparing financial statements. Using a work sheet lessens the possibility of leaving out an adjustment and helps the accountant check the arithmetical accuracy of the accounts. The work sheet is never published and is rarely seen by management. It is a tool for the accountant.

Because preparing a work sheet is a mechanical process, many accountants use a computer for this purpose. Some accountants use a spreadsheet program to prepare the work sheet. Others use a general ledger system to prepare financial statements from the adjusted trial balance.

 *Study Note*

The work sheet is extremely useful when an accountant must make numerous adjustments. It is not a financial statement, it is not required, and it is not made public.

Preparing the Work Sheet

A common form of work sheet has one column for account names and/or account numbers and multiple columns with headings like the ones shown in Exhibit S-7. A heading that includes the name of the company and the period of time covered (as on the income statement) identifies the work sheet. As Exhibit S-7 shows, preparation of a work sheet involves five steps.

▼ EXHIBIT S-7

The Work Sheet

Treadle Website Design, Inc.
Work Sheet
For the Month Ended July 31, 20xx

Account Name	Trial Balance Debit	Trial Balance Credit	Adjustments Debit	Adjustments Credit	Adjusted Trial Balance Debit	Adjusted Trial Balance Credit	Income Statement Debit	Income Statement Credit	Balance Sheet Debit	Balance Sheet Credit
Cash	22,480				22,480				22,480	
Accounts Receivable	4,600		(g) 400		5,000				5,000	
Office Supplies	5,200			(b) 1,540	3,660				3,660	
Prepaid Rent	3,200			(a) 1,600	1,600				1,600	
Office Equipment	16,320				16,320				16,320	
Accumulated Depreciation–Office Equipment		—		(c) 300		300				300
Accounts Payable		6,280				6,280				6,280
Unearned Design Revenue		1,400	(f) 800			600				600
Common Stock		40,000				40,000				40,000
Dividends	2,800				2,800				2,800	
Design Revenue		12,400		(f) 800 (g) 400		13,600		13,600		
Wages Expense	4,800		(d) 720		5,520		5,520			
Utilities Expense	680				680		680			
	60,080	60,080								
Rent Expense			(a) 1,600		1,600		1,600			
Office Supplies Expense			(b) 1,540		1,540		1,540			
Depreciation Expense–Office Equipment			(c) 300		300		300			
Wages Payable				(d) 720		720				720
Income Taxes Expense			(e) 800		800		800			
Income Taxes Payable				(e) 800		800				800
			6,160	6,160	62,300	62,300	10,440	13,600	51,860	48,700
Net Income							3,160			3,160
							13,600	13,600	51,860	51,860

Note: The columns of the work sheet are prepared in the following order: (1) Trial Balance, (2) Adjustments, (3) Adjusted Trial Balance, and (4) Income Statement and Balance Sheet columns. In the fifth step, the Income Statement and Balance Sheet columns are totaled.

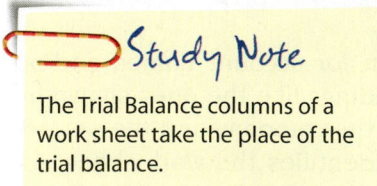

Study Note

The Trial Balance columns of a work sheet take the place of the trial balance.

Step 1. Enter and total the account balances in the Trial Balance columns. The debit and credit balances of the accounts as of the last day of an accounting period are copied directly from the ledger into the Trial Balance columns, as shown in Exhibit S-7. When accountants use a work sheet, they do not have to prepare a separate trial balance.

Step 2. **Enter and total the adjustments in the Adjustments columns.** The required adjustments are entered in the Adjustments columns of the work sheet. As each adjustment is entered, a letter is used to identify its debit and credit parts. For example, in Exhibit S-7, the letter **a** identifies the adjustment made for the rent that Treadle Website Design prepaid on July 3, which results in a debit to Rent Expense and a credit to Prepaid Rent. These identifying letters may be used to reference supporting computations or documentation for the related adjusting entries and can simplify the recording of adjusting entries in the general journal.

A trial balance includes only accounts that have balances; if an adjustment involves an account that does not appear in the trial balance, the new account is added below the accounts listed on the work sheet. For example, Rent Expense has been added to Exhibit S-7. Accumulated depreciation accounts, which have a zero balance only in the initial period of operation, are the only exception to this rule. They are listed immediately after their associated asset accounts.

When all the adjustments have been made, the two Adjustments columns must be totaled. This procedure proves that the debits and credits of the adjustments are equal, and it generally reduces errors in the work sheet.

Step 3. **Enter and total the adjusted account balances in the Adjusted Trial Balance columns.** The adjusted trial balance in the work sheet is prepared by combining the amount of each account in the Trial Balance columns with the corresponding amount in the Adjustments columns and entering each result in the Adjusted Trial Balance columns.

Exhibit S-7 contains examples of *crossfooting*, or adding and subtracting a group of numbers horizontally. The first line shows Cash with a debit balance of $22,480. Because there are no adjustments to the Cash account, $22,480 is entered in the debit column of the Adjusted Trial Balance columns. On the second line, Accounts Receivable shows a debit of $4,600 in the Trial Balance columns. Because there is a debit of $400 from adjustment **g** in the Adjustments columns, it is added to the $4,600 and carried over to the debit column of the Adjusted Trial Balance columns at $5,000. On the next line, Office Supplies shows a debit of $5,200 in the Trial Balance columns and a credit of $1,540 from adjustment **b** in the Adjustments columns. Subtracting $1,540 from $5,200 results in a $3,660 debit balance in the Adjusted Trial Balance columns. This process is followed for all the accounts, including those added below the trial balance totals. The Adjusted Trial Balance columns are then *footed* (totaled) to check the accuracy of the crossfooting.

Step 4. **Extend the account balances from the Adjusted Trial Balance columns to the Income Statement or Balance Sheet columns.** Every account in the adjusted trial balance is an income statement account or a balance sheet account. Each account is extended to its proper place as a debit or credit in either the Income Statement columns or the Balance Sheet columns. As shown in Exhibit S-7, revenue and expense accounts are extended to the Income Statement columns, and asset, liability, and the Common Stock and Dividends accounts are extended to the Balance Sheet columns.

To avoid overlooking an account, the accounts are extended line by line, beginning with the first line (Cash) and not omitting any subsequent lines. For instance, the Cash debit balance of $22,480 is extended to the debit column of the Balance Sheet columns; then, the Accounts Receivable debit balance of $5,000 is extended to the debit column of the Balance Sheet columns; and so forth.

Step 5. **Total the Income Statement columns and the Balance Sheet columns. Enter the net income or net loss in both pairs of columns as a balancing figure, and recompute the column totals.** This last step, shown in Exhibit S-7, is necessary to compute net income or net loss and to prove the arithmetical accuracy of the work sheet.

Net income (or net loss) is equal to the difference between the total debits and credits of the Income Statement columns. It is also equal to the difference between the total debits and credits of the Balance Sheet columns.

Revenues (Income Statement credit column total)	$13,600
Expenses (Income Statement debit column total)	(10,440)
Net Income	$ 3,160

In this case, revenues (credit column) exceed expenses (debit column). Thus, Treadle Website Design has a net income of $3,160. The same difference occurs between the total debits and credits of the Balance Sheet columns.

The $3,160 is entered in the debit side of the Income Statement columns and in the credit side of the Balance Sheet columns to balance the columns. Remember that the excess of revenues over expenses (net income) increases stockholders' equity and that increases in stockholders' equity are recorded by credits.

When a net loss occurs, the opposite rule applies. The excess of expenses over revenues—net loss—is placed in the credit side of the Income Statement columns as a balancing figure. It is then placed in the debit side of the Balance Sheet columns because a net loss decreases stockholders' equity, and decreases in stockholders' equity are recorded by debits.

As a final check, the four columns are totaled again. If the Income Statement columns and the Balance Sheet columns do not balance, an account may have been extended or sorted to the wrong column, or an error may have been made in adding the columns. Of course, equal totals in the two pairs of columns are not absolute proof of accuracy. If an asset has been carried to the Income Statement debit column (or an expense has been carried to the Balance Sheet debit column) or a similar error with revenues or liabilities has been made, the work sheet will balance, but the net income figure will be wrong.

Using the Work Sheet

Accountants use the completed work sheet in performing three principal tasks:

1. **Recording the adjusting entries in the general journal.** Because the information needed to record the adjusting entries can be copied from the work sheet, entering the adjustments in the journal is an easy step, as shown in Exhibit S-8. The adjusting entries are then posted to the general ledger.

2. **Recording the closing entries in the general journal.** The Income Statement columns of the work sheet show all the accounts that need to be closed, except for the Dividends account. Exhibits S-1 through S-5 show how the closing entries are entered in the journal and posted to the ledger.

 **Study Note**

Theoretically, adjusting entries can be recorded in the accounting records before the financial statements are prepared, or even before the work sheet is completed. However, they always precede the preparation of closing entries.

▼ **EXHIBIT S-8**

Adjustments from the Work Sheet Entered in the General Journal

	General Journal			Page 3
Date	Description	Post. Ref.	Debit	Credit
20xx				
July 31	Rent Expense	514	1,600	
	Prepaid Rent	117		1,600
	To recognize expiration of one month's rent			
	Office Supplies Expense	517	1,540	
	Office Supplies	116		1,540
	To recognize office supplies used during the month			
	Depreciation Expense–Office Equipment	520	300	
	Accumulated Depreciation–Office Equipment	147		300
	To record depreciation of office equipment for a month			
	Wages Expense	511	720	
	Wages Payable	214		720
	To accrue unrecorded wages			
	Income Taxes Expense	521	800	
	Income Taxes Payable	215		800
	To accrue estimated income taxes			
	Unearned Design Revenue	213	800	
	Design Revenue	411		800
	To recognize payment for services not yet performed			
	Accounts Receivable	113	400	
	Design Revenue	411		400
	To accrue website design fees earned but unrecorded			

3. **Preparing the financial statements.** Once the work sheet has been completed, preparing the financial statements is simple because the account balances have been sorted into the Income Statement and Balance Sheet columns.

Supplement Assignments

Questions

1. Which of the following accounts would you expect to find in the post-closing trial balance?

   a. Insurance Expense   e. Dividends
   b. Accounts Receivable   f. Supplies
   c. Commission Revenue   g. Supplies Expense
   d. Prepaid Insurance   h. Retained Earnings

2. Why are working papers important to accountants?
3. Why are work sheets never published and rarely seen by management?
4. Can the work sheet be used as a substitute for the financial statements? Explain your answer.

5. Why should the Adjusted Trial Balance columns of the work sheet be totaled before the adjusted amounts are carried to the Income Statement and Balance Sheet columns?

6. What sequence should be followed in extending the amounts in the Adjusted Trial Balance columns to the Income Statement and Balance Sheet columns? Discuss your answer.

7. Do the Income Statement columns and the Balance Sheet columns of the work sheet balance after the amounts from the Adjusted Trial Balance columns are extended? Why or why not?

8. Do the totals of the Balance Sheet columns of the work sheet agree with the totals on the balance sheet? Explain your answer.

9. Should adjusting entries be posted to the ledger accounts before or after the closing entries? Explain your answer.

10. At the end of the accounting period, does the posting of adjusting entries to the ledger precede or follow preparation of the work sheet?

Exercises

Preparation of Closing Entries

E 1. The items below are from the Income Statement columns of the work sheet for Best Repair Shop, Inc., for the year ended December 31, 20xx.

| | Income Statement | |
Account Name	Debit	Credit
Repair Revenue		25,620
Wages Expense	8,110	
Rent Expense	1,200	
Supplies Expense	4,260	
Insurance Expense	915	
Depreciation Expense–Repair Equipment	1,345	
Income Taxes Expense	1,000	1,000
	16,830	25,620
Net Income	8,790	
	25,620	25,620

Prepare entries to close the revenue, expense, Income Summary, and Dividends accounts. Dividends of $5,000 were paid during the year.

Completion of a Work Sheet

E 2. The following is a highly simplified list of trial balance accounts and their normal balances for the month ended October 31, 20xx, which was the company's first month of operation:

Trial Balance Accounts and Balances

Cash	$4	Unearned Revenue	$ 3
Accounts Receivable	7	Common Stock	12
Prepaid Insurance	2	Retained Earnings	7
Supplies	4	Dividends	6
Office Equipment	8	Service Revenue	23
Accumulated Depreciation–		Wages Expense	10
Office Equipment	1	Utilities Expense	2
Accounts Payable	4		

1. Prepare a work sheet, entering the trial balance accounts in the order they would normally appear and putting the balances in the correct columns.
2. Complete the work sheet using the following information:
   a. Expired insurance, $1.
   b. Of the unearned revenue balance, $2 has been earned by the end of the month.
   c. Estimated depreciation on office equipment, $1.
   d. Accrued wages, $1.
   e. Unused supplies on hand, $1.
   f. Estimated federal income taxes, $1.

Problems

Closing Entries Using T Accounts and Preparation of Financial Statements

P 1. The adjusted trial balance for Settles Tennis Club, Inc., at the end of the company's fiscal year appears below.

Settles Tennis Club, Inc.
Adjusted Trial Balance
June 30, 20x8

Cash	$ 26,200	
Prepaid Advertising	9,600	
Supplies	1,200	
Land	100,000	
Building	645,200	
Accumulated Depreciation–Building		$ 260,000
Equipment	156,000	
Accumulated Depreciation–Equipment		50,400
Accounts Payable		73,000
Wages Payable		9,000
Property Taxes Payable		22,500
Unearned Revenues–Locker Fees		3,000
Income Taxes Payable		20,000
Common Stock		200,000
Retained Earnings		271,150
Dividends	54,000	
Revenues from Court Fees		678,100
Revenues from Locker Fees		9,600
Wages Expense	351,000	
Maintenance Expense	51,600	
Advertising Expense	39,750	
Utilities Expense	64,800	
Supplies Expense	6,000	
Depreciation Expense–Building	30,000	
Depreciation Expense–Equipment	12,000	
Property Taxes Expense	22,500	
Miscellaneous Expense	6,900	
Income Taxes Expense	20,000	
	$1,596,750	$1,596,750

Required

1. Prepare T accounts and enter the balances for Retained Earnings, Dividends, Income Summary, and all revenue and expense accounts.
2. Enter the four required closing entries in the T accounts, labeling the components *a, b, c,* and *d,* as appropriate.
3. Prepare an income statement, a statement of retained earnings, and a balance sheet for Settles Tennis Club, Inc.
4. Explain why closing entries are necessary at the end of the accounting period.

The Complete Accounting Cycle Without a Work Sheet: Two Months

(*second month optional*)

 P 2. On May 1, 20xx, Javier Munoz opened Javier's Repair Service, Inc. During the month, he completed the following transactions for the company:

May	1	Began business by depositing $5,000 in a bank account in the name of the company in exchange for 500 shares of $10 par value common stock.
	1	Paid the rent for a store for current month, $425.
	1	Paid the premium on a one-year insurance policy, $480.
	2	Purchased repair equipment from Motley Company, $4,200. Terms were $600 down and $300 per month for one year. First payment is due June 1.
	5	Purchased repair supplies from AWD Company on credit, $468.
	8	Paid cash for an advertisement in a local newspaper, $60.
	15	Received cash repair revenue for the first half of the month, $400.
	21	Paid AWD Company on account, $225.
	31	Received cash repair revenue for the second half of May, $975.
	31	Declared and paid a cash dividend, $300.

Required for **May**

1. Prepare journal entries to record the May transactions.
2. Open the following accounts: Cash (111); Prepaid Insurance (117); Repair Supplies (119); Repair Equipment (144); Accumulated Depreciation–Repair Equipment (145); Accounts Payable (212); Income Taxes Payable (213); Common Stock (311); Retained Earnings (312); Dividends (313); Income Summary (314); Repair Revenue (411); Store Rent Expense (511); Advertising Expense (512); Insurance Expense (513); Repair Supplies Expense (514); Depreciation Expense–Repair Equipment (515); and Income Taxes Expense (516). Post the May journal entries to the ledger accounts.
3. Using the following information, record adjusting entries in the general journal and post to the ledger accounts:
   a. One month's insurance has expired.
   b. The remaining inventory of unused repair supplies is $169.
   c. The estimated depreciation on repair equipment is $70.
   d. Estimated income taxes are $50.
4. From the accounts in the ledger, prepare an adjusted trial balance. (**Note:** Normally a trial balance is prepared before adjustments but is omitted here to save time.)
5. From the adjusted trial balance, prepare an income statement, a statement of retained earnings, and a balance sheet for May.
6. Prepare and post closing entries.
7. Prepare a post-closing trial balance.

(Optional)

During June, Javier Munoz completed these transactions for Javier's Repair Service, Inc.:

June 1   Paid the monthly rent, $425.
    1   Made the monthly payment to Motley Company, $300.
    6   Purchased additional repair supplies on credit from AWD Company, $863.
  15   Received cash repair revenue for the first half of the month, $914.
  20   Paid cash for an advertisement in the local newspaper, $60.
  23   Paid AWD Company on account, $600.
  30   Received cash repair revenue for the last half of the month, $817.
  30   Declared and paid a cash dividend, $300.

8. Prepare and post journal entries to record the June transactions.
9. Using the following information, record adjusting entries in the general journal and post to the ledger accounts:

   a. One month's insurance has expired.
   b. The inventory of unused repair supplies is $413.
   c. The estimated depreciation on repair equipment is $70.
   d. Estimated income taxes are $50.

10. From the accounts in the ledger, prepare an adjusted trial balance.
11. From the adjusted trial balance, prepare the June income statement, statement of retained earnings, and balance sheet.
12. Prepare and post closing entries.
13. Prepare a post-closing trial balance.

Preparation of a Work Sheet, Financial Statements, and Adjusting and Closing Entries

P 3. Beauchamp Theater Corporation's trial balance at the end of its current fiscal year appears at the top of the next page.

Required

1. Enter Beauchamp Theater Corporation's trial balance amounts in the Trial Balance columns of a work sheet and complete the work sheet using the following information:

   a. Expired insurance, $17,400.
   b. Inventory of unused office supplies, $244.
   c. Inventory of unused cleaning supplies, $468.
   d. Estimated depreciation on the building, $14,000.
   e. Estimated depreciation on the theater furnishings, $36,000.
   f. Estimated depreciation on the office equipment, $3,160.
   g. The company credits all gift books sold during the year to the Gift Books Liability account. A gift book is a booklet of ticket coupons that is purchased in advance as a gift. The recipient redeems the coupons at some point in the future. On June 30 it was estimated that $37,800 worth of the gift books had been redeemed.
   h. Accrued but unpaid usher wages at the end of the accounting period, $860.
   i. Estimated federal income taxes, $20,000.

2. Prepare an income statement, a statement of retained earnings, and a balance sheet.
3. Prepare adjusting and closing entries.

Beauchamp Theater Corporation
Trial Balance
June 30, 20x7

Cash	$ 31,800	
Accounts Receivable	18,544	
Prepaid Insurance	19,600	
Office Supplies	780	
Cleaning Supplies	3,590	
Land	20,000	
Building	400,000	
Accumulated Depreciation–Building		$ 39,400
Theater Furnishings	370,000	
Accumulated Depreciation–Theater Furnishings		65,000
Office Equipment	31,600	
Accumulated Depreciation–Office Equipment		15,560
Accounts Payable		45,506
Gift Books Liability		41,900
Mortgage Payable		300,000
Common Stock		200,000
Retained Earnings		112,648
Dividends	60,000	
Ticket Sales Revenue		411,400
Theater Rental Revenue		45,200
Usher Wages Expense	157,000	
Office Wages Expense	24,000	
Utilities Expense	112,700	
Interest Expense	27,000	
	$1,276,614	$1,276,614

Preparation of a Work Sheet, Financial Statements, and Adjusting and Closing Entries

P 4. The trial balance on the opposite page was taken from the ledger of Wylie Package Delivery Corporation on August 31, 20x7, the end of the company's fiscal year.

Required

1. Enter the trial balance amounts in the Trial Balance columns of a work sheet and complete the work sheet using the following information:

   a. Expired insurance, $1,530.
   b. Inventory of unused delivery supplies, $715.
   c. Inventory of unused office supplies, $93.
   d. Estimated depreciation, building, $7,200.
   e. Estimated depreciation, trucks, $7,725.
   f. Estimated depreciation, office equipment, $1,350.
   g. The company credits the lockbox fees of customers who pay in advance to the Unearned Lockbox Fees account. Of the amount credited to this account during the year, $2,815 had been earned by August 31.

Wylie Package Delivery Corporation
Trial Balance
August 31, 20x7

Cash	$ 5,036	
Accounts Receivable	14,657	
Prepaid Insurance	2,670	
Delivery Supplies	7,350	
Office Supplies	1,230	
Land	7,500	
Building	98,000	
Accumulated Depreciation–Building		$ 26,700
Trucks	51,900	
Accumulated Depreciation––Trucks		15,450
Office Equipment	7,950	
Accumulated Depreciation–Office Equipment		5,400
Accounts Payable		4,698
Unearned Lockbox Fees		4,170
Mortgage Payable		36,000
Common Stock		20,000
Retained Earnings		44,365
Dividends	15,000	
Delivery Services Revenue		141,735
Lockbox Fees Earned		14,400
Truck Drivers' Wages Expense	63,900	
Office Salaries Expense	22,200	
Gas, Oil, and Truck Repairs Expense	15,525	
	$312,918	$312,918

h. Lockbox fees earned but unrecorded and uncollected at the end of the accounting period, $408.
i. Accrued but unpaid truck drivers' wages at the end of the year, $960.
j. Management estimates federal income taxes to be $6,000.
2. Prepare an income statement, a statement of retained earnings, and a balance sheet.
3. Prepare adjusting and closing entries.

CHAPTER

4

Financial Reporting and Analysis

Stockholders, investors, creditors, and other interested parties rely on the integrity of a company's financial reports. A company's managers and accountants therefore have a responsibility to act ethically in the reporting process. However, what is often overlooked is that the users of financial reports also have a responsibility to recognize and understand the types of judgments and estimates that underlie these reports.

LEARNING OBJECTIVES

Making a Statement

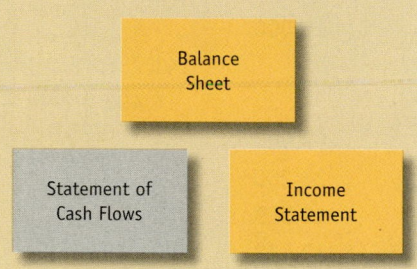

Grouping like accounts on the balance sheet and income statement aids analysis.

LO1 Describe the objectives and qualitative characteristics of financial reporting and the ethical responsibilities that financial reporting involves.

LO2 Define and describe the conventions of *comparability* and *consistency, materiality, conservatism, full disclosure,* and *cost-benefit.*

LO3 Identify and describe the basic components of a classified balance sheet.

LO4 Describe the features of multistep and single-step classified income statements.

LO5 Use classified financial statements to evaluate liquidity and profitability.

- How should financial statements be organized to provide the best information?

- What key measures best capture a company's financial performance?

In its annual report, **Dell's** management states that the company's objective is "to maximize stockholder value by executing a strategy based on ... a balance of three priorities: liquidity, profitability, and growth."[1] In judging whether a company has achieved its objectives, investors, creditors, managers, and others analyze relationships between key numbers in the financial statements that appear in the company's annual report.

Dell's annual report summarizes the company's financial performance by condensing a tremendous amount of information to a few numbers that managers and external users of financial statements consider most important. As shown in the Financial Highlights below, Dell uses just four measures to summarize its operating results and the change in those results from one fiscal year to the next.

DELL'S FINANCIAL HIGHLIGHTS
Operating Results (In millions)

	2004	2003	Change
Net revenue	$41,444	$35,404	17.1%
Gross profit	7,552	6,349	18.9%
Operating income	3,544	2,844	24.6%
Net income	2,645	2,122	24.6%

Foundations of Financial Reporting

LO1 Describe the objectives and qualitative characteristics of financial reporting and the ethical responsibilities that financial reporting involves.

By issuing stocks and bonds that are traded in financial markets, corporations can raise the cash they need to carry out current and future business activities. Investors in stocks and bonds expect increases in the firm's stock price and returns from dividends. Creditors want to know if the firm can repay a loan plus interest in accordance with specified terms. Very importantly, both investors and creditors need to know if the firm can generate adequate cash flows to maintain its liquidity. Information pertaining to all these matters appears in the financial statements published in a company's annual report.

In the following sections, we describe the objectives of financial reporting and the qualitative characteristics and ethical considerations that are involved. Figure 1 illustrates these factors.

Objectives of Financial Reporting

The Financial Accounting Standards Board (FASB) emphasizes the needs of users when it defines the objectives of financial reporting as follows:[2]

Study Note

Although reading financial reports requires some understanding of business, it does not require the skills of a CPA.

1. *To furnish information useful in making investment and credit decisions.* Financial reporting should offer information that can help current and potential investors and creditors make rational investment and credit decisions. The reports should be in a form that makes sense to anyone who has some understanding of business and is willing to study the information carefully.

2. *To provide information useful in assessing cash flow prospects.* Financial reporting should supply information that can help current and potential investors and creditors judge the amount, timing, and risk of expected cash receipts from dividends or interest and the proceeds from the sale, redemption, or maturity of stocks or loans.

3. *To provide information about business resources, claims to those resources, and changes in them.* Financial reporting should provide information about a company's assets, liabilities, and stockholders' equity, and the effect that transactions have on them.

Financial statements periodically present to parties outside the business the information that has been gathered and processed in the accounting system. These statements—the balance sheet, the income statement, the statement of retained earnings, and the statement of cash flows—are the most important output of the accounting system. They are "general purpose" because of their wide audience. They are "external" because their users are outside the business. Because of a potential conflict of interest between managers, who must prepare the statements, and investors or creditors, who invest in or lend money to the business, financial statements usually are audited by outside accountants to ensure their reliability.

Qualitative Characteristics of Accounting Information

Students in their first accounting course often get the idea that accounting is 100 percent accurate. Contributing to this perception is that introductory textbooks like this one present the basics of accounting in a simple form to help

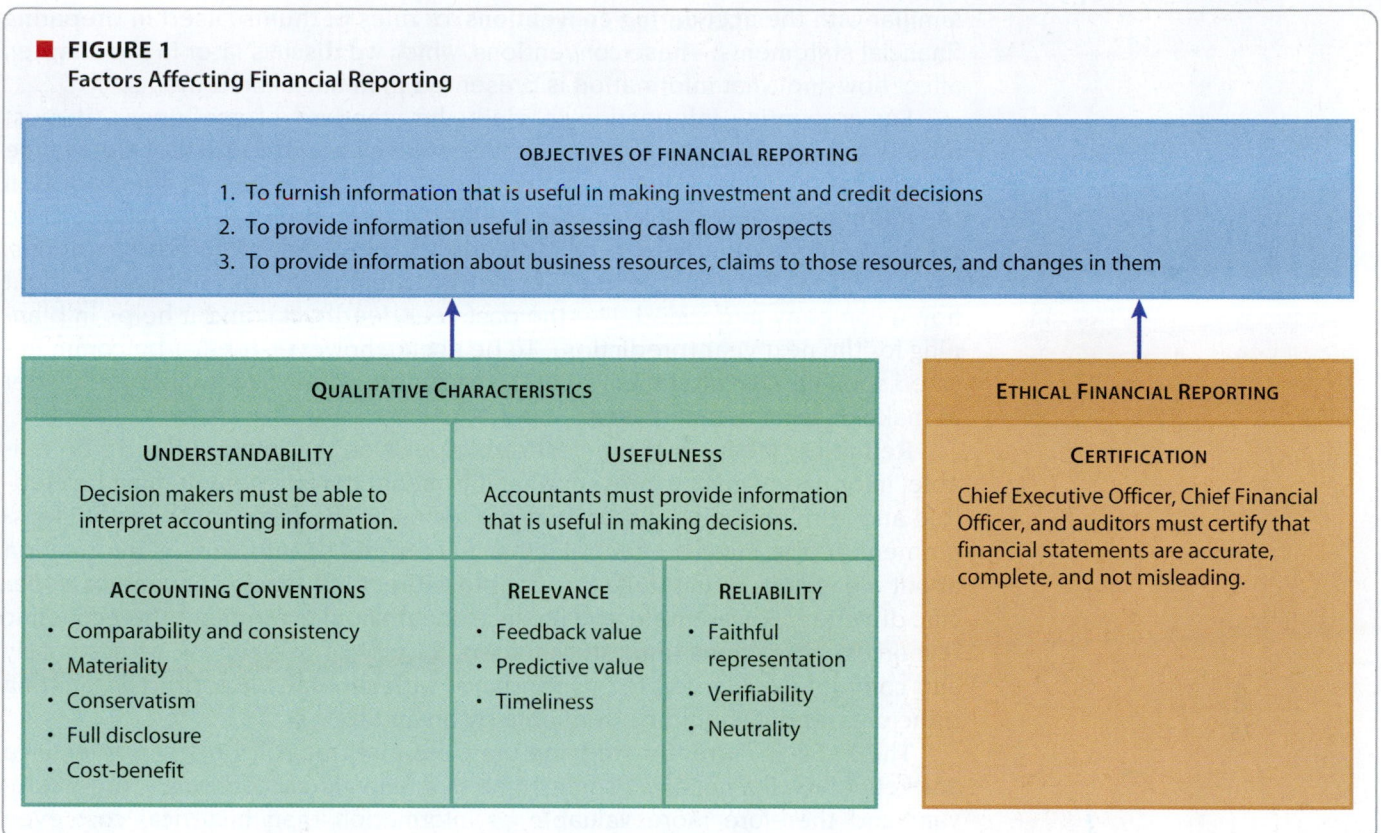

■ **FIGURE 1**
Factors Affecting Financial Reporting

OBJECTIVES OF FINANCIAL REPORTING

1. To furnish information that is useful in making investment and credit decisions
2. To provide information useful in assessing cash flow prospects
3. To provide information about business resources, claims to those resources, and changes in them

QUALITATIVE CHARACTERISTICS

UNDERSTANDABILITY

Decision makers must be able to interpret accounting information.

USEFULNESS

Accountants must provide information that is useful in making decisions.

ACCOUNTING CONVENTIONS

- Comparability and consistency
- Materiality
- Conservatism
- Full disclosure
- Cost-benefit

RELEVANCE

- Feedback value
- Predictive value
- Timeliness

RELIABILITY

- Faithful representation
- Verifiability
- Neutrality

ETHICAL FINANCIAL REPORTING

CERTIFICATION

Chief Executive Officer, Chief Financial Officer, and auditors must certify that financial statements are accurate, complete, and not misleading.

students understand them. All the problems can be solved, and all the numbers add up; what is supposed to equal something else does. Accounting seems very much like mathematics in its precision. In practice, however, accounting information is neither simple nor precise, and it rarely satisfies all criteria. The FASB emphasizes this fact in the following statement:

> The information provided by financial reporting often results from approximate, rather than exact, measures. The measures commonly involve numerous estimates, classifications, summarizations, judgments and allocations. The outcome of economic activity in a dynamic economy is uncertain and results from combinations of many factors. Thus, despite the aura of precision that may seem to surround financial reporting in general and financial statements in particular, with few exceptions the measures are approximations, which may be based on rules and conventions, rather than exact amounts.[3]

The goal of generating accounting information is to provide the data that different users need to make informed decisions for their unique situations. The ways this goal is accomplished provide much of the interest and controversy in accounting. To facilitate interpretation of accounting information, the FASB has established standards, or **qualitative characteristics**, by which to judge the information.

The most important qualitative characteristics are understandability and usefulness. **Understandability** depends on both the accountant and the decision maker. The accountant prepares the financial statements in accordance with accepted practices that are intended to make the information understandable. But the decision maker must know how to interpret the information; in making decisions, he or she must judge what information to use, how to use it, and what it means. To understand accounting information, users must be familiar with the **accounting conventions**, or rules of thumb, used in preparing financial statements. These conventions, which we discuss later in the chapter, affect how and what information is presented in financial statements.

For accounting information to meet the standard of **usefulness**, it must have two major qualitative characteristics: relevance and reliability. **Relevance** means that the information has a direct bearing on a decision. In other words, if the information were not available, a different decision would be made. To be relevant, information must provide feedback, help predict future conditions, and be timely. For example, the income statement provides information about how a company performed over the past year (feedback), and it helps in planning for the next year (prediction). To be useful, however, it must be communicated soon enough after the end of the accounting period to enable the reader to make decisions (timeliness).

Reliability means that the user can depend on the information. To be reliable, information must represent what it is meant to represent. It must be credible and verifiable by independent parties using the same methods of measurement. It also must be neutral. Financial reports should convey information about a business as faithfully as possible without influencing anyone in a specific direction. For example, the balance sheet should represent the economic resources, obligations, and stockholders' equity of a business as accurately and completely as possible in accordance with generally accepted accounting principles, and it should be verifiable by an auditor.

The FASB is currently studying the potential tradeoff between relevance and reliability. For instance, some argue that fair value accounting is more relevant and therefore more valuable as information than historical cost even though it may be a less reliable measure. Others argue that historical cost is more valuable because of its reliability.[4]

Management's Certification of the Financial Statements

As we noted earlier in the text, in 2002, in the wake of accounting scandals at **Enron** and **WorldCom**, Congress passed the Sarbanes-Oxley Act. One of the important outcomes of this legislation was that the Securities and Exchange Commission instituted rules requiring the chief executive officers and chief financial officers of all publicly traded companies to certify that, to their knowledge, the quarterly and annual statements that their companies file with the SEC are accurate and complete. An example of this type of management certification appears in the 2003 10-K form that **Dell Computer Corporation** filed with the SEC. In that report, Michael Dell, then the company's chief executive officer, made the following statement:

> Based on my knowledge, this annual report does not contain any untrue statement of material fact or omit to state a material fact necessary to make the statements . . . not misleading with respect to the period covered. . . . Based on my knowledge, the financial statements and other financial information . . . fairly present in all material respects the financial condition, results of operations and cash flows of the registrant as of, and for the periods presented in the annual report.[5]

Dell's chief financial officer signed a similar statement.

As the Enron and WorldCom scandals demonstrated, fraudulent financial reporting can have high costs for investors, lenders, employees, and customers. It can also have high costs for the people who condone, authorize, or prepare misleading reports—even those at the highest corporate levels. In

March 2005, Bernard J. Ebbers, former CEO of WorldCom, was convicted of seven counts of filing false reports with the SEC and one count each of securities fraud and conspiracy. Each count could carry a prison sentence of five to ten years. In 2005, both Kenneth Lay, former chairman of Enron Corporation, and Jeffrey Skilling, Enron's former CEO, were awaiting trial on charges similar to the ones of which Ebbers was convicted.[6]

STOP • REVIEW • APPLY

1-1. What are the three objectives of financial reporting?

1-2. What are the qualitative characteristics of accounting information? Explain their significance.

1-3. Who are the people responsible for preparing financial statements? What does the preparation of reliable financial statements entail?

Suggested answers to all Stop, Review, and Apply questions follow the appendixes.

Accounting Conventions

LO2 Define and describe the conventions of *comparability* and *consistency, materiality, conservatism, full disclosure,* and *cost-benefit.*

Financial statements are based largely on estimates and the application of accounting rules for recognition and allocation. To facilitate interpretation, accountants depend on five conventions, or rules of thumb, in recording transactions and preparing financial statements: comparability and consistency, materiality, conservatism, full disclosure, and cost-benefit.

Comparability and Consistency

Information about a company is more useful when it can be compared over several periods or when it can be compared with information about other companies. **Comparability** means that information is presented in such a way that a decision maker can recognize similarities, differences, and trends over different periods in the same company and among different companies.

Consistent use of accounting measures and procedures is important in achieving comparability. The **consistency** convention requires that once a company has adopted an accounting procedure, it must use it from one period to the next unless a note to the financial statements informs users of a change in procedure. Generally accepted accounting principles specify what the note must contain:

> The nature of and justification for a change in accounting principle and its effect on income should be disclosed in the financial statements of the period in which the change is made. The justification for the change should explain clearly why the newly adopted accounting principle is preferable.[7]

For example, in the notes to its financial statements, **Goodyear Tire & Rubber Company** disclosed that it had changed its method of accounting for inventories because management felt the new method improved the matching of

Like any other company, Goodyear must ensure that the quality of its products is consistent and that its accounting methods are as well. When a company changes an accounting method, it has a duty to inform users of its financial statements of the change. Such information is essential in making effective comparisons of a company's performance over several periods or in comparing its performance with that of other companies.

revenues and costs. Without such an acknowledgment, users of financial statements can assume that the treatment of a particular transaction, account, or item has not changed since the last period.

Materiality

Materiality refers to the relative importance of an item or event. In general, an item or event is material if there is a reasonable expectation that knowing about it would influence the decisions of users of financial statements. Some items or events are so small or insignificant that they would make little difference to decision makers no matter how they are handled. Thus, a large company, like **Dell Computer Corporation**, may decide that expenditures for durable items of less than $500 should be charged as expenses rather than recorded as long-term assets and depreciated.

FOCUS ON BUSINESS PRACTICE

Are Yahoo! and Google Comparable? Can an Internet Company Be Conservative?

In a recent quarter, **Yahoo! Inc.** reported revenue of $758 million, but looked at another way, the revenue could be $550 million. In the same quarter, Yahoo!'s rival, **Google Inc.**, reported revenue of $390 million, but that could be $652 million. What's going on?

Both Yahoo! and Google follow GAAP in reporting revenue, but their interpretations differ. The difference involves how they account for revenue from advertisements that they place on other companies' websites. Yahoo! and Google are paid each time an Internet user clicks on one of their ads, but they pay some of that money to the company on whose site the ad appears. Yahoo! counts the revenue at the gross amount (and shows the payment as an operating expense); hence, its reported revenue of $758 million. Google counts the revenues at the net amount (gross minus the payment); hence, the reported revenue of $390 million. Analysts consider the way Google reports to be the more conservative practice, and in fact, when Yahoo! communicates with users, it shows the net amount also because it "conveys more transparent economic value to the investor."[8]

How Much Is Material? It's Not Only a Matter of Numbers.

The materiality issue was long a pet peeve of the SEC, which contended that companies were increasingly abusing the convention to protect their stocks from taking a pounding when earnings did not reach their targets. In consequence, the SEC issued a rule that put stricter requirements on the use of materiality. In addition to providing quantitative guides, the rule includes qualitative considerations. The percentage assessment of material-ity—the rule of thumb of 5 percent or more of net income that accountants and companies have traditionally used—is acceptable as an initial screening. However, the rule states that companies cannot decline to book items in the interest of meeting earnings estimates, preserving a growing earnings trend, converting a loss to a profit, increasing management compensation, or hiding an illegal transaction, such as a bribe.[9]

Theoretically, a $10 stapler is a long-term asset and should therefore be capitalized and depreciated over its useful life. However, the convention of materiality allows the stapler to be expensed entirely in the year of purchase because its cost is small and writing it off in one year will have no effect on anyone's decision making.

The materiality of an item normally is determined by relating its dollar value to an element of the financial statements, such as net income or total assets. As a rule, when an item is worth 5 percent or more of net income, accountants treat it as material. However, materiality depends not only on the value of an item, but also on its nature. For example, in a multimillion-dollar company, a mistake of $5,000 in recording an item may not be important, but the discovery of a $5,000 bribe or theft can be very important. Moreover, many small errors can add up to a material amount.

Conservatism

Study Note

The purpose of conservatism is not to produce the lowest net income and lowest asset value. It is a guideline for choosing among GAAP alternatives, and it should be used with care.

When accountants are uncertain about the judgments or estimates they must make, which is often the case, they look to the convention of **conservatism**. This convention holds that when faced with choosing between two equally acceptable procedures, accountants should choose the one that is least likely to overstate assets and income.

One of the most common applications of the conservatism convention is the use of the lower-of-cost-or-market method in accounting for inventories. Under this method, if an item's market value is greater than its original cost, the more conservative cost figure is used. If the market value is below the original cost, the more conservative market value is used. The latter situation often occurs in the computer industry.

Study Note

Expensing a long-term asset in the period of purchase is not an alternative allowed under GAAP.

Conservatism can be a useful tool in doubtful cases, but when it is abused, it can lead to incorrect and misleading financial statements. For example, there is no uncertainty about how a long-term asset of material cost should be treated. When conservatism is used to justify expensing such an asset in the period of purchase, income and assets for the current period will be understated, and income in future periods will be overstated. Its cost should be recorded as an asset and spread over the useful life of the asset, as explained in Chapter 3. Accountants therefore depend on the conservatism convention only when uncertain about which accounting procedure to use.

Full Disclosure

The convention of **full disclosure** requires that financial statements present all the information relevant to users' understanding of the statements. That is, the statements must offer any explanation needed to keep them from being misleading. Explanatory notes are therefore an integral part of the financial statements. For instance, as we have already mentioned, the notes should disclose any change that a company has made in its accounting procedures.

A company must also disclose significant events arising after the balance sheet date in the financial statements. Suppose a firm has purchased a piece of land for a future subdivision. Shortly after the end of its fiscal year, the firm is served papers to halt construction because the Environmental Protection Agency asserts that the land was once a toxic waste dump. This information, which obviously affects the users of the financial statements, must be disclosed in the statements for the fiscal year just ended.

Additional note disclosures required by the FASB and other official bodies include the accounting procedures used in preparing the financial statements; and important terms of a company's debt, commitments, and contingencies. However, the statements can become so cluttered with notes that they impede rather than help understanding. Beyond the required disclosures, the application of the full-disclosure convention is based on the judgment of management and of the accountants who prepare the financial statements.

In recent years, investors and creditors also have had an influence on full disclosure. To protect them, independent auditors, the stock exchanges, and the SEC have made more demands for disclosure by publicly owned companies. The SEC has pushed especially hard for the enforcement of full disclosure. As a result, more and better information about corporations is available to the public today than ever before.

Cost-Benefit

The **cost-benefit** convention holds that the benefits to be gained from providing accounting information should be greater than the costs of providing it. Of course, minimum levels of relevance and reliability must be reached if accounting information is to be useful. Beyond the minimum levels, however, it is up to the FASB and the SEC, which stipulate the information that must be reported, and the accountant, who provides the information, to judge the costs and benefits in each case.

Firms use the cost-benefit convention for both accounting and nonaccounting decisions. Department stores could almost completely eliminate shoplifting if they hired five times as many clerks as they now have and assigned them to watching customers. The benefit would be reduced shoplifting. The cost would be reduced sales (customers do not like being closely watched) and increased wages expense. Although shoplifting is a serious problem for department stores, the benefit of reducing shoplifting in this way does not outweigh the cost.

FOCUS ON BUSINESS PRACTICE

When Is "Full Disclosure" Too Much? It's a Matter of Cost and Benefits.

The large accounting firm of **Ernst & Young** reported that over a 20-year period, the total number of pages in the annual reports of 25 large, well-known companies increased an average of 84 percent, and the number of pages of notes increased 325 percent—from 4 to 17 pages. Management's discussion and analysis increased 300 percent, from 3 pages to 12.[10] Because some people feel that "these documents are so daunting that people don't read them at all," the SEC allows companies to issue to the public "summary reports" in which the bulk of the notes can be reduced.

Although more accessible and less costly, summary reports are controversial because many analysts feel that it is in the notes that one gets the detailed information necessary to understand complex business operations. One analyst remarked, "To banish the notes for fear they will turn off readers would be like eliminating fractions from math books on the theory that the average student prefers to work with whole numbers."[11] Where this controversy will end, nobody knows. Detailed reports still must be filed with the SEC, but more and more companies are providing summary reports to the public.

The costs and benefits of a requirement for accounting disclosure are both immediate and deferred. Judging the final costs and benefits of a far-reaching and costly requirement for accounting disclosure is difficult. For instance, the FASB allows certain large companies to make a supplemental disclosure in their financial statements of the effects of changes in consumer price levels. Most companies choose not to present this information because they believe the costs of producing and providing it exceed its benefits to the readers of their financial statements. Cost-benefit is a question that the FASB, SEC, and all other regulators face. Even though there are no definitive ways of measuring costs and benefits, much of an accountant's work deals with these concepts.

S T O P • R E V I E W • A P P L Y

2-1. What are accounting conventions, and why are they important to users of financial statements?

2-2. Explain how each of the five accounting conventions helps users interpret financial information.

Examples of Accounting Conventions   Each item in the numbered list below pertains to one of the five accounting conventions listed on the right. Match each item to the letter of the appropriate convention.

1. A note to the financial statements explains the company's method of revenue recognition.

2. Inventory is accounted for at its market value, which is less than its original cost.

3. A company uses the same method of revenue recognition year after year.

4. Several accounts are grouped into one category because the total amount of each account is small.

5. A company does not keep detailed records of certain operations because the information gained from the detail is not deemed useful.

a. Comparability and consistency

b. Materiality

c. Conservatism

d. Full disclosure

e. Cost-benefit

SOLUTION

1. d   2. c   3. a   4. b   5. e

Classified Balance Sheet

LO3   Identify and describe the basic components of a classified balance sheet.

As you know, a balance sheet presents a company's financial position at a particular time. The balance sheets we have presented thus far categorize accounts as assets, liabilities, and stockholders' equity. Because even a fairly small company can have hundreds of accounts, simply listing accounts in these broad categories is not particularly helpful to a statement user. Setting up subcategories within the major categories can make financial statements much more useful. This format enables investors and creditors to study and evaluate relationships among the subcategories.

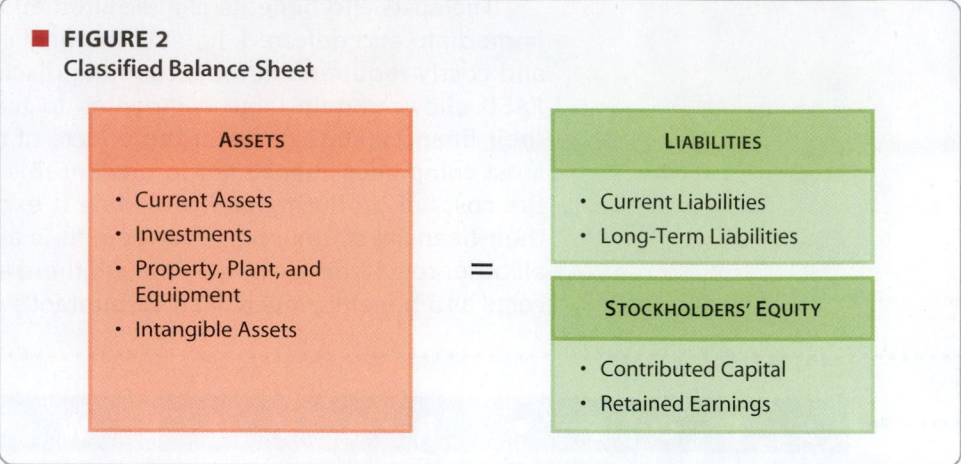

■ **FIGURE 2**
Classified Balance Sheet

ASSETS
• Current Assets
• Investments
• Property, Plant, and Equipment
• Intangible Assets

=

LIABILITIES
• Current Liabilities
• Long-Term Liabilities

STOCKHOLDERS' EQUITY
• Contributed Capital
• Retained Earnings

General-purpose external financial statements that are divided into sub-categories are called **classified financial statements**. Figure 2 depicts the sub-categories into which assets, liabilities, and stockholders' equity are usually broken down.

The subcategories of Ling Auto Supply Corporation's classified balance sheet, shown in Exhibit 1, typify those used by most corporations in the United States. The subcategories under stockholders' equity would, of course, be different if Ling Auto Supply was a sole proprietorship or partnership rather than a corporation.

Assets

As you can see in Exhibit 1, the classified balance sheet of a U.S. company typically divides assets into four categories:

1. Current assets

2. Investments

3. Property, plant, and equipment

4. Intangible assets

These categories are listed in the order of their presumed ease of conversion into cash. For example, current assets are usually more easily converted to cash than are property, plant, and equipment. For simplicity, some companies group investments, intangible assets, and other miscellaneous assets into a category called **other assets**.

FOCUS ON BUSINESS PRACTICE
There's More Than One Way to Balance a Balance Sheet.

In the United Kingdom and in countries influenced by U.K. practices, such as Australia and South Africa, some companies use a balance sheet formula that differs from the one used in the United States. Instead of equating total assets with total liabilities and stockholders' equity (A = L + SE), these companies equate net worth with stockholders' equity in the following way:

Total Assets − Total Liabilities = Net Worth = Stockholders' Equity

Interestingly, in contrast to U.S. practice, the accounts in the total assets category are listed from least liquid to most liquid. Long-term assets are listed first and start with intangible assets; current assets are listed last and end with Cash.

EXHIBIT 1 ▶ | Classified Balance Sheet for Ling Auto Supply Corporation

Ling Auto Supply Corporation
Balance Sheet
December 31, 20xx

Assets

Current assets

Cash		$ 20,720	
Short-term investments		4,000	
Notes receivable		16,000	
Accounts receivable		70,600	
Merchandise inventory		120,800	
Prepaid insurance		13,200	
Supplies		3,392	
Total current assets			$248,712

Investments

Land held for future use			10,000

Property, plant, and equipment

Land		$ 9,000	
Building	$41,300		
Less accumulated depreciation	17,280	24,020	
Equipment	$54,000		
Less accumulated depreciation	28,900	25,100	
Total property, plant, and equipment			58,120

Intangible assets

Trademark			1,000
Total assets			$317,832

Liabilities

Current liabilities

Notes payable		$ 30,000
Accounts payable		51,366
Salaries payable		4,000
Total current liabilities		$ 85,366

Long-term liabilities

Mortgage payable		35,600
Total liabilities		$120,966

Stockholders' Equity

Contributed capital

Common stock, $20 par value, 5,000 shares authorized, issued, and outstanding		$100,000
Additional paid-in capital		20,000
Total contributed capital		$120,000
Retained earnings		76,866
Total stockholders' equity		196,866
Total liabilities and stockholders' equity		$317,832

Current Assets

Current assets are cash and other assets that a company can reasonably expect to convert to cash, sell, or consume within one year or its *normal operating cycle*, whichever is longer. A company's **normal operating cycle** is the average time it needs to go from spending cash to receiving cash. For example, suppose a company uses cash to buy inventory and sells the inventory to a customer on credit. The resulting receivable must be collected in cash before the normal operating cycle ends.

The normal operating cycle for most companies is less than one year, but there are exceptions. For example, because of the length of time it takes **The Boeing Company** to build aircraft, its normal operating cycle exceeds one year. The inventory used in building the planes is nonetheless considered a current asset because the planes will be sold within the normal operating cycle. Another example is a company that sells on an installment basis. The payments for a television set or a refrigerator can extend over 24 or 36 months, but these receivables are still considered current assets.

Cash is obviously a current asset. Short-term investments, notes and accounts receivable, and inventory that a company expects to convert to cash within the next year or the normal operating cycle are also current assets. On the balance sheet, they are listed in the order of their ease of conversion to cash.

Prepaid expenses, such as rent and insurance paid in advance, and inventories of supplies bought for use rather than for sale should be classified as current assets. These assets are current in the sense that if they had not been bought earlier, a current outlay of cash would be needed to obtain them.

In deciding whether an asset is current or noncurrent, the idea of "reasonable expectation" is important. For example, Short-Term Investments, also called *Marketable Securities*, is an account used for temporary investments, such as U.S. Treasury bills, of "idle" cash—that is, cash that is not immediately required for operating purposes. Management can reasonably expect to sell these securities as cash needs arise over the next year or within the company's current operating cycle. Investments in securities that management does not expect to sell within the next year and that do not involve the temporary use of idle cash should be shown in the investments category of a classified balance sheet.

Investments

The **investments** category includes assets, usually long term, that are not used in normal business operations and that management does not plan to convert to cash within the next year. Items in this category are securities held for long-term investment, long-term notes receivable, land held for future use, plant or equipment not used in the business, and special funds established to pay off a debt or buy a building. Also included are large permanent investments in another company for the purpose of controlling that company.

> *Study Note*
>
> For an investment to be classified as current, management must expect to sell it within the next year or the current operating cycle, so it must be readily marketable.

Property, Plant, and Equipment

Property, plant, and equipment are tangible long-term assets used in a business's day-to-day operations. They represent a place to operate (land and buildings) and the equipment used to produce, sell, and deliver goods or services. They are therefore also called *operating assets* or, sometimes, *fixed assets, tangible assets, long-lived assets,* or *plant assets*. Through depreciation, the costs of these assets (except land) are spread over the periods they benefit. Past depreciation is recorded in the Accumulated Depreciation accounts.

To reduce clutter on the balance sheet, property, plant, and equipment are often combined—for example:

Property, plant, and equipment (net) $58,120

The company provides the details in a note to the financial statements.

The property, plant, and equipment category also includes natural resources owned by the company, such as forest lands, oil and gas properties, and coal mines, if they are used in the regular course of business. If they are not, they are listed in the investments category.

Intangible Assets

Intangible assets are long-term assets with no physical substance whose value stems from the rights or privileges they extend to their owners. Examples are patents, copyrights, goodwill, franchises, and trademarks. These assets are recorded at cost, which is spread over the expected life of the right or privilege. Goodwill, which arises in an acquisition of another company, is an intangible asset that is recorded at cost but is not amortized. It is reviewed each year for possible loss of value.

Liabilities

Liabilities are divided into two categories that are based on when the liabilities fall due: current liabilities and long-term liabilities.

Current Liabilities

Current liabilities are obligations that must be satisfied within one year or within the company's normal operating cycle, whichever is longer. These liabilities are typically paid out of current assets or by incurring new short-term liabilities. They include notes payable, accounts payable, the current portion of long-term debt, salaries and wages payable, taxes payable, and customer advances (unearned revenues).

Long-Term Liabilities

Debts that fall due more than one year in the future or beyond the normal operating cycle, which will be paid out of noncurrent assets, are **long-term liabilities**. Mortgages payable, long-term notes, bonds payable, employee pension obligations, and long-term lease liabilities generally fall into this category. Deferred income taxes are often disclosed as a separate category in the long-term liability section of the balance sheet of publicly held corporations. This liability arises because the rules for measuring income for tax purposes differ from those for financial reporting. The cumulative annual difference between the income taxes payable to governments and the income taxes expense reported on the income statement is included in the account Deferred Income Taxes.

Study Note

The portion of a mortgage that is due during the next year or the current operating cycle would be classified as a current liability; the portion due after the next year or the current operating cycle would be classified as a long-term liability.

Stockholders' Equity

As you know, corporations are owned by their stockholders and are separate legal entities. Exhibit 1 shows the stockholders' equity section of a corporation's balance sheet. This section has two parts: contributed capital and retained earnings. Generally, contributed capital is shown on a corporate balance sheet as two amounts: the par value of the issued stock, and additional paid-in capital, which is the amount paid in above par value.

Owner's Equity and Partners' Equity

Although the form of business organization does not usually affect the accounting treatment of assets and liabilities, the equity section of the balance sheet of a sole proprietorship or partnership is very different from the equity section of a corporation's balance sheet.

Sole Proprietorship The equity section of a sole proprietorship's balance sheet simply shows the capital in the owner's name at an amount equal to the net assets of the company. It might appear as follows:

Owner's Equity

Thomas Ling, Capital $196,866

EXHIBIT 2 ▶

Classified Balance Sheet for Dell Computer Corporation

Dell Computer Corporation
Consolidated Statement of Financial Position
(In millions)

	January 30, 2004	January 31, 2003
Assets		
Current assets:		
Cash and cash equivalents	$ 4,317	$ 4,232
Short-term investments	835	406
Accounts receivable, net	3,635	2,586
Inventories	327	306
Other	1,519	1,394
Total current assets	10,633	8,924
Property, plant, and equipment, net	1,517	913
Investments	6,770	5,267
Other non-current assets	391	366
Total assets	$19,311	$15,470
Liabilities and Stockholders' Equity		
Current liabilities:		
Accounts payable	$ 7,316	$ 5,989
Accrued and other	3,580	2,944
Total current liabilities	10,896	8,933
Long-term debt	505	506
Other non-current liabilities	1,630	1,158
Commitments and contingent liabilities (Note 7)	—	—
Total liabilities	13,031	10,597
Stockholders' equity:		
Preferred stock and capital in excess of $.01 par value; shares issued and outstanding: none	—	—
Common stock and capital in excess of $.01 par value; shares authorized: 7,000; shares issued: 2,721 and 2,681 respectively	6,823	6,018
Treasury stock, at cost; 165 and 102 shares, respectively	(6,539)	(4,539)
Retained earnings	6,131	3,486
Other comprehensive loss	(83)	(33)
Other	(52)	(59)
Total stockholders' equity	6,280	4,873
Total liabilities and stockholders' equity	$19,311	$15,470

Source: Dell Computer Corporation, *Annual Report*, 2004.

Because in a sole proprietorship, there is no legal separation between the owner and the business, there is no need to separate contributed capital from earnings retained for use in the business. The Capital account is increased by both the owner's investments and net income. It is decreased by net losses and withdrawals of assets from the business for personal use by the owner. In this kind of business, the formality of declaring and paying dividends is not required.

In fact, the terms *owner's equity*, *proprietorship*, *capital*, and *net worth* are used interchangeably. They all stand for the owner's interest in the company. The first three terms are preferred to *net worth* because most assets are recorded at original cost rather than at current value. For this reason, the ownership section does not represent "worth." It is really a claim against the assets of the company.

Partnership   The equity section of a partnership's balance sheet is called *partners' equity*. It is much like that of a sole proprietorship's balance sheet. It might appear as follows:

Partners' Equity

A. J. Martin, Capital	$ 84,375	
Thomas Ling, Capital	112,491	
Total partners' equity		$196,866

Dell's Balance Sheets

Although balance sheets generally resemble the one shown in Exhibit 1 for Ling Auto Supply Corporation, no two companies have financial statements that are exactly alike. The balance sheet of **Dell Computer Corporation** is a good example of some of the variations. As shown in Exhibit 2, it provides data for two years so that users can evaluate the change from one year to the next. Note that its major classifications are similar but not identical to those of Ling Auto Supply. For instance, Ling Auto Supply has asset categories for investments and intangibles, and Dell has an asset category called "other non-current assets," which is a small amount of its total assets. Also note that Dell has a category called "other non-current liabilities." Because this category is listed after long-term debt, it represents longer-term liabilities, due more than one year after the balance sheet date.

Dell's stockholders' equity section also differs from that of Ling Auto Supply in that it subtracts a category called "other" from common stock, treasury stock, retained earnings, and other comprehensive loss.

STOP • REVIEW • APPLY

3-1. What purpose do classified financial statements serve?

3-2. What are four common categories of assets on a classified balance sheet?

3-3. What criteria must an asset meet to be classified as current? Under what condition is an asset considered current even if it will not be realized as cash within a year? What are two examples of assets that fall into this category?

3-4. In what order should current assets be listed?

3-5. What is the difference between a short-term investment in the current assets section of a balance sheet and a security in the investments section?

3-6. What is an intangible asset? Give at least three examples.

3-7. Name the two major categories of liabilities.

3-8. What are the primary differences between the equity section of the balance sheet of a sole proprietorship or partnership and the equity section of a corporation's balance sheet?

Balance Sheet Classifications   The lettered items below represent a classification scheme for a balance sheet. The numbered items are account titles. Match each account with the letter of the category in which it belongs, or indicate that it does not appear on the balance sheet.

a. Current assets

b. Investments

c. Property, plant, and equipment

d. Intangible assets

e. Current liabilities

f. Long-term liabilities

g. Stockholders' equity

h. Not on balance sheet

1. Trademark

2. Marketable Securities

3. Land Held for Future Use

4. Taxes Payable

5. Bond Payable in Five Years

6. Common Stock

7. Land Used in Operations

8. Accumulated Depreciation

9. Accounts Receivable

10. Interest Expense

11. Unearned Revenue

12. Prepaid Rent

SOLUTION

1. d		7. c	
2. a		8. c	
3. b		9. a	
4. e		10. h	
5. f		11. e	
6. g		12. a	

Forms of the Income Statement

LO4   Describe the features of multistep and single-step classified income statements.

In the income statements we have presented thus far, expenses have been deducted from revenue in a single step to arrive at net income. Here, we look at a multistep income statement and a single-step format more complex than the one we presented in earlier chapters.

Multistep Income Statement

A **multistep income statement** goes through a series of steps, or subtotals, to arrive at net income. Figure 3 compares the multistep income statement of a

■ **FIGURE 3**

The Components of Multistep Income Statements for Service and Merchandising or Manufacturing Companies

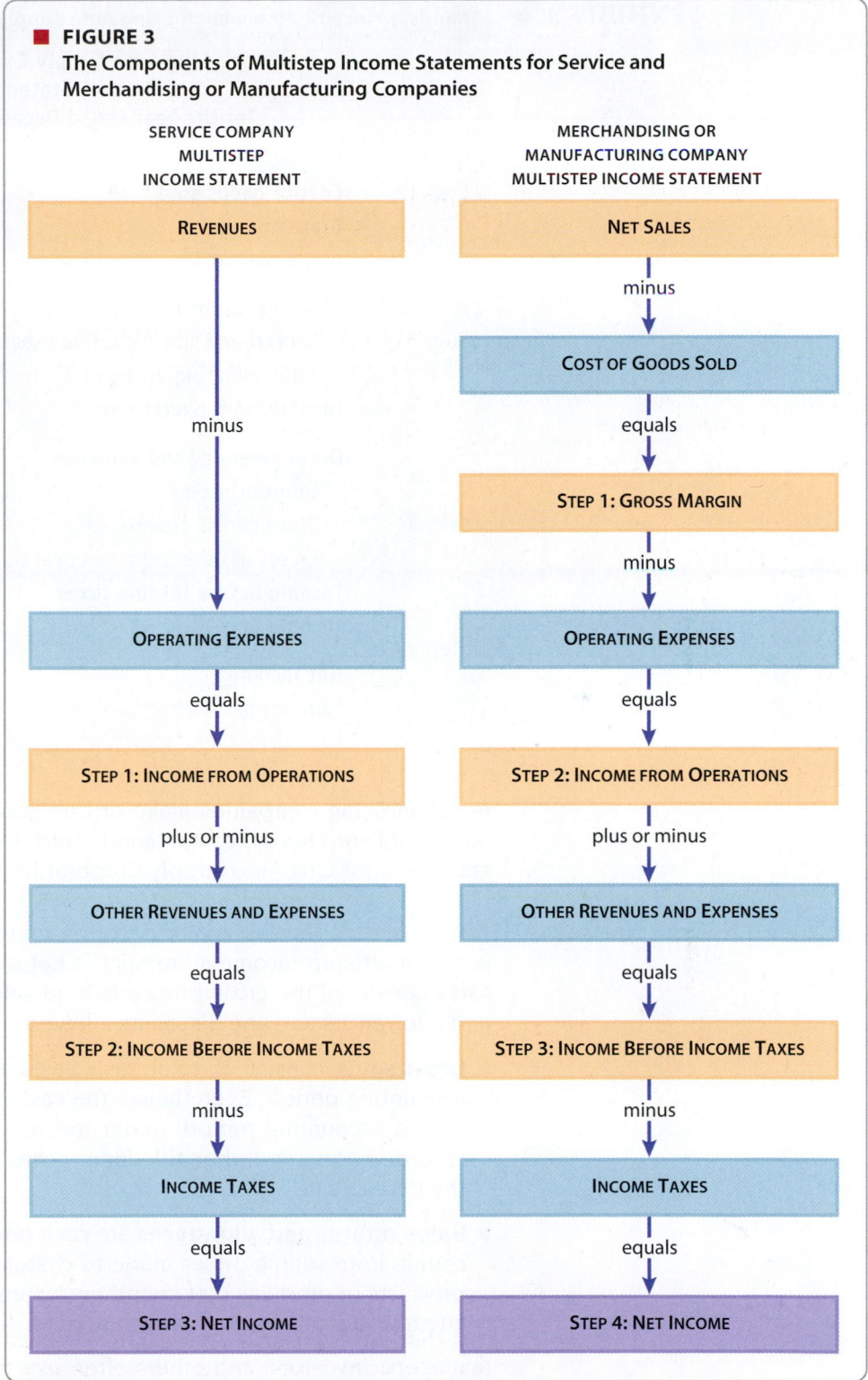

service company with that of a **merchandising company**, which buys and sells products, and a **manufacturing company**, which makes and sells products.

As you can see in Figure 3, in a service company's multistep income statement, the operating expenses are deducted from revenues in a single step to arrive at income from operations. In contrast, because manufacturing and

EXHIBIT 3 ▶

Multistep Income Statement for Ling Auto Supply Corporation

Ling Auto Supply Corporation
Income Statement
For the Year Ended December 31, 20xx

Step 1	Net sales		$579,312
	Cost of goods sold		362,520
	Gross margin		$216,792
	Operating expenses		
Step 2	Selling expenses	$109,560	
	General and administrative expenses	69,008	
	Total operating expenses		178,568
	Income from operations		$ 38,224
	Other revenues and expenses		
Step 3	Interest income	$ 2,800	
	Less interest expense	5,262	
	Excess of other expenses over other revenues		2,462
	Income before income taxes		$ 35,762
Step 4	Income taxes		6,762
	Net income		$ 29,000
	Earnings per share		$ 5.80

merchandising companies make or buy goods for sale, they must include an additional step for the cost of goods sold. Exhibit 3 shows a multistep income statement for Ling Auto Supply Corporation, a merchandising company.

Net Sales   The first major part of a merchandising or manufacturing company's multistep income statement is **net sales**, often simply called *sales*. Net sales consist of the gross proceeds from sales (gross sales) less sales returns and allowances and any discounts allowed.

▶ **Gross sales** consist of total cash sales and total credit sales during an accounting period. Even though the cash may not be collected until the following accounting period, under the revenue recognition rule, revenue is recorded as earned when title for merchandise passes from seller to buyer at the time of sale.

▶ **Sales returns and allowances** are cash refunds, credits on account, and discounts from selling prices made to customers who have received defective products or products that are otherwise unsatisfactory. If other discounts are given to customers, they also should be deducted from gross sales.

Managers, investors, and others often use the amount of sales and trends in sales as indicators of a firm's progress. To detect trends, they compare the net sales of different accounting periods. Increasing sales suggest growth; decreasing sales indicate the possibility of decreased future earnings and other financial problems.

 **Study Note**

The matching rule precludes the cost of inventory from being expensed until the inventory has been sold.

Cost of Goods Sold   The second part of a multistep income statement for a merchandiser or manufacturer is **cost of goods sold**, also called *cost of sales*.

Cost of goods sold (an expense) is the amount a merchandiser paid for the merchandise it sold during an accounting period. For a manufacturer, it is the cost of making the products it sold during an accounting period.

Gross Margin

The third major part of a multistep income statement for a merchandiser or manufacturer is **gross margin**, or *gross profit*, which is the difference between net sales and the cost of goods sold (Step 1 in Exhibit 3). To be successful, companies must achieve a gross margin sufficient to cover operating expenses and provide an adequate after-tax income.

Managers are interested in both the amount and percentage of gross margin. The percentage is computed by dividing the amount of gross margin by net sales. In the case of Ling Auto Supply Corporation, the amount of gross margin is $216,792, and the percentage of gross margin is 37.4 percent ($216,792 ÷ $579,312). This information is useful in planning business operations. For instance, management may try to increase total sales by reducing the selling price. Although this strategy reduces the percentage of gross margin, it will work if the total of items sold increases enough to raise the absolute amount of gross margin. This is the strategy followed by discount warehouse stores like **Sam's Club** and **Costco Wholesale Corporation**.

On the other hand, management may decide to keep a high gross margin from sales and try to increase sales and the amount of gross margin by increasing operating expenses, such as advertising. This is the strategy used by upscale specialty stores like **Neiman Marcus** and **Tiffany & Co**.

Other strategies to increase gross margin from sales include using better purchasing methods to reduce cost of goods sold.

Operating Expenses

Operating expenses—expenses incurred in running a business other than the cost of goods sold—are the next major part of a multistep income statement. Operating expenses are often grouped into the categories of selling expenses and general and administrative expenses.

- Selling expenses include the costs of storing goods and preparing them for sale; preparing displays, advertising, and otherwise promoting sales; and delivering goods to a buyer if the seller has agreed to pay the cost of delivery.

- General and administrative expenses include expenses for accounting, personnel, credit checking, collections, and any other expenses that apply to overall operations. Although occupancy expenses, such as rent expense, insurance expense, and utilities expense, are often classified as general and administrative expenses, they can also be allocated between selling expenses and general and administrative expenses.

Careful planning and control of operating expenses can improve a company's profitability.

Income from Operations

Income from operations, or *operating income*, is the difference between gross margin and operating expenses (Step 2 in Exhibit 3). It represents the income from a company's main business. Income from operations is often used to compare the profitability of two or more companies or divisions within a company.

Other Revenues and Expenses

Other revenues and expenses, also called *nonoperating revenues and expenses*, are not related to a company's operating

---

Study Note

Gross margin is an important measure of profitability. When it is less than operating expenses, the company has suffered a net loss from operations.

Study Note

The most common operating expenses are selling expenses and general and administrative expenses. They are deducted from gross margin on the income statement.

activities. This section of a multistep income statement includes revenues from investments (such as dividends and interest on stocks, bonds, and savings accounts) and interest earned on credit or notes extended to customers. It also includes interest expense and other expenses that result from borrowing money or from credit extended to the company. If a company has other kinds of revenues and expenses not related to its normal business operations, they, too, are included in this part of the income statement.

An analyst who wants to compare two companies independent of their financing methods—that is, *before* considering other revenues and expenses— would focus on income from operations.

Income Before Income Taxes

Income before income taxes is the amount a company has earned from all activities—operating and nonoperating—before taking into account the amount of income taxes it incurred (Step 3 in Exhibit 3). Because companies may be subject to different income tax rates, income before income taxes is often used to compare the profitability of two or more companies or divisions within a company.

Income Taxes

Income taxes, also called *provision for income taxes*, represent the expense for federal, state, and local taxes on corporate income. Income taxes are shown as a separate item on the income statement. Usually, the word *expense* is not used on the statement. Income taxes do not appear on the income statements of sole proprietorships and partnerships because the individuals who own these businesses are the tax-paying units; they pay income taxes on their share of the business income. Corporations, however, must report and pay income taxes on their earnings.

Because federal, state, and local income taxes for corporations are substantial, they have a significant effect on business decisions. Current federal income tax rates for corporations vary from 15 percent to 35 percent depending on the amount of income before income taxes and other factors. Most other taxes, such as property and employment taxes, are included in operating expenses.

Net Income

Net income is the final figure, or "bottom line," of an income statement. It is what remains of gross margin after operating expenses have been deducted, other revenues and expenses have been added or deducted, and income taxes have been deducted (Step 4 in Exhibit 3).

Net income is an important performance measure because it represents the amount of earnings that accrue to stockholders. It is the amount transferred to retained earnings from all the income that business operations have generated during an accounting period. Both managers and investors often use net income to measure a business's financial performance over the past accounting period.

Earnings per Share

Earnings per share, often called *net income per share*, is the net income earned on each share of common stock. Shares of stock represent ownership in corporations, and the net income per share is reported immediately below net income on the income statement. In the simplest case, it is computed by dividing the net income by the average number of shares of common stock outstanding during the year. For example, Ling Auto Supply Corporation's earnings per share of $5.80 was computed by dividing the net

▼ **EXHIBIT 4**

Multistep Income Statement for Dell Computer Corporation

Dell Computer Corporation
Consolidated Statement of Income
(In millions, except per share amounts)

	Fiscal Year Ended		
	January 30, 2004	January 31, 2003	February 1, 2002
Net revenue	$41,444	$35,404	$31,168
Cost of revenue	33,892	29,055	25,661
Gross margin	7,552	6,349	5,507
Operating expenses:			
Selling, general and administration	3,544	3,050	2,784
Research, development and engineering	464	455	452
Special charges	—	—	482
Total operating expenses	4,008	3,505	3,718
Operating income	3,544	2,844	1,789
Investment and other income (loss), net	180	183	(58)
Income before income taxes	3,724	3,027	1,731
Income tax provision	1,079	905	485
Net income	$ 2,645	$ 2,122	$ 1,246

Source: Dell Computer Corporation, *Annual Report*, 2004.

income of $29,000 by the 5,000 shares of common stock outstanding (see the stockholders' equity section in Exhibit 1). Investors find the figure useful as a quick way of assessing both a company's profitability and its earnings in relation to the market price of its stock.

Dell's Income Statements

Like balance sheets, income statements vary among companies. You will rarely, if ever, find an income statement exactly like the one we have presented for Ling Auto Supply Corporation. Companies use both different terms and different structures. For example, as you can see in Exhibit 4, in its multistep income statement, **Dell Computer Corporation** provided three years of data for purposes of comparison.

Single-Step Income Statement

Study Note

If you encounter income statement components not covered in this chapter, refer to the index at the end of the book to find the topic and read about it.

Exhibit 5 shows a **single-step income statement** for Ling Auto Supply Corporation. In this type of statement, income before income taxes is derived in a single step by putting the major categories of revenues in the first part of the statement and the major categories of costs and expenses in the second part. Income taxes are shown as a separate item, as on the multistep income statement. Both the multistep form and the single-step form have advantages: the multistep form shows the components used in deriving net income, and the single-step form has the advantage of simplicity.

EXHIBIT 5 ▶ | **Single-Step Income Statement for Ling Auto Supply Corporation**

Ling Auto Supply Corporation
Income Statement
For the Year Ended December 31, 20xx

Revenues		
Net sales		$579,312
Interest income		2,800
Total revenues		$582,112
Costs and expenses		
Cost of goods sold	$362,520	
Selling expenses	109,560	
General and administrative expenses	69,008	
Interest expense	5,262	
Total costs and expenses		546,350
Income before income taxes		$ 35,762
Income taxes		6,762
Net income		$ 29,000
Earnings per share		$ 5.80

S T O P • R E V I E W • A P P L Y

4-1. What is the primary difference between the operations of a merchandising business and those of a service business? How is this difference reflected on the income statement?

4-2. Define *gross margin*. Why is it important?

4-3. Why are other revenues and expenses separated from operating revenues and expenses in a multistep income statement?

4-4. Define *earnings per share*, and describe how this figure appears on the income statement.

4-5. Explain how a multistep income statement differs from a single-step income statement. What are the merits of each form?

Income Statement Classification A classification scheme for a multistep income statement appears below, and at the top of the opposite page is a list of accounts. Match each account with the category in which it belongs, or indicate that it is not on the income statement.

a. Net sales

b. Cost of goods sold

c. Selling expenses

d. General and administrative expenses

e. Other revenues and expenses

f. Not on income statement

1. Sales Returns and allowances
2. Cost of Sales
3. Dividend Income
4. Delivery Expense
5. Office Salaries Expense

6. Wages Payable
7. Sales Salaries Expense
8. Advertising Expense
9. Interest Expense
10. Commissions Expense

SOLUTION

1. a	6. f
2. b	7. c
3. e	8. c
4. c	9. e
5. d	10. c

Using Classified Financial Statements

LO5 Use classified financial statements to evaluate liquidity and profitability.

Study Note

Accounts must be classified correctly before the ratios are computed. If they are not classified correctly, the ratios will be incorrect.

Investors and creditors base their decisions largely on their assessments of a firm's potential liquidity and profitability, and in making those assessments, they often rely on ratios. As you will see in the following pages, ratios use the components of classified financial statements to reflect how well a firm has performed in terms of maintaining liquidity and achieving profitability.

Evaluation of Liquidity

As you know, *liquidity* means having enough money on hand to pay bills when they are due and to take care of unexpected needs for cash. In an earlier chapter, we introduced the cash return on assets ratio, a liquidity measure that is computed by dividing net cash flows from operating activities by average total assets. Here, we introduce two additional measures of liquidity: working capital and the current ratio.

Working Capital **Working capital** is the amount by which current assets exceed current liabilities. It is an important measure of liquidity because current liabilities must be satisfied within one year or one operating cycle, whichever is longer, and current assets are used to pay the current liabilities. Thus, the excess of current assets over current liabilities—the working capital—is what is on hand to continue business operations.

For Ling Auto Supply Corporation, working capital is computed as follows:

Current assets	$248,712
Less current liabilities	85,366
Working capital	$163,346

Working capital can be used to buy inventory, obtain credit, and finance expanded sales. Lack of working capital can lead to a company's failure.

Current Ratio The current ratio is closely related to working capital. Many bankers and other creditors believe it is a good indicator of a company's ability

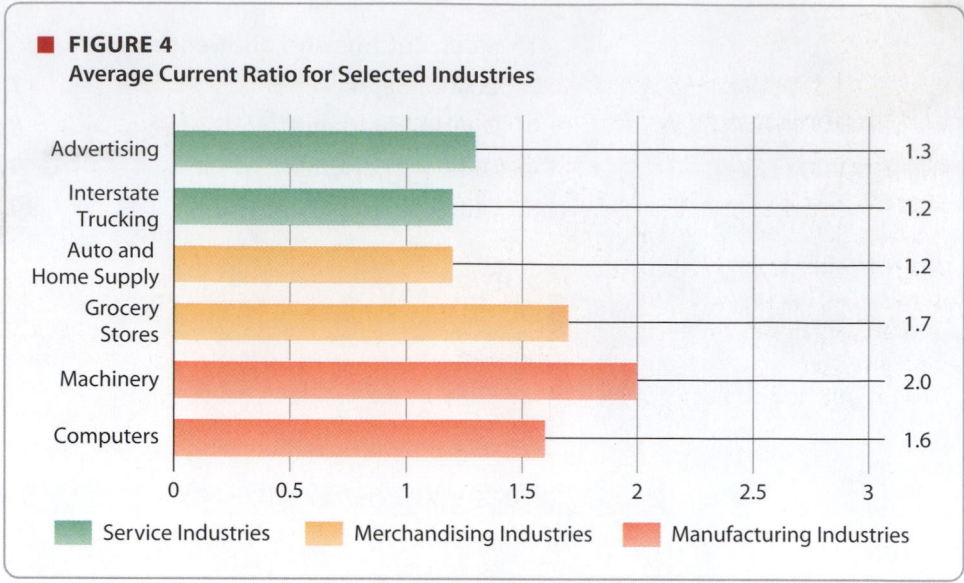

■ FIGURE 4
Average Current Ratio for Selected Industries

Service Industries · Merchandising Industries · Manufacturing Industries

Source: Data from Dun & Bradstreet, *Industry Norms and Key Business Ratios,* 2003–2004

to pay its debts on time. The **current ratio** is the ratio of current assets to current liabilities. For Ling Auto Supply Corporation, it is computed like this:

$$\text{Current Ratio} = \frac{\text{Current Assets}}{\text{Current Liabilities}} = \frac{\$248{,}712}{\$85{,}366} = 2.9$$

Thus, Ling Auto Supply has $2.90 of current assets for each $1.00 of current liabilities. Is that good or bad? The answer requires a comparison of this year's current ratio with ratios for earlier years and with similar measures for companies in the same industry.

As Figure 4 illustrates, the average current ratio varies from industry to industry. For the advertising industry, which has no merchandise inventory, the current ratio is 1.3. The auto and home supply industry, in which companies carry large merchandise inventories, has an average current ratio of 1.2. The current ratio for Ling Auto Supply Corporation, 2.9, exceeds the average for its industry.

A very low current ratio, of course, can be unfavorable, indicating that a company will not be able to pay its debts on time. But that is not always the case. For example, **McDonald's** and various other successful companies have very low current ratios because they carefully plan their cash flows.

A very high current ratio may indicate that a company is not using its assets to the best advantage. In other words, it could probably use its excess funds more effectively to increase its overall profit.

Evaluation of Profitability

Just as important as paying bills on time is *profitability*—the ability to earn a satisfactory income. As a goal, profitability competes with liquidity for managerial attention because liquid assets, although important, are not the best profit-producing resources. Cash, of course, means purchasing power, but a satisfactory profit can be made only if purchasing power is used to buy profit-producing (and less liquid) assets, such as inventory and long-term assets.

To evaluate a company's profitability, you must relate its current performance to its past performance and prospects for the future, as well as to the

averages of other companies in the same industry. The following are the ratios commonly used to evaluate a company's ability to earn income:

1. Profit margin

2. Asset turnover

3. Return on assets

4. Debt to equity ratio

5. Return on equity

In previous chapters, we introduced the profit margin and return on assets ratios. Here, we review these ratios, introduce the other profitability ratios, and show their interrelationships.

Profit Margin The **profit margin** shows the percentage of each sales dollar that results in net income. It should not be confused with gross margin, which is not a ratio but rather the amount by which revenues exceed the cost of goods sold. Ling Auto Supply Corporation has a profit margin of 5.0 percent. It is computed as follows:

$$\text{Profit Margin} = \frac{\text{Net Income}}{\text{Net Sales}} = \frac{\$29,000}{\$579,312} = .050, \text{ or } 5.0\%$$

Thus, on each dollar of net sales, Ling Auto Supply makes 5 cents. A difference of 1 or 2 percent in a company's profit margin can be the difference between a fair year and a very profitable one.

Asset Turnover The **asset turnover** ratio measures how efficiently assets are used to produce sales. In other words, it shows how many dollars of sales are generated by each dollar of assets. A company with a higher asset turnover uses its assets more productively than one with a lower asset turnover.

The asset turnover ratio is computed by dividing net sales by average total assets. Average total assets are the sum of assets at the beginning of an accounting period and at the end of the period divided by 2. For example, if Ling Auto Supply Corporation had assets of $297,240 at the beginning of the year, its asset turnover would be computed as follows:

$$\text{Asset Turnover} = \frac{\text{Net Sales}}{\text{Average Total Assets}}$$

$$= \frac{\$579,312}{(\$317,832 + \$297,240) \div 2} = \frac{\$579,312}{\$307,536} = 1.9 \text{ times}$$

Thus, Ling Auto Supply would produce $1.90 in sales for each dollar invested in assets. This ratio shows a relationship between an income statement figure (net sales) and a balance sheet figure (total assets).

Return on Assets

Both the profit margin and asset turnover ratios have limitations. The profit margin ratio does not consider the assets necessary to produce income, and the asset turnover ratio does not take into account the amount of income produced. The **return on assets** ratio overcomes these deficiencies by relating net income to average total assets. For Ling Auto Supply, it is computed like this:

$$\text{Return on Assets} = \frac{\text{Net Income}}{\text{Average Total Assets}}$$

$$= \frac{\$29,000}{(\$317,832 + \$297,240) \div 2} = \frac{\$29,000}{\$307,536} = .094, \text{ or } 9.4\%$$

For each dollar invested, Ling's assets generate 9.4 cents of net income. This ratio indicates the income-generating strength (profit margin) of the company's resources and how efficiently the company is using all its assets (asset turnover).

Return on assets, then, combines profit margin and asset turnover:

$$\frac{\text{Net Income}}{\text{Net Sales}} \times \frac{\text{Net Sales}}{\text{Average Total Assets}} = \frac{\text{Net Income}}{\text{Average Total Assets}}$$

$$\text{Profit Margin} \times \text{Asset Turnover} = \text{Return on Assets}$$

$$5.0\% \times 1.9 \text{ times} = 9.5\%^*$$

*The slight difference between 9.4 and 9.5 percent is due to rounding.

Thus, a company's management can improve overall profitability by increasing the profit margin, the asset turnover, or both. Similarly, in evaluating a company's overall profitability, a financial statement user must consider how these two ratios interact to produce return on assets.

By studying Figures 5, 6, and 7, you can see the different ways in which various industries combine profit margin and asset turnover to produce return on assets. For instance, by comparing the return on assets for grocery stores and

> **Study Note**
>
> Return on assets is one of the most widely used measures of profitability because it reflects both the profit margin and asset turnover.

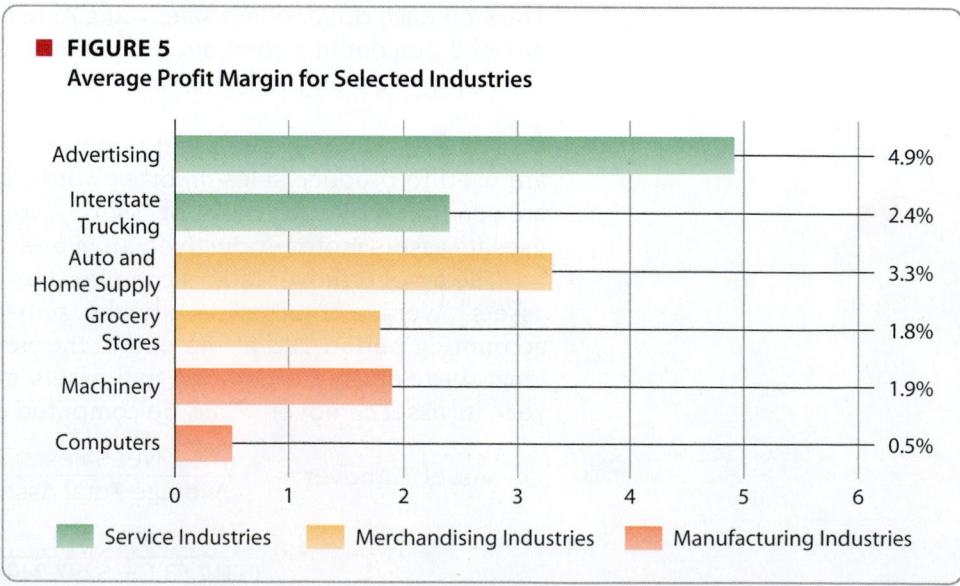

■ FIGURE 5
Average Profit Margin for Selected Industries

- Advertising — 4.9%
- Interstate Trucking — 2.4%
- Auto and Home Supply — 3.3%
- Grocery Stores — 1.8%
- Machinery — 1.9%
- Computers — 0.5%

Service Industries   Merchandising Industries   Manufacturing Industries

Source: Data from Dun & Bradstreet, *Industry Norms and Key Business Ratios, 2003–2004*

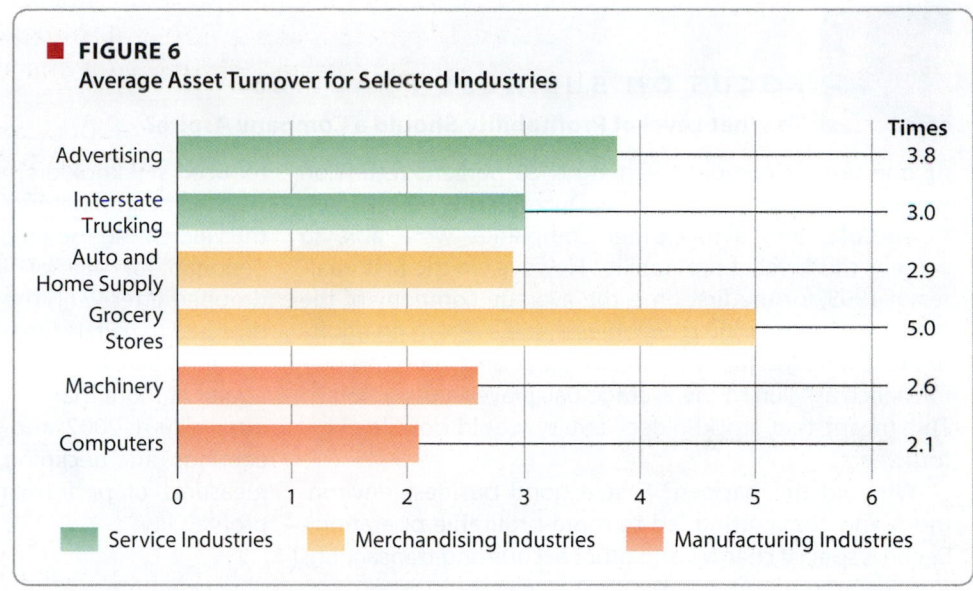

FIGURE 6
Average Asset Turnover for Selected Industries

Source: Data from Dun & Bradstreet, *Industry Norms and Key Business Ratios*, 2003–2004

auto and home supply companies, you can see how they achieve that return in very different ways. The grocery store industry has a profit margin of 1.8 percent, which when multiplied by an asset turnover of 5.0 times gives a return on assets of 9.0 percent. The auto and home supply industry has a higher profit margin, 3.3 percent, and a lower asset turnover, 2.9 times, and produces a return on assets of 9.6 percent.

Ling Auto Supply's profit margin of 5.0 percent is well above the auto and home supply industry's average, but its asset turnover of 1.9 times lags behind the industry average. Ling is sacrificing asset turnover to achieve a higher profit margin. It is not clear that this strategy is working, because Ling's return on assets of 9.4 percent is less than the industry average.

Debt to Equity Ratio Another useful measure of profitability is the **debt to equity ratio**, which shows the proportion of a company's assets that is

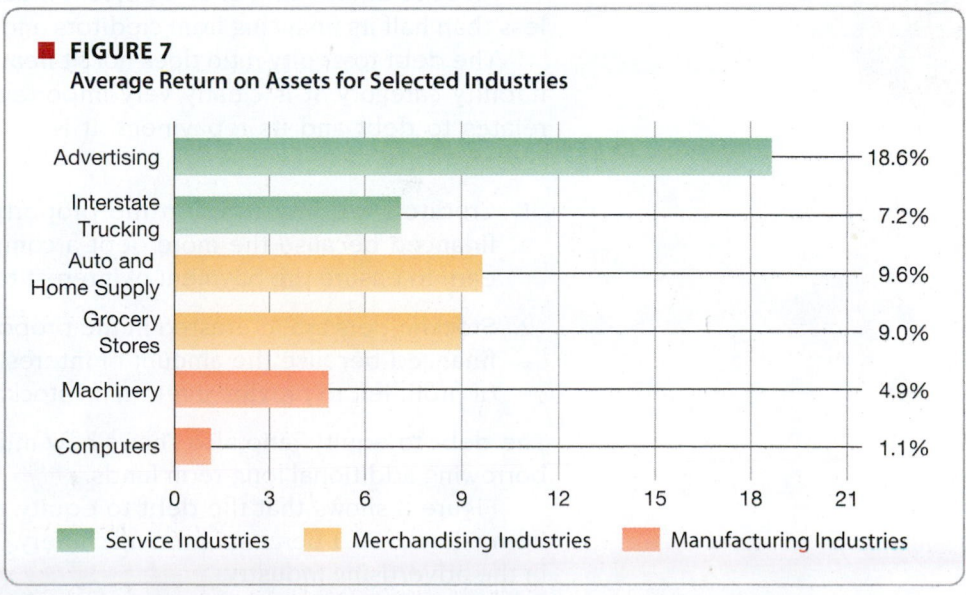

FIGURE 7
Average Return on Assets for Selected Industries

Source: Data from Dun & Bradstreet, *Industry Norms and Key Business Ratios*, 2003–2004

financed by creditors and the proportion that is financed by stockholders. This ratio is computed by dividing total liabilities by stockholders' equity. The balance sheets of most public companies do not show total liabilities; a short way of determining them is to deduct the total stockholders' equity from total assets.

A debt to equity ratio of 1.0 means that total liabilities equal stockholders' equity—that half of a company's assets are financed by creditors. A ratio of .5 means that one-third of a company's total assets are financed by creditors. A company with a high debt to equity ratio is at risk in poor economic times because it must continue to repay creditors. Stockholders' investments, on the other hand, do not have to be repaid, and dividends can be deferred when a company suffers because of a poor economy.

Ling Auto Supply's debt to equity ratio is computed as follows:

$$\text{Debt to Equity} = \frac{\text{Total Liabilities}}{\text{Stockholders' Equity}} = \frac{\$120,966}{\$196,866} = .614, \text{ or } 61.4\%$$

The debt to equity ratio of 61.4 percent means that Ling Auto Supply receives less than half its financing from creditors and more than half from investors.

The debt to equity ratio does not fit neatly into either the liquidity or profitability category. It is clearly very important to liquidity analysis because it relates to debt and its repayment. It is also relevant to profitability for two reasons:

1. Creditors are interested in the proportion of the business that is debt-financed because the more debt a company has, the more profit it must earn to ensure the payment of interest to creditors.

2. Stockholders are interested in the proportion of the business that is debt-financed because the amount of interest paid on debt affects the amount of profit left to provide a return on stockholders' investments.

The debt to equity ratio also shows how much expansion is possible through borrowing additional long-term funds.

Figure 8 shows that the debt to equity ratio in selected industries varies from a low of 90.3 percent in the machinery industry to a high of 202.4 percent in the advertising industry.

Return on equity—the ratio of net income to average stockholder's equity—is an important measure of a company's profitablility. It indicates how much stockholders have earned on their investments. At one time, Coca-Cola Company was among a few companies that earned a 20 percent return on equity.

Return on Equity   Of course, stockholders are interested in how much they have earned on their investment in the business. Their **return on equity** is measured by the ratio of net income to average stockholders' equity. Taking the ending stockholders' equity from the balance sheet and assuming that beginning stockholders' equity is $201,106, Ling Auto Supply Corporation's return on equity is computed as follows:

$$\text{Return on Equity} = \frac{\text{Net Income}}{\text{Average Stockholder's Equity}}$$

$$= \frac{\$29,000}{(\$196,866 + \$201,106) \div 2} = \frac{\$29,000}{\$198,986} = .146, \text{ or } 14.6\%$$

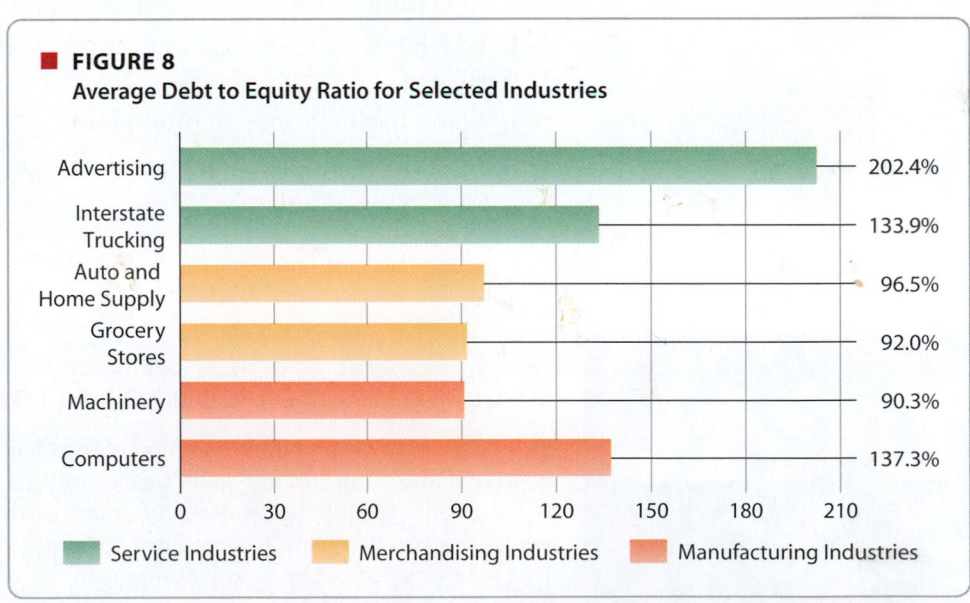

■ **FIGURE 8**
Average Debt to Equity Ratio for Selected Industries

Industry	Ratio
Advertising	202.4%
Interstate Trucking	133.9%
Auto and Home Supply	96.5%
Grocery Stores	92.0%
Machinery	90.3%
Computers	137.3%

Service Industries   Merchandising Industries   Manufacturing Industries

Source: Data from Dun & Bradstreet, *Industry Norms and Key Business Ratios,* 2003–2004

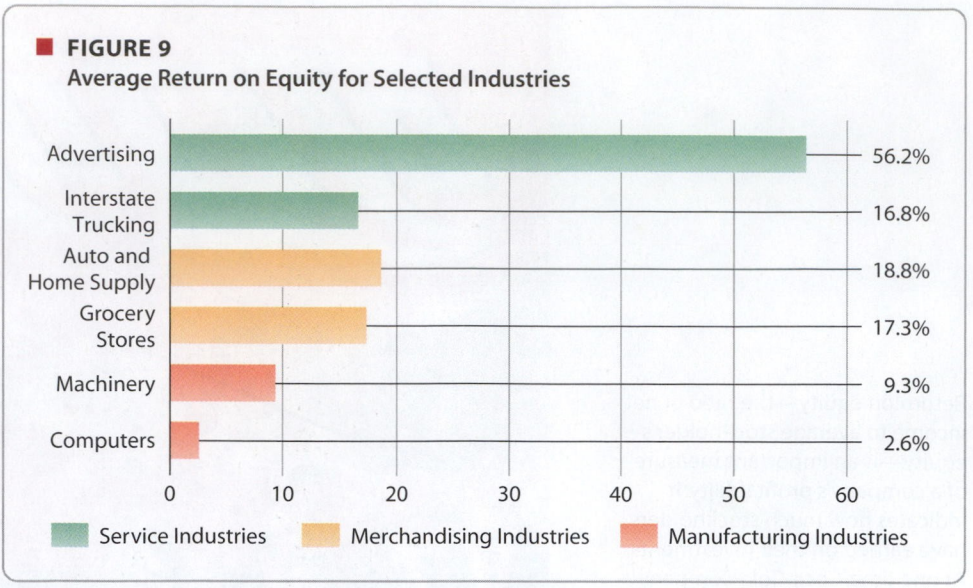

FIGURE 9
Average Return on Equity for Selected Industries

Advertising	56.2%
Interstate Trucking	16.8%
Auto and Home Supply	18.8%
Grocery Stores	17.3%
Machinery	9.3%
Computers	2.6%

Service Industries   Merchandising Industries   Manufacturing Industries

Source: **Data from Dun & Bradstreet,** *Industry Norms and Key Business Ratios,* 2003–2004

Thus, in 20xx, Ling earned 14.6 cents for every dollar invested by stockholders. Whether this is an acceptable return depends on several factors, such as how much the company earned in previous years and how much other companies in the same industry earned. As measured by return on equity, the advertising industry is the most profitable of our sample industries, with a return on equity of 56.2 percent (see Figure 9). Ling Auto Supply Corporation's average return on equity of 14.6 percent is less than the average of 18.8 percent for the auto and home supply industry.

S T O P • R E V I E W • A P P L Y

5-1. Define *liquidity*, and name two measures of liquidity.

5-2. How is the current ratio computed, and why is it important?

5-3. Which is the more important goal, liquidity or profitability? Explain your answer.

5-4. Name five measures of profitability.

5-5. What is the relationship among profit margin, asset turnover, and return on assets?

A LOOK BACK AT

DELL COMPUTER CORPORATION

In the Decision Point at the beginning of the chapter, we noted that **Dell's** objective is "to maximize stockholder value by executing a strategy based on . . . a balance of three priorities: liquidity, profitability, and growth."[14] We also noted that in judging whether a company has achieved its objectives, investors, creditors, and others analyze relationships between key numbers in the company's financial statements. We asked these questions:

- How should financial statements be organized to provide the best information?
- What key measures best capture a company's financial performance?

As you saw in Exhibits 2 and 4, Dell uses a classified balance sheet and a multi-step income statement to communicate its financial results to users. The Financial Highlights from Dell's annual report that we presented in the Decision Point show that the company increased its revenues by 17.1 percent between 2003 and 2004. More significantly, it increased both its operating income and net income by 24.6 percent.

Using data from Dell's balance sheets and income statements, we can analyze how the company achieved this growth by computing its profitability ratios (dollars are in millions):

	2004	2003
$\dfrac{\text{Net Income}}{\text{Net Revenues}}$	$\dfrac{\$2,645}{\$41,444}$	$\dfrac{\$2,122}{\$35,404}$
K/R Profit Margin:	6.4%	6.0%
$\dfrac{\text{Net Revenues}}{\text{Average Total Assets}}$	$\dfrac{\$41,444}{(\$19,311 + \$15,470) \div 2}$	$\dfrac{\$35,404}{(\$15,470 + \$13,535) \div 2}$
	$\dfrac{\$41,444}{\$17,390.5}$	$\dfrac{\$35,404}{\$14,502.5}$
K/R Asset Turnover:	2.4 times	2.4 times
$\dfrac{\text{Net Income}}{\text{Average Total Assets}}$	$\dfrac{\$2,645}{(\$19,311 + \$15,470) \div 2}$	$\dfrac{\$2,122}{(\$15,470 + \$13,535)^* \div 2}$
	$\dfrac{\$2,645}{\$17,390.5}$	$\dfrac{\$2,122}{\$14,502.5}$
K/R Return on Assets:	15.2, or 15.2%	14.6, or 14.6%

* From Dell Computer Corporation's 2003 annual report.

By relating these three ratios to each other and to the computer industry averages in Figures 5, 6, and 7, we can see that Dell's profitability is clearly superior:

	Profit Margin	×	Asset Turnover	=	Return on Assets
2003:	6.0%	×	2.4 times	=	14.6%*
2004:	6.4%	×	2.4 times	=	15.2%*
Industry Average:	.5%	×	2.1 times	=	1.1%

*The differences are due to rounding.

Dell improved its return on assets in 2004 by improving its profit margin. It did better than its industry competitors by a substantial margin on both its profit margin and return on assets. Its asset turnover was stable and very close to the industry average.

Dell also took advantage of debt financing to leverage its profitability into a very high return on equity, as shown by its debt to equity and return on equity ratios:

	2004	2003
$\dfrac{\text{Total Liabilities}}{\text{Total Stockholders' Equity}}$	$\dfrac{\$13,031}{\$6,280}$	$\dfrac{\$10,597}{\$4,873}$
K/R Debt to Equity Ratio:	2.08, or 208%	2.17, or 217%
Industry Average:	1.37, or 137%	

$\dfrac{\text{Net Income}}{\text{Average Stockholders' Equity}}$	$\dfrac{\$2,645}{(\$6,280 + \$4,873) \div 2}$	$\dfrac{\$2,122}{(\$4,873 + \$4,694)^* \div 2}$
	$\dfrac{\$2,645}{\$5,576.5}$	$\dfrac{\$2,122}{\$4,783.5}$
K/R Return on Equity: 47.4%		44.4%
Industry Average: 2.6%		

_____

* From Dell Computer Corporation's 2003 annual report.

By astute management of average assets, debt, and equity, Dell transformed a profit margin of 6.4 percent into a return to its stockholders of 47.4 percent, a performance almost 18 times better than that of its competitors.

CHAPTER REVIEW

Review of Learning Objectives

LO1 Describe the objectives and qualitative characteristics of financial reporting and the ethical responsibilities that financial reporting involves.

The objectives of financial reporting are to provide information useful in making investment and credit decisions, judging cash flow prospects, and understanding business resources, claims to those resources, and changes in them.

The most important qualitative characteristics of accounting information are understandability and usefulness. Understandability depends on the knowledge of the user and the ability of the accountant to provide useful information. Usefulness is a function of two primary characteristics, relevance and reliability. Information is relevant when it has an effect on a decision. Information that is relevant has both feedback and predictive value and is timely. To be reliable, information must represent what it is supposed to represent and be verifiable and neutral. Since the passage of the Sarbanes-Oxley Act in 2002, CEOs and CFOs have been required to certify to the accuracy and completeness of their companies' financial statements.

LO2 Define and describe the conventions of *comparability and consistency, materiality, conservatism, full disclosure,* and *cost-benefit.*

Because accountants' measurements are not exact, certain conventions are applied to help users interpret financial statements. The first of these conventions is comparability and consistency. Consistency requires the use of the same accounting procedures from period to period and enhances the comparability of financial statements. The materiality convention has to do with determining the relative importance of an item. Conservatism entails using the procedure that is least likely to overstate assets and income. Full disclosure means including all relevant information in the financial statements. The cost-benefit convention holds that the benefits to be gained from providing accounting information should be greater than the costs of providing it.

LO3 Identify and describe the basic components of a classified balance sheet.

The basic components of a classified balance sheet are as follows:

Assets	Liabilities
Current assets	Current liabilities
Investments	Long-term liabilities
Property, plant, and equipment	**Stockholders' Equity**
Intangible assets	Contributed capital
(Other assets)	Retained earnings

Current assets are cash and other assets that a firm can reasonably expect to convert to cash or use up during the next year or the normal operating cycle, whichever is longer. Investments are assets, usually long term, that are not used in the normal operation of a business. Property, plant, and equipment are tangible long-term assets used in day-to-day operations. Intangible assets are long-term assets with no physical substance whose value stems from the rights or privileges they extend to stockholders.

A current liability is an obligation due to be paid or performed during the next year or the normal operating cycle, whichever is longer. Long-term liabilities are debts that fall due more than one year in the future or beyond the normal operating cycle.

The equity section of a corporation's balance sheet differs from the balance sheet of a proprietorship or partnership in that it has subcategories for contributed capital (the assets invested by stockholders) and retained earnings (stockholders' claim to assets earned from operations and reinvested in operations).

LO4 Describe the features of multistep and single-step classified income statements.

Classified income statements for external reporting can be in multistep or single-step form. The multistep form arrives at income before income taxes through a series of steps; the single-step form arrives at income before income taxes in a single step. A multistep income statement usually has a separate section for other revenues and expenses.

LO5 Use classified financial statements to evaluate liquidity and profitability.

In evaluating a company's liquidity and profitability, investors and creditors rely on the data provided in classified financial statements. Two measures of liquidity are working capital and the current ratio. Five measures of profitability are profit margin, asset turnover, return on assets, debt to equity ratio, and return on equity. Industry averages are useful in interpreting these ratios.

REVIEW of Concepts and Terminology

The following concepts and terms were introduced in this chapter:

Accounting conventions: Rules of thumb, or general principles, for recording transactions and preparing financial statements. **(LO1)**

Classified financial statements: General-purpose external financial statements that are divided into subcategories. **(LO3)**

Comparability: The convention of presenting information in a way that enables decision makers to recognize similarities, differences, and trends over different periods in the same company and among different companies. **(LO2)**

Conservatism: The convention that when faced with two equally acceptable alternatives, the accountant chooses the one least likely to overstate assets and income. **(LO2)**

Consistency: The convention requiring that once a company has adopted an accounting procedure, it must use it from one period to the next unless a note to the financial statements informs users of a change in procedure. **(LO2)**

Cost-benefit: The convention that the benefits gained from providing accounting information should be greater than the costs of providing that information. **(LO2)**

Cost of goods sold: The amount a merchandiser paid for the merchandise it sold during an accounting period or the cost to a manufacturer of making the products it sold during an accounting period. Also called *cost of sales*. **(LO4)**

Current assets: Cash and other assets that a company can reasonably expect to convert to cash, sell, or consume within one year or its normal operating cycle, whichever is longer. **(LO3)**

Current liabilities: Obligations due to be paid or performed within one year or within the normal operating cycle, whichever is longer. **(LO3)**

Earnings per share: Net income earned on each share of common stock; net income divided by the average number of common shares outstanding during the year. Also called *net income per share*. **(LO4)**

Full disclosure: The convention requiring that a company's financial statements and their notes present all information relevant to the users' understanding of the statements. **(LO2)**

Gross margin: The difference between net sales and cost of goods sold. Also called *gross profit*. **(LO4)**

Gross sales: Total sales for cash and on credit during an accounting period. **(LO4)**

Income before income taxes: The amount a company has earned from all activities—operating and nonoperating—before taking into account the amount of income taxes incurred. **(LO4)**

Income from operations: Gross margin minus operating expenses. Also called *operating income*. **(LO4)**

Income taxes: A category for the expense of federal, state, and local taxes that appears only on the income statements of corporations. Also called *provision for income taxes*. **(LO4)**

Intangible assets: Long-term assets with no physical substance whose value stems from the rights or privileges they extend to their owners. **(LO3)**

Investments: Assets, usually long term, that are not used in the normal operation of a business and that management does not intend to convert to cash within the next year. **(LO3)**

Long-term liabilities: Debts that fall due more than one year in the future or beyond the normal operating cycle. **(LO3)**

Manufacturing company: A company that makes and sells products. **(LO4)**

Materiality: The convention that refers to the relative importance of an item or event in a financial statement and its influence on the decisions of the users of financial statements. **(LO2)**

Merchandising company: A company, either a wholesaler or retailer, that buys and sells products. **(LO4)**

Multistep income statement: An income statement that goes through a series of steps to arrive at net income. **(LO4)**

Net income: What remains of gross margin after operating expenses have been deducted, other revenues and expenses have been added or deducted, and income taxes have been deducted. **(LO4)**

Net sales: The gross proceeds from sales of merchandise (gross sales) less sales returns and allowances and any discounts allowed. Often called *sales*. **(LO4)**

Normal operating cycle: The average time a company needs to go from spending cash to receiving cash. **(LO3)**

Operating expenses: Expenses other than cost of goods sold incurred in running a business. **(LO4)**

Other assets: A balance sheet category that some companies use to group all assets other than current assets and property, plant, and equipment. **(LO3)**

Other revenues and expenses: The section of a multistep income statement that includes revenues and expenses not related to business operations. Also called *nonoperating revenues and expenses*. **(LO4)**

Property, plant, and equipment: Tangible long-term assets used in the continuing operation of a business. Also called *operating assets, fixed assets, tangible assets, long-lived assets,* or *plant assets*. **(LO3)**

Qualitative characteristics: Standards for judging accounting information. **(LO1)**

Relevance: The qualitative characteristic of information that has a direct effect on a decision. **(LO1)**

Reliability: The qualitative characteristic of information that represents what it is supposed to represent and is verifiable and neutral. **(LO1)**

Sales returns and allowances: Refunds, credits, and discounts given to customers who have received defective goods. **(LO4)**

Single-step income statement: An income statement that arrives at income before income taxes in a single step. **(LO4)**

Understandability: The qualitative characteristic of information that enables users to perceive its meaning. **(LO1)**

Usefulness: The qualitative characteristic of information that is relevant and reliable. **(LO1)**

Working capital: A measure of liquidity that shows the net current assets on hand to continue business operations; Total Current Assets − Total Current Liabilities. **(LO5)**

Key Ratios

Asset turnover: A measure of profitability that shows how efficiently assets are used to produce sales; Net Sales ÷ Average Total Assets. **(LO5)**

Current ratio: A measure of liquidity; Current Assets ÷ Current Liabilities. **(LO5)**

Debt to equity ratio: A measure of profitability that shows the proportion of a company's assets that is financed by creditors and the proportion financed by stockholders; Total Liabilities ÷ Stockholders' Equity. **(LO5)**

Profit margin: A measure of profitability that shows the percentage of each sales dollar that results in net income; Net Income ÷ Net Sales. **(LO5)**

Return on assets: A measure of profitability that shows how efficiently a company uses its assets to produce income; Net Income ÷ Average Total Assets. **(LO5)**

Return on equity: A measure of profitability that relates the amount earned by a business to the stockholders' investment in the business; Net Income ÷ Average Stockholders' Equity. **(LO5)**

REVIEW Problem

LO5 Using Ratios to Analyze Liquidity and Profitability

 Flavin Shirt Company has been facing increased competition from overseas shirtmakers. Its total assets and stockholders' equity at the beginning of 20x6 were $690,000 and $590,000, respectively. A summary of the firm's data for 2006 and 2007 follows.

	20x7	20x6
Current assets	$ 200,000	$ 170,000
Total assets	880,000	710,000
Current liabilities	90,000	50,000
Long-term liabilities	150,000	50,000
Stockholders' equity	640,000	610,000
Sales	1,200,000	1,050,000
Net income	60,000	80,000

Required

Use (1) liquidity analysis and (2) profitability analysis to document Flavin Shirt Company's declining financial position.

Answer to Review Problem

1. Liquidity analysis:

	A	B	C	D	E
1		Current Assets	Current Liabilities	Working Capital	Current Ratio
2	20X6	$ 170,000	$ 50,000	$ 120,000	3.40
3	20X7	200,000	90,000	110,000	2.22
4	Decrease in				
5	working capital			$ 10,000	
6	Decrease in current ratio				1.18

Both working capital and the current ratio declined between 20x6 and 20x7 because the $40,000 increase in current liabilities ($90,000 − $50,000) was greater than the $30,000 increase in current assets.

2. Profitability analysis:

	A	B	C	D	E	F	G	H	I
1		Net Income	Sales	Profit Margin	Average Total Assets	Asset Turnover	Return on Assets	Average Stock-holders' Equity	Return on Equity
2	20X6	$ 80,000	$1,050,000	7.6%	$700,000[1]	1.50	11.4%	$ 600,000[3]	13.3%
3	20X7	60,000	1,200,000	5.0%	795,000[2]	1.51	7.5%	625,000[4]	9.6%
4	Increase								
5	(decrease)	$ (20,000)	$ 150,000	(2.6%)	$ 95,000	0.01	(3.9%)	$ 25,000	(3.7%)
6									
7									
8									
9	[1] ($710,000 + $690,000) ÷ 2				[3] ($610,000 + $590,000) ÷ 2				
10	[2] ($880,000 + $710,000) ÷ 2				[4] ($640,000 + $610,000) ÷ 2				

Net income decreased by $20,000 despite an increase in sales of $150,000 and an increase in average total assets of $95,000. Thus, the profit margin fell from 7.6 percent to 5.0 percent, and return on assets fell from 11.4 percent to 7.5 percent. Asset turnover showed almost no change and so did not contribute to the decline in profitability. The decrease in return on equity, from 13.3 percent to 9.6 percent, was not as great as the decrease in return on assets because the growth in total assets was financed mainly by debt rather than by stockholders' equity, as shown in the capital structure analysis below.

	A	B	C	D
1		Total Liabilities	Stockholders' Equity	Debt to Equity Ratio
2	20X6	$ 100,000	$ 610,000	16.4%
3	20X7	240,000	640,000	37.5%
4	Increase	$ 140,000	$ 30,000	21.1%

Total liabilities increased by $140,000, while stockholders' equity increased by $30,000. Thus, the amount of the business financed by debt in relation to the amount financed by stockholders' equity increased between 20x6 and 20x7.

CHAPTER ASSIGNMENTS

≡ BUILDING Your Basic Knowledge and Skills

Short Exercises

LO1 **Objectives and Qualitative Characteristics**

SE 1. Identify each of the following statements as either an objective (O) of financial information or as a qualitative (Q) characteristic of accounting information:

1. Information about business resources, claims to those resources, and changes in them should be provided.
2. Decision makers must be able to interpret accounting information.
3. Information that is useful in making investment and credit decisions should be furnished.
4. Accounting information must be relevant and reliable.
5. Information useful in assessing cash flow prospects should be provided.

LO2 **Accounting Conventions**

SE 2. State which of the accounting conventions—comparability and consistency, materiality, conservatism, full disclosure, or cost-benefit—is being followed in each of the cases listed below.

1. Management provides detailed information about the company's long-term debt in the notes to the financial statements.
2. A company does not account separately for discounts received for prompt payment of accounts payable because few of these transactions occur and the total amount of the discounts is small.

3. Management eliminates a weekly report on property, plant, and equipment acquisitions and disposals because no one finds it useful.
4. A company follows the policy of recognizing a loss on inventory when the market value of an item falls below its cost but does nothing if the market value rises.
5. When several accounting methods are acceptable, management chooses a single method and follows that method from year to year.

LO3   Classification of Accounts: Balance Sheet

SE 3. Tell whether each of the following accounts is a current asset; an investment; property, plant, and equipment; an intangible asset; a current liability; a long-term liability; stockholders' equity; or not on the balance sheet:

1. Delivery Trucks
2. Accounts Payable
3. Note Payable (due in 90 days)
4. Delivery Expense
5. Common Stock

6. Prepaid Insurance
7. Trademark
8. Investment to Be Held Six Months
9. Income Taxes Payable
10. Factory Not Used in Business

LO3   Classified Balance Sheet

SE 4. Using the following accounts, prepare a classified balance sheet at year end, May 31, 20xx: Accounts Payable, $800; Accounts Receivable, $1,100; Accumulated Depreciation–Equipment, $700; Cash, $200; Common Stock, $1,000; Equipment, $3,000; Franchise, $200; Investments (long-term), $500; Merchandise Inventory, $600; Notes Payable (long-term), $400; Retained Earnings, ?; Wages Payable, $100.

LO4   Classification of Accounts: Income Statement

SE 5. Tell whether each of the following accounts is part of net sales, cost of goods sold, operating expenses, or other revenues and expenses, or is not on the income statement:

1. Delivery Expense
2. Interest Expense
3. Unearned Revenue
4. Sales Returns and Allowances

5. Cost of Goods Sold
6. Depreciation Expense
7. Investment Income
8. Retained Earnings

LO4   Single-Step Income Statement

SE 6. Using the following accounts, prepare a single-step income statement at year end, May 31, 20xx: Cost of Goods Sold, $840; General Expenses, $450; Income Taxes, $105; Interest Expense, $210; Interest Income, $90; Net Sales, $2,400; Selling Expenses, $555. Ignore earnings per share.

LO4   Multistep Income Statement

SE 7. Using the accounts presented in **SE 6**, prepare a multistep income statement.

LO4   Liquidity Ratios

SE 8. Using the following accounts and balances taken from a year-end balance sheet, compute working capital and the current ratio:

Accounts Payable	$ 3,500
Accounts Receivable	5,000
Cash	2,000
Common Stock	10,000
Marketable Securities	1,000

Merchandise Inventory	$ 6,000
Notes Payable in Three Years	6,500
Property, Plant, and Equipment	20,000
Retained Earnings	14,000

LO5 Profitability Ratios

 SE 9. Using the following information from a balance sheet and an income statement, compute the (1) profit margin, (2) asset turnover, (3) return on assets, (4) debt to equity ratio, and (5) return on equity. (The previous year's total assets were $200,000, and stockholders' equity was $140,000.)

Total assets	$240,000
Total liabilities	60,000
Total stockholders' equity	180,000
Net sales	260,000
Cost of goods sold	140,000
Operating expenses	80,000
Income taxes	10,000

LO5 Profitability Ratios

 SE 10. Assume that a company has a profit margin of 6.0 percent, an asset turnover of 3.2 times, and a debt to equity ratio of 50 percent. What are the company's return on assets and return on equity?

Exercises

LO1, LO2, LO3 Discussion Questions

E 1. Develop a brief answer to each of the following questions:

1. How do the four basic financial statements meet the third objective of financial reporting?
2. What are some areas that require estimates to record transactions under the matching rule?
3. How can financial information be consistent but not comparable?
4. When might an amount be material to management but not to the CPA auditing the financial statements?

LO4, LO5 Discussion Questions

E 2. Develop a brief answer to each of the following questions:

1. Why is it that land held for future use and equipment not currently used in the business are classified as investments rather than as property, plant, and equipment?
2. Which is the better measure of a company's performance—income from operations or net income?
3. Why is it important to compare a company's financial performance with industry standards?
4. Is the statement "Return on assets is a better measure of profitability than profit margin" true or false and why?

LO1, LO2 Financial Accounting Concepts

E 3. The lettered items below represent a classification scheme for the concepts of financial accounting. Match each numbered term in the list that follows with the letter of the category in which it belongs.

a. Decision makers (users of accounting information)
b. Business activities or entities relevant to accounting measurement

c. Objectives of accounting information
d. Accounting measurement considerations
e. Accounting processing considerations
f. Qualitative characteristics
g. Accounting conventions
h. Financial statements

1. Conservatism	13. Specific business entities
2. Verifiability	14. Classification
3. Statement of cash flows	15. Management
4. Materiality	16. Neutrality
5. Reliability	17. Internal accounting control
6. Recognition	18. Valuation
7. Cost-benefit	19. Investors
8. Understandability	20. Timeliness
9. Business transactions	21. Relevance
10. Consistency	22. Furnishing information that is useful in assessing cash flow prospects
11. Full disclosure	
12. Furnishing information that is useful to investors and creditors	

LO2   **Accounting Concepts and Conventions**

E 4. Each of the statements below violates a convention in accounting. State which of the following accounting conventions is violated: comparability and consistency, materiality, conservatism, full disclosure, or cost-benefit.

1. A series of reports that are time-consuming and expensive to prepare are presented to the board of directors each month, even though the reports are never used.
2. A company changes its method of accounting for depreciation.
3. The company in **2** does not indicate in the financial statements that the method of depreciation was changed; nor does it specify the effect of the change on net income.
4. A company's new office building, which is built next to the company's existing factory, is debited to the Factory account because it represents a fairly small dollar amount in relation to the factory.
5. The asset account for a pickup truck still used in the business is written down to what the truck could be sold for, even though the carrying value under conventional depreciation methods is higher.

LO3   **Classification of Accounts: Balance Sheet**

E 5. The lettered items below represent a classification scheme for a balance sheet, and the numbered items in the list at the top of the opposite page are account titles. Match each account with the letter of the category in which it belongs.

a. Current assets
b. Investments
c. Property, plant, and equipment
d. Intangible assets
e. Current liabilities
f. Long-term liabilities
g. Stockholders' equity
h. Not on balance sheet

1. Patent
2. Building Held for Sale
3. Prepaid Rent
4. Wages Payable
5. Note Payable in Five Years
6. Building Used in Operations
7. Fund Held to Pay Off Long-Term Debt
8. Inventory
9. Prepaid Insurance
10. Depreciation Expense
11. Accounts Receivable
12. Interest Expense
13. Unearned Revenue
14. Short-Term Investments
15. Accumulated Depreciation
16. Retained Earnings

LO3 Classified Balance Sheet Preparation

E 6. The following data pertain to Kabli, Inc.: Accounts Payable, $20,400; Accounts Receivable, $15,200; Accumulated Depreciation–Building, $5,600; Accumulated Depreciation–Equipment, $6,800; Bonds Payable, $24,000; Building, $28,000; Cash, $12,480; Common Stock, $10 par, 4,000 shares authorized, issued, and outstanding, $40,000; Copyright, $2,480; Equipment, $60,800; Inventory, $16,000; Investment in Corporate Securities (long-term), $8,000; Investment in Six-Month Government Securities, $6,560; Land, $3,200; Paid-in Capital in Excess of Par Value, $20,000; Prepaid Rent, $480; Retained Earnings, $35,280; and Revenue Received in Advance, $1,120.

Prepare a classified balance sheet at December 31, 20xx.

LO4 Classification of Accounts: Income Statement

E 7. Using the classification scheme below for a multistep income statement, match each account with the letter of the category in which it belongs.

a. Net sales
b. Cost of goods sold
c. Selling expenses
d. General and administrative expenses
e. Other revenues and expenses
f. Not on income statement

1. Sales Discounts
2. Cost of Goods Sold
3. Dividend Income
4. Advertising Expense
5. Office Salaries Expense
6. Freight Out Expense
7. Prepaid Insurance
8. Utilities Expense
9. Sales Salaries Expense
10. Rent Expense
11. Depreciation Expense–Delivery Equipment
12. Taxes Payable
13. Interest Expense

LO4 Preparation of Income Statements

E 8. The following data pertain to a corporation: net sales, $405,000; cost of goods sold, $220,000; selling expenses, $90,000; general and administrative expenses, $60,000; income taxes, $7,500; interest expense, $4,000; interest income, $3,000; and common stock outstanding, 50,000 shares.

1. Prepare a single-step income statement.
2. Prepare a multistep income statement.

LO4 Multistep Income Statement

E 9. A single-step income statement appears at the top of the following page. Present the information in a multistep income statement, and indicate what insights can be obtained from the multistep form as opposed to the single-step form.

Pasica Linens Corporation
Income Statement
For the Year Ended December 31, 20xx

Revenues		
Net sales		$1,197,132
Interest income		5,720
Total revenues		$1,202,852
Costs and expenses		
Cost of goods sold	$777,080	
Selling expenses	203,740	
General and administrative expenses	100,688	
Interest expense	13,560	
Total costs and expenses		1,095,068
Income before income taxes		$ 107,784
Income taxes		24,000
Net income		$ 83,784
Earnings per share		$ 8.38

LO5 Liquidity Ratios

E 10. The accounts and balances that follow are from the general ledger of Fields Corporation. Compute the (1) working capital and (2) current ratio.

Accounts Payable	$13,280
Accounts Receivable	8,160
Cash	1,200
Current Portion of Long-Term Debt	8,000
Long-Term Investments	8,320
Marketable Securities	10,080
Merchandise Inventory	20,320
Notes Payable (90 days)	12,000
Notes Payable (2 years)	16,000
Notes Receivable (90 days)	20,800
Notes Receivable (2 years)	8,000
Prepaid Insurance	320
Property, Plant, and Equipment	48,000
Property Taxes Payable	1,000
Retained Earnings	22,640
Salaries Payable	680
Supplies	280
Unearned Revenue	600

LO5 Profitability Ratios

E 11. The following end-of-year amounts are from the financial statements of Konstan Corporation: total assets, $213,000; total liabilities, $86,000; stockholders' equity, $127,000; net sales, $391,000; cost of goods sold, $243,000; operating expenses, $89,000; income taxes, $12,000; and dividends, $20,000. During the past year, total assets increased by $37,500. Total stockholders' equity was affected only by net income and dividends. Compute the (1) profit margin, (2) asset turnover, (3) return on assets, (4) debt to equity ratio, and (5) return on equity.

LO5 **Liquidity and Profitability**

E 12. The simplified balance sheet and income statement for a corporation appear below.

Balance Sheet
December 31, 20xx

Assets		Liabilities	
Current assets	$ 50,000	Current liabilities	$ 20,000
Investments	10,000	Long-term liabilities	30,000
Property, plant, and		Total liabilities	$ 50,000
equipment	146,500		
Intangible assets	13,500	**Stockholders' Equity**	
		Common stock	$100,000
		Retained earnings	70,000
		Total stockholders' equity	$170,000
		Total liabilities and	
Total assets	$220,000	stockholders' equity	$220,000

Income Statement
For the Year Ended December 31, 20xx

Net sales	$410,000
Cost of goods sold	250,000
Gross margin	$160,000
Operating expenses	130,000
Income before income taxes	$ 30,000
Income taxes	5,000
Net income	$ 25,000

Total assets and stockholders' equity at the beginning of 20xx were $180,000 and $140,000, respectively.

1. Compute the following liquidity measures: (a) working capital and (b) current ratio.
2. Compute the following profitability measures: (a) profit margin, (b) asset turnover, (c) return on assets, (d) debt to equity ratio, and (e) return on equity.

Problems

LO2 **Accounting Conventions**

P 1. In each case below, accounting conventions may have been violated.

1. Hastings Manufacturing Company uses the cost method for computing the balance sheet amount of inventory unless the market value of the inventory is less than the cost, in which case the market value is used. At the end of the current year, the market value is $154,000 and the cost is $160,000. Hastings uses the $154,000 figure to compute current assets because management believes it is the more cautious approach.

2. Gormanus Company has annual sales of $20,000,000. It follows the practice of recording any items costing less than $500 as expenses in the year purchased. During the current year, it purchased several chairs for the executive conference room at $490 each, including freight. Although the chairs were expected to last for at least ten years, they were recorded as an expense in accordance with company policy.

3. Nogel Company closed its books on October 31, 20x6, before preparing its annual report. On November 3, 20x6, a fire destroyed one of the company's two factories. Although the company had fire insurance and would not suffer a loss on the building, a significant decrease in sales in 20x7 was expected because of the fire. The fire damage was not reported in the 20x6 financial statements because the fire had not affected the company's operations during that year.

4. Ex-Act Drug Company spends a substantial portion of its profits on research and development. The company had been reporting its $5,000,000 expenditure for research and development as a lump sum, but management recently decided to begin classifying the expenditures by project, even though its recordkeeping costs will increase.

5. During the current year, RBI Company changed from one generally accepted method of accounting for inventories to another method.

Required

User Insight: For each of these cases, identify the accounting convention that applies, state whether or not the treatment is in accord with the convention and GAAP, and briefly explain why.

LO4 Forms of the Income Statement

P 2. Ramos Nursery Corporation's single-step income statements for 20x7 and 20x6 follow.

Ramos Nursery Corporation Income Statements For the Years Ended April 30, 20x7 and 20x6		
	20x7	**20x6**
Revenues		
Net sales	$525,932	$475,264
Interest income	800	700
Total revenues	$526,732	$475,964
Costs and expenses		
Cost of goods sold	$234,948	$171,850
Selling expenses	161,692	150,700
General and administrative expenses	62,866	42,086
Interest expense	3,600	850
Total costs and expenses	$463,106	$365,486
Income before income taxes	$ 63,626	$110,478
Income taxes	15,000	27,600
Net income	$ 48,626	$ 82,878
Earnings per share	$ 2.43	$ 4.14

Ramos Nursery Corporation had 20,000 shares of common stock outstanding during both 20x7 and 20x6.

Required

1. From the information provided, prepare multistep income statements for 20x6 and 20x7 showing percentages of net sales for each component.
2. **User Insight:** Did income from operations increase or decrease from 20x6 to 20x7? Write a short explanation of why this change occurred.
3. **User Insight:** What effect did other revenues and expenses have on the change in income before income taxes? What action by management probably caused this change?

LO3, LO5 **Classified Balance Sheet**

  P 3. The following information is from the June 30, 20x7, post-closing trial balance of Kissell Hardware Corporation.

Account Name	Debit	Credit
Cash	$ 31,000	
Short-Term Investments	33,000	
Notes Receivable	10,000	
Accounts Receivable	276,000	
Merchandise Inventory	145,000	
Prepaid Rent	1,600	
Prepaid Insurance	4,800	
Sales Supplies	1,280	
Office Supplies	440	
Deposit for Future Advertising	3,680	
Building, Not in use	49,600	
Land	22,400	
Delivery Equipment	41,200	
Accumulated Depreciation–Delivery Equipment		$ 28,400
Trademark	4,000	
Accounts Payable		114,600
Salaries Payable		5,200
Interest Payable		840
Long-Term Notes Payable		80,000
Common Stock ($1 par value)		20,000
Paid-in Capital in Excess of Par Value		160,000
Retained Earnings		214,960

Required

1. From the information provided, prepare a classified balance sheet for Kissell Hardware Corporation.
2. Compute Kissell Hardware's current ratio and debt to equity ratio.
3. **User Insight:** As a user of the classified balance sheet, why would you want to know the current ratio or the debt to equity ratio?

LO5 **Liquidity and Profitability**

 P 4. A summary of data from the income statements and balance sheets for Okumura Construction Supply, Inc., for 20x7 and 20x6 appears at the top of the next page.

	20x7	20x6
Current assets	$ 366,000	$ 310,000
Total assets	2,320,000	1,740,000
Current liabilities	180,000	120,000
Long-term liabilities	800,000	580,000
Stockholders' equity	1,340,000	1,040,000
Net sales	4,600,000	3,480,000
Net income	300,000	204,000

Total assets and stockholders' equity at the beginning of 20x6 were $1,360,000 and $840,000, respectively.

Required

1. Compute the following liquidity measures for 20x6 and 20x7: (a) working capital and (b) current ratio. **User Insight:** Comment on the differences between the years.
2. Compute the following measures of profitability for 20x6 and 20x7: (a) profit margin, (b) asset turnover, (c) return on assets, (d) debt to equity ratio, and (e) return on equity. **User Insight:** Comment on the change in performance from 20x6 to 20x7.

LO3, LO4, LO5 **Classified Financial Statement Preparation and Analysis**

P 5. Wu Corporation sells outdoor sports equipment. At the December 31, 20x6, year end, the following financial information was available from the income statement: administrative expenses, $161,600; cost of goods sold, $700,840; income taxes, $14,000; interest expense, $45,280; interest income, $5,600; net sales, $1,428,780; and selling expenses, $440,400.

The following information was available from the balance sheet (after closing entries were made): accounts payable, $65,200; accounts receivable, $209,600; accumulated depreciation–delivery equipment, $34,200; accumulated depreciation–store fixtures, $84,440; cash, $56,800; common stock, $1 par value, 20,000 shares authorized, issued, and outstanding, $20,000; delivery equipment, $177,000; inventory, $273,080; investment in securities (long-term), $112,000; investment in U.S. government securities (short-term), $79,200; long-term notes payable, $200,000; paid-in capital in excess of par value, $180,000; retained earnings, $518,600 (ending balance); notes payable (short-term), $100,000; prepaid expenses (short-term), $11,520; and store fixtures, $283,240.

Total assets and total stockholders' equity at December 31, 20x5, were $1,048,800 and $766,340, respectively, and dividends for the year were $120,000.

Required

1. From the information above, prepare (a) an income statement in single-step form, (b) a statement of retained earnings, and (c) a classified balance sheet.
2. **User Insight:** From the statements you have prepared, compute the following measures: (a) working capital and current ratio (for liquidity); and (b) profit margin, asset turnover, return on assets, debt to equity ratio, and return on equity (for profitability).
3. **User Insight:** Using the industry averages for the auto and home supply business in Figures 4 through 9 in this chapter, determine whether Wu Corporation needs to improve its liquidity or its profitability. Explain your answer, making recommendations as to specific areas on which Wu Corporation should concentrate.

Alternate Problems

LO2 **Accounting Conventions**

P 6. In each case below, accounting conventions may have been violated.

1. After careful study, Kipling Company, which has offices in 40 states, has determined that its method of depreciating office furniture should be changed. The new method is adopted for the current year, and the change is noted in the financial statements.

2. In the past, Cortes Corporation has recorded operating expenses in general accounts (e.g., Salaries Expense and Utilities Expense). Management has determined that despite the additional recordkeeping costs, the company's income statement should break down each operating expense into its components of selling expense and administrative expense.

3. Fitz Corporation's auditor discovered that a company official had authorized the payment of an $800 bribe to a local official. Management argued that because the item was so small in relation to the size of the company ($1,500,000 in sales), the illegal payment should not be disclosed.

4. Glowacki's Bookstore built a small addition to its main building to house a new computer games section. Because no one could be sure that the computer games section would succeed, the accountant took a conservative approach and recorded the addition as an expense.

5. Since it began operations ten years ago, Xu Company has used the same generally accepted inventory method. The company does not disclose in its financial statements what inventory method it uses.

Required

User Insight: In each of these cases, identify the accounting convention that applies, state whether or not the treatment is in accord with the convention and generally accepted accounting principles, and briefly explain why.

LO4 **Forms of the Income Statement**

P 7. The income statements that follow are for Loury Hardware Corporation.

Loury Hardware Corporation
Income Statements
For the Years Ended July 31, 20x8 and 20x7

	20x8	20x7
Revenues		
Net sales	$464,200	$388,466
Interest income	420	500
Total revenues	$464,620	$388,966
Costs and expenses		
Cost of goods sold	$243,880	$198,788
Selling expenses	95,160	55,644
General and administrative expenses	90,840	49,286
Interest expense	5,600	1,100
Total costs and expenses	$435,480	$304,818
Income before income taxes	$ 29,140	$ 84,148
Income taxes	7,000	21,000
Net income	$ 22,140	$ 63,148
Earnings per share	$ 2.21	$ 6.31

Required

1. From the information provided, prepare a multistep income statement for 20x7 and 20x8 showing percentages of net sales for each component.
2. **User Insight:** Did income from operations increase or decrease from 20x7 to 20x8? Write a short explanation of why this change occurred.
3. **User Insight:** What effect did other revenues and expenses have on the change in income before income taxes? What action by Loury Hardware's management probably accounted for this change?

LO5   Liquidity and Profitability

 P 8. Rollins Products has had poor operating results for the past two years. As the accountant for Rollins Products Corporation, you have the following information available to you:

	20x7	20x6
Current assets	$ 45,000	$ 35,000
Total assets	145,000	110,000
Current liabilities	20,000	10,000
Long-term liabilities	20,000	—
Stockholders' equity	105,000	100,000
Net sales	262,000	200,000
Net income	16,000	11,000

Total assets and stockholders' equity at the beginning of 20x6 were $90,000 and $80,000, respectively.

Required

1. Compute the following measures of liquidity for 20x6 and 20x7: (a) working capital and (b) current ratio. **User Insight:** Comment on the differences between the years.
2. Compute the following measures of profitability for 20x6 and 20x7: (a) profit margin, (b) asset turnover, (c) return on assets, (d) debt to equity ratio, and (e) return on equity. **User Insight:** Comment on the change in performance from 20x6 to 20x7.

≡ ENHANCING Your Knowledge, Skills, and Critical Thinking

Conceptual Understanding Cases

LO2   Consistency and Full Disclosure

C 1. Cuyahoga Parking, which operates a seven-story parking building in downtown Cleveland, has a calendar year end. It serves daily and hourly parkers, as well as monthly parkers who pay a fixed monthly rate in advance. The company traditionally has recorded all cash receipts as revenues when received. Most monthly parkers pay in full during the month prior to that in which they have the right to park. The company's auditors have said that beginning in 20x6, the company should consider recording the cash receipts from monthly parking on an accrual basis, crediting Unearned Revenues. Total cash receipts for 20x6 were $1,250,000, and the cash receipts received in 20x6 and applicable to January 20x7 were $62,500. Discuss the relevance of the accounting conventions of consistency and full disclosure to the decision to record the monthly parking revenues on an accrual basis.

LO2 **Materiality**

C 2. Hagia Electronics, Inc., operates a chain of consumer electronics stores in the Dallas area. This year the company achieved annual sales of $75 million, on which it earned a net income of $3 million. At the beginning of the year, management implemented a new inventory system that enabled it to track all purchases and sales. At the end of the year, a physical inventory reveals that the actual inventory was $120,000 below what the new system indicated it should be. The inventory loss, which probably resulted from shoplifting, is reflected in a higher cost of goods sold. The problem concerns management but seems to be less important to the company's auditors. What is materiality? Why might the inventory loss concern management more than it does the auditors? Do you think the amount of inventory loss is material?

Interpreting Financial Reports

LO5 **Comparison of Profitability**

K/R

C 3. Two of the largest chains of grocery stores in the United States are **Albertson's Inc.** and the **Great Atlantic & Pacific Tea Company (A&P).** In a recent fiscal year, Albertson's had a net income of $765 million, and A&P had a net income of $14 million. It is difficult to judge which company is more profitable from those figures alone because they do not take into account the relative sales, sizes, and investments of the companies. Data (in millions) to complete a financial analysis of the two companies follow:[15]

	Albertson's	A&P
Net sales	$36,762	$10,151
Beginning total assets	15,719	3,335
Ending total assets	16,078	3,309
Beginning total liabilities	10,017	2,489
Ending total liabilities	10,394	2,512
Beginning stockholders' equity	5,702	846
Ending stockholders' equity	5,684	797

1. Determine which company was more profitable by computing profit margin, asset turnover, return on assets, debt to equity ratio, and return on equity for the two companies. Comment on the relative profitability of the two companies.
2. What do the ratios tell you about the factors that go into achieving an adequate return on assets in the grocery industry? For industry data, refer to Figures 4 through 9 in this chapter.
3. How would you characterize the use of debt financing in the grocery industry and the use of debt by these two companies?

LO5 **Evaluation of Profitability**

K/R

C 4. Monique Smith is the principal stockholder and president of Monique Tapestries, Inc., which wholesales fine tapestries to retail stores. Because Smith was not satisfied with the company earnings in 20x6, she raised prices in 20x7, increasing gross margin from sales from 30 percent in 20x6 to 35 percent in 20x7. Smith is pleased that net income went up from 20x6 to 20x7, as shown in the comparative income statements on the next page. Total assets for Monique Tapestries, Inc., at year end for 20x5, 20x6, and 20x7 were $1,246,780, $1,386,810, and $1,536,910, respectively.

Has Monique Tapestries' profitability really improved? (**Hint:** Compute profit margin and return on assets.) What factors has Smith overlooked in evaluating

	20x7	20x6
Revenues		
Net sales	$1,222,600	$1,386,400
Costs and expenses		
Cost of goods sold	$ 794,690	$ 970,480
Selling and administrative expenses	308,398	305,008
Total costs and expenses	$1,103,088	$1,275,488
Income before income taxes	$ 119,512	$ 110,912
Income taxes	30,000	28,000
Net income	$ 89,512	$ 82,912

the profitability of the company? (**Hint:** Compute asset turnover and comment on the role it plays in profitability.)

Decision Analysis Using Excel

LO5   **Financial Analysis for Loan Decision**

 C 5. Esteban Almada was recently promoted to loan officer at First Federal Bank. He has authority to issue loans up to $75,000 without approval from a higher bank official. This week two small companies, Dubrovnik Supplies, Inc., and Shimano Fashions, Inc., have each submitted a proposal for a six-month, $75,000 loan. To prepare financial analyses of the two companies, Almada has obtained the information summarized below.

Dubrovnik Supplies, Inc., is a local lumber and home improvement company. Because sales have increased so much during the past two years, Dubrovnik Supplies has had to raise additional working capital, especially as represented by receivables and inventory. The $75,000 loan is needed to assure the company of enough working capital for the next year. Dubrovnik Supplies began the year with total assets of $1,110,000 and stockholders' equity of $390,000. During the past year, the company had a net income of $60,000 on net sales of $1,140,000. Dubrovnik Supplies' unclassified balance sheet as of the current date appears as follows:

Assets		Liabilities and Stockholders' Equity	
Cash	$ 45,000	Accounts payable	$ 300,000
Accounts receivable (net)	225,000	Notes payable (short term)	150,000
Inventory	375,000	Notes payable (long term)	300,000
Land	75,000	Common stock	375,000
Buildings (net)	375,000	Retained earnings	75,000
Equipment (net)	105,000	Total liabilities and	
Total assets	$1,200,000	stockholders' equity	$1,200,000

Shimano Fashions, Inc., has for three years been a successful clothing store for young professional women. The leased store is located in the downtown financial district. Shimano's loan proposal asks for $75,000 to pay for stocking a new line of women's suits during the coming season. At the beginning of the year, the company had total assets of $300,000 and total stockholders' equity of $171,000. Over the past year, the company earned a net income of $54,000 on net sales of $720,000. The firm's unclassified balance sheet at the current date is as follows:

Assets		Liabilities and Stockholders' Equity	
Cash	$ 15,000	Accounts payable	$120,000
Accounts receivable (net)	75,000	Accrued liabilities	15,000
Inventory	202,500	Common stock	75,000
Prepaid expenses	7,500	Retained earnings	150,000
Equipment (net)	60,000	Total liabilities and	
Total assets	$360,000	stockholders' equity	$360,000

1. Prepare a financial analysis of each company's liquidity before and after receiving the proposed loan. Also compute profitability ratios before and after, as appropriate. Write a brief summary of the effect of the proposed loan on each company's financial position.
2. Assume you are Esteban Almada and can make a loan to only one of these companies. Write a memorandum to the bank's vice president outlining your decision and naming the company to which you would lend $75,000. Be sure to state what positive and negative factors could affect each company's ability to pay back the loan in the next year. Also indicate what other information of a financial or nonfinancial nature would be helpful in making a final decision.

Annual Report Case: CVS Corporation

LO3, LO4, LO5   Classified Balance Sheet and Multistep Income Statement

C 6. Refer to **CVS Corporation's** annual report in the Supplement to Chapter 1 to answer the following questions. (Note that 2004 refers to the year ended January 1, 2005, and 2003 refers to the year ended January 3, 2004.)

1. Consolidated balance sheets: (a) Did the amount of working capital increase or decrease from 2003 to 2004? By how much? (b) Did the current ratio improve from 2003 to 2004? (c) Does the company have long-term investments or intangible assets? (d) Did the debt to equity ratio of CVS change from 2003 to 2004? (e) What is the contributed capital for 2004? How does contributed capital compare with retained earnings?
2. Consolidated statements of operations: (a) Does CVS use a multistep or single-step income statement? (b) Is it a comparative statement? (c) What is the trend of net earnings? (d) How significant are income taxes for CVS?

Comparison Case: CVS versus Southwest

LO5   Financial Analysis

C 7. Compare the financial performance of **CVS Corporation** and **Southwest Airlines Co.** on the basis of liquidity and profitability for 2004 and 2003. Use the following ratios: working capital, current ratio, debt to equity ratio, profit margin, asset turnover, return on assets, and return on equity. In 2002, total assets and total stockholder's equity for CVS were $9,645.3 million and $5.197.0 million, respectively. Southwest's total assets were $8,954 million, and total stockholders' equity was $4,422 million in 2002. Comment on the relative performance of the two companies. In general, how does Southwest's performance compare to CVS's with respect to liquidity and profitability? What distinguishes Southwest's profitability performance from that of CVS?

Ethical Dilemma Case

LO1   **Ethics and Financial Reporting**

C 8. Beacon Systems, located outside Atlanta, develops computer software and licenses it to financial institutions. The firm uses an aggressive accounting method that records revenues from the software it has developed on a percentage of completion basis. Consequently, revenue for partially completed projects is recognized based on the portion of the project that has been completed. If a project is 50 percent completed, then 50 percent of the contracted revenue is recognized. In 20x7, preliminary estimates for a $7 million project are that the project is 75 percent complete. Because the estimate of completion is a matter of judgment, management asks for a new report showing the project to be 90 percent complete. The change will enable senior managers to meet their financial goals for the year and thus receive substantial year-end bonuses. Do you think management's action is ethical? If you were the company controller and were asked to prepare the new report, would you do it? What action would you take?

Internet Case

LO5   **Annual Reports and Financial Analysis**

C 9. Select a large, well-known company and access its annual report online. In the annual report of the company you have chosen, find the four basic financial statements and the notes to the financial statements. Perform a liquidity analysis, including the calculation of working capital and the current ratio. Perform a profitability analysis, calculating profit margin, asset turnover, return on assets, debt to equity ratio, and return on equity. Be prepared to present your findings in class.

Group Activity Case

LO1   **Qualitative Characteristics of Accounting Information**

C 10. Review the multistep income statement presented in Exhibits 3 and 4. In your group, discuss how this form of the income statement meets each of these qualitative characteristics of accounting information: understandability, usefulness, relevance, and reliability. Be prepared to present your conclusions in class.

Business Communication Case

LO5   **Financial Analysis with Industry Comparison**

C 11. Refer to the "Look Back" section in this chapter and to Dell's classified balance sheet in Exhibit 2. Write a memorandum to the board of directors that summarizes Dell's profitability performance from 2003 to 2004. (Total assets and total stockholders' equity for Dell in 2002 were $13,535 million and $4,694 million, respectively.) Include an assessment of that performance and compare Dell's performance with the industry averages in Figures 4 to 9.

The Annual Report Project

Many instructors assign a term project that requires reading and analyzing an annual report. The Annual Report Project described here has been successful in our classes. It may be used with the annual report of any company, including CVS Corporation's annual report and the financial statements from Southwest Airlines Co.'s annual report that appear in the Supplement to Chapter 1.

The extent to which financial analysis is required depends on the point in the course at which the Annual Report Project is assigned. Instruction 3E, below, provides several options.

Instructions:

1. Choose a company, and obtain its most recent annual report online or through your library or another source.

2. Use the Internet or your library to locate at least two articles about the company and the industry in which it operates. Read the articles, as well as the annual report, and summarize your findings. In addition, access the company's Internet home page directly or through the Needles Accounting Resource Center Website (http://accounting.college.hmco.com/students). Review the company's products and services and its financial information. Summarize what you have learned.

3. Your analysis should consist of five or six double-spaced pages organized according to the following outline:

   A. **Introduction**
   Identify the company by writing a summary that includes the following elements:

   ◗ Name of the chief executive officer

   ◗ Location of the home office

   ◗ Ending date of latest fiscal year

   ◗ Description of the company's principal products or services

   ◗ Main geographic area of activity

   ◗ Name of the company's independent accountants (auditors). In your own words, explain what the accountants said about the company's financial statements.

   ◗ The most recent price of the company's stock and its dividend per share. Be sure to provide the date for this information.

   B. **Industry Situation and Company Plans**
   Describe the industry and its outlook. Then summarize the company's future plans based on what you learned from the annual report and your other research. Be sure to include any relevant information from management's letter to the stockholders.

   C. **Financial Statements**
   Income Statement: Is the format most like a single-step or multistep format? Determine gross profit, income from operations, and net income

for the last two years. Comment on the increases or decreases in these amounts.

Balance Sheet: Show that Assets = Liabilities + Stockholders' Equity for the past two years.

Statement of Cash Flows: Indicate whether the company's cash flows from operations for the past two years were more or less than net income. Also indicate whether the company is expanding through investing activities. Identify the company's most important source of financing. Overall, has cash increased or decreased over the past two years?

D. Accounting Policies

Describe the company's significant accounting policies, if any, relating to revenue recognition, cash, short-term investments, merchandise inventories, and property and equipment. Identify the topics of the notes to the financial statements.

E. Financial Analysis

For the past two years, calculate and discuss the significance of the following ratios:

Option (a): Basic (After Completing Chapter 4)

Liquidity Ratios
> Working capital
> Current ratio

Profitability Ratios
> Profit margin
> Asset turnover
> Return on assets
> Debt to equity ratio
> Return on equity

Option (b): Basic with Enhanced Liquidity Analysis (After Completing Chapter 8)

Liquidity Ratios
> Working capital
> Current ratio
> Receivable turnover
> Days' sales uncollected
> Inventory turnover
> Days' inventory on hand
> Payables turnover
> Days' payable
> Operating cycle
> Financing period

Profitability Ratios
> Profit margin
> Asset turnover
> Return on assets
> Debt to equity ratio
> Return on equity

Option (c): Comprehensive (After Completing Chapter 13 or 14)

Liquidity Ratios
> Working capital
> Current ratio

Receivable turnover
Days' sales uncollected
Inventory turnover
Days' inventory on hand
Payables turnover
Days' payable
Operating cycle
Financing period

Profitability Ratios
Profit margin
Asset turnover
Return on assets
Return on equity

Long-Term Solvency Ratios
Debt to equity ratio
Interest coverage

Cash Flow Adequacy
Cash flow yield
Cash flows to sales
Cash flows to assets
Free cash flow

Market Strength Ratios
Price/earnings per share
Dividends yield

The Operating Cycle and Merchandising Operations

In the last chapter, we pointed out management's responsibility for ensuring the accuracy and fairness of financial statements. To fulfill that responsibility, management must see that transactions are properly recorded and that the company's assets are protected. That, in turn, requires a system of internal controls. In this chapter, we examine internal controls over the transactions of merchandising companies and the operating cycle in which such transactions take place. The internal controls and other issues that we describe here also apply to manufacturing companies.

LEARNING OBJECTIVES

Making a Statement

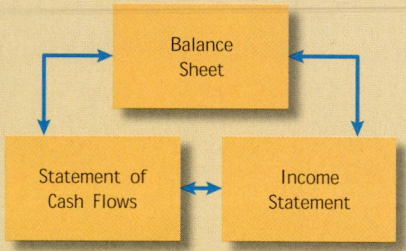

Merchandising transactions can impact all the financial statements.

LO1 Identify the management issues related to merchandising businesses.

LO2 Describe the terms of sale related to merchandising transactions.

LO3 Prepare an income statement and record merchandising transactions under the perpetual inventory system.

LO4 Prepare an income statement and record merchandising transactions under the periodic inventory system.

LO5 Describe the components of internal control, control activities, and limitations on internal control.

LO6 Apply internal control activities to common merchandising transactions.

- How can the company efficiently manage its cycle of merchandising operations?

- How can merchandising transactions be recorded to reflect the company's performance?

- How can the company maintain control over its merchandising operations?

Costco is a highly successful and fast-growing merchandising company. Like all other merchandisers, Costco has two key decisions to make: the price at which it will sell goods and the level of service it will provide. A department store may set the price of its merchandise at a relatively high level and provide a great deal of service. A discount store, on the other hand, may price its merchandise at a relatively low level and provide limited service. In the type of discount stores that Costco operates, customers buy memberships that allow them to buy in bulk at wholesale prices. Costco purchases merchandise in large quantities from many suppliers, places the goods on racks in its warehouse-like stores, and sells the goods to customers at very low prices, with less personal service.

Costco's large scale, reflected in its Financial Highlights,[1] presents management with many challenges.

COSTCO'S FINANCIAL HIGHLIGHTS
Operating Results (In millions)

Fiscal-Year Ended	August 31, 2004	August 31, 2003	Change
Net revenue	$48,107	$42,546	13.1%
Cost of sales	42,092	37,235	13.0
Gross margin	$ 6,015	$ 5,311	13.3
Operating expenses	4,630	4,154	11.5
Operating income	$ 1,385	$ 1,157	19.7

Managing Merchandising Businesses

A **merchandising business** earns income by buying and selling goods, which are called **merchandise inventory**. Whether a merchandiser is a wholesaler or a retailer, it uses the same basic accounting methods as a service company. However, the buying and selling of goods adds to the complexity of the business and of the accounting process. To understand the issues involved in accounting for a merchandising business, one must be familiar with the issues involved in managing such a business.

Operating Cycle

Merchandising businesses engage in a series of transactions called the **operating cycle**. Figure 1 shows the transactions that make up this cycle:

1. Purchase of merchandise inventory for cash or on credit
2. Payment for purchases made on credit
3. Sales of merchandise inventory for cash or on credit
4. Collection of cash from credit sales

Study Note

The operating cycle is the average days' inventory on hand plus the average number of days to collect credit sales.

When merchandisers purchase inventory on credit, which they usually do, they have a period of time before payment is due. However, this period is generally less than the time it takes them to sell the goods. To finance the inventory until they sell it and collect payment for it, merchandisers must rely on cash flows from within the company or from borrowing. If they lack the cash to pay bills when they come due, they can be forced out of business. Thus, managing cash flow is a critical concern.

A merchandiser's need to manage cash flow is demonstrated in Figure 2, which shows the financing period. Sometimes referred to as the *cash gap*, the

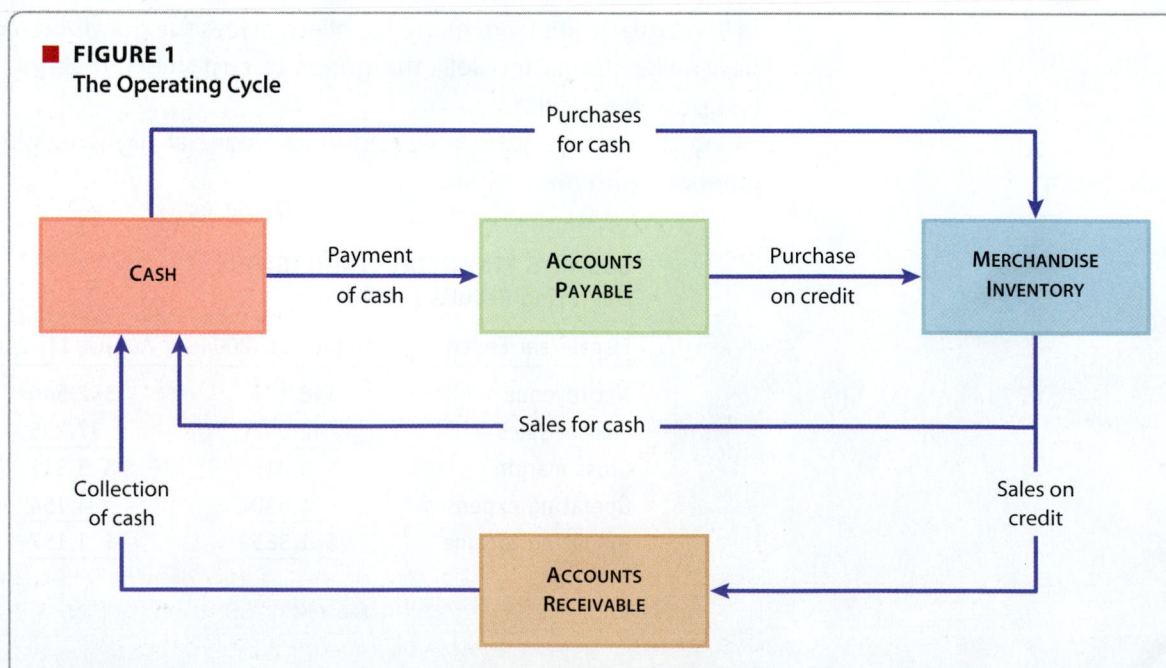

■ **FIGURE 1**
The Operating Cycle

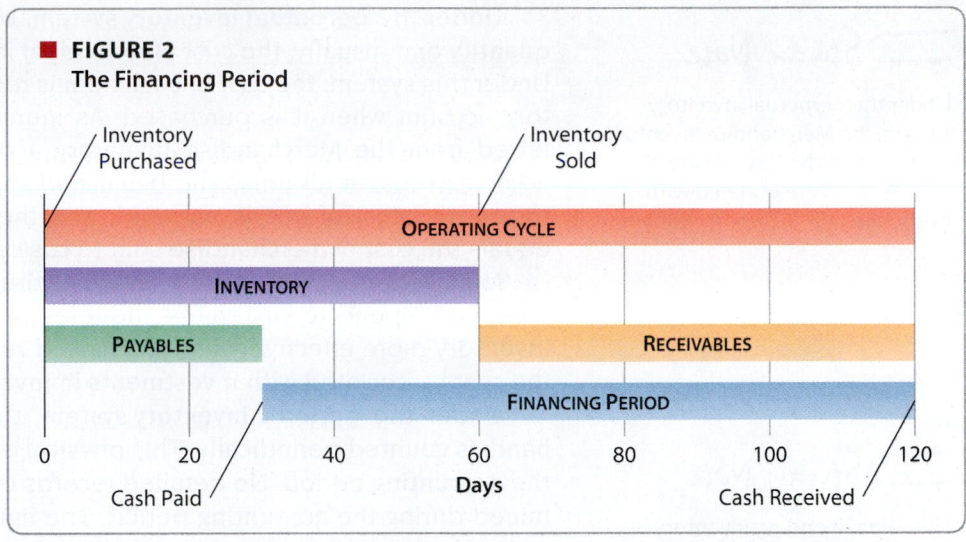

■ **FIGURE 2**
The Financing Period

financing period is the amount of time from the purchase of inventory until it is sold and payment is collected, less the amount of time creditors give the company to pay for the inventory. Thus, if it takes 60 days to sell the inventory, 60 days to collect for the sale, and creditors' payment terms are 30 days, the financing period is 90 days. During the financing period, the company will be without cash from this series of transactions and will need either to have funds available internally or to borrow from a bank.

The type of merchandising operation in which a company engages can affect the financing period. For example, compare **Costco's** financing period with that of a traditional department store chain, **Dillard's, Inc.**:

	Dillard's	Costco	Difference
Days' inventory on hand	102 days	30 days	−72 days
Days' receivable	42	3	−39
Less days' payable	−43	−29	−(14)
Financing period	**101 days**	**4 days**	**−97 days**

Costco has a significant advantage over Dillard's because it holds its inventory for a far shorter period before it sells it and collects receivables much faster. Its very short financing period is one of the reasons Costco can charge such low prices.

By reducing its financing period, a company can improve its cash flow. Many merchandisers, including Costco, do this by selling as much as possible for cash. Cash sales include sales on bank *credit cards*, such as Visa or Master-Card, and on *debit cards*, which draw directly on the purchaser's bank account. They are considered cash sales because funds from them are available to the merchandiser immediately. Small retail stores may have mostly cash sales and very few credit sales, whereas large wholesale concerns may have almost all credit sales.

Study Note

A sale takes place when title to the goods transfers to the buyer.

Choice of Inventory System

Another issue in managing a merchandising business is the choice of inventory system. Management must choose the system or combination of systems that best achieves the company's goals. The two basic systems of accounting for the many items in merchandise inventory are the perpetual inventory system and the periodic inventory system.

Study Note

Under the perpetual inventory system, the Merchandise Inventory account and the Cost of Goods Sold account are updated with every sale.

Under the **perpetual inventory system**, continuous records are kept of the quantity and, usually, the cost of individual items as they are bought and sold. Under this system, the cost of each item is recorded in the Merchandise Inventory account when it is purchased. As merchandise is sold, its cost is transferred from the Merchandise Inventory account to the Cost of Goods Sold account. Thus, at all times the balance of the Merchandise Inventory account equals the cost of goods on hand, and the balance in Cost of Goods Sold equals the cost of merchandise sold to customers.

Managers use the detailed data that the perpetual inventory system provides to respond to customers' inquiries about product availability, to order inventory more effectively and thus avoid running out of stock, and to control the costs associated with investments in inventory.

Under the **periodic inventory system**, the inventory not yet sold, or on hand, is counted periodically. This physical count is usually taken at the end of the accounting period. No detailed records of the inventory on hand are maintained during the accounting period. The figure for inventory on hand is accurate only on the balance sheet date. As soon as any purchases or sales are made, the inventory figure becomes a historical amount, and it remains so until the new ending inventory amount is entered at the end of the next accounting period.

Study Note

The value of ending inventory on the balance sheet is determined by multiplying the quantity of each inventory item by its unit cost.

Some retail and wholesale businesses use the periodic inventory system because it reduces the amount of clerical work. If a business is fairly small, management can maintain control over its inventory simply through observation or by using an offline system of cards or computer records. But for larger businesses, the lack of detailed records may lead to lost sales or high operating costs.

Because of the difficulty and expense of accounting for the purchase and sale of each item, companies that sell items of low value in high volume have traditionally used the periodic inventory system. Examples of such companies include drugstores, automobile parts stores, department stores, and discount stores. In contrast, companies that sell items that have a high unit value, such as appliances or automobiles, have tended to use the perpetual inventory system.

The distinction between high and low unit value for inventory systems has blurred considerably in recent years. Although the periodic inventory system is still widely used, computerization has led to a large increase in the use of the perpetual inventory system. It is important to note that the perpetual inventory system does not eliminate the need for a physical count of the inventory; one should be taken periodically to ensure that the actual number of goods on hand matches the quantity indicated by the computer records.

FOCUS ON BUSINESS PRACTICE

How Have Bar Codes Influenced the Choice of Inventory Systems?

Most grocery stores, which traditionally used the periodic inventory system, now employ bar coding to update the physical inventory as items are sold. At the checkout counter, the cashier scans the electronic marking on each product, called a *bar code* or *universal product code* (UPC), into the cash register, which is linked to a computer that records the sale. Bar coding has become common in all types of retail companies, and in manufacturing firms and hospitals as well. It has also become a major factor in the increased use of the perpetual inventory system. Interestingly, some retail businesses now use the perpetual inventory system for keeping track of the physical flow of inventory and the periodic inventory system for preparing their financial statements.

Foreign Business Transactions

Most large merchandising and manufacturing firms and even many small ones transact some of their business overseas. For example, a U.S. manufacturer may expand by selling its product to foreign customers, or it may lower its product cost by buying a less expensive part from a source in another country. Such sales and purchase transactions may take place in Japanese yen, British pounds, or some other foreign currency.

When an international transaction involves two different currencies, as most such transactions do, one currency has to be translated into another by using an exchange rate. As we noted earlier in the text, an *exchange rate* is the value of one currency stated in terms of another. We also noted that the values of other currencies in relation to the dollar rise and fall daily according to supply and demand. Thus, if there is a delay between the date of sale or purchase and the date of receipt of payment, the amount of cash involved in an international transaction may differ from the amount originally agreed on.

If the billing of an international sale and the payment for it are both in the domestic currency, no accounting problem arises. For example, if a U.S. maker of precision tools sells $160,000 worth of its products to a British company and bills the British company in dollars, the U.S. company will receive $160,000 when it collects payment. However, if the U.S. company bills the British company in British pounds and accepts payment in pounds, it will incur an **exchange gain or loss** if the exchange rate between dollars and pounds changes between the date of sale and the date of payment.

For example, assume that the U.S. company billed the sale of $160,000 at £100,000, reflecting an exchange rate of 1.60 (that is, $1.60 per pound) on the sale date. Now assume that by the date of payment, the exchange rate has fallen to 1.50. When the U.S. company receives its £100,000, it will be worth only $150,000 (£100,000 × $1.50 = $150,000). It will have incurred an exchange loss of $10,000 because it agreed to accept a fixed number of British pounds in payment for its products, and the value of each pound dropped before the payment was made. Had the value of the pound in relation to the dollar increased, the company would have made an exchange gain.

The same logic applies to purchases as to sales, except that the relationship of exchange gains and losses to changes in exchange rates is reversed. For example, assume that the U.S company purchases products from the British company for $160,000. If the payment is to be made in U.S. dollars, no accounting problem arises. However, if the British company expects to be paid in pounds, the U.S. company will have an exchange gain of $10,000 because it agreed to pay a fixed £100,000, and between the dates of purchase and payment, the exchange value of the pound decreased from $1.60 to $1.50. To make the £100,000 payment, the U.S. company has to expend only $150,000.

Exchange gains and losses are reported on the income statement. Because of their bearing on a company's financial performance, they are of considerable interest to managers and investors. Lack of uniformity in international accounting standards is another matter of which investors must be wary.

The Need for Internal Controls

Buying and selling, the principal transactions of merchandising businesses, involve assets—cash, accounts receivable, and merchandise inventory—that are vulnerable to theft and embezzlement. Cash and inventory can, of course, be fairly easy to steal. The potential for embezzlement exists because the

Merchandise inventory includes all goods intended for sale wherever they are located—on store shelves, in warehouses, on car lots, or in transit from suppliers if title to the goods has passed to the merchandiser. To prevent loss of inventory, a merchandiser must have an effective system of internal control.

Study Note

Inventory shortages can result from honest mistakes, such as accidentally tagging inventory with the wrong number.

large number of transactions that are usually involved in a merchandising business (e.g., cash receipts, receipts on account, payments for purchases, and receipts and shipments of inventory) makes monitoring the accounting records difficult.

If a merchandising company does not take steps to protect its assets, it can suffer high losses of both cash and inventory. Management's responsibility is to establish an environment, accounting systems, and control procedures that will protect the company's assets. These systems and procedures are called **internal controls**.

Taking a **physical inventory** facilitates control over merchandise inventory. This process involves an actual count of all merchandise on hand. It can be a difficult task because it is easy to accidentally omit items or count them twice. As we noted earlier, a physical inventory must be taken under both the periodic and the perpetual inventory systems.

A company's merchandise inventory includes all goods intended for sale regardless of where they are located—on shelves, in storerooms, in warehouses, or in trucks between warehouses and stores. It also includes goods in transit from suppliers if title to the goods has passed to the merchandiser. Ending inventory does not include merchandise that a company has sold but not yet delivered to customers. Nor does it include goods that it cannot sell because they are damaged or obsolete. If damaged or obsolete goods can be sold at a reduced price, however, they should be included in ending inventory at their reduced value.

Merchandisers usually take a physical inventory after the close of business on the last day of their fiscal year. To facilitate the process, they often end the fiscal year in a slow season, when inventories are at relatively low levels. For example, many department stores end their fiscal year in January or February. After hours—at night, on a weekend, or when the store closes for all or part of a day for taking inventory—employees count all items and record the results on numbered inventory tickets or sheets, following procedures to ensure that no items will be missed. Using bar coding to take inventory electronically has greatly facilitated the process in many companies.

Most companies experience losses of merchandise inventory from spoilage, shoplifting, and theft by employees. When such losses occur, the periodic inventory system provides no means of identifying them because the costs are automatically included in the cost of goods sold. For example, suppose a company has lost $1,250 in stolen merchandise during an accounting period. When the physical inventory is taken, the missing items are not in stock, so they cannot be counted. Because the ending inventory does not contain these items, the amount subtracted from goods available for sale is less than it would be if the goods were in stock. The cost of goods sold, then, is overstated by $1,250. In a sense, the cost of goods sold is inflated by the amount of merchandise that has been lost.

The perpetual inventory system makes it easier to identify such losses. Because the Merchandise Inventory account is continuously updated for sales, purchases, and returns, the loss will show up as the difference between the inventory records and the physical inventory taken at the end of the accounting period. Once the amount of the loss has been identified, the ending inventory is updated by crediting the Merchandise Inventory account. The offsetting debit is usually an increase in Cost of Goods Sold because the loss is considered a cost that reduces the company's gross margin.

Management's Responsibility for Internal Control

Management is responsible for establishing a satisfactory system of internal controls. Such a system includes all the policies and procedures needed to ensure the reliability of financial reporting, compliance with laws and regulations, and the effectiveness and efficiency of operations. In other words, management must safeguard the firm's assets, ensure the reliability of its accounting records, and see that its employees comply with all legal requirements and operate the firm to the best advantage of its owners.

Section 404 of the Sarbanes-Oxley act of 2002 requires that the chief executive officer, the chief financial officer, and the auditors of a public company fully document and certify the company's system of internal controls. For example, in its annual report, **Costco's** management acknowledges its responsibility for internal control as follows:

> [We] are responsible for establishing and maintaining disclosure controls and procedures and internal controls for financial reporting [on behalf of the company].[2]

FOCUS ON BUSINESS PRACTICE
How Hard Is Financial Fraud to Detect When Its Effects Are Not Material?

In some companies, management works hard to fool the auditors. Several former chief financial officers of **Health-South** pleaded guilty to a massive fraud that did manage to fool the auditors for a number of years. To meet the expectations of financial analysts, these executives manipulated the company's revenue line so that revenue and earnings appeared greater than they were. The fraud involved making adjustments for the difference between what HealthSouth charged a patient and the amount the company could collect from the patient's health insurer. By improperly recording these amounts, HealthSouth's CFOs improved revenue and earnings. For every dollar of illicit revenue they recorded as a credit, they had to make a corresponding debit entry on the balance sheet. Knowing the materiality convention and that the auditors look for material differences, they spread the adjustments around the balance sheet in small pieces so that the auditors wouldn't notice. In effect, the balance sheet looked right because every account, even cash, was artificially increased by a small, or immaterial, amount. In the end, total assets were overstated by $1.5 billion.[3]

S T O P • R E V I E W • A P P L Y

1-1. What is the operating cycle of a merchandising business, and why is it important?

1-2. What is the financing period, and what are its components?

1-3. What is the difference between the perpetual inventory system and the periodic inventory system?

1-4. What conditions cause an exchange gain or loss?

1-5. Why are internal controls needed, and what is management's responsibility for implementing them?

Suggested answers to all Stop, Review, and Apply questions follow the appendixes.

Terms of Sale

LO2 Describe the terms of sale related to merchandising transactions.

When goods are sold on credit, both parties should understand the amount and timing of payment as well as other terms of the purchase, such as who pays delivery charges and what warranties or rights of return apply. Sellers quote prices in different ways. Many merchants quote the price at which they expect to sell their goods. Others, particularly manufacturers and wholesalers, quote prices as a percentage (usually 30 percent or more) off their list or catalogue prices. Such a reduction is called a **trade discount**.

For example, if an article is listed at $1,000 with a trade discount of 40 percent, or $400, the seller records the sale at $600, and the buyer records the purchase at $600. The seller may raise or lower the trade discount depending on the quantity purchased. The list or catalogue price and related trade discount are used only to arrive at an agreed-on price; they do not appear in the accounting records.

Sales and Purchases Discounts

Study Note

A trade discount applies to the list or catalogue price. A sales discount applies to the sales price.

The terms of sale are usually printed on the sales invoice and thus constitute part of the sales agreement. Terms differ from industry to industry. In some industries, payment is expected in a short period of time, such as 10 or 30 days. In these cases, the invoice is marked "n/10" ("net 10") or "n/30" ("net 30"), meaning that the amount of the invoice is due either 10 days or 30 days after the invoice date. If the invoice is due 10 days after the end of the month, it is marked "n/10 eom."

Study Note

Early collection also has the advantage of reducing the probability of a customer's defaulting.

In some industries, it is customary to give a discount for early payment. This discount, called a **sales discount**, is intended to increase the seller's liquidity by reducing the amount of money tied up in accounts receivable. An invoice that offers a sales discount might be labeled "2/10, n/30," which means that the buyer either can pay the invoice within 10 days of the invoice date and take a 2 percent discount or can wait 30 days and pay the full amount of the invoice. It is often advantageous for a buyer to take the discount because the saving of 2 percent over a period of 20 days (from the 11th day to the 30th day) represents an effective annual rate of 36.5 percent (365 days ÷ 20 days × 2% = 36.5%). Most companies would be better off borrowing money to take the discount. The practice of giving sales discounts has been declining because it is costly to the seller and because, from the buyer's viewpoint, the amount of the discount is usually very small in relation to the price of the purchase.

Because it is not possible to know at the time of a sale whether the customer will pay in time to take advantage of a sales discount, the discounts are recorded only at the time the customer pays. For example, suppose Laboda Sportswear Corporation sells merchandise to a customer on September 20 for $600 on terms of 2/10, n/30. Laboda records the sale on September 20 for the full amount of $600. If the customer takes advantage of the discount by paying on or before September 30, Laboda will receive $588 in cash and will reduce its accounts receivable by $600. The difference of $12 ($600 × .02) will be debited to an account called *Sales Discounts*. Sales Discounts is a contra-revenue account with a normal debit balance that is deducted from sales on the income statement.

The same logic applies to **purchases discounts**, which are discounts that a buyer takes for the early payment of merchandise. For example, the buyer in the transaction described above will record the purchase on September 20 at $600. If the buyer pays on or before September 30, it will record cash paid of $588 and reduce its accounts payable by $600. The difference of $12 is recorded as a credit to an account called Purchases Discounts. The *Purchases Discounts account* reduces cost of goods sold or purchases depending on the inventory method used.

Transportation Costs

In some industries, the seller usually pays transportation costs and charges a price that includes those costs. In other industries, it is customary for the purchaser to pay transportation charges. Special terms designate whether the seller or the purchaser pays the freight charges.

FOB shipping point means that the seller places the merchandise "free on board" at the point of origin and the buyer bears the shipping costs. The title

Shipping terms affect the financial statements. *FOB shipping point* means the buyer pays the freight charges; when relatively small, these charges are usually included in cost of goods sold on the buyer's income statement. *FOB destination* means the seller pays the frieght charges; they are included in selling expenses on the seller's income statement.

to the merchandise passes to the buyer at that point. For example, when the sales agreement for the purchase of a car says "FOB factory," the buyer must pay the freight from the factory where the car was made to wherever he or she is located, and the buyer owns the car from the time it leaves the factory.

FOB destination means that the seller bears the transportation costs to the place where the merchandise is delivered. The seller retains title until the merchandise reaches its destination and usually prepays the shipping costs, in which case the buyer makes no accounting entry for freight.

The effects of these special shipping terms are summarized as follows:

Shipping Term	Where Title Passes	Who Pays the Cost of Transportation
FOB shipping point	At origin	Buyer
FOB destination	At destination	Seller

When the buyer pays the transportation charge, it is called **freight-in**, and it is added to the cost of merchandise purchased. Thus, freight-in increases the buyer's cost of merchandise inventory, as well as the cost of goods sold after they are sold. When freight-in is a relatively small amount, most companies include the cost in the cost of goods sold on the income statement rather than going to the trouble of allocating part of it to merchandise inventory.

When the seller pays the transportation charge, it is called **delivery expense**, or *freight-out*. Because the seller incurs this cost to facilitate the sale of its product, the cost is included in selling expenses on the income statement.

Terms of Debit and Credit Card Sales

Many retailers allow customers to use debit or credit cards to charge their purchases. Debit cards deduct directly from a person's bank account, whereas a credit card allows for payment later. Five of the most widely used credit cards are American Express, Discover Card, Diners Club, MasterCard, and Visa. The customer establishes credit with the lender (the credit card issuer) and receives a plastic card to use in making charges. If a seller accepts the card, the customer signs an invoice at the time of the sale. The sale is communicated to the seller's bank, resulting in a cash deposit in the seller's bank account. Thus, the seller does not have to establish the customer's credit, collect from the customer, or tie up money in accounts receivable. As payment, the lender, rather than paying the total amount of the credit card sales, takes a discount of 2 to 6 percent. The discount is a selling expense for the merchandiser. For example, if a restaurant makes sales of $1,000 on Visa credit cards and Visa takes a 4 percent discount on the sales, the restaurant would record Cash in the amount of $960 and Credit Card Expense in the amount of $40.

FOCUS ON BUSINESS PRACTICE
How Are Buying Habits Changing?

Cash and checks are becoming an increasingly rare method of paying for purchases. Approximately 73 percent of Americans have credit or debit cards, and the purchases they make with these cards total $2.2 trillion annually. In 2003, for the first time, credit and debit cards accounted for more than half of all in-store payments . Although retailers that accept these cards must pay the fees charged by the card issuers, the evidence shows that acceptance of the cards increases the amount of sales. For instance, when **McDonald's** started accepting credit and debit cards, its average transaction went from $4.50 to $7.00.[4]

STOP • REVIEW • APPLY

2-1. What is the difference between a trade discount and a sales discount?

2-2. Is Sales Discounts an asset, liability, expense, or contra-revenue account? Is the normal balance of the Sales Discounts account a debit or a credit balance?

2-3. Two suppliers quoted these prices and terms on 50 units of a product:

	Price	Terms
Supplier A	$20 per unit	FOB shipping point
Supplier B	$21 per unit	FOB destination

Which supplier is quoting the better deal? Explain your answer.

2-4. Is freight-in an operating expense? Explain your answer.

Perpetual Inventory System

LO3 Prepare an income statement and record merchandising transactions under the perpetual inventory system.

Exhibit 1 shows how an income statement appears when a company uses the perpetual inventory system. The focal point of the statement is cost of goods sold, which is deducted from net sales to arrive at gross margin. Under the perpetual inventory system, the Merchandise Inventory and Cost of Goods Sold accounts are continually updated during the accounting period as purchases, sales, and other inventory transactions that affect these accounts occur.

Purchases of Merchandise

Figure 3 shows how transactions involving purchases of merchandise are recorded under the perpetual inventory system. As you can see, the focus of

EXHIBIT 1 ▶

Income Statement Under the Perpetual Inventory System

Laboda Sportswear Corporation
Income Statement
For the Year Ended December 31, 20x7

Net sales	$478,650
Cost of goods sold*	262,720
Gross margin	$215,930
Operating Expenses	156,968
Income before income taxes	$ 58,962
Income taxes	10,000
Net income	$ 48,962

*Freight-in has been included in cost of goods sold.

> **Study Note**
>
> On the income statement, freight-in is included as part of cost of goods sold, and delivery expense (freight-out) is included as an operating (selling) expense.

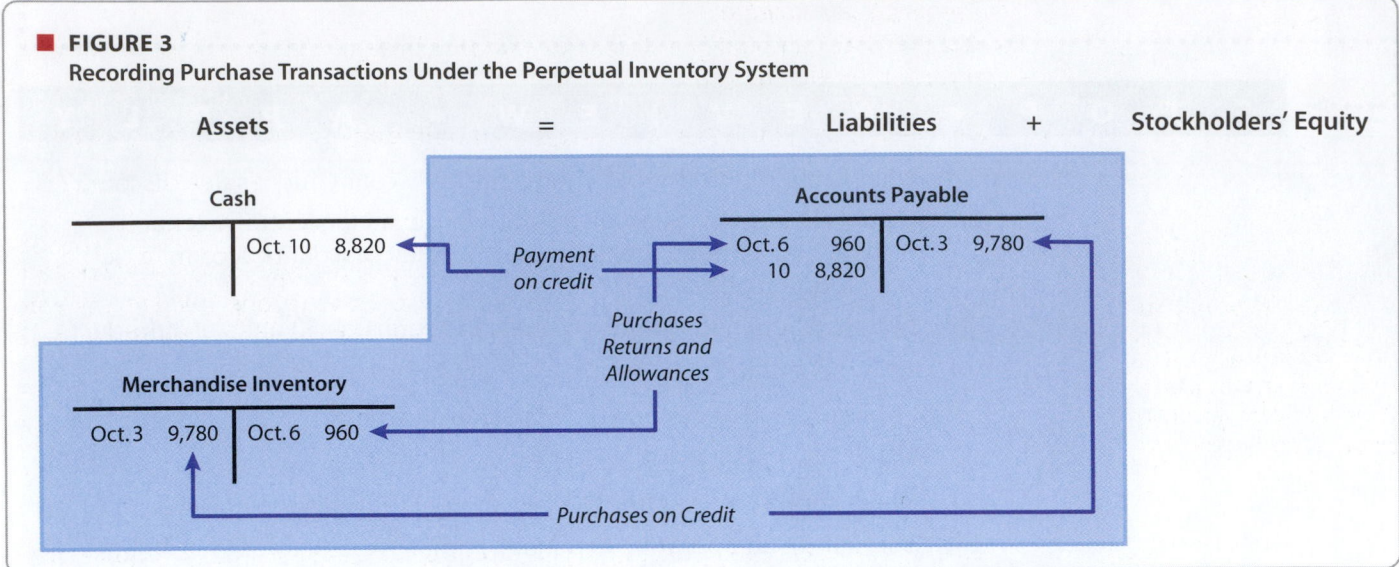

■ **FIGURE 3**
Recording Purchase Transactions Under the Perpetual Inventory System

these journal entries is Accounts Payable. These entries are summarized below. (For a comparison of complete journal entries made under the perpetual and periodic inventory systems, see the Review Problem in this chapter.)

Purchases on Credit
Oct. 3: Received merchandise purchased on credit, invoice dated Oct. 1, terms n/10, $9,780.

Comment: Under the perpetual inventory system, the cost of merchandise is recorded in the Merchandise Inventory account at the time of purchase. In the transaction described here, payment is due ten days from the invoice date. If an invoice includes a charge for shipping or if shipping is billed separately, it should be debited to Freight-In.

Purchases Returns and Allowances
Oct. 6: Returned part of merchandise received on Oct. 3 for credit, $960.

Comment: Under the perpetual inventory system, when a buyer is allowed to return all or part of a purchase or is given an allowance—a reduction in the amount to be paid, Merchandise Inventory is reduced, as is Accounts Payable.

> *Study Note*
>
> The Merchandise Inventory account increases when a purchase is made.

FOCUS ON BUSINESS PRACTICE

Are Purchase Allowances Revenues?

Food companies like **Sara Lee, Kraft, Georgia-Pacific,** and **Nestlé** commonly give rebates, a type of purchase allowance, to supermarket chains that allow them more room to display their products. Another common practice among companies in the food industry is to grant customers rebates ranging from 8.5 percent to 48 percent depending on the customer's annual volume of purchases. A division of **Ahold,** the large Dutch supermarket operator, booked the rebates it anticipated receiving from food companies as revenue at the time it placed its orders. Simply by buying more, which it did—to the point that its warehouses were filled with unsold goods—it was able to inflate revenues. Regional managers said it was clear that if they didn't place large orders, their jobs would be on the line. As it turned out, by prematurely recognizing the rebates, Ahold overstated it profits over two years by more than $500 million. The correct accounting practice would have been to wait until the rebate was granted at the time of payment and to show it as a reduction in cost of goods sold, not as an increase in revenue.[5]

Payments on Account

Oct. 10: Paid amount in full due for the purchase of Oct. 3, part of which was returned on Oct. 6, $8,820.

Comment: Payment is made for the net amount due of $8,820 ($9,780 − $960).

Sales of Merchandise

Study Note

The Cost of Goods Sold account is increased and the Merchandise Inventory account is decreased when a sale is made.

Figure 4 shows how transactions involving sales of merchandise are recorded under the perpetual inventory system. These transactions involve several accounts, including Cash, Accounts Receivable, Merchandise Inventory, and Cost of Goods Sold.

Sales on Credit

Oct. 7: Sold merchandise on credit, terms n/30, FOB destination, $2,400; the cost of the merchandise was $1,440.

Comment: Under the perpetual inventory system, sales always require two entries, as shown in Figure 4. First, the sale is recorded by increasing Accounts Receivable and Sales. Second, Cost of Goods Sold is updated by a transfer from Merchandise Inventory. In the case of cash sales, Cash rather than Accounts Receivable is debited for the amount of the sale. If the seller pays for the shipping, it should be debited to Delivery Expense.

Sales Returns and Allowances

Oct. 9: Accepted return of part of merchandise sold on Oct. 7 for full credit and returned it to merchandise inventory, $600; the cost of the merchandise was $360.

■ **FIGURE 4**
Recording Sales Transactions Under the Perpetual Inventory System

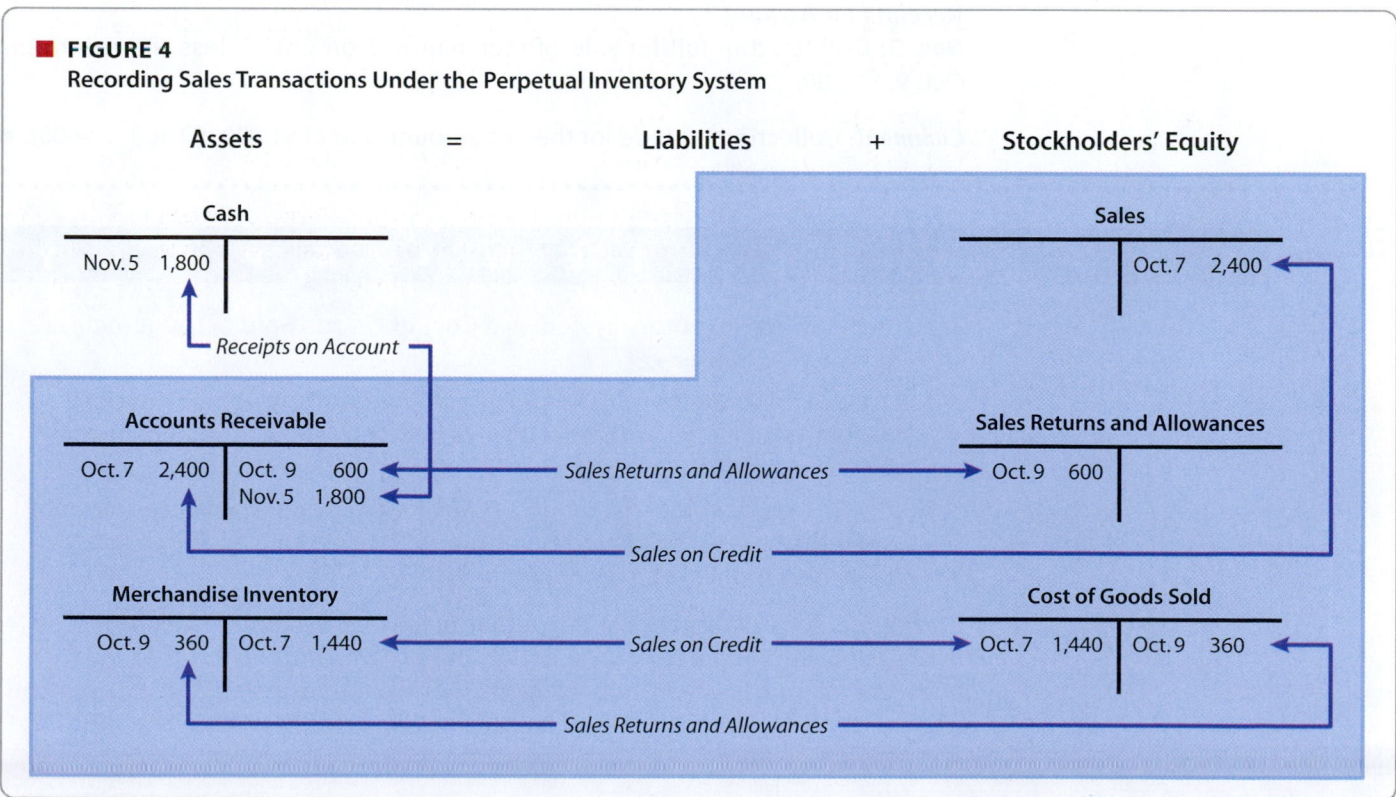

Comment: Under the perpetual inventory system, when a seller allows the buyer to return all or part of a sale or gives an allowance—a reduction in amount, two entries are again necessary. First, the original sale is reversed by reducing Accounts Receivable and debiting Sales Returns and Allowances. The **Sales Returns and Allowances account** gives management a readily available measure of unsatisfactory products and dissatisfied customers. It is a contra-revenue account with a normal debit balance and is deducted from sales on the income statement. Second, the cost of the merchandise must also be transferred from the Cost of Goods Sold account back into the Merchandise Inventory account. If the company makes an allowance instead of accepting a return, or if the merchandise cannot be returned to inventory and resold, this transfer is not made.

> **Study Note**
>
> Because the Sales account is established with a credit, its contra account, Sales Returns and Allowances, is established with a debit.

Receipts on Account
Nov. 5: Collected in full for sale of merchandise on Oct. 7, less the return on Oct. 9, $1,800.

Comment: Collection is made for the net amount due of $1,800 ($2,400 − $600).

S T O P • R E V I E W • A P P L Y

3-1. Under which inventory system is a Cost of Goods Sold account maintained? Explain why.

3-2. Discuss this statement: "The perpetual inventory system is the best system because management always needs to know how much inventory is on hand."

3-3. Why is it advisable to maintain a Sales Returns and Allowances account when the same result could be obtained by debiting each return or allowance to the Sales account?

Merchandising Transactions: Perpetual Inventory System The numbered items at the top of the next page are account titles, and the lettered items are types of merchandising transactions. For each transaction, indicate which accounts are debited or credited by placing the account numbers in the appropriate columns.

1. Cash
2. Accounts Receivable
3. Merchandise Inventory
4. Accounts Payable
5. Sales
6. Sales Returns and Allowances
7. Cost of Goods Sold

	Account Debited	Account Credited
a. Purchase on credit	3	4
b. Purchase return for credit	4	3
c. Purchase for cash	3	1
d. Sale on credit	2	3
e. Sale for cash	1	3
f. Sales return for credit	3	2
g. Payment on account	4	1
h. Receipt on account	1	2

SOLUTION

	Account Debited	Account Credited
a. Purchase on credit	3	4
b. Purchase return for credit	4	3
c. Purchase for cash	3	1
d. Sale on credit	2, 7	3, 5
e. Sale for cash	1, 7	3, 5
f. Sales return for credit	3, 6	2, 7
g. Payment on account	4	1
h. Receipt on account	1	2

Periodic Inventory System

LO4 Prepare an income statement and record merchandising transactions under the periodic inventory system.

Exhibit 2 shows how an income statement appears when a company uses the periodic inventory system. A major feature of this statement is the computation of cost of goods sold. Cost of goods sold must be computed on the income statement because it is not updated for purchases, sales, and other transactions during the accounting period, as it is under the perpetual inventory system. Figure 5 illustrates the components of cost of goods sold.

EXHIBIT 2 ▶

Income Statement Under the Periodic Inventory System

Laboda Sportswear Corporation
Income Statement
For the Year Ended December 31, 20x7

Net sales			$478,650
Cost of goods sold			
Merchandise inventory, December 31, 20x6		$105,600	
Purchases	$252,800		
Less purchases returns and allowances	15,552		
Net purchases	$237,248		
Freight-in	16,472		
Net cost of purchases		253,720	
Goods available for sale		$359,320	
Less merchandise inventory, December 31, 20x7		96,600	
Cost of goods sold			262,720
Gross margin			$215,930
Operating expenses			156,968
Income before income taxes			$ 58,962
Income taxes			10,000
Net income			$ 48,962

To calculate cost of goods sold, the **goods available for sale** must first be determined. The goods available for sale during an accounting period is the sum of two factors: beginning inventory and the net cost of purchases during the period. As you can see in Exhibit 2, the goods that Laboda Sportswear Corporation has available for sale during the period amount to $359,320 ($105,600 + $253,720).

If a company sold all the goods available for sale during an accounting period, the cost of goods sold would equal the goods available for sale. In most

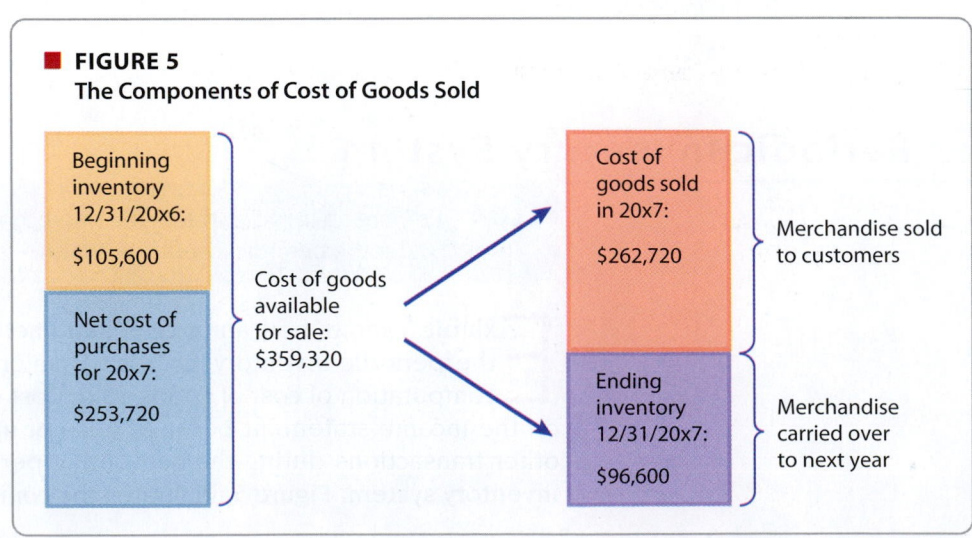

■ FIGURE 5
The Components of Cost of Goods Sold

businesses, however, some merchandise remains unsold and on hand at the end of the period. This ending inventory must be deducted from the goods available for sale to determine the cost of goods sold. In Exhibit 2, the company's ending inventory on December 31, 20x7, is $96,600. Thus, its cost of goods sold is $262,720 ($359,320 − $96,600).

An important component of the cost of goods sold section is **net cost of purchases**. As you can see in Exhibit 2, net cost of purchases is the sum of net purchases and freight-in. **Net purchases** equal total purchases less any deductions, such as purchases returns and allowances and any discounts allowed by suppliers for early payment. Freight-in is added to net purchases because transportation charges are a necessary cost of receiving merchandise for sale.

Purchases of Merchandise

Figure 6 shows how transactions involving purchases of merchandise are recorded under the periodic inventory system. A primary difference between the perpetual and periodic inventory systems is that in the perpetual inventory system, the Merchandise Inventory account is adjusted each time a purchase, sale, or other inventory transaction occurs, whereas in the periodic inventory system, the Merchandise Inventory account stays at its beginning balance until the physical inventory is recorded at the end of the period. The periodic system uses a Purchases account to accumulate purchases during an accounting period and a Purchases Returns and Allowances account to accumulate returns of and allowances on purchases.

The following sections illustrate how Laboda Sportswear Corporation would record purchase transactions under the periodic inventory system.

Purchases on Credit

Oct. 3: Received merchandise purchased on credit, invoice dated Oct. 1, terms n/10, $9,780.

Comment: Under the periodic inventory system, the cost of merchandise is recorded in the **Purchases account** at the time of purchase. This account is a temporary one used only with the periodic inventory system. Its sole purpose is to accumulate the total cost of merchandise purchased for resale during an

Study Note

Purchases accounts and Purchases Returns and Allowances accounts are used only in conjunction with a periodic inventory system.

Study Note

Under the periodic inventory system, the Purchases account increases when a company makes a purchase.

■ **FIGURE 6**
Recording Purchase Transactions Under the Periodic Inventory System

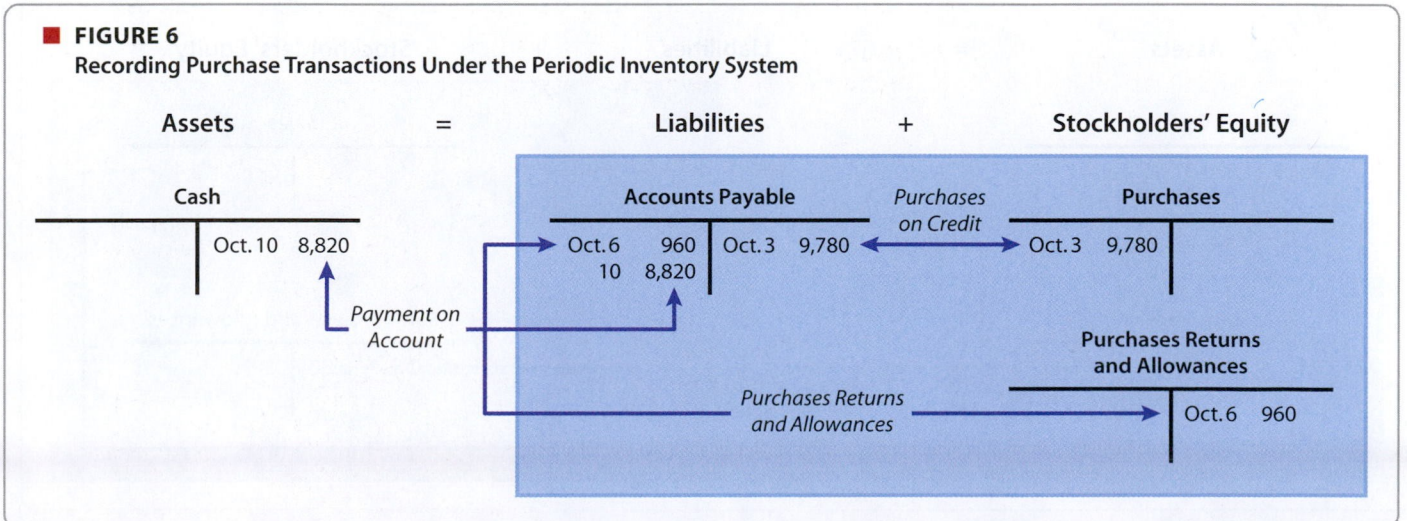

accounting period. (Purchases of other assets, such as equipment, are recorded in the appropriate asset account, not in the Purchases account.) The Purchases account does not indicate whether merchandise has been sold or is still on hand.

Purchases Returns and Allowances

Oct. 6: Returned part of merchandise received on Oct. 3 for credit, $960.

Comment: Under the periodic inventory system, the amount of a return or allowance is recorded in the **Purchases Returns and Allowances account**. This account is a contra-purchases account with a normal credit balance, and it is deducted from purchases on the income statement. Accounts Payable is also reduced.

Payments on Account

Oct. 10: Paid amount in full due for the purchase of Oct. 3, part of which was returned on Oct. 6, $8,820.

Comment: Payment is made for the net amount due of $8,820 ($9,780 − $960).

Sales of Merchandise

Figure 7 shows how transactions involving sales of merchandise are recorded under the periodic inventory system.

Sales on Credit

Oct. 7: Sold merchandise on credit, terms n/30, FOB destination, $2,400; the cost of the merchandise was $1,440.

Comment: As shown in Figure 7, under the periodic inventory system, sales require only one entry to increase Sales and Accounts Receivable. In the case of cash sales, Cash rather than Accounts Receivable is debited for the amount of the sale. If the seller pays for the shipping, the amount should be debited to Delivery Expense.

Study Note

Because the Purchases account is established with a debit, its contra account, Purchases Returns and Allowances, is established with a credit.

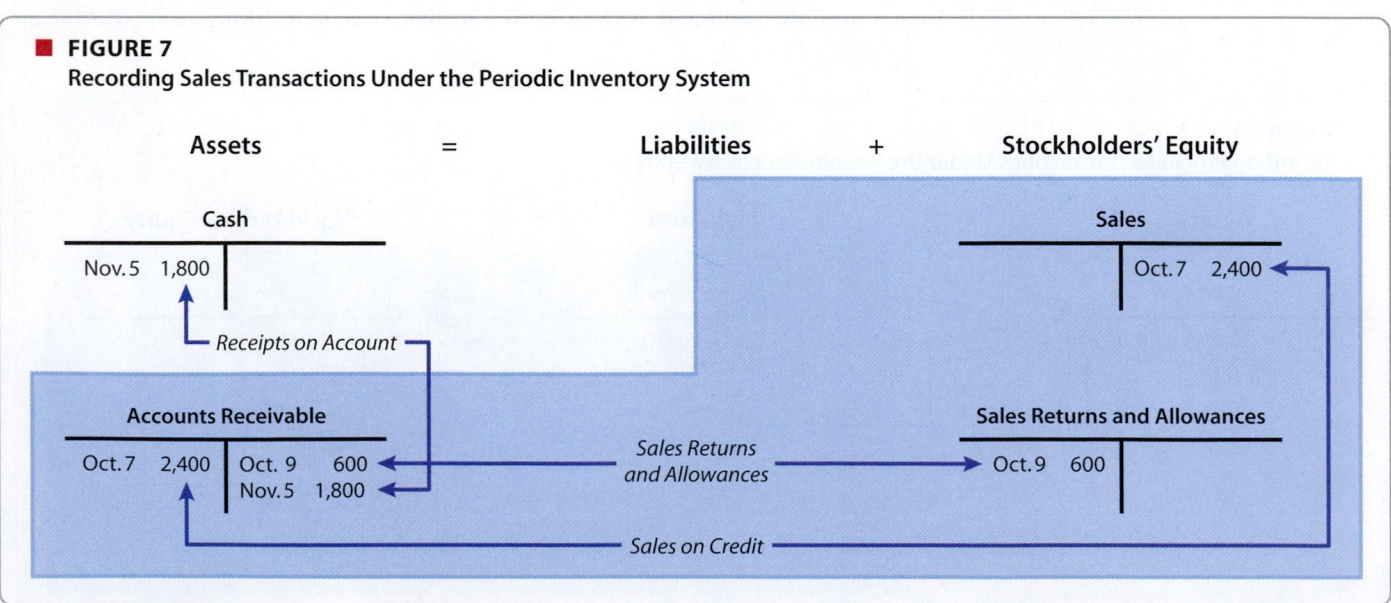

■ **FIGURE 7**
Recording Sales Transactions Under the Periodic Inventory System

Sales Returns and Allowances

Oct. 9: Accepted return of part of merchandise sold on Oct. 7 for full credit and returned it to merchandise inventory, $600; the cost of the merchandise was $360.

Comment: Under the periodic inventory system, when a seller allows the buyer to return all or part of a sale or gives an allowance, only one entry is needed to reduce Accounts Receivable and debit Sales Returns and Allowances. The Sales Returns and Allowances account is a contra-revenue account with a normal debit balance and is deducted from sales on the income statement.

Receipts on Account

Nov. 5: Collected in full for sale of merchandise on Oct. 7, less the return on Oct. 9, $1,800.

Comment: Collection is made for the net amount due of $1,800 ($2,400 − $600).

STOP • REVIEW • APPLY

4-1. Under the periodic inventory system, an important figure in computing cost of goods sold is goods available for sale. What are the two main components of goods available for sale, and what is the relationship of ending inventory to goods available for sale?

4-2. Under the periodic inventory system, how must the amount of inventory at the end of the year be determined?

4-3. Hornberger Hardware purchased the following items: (a) a delivery truck, (b) two dozen hammers, (c) supplies for its office workers, and (d) a broom for the janitor. Which items should be debited to the Purchases account under the periodic inventory system?

4-4. What are the principal differences in the way merchandise transactions are recorded under the perpetual inventory system and the periodic inventory system?

Merchandising Transactions: Periodic Inventory System   The numbered items at the top of the next page are account titles, and the lettered items are types of merchandising transactions. For each transaction, indicate which accounts are debited or credited by placing the account numbers in the appropriate columns.

1. Cash
2. Accounts Receivable
3. Merchandise Inventory
4. Accounts Payable
5. Sales
6. Sales Returns and Allowances
7. Purchases
8. Purchases Returns and Allowances

	Account Debited	Account Credited
a. Purchase on credit		
b. Purchase return for credit		
c. Purchase for cash		
d. Sale on credit		
e. Sale for cash		
f. Sales return for credit		
g. Payment on account		
h. Receipt on account		

SOLUTION

	Account Debited	Account Credited
a. Purchase on credit	7	4
b. Purchase return for credit	4	8
c. Purchase for cash	7	1
d. Sale on credit	2	5
e. Sale for cash	1	5
f. Sales return for credit	6	2
g. Payment on account	4	1
h. Receipt on account	1	2

Internal Control: Components, Activities, and Limitations

LO5 Describe the components of internal control, control activities, and limitations on internal control.

As mentioned earlier, if a merchandising company does not take steps to protect its assets, it can suffer high losses of cash and inventory through embezzlement and theft. To avoid such occurrences, management must set up and maintain a good system of internal control.

FOCUS ON BUSINESS PRACTICE
Which Frauds Are Most Common?

A survey of 5,000 large U.S. businesses disclosed that 36 percent suffered losses in excess of $1 million (up from 21 percent in 1998) due to fraud or inventory theft. The frauds most commonly cited were credit card fraud, check fraud, false invoices and phantom vendors, and expense account abuse. The most common reasons for the occurrences of these frauds were poor internal controls, management override of internal controls, and collusion. The most common methods of detecting them were notification by an employee, internal controls, internal auditor review, notification by a customer, and accidental discovery.

Companies that are successful in preventing fraud have a good system of internal control, a formal code of ethics, and a program to monitor compliance that includes a system for reporting incidents of fraud. These companies routinely communicate the existence of the program to their employees.[9]

Components of Internal Control

An effective system of internal control has five interrelated components:[10]

1. *Control environment* The **control environment** is created by management's overall attitude, awareness, and actions. It encompasses a company's ethics, philosophy and operating style, organizational structure, method of assigning authority and responsibility, and personnel policies and practices. Personnel should be qualified to handle responsibilities, which means that they must be trained and informed about what is expected of them. For example, the manager of a retail store should train employees to follow prescribed procedures for handling cash sales, credit card sales, and returns and refunds.

2. *Risk assessment* **Risk assessment** involves identifying areas in which risks of loss of assets or inaccuracies in accounting records are high so that adequate controls can be implemented. Among the greater risks in a retail store are that employees may steal cash and customers may steal goods.

3. *Information and communication* **Information and communication** pertains to the accounting system established by management—to the way the system gathers and treats information about the company's transactions and to how it communicates individual responsibilities within the system. Employees must understand exactly what their functions are.

4. *Control activities* **Control activities** are the policies and procedures management puts in place to see that its directives are carried out. (Control activities are discussed in more detail below.)

5. *Monitoring* **Monitoring** involves management's regular assessment of the quality of internal control, including periodic review of compliance with all policies and procedures. Large companies often have a staff of internal auditors who review the company's system of internal control to determine if it is working properly and if procedures are being followed. In smaller businesses, owners and managers conduct these reviews.

Control Activities

Control activities are a very important way of implementing internal control. The goal of these activities is to safeguard a company's assets and ensure the reliability of its accounting records.

Control activities including the following:

1. *Authorization* Managers should authorize certain transactions and activities. In a retail store, for example, cashiers customarily authorize cash sales, but other transactions, such as issuing a refund, may require a manager's approval.

2. *Recording transactions* To establish accountability for assets, all transactions should be recorded. For example, if a retail store uses a cash register that records sales, refunds, and other transactions on a paper tape or computer disk, the cashier can be held accountable for the cash received and the merchandise removed during his or her shift.

3. *Documents and records* Well-designed documents help ensure that transactions are properly recorded. For example, using prenumbered invoices and other documents is a way of ensuring that all transactions are recorded.

4. *Physical controls* Managers should specify who has access to assets. For example, in a retail store, only the person responsible for the cash register should have access to it. Other employees should not be able to open the cash drawer when the cashier is not present. Similarly, only authorized personnel should have access to warehouses and storerooms. Access to accounting records, including those stored in company computers, should also be controlled.

5. *Periodic independent verification* Someone other than the persons responsible for the accounting records and assets should periodically check the records against the assets. For example, at the end of each shift or day in a retail store, the owner or manager should count the cash in the cash drawer and compare the amount with the amount recorded on the tape or computer disk in the cash register. Other examples of independent verification are periodic counts of physical inventory and reconciliations of monthly bank statements.

6. *Separation of duties* No one person should be in charge of authorizing transactions, handling assets, or keeping records of assets. For example, in a well-managed electronics store, each employee oversees only a single part of a transaction. A sales employee takes the order and creates an invoice. Another employee receives the customer's cash or credit card payment and issues a receipt. Once the customer has a receipt, and only then, a third employee obtains the item from the warehouse and gives it to the customer. A person in the accounting department subsequently compares all sales recorded on the tape or disk in the cash register with the sales invoices and updates the inventory in the accounting records. The separation of duties means that a mistake, careless or not, cannot be made without being seen by at least one other person.

7. *Sound personnel practices* Personnel practices that promote internal control include adequate supervision, rotation of key people among different jobs, insistence that employees take vacations, and bonding of personnel who handle cash or inventory. **Bonding** is the process of carefully checking an employee's background and insuring the company against theft by that person. Bonding does not guarantee against theft, but it does prevent or reduce loss if theft occurs. Prudent personnel practices help ensure that

employees know their jobs, are honest, and will find it difficult to carry out and conceal embezzlement over time.

Limitations on Internal Control

No system of internal control is without weaknesses. As long as people perform control procedures, an internal control system will be vulnerable to human error. Errors can arise from misunderstandings, mistakes in judgment, carelessness, distraction, or fatigue. And separation of duties can be defeated through collusion by employees who secretly agree to deceive a company. In addition, established procedures may be ineffective against employees' errors or dishonesty, and controls that were initially effective may become ineffective when conditions change. In some cases, the costs of establishing and maintaining elaborate control systems may exceed the benefits. In a small business, for example, active involvement by the owner can be a practical substitute for the separation of some duties.

 *Study Note*

No control procedure can guarantee the prevention of theft. However, the more procedures that are in place, the less likely it is that a theft will occur.

S T O P • R E V I E W • A P P L Y

5-1. Most people think of internal control as a means of making fraud harder to commit and easier to detect. What are some other important purposes of internal control?

5-2. What are the five components of internal control?

5-3. What are some examples of control activities?

5-4. Why is the separation of duties necessary to ensure sound internal control? What does this principle assume about the relationships of employees in a company and the possibility of two or more of them stealing from the company?

5-5. In a small business, it is sometimes impossible to separate duties completely. What are three other procedures that a small business can use to achieve internal control over cash?

Internal Control over Merchandising Transactions

LO6 Apply internal control activities to common merchandising transactions.

Sound internal control activities are needed in all aspects of a business, but particularly when assets are involved. Assets are especially vulnerable when they enter and leave a business. When sales are made, for example, cash or other assets enter the business, and goods or services leave. Controls must be set up to prevent theft during those transactions. Purchases of assets and payments of liabilities must also be controlled; adequate purchasing and payment systems can safeguard most such transactions. In addition, assets on hand, such as cash, investments, inventory, plant, and equipment, must be protected.

In this section of the text, you will see how merchandising companies apply internal control activities to such transactions as cash sales, receipts, purchases, and cash payments. Service and manufacturing businesses use similar procedures.

Internal Control and Management Goals

When a system of internal control is applied effectively to merchandising transactions, it can achieve important management goals. As we have noted, it can prevent losses of cash and inventory due to theft or fraud, and it can ensure that records of transactions and account balances are accurate. It can also help managers achieve three broader goals:

1. Keeping enough inventory on hand to sell to customers without overstocking merchandise

2. Keeping sufficient cash on hand to pay for purchases in time to receive discounts

3. Keeping credit losses as low as possible by making credit sales only to customers who are likely to pay on time

One control that managers use to meet these broad goals is the cash budget, which projects future cash receipts and disbursements. By maintaining adequate cash balances, a company is able to take advantage of discounts on purchases, prepare to borrow money when necessary, and avoid the damaging effects of being unable to pay bills when they are due. By investing excess cash, the company can earn interest until the cash is needed.

A more specific control is the separation of duties that involve the handling of cash. Such separation makes theft without detection extremely unlikely unless two or more employees conspire. The separation of duties is easier in large businesses than in small ones, where one person may have to carry out several duties. The effectiveness of internal control over cash varies, based on the size and nature of the company. Most firms, however, should use the following procedures:

1. Separate the functions of authorization, recordkeeping, and custodianship of cash.

2. Limit the number of people who have access to cash, and designate who those people are.

3. Bond all employees who have access to cash.

4. Keep the amount of cash on hand to a minimum by using banking facilities as much as possible.

5. Physically protect cash on hand by using cash registers, cashiers' cages, and safes.

6. Record and deposit all cash receipts promptly, and make payments by check rather than by currency.

7. Have a person who does not handle or record cash make unannounced audits of the cash on hand.

8. Have a person who does not authorize, handle, or record cash transactions reconcile the Cash account each month.

Notice that each of these procedures helps safeguard cash by making it more difficult for any one individual who has access to cash to steal or misuse it without being detected.

Study Note

Maintaining internal control is especially difficult for a merchandiser. Management must not only establish controls for cash sales receipts, purchases, and cash payments, but also go to great lengths to manage and protect its inventory.

Control of Cash Receipts

Cash payments for sales of goods and services can be received by mail or over the counter in the form of checks, credit or debit cards, or currency. Whatever the source of the payments, cash should be recorded immediately upon receipt. Such a journal establishes a written record of cash receipts that should prevent errors and make theft more difficult.

Control of Cash Received by Mail

Cash received by mail is vulnerable to theft by the employees who handle it. For that reason, companies that deal in mail-order sales generally ask customers to pay by credit card, check, or money order instead of with currency.

When cash is received in the mail, two or more employees should handle it. The employee who opens the mail should make a list in triplicate of the money received. The list should contain each payer's name, the purpose for which the money was sent, and the amount. One copy goes with the cash to the cashier, who deposits the money. The second copy goes to the accounting department for recording. The person who opens the mail keeps the third copy. Errors can be easily caught because the amount deposited by the cashier must agree with the amount received and the amount recorded in the cash receipts journal.

Control of Cash Received over the Counter

Cash registers and prenumbered sales tickets are common tools for controlling cash received over the counter. The amount of a cash sale is rung up on the cash register at the time of the sale. The register should be placed so that the customer can see the amount recorded. Each cash register should have a locked-in tape on which it prints the day's transactions. At the end of the day, the cashier counts the cash in the register and turns it in to the cashier's office. Another employee takes the tape out of the cash register and records the cash receipts for the day in the cash receipts journal. The amount of cash turned in and the amount recorded on the tape should agree; if not, any differences must be explained.

Large retail chains like **Costco** commonly monitor cash receipts by having each cash register tied directly into a computer that records each transaction as it occurs. Whether the elements are performed manually or by computer, separating responsibility for cash receipts, cash deposits, and recordkeeping is necessary to ensure good internal control.

> *Study Note*
>
> The cashier should not be allowed to remove the cash register tape or to record the day's cash receipts.

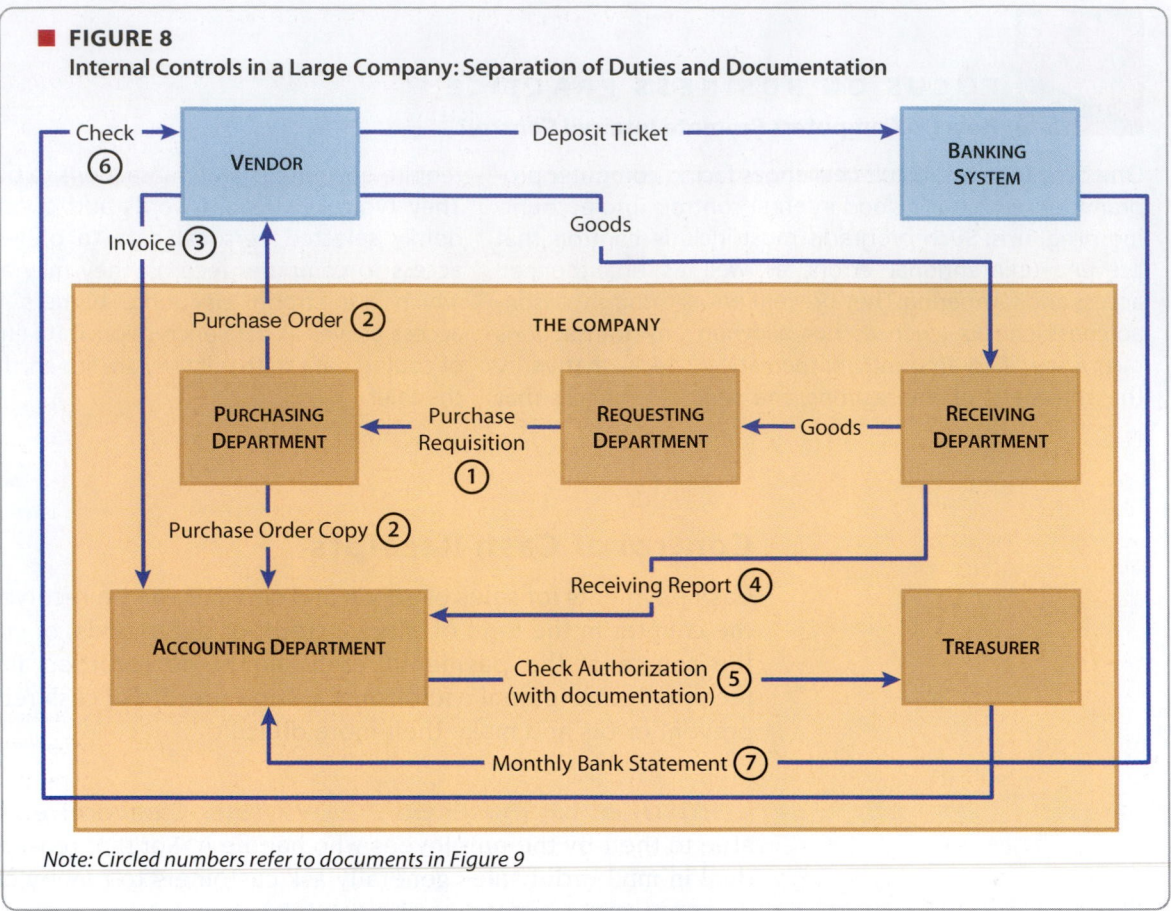

■ **FIGURE 8**
Internal Controls in a Large Company: Separation of Duties and Documentation

Note: Circled numbers refer to documents in Figure 9

In some stores, internal control is further strengthened by the use of prenumbered sales tickets and a central cash register or cashier's office, where all sales are rung up and collected by a person who does not participate in the sale. The salesperson completes a prenumbered sales ticket at the time of the sale, giving one copy to the customer and keeping a copy. At the end of the day, all sales tickets must be accounted for, and the sales total computed from the sales tickets must equal the total sales recorded on the cash register.

Control of Purchases and Cash Disbursements

Cash disbursements are particularly vulnerable to fraud and embezzlement. In one case, the treasurer of one of the nation's largest jewelry retailers was charged with having stolen over $500,000 by systematically overpaying the company's federal income taxes and keeping the refund checks as they came back to the company.

To avoid this type of theft, cash payments should be made only after they have been specifically authorized and supported by documents that establish the validity and amount of the claims. A company should also separate the duties involved in purchasing goods and services and the duties involved in paying for them. The degree of separation that is possible varies, depending on the size of the business.

Figure 8 shows how a large company can maximize the separation of duties. Five internal units (the requesting department, the purchasing department, the accounting department, the receiving department, and the treasurer) and two firms outside the company (the vendor and the bank) play a role in this control plan. Notice that business documents are crucial components of the plan.

Figure 9 illustrates the typical sequence in which documents are used in an internal control plan for purchases and cash disbursements. To begin, the credit office (requesting department) of Laboda Sportswear Corporation fills out a formal request for a purchase, or **purchase requisition**, for office supplies (item 1). The department head approves it and forwards it to the purchasing department. The people in the purchasing department prepare a **purchase order** (item 2). The purchase order is addressed to the vendor (seller) and contains a description of the quantity and type of items ordered, the expected price, the shipping date and terms, and other instructions. The purchase order indicates that Laboda will not pay any bill that does include a purchase order number.

After receiving the purchase order, the vendor, Henderson Supply Company, ships the goods and sends an **invoice** (item 3) to Laboda Sportswear. The invoice shows the quantity of goods delivered, describes what they are, and lists the price and terms of payment. If all the goods cannot be shipped immediately, the invoice indicates the estimated date of shipment for the remainder.

When the goods reach Laboda's receiving department, an employee notes the quantity, type of goods, and their condition on a **receiving report** (item 4). The receiving department does not receive a copy of the purchase order or the invoice, so its employees don't know what should be received or its value. Thus, they are not tempted to steal any excess that may be delivered.

The receiving report goes to the accounting department, where it is compared with the purchase order and the invoice. If everything is correct, the accounting department completes a **check authorization** and attaches it to the three supporting documents. The check authorization form shown in item 5 has a space for each item to be checked off as it is examined. Notice that the accounting department has all the documentary evidence for the transaction but does not have access to the assets purchased. Nor does it write the check for payment. This means that the people doing the accounting cannot conceal fraud by falsifying documents.

Finally, the treasurer examines all the documents. If the treasurer approves them, he or she signs a check (item 6) made out to the vendor in the amount of the invoice less any applicable discount. In some systems, the accounting department fills out the check so that all the treasurer has to do is inspect and sign it. The check is then sent to the vendor, with a remittance advice showing what the check is for. A vendor that is not paid the proper amount will complain, of course, thus providing a form of outside control over the payment. The vendor deposits the check in its bank, and the canceled check appears in Laboda Sportswear's next bank statement (item 7). If the treasurer has made the check out for the wrong amount (or altered an amount that was already filled in), the problem will show up in the company's bank reconciliation.

As shown in Figure 9, every action is documented and verified by at least one other person. Thus, the requesting department cannot work out a kickback scheme to make illegal payments to the vendor because the receiving department independently records receipts and the accounting department verifies prices. The receiving department cannot steal goods because the receiving report must equal the invoice. For the same reason, the vendor cannot bill for more goods than it ships. The treasurer verifies the accounting department's work, and the accounting department ultimately checks the treasurer's work.

The system we have described is a simple one that provides adequate internal control. There are many variations on it.

Study Note

A purchase requisition is not the same as a purchase order. A purchase requisition is sent to the purchasing department; a purchase order is sent to the vendor.

Study Note

Invoice is the business term for *bill*. Every business document must have a number for purposes of reference.

■ **FIGURE 9**

Internal Control Plan for Purchases and Cash Disbursements

Business Document	Prepared by	Sent to	Verification and Related Procedures
① Purchase requisition	Requesting department	Purchasing department	Purchasing verifies authorization.
② Purchase order	Purchasing department	Vendor	Vendor sends goods or services in accordance with purchase order.
③ Invoice	Vendor	Accounting department	Accounting receives invoice from vendor.
④ Receiving report	Receiving department	Accounting department	Accounting compares invoice, purchase order, and receiving report. Accounting verifies prices.
⑤ Check authorization	Accounting department	Treasurer	Accounting attaches check authorization to invoice, purchase order, and receiving report.
⑥ Check	Treasurer	Vendor	Treasurer verifies all documents before preparing check.
⑦ Bank statement	Buyer's bank	Accounting department	Accounting compares amount and payee's name on returned check with check authorization.

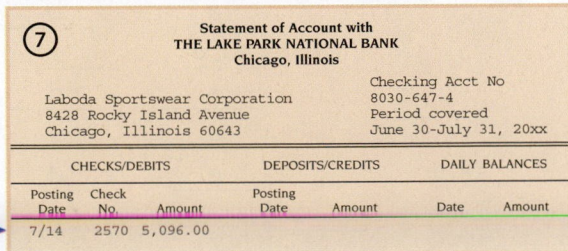

S T O P • R E V I E W • A P P L Y

6-1. At Thrifty Variety Store, sales clerks count the currency in their cash registers at the end of each day. They then remove the tape from their registers and fill in a daily cash form, in which they note any discrepancies. An employee in the cashier's office counts the cash, compares the total with the daily cash form, and then gives the cash to the company's cashier. What is the weakness in this system of internal control?

6-2. How does a movie theater control cash receipts?

Business Documents for Purchases and Cash Disbursements Items **a–e** below are a company's departments. Items **f** and **g** are firms with which the company has transactions:

a. Requesting department

b. Purchasing department

c. Receiving department

d. Accounting department

e. Treasurer

f. Vendor

g. Bank

Use the letter of the department or firm to indicate which one prepares and sends the following business documents:

	Prepared by	Received by
1. Receiving report	_____	_____
2. Purchase order	_____	_____
3. Purchase requisition	_____	_____
4. Check	_____	_____
5. Invoice	_____	_____
6. Check authorization	_____	_____
7. Bank statement	_____	_____

SOLUTION

	Prepared by	Received by
1. Receiving report	c	d
2. Purchase order	b	f
3. Purchase requisition	a	b
4. Check	d, e	f
5. Invoice	f	d
6. Check authorization	d	e
7. Bank statement	g	d

COSTCO WHOLESALE CORPORATION

In this chapter's Decision Point, we noted that **Costco's** managers face many challenges. To ensure the company's success, they must address the following questions:

- **How can the company efficiently manage its cycle of merchandising operations?**
- **How can merchandising transactions be recorded to reflect the company's performance?**
- **How can the company maintain control over its merchandising operations?**

Costco is a very efficiently run organization as reflected by its operating cycle. It sells its inventory every 30 days on average and has almost no receivables. The Financial Highlights at the beginning of the chapter also demonstrate operating efficiency. They show that Costco's operating expenses increased by only 11.5 percent at the same time that net revenue and gross margin increased by about 13 percent. These relationships resulted in a 19.7 percent jump in operating income. Costco's chief executive officer commented on these results as follows:

> Fiscal 2004 was an exciting year for Costco, where we were able to show solid growth, not only in our merchandising and sales efforts, but also substantial progress in operational controls, which when combined, resulted in an improved bottom line. [11]

By buying and selling merchandise in bulk, providing very little service, and keeping its financing period to a minimum, Costco is able to offer its customers wholesale prices. A comparison of gross margin with net revenue in fiscal 2004 shows that Costco made only 12.5 percent ($6,015 ÷ $48,107) on each dollar of sales.

To sell for less and still make a profit, Costco must have a system of recording sales and purchase transactions that gives a fair view of its financial performance. It must also maintain a system of internal control that will not only ensure that these transactions are properly recorded, but will also protect the company's assets. In his certification of Costco's financial statements, the CEO stated that the company has "designed such internal control over financial reporting . . . to provide reasonable assurance regarding the reliability of financial reporting and the preparation of financial statements." [12]

CHAPTER REVIEW

REVIEW of Learning Objectives

LO1 Identify the management issues related to merchandising businesses.

Merchandising companies differ from service companies in that they earn income by buying and selling goods. The buying and selling of goods adds to the complexity of the business and raises four issues that management must address. First, the series of transactions in which merchandising companies engage (the operating cycle) requires careful cash flow management. Second, management must choose whether to use the perpetual or the periodic inventory system. Third, if a company has international transactions, it must deal with changing exchange rates. Fourth, management must establish an internal control structure that protects the company's assets—its cash, merchandise inventory, and accounts receivable.

LO2 Describe the terms of sale related to merchandising transactions.

A trade discount is a reduction from the list or catalogue price of a product. A sales discount is a discount given for early payment of a sale on credit. Terms of 2/10, n/30 mean that the buyer can take a 2 percent discount if the invoice is paid within ten days of the invoice date. Otherwise, the buyer is obligated to pay the full amount in 30 days. Discounts on sales are recorded in the Sales Discounts account, and discounts on purchases are recorded in the Purchases Discounts account. FOB shipping point means that the buyer bears the cost of transportation and that title to the goods passes to the buyer at the shipping origin. FOB destination means that the seller bears the cost of transportation and that title does not pass to the buyer until the goods reach their destination. To the seller, debit and credit card sales are similar to cash sales.

LO3 Prepare an income statement and record merchandising transactions under the perpetual inventory system.

Under the perpetual inventory system, the Merchandise Inventory account is continuously adjusted by entering purchases, sales, and other inventory transactions as they occur. Purchases increase the Merchandise Inventory account, and purchases returns decrease it. As goods are sold, their cost is transferred from the Merchandise Inventory account to the Cost of Goods Sold account.

LO4 Prepare an income statement and record merchandising transactions under the periodic inventory system.

When the periodic inventory system is used, the cost of goods sold section of the income statement must include the following elements:

$$\text{Purchases} - \frac{\text{Purchases returns and}}{\text{allowances}} + \text{Freight-in} = \frac{\text{Net cost of}}{\text{purchases}}$$

$$\frac{\text{Beginning}}{\text{merchandise inventory}} + \frac{\text{Net cost of}}{\text{purchases}} = \frac{\text{Goods}}{\text{available for sale}}$$

$$\frac{\text{Goods}}{\text{available for sale}} - \frac{\text{Ending}}{\text{merchandise inventory}} = \frac{\text{Cost of}}{\text{goods sold}}$$

Under the periodic inventory system, the Merchandise Inventory account stays at the beginning level until the physical inventory is recorded at the end of the accounting period. A Purchases account is used to accumulate purchases of merchandise during the accounting period, and a Purchases Returns and Allowances account is used to accumulate returns of purchases and allowances on purchases.

LO5 Describe the components of internal control, control activities, and limitations on internal control.

Internal control consists of all the policies and procedures a company uses to ensure the reliability of financial reporting, compliance with laws and regulations, and the effectiveness and efficiency of operations. Internal control has five components: the control environment, risk assessment, information and communication, control activities, and monitoring. Control activities include having managers authorize certain transactions; recording all transactions to establish accountability for assets; using well-designed documents to ensure proper recording of transactions; instituting physical controls; periodically checking records and assets; separating duties; and using sound personnel policies. A system of internal control relies on the people who implement it. Thus, the effectiveness of internal control is limited by the people involved. Human error, collusion, and failure to recognize changed conditions can contribute to a system's failure.

LO6 Apply internal control activities to common merchandising transactions.

To implement internal control over cash sales, receipts, purchases, and disbursements, the functions of authorization, recordkeeping, and custodianship of cash should be kept separate. The people who have access to cash should be specifically designated and their number limited. Employees who have access to cash should be bonded. The control system should also provide for the use of banking services, physical protection of assets, prompt recording and deposit of cash receipts, and payment by check. A person who does not authorize, handle, or record cash transactions should make unannounced audits of the cash on hand, and the Cash account should be reconciled each month.

REVIEW of Concepts and Terminology

The following concepts and terms were introduced in this chapter:

Bonding: The process of carefully checking an employee's background and insuring the company against theft by that person. **(LO5)**

Check authorization: A form that an accounting department prepares after it has compared a receiving report with a purchase order and invoice and that authorizes the issuance of a check to pay the invoice. **(LO6)**

Control activities: Policies and procedures that management establishes to ensure that the objectives of internal control are met. **(LO5)**

Control environment: A company's ethics, philosophy and operating style, organizational structure, method of assigning authority and responsibility, and personnel policies and practices. **(LO5)**

Delivery expense: The transportation cost of delivering merchandise. Also called *freight-out*. **(LO2)**

Exchange gain or loss: A gain or loss due to exchange rate fluctuation, which is reported on the income statement. **(LO1)**

Financing period: The amount of time from the purchase of inventory until it is sold and payment is collected, less the amount of time creditors give the company to pay for the inventory. **(LO1)**

FOB destination: A term indicating that the seller retains title to the merchandise until it reaches its destination and that the seller bears the shipping costs. **(LO2)**

FOB shipping point: A term indicating that the buyer assumes title to the merchandise at the shipping point and bears the shipping costs. **(LO2)**

Freight-in: The transportation cost of receiving merchandise. **(LO2)**

Goods available for sale: The sum of beginning inventory and the net cost of purchases during an accounting period. **(LO4)**

Information and communication: A component of internal control that refers to the way in which the accounting system gathers and treats information and how it communicates responsibilities within the system. **(LO5)**

Internal controls: The systems and procedures that management uses to protect a company's assets. **(LO1)**

Invoice: A form that a vendor sends to a purchaser describing the goods delivered and the quantity, price, and terms of payment. **(LO6)**

Merchandise inventory: The goods on hand at any one time that are available for sale to customers. **(LO1)**

Merchandising business: A business that earns income by buying and selling goods. **(LO1)**

Monitoring: Management's regular assessment of the quality of internal control. **(LO5)**

Net cost of purchases: Net purchases plus any freight charges on the purchases. **(LO4)**

Net purchases: Total purchases less any deductions, such as purchases returns and allowances and discounts on purchases. **(LO4)**

Operating cycle: A series of transactions that includes purchases of merchandise inventory for cash or on credit, payment for purchases made on credit, sales of merchandise inventory for cash or on credit, and collection of cash from credit sales. **(LO1)**

Periodic inventory system: A system for determining inventory on hand by periodically taking a physical count. **(LO1)**

Perpetual inventory system: A system for determining inventory on hand by keeping continuous records of the quantity and, usually, the cost of individual items as they are bought and sold. **(LO1)**

Physical inventory: An actual count of all merchandise on hand. **(LO1)**

Purchase order: A form that a company's purchasing department sends to a vendor describing the items ordered and the quantity, price, terms, and shipping date. **(LO6)**

Purchase requisition: A formal written request for a purchase that a company's credit office (requesting department) sends to the purchasing department. **(LO6)**

Purchases account: A temporary account used under the periodic inventory system to accumulate the cost of merchandise purchased for resale during an accounting period. **(LO4)**

Purchases discounts: Discounts that buyers take for early payment of merchandise; the Purchases Discounts account is a contra-purchases account used under the periodic inventory system. **(LO2)**

Purchases Returns and Allowances account: A contra-purchases account used under the periodic inventory system to accumulate cash refunds, credits on account, and other allowances made by suppliers. **(LO4)**

Receiving report: A form on which an employee in a company's receiving department notes the quantity, type of goods, and their condition upon delivery from the vendor. **(LO6)**

Risk assessment: The identification of areas in which risk of loss of assets or inaccuracies in accounting records is high. **(LO5)**

Sales discount: A discount given to a buyer for early payment of a sale made on credit; the Sales Discounts account is a contra-revenue account. **(LO2)**

Sales Returns and Allowances account: A contra-revenue account used to accumulate cash refunds, credits on account, and other allowances made to customers who have received defective or otherwise unsatisfactory products. **(LO3)**

Trade discount: A deduction (usually 30 percent or more) off a list or catalogue price, which is not recorded in the accounting records. **(LO2)**

REVIEW Problem

Merchandising Transactions: Perpetual and Periodic Inventory Systems

LO3, LO4   Dawkins Company engaged in the following transactions during October:

Oct. 1 Sold merchandise to Ernie Devlin on credit, terms n/30, FOB shipping point, $1,050 (cost, $630).

2 Purchased merchandise on credit from Ruland Company, terms n/30, FOB shipping point, $1,900.

2 Paid Custom Freight $145 for freight charges on merchandise received.

9 Purchased merchandise on credit from LNP Company, terms n/30, FOB shipping point, $1,800, including $100 freight costs paid by LNP Company.

11 Accepted from Ernie Devlin a return of merchandise, which was returned to inventory, $150 (cost, $90).

14 Returned for credit $300 of merchandise purchased on October 2.

16 Sold merchandise for cash, $500 (cost, $300).

22 Paid Ruland Company for purchase of October 2 less return on October 14.

Oct. 23 Received full payment from Ernie Devlin for his October 1 purchase, less return on October 11.

Required

1. Record these transactions in journal form, assuming Dawkins Company uses the perpetual inventory system.
2. Record the transactions in journal form, assuming Dawkins Company uses the periodic inventory system.

Answer to Review Problem

Accounts that differ under the two systems are highlighted.

	A	B	C	D	E	F	G	H	I	J
1				**1. Perpetual Inventory System**				**2. Periodic Inventory System**		
2	Oct.	1		Accounts Receivable	1,050			Accounts Receivable	1,050	
3				Sales		1,050		Sales		1,050
4				Sold merchandise on account to Ernie Devlin, terms n/30, FOB shipping point				Sold merchandise on account to Ernie Devlin, terms n/30, FOB shipping point		
5				Cost of Goods Sold	630					
6				Merchandise Inventory		630				
7				Transferred cost of merchandise sold to Cost of Goods Sold account						
8		2		Merchandise Inventory	1,900			Purchases	1,900	
9				Accounts Payable		1,900		Accounts Payable		1,900
10				Purchased merchandise on account from Ruland Company, terms n/30, FOB shipping point				Purchased merchandise on account from Ruland Company, terms n/30, FOB shipping point		
11				Freight-In	145			Freight-In	145	
12				Cash		145		Cash		145
13				Paid freight on previous purchase				Paid freight on previous purchase		
14		9		Merchandise Inventory	1,700			Purchases	1,700	
15				Freight-In	100			Freight-In	100	
16				Accounts Payable		1,800		Accounts Payable		1,800
17				Purchased merchandise on account from LNP Company, terms n/30, FOB shipping point, freight paid by supplier				Purchased merchandise on account from LNP Company, terms n/30, FOB shipping point, freight paid by supplier		
18		11		Sales Returns and Allowances	150			Sales Returns and Allowances	150	
19				Accounts Receivable		150		Accounts Receivable		150
20				Accepted return of merchandise from Ernie Devlin				Accepted return of merchandise from Ernie Devlin		
21				Merchandise Inventory	90					
22				Cost of Goods Sold		90				
23				Transferred cost of merchandise returned to Merchandise Inventory account						

(Continued)

	A	B	C	D	E	F	G	H	I	J
24				**1. Perpetual Inventory System**				**2. Periodic Inventory System**		
25	Oct.	14		Accounts Payable	300			Accounts Payable	300	
26				Merchandise Inventory		300		Purchases Returns and Allowances		300
27				Returned portion of merchandise purchased from Ruland Company				Returned portion of merchandise purchased from Ruland Company		
28		16		Cash	500			Cash	500	
29				Sales		500		Sales		500
30				Sold merchandise for cash				Sold merchandise for cash		
31				Cost of Goods Sold	300					
32				Merchandise Inventory		300				
33				Transferred cost of merchandise sold to Cost of Goods Sold account						
34		22		Accounts Payable	1,600			Accounts Payable	1,600	
35				Cash		1,600		Cash		1,600
36				Made payment on account to Ruland Company $1,900 − $300 = $1,600				Made payment on account to Ruland Company $1,900 − $300 = $1,600		
37		23		Cash	900			Cash	900	
38				Accounts Receivable		900		Accounts Receivable		900
39				Received payment on account from Ernie Devlin $1,050 − $150 = $900				Received payment on account from Ernie Devlin $1,050 − $150 = $900		

CHAPTER ASSIGNMENTS

BUILDING Your Knowledge and Skills

Short Exercises

LO1 **Identification of Management Issues**

SE 1. Identify each of the following decisions as most directly related to (a) cash flow management, (b) choice of inventory system, (c) foreign merchandising transactions, or (d) internal controls:

1. Determination of how to protect cash from theft or embezzlement
2. Determination of the effects of changes in exchange rates
3. Determination of policies governing sales of merchandise on credit
4. Determination of whether to use the periodic or the perpetual inventory system

LO1 **Operating Cycle**

SE 2. On average, Mason Company holds its inventory 40 days before it is sold, waits 25 days for customers' payments, and takes 33 days to pay suppliers. For how many days must it provide financing in its operating cycle?

LO2 **Terms of Sale**

SE 3. A dealer buys tooling machines from a manufacturer and resells them to its customers.

a. The manufacturer sets a list or catalogue price of $12,000 for a machine. The manufacturer offers its dealers a 40 percent trade discount.

b. The manufacturer sells the machine under terms of FOB shipping point. The cost of shipping is $700.

c. The manufacturer offers a sales discount of 2/10, n/30. The sales discount does not apply to shipping costs.

What is the net cost of the tooling machine to the dealer, assuming it is paid for within ten days of purchase?

LO2 **Sales and Purchases Discounts**

SE 4. On April 15, Campeche Company sold merchandise to Walters Company for $3,000 on terms of 2/10, n/30. Assume a return of merchandise on April 20 of $600, and payment in full on April 25. What is the payment by Walters to Campeche on April 25?

LO3 **Purchases of Merchandise: Perpetual Inventory System**

SE 5. Record in T account form each of the following transactions, assuming the perpetual inventory system is used:

Aug. 2 Purchased merchandise on credit from Indio Company, invoice dated August 1, terms n/10, FOB shipping point, $1,150.

3 Received bill from Lee Shipping Company for transportation costs on August 2 shipment, invoice dated August 1, terms n/30, $105.

7 Returned damaged merchandise received from Indio Company on August 2 for credit, $180.

10 Paid in full the amount due to Indio Company for the purchase of August 2, part of which was returned on August 7.

LO4 **Purchases of Merchandise: Periodic Inventory System**

SE 6. Record in T account form the transactions in **SE 5**, assuming the periodic inventory system is used.

LO4 **Cost of Goods Sold: Periodic Inventory System**

SE 7. Using the following data and assuming cost of goods sold is $273,700, prepare the cost of goods sold section of a merchandising income statement (periodic inventory system). Include the amount of purchases for the month of October.

Freight-in	$13,800
Merchandise inventory, Sept. 30, 20xx	37,950
Merchandise inventory, Oct. 31, 20xx	50,600
Purchases	?
Purchases returns and allowances	10,350

LO4 **Sales of Merchandise: Periodic Inventory System**

SE 8. Record in T account form the following transactions, assuming the periodic inventory system is used:

Aug. 4 Sold merchandise on credit to Jing Corporation, terms n/30, FOB destination, $2,520.

5 Paid transportation costs for sale of August 4, $231.

9 Part of the merchandise sold on August 4 was accepted back from Jing Corporation for full credit and returned to the merchandise inventory, $735.

Sept. 3 Received payment in full from Jing Corporation for merchandise sold on August 4, less the return on August 9.

LO5, LO6   **Internal Control Activities**

SE 9. Match the check-writing policies for a small business described below to the following control activities:

a. Authorization
b. Recording transactions
c. Documents and records
d. Physical controls

e. Periodic independent check
f. Separation of duties
g. Sound personnel policies

1. The person who writes the checks to pay bills is different from the people who authorize the payments and keep records of the payments.
2. The checks are kept in a locked drawer. The only person who has the key is the person who writes the checks.
3. The person who writes the checks is bonded.
4. Once each month the owner compares and reconciles the amount of money shown in the accounting records with the amount in the bank account.
5. The owner of the business approves each check before it is mailed.
6. Information pertaining to each check is recorded on the check stub.
7. Every day, all checks are recorded in the accounting records, using the information on the check stubs.

LO5   **Limitations of Internal Control**

SE 10. Internal control is subject to several inherent limitations. Indicate whether each of the following situations is an example of (a) human error, (b) collusion among employees, (c) changed conditions, or (d) cost-benefit considerations:

1. Effective separation of duties in a restaurant is impractical because the business is too small.
2. The cashier and the manager of a retail shoe store work together to avoid the internal controls for the purpose of embezzling funds.
3. The cashier in a pizza shop does not understand the procedures for operating the cash register and thus fails to ring up all the sales and count the cash at the end of the day.
4. At a law firm, computer supplies are mistakenly delivered to the reception area instead of the receiving area because the supplier began using a different system of shipment. As a result, the receipt of supplies is not recorded.

Exercises

LO1, LO2   **Discussion Questions**

E 1. Develop a brief answer to each of the following questions:

1. Can a company have a "negative" financing period?
2. If you sold goods to a company in Europe and the exchange rate for the dollar is declining as it relates to the euro, would you want the eventual payment to be made in dollars or euros?
3. Who has ultimate responsibility for safeguarding a company's assets with a system of internal control?
4. Assume a large shipment of uninsured merchandise to your company is destroyed when the delivery truck has an accident and burns. Would you want the terms to be FOB shipping point or FOB destination?

LO3, LO4, LO5, LO6 **Discussion Questions**

E 2. Develop a brief answer to each of the following questions:

1. Under the perpetual inventory system, the Merchandise Inventory account is constantly updated. What would cause it to have the wrong balance?
2. Why is a physical inventory needed under both the periodic and perpetual inventory systems?
3. Which of the following accounts would be assigned a higher level of risk: Building or Merchandising Inventory?
4. Why is it important to write down the amount of cash received through the mail or over the counter?

LO1 **Management Issues and Decisions**

E 3. The decisions that follow were made by the management of Posad Cotton Company. Indicate whether each decision pertains primarily to (a) cash flow management, (b) choice of inventory system, (c) foreign transactions, or (d) control of merchandising operations.

1. Decided to mark each item of inventory with a magnetic tag that sets off an alarm if the tag is removed from the store before being deactivated.
2. Decided to reduce the credit terms offered to customers from 30 days to 20 days to speed up collection of accounts.
3. Decided that the benefits of keeping track of each item of inventory as it is bought and sold would exceed the costs of such a system.
4. Decided to purchase goods made by a Chinese supplier.
5. Decided to purchase a new type of cash register that can be operated only by a person who knows a predetermined code.
6. Decided to switch to a new cleaning service that will provide the same service at a lower cost with payment due in 30 days instead of 20 days.

LO1 **Foreign Merchandising Transactions**

E 4. Wooster Corporation purchased a special-purpose machine from Konigsberg Corporation on credit for € 50,000. At the date of purchase, the exchange rate was $1.00 per euro. On the date of the payment, which was made in euros, the value of the euro was $1.25. Did Wooster incur an exchange gain or loss? How much was it?

LO2 **Terms of Sale**

E 5. A household appliance dealer buys refrigerators from a manufacturer and resells them to its customers.

a. The manufacturer sets a list or catalogue price of $1,500 for a refrigerator. The manufacturer offers its dealers a 30 percent trade discount.
b. The manufacturer sells the machine under terms of FOB destination. The cost of shipping is $150.
c. The manufacturer offers a sales discount of 2/10, n/30. Sales discounts do not apply to shipping costs.

What is the net cost of the refrigerator to the dealer, assuming it is paid for within ten days of purchase?

LO2, LO4 **Sales Involving Discounts: Periodic Inventory System**

E 6. Prepare journal entries for the transactions of Sasina Company, and determine the total amount received from Borsa Company:

Mar. 1 Sold merchandise on credit to Borsa Company, terms 2/10, n/30, FOB shipping point, $500.

Mar.	3	Accepted a return from Borsa Company for full credit, $200.
	10	Received payment from Borsa Company for the sale, less the return and discount.
	11	Sold merchandise on credit to Borsa Company, terms 2/10, n/30, FOB shipping point, $800.
	31	Received payment from Borsa Company for the sale of March 11.

LO2, LO3 **Purchases Involving Discounts: Perpetual Inventory System**

E 7. Washington Company engaged in the following transactions:

July	2	Purchased merchandise on credit from Zapala Company, terms 2/10, n/30, FOB destination, invoice dated July 1, $2,000.
	6	Returned some merchandise to Zapala Company for full credit, $250.
	11	Paid Zapala Company for purchase of July 2 less return and discount.
	14	Purchased merchandise on credit from Zapala Company, terms 2/10, n/30, FOB destination, invoice dated July 12, $2,250.
	31	Paid amount owed Zapala Company for purchase of July 14.

Prepare journal entries and determine the total amount paid to Zapala Company.

LO3 **Preparation of the Income Statement: Perpetual Inventory System**

E 8. Using the selected account balances at December 31, 20xx, for Weddings, Etc. that follow, prepare an income statement for the year ended December 31, 20xx. Show detail of net sales. The company uses the perpetual inventory system, and Freight-In has not been included in Cost of Goods Sold.

Account Name	Debit	Credit
Sales		$475,000
Sales Returns and Allowances	$ 23,500	
Cost of Goods Sold	280,000	
Freight-In	13,500	
Selling Expenses	43,000	
General and Administrative Expenses	87,000	
Income Taxes	10,000	

LO3 **Recording Purchases: Perpetual Inventory System**

E 9. Give the entries in T account form to record each of the following transactions under the perpetual inventory system:

a. Purchased merchandise on credit, terms n/30, FOB shipping point, $5,000.
b. Paid freight on the shipment in transaction a, $270.
c. Purchased merchandise on credit, terms n/30, FOB destination, $2,800.
d. Purchased merchandise on credit, terms n/30, FOB shipping point, $5,200, which includes freight paid by the supplier of $400.
e. Returned part of the merchandise purchased in transaction c, $1,000.
f. Paid the amount owed on the purchase in transaction a.
g. Paid the amount owed on the purchase in transaction d.
h. Paid the amount owed on the purchase in transaction c less the return in e.

LO3 **Recording Sales: Perpetual Inventory System**

E 10. On June 15, Dej Company sold merchandise for $2,600 on terms of n/30 to Musan Company. On June 20, Musan Company returned some of the merchandise for a credit of $600, and on June 25, Musan paid the balance owed. Give Dej's entries in T account form to record the sale, return, and receipt of payment under the perpetual inventory system. The cost of the merchandise sold on June 15 was $1,500, and the cost of the merchandise returned to inventory on June 20 was $350.

LO4 **Preparation of the Income Statement: Periodic Inventory System**

E 11. Using the selected year-end account balances at December 31, 20x6, for the Yacuma General Store shown below, prepare a 20x6 income statement. Show detail of net sales. The company uses the periodic inventory system. Beginning merchandise inventory was $26,000; ending merchandise inventory is $22,000.

Account Name	Debit	Credit
Sales		$297,000
Sales Returns and Allowances	$ 15,200	
Purchases	114,800	
Purchases Returns and Allowances		4,000
Freight-In	5,600	
Selling Expenses	48,500	
General and Administrative Expenses	37,200	
Income Taxes	15,000	

LO4 **Merchandising Income Statement: Missing Data, Multiple Years**

E 12. Determine the missing data for each letter in the following three income statements for Sampson Paper Company (in thousands):

	20x7	20x6	20x5
Sales	$ p	$ h	$572
Sales returns and allowances	48	38	a
Net sales	q	634	b
Merchandise inventory, beginning	r	i	76
Purchases	384	338	c
Purchases returns and allowances	62	j	34
Freight-in	s	58	44
Net cost of purchases	378	k	d
Goods available for sale	444	424	364
Merchandise inventory, ending	78	l	84
Cost of goods sold	t	358	e
Gross margin	284	m	252
Selling expenses	u	156	f
General and administrative expenses	78	n	66
Total operating expenses	260	256	g
Income before income taxes	v	o	54
Income taxes	6	4	10
Net income	w	16	44

LO4 **Recording Purchases: Periodic Inventory System**

E 13. Using the data in **E 9**, give the entries in T-account form to record each of the transactions under the periodic inventory system.

LO4 **Recording Sales: Periodic Inventory System**

E 14. Using the relevant data in **E 10**, give the entries in T-account form to record each of the transactions under the periodic inventory system.

LO5 **Use of Accounting Records in Internal Control**

E 15. Careful scrutiny of accounting records and financial statements can lead to the discovery of fraud or embezzlement. Each of the situations that follows may indicate a breakdown in internal control. Indicate the nature of the possible fraud or embezzlement in each of these situations.

1. Wages expense for a branch office was 30 percent higher in 20x7 than in 20x6, even though the office was authorized to employ only the same four employees and raises were only 5 percent in 20x7.
2. Sales returns and allowances increased from 5 percent to 20 percent of sales in the first two months of 20x7, after record sales in 20x6 resulted in large bonuses for the sales staff.
3. Gross margin decreased from 40 percent of net sales in 20x6 to 20 percent in 20x7, even though there was no change in pricing. Ending inventory was 50 percent less at the end of 20x7 than it was at the beginning of the year. There is no immediate explanation for the decrease in inventory.
4. A review of daily records of cash register receipts shows that one cashier consistently accepts more discount coupons for purchases than do the other cashiers.

LO5, LO6 **Control Procedures**

E 16. Alina Sadofsky, who operates a small grocery store, has established the following policies with regard to the checkout cashiers:

1. Each Cashier has his or her own cash drawer, to which no one else has access.
2. Cashiers may accept checks for purchases under $50 with proper identification. For checks over $50, they must receive approval from Sadofsky.
3. Every sale must be rung up on the cash register and a receipt given to the customer. Each sale is recorded on a tape inside the cash register.
4. At the end of each day, Sadofsky counts the cash in the drawer and compares it with the amount on the tape inside the cash register.

Match the following conditions for internal control to each of the policies listed above:

a. Transactions are executed in accordance with management's general or specific authorization.
b. Transactions are recorded as necessary to permit preparation of financial statements and maintain accountability for assets.
c. Access to assets is permitted only as allowed by management.
d. At reasonable intervals, the records of assets are compared with the existing assets.

LO5, LO6 **Internal Control Procedures**

E 17. Adelphi Video Store maintains the following policies with regard to purchases of new videotapes at each of its branch stores:

1. Employees are required to take vacations, and the duties of employees are rotated periodically.
2. Once each month a person from the home office visits each branch store to examine the receiving records and to compare the inventory of videos with the accounting records.
3. Purchases of new videos must be authorized by purchase order in the home office and paid for by the treasurer in the home office. Receiving reports are prepared in each branch and sent to the home office.
4. All new personnel receive one hour of training in how to receive and catalogue new videos.
5. The company maintains a perpetual inventory system that keeps track of all videos purchased, sold, and on hand.

Match the following control procedures to each of the above policies. (Some may have several answers.)

a. Authorization
b. Recording transactions
c. Documents and records
d. Limited accessi

e. Periodic independent verification
f. Separation of duties
g. Sound personnel policies

Problems

LO1, LO3   **Merchandising Income Statement: Perpetual Inventory System**

P 1. At the end of the fiscal year, August 31, 20x6, selected accounts from the adjusted trial balance for Mikhail's Delivery, Inc., appeared as follows:

Mikhail's Delivery, Inc.		
Partial Adjusted Trial Balance		
August 31, 20x6		
Sales		$162,000
Sales Returns and Allowances	$ 2,000	
Cost of Goods Sold	61,400	
Freight-In	2,300	
Store Salaries Expense	32,625	
Office Salaries Expense	12,875	
Advertising Expense	24,300	
Rent Expense	2,400	
Insurance Expense	1,200	
Utilities Expense	1,560	
Store Supplies Expense	2,880	
Office Supplies Expense	1,175	
Depreciation Expense–Store Equipment	1,050	
Depreciation Expense–Office Equipment	800	
Income Taxes	2,000	

Required

1. Using the information given, prepare an income statement for Mikhail's Delivery, Inc. Store Salaries Expense; Advertising Expense; Stores Supplies Expense; and Depreciation Expense–Store Equipment are selling expenses. The other expenses are general and administrative expenses. The company uses the perpetual inventory system. Show details of net sales and operating expenses.

2. **User Insight:** Based on your knowledge at this point in the course, how would you use the income statement for Mikhail's Delivery, Inc. to evaluate the company's profitability? What other financial statement should be considered and why?

LO3   **Merchandising Transactions: Perpetual Inventory System**

P 2. Tonia Company engaged in the following transactions in July 20xx:

July   1   Sold merchandise to Su Long on credit, terms n/30, FOB shipping point, $4,200 (cost, $2,520).

      3   Purchased merchandise on credit from Angier Company, terms n/30, FOB shipping point, $7,600.

      5   Paid Mix Freight for freight charges on merchandise received, $580.

July 8 Purchased merchandise on credit from Exto Supply Company, terms n/30, FOB shipping point, $7,200, which includes $400 freight costs paid by Exto Supply Company.

   12 Returned some of the merchandise purchased on July 3 for credit, $1,200.

   15 Sold merchandise on credit to Pete Smith, terms n/30, FOB shipping point, $2,400 (cost, $1,440).

   17 Sold merchandise for cash, $2,000 (cost, $1,200).

   18 Accepted for full credit a return from Su Long and returned merchandise to inventory, $400 (cost, $240).

   24 Paid Angier Company for purchase of July 3 less return of July 12.

   25 Received check from Su Long for July 1 purchase less the return on July 18.

Required

1. Prepare entries in journal form (refer to the review problem) to record the transactions, assuming use of the perpetual inventory system.

2. **User Insight:** In their published financial statements, most companies call the first line on their income statement "net sales." Other companies simply say "sales." Do you think these terms are equivalent and comparable? What would be the content of "net sales"? What might be the reason a company would use "sales" instead of "net sales"?

LO1, LO4 **Merchandising Income Statement: Periodic Inventory System**

P 3. The data below are selected accounts from the adjusted trial balance of Dan's Sports Equipment, Inc., on September 30, 20x6, the fiscal year end. The company's beginning merchandise inventory was $81,222 and ending merchandise inventory is $76,664 for the period.

Dan's Sports Equipment, Inc. Partial Adjusted Trial Balance September 30, 20x6		
Sales		$433,912
Sales Returns and Allowances	$ 11,250	
Purchases	221,185	
Purchases Returns and Allowances		30,238
Freight-In	10,078	
Store Salaries Expense	107,550	
Office Salaries Expense	26,500	
Advertising Expense	18,200	
Rent Expense	14,400	
Insurance Expense	2,800	
Utilities Expense	18,760	
Store Supplies Expense	464	
Office Supplies Expense	814	
Depreciation Expense, Store Equipment	1,800	
Depreciation Expense, Office Equipment	1,850	
Income Taxes	5,000	

Required

1. Prepare a multistep income statement for Dan's Sports Equipment, Inc. Store Salaries Expense; Advertising Expense; Store Supplies Expense; and

Depreciation Expense–Store Equipment are selling expenses. The other expenses are general and administrative expenses. The company uses the periodic inventory system. Show details of net sales and operating expenses.

2. **User Insight:** Based on your knowledge at this point in the course, how would you use the income statement for Dan's Sports Equipment to evaluate the company's profitability? What other financial statements should you consider and why?

LO4   **Merchandising Transactions: Periodic Inventory System**

P 4. Use the data in **P 2** for this problem.

Required

1. Prepare entries in journal form (refer to the review problem) to record the transactions, assuming use of the periodic inventory system.
2. **User Insight:** Receiving cash rebates from suppliers based on the past year's purchases is common in some industries. If at the end of the year, Tonia Company receives rebates in cash from a supplier, should these cash rebates be reported as revenue? Why or why not?

LO5, LO6   **Internal Control**

P 5. Industrial Services Company provides maintenance services to factories in the West Bend, Wisconsin, area. The company, which buys a large amount of cleaning supplies, consistently has been over budget in its expenditures for these items. In the past, supplies were left open in the warehouse to be taken each evening as needed by the onsite supervisors. A clerk in the accounting department periodically ordered additional supplies from a long-time supplier. No records were maintained other than to record purchases. Once a year, an inventory of supplies was made for the preparation of the financial statements.

To solve the budgetary problem, management decides to implement a new system for purchasing and controlling supplies. The following actions take place:

1. Management places a supplies clerk in charge of a secured storeroom for cleaning supplies.
2. Supervisors use a purchase requisition to request supplies for the jobs they oversee.
3. Each job receives a predetermined amount of supplies based on a study of each job's needs.
4. In the storeroom, the supplies clerk notes the levels of supplies and completes the purchase requisition when new supplies are needed.
5. The purchase requisition goes to the purchasing clerk, a new position. The purchasing clerk is solely responsible for authorizing purchases and preparing the purchase orders.
6. Supplier prices are monitored constantly by the purchasing clerk to ensure that the lowest price is obtained.
7. When supplies are received, the supplies clerk checks them in and prepares a receiving report. The supplies clerk sends the receiving report to accounting, where each payment to a supplier is documented by the purchase requisition, the purchase order, and the receiving report.
8. The accounting department also maintains a record of supplies inventory, supplies requisitioned by supervisors, and supplies received.
9. Once each month, the warehouse manager takes a physical inventory of cleaning supplies in the storeroom and compares it against the supplies inventory records that the accounting department maintains.

Required

1. Indicate which of the following control activities applies to each of the improvements in the internal control system (more than one may apply):

a. Authorization
b. Recording transactions
c. Documents and records
d. Physical controls
e. Periodic independent verification
f. Separation of duties
g. Sound personnel policies

2. **User Insight:** Explain why each new control activity is an improvement over the activities of the old system.

Alternate Problems

LO1, LO3   **Merchandising Income Statement: Perpetual Inventory System**

 P 6. At the end of the fiscal year, June 30, 20x6, selected accounts from the adjusted trial balance for Hans' Video Store, Inc., appeared as shown below.

Hans' Video Store, Inc. Partial Adjusted Trial Balance June 30, 20x6		
Sales		$867,824
Sales Returns and Allowances	$ 22,500	
Cost of Goods Sold	442,370	
Freight-In	20,156	
Store Salaries Expense	215,100	
Office Salaries Expense	53,000	
Advertising Expense	36,400	
Rent Expense	28,800	
Insurance Expense	5,600	
Utilities Expense	17,520	
Store Supplies Expense	4,928	
Office Supplies Expense	3,628	
Depreciation Expense–Store Equipment	3,600	
Depreciation Expense–Office Equipment	3,700	
Income Taxes	5,000	

Required

1. Prepare a multistep income statement for Hans' Video Store, Inc. Freight-In should be combined with Cost of Goods Sold. Store Salaries Expense; Advertising Expense; Store Supplies Expense; and Depreciation Expense–Store Equipment are selling expenses. The other expenses are general and administrative expenses. The company uses the perpetual inventory system. Show details of net sales and operating expenses.

2. **User Insight:** Based on your knowledge at this point in the course, how would you use the income statement for Hans' Video Store to evaluate the company's profitability? What other financial statement should you consider and why?

LO3   **Merchandising Transactions: Perpetual Inventory System**

P 7. Tattle Company engaged in the following transactions in October 20xx:

Oct. 7 Sold merchandise on credit to Lina Ortiz, terms n/30, FOB shipping point, $6,000 (cost, $3,600).

8 Purchased merchandise on credit from Ruff Company, terms n/30, FOB shipping point, $12,000.

9 Paid Curry Company for shipping charges on merchandise purchased on October 8, $508.

10 Purchased merchandise on credit from Sewall Company, terms n/30, FOB shipping point, $19,200, including $1,200 freight costs paid by Sewall.

14 Sold merchandise on credit to Peter Watts, terms n/30, FOB shipping point, $4,800 (cost, $2,880).

14 Returned damaged merchandise received from Ruff Company on October 8 for credit, $1,200.

17 Received check from Lina Ortiz for her purchase of October 7.

19 Sold merchandise for cash, $3,600 (cost, $2,160).

20 Paid Sewall Company for purchase of October 10.

21 Paid Ruff Company the balance from the transactions of October 8 and October 14.

24 Accepted from Peter Watts a return of merchandise, which was put back in inventory, $400 (cost, $240).

Required

1. Prepare entries in journal form (refer to the review problem) to record the transactions, assuming use of the perpetual inventory system.

2. **User Insight:** Receiving cash rebates from suppliers based on the past year's purchases is a common practice in some industries. If at the end of the year Tattle Company receives rebates in cash from a supplier, should these cash rebates be reported as revenue? Why or why not?

LO1, LO4 **Merchandising Income Statement: Periodic Inventory System**

P 8. Selected accounts from the adjusted trial balance for Pierre's Gourmet Shop, Inc., as of March 31, 20x7, the end of the fiscal year, are shown below.

Pierre's Gourmet Shop, Inc.
Partial Adjusted Trial Balance
March 31, 20x7

Sales		$165,000
Sales Returns and Allowances	$ 2,000	
Purchases	70,200	
Purchases Returns and Allowances		2,600
Freight-In	2,300	
Store Salaries Expense	32,625	
Office Salaries Expense	12,875	
Advertising Expense	24,300	
Rent Expense	2,400	
Insurance Expense	1,200	
Utilities Expense	1,560	
Store Supplies Expense	2,880	
Office Supplies Expense	1,175	
Depreciation Expense–Store Equipment	1,050	
Depreciation Expense–Office Equipment	800	
Income Taxes	1,000	

The merchandise inventory for Pierre's Gourmet Shop was $38,200 at the beginning of the year and $29,400 at the end of the year.

1. Using the information given, prepare an income statement for Pierre's Gourmet Shop, Inc. Store Salaries Expense; Advertising Expense; Store Supplies Expense; and Depreciation Expense–Store Equipment are selling expenses. The other expenses are general and administrative expenses. The company uses the periodic inventory system. Show details of net sales and operating expenses.

2. **User Insight:** Based on your knowledge at this point in the course, how would you use the income statement for Pierre's Gourmet Shop to evaluate the company's profitability? What other financial statements should you consider and why?

LO4   **Merchandising Transactions: Periodic Inventory System**

P 9. Use the data in **P 7** for this problem.

Required

1. Prepare entries in journal form (refer to the review problem) to record the transactions, assuming use of the periodic inventory system.

2. **User Insight:** In their published financial statements most companies call the first line on their income statement "net sales." Other companies simply say "sales." Do you think these terms are equivalent and comparable? What would be the content of "net sales"? What might be the reason a company would use "sales" instead of "net sales"?

ENHANCING Your Knowledge, Skills, and Critical Thinking

Conceptual Understanding Cases

LO1   **Cash Flow Management**

C 1. Roman Sound Source, Inc., has operated in Kansas for 30 years. The company has always prided itself on providing individual attention to its customers. It carries a large inventory so it can offer a good selection and deliver purchases quickly. It accepts credit cards and checks but also provides 90 days credit to reliable customers who have purchased from the company in the past. It maintains good relations with suppliers by paying invoices quickly.

During the past year, the company has been strapped for cash and has had to borrow from the bank to pay its bills. An analysis of its financial statements reveals that, on average, inventory is on hand for 70 days before being sold, and receivables are held for 90 days before being paid. Accounts payable are paid, on average, in 20 days. What are the operating cycle and the financing period? How long are Roman's operating cycle and financing period? Describe three ways in which Roman can improve its cash flow management.

LO1   **Periodic Versus Perpetual Inventory Systems**

C 2. Books Unlimited is a well-established chain of 20 bookstores in western Ohio. In recent years the company has grown rapidly, adding five new stores in regional malls. The manager of each store selects stock based on the market in his or her region. Managers select items from a master list of available titles that the central office provides. Every six months, a physical inventory is taken, and financial statements are prepared using the periodic inventory system. At that time, books that have not sold well are placed on sale or, whenever possible, returned to the publisher.

Management has found that when selecting books, the new managers are not judging the market as well as the managers of the older, established stores. Thus, management is thinking about implementing a perpetual inventory system and carefully monitoring sales from the central office. Do you think Books Unlimited should switch to the perpetual inventory system or stay with the periodic inventory system? Discuss the advantages and disadvantages of each system.

LO3   **Effects of Weak Dollar**

C 3. In 2004, **McDonald's** reported that its sales in Europe exceeded its sales in the United States for the first time. This result, while reflective of the company's phenomenal success in Europe, was also attributed to the weak dollar in relation to the euro in 2004. McDonald's reports its sales wherever they take place in U.S. dollars. Explain why a weak dollar relative to the euro would lead to an increase in McDonald's reported European sales. Why is a weak dollar not relevant to a discussion of McDonald's sales in the United States?

Interpreting Financial Reports

LO5   **Internal Control Lapse**

C 4. **Starbucks Corporation** has accused an employee and her husband of embezzling $3.7 million by billing the company for services from a fictitious consulting firm. The couple created a phony company called RAD Services Inc. and charged Starbucks for work they never provided. The employee worked in Starbucks' Information Technology Department. RAD Services Inc. charged Starbucks as much as $492,800 for consulting services in a single week.[13] For such a fraud to have taken place, certain control activities were likely not implemented. Identify and describe these activities.

Decision Analysis Using Excel

LO1, LO3, LO4, LO5   **Analysis of Merchandising Income Statement**

C 5. In 20x6, Alisa Harper opened a small retail store in a suburban mall. Called Harper Jeans Company, the shop sold designer jeans. Alisa Harper worked 14 hours a day and controlled all aspects of the operation. All sales were for cash or bank credit card. Harper Jeans Company was such a success that in 20x7, Harper decided to open a second store in another mall. Because the new shop needed her attention, she hired a manager to work in the original store with its two existing sales clerks. During 20x7, the new store was successful, but the operations of the original store did not match the first year's performance.

Concerned about this turn of events, Harper compared the two years' results for the original store. The figures are as follows:

	20x7	20x6
Net sales	$325,000	$350,000
Cost of goods sold	225,000	225,000
Gross margin	$100,000	$125,000
Operating expenses	75,000	50,000
Income before income taxes	$ 25,000	$ 75,000

In addition, Harper's analysis revealed that the cost and selling price of jeans were about the same in both years and that the level of operating expenses was roughly the same in both years, except for the new manager's $25,000 salary. Sales returns and allowances were insignificant amounts in both years.

Studying the situation further, Harper discovered the following facts about the cost of goods sold:

	20x7	20x6
Purchases	$200,000	$271,000
Total purchases allowances	15,000	20,000
Freight-in	19,000	27,000
Physical inventory, end of year	32,000	53,000

Still not satisfied, Harper went through all the individual sales and purchase records for the year. Both sales and purchases were verified. However, the 20x7 ending inventory should have been $57,000, given the unit purchases and sales during the year. After puzzling over all this information, Harper comes to you for accounting help.

1. Using Harper's new information, recompute the cost of goods sold for 20x6 and 20x7, and account for the difference in income before income taxes between 20x6 and 20x7.

2. Suggest at least two reasons for the discrepancy in the 20x7 ending inventory. How might Harper improve the management of the original store?

Annual Report Case: CVS Corporation

LO1 **Operating Cycle and Financing Period**

C 6. Refer to **CVS Corporation's** annual report in the Supplement to Chapter 1 and to Figures 1 and 2 in this chapter. Write a memorandum to your instructor briefly describing CVS's operating cycle and financing period. This memorandum should identify the most common transactions in the operating cycle as it applies to CVS. It should refer to the importance of accounts receivable, accounts payable, and merchandise inventory in the CVS financial statements. Complete the memorandum by explaining why the operating cycle and financing period are favorable to the company.

Comparison Case: CVS Versus Walgreens

LO1 **Income Statement Analysis**

C 7. Refer to **CVS's** annual report in the Supplement to Chapter 1 and to the following data (in millions) for **Walgreens** in 2004: net sales, $37,508.2; cost of sales, $27,310.4; total operating expenses, $8,071.7; and inventories, $4,738.6. Determine which company—CVS or Walgreens—had more profitable merchandising operations in fiscal 2004 by preparing a schedule that compares the companies based on net sales, cost of sales, gross margin, total operating expenses, and income from operations as a percentage of sales. (**Hint:** You should put the income statements in comparable formats.) In addition, for each company, compute inventories as a percentage of the cost of sales. Which company has the highest prices in relation to costs of sales? Which company is more efficient in its operating expenses? Which company manages its inventories better? Overall, on the basis of the income statement, which company is more profitable? Explain your answers.

Ethical Dilemma Case

LO1, LO3 **Barter Transactions**

C 8. Barter transactions in which one company trades goods or services to another company for other goods and services are becoming more common.

Broadcasters, for example, often barter advertising air time for goods or services. In such good-faith transactions, the broadcaster will credit revenue for the fair value of on-air advertising while debiting accounts in equal amounts for the nonmonetary goods and services it receives. **Dynergy,** an energy company, and another company agreed to buy and sell power to each other for the same price, terms, and volume. This resulted in no profit for Dynergy but increased its sales for the year, which perhaps helped it meet its sales goals and management's annual incentive bonus plans.[14] Do you think barter transactions that result in little or no profit for either company are ethical? Are they ethical in certain situations but not in others? How could you tell the difference?

Internet Case

LO1, LO3 Comparison of Traditional Merchandising with Ecommerce

C 9. E*commerce* is a word coined to describe business conducted over the Internet. Ecommerce is similar in some ways to traditional retailing, but it presents new challenges. Go to the website of **Amazon.com.** Investigate and list the steps a customer makes to purchase an item on the site. How do these steps differ from those in a traditional retail store such as **Borders** or **Barnes & Noble**? What are some of the accounting challenges in recording Internet transactions? Be prepared to discuss your results in class.

Group Activity Case

LO5, LO6 Merchandise Inventory and Internal Controls

C 10. Go to a retail business, such as a bookstore, clothing shop, gift shop, grocery, hardware store, or car dealership in your local shopping area or a shopping mall. Ask to speak to someone who is knowledgeable about the store's inventory methods. Your instructor will assign groups to find the answers to the following questions. Be prepared to discuss your findings in class.

1. *Inventory systems*   How is each item of inventory identified? Does the business have a computerized or a manual inventory system? Which inventory system, periodic or perpetual, is used? How often do employees take a physical inventory? What procedures are followed in taking a physical inventory? What kinds of inventory reports are prepared or received?
2. *Internal control structure*   How does the company protect itself against inventory theft and loss? What control activities, including authorization, recording transactions, documents and records, physical controls, periodic checks, separation of duties, and sound personnel policies, does the company use? Can you see these control procedures in use?

Business Communication Case

LO5, LO6 Internal Control in a Small Business

C 11. Gina Limke runs a small company, called Limke Construction Company. In the past, Gina's various site managers have each purchased construction materials for their jobs. She thinks that if she establishes a centralized purchasing department, it would help reduce waste and possibly theft. She has asked you, the company's accountant, to write a short memorandum that describes how such a purchasing system and the accompanying internal controls would work, and what forms would be needed to implement it. Assume the company has a central warehouse where material could be received.

Inventories

For any company that makes or sells merchandise, inventory is an extremely important asset. Managing this asset is a challenging task. It requires not only protecting goods from theft or loss, but also ensuring that operations are highly efficient. Further, as you will see in this chapter, proper accounting of inventory is essential because misstatements will affect net income in at least two years.

LEARNING OBJECTIVES

LO1 Explain the management decisions related to inventory accounting, evaluation of inventory level, and the effects of inventory misstatements on income measurement.

LO2 Define *inventory cost,* contrast goods flow and cost flow, and explain the lower-of-cost-or-market (LCM) rule.

LO3 Calculate inventory cost under the periodic inventory system using various costing methods.

LO4 Explain the effects of inventory costing methods on income determination and income taxes.

SUPPLEMENTAL OBJECTIVES

SO5 Calculate inventory cost under the perpetual inventory system using various costing methods.

SO6 Use the retail method and gross profit method to estimate the cost of ending inventory.

Making a Statement

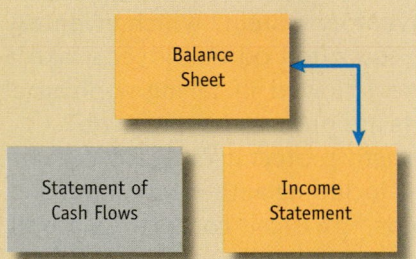

Valuation of inventories affects the amount of inventories on the balance sheet and the cost of goods sold on the income statement.

- What is the impact of inventory decisions on operating results?
- How should inventory be valued?
- How should the level of inventory be evaluated?

Cisco Systems manufactures and sells networking and communications products. It is the world's leading producer of the switches, hubs, gateways, and firewalls that make the Internet possible. As you can see in Cisco's Financial Highlights,[1] inventory is an important component of the company's total assets.

CISCO'S FINANCIAL HIGHLIGHTS
(In millions)

	2004	2003	2002
Product sales	$18,550	$15,565	$15,669
Cost of goods sold	5,766	4,594	5,914
Operating income	6,292	4,882	2,919
Inventories	1,207	873	856
Total assets	35,594	37,107	37,795

Managing Inventories

nventory is considered a current asset because a company normally sells it within a year or within its operating cycle. For a merchandising company like **CVS** or **Walgreens**, inventory consists of all goods owned and held for sale in the regular course of business. Because manufacturing companies like **Cisco** are engaged in making products, they have three kinds of inventory:

- Raw materials (goods used in making products)

- Work in process (partially completed products)

- Finished goods ready for sale

In a note to its financial statements, Cisco showed the following breakdown of its inventories (figures are in millions):[2]

Inventories	2004	2003
Raw materials	$ 58	$ 38
Work in process	459	291
Finished goods	690	544
Total inventories	$1,207	$873

The work in process and the finished goods inventories have three cost components:

- Cost of the raw materials that go into the product

- Cost of the labor used to convert the raw materials to finished goods

- Overhead costs that support the production process

Overhead costs include the costs of indirect materials (such as packing materials), indirect labor (such as the salaries of supervisors), factory rent, depreciation of plant assets, utilities, and insurance.

Inventory Decisions

Study Note

Management considers the behavior of inventory prices over time when selecting inventory costing methods.

The primary objective of inventory accounting is to determine income properly by matching costs of the period against revenues for the period. As you can see in Figure 1, in accounting for inventory, management must choose among different processing systems, costing methods, and valuation methods. These different systems and methods usually result in different amounts of reported net income. Thus, management's choices affect investors' and creditors' evaluations of a company, as well as internal evaluations, such as the performance reviews on which bonuses and executive compensation are based.

The consistency convention requires that once a company has decided on the systems and methods it will use in accounting for inventory, it must use them from one accounting period to the next unless management can justify a change. When a change is justifiable, the full disclosure convention requires that the company clearly describe the change and its effects in the notes to its financial statements.

Because the valuation of inventory affects income, it can have a considerable impact on the amount of income taxes a company pays—and the amount of taxes it pays can have a considerable impact on its cash flows. Federal

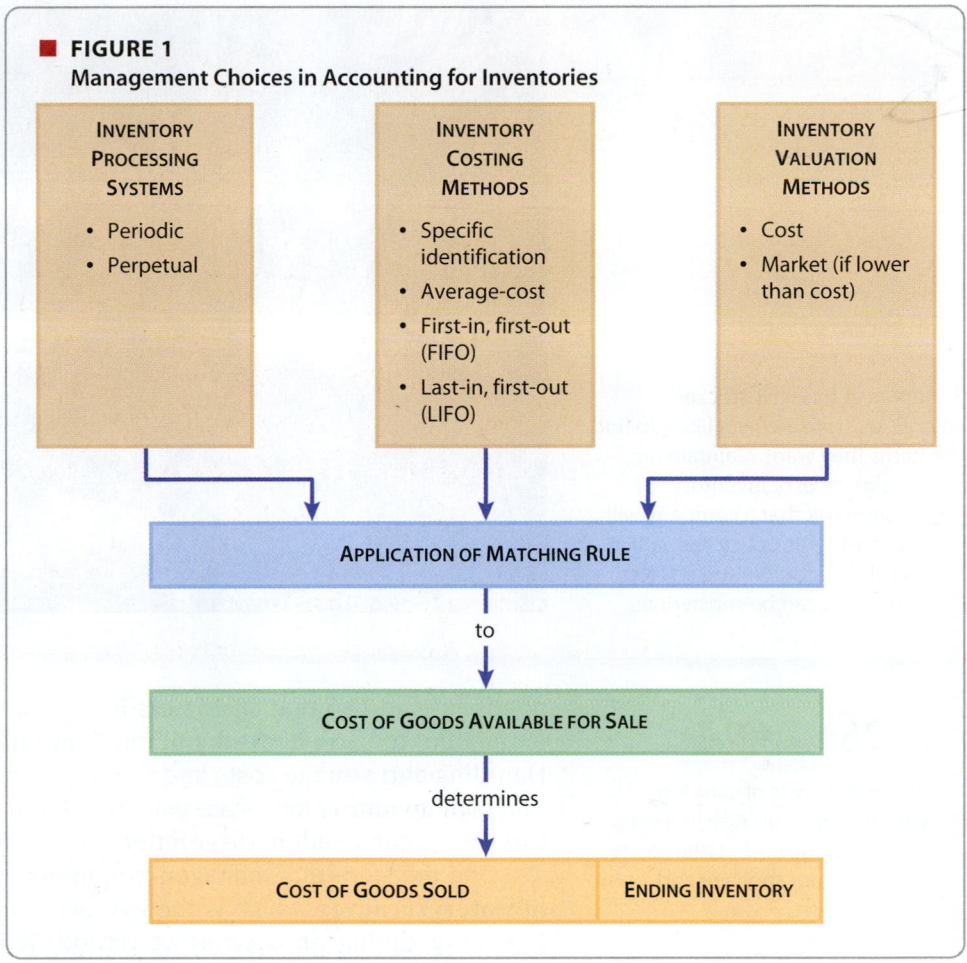

■ FIGURE 1
Management Choices in Accounting for Inventories

INVENTORY PROCESSING SYSTEMS	INVENTORY COSTING METHODS	INVENTORY VALUATION METHODS
• Periodic • Perpetual	• Specific identification • Average-cost • First-in, first-out (FIFO) • Last-in, first-out (LIFO)	• Cost • Market (if lower than cost)

APPLICATION OF MATCHING RULE

to

COST OF GOODS AVAILABLE FOR SALE

determines

| COST OF GOODS SOLD | ENDING INVENTORY |

income tax regulations are specific about the valuation methods a company may use. As a result, management is sometimes faced with the dilemma of how to apply GAAP to income determination and still minimize income taxes.

Evaluating the Level of Inventory

The level of inventory a company maintains has important economic consequences. Ideally, management wants to have a great variety and quantity of

FOCUS ON BUSINESS PRACTICE
A Whirlwind Inventory Turnover—How Does Dell Do It?

Dell Computer Corporation turns its inventory over every six days. How can it do this when other computer companies have inventory on hand for 60 days or even longer? Technology and good inventory management are a big part of the answer.

Dell's speed from order to delivery sets the standard for the computer industry. Consider that a computer ordered by 9 A.M. can be delivered the next day by 9 P.M. How can Dell do this when it does not start ordering components and assembling computers until a customer places an order? First, Dell's suppliers keep components warehoused just

minutes from Dell's factories, making efficient, just-in-time operations possible. Another time and money saver is the handling of computer monitors. Monitors are no longer shipped first to Dell and then on to buyers. Dell sends an email message to a shipper, such as **United Parcel Service**, and the shipper picks up a monitor from a supplier and schedules it to arrive with the PC. In addition to contributing to a high inventory turnover, this practice saves Dell about $30 per monitor in freight costs. Dell is showing the world how to run a business in the cyber age by selling more than $1 million worth of computers a day on its website.[3]

Shoppers at this well-stocked Toys "R" Us store are very likely to find the items they want. Maintaining such a high level of inventory reduces the risk that a company will lose sales, but this policy has a price. The handling, storage, and interest costs involved can be substantial.

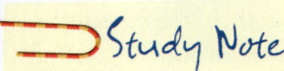

Study Note

Some of the costs of carrying inventory are insurance, property tax, and storage costs. Other costs may result from spoilage and employee theft.

goods on hand so that customers have a large choice and do not have to wait for an item to be restocked. But implementing such a policy can be expensive. Handling and storage costs and the interest cost of the funds needed to maintain high inventory levels are usually substantial. On the other hand, low inventory levels can result in disgruntled customers and lost sales.

One measure that managers commonly use to evaluate inventory levels is **inventory turnover**, which is the average number of times a company sells its inventory during an accounting period. It is computed by dividing cost of goods sold by average inventory. For example, using the data presented in this chapter's Decision Point, we can compute **Cisco's** inventory turnover for 2004 as follows (figures are in millions):

$$\text{Inventory Turnover} = \frac{\text{Cost of Goods Sold}}{\text{Average Inventory}}$$

$$= \frac{\$5,766}{(\$1,207 + \$873) \div 2}$$

$$= \frac{\$5,766}{\$1,040} = 5.5 \text{ times}$$

Another common measure of inventory levels is **days' inventory on hand**, which is the average number of days it takes a company to sell the inventory it has in stock. For Cisco, it is computed as follows:

$$\text{Days' Inventory on Hand} = \frac{\text{Number of Days in a Year}}{\text{Inventory Turnover}}$$

$$= \frac{365 \text{ days}}{5.5 \text{ times}} = 66.4 \text{ days}$$

Cisco turned its inventory over 5.5 times in 2004 or, on average, every 66.4 days. Thus, it had to provide financing for the inventory for more than two months before it sold it.

As you can see in Figures 2 and 3, inventory turnover and days' inventory on hand vary by industry. Nonetheless, companies that maintain their inventories at low levels and still satisfy customers' needs are the most successful.

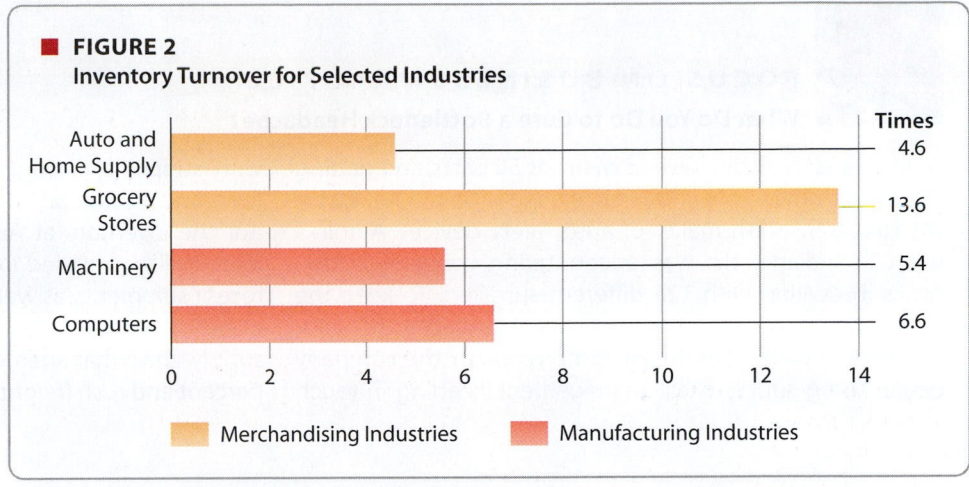

■ **FIGURE 2**
Inventory Turnover for Selected Industries

Source: Data from Dun & Bradstreet, *Industry Norms and Key Business Ratios*, 2003–2004

To reduce their levels of inventory, many merchandisers and manufacturers use supply-chain management in conjunction with a just-in-time operating environment. With **supply-chain management**, a company uses the Internet to order and track goods that it needs immediately. A **just-in-time operating environment** is one in which goods arrive just at the time they are needed.

Cisco uses supply-chain management to increase inventory turnover. It manages its inventory purchases through business-to-business transactions that it conducts over the Internet. It also uses a just-in-time operating environment in which it works closely with suppliers to coordinate and schedule shipments so that the shipments arrive exactly when needed. The benefits of using supply-chain management in a just-in-time operating environment are that Cisco has less money tied up in inventory and its cost of carrying inventory is reduced.

Effects of Inventory Misstatements on Income Measurement

The reason inventory accounting is so important to income measurement is the way income is measured on the income statement. Recall that gross margin is the difference between net sales and cost of goods sold and that cost of goods

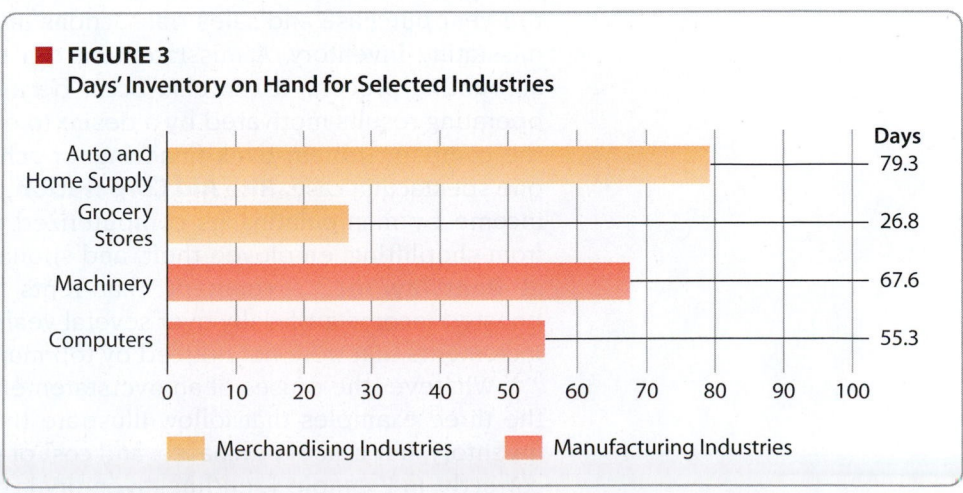

■ **FIGURE 3**
Days' Inventory on Hand for Selected Industries

Source: Data from Dun & Bradstreet, *Industry Norms and Key Business Ratios*, 2003–2004

sold depends on the portion of cost of goods available for sale assigned to ending inventory. These relationships lead to the following conclusions:

- The higher the value of ending inventory, the lower the cost of goods sold and the higher the gross margin.

- Conversely, the lower the value of ending inventory, the higher the cost of goods sold and the lower the gross margin.

Because the amount of gross margin has a direct effect on net income, the value assigned to ending inventory also affects net income. In effect, the value of ending inventory determines what portion of the cost of goods available for sale is assigned to cost of goods sold and what portion is assigned to the balance sheet as inventory to be carried over into the next accounting period.

The basic issue in separating goods available for sale into two components—goods sold and goods not sold—is to assign a value to the goods not sold, the ending inventory. The portion of goods available for sale not assigned to the ending inventory is used to determine the cost of goods sold. Because the figures for ending inventory and cost of goods sold are related, a misstatement in the inventory figure at the end of an accounting period will cause an equal misstatement in gross margin and income before income taxes in the income statement. The amount of assets and stockholders' equity on the balance sheet will be misstated by the same amount.

Inventory is particularly susceptible to fraudulent financial reporting. For example, it is easy to overstate or understate inventory by including end-of-the-year purchase and sales transactions in the wrong fiscal year or by simply misstating inventory. A misstatement can occur because of mistakes in the accounting process. It can also occur because of deliberate manipulation of operating results motivated by a desire to enhance the market's perception of the company, obtain bank financing, or achieve compensation incentives. In one spectacular case, **Rite Aid Corporation**, the large drugstore chain, falsified income by manipulating its computerized inventory system to cover losses from shoplifting, employee theft, and spoilage. In another case, bookkeepers at **RentWay, Inc.,** a company that rents furniture to apartment dwellers, boosted income artificially over several years by overstating inventory in small increments that were not noticed by top management.

Whatever the causes of an overstatement or understatement of inventory, the three examples that follow illustrate the effects. In each case, beginning inventory, net cost of purchases, and cost of goods available for sale are stated correctly. In Example 1, ending inventory is correctly stated; in Example 2, it is overstated by $6,000; and in Example 3, it is understated by $6,000.

Autoliv's use of supply-chain management is an example of how this system has benefited businesses. By using the Internet to order and track the numerous parts involved in the manufacture of the seat belts pictured here, Autoliv prevented delays in the shipments of parts by allowing its suppliers to monitor inventory and thus to anticipate problems. The firm also drastically reduced its inventory and freight costs.

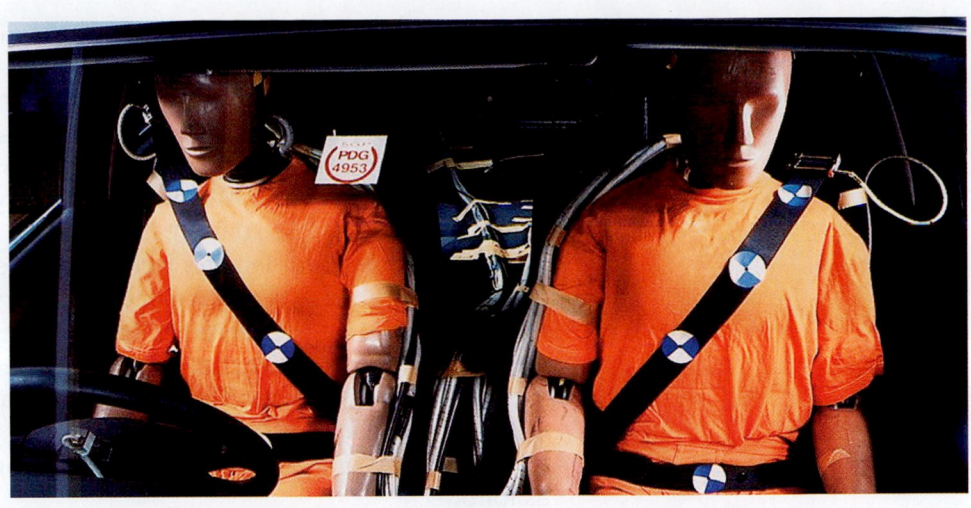

Example 1. Ending Inventory Correctly Stated at $10,000

Cost of Goods Sold for the Year		Income Statement for the Year	
Beginning inventory	$12,000	Net sales	$100,000
Net cost of purchases	58,000	Cost of goods sold	60,000
Cost of goods available for sale	$70,000	Gross margin	$ 40,000
Ending inventory	10,000	Operating expenses	32,000
		Income before income	
Cost of goods sold	$60,000	taxes	$ 8,000

Example 2. Ending Inventory Overstated by $6,000

Cost of Goods Sold for the Year		Income Statement for the Year	
Beginning inventory	$12,000	Net sales	$100,000
Net cost of purchases	58,000	Cost of goods sold	54,000
Cost of goods available for sale	$70,000	Gross margin	$ 46,000
Ending inventory	16,000	Operating expenses	32,000
		Income before income	
Cost of goods sold	$54,000	taxes	$ 14,000

Example 3. Ending Inventory Understated by $6,000

Cost of Goods Sold for the Year		Income Statement for the Year	
Beginning inventory	$12,000	Net sales	$100,000
Net cost of purchases	58,000	Cost of goods sold	66,000
Cost of goods available for sale	$70,000	Gross margin	$ 34,000
Ending inventory	4,000	Operating expenses	32,000
		Income before income	
Cost of goods sold	$66,000	taxes	$ 2,000

In all three examples, the cost of goods available for sale was $70,000. The difference in income before income taxes resulted from how this $70,000 was divided between ending inventory and cost of goods sold.

Study Note

A misstatement of inventory has the opposite effect in two successive accounting periods.

Because the ending inventory in one period becomes the beginning inventory in the following period, a misstatement in inventory valuation affects not only the current period but the following period as well. Over two periods, the errors in income before income taxes will offset, or counterbalance, each other. For instance, in Example 2, the overstatement of ending inventory will cause a $6,000 overstatement of beginning inventory in the following year, which will result in a $6,000 understatement of income.

Because the total income before income taxes for the two periods is the same, it may appear that one need not worry about inventory misstatements. However, the misstatements violate the matching rule. In addition, management, creditors, and investors base many decisions on the accountant's determination of net income. The accountant has an obligation to make the net income figure for each period as useful as possible.

The effects of inventory misstatements on income before income taxes are as follows:

Year 1	Year 2
Ending inventory overstated	**Beginning inventory overstated**
Cost of goods sold understated	Cost of goods sold overstated
Income before income taxes overstated	Income before income taxes understated
Ending inventory understated	**Beginning inventory understated**
Cost of goods sold overstated	Cost of goods sold understated
Income before income taxes understated	Income before income taxes overstated

STOP • REVIEW • APPLY

1-1. How does a manufacturing company's inventory differ from that of a merchandising company?

1-2. What is the primary objective of inventory accounting?

1-3. Why is the level of inventory important, and what are two common measures of inventory level?

1-4. Why is inventory particularly vulnerable to fraudulent financial reporting?

1-5. If inventory is overstated at the end of 20x5, what is the effect on the (a) 20x5 net income, (b) 20x5 year-end balance sheet value, (c) 20x6 net income, and (d) 20x6 year-end balance sheet value?

Suggested answers to all Stop, Review, and Apply questions follow the appendixes.

Inventory Cost and Valuation

LO2 Define *inventory cost,* contrast goods flow and cost flow, and explain the lower-of-cost-or-market (LCM) rule.

The primary basis of accounting for inventories is cost, the price paid to acquire an asset. **Inventory cost** includes the following:

▶ Invoice price less purchases discounts

▶ Freight-in, including insurance in transit

▶ Applicable taxes and tariffs

Other costs—for ordering, receiving, and storing—should in principle be included in inventory cost. In practice, however, it is so difficult to allocate such costs to specific inventory items that they are usually considered expenses of the accounting period rather than inventory costs.

Inventory costing and valuation depend on the prices of the goods in inventory. The prices of most goods vary during the year. A company may have purchased identical lots of merchandise at different prices. Also, when a company deals in identical items, it is often impossible to tell which have been sold and which are still in inventory. When that is the case, it is necessary to make an assumption about the order in which items have been sold. Because the assumed order of sale may or may not be the same as the actual order of sale, the assumption is really about the *flow of costs* rather than the *flow of physical inventory*.

Goods Flows and Cost Flows

Goods flow refers to the actual physical movement of goods in the operations of a company. **Cost flow** refers to the association of costs with their *assumed* flow in the operations of a company. The assumed cost flow may or may not be the same as the actual goods flow. The possibility of a difference between cost flow and goods flow may seem strange at first, but it arises because several choices of assumed cost flow are available under generally accepted accounting principles. In fact, it is sometimes preferable to use an assumed cost flow that bears no relationship to goods flow because it gives a better estimate of income, which is the main goal of inventory valuation.

Merchandise in Transit   Because merchandise inventory includes all items that a company owns and holds for sale, the status of any merchandise in transit, whether the company is selling it or buying it, must be evaluated to see if the merchandise should be included in the inventory count. Neither the seller nor the buyer has *physical* possession of merchandise in transit. As Figure 4 shows, ownership is determined by the terms of the shipping agreement,

Study Note

The assumed flow of inventory costs does not have to correspond to the physical flow of goods.

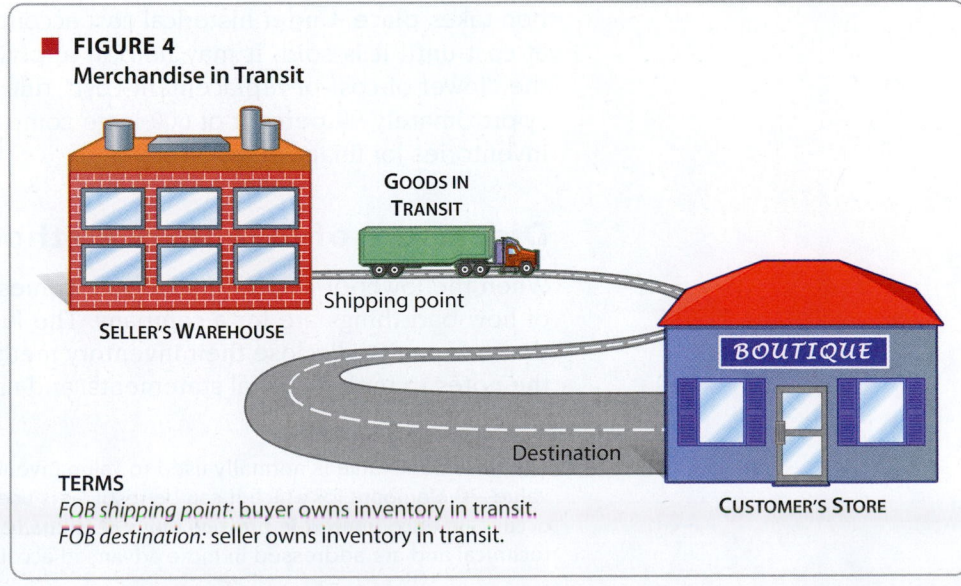

■ **FIGURE 4**
Merchandise in Transit

GOODS IN TRANSIT

Shipping point

SELLER'S WAREHOUSE

Destination

BOUTIQUE

CUSTOMER'S STORE

TERMS
FOB shipping point: buyer owns inventory in transit.
FOB destination: seller owns inventory in transit.

which indicate when title passes. Outgoing goods shipped FOB (free on board) destination are included in the seller's merchandise inventory, whereas those shipped FOB shipping point are not. Conversely, incoming goods shipped FOB shipping point are included in the buyer's merchandise inventory, but those shipped FOB destination are not.

Merchandise on Hand Not Included in Inventory At the time a company takes a physical inventory, it may have merchandise on hand to which it does not hold title. For example, it may have sold goods but not yet delivered them to the buyer, but because the sale has been completed, title has passed to the buyer. Thus, the merchandise should be included in the buyer's inventory, not the seller's. Goods held on consignment also fall into this category.

A **consignment** is merchandise that its owner (the consignor) places on the premises of another company (the consignee) with the understanding that payment is expected only when the merchandise is sold and that unsold items may be returned to the consignor. Title to consigned goods remains with the consignor until the consignee sells the goods. Consigned goods should not be included in the consignee's physical inventory because they still belong to the consignor.

Lower-of-Cost-or-Market (LCM) Rule

Although cost is usually the most appropriate basis for valuation of inventory, inventory may at times be properly shown in the financial statements at less than its historical, or original, cost. If the market value of inventory falls below its historical cost because of physical deterioration, obsolescence, or decline in price level, a loss has occurred. This loss is recognized by writing the inventory down to **market**—that is, to its current replacement cost. For a merchandising company, market is the amount that it would pay at the present time for the same goods, purchased from the usual suppliers and in the usual quantities.

When the replacement cost of inventory falls below its historical cost (as determined by an inventory costing method), the **lower-of-cost-or-market (LCM) rule** requires that the inventory be written down to the lower value and that a loss be recorded. This rule is an example of the application of the conservatism convention because the loss is recognized before an actual transaction takes place. Under historical cost accounting, the inventory would remain at cost until it is sold. It may help in applying the LCM rule to think of it as the "lower-of-cost-or-replacement-cost" rule.* According to an AICPA survey, approximately 90 percent of 600 large companies apply the LCM rule to their inventories for financial reporting.[5]

Disclosure of Inventory Methods

When the lower-of-cost-or-market rule comes into play, it can be an indication of how bad things are for a company. The full disclosure convention requires that companies disclose their inventory methods, including the use of LCM, in the notes to their financial statements, and users should pay close attention to

Study Note

Cost must be determined by one of the inventory costing methods before it can be compared with the market value.

---

*Replacement value is normally used to value inventory, but in some cases, the realizable value—the amount for which it can be resold—is used. The circumstances in which this occurs are encountered in practice only occasionally. The valuation procedures are quite technical and are addressed in more advanced accounting courses.

them. For example, in 2001, when the market for Internet and telecommunications equipment had soured, **Cisco's** annual report contained this note:

> Inventories are stated at the lower of cost or market. Cost is computed . . . on a first-in, first-out basis. The company provides allowances on excess and obsolete inventories.[6]

In 2001, Cisco found itself faced with probably the largest inventory loss in history. It had to write down to zero almost two-thirds of its $2.5 billion inventory, 80 percent of which consisted of raw materials that would never be made into final product.[7]

In another case in which the LCM rule came into play, **Kmart**, through poor management, a downturn in the economy, and underperforming stores, found itself with a huge amount of excess merchandise, including more than 5,000 truckloads of goods stored in parking lots, which it could not sell except at drastically reduced prices. The company had to mark down its inventory by $1 billion in order to sell it, which resulted in a debilitating loss.[8]

STOP • REVIEW • APPLY

2-1. What items should be included in the cost of inventory?

2-2. What is the difference between goods flow and cost flow?

2-3. At the end of its fiscal year on June 30, Fargo Sales Company has an order for 130 units of product in its warehouse. Although the shipping department tries, it cannot ship the product by June 30, and title to the goods has not yet passed. Should the 130 units be included in the year-end count of inventory? Why or why not?

2-4. In the phrase *lower of cost or market*, what does *market* mean?

2-5. Why is it important for a company to disclose its method of accounting for inventory costs?

Inventory Costs and Valuation Concepts   Match the letter of each item below with the numbers of the related items:

a. An inventory cost

b. An assumption used in the valuation of inventory

c. Full disclosure convention

d. Conservatism convention

e. Consistency convention

f. Not an inventory cost or assumed flow

1. Cost of consigned goods

2. A note to the financial statements explaining inventory policies

3. Application of the LCM rule

4. Goods flow

5. Transportation charge for merchandise shipped FOB shipping point

6. Cost flow

7. Choosing a method and sticking with it

8. Transportation charge for merchandise shipped FOB destination

Inventory Cost Under the Periodic Inventory System

LO3 Calculate inventory cost under the periodic inventory system using various costing methods.

The value assigned to ending inventory is the result of two measurements: quantity and cost. As you know, under the periodic inventory system, quantity is determined by taking a physical inventory; under the perpetual inventory system, quantities are updated as purchases and sales take place. Cost is determined by using one of the following methods, each based on a different assumption of cost flow:

1. Specific identification method

2. Average-cost method

3. First-in, first-out (FIFO) method

4. Last-in, first-out (LIFO) method

The choice of method depends on the nature of the business, the financial effects of the method, and the cost of implementing the method.

To illustrate how each method is used under the periodic inventory system, we use the following data for June, a month in which prices were rising:

June 1	Inventory	80 units @ $10.00	$ 800
6	Purchase	220 units @ $12.50	2,750
25	Purchase	200 units @ $14.00	2,800
	Goods available for sale	500 units	$6,350
	Sales	280 units	
	On hand June 30	220 units	

The problem of inventory costing is to divide the cost of the goods available for sale ($6,350) between the 280 units sold and the 220 units on hand.

Specific Identification Method

The **specific identification method** identifies the cost of each item in ending inventory. It can be used only when it is possible to identify the units in ending inventory as coming from specific purchases. For instance, if the June 30 inventory consisted of 50 units from the June 1 inventory, 100 units from the June 6 purchase, and 70 units from the June 25 purchase, the specific identification method would assign the costs as follows:

Periodic Inventory System—Specific Identification Method

50 units @ $10.00	$ 500	Cost of goods available	
100 units @ $12.50	1,250	for sale	$6,350
70 units @ $14.00	980	Less June 30 inventory	2,730
220 units at a cost of	$2,730	Cost of goods sold	$3,620

The specific identification method may appear logical, and it can be used by companies that deal in high-priced articles, such as works of art, precious gems, or rare antiques. However, most companies do not use it for the following reasons:

1. It is usually impractical, if not impossible, to keep track of the purchase and sale of individual items.

2. When a company deals in items that are identical but that it bought at different prices, deciding which items were sold becomes arbitrary. If the company were to use the specific identification method, it could raise or lower income by choosing the lower- or higher-priced items.

Average-Cost Method

Under the **average-cost method**, inventory is priced at the average cost of the goods available for sale during the accounting period. Average cost is computed by dividing the total cost of goods available for sale by the total units available for sale. This gives an average unit cost that is applied to the units in ending inventory.

In our illustration, the ending inventory would be $2,794, or $12.70 per unit, determined as follows:

Periodic Inventory System—Average-Cost Method

Cost of Goods Available for Sale ÷ Units Available for Sale = Average Unit Cost
$6,350 ÷ 500 units = $12.70

→ Ending inventory: 220 units @ $12.70 =	$2,794
Cost of goods available for sale	$6,350
↳ Less June 30 inventory	2,794
Cost of goods sold	$3,556

The average-cost method tends to level out the effects of cost increases and decreases because the cost of the ending inventory is influenced by all the prices paid during the year and by the cost of beginning inventory. Some analysts, however, criticize this method because they believe recent costs are more relevant for income measurement and decision making.

First-In, First-Out (FIFO) Method

The **first-in, first-out (FIFO) method** assumes that the costs of the first items acquired should be assigned to the first items sold. The costs of the goods on hand at the end of a period are assumed to be from the most recent purchases, and the costs assigned to goods that have been sold are assumed to be from the earliest purchases. Any business, regardless of its goods flow, can use the FIFO method because the assumption underlying it is based on the flow of costs, not the flow of goods.

In our illustration, the FIFO method would result in an ending inventory of $3,050, computed as follows:

Periodic Inventory System—FIFO Method

200 units @ $14.00 from purchase of June 25	$2,800
20 units @ $12.50 from purchase of June 6	250
→ 220 units at a cost of	$3,050
Cost of goods available for sale	$6,350
↳ Less June 30 inventory	3,050
Cost of goods sold	$3,300

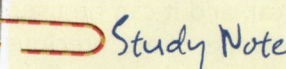

Thus, the FIFO method values ending inventory at the most recent costs and includes earlier costs in cost of goods sold. During periods of rising prices, FIFO yields the highest possible amount of net income because cost of goods sold shows the earliest costs incurred, which are lower during periods of inflation. Another reason for this is that businesses tend to raise selling prices as costs increase, even when they purchased the goods before the cost increase. In periods of declining prices, FIFO tends to charge the older and higher prices against revenues, thus reducing income. Consequently, a major criticism of FIFO is that it magnifies the effects of the business cycle on income.

Last-In, First-Out (LIFO) Method

The **last-in, first-out (LIFO) method** of costing inventories assumes that the costs of the last items purchased should be assigned to the first items sold and that the cost of ending inventory should reflect the cost of the goods purchased earliest. Under LIFO, the June 30 inventory would be $2,550:

Periodic Inventory System—LIFO Method

80 units @ $10.00 from June 1 inventory	$ 800
140 units @ $12.50 from purchase of June 6	1,750
220 units at a cost of	$2,550
Cost of goods available for sale	$6,350
Less June 30 inventory	2,550
Cost of goods sold	$3,800

The effect of LIFO is to value inventory at the earliest prices and to include the cost of the most recently purchased goods in the cost of goods sold. This assumption, of course, does not agree with the actual physical movement of goods in most businesses.

There is, however, a strong logical argument to support LIFO. A certain size of inventory is necessary in a going concern—when inventory is sold, it must be replaced with more goods. The supporters of LIFO reason that the fairest determination of income occurs if the current costs of merchandise are matched against current sales prices, regardless of which physical units of merchandise are sold. When prices are moving either up or down, the cost of goods sold will, under LIFO, show costs closer to the price level at the time the goods are sold. Thus, the LIFO method tends to show a smaller net income during inflationary times and a larger net income during deflationary times than other methods of inventory valuation. The peaks and valleys of the business cycle tend to be smoothed out. In inventory valuation, the flow of costs—and hence

FOCUS ON BUSINESS PRACTICE

What's a "Category Killer"?

A type of retail company called the "category killer" seems to ignore the tenets of good inventory management. The category killers include **Home Depot, Barnes & Noble, Wal-Mart, Toys "R" Us,** and **Blockbuster Entertainment Corporation.** These retailers maintain huge inventories of the goods in which they specialize and sell them at such low prices that other firms find it hard to compete. Although the category killers have large amounts of money tied up in inventories, they maintain very sophisticated just-in-time operating environments that require suppliers to meet demanding standards for delivery of products and reduction of inventory costs. Some suppliers are required to stock the shelves and keep track of inventory levels. By minimizing handling and overhead costs and buying at favorably low prices, the category killers have realized large profits.

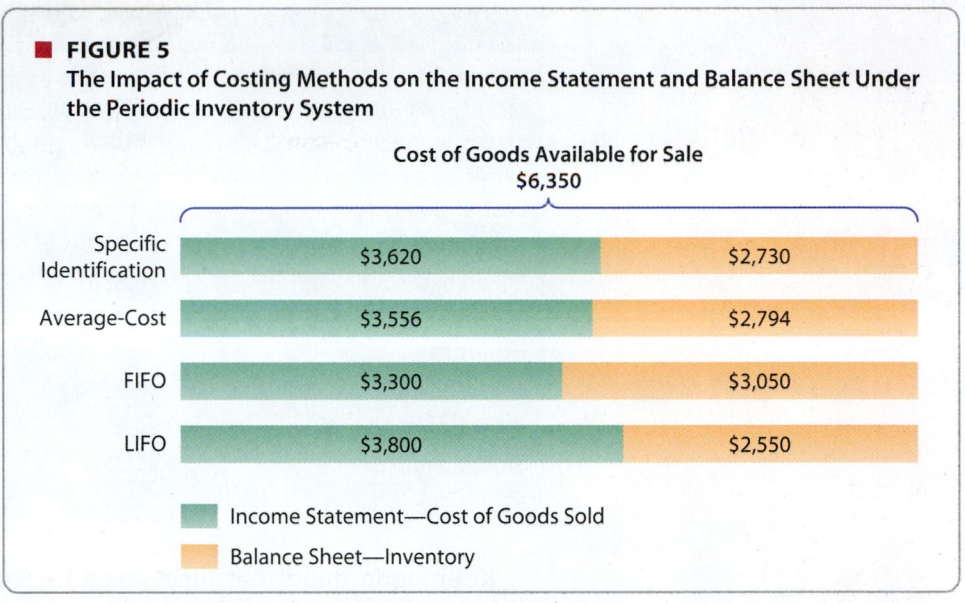

■ **FIGURE 5**
The Impact of Costing Methods on the Income Statement and Balance Sheet Under the Periodic Inventory System

Cost of Goods Available for Sale
$6,350

	Income Statement—Cost of Goods Sold	Balance Sheet—Inventory
Specific Identification	$3,620	$2,730
Average-Cost	$3,556	$2,794
FIFO	$3,300	$3,050
LIFO	$3,800	$2,550

■ Income Statement—Cost of Goods Sold
■ Balance Sheet—Inventory

income determination—is more important than the physical movement of goods and balance sheet valuation.

An argument can also be made against LIFO. Because the inventory valuation on the balance sheet reflects earlier prices, it often gives an unrealistic picture of the inventory's current value. Balance sheet measures like working capital and current ratio may be distorted and must be interpreted carefully.

Figure 5 summarizes how the four inventory costing methods affect the cost of goods sold on the income statement and inventory on the balance sheet when a company uses the periodic inventory system. In periods of rising prices, FIFO yields the highest inventory valuation, the lowest cost of goods sold, and hence a higher net income; LIFO yields the lowest inventory valuation, the highest cost of goods sold, and thus a lower net income.

S T O P • R E V I E W • A P P L Y

3-1. Do the FIFO and LIFO inventory costing methods result in different quantities of ending inventory? Explain your answer.

3-2. Under which inventory costing methods are (a) the earliest costs assigned to inventory, (b) the latest costs assigned to inventory, and (c) the average costs assigned to inventory?

3-3. What are the relative advantages and disadvantages of FIFO and LIFO from management's point of view?

Impact of Inventory Decisions

LO4 Explain the effects of inventory costing methods on income determination and income taxes

Table 1 shows how the specific identification, average-cost, FIFO, and LIFO methods of pricing inventory affect gross margin. The table uses the same data as in the previous section and assumes June sales of $5,000.

TABLE 1. Effects of Inventory Costing Methods on Gross Margin

	Specific Identification Method	Average-Cost Method	FIFO Method	LIFO Method
Sales	$5,000	$5,000	$5,000	$5,000
Cost of goods sold				
Beginning inventory	$ 800	$ 800	$ 800	$ 800
Purchases	5,550	5,550	5,550	5,550
Cost of goods available for sale	$6,350	$6,350	$6,350	$6,350
Less ending inventory	2,730	2,794	3,050	2,550
Cost of goods sold	$3,620	$3,556	$3,300	$3,800
Gross margin	$1,380	$1,444	$1,700	$1,200

Keeping in mind that June was a period of rising prices, you can see in Table 1 that LIFO, which charges the most recent—and, in this case, the highest—prices to cost of goods sold, resulted in the lowest gross margin. Conversely, FIFO, which charges the earliest—and, in this case, the lowest—prices to cost of goods sold, produced the highest gross margin. The gross margin under the average-cost method falls between the gross margins produced by LIFO and FIFO, so this method clearly has a less pronounced effect.

During a period of declining prices, the LIFO method would produce a higher gross margin than the FIFO method. It is apparent that both these methods have the greatest impact on gross margin during prolonged periods of price changes, whether up or down. Because the specific identification method depends on the particular items sold, no generalization can be made about the effect of changing prices on gross margin.

Effects on the Financial Statements

As Figure 6 shows, the FIFO, LIFO, and average-cost methods of inventory costing are widely used. Each method has its advantages and disadvantages—none is perfect. Among the factors managers should consider in choosing an inventory costing method are the trend of prices and the effects of each method on financial statements, income taxes, and cash flows.

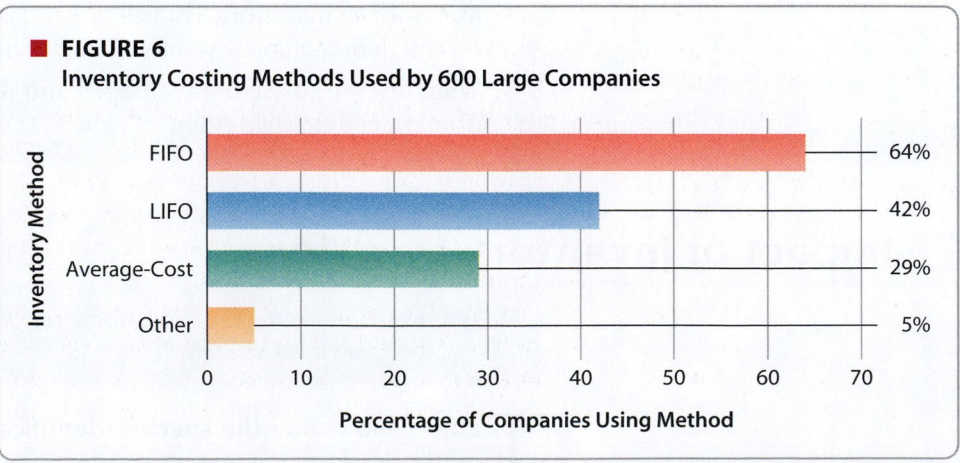

■ **FIGURE 6**
Inventory Costing Methods Used by 600 Large Companies

Source: "Industry Costing Methods Used by 600 Large Companies." Copyright © 2004 by AICPA. Reproduced with permission.

As we have pointed out, inventory costing methods have different effects on the income statement and balance sheet. The LIFO method is best suited for the income statement because it matches revenues and cost of goods sold. But it is not the best method for valuation of inventory on the balance sheet, particularly during a prolonged period of price increases or decreases. FIFO, on the other hand, is well suited to the balance sheet because the ending inventory is closest to current values and thus gives a more realistic view of a company's current assets. Readers of financial statements must be alert to the inventory methods a company uses and be able to assess their effects.

Effects on Income Taxes

The Internal Revenue Service governs how inventories must be valued for federal income tax purposes. IRS regulations give companies a wide choice of inventory costing methods, including specific identification, average-cost, FIFO, and LIFO, and, except when the LIFO method is used, it allows them to apply the lower-of-cost-or-market rule. However, if a company wants to change the valuation method it uses for income tax purposes, it must have advance approval from the IRS.* This requirement conforms to the consistency convention. Because changes in inventory costing method can cause sizable fluctuations in income and make income statements hard to interpret from year to year, a company should change its inventory method only if there is a good reason to do so. The company must show the nature and effect of the change in its financial statements.

Many accountants believe that using the FIFO and average-cost methods in periods of rising prices causes businesses to report more than their actual profit, resulting in excess payment of income tax. Profit is overstated because cost of goods sold is understated relative to current prices. Thus, the company must buy replacement inventory at higher prices, while additional funds are needed to pay income taxes. During the rapid inflation of 1979 to 1982, billions of dollars reported as profits and paid in income taxes were believed to be the result of poor matching of current costs and revenues under the FIFO and average-cost methods. Consequently, many companies, believing that prices would continue to rise, switched to the LIFO inventory method.

When a company uses the LIFO method to report income for tax purposes, the IRS requires that it use the same method in its accounting records, and, as we have noted, it disallows use of the LCM rule. The company may, however, use the LCM rule for financial reporting purposes.

Over a period of rising prices, a business that uses the LIFO method may find that for balance sheet purposes, its inventory is valued at a figure far below what it currently pays for the same items. Management must monitor such a situation carefully, because if it lets the inventory quantity at year end fall below the level at the beginning of the year, the company will find itself paying higher income taxes. Higher income before taxes results because the company expenses the historical costs of inventory, which are below current costs. When sales have reduced inventories below the levels set in prior years, it is called a **LIFO liquidation**—that is, units sold exceed units purchased for the period.

Managers can prevent a LIFO liquidation by making enough purchases before the end of the year to restore the desired inventory level. Sometimes, however, a LIFO liquidation cannot be avoided because products are discontinued or supplies are interrupted, as in the case of a strike. In 2004, 26 out of

> **Study Note**
>
> In periods of rising prices, LIFO results in lower net income and thus lower taxes.

---

* A single exception to this rule is that when companies change to LIFO from another method, they do not need advance approval from the IRS.

FOCUS ON BUSINESS PRACTICE

Does a Company's Inventory Costing Method Affect Its Operating Decisions?

It certainly does when taxes are involved. Research has shown that among firms that use the LIFO inventory method, those with high tax rates are more likely to buy extra inventory at year end than are those with low tax rates.[9] This behavior is predictable because in determining taxable income, LIFO deducts the costs of the most recent purchases, which are likely to be higher than the costs of earlier purchases. By buying extra inventory at year end, a company can lower its income taxes.

600 large companies reported a LIFO liquidation in which their net income increased due to the matching of historical costs with present sales dollars.[10]

Effects on Cash Flows

Generally speaking, the choice of accounting methods does not affect cash flows. For example, a company's choice of average cost, FIFO, or LIFO does not affect what it pays for goods or the price at which it sells them. However, the fact that income tax law requires a company to use the same method for income tax purposes and financial reporting means that the choice of inventory method will affect the amount of income tax paid. Therefore, choosing a method that results in lower income will result in lower income taxes due. In most other cases where there is a choice of accounting method, a company may choose different methods for income tax computations and financial reporting.

S T O P • R E V I E W • A P P L Y

4-1. In periods of steadily rising prices, which inventory method—average-cost, FIFO, or LIFO—will give the (a) highest ending inventory cost, (b) lowest ending inventory cost, (c) highest net income, and (d) lowest net income?

4-2. What is the relationship between income tax rules and the inventory valuation methods?

Characteristics of Inventory Costing Methods   Match each of the descriptions listed below to these inventory costing methods:

a. Specific identification

b. Average-cost

c. First-in, first-out (FIFO)

d. Last-in, first-out (LIFO)

  1. Matches recent costs with recent revenues

  2. Assumes that each item of inventory is identifiable

  3. Results in the most realistic balance sheet valuation

  4. Results in the lowest net income in periods of deflation

  5. Results in the lowest net income in periods of inflation

  6. Matches the oldest costs with recent revenues

  7. Results in the highest net income in periods of inflation

  8. Results in the highest net income in periods of deflation

  9. Tends to level out the effects of inflation

  10. Is unpredictable as to the effects of inflation

Inventory Cost Under the Perpetual Inventory System

SO5 Calculate inventory cost under the perpetual inventory system using various costing methods.

> **Study Note**
>
> The costs of an automated perpetual system are considerable. They include the costs of automating the system, maintaining the system, and taking a physical inventory.

Under the perpetual inventory system, cost of goods sold is accumulated as sales are made and costs are transferred from the Inventory account to the Cost of Goods Sold account. The cost of the ending inventory is the balance of the Inventory account. To illustrate costing methods under the perpetual inventory system, we use the following data:

Inventory Data—June 30

June	1	Inventory	80 units @ $10.00
	6	Purchase	220 units @ $12.50
	10	Sale	280 units
	25	Purchase	200 units @ $14.00
	30	Inventory	220 units

The specific identification method produces the same inventory cost and cost of goods sold under the perpetual system as under the periodic system because cost of goods sold and ending inventory are based on the cost of the identified items sold and on hand. The detailed records of purchases and sales maintained under the perpetual system facilitate the use of the specific identification method.

The average-cost method uses a different approach under the perpetual and periodic systems, and it produces different results. Under the periodic system, the average cost is computed for all goods available for sale during the period. Under the perpetual system, an average is computed after each purchase or series of purchases, as follows:

Perpetual Inventory System—Average-Cost Method

June	1	Inventory	80 units @ $10.00	$ 800
	6	Purchase	220 units @ $12.50	2,750
	6	Balance	300 units @ $11.83*	$3,550
				(new average computed)
	10	Sale	280 units @ $11.83*	(3,313)
	10	Balance	20 units @ $11.83*	$ 237
	25	Purchase	200 units @ $14.00	2,800
	30	Inventory	220 units @ $13.80*	$3,037
				(new average computed)
Cost of goods sold				$3,313

*Rounded.

The costs applied to sales become the cost of goods sold, $3,313. The ending inventory is the balance, $3,037.

When costing inventory with the FIFO and LIFO methods, it is necessary to keep track of the components of inventory at each step of the way because as sales are made, the costs must be assigned in the proper order. The FIFO method is applied as follows:

Perpetual Inventory System—FIFO Method

June	1	Inventory	80 units @ $10.00		$ 800
	6	Purchase	220 units @ $12.50		2,750
	10	Sale	80 units @ $10.00	($ 800)	
			200 units @ $12.50	(2,500)	(3,300)
	10	Balance	20 units @ $12.50		$ 250
	25	Purchase	200 units @ $14.00		2,800
	30	Inventory	20 units @ $12.50	$ 250	
			200 units @ $14.00	2,800	$3,050
Cost of goods sold					$3,300

Note that the ending inventory of $3,050 and the cost of goods sold of $3,300 are the same as the figures computed earlier under the periodic inventory system. This will always occur because the ending inventory under both systems consists of the last items purchased—in this case, the entire purchase of June 25 and 20 units from the purchase of June 6.

The LIFO method is applied as follows:

Perpetual Inventory System—LIFO Method

June	1	Inventory	80 units @ $10.00		$ 800
	6	Purchase	220 units @ $12.50		2,750
	10	Sale	220 units @ $12.50	($2,750)	
			60 units @ $10.00	(600)	(3,350)
	10	Balance	20 units @ $10.00		$ 200
	25	Purchase	200 units @ $14.00		2,800
	30	Inventory	20 units @ $10.00	$ 200	
			200 units @ $14.00	2,800	$3,000
Cost of goods sold					$3,350

Notice that the ending inventory of $3,000 includes 20 units from the beginning inventory and 200 units from the June 25 purchase.

Figure 7 compares the average-cost, FIFO, and LIFO methods under the perpetual inventory system. The rank of the results is the same as under the periodic inventory system, but some amounts have changed. For example, LIFO has the lowest balance sheet inventory valuation regardless of the inven-

FOCUS ON BUSINESS PRACTICE

More Companies Enjoy LIFO!

The availability of better technology may partially account for the increasing use of LIFO in the United States. Using the LIFO method under the perpetual inventory system has always been a tedious process, especially if done manually. The development of faster and less expensive computer systems has made it easier for companies that use the perpetual inventory system to switch to LIFO and enjoy that method's economic benefits.

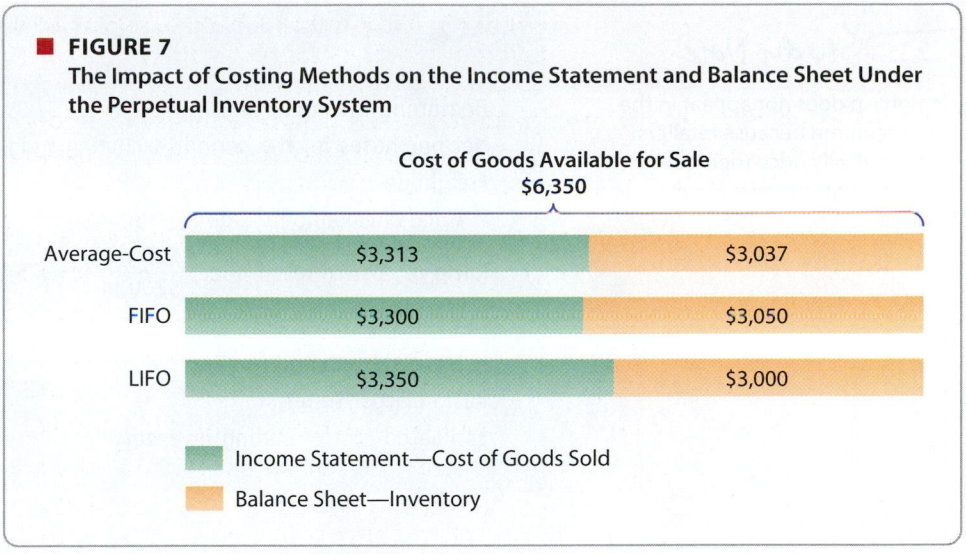

■ FIGURE 7
The Impact of Costing Methods on the Income Statement and Balance Sheet Under the Perpetual Inventory System

tory system used, but the amount is $3,000 using the perpetual system versus $2,550 using the periodic system.

STOP • REVIEW • APPLY

5-1. Why would it be more expensive to maintain a perpetual inventory system than a periodic inventory system?

5-2. Under the perpetual inventory system, why should a physical inventory be taken periodically?

Valuing Inventory by Estimation

> **SO6** Use the retail method and gross profit method to estimate the cost of ending inventory.

t is sometimes necessary or desirable to estimate the value of ending inventory. The retail method and gross profit method are most commonly used for this purpose.

Retail Method

The **retail method** estimates the cost of ending inventory by using the ratio of cost to retail price. Retail merchandising businesses use this method for two main reasons:

1. To prepare financial statements for each accounting period, one must know the cost of inventory; the retail method can be used to estimate the cost without taking the time or going to the expense of determining the cost of each item in the inventory.

2. Because items in a retail store normally have a price tag or a universal product code, it is common practice to take the physical inventory at retail

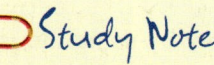
TABLE 2.   Retail Method of Inventory Estimation

	Cost	Retail
Beginning inventory	$ 40,000	$ 55,000
Net purchases for the period (excluding freight-in)	107,000	145,000
Freight-in	3,000	
Goods available for sale	$150,000	$200,000
Ratio of cost to retail price: $\dfrac{\$150,000}{\$200,000} = 75\%$		
Net sales during the period		160,000
Estimated ending inventory at retail		$ 40,000
Ratio of cost to retail	75%	
Estimated cost of ending inventory	$ 30,000	

from these price tags or codes and to reduce the total value to cost by using the retail method. The term *at retail* means the amount of the inventory at the marked selling prices of the inventory items.

When the retail method is used to estimate ending inventory, the records must show the beginning inventory at cost and at retail. They must also show the amount of goods purchased during the period at cost and at retail. The net sales at retail is the balance of the Sales account less returns and allowances. A simple example of the retail method is shown in Table 2.

Goods available for sale is determined at cost and at retail by listing beginning inventory and net purchases for the period at cost and at their expected selling price, adding freight-in to the cost column, and totaling. The ratio of these two amounts (cost to retail price) provides an estimate of the cost of each dollar of retail sales value. The estimated ending inventory at retail is then determined by deducting sales for the period from the retail price of the goods that were available for sale during the period. The inventory at retail is then converted to cost on the basis of the ratio of cost to retail.

The cost of ending inventory can also be estimated by applying the ratio of cost to retail price to the total retail value of the physical count of the ending inventory. Applying the retail method in practice is often more difficult than this simple example because of such complications as changes in retail price during the period, different markups on different types of merchandise, and varying volumes of sales for different types of merchandise.

Gross Profit Method

The **gross profit method** (also known as the *gross margin method*) assumes that the ratio of gross margin for a business remains relatively stable from year to year. The gross profit method is used in place of the retail method when records of the retail prices of beginning inventory and purchases are not available. It is a useful way of estimating the amount of inventory lost or destroyed by theft, fire, or other hazards; insurance companies often use it to verify loss claims. The gross profit method is acceptable for estimating the cost of inventory for interim reports, but it is not acceptable for valuing inventory in the annual financial statements.

As Table 3 shows, the gross profit method is simple to use. First, figure the cost of goods available for sale in the usual way (add purchases to beginning

TABLE 3.   Gross Profit Method of Inventory Estimation

1. Beginning inventory at cost		$ 50,000
Purchases at cost (including freight-in)		290,000
Cost of goods available for sale		$340,000
2. Less estimated cost of goods sold		
Sales at selling price	$400,000	
Less estimated gross margin		
(400,000 × 30%)	120,000	
Estimated cost of goods sold		280,000
3. Estimated cost of ending inventory		$ 60,000

inventory). Second, estimate the cost of goods sold by deducting the estimated gross margin of 30 percent from sales. Finally, deduct the estimated cost of goods sold from the goods available for sale to arrive at the estimated cost of ending inventory.

S T O P • R E V I E W • A P P L Y

6-1. Does using the retail method mean that inventories are measured at retail value on the balance sheet? Explain your answer.

6-2. For what reasons might managers use the gross profit method of estimating inventory?

A LOOK BACK AT

CISCO SYSTEMS, INC.

In this chapter's Decision Point, we posed the following questions:

- **What is the impact of inventory decisions on operating results?**
- **How should inventory be valued?**
- **How should the level of inventory be evaluated?**

As we pointed out in the chapter, Cisco uses supply-chain management and a just-in-time operating environment to manage its inventory. By doing so, it reduces its operating costs. We also pointed out that in 2001, a time when the market for Cisco's products had soured, a note in Cisco's annual report disclosed that the company used the first-in, first-out costing method and applied the lower-of-cost-or-market rule to its inventories. Cisco's approach to valuation adheres to the conservatism convention because it recognizes losses in value before the products are sold. As a result, Cisco recognized a loss of more than $1.5 billion. Such losses are common in the rapidly changing Internet environment in which Cisco operates.

Using data from Cisco's Financial Highlights, we can evaluate the company's success in managing its inventories by comparing its inventory turnover ratio and days' inventory on hand in 2004 and 2003 (dollar amounts are in millions):

		2004	2003
$\dfrac{\text{Cost of Goods Sold}}{\text{Average Inventory}}$		$\dfrac{\$5,766}{(\$1,207 + \$873) \div 2}$	$\dfrac{\$4,594}{(\$873 + \$856) \div 2}$
		$\dfrac{\$5,766}{\$1,040}$	$\dfrac{\$4,594}{\$864.5}$
K/R	Inventory Turnover:	5.5 times	5.3 times
	$\dfrac{\text{Number of Days in a Year}}{\text{Inventory Turnover}}$	$\dfrac{365 \text{ days}}{5.5 \text{ times}}$	$\dfrac{365 \text{ days}}{5.3 \text{ times}}$
K/R	Days' Inventory on Hand:	66.4 days	68.9 days

Thus, in 2004, Cisco achieved a small improvement in its inventory turnover, as well as a reduction in the number of days it had inventory on hand.

CHAPTER REVIEW

REVIEW of Learning Objectives

LO1 Explain the management decisions related to inventory accounting, evaluation of inventory level, and the effects of inventory misstatements on income measurement.

The objective of inventory accounting is the proper determination of income through the matching of costs and revenues. In accounting for inventories, management must choose the type of processing system, costing method, and valuation method the company will use. Because the value of inventory affects a company's net income, management's choices will affect not only external and internal evaluations of the company, but also the amount of income taxes the company pays and its cash flows.

The level of inventory a company maintains has important economic consequences. To evaluate inventory levels, managers commonly use inventory turnover and its related measure, days' inventory on hand. Supply-chain management and a just-in-time operating environment are a means of increasing inventory turnover and reducing inventory carrying costs.

If the value of ending inventory is understated or overstated, a corresponding error—dollar for dollar—will be made in income before income taxes. Furthermore, because the ending inventory of one period is the beginning inventory of the next, the misstatement affects two accounting periods, although the effects are opposite.

LO2 Define *inventory cost,* contrast goods flow and cost flow, and explain the lower-of-cost-or-market (LCM) rule.

Inventory cost includes the invoice price less purchases discounts; freight-in, including insurance in transit; and applicable taxes and tariffs. Goods flow refers to the actual physical flow of merchandise in a business, whereas cost flow refers to the assumed flow of costs. The lower-of-cost-or-market rule states that if the replacement cost (market cost) of the inventory is lower than the original cost, the lower figure should be used.

LO3 Calculate inventory cost under the periodic inventory system using various costing methods.

The value assigned to ending inventory is the result of two measurements: quantity and cost. Quantity is determined by taking a physical inventory. Cost is determined by using one of four inventory methods, each based on a different assumption of cost flow. Under the periodic inventory system, the specific identification method identifies the actual cost of each item in inventory. The average-cost method assumes that the cost of inventory is the average cost of goods available for sale during the period. The first-in, first-out (FIFO) method assumes that the costs of the first items acquired should be assigned to the first items sold. The last-in, first-out (LIFO) method assumes that the costs of the last items acquired should be assigned to the first items sold. The inventory method used may or may not correspond to the actual physical flow of goods.

LO4 Explain the effects of inventory costing methods on income determination and income taxes.

During periods of rising prices, the LIFO method will show the lowest net income; FIFO, the highest; and average-cost, in between. LIFO and FIFO have the opposite effects in periods of falling prices. No generalization can be made regarding the specific identification method. The Internal Revenue Service requires that if LIFO is used for tax purposes, it must be used for financial statements; it also does not allow the lower-of-cost-or-market rule to be applied to the LIFO method.

Supplemental Objectives

SO5 Calculate inventory cost under the perpetual inventory system using various costing methods.

Under the perpetual inventory system, cost of goods sold is accumulated as sales are made and costs are transferred from the Inventory account to the Cost of Goods Sold account. The cost of the ending inventory is the balance of the Inventory account. The specific identification method and the FIFO method produce the same results under both the perpetual and periodic inventory systems. The results differ for the average-cost method because an average is calculated after each sale rather than at the end of the accounting period. Results also differ for the LIFO method because the cost components of inventory change constantly as goods are bought and sold.

SO6 Use the retail method and gross profit method to estimate the cost of ending inventory.

Two methods of estimating the value of inventory are the retail method and the gross profit method. Under the retail method, inventory is determined at retail prices and is then reduced to estimated cost by applying a ratio of cost to retail price. Under the gross profit method, cost of goods sold is estimated by reducing sales by estimated gross margin. The estimated cost of goods sold is then deducted from the cost of goods available for sale to estimate the cost of ending inventory.

REVIEW of Concepts and Terminology

The following concepts and terms were introduced in this chapter:

Average-cost method: An inventory costing method in which inventory is priced at the average cost of the goods available for sale during the period. **(LO3)**

Consignment: Merchandise that its owner (the con-signor) places on the premises of another company (the consignee) with the understanding that payment is expected only when the merchandise is sold and that unsold items may be returned to the consignor. **(LO2)**

Cost flow: The association of costs with their assumed flow in the operations of a company. **(LO2)**

First-in, first-out (FIFO) method: An inventory costing method based on the assumption that the costs of the first items acquired should be assigned to the first items sold. **(LO3)**

Goods flow: The actual physical movement of goods in the operations of a company. **(LO2)**

Gross profit method: A method of inventory estimation based on the assumption that the ratio of gross margin for a business remains relatively stable from year to year. Also called *gross margin method*. **(SO6)**

Inventory cost: The invoice price of an asset less purchases discounts, plus freight in, plus applicable taxes and tariffs. **(LO2)**

Just-in-time operating environment: A method of reducing levels of inventory by working closely with suppliers to coordinate and schedule deliveries so that goods arrive just at the time they are needed. **(LO1)**

Last-in, first-out (LIFO) method: An inventory costing method based on the assumption that the costs of

the last items purchased should be assigned to the first items sold. **(LO3)**

LIFO liquidation: The reduction of inventory below previous levels because sales of older, lower-priced units have exceeded the purchases of units for the current period. **(LO4)**

Lower-of-cost-or-market (LCM) rule: A method of valuing inventory at an amount less than cost when the replacement cost falls below historical cost. **(LO2)**

Market: Current replacement cost of inventory. **(LO2)**

Retail method: A method of inventory estimation, used in retail merchandising businesses, in which inventory at retail value is reduced by the ratio of cost to retail price. **(SO6)**

Specific identification method: An inventory costing method in which the cost of each item in ending inventory is identified as coming from a specific purchase. **(LO3)**

Supply-chain management: A system of managing inventory and purchasing through business-to-business transactions conducted over the Internet. **(LO1)**

Key Ratios

Days' inventory on hand: The average number of days required to sell the inventory on hand; Number of Days in a Year ÷ Inventory Turnover. **(LO1)**

Inventory turnover: A ratio indicating the number of times a company's average inventory is sold during an accounting period; Cost of Goods Sold ÷ Average Inventory. **(LO1)**

REVIEW Problem

Periodic and Perpetual Inventory Systems

The following table summarizes the beginning inventory, purchases, and sales of Psi Company's single product during January:

	A	B	C	D	E	F	G	H
1					**Beginning Inventory and Purchases**			
2	Date				Units	Cost	Total	Sales Units
3	Jan.	1		Inventory	1,400	$20	$28,000	
4		8		Purchase	600	22	13,200	
5		10		Sale				1,600
6		24		Purchase	800	24	19,200	
7								
8	Totals				2,800		$60,400	1,600

Required

1. Assuming that the company uses the periodic inventory system, compute the cost that should be assigned to ending inventory and to cost of goods sold using (a) the average-cost method, (b) the FIFO method, and (c) the LIFO method.
2. Assuming that the company uses the perpetual inventory system, compute the cost that should be assigned to ending inventory and to cost of goods sold using (a) the average-cost method, (b) the FIFO method, and (c) the LIFO method.
3. Compute inventory turnover and days' inventory on hand under each of the inventory cost flow assumptions in 1. What conclusion can you draw from this comparison?

Answer to Review Problem

	Units	Amount
Beginning inventory	1,400	$28,000
Purchases	1,400	32,400
Available for sale	2,800	$60,400
Sales	1,600	
Ending inventory	1,200	

1. Periodic inventory system:

   a. Average-cost method

Cost of goods available for sale		$60,400
Less ending inventory consisting of		
1,200 units at $21.57*		25,884
Cost of goods sold		$34,516

   *$60,400 ÷ 2,800 units = $21.57 (rounded).

   b. FIFO method

Cost of goods available for sale		$60,400
Less ending inventory consisting of		
Jan. 24 purchase (800 × $24)	$19,200	
Jan. 8 purchase (400 × $22)	8,800	28,000
Cost of goods sold		$32,400

c. LIFO method

Cost of goods available for sale	$60,400
Less ending inventory consisting of	
beginning inventory (1,200 × $20)	24,000
Cost of goods sold	$36,400

2. Perpetual inventory system:

a. Average-cost method

Date			Units	Cost	Amount
Jan.	1	Inventory	1,400	$20.00	$28,000
	8	Purchase	600	22.00	13,200
	8	Balance	2,000	20.60	$41,200
	10	Sale	(1,600)	20.60	(32,960)
	10	Balance	400	20.60	$ 8,240
	24	Purchase	800	24.00	19,200
	31	Inventory	1,200	22.87*	$27,440
Cost of goods sold					$32,960

*Rounded.

b. FIFO method

Date			Units	Cost	Amount
Jan.	1	Inventory	1,400	$20	$28,000
	8	Purchase	600	22	13,200
	8	Balance	1,400	20	
			600	22	$41,200
	10	Sale	(1,400)	20	
			(200)	22	(32,400)
	10	Balance	400	22	$ 8,800
	24	Purchase	800	24	19,200
	31	Inventory	400	22	
			800	24	$28,000
Cost of goods sold					$32,400

c. LIFO method

Date			Units	Cost	Amount
Jan.	1	Inventory	1,400	$20	$28,000
	8	Purchase	600	22	13,200
	8	Balance	1,400	20	
			600	22	$41,200
	10	Sale	(600)	22	
			(1,000)	20	(33,200)
	10	Balance	400	20	$ 8,000
	24	Purchase	800	24	19,200
	31	Inventory	400	20	
			800	24	$27,200
Cost of goods sold					$33,200

3. Ratios computed:

	Average-Cost	**FIFO**	**LIFO**
Cost of Goods Sold	$34,516	$32,400	$36,400
Average Inventory	$26,942	$28,000	$26,000
	($25,884 + $28,000) ÷ 2	($28,000 + $28,000) ÷ 2	($24,000 + $28,000) ÷ 2
Inventory Turnover:	1.3 times	1.2 times	1.4 times
Days' Inventory on Hand:	(365 days ÷ 1.3 times)	(365 days ÷ 1.2 times)	(365 days ÷ 1.4 times)
	280.8 days	304.2 days	260.7 days

In periods of rising prices, the LIFO method will always result in a higher inventory turnover and lower days' inventory on hand than the other costing methods. When comparing inventory ratios for two or more companies, their inventory methods should be considered.

CHAPTER ASSIGNMENTS

BUILDING Your Basic Knowledge and Skills

Short Exercises

LO1 **Management Issues**

SE 1. Indicate whether each of the following items is associated with (a) allocating the cost of inventories in accordance with the matching rule, (b) assessing the impact of inventory decisions, (c) evaluating the level of inventory, or (d) engaging in an unethical practice.

1. Calculating days' inventory on hand
2. Ordering a supply of inventory to satisfy customer needs
3. Valuing inventory at an amount to achieve a specific profit objective
4. Calculating the income tax effect of an inventory method
5. Deciding the cost to place on ending inventory

LO1 **Inventory Turnover and Days' Inventory on Hand**

SE 2. During 20x6, Chauncey Clothiers had beginning inventory of $480,000, ending inventory of $560,000, and cost of goods sold of $2,200,000. Compute the inventory turnover and days' inventory on hand.

LO3 **Specific Identification Method**

SE 3. Assume the following data with regard to inventory for Caciato Company:

Aug. 1	Inventory	40 units @ $10 per unit	$ 400
8	Purchase	50 units @ $11 per unit	550
22	Purchase	35 units @ $12 per unit	420
Goods available for sale		125 units	$1,370
Aug. 15	Sale	45 units	
28	Sale	25 units	
Inventory, Aug. 31		55 units	

Assuming that the inventory consists of 30 units from the August 8 purchase and 25 units from the purchase of August 22, calculate the cost of ending inventory and cost of goods sold.

LO3 **Average-Cost Method: Periodic Inventory System**

SE 4. Using the data in **SE 3**, calculate the cost of ending inventory and cost of goods sold according to the average-cost method under the periodic inventory system.

LO3 **FIFO Method: Periodic Inventory System**

SE 5. Using the data in **SE 3**, calculate the cost of ending inventory and cost of goods sold according to the FIFO method under the periodic inventory system.

LO3 **LIFO Method: Periodic Inventory System**

SE 6. Using the data in **SE 3**, calculate the cost of ending inventory and cost of goods sold according to the LIFO method under the periodic inventory system.

LO4 **Effects of Inventory Costing Methods and Changing Prices**

SE 7. Using Table 1 as an example, prepare a table with four columns that shows the ending inventory and cost of goods sold for each of the results from your calculations in **SE 3** through **SE 6**, including the effects of the different prices at which the merchandise was purchased. Which method(s) would result in the lowest income taxes?

SO5 **Average-Cost Method: Perpetual Inventory System**

SE 8. Using the data in **SE 3**, calculate the cost of ending inventory and cost of goods sold according to the average-cost method under the perpetual inventory system.

SO5 **FIFO Method: Perpetual Inventory System**

SE 9. Using the data in **SE 3**, calculate the cost of ending inventory and cost of goods sold according to the FIFO method under the perpetual inventory system.

SO5 **LIFO Method: Perpetual Inventory System**

SE 10. Using the data in **SE 3**, calculate the cost of ending inventory and cost of goods sold according to the LIFO method under the perpetual inventory system.

Exercises

LO1, LO2 **Discussion Questions**

E 1. Develop a brief answer to each of the following questions:

1. Is it good or bad for a retail store to have a large inventory?
2. Which is more important from the standpoint of inventory costing: the flow of goods or the flow of costs?
3. Why is misstatement of inventory one of the most common means of financial statement fraud?
4. Given that the LCM rule is an application of the conservatism convention in the current accounting period, is the effect of this application also conservative in the next period?

LO4, SO5, SO6   **Discussion Questions**

E 2. Develop a brief answer to each of the following questions:

1. Under what condition would all four methods of inventory pricing produce exactly the same results?
2. Under the perpetual inventory system, why is the cost of goods sold not determined by deducting the ending inventory from goods available for sale, as it is under the periodic method?
3. Which of the following methods do not require a physical inventory: periodic inventory system, perpetual inventory method, retail method, or gross profit method?

LO1   **Management Issues**

E 3. Indicate whether each of the following items is associated with (a) allocating the cost of inventories in accordance with the matching rule, (b) assessing the impact of inventory decisions, (c) evaluating the level of inventory, or (d) engaging in an unethical action.

1. Computing inventory turnover
2. Valuing inventory at an amount to meet management's targeted net income
3. Application of the just-in-time operating environment
4. Determining the effects of inventory decisions on cash flows
5. Apportioning the cost of goods available for sale to ending inventory and cost of goods sold
6. Determining the effects of inventory methods on income taxes
7. Determining the assumption about the flow of costs into and out of the company

LO1   **Inventory Ratios**

E 4. Just a Buck Discount Stores is assessing its levels of inventory for 20x6 and 20x7 and has gathered the following data:

	20x7	20x6	20x5
Ending inventory	$ 96,000	$ 81,000	$69,000
Cost of goods sold	480,000	450,000	

Compute the inventory turnover and days' inventory on hand for 20x6 and 20x7 and comment on the results.

LO1   **Effects of Inventory Errors**

E 5. Condensed income statements for Cozumel Company for two years are shown below.

	20x7	20x6
Sales	$252,000	$210,000
Cost of goods sold	150,000	108,000
Gross margin	$102,000	$102,000
Operating expenses	60,000	60,000
Income before income taxes	$ 42,000	$ 42,000

After the end of 20x7, the company discovered that an error had resulted in an $18,000 understatement of the 20x6 ending inventory.

Compute the corrected income before income taxes for 20x6 and 20x7. What effect will the error have on income before income taxes and stockholders' equity for 20x8?

LO1, LO2, LO3 Accounting Conventions and Inventory Valuation

E 6. Turnbow Company, a telecommunications equipment company, has used the LIFO method adjusted for lower of cost or market for a number of years. Due to falling prices of its equipment, it has had to adjust (reduce) the cost of inventory to market each year for two years. The company is considering changing its method to FIFO adjusted for lower of cost or market in the future. Explain how the accounting conventions of consistency, full disclosure, and conservatism apply to this decision. If the change were made, why would management expect fewer adjustments to market in the future?

LO3 Periodic Inventory System and Inventory Costing Methods

E 7. Martha's Grain Shop recorded the following purchases and sales of fertilizer during the past year:

Jan. 1	Beginning inventory	125 cases @ $23	$ 2,875
Feb. 25	Purchase	100 cases @ $26	2,600
June 15	Purchase	200 cases @ $28	5,600
Oct. 15	Purchase	150 cases @ $28	4,200
Dec. 15	Purchase	100 cases @ $30	3,000
Goods available for sale		675	$18,275
Total sales		500 cases	
Dec. 31	Ending inventory	175 cases	

Assume that Martha's Grain Shop sold all of the June 15 purchase and 100 cases each from the January 1 beginning inventory, the October 15 purchase, and the December 15 purchase.

Determine the costs that should be assigned to ending inventory and cost of goods sold under each of the following assumptions: (1) costs are assigned by the specific identification method; (2) costs are assigned by the average-cost method; (3) costs are assigned by the FIFO method; (4) costs are assigned by the LIFO method. What conclusions can be drawn about the effect of each method on the income statement and the balance sheet of Martha's Grain Shop? Round your answers to the nearest whole number and assume the periodic inventory system.

LO3 Periodic Inventory System and Inventory Costing Methods

E 8. During its first year of operation, Krabna Company purchased 5,600 units of a product at $42 per unit. During the second year, it purchased 6,000 units of the same product at $48 per unit. During the third year, it purchased 5,000 units at $60 per unit. Krabna Company managed to have an ending inventory each year of 1,000 units. The company uses the periodic inventory system.

Prepare cost of goods sold statements that compare the value of ending inventory and the cost of goods sold for each of the three years using (1) the FIFO inventory costing method and (2) the LIFO method. From the resulting data, what conclusions can you draw about the relationships between the changes in unit price and the changes in the value of ending inventory?

LO3 Periodic Inventory System and Inventory Costing Methods

E 9. In chronological order, the inventory, purchases, and sales of a single product for a recent month are as follows:

			Units	Amount per Unit
June	1	Beginning inventory	150	$30
	4	Purchase	400	33
	12	Purchase	800	36
	16	Sales	1,300	60
	24	Purchase	300	39

Using the periodic inventory system, compute the cost of ending inventory, cost of goods sold, and gross margin. Use the average-cost, FIFO, and LIFO inventory costing methods. Explain the differences in gross margin produced by the three methods. Round unit costs to cents and totals to dollars.

LO4 ## Effects of Inventory Costing Methods on Cash Flows

E 10. Hart Products, Inc., sold 120,000 cases of glue at $20 per case during 20x7. Its beginning inventory consisted of 20,000 cases at a cost of $12 per case. During 20x7, it purchased 60,000 cases at $14 per case and later 50,000 cases at $15 per case. Operating expenses were $550,000, and the applicable income tax rate was 30 percent.

Using the periodic inventory system, compute net income using the FIFO method and the LIFO method for costing inventory. Which alternative produces the larger cash flow? The company is considering a purchase of 10,000 cases at $15 per case just before the year end. What effect on net income and on cash flow will this proposed purchase have under each method? (**Hint:** What are the income tax consequences?)

SO5 ## Perpetual Inventory System and Inventory Costing Methods

E 11. Referring to the data provided in **E 9** and using the perpetual inventory system, compute the cost of ending inventory, cost of goods sold, and gross margin. Use the average-cost, FIFO, and LIFO inventory costing methods. Explain the reasons for the differences in gross margin produced by the three methods. Round unit costs to cents and totals to dollars.

LO3, SO5 ## Periodic and Perpetual Systems and Inventory Costing Methods

E 12. During July 20x7, Fan-Qi, Inc., sold 500 units of its product Ultima for $8,000. The following units were available:

	Units	Cost
Beginning inventory	200	$ 2
Purchase 1	80	4
Purchase 2	120	6
Purchase 3	300	9
Purchase 4	180	12

A sale of 500 units was made after purchase 3. Of the units sold, 200 came from beginning inventory and 300 came from purchase 3.

Determine cost of goods available for sale and ending inventory in units. Then determine the costs that should be assigned to cost of goods sold and ending inventory under each of the following assumptions: (1) Costs are assigned under the periodic inventory system using (a) the specific identification method, (b) the average-cost method, (c) the FIFO method, and (d) the LIFO method. (2) Costs are assigned under the perpetual inventory system using (a) the average-cost method, (b) the FIFO method, and (c) the LIFO method. For each alternative, show the gross margin. Round unit costs to cents and totals to dollars.

SO6 Retail Method

E 13. Corabia Dress Shop had net retail sales of $250,000 during the current year. The following additional information was obtained from the company's accounting records:

	At Cost	At Retail
Beginning inventory	$ 40,000	$ 60,000
Net purchases (excluding freight-in)	140,000	220,000
Freight-in	10,400	

1. Using the retail method, estimate the company's ending inventory at cost.
2. Assume that a physical inventory taken at year end revealed an inventory on hand of $18,000 at retail value. What is the estimated amount of inventory shrinkage (loss due to theft, damage, etc.) at cost using the retail method?

SO6 Gross Profit Method

E 14. Chen Mo-Wan was at home when he received a call from the fire department telling him his store had burned. His business was a total loss. The insurance company asked him to prove his inventory loss. For the year, until the date of the fire, Chen's company had sales of $900,000 and purchases of $560,000. Freight-in amounted to $27,400, and beginning inventory was $90,000. Chen always priced his goods to achieve a gross margin of 40 percent. Compute Chen's estimated inventory loss.

Problems

LO1, LO3 Periodic Inventory System and Inventory Costing Methods

P 1. The Midori Cabinet Company sold 2,200 cabinets during 20x7 at $160 per cabinet. Its beginning inventory on January 1 was 130 cabinets at $56. Purchases made during the year were as follows:

February	225 cabinets @ $62
April	350 cabinets @ $65
June	700 cabinets @ $70
August	300 cabinets @ $66
October	400 cabinets @ $68
November	250 cabinets @ $72

The company's selling and administrative expenses for the year were $101,000. The company uses the periodic inventory system.

Required

1. Prepare a schedule to compute the cost of goods available for sale.
2. Compute income before income taxes under each of the following inventory cost flow assumptions: (a) the average-cost method, (b) the FIFO method, and (c) the LIFO method.
3. **User Insight:** Compute inventory turnover and days' inventory on hand under each of the inventory cost flow assumptions in requirement **2**. What conclusion can you draw from this comparison?

LO1, LO3 Periodic Inventory System and Inventory Costing Methods

P 2. The inventory, purchases, and sales of Product ISO for March and April are listed below. The company closes its books at the end of each month. It uses the periodic inventory system.

Mar.	1	Beginning inventory	60 units @ $49
	10	Purchase	100 units @ $52

Mar.	19	Sale	90 units
	31	Ending inventory	70 units
Apr.	4	Purchase	120 units @ $53
	15	Purchase	50 units @ $54
	23	Sale	200 units
	25	Purchase	100 units @ $55
	30	Ending inventory	140 units

Required

1. Compute the cost of the ending inventory on March 31 and April 30 using the average-cost method. In addition, determine cost of goods sold for March and April. Round unit costs to cents and totals to dollars.
2. Compute the cost of the ending inventory on March 31 and April 30 using the FIFO method. Also determine cost of goods sold for March and April.
3. Compute the cost of the ending inventory on March 31 and April 30 using the LIFO method. Also determine cost of goods sold for March and April.
4. **User Insight:** Do the cash flows from operations for March and April differ depending on which inventory costing method is used—average-cost, FIFO, or LIFO? Explain.

LO4, SO5 | **Perpetual Inventory System and Inventory Costing Methods**

 P 3. Use the data provided in **P 2**, but assume that the company uses the perpetual inventory system. (**Hint:** In preparing the solutions required below, it is helpful to determine the balance of inventory after each transaction, as shown in the Review Problem in this chapter.)

Required

1. Determine the cost of ending inventory and cost of goods sold for March and April using the average-cost method. Round unit costs to cents and totals to dollars.
2. Determine the cost of ending inventory and cost of goods sold for March and April using the FIFO method.
3. Determine the cost of ending inventory and cost of goods sold for March and April using the LIFO method.
4. **User Insight:** Assume that this company grows for many years in a long period of rising prices. How realistic do you think the balance sheet value for inventory would be and what effect would it have on the inventory turnover ratio?

SO6 | **Retail Method**

P 4. Fuentes Company operates a large discount store and uses the retail method to estimate the cost of ending inventory. Management suspects that in recent weeks there have been unusually heavy losses from shoplifting or employee pilferage. To estimate the amount of the loss, the company has taken a physical inventory and will compare the results with the estimated cost of inventory. Data from the accounting records of Fuentes Company are as follows:

	At Cost	At Retail
October 1 beginning inventory	$51,488	$ 74,300
Purchases	71,733	108,500
Purchases returns and allowances	(2,043)	(3,200)
Freight-in	950	
Sales		109,183
Sales returns and allowances		(933)
October 31 physical inventory at retail		62,450

Required

1. Using the retail method, prepare a schedule to estimate the dollar amount of the store's month-end inventory at cost.
2. Use the store's cost to retail ratio to reduce the retail value of the physical inventory to cost.
3. Calculate the estimated amount of inventory shortage at cost and at retail.
4. **User Insight:** Many retail chains use the retail method because it is efficient. Why do you think using this method is an efficient way for these companies to operate?

SO6 **Gross Profit Method**

P 5. Oakley Sisters is a large retail furniture company that operates in two adjacent warehouses. One warehouse is a showroom, and the other is used to store merchandise. On the night of April 22, 20x6, a fire broke out in the storage warehouse and destroyed the merchandise stored there. Fortunately, the fire did not reach the showroom, so all the merchandise on display was saved.

Although the company maintained a perpetual inventory system, its records were rather haphazard, and the last reliable physical inventory had been taken on December 31. In addition, there was no control of the flow of goods between the showroom and the warehouse. Thus, it was impossible to tell what goods should have been in either place. As a result, the insurance company required an independent estimate of the amount of loss. The insurance company examiners were satisfied when they received the following information:

Merchandise inventory on December 31, 20x5	$ 727,400
Purchases, January 1 to April 22, 20x6	1,206,100
Purchases returns, January 1 to April 22, 20x6	(5,353)
Freight-in, January 1 to April 22, 20x6	26,550
Sales, January 1 to April 22, 20x6	1,979,525
Sales returns, January 1 to April 22, 20x6	(14,900)
Merchandise inventory in showroom on April 22, 20x6	201,480
Average gross margin	44%

Required

1. Prepare a schedule that estimates the amount of the inventory lost in the fire.
2. **User Insight:** What are some other reasons management might need to estimate the amount of inventory?

Alternate Problems

LO1, LO3 **Periodic Inventory System and Inventory Costing Methods**

P 6. MacRae Company merchandises a single product called Sooto. The following data represent beginning inventory and purchases of Sooto during the past year: January 1 inventory, 68,000 units at $11.00; February purchases, 80,000 units at $12.00; March purchases, 160,000 units at $12.40; May purchases, 120,000 units at $12.60; July purchases, 200,000 units at $12.80; September purchases, 160,000 units at $12.60; and November purchases, 60,000 units at $13.00. Sales of Sooto totaled 786,000 units at $20.00 per unit. Selling and administrative expenses totaled $5,102,000 for the year. MacRae Company uses the periodic inventory system.

Required

1. Prepare a schedule to compute the cost of goods available for sale.
2. Compute income before income taxes under each of the following inventory cost flow assumptions: (a) the average-cost method; (b) the FIFO method; and (c) the LIFO method.
3. **User Insight:** Compute inventory turnover and days' inventory on hand under each of the inventory cost flow assumptions listed in requirement **2**. What conclusion can you draw?

LO1, LO3 **Periodic Inventory System and Inventory Costing Methods**

P 7. The inventory of Product B and data on purchases and sales for a two-month period follow. The company closes its books at the end of each month. It uses the periodic inventory system.

Apr.	1	Beginning inventory	50 units @ $102
	10	Purchase	100 units @ $110
	17	Sale	90 units
	30	Ending inventory	60 units
May	2	Purchase	100 units @ $108
	14	Purchase	50 units @ $112
	22	Purchase	60 units @ $117
	30	Sale	200 units
	31	Ending inventory	70 units

Required

1. Compute the cost of ending inventory of Product B on April 30 and May 31 using the average-cost method. In addition, determine cost of goods sold for April and May. Round unit costs to cents and totals to dollars.
2. Compute the cost of the ending inventory on April 30 and May 31 using the FIFO method. In addition, determine cost of goods sold for April and May.
3. Compute the cost of the ending inventory on April 30 and May 31 using the LIFO method. In addition, determine cost of goods sold for April and May.
4. **User Insight:** Do the cash flows from operations for April and May differ depending on which inventory costing method is used—average-cost, FIFO, or LIFO? Explain.

LO4, SO5 **Perpetual Inventory System and Inventory Costing Methods**

P 8. Use the data provided in **P 7**, but assume that the company uses the perpetual inventory system. (**Hint:** In preparing the solutions required below, it is helpful to determine the balance of inventory after each transaction, as shown in the Review Problem in this chapter.)

Required

1. Determine the cost of ending inventory and cost of goods sold for April and May using the average-cost method. Round unit costs to cents and totals to dollars.
2. Determine the cost of ending inventory and cost of goods sold for April and May using the FIFO method.
3. Determine the cost of ending inventory and cost of goods sold for April and May using the LIFO method.
4. **User Insight:** Do the cash flows from operations for April and May differ depending on which inventory costing method is used—average-cost, FIFO, or LIFO? Explain.

≡ ENHANCING Your Knowledge, Skills, and Critical Thinking

Conceptual Understanding Cases

LO1 Evaluation of Inventory Levels

C 1. J. C. Penney, a large retail company with many stores, has an inventory turnover of 4.1 times. **Dell Computer Corporation,** an Internet mail-order company, has an inventory turnover of 60.0. Dell achieves its high turnover through supply-chain management in a just-in-time operating environment. Why is inventory turnover important to companies like J. C. Penney and Dell? Why are comparisons among companies important? Are J. C. Penney and Dell a good match for comparison? Describe supply-chain management and a just-in-time operating environment. Why are they important to achieving a favorable inventory turnover?

LO1 Misstatement of Inventory

C 2. Crazy Eddie, Inc., a discount consumer electronics chain, seemed to be missing $52 million in merchandise inventory. "It was a shock," the new management was quoted as saying. It was also one of the nation's largest swindles. Investors lost $145.6 million when the company declared bankruptcy. A count turned up only $75 million in inventory, compared with $126.7 million reported by former management. Net sales could account for only $6.7 million of the difference. At the time, it was not clear whether bookkeeping errors in prior years or an actual physical loss created the shortfall, although at least one store manager felt it was a bookkeeping error because security was strong. "It would be hard for someone to steal anything," he said. Former management was eventually fined $72.7 million.[11]

1. What is the effect of the misstatement of inventory on Crazy Eddie's reported earnings in prior accounting periods?
2. Is this a situation you would expect in a company that is experiencing financial difficulty? Explain.

LO4 LIFO Inventory Method

C 3. Eighty-nine percent of chemical companies use the LIFO inventory method for the costing of inventories, whereas only 8 percent of computer equipment companies use LIFO.[12] Describe the LIFO inventory method. What effects does it have on reported income, cash flows, and income taxes during periods of price changes? Why do you think so many chemical companies use LIFO while most companies in the computer industry do not?

Interpreting Financial Reports

LO2 LCM and Conservatism

C 4. Exxon Mobil Corporation, the world's largest company, uses the LIFO inventory method for most of its inventories. Its inventory costs are heavily dependent on the cost of oil. In a recent year when the price of oil was down, Exxon Mobil, following the lower-of-cost-or-market (LCM) rule, wrote down its inventory by $325 million. In the next year, when the price of oil recovered, the company reported that market price exceeded the LIFO carrying values by $6.8 billion.[13] Explain why the LCM rule resulted in a write-down in the first year. What is the inconsistency between the first- and second-year treatments of the change in the price of oil? How does the accounting convention of conservatism explain the inconsistency? If the price of oil declined substantially in a third year, what would be the likely consequence?

LO1, LO4 **FIFO and LIFO**

C 5. Exxon Mobil Corporation, had net sales of $237,054 million, cost of goods sold of $107,658 million, and net income of $21,510 million in 2003. Inventories under the LIFO method used by the company were $8,136 million in 2004 and $7,665 million in 2003. Inventory would have been considerably higher in both years if the company had used FIFO.[14] Why do you suppose Exxon Mobil's management chooses to use the LIFO inventory method? On what economic conditions, if any, do those reasons depend?

Decision Analysis Using Excel

LO3, LO4 **FIFO versus LIFO Analysis**

C 6. Refrigerated Truck Sales Company (RTS Company) buys large refrigerated trucks from the manufacturer and sells them to companies and independent truckers who haul perishable goods over long distances. RTS has been successful in this specialized niche of the industry. Because of the high cost of the trucks and of financing inventory, RTS tries to maintain as small an inventory as possible. In fact, at the beginning of July the company had no inventory or liabilities, as shown on the balance sheet below.

On July 9, RTS took delivery of a truck at a price of $150,000. On July 19, an identical truck was delivered to the company at a price of $160,000. On July 28, the company sold one of the trucks for $195,000. During July, expenses totaled $15,000. All transactions were paid in cash.

RTS Company
Balance Sheet
July 1, 20x7

Assets		Stockholders' Equity	
Cash	$400,000	Common stock	$400,000
Total assets	$400,000	Total stockholders' equity	$400,000

1. Prepare income statements and balance sheets for RTS on July 31 using (a) the FIFO method of inventory valuation and (b) the LIFO method of inventory valuation. Assume an income tax rate of 40 percent. Explain the effects of each method on the financial statements.
2. Assume that the management of RTS Company has a policy of declaring a cash dividend each period that is exactly equal to net income. What effects does this action have on each balance sheet prepared in requirement 1? How do the resulting balance sheets compare with the balance sheet at the beginning of the month? Which inventory method, if either, do you feel is more realistic in representing RTS's income?
3. Assume that RTS receives notice of another price increase of $10,000 on refrigerated trucks, to take effect on August 1. How does this information relate to management's dividend policy, and how will it affect next month's operations?

Annual Report Case: CVS Corporation

LO1, LO4, SO5, SO6 **Inventory Costing Methods and Ratios**

C 7. Refer to the note related to inventories in **CVS Corporation's** annual report in the Supplement to Chapter 1 to answer the following questions: What inventory method(s) does CVS use? If LIFO inventories had been valued at FIFO, why would there be no difference? Do you think many of the company's inventories are valued at market? Few companies use the retail method, so why do you think CVS uses it? Compute and compare the inventory turnover and days' inventory on hand for CVS for 2004 and 2003. Ending 2002 inventories were $4,018.6 million.

Comparison Case: CVS Versus Walgreens

LO1

Inventory Efficiency

K/R

C 8. Refer to **CVS's** annual report in the Supplement to Chapter 1 and to the following data (in millions) for **Walgreens**: cost of goods sold, $27,310.4 and $23,706.2 for 2004 and 2003, respectively; inventories, $4,738.6, $4,202.7 and $3,645.2 for 2004, 2003, and 2002, respectively. Ending inventories for 2002 for CVS were $4,018.6 million. Calculate inventory turnover and days' inventory on hand for 2004 and 2003. If you did **C 7**, refer to your answer there for CVS. Has either company improved its performance over the past two years? What advantage does the superior company's performance provide to it? Which company appears to make the most efficient use of inventories? Explain your answers.

Ethical Dilemma Case

LO1, LO4

Inventories, Income Determination, and Ethics

C 9. Flare, Inc., which has a December 31 year end, designs and sells fashions for young professional women. Sandra Mason, president of the company, fears that the forecasted 20x7 profitability goals will not be reached. She is pleased when Flare receives a large order on December 30 from The Executive Woman, a retail chain of upscale stores for businesswomen. Mason immediately directs the controller to record the sale, which represents 13 percent of Flare's annual sales. At the same time, she directs the inventory control department not to separate the goods for shipment until after January 1. Separated goods are not included in inventory because they have been sold.

On December 31, the company's auditors arrive to observe the year-end taking of the physical inventory under the periodic inventory system. How will Sandra Mason's actions affect Flare's 20x7 profitability? How will they affect Flare's 20x8 profitability? Were Mason's actions ethical? Why or why not?

Internet Case

LO4, SO5

Effect of LIFO on Income and Cash Flows

C 10. Maytag Corporation, an appliance manufacturer, uses the LIFO inventory method. Go to its website and select "About Maytag." Then select "Financial Center." After finding the income statement and inventory note, calculate what net income would have been had the company used FIFO. Calculate how much cash the company saved for the year and cumulatively by using LIFO. What is the difference between the LIFO and FIFO gross margin and profit margin results? Which reporting alternative is better for the company?

Group Activity Case

LO2, LO4

Retail Business Inventories

C 11. Assign teams to various types of stores in your community—a grocery, clothing, book, music, or appliance store. Make an appointment to interview the manager for 30 minutes to discuss the company's inventory accounting system. The store may be a branch of a larger company. Ask the following questions, summarize your findings in a paper, and be prepared to discuss your results in class:

1. What is the physical flow of merchandise into the store, and what documents are used in connection with this flow?
2. What documents are prepared when merchandise is sold?
3. Does the store keep perpetual inventory records? If so, does it keep the records in units only, or does it keep track of cost as well? If not, what system does the store use?
4. How often does the company take a physical inventory?
5. How are financial statements generated for the store?
6. What method does the company use to cost its inventory for financial statements?

Business Communication Case

LO1, LO2, LO3   Inventory Ratio Analysis

 C 12. Yamaha Corporation and **Pioneer Corporation** are two large, diversified Japanese electronics companies. Both use the average-cost method and the lower-of-cost-or-market rule to account for inventories. The following data are for their 2004 fiscal years (in millions of yen):[15]

	Yamaha	Pioneer
Beginning inventory	¥ 78,492	¥ 93,620
Ending inventory	72,146	107,806
Cost of goods sold	337,813	442,924

Assume you have been asked to analyze the inventory efficiency of the two companies. Prepare a memorandum to your boss that compares the inventory efficiency of Yamaha and Pioneer by computing the inventory turnover and days' inventory on hand for both companies in 2004. Show and comment on the relative efficiency of the two companies. Also comment on how the inventory method would affect your evaluation if you were to compare Yamaha and Pioneer to each other and to a U.S. company given the fact that most companies in the United States use the LIFO inventory method. Mention what could be done to make the results comparable.

Cash and Receivables

Cash and receivables require careful oversight to ensure that they are ethically handled. If cash is mismanaged or stolen, it can bring about the downfall of a business. Because accounts receivable and notes receivable require estimates of future losses, they can be easily manipulated to show improvement in reported earnings. Improved earnings can, of course, enhance a company's stock price, as well as the bonuses of its executives. In this chapter, we address the management of cash and demonstrate the importance of estimates in accounting for receivables.

LEARNING OBJECTIVES

Making a Statement

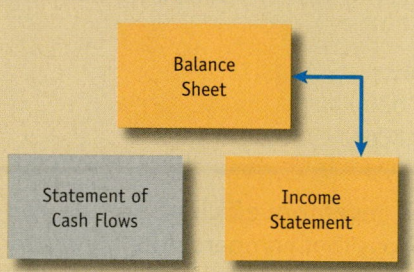

Estimation of uncollectible credit sales affects the amount of accounts receivable on the balance sheet and operating expenses on the income statement.

LO1 Identify and explain the management and ethical issues related to cash and receivables.

LO2 Define *cash equivalents,* and explain methods of controlling cash, including bank reconciliations.

LO3 Apply the allowance method of accounting for uncollectible accounts.

LO4 Define *promissory note,* and make common calculations for promissory notes receivable.

- How can the company control its cash needs?

- How can the company evaluate credit policies and the level of its receivables?

- How should the company estimate the value of its receivables?

Nike, one of the world's largest and best-known athletic sportswear companies, must give the retail stores that buy its products time to pay for their purchases. At the same time, however, Nike must have enough cash on hand to pay its suppliers. As you can see in Nike's Financial Highlights, cash and accounts receivable have made up roughly 50 percent of its current assets in recent years.[1] The company must therefore plan and control its cash flows very carefully.

NIKE'S FINANCIAL HIGHLIGHTS
(In millions)

	2004	2003	2002
Cash	$ 828.0	$ 634.0	$ 575.5
Accounts receivable, net	2,120.2	2,083.9	1,948.7
Total current assets	5,512.0	4,787.1	4,550.4
Net sales	12,253.1	10,697.0	9,893.0

Management Issues Related to Cash and Receivables

LO1 Identify and explain the management and ethical issues related to cash and receivables.

The management of cash and accounts and notes receivable is critical to maintaining adequate liquidity. These assets are important components of the operating cycle, which also includes inventories and accounts payable. In dealing with cash and receivables, management must address five key issues: managing cash needs, setting credit policies, evaluating the level of accounts receivable, financing receivables, and making ethical estimates of credit losses.

Cash Needs

On the balance sheet, **cash** usually consists of currency and coins on hand, checks and money orders from customers, and deposits in checking and savings accounts. Cash is the most liquid of all assets and the most readily available to pay debts. It is central to the operating cycle because all operating transactions eventually use or generate cash.

Cash may include a *compensating balance*, an amount that is not entirely free to be spent. A **compensating balance** is a minimum amount that a bank requires a company to keep in its bank account as part of a credit-granting arrangement. Such an arrangement restricts cash; in effect, it increases the interest on the loan and reduces a company's liquidity. The Securities and Exchange Commission therefore requires companies that have compensating balances to disclose the amounts involved.

Most companies experience seasonal cycles of business activity during the year. During some periods, sales are weak; during others, they are strong. There are also periods when expenditures are high, and periods when they are low. For toy companies, college textbook publishers, amusement parks, construction companies, and manufacturers of sports equipment, the cycles are dramatic, but all companies experience them to some degree.

Seasonal cycles require careful planning of cash inflows, cash outflows, borrowing, and investing. Figure 1 shows the seasonal cycles typical of an athletic sportswear company like **Nike**. As you can see, cash receipts from sales are highest in the late spring, summer, and fall because that is when most people engage in outdoor sports. Sales are relatively low in the winter months. On the other hand, cash expenditures are highest in late winter and spring as the com-

FOCUS ON BUSINESS PRACTICE

How Do Good Companies Deal with Bad Times?

Good companies manage their cash well even in bad times. When a slump in the technology market caused **Texas Instrument's** sales to decline by more than 40 percent, resulting in a loss of nearly $120 million, this large electronics firm actually increased its cash by acting quickly to cut its purchases of plant assets by two-thirds. It also reduced its payroll and lowered the average number of days it had inventory on hand from 71 to 58.[2]

In similar circumstances, some companies have not reacted as quickly as Texas Instruments. For example,

before 9/11, the Big Three automakers—**General Motors**, **Ford**, and **DaimlerChrysler**—were awash in cash. However, in little over a year, the three companies went through $28 billion in cash through various purchases, losses, dividends, and share buybacks. Then, with increasing losses from rising costs, big rebates, and zero percent financing, they were suddenly faced with a shortage of cash. As a result, Standard & Poor's lowered their credit ratings, which raises the interest cost of borrowing money. Perhaps the Big Three should have held on to some of that cash.[3]

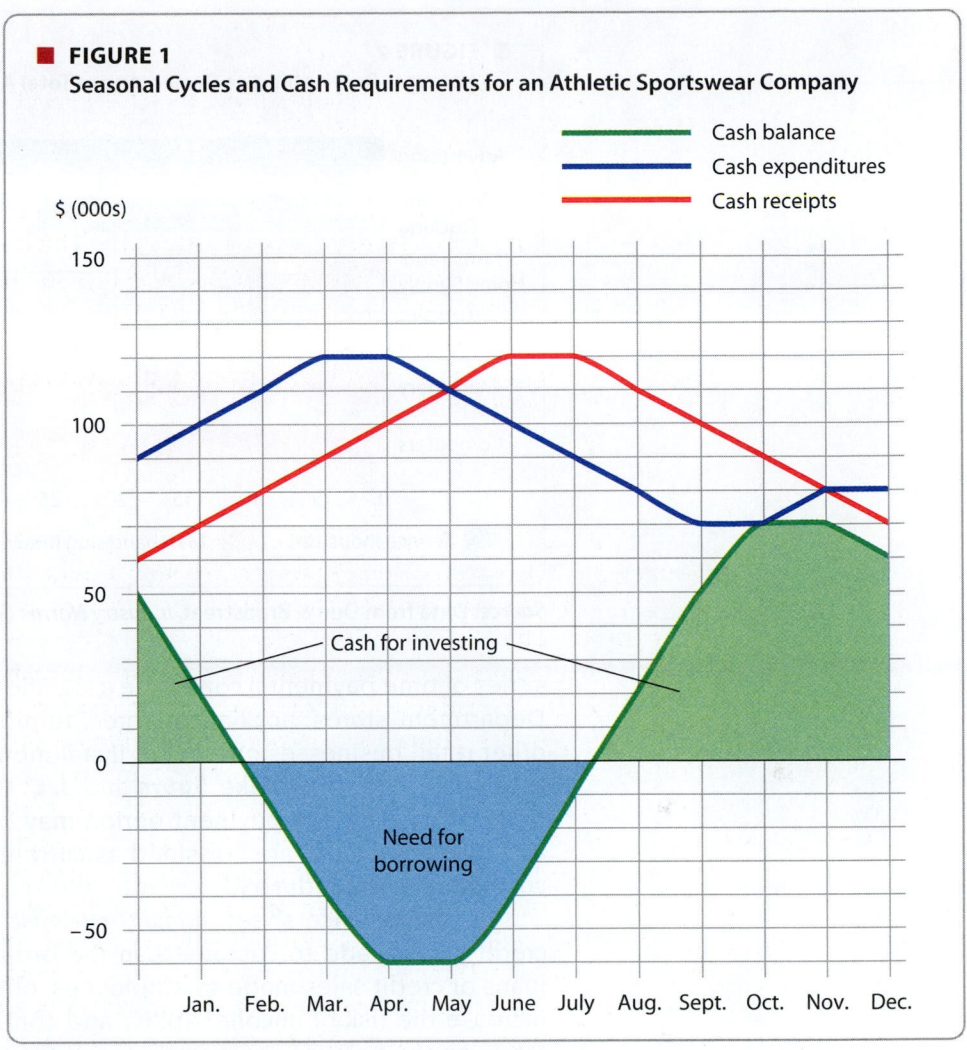

FIGURE 1

Seasonal Cycles and Cash Requirements for an Athletic Sportswear Company

Legend:
- Cash balance
- Cash expenditures
- Cash receipts

$ (000s)

Cash for investing

Need for borrowing

Jan. Feb. Mar. Apr. May June July Aug. Sept. Oct. Nov. Dec.

pany builds up inventory for spring and summer selling. During the late summer, fall, and winter, the company has excess cash on hand that it needs to invest in a way that will earn a return but still permit access to cash as needed. During late spring and early summer, the company needs to plan for short-term borrowing to tide it over until cash receipts pick up later in the year.

Accounts Receivable and Credit Policies

Like cash, accounts receivable and notes receivable are major types of **short-term financial assets**. Both kinds of receivables result from extending credit to individual customers or to other companies. Retailers like **Sears** (recently merged with **Kmart**) have made credit available to nearly every responsible person in the United States. Every field of retail trade has expanded by allowing customers to make payments a month or more after the date of sale. What is not so apparent is that credit has expanded even more among wholesalers and manufacturers like **Nike** than at the retail level. Figure 2 shows the levels of accounts receivable in selected industries.

As we have indicated, **accounts receivable** are the short-term financial assets of a wholesaler or retailer that arise from sales on credit. This type of credit is often called **trade credit**. Terms of trade credit usually range from 5 to 60 days, depending on industry practice. For some companies that sell to consumers, **installment accounts receivable**, which allow the buyer to make a

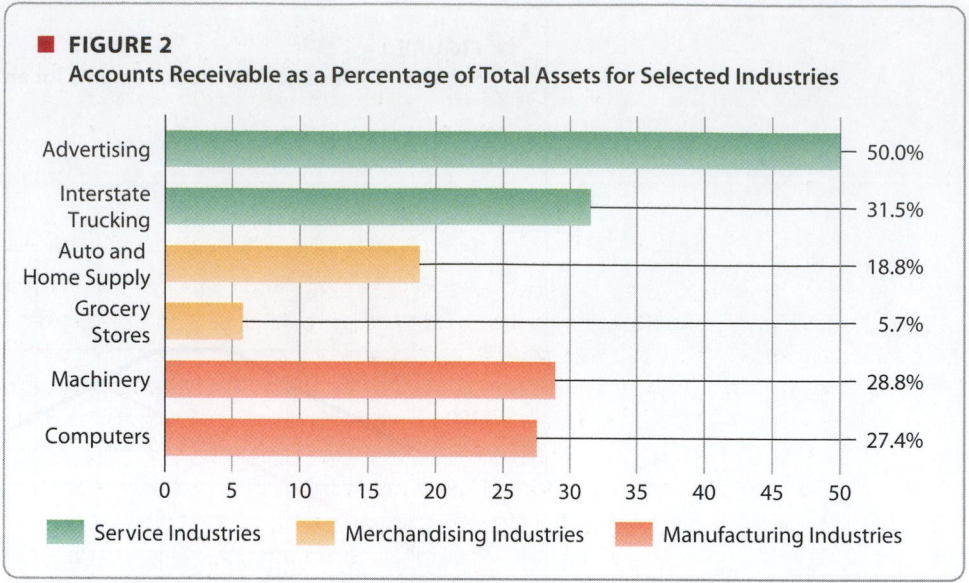

■ **FIGURE 2**
Accounts Receivable as a Percentage of Total Assets for Selected Industries

Source: Data from Dun & Bradstreet, *Industry Norms and Key Business Ratios,* 2003–2004.

series of time payments, constitute a significant portion of accounts receivable. Department stores, appliance stores, furniture stores, used car dealers, and other retail businesses often offer installment credit. The installment accounts receivable of retailers like **Sears** and **J. C. Penney** can amount to millions of dollars. Although the payment period may be 24 months or more, installment accounts receivable are classified as current assets if such credit policies are customary in the industry.

On the balance sheet, *accounts receivable* designates amounts arising from credit sales made to customers in the ordinary course of business. Because loans or credit sales made to employees, officers, or owners of the corporation increase the risk of uncollectibility and conflict of interest, they appear separately on the balance sheet under asset titles like *receivables from employees*.

Normally, individual accounts receivable have debit balances, but sometimes customers overpay their accounts either by mistake or in anticipation of making future purchases. When these accounts show credit balances, the company should show the total credits on its balance sheet as a current liability. The reason for this is that if the customers make no future purchases, the company will have to grant them refunds.

Companies that sell on credit do so to be competitive and to increase sales. In setting credit terms, a company must keep in mind the credit terms of its competitors and the needs of its customers. Obviously, any company that sells on credit wants customers who will pay their bills on time. To increase the likelihood of selling only to customers who will pay on time, most companies develop control procedures and maintain a credit department. The credit department's responsibilities include examining each person or company that applies for credit and approving or rejecting a credit sale to that customer. Typically, the credit department asks for information about the customer's financial resources and debts. It may also check personal references and credit bureaus for further information. Then, based on the information it has gathered, it decides whether to extend credit to the customer.

Companies that are too lenient in granting credit can run into difficulties when customers don't pay. For example, **Capital One**, an aggressive credit card company, attracted 8.1 million new customers, but many of them had poor credit ratings. As a result, the company's unpaid accounts rose from less than 4 percent to 4.96 percent and in 2004 were headed toward 6 percent.[4] **Sprint**, one of the weaker companies in the highly competitive cell phone industry, targeted customers with poor credit histories. It attracted so many who failed to pay their bills that its stock dropped by 50 percent to $2.50 because of the losses that resulted.[5]

Evaluating the Level of Accounts Receivable

Two common measures of the effect of a company's credit policies are receivable turnover and days' sales uncollected. The **receivable turnover** shows how many times, on average, a company turned its receivables into cash during an accounting period. It reflects the relative size of a company's accounts receivable and the success of its credit and collection policies. It may also be affected by external factors, such as seasonal conditions and interest rates. **Days' sales uncollected** is a related measure that shows, on average, how long it takes to collect accounts receivable.

The receivable turnover is computed by dividing net sales by average accounts receivable (net of allowances). Theoretically, the numerator should be net credit sales, but the amount of net credit sales is rarely available in public reports, so investors use total net sales. Using data from **Nike's** Financial Highlights at the beginning of the chapter, we can compute the company's receivable turnover as follows (dollar amounts are in millions):

$$\text{Receivable Turnover} = \frac{\text{Net Sales}}{\text{Average Accounts Receivable}}$$

$$= \frac{\$12,253.1}{(\$2,120.2 + \$2,083.9) \div 2}$$

$$= \frac{\$12,253.1}{\$2,102.1} = 5.8 \text{ times}$$

To find days' sales uncollected, the number of days in a year is divided by the receivable turnover, as follows:

$$\text{Days' Sales Uncollected} = \frac{365 \text{ days}}{\text{Receivable Turnover}} = \frac{365 \text{ days}}{5.8} = 62.9 \text{ days}$$

Thus, Nike turned its receivables 5.8 times a year, or an average of every 62.9 days. A turnover period of this length is not unusual among apparel companies because their credit terms allow retail outlets time to sell products before paying for them. However, it is longer than the turnover period of many companies in other industries. To interpret a company's ratios, you must take into consideration the norms of the industry in which it operates.

FOCUS ON BUSINESS PRACTICE

How Do Powerful Buyers Cause Problems for Small Suppliers?

Big buyers often have significant power over small suppliers, and their cash management decisions can cause severe cash flow problems for the little companies that depend on them. For instance, in an effort to control costs and optimize cash flow, **Ameritech Corp**. told 70,000 suppliers that it would begin paying its bills in 45 days instead of 30. Other large companies routinely take 90 days or more to pay. Some small suppliers are so anxious to get the big companies' business that they fail to realize the implications of the deals they make until it is too late. When **Earthly Elements, Inc.**, accepted a $10,000 order for dried floral gifts from a national home shopping network, its management was ecstatic because the deal increased sales by 25 percent. But in four months, the resulting cash crunch forced the company to close down. When the shopping network finally paid for the order six months later, it was too late to revive Earthly Elements.[6]

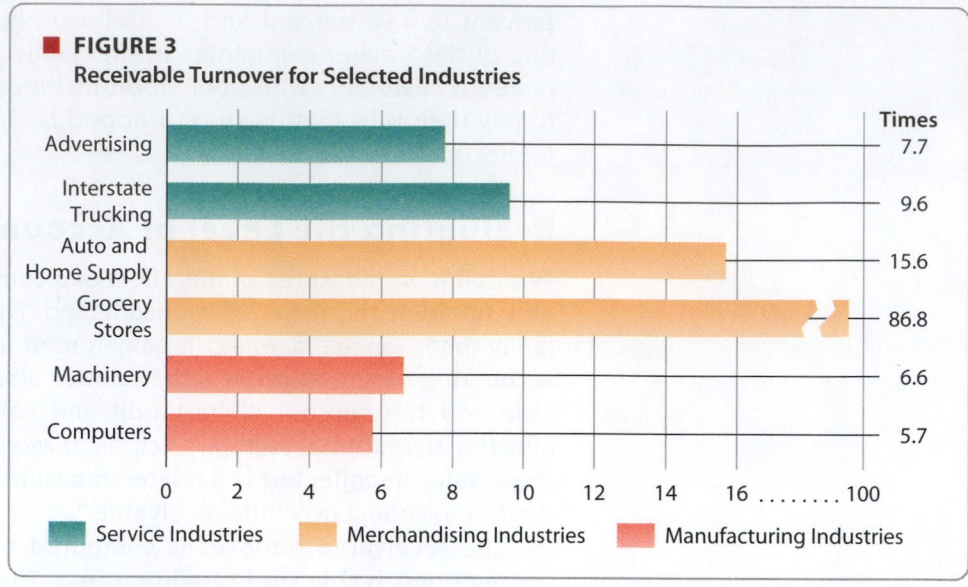

Source: Data from Dun & Bradstreet, *Industry Norms and Key Business Ratios,* 2003–2004.

As Figure 3 shows, the receivable turnover ratio varies substantially from industry to industry. Because grocery stores have few receivables, they have a very quick turnover. The turnover in interstate trucking is 9.6 times because the typical credit terms in that industry are 30 days. The turnover in the machinery and computer industries is lower because those industries tend to have longer credit terms.

Figure 4 shows the days' sales uncollected for the industries listed in Figure 3. Grocery stores, which have the lowest ratio (4.2 days) require the least amount of receivables financing; the computer industry, with days' sales uncollected of 64.0 days, requires the most.

Financing Receivables

Financial flexibility is important to most companies. Companies that have significant amounts of assets tied up in accounts receivable may be unwilling or

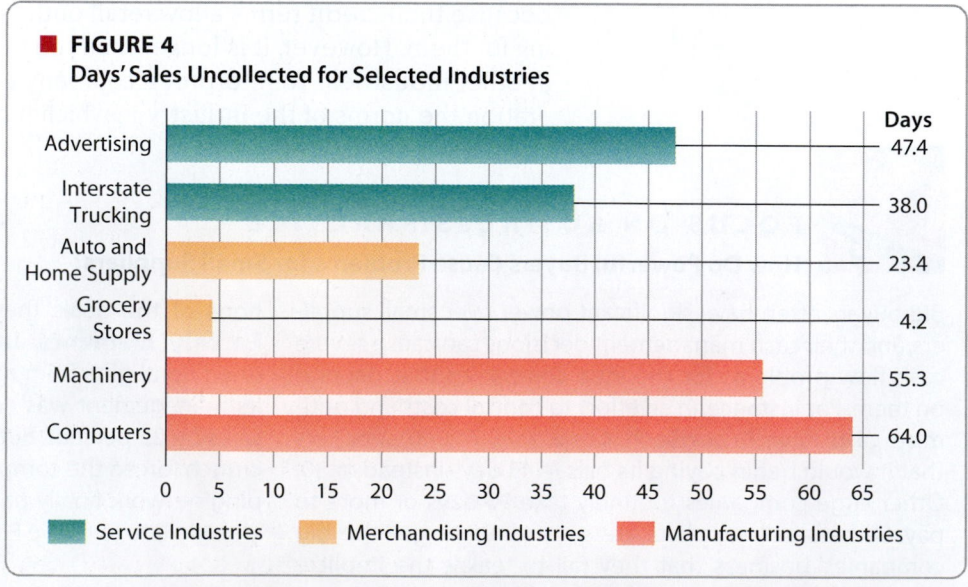

Source: Data from Dun & Bradstreet, *Industry Norms and Key Business Ratios,* 2003–2004.

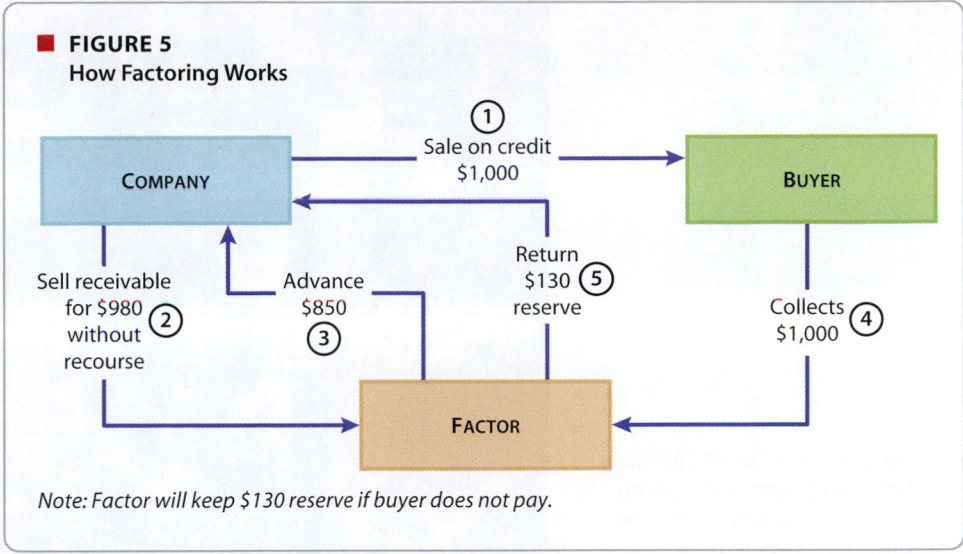

■ **FIGURE 5**
How Factoring Works

Note: Factor will keep $130 reserve if buyer does not pay.

unable to wait until they collect cash from their receivables. Many corporations have set up finance companies to help their customers pay for the purchase of their products. For example, **Ford** has set up Ford Motor Credit Company (FMCC), **General Motors** has set up General Motors Acceptance Corporation (GMAC), and **Sears** has set up Sears Roebuck Acceptance Corporation (SRAC). Other companies borrow funds by pledging their accounts receivable as collateral. If a company does not pay back its loan, the creditor can take the collateral (in this case, the accounts receivable) and convert it to cash to satisfy the loan.

Companies can also raise funds by selling or transferring accounts receivable to another entity, called a **factor**, as illustrated in Figure 5. The sale or transfer of accounts receivable, called **factoring**, can be done with or without recourse. *With recourse* means that the seller of the receivables is liable to the factor (i.e., the purchaser) if a receivable cannot be collected. *Without recourse* means that the factor bears any losses from unpaid accounts. A company's acceptance of credit cards like Visa, MasterCard, or American Express is an example of factoring without recourse because the issuers of the cards accept the risk of nonpayment.

The factor, of course, charges a fee for its service. The fee for sales with recourse is usually about 2 percent of the accounts receivable. The fee is higher for sales without recourse because the factor's risk is greater. In accounting terminology, a seller of receivables with recourse is said to be contingently liable. A **contingent liability** is a potential liability that can develop into a real liability if a particular event occurs. In this case, the event would be a customer's nonpayment of a receivable. A contingent liability generally requires disclosure in the notes to the financial statements.

Nike does not factor or otherwise directly finance its receivables, but **Circuit City Stores**, one of the nation's largest electronics and appliance retailers, does. To promote sales, Circuit City offers generous terms through its installment programs, under which customers pay over a number of months. However, because of its rapid growth, the company needs the cash from these installment receivables sooner than the customers have agreed to pay. To generate cash immediately from these receivables, Circuit City sells them through a process called *securitization*.

Under **securitization**, a company groups its receivables in batches and sells them at a discount to companies and investors. When the receivables are

> **Study Note**
>
> A company that factors its receivables will have a better receivable turnover and days' sales uncollected than a company that does not factor them.

To encourage sales, Circuit City offers installment programs, under which customers pay over time. When the company needs cash from these installment receivables sooner than customers have agreed to pay, Circuit City sells the receivables in batches at a discount to companies and investors—a process called *securitization*.

paid, the buyers get the full amount; their profit depends on the amount of the discount. Circuit City sells all its receivables without recourse, which means that after selling them, it has no further liability, even if no customers were to pay. If Circuit City sold its receivables with recourse and a customer did not pay, it would have to make good on the debt.[7]

Another method of financing receivables is to sell promissory notes held as notes receivable to a financial lender, usually a bank. This practice is called **discounting** because the bank derives its profit by deducting the interest from the maturity value of the note. The holder of the note (usually the payee) endorses the note and turns it over it to the bank. The bank expects to collect the maturity value of the note (principal plus interest) on the maturity date, but it also has recourse against the note's endorser.

For example, if Company A holds a $10,000 note from Company B and the note will pay $600 in interest, a bank may be willing to buy the note for $9,600. If Company B pays, the bank will receive $10,600 at maturity and realize a $1,000 profit. If it fails to pay, Company A is liable to the bank for payment. In the meantime, Company A has a contingent liability in the amount of the discounted note plus interest that it must disclose in the notes to its financial statements.

Ethics and Estimates in Accounting for Receivables

As we have noted, companies extend credit to customers because they expect it will increase their sales and earnings, but they know they will always have some credit customers who cannot or will not pay. The accounts of such customers are called **uncollectible accounts**, or *bad debts*, and they are expenses of selling on credit. To match these expenses, or losses, to the revenues they help generate, they should be recognized at the time credit sales are made.

Of course, at the time a company makes credit sales, it cannot identify which customers will not pay their bills, nor can it predict the exact amount of money it will lose. Therefore, to adhere to the matching rule, it must estimate losses from uncollectible accounts. The estimate becomes an expense in the fiscal year in which the sales are made.

Because the amount of uncollectible accounts can only be estimated and the exact amount will not be known until later, a company's earnings can be easily manipulated. Earnings can be overstated by underestimating the amount of losses from uncollectible accounts, and they can be understated by overestimating the amount of the losses. Misstatements of earnings can occur simply because of a bad estimate. But, as we have noted elsewhere, they can be deliberately made to meet analysts' estimates of earnings, reduce income taxes, or meet benchmarks for bonuses.

Among the many examples of unethical or questionable practices in dealing with uncollectible accounts are the following:

- **WorldCom** (now **MCI**) increased revenues and hid losses by continuing to bill customers for service for years after the customers had quit paying.

- The policy of **Household International**, a large personal finance company, seems to be flexible about when to declare loans delinquent. As a result, the company can vary its estimates of uncollectible accounts from year to year.[8]

- By making large allowances for estimated uncollectible accounts and then gradually reducing them, **Bank One** improved its earnings over several years.[9]

- **HealthSouth** manipulated its income by varying its estimates of the difference between what it charged patients and what it could collect from insurance companies.[10]

Companies with high ethical standards try to be accurate in their estimates of uncollectible accounts, and they disclose the basis of their estimates. For example, **Nike's** management describes its estimates as follows:

> We make ongoing estimates relating to the collectibility of our accounts receivable and maintain [an allowance] for estimated losses resulting from the inability of our customers to make required payments. In determining the amount of the [allowance], we consider our historical level of credit losses and make judgments about the creditworthiness of significant customers based on ongoing credit evaluations. Since we cannot predict future changes in the financial stability of our customers, actual future losses from uncollectible accounts may differ from our estimates.[11]

STOP • REVIEW • APPLY

1-1. What items are included in the Cash account? What is a compensating balance?

1-2. Why does a company sell on credit if it expects that some of its accounts receivable will not be paid? What role does a credit department play in selling on credit?

1-3. Indicate which of the following items should be included in accounts receivable on the balance sheet (if an item does not belong there, indicate where on the balance sheet it should appear): (a) installment accounts receivable from regular customers, due monthly for three years; (b) debit balances in customers' accounts; (c) receivables from employees; (d) credit balances in customers' accounts; and (e) receivables from officers of the company.

1-4. How does the receivable turnover ratio help in evaluating the level of receivables?

1-5. What is a factor, and what do the terms *factoring with recourse* and *factoring without recourse* mean?

1-6. How is accounting for receivables susceptible to unethical financial reporting?

Suggested answers to all Stop, Review, and Apply questions follow the appendixes.

Cash Equivalents and Cash Control

> **LO2** Define *cash equivalents,* and explain methods of controlling cash, including bank reconciliations.

Cash Equivalents

As we noted earlier, cash is the asset most readily available to pay debts, but at times a company may have more cash on hand than it needs to pay its debts. Excess cash should not remain idle, especially during periods of high interest rates. Management may decide to invest the excess cash in short-term interest-bearing accounts or certificates of deposit (CDs) at banks and other financial institutions, in government securities (such as U.S. Treasury notes), or in other securities. If these investments have a term of 90 days or less when they are purchased, they are called **cash equivalents** because the funds revert to cash so quickly they are treated as cash on the balance sheet.

Nike describes its treatment of cash and cash equivalents as follows:

> Cash and equivalents represent cash and short-term, highly liquid investments with original maturities of three months or less at the time of purchase. The carrying amounts reflected in the consolidated balance sheet for cash and equivalents approximate fair value due to their short maturities.[12]

According to a recent survey of 600 large U.S. corporations, 6 percent use the term *cash* as the balance sheet caption, and 89 percent use either *cash and cash equivalents* or *cash and equivalents*. The rest either combine cash with marketable securities or have no cash.[13]

Cash Control Methods

In an earlier chapter, we discussed the concept of internal control and how it applies to cash transactions. Here, we address three additional ways of controlling cash: imprest systems; banking services, including electronic funds transfer; and bank reconciliations.

Imprest Systems Most companies need to keep some currency and coins on hand. Currency and coins are needed for cash registers, for paying expenses that are impractical to pay by check, and for situations that require cash advances—for example, when sales representatives need cash for travel expenses. One way to control a cash fund and cash advances is by using an **imprest system**.

A common form of imprest system is a petty cash fund, which is established at a fixed amount. A receipt documents each cash payment made from the fund. The fund is periodically reimbursed, based on the documented expenditures, by the exact amount necessary to restore its original cash balance. The person responsible for the petty cash fund must always be able to account for its contents by showing that total cash and receipts equal the original fixed amount.

Banking Services

All businesses rely on banks to control cash receipts and cash disbursements. Banks serve as safe depositories for cash, negotiable instruments, and other valuable business documents, such as stocks and bonds. The checking accounts that banks provide improve control by minimizing the amount of currency a company needs to keep on hand and by supplying permanent records of all cash payments. Banks also serve as agents in a variety of transactions, such as the collection and payment of certain kinds of debts and the exchange of foreign currencies.

Electronic funds transfer (EFT) is a method of conducting business transactions that does not involve the actual transfer of cash. With EFT, a company electronically transfers cash from its bank to another company's bank. For the banks, the electronic transfer is simply a bookkeeping entry. Companies today rely heavily on this method of payment. **Wal-Mart**, for example, makes 75 percent of its payments to suppliers through EFT.

Because of EFT and other electronic banking services, we are rapidly becoming a cashless society. Automated teller machines (ATMs) allow bank customers to make deposits, withdraw cash, transfer funds among accounts, and pay bills. Large consumer banks like **Citibank**, **Chase**, and **Bank of America** process hundreds of thousands of ATM transactions each week. Many banks also give customers the option of paying bills over the telephone and with *debit cards*. In 2003, debit cards accounted for more than 16 billion transactions.[14] When a customer makes a retail purchase using a debit card, the amount of the purchase is deducted directly from the buyer's bank account. The bank usually documents debit card transactions for the retailer, but the retailer must develop new internal controls to ensure that the transactions are recorded properly and that unauthorized transfers do not occur. It is expected that within a few years, a majority of all retail activity will be handled electronically.

Bank Reconciliations

Rarely does the balance of a company's Cash account exactly equal the cash balance on its bank statement. The bank may not yet have recorded certain transactions that appear in the company's records, and the company may not yet have recorded certain bank transactions. A bank reconciliation is therefore a necessary step in internal control. A **bank reconciliation** is the process of accounting for the difference between the balance on a company's bank statement and the balance in its Cash account. This process involves making additions to and subtractions from both balances to arrive at the adjusted cash balance.

The following are the transactions that most commonly appear in a company's records but not on its bank statement :

1. *Outstanding checks.* These are checks that a company has issued and recorded but that do not yet appear on its bank statement.

2. *Deposits in transit*: These are deposits a company has sent to its bank but that the bank did not receive in time to enter on the bank statement.

Transactions that may appear on the bank statement but not in the company's records include the following:

1. *Service charges* (SC): Banks often charge a fee, or service charge, for the use of a checking account. Many banks base the service charge on a number of factors, such as the average balance of the account during the month or the number of checks drawn.

2. *NSF (nonsufficient funds) checks*: An NSF check is a check that a company has deposited but that is not paid when the bank presents it to the issuer's bank. The bank charges the company's account and returns the check so that the company can try to collect the amount due. If the bank has deducted the NSF check on the bank statement but the company has not deducted it from its book balance, an adjustment must be made in the bank reconciliation. The company usually reclassifies the NSF check from Cash to Accounts Receivable because it must now collect from the person or company that wrote the check.

3. *Miscellaneous debits and credits*: Banks also charge for other services, such as stopping payment on checks and printing checks. The bank notifies the depositor of each deduction by including a debit memorandum with the monthly statement. A bank also sometimes serves as an agent in collecting on promissory notes for the depositor. When it does, it includes a credit memorandum in the bank statement, along with a debit memorandum for the service charge.

4. *Interest income*: Banks commonly pay interest on a company's average balance. Accounts that pay interest are sometimes called NOW or money market accounts.

An error by either the bank or the depositor will, of course, require immediate correction.

To illustrate the preparation of a bank reconciliation, suppose that Kim Maintenance Company's bank statement for October shows a balance of $3,471.07 on October 31 and that on the same date, the company's records show a cash balance of $2,415.91. The purpose of a bank reconciliation is to identify the items that make up the difference between these amounts and to determine the correct cash balance. Exhibit 1 shows Kim Maintenance Company's bank reconciliation for October. The circled numbers in the exhibit refer to the following:

1. The bank has not recorded a deposit in the amount of $276.00 that the company mailed to the bank on October 31.

2. The bank has not paid the five checks that the company issued in September and October: Even though the September 14 check was deducted in the September 30 reconciliation, it must be deducted again in each subsequent month in which it remains outstanding.

3. The company incorrectly recorded a $300 deposit from cash sales as $330.00. On October 6, the bank received the deposit and corrected the amount.

4. Among the returned checks was a credit memorandum showing that the bank had collected a promissory note from A. Jacobs in the amount of $280.00, plus $20.00 in interest on the note. A debit memorandum was also

> ### Study Note
>
> A credit memorandum means that an amount was *added* to the bank balance; a debit memorandum means that an amount was *deducted*.

EXHIBIT 1 ▶ | Bank Reconciliation

Kim Maintenance Company
Bank Reconciliation
October 31, 20xx

Balance per bank, October 31		$3,471.07
① Add deposit of October 31 in transit		276.00
		$3,747.07
② Less outstanding checks:		
No. 551, issued on Sept. 14	$150.00	
No. 576, issued on Oct. 30	40.68	
No. 578, issued on Oct. 31	500.00	
No. 579, issued on Oct. 31	370.00	
No. 580, issued on Oct. 31	130.50	1,191.18
Adjusted bank balance, October 31		**$2,555.89**
Balance per books, October 31		$2,415.91
Add:		
④ Note receivable collected by bank	$280.00	
④ Interest income on note	20.00	
⑦ Interest income	15.62	315.62
		$2,731.53
Less:		
③ Overstatement of deposit of October 6	$ 30.00	
④ Collection fee	5.00	
⑤ NSF check of Arthur Clubb	128.14	
⑥ Service charge	12.50	175.64
Adjusted book balance, October 31		**$2,555.89**

Study Note

It is possible to place an item in the wrong section of a bank reconciliation and still have it balance. The *correct* adjusted balance must be obtained.

enclosed for the $5.00 collection fee. The company had not entered these amounts in its records.

5. Also returned with the bank statement was an NSF check for $128.14 that the company had received from a customer named Arthur Clubb. The NSF check was not reflected in the company's records.

6. A debit memorandum was enclosed for the regular monthly service charge of $12.50. The company had not yet recorded this charge.

7. Interest earned on the company's average balance was $15.62.

As you can see in Exhibit 1, starting from their separate balances, both the bank and book amounts are adjusted to the amount of $2,555.89. This adjusted balance is the amount of cash the company owns on October 31 and thus is the amount that should appear on its October 31 balance sheet.

When outstanding checks are presented to the bank for payment and the bank receives and records the deposit in transit, the bank balance will automatically become correct. However, the company must update its book balance by recording all the items reported by the bank. Thus, Kim Maintenance Company would record an increase in Cash with the following items:

◆ Increase (debit) in Notes Receivable, $280

◆ Increase (credit) in Interest Income, $20.00 (interest on note)

▸ Increase (credit) in Interest Income, $15.62 (interest on average bank balance)

The company would record a reduction in Cash with these items:

▸ Decrease (debit) in Sales, $30 (error in recording deposit)

▸ Increase (debit) in Accounts Receivable, $128.14 (return of NSF check)

▸ Increase (debit) in Bank Service Charges, $17.50 ($12.50 + $5.00)

As the use of electronic funds transfer, automatic payments, and debit cards increases, the items that most businesses will have to deal with in their bank reconciliations will undoubtedly grow.

S T O P • R E V I E W • A P P L Y

2-1. How do cash equivalents differ from cash?

2-2. Why is an imprest system an effective control over cash?

2-3. What is a bank reconciliation? What two amounts need to be reconciled?

Uncollectible Accounts

LO3 Apply the allowance method of accounting for uncollectible accounts.

Study Note

The direct charge-off method does not conform to the matching rule.

Some companies recognize a loss at the time they determine that an account is uncollectible by reducing Accounts Receivable and increasing Uncollectible Accounts Expense. Federal regulations require companies to use this method of recognizing a loss—called the **direct charge-off method** —in computing taxable income. Although small companies may use this method for all purposes, companies that follow generally accepted accounting principles do not use it in their financial statements. The reason they do not is that a direct charge-off is usually recorded in a different accounting period from the one in which the sale takes place, and the method therefore does not conform to the matching rule. Companies that follow GAAP prefer the allowance method.

The Allowance Method

Study Note

The allowance method relies on an estimate of uncollectible accounts but is in accord with the matching rule.

Under the **allowance method**, losses from bad debts are matched against the sales they help to produce. As mentioned earlier, when management extends credit to increase sales, it knows it will incur some losses from uncollectible accounts. Losses from credit sales should be recognized at the time the sales are made so that they are matched to the revenues they help generate. Of course, at the time a company makes credit sales, management cannot identify which customers will not pay their debts, nor can it predict the exact amount of money the company will lose. Therefore, to observe the matching rule, losses from uncollectible accounts must be estimated, and the estimate becomes an expense in the period in which the sales are made.

For example, suppose that Cottage Sales Company made most of its sales on credit during its first year of operation, 20x6. At the end of the year, accounts receivable amounted to $100,000. On December 31, 20x6, management reviewed the collectible status of the accounts receivable. Approximately $6,000 of the $100,000 of accounts receivable were estimated to be uncollectible. The following adjusting entry would be made on December 31 of that year:

A	= L +	SE	20x6		
−6,000		−6,000	Dec. 31	Uncollectible Accounts Expense	6,000	
				Allowance for Uncollectible Accounts		6,000
				To record the estimated uncollectible accounts expense for the year		

Disclosure of Uncollectible Accounts

Uncollectible Accounts Expense appears on the income statement as an operating expense. **Allowance for Uncollectible Accounts** appears on the balance sheet as a contra account that is deducted from accounts receivable. It reduces the accounts receivable to the amount expected to be collected in cash, as follows:

Current assets		
Cash		$ 10,000
Short-term investments		15,000
Accounts receivable	$100,000	
Less allowance for uncollectible accounts	6,000	94,000
Inventory		56,000
Total current assets		$175,000

Accounts receivable may also be shown on the balance sheet as follows:

Accounts receivable (net of allowance for uncollectible accounts of $6,000)	$94,000

Or accounts receivable may be shown at "net," with the amount of the allowance for uncollectible accounts identified in a note to the financial statements. The allowance account is necessary because the specific uncollectible accounts will not be identified until later.

The allowance account often has other titles, such as *Allowance for Doubtful Accounts* and *Allowance for Bad Debts*. Once in a while, the older phrase *Reserve for Bad Debts* will be seen, but in modern practice it should not be used. *Bad Debts Expense* is a title often used for Uncollectible Accounts Expense.

Estimating Uncollectible Accounts Expense

As noted, expected losses from uncollectible accounts must be estimated. Of course, estimates can vary widely. If management takes an optimistic view and projects a small loss from uncollectible accounts, the resulting net accounts receivable will be larger than if management takes a pessimistic view. The net income will also be larger under the optimistic view because the estimated expense will be smaller. The company's accountant makes an estimate based on past experience and current economic conditions. For example, losses from uncollectible accounts are normally expected to be greater in a recession than during a period of economic growth. The final decision, made by management, on the amount of the expense will depend on objective information, such as

Study Note

The purpose of Allowance for Uncollectible Accounts is to reduce the gross accounts receivable to the amount estimated to be collectible (net realizable value). The purpose of another contra account, Accumulated Depreciation, is *not* to reduce the gross plant and equipment accounts to realizable value. Rather, its purpose is to show how much of the cost of the plant and equipment has been allocated as an expense to previous accounting periods.

Study Note

The accountant looks at both local and national economic conditions in determining the estimated uncollectible accounts expense.

FOCUS ON BUSINESS PRACTICE

Why Are Estimates Difficult to Make?

To be profitable, a company must not only sell goods and services; it must also generate cash flows by collecting on those sales. The latter has sometimes been a problem for leading North American manufacturers of telecommunications equipment. In the late 1990s, to make sales to start-up telecom companies, these manufacturers lent many billions of dollars to their customers. **Nortel Networks** had $4.1 billion in customer financing; **Cisco Systems**, $2.4 billion; and **Lucent Technologies**, $5.4 billion. Many of these loans became bad debts when the telecom industry experienced a major recession in 2001. As a result, all three companies increased their estimates of allowances for uncollectible accounts, actions that eliminated previously reported earnings and caused the companies' stock prices to fall.[15] However, it turned out that these companies had overestimated how bad the losses would be. In later years, they reduced their allowances for credit losses, thereby increasing their reported earnings.[16]

the accountant's analyses, and on certain qualitative factors, such as how investors, bankers, creditors, and others view the performance of the debtor company. Regardless of the qualitative considerations, the estimated losses from uncollectible accounts should be realistic.

Two common methods of estimating uncollectible accounts expense are the percentage of net sales method and the accounts receivable aging method.

Percentage of Net Sales Method The **percentage of net sales method** asks the question, How much of this year's *net sales* will not be collected? The answer determines the amount of uncollectible accounts expense for the year. For example, the following balances represent Hassel Company's ending figures for 20x9:

SALES		SALES RETURNS AND ALLOWANCES	
	Dec. 31 645,000	Dec. 31 40,000	

SALES DISCOUNTS		ALLOWANCE FOR UNCOLLECTIBLE ACCOUNTS	
Dec. 31 5,000			Dec. 31 3,600

The following are Hassel's actual losses from uncollectible accounts for the past three years:

Year	Net Sales	Losses from Uncollectible Accounts	Percentage
20x6	$ 520,000	$10,200	1.96
20x7	595,000	13,900	2.34
20x8	585,000	9,900	1.69
Total	$1,700,000	$34,000	2.00

Credit sales often constitute most of a company's sales. If a company has substantial cash sales, it should use only its net credit sales in estimating uncollectible accounts.

Hassel's management believes that its uncollectible accounts will continue to average about 2 percent of net sales. The uncollectible accounts expense for the year 20x9 is therefore estimated as follows:

$$.02 \times (\$645,000 - \$40,000 - \$5,000) = .02 \times \$600,000 = \$12,000$$

The following entry would be made to record the estimate:

> **Study Note**
>
> Unlike the direct charge-off method, the percentage of net sales method matches revenues with expenses.

A	= L +	SE
−12,000		−12,000

20x9

Dec. 31	Uncollectible Accounts Expense	12,000	
	Allowance for Uncollectible Accounts		12,000
	To record uncollectible accounts expense at 2 percent of $600,000 net sales		

After this entry is posted, Allowance for Uncollectible Accounts will have a balance of $15,600:

ALLOWANCE FOR UNCOLLECTIBLE ACCOUNTS	
	Dec. 31 3,600
	Dec. 31 Adj. 12,000
	Dec. 31 Bal. 15,600

The balance consists of the $12,000 estimated uncollectible accounts receivable from 20x9 sales and the $3,600 estimated uncollectible accounts receivable from previous years.

Accounts Receivable Aging Method

The **accounts receivable aging method** asks the question, How much of the *ending balance of accounts receivable* will not be collected? With this method, the ending balance of Allowance for Uncollectible Accounts is determined directly through an analysis of accounts receivable. The difference between the amount determined to be uncollectible and the actual balance of Allowance for Uncollectible Accounts is the expense for the period. In theory, this method should produce the same result as the percentage of net sales method, but in practice it rarely does.

The **aging of accounts receivable** is the process of listing each customer's receivable account according to the due date of the account. If the customer's account is past due, there is a possibility that the account will not be paid. And that possibility increases as the account extends further beyond the due date. The aging of accounts receivable helps management evaluate its credit and collection policies and alerts it to possible problems.

Exhibit 2 illustrates the aging of accounts receivable for Myer Company. Each account receivable is classified as being not yet due or as being 1–30 days, 31–60 days, 61–90 days, or over 90 days past due. Based on past experience, the estimated percentage for each category is determined and multiplied by the amount in each category to determine the estimated, or target, balance of Allowance for Uncollectible Accounts. In total, it is estimated that $2,459 of the $44,400 in accounts receivable will not be collected.

Once the target balance for Allowance for Uncollectible Accounts has been found, it is necessary to determine the amount of the adjustment. The amount depends on the current balance of the allowance account. Let us assume two cases for the December 31 balance of Myer Company's Allowance for Uncollectible Accounts: (1) a credit balance of $800 and (2) a debit balance of $800.

In the first case, an adjustment of $1,659 is needed to bring the balance of the allowance account to a $2,459 credit balance:

> **Study Note**
>
> When the write-offs in an accounting period exceed the amount of the allowance, a debit balance in the Allowance for Uncollectible Accounts account results.

Targeted balance for allowance for uncollectible accounts	$2,459
Less current credit balance of allowance for uncollectible accounts	800
Uncollectible accounts expense	$1,659

▼ **EXHIBIT 2**

Analysis of Accounts Receivable by Age

**Myer Company
Analysis of Accounts Receivable by Age
December 31, 20x6**

Customer	Total	Not Yet Due	1–30 Days Past Due	31–60 Days Past Due	61–90 Days Past Due	Over 90 Days Past Due
A. Arnold	$ 150		$ 150			
M. Benoit	400			$ 400		
J. Connolly	1,000	$ 900	100			
R. Deering	250				$ 250	
Others	42,600	21,000	14,000	3,800	2,200	$1,600
Totals	$44,400	$21,900	$14,250	$4,200	$2,450	$1,600
Estimated percentage uncollectible		1.0	2.0	10.0	30.0	50.0
Allowance for Uncollectible Accounts	$ 2,459	$ 219	$ 285	$ 420	$ 735	$ 800

The uncollectible accounts expense is recorded as follows:

A = L + SE		
−1,659 −1,659		

20x6			
Dec. 31	Uncollectible Accounts Expense	1,659	
	Allowance for Uncollectible Accounts		1,659
	To bring the allowance for uncollectible accounts to the level of estimated losses		

The resulting balance of Allowance for Uncollectible Accounts is $2,459:

ALLOWANCE FOR UNCOLLECTIBLE ACCOUNTS	
	Dec. 31 800
	Dec. 31 Adj. 1,659
	Dec. 31 Bal. **2,459**

In the second case, because Allowance for Uncollectible Accounts has a debit balance of $800, the estimated uncollectible accounts expense for the year will have to be $3,259 to reach the targeted balance of $2,459. This calculation is as follows:

Targeted balance for allowance for uncollectible accounts	$2,459
Plus current debit balance of allowance for uncollectible accounts	800
Uncollectible accounts expense	$3,259

The uncollectible accounts expense is recorded as follows:

A = L + SE	20x6	
−3,259 −3,259	Dec. 31 Uncollectible Accounts Expense	3,259
	Allowance for Uncollectible Accounts	3,259
	To bring the allowance for	
	uncollectible accounts to the	
	level of estimated losses	

After this entry, Allowance for Uncollectible Accounts has a credit balance of $2,459:

ALLOWANCE FOR UNCOLLECTIBLE ACCOUNTS		
Dec. 31 800	Dec. 31 Adj.	3,259
	Dec. 31 Bal.	**2,459**

Study Note

Describing the aging method as the balance sheet method emphasizes that the computation is based on ending accounts receivable rather than on net sales for the period.

Comparison of the Two Methods

Both the percentage of net sales method and the accounts receivable aging method estimate the uncollectible accounts expense in accordance with the matching rule, but as shown in Figure 6, they do so in different ways. The percentage of net sales method is an income statement approach. It assumes that a certain proportion of sales will not be collected, and this proportion is the *amount of Uncollectible Accounts Expense* for the accounting period. The accounts receivable aging method is a balance sheet approach. It assumes that a certain proportion of accounts receivable outstanding will not be collected. This proportion is the *targeted balance of the Allowance for Uncollectible Accounts account.* The expense

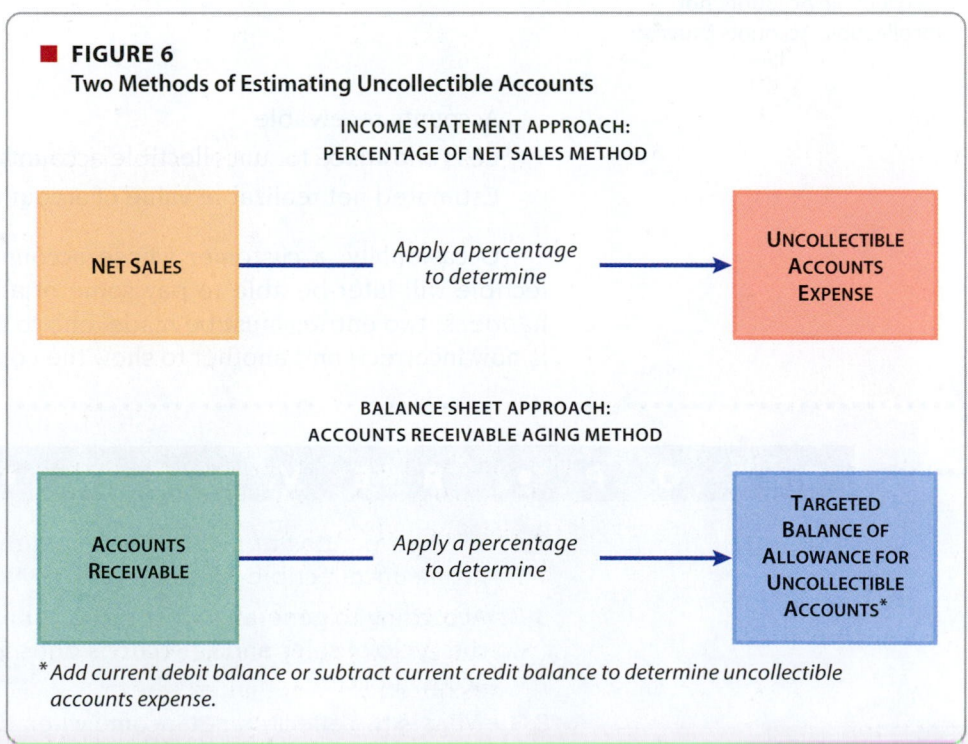

■ **FIGURE 6**
Two Methods of Estimating Uncollectible Accounts

INCOME STATEMENT APPROACH:
PERCENTAGE OF NET SALES METHOD

NET SALES → Apply a percentage to determine → UNCOLLECTIBLE ACCOUNTS EXPENSE

BALANCE SHEET APPROACH:
ACCOUNTS RECEIVABLE AGING METHOD

ACCOUNTS RECEIVABLE → Apply a percentage to determine → TARGETED BALANCE OF ALLOWANCE FOR UNCOLLECTIBLE ACCOUNTS*

*Add current debit balance or subtract current credit balance to determine uncollectible accounts expense.

for the accounting period is the difference between the targeted balance and the current balance of the allowance account.

Writing Off Uncollectible Accounts

Regardless of the method used to estimate uncollectible accounts, the total of accounts receivable written off in an accounting period will rarely equal the estimated uncollectible amount. The allowance account will show a credit balance when the total of accounts written off is less than the estimated uncollectible amount. It will show a debit balance when the total of accounts written off is greater than the estimated uncollectible amount.

When it becomes clear that a specific account receivable will not be collected, the amount should be written off to Allowance for Uncollectible Accounts. Remember that the uncollectible amount was already accounted for as an expense when the allowance was established. For example, assume that on January 15, 20x7, R. Deering, who owes Myer Company $250, is declared bankrupt by a federal court. The entry to *write off* this account is as follows:

A = L + SE				
+250	20x7			
−250	Jan. 15	Allowance for Uncollectible Accounts	250	
		Accounts Receivable		250
		To write off receivable		
		from R. Deering as uncollectible		
		because of his bankruptcy		

Study Note

When writing off an individual account, debit Allowance for Uncollectible Accounts, not Uncollectible Accounts Expense.

Although the write-off removes the uncollectible amount from Accounts Receivable, it does not affect the estimated net realizable value of accounts receivable. It simply reduces R. Deering's account to zero and reduces Allowance for Uncollectible Accounts by $250, as shown below:

	Balances Before Write-off	Balances After Write-off
Accounts receivable	$44,400	$44,150
Less allowance for uncollectible accounts	2,459	2,209
Estimated net realizable value of accounts receivable	$41,941	$41,941

Occasionally, a customer whose account has been written off as uncollectible will later be able to pay some or all of the amount owed. When that happens, two entries must be made: one to reverse the earlier write-off (which is now incorrect) and another to show the collection of the account.

S T O P • R E V I E W • A P P L Y

3-1. What accounting principle does the direct charge-off method of recognizing uncollectible accounts violate? Why?

3-2. According to generally accepted accounting principles, at what point in the cycle of sales and collections does a loss on an uncollectible account occur?

3-3. What is the effect on net income when management takes an optimistic rather than a pessimistic view of estimated uncollectible accounts?

3-4. Why is the percentage of net sales method of estimating uncollectible accounts called an income statement approach, and why is the accounts receivable aging method called a balance sheet approach?

3-5. What is the reasoning behind the percentage of net sales method and the accounts receivable aging method?

3-6. Suppose that after adjusting and closing accounts at the end of a fiscal year, Accounts Receivable is $176,000 and Allowance for Uncollectible Accounts is $14,500. (a) What is the collectible value of Accounts Receivable? (b) If the $450 account of a bankrupt customer is written off in the first month of the new year, what will the collectible value of Accounts Receivable be?

Aging and Net Sales Methods Contrasted   A & A Musical Instrument, Inc., sells its merchandise on credit. In the company's last fiscal year, which ended July 31, it had net sales of $3,500,000. At the end of the fiscal year, it had Accounts Receivable of $900,000 and a credit balance in Allowance for Uncollectible Accounts of $5,600. In the past, the company has been unable to collect on approximately 1 percent of its net sales. An aging analysis of accounts receivable has indicated that $40,000 of current receivables are uncollectible.

1. Calculate the amount of uncollectible accounts expense, and use T accounts to determine the resulting balance of Allowance for Uncollectible Accounts under the percentage of net sales method and the accounts receivable aging method.

2. How would your answers change if Allowance for Uncollectible Accounts had a debit balance of $5,600 instead of a credit balance?

SOLUTION

1. **Percentage of net sales method:**

ALLOWANCE FOR UNCOLLECTIBLE ACCOUNTS

	July 31 5,600
	31 UA Exp. 35,000*
	July 31 Bal. 40,600

*Uncollectible Accounts Expense = $3,500,000 × .01

Aging Method:

ALLOWANCE FOR UNCOLLECTIBLE ACCOUNTS

	July 31 5,600
	31 UA Exp. 34,400*
	July 31 Bal. 40,000

*Uncollectible Accounts Expense = $40,000 − $5,600

2. Under the percentage of net sales method, the amount of the expense is the same in 1 and 2 but the ending balance will be $29,400 ($35,000 − $5,600). Under the aging method, the ending balance is the same, but the amount of the expense will be $45,600 ($40,000 + $5,600).

≡ Notes Receivable

LO4 Define *promissory note,* and make common calculations for promissory notes receivable.

A **promissory note** is an unconditional promise to pay a definite sum of money on demand or at a future date. The person or company that signs the note and thereby promises to pay is the *maker* of the note. The entity to whom payment is to be made is the *payee.*

The promissory note shown in Figure 7 is an unconditional promise by the maker, Samuel Mason, to pay a definite sum—or principal ($1,000)—to the payee, Cook County Bank & Trust, on August 18, 20x6. As you can see, this promissory note is dated May 20, 20x6, and bears an interest rate of 8 percent.

A payee includes all the promissory notes it holds that are due in less than one year in **notes receivable** in the current assets section of its balance sheet. A maker includes them in **notes payable** in the current liabilities section of its balance sheet.

The nature of a company's business generally determines how frequently it receives promissory notes from customers. Firms that sell durable goods of high value, such as farm machinery and automobiles, often accept promissory notes. Among the advantages of these notes are that they produce interest income and represent a stronger legal claim against a debtor than do accounts receivable. In addition, selling—or discounting—promissory notes to banks is a common financing method. Almost all companies occasionally accept promissory notes, and many companies obtain them in settlement of past-due accounts.

Maturity Date

The **maturity date** is the date on which a promissory note must be paid. This date must be stated on the note or be determinable from the facts stated on

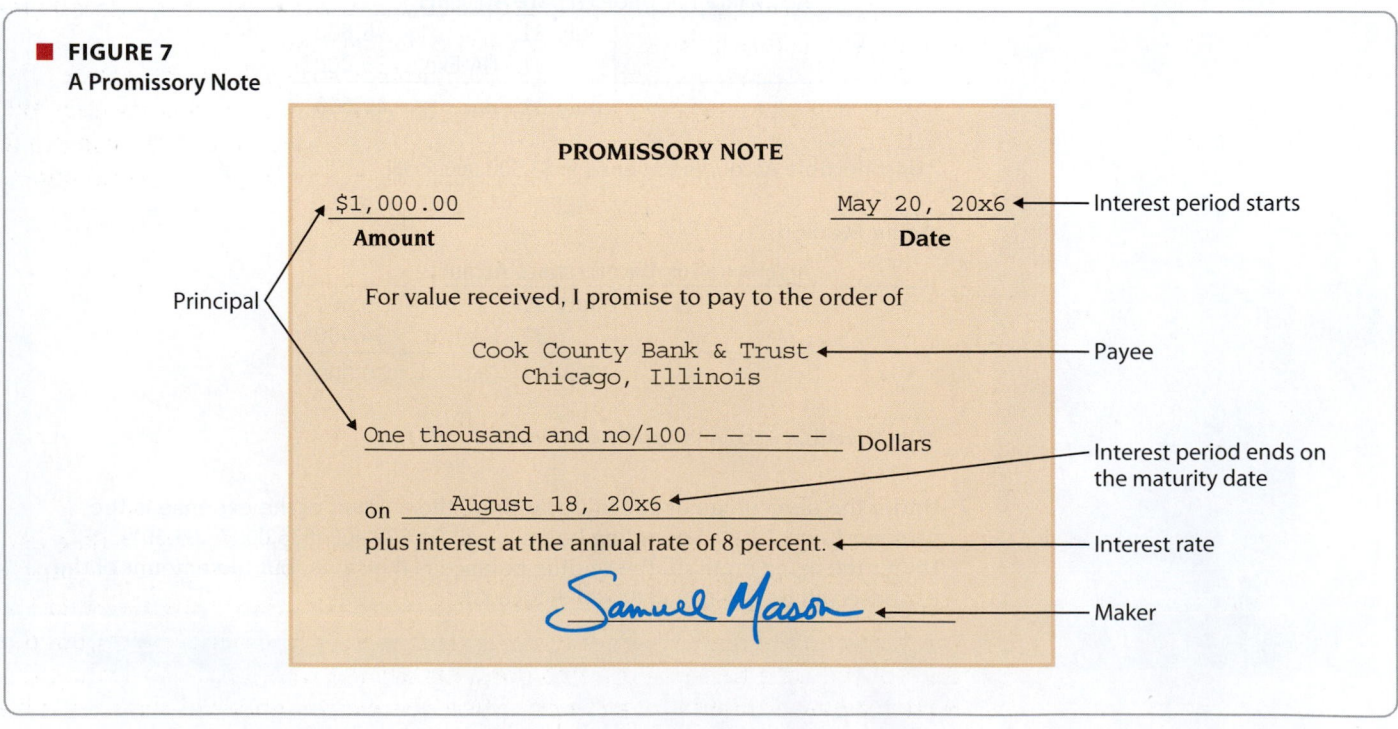

■ **FIGURE 7**
A Promissory Note

Automobile manufacturers like Toyota, whose assembly line is pictured here, often accept promissory notes, which are unconditional promises to pay a definite sum of money on demand or at a future date. These notes produce interest income and represent a stronger legal claim against a debtor than do accounts receivable. In addition, firms commonly raise money by selling—or discounting—promissory notes to banks.

the note. The following are among the most common statements of maturity date:

1. A specific date, such as "November 14, 20xx"

2. A specific number of months after the date of the note, such as "three months after November 14, 20xx"

3. A specific number of days after the date of the note, such as "60 days after November 14, 20xx"

The maturity date is obvious when a specific date is stated. And when the maturity date is a number of months from the date of the note, one simply uses the same day in the appropriate future month. For example, a note dated January 20 that is due in two months would be due on March 20.

When the maturity date is a specific number of days from the date of the note, however, the exact maturity date must be determined. In computing the maturity date, it is important to exclude the date of the note. For example, a note dated May 20 and due in 90 days would be due on August 18, determined as follows:

Days remaining in May (31 − 20)	11
Days in June	30
Days in July	31
Days in August	18
Total days	90

Duration of a Note

The **duration of a note** is the time between a promissory note's issue date and its maturity date. Knowing the exact number of days in the duration of a note is important because interest is calculated on that basis. Identifying the duration is easy when the maturity date is stated as a specific number of days from the date of the note because the two numbers are the same. However, when the maturity date is stated as a specific date, the exact number of days must be

determined. Assume that a note issued on May 10 matures on August 10. The duration of the note is 92 days:

Days remaining in May (31 − 10)	21
Days in June	30
Days in July	31
Days in August	10
Total days	92

Interest and Interest Rate

Interest is the cost of borrowing money or the return on lending money, depending on whether one is the borrower or the lender. The amount of interest is based on three factors: the principal (the amount of money borrowed or lent), the rate of interest, and the loan's length of time. The formula used in computing interest is as follows:

$$\text{Principal} \times \text{Rate of Interest} \times \text{Time} = \text{Interest}$$

Interest rates are usually stated on an annual basis. For example, the interest on a one-year, 8 percent, \$1,000 note would be \$80 (\$1,000 × 8/100 × 1 = \$80). If the term, or time period, of the note is three months instead of a year, the interest charge would be \$20 (\$1,000 × 8/100 × 3/12 = \$20).

When the term of a note is expressed in days, the exact number of days must be used in computing the interest. Thus, if the term of the note described above was 45 days, the interest would be \$10, computed as follows: \$1,000 × 8/100 × 45/365 = \$9.86.

Maturity Value

The **maturity value** is the total proceeds of a promissory note—face value plus interest—at the maturity date. The maturity value of a 90-day, 8 percent, \$1,000 note is computed as follows:

$$
\begin{aligned}
\text{Maturity Value} &= \text{Principal} + \text{Interest} \\
&= \$1,000 + (\$1,000 \times 8/100 \times 90/365) \\
&= \$1,000 + \$19.73 \\
&= \$1,019.73
\end{aligned}
$$

There are also so-called non-interest-bearing notes. The maturity value is the face value, or principal amount. In this case, the principal includes an implied interest cost.

Accrued Interest

A promissory note received in one accounting period may not be due until a later period. The interest on a note accrues by a small amount each day of the note's duration. As we described in an earlier chapter, the matching rule requires that the accrued interest be apportioned to the periods in which it belongs. For example, assume that the \$1,000, 90-day, 8 percent note discussed above was received on August 31 and that the fiscal year ended on September 30. In this case, 30 days interest, or \$6.58 (\$1,000 × 8/100 × 30/365 = \$6.58), would be earned in the fiscal year that ends on September 30. An adjusting entry would be made to record the interest receivable as an asset and the interest income as revenue. The remainder of the interest income, \$13.15

($1,000 × 8/100 × 60/365), would be recorded as income, and the interest receivable ($6.58) would be shown as received when the note is paid. Note that all the cash for the interest is received when the note is paid, but the interest income is apportioned to two fiscal years.

Dishonored Note

When the maker of a note does not pay the note at maturity, it is said to be a **dishonored note**. The holder, or payee, of a dishonored note should make an entry to transfer the total amount due (including interest income) from Notes Receivable to an account receivable from the debtor. Two objectives are accomplished by transferring a dishonored note into an Accounts Receivable account. First, it leaves only notes that have not matured and are presumably negotiable and collectible in the Notes Receivable account. Second, it establishes a record in the borrower's accounts receivable account that the customer has dishonored a note receivable. Such information may be helpful in deciding whether to extend credit to the customer in the future.

S T O P • R E V I E W • A P P L Y

4-1. What is a promissory note?

4-2. Who is the maker of a promissory note? Who is the payee?

4-3. What is the difference between interest and interest rate?

4-4. What are the maturity dates of the following notes: (a) a three-month note that is dated August 16, (b) a 90-day note that is dated August 16, and (c) a 60-day note that is dated March 25?

Promissory Note Calculations Assume that on December 1, 20x6, a company receives a 90-day, 8 percent, $5,000 note and that the company prepares financial statements monthly.

1. What is the maturity date of the note?

2. How much interest will be earned on the note if it is paid when due?

3. What is the maturity value of the note?

4. If the company's fiscal year ends on December 31, describe the adjusting entry that would be made, including the amount.

5. How much interest will be earned on this note in 20x7?

SOLUTION

1. Maturity date is March 1, determined as follows:

Days remaining in December (31 − 1)	30
Days in January	31
Days in February	28
Days in March	1
Total days	90

2. Interest: $5,000 × 8/100 × 90/365 = $98.63

3. Maturity value: $5,000 + $98.63 = $5,098.63

4. An adjusting entry to accrue 30 days of interest income in the amount of $32.88 ($5,000 × 8/100 × 30/365) would be needed.

5. Interest earned in 20x7: $65.75 ($98.63 − $32.88)

A LOOK BACK AT

NIKE, INC.

In this chapter's Decision Point, we noted that Nike must give the retailers that buy its products time to pay for their purchases, but at the same time, Nike must have enough cash on hand to pay its suppliers. To plan the company's cash flows, Nike's management must address the following questions:

- **How can the company control its cash needs?**
- **How can the company evaluate credit policies and the level of its receivables?**
- **How should the company estimate the value of its receivables?**

As you saw in Figure 1, companies like Nike go through seasonal cycles that affect their cash flows. At times, Nike may have excess cash available that it can invest in a way that earns a return but still permits ready access to cash. At other times, it may have to borrow funds. To ensure that it can borrow funds when it needs to, Nike maintains good relations with its banks.

To evaluate the company's credit policies and the level of its accounts receivable, management can compare the current year's receivable turnover and days' sales uncollected with those ratios in previous years. Using data from Nike's Financial Highlights, we can compute these ratios for 2003 and 2004 as follows (dollars are in millions):

		2004	2003
Receivable Turnover:	$\dfrac{\text{Net Sales}}{\text{Average Accounts Receivable}}$	$\dfrac{\$12,253.1}{(\$2,120.2 + \$2,083.9) \div 2}$	$\dfrac{\$10,697.0}{(\$2,083.9 + \$1,948.7) \div 2}$
		$\dfrac{\$12,253.1}{\$2,102.1}$	$\dfrac{\$10,697.0}{\$2,016.3}$
		5.8 times	5.3 times
Days' Sales Uncollected:	$\dfrac{\text{Number of Days in a Year}}{\text{Receivable Turnover}}$	$\dfrac{365 \text{ days}}{5.8 \text{ times}}$	$\dfrac{365 \text{ days}}{5.3 \text{ times}}$
		62.9 days	68.9 days

Thus, in 2004, Nike achieved a small improvement in its receivable turnover. It also reduced the number of days it takes to collect accounts receivable.

A note in Nike's report to the SEC provides insight into management's ability to estimate losses from uncollectible accounts (amounts are in millions):

	2004	2003	2002	Totals
Uncollectible Accounts Expense	$36.4	$25.8	$23.7	$85.9
Write-off net of recoveries	23.1	25.5	19.6	68.2
Difference	$12.7	$ .3	$ 4.1	$17.7

From this analysis, you can see that management was generally conservative in its estimates. That is, it tended to overestimate the amount of loss from customers who did not pay. This was especially so in 2004. Nike's management explained the over-estimate of expense in 2004 as follows: "Accounts receivable provided cash to the Company due to the improved account management through better utilization of supply chain systems."[17]

CHAPTER REVIEW

REVIEW of Learning Objectives

LO1 Identify and explain the management and ethical issues related to cash and receivables.

The management of cash and receivables is critical to maintaining adequate liquidity. In dealing with these assets, management must (1) consider the need for short-term investing and borrowing as the business's balance of cash fluctuates during seasonal cycles, (2) establish credit policies that balance the need for sales with the ability to collect, (3) evaluate the level of receivables using receivable turnover and days' sales uncollected, (4) assess the need to increase cash flows through the financing of receivables, and (5) understand the importance of ethics in estimating credit losses.

LO2 Define *cash equivalents*, and explain methods of controlling cash, including bank reconciliations.

Cash equivalents are investments that have a term of 90 days or less. Methods of controlling cash include imprest systems; banking services, including electronic funds transfer; and bank reconciliations. A bank reconciliation accounts for the difference between the balance on a company's bank statement and the balance in its Cash account. It involves adjusting for outstanding checks, deposits in transit, service charges, NSF checks, miscellaneous debits and credits, and interest income.

LO3 Apply the allowance method of accounting for uncollectible accounts.

Because of the time lag between credit sales and the time accounts are judged uncollectible, the allowance method is used to match the amount of uncollectible accounts against revenues in any given period. Uncollectible accounts expense is estimated by using either the percentage of net sales method or the accounts receivable aging method. When the first method is used, bad debts are judged to be a certain percentage of sales during the period. When the second method is used, certain percentages are applied to groups of accounts receivable that have been arranged by due dates.

Allowance for Uncollectible Accounts is a contra-asset account to Accounts Receivable. The estimate of uncollectible accounts is debited to Uncollectible Accounts Expense and credited to the allowance account. When an individual account is determined to be uncollectible, it is removed from Accounts Receivable by debiting the allowance account and crediting Accounts Receivable. If the written-off account is later collected, the earlier entry is reversed and the collection is recorded in the normal way.

LO4 Define *promissory note* and make common calculations for promissory notes receivable.

A promissory note is an unconditional promise to pay a definite sum of money on demand or at a future date. Companies that sell durable goods of high value, such as farm machinery and automobiles, often accept promissory notes. Selling these notes to banks is a common financing method. In accounting for promissory notes, it is important to know how to calculate the maturity date, duration of a note, interest and interest rate, and maturity value.

REVIEW of Concepts and Terminology

The following concepts and terms were introduced in this chapter:

Accounts receivable: Short-term financial assets that arise from sales on credit at the wholesale or retail level. **(LO1)**

Accounts receivable aging method: A method of estimating uncollectible accounts based on the assumption that a predictable proportion of each dollar of accounts receivable outstanding will not be collected. **(LO3)**

Aging of accounts receivable: The process of listing each customer's receivable account according to the due date of the account. **(LO3)**

Allowance for Uncollectible Accounts: A contra-asset account that reduces accounts receivable to the amount expected to be collected in cash. Also called *Allowance for Doubtful Accounts* and *Allowance for Bad Debts*. **(LO3)**

Allowance method: A method of accounting for uncollectible accounts by expensing estimated uncollectible accounts in the period in which the related sales take place. **(LO3)**

Bank reconciliation: The process of accounting for the difference between the balance appearing on a company's bank statement and the balance in its Cash account. **(LO2)**

Cash: Coins and currency on hand, checks and money orders from customers, and deposits in checking and savings accounts. **(LO1)**

Cash equivalents: Short-term investments that will revert to cash in 90 days or less from the time they are purchased. **(LO2)**

Compensating balance: A minimum amount that a bank requires a company to keep in its bank account as part of a credit-granting arrangement. **(LO1)**

Contingent liability: A potential liability that can develop into a real liability if a particular event occurs. **(LO1)**

Direct charge-off method: A method of accounting for uncollectible accounts by directly debiting an expense account when bad debts are discovered; it violates the matching rule but is required for computing federal income tax. **(LO3)**

Discounting: A method of selling notes receivable to a bank in which the bank derives its profit by deducting the interest from the maturity value of the note. **(LO1)**

Dishonored note: A promissory note that the maker cannot or will not pay at the maturity date. **(LO4)**

Duration of a note: The time between a promissory note's issue date and its maturity date. **(LO4)**

Electronic funds transfer (EFT): The transfer of funds from one bank to another through electronic communication. **(LO2)**

Factor: An entity that buys accounts receivable. **(LO1)**

Factoring: The sale or transfer of accounts receivable. **(LO1)**

Imprest system: A system for controlling small cash disbursements by establishing a fund at a fixed amount and periodically reimbursing the fund by the amount necessary to restore its original cash balance. **(LO2)**

Installment accounts receivable: Accounts receivable that are payable in a series of time payments. **(LO1)**

Interest: The cost of borrowing money or the return on lending money, depending on whether one is the borrower or the lender. **(LO4)**

Maturity date: The date on which a promissory note must be paid. **(LO4)**

Maturity value: The total proceeds of a promissory note—face value plus interest—at the maturity date. **(LO4)**

Notes payable: Collective term for promissory notes owed by the entity (maker) who promises payment to other entities. **(LO4)**

Notes receivable: Collective term for promissory notes held by the entity to whom payment is promised (payee). **(LO4)**

Percentage of net sales method: A method of estimating uncollectible accounts based on the assumption that a predictable proportion of each dollar of sales will not be collected. **(LO3)**

Promissory note: An unconditional promise to pay a definite sum of money on demand or at a future date. **(LO4)**

Securitization: The grouping of receivables into batches for sale at a discount to companies and investors. **(LO1)**

Short-term financial assets: Assets that arise from cash transactions, the investment of cash, and the extension of credit. **(LO1)**

Trade credit: Credit granted to customers by wholesalers or retailers. **(LO1)**

Uncollectible accounts: Accounts receivable owed by customers who cannot or will not pay. Also called *bad debts*. **(LO1)**

Key Ratios

Days' sales uncollected: A ratio that shows on average how long it takes to collect accounts receivable; 365 Days ÷ Receivable Turnover. **(LO1)**

Receivable turnover: A ratio for measuring the average number of times receivables are turned into cash during an accounting period; Net Sales ÷ Average Accounts Receivable. **(LO1)**

REVIEW Problem

LO1, LO3   **Estimating Uncollectible Accounts and Receivables Analysis**

K/R   Farm Implement Corporation sells merchandise on credit and also accepts notes as payment. During the year ended June 30, the company had net sales of $1,200,000. At the end of the year, it had Accounts Receivable of $400,000 and a debit balance in Allowance for Uncollectible Accounts of $2,100. In the past, approximately 1.5 percent of net sales has been uncollectible. Also, an aging analysis of accounts receivable reveals that $17,000 in accounts receivable appears to be uncollectible.

Required

1. Compute Uncollectible Accounts Expense, and determine the ending balance of Allowance for Uncollectible Accounts and Accounts Receivable, Net, under (a) the percentage of net sales method and (b) the accounts receivable aging method.
2. Compute the receivable turnover and days' sales uncollected using the data from the accounts receivable aging method in requirement 1 and assuming that the prior year's net accounts receivable were $353,000.

Answer to Review Problem

1. Uncollectible Accounts Expense and ending account balances

   a. Percentage of net sales method:
      Uncollectible Accounts Expense = 1.5 percent × $1,200,000 = $18,000
      Allowance for Uncollectible Accounts = $18,000 − $2,100 = $15,900
      Accounts Receivable, Net = $400,000 − $15,900 = $384,100
   b. Accounts receivable aging method:
      Uncollectible Accounts Expense = $2,100 + $17,000 = $19,100
      Allowance for Uncollectible Accounts = $17,000
      Accounts Receivable, Net = $400,000 − $17,000 = $383,000
2. Receivable turnover and days' sales uncollected

$$\text{Receivable Turnover} = \frac{\$1,200,000}{(\$383,000 + \$353,000) \div 2} = 3.3 \text{ times}$$

$$\text{Days' Sales Uncollected} = \frac{365 \text{ days}}{3.3 \text{ times}} = 110.6 \text{ days}$$

CHAPTER ASSIGNMENTS

BUILDING Your Basic Knowledge and Skills

Short Exercises

LO1   **Management Issues**

SE 1. Indicate whether each of the following actions is related to (a) managing cash needs, (b) setting credit policies, (c) financing receivables, or (d) ethically reporting receivables:

1. Selling accounts receivable to a factor
2. Borrowing funds for short-term needs during slow periods
3. Conducting thorough checks of new customers' ability to pay
4. Making every effort to reflect possible future losses accurately

LO1   **Short-Term Liquidity Ratios**

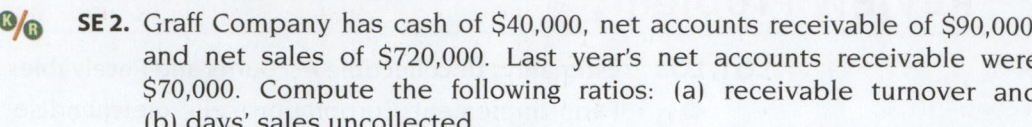

SE 2. Graff Company has cash of $40,000, net accounts receivable of $90,000, and net sales of $720,000. Last year's net accounts receivable were $70,000. Compute the following ratios: (a) receivable turnover and (b) days' sales uncollected.

LO2   **Cash and Cash Equivalents**

SE 3. Compute the amount of cash and cash equivalents on Balsas Company's balance sheet if, on the balance sheet date, it has currency and coins on hand of $250, deposits in checking accounts of $1,500, U.S. Treasury bills due in 80 days of $15,000, and U.S. Treasury bonds due in 200 days of $25,000.

LO2   **Bank Reconciliation**

SE 4. Prepare a bank reconciliation from the following information:

a. Balance per bank statement as of June 30, $4,862.77
b. Balance per books as of June 30, $2,479.48
c. Deposits in transit, $654.24
d. Outstanding checks, $3,028.89
e. Interest on average balance, $8.64

LO3   **Percentage of Net Sales Method**

SE 5. At the end of October, Murphy Company's management estimates the uncollectible accounts expense to be 1 percent of net sales of $1,385,000. Prepare the entry to record the uncollectible accounts expense, assuming the Allowance for Uncollectible Accounts has a debit balance of $7,000.

LO3   **Accounts Receivable Aging Method**

SE 6. An aging analysis on June 30 of the accounts receivable of Sung Corporation indicates that uncollectible accounts amount to $86,000. Prepare the entry to record uncollectible accounts expense under each of the following independent assumptions:

a. Allowance for Uncollectible Accounts has a credit balance of $18,000 before adjustment.
b. Allowance for Uncollectible Accounts has a debit balance of $14,000 before adjustment.

LO3   **Write-off of Accounts Receivable**

SE 7. Koude Corporation, which uses the allowance method, has accounts receivable of $25,400 and an allowance for uncollectible accounts of $4,900. An account receivable from Eva Stursa of $2,200 is deemed to be uncollectible and is written off. What is the amount of net accounts receivable before and after the write-off?

LO4   **Notes Receivable Calculations**

SE 8. On August 25, Champion Company received a 90-day, 9 percent note in settlement of an account receivable in the amount of $20,000. Determine the maturity date, amount of interest on the note, and maturity value.

Exercises

LO1, LO2   **Discussion Questions**

E 1. Develop a brief answer to each of the following questions:

1. Name some businesses whose needs for cash fluctuate during the year. Name some whose needs for cash are relatively stable over the year.

2. Why is it advantageous for a company to finance its receivables?
3. To increase its sales, a company decides to increase its credit terms from 15 to 30 days. What effect will this change in policy have on receivable turnover and days' sales uncollected?
4. How might the receivable turnover and days' sales uncollected reveal that management is consistently underestimating the amount of losses from uncollectible accounts? Is this action ethical?

LO3, LO4   **Discussion Questions**

E 2. Develop a brief answer to each of the following questions:

1. What accounting rule is violated by the direct charge-off method of recognizing uncollectible accounts? Why?
2. In what ways is Allowance for Uncollectible Accounts similar to Accumulated Depreciation? In what ways is it different?
3. Under what circumstances would an accrual of interest income on an interest-bearing note receivable not be required at the end of an accounting period?

LO1   **Management Issues**

E 3. Indicate whether each of the following actions is primarily related to (a) managing cash needs, (b) setting credit policies, (c) financing receivables, or (d) ethically reporting accounts receivable:

1. Buying a U.S. Treasury bill with cash that is not needed for a few months
2. Comparing receivable turnovers for two years
3. Setting a policy that allows customers to buy on credit
4. Selling notes receivable to a financing company
5. Making careful estimates of losses from uncollectible accounts
6. Borrowing funds for short-term needs in a period when sales are low
7. Changing the terms for credit sales in an effort to reduce the days' sales uncollected
8. Revising estimated credit losses in a timely manner when conditions change
9. Establishing a department whose responsibility is to approve customers' credit

LO1   **Short-Term Liquidity Ratios**

   E 4. Using the following data from Kalel Corporation's financial statements, compute the receivable turnover and the days' sales uncollected:

Current assets	
Cash	$ 35,000
Short-term investments	85,000
Notes receivable	120,000
Accounts receivable, net	100,000
Inventory	250,000
Prepaid assets	25,000
Total current assets	$615,000
Current liabilities	
Notes payable	$150,000
Accounts payable	75,000
Accrued liabilities	10,000
Total current liabilities	$235,000
Net sales	$800,000
Last period's accounts receivable, net	$ 90,000

LO2   Cash and Cash Equivalents

E 5. At year end, Sarong Company had currency and coins in cash registers of $5,600, money orders from customers of $10,000, deposits in checking accounts of $64,000, U.S. Treasury bills due in 80 days of $180,000, certificates of deposit at the bank that mature in six months of $200,000, and U.S. Treasury bonds due in one year of $100,000. Calculate the amount of cash and cash equivalents that will be shown on the company's year-end balance sheet.

LO2   Bank Reconciliation

E 6. Prepare a bank reconciliation from the following information:

a. Balance per bank statement as of May 31, $16,655.44
b. Balance per books as of May 31, $12,091.94
c. Deposits in transit, $2,234.81
d. Outstanding checks, $6,808.16
e. Bank service charge, $9.85

LO3   Percentage of Net Sales Method

E 7. At the end of the year, Jung Enterprises estimates the uncollectible accounts expense to be .7 percent of net sales of $15,150,000. The current credit balance of Allowance for Uncollectible Accounts is $25,800. Prepare the entry to record the uncollectible accounts expense. What is the balance of Allowance for Uncollectible Accounts after this adjustment?

LO3   Accounts Receivable Aging Method

E 8. The Accounts Receivable account of Helmond Company shows a debit balance of $104,000 at the end of the year. An aging analysis of the individual accounts indicates estimated uncollectible accounts to be $6,700.

Prepare the entry to record the uncollectible accounts expense under each of the following independent assumptions: (a) Allowance for Uncollectible Accounts has a credit balance of $800 before adjustment, and (b) Allowance for Uncollectible Accounts has a debit balance of $800 before adjustment. What is the balance of Allowance for Uncollectible Accounts after each of these adjustments?

LO3   Aging Method and Net Sales Method Contrasted

E 9. At the beginning of 20xx, the balances for Accounts Receivable and Allowance for Uncollectible Accounts were $215,000 and $15,700 (credit), respectively. During the year, credit sales were $1,600,000, and collections on account were $1,475,000. In addition, $17,500 in uncollectible accounts was written off.

Using T accounts, determine the year-end balances of Accounts Receivable and Allowance for Uncollectible Accounts. Then prepare the year-end adjusting entry to record the uncollectible accounts expense under each of the following conditions. Also show the year-end balance sheet presentation of accounts receivable and allowance for uncollectible accounts.

a. Management estimates the percentage of uncollectible credit sales to be 1.2 percent of total credit sales.
b. Based on an aging of accounts receivable, management estimates the end-of-year uncollectible accounts receivable to be $19,350.

Post the results of each of the entries to the T account for Allowance for Uncollectible Accounts.

LO3 **Aging Method and Net Sales Method Contrasted**

E 10. During 20x7, Luna Supply Company had net sales of $5,700,000. Most of the sales were on credit. At the end of 20x7, the balance of Accounts Receivable was $700,000, and Allowance for Uncollectible Accounts had a debit balance of $24,000. Luna Supply Company's management uses two methods of estimating uncollectible accounts expense: the percentage of net sales method and the accounts receivable aging method. The percentage of uncollectible sales is 1.5 percent of net sales, and based on an aging of accounts receivable, the end-of-year uncollectible accounts total $70,000.

Prepare the end-of-year adjusting entry to record the uncollectible accounts expense under each method. What will the balance of Allowance for Uncollectible Accounts be after each adjustment? Why are the results different? Which method is likely to be more reliable? Why?

LO3 **Aging Method and Net Sales Method Contrasted**

E 11. The Rosewood Parts Company sells merchandise on credit. During the fiscal year ended July 31, the company had net sales of $2,300,000. At the end of the year, it had Accounts Receivable of $600,000 and a debit balance in Allowance for Uncollectible Accounts of $3,400. In the past, approximately 1.4 percent of net sales have proved to be uncollectible. Also, an aging analysis of accounts receivable reveals that $30,000 of the receivables appears to be uncollectible.

Prepare entries in journal form to record uncollectible accounts expense using (a) the percentage of net sales method and (b) the accounts receivable aging method. What is the resulting balance of Allowance for Uncollectible Accounts under each method? How would your answers under each method change if Allowance for Uncollectible Accounts had a credit balance of $3,400 instead of a debit balance? Why do the methods result in different balances?

LO3 **Write-off of Accounts Receivable**

E 12. Calvin Company, which uses the allowance method, has Accounts Receivable of $32,500 and an allowance for uncollectible accounts of $3,200 (credit). The company sold merchandise to Mariko Kimura for $3,600 and later received $1,200 from Kimura. The rest of the amount due from Kimura had to be written off as uncollectible. Using T accounts, show the beginning balances and the effects of the Kimura transactions on Accounts Receivable and Allowance for Uncollectible Accounts. What is the amount of net accounts receivable before and after the write-off?

LO4 **Interest Computations**

E 13. Determine the interest on the following notes:

a. $38,760 at 10 percent for 90 days
b. $27,200 at 12 percent for 60 days
c. $30,600 at 9 percent for 30 days
d. $51,000 at 15 percent for 120 days
e. $18,360 at 6 percent for 60 days

LO4 **Notes Receivable Calculations**

E 14. Determine the maturity date, interest at maturity, and maturity value for a 90-day, 10 percent, $18,000 note from Baptiste Corporation dated February 15.

LO4 **Notes Receivable Calculations**

E 15. Determine the maturity date, interest in 2007 and 2008, and maturity value for a 90-day, 12 percent, $15,000 note from a customer dated December 1, 20x7, assuming a December 31 year-end.

LO4 **Notes Receivable Calculations**

E 16. Determine the maturity date, interest at maturity, and maturity value for each of the following notes:

a. A 60-day, 10 percent, $2,400 note dated January 5 received from J. Gibbs for granting a time extension on a past-due account.

b. A 60-day, 12 percent, $1,500 note dated March 9 received from L. Varela for granting a time extension on a past-due account.

Problems

LO2 **Bank Reconciliation**

P 1. The following information is available for Rosemary Corporation as of April 30, 20xx:

a. Cash on the books as of April 30 amounted to $114,175.28. Cash on the bank statement for the same date was $141,717.08.

b. A deposit of $14,249.84, representing cash receipts of April 30, did not appear on the bank statement.

c. Outstanding checks totaled $7,293.64.

d. A check for $2,420.00 returned with the statement was recorded as $2,024.00. The check was for advertising.

e. The bank service charge for April amounted to $26.00.

f. The bank collected $36,400.00 for Rosemary Corporation on a note. The face value of the note was $36,000.00

g. An NSF check for $1,140.00 from a customer, Chad Altier, was returned with the statement.

h. The bank mistakenly deducted a check for $800.00 that was drawn by Fox Corporation.

i. The bank reported a credit of $460.00 for interest on the average balance.

Required

1. Prepare a bank reconciliation for Rosemary Corporation as of April 30, 20xx.

2. Prepare the necessary entries in journal form from the reconciliation.

3. State the amount of cash that should appear on Rosemary Corporation's balance sheet as of April 30.

4. **User Insight:** Why is a bank reconciliation a necessary internal control?

LO1, LO3 **Methods of Estimating Uncollectible Accounts and Receivables Analysis**

P 2. On December 31 of last year, the balance sheet of Vaslor Company had Accounts Receivable of $298,000 and a credit balance in Allowance for Uncollectible Accounts of $20,300. During the current year, Vaslor Company's records included the following selected activities: (a) sales on account, $1,195,000; (b) sales returns and allowances, $73,000; (c) collections from customers, $1,150,000; and (d) accounts written off as worthless, $16,000. In the past, 1.6 percent of Vaslor Company's net sales have been uncollectible.

Required

1. Prepare T accounts for Accounts Receivable and Allowance for Uncollectible Accounts. Enter the beginning balances, and show the effects on

these accounts of the items listed above, summarizing the year's activity. Determine the ending balance of each account.

2. Compute Uncollectible Accounts Expense and determine the ending balance of Allowance for Uncollectible Accounts under (a) the percentage of net sales method and (b) the accounts receivable aging method. Assume that an aging of the accounts receivable shows that $20,000 may be uncollectible.

3. Compute the receivable turnover and days' sales uncollected, using the data from the accounts receivable aging method in requirement **2**.

4. **User Insight:** How do you explain that the two methods used in requirement **2** result in different amounts for Uncollectible Accounts Expense? What rationale underlies each method?

LO3 Accounts Receivable Aging Method

 P 3. Thant Company uses the accounts receivable aging method to estimate uncollectible accounts. At the beginning of the year, the balance of the Accounts Receivable account was a debit of $88,430, and the balance of Allowance for Uncollectible Accounts was a credit of $7,200. During the year, the store had sales on account of $473,000, sales returns and allowances of $4,200, worthless accounts written off of $7,900, and collections from customers of $450,730. At the end of year (December 31), a junior accountant for Thant Company was preparing an aging analysis of accounts receivable. At the top of page 6 of the report, the following totals appeared:

Customer Account	Total	Not Yet Due	1–30 Days Past Due	31–60 Days Past Due	61–90 Days Past Due	Over 90 Days Past Due
Balance Forward	$89,640	$49,030	$24,110	$9,210	$3,990	$3,300

To finish the analysis, the following accounts need to be classified:

Account	Amount	Due Date
B. Singh	$ 930	Jan. 14 (next year)
L. Wells	620	Dec. 24
A. Roc	1,955	Sept. 28
T. Cila	2,100	Aug. 16
M. Mix	375	Dec. 14
S. Price	2,685	Jan. 23 (next year)
J. Wendt	295	Nov. 5
	$8,960	

From past experience, the company has found that the following rates are realistic for estimating uncollectible accounts:

Time	Percentage Considered Uncollectible
Not yet due	2
1–30 days past due	5
31–60 days past due	15
61–90 days past due	25
Over 90 days past due	50

Required

1. Complete the aging analysis of accounts receivable.
2. Compute the end-of-year balances (before adjustments) of Accounts Receivable and Allowance for Uncollectible Accounts.
3. Prepare an analysis computing the estimated uncollectible accounts.

4. Calculate Thant Company's estimated uncollectible accounts expense for the year (round the amount to the nearest whole dollar).

5. **User Insight:** What role do estimates play in applying the aging analysis? What factors might affect these estimates?

LO4 **Notes Receivable Calculations**

P 4. Abraham Importing Company engaged in the following transactions involving promissory notes:

May 3 Sold engines to Anton Company for $60,000 in exchange for a 90-day, 12 percent promissory note.

16 Sold engines to Yu Company for $32,000 in exchange for a 60-day, 13 percent note.

31 Sold engines to Yu Company for $30,000 in exchange for a 90-day, 11 percent note.

Required

1. For each of the notes, determine the (a) maturity date, (b) interest on the note, and (c) maturity value.

2. Assume that the fiscal year for Abraham Importing Company ends on June 30. How much interest income should be recorded on that date?

3. **User Insight:** What are the effects of the transactions in May on cash flows for the year ended June 30?

Alternate Problems

LO2 **Bank Reconciliation**

P 5. The following information is available for Abdul Saleem, Inc., as of May 31, 20xx:

a. Cash on the books as of May 31 amounted to $42,754.16. Cash on the bank statement for the same date was $52,351.46.

b. A deposit of $5,220.94, representing cash receipts of May 31, did not appear on the bank statement.

c. Outstanding checks totaled $3,936.80.

d. A check for $1,920.00 returned with the statement was recorded incorrectly in the check register as $1,380.00. The check was for a cash purchase of merchandise.

e. The bank service charge for May amounted to $25.

f. The bank collected $12,240.00 for Abdul Saleem, Inc., on a note. The face value of the note was $12,000.00.

g. An NSF check for $183.56 from a customer, Ann Greeno, was returned with the statement.

h. The bank mistakenly charged to the company account a check for $850.00 drawn by another company.

i. The bank reported that it had credited the account for $240.00 in interest on the average balance for May.

Required

1. Prepare a bank reconciliation for Abdul Saleem, Inc., as of May 31, 20xx.

2. Prepare the entries in journal form necessary to adjust the accounts.

3. What amount of cash should appear on Abdul Saleem, Inc.'s balance sheet as of May 31?

4. **User Insight:** Why is a bank reconciliation considered an important control over cash?

LO1, LO3 **Methods of Estimating Uncollectible Accounts and Receivables Analysis**

P 6. Hernandez Company had an Accounts Receivable balance of $320,000 and a credit balance in Allowance for Uncollectible Accounts of $16,700 at January 1, 20xx. During the year, the company recorded the following transactions:

a. Sales on account, $1,052,000
b. Sales returns and allowances by credit customers, $53,400
c. Collections from customers, $993,000
d. Worthless accounts written off, $19,800

The company's past history indicates that 2.5 percent of its net credit sales will not be collected.

Required

1. Prepare T accounts for Accounts Receivable and Allowance for Uncollectible Accounts. Enter the beginning balances, and show the effects on these accounts of the items listed above, summarizing the year's activity. Determine the ending balance of each account.

2. Compute Uncollectible Accounts Expense and determine the ending balance of Allowance for Uncollectible Accounts under (a) the percentage of net sales method and (b) the accounts receivable aging method, assuming an aging of the accounts receivable shows that $24,000 may be uncollectible.

3. Compute the receivable turnover and days' sales uncollected, using the data from the accounts receivable aging method in requirement **2**.

4. **User Insight:** How do you explain that the two methods used in requirement **2** result in different amounts for Uncollectible Accounts Expense? What rationale underlies each method?

LO 3 **Accounts Receivable Aging Method**

P 7. The Fossell Fashions Store uses the accounts receivable aging method to estimate uncollectible accounts. On February 1, 20x7, the balance of the Accounts Receivable account was a debit of $446,341, and the balance of Allowance for Uncollectible Accounts was a credit of $43,000. During the year, the store had sales on account of $3,724,000, sales returns and allowances of $63,000, worthless accounts written off of $44,300, and collections from customers of $3,214,000. As part of the end-of-year (January 31, 20x8) procedures, an aging analysis of accounts receivable is prepared. The analysis, which is partially complete, is as follows:

Customer Account	Total	Not Yet Due	1–30 Days Past Due	31–60 Days Past Due	61–90 Days Past Due	Over 90 Days Past Due
Balance Forward	$793,791	$438,933	$149,614	$106,400	$57,442	$41,402

To finish the analysis, the following accounts need to be classified:

Account	Amount	Due Date
J. Curtis	$10,977	Jan. 15
T. Dawson	9,314	Feb. 15 (next fiscal year)
L. Zapata	8,664	Dec. 20
R. Copa	780	Oct. 1
E. Land	14,810	Jan. 4
S. Qadri	6,316	Nov. 15
A. Rosenthal	4,389	Mar. 1 (next fiscal year)
	$55,250	

From past experience, the company has found that the following rates are realistic for estimating uncollectible accounts:

Time	Percentage Considered Uncollectible
Not yet due	2
1–30 days past due	5
31–60 days past due	15
61–90 days past due	25
Over 90 days past due	50

Required

1. Complete the aging analysis of accounts receivable.
2. Compute the end-of-year balances (before adjustments) of Accounts Receivable and Allowance for Uncollectible Accounts.
3. Prepare an analysis computing the estimated uncollectible accounts.
4. How much is Fossell Fashion Store's estimated uncollectible accounts expense for the year? (Round the adjustment to the nearest whole dollar.)
5. **User Insight:** What role do estimates play in applying the aging analysis? What factors might affect these estimates?

≡ ENHANCING Your Knowledge, Skills, and Critical Thinking

Conceptual Understanding Cases

LO1 **Role of Credit Sales**

C 1. Mitsubishi Corp., a broadly diversified Japanese corporation, instituted a credit plan called Three Diamonds for customers who buy its major electronic products, such as large-screen televisions and videotape recorders, from specified retail dealers.[18] Under the plan, approved customers who make purchases in July of one year do not have to make any payments until September of the next year. Nor do they have to pay interest during the intervening months. Mitsubishi pays the dealer the full amount less a small fee, sends the customer a Mitsubishi credit card, and collects from the customer at the specified time.

What was Mitsubishi's motivation for establishing such generous credit terms? What costs are involved? What are the accounting implications?

LO1, LO3 **Role of Estimates in Accounting for Receivables**

C 2. CompuCredit is a credit card issuer in Atlanta. It prides itself on making credit cards available to almost anybody in a matter of seconds over the Internet. The cost to the consumer is an interest rate of 28 percent, about double that of companies that provide cards only to customers with good credit. Despite its high interest rate, CompuCredit has been successful, reporting 1.9 million accounts and an income of approximately $100 million in a recent year. To calculate its income, the company estimates that 10 percent of its $1.3 billion in accounts receivable will not be paid; the industry average is 7 percent. Some analysts have been critical of CompuCredit for being too optimistic in its projections of losses.[19]

Why are estimates necessary in accounting for receivables? If CompuCredit were to use the same estimate of losses as other companies in its industry, what would its income have been for the year? How would one determine if CompuCredit's estimate of losses is reasonable?

LO1 **Receivables Financing**

C 3. Gellis Appliances, Inc., located in central Michigan, is a small manufacturer of washing machines and dryers. Gellis sells most of its appliances to large, established discount retail companies that market the appliances under their own names. Gellis sells the appliances on trade credit terms of n/60. If a customer wants a longer term, however, Gellis will accept a note with a term of up to nine months. At present, the company is having cash flow troubles and needs $10 million immediately. Its cash balance is $400,000, its accounts receivable balance is $4.6 million, and its notes receivable balance is $7.4 million.

How might Gellis Appliance's management use its accounts receivable and notes receivable to raise the cash it needs? What are the company's prospects for raising the needed cash?

Interpreting Financial Reports

LO1 **Comparison and Interpretation of Ratios**

C 4. **Fosters Group Limited** and **Heineken N.V.** are two well-known beer companies. Fosters is an Australian company, and Heineken is Dutch. Fosters is about half the size of Heineken.

Ratios can help in comparing and understanding companies that are different in size and that use different currencies. For example, the receivable turnovers for Fosters and Heineken in 2003 and 2002 were as follows:[20]

	2003	2002
Fosters	5.6 times	3.2 times
Heineken	6.7 times	6.7 times

What do the ratios tell you about the credit policies of the two companies? How long does it take each, on average, to collect a receivable? What do the ratios tell you about the companies' relative needs for capital to finance receivables? Which company is improving? Can you tell which company has a better credit policy? Explain your answers.

Decision Analysis Using Excel

LO1, LO3 **Accounting for Accounts Receivable**

C 5. Mirador Products Co. is a major consumer goods company that sells over 3,000 products in 135 countries. The company's annual report to the Securities and Exchange Commission presented the following data (in thousands) pertaining to net sales and accounts related to accounts receivable for 2007, 2006, and 2005.

	2007	2006	2005
Net sales	$9,820,000	$9,730,000	$9,888,000
Accounts receivable	1,046,000	1,048,000	1,008,000
Allowance for uncollectible accounts	37,200	42,400	49,000
Uncollectible accounts expense	30,000	33,400	31,600
Uncollectible accounts written off	38,600	40,200	35,400
Recoveries of accounts previously written off	3,400	200	2,000

1. Compute the ratio of uncollectible accounts expense to net sales and to accounts receivable, and the ratio of allowance for uncollectible accounts to accounts receivable for 2007, 2006, and 2005.
2. Compute the receivable turnover and days' sales uncollected for each year, assuming 2004 net accounts receivable were $930,000,000.

3. What is your interpretation of the ratios? Describe management's attitude toward the collectibility of accounts receivable over the three-year period.

Annual Report Case: CVS Corporation

LO1, LO2, LO3   **Cash and Receivables**

C 6. Refer to **CVS Corporation's** annual report in the Supplement to Chapter 1 to answer the following questions:

1. What amount of cash and cash equivalents did CVS Corporation have in 2004? Do you suppose most of that amount is cash in the bank or cash equivalents?
2. CVS does not disclose an allowance for uncollectible accounts. How do you explain the lack of disclosure?
3. What do you think CVS's seasonal needs for cash are? Where in CVS's financial statements is the seasonality of sales discussed?

Comparison Case: CVS Versus Walgreens

LO1   **Accounts Receivable Analysis**

    C 7. Refer to the **CVS** annual report in the Supplement to Chapter 1 and to the following data (in millions) for Walgreens: net sales, $37,508.2 and $32,505.4 for 2004 and 2003, respectively; accounts receivable, net, $1,169.1 and $1,017.8 for 2004 and 2003, respectively.

1. Compute receivable turnover and days' sales uncollected for 2004 and 2003 for CVS and Walgreens. Accounts Receivable in 2002 were $1,019.3 million for CVS and $954.8 million for Walgreens.
2. Do you discern any differences in the two companies' credit policies? Explain your answer.

Ethical Dilemma Case

LO1, LO3   **Ethics and Uncollectible Accounts**

C 8. Anderson Interiors, a successful retail furniture company, is located in an affluent suburb where a major insurance company has just announced a restructuring that will lay off 4,000 employees. Anderson Interiors sells quality furniture, usually on credit. Accounts Receivable is one of its major assets. Although the company's annual uncollectible accounts losses are not out of line, they represent a sizable amount. The company depends on bank loans for its financing. Sales and net income have declined in the past year, and some customers are falling behind in paying their accounts.

Lucretia Anderson, the owner of the business, knows that the bank's loan officer likes to see a steady performance. She has therefore instructed the company's controller to underestimate the uncollectible accounts this year to show a small growth in earnings. Anderson believes this action is justified because earnings in future years will average out the losses, and since the company has a history of success, she believes the adjustments are meaningless accounting measures anyway.

Are Anderson's actions ethical? Would any parties be harmed by her actions? How important is it to try to be accurate in estimating losses from uncollectible accounts?

Internet Case

LO1, LO3   Comparison of J.C. Penney, Inc., and Dillard's, Inc.

C 9. Access the annual reports of **J.C. Penney** and **Dillard's**. Find the accounts receivable on each company's balance sheet and the notes to the financial statements that are related to those accounts. Which company has the most accounts receivable as a percentage of total assets? What is the percentage of the allowance account to gross accounts receivable for each company? Which company experienced the highest loss rate on its receivables? Why do you think there is a difference? Do the companies finance their receivables? Be prepared to discuss your findings in class.

Group Activity Case

LO1   Effects of Credit Policies

C 10. **Tenet Healthcare Corp.**, the second largest publicly traded hospital chain in the United States, had a large amount of uncollectible accounts expense because so many patients were unable to pay their medical bills. Its uncollectible accounts expense amounted to about 11 percent of its revenues. After management analyzed the problem, they found that 70 percent of the losses came from uninsured patients and 30 percent from those who had insurance. The company realized that many of the uninsured could not be expected to pay and that the large amount of the bills simply discouraged patients from seeking health care. The company decided to start charging these patients less, hoping it could eliminate 40 to 60 percent of its bad debts loss. The company's chief financial officer said, "A significant amount of the revenue will never be recorded in the first place due to this pricing, so that it will not have to be written off as bad debt.[21]

In informal groups in class, discuss and report on the following questions: What effect will the new pricing policy have on the company's reported earnings? Why would the company want to show lower uncollectible accounts expense? Do you think the new policy has ethical ramifications?

Business Communication Case

LO1, LO2   Cash Management and Cash Equivalents

C 11. Collegiate Publishing Company publishes college textbooks in the sciences and humanities. More than 50 percent of Collegiate Publishing's sales occur in July, August, and December. The company's cash balance builds up until sometime after the sales take place and the books are paid for. During the rest of the year, its sales are low. The company's treasurer keeps the cash in a bank checking account earning little or no interest and pays bills from this account as they come due. To survive periods when cash receipts are low, Collegiate Publishing Company sometimes borrows money, and it repays the loans in the months when cash receipts are largest.

The company is currently considering two plans of action. First, it would work with the bookstores to implement electronic funds transfer (EFT) for payment. Second, it would invest in short-term (less than 90 days) securities that pay a higher rate of interest than the checking account.

Write a memorandum to the president that lays out the advantages of EFT and states the accounting implications (if any) of the plan to invest in short-term securities.

Current Liabilities and the Time Value of Money

Although some current liabilities, such as accounts payable, are recorded when a company makes a purchase, others accrue during an accounting period and are not recorded until adjusting entries are made at the end of the period. In addition, the value of some accruals must be estimated. If accrued liabilities are not recognized and valued properly, both liabilities and expenses will be understated on the financial statements, making the company's performance look better than it actually is. The time value of money is a concept that underlies both assets and liabilities.

LEARNING OBJECTIVES

Making a Statement

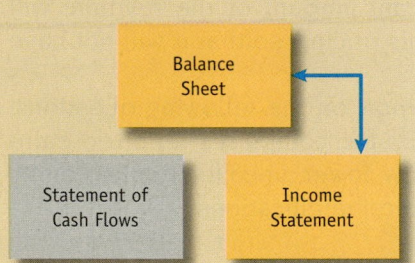

Measurement of unearned revenues and accrued expenses impacts the amount of current liabilities on the balance sheet and revenues and expenses on the income statement.

LO1 Identify the management issues related to current liabilities.

LO2 Identify, compute, and record definitely determinable and estimated current liabilities.

LO3 Distinguish *contingent liabilities* from *commitments*.

LO4 Define the *time value of money,* and apply it to future and present values.

LO5 Apply the time value of money to simple accounting situations.

- How does Amazon.com's decision to incur heavy debt relate to the goals of the business?
- Is the level of accounts payable in the operating cycle satisfactory?
- Has the company properly identified and accounted for all its current liabilities?

Amazon.com is one of the few Internet companies that survived the dot.com crash of 2001. Its management of cash flows and liabilities played a big role in its survival. As you can see in Amazon.com's Financial Highlights, its total liabilities in 2004 were almost $3.5 billion. At that time, its total assets were not quite $3.3 billion. The deficit in stockholders' equity was the result of losses that the high-flying company accumulated in its start-up years.[1]

Managing liabilities is obviously important to achieving profitability and liquidity. A company must incur liabilities to support its operating and financing activities, but payment of these obligations requires an outflow of cash. Achieving the appropriate level of liabilities is critical to a company's success, especially for a new company. If a company has too few liabilities, it may not be earning up to its potential. If it has too many liabilities, it may be incurring excessive risks. A company with heavy debt is vulnerable to failure.

AMAZON.COM'S FINANCIAL HIGHLIGHTS
(In thousands)

Current Liabilities	2004	2003
Accounts payable	$1,141,733	$ 819,811
Accrued expenses and other current liabilities	361,128	317,730
Unearned revenue	41,099	37,844
Interest payable	74,059	73,100
Current maturities of long-term debt	2,381	4,216
Total current liabilities	$1,620,400	$1,252,701
Long-term debt	1,855,319	1,945,439
Total liabilities	$3,475,719	$3,198,140

Management Issues Related to Current Liabilities

LO1 Identify the management issues related to current liabilities.

Current liabilities require careful management of liquidity and cash flows, as well as close monitoring of accounts payable. In reporting on current liabilities, managers must understand how they should be recognized, valued, classified, and disclosed.

Managing Liquidity and Cash Flows

The primary reason a company incurs current liabilities is to meet its needs for cash during the operating cycle. The operating cycle is the process of converting cash to cash through a series of purchases, sales, and collection of accounts receivable. Most current liabilities arise in support of this cycle, as when accounts payable arise from purchases of inventory, accrued expenses arise from operating costs, and unearned revenues arise from customers' advance payments. Companies incur short-term debt to raise cash during periods of inventory build-up or while waiting for collection of receivables. They use the cash to pay the portion of long-term debt that is currently due and to pay liabilities arising from operations.

Failure to manage the cash flows related to current liabilities can have serious consequences for a business. For instance, if suppliers are not paid on time, they may withhold shipments that are vital to a company's operations. Continued failure to pay current liabilities can lead to bankruptcy. To evaluate a company's ability to pay its current liabilities, analysts often use two measures of liquidity—working capital and the current ratio, both of which we defined in an earlier chapter. Current liabilities are a key component of both these measures. They typically equal from 25 to 50 percent of total assets.

As shown below (in thousands), **Amazon.com's** short-term liquidity as measured by working capital was positive in 2003 and improved in 2004:

	Current Assets	−	Current Liabilities	=	Working Capital
2003	$1,820,809	−	$1,252,701	=	$568,108
2004	$2,539,396	−	$1,620,400	=	$918,996

Amazon.com's current ratio (current assets divided by current liabilities) also improved, from 1.5 times in 2003 to 1.6 times in 2004.

Thus, despite its deficit in stockholders' equity, Amazon.com was able to maintain short-term liquidity. Companies commonly have problems maintaining liquidity in their early years, but Amazon.com managed its debt well. Further, as shown in its Financial Highlights, Amazon.com was able to raise funds by incurring long-term debt, which allowed it to acquire the facilities and software it needed in its operations.

Evaluating Accounts Payable

Another consideration in managing liquidity and cash flows is the time suppliers give a company to pay for purchases. Measures commonly used to assess a company's ability to pay within a certain time frame are **payables turnover** and **days' payable**. Payables turnover is the number of times, on average, that a company pays its accounts payable in an accounting period. Days' payable shows how long, on average, a company takes to pay its accounts payables.

To measure payables turnover for **Amazon.com**, we must first calculate purchases by adjusting cost of goods sold for the change in inventory. An increase in inventory means purchases were more than cost of goods sold; a

FOCUS ON BUSINESS PRACTICE

Debt Problems Can Plague Even Well-Known Companies.

In a Wall Street horror story that illustrates the importance of managing current liabilities, **Xerox Corporation**, one of the most storied names in American business, found itself combating rumors that it was facing bankruptcy. Following a statement by Xerox's CEO that the company's financial model was "unsustainable," management was forced to defend the company's liquidity by saying it had adequate funds to continue operations. But in a report filed with the SEC, management acknowledged that it had tapped into its $7 billion line of bank credit for more than $3 billion to pay off short-term debt that was coming due. Unable to secure more money from any other source to pay these debts, Xerox had no choice but to turn to the line of credit from its bank. Had it run out, the company might well have gone bankrupt.[2] Fortunately, Xerox was able to restructure its line of credit to stay in business.

decrease means purchases were less than cost of goods sold. Amazon.com's cost of goods sold in 2004 was $5,319,127 thousand, and its inventory increased by $185,792 thousand. Its payables turnover is computed as follows:

$$\text{Payables Turnover} = \frac{\text{Cost of Goods Sold} + \text{Change in Merchandise Inventory}}{\text{Average Accounts Payable}}$$

$$= \frac{\$5,319,127 + \$185,792}{(\$1,141,733 + \$819,811) \div 2}$$

$$= \frac{\$5,504,919}{\$980,772} = 5.6 \text{ times}$$

To find the days' payable, the number of days in a year is divided by the payables turnover:

$$\text{Days' Payable} = \frac{365 \text{ days}}{\text{Payables Turnover}} = \frac{365 \text{ days}}{5.6} = 65.2 \text{ days}$$

The payables turnover of 5.6 times and days' payable of 65.2 days indicate that the credit terms Amazon.com receives from its suppliers are excellent. In other industries, the credit terms are not nearly as favorable. As you can see in Figures 1 and 2, companies in other industries have higher payables turnover and

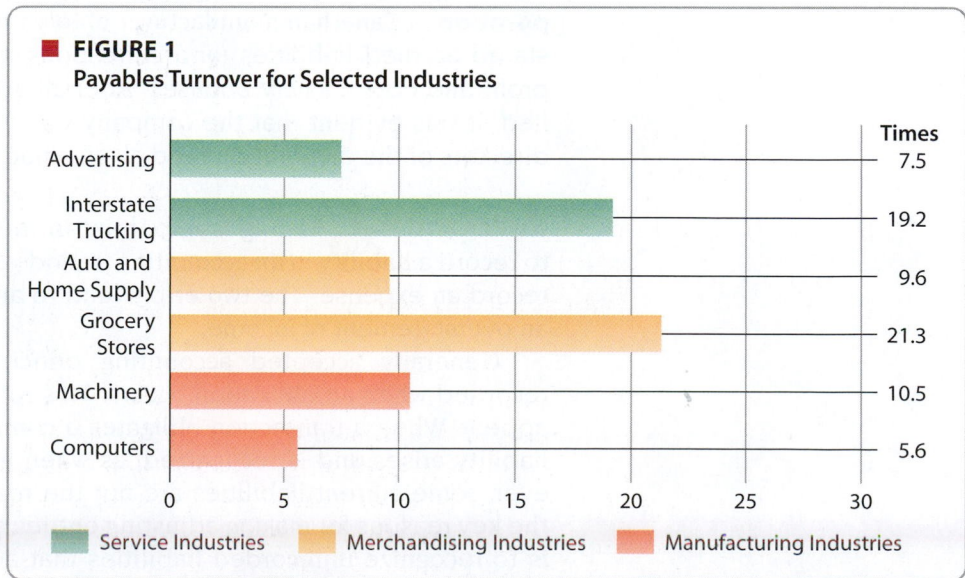

■ **FIGURE 1**
Payables Turnover for Selected Industries

Industry	Times
Advertising	7.5
Interstate Trucking	19.2
Auto and Home Supply	9.6
Grocery Stores	21.3
Machinery	10.5
Computers	5.6

Service Industries   Merchandising Industries   Manufacturing Industries

Source: Data from Dun & Bradstreet, *Industry Norms and Key Business Ratios,* 2003–2004.

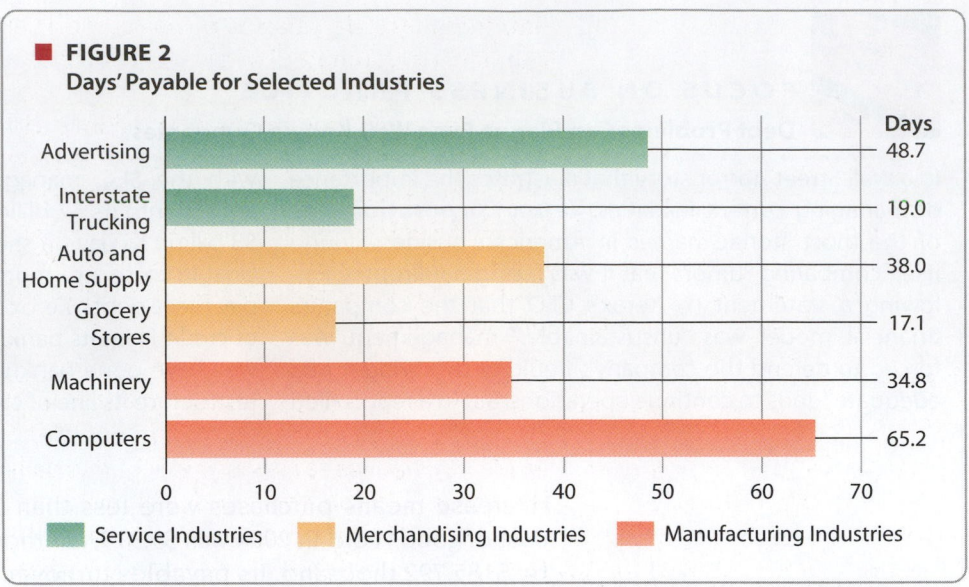

FIGURE 2
Days' Payable for Selected Industries

Source: Data from Dun & Bradstreet, *Industry Norms and Key Business Ratios,* 2003–2004.

lower days' payable than Amazon.com. The company's inventory turnover ratio of approximately 13 day is also extraordinary. These ratios have been a major factor in Amazon.com's ability to maintain adequate liquidity. To get a full picture of a company's operating cycle and liquidity, you should consider payables turnover and days' payable in relation to inventory and receivable turnovers and their related number of days' ratios.

Reporting Liabilities

In deciding whether to buy stock in a company or lend money to it, investors and creditors must evaluate not only the company's current liabilities, but its future obligations as well. In doing so, they have to rely on the integrity of the company's financial statements.

Ethical reporting of liabilities requires that they be properly recognized, valued, classified, and disclosed. In one notable case involving unethical reporting of liabilities, the CEO and other employees of **Nortel Networks Corporation**, a Canadian manufacturer of telecommunications equipment, understated accrued liabilities (and corresponding expenses) in order to report a profit and obtain salary bonuses. After all accrued liabilities had been identified, it was evident that the company was in fact losing money. The board of directors of the corporation fired all who had been involved.[3]

Recognition   Timing is important in the recognition of liabilities. Failure to record a liability in an accounting period very often goes along with failure to record an expense. The two errors lead to an understatement of expense and an overstatement of income.

Generally accepted accounting principles require that a liability be recorded when an obligation occurs. This rule is harder to apply than it might appear. When a transaction obligates a company to make future payments, a liability arises and is recognized, as when goods are bought on credit. However, some current liabilities are not the result of direct transactions. One of the key reasons for making adjusting entries at the end of an accounting period is to recognize unrecorded liabilities that accrue during the period. Accrued liabilities include salaries payable and interest payable. Other liabilities that can only be estimated, such as taxes payable, must also be recognized through adjusting entries.

Agreements for future transactions do not have to be recognized. For instance, **Amazon.com** might agree to pay an executive $250,000 a year for a period of three years, or it might agree to buy an unspecified amount of advertising at a certain price over the next five years. Such contracts, though they are definite commitments, are not considered liabilities because they are for future—not past—transactions. Because there is no current obligation, no liability is recognized.

Valuation   On the balance sheet, a liability is generally valued at the amount of money needed to pay the debt or at the fair market value of the goods or services to be delivered. Disclosure of the fair value of liabilities may be required in the notes to the financial statements.

The amount of most liabilities is definitely known. For example, **Amazon.com** sells a large number of gift certificates that are redeemable in the future. The amount of the liability (unearned revenue) is known, but the exact timing is not known.

Some companies, however, must estimate future liabilities. For example, an automobile dealer that sells a car with a one-year warranty must provide parts and service during the year. The obligation is definite because the sale has occurred, but the amount of the obligation can only be estimated. Such estimates are usually based on past experience and anticipated changes in the business environment.

Classification   As you may recall from our discussion of classified balance sheets in an earlier chapter, **current liabilities** are debts and obligations that a company expects to satisfy within one year or within its normal operating cycle, whichever is longer. These liabilities are normally paid out of current assets or with cash generated by operations. **Long-term liabilities** are liabilities due beyond one year or beyond the normal operating cycle. The purpose of incurring long-term liabilities is to finance long-term assets. For example, **Amazon.com** incurs long-term debt to finance its warehouse and distribution system. The distinction between current and long-term liabilities is important because it affects the evaluation of a company's liquidity.

Disclosure   A company may have to include additional explanation of some liability accounts in the notes to its financial statements. For example, if a company's Notes Payable account is large, it should disclose the balances, maturity dates, interest rates, and other features of the debts in an explanatory note. Any special credit arrangements should also be disclosed. For example, in a note to its financial statements, **Hershey Foods Corporation**, the famous candy company, discloses a portion of its credit arrangements:

> **Short-Term Debt and Financing Arrangements**
> The company maintained short-term and long-term credit facilities with a syndicate of banks in the amount of $400 million.[4]

Unused lines of credit allow a company to borrow on short notice up to the credit limit, with little or no negotiation. Thus, the type of disclosure in Hershey's note is helpful in assessing whether a company has additional borrowing power.

STOP • REVIEW • APPLY

1-1. What are three examples of current liabilities?

1-2. What are two measures of liquidity used in evaluating a firm's ability to pay its current liabilities?

1-3. What does payables turnover tell you about a company's liquidity?

1-4. Why is the timing of liability recognition important?

1-5. What is the rule for classifying a liability as current?

1-6. Manly Company has an unused line of bank credit of $100,000. Should Manly record this line of credit as a liability and disclose it in its financial statements?

Suggested answers to all Stop, Review, and Apply questions follow the appendixes.

Common Types of Current Liabilities

> **LO2**   Identify, compute, and record definitely determinable and estimated current liabilities.

As noted earlier, a company incurs current liabilities to meet its needs for cash during the operating cycle. These liabilities fall into two major groups: definitely determinable liabilities and estimated liabilities.

Definitely Determinable Liabilities

Study Note

On the balance sheet, the order of presentation for current liabilities is not as strict as for current assets. Generally, accounts payable or notes payable appear first, and the rest of current liabilities follow.

Current liabilities that are set by contract or statute and that can be measured exactly are called **definitely determinable liabilities**. The problems in accounting for these liabilities are to determine their existence and amount and to see that they are recorded properly. The most common definitely determinable liabilities are described below.

Accounts Payable   Accounts payable (sometimes called *trade accounts payable*) are short-term obligations to suppliers for goods and services. The amount in the Accounts Payable account is generally supported by an accounts payable subsidiary ledger, which contains an individual account for each person or company to which money is owed. As shown in the Financial Highlights at the beginning of the chapter, accounts payable make up more than half of **Amazon.com's** current liabilities.

Bank Loans and Commercial Paper   Management often establishes a **line of credit** with a bank. This arrangement allows the company to borrow funds when they are needed to finance current operations. In a note to its financial statements, **Goodyear Tire & Rubber Company** describes its lines of credit as follows: "At December 31, 2004, we had credit arrangements totaling $7.30 billion, of which $1.12 billion were unused."[5]

Although a company signs a promissory note for the full amount of a line of credit, it has great flexibility in using the available funds. It can increase its borrowing up to the limit when it needs cash and reduce the amount borrowed when it generates enough cash of its own. Both the amount borrowed and the interest rate charged by the bank may change daily. The bank may require the company to meet certain financial goals (such as maintaining specific profit margins, current ratios, or debt to equity ratios) to retain its line of credit.

Companies with excellent credit ratings can borrow short-term funds by issuing **commercial paper**, which are unsecured loans (i.e., loans not backed up by any specific assets) that are sold to the public, usually through professionally managed investment firms. Highly rated companies rely heavily on commercial paper to raise short-term funds, but they can quickly lose access to this means of borrowing if their credit rating drops. Because of disappointing operating results in recent years, well-known companies like **DaimlerChrysler**, **Lucent Technologies**, and **Motorola** have lost some or all of their ability to issue commercial paper.

The portion of a line of credit currently borrowed and the amount of commercial paper issued are usually combined with notes payable in the current liabilities section of the balance sheet. Details are disclosed in a note to the financial statements.

Notes Payable Short-term notes payable are obligations represented by promissory notes. A company may sign promissory notes to obtain bank loans, pay suppliers for goods and services, or secure credit from other sources.

Interest is usually stated separately on the face of the note, as shown in Figure 3. The entries to record the note in Figure 3 are as follows:

> **Study Note**
>
> Only the used portion of a line of credit is recognized as a liability in the financial statements.

ISSUANCE

A	=	L	+	SE
+5,000		+5,000		

Oct. 30	Cash	5,000	
	Notes Payable		5,000
	Issued 60-day, 12% promissory note		

PAYMENT

A	=	L	+	SE
−5,098.63		−5,000		−98.63

Oct. 30	Notes Payable	5,000.00	
	Interest Expense	98.63	
	Cash		5,098.63
	Payment of promissory note with $100 interest		

$$\$5,000 \times \frac{12}{100} \times \frac{60}{365} = \$98.63$$

■ **FIGURE 3**
Promissory Note

> Chicago, Illinois _____ August 31, 20xx _____
>
> Sixty days after date I promise to pay First Federal Bank the sum of $5,000 with interest at the rate of 12% per annum.
>
> *Sandra Caron*
> Caron Corporation

Accrued Liabilities

As we noted earlier, a key reason for making adjusting entries at the end of an accounting period is to recognize liabilities that are not already in the accounting records. This practice applies to any type of liability. As you will see, accrued liabilities (also called *accrued expenses*) can include estimated liabilities.

Here, we focus on interest payable, a definitely determinable liability. Interest accrues daily on interest-bearing notes. In accordance with the matching rule, an adjusting entry is made at the end of each accounting period to record the interest obligation up to that point. For example, if the accounting period of the maker of the note in Figure 3 ends on September 30, or 30 days after the issuance of the 60-day note, the adjusting entry would be as follows:

A = L + SE		
+49.32 −49.32		

Sept. 30	Interest Expense	49.32	
	Interest Payable		49.32
	To record 30 days' interest expense on promissory note		

$$\$5,000 \times \frac{12}{100} \times \frac{30}{365} = \$49.32$$

As can be seen in **Amazon.com's** Financial Highlights, the company had accrued interest payable of over $70 million in both 2003 and 2004.

Dividends Payable

As you know, cash dividends are a distribution of earnings to a corporation's stockholders, and a corporation's board of directors has the sole authority to declare them. The corporation has no liability for dividends until the date of declaration. The time between that date and the date of payment of dividends is usually short. During this brief interval, the dividends declared are considered current liabilities of the corporation.

Sales and Excise Taxes Payable

Most states and many cities levy a sales tax on retail transactions, and the federal government imposes an excise tax on some products, such as gasoline. A merchant that sells goods subject to these taxes must collect the taxes and forward them periodically to the appropriate government agency. Until the merchant remits the amount it has collected to the government, that amount represents a current liability. For example, suppose a merchant makes a $100 sale that is subject to a 5 percent sales tax and a 10 percent excise tax. If the sale takes place on June 1, the entry to record it is as follows:

A = L + SE			
+115 +5 +100			
+10			

June 1	Cash	115	
	Sales		100
	Sales Tax Payable		5
	Excise Tax Payable		10
	Sales of merchandise and collection of sales and excise tax		

The sale is properly recorded at $100, and the taxes collected are recorded as liabilities to be remitted to the appropriate government agencies.

Companies that have a physical presence in many cities and states require a complex accounting system for sales taxes because the rates vary from state to state and city to city. Because **Amazon.com** is an Internet company without a physical presence in most states and thus does not always have to collect sales tax from its customers, its sales tax situation is simpler. This situation may change in the future, but so far Congress has exempted most Internet sales from sales tax.

Current Portion of Long-Term Debt

If a portion of long-term debt is due within the next year and is to be paid from current assets, that portion is classified as a current liability. For example, **Amazon.com's** Financial Highlights show the following amounts (in thousands):

Current liabilities:
Current maturities of long-term debt $ 2,381
Long-term liabilities:
Long-term debt   1,855,319

In this case, no journal entry is necessary. The total debt of $1,857,700 is simply reclassified into two categories when the company prepares its financial statements.

Payroll Liabilities

For most organizations, the cost of labor and payroll taxes is a major expense. In the banking and airlines industries, payroll costs represent more than half of all operating costs. Payroll accounting is important because complex laws and significant liabilities are involved. The employer is liable to employees for wages and salaries and to various agencies for amounts withheld from wages and salaries and for related taxes. **Wages** are compensation of employees at an hourly rate; **salaries** are compensation of employees at a monthly or yearly rate.

Because payroll accounting applies only to an organization's employees, it is important to distinguish between employees and independent contractors. Employees are paid a wage or salary by the organization and are under its direct supervision and control. Independent contractors are not employees of the organization and so are not accounted for under the payroll system. They offer services to the organization for a fee, but they are not under its direct control or supervision. Certified public accountants, advertising agencies, and lawyers, for example, often act as independent contractors.

FOCUS ON BUSINESS PRACTICE

Small Businesses Offer Benefits, Too.

A survey of small business in the Midwest focused on the employee benefits that these companies offer. The graph at the right presents the results. As you can see, 77 percent of respondents provided both paid vacation and health/medical benefits, and 23 percent even offered their employees tuition reimbursement.[6]

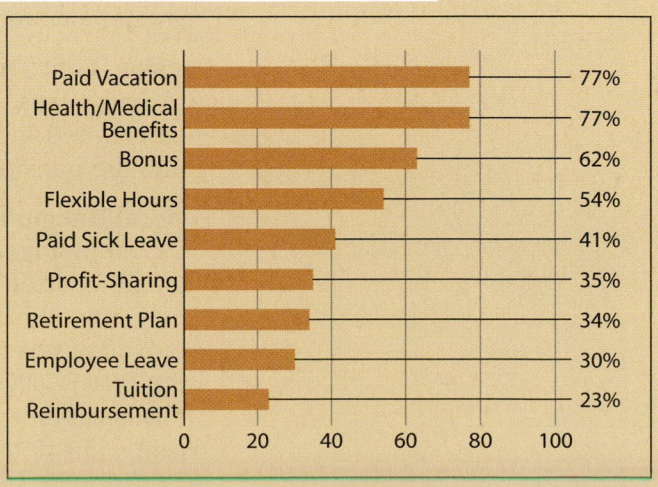

Benefit	Percentage
Paid Vacation	77%
Health/Medical Benefits	77%
Bonus	62%
Flexible Hours	54%
Paid Sick Leave	41%
Profit-Sharing	35%
Retirement Plan	34%
Employee Leave	30%
Tuition Reimbursement	23%

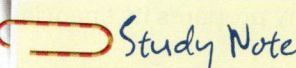

Figure 4 shows how payroll liabilities relate to employee earnings and employer taxes and other costs. When accounting for payroll liabilities, it is important to keep the following in mind:

▶ The amount payable to employees is less than the amount of their earnings. This occurs because employers are required by law or are requested by employees to withhold certain amounts from wages and send them directly to government agencies or other organizations.

▶ An employer's total liabilities exceed employees' earnings because the employer must pay additional taxes and make other contributions (e.g., for pensions and medical care) that increase the cost and liabilities.

The most common withholdings, taxes, and other payroll costs are described below.

Federal Income Taxes Employers are required to withhold federal income taxes from employees' paychecks and pay them to the United States Treasury. These taxes are collected each time an employee is paid.

State and Local Income Taxes Most states and some local governments levy income taxes. In most cases, the procedures for withholding are similar to those for federal income taxes.

Social Security (FICA) Tax The social security program (the Federal Insurance Contribution Act) provides retirement and disability benefits and survivor's benefits. About 90 percent of the people working in the United States fall under the provisions of this program. The 2005 social security tax rate of 6.2 percent was paid by *both* employee and employer on the first $90,000 earned by an employee during the calendar year. Both the rate and the base to which it applies are subject to change in future years.

Medicare Tax A major extension of the social security program is Medicare, which provides hospitalization and medical insurance for persons over age 65. In 2005, the Medicare tax rate was 1.45 percent of gross income, with no limit, paid by *both* employee and employer.

Medical Insurance Many organizations provide medical benefits to employees. Often, the employee contributes a portion of the cost through withholdings from income and the employer pays the rest—usually a greater amount—to the insurance company.

Pension Contributions Many organizations also provide pension benefits to employees. A portion of the pension contribution is withheld from the employee's income, and the organization pays the rest of the amount into the pension fund.

Federal Unemployment Insurance (FUTA) Tax This tax pays for programs for unemployed workers. It is paid *only* by employers and recently was 6.2 percent of the first $7,000 earned by each employee (this amount may vary from state to state). The employer is allowed a credit for unemployment taxes it pays to the state. The maximum credit is 5.4 percent of the first $7,000 earned by each employee. Most states set their rate at this maximum. Thus, the FUTA tax most often paid is .8 percent (6.2 percent − 5.4 percent) of the taxable wages.

State Unemployment Insurance Tax State unemployment programs provide compensation to eligible unemployed workers. The compensation

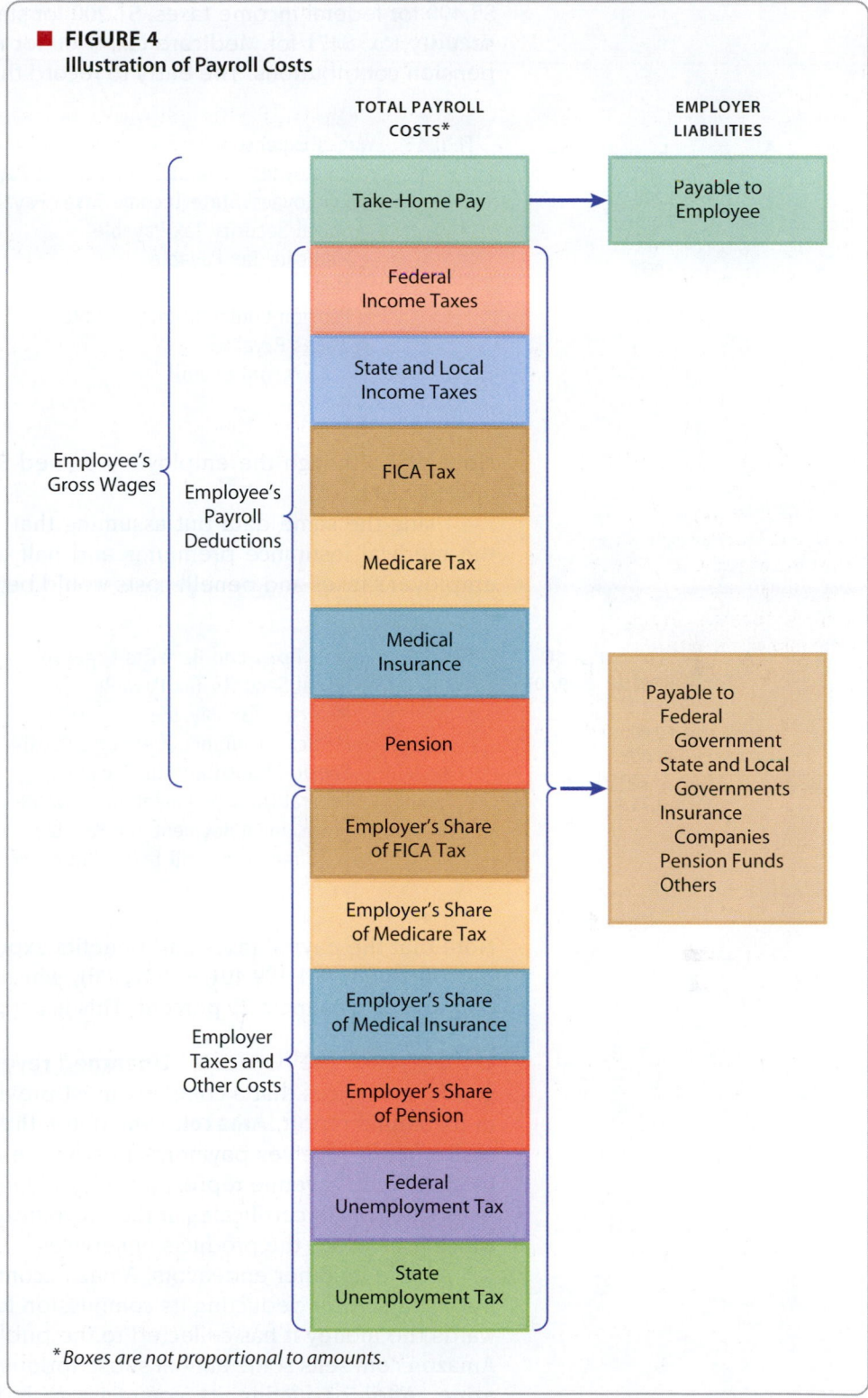

■ **FIGURE 4**
Illustration of Payroll Costs

Boxes are not proportional to amounts.

is paid out of the fund provided by the 5.4 percent of the first $7,000 (or whatever amount the state sets) earned by each employee. In some states, employers with favorable employment records may be entitled to pay less than 5.4 percent.

To illustrate the recording of a payroll, suppose that on February 15, a company's wages for employees are $32,500 and withholdings for employees are

$5,400 for federal income taxes, $1,200 for state income taxes, $2,015 for social security tax, $471 for Medicare tax, $900 for medical insurance, and $1,300 for pension contributions. The entry to record this payroll is as follows:

A	=	L	+	SE
		+5,400		−32,500
		+1,200		
		+2,015		
		+471		
		+900		
		+1,300		
		+21,214		

Feb. 15	Wages Expense	32,500	
	Employees' Federal Income Taxes Payable		5,400
	Employees' State Income Taxes Payable		1,200
	Social Security Tax Payable		2,015
	Medicare Tax Payable		471
	Medical Insurance Premiums Payable		900
	Pension Contributions Payable		1,300
	Wages Payable		21,214
	To record payroll		

Note that although the employees earned $32,500, their take-home pay was only $21,214.

Using the same data but assuming that the employer pays 80 percent of the medical insurance premiums and half of the pension contributions, the employer's taxes and benefit costs would be recorded as follows:

A	=	L	+	SE
		+2,015		−9,401
		+471		
		+3,600		
		+1,300		
		+260		
		+1,755		

Feb. 15	Payroll Taxes and Benefits Expense	9,401	
	Social Security Tax Payable		2,015
	Medicare Tax Payable		471
	Medical Insurance Premiums Payable		3,600
	Pension Contributions Payable		1,300
	Federal Unemployment Tax Payable		260
	State Unemployment Tax Payable		1,755
	To record payroll taxes and other costs		

Note that the payroll taxes and benefits expense increase the total cost of the payroll to $41,901 ($9,401 + $32,500), which exceeds the amount earned by employees by almost 29 percent. This is a typical situation.

Unearned Revenues   **Unearned revenues** are advance payments for goods or services that a company must provide in a future accounting period. In its annual report, **Amazon.com** states that it records unearned revenue as cash when it receives payments in advance and as accounts receivable when the unearned revenue represents a legally enforceable contract, as is the case in its sales of gift certificates. It then recognizes the revenue over the period in which it provides the products or services.

Among its other endeavors, Amazon.com sells subscriptions for magazine publishers. After deducting its commission for selling the subscriptions, it forwards the money it has collected to the publisher. Suppose, for example, that Amazon.com sells some annual subscriptions for a publisher of a monthly magazine. After deducting its commission, it forwards $240 to the publisher. Because the publisher has not yet delivered the 12 issues of the magazine, the $240 is unearned revenue. The publisher would make the following entry:

A	=	L	+	SE
+240		+240		

Cash		240	
Unearned Subscriptions			240
Receipt of annual subscriptions in advance			

The publisher now has a liability of $240 that will be gradually reduced over the year as it sends out monthly issues of the magazine, which it will record as follows:

A = L + SE
      −20 +20

Unearned Subscriptions	20	
Subscription Revenues		20
Delivery of monthly magazine issues		

Many businesses, including repair companies, construction companies, and special-order firms, ask for a deposit before they will begin work. Until they deliver the goods or services, these deposits are current liabilities.

Estimated Liabilities

Estimated liabilities are definite debts or obligations whose exact dollar amount cannot be known until a later date. Because there is no doubt that a legal obligation exists, the primary accounting problem is to estimate and record the amount of the liability. Examples of estimated liabilities are described below.

Income Taxes Payable   The federal government, most state governments, and some cities and towns levy a tax on a corporation's income. The amount of the liability depends on the results of a corporation's operations, which are often not known until after the end of the corporation's fiscal year. However, because income taxes are an expense in the year in which income is earned, an adjusting entry is necessary to record the estimated tax liability. The format of a typical entry is as follows:

A = L + SE
   +53,000 −53,000

Dec. 31	Income Taxes Expense	53,000	
	Income Taxes Payable		53,000
	To record estimated federal income taxes		

Sole proprietorships and partnerships do *not* pay income taxes. However, their owners must report their share of the firm's income on their individual tax returns.

Property Taxes Payable   Property taxes are a main source of revenue for local governments. They are levied annually on real property, such as land and buildings, and on personal property, such as inventory and equipment. Because the fiscal years of local governments rarely correspond to a company's fiscal year, it is necessary to estimate the amount of property taxes that applies to each month of the year.

Promotional Costs   You are no doubt familiar with the coupons and rebates that are part of many companies' marketing programs and with the frequent flyer programs that airlines have been offering for more than 20 years. Companies usually record the costs of these programs as a reduction in sales (a contra-sales account) rather than as an expense with a corresponding current liability. As **Hershey Foods Corporation** acknowledges in its annual report, promotional costs are hard to estimate:

Accrued liabilities represent the most difficult or subjective judgments involving liabilities associated with marketing programs. The company utilizes numerous trade promotion and customer coupon programs. The costs of these programs are recognized as a reduction to net sales with the recording of the corresponding liability. . . . The accrued liability is determined through analysis of programs offered, historical trends, [and other means].[8]

Hershey accrues about $500 million in promotional costs each year and reports that its estimates are usually accurate within about 4 percent, or $20 million.

Product Warranty Liability

When a firm sells a product or service with a warranty, it has a liability for the length of the warranty. The warranty is a feature of the product and is included in the selling price; its cost should therefore be debited to an expense account in the period of the sale. Based on past experience, it should be possible to estimate the amount the warranty will cost in the future. Some products will require little warranty service; others may require much. Thus, there will be an average cost per product.

For example, suppose a muffler company like **Midas** guarantees that it will replace free of charge any muffler it sells that fails during the time the buyer owns the car. The company charges a small service fee for replacing the muffler. In the past, 6 percent of the mufflers sold have been returned for replacement under the warranty. The average cost of a muffler is $50. If the company sold 350 mufflers during July, the accrued liability would be recorded as an adjustment at the end of July, as shown below:

Study Note

Recording a product warranty expense in the period of the sale is an application of the matching rule.

A =	L	+	SE
	+1,050		−1,050

July 31	Product Warranty Expense	1,050	
	Estimated Product Warranty Liability		1,050
	To record estimated product warranty expense:		
	Number of units sold	350	
	Rate of replacement under warranty	× .06	
	Estimated units to be replaced	21	
	Estimated cost per unit	$ 50	
	Estimated liability for product warranty	$1,050	

When a muffler is returned for replacement under the warranty, the cost of the muffler is charged against the Estimated Product Warranty Liability

Today, because of frequent flyer programs, U.S. airlines have more than 4 trillion "free miles" outstanding. What are the accounting implications of these programs? Companies usually record the costs as a reduction in sales (a contra-sales account) rather than as an expense with a corresponding current liability.

account. For example, suppose that on December 5, a customer returns with a defective muffler, which cost $40, and pays a $20 service fee to have it replaced. The entry is as follows:

A	=	L	+	SE				
+20		−40		+20	Dec. 5	Cash	20	
−40						Estimated Product Warranty Liability	40	
						Service Revenue		20
						Merchandise Inventory		40
						Replacement of muffler under warranty		

Vacation Pay Liability In most companies, employees accrue paid vacation as they work during the year. For example, an employee may earn two weeks of paid vacation for each 50 weeks of work. Thus, the person is paid 52 weeks' salary for 50 weeks' work. The cost of the two weeks' vacation should be allocated as an expense over the whole year so that month-to-month costs will not be distorted. The vacation pay represents 4 percent (two weeks' vacation divided by 50 weeks) of a worker's pay. Every week worked earns the employee a small fraction (2 percent) of vacation pay, which is 4 percent of total annual salary.

FOCUS ON BUSINESS PRACTICE

What Is the Cost of Frequent Flyer Miles?

In the early 1980s, **American Airlines** developed a frequent flyer program that awards free trips and other bonuses to customers based on the number of miles they fly on the airline. Since then, many other airlines have instituted similar programs, and it is estimated that 40 million people now participate in them. Today, U.S. airlines have more than 4 trillion "free miles" outstanding, and 8 percent of passengers travel on "free" tickets. Estimated liabilities for these tickets have become an important consideration in evaluating an airline's financial position. Complicating the estimate is that almost half the miles have been earned through purchases from hotels, car rental and telephone companies, Internet service providers like **AOL**, and bank credit cards.[9]

Vacation pay liability can represent a substantial amount of money. For example, in the 10-K form that it submitted to the SEC for 2004, **US Airways** reported accrued salaries, wages, and vacation liabilities of $167 million.

Suppose that a company with a vacation policy of two weeks of paid vacation for each 50 weeks of work has a payroll of $21,000 and that it paid $1,000 of that amount to employees on vacation for the week ended April 20. Because of turnover and rules regarding term of employment, the company assumes that only 75 percent of employees will ultimately collect vacation pay. The computation of vacation pay expense based on the payroll of employees not on vacation ($21,000 − $1,000) is as follows: $20,000 × 4 percent × 75 percent = $600. The company would make the following entry to record vacation pay expense for the week ended April 20:

A = L + SE
+600 −600

Apr. 20	Vacation Pay Expense	600	
	Estimated Liability for Vacation Pay		600
	Estimated vacation pay expense		

At the time employees receive their vacation pay, an entry is made debiting Estimated Liability for Vacation Pay and crediting Cash or Wages Payable. This entry records the $1,000 paid to employees on vacation during August:

A* = L + SE
−1,000 −1,000

* Assumes cash paid.

Aug. 31	Estimated Liability for Vacation Pay	1,000	
	Cash (or Wages Payable)		1,000
	Wages of employees on vacation		

The treatment of vacation pay presented here can also be applied to other payroll costs, such as bonus plans and contributions to pension plans.

S T O P • R E V I E W • A P P L Y

2-1. What is the difference between a line of credit and commercial paper?

2-2. When can a portion of long-term debt be classified as a current liability?

2-3. What are three types of employer-related payroll liabilities?

2-4. Who pays social security and Medicare taxes?

2-5. Why are unearned revenues classified as liabilities?

2-6. What is definite about an estimated liability?

2-7. Why are income taxes payable considered to be estimated liabilities?

2-8. In accounting for discount coupons, how is recording the estimate of how much will be redeemed as a contra-sales account similar to and different from recording it as a promotional expense?

2-9. When does a company incur a liability for a product warranty?

Identification of Current Liabilities Identify each of the following as either (1) a definitely determinable liability or (2) an estimated liability:

_____ a. Bank loan

_____ b. Dividends payable

_____ c. Product warranty liabilities

_____ d. Interest payable

_____ e. Income taxes payable

_____ f. Vacation pay liability

_____ g. Notes payable

_____ h. Property taxes payable

_____ i. Commercial paper

_____ j. Gift certificate liability

SOLUTION

a.	1	f.	2
b.	1	g.	1
c.	2	h.	2
d.	1	i.	1
e.	2	j.	2

Contingent Liabilities and Commitments

LO3   Distinguish *contingent liabilities* from *commitments*.

The FASB requires companies to disclose in a note to their financial statements any contingent liabilities and commitments they may have. A **contingent liability** is not an *existing* obligation. Rather, it is a *potential* liability because it depends on a future event arising out of a past transaction. Contingent liabilities often involve lawsuits, income tax disputes, discounted notes receivable, guarantees of debt, and failure to follow government regulations. For instance, a construction company that built a bridge may have been sued by the state for using poor materials. The past transaction is the building of the bridge under contract. The future event is the outcome of the lawsuit, which is not yet known.

The FASB has established two conditions for determining when a contingency should be entered in the accounting records:

1. The liability must be probable.

2. The liability can be reasonably estimated.[10]

Estimated liabilities like the income tax, warranty, and vacation pay liabilities that we have described meet those conditions. They are therefore accrued in the accounting records.

In a survey of 600 large companies, the most common types of contingencies reported were litigation, which can involve many different issues, and environmental concerns, such as toxic waste cleanup.[11] In a note to its 2003 annual report, **Amazon.com** described a contingent liability involving litigation:

> On July 17, 2003, Pinpoint, Inc. filed a complaint for patent infringement in the United States District Court. . . . We dispute the allegations of wrongdoing in this complaint and intend to vigorously defend ourselves in the matter.

A **commitment** is a legal obligation that does not meet the technical requirements for recognition as a liability and so is not recorded. The most common examples are purchase agreements and leases.[12] For example, in its

Study Note

Contingencies are recorded when they are probable and can be reasonably estimated.

2003 annual report, Amazon.com notes that "we currently lease office and ful-fillment center facilities and fixed assets under non-cancelable operating and capital leases."

STOP • REVIEW • APPLY

3-1. What is a contingent liability, and how does it differ from a commitment?

3-2. What are two examples of contingent liabilities? Why is each a contingent liability?

3-3. What is an example of a commitment?

The Time Value of Money

LO4 Define the *time value of money,* and apply it to future and present values.

"Time is money" is a common expression. It derives from the concept of the **time value of money**, which refers to the costs or benefits derived from holding or not holding money over time. **Interest** is the cost of using money for a specific period.

The interest associated with the time value of money is an important consideration in any kind of business decision. For example, if you sell a bicycle for $100 and hold that amount for one year without putting it in a savings account, you have forgone the interest that the money would have earned. However, if you accept a note payable instead of cash and add the interest to the price of the bicycle, you will not forgo the interest that the cash could have earned.

Simple interest is the interest cost for one or more periods when the principal sum—the amount on which interest is computed—stays the same from period to period. **Compound interest** is the interest cost for two or more periods when after each period, the interest earned in that period is added to the amount on which interest is computed in future periods. In other words, the principal sum is increased at the end of each period by the interest earned in that period. The following two examples illustrate these concepts:

Study Note

In business, compound interest is the most useful concept of interest because it helps decision makers choose among alternative courses of action.

Example of Simple Interest Joe Sanchez accepts an 8 percent, $30,000 note due in 90 days. How much will he receive at that time? The interest is calculated as follows:

$$\text{Interest} = \text{Principal} \times \text{Rate} \times \text{Time}$$
$$= \$30,000 \times 8/100 \times 90/365$$
$$= \$591.78$$

Therefore, the total that Sanchez will receive is $30,591.78, calculated as follows:

$$\text{Total} = \text{Principal} + \text{Interest}$$
$$= \$30,000 + \$591.78$$
$$= \$30,591.78$$

Example of Compound Interest Anna Wang deposits $5,000 in an account that pays 6 percent interest. She expects to leave the principal and accumulated interest in the account for three years. How much will the account total at the end of three years? Assume that the interest is paid at the end of the year and is added to the principal at that time, and that this total in turn earns interest. The amount at the end of three years is computed as follows:

(1) Year	(2) Principal Amount at Beginning of Year	(3) Annual Amount of Interest (Col. 2 × 6%)	(4) Accumulated Amount at End of Year (Col. 2 + Col. 3)
1	$5,000.00	$300.00	$5,300.00
2	5,300.00	318.00	5,618.00
3	5,618.00	337.08	5,955.08

At the end of three years, Wang will have $5,955.08 in her account. Note that the amount of interest increases each year by the interest rate times the interest of the previous year. For example, between year 1 and year 2, the interest increased by $18, which equals 6 percent times $300.

Future Value

Another way to ask the question we posed in our example of compound interest is, What is the future value of a single sum ($5,000) at compound interest (6 percent) for three years? **Future value** is the amount an investment will be worth at a future date if invested at compound interest. Managers often want to know future value, but the method of computing future value that we just illustrated is too time-consuming in practice. Imagine how tedious the calculation would be if the example were ten years instead of three. Fortunately, there are tables that simplify solving problems involving compound interest. Table 1, which shows the future value of $1 after a given number of periods, is an example. This table and the others in this chapter are excerpts from larger tables in the appendix on future value and present value tables.

Future Value of a Single Sum Invested at Compound Interest
Using Table 1 to compute the future value of Anna Wang's savings account, we simply look down the 6 percent column until we reach the line for three periods and find the factor 1.191. This factor, when multiplied by $1, gives the

TABLE 1. Future Value of $1 After a Given Number of Periods

Period	1%	2%	3%	4%	5%	6%	7%	8%	9%	10%	12%	14%	15%
1	1.010	1.020	1.030	1.040	1.050	1.060	1.070	1.080	1.090	1.100	1.120	1.140	1.150
2	1.020	1.040	1.061	1.082	1.103	1.124	1.145	1.166	1.188	1.210	1.254	1.300	1.323
3	1.030	1.061	1.093	1.125	1.158	1.191	1.225	1.260	1.295	1.331	1.405	1.482	1.521
4	1.041	1.082	1.126	1.170	1.216	1.262	1.311	1.360	1.412	1.464	1.574	1.689	1.749
5	1.051	1.104	1.159	1.217	1.276	1.338	1.403	1.469	1.539	1.611	1.762	1.925	2.011
6	1.062	1.126	1.194	1.265	1.340	1.419	1.501	1.587	1.677	1.772	1.974	2.195	2.313
7	1.072	1.149	1.230	1.316	1.407	1.504	1.606	1.714	1.828	1.949	2.211	2.502	2.660
8	1.083	1.172	1.267	1.369	1.477	1.594	1.718	1.851	1.993	2.144	2.476	2.853	3.059
9	1.094	1.195	1.305	1.423	1.551	1.689	1.838	1.999	2.172	2.358	2.773	3.252	3.518
10	1.105	1.219	1.344	1.480	1.629	1.791	1.967	2.159	2.367	2.594	3.106	3.707	4.046

future value of that $1 at compound interest of 6 percent for three periods (years in this case). Thus, we solve the problem as follows:

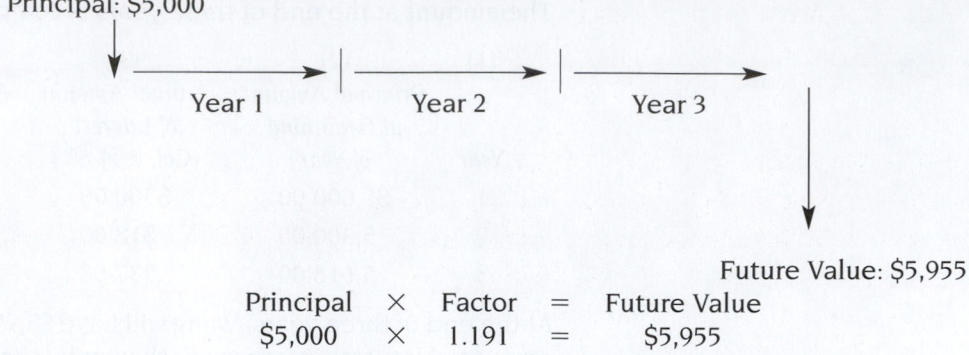

Principal: $5,000

Future Value: $5,955

$$
\begin{array}{cccc}
\text{Principal} & \times & \text{Factor} & = & \text{Future Value} \\
\$5,000 & \times & 1.191 & = & \$5,955
\end{array}
$$

Except for a rounding difference of $.08, the answer is the same as our earlier one.

Future Value of an Ordinary Annuity

Another common problem involves an **ordinary annuity**, which is a series of equal payments made at the end of equal intervals of time, with compound interest on these payments. For example, suppose that at the end of each of the next three years, Ben Katz puts $200 into a savings account that pays 5 percent interest. How much money will he have in his account at the end of the three years? The following is one way of computing the amount:

(1) Year	(2) Beginning Balance	(3) Interest Earned (5% × Col. 2)	(4) Periodic Payment	(5) Accumulated at End of Period (Col. 2 + Col. 3 + Col. 4)
1	—	—	$200	$200.00
2	$200.00	$10.00	200	410.00
3	410.00	20.50	200	630.50

Katz would have $630.50 in his account at the end of three years, consisting of $600.00 in periodic payments and $30.50 in interest.

We can simplify this calculation by using Table 2. Looking down the 5 percent column and across the row for the third period, we find the factor 3.153. This factor, when multiplied by $1, gives the future value of a series of three $1 payments at compound interest of 5 percent. Thus, we solve the problem as follows:

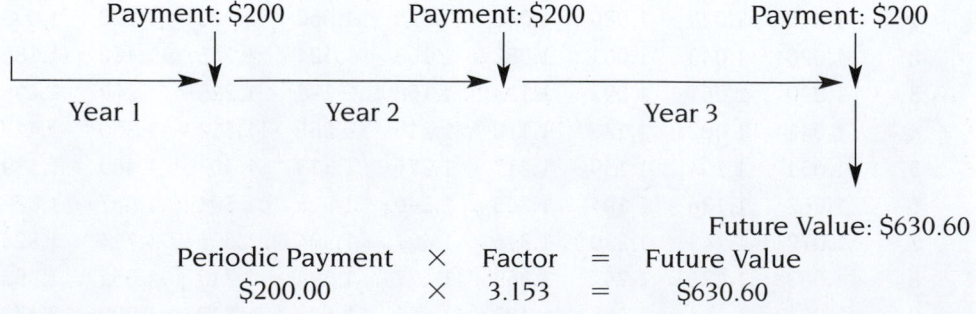

Payment: $200   Payment: $200   Payment: $200

Year 1   Year 2   Year 3

Future Value: $630.60

$$
\begin{array}{cccc}
\text{Periodic Payment} & \times & \text{Factor} & = & \text{Future Value} \\
\$200.00 & \times & 3.153 & = & \$630.60
\end{array}
$$

Except for a rounding difference of $.10, the result is the same as our earlier one.

TABLE 2. **Future Value of an Ordinary Annuity of $1 Paid in Each Period for a Given Number of Periods**

Period	1%	2%	3%	4%	5%	6%	7%	8%	9%	10%	12%	14%	15%
1	1.000	1.000	1.000	1.000	1.000	1.000	1.000	1.000	1.000	1.000	1.000	1.000	1.000
2	2.010	2.020	2.030	2.040	2.050	2.060	2.070	2.080	2.090	2.100	2.120	2.140	2.150
3	3.030	3.060	3.091	3.122	3.153	3.184	3.215	3.246	3.278	3.310	3.374	3.440	3.473
4	4.060	4.122	4.184	4.246	4.310	4.375	4.440	4.506	4.573	4.641	4.779	4.921	4.993
5	5.101	5.204	5.309	5.416	5.526	5.637	5.751	5.867	5.985	6.105	6.353	6.610	6.742
6	6.152	6.308	6.468	6.633	6.802	6.975	7.153	7.336	7.523	7.716	8.115	8.536	8.754
7	7.214	7.434	7.662	7.898	8.142	8.394	8.654	8.923	9.200	9.487	10.090	10.730	11.070
8	8.286	8.538	8.892	9.214	9.549	9.897	10.260	10.640	11.030	11.440	12.300	13.230	13.730
9	9.369	9.755	10.160	10.580	11.030	11.490	11.980	12.490	13.020	13.580	14.780	16.090	16.790
10	10.460	10.950	11.460	12.010	12.580	13.180	13.820	14.490	15.190	15.940	17.550	19.340	20.300

Present Value

Study Note

Present value is a method of valuing future cash flows. Financial analysts commonly compute present value to determine the value of potential investments.

Suppose you had the choice of receiving $100 today or one year from today. No doubt, you would choose to receive it today. Why? If you have the money today, you can put it in a savings account to earn interest so you will have more than $100 a year from today. In other words, an amount to be received in the future (future value) is not worth as much today as an amount received today (present value). **Present value** is the amount that must be invested today at a given rate of interest to produce a given future value. Thus, present value and future value are closely related.

For example, suppose Sue Dapper needs $1,000 one year from now. How much does she have to invest today to achieve that goal if the interest rate is 5 percent? From earlier examples, we can establish the following equation:

Present Value	×	(1.0 + Interest Rate)	=	Future Value
Present Value	×	1.05	=	$1,000.00
Present Value			=	$1,000.00 ÷ 1.05
Present Value			=	$952.38

To achieve a future value of $1,000, Dapper must invest a present value of $952.38. Interest of 5 percent on $952.38 for one year equals $47.62, and these two amounts added together equal $1,000.

Present Value of a Single Sum Due in the Future

When more than one period is involved, the calculation of present value is more complicated. For example, suppose Don Riley wants to be sure of having $4,000 at the end of three years. How much must he invest today in a 5 percent savings account to achieve this goal? We can compute the present value of $4,000 at compound interest of 5 percent for three years by adapting the above equation:

Year	Amount at End of Year	Divide by		Present Value at Beginning of Year
3	$4,000.00	÷ 1.05	=	$3,809.52
2	3,809.52	÷ 1.05	=	3,628.11
1	3,628.11	÷ 1.05	=	3,455.34

Riley must invest $3,455.34 today to achieve a value of $4,000 in three years.

TABLE 3. Present Value of $1 to Be Received at the End of a Given Number of Periods

Period	1%	2%	3%	4%	5%	6%	7%	8%	9%	10%
1	0.990	0.980	0.971	0.962	0.952	0.943	0.935	0.926	0.917	0.909
2	0.980	0.961	0.943	0.925	0.907	0.890	0.873	0.857	0.842	0.826
3	0.971	0.942	0.915	0.889	0.864	0.840	0.816	0.794	0.772	0.751
4	0.961	0.924	0.888	0.855	0.823	0.792	0.763	0.735	0.708	0.683
5	0.951	0.906	0.863	0.822	0.784	0.747	0.713	0.681	0.650	0.621
6	0.942	0.888	0.837	0.790	0.746	0.705	0.666	0.630	0.596	0.564
7	0.933	0.871	0.813	0.760	0.711	0.665	0.623	0.583	0.547	0.513
8	0.923	0.853	0.789	0.731	0.677	0.627	0.582	0.540	0.502	0.467
9	0.914	0.837	0.766	0.703	0.645	0.592	0.544	0.500	0.460	0.424
10	0.905	0.820	0.744	0.676	0.614	0.558	0.508	0.463	0.422	0.386

Again, we can simplify the calculation by using the appropriate table. In Table 3, the point at which the 5 percent column and the row for period 3 intersect shows a factor of .864. This factor, when multiplied by $1, gives the present value of $1 to be received three years from now at 5 percent interest. Thus, we solve the problem as follows:

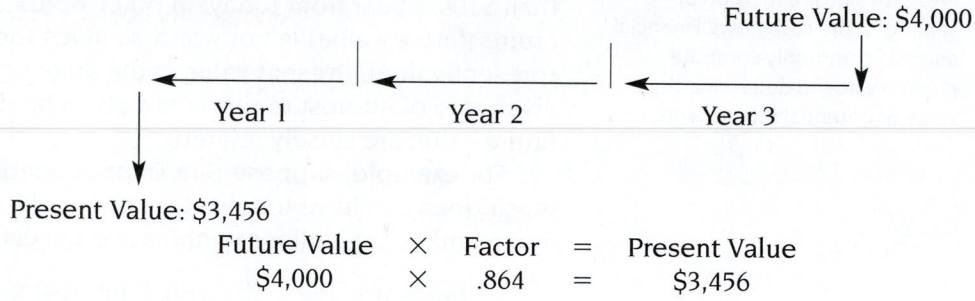

Present Value: $3,456

Future Value	×	Factor	=	Present Value
$4,000	×	.864	=	$3,456

Except for a rounding difference of $.66, this result is the same as our earlier one.

Present Value of an Ordinary Annuity

It is often necessary to compute the present value of a series of receipts or payments equally spaced over time—in other words, the present value of an ordinary annuity. For example, suppose Kathy Casal has sold a piece of property and is to receive $15,000 in three equal annual payments of $5,000 beginning one year from today. What is the present value of this sale if the current interest rate is 5 percent?

Using Table 3, we can compute the present value by calculating a separate value for each of the three payments and summing the results, as follows:

Future Receipts (Annuity)				Present Value Factor at 5 Percent (from Table 3)		Present Value
Year 1	Year 2	Year 3				
$5,000			×	.952	=	$ 4,760
	$5,000		×	.907	=	4,535
		$5,000	×	.864	=	4,320
Total Present Value						$13,615

The present value of the sale is $13,615. Thus, there is an implied interest cost (given the 5 percent rate) of $1,385 associated with the payment plan that allows the purchaser to pay in three installments.

TABLE 4. **Present Value of an Ordinary $1 Annuity Received in Each Period for a Given Number of Periods**

Period	1%	2%	3%	4%	5%	6%	7%	8%	9%	10%
1	0.990	0.980	0.971	0.962	0.952	0.943	0.935	0.926	0.917	0.909
2	1.970	1.942	1.913	1.886	1.859	1.833	1.808	1.783	1.759	1.736
3	2.941	2.884	2.829	2.775	2.723	2.673	2.624	2.577	2.531	2.487
4	3.902	3.808	3.717	3.630	3.546	3.465	3.387	3.312	3.240	3.170
5	4.853	4.713	4.580	4.452	4.329	4.212	4.100	3.993	3.890	3.791
6	5.795	5.601	5.417	5.242	5.076	4.917	4.767	4.623	4.486	4.355
7	6.728	6.472	6.230	6.002	5.786	5.582	5.389	5.206	5.033	4.868
8	7.652	7.325	7.020	6.733	6.463	6.210	5.971	5.747	5.535	5.335
9	8.566	8.162	7.786	7.435	7.108	6.802	6.515	6.247	5.995	5.759
10	9.471	8.983	8.530	8.111	7.722	7.360	7.024	6.710	6.418	6.145

We can make this calculation more easily by using Table 4. The point at which the 5 percent column intersects the row for period 3 shows a factor of 2.723. When multiplied by $1, this factor gives the present value of a series of three $1 payments (spaced one year apart) at compound interest of 5 percent. Thus, we solve the problem as follows:

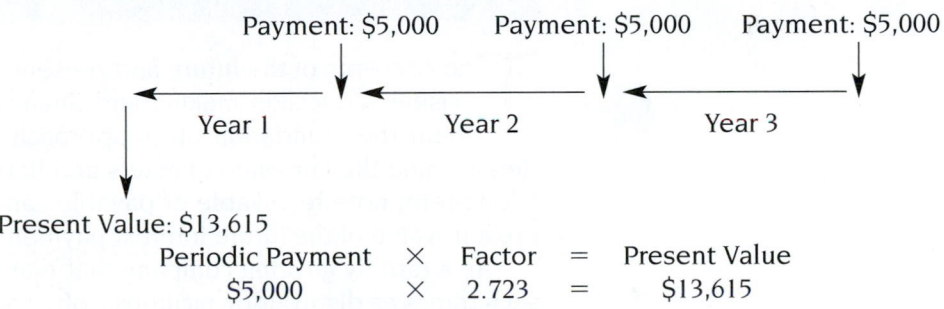

Present Value: $13,615

	Periodic Payment	×	Factor	=	Present Value
	$5,000	×	2.723	=	$13,615

This result is the same as the one we computed earlier.

Time Periods As in all our examples, the compounding period is in most cases one year, and the interest rate is stated on an annual basis. However, the left-hand column in Tables 1 to 4 refers not to years but to periods. This wording accommodates compounding periods of less than one year. Savings accounts that record interest quarterly and bonds that pay interest semiannually are cases in which the compounding period is less than one year. To use the tables in these cases, it is necessary to (1) divide the annual interest rate by the number of periods in the year, and (2) multiply the number of periods in one year by the number of years.

For example, suppose we want to compute the future (maturity) value of a $6,000 note that is to be paid in two years and that carries an annual interest rate of 8 percent. The compounding period is semiannual. Before using Table 1 in this computation, we must compute the interest rate that applies to each compounding period and the total number of compounding periods. First, the interest rate to use is 4 percent (8% annual rate ÷ 2 periods per year). Second, the total number of compounding periods is 4 (2 periods per year × 2 years). From Table 1, therefore, the maturity value of the note is computed as follows:

<aside>
Study Note

The interest rate used when compounding interest for less than one year is the annual rate divided by the number of periods in a year.
</aside>

Principal	×	Factor	=	Future Value
$6,000	×	1.170	=	$7,020

The note will be worth $7,020 in two years.

This method of determining the interest rate and the number of periods when the compounding period is less than one year can be used with all four tables.

Applications of the Time Value of Money

LO5 Apply the time value of money to simple accounting situations.

The concepts of the future and present value of money are widely used in business decision making and financial reporting. The FASB has made them the foundation of its approach to using cash flow information in determining the fair value of assets and liabilities.[13] For example, the value of a long-term note receivable or payable can be determined by calculating the present value of the future interest payments.

As a rapidly growing company that makes many long-term investments in such things as distribution facilities, software, and the acquisition of other companies, **Amazon.com** finds many uses for the time value of money. For example, Amazon.com's management will compare the expected present value of the future cash flows of an investment with the current outlay that the investment requires, and it will use a target interest rate that it wants to earn on the investment. If the present value of the investment exceeds the current outlay, Amazon.com will earn at least its target interest rate if management's projections of cash are accurate.

In the sections that follow, we illustrate some simple, useful applications of the time value of money.

Valuing an Asset

An asset is something that will provide future benefits to the company that owns it. Usually, the purchase price of an asset represents the present value of those future benefits. It is possible to evaluate a proposed purchase price by comparing it with the present value of the asset to the company.

For example, Sam Hurst is thinking of buying a new machine that will reduce his annual labor cost by $700 per year. The machine will last eight years. The interest rate that Hurst assumes for making managerial decisions is 10 percent. What is the maximum amount (present value) that Hurst should pay for the machine?

The present value of the machine to Hurst is equal to the present value of an ordinary annuity of $700 per year for eight years at compound interest of 10 percent. Using the factor from Table 4, we compute the value as follows:

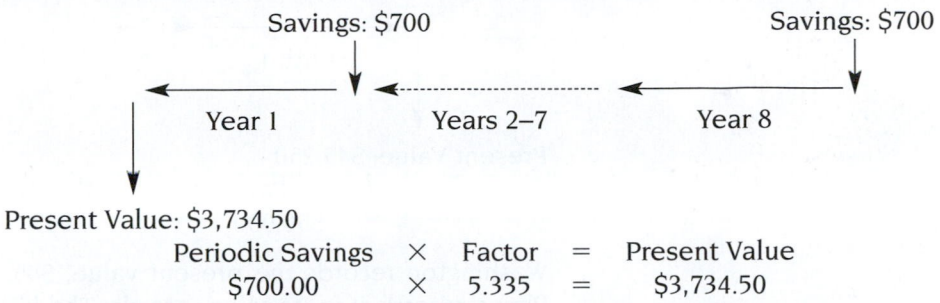

Savings: $700   Savings: $700

Year 1   Years 2–7   Year 8

Present Value: $3,734.50

Periodic Savings	×	Factor	=	Present Value
$700.00	×	5.335	=	$3,734.50

Hurst should not pay more than $3,734.50 for the machine because this amount equals the present value of the benefits he would receive from owning it.

Deferred Payment

To encourage buyers to make a purchase, sellers sometimes agree to defer payment for a sale. This practice is common among companies that sell agricultural equipment; to accommodate farmers who often need new equipment in the spring but cannot pay for it until they sell their crops in the fall, these companies are willing to defer payment.

Suppose Plains Implement Corporation sells a tractor to Dana Washington for $50,000 on February 1 and agrees to take payment ten months later, on December 1. When such an agreement is made, the future payment includes not only the selling price, but also an implied (imputed) interest cost. If the prevailing annual interest rate for such transactions is 12 percent compounded monthly, the actual price of the tractor would be the present value of the future

Companies that sell agricultural equipment like these combine harvesters often agree to defer payment for a sale. This practice is common because farmers often need new equipment in the spring but cannot pay for it until they sell their crops in the fall. Deferred payment is a useful application of the time value of money.

payment, computed using the factor from Table 3 (10 periods, 1 percent [12 percent divided by 12 months]), as follows:

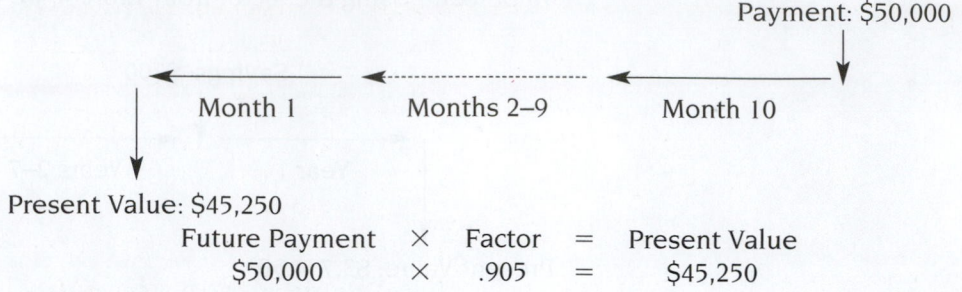

Future Payment × Factor = Present Value
$50,000 × .905 = $45,250

Washington records the present value, $45,250, in his purchase records, and Plains records it in its sales records. The balance consists of interest expense or interest income.

Investment of Idle Cash

Suppose Childware Corporation, a toy manufacturer, needs funds for a future expansion. At present, it has $10,000,000 in cash that it does not expect to need for one year. It places the cash in an account that pays 4 percent annual interest. Interest is compounded and credited to the company's account quarterly. How much cash will Childware have at the end of the year?

The future value factor from Table 1 is based on four quarterly periods of 1 percent (4 percent divided by 4 quarters), and the future value is computed as follows:

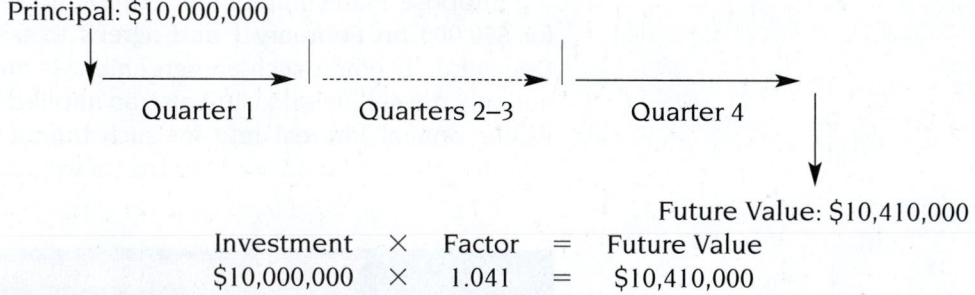

Investment × Factor = Future Value
$10,000,000 × 1.041 = $10,410,000

The initial investment is recorded with a debit to Short-Term Investments. Each quarter, the company increases Short-Term Investments by the amount of the interest earned. Interest Income is credited. Similar entries would be made for four more months, at which time the balance of Short-Term Investments would be about $110,410,000. The actual amount accumulated might vary from this total because the interest rate paid may vary over time as a result of changes in market conditions.

Accumulation of a Fund for Loan Repayment

When a company owes a large fixed amount due in several years, management would be wise to accumulate a fund to pay off the debt at maturity. As part of a loan agreement, creditors sometimes require that such a fund be established. In establishing the fund, management must determine how much cash must be set aside each period to pay the debt. The amount will depend on the estimated rate of interest the fund will earn.

Suppose Aloha Corporation agrees with a creditor to set aside cash at the end of each year to accumulate enough to pay off a $100,000 note due in six years. It will make five annual contributions by the time the note is due. The fund is projected to earn 8 percent, compounded annually. We can calculate the amount of each annual payment by using Table 2 (5 periods, 8 percent):

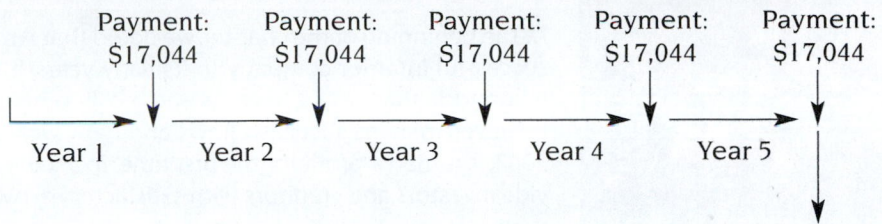

	Payment: $17,044	Payment: $17,044	Payment: $17,044	Payment: $17,044	Payment: $17,044
	Year 1	Year 2	Year 3	Year 4	Year 5

Future Value: $100,000

Future Value of Fund	÷	Factor	=	Annual Investment
$100,000	÷	5.867	=	$17,044 (rounded)

Other Applications

There are many other applications of present value in accounting, including computing imputed interest on non-interest-bearing notes, accounting for installment notes, valuing a bond, and recording lease obligations. Present value is also applied in accounting for pension obligations; valuing debt; depreciating property, plant, and equipment; making capital expenditure decisions; and generally in accounting for any item in which time is a factor.

S T O P • R E V I E W • A P P L Y

5-1. Why is the time value of money important in making business decisions?

5-2. What are the applications of present value to financial reporting?

5-3. What are some of the ways in which businesses use present value?

Valuing an Asset When Making a Purchasing Decision   Jerry owns a restaurant and has the opportunity to buy a high-quality espresso coffee machine for $5,000. After carefully studying projected costs and revenues, Jerry estimates that the machine will produce a net cash flow of $1,600 annually and will last for five years. He determines that an interest rate of 10 percent is an adequate return on investment for his business.

Calculate the present value of the machine to Jerry. Based on your calculation, do you think a decision to purchase the machine would be wise?

SOLUTION

Calculation of the present value:

Annual cash flow	$1,600.00
Factor from Table 4 (5 years at 10%)	× 3.791
Present value of net cash flows	6,065.60
Less purchase price	− 5,000.00
Net present value	$1,065.60

The present value of the net cash flows from the machine exceeds the purchase price. Thus, the investment will return more than 10 percent to Jerry's business. A decision to purchase the machine would therefore be wise.

AMAZON.COM, INC.

At the beginning of the chapter, we noted that **Amazon.com** has been an unusually successful Internet company. In its early years, it experienced operating losses of a magnitude that would have caused most companies to go bankrupt. Amazon.com, however, managed its cash flows and debt well enough to stay in business, and in 2003, it turned a profit for the first time. To accomplish this, the company had to provide investors and creditors with satisfactory answers to these questions:

- **How does Amazon.com's decision to incur heavy debt relate to the goals of the business?**
- **Is the level of accounts payable in the operating cycle satisfactory?**
- **Has the company properly identified and accounted for all its current liabilities?**

As a new company, Amazon.com had to make extensive investments in Internet software and distribution facilities. This required a lot of capital, much of which the company raised by borrowing money. It analyzed its future cash flows in terms of present value and carefully planned its cash needs by making very good use of the operating cycle. By selling mostly for cash, keeping inventories low, and making maximum use of credit from its suppliers, it was able to keep its cash needs to a minimum. This is particularly evident when we compare its payables turnover and days' payable for 2003 and 2004 (dollar amounts are in thousands):

		2004	2003
$\dfrac{\text{Cost of Goods} \pm \text{Change in Merchandise}}{\text{Sold}\ \qquad\ \text{Inventory}}$ $\overline{\text{Average Accounts Payable}}$	=	$\dfrac{\$5,319,127 + \$185,792}{(\$1,141,733 + \$819,811) \div 2}$	$\dfrac{\$4,006,531 + \$91,492}{(\$819,811 + \$618,128) \div 2}$
	=	$\dfrac{\$5,504,919}{\$980,772}$	$\dfrac{\$4,098,023}{\$718,969.5}$
K/R Payables Turnover	=	5.6 times	5.7 times
$\dfrac{\text{365 days}}{\text{Payables Turnover}}$	=	$\dfrac{\text{365 days}}{5.6}$	$\dfrac{\text{365 days}}{5.7}$
K/R Days' Payable	=	65.2 days	64.0 days

Clearly, Amazon.com maintained a favorable payables turnover and days' payable ratio over the two-year period and experienced a small improvement in 2004. The comprehensive list of current liabilities that it presents in its 2004 annual report gives readers a clear picture of the company's short-term obligations. Now that Amazon.com has achieved profitable operations, it will be interesting to see how it manages it liabilities in the future.

CHAPTER REVIEW

REVIEW of Learning Objectives

LO1 Identify the management issues related to current liabilities.

Current liabilities are an important consideration in managing a company's liquidity and cash flows. Key measures of liquidity are working capital, payables turnover, and days' payable. Liabilities result from past transactions and should be recognized at the time a transaction obligates a company to make future payments. They are valued at the amount of money necessary to satisfy the obligation or at the fair value of the goods or services to be delivered. Liabilities are classified as current or long term. Supplemental disclosure is required when the nature or details of the obligations would help in understanding the liability.

LO2 Identify, compute, and record definitely determinable and estimated current liabilities.

The two major categories of current liabilities are definitely determinable liabilities and estimated liabilities. Definitely determinable liabilities can be measured exactly. They include accounts payable, bank loans and commercial paper, notes payable, accrued liabilities, dividends payable, sales and excise taxes payable, the current portion of long-term debt, payroll liabilities, and unearned revenues.

Estimated liabilities definitely exist, but their amounts are uncertain and must be estimated. They include liabilities for income taxes, property taxes, promotional costs, product warranties, and vacation pay.

LO3 Distinguish *contingent liabilities* from *commitments*.

A contingent liability is a potential liability that arises from a past transaction and is dependent on a future event. Contingent liabilities often involve lawsuits, income tax disputes, discounted notes receivable, guarantees of debt, and failure to follow government regulations. A commitment is a legal obligation, such as a purchase agreement, that is not recorded as a liability.

LO4 Define the *time value of money,* and apply it to future and present values.

The time value of money refers to the costs or benefits derived from holding or not holding money over time. Interest is the cost of using money for a specific period. In computing simple interest, the amount on which the interest is computed stays the same from period to period. In computing compound interest, the interest for a period is added to the principal amount before the interest for the next period is computed.

Future value is the amount an investment will be worth at a future date if invested at compound interest. An ordinary annuity is a series of equal payments made at the end of equal intervals of time, with compound interest on the payments. Present value is the amount that must be invested today at a given rate of interest to produce a given future value. The present value of an ordinary annuity is the present value of a series of payments. Calculations of future and present values are simplified by using the appropriate tables, which appear in an appendix to the book.

LO5 Apply the time value of money to simple accounting situations.

Present value may be used in evaluating the proposed purchase price of an asset, in computing the present value of deferred payments, in determining the future value of an investment of idle cash, in establishing a fund for loan repayment, and in numerous other accounting situations in which time is a factor.

REVIEW of Concepts and Terminology

The following concepts and terms were introduced in this chapter:

Commercial paper: Unsecured loans sold to the public, usually through professionally managed investment firms, as a means of borrowing short-term funds. **(LO2)**

Commitment: A legal obligation that does not meet the technical requirements for recognition as a liability. **(LO3)**

Compound interest: The interest cost for two or more periods when after each period, the interest of that period is added to the amount on which interest is computed in future periods. **(LO4)**

Contingent liability: A potential liability that arises from a past transaction and is dependent on a future event. **(LO3)**

Current liabilities: Debts and obligations that a company expects to satisfy within one year or within the normal operating cycle, whichever is longer. **(LO1)**

Definitely determinable liabilities: Current liabilities that are set by contract or statute and that can be measured exactly. **(LO2)**

Estimated liabilities: Definite debts or obligations whose exact amounts cannot be known until a later date. **(LO2)**

Future value: The amount an investment will be worth at a future date if invested at compound interest. **(LO4)**

Interest: The cost of using money for a specific period. **(LO4)**

Line of credit: An arrangement with a bank that allows a company to borrow funds as needed. **(LO2)**

Long-term liabilities: Debts and obligations due beyond one year or beyond the normal operating cycle. **(LO1)**

Ordinary annuity: A series of equal payments made at the end of equal intervals of time, with compound interest on the payments. **(LO4)**

Present value: The amount that must be invested today at a given rate of interest to produce a given future value. **(LO4)**

Salaries: Compensation of employees at a monthly or yearly rate. **(LO2)**

Simple interest: The interest cost for one or more periods when the amount on which the interest is computed stays the same from period to period. **(LO4)**

Time value of money: The costs or benefits derived from holding or not holding money over time. **(LO4)**

Unearned revenues: Revenues received in advance for goods or services that will not be delivered during the current accounting period. **(LO2)**

Wages: Compensation of employees at an hourly rate. **(LO2)**

Key Ratios

Days' payable: How long, on average, a company takes to pay its accounts payable; 365 days ÷ Payables Turnover. **(LO1)**

Payables turnover: The number of times, on average, that a company pays its accounts payable in an accounting period; (Cost of Goods Sold +/− Change in Merchandise Inventory) ÷ Average Accounts Payable. **(LO1)**

REVIEW Problem

LO1 **Identification and Evaluation of Current Liabilities**

 Sara Jones started a small fitness business, Sara's Fitness Center, last year. In addition to offering exercise classes, she sells nutritional supplements. She has not yet filed any tax reports for her business and therefore owes taxes. Because she has limited experience in running a business, she has brought you all her business records—a checkbook, canceled checks, deposit slips, suppliers' invoices, a notice of annual property taxes of $1,800 due to the city, and a promissory note to her bank for $8,000. She wants you to determine what her business owes the government and other parties.

You analyze all her records and determine the following as of December 31, 20x5:

Unpaid invoices for supplements	$ 6,000
Sales of supplements (excluding sales tax)	28,500
Cost of supplements sold	16,800
Exercise instructor salaries	11,400
Exercise revenues	40,700
Current assets	20,000
Supplements inventory (12/31/05)	13,500
Supplements inventory (12/31/04)	10,500

You learn that the company has sold gift certificates in the amount of $350 that have not been redeemed and that it has deducted $687 from its two employees' salaries for federal income taxes owed to the government. The current social security tax is 6.2 percent on maximum earnings of $90,000 for each employee, and the current Medicare tax is 1.45 percent (no maximum earnings). The FUTA tax is 5.4 percent to the state and .8 percent to the federal government on the first $7,000 earned by each employee; no employee earned more than $7,000. Jones has not filed a sales tax report to the state (6 percent of supplements sales).

Required

1. Given these facts, determine the company's current liabilities as of December 31, 20x5.
2. **User Insight:** Your analysis of the company's current liabilities has been based on documents that the owner showed you. What liabilities may be missing from your analysis?
3. **User Insight:** Evaluate the company's liquidity by calculating working capital, payables turnover, and days' payable. Comment on the results. (Assume average accounts payable were the same as year-end accounts payable.)

Answer to Review Problem

1. The current liabilities of Sara's Fitness Center as of December 31, 20x5, are as follows:

	A	B	C
1	Accounts payable		$ 6,000.00
2	Notes payable		8,000.00
3	Property tax liability		1,800.00
4	Sales tax payable	($28,500 x 0.06)	1,710.00
5	Social security tax payable	($11,400 x 0.062)	706.80
6	Medicare tax payable	($11,400 x 0.0145)	165.30
7	State unemployment tax payable	($11,400 x 0.054)	615.60
8	Federal unemployment tax payable	($11,400 x 0.008)	91.20
9	Federal income tax withholding		687.00
10	Unearned revenues		350.00
11	Total current liabilities		20,125.90

2. The company may have current liabilities for which you have not seen any documentary evidence. For instance, invoices for accounts payable could be missing. In addition, the company may have accrued liabilities, such as vacation pay for its two employees, which would require establishing an

estimated liability. If the promissory note to Jones's bank is interest-bearing, it also would require an adjustment to accrue interest payable, and the company could have other loans outstanding for which you have not seen documentary evidence. Moreover, it may have to pay penalties and interest to the federal and state governments because of its failure to remit tax payments on a timely basis. City and state income tax withholding for the employees could be another overlooked liability.

3. Liquidity ratios computed and evaluated:

	A	B	C	D	E	F	G	H
1	Working Capital	=		Current Assets − Current Liabilities				
3		=		$20,000.00 − $20,125.90				
5		=		($125.90)				
6								
7	Payables Turnover	=	Cost of Goods Sold +/− Change in Merchandise Inventory					
8			Accounts Payable					
10		=		$16,800 + $3,000				
11				$6,000				
13		=		$19,800				
14				$6,000				
16		=		3.3 times				
17								
18	Days' Payable	=		365 days				
19				Payables Turnover				
21		=		365 days				
22				3.3 times				
24		=		110.6 days				

Sara's Fitness Center has a negative working capital of $125.90, its payables turnover is only 3.3 times, and it takes an average of 110.6 days to pay its accounts payable. Its liquidity is therefore highly questionable. Many of its current assets are inventory, which it must sell to generate cash, and it must pay most of its current liabilities sooner than the 110.6 days would indicate.

CHAPTER ASSIGNMENTS

BUILDING Your Basic Knowledge and Skills

Short Exercises

LO1 **Issues in Accounting for Liabilities**

SE 1. Indicate whether each of the following actions relates to (a) managing liquidity and cash flow, (b) recognition of liabilities, (c) valuation of liabilities, (d) classification of liabilities, or (e) disclosure of liabilities:

1. Determining that a liability will be paid in less than one year
2. Estimating the amount of a liability

3. Providing information about when liabilities are due and their interest rates
4. Determining when a liability arises
5. Assessing working capital and payables turnover

LO1 **Measuring Short-Term Liquidity**

 SE 2. Robinson Company has current assets of $65,000 and current liabilities of $40,000, of which accounts payable are $35,000. Robinson's cost of goods sold is $230,000, its merchandise inventory increased by $10,000, and accounts payable were $25,000 the prior year. Calculate Robinson's working capital, payables turnover, and days' payable.

LO2, LO3 **Types of Liabilities**

SE 3. Indicate whether each of the following is (a) a definitely determinable liability, (b) an estimated liability, (c) a commitment, or (d) a contingent liability:

1. Dividends Payable
2. Pending litigation
3. Income Taxes Payable
4. Current portion of long-term debt
5. Vacation Pay Liability
6. Guaranteed loans of another company
7. Purchase agreement

LO2 **Interest Expense on Note Payable**

SE 4. On the last day of August, Navarro Company borrowed $120,000 on a bank note for 60 days at 10 percent interest. Assume that interest is stated separately. Prepare the following entries in journal form: (1) August 31, recording of note; and (2) October 30, payment of note plus interest.

LO2 **Payroll Expenses**

SE 5. The following payroll totals for the month of April are from the payroll register of Ha Corporation: salaries, $446,000; federal income taxes withheld, $62,880; social security tax withheld, $27,652; Medicare tax withheld, $6,467; medical insurance deductions, $13,160; and salaries subject to unemployment taxes, $313,200.

Determine the total and components of (1) the monthly payroll and (2) employer's payroll expense, assuming social security and Medicare taxes equal to the amounts for employees, a federal unemployment insurance tax of .8 percent, a state unemployment tax of 5.4 percent, and medical insurance premiums for which the employer pays 80 percent of the cost.

LO2 **Product Warranty Liability**

SE 6. Harper Corp. manufactures and sells travel clocks. Each clock costs $12.50 to produce and sells for $25. In addition, each clock carries a warranty that provides for free replacement if it fails during the two years following the sale. In the past, 5 percent of the clocks sold have had to be replaced under the warranty. During October, Harper sold 52,000 clocks, and 2,800 clocks were replaced under the warranty. Prepare entries in journal form to record the estimated liability for product warranties during the month and the clocks replaced under wring the month.

Note: Tables 1 to 4 in the appendix on future value and present value tables may be used where appropriate to solve **SE 7** through **SE 10.**

LO4   **Simple and Compound Interest**

SE 7. Murad Motors, Inc., receives a one-year note that carries a 12 percent annual interest rate on $3,000 for the sale of a used car. Compute the maturity value under each of the following assumptions: (1) Simple interest is charged. (2) The interest is compounded semiannually. (3) The interest is compounded quarterly. (4) The interest is compounded monthly.

LO4   **Future Value Calculations**

SE 8. Find the future value of (1) a single payment of $5,000 at 7 percent for ten years, (2) ten annual payments of $500 at 7 percent, (3) a single payment of $1,500 at 9 percent for seven years, and (4) seven annual payments of $1,500 at 9 percent.

LO4   **Present Value Calculations**

SE 9. Find the present value of (1) a single payment of $24,000 at 6 percent for 12 years, (2) 12 annual payments of $2,000 at 6 percent, (3) a single payment of $5,000 at 9 percent for five years, and (4) five annual payments of $5,000 at 9 percent.

LO5   **Valuing an Asset for the Purpose of Making a Purchasing Decision**

SE 10. Hogan Whitner owns a machine shop and has the opportunity to purchase a new machine for $30,000. After carefully studying projected costs and revenues, Whitner estimates that the new machine will produce a net cash flow of $7,200 annually and will last for eight years. Whitner believes that an interest rate of 10 percent is adequate for his business.

Calculate the present value of the machine to Whitner. Does the purchase appear to be a smart business decision?

Exercises

LO1, LO2, LO3   **Discussion Questions**

E 1. Develop a brief answer to each of the following questions:

1. Ned Johnson, a star college basketball player, received a contract from the Midwest Blazers to play professional basketball. The contract calls for a salary of $300,000 a year for four years, dependent on his making the team in each of those years. Should this contract be considered a liability and recorded on the books of the basketball team?
2. Is increasing payables turnover good or bad for a company? Why or why not?
3. Do adjusting entries involving estimated liabilities and accruals ever affect cash flows?
4. When would a commitment be recognized in the accounting records?

LO4   **Discussion Questions**

E 2. Develop a brief answer to each of the following questions:

1. Is a friend who borrows money from you for three years and agrees to pay you interest after each year paying you simple or compound interest?
2. Ordinary annuities assume that the first payment is made at the end of each year. In a transaction, who is better off in this arrangement, the payer or the receiver? Why?
3. Why is present value one of the most useful concepts in making business decisions?

LO1   **Issues in Accounting for Liabilities**

E 3. Indicate whether each of the following actions relates to (a) managing liquidity and cash flows, (b) recognition of liabilities, (c) valuation of liabilities, (d) classification of liabilities, or (e) disclosure of liabilities:

1. Setting a liability at the fair market value of goods to be delivered
2. Relating the payment date of a liability to the length of the operating cycle
3. Recording a liability in accordance with the matching rule
4. Providing information about financial instruments on the balance sheet
5. Estimating the amount of "cents-off" coupons that will be redeemed
6. Categorizing a liability as long-term debt
7. Measuring working capital
8. Comparing days' payable with last year

LO1   **Measuring Short-Term Liquidity**

E 4. In 20x7, Michaud Company had current assets of $155,000 and current liabilities of $100,000, of which accounts payable were $65,000. Cost of goods sold was $425,000, merchandise inventory increased by $40,000, and accounts payable were $55,000 in the prior year. In 20x8, Michaud had current assets of $210,000 and current liabilities of $160,000, of which accounts payable were $75,000. Cost of goods sold was $475,000, and merchandise inventory decreased by $15,000. Calculate Michaud working capital, payables turnover, and days' payable for 20x7 and 20x8. Assess Michaud liquidity and cash flows in relation to the change in payables turnover from 20x7 to 20x8.

LO2   **Interest Expense on Note Payable**

E 5. On the last day of October, Thornton Company borrows $60,000 on a bank note for 60 days at 12 percent interest. Interest is not included in the face amount. Prepare the following entries in journal form: (1) October 31, recording of note; (2) November 30, accrual of interest expense; and (3) December 30, payment of note plus interest.

LO2   **Sales and Excise Taxes**

E 6. Web Design Services billed its customers a total of $490,200 for the month of August, including 9 percent federal excise tax and 5 percent sales tax.

1. Determine the proper amount of service revenue to report for the month.
2. Prepare an entry in journal form to record the revenue and related liabilities for the month.

LO2   **Payroll Expenses**

E 7. At the end of October, the payroll register for Symphony Tool and Die Corporation contained the following totals: wages, $371,000; federal income taxes withheld, $94,884; state income taxes withheld, $15,636; social security tax withheld, $23,002; Medicare tax withheld, $5,379.50; medical insurance deductions, $12,870; and wages subject to unemployment taxes, $57,240.

Determine the total and components of the (1) monthly payroll and (2) employer payroll expenses, assuming social security and Medicare taxes equal to the amount for employees, a federal unemployment insurance tax of .8 percent, a state unemployment tax of 5.4 percent, and medical insurance premiums for which the employer pays 80 percent of the cost.

LO2   **Product Warranty Liability**

E 8. Snapz Company manufactures and sells electronic games. Each game costs $25 to produce, sells for $45, and carries a warranty that provides for free replacement if it fails during the two years following the sale. In the past, 7 percent of the games sold had to be replaced under the warranty. During July, Snapz sold 13,000 games, and 1,400 games were replaced under the warranty.

1. Prepare an entry in journal form to record the estimated liability for product warranties during the month.
2. Prepare an entry in journal form to record the games replaced under warranty during the month.

LO2 **Vacation Pay Liability**

E 9. Bivens Corporation gives three weeks' paid vacation to each employee who has worked at the company for one year. Based on studies of employee turnover and previous experience, management estimates that 65 percent of the employees will qualify for vacation pay this year.

1. Assume that Bivens's July payroll is $300,000, of which $20,000 is paid to employees on vacation. Figure the estimated employee vacation benefit for the month.
2. Prepare an entry in journal form to record the employee benefit for July.
3. Prepare an entry in journal form to record the pay to employees on vacation.

Note: Tables 1 to 4 in the appendix on future value and present value tables may be used where appropriate to solve **E 10** through **E 20**.

LO4 **Future Value Calculations**

E 10. Song receives a one-year note for $6,000 that carries a 12 percent annual interest rate for the sale of a used car. Compute the maturity value under each of the following assumptions: (1) The interest is simple interest. (2) The interest is compounded semiannually. (3) The interest is compounded quarterly. (4) The interest is compounded monthly.

LO4 **Future Value Calculations**

E 11. Find the future value of (1) a single payment of $40,000 at 7 percent for ten years, (2) ten annual payments of $4,000 at 7 percent, (3) a single payment of $12,000 at 9 percent for seven years, and (4) seven annual payments of $12,000 at 9 percent.

LO4, LO5 **Determining an Advance Payment**

E 12. Denise Davis is contemplating paying five years' rent in advance. Her annual rent is $12,600. Calculate the single sum that would have to be paid now for the advance rent if we assume compound interest of 8 percent.

LO4 **Present Value Calculations**

E 13. Find the present value of (1) a single payment of $12,000 at 6 percent for 12 years, (2) 12 annual payments of $1,000 at 6 percent, (3) a single payment of $2,500 at 9 percent for five years, and (4) five annual payments of $2,500 at 9 percent.

LO4, LO5 **Present Value of a Lump-Sum Contract**

E 14. A contract calls for a lump-sum payment of $30,000. Find the present value of the contract, assuming that (1) the payment is due in five years, and the current interest rate is 9 percent; (2) the payment is due in ten years, and the current interest rate is 9 percent; (3) the payment is due in five years, and the current interest rate is 5 percent; and (4) the payment is due in ten years, and the current interest rate is 5 percent.

LO4, LO5   Present Value of an Annuity Contract

E 15. A contract calls for annual payments of $2,400. Find the present value of the contract, assuming that (1) the number of payments is seven, and the current interest rate is 6 percent; (2) the number of payments is 14, and the current interest rate is 6 percent; (3) the number of payments is seven, and the current interest rate is 8 percent; and (4) the number of payments is 14, and the current interest rate is 8 percent.

LO4, LO5   Valuing an Asset for the Purpose of Making a Purchasing Decision

E 16. Charles Ogden owns a service station and has the opportunity to purchase a car wash machine for $15,000. After carefully studying projected costs and revenues, Ogden estimates that the car wash machine will produce a net cash flow of $2,600 annually and will last for eight years. He determines that an interest rate of 14 percent is adequate for his business. Calculate the present value of the machine to Ogden. Does the purchase appear to be a smart business decision?

LO4, LO5   Deferred Payment

E 17. Antwone Equipment Corporation sold a precision tool machine with computer controls to Trudeau Corporation for $400,000 on January 2 and agreed to take payment nine months later on October 2. Assuming that the prevailing annual interest rate for such a transaction is 16 percent compounded quarterly, what is the actual sale (purchase) price of the machine tool?

LO4, LO5   Investment of Idle Cash

E 18. Playwright Publishing Company, a publisher of college textbooks, has just completed a successful fall selling season and has $2,500,000 in cash to invest for nine months, beginning on January 1. The company places the cash in an account that is expected to pay 4 percent annual interest compounded quarterly. Interest is credited to the company's account each quarter. How much cash will the company have at the end of nine months?

LO4, LO5   Accumulation of a Fund

E 19. Semma Corporation borrows $1,500,000 from an insurance company on a five-year note. Management agrees to set aside enough cash at the end of each year to accumulate the amount needed to pay off the note at maturity. Since the first contribution to the fund will be made in one year, four annual contributions are needed. Assuming that the fund will earn 10 percent compounded annually, how much will the annual contribution to the fund be? (Round to nearest dollar.)

LO4, LO5   Negotiating the Sale of a Business

E 20. Andrea Lima is attempting to sell her business to Alfonso Moreno. The company has assets of $1,800,000, liabilities of $1,600,000, and stockholders' equity of $200,000. Both parties agree that the proper rate of return to expect is 12 percent; however, they differ on other assumptions. Lima believes that the business will generate at least $200,000 per year of cash flows for 20 years. Moreno thinks that $160,000 in cash flows per year is more reasonable and that only ten years in the future should be considered. Using Table 4 in the appendix on future value and present value tables, determine the range for negotiation by computing the present value of Lima's offer to sell and of Moreno's offer to buy.

Problems

LO1, LO2, LO3 Identification of Current Liabilities, Contingencies, and Commitments

P 1. Listed below are common types of current liabilities, contingencies, and commitments:

a. Accounts payable
b. Bank loans and commercial paper
c. Notes payable
d. Dividends payable
e. Sales and excise taxes payable
f. Current portion of long-term debt
g. Payroll liabilities
h. Unearned revenues

i. Income taxes payable
j. Property taxes payable
k. Promotional costs
l. Product warranty liability
m. Vacation pay liability
n. Contingent liability
o. Commitment

Required

1. For each of the following statements, identify the category above to which it gives rise or with which it is most closely associated:

    1. A company agrees to replace parts of a product if they fail.
    2. An employee earns one day off for each month worked.
    3. A company signs a contract to lease a building for five years.
    4. A company puts discount coupons in the newspaper.
    5. A company agrees to pay insurance costs for employees.
    6. A portion of a mortgage on a building is due this year.
    7. The board of directors declares a dividend.
    8. A company has trade payables.
    9. A company has a pending lawsuit against it.
    10. A company arranges for a line of credit.
    11. A company signs a note due in 60 days.
    12. A company operates in a state that has a sales tax.
    13. A company earns a profit that is taxable.
    14. A company owns buildings that are subject to property taxes.

2. **User Insight:** Of the items listed from **a** to **o** above, which ones would you not expect to see listed on the balance sheet with a dollar amount? Of those items that would be listed on the balance sheet with a dollar amount, which ones would you consider to involve the most judgment or discretion on the part of management?

LO2 Notes Payable and Wages Payable

P 2. Part A: Alhara Corporation, whose fiscal year ended June 30, 20xx, completed the following transactions involving notes payable:

May 21 Obtained a 60-day extension on a $36,000 trade account payable owed to a supplier by signing a 60-day, $36,000 note. Interest is in addition to the face value, at the rate of 14 percent.
June 30 Made the end-of-year adjusting entry to accrue interest expense.
July 20 Paid off the note plus interest due the supplier.

Required

1. Prepare journal entries for the notes payable transactions.
2. **User Insight:** When notes payable appears on the balance sheet, what other current liability would you look for to be associated with the notes? What would it mean if this other current liability did not appear?

Part B: The payroll register for Alhara Corporation contained the following totals at the end of July: wages, $278,250; federal income taxes withheld,

$71,163; state income taxes withheld, $11,727; social security tax withheld, $17,253; Medicare tax withheld, $4,035; medical insurance deductions, $9,600; and wages subject to unemployment taxes, $171,720.

Required

Prepare entries to record the (1) monthly payroll and (2) employer payroll expenses, assuming social security and Medicare taxes equal to the amount for employees, a federal unemployment insurance tax of .8 percent, a state unemployment tax of 5.4 percent, and medical insurance premiums for which the employer pays 80 percent of the cost.

LO2 **Product Warranty Liability**

P 3. Visicorp Company is engaged in the retail sale of high-definition televisions (HDTVs). Each HDTV has a 24-month warranty on parts. If a repair under warranty is required, a charge for the labor is made. Management has found that 20 percent of the HDTVs sold require some work before the warranty expires. Furthermore, the average cost of replacement parts has been $120 per repair. At the beginning of January, the account for the estimated liability for product warranties had a credit balance of $28,600. During January, 112 HDTVs were returned under the warranty. The cost of the parts used in repairing the HDTVs was $17,530, and $18,884 was collected as service revenue for the labor involved. During January, the month before the Super Bowl, Visicorp Company sold 450 new HDTVs.

Required

1. Prepare entries in journal form to record each of the following: (a) the warranty work completed during the month, including related revenue; (b) the estimated liability for product warranties for HDTVs sold during the month.

2. Compute the balance of the Estimated Product Warranty Liability account at the end of the month.

3. **User Insight:** If the company's product warranty liability is overestimated, what are the effects on current and future years' income?

LO1 **Identification and Evaluation of Current Liabilities**

P 4. Jose Hernandez opened a small motorcycle repair shop, Hernandez Cycle Repair, on January 2, 20x6. The shop also sells a limited number of motorcycle parts. In January 20x7, Hernandez realized he had never filed any tax reports for his business and therefore probably owes a considerable amount of taxes. Since he has limited experience in running a business, he has brought you all his business records, including a checkbook, canceled checks, deposit slips, suppliers' invoices, a notice of annual property taxes of $4,620 due to the city, and a promissory note to his father-in-law for $5,000. He wants you to determine what his business owes the government and other parties.

You analyze all his records and determine the following as of December 31, 20x6:

Unpaid invoices for motorcycle parts	$ 18,000
Parts sales (excluding sales tax)	88,540
Cost of Parts Sold	62,250
Workers' salaries	20,400
Repair revenues	120,600
Current assets	32,600
Motorcycle parts inventory	23,500

You learn that the company has deducted $952 from the two employees' salaries for federal income taxes owed to the government. The current social security tax is 6.2 percent on maximum earnings of $90,000 for each employee, and the current Medicare tax is 1.45 percent (no maximum earnings). The FUTA tax is 5.4 percent to the state and .8 percent to the federal government on the first $7,000 earned by each employee, and each employee earned more than $7,000. Hernandez has not filed a sales tax report to the state (5 percent of sales).

Required

1. Given these limited facts, determine Hernandez Cycle Repair's current liabilities as of December 31, 20x6.
2. **User Insight:** What additional information would you want from Hernandez to satisfy yourself that all current liabilities have been identified?
3. **User Insight:** Evaluate Hernandez's liquidity by calculating working capital, payables turnover, and days' payable. Comment on the results. (Assume average accounts payable were the same as year-end accounts payable.)

LO4, LO5 **Applications of Time Value of Money**

P 5. The management of Pzazz, Inc., took the following actions that went into effect on January 2, 20x7. Each action involved an application of the time value of money.

a. Established in one payment of $50,000 a contingency fund for the possible settlement of a lawsuit. The suit is expected to be settled in two years.
b. Asked for another fund to be established by a single payment to accumulate to $150,000 in four years.
c. Approved the purchase of a parcel of land for future plant expansion. Payments are to start January 2, 20x8, at $100,000 per year for five years.
d. Determined that a new building to be built on the property in **c** would cost $800,000 and authorized five annual payments to be paid starting January 2, 20x8, into a fund for its construction.

Required

1. Assuming an annual interest rate of 8 percent and using Tables 1 to 4 in this chapter, answer the following questions:
   a. In action **a**, how much will the fund total in two years?
   b. In action **b**, how much will need to be deposited initially to accumulate the desired amount?
   c. In action **c**, what is the purchase price (present value) of the land?
   d. In action **d**, how much would the equal annual payments need to be to accumulate enough money to construct the building?
2. **User Insight:** What is the fundamental reason time value of money analysis is a useful tool in making business decisions?

Alternate Problems

LO2 **Notes Payable and Wages Payable**

P 6. Part A: Green T Company, whose fiscal year ends December 31, completed the following transactions involving notes payable:

20x7
Nov. 25   Purchased a new loading cart by issuing a 60-day, 10 percent note for $43,200.
Dec. 31   Made the end-of-year adjusting entry to accrue interest expense.

20x8

Jan. 24 Paid off the loading cart note.

*R*equired

1. Prepare entries in journal form for Green T Company's notes payable transactions.

2. **User Insight:** When notes payable appears on the balance sheet, what other current liability would you look for to be associated with the notes? What would it mean if this other current liability did not appear?

Part B: At the end of October, the payroll register for Green T Company contained the following totals: wages, $92,750; federal income taxes withheld, $23,721; state income taxes withheld, $3,909; social security tax withheld, $5,751; Medicare tax withheld, $1,345; medical insurance deductions, $3,200; and wages subject to unemployment taxes, $57,240.

*R*equired

Prepare entries to record the (1) monthly payroll and (2) employer payroll expenses, assuming social security and Medicare taxes equal to the amount for employees, a federal unemployment insurance tax of .8 percent, a state unemployment tax of 5.4 percent, and medical insurance premiums for which the employer pays 80 percent of the cost.

LO2 **Product Warranty Liability**

 P 7. The Kow Long Products Company manufactures and sells wireless video cell phones, which it guarantees for five years. If a cell phone fails, it is replaced free, but the customer is charged a service fee for handling. In the past, management has found that only 3 percent of the cell phones sold required replacement under the warranty. The average cell phone costs the company $240. At the beginning of September, the account for estimated liability for product warranties had a credit balance of $208,000. During September, 250 cell phones were returned under the warranty. The company collected $9,860 of service fees for handling. During the month, the company sold 2,800 cell phones.

*R*equired

1. Prepare entries in journal form to record (a) the cost of cell phones replaced under warranty and (b) the estimated liability for product warranties for cell phones sold during the month.

2. Compute the balance of the Estimated Product Warranty Liability account at the end of the month.

3. **User Insight:** If the company's product warranty liability is underestimated, what are the effects on current and future years' income?

LO4, LO5 **Applications of Time Value of Money**

P 8. Rothberg Corporation's management took the following actions, which went into effect on January 2, 20x7. Each action involved an application of the time value of money.

a. Established a new retirement plan to take effect in three years and authorized three annual payments of $1,000,000, starting January 2, 20x8, to establish the retirement fund.

b. Approved plans for a new distribution center to be built for $2,000,000 and authorized five annual payments, starting January 2, 20x8, to accumulate the funds for the new center.

c. Bought out the contract of a member of top management for a payment of $100,000 per year for four years beginning January 2, 20x8.

d. Set aside $600,000 for possible losses from lawsuits over a defective product. The lawsuits are not expected to be settled for three years.

Required

1. Assuming an annual interest rate of 10 percent and using Tables 1 to 4 in this chapter, answer the following questions:
   a. In action **a**, how much will the retirement fund total after the three payments are made?
   b. In action **b**, how much must the annual payment be to reach the goal?
   c. In action **c**, what is the cost (present value) of the buyout?
   d. In action **d**, how much will the fund total in three years?
2. **User Insight:** Many businesses analyze the time value of money extensively when making decisions about investing in long-term assets. Why is this type of analysis particularly appropriate for such decisions?

≡ ENHANCING Your Knowledge, Skills, and Critical Thinking

Conceptual Understanding Cases

LO2 Frequent Flyer Plan

C 1. JetGreen Airways instituted a frequent flyer program in which passengers accumulate points toward a free flight based on the number of miles they fly on the airline. One point was awarded for each mile flown, with a minimum of 750 miles being given for any flight. Because of competition in 2006, the company began a bonus plan in which passengers receive triple the normal mileage points. In the past, about 1.5 percent of passenger miles were flown by passengers who had converted points to free flights. With the triple mileage program, JetGreen expects that a 2.5 percent rate will be more appropriate for future years.

During 2006, the company had passenger revenues of $966.3 million and passenger transportation operating expenses of $802.8 million before depreciation and amortization. Operating income was $86.1 million. What is the appropriate rate to use to estimate free miles? What would be the effect of the estimated liability for free travel by frequent fliers on 2006 net income? Describe several ways to estimate the amount of this liability. Be prepared to discuss the arguments for and against recognizing this liability.

LO3 Lawsuits and Contingent Liabilities

C 2. When faced with lawsuits, many companies recognize a loss and therefore credit a liability or reserve account for any future losses that may result. For instance, in the famous **WorldCom** case, **Citibank**, the world's largest financial services firm, announced it was setting up reserves or liabilities of $5.6 billion in connection with pending lawsuits related to its relationship with World-Com.[14] Are these lawsuits contingent liabilities? Using the two criteria established by the FASB for recording a contingency, what conditions must exist for Citibank to record these lawsuits when they have not yet been heard in court?

LO4, LO5 Time Value of Money

C 3. **Mitsubishi**, the large Japanese electronics company, advertised its $4,499 Diamond Series 65-inch-wide screen Projection TV with no payments and no interest for 12 months.[15] What role does the time value of money play in this promotion? Assuming that Mitsubishi is able to borrow funds at 8 percent interest, what is the cost to Mitsubishi of every customer who takes advantage of this offer? If you were able to borrow to pay cash for this TV, which rate would be more relevant in determining how much you might offer for the TV—the rate at which you borrow money or the rate Mitsubishi borrows money?

Interpreting Financial Reports

LO1 **Comparison of Two Companies' Ratios with Industry Ratios**

C 4. Both **Sun Microsystems Inc**. and **Cisco Systems** are in the computer industry. These data (in thousands) are for their fiscal year ends:[16]

	Sun	Cisco
Accounts payable	$1,057,000	$ 657,000
Cost of goods sold	6,669,000	15,126,000
Increase (decrease) in inventory	48,000	334,000

Compare the payables turnover ratio and days' payable for both companies. Comment on the results. How are cash flows affected by days' payable? How do Sun Microsystems' and Cisco Systems' ratios compare with the computer industry ratios shown in Figures 1 and 2 in this chapter? (Use year-end amounts for ratios.)

LO2 **Nature and Recognition of an Estimated Liability**

C 5. The decision to recognize and record a liability is sometimes a matter of judgment. People who use **General Motors** credit cards earn rebates toward the purchase or lease of GM vehicles in relation to the amount of purchases they make with their cards. General Motors chooses to treat these outstanding rebates as a commitment in the notes to its financial statements:

> GM sponsors a credit card program . . . which offers rebates that can be applied primarily against the purchase or lease of GM vehicles. The amount of rebates available to qualified cardholders (net of deferred program income) was $4.5 billion, $4.1 billion, and $4.0 billion at December 31, 2004, 2003, and 2002, respectively.[17]

Using the two criteria established by the FASB for recording a contingency, explain GM's reasoning in treating this liability as a commitment in the notes, where it will likely receive less attention by analysts, rather than including it on the income statement as an expense and on the balance sheet as an estimated liability. Do you agree with this position? (**Hint:** Apply the matching rule.)

Decision Analysis Using Excel

LO4, LO5 **Baseball Contract**

C 6. The St. Louis Titans' fifth-year shortstop Devon Turner made the All-Star team in 2007. Turner has three years left on a contract that is to pay him $2.4 million a year. He wants to renegotiate his contract because other players who have equally outstanding records (although they also have more experience) are receiving as much as $10.5 million per year for five years. Management has a policy of never renegotiating a current contract but is willing to consider extending the contract to additional years. In fact, the Titans have offered Turner an additional three years at $6.0 million, $9.0 million, and $12.0 million, respectively. In addition, they have added an option year at $15.0 million. Management points out that this package is worth $42.0 million, or $10.5 million per year on average. Turner is considering this offer and is also considering asking for a bonus to be paid upon signing the contract. Write a memorandum to Turner that comments on management's position and evaluates the offer, assuming a current interest rate of 10 percent. (**Hint:** Use present values.) Propose a range for the signing bonus. Finally, include other considerations that may affect the value of the offer.

Annual Report Case: CVS Corporation

LO1, LO3 **Short-Term Liabilities and Seasonality; Commitments and Contingencies**

C 7. Refer to the quarterly financial report near the end of the notes to the financial statements in **CVS's** annual report. Is CVS a seasonal business? Would you expect short-term borrowings and accounts payable to be unusually high or unusually low at the balance sheet date of January 1, 2005?

Read CVS's note on commitments and contingencies. What commitments and contingencies does the company have? Why is it important to consider this information in connection with payables analysis?

Comparison Case: CVS Corporation Versus Walgreens

LO1 **Payables Analysis**

K/R **C 8.** Refer to **CVS's** financial statements in the Supplement to Chapter 1 and to the following data for **Walgreens**:

	2004	2003	2002
Cost of sales	$27,310.4	$23,706.2	$21,076.1
Trade accounts payable	2,641.5	2,407.8	1,836.4
Increase in inventories	536.0	557.5	162.8

Compute the payables turnover and days' payable for CVS and Walgreens for the past two years. In 2002, CVS had accounts payable of $1,707.9 million, and its inventories were $4,018.6. Which company do you think makes the most use of creditors for financing the needs of the operating cycle? Has the trend changed?

Ethical Dilemma Case

LO2 **Known Legal Violations**

C 9. Surf and Turf Restaurant is a large steak restaurant in the suburbs of Chicago. Don O'Shannon, an accounting student at a nearby college, recently secured a full-time accounting job at the restaurant. He felt fortunate to have a good job that accommodated his class schedule because the local economy was very bad. After a few weeks on the job, O'Shannon realized that his boss, the owner of the business, was paying the kitchen workers in cash and was not withholding federal and state income taxes or social security and Medicare taxes. O'Shannon understands that federal and state laws require these taxes to be withheld and paid to the appropriate agency in a timely manner. He also realizes that if he raises this issue, he could lose his job. What alternatives are available to O'Shannon? What action would you take if you were in his position? Why did you make this choice?

Internet Case

LO2, LO3 **Pain in the Drug Industry**

C 10. Pain medications have been in the news. The big drug company **Merck** had to withdraw its pain killer Vioxx from the market when it became known that the drug increased the risk of heart attacks. Other drugs are under scrutiny, like Celebrex from **Pfizer**. Do an Internet search on these terms and companies. Find out if any lawsuits have been initiated and how these companies are reacting. Access their annual reports and find out what they report under contingent liabilities in the notes to the financial statements and elsewhere. Have they set aside any reserves for liabilities? What are the criteria for recognizing potential liabilities in the accounting records?

Group Activity Case

LO2, LO5   **Nature and Recognition of an Estimated Liability**

C 11. Assume that you work for Relax-A-Pools, Inc., a retail company that sells backyard above-ground swimming pools for $10,000. Your boss is considering two types of promotions:

1. Offering customers a $1,000 coupon that they can apply to future purchases, including the purchase of annual pool maintenance.
2. Offering credit terms that allow payments of $2,000 down and $2,000 per year for four years starting one year after the purchase. Relax-A-Pools would have to borrow money at 7 percent interest to finance these credit arrangements.

Divide the class into groups. After discussing the relative merits of these two plans, including their implications for accounting and the time value of money, each group should decide on the best alternative. The groups may recommend changes in the plans. A representative of each group should report the group's findings to the class.

Business Communication Case

LO5   **Evaluation of an Auto Lease**

C 12. Ford Credit ran an advertisement offering three alternatives for a 24-month lease on a new Lincoln automobile. The three alternatives were zero dollars down and $587 per month for 24 months, $1,975 down and $499 per month for 24 months, or $12,283 down and no monthly payments.[18] Your boss asks you to prepare an analysis of the three alternatives assuming a 12 percent annual return compounded monthly is the relevant interest rate for the company. Present your analysis and make a recommendation to your boss in a one-page business memorandum. Use Table 4 in the appendix on future value and present value tables to determine which is the best deal. How would your recommendation change if the interest rate were higher? If it were lower?

Long-Term Assets

Long-term assets include tangible assets, such as land, buildings, and equipment; natural resources, such as timberland and oil fields; and intangible assets, such as patents and copyrights. These assets represent a company's strategic commitments well into the future. The judgments related to their acquisition, operation, and disposal and to the allocation of their costs will affect a company's performance for years to come. Investors and creditors rely on accurate and full reporting of the assumptions and judgments that underlie the measurement of long-term assets.

LEARNING OBJECTIVES

Making a Statement

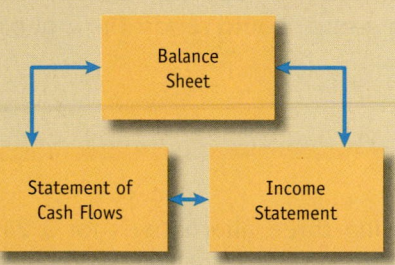

Purchase, use, and disposal of long-term assets affect all financial statements.

LO1 Define *long-term assets,* and explain the management issues related to them.

LO2 Distinguish between *capital expenditures* and *revenue expenditures,* and account for the cost of property, plant, and equipment.

LO3 Compute depreciation under the straight-line, production, and declining-balance methods.

LO4 Account for the disposal of depreciable assets.

LO5 Identify the issues related to accounting for natural resources, and compute depletion.

LO6 Identify the issues related to accounting for intangible assets, including research and development costs and goodwill.

- **What are Apple's long-term assets?**

- **What are its policies in accounting for long-term assets?**

- **Does the company generate enough cash flow to finance its continued growth?**

Long known for its innovative technology and design of computers, **Apple** revolutionized the music industry with its digital iPod music player. The company's success stems from its willingness to invest in research and development and long-term assets to create new products. Each year, it spends almost $500 million on research and development and about $175 million on new long-term assets. Almost 40 percent of its assets are long term. You can get an idea of the extent and importance of Apple's long-term assets by looking at the Financial Highlights from its balance sheet.[1]

APPLE COMPUTER'S FINANCIAL HIGHLIGHTS
(In millions)

	2004	2003
Property, Plant, and Equipment:		
Land and buildings	$ 351	$ 350
Machinery, equipment, and internal-use software	422	393
Office furniture and equipment	79	74
Leasehold improvements	446	357
	1,298	1,174
Less accumulated depreciation and amortization	591	505
Total property, plant, and equipment, net	$ 707	$ 669
Other Noncurrent Assets:		
Goodwill	80	85
Acquired intangible assets	17	24
Other noncurrent assets	191	150
Total other noncurrent assets	$ 288	$ 259

Management Issues Related to Long-Term Assets

LO1 Define *long-term assets*, and explain the management issues related to them.

Long-term assets were once called fixed assets, but this term has fallen out of favor because it implies that the assets last forever, which they do not. Long-term assets have the following characteristics:

▸ *They have a useful life of more than one year.* This distinguishes them from current assets, which a company expects to use up or convert to cash within one year or during its operating cycle, whichever is longer. They also differ from current assets in that they support the operating cycle, rather than being part of it. Although there is no strict rule for defining the useful life of a long-term asset, the most common criterion is that the asset be capable of repeated use for at least a year. Included in this category is equipment used only in peak or emergency periods, such as electric generators.

▸ *They are used in the operation of a business.* Assets not used in the normal course of business, such as land held for speculative reasons or buildings no longer used in ordinary business operations, should be classified as long-term investments, not as long-term assets.

▸ *They are not intended for resale to customers.* An asset that a company intends to resell to customers should be classified as inventory—not as a long-term asset—no matter how durable it is. For example, a printing press that a manufacturer offers for sale is part of the manufacturer's inventory, but it is a long-term asset for a printing company that buys it to use in its operations.

Figure 1 shows the relative importance of long-term assets in various industries. Figure 2 shows how long-term assets are classified and defines the methods of accounting for them. Plant assets, which are **tangible assets**, are accounted for through **depreciation**. (Although land is a tangible asset, it is not depreciated because it has an unlimited life.) **Natural resources**, which are also tangible assets, are accounted for through **depletion**. **Intangible assets**

Study Note

For an asset to be classified as property, plant, and equipment, it must be "put in use," which means it is available for its intended purpose. An emergency generator is "put in use" when it is available for emergencies, even if it is never used.

Study Note

A computer that a company uses in an office is a long-term plant asset. An identical computer that a company sells to customers is considered inventory.

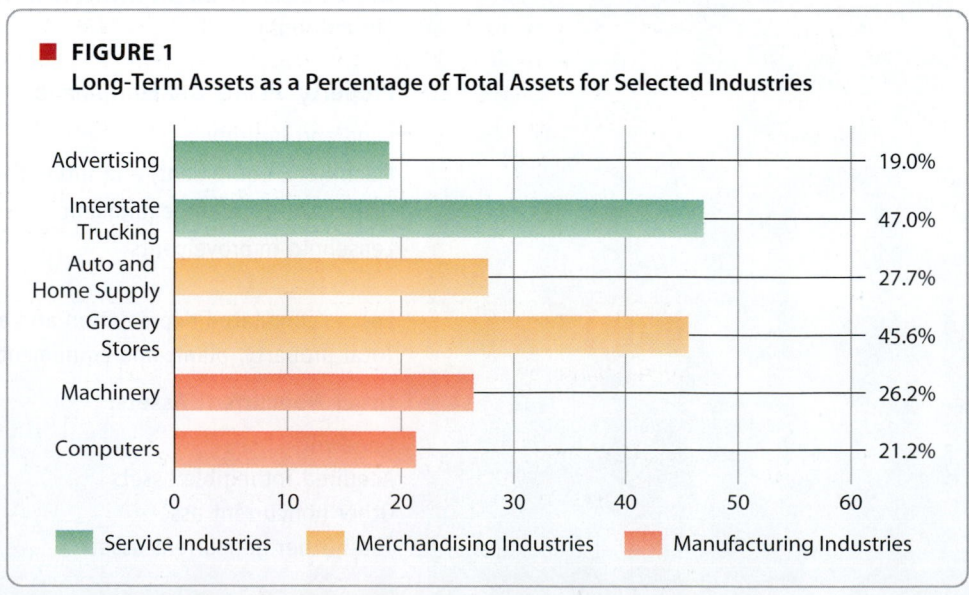

■ **FIGURE 1**
Long-Term Assets as a Percentage of Total Assets for Selected Industries

Industry	Percentage
Advertising	19.0%
Interstate Trucking	47.0%
Auto and Home Supply	27.7%
Grocery Stores	45.6%
Machinery	26.2%
Computers	21.2%

■ Service Industries   ■ Merchandising Industries   ■ Manufacturing Industries

Source: Data from Dun & Bradstreet, *Industry Norms and Key Business Ratios,* 2003–2004

■ **FIGURE 2**
Classification of Long-Term Assets and Methods of Accounting for Them

BALANCE SHEET	INCOME STATEMENT
Long-Term Assets	**Expenses**

Tangible Assets: long-term assets that have physical substance

Land

Plant, Buildings, Equipment (plant assets)

Land is not expensed because it has an unlimited life.

Depreciation: periodic allocation of the cost of a tangible long-lived asset (other than land and natural resources) over its estimated useful life

Natural Resources: long-term assets purchased for the economic value that can be taken from the land and used up, as with ore, lumber, oil, and gas or other resources contained in the land

Mines

Timberland

Oil and Gas Fields

Depletion: exhaustion of a natural resource through mining, cutting, pumping, or other extraction, and the way in which the cost is allocated

Intangible Assets: long-term assets that have no physical substance but have a value based on rights or advantages accruing to the owner

Patents, Copyrights, Trademarks, Franchises, Leaseholds, Goodwill

Amortization: periodic allocation of the cost of an intangible asset to the periods it benefits

Goodwill is not expensed, but its value is reviewed annually.

Study Note

To be classified as intangible, an asset must lack physical substance, be long term, and represent a legal right or advantage.

are accounted for through **amortization**. (Although goodwill is an intangible asset, it is not expensed; however, it is reviewed for impairment each year.)

Long-term assets are generally reported at carrying value. As shown in Figure 3, **carrying value** (also called *book value*) is the unexpired part of an asset's cost. If a long-term asset loses some or all of its potential to generate revenue before the end of its useful life, it is deemed *impaired*, and its carrying value is reduced.

All long-term assets are subject to an annual impairment evaluation. **Asset impairment** occurs when the carrying value of a long-term asset exceeds

■ **FIGURE 3**
Carrying Value of Long-Term Assets on the Balance Sheet

Plant Assets	Natural Resources	Intangible Assets
Less Accumulated Depreciation	Less Accumulated Depletion	Less Accumulated Amortization
Carrying Value	Carrying Value	Carrying Value

its fair value.[2] *Fair value* is the amount for which the asset could be bought or sold in a current transaction. For example, if the sum of the expected cash flows from an asset is less than its carrying value, the asset would be impaired. Reducing carrying value to fair value, as measured by the present value of future cash flows, is an application of conservatism. A reduction in carrying value as the result of impairment is recorded as a loss. When the market prices used to establish fair value are not available, the amount of an impairment must be estimated from the best available information.

In 2004, **Apple** recognized losses of $5.5 million in asset impairments. A few years earlier, in the midst of an economic slowdown in the telecommunications industry, **WorldCom** recorded asset impairments that totaled $79.8 billion, the largest impairment write-down in history. Since then, other telecommunications companies, including **AT&T** and **Qwest Communications**, have taken large impairment write-downs. Due to these companies' declining revenues, the carrying value of some of their long-term assets no longer exceeded the cash flows that they were meant to help generate.[3] Because of the write-downs, these companies reported large operating losses.

Taking a large write-down in a bad year is often called "taking a big bath" because it "cleans" future years of the bad year's costs and thus can help a company return to a profitable status. In other words, by taking the largest possible loss on a long-term asset in a bad year, companies hope to reduce the costs of depreciation or amortization on the asset in subsequent years.

In the next few pages, we discuss the management issues related to long-term assets—how management decides whether it will acquire them, how it will finance them, and how it will account for them.

Acquiring Long-Term Assets

The decision to acquire a long-term asset is a complex process. For example, **Apple's** decision to invest capital in establishing its own retail stores throughout the country required very careful analysis. Methods of evaluating data to make rational decisions about acquiring long-term assets are grouped under a topic called capital budgeting, which is usually covered as a managerial accounting topic. However, an awareness of the general nature of the problem is helpful in understanding the management issues related to long-term assets.

To illustrate an acquisition decision, suppose that Apple's management is considering the purchase of a $50,000 customer-relations software package. Management estimates that the new software will save net cash flows of $20,000 per year for four years, the usual life of new software, and that the software will be worth $10,000 at the end of that period. These data are summarized as follows:

	20x5	20x6	20x7	20x8
Acquisition cost	($50,000)			
Net annual savings in cash flows	$20,000	$20,000	$20,000	$20,000
Disposal price				10,000
Net cash flows	($30,000)	$20,000	$20,000	$30,000

To put the cash flows on a comparable basis, it is helpful to use present value tables, such as Tables 3 and 4 in the appendix on future value and present value tables. If the interest rate set by management as a desirable return is 10 percent compounded annually, the purchase decision would be evaluated as follows:

		Present Value
Acquisition cost	Present value factor = 1.000	
	1.000 × $50,000	($50,000)
Net annual savings in cash flows	Present value factor = 3.170 (Table 4: 4 periods, 10%)	
	3.170 × $20,000	63,400
Disposal price	Present value factor = .683 (Table 3: 4 periods, 10%)	
	.683 × $10,000	6,830
Net present value		$20,230

As long as the net present value is positive, Apple will earn at least 10 percent on the investment. In this case, the return is greater than 10 percent because the net present value is a positive $20,230. Moreover, the net present value is large relative to the investment. Based on this analysis, it appears that Apple's management should make the decision to purchase. However, in making its decision, it should take other important considerations into account, including the costs of training personnel to use the software. It should also allow for the possibility that because of unforeseen circumstances, the savings may not be as great as expected.

Information about acquisitions of long-term assets appears in the investing activities section of the statement of cash flows. In referring to this section of its 2004 annual report, Apple's management makes the following statement:

> The company's total capital expenditures were $176 million during fiscal 2004. . . . The company currently anticipates it will utilize approximately $240 million for capital expenditures during 2005, approximately $125 million of which is expected to be utilized for further expansion of the Company's Retail segment and the remainder utilized to support normal replacement of existing capital assets.

Financing Long-Term Assets

When management decides to acquire a long-term asset, it must also decide how to finance the purchase. Many financing arrangements are based on the life of the asset. For example, an automobile loan generally spans 4 or 5 years, whereas a mortgage on a house may span 30 years. For a major long-term acquisition, a company may issue stock, long-term notes, or bonds. Some companies are profitable enough to pay for long-term assets out of cash flows from operations. A good place to study a company's investing and financing activities is its statement of cash flows, and a good measure of its ability to finance long-term assets is free cash flow.

Free cash flow is the amount of cash that remains after deducting the funds a company must commit to continue operating at its planned level. The commitments to be covered include current or continuing operations, interest, income taxes, dividends, and net capital expenditures (purchases of plant assets minus sales of plant assets). If a company fails to pay for current or continuing operations, interest, and income taxes, its creditors and the government can take legal action. Although the payment of dividends is not strictly required, dividends normally represent a commitment to stockholders. If they are reduced or eliminated, stockholders will be unhappy, and the price of the company's stock will fall. Net capital expenditures represent management's plans for the future.

A positive free cash flow means that a company has met all its cash commitments and has cash available to reduce debt or to expand its operations. A negative free cash flow means that it will have to sell investments, borrow money, or issue stock in the short term to continue at its planned level. If free cash flow remains negative for several years, a company may not be able to raise cash by issuing stock or bonds.

Using data from **Apple's** statement of cash flows in its 2004 annual report, we can compute the company's free cash flow as follows (in millions):

$$\begin{aligned}
\text{Free Cash Flow} &= \text{Net Cash Flows from Operating Activities} - \text{Dividends} - \\
&\quad \text{(Purchases of Plant Assets} - \text{Sales of Plant Assets)} \\
&= \$934 - \$0 - (\$176 - \$0) \\
&= \$758
\end{aligned}$$

Study Note

The computation of free cash flow uses *net capital expenditures* in place of (*purchases of plant assets* − *sales of plant assets*) when plant assets are small or immaterial.

This analysis confirms Apple's strong financial position. Its cash flow from operating activities far exceeds its net capital expenditures of $176 million. A factor that contributes to its positive free cash flow of $758 million is that the company pays no dividends. The financing activities section of Apple's statement of cash flows also indicates that the company, rather than incurring debt for expansion, actually reduced its long-term debt by $300 million.

Applying the Matching Rule

When a company records an expenditure as a long-term asset, it is deferring an expense until a later period. Thus, the current period's profitability looks better than it would if the expenditure had been expensed immediately. Management has considerable latitude in making the judgments and estimates necessary to account for all types and aspects of long-term assets. Sometimes, this latitude is used unwisely and unethically. For example, in the infamous **WorldCom** accounting fraud, management ordered that certain expenditures that should have been recorded as operating expenses be capitalized as long-term assets and written off over several years. The result was an overstatement of income by about $10 billion, which ultimately led to the largest bankruptcy in the history of U.S. business.

To avoid fraudulent reporting of long-term assets, a company's management must apply the matching rule in resolving two important issues. The first is how much of the total cost of a long-term asset to allocate to expense in the current accounting period. The second is how much to retain on the balance sheet as an asset that will benefit future periods. To resolve these issues, management must answer four important questions about the acquisition, use, and disposal of each long-term asset (see Figure 4):

1. How is the cost of the long-term asset determined?

2. How should the expired portion of the cost of the long-term asset be allocated against revenues over time?

3. How should subsequent expenditures, such as repairs and additions, be treated?

4. How should disposal of the long-term asset be recorded?

Management's answers to these questions can be found in the company's annual report under management's discussion and analysis and in the notes to the financial statements.

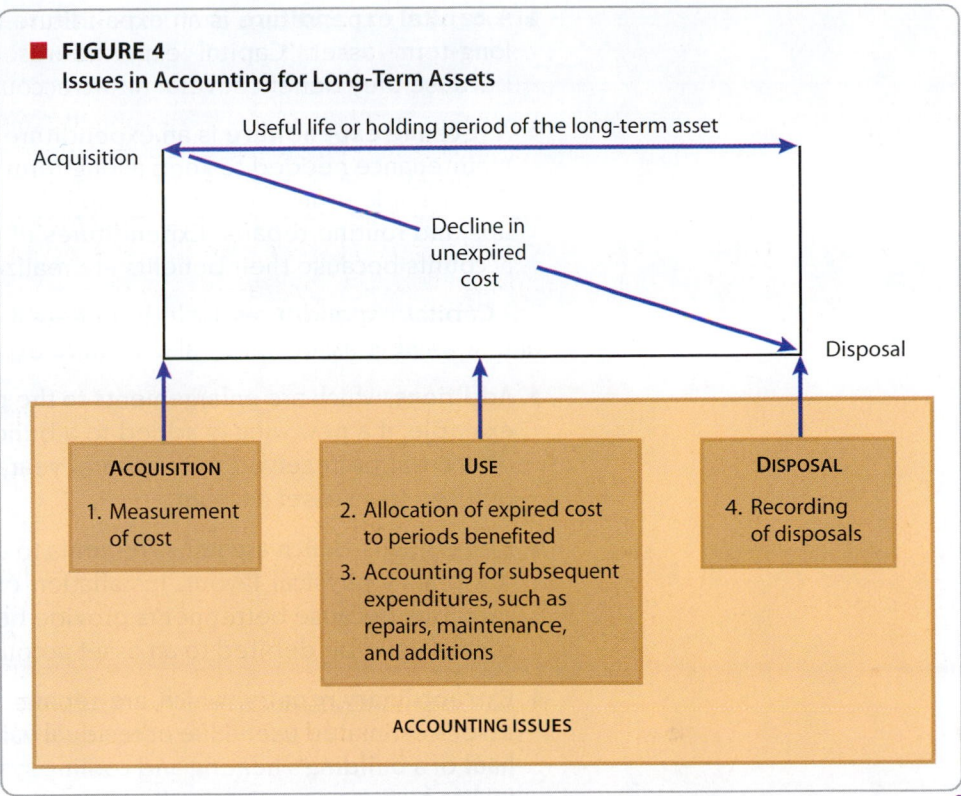

■ **FIGURE 4**
Issues in Accounting for Long-Term Assets

S T O P • R E V I E W • A P P L Y

1-1. What are the characteristics of long-term assets?

1-2. Why is land different from other long-term assets?

1-3. What do accountants mean by *depreciation*, and how does depreciation differ from depletion and amortization?

1-4. What is asset impairment, and how does it affect the valuation of long-term assets?

1-5. How do cash flows relate to the decision to acquire a long-term asset, and how does an asset's useful life relate to the means of financing it?

1-6. Define *free cash flow*, and identify its components. What do *positive free cash flow* and *negative free cash flow* mean?

1-7. What four questions are important in accounting for long-term assets?

Suggested answers to all Stop, Review, and Apply questions follow the appendixes.

Acquisition Cost of Property, Plant, and Equipment

LO2 Distinguish between *capital expenditures* and *revenue expenditures,* and account for the cost of property, plant, and equipment.

Expenditure refers to a payment or an obligation to make a future payment for an asset, such as a truck, or for a service, such as a repair. Expenditures are classified as capital expenditures or revenue expenditures.

- A **capital expenditure** is an expenditure for the purchase or expansion of a long-term asset. Capital expenditures are recorded in asset accounts because they benefit several future accounting periods.

- A **revenue expenditure** is an expenditure made for the ordinary repairs and maintenance needed to keep a long-term asset in good operating condition. For example, trucks, machines, and other equipment require periodic tune-ups and routine repairs. Expenditures of this type are recorded in expense accounts because their benefits are realized in the current period.

Capital expenditures include outlays for plant assets, natural resources, and intangible assets. They also include expenditures for the following:

- **Additions**, which are enlargements to the physical layout of a plant asset. For example, if a new wing is added to a building, the benefits from the expenditure will be received over several years, and the amount paid should be debited to an asset account.

- **Betterments**, which are improvements to a plant asset but that do not add to the plant's physical layout. Installation of an air-conditioning system is an example. Because betterments provide benefits over a period of years, their costs should be debited to an asset account.

- **Extraordinary repairs**, which are repairs that significantly enhance a plant asset's estimated useful life or residual value. For example, a complete overhaul of a building's heating and cooling system may extend the system's useful life by five years. Extraordinary repairs are typically recorded by reducing the Accumulated Depreciation account; the assumption in doing so is that some of the depreciation previously recorded on the asset has now been eliminated. The effect of the reduction is to increase the asset's carrying value by the cost of the extraordinary repair. The new carrying value should be depreciated over the asset's new estimated useful life.

The distinction between capital and revenue expenditures is important in applying the matching rule. For example, if the purchase of a machine that will benefit a company for several years is mistakenly recorded as a revenue expenditure, the total cost of the machine becomes an expense on the income statement in the current period. As a result, current net income will be reported at a lower amount (understated), and in future periods, net income will be reported at a higher amount (overstated). If, on the other hand, a revenue expenditure, such as the routine overhaul of a piece of machinery, is charged to an asset account, the expense of the current period will be understated. Current net income will be overstated by the same amount, and the net income of future periods will be understated.

General Approach to Acquisition Costs

The acquisition cost of property, plant, and equipment includes all expenditures reasonable and necessary to get an asset in place and ready for use. For example, the cost of installing and testing a machine is a legitimate cost of acquiring the machine. However, if the machine is damaged during installation, the cost of repairs is an operating expense, not an acquisition cost.

Acquisition cost is easiest to determine when a purchase is made for cash. In that case, the cost of the asset is equal to the cash paid for it plus expenditures for freight, insurance while in transit, installation, and other necessary related costs. Expenditures for freight, insurance while in transit, and installation are included in the cost of the asset because they are necessary if the asset is to function. In accordance with the matching rule, these expenditures

Study Note

Expenditures necessary to prepare an asset for its intended use are a cost of the asset.

are allocated over the asset's useful life rather than charged as expenses in the current period.

Any interest charges incurred in purchasing an asset are not a cost of the asset; they are a cost of borrowing the money to buy the asset and are therefore an operating expense. An exception to this rule is that interest costs incurred during the construction of an asset are properly included as a cost of the asset.[4]

As a matter of practicality, many companies establish policies that define when an expenditure should be recorded as an expense or as an asset. For example, small expenditures for items that qualify as long-term assets may be treated as expenses because the amounts involved are not material in relation to net income. Thus, although a wastebasket may last for years, it would be recorded as supplies expense rather than as a depreciable asset.

Specific Applications

In the sections that follow, we discuss some of the problems of determining the cost of long-term plant assets.

Land   The purchase price of land should be debited to the Land account. Other expenditures that should be debited to the Land account include commissions to real estate agents; lawyers' fees; accrued taxes paid by the purchaser; costs of preparing the land to build on, such as the costs of tearing down old buildings and grading the land; and assessments for local improvements, such as putting in streets and sewage systems. The cost of landscaping is usually debited to the Land account because such improvements are relatively permanent. Land is not subject to depreciation because it has an unlimited useful life.

Let us assume that a company buys land for a new retail operation. The net purchase price is $170,000. The company also pays brokerage fees of $6,000, legal fees of $2,000, $10,000 to have an old building on the site torn down, and

To make way for its new headquarters in Birmingham, Alabama, Energen Corporation had this ten-story building imploded. Like other costs involved in preparing land for use, the cost of implosion is debited to the Land account. Other expenditures debited to the Land account include the purchase price of the land, brokerage and legal fees involved in the purchase, taxes paid by the purchaser, and landscaping.

$1,000 to have the site graded. It receives $4,000 in salvage from the old building. The cost of the land is $185,000, calculated as follows:

Net purchase price		$170,000
Brokerage fees		6,000
Legal fees		2,000
Tearing down old building	$10,000	
Less salvage	4,000	6,000
Grading		1,000
Total cost		$185,000

Land Improvements Some improvements to real estate, such as driveways, parking lots, and fences, have a limited life and thus are subject to depreciation. They should be recorded in an account called Land Improvements rather than in the Land account.

Buildings When a company buys a building, the cost includes the purchase price and all repairs and other expenditures required to put the building in usable condition. When a company uses a contractor to construct a building, the cost includes the net contract price plus other expenditures necessary to put the building in usable condition. When a company constructs its own building, the cost includes all reasonable and necessary expenditures, including the costs of materials, labor, part of the overhead and other indirect costs, architects' fees, insurance during construction, interest on construction loans during the period of construction, lawyers' fees, and building permits. Because buildings have a limited useful life, they are subject to depreciation.

Leasehold Improvements Improvements to leased property that become the property of the lessor (the owner of the property) at the end of the lease are called **leasehold improvements**. For example, a tenant's installation of light fixtures, carpets, or walls would be considered a leasehold improvement. These improvements are usually classified as tangible assets in the property, plant, and equipment section of the balance sheet. Sometimes, they are included in the intangible assets section; the theory in reporting them as intangibles is that because they revert to the lessor at the end of the lease, they are more of a right than a tangible asset. The cost of a leasehold improvement is depreciated or amortized over the remaining term of the lease or the useful life of the improvement, whichever is shorter.

Leasehold improvements are fairly common in large businesses. A study of large companies showed that 19 percent report leasehold improvements. The percentage is likely to be much higher for small businesses because they generally operate in leased premises.[5]

Equipment The cost of equipment includes all expenditures connected with purchasing the equipment and preparing it for use. Among these expenditures are the invoice price less cash discounts; freight, including insurance; excise taxes and tariffs; buying expenses; installation costs; and test runs to ready the equipment for operation. Equipment is subject to depreciation.

Group Purchases Companies sometimes purchase land and other assets for a lump sum. Because land has an unlimited life and is a nondepreciable asset, it must have a separate ledger account, and the lump-sum purchase price must be apportioned between the land and the other assets. For example, suppose a company buys a building and the land on which it is situated for a lump sum of $85,000. The company can apportion the costs by determining what it would have paid for the building and for the land if it had purchased them separately and applying the appropriate percentages to the lump-sum price. Assume that appraisals yield estimates of $10,000 for the land and $90,000 for the building if purchased separately. In that case, 10 percent of the lump-sum price, or $8,500, would be allocated to the land, and 90 percent, or $76,500, would be allocated to the building, as follows:

	Appraisal	*Percentage*		*Apportionment*	
Land	$ 10,000	10%	($10,000 ÷ $100,000)	$ 8,500	($85,000 × 10%)
Building	90,000	90%	($90,000 ÷ $100,000)	76,500	($85,000 × 90%)
Totals	$100,000	100%		$85,000	

S T O P • R E V I E W • A P P L Y

2-1. What is the difference between revenue expenditures and capital expenditures, and why is it important?

2-2. In what ways do an addition, a betterment, and an extraordinary repair differ?

2-3. When an addition to a building is charged as a repair expense, how will it affect income in future years?

2-4. What, in general, is included in the acquisition cost of a long-term asset?

2-5. The following expenditures relate to the purchase of a computer system: (a) purchase price, (b) interest charges incurred in purchasing the equipment, (c) freight charges, (d) installation charges, (e) cost of special communications outlets at the computer site, (f) cost of repairing a part damaged during installation, and (g) cost of adjustments to the system during the first month of operation. Which of these expenditures should be charged to an asset account?

2-6. Hale's Grocery obtained bids on the construction of a receiving dock at the back of its store. The lowest bid was $22,000. The company decided to build the dock itself and was able to do so for $20,000, which it borrowed. It recorded the expenditures by debiting its Buildings account for $22,000 and crediting its Notes Payable account for $20,000 and its Gain on Construction account for $2,000. Do you agree with this entry? Why or why not?

Identification of Capital Expenditures Match each term below with the corresponding action in the list that follows by writing the appropriate numbers in the blanks:

1. Addition
2. Betterment
3. Extraordinary repair
4. Land
5. Land improvement

6. Leasehold improvement
7. Buildings
8. Equipment
9. Not a capital expenditure

_____ a. Purchase of a computer

_____ b. Purchase of a lighting system for a parking lot

_____ c. Repainting of an existing building

_____ d. Installation of a new roof that extends an existing building's useful life

_____ e. Construction of a foundation for a new building

_____ f. Erection of a new storage facility at the back of an existing building

_____ g. Installation of partitions and shelves in a leased space

_____ h. Clearing of land in preparation for construction of a new building

_____ i. Installation of a new heating system in an existing building

SOLUTION

a. 8	f. 1
b. 5	g. 6
c. 9	h. 4
d. 3	i. 2
e. 7	

≡ Depreciation

LO3 Compute depreciation under the straight-line, production, and declining-balance methods.

As we noted earlier, _depreciation_ is the periodic allocation of the cost of a tangible asset (other than land and natural resources) over the asset's estimated useful life. In accounting for depreciation, it is important to keep the following points in mind:

▶ _All tangible assets except land have a limited useful life, and the costs of these assets must be distributed as expenses over the years they benefit._ Physical deterioration and obsolescence are the major factors in limiting a depreciable asset's useful life.

— **Physical deterioration** results from use and from exposure to the elements, such as wind and sun. Periodic repairs and a sound maintenance policy may keep buildings and equipment in good operating order and extract the maximum useful life from them, but every machine or building must at some point be discarded. Repairs do not eliminate the need for depreciation.

— **Obsolescence** refers to the process of going out of date. Because of fast-changing technology and fast-changing demands, machinery and even buildings often become obsolete before they wear out.

Accountants do not distinguish between physical deterioration and obsolescence because they are interested in the length of an asset's useful life, not in what limits its useful life.

▶ _Depreciation refers to the allocation of the cost of a plant asset to the periods that benefit from the asset, not to the asset's physical deterioration or decrease in market value._ The term _depreciation_ describes the gradual conversion of the cost of the asset into an expense.

▶ _Depreciation is not a process of valuation._ Accounting records are not indicators of changing price levels; they are kept in accordance with the cost principle. Because of an advantageous purchase price and market conditions, the

Study Note

A computer may be functioning as well as it did on the day it was purchased four years ago, but because much faster, more efficient computers have become available, the old computer is now obsolete.

Study Note

Depreciation is the allocation of the acquisition cost of a plant asset, and any similarity between undepreciated cost and current market value is pure coincidence.

value of a building may increase. Nevertheless, because depreciation is a process of allocation, not valuation, depreciation on the building must con-tinue to be recorded. Eventually, the building will wear out or become obso-lete regardless of interim fluctuations in market value.

Factors in Computing Depreciation

Four factors affect the computation of depreciation:

1. *Cost.* As explained earlier, cost is the net purchase price of an asset plus all reasonable and necessary expenditures to get it in place and ready for use.

2. *Residual value.* **Residual value** is an asset's estimated scrap, salvage, or trade-in value on the estimated date of its disposal. Other terms used to describe residual value are *salvage value* and *disposal value*.

3. *Depreciable cost.* **Depreciable cost** is an asset's cost less its residual value. For example, a truck that cost $12,000 and that has a residual value of $3,000 would have a depreciable cost of $9,000. Depreciable cost must be allocated over the useful life of the asset.

4. *Estimated useful life.* **Estimated useful life** is the total number of service units expected from a long-term asset. Service units may be measured in terms of the years an asset is expected to be used, the units it is expected to pro-duce, the miles it is expected to be driven, or similar measures. In com-puting an asset's estimated useful life, an accountant should consider all relevant information, including past experience with similar assets, the asset's present condition, the company's repair and maintenance policy, and current technological and industry trends.

Depreciation is recorded at the end of an accounting period with an adjust-ing entry that takes the following form:

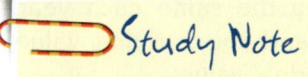

A	= L +	SE	
−XXX		−XXX	

Depreciation Expense, Asset Name	XXX	
Accumulated Depreciation, Asset Name		XXX
To record depreciation for the period		

Methods of Computing Depreciation

Many methods are used to allocate the cost of plant assets to accounting peri-ods through depreciation. Each is appropriate in certain circumstances. The most common methods are the straight-line method, the production method, and an accelerated method known as the declining-balance method.

Straight-Line Method

When the **straight-line method** is used to calculate depreciation, the asset's depreciable cost is spread evenly over the estimated useful life of the asset. The straight-line method is based on the assumption that depreciation depends only on the passage of time. The depreciation expense for each period is computed by dividing the depreciable cost (cost of the depreciating asset less its estimated residual value) by the number of accounting periods in the asset's estimated useful life. The rate of depreciation is the same in each year.

Suppose, for example, that a delivery truck cost $10,000 and has an estimated residual value of $1,000 at the end of its estimated useful life of five years. Under the straight-line method, the annual depreciation would be $1,800, calculated as follows:

Study Note

Residual value and useful life are, at best, educated guesses.

$$\frac{\text{Cost} - \text{Residual Value}}{\text{Estimated Useful Life}} = \frac{\$10,000 - \$1,000}{5 \text{ years}} = \$1,800 \text{ per year}$$

The depreciation schedule for the five years would be as follows:

Depreciation Schedule, Straight-Line Method

	Cost	Annual Depreciation	Accumulated Depreciation	Carrying Value
Date of purchase	$10,000	—	—	$10,000
End of first year	10,000	$1,800	$1,800	8,200
End of second year	10,000	1,800	3,600	6,400
End of third year	10,000	1,800	5,400	4,600
End of fourth year	10,000	1,800	7,200	2,800
End of fifth year	10,000	1,800	9,000	1,000

Note that in addition to annual depreciation's being the same each year, the accumulated depreciation increases uniformly, and the carrying value decreases uniformly until it reaches the estimated residual value.

Production Method

The **production method** is based on the assumption that depreciation is solely the result of use and that the passage of time plays no role in the process. If we assume that the delivery truck in the previous example has an estimated useful life of 90,000 miles, the depreciation cost per mile would be determined as follows:

Study Note

The production method is appropriate when a company has widely fluctuating rates of production. For example, carpet mills often close during the first two weeks in July but may run double shifts in September. With the production method, depreciation would be in direct relation to a mill's units of output.

$$\frac{\text{Cost} - \text{Residual Value}}{\text{Estimated Units of Useful Life}} = \frac{\$10,000 - \$1,000}{90,000 \text{ miles}} = \$0.10 \text{ per mile}$$

If the truck was driven 20,000 miles in the first year, 30,000 miles in the second, 10,000 miles in the third, 20,000 miles in the fourth, and 10,000 miles in the fifth, the depreciation schedule for the truck would be as follows:

Depreciation Schedule, Production Method

	Cost	Miles	Annual Depreciation	Accumulated Depreciation	Carrying Value
Date of purchase	$10,000	—	—	—	$10,000
End of first year	10,000	20,000	$2,000	$2,000	8,000
End of second year	10,000	30,000	3,000	5,000	5,000
End of third year	10,000	10,000	1,000	6,000	4,000
End of fourth year	10,000	20,000	2,000	8,000	2,000
End of fifth year	10,000	10,000	1,000	9,000	1,000

As you can see, the amount of depreciation each year is directly related to the units of use. The accumulated depreciation increases annually in direct relation to these units, and the carrying value decreases each year until it reaches the estimated residual value.

The production method should be used only when the output of an asset over its useful life can be estimated with reasonable accuracy. In addition, the unit used to measure the estimated useful life of an asset should be appropriate for the asset. For example, the number of items produced may be an appropriate measure for one machine, but the number of hours of use may be a better measure for another.

Declining-Balance Method

An **accelerated method** of depreciation results in relatively large amounts of depreciation in the early years of an asset's life and smaller amounts in later years. This type of method, which is based on the passage of time, assumes that many plant assets are most efficient when new and so provide the greatest benefits in their first years. It is consistent with the matching rule to allocate more depreciation to an asset in its earlier years than to later ones if the benefits it provides in its early years are greater than those it provides later on.

Fast-changing technologies often cause equipment to become obsolescent and lose service value rapidly. In such cases, using an accelerated method is appropriate because it allocates more depreciation to earlier years than to later ones. Another argument in favor of using an accelerated method is that repair expense is likely to increase as an asset ages. Thus, the total of repair and depreciation expense will remain fairly constant over the years. This result naturally assumes that the services received from the asset are roughly equal from year to year.

The **declining-balance method** is the most common accelerated method of depreciation. With this method, depreciation is computed by applying a fixed rate to the carrying value (the declining balance) of a tangible long-term asset. It therefore results in higher depreciation charges in the early years of the asset's life. Though any fixed rate can be used, the most common rate is a percentage equal to twice the straight-line depreciation percentage. When twice the straight-line rate is used, the method is usually called the **double-declining-balance method**.

In our example of the straight-line method, the delivery truck had an estimated useful life of five years, and the annual depreciation rate for the truck was therefore 20 percent (100 percent ÷ 5 years). Under the double-declining-balance method, the fixed rate would be 40 percent (2 × 20 percent). This fixed rate is applied to the carrying value that remains at the end of each year. With this method, the depreciation schedule would be as follows:

Study Note

Accelerated depreciation is appropriate for assets that provide the greatest benefits in their early years. Under an accelerated method, depreciation charges will be highest in years when revenue generation from the asset is highest.

Study Note

The double-declining-balance method is the only method presented here in which the residual value is not deducted before beginning the depreciation calculation.

Depreciation Schedule, Double-Declining-Balance Method

	Cost	Annual Depreciation		Accumulated Depreciation	Carrying Value
Date of purchase	$10,000		—	—	$10,000
End of first year	10,000	(40% × $10,000)	$4,000	$4,000	6,000
End of second year	10,000	(40% × $6,000)	2,400	6,400	3,600
End of third year	10,000	(40% × $3,600)	1,440	7,840	2,160
End of fourth year	10,000	(40% × $2,160)	864	8,704	1,296
End of fifth year	10,000		296*	9,000	1,000

*Depreciation is limited to the amount necessary to reduce carrying value to residual value: $296 = $1,296 (previous carrying value) − $1,000 (residual value).

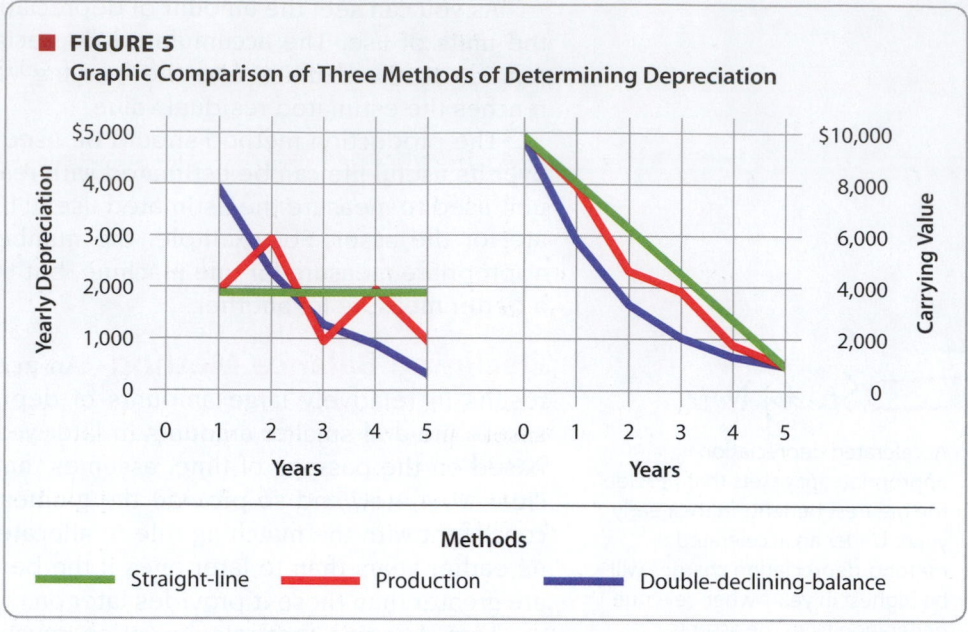

FIGURE 5

Graphic Comparison of Three Methods of Determining Depreciation

Methods
— Straight-line   — Production   — Double-declining-balance

Note that the fixed rate is always applied to the carrying value at the end of the previous year. Depreciation is greatest in the first year and declines each year after that. The depreciation in the last year is limited to the amount necessary to reduce carrying value to residual value.

Comparison of the Three Methods

Figure 5 compares yearly depreciation and carrying value under the three methods. The graph on the left shows yearly depreciation. As you can see, straight-line depreciation is uniform at $1,800 per year over the five-year period. The double-declining-balance method begins at $4,000 and decreases each year to amounts that are less than straight-line (ultimately, $296). The production method does not generate a regular pattern because of the random fluctuation of the depreciation from year to year.

The graph on the right shows the carrying value under the three methods. Each method starts in the same place (cost of $10,000) and ends at the same place (residual value of $1,000). However, the patterns of carrying value during the asset's useful life differ. For instance, the carrying value under the straight-line method is always greater than under the double-declining-balance method, except at the beginning and end of the asset's useful life.

FOCUS ON BUSINESS PRACTICE

Accelerated Methods Save Money!

As shown in Figure 6, an AICPA study of 600 large companies found that the overwhelming majority used the straight-line method of depreciation for financial reporting. Only about 11 percent used some type of accelerated method, and 5 percent used the production method. These figures tend to be misleading about the importance of accelerated depreciation methods, however, especially when it comes to income taxes. Federal income tax laws allow either the straight-line method or an accelerated method, and for tax purposes, about 75 percent of the 600 companies studied preferred an accelerated method. Companies use different methods of depreciation for good reason. The straight-line method can be advantageous for financial reporting because it can produce the highest net income, and an accelerated method can be beneficial for tax purposes because it can result in lower income taxes.

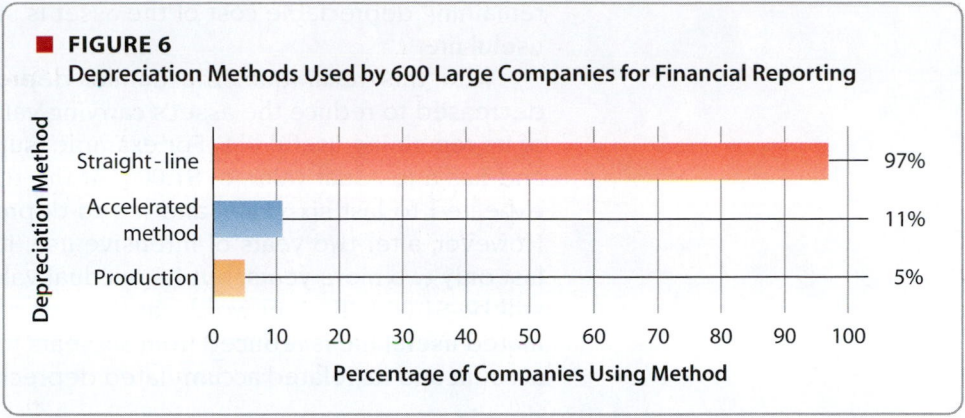

FIGURE 6

Depreciation Methods Used by 600 Large Companies for Financial Reporting

Total percentage exceeds 100 because some companies used different methods for different types of depreciable assets.

"Depreciation Methods Used by 600 Large Companies." Copyright © 2004 by AICPA. Reproduced with permission.

Special Issues in Depreciation

Other issues in depreciating assets include group depreciation, depreciation for partial years, revision of depreciation rates, and accelerated cost recovery for tax purposes.

Group Depreciation   The estimated useful life of an asset is the average length of time assets of the same type are expected to last. For example, the average useful life of a particular type of machine may be six years, but some machines in this category may last only two or three years, while others may last eight or nine years or longer. For this reason, and for convenience, large companies group similar assets, such as machines, trucks, and pieces of office equipment, to calculate depreciation. This method, called **group depreciation**, is widely used in all fields of industry and business. A survey of large businesses indicated that 65 percent used group depreciation for all or part of their plant assets.[6]

Depreciation for Partial Years   To simplify our examples of depreciation, we have assumed that plant assets were purchased at the beginning or end of an accounting period. Usually, however, businesses buy assets when they are needed and sell or discard them when they are no longer needed or useful. The time of year is normally not a factor in the decision. Thus, it is often necessary to calculate depreciation for partial years. Some companies compute depreciation to the nearest month. Others use the half-year convention, in which one-half year of depreciation is taken in the year the asset is purchased and one-half year is taken in the year the asset is sold.

Revision of Depreciation Rates   Because a depreciation rate is based on an estimate of an asset's useful life, the periodic depreciation charge is seldom precise. It is sometimes very inadequate or excessive. Such a situation may result from an underestimate or overestimate of the asset's useful life or from a wrong estimate of its residual value. What should a company do when it discovers that a piece of equipment that it has used for several years will last a shorter—or longer—time than originally estimated? Sometimes, it is necessary to revise the estimate of useful life so that the periodic depreciation expense increases or decreases. Then, to reflect the revised situation, the remaining depreciable cost of the asset is spread over the remaining years of useful life.

With this technique, the annual depreciation expense is increased or decreased to reduce the asset's carrying value to its residual value at the end of its remaining useful life. For example, suppose a delivery truck cost $7,000 and has a residual value of $1,000. At the time of the purchase, the truck was expected to last six years, and it was depreciated on the straight-line basis. However, after two years of intensive use, it is determined that the truck will last only two more years, but its residual value at the end of the two years will still be $1,000. In other words, at the end of the second year, the truck's estimated useful life is reduced from six years to four years. At that time, the asset account and its related accumulated depreciation account would be as follows:

DELIVERY TRUCK		ACCUMULATED DEPRECIATION, DELIVERY TRUCK	
Cost 7,000		Depreciation, Year 1	1,000
		Depreciation, Year 2	1,000

The remaining depreciable cost is computed as follows:

Cost	−	**Depreciation Already Taken**	−	**Residual Value**	
$7,000	−	$2,000	−	$1,000	= $4,000

The new annual periodic depreciation charge is computed by dividing the remaining depreciable cost of $4,000 by the remaining useful life of two years. Therefore, the new periodic depreciation charge is $2,000. This method of revising depreciation is used widely in industry. It is also supported by *Opinion No. 9* and *Opinion No. 20* of the Accounting Principles Board of the AICPA.

Accelerated Cost Recovery for Tax Purposes
Over the years, to encourage businesses to invest in new plant and equipment, Congress has revised the federal income tax law to allow rapid write-offs of plant assets. Depreciation allowed for tax purposes differs considerably from depreciation calculated for financial statements. Tax methods of depreciation are usually not acceptable for financial reporting because the periods over which deductions may be taken are often shorter than the assets' estimated useful lives.

Recent changes in the federal income tax law allow a small company to expense the first $100,000 of equipment expenditures rather than recording them as assets. The law also allows an accelerated method of writing off expenditures that are recorded as assets. This method discards the concepts of estimated useful life and residual value. For most property other than real estate, it uses a 200 percent declining balance with a half-year convention (only one half-year's depreciation is allowed in the year of purchase, and one half-year's depreciation is taken in the last year). This method enables businesses to recover most of the cost of their investments early in the depreciation process.

Study Note

For financial reporting purposes, the objective is to measure performance accurately. For tax purposes, the objective is to minimize tax liability.

STOP • REVIEW • APPLY

3-1. Why is it useful to think of a plant asset as a bundle of service units?

3-2. A firm buys technical equipment that is expected to last 12 years. Why might the firm have to depreciate the equipment over a shorter time?

3-3. A company purchased a building five years ago. The building's market value is now greater than when the building was purchased. Should the company stop depreciating the building?

3-4. Evaluate the following statement: "A parking lot should not be depreciated because adequate repairs will make it last for an indefinite period."

3-5. Is the purpose of depreciation to determine the value of equipment? Explain your answer.

3-6. How do the assumptions underlying the straight-line and production methods of depreciation differ?

3-7. What is the principal argument in favor of an accelerated depreciation method?

3-8. On what basis is depreciation taken on a group of assets rather than on individual items?

3-9. What procedure should be followed in revising a depreciation rate?

Disposal of Depreciable Assets

LO4   Account for the disposal of depreciable assets.

When plant assets are no longer useful because they have physically deteriorated or become obsolete, a company can dispose of them by discarding them, selling them for cash, or trading them in on the purchase of a new asset. Regardless of how a company disposes of a plant asset, it must record depreciation expense for the partial year up to the date of disposal. This step is required because the company used the asset until that date and, under the matching rule, the accounting period should receive the proper allocation of depreciation expense.

In the next sections, we show how a company records each type of disposal. As our example, we assume that MGC Company purchased a machine on January 2, 20x2, for $6,500 and planned to depreciate it on a straight-line basis over an estimated useful life of eight years. The machine's residual value at the end of eight years was estimated to be $300. On December 31, 20x7, the balances of the relevant accounts were as follows:

Study Note

When it disposes of an asset, a company must bring the depreciation up to date and remove all evidence of ownership of the asset, including the contra account Accumulated Depreciation.

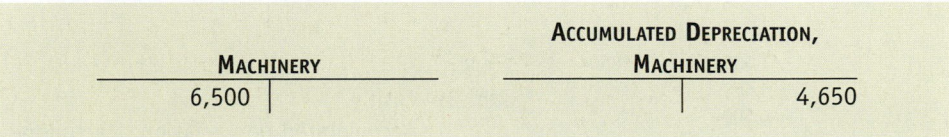

	MACHINERY		ACCUMULATED DEPRECIATION, MACHINERY	
	6,500			4,650

On January 2, 20x8, management disposed of the asset.

Discarded Plant Assets

A plant asset rarely lasts exactly as long as its estimated life. If it lasts longer than its estimated life, it is not depreciated past the point at which its carrying value equals its residual value. The purpose of depreciation is to spread the depreciable cost of an asset over its estimated life. Thus, the total accumulated depreciation should never exceed the total depreciable cost. If an asset remains in use beyond the end of its estimated life, its cost and accumulated depreciation remain in the ledger accounts. Proper records will thus be available for maintaining control over plant assets. If the residual value is zero, the carrying value of a fully depreciated asset is zero until the asset is disposed of. If such an asset is discarded, no gain or loss results.

In our example, however, the discarded equipment has a carrying value of $1,850 at the time of its disposal. The carrying value is computed from the T accounts above as machinery of $6,500 less accumulated depreciation of $4,650. A loss equal to the carrying value should be recorded when the machine is discarded, as follows:

A	= L +	SE
+ 4,650		
− 6,500		− 1,850

20x8			
Jan. 2	Accumulated Depreciation, Machinery	4,650	
	Loss on Disposal of Machinery	1,850	
	Machinery		6,500
	Discarded machine no longer		
	used in the business		

Gains and losses on disposals of plant assets are classified as other revenues and expenses on the income statement.

Plant Assets Sold for Cash

Study Note

When an asset is discarded or sold for cash, the gain or loss equals cash received minus carrying the value.

The entry to record a plant asset sold for cash is similar to the one just illustrated, except that the receipt of cash should also be recorded. The following entries show how to record the sale of a machine under three assumptions about the selling price. In the first case, the $1,850 cash received is exactly equal to the $1,850 carrying value of the machine; therefore, no gain or loss occurs:

A	= L + SE
+ 1,850	
+ 4,650	
− 6,500	

20x8			
Jan. 2	Cash	1,850	
	Accumulated Depreciation, Machinery	4,650	
	Machinery		6,500
	Sale of machine for carrying		
	value; no gain or loss		

In the second case, the $1,000 cash received is less than the carrying value of $1,850, so a loss of $850 is recorded:

A	= L +	SE
+ 1,000		− 850
+ 4,650		
− 6,500		

20x8			
Jan. 2	Cash	1,000	
	Accumulated Depreciation, Machinery	4,650	
	Loss on Sale of Machinery	850	
	Machinery		6,500
	Sale of machine at less than		
	carrying value; loss of $850		
	($1,850 − $1,000) recorded		

In the third case, the $2,000 cash received exceeds the carrying value of $1,850, so a gain of $150 is recorded:

A	= L +	SE
+ 2,000		+150
+ 4,650		
− 6,500		

20x8			
Jan. 2	Cash	2,000	
	Accumulated Depreciation, Machinery	4,650	
	Gain on Sale of Machinery		150
	Machinery		6,500
	Sale of machine at more than the carrying value; gain of $150 ($2,000 − $1,850) recorded		

Exchanges of Plant Assets

As we have noted, businesses can dispose of plant assets by trading them in on the purchase of other plant assets. Exchanges may involve similar assets, such as an old machine traded in on a newer model, or dissimilar assets, such as a cement mixer traded in on a truck. In either case, the purchase price is reduced by the amount of the trade-in allowance.

Basically, accounting for exchanges of plant assets is similar to accounting for sales of plant assets for cash. If the trade-in allowance is greater than the asset's carrying value, the company realizes a gain. If the allowance is less, it suffers a loss. (Some special rules apply and are addressed in more advanced courses.)

S T O P • R E V I E W • A P P L Y

4-1. If a company sells a plant asset during its fiscal year, why should it compute depreciation on the asset for the part of the year that precedes the date of the sale?

4-2. If a plant asset is discarded before the end of its useful life, how is the amount of loss measured?

4-3. When a company sells an asset for cash, how is the gain or loss on the sale determined?

Natural Resources

LO5 Identify the issues related to accounting for natural resources, and compute depletion.

Study Note

Natural resources are not intangible assets. They are correctly classified as components of property, plant, and equipment.

Natural resources are long-term assets that appear on a balance sheet with descriptive titles like Timberlands, Oil and Gas Reserves, and Mineral Deposits. The distinguishing characteristic of these assets is that they are converted to inventory by cutting, pumping, mining, or other extraction methods. They are recorded at acquisition cost, which may include some costs of development. As a natural resource is extracted and converted to inventory, its asset account must be proportionally reduced. For example, the carrying value of oil reserves on the balance sheet is reduced by the proportional cost of the barrels pumped during the period. As a result, the original cost of the oil reserves is gradually reduced, and depletion is recognized in the amount of the decrease.

When you season your food with salt, you probably don't think of it as using a natural resource, but that is what salt is. Table salt is produced by evaporation methods; rock salt, which is used for highway maintenance, is mined. Natural resources are considered components of property, plant, and equipment. These long-term assets are recorded at acquistion cost, which may include some costs of development.

Depletion

Depletion refers not only to the exhaustion of a natural resource, but also to the proportional allocation of the cost of a natural resource to the units extracted. The way in which the cost of a natural resource is allocated closely resembles the production method of calculating depreciation. When a natural resource is purchased or developed, the total units that will be available, such as barrels of oil, tons of coal, or board-feet of lumber, must be estimated. The depletion cost per unit is determined by dividing the cost of the natural resource (less residual value, if any) by the estimated number of units available. The amount of the depletion cost for each accounting period is then computed by multiplying the depletion cost per unit by the number of units extracted and sold.

For example, suppose a mine was purchased for $1,800,000 and that it has an estimated residual value of $300,000 and contains an estimated 1,500,000 tons of coal. The depletion charge per ton of coal is $1, calculated as follows:

$$\frac{\$1,800,000 - \$300,000}{1,500,000 \text{ tons}} = \$1 \text{ per ton}$$

Thus, if 115,000 tons of coal are mined and sold during the first year, the depletion charge for the year is $115,000. This charge would be recorded as follows:

A	= L +	SE	
−115,000		−115,000	

Dec. 31	Depletion Expense, Coal Deposits	115,000	
	Accumulated Depletion, Coal Deposits		115,000
	To record depletion of coal mine: $1 per ton for 115,000 tons mined and sold		

On the balance sheet, data for the mine would be presented as follows:

Coal deposits		$1,800,000	
Less accumulated depletion		115,000	$1,685,000

Sometimes, a natural resource is not sold in the year it is extracted. It is important to note that it would then be recorded as a depletion *expense* in the year it is *sold*. The part not sold is considered inventory.

Depreciation of Related Plant Assets

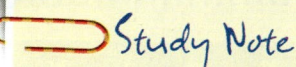

The extraction of natural resources generally requires special on-site buildings and equipment (e.g., conveyors, drills, and pumps). The useful life of these plant assets may be longer than the estimated time it will take to deplete the resources. However, a company may plan to abandon these assets after all the resources have been extracted because they no longer serve a useful purpose. In this case, they should be depreciated on the same basis as the depletion.

For example, if machinery with a useful life of ten years is installed on an oil field that is expected to be depleted in eight years, the machinery should be depreciated over the eight-year period, using the production method. That way, each year's depreciation will be proportional to the year's depletion. If one-sixth of the oil field's total reserves is pumped in one year, then the depreciation should be one-sixth of the machinery's cost minus the residual value.

If the useful life of a long-term plant asset is less than the expected life of the resource, the shorter life should be used to compute depreciation. In such cases, or when an asset will not be abandoned after all reserves have been depleted, other depreciation methods, such as straight-line or declining-balance, are appropriate.

Development and Exploration Costs in the Oil and Gas Industry

The costs of exploring and developing oil and gas resources can be accounted for under one of two methods. Under **successful efforts accounting**, the cost of successful exploration—for example, producing an oil well—is a cost of the resource. It should be recorded as an asset and depleted over the estimated life of the resource. The cost of an unsuccessful exploration—such as the cost of a dry well—is written off immediately as a loss. Because of these immediate write-offs, successful efforts accounting is considered the more conservative method and is used by most large oil companies.

On the other hand, smaller, independent oil companies argue that the cost of dry wells is part of the overall cost of the systematic development of an oil field and is thus a part of the cost of producing wells. Under the **full-costing method**, all costs, including the cost of dry wells, are recorded as assets and depleted over the estimated life of the producing resources. This method tends to improve a company's earnings performance in its early years.

The Financial Accounting Standards Board permits the use of either method.[7]

FOCUS ON BUSINESS PRACTICE
How Do You Measure What's Underground? With a Good Guess.

Accounting standards require publicly traded energy companies to disclose in their annual reports their production activities, estimates of their proven oil and gas reserves, and estimates of the present value of the future cash flows those reserves are expected to generate. The figures are not easy to estimate. After all, the reserves are often miles underground or beneath deep water. As a result, these figures are considered "supplementary" and not reliable enough to be audited independently. Nevertheless, it appears that some companies, including **Royal Dutch/Shell Group**, have overestimated their reserves and thus overestimated their future prospects. Apparently, some managers at Royal Dutch/Shell Group receive bonuses based on the amount of new reserves added to the annual report. When the company recently announced that it was reducing its reported reserves by 20 percent, the price of its stock dropped.[8]

S T O P • R E V I E W • A P P L Y

5-1. What circumstance would cause the amount of annual depletion to differ from the amount of depletion expense?

5-2. Under what circumstances can a mining company depreciate its plant assets over a period that is less than the assets' useful lives?

5-3. What is the difference between successful efforts accounting and full-costing accounting?

Natural Resource Depletion and Depreciation of Related Plant Assets
Maase Mining Company paid $4,400,000 for land containing an estimated 20 million tons of ore. The land without the ore is estimated to be worth $1,000,000. The company spent $690,000 to erect buildings on the site and $1,200,000 on installing equipment. The buildings have an estimated useful life of 30 years, and the equipment has an estimated useful life of 10 years. Because of the remote location, neither the buildings nor the equipment has a residual value. The company expects that it can mine all the usable ore in 10 years. During its first year of operation, it mined and sold 1,400,000 tons of ore.

1. Compute the depletion charge per ton.

2. Compute the depletion expense that Maase Mining should record for its first year of operation.

3. Determine the depreciation expense for the year for the buildings, making it proportional to the depletion.

4. Determine the depreciation expense for the year for the equipment under two alternatives: (a) making the expense proportional to the depletion, and (b) using the straight-line method.

SOLUTION

1. $\dfrac{\$4,400,000 - \$1,000,000}{20,000,000 \text{ tons}} = \$.0.17 \text{ per ton}$

2. $1,400,000 \text{ tons} \times \$0.17 \text{ per ton} = \$238,000$

3. $\dfrac{1,400,000 \text{ tons}}{20,000,000 \text{ tons}} \times \$690,000 = \$48,300$

4. a. $\dfrac{1,400,000 \text{ tons}}{20,000,000 \text{ tons}} \times \$1,200,000 = \$84,000$

   b. $\dfrac{\$1,200,000}{10 \text{ years}} \times 1 \text{ year} = \$120,000$

≡ Intangible Assets

LO6 Identify the issues related to accounting for intangible assets, including research and development costs and goodwill.

An intangible asset is both long term and nonphysical. Its value comes from the long-term rights or advantages it affords its owner. Table 1 describes the most common types of intangible assets—goodwill, trademarks and brand names, copyrights, patents, franchises and licenses, leaseholds, software, noncompete covenants, and customer lists—and their accounting treatment.

TABLE 1. Accounting for Intangible Assets

Type	Description	Usual Accounting Treatment*
Goodwill	The excess of the amount paid for a business over the fair market value of the business's net assets	Debit Goodwill for the acquisition cost, and review impairment annually.
Trademark, brand name	A registered symbol or name that can be used only by its owner to identify a product or service	Debit Trademark or Brand Name for the acquisition cost, and review impairment annually.
Copyright	An exclusive right granted by the federal government to reproduce and sell literary, musical, and other artistic materials and computer programs for a period of the author's life plus 70 years	Record at acquisition cost, and amortize over the asset's useful life, which is often much shorter than its legal life. For example, the cost of paperback rights to a popular novel would typically be amortized over a useful life of two to four years.
Patent	An exclusive right granted by the federal government for a period of 20 years to make a particular product or use a specific process. A design may be granted a patent for 14 years.	The cost of successfully defending a patent in a patent infringement suit is added to the acquisition cost of the patent. Amortize over the asset's useful life, which may be less than its legal life.
Franchise, license	A right to an exclusive territory or market, or the right to use a formula, technique, process, or design	Debit Franchise or License for the acquisition cost, and amortize over the asset's useful life since it is likely that these types of assets would have a definite useful life; review impairment annually.
Leasehold	A right to occupy land or buildings under a long-term rental contract. For example, if Company A sells or subleases its right to use a retail location to Company B for ten years in return for one or more rental payments, Company B has purchased a leasehold.	The lessor (Company A) debits Leasehold for the amount of the rental payment and amortizes it over the remaining life of the lease. The lessee (Company B) debits payments to Lease Expense.
Software	Capitalized costs of computer programs developed for sale, lease, or internal use	Record the amount of capitalizable production costs, and amortize over the estimated economic life of the product.
Noncompete covenant	A contract limiting the rights of others to compete in a specific industry or line of business for a specified period	Record at acquisition cost, and amortize over the contract period.
Customer list	A list of customers or subscribers	Debit Customer Lists for amount paid, and amortize over the asset's expected life.

*All intangible assets are subject to annual impairment test.

Like intangible assets, some current assets—for example, accounts receivable and certain prepaid expenses—have no physical substance, but because current assets are short term, they are not classified as intangible assets.

Figure 7 shows the percentage of companies that report the various types of intangible assets. For some companies, intangible assets make up a substantial portion of total assets. As noted in the Decision Point, **Apple Computer's** goodwill and other acquired intangible assets amounted to $97 million in 2004. How these assets are accounted for has a major effect on Apple's performance.

The purchase of an intangible asset is a special kind of capital expenditure. Such assets are accounted for at acquisition cost—that is, the amount that a company paid for them. Some intangible assets, such as goodwill and trademarks, may be acquired at little or no cost. Even though these assets may have

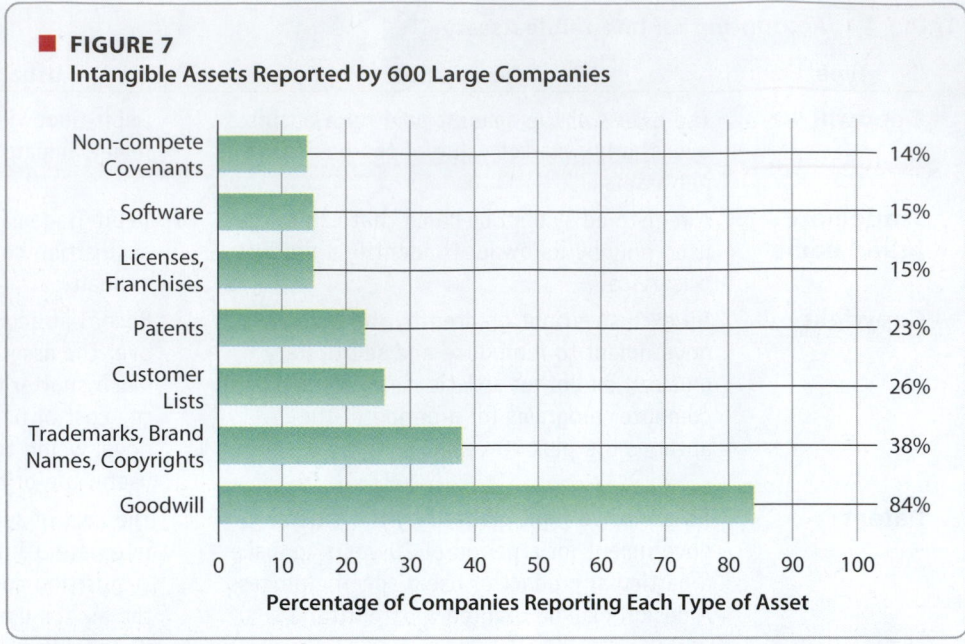

FIGURE 7
Intangible Assets Reported by 600 Large Companies

Percentage of Companies Reporting Each Type of Asset

Non-compete Covenants — 14%
Software — 15%
Licenses, Franchises — 15%
Patents — 23%
Customer Lists — 26%
Trademarks, Brand Names, Copyrights — 38%
Goodwill — 84%

Source: Data from American Institute of Certified Public Accountants, *Accounting Trends & Techniques* (New York: AICPA, 2004).

great value and be needed for profitable operations, a company should include them on its balance sheet only if it purchased them from another party at a price established in the marketplace. When a company develops its own intangible assets, it should record the costs of development as expenses. An exception is the cost of internally developed computer software after a working prototype of the software has been developed.

Purchased intangible assets are recorded at cost, or at fair value when purchased as part of a group of assets. The useful life of an intangible asset is the period over which the asset is expected to contribute to future cash flows of the entity. The useful life may be definite or indefinite:[11]

▸ Definite useful life: A definite useful life means the useful life is subject to a legal limit or can be reasonably estimated. Examples include patents, copyrights, and leaseholds. Often the estimated useful lives of these assets are less than their legal limits. The cost of an intangible asset with a definite useful life should be allocated to expense through periodic amortization over the asset's useful life in much the same way that a building is depreciated.

FOCUS ON BUSINESS PRACTICE

Who's Number One in Brands?

Brands are intangible assets that often do not appear on a company's balance sheet because rather than purchasing them, the company has developed them over time. A recent report attempted to value brands by the discounted present value of future cash flows.[9] According to the report, the ten most valuable brands in the world were as follows:

Coca-Cola's brand was valued at almost $70 billion, whereas the Mercedes brand was valued at $21 billion. Where did **Apple** stand? It was number 50 at $5.3 billion, but this analysis was made before taking into account Apple's successful iPod, which has certainly increased its brand power.

Coca-Cola	**Intel**	**McDonald's**
Microsoft	**Nokia**	**Marlboro**
IBM	**Disney**	**Mercedes**
GE		

One of the most valuable intangible assets some companies have is a list of customers. For example, the **Newark Morning Ledger Company**, a newspaper chain, purchased a chain of Michigan newspapers whose list of 460,000 subscribers was valued at $68 million. The U.S. Supreme Court upheld the company's right to amortize the value of the subscriber list because the company showed that the list had a limited useful life. The Internal Revenue Service had argued that the list had an indefinite life and therefore could not provide tax deductions through amortization. This ruling has benefited other types of businesses that purchase everything from bank deposits to pharmacy prescription files.[10]

Study Note

The cost of mailing lists may be recorded as an asset because the mailing lists will be used over and over and will benefit future accounting periods.

▶ **Indefinite useful life:** An indefinite useful life means that the useful life of the asset is not limited by legal, regulatory, contractual, competitive, economic, or other factors. This definition does not imply that these assets last forever. Examples can include trademarks and brands. The costs of intangible assets with an indefinite life are not amortized as long as circumstances continue to support an indefinite life.

All intangible assets, whether definite or indefinite, are subject to an annual impairment test to determine if the assets justify their value of the balance sheet. If it is determined that they have lost some or all of their value in producing future cash flows they should be written down to their fair value or to zero if they have no fair value. The amount of the write down is shown on the income statement as an impairment charge (deduction) in income from operations.

To illustrate these procedures, suppose Soda Bottling Company purchases a patent on a unique bottle cap for $18,000. The purchase would be recorded with an entry of $18,000 in the asset account Patents. (Note that if the company developed the bottle cap internally instead of purchasing the patent, the costs of developing the cap—such as researchers' salaries and the costs of supplies and equipment used in testing—would be expensed as incurred.) Although the patent for the bottle cap will last for 20 years, Soda determines that it will sell the product that uses the cap for only six years.

The entry to record the annual amortization expense is for $3,000 ($18,000 ÷ 6 years). The Patents account is reduced directly by the amortization expense in contrast to the treatment of other long-term asset accounts, for which depreciation or depletion is accumulated in separate contra accounts.

If the patent becomes worthless before it is fully amortized, the remaining carrying value is written off as a loss by removing it from the Patents account.

Research and Development Costs

Most successful companies carry out research and development (R&D) activities, often within a separate department. Among these activities are development of new products, testing of existing and proposed products, and pure research. The costs of these activities are substantial for many companies. In a recent year, **General Motors** spent $5.7 billion, or about 3 percent of its revenues, on R&D.[12] R&D costs can be even greater in high-tech fields like pharmaceuticals. For example, **Abbott Laboratories** recently spent $1.7 billion, or 8.6 percent of its revenues, on R&D.[13]

The Financial Accounting Standards Board requires that all R&D costs be treated as revenue expenditures and charged to expense in the period in which they are incurred.[14] The reasoning behind this requirement is that it is too hard to trace specific costs to specific profitable developments. Also, the costs of research and development are continuous and necessary for the success of a business and so should be treated as current expenses. To support this conclusion, the FASB cited studies showing that 30 to 90 percent of all new products fail and that 75 percent of new-product expenses go to unsuccessful products. Thus, their costs do not represent future benefits.

Computer Software Costs

The costs that companies incur in developing computer software for sale or lease or for their own internal use are considered research and development costs until the product has proved technologically feasible. Thus, costs incurred before that point should be charged to expense as they are incurred. A product is deemed technologically feasible when a detailed working program has been designed. Once that occurs, all software production costs are recorded as assets and are amortized over the software's estimated economic life using the straight-line method. If at any time the company cannot expect to realize from the software the amount of the unamortized costs on the balance sheet, the asset should be written down to the amount expected to be realized.[15]

Goodwill

Goodwill means different things to different people. Generally, it refers to a company's good reputation. From an accounting standpoint, goodwill exists when a purchaser pays more for a business than the fair market value of the business's net assets. In other words, the purchaser would pay less if it bought the assets separately. Most businesses are worth more as going concerns than as collections of assets.

When the purchase price of a business is more than the fair market value of its physical assets, the business must have intangible assets. If it does not have patents, copyrights, trademarks, or other identifiable intangible assets of value, the excess payment is assumed to be for goodwill. Goodwill reflects all the factors that allow a company to earn a higher-than-market rate of return on its assets, including customer satisfaction, good management, manufacturing efficiency, the advantages of having a monopoly, good locations, and good employee relations. The payment above and beyond the fair market value of the tangible assets and other specific intangible assets is properly recorded in the Goodwill account.

The FASB requires that purchased goodwill be reported as a separate line item on the balance sheet and that it be reviewed annually for impairment. If the fair value of goodwill is less than its carrying value on the balance sheet, goodwill is considered impaired. In that case, it is reduced to its fair value, and the impairment charge is reported on the income statement. A company can perform the fair value measurement for each reporting unit at any time as long as the measurement date is consistent from year to year.[16]

FOCUS ON BUSINESS PRACTICE
Wake up, Goodwill Is Growing!

As Figure 7 shows, 84 percent of 600 large companies separately report goodwill as an asset. Because much of the growth of these companies has come through purchasing other companies, goodwill as a percentage of total assets has also grown. As the table at the right shows, the amount of goodwill can be material.[17]

	Goodwill (in billions)	Percentage of Total Assets
General Mills	$6,684	36
Heinz	$1,956	20
Tribune Company	$5,467	38

A company should record goodwill only when it acquires a controlling interest in another business. The amount to be recorded as goodwill can be determined by writing the identifiable net assets up to their fair market values at the time of purchase and subtracting the total from the purchase price. For example, suppose a company pays $11,400,000 to purchase another business. If the net assets of the business (total assets − total liabilities) are fairly valued at $10,000,000, then the amount of the goodwill is $1,400,000 ($11,400,000 − $10,000,000). If the fair market value of the net assets is more or less than $10,000,000, an entry is made in the accounting records to adjust the assets to the fair market value. The goodwill would then represent the difference between the adjusted net assets and the purchase price of $11,400,000.

S T O P • R E V I E W • A P P L Y

6-1. Accounts receivable have no physical substance. Why are they then not classified as intangible assets?

6-2. Under what circumstances can a company have intangible assets that do not appear on the balance sheet?

6-3. What is the FASB's rule for treating research and development costs?

6-4. How is accounting for software development costs similar to and different from accounting for research and development costs?

6-5. Under what conditions should goodwill be recorded? Should it remain in the records permanently once it is recorded?

A LOOK BACK AT

APPLE COMPUTER, INC.

We began the chapter by emphasizing that **Apple's** success as an innovator and marketer comes from wise and steady investments in long-term assets and related expenditures like research and development. In evaluating Apple's performance, investors and creditors look for answers to the following questions:

- **What are Apple's long-term assets?**
- **What are its policies in accounting for long-term assets?**
- **Does the company generate enough cash flow to finance its continued growth?**

Apple's tangible long-term assets include land, manufacturing facilities, office buildings, machinery, equipment, and leasehold improvements to its retail stores. Its balance sheet also includes goodwill and intangible assets that it acquired through acquisitions. Because internally developed intangible assets are not recorded as assets, the value of Apple's own brand name is not reflected on the balance sheet. Clearly, however, it far exceeds the value of the intangible assets that are listed.

In accordance with GAAP, Apple's accounting policies include using the straight-line depreciation method for tangible assets, amortizing intangible assets over a reasonable useful life, and expensing research and development costs. In addition, it evaluates its long-term assets for impairment each year to ensure that it is not carrying assets on its balance sheet at amounts that exceed their value.

A good measure of the funds that Apple has available for growth is its free cash flow:

Free Cash Flow = Net Cash Flows from Operating Activities − Dividends − (Purchases of Plant Assets − Sales of Plant Assets)

	2004	2003
Free Cash Flow	= $934 − $0 − ($176 − $0)	$289 − $0 − ($164 − $0)
	= $758	= $125

This two-year view of Apple's free cash flow shows great improvement in 2004. The company obviously generated enough cash to finance its continued growth. Its policy of not paying dividends contributes to the amount of cash it has available for this purpose. Although Apple may have sold some plant assets, the amounts were sufficiently immaterial that it did not report them separately.

CHAPTER REVIEW

REVIEW of Learning Objectives

LO1 Define *long-term assets,* and explain the management issues related to them.

Long-term assets have a useful life of more than one year, are used in the operation of a business, and are not intended for resale. They can be tangible or intangible. In the former category are land, plant assets, and natural resources. In the latter are patents, trademarks, franchises, and other rights, as well as goodwill. The management issues related to long-term assets include decisions about whether to acquire the assets, how to finance them, and how to account for them.

LO2 Distinguish between *capital expenditures* and *revenue expenditures,* and account for the cost of property, plant, and equipment.

Capital expenditures are recorded as assets, whereas revenue expenditures are recorded as expenses of the current period. Capital expenditures include not only outlays for plant assets, natural resources, and intangible assets, but also expenditures for additions, betterments, and extraordinary repairs that increase an asset's residual value or extend its useful life. Revenue expenditures are made for ordinary repairs and maintenance. The error of classifying a capital expenditure as a revenue expenditure, or vice versa, has an important effect on net income.

The acquisition cost of property, plant, and equipment includes all expenditures reasonable and necessary to get the asset in place and ready for use. Among these expenditures are purchase price, installation cost, freight charges, and insurance during transit. The acquisition cost of a plant asset is allocated over the asset's useful life.

LO3 Compute depreciation under the straight-line, production, and declining-balance methods.

Depreciation—the periodic allocation of the cost of a plant asset over its estimated useful life—is commonly computed by using the straight-line method, the production method, or an accelerated method. The straight-line method is related directly to the passage of time, whereas the production method is related directly to use or output. An accelerated method, which results in relatively large amounts of depreciation in earlier years and reduced amounts in later years, is based on the assumption that plant assets provide greater economic benefits in their earlier years than in later ones. The most common accelerated method is the declining-balance method.

LO4 Account for the disposal of depreciable assets.

A company can dispose of a long-term plant asset by discarding or selling it or exchanging it for another asset. Regardless of the way in which a company disposes of such an asset, it must record depreciation up to the date of disposal. To do so, it must remove the carrying value from the asset account and the depreciation to date from the accumulated depreciation account. When a company sells a depreciable long-term asset at a price that differs from its carrying value, it should report the gain or loss on its income statement. In recording exchanges of similar plant assets, a gain or loss may arise.

LO5 Identify the issues related to accounting for natural resources, and compute depletion.

Natural resources are depletable assets that are converted to inventory by cutting, pumping, mining, or other forms of extraction. They are recorded at cost as long-term assets. As natural resources are sold, their costs are allocated as expenses through depletion charges. The depletion charge is based on the ratio of the resource extracted to the total estimated resource. A major issue related to this subject is accounting for oil and gas reserves.

LO6 Identify the issues related to accounting for intangible assets, including research and development costs and goodwill.

The purchase of an intangible asset should be treated as a capital expenditure and recorded at acquisition cost, which in turn should be amortized over the useful life of the asset. The FASB requires that research and development costs be treated as revenue expenditures and charged as expenses in the periods of expenditure. Software costs are treated as research and development costs and expensed until a feasible working program is developed, after which time the costs may be capitalized and amortized over a reasonable estimated life. Goodwill is the excess of the amount paid for a business over the fair market value of the net assets and is usually related to the business's superior earning potential. It should be recorded only when a company purchases an entire business, and it should be reviewed annually for possible impairment.

REVIEW of Concepts and Terminology

The following concepts and terms were introduced in this chapter:

Accelerated method: A method of depreciation that allocates relatively large amounts of the depreciable cost of an asset to earlier years and smaller amounts to later years. **(LO3)**

Additions: Enlargements to the physical layout of a plant asset. **(LO2)**

Amortization: The periodic allocation of the cost of an intangible asset to the periods it benefits. **(LO1)**

Asset impairment: Loss of revenue-generating potential of a long-lived asset before the end of its useful life; the difference between an asset's carrying value and its fair value, as measured by the present value of the expected cash flows. **(LO1)**

Betterments: Improvements that do not add to the physical layout of a plant asset. **(LO2)**

Brand name: A registered name that can be used only by its owner to identify a product or service. **(LO6)**

Capital expenditure: An expenditure for the purchase or expansion of a long-term asset, which is recorded in an asset account. **(LO2)**

Carrying value: The unexpired part of an asset's cost. Also called *book value*. **(LO1)**

Copyright: An exclusive right granted by the federal government to reproduce and sell literary, musical, and other artistic materials and computer programs for a period of the author's life plus 70 years. **(LO6)**

Customer list: A list of customers or subscribers. **(LO6)**

Declining-balance method: An accelerated method of depreciation in which depreciation is computed by applying a fixed rate to the carrying value (the declining balance) of a tangible long-lived asset. **(LO3)**

Depletion: The exhaustion of a natural resource through mining, cutting, pumping, or other extraction, and the way in which the cost is allocated. **(LO1)**

Depreciable cost: The cost of an asset less its residual value. **(LO3)**

Depreciation: The periodic allocation of the cost of a tangible long-lived asset (other than land and natural resources) over its estimated useful life. **(LO1)**

Double-declining-balance method: An accelerated method of depreciation in which a fixed rate equal to twice the straight-line percentage is applied to the carrying value (the declining balance) of a tangible long-lived asset. **(LO3)**

Estimated useful life: The total number of service units expected from a long-term asset. **(LO3)**

Expenditure: A payment or an obligation to make future payment for an asset or a service. **(LO2)**

Extraordinary repairs: Repairs that significantly enhance a plant asset's estimated useful life or residual value and thereby increase its carrying value. **(LO2)**

Franchise: The right to an exclusive territory or market. **(LO6)**

Free cash flow: Amount of cash that remains after deducting the funds a company must commit to continue operating at its planned level; Net Cash Flows from Operating Activities − Dividends − (Purchases of Plant Assets − Sales of Plant Assets). **(LO1)**

Full-costing method: A method of accounting for the costs of exploring and developing oil and gas resources in which all costs are recorded as assets and depleted over the estimated life of the producing resources. **(LO5)**

Goodwill: The excess of the amount paid for a business over the fair market value of the business's net assets. **(LO6)**

Group depreciation: The grouping of similar items to calculate depreciation. **(LO3)**

Intangible assets: Long-term assets with no physical substance whose value is based on rights or advantages accruing to the owner. **(LO1)**

Leasehold: A right to occupy land or buildings under a long-term rental contract. **(LO6)**

Leasehold improvements: Improvements to leased property that become the property of the lessor at the end of the lease. **(LO2)**

License: The right to use a formula, technique, process, or design. **(LO6)**

Long-term assets: Assets that have a useful life of more than one year, are used in the operation of a business, and are not intended for resale. Less commonly called *fixed assets*. **(LO1)**

Natural resources: Long-term assets purchased for the economic value that can be taken from the land and used up. **(LO1)**

Noncompete covenant: A contract limiting the rights of others to compete in a specific industry or line of business for a specified period. **(LO6)**

Obsolescence: The process of becoming out of date, which is a factor in the limited useful life of tangible assets. **(LO3)**

Patent: An exclusive right granted by the federal government for a period of 20 years to make a particular product or use a specific process. **(LO6)**

Physical deterioration: A decline in the useful life of a depreciable asset resulting from use and from exposure to the elements. **(LO3)**

Production method: A method of depreciation that assumes depreciation is solely the result of use and that allocates depreciation based on the units of use or output during each period of an asset's useful life. **(LO3)**

Residual value: The estimated net scrap, salvage, or trade-in value of a tangible asset at the estimated date of its disposal. Also called *salvage value* or *disposal value*. **(LO3)**

Revenue expenditure: An expenditure for ordinary repairs and maintenance of a long-term asset, which is recorded by a debit to an expense account. **(LO2)**

Software: Capitalized costs associated with computer programs developed for sale, lease, or internal use and amortized over the estimated economic life of the programs. **(LO6)**

Straight-line method: A method of depreciation that assumes depreciation depends only on the passage of time and that allocates an equal amount of depreciation to each accounting period in an asset's useful life. **(LO3)**

Successful efforts accounting: A method of accounting for the costs of exploring and developing oil and gas resources in which successful exploration is recorded as an asset and depleted over the estimated life of the resource and all unsuccessful efforts are immediately written off as losses. **(LO5)**

Tangible assets: Long-term assets that have physical substance. **(LO1)**

Trademark: A registered symbol that can be used only by its owner to identify a product or service. **(LO6)**

≡ REVIEW Problem

LO3   **Comparison of Depreciation Methods**

Norton Construction Company purchased a cement mixer on January 2, 20x5, for $14,500. The mixer was expected to have a useful life of five years and a residual value of $1,000. The company's engineers estimated that the mixer would have a useful life of 7,500 hours. It was used for 1,500 hours in 20x5, 2,625 hours in 20x6, 2,250 hours in 20x7, 750 hours in 20x8, and 375 hours in 20x9. The company's fiscal year ends on December 31.

Required

1. Compute the depreciation expense and carrying value for 20x5 to 20x9, using the following methods: (a) straight-line, (b) production, and (c) double-declining-balance.

2. Show the balance sheet presentation for the cement mixer on December 31, 20x5. Assume the straight-line method.
3. What conclusions can you draw from the patterns of yearly depreciation?

Answer to Review Problem

1. Depreciation computed:

	A	B	C	D	E
1	Depreciation Method	Year	Computation	Depreciation	Carrying Value
2	a. Straight-line	20x5	$13,500 ÷ 5	$2,700	$11,800
3		20x6	13,500 ÷ 5	2,700	9,100
4		20x7	13,500 ÷ 5	2,700	6,400
5		20x8	13,500 ÷ 5	2,700	3,700
6		20x9	13,500 ÷ 5	2,700	1,000
7					
8	b. Production	20x5	$13,500 × 1,500/7,500	$2,700	$11,800
9		20x6	13,500 × 2,625/7,500	4,725	7,075
10		20x7	13,500 × 2,250/7,500	4,050	3,025
11		20x8	13,500 × 750/7,500	1,350	1,675
12		20x9	13,500 × 375/7,500	675	1,000
13					
	c. Double-declining-				
14	balance	20x5	$14,500 × .4	$5,800	$8,700
15		20x6	8,700 × .4	3,480	5,220
16		20x7	5,220 × .4	2,088	3,132
17		20x8	3,132 × .4	1,253*	1,879
18		20x9		879†	1,000
19					
20	* Rounded.				
21	† Remaining depreciation to reduce carrying value to residual value ($1,879 – $879).				

2. Balance sheet presentation on December 31, 20x5:

Property, plant, and equipment	
Cement mixer	$14,500
Less accumulated depreciation	2,700
	$11,800

3. The pattern of depreciation for the straight-line method differs significantly from the pattern for the double-declining-balance method. In the earlier years, the amount of depreciation under the double-declining-balance method is significantly greater than the amount under the straight-line method. In the later years, the opposite is true. The carrying value under the straight-line method is greater than under the double-declining-balance method at the end of all years except the fifth year. Depreciation under the production method differs from depreciation under the other methods in that it follows no regular pattern. It varies with the amount of use. Consequently, depreciation is greatest in 20x6 and 20x7, which are the years of greatest use. Use declined significantly in the last two years.

CHAPTER ASSIGNMENTS

BUILDING Your Basic Knowledge and Skills

Short Exercises

LO1 **Management Issues**

SE 1. Indicate whether each of the following actions is primarily related to (a) acquisition of long-term assets, (b) evaluating the adequacy of financing of long-term assets, or (c) applying the matching rule to long-term assets.

1. Deciding between common stock and long-term notes for the raising of funds
2. Relating the acquisition cost of a long-term asset to the cash flows generated by the asset
3. Determining how long an asset will benefit the company
4. Deciding to use cash flows from operations to purchase long-term assets
5. Determining how much an asset will sell for when it is no longer useful to the company
6. Calculating free cash flow

LO1 **Free Cash Flow**

SE 2. Sebel Corporation had cash flows from operating activities during the past year of $194,000. During the year, the company expended $25,000 for dividends; expended $158,000 for property, plant, and equipment; and sold property, plant, and equipment for $12,000. Calculate the company's free cash flow. What does the result tell you about the company?

LO2 **Determining Cost of Long-Term Assets**

SE 3. Watts Auto purchased a neighboring lot for a new building and parking lot. Indicate whether each of the following expenditures is properly charged to (a) Land, (b) Land Improvements, or (c) Buildings.

1. Paving costs
2. Architects' fee for building design
3. Cost of clearing the property
4. Cost of the property
5. Building construction costs
6. Lights around the property
7. Building permit
8. Interest on the construction loan

LO2 **Group Purchase**

SE 4. Lian Company purchased property with a warehouse and parking lot for $1,500,000. An appraiser valued the components of the property if purchased separately as follows:

Land	$ 400,000
Land improvements	200,000
Building	1,000,000
Total	$1,600,000

Determine the cost to be assigned to each component.

LO3 **Straight-Line Method**

SE 5. Willowbrook Fitness Center purchased a new step machine for $8,250. The apparatus is expected to last four years and have a residual value of $750. What will the depreciation expense be for each year under the straight-line method?

LO3 **Production Method**

SE 6. Assume that the step machine in **SE 5** has an estimated useful life of 8,000 hours and was used for 2,400 hours in year 1, 2,000 hours in year 2, 2,200 hours in year 3, and 1,400 hours in year 4. How much would depreciation expense be in each year?

LO3 **Double-Declining-Balance Method**

SE 7. Assume that the step machine in **SE 5** is depreciated using the double-declining-balance method. How much would depreciation expense be in each year?

LO4 **Disposal of Plant Assets: No Trade-In**

SE 8. Alarico Printing owned a piece of equipment that cost $16,200 and on which it had recorded $9,000 of accumulated depreciation. The company disposed of the equipment on January 2, the first day of business of the current year.

1. Calculate the carrying value of the equipment.
2. Calculate the gain or loss on the disposal under each of the following assumptions:

   a. The equipment was discarded as having no value.
   b. The equipment was sold for $3,000 cash.
   c. The equipment was sold for $8,000 cash.

LO5 **Natural Resources**

SE 9. Narda Company purchased land containing an estimated 4,000,000 tons of ore for $16,000,000. The land will be worth $2,400,000 without the ore after eight years of active mining. Although the equipment needed for the mining will have a useful life of 20 years, it is not expected to be usable and will have no value after the mining on this site is complete. Compute the depletion charge per ton and the amount of depletion expense for the first year of operation, assuming that 600,000 tons of ore are mined and sold. Also, compute the first-year depreciation on the mining equipment using the production method, assuming a cost of $19,200,000 with no residual value.

LO6 **Intangible Assets: Computer Software**

SE 10. Danya Company has created a new software application for PCs. Its costs during research and development were $250,000. Its costs after the working program was developed were $175,000. Although the company's copyright may be amortized over 40 years, management believes that the product will be viable for only five years. How should the costs be accounted for? At what value will the software appear on the balance sheet after one year?

Exercises

LO1, LO2, LO3 **Discussion Questions**

E 1. Develop a brief answer for each of the following questions:

1. Is carrying value ever the same as market value?
2. What major advantage does a company that has positive free cash flow have over a company that has negative free cash flow?
3. What incentive does a company have to allocate more of a group purchase price to land than to building?

4. Which depreciation method would best reflect the risk of obsolescence from rapid technological changes?

LO4, LO5, LO6 **Discussion Questions**

E 2. Develop a brief answer for each of the following questions:

1. When would the disposal of a long-term asset result in no gain or loss?
2. When would annual depletion not equal depletion expense?
3. Why would a firm amortize a patent over fewer years than the patent's life?
4. Why would a company spend millions of dollars on goodwill?

LO1 **Management Issues**

E 3. Indicate whether each of the following actions is primarily related to (a) acquisition of long-term assets, (b) evaluating the financing of long-term assets, or (c) applying the matching rule to long-term assets.

1. Deciding to use the production method of depreciation
2. Allocating costs on a group purchase
3. Determining the total units a machine will produce
4. Deciding to borrow funds to purchase equipment
5. Estimating the savings a new machine will produce and comparing that amount to cost
6. Examining the trend of free cash flow over several years
7. Deciding whether to rent or buy a piece of equipment

LO1 **Purchase Decision—Present Value Analysis**

E 4. Management is considering the purchase of a new machine for a cost of $6,000. It is estimated that the machine will generate positive net cash flows of $1,500 per year for five years and will have a disposal price at the end of that time of $500. Assuming an interest rate of 9 percent, determine if management should purchase the machine. Use Tables 3 and 4 in the appendix on future value and present value tables to determine the net present value of the new machine.

LO1 **Free Cash Flow**

E 5. Zedek Corporation had cash flows from operating activities during the past year of $216,000. During the year, the company expended $462,000 for property, plant, and equipment; sold property, plant, and equipment for $54,000; and paid dividends of $50,000. Calculate the company's free cash flow. What does the result tell you about the company?

LO2 **Special Types of Capital Expenditures**

E 6. Tell whether each of the following transactions related to an office building is a revenue expenditure (RE) or a capital expenditure (CE). In addition, indicate whether each transaction is an ordinary repair (OR), an extraordinary repair (ER), an addition (A), a betterment (B), or none of these (N).

1. The hallways and ceilings in the building are repainted at a cost of $4,150.
2. The hallways, which have tile floors, are carpeted at a cost of $14,000.
3. A new wing is added to the building at a cost of $87,500.
4. Furniture is purchased for the entrance to the building at a cost of $8,250.
5. The air-conditioning system is overhauled at a cost of $14,250. The overhaul extends the useful life of the air-conditioning system by ten years.
6. A cleaning firm is paid $100 per week to clean the newly installed carpets.

LO2 **Determining Cost of Long-Term Assets**

E 7. Sakai Manufacturing purchased land next to its factory to be used as a parking lot. The expenditures incurred by the company were as follows:

purchase price, $300,000; broker's fees, $24,000; title search and other fees, $2,200; demolition of a cottage on the property, $8,000; general grading of property, $4,200; paving parking lots, $40,000; lighting for parking lots, $32,000; and signs for parking lots, $6,400. Determine the amounts that should be debited to the Land account and the Land Improvements account.

LO2 Group Purchase

E 8. Ebra Allen purchased a car wash for $240,000. If purchased separately, the land would have cost $60,000, the building $135,000, and the equipment $105,000. Determine the amount that should be recorded in the new business's records for land, building, and equipment.

LO2, LO3 Cost of Long-Term Asset and Depreciation

E 9. Demarco Phipps purchased a used tractor for $17,500. Before the tractor could be used, it required new tires, which cost $1,100, and an overhaul, which cost $1,400. Its first tank of fuel cost $75. The tractor is expected to last six years and have a residual value of $2,000. Determine the cost and depreciable cost of the tractor and calculate the first year's depreciation under the straight-line method.

LO3 Depreciation Methods

E 10. On January 13, 2006, Silverio Oil Company purchased a drilling truck for $45,000. Silverio expects the truck to last five years or 200,000 miles, with an estimated residual value of $7,500 at the end of that time. During 20x7, the truck is driven 48,000 miles. Silverio's year end is December 31. Compute the depreciation for 20x7 under each of the following methods: (1) straight-line, (2) production, and (3) double-declining-balance. Using the amount computed in **(3)**, prepare the entry in journal form to record depreciation expense for the second year, and show how the Drilling Truck account would appear on the balance sheet.

LO3 Double-Declining-Balance Method

E 11. Percival Burglar Alarm Systems Company purchased a computer for $1,120. It has an estimated useful life of four years and an estimated residual value of $120. Compute the depreciation charge for each of the four years using the double-declining-balance method.

LO3 Revision of Depreciation Rates

E 12. Feld Hospital purchased a special x-ray machine. The machine, which cost $623,120, was expected to last ten years, with an estimated residual value of $63,120. After two years of operation (and depreciation charges using the straight-line method), it became evident that the x-ray machine would last a total of only seven years. The estimated residual value, however, would remain the same. Given this information, determine the new depreciation charge for the third year on the basis of the revised estimated useful life.

LO4 Disposal of Plant Assets

E 13. A piece of equipment that cost $64,800 and on which $36,000 of accumulated depreciation had been recorded was disposed of on January 2, the first day of business of the current year. For each of the following assumptions, compute the gain or loss on the disposal.

1. The equipment was discarded as having no value.
2. The equipment was sold for $12,000 cash.
3. The equipment was sold for $36,000 cash.

LO4 **Disposal of Plant Assets**

E 14. King Company purchased a computer on January 2, 20x6, at a cost of $2,500. The computer is expected to have a useful life of five years and a residual value of $250. Assume that the computer is disposed of on July 1, 20x9. Record the depreciation expense for half a year and the disposal under each of the following assumptions:

1. The computer is discarded.
2. The computer is sold for $400.
3. The computer is sold for $1,100.

LO5 **Natural Resource Depletion and Depreciation of Related Plant Assets**

E 15. Cooby Company purchased land containing an estimated 5 million tons of ore for a cost of $8,800,000. The land without the ore is estimated to be worth $500,000. During its first year of operation, the company mined and sold 750,000 tons of ore. Compute the depletion charge per ton. Compute the depletion expense that Cooby should record for the year.

LO6 **Amortization of Copyrights and Trademarks**

E 16. The following exercise is about amortizing copyrights and trademarks.

1. Akram Publishing Company purchased the copyright to a basic computer textbook for $40,000. The usual life of a textbook is about four years. However, the copyright will remain in effect for another 50 years. Calculate the annual amortization of the copyright.
2. Saui Company purchased a trademark from a well-known supermarket for $320,000. The management of the company argued that the trademark's useful life was indefinite. Explain how the cost should be accounted for.

LO6 **Accounting for a Patent**

E 17. At the beginning of the fiscal year, Ricks Company purchased for $1,030,000 a patent that applies to the manufacture of a unique tamper-proof lid for medicine bottles. Ricks incurred legal costs of $450,000 in successfully defending use of the lid by a competitor. Ricks estimated that the patent would be valuable for at least ten years. During the first two years of operations, Ricks successfully marketed the lid. At the beginning of the third year, a study appeared in a consumer magazine showing that children could in fact remove the lid. As a result, all orders for the lids were canceled, and the patent was rendered worthless.

Prepare entries in journal form to record the following: (a) purchase of the patent; (b) successful defense of the patent; (c) amortization expense for the first year; and (d) write-off of the patent as worthless.

Problems

LO1, LO2 **Identification of Long-Term Assets Terminology**

P 1. Listed below are common terms associated with long-term assets:

a. Tangible assets
b. Natural resources
c. Intangible assets
d. Additions
e. Betterments
f. Extraordinary repair
g. Depreciation
h. Depletion
i. Amortization
j. Revenue expenditure
k. Free cash flow

Required

1. For each of the following statements, identify the term listed above with which it is associated. (If two terms apply, choose the one that is most closely associated.)

   1. Periodic cost associated with intangible assets
   2. Cost of constructing a new wing on a building
   3. A measure of funds available for expansion
   4. A group of assets encompassing property, plant, and equipment
   5. Cost associated with enhancing a building but not expanding it
   6. Periodic cost associated with tangible assets
   7. A group of assets that gain their value from contracts or rights
   8. Cost of normal repairs to a building
   9. Assets whose value derives from what can be extracted from them
   10. Periodic cost associated with natural resources
   11. Cost of a repair that extends the useful life of a building

2. **User Insight:** Assuming the company uses cash for all its expenditures, which of the items listed above would you expect to see on the income statement? Which ones would not result in an outlay of cash?

LO2   **Determining Cost of Assets**

P 2. Oslo Company was formed on January 1, 2007, and began constructing a new plant. At the end of 2007, its auditor discovered that all expenditures involving long-term assets had been debited to an account called Fixed Assets. An analysis of the Fixed Assets account, which had a year-end balance of $2,644,972, disclosed that it contained the following items:

Cost of land	$ 316,600
Surveying costs	4,100
Transfer of title and other fees required by the county	920
Broker's fees for land	21,144
Attorney's fees associated with land acquisition	7,048
Cost of removing timber from land	50,400
Cost of grading land	4,200
Cost of digging building foundation	34,600
Architect's fee for building and land improvements (80 percent building)	64,800
Cost of building construction	710,000
Cost of sidewalks	11,400
Cost of parking lots	54,400
Cost of lighting for grounds	80,300
Cost of landscaping	11,800
Cost of machinery	989,000
Shipping cost on machinery	55,300
Cost of installing machinery	176,200
Cost of testing machinery	22,100
Cost of changes in building to comply with safety regulations pertaining to machinery	12,540
Cost of repairing building that was damaged in the installation of machinery	8,900
Cost of medical bill for injury received by employee while installing machinery	2,400
Cost of water damage to building during heavy rains prior to opening the plant for operation	6,820
Account balance	$2,644,972

Oslo Company sold the timber it cleared from the land to a firewood dealer for $5,000. This amount was credited to Miscellaneous Income.

During the construction period, two of Oslo's supervisors devoted full time to the construction project. Their annual salaries were $48,000 and $42,000, respectively. They spent two months on the purchase and preparation of the land, six months on the construction of the building (approximately one-sixth of which was devoted to improvements on the grounds), and one month on machinery installation. When the plant began operation on October 1, the supervisors returned to their regular duties. Their salaries were debited to Factory Salaries Expense.

Required

1. Prepare a schedule with the following column headings: Land, Land Improvements, Buildings, Machinery, and Expense. Place each of the above expenditures in the appropriate column. Negative amounts should be shown in parentheses. Total the columns.
2. **User Insight:** What impact does the classification of the items among several accounts have on evaluating the profitability performance of the company?

LO3, LO4 **Comparison of Depreciation Methods**

P 3. Laughlin Designs, Inc., purchased a computerized blueprint printer that will assist in the design and display of plans for factory layouts. The cost of the printer was $22,500, and its expected useful life is four years. The company can probably sell the printer for $2,500 at the end of six years. The printer is expected to last 6,000 hours. It was used 1,200 hours in year 1; 1,800 hours in year 2; 2,400 hours in year 3; and 600 hours in year 4.

Required

1. Compute the annual depreciation and carrying value for the new blueprint printer for each of the four years (round to the nearest dollar where necessary) under each of the following methods: (a) straight-line, (b) production, and (c) double-declining-balance.
2. If the printer is sold for $12,000 after year 2, what would be the gain or loss under each method?
3. **User Insight:** What conclusions can you draw from the patterns of yearly depreciation and carrying value in requirement 1? Do the three methods differ in their impact on profitability? Do they differ in their effect on the company's operating cash flows? Explain.

LO3, LO4 **Comparison of Depreciation Methods**

P 4. Myles Construction Company purchased a new crane for $360,500 at the beginning of year 1. The crane has an estimated residual value of $35,000 and an estimated useful life of six years. The crane is expected to last 10,000 hours. It was used 1,800 hours in year 1; 2,000 in year 2; 2,500 in year 3; 1,500 in year 4; 1,200 in year 5; and 1,000 in year 6.

Required

1. Compute the annual depreciation and carrying value for the new crane for each of the six years (round to the nearest dollar where necessary) under each of the following methods: (a) straight-line, (b) production, and (c) double-declining-balance.
2. If the crane is sold for $250,000 after year 3, what would be the amount of gain or loss under each method?

3. **User Insight:** Do the three methods differ in their effect on the company's profitability? Do they differ in their effect on the company's operating cash flows? Explain.

LO5 Natural Resource Depletion and Depreciation of Related Plant Assets

P 5. Dombrad Mining Company purchased land containing an estimated 10 million tons of ore for a cost of $4,400,000. The land without the ore is estimated to be worth $800,000. The company expects that all the usable ore can be mined in 10 years. Buildings costing $400,000 with an estimated useful life of 30 years were erected on the site. Equipment costing $480,000 with an estimated useful life of 10 years was installed. Because of the remote location, neither the buildings nor the equipment has an estimated residual value. During its first year of operation, the company mined and sold 800,000 tons of ore.

Required

1. Compute the depletion charge per ton.
2. Compute the depletion expense that Dombrad Mining should record for the year.
3. Determine the depreciation expense for the year for the buildings, making it proportional to the depletion.
4. Determine the depreciation expense for the year for the equipment under two alternatives: (a) making the expense proportional to the depletion and (b) using the straight-line method.
5. **User Insight:** Suppose the company mined and sold 1,000,000 tons of ore (instead of 800,000) during the first year. Would the change in the results in requirements **2** or **3** affect earnings or cash flows? Explain.

Alternate Problems

LO2 Determining Cost of Assets

P 6. Pappas Computers constructed a new training center in 20x7. You have been hired to manage the training center. A review of the accounting records shows the following expenditures debited to an asset account called Training Center:

Attorney's fee, land acquisition	$ 34,900
Cost of land	598,000
Architect's fee, building design	102,000
Building	1,020,000
Parking lot and sidewalk	135,600
Electrical wiring, building	164,000
Landscaping	55,000
Cost of surveying land	9,200
Training equipment, tables, and chairs	136,400
Installation of training equipment	68,000
Cost of grading the land	14,000
Cost of changes in building to soundproof rooms	59,200
Total account balance	$2,396,300

During the center's construction, an employee of Pappas Computers worked full time overseeing the project. He spent two months on the purchase and preparation of the site, six months on the construction, one month on land improvements, and one month on equipment installation and training room furniture purchase and setup. His salary of $64,000 during this ten-month period was charged to Administrative Expense. The training center was placed in operation on November 1.

Required

1. Prepare a schedule with the following four column (account) headings: Land, Land Improvements, Building, and Equipment. Place each of the above expenditures in the appropriate column. Total the columns.
2. **User Insight:** What impact does the classification of the items among several accounts have on evaluating the profitability performance of the company?

LO3, LO4 ### Comparison of Depreciation Methods

P 7. Gent Manufacturing Company purchased a robot for $720,000 at the beginning of year 1. The robot has an estimated useful life of four years and an estimated residual value of $60,000. The robot, which should last 20,000 hours, was operated 6,000 hours in year 1; 8,000 hours in year 2; 4,000 hours in year 3; and 2,000 hours in year 4.

Required

1. Compute the annual depreciation and carrying value for the robot for each year assuming the following depreciation methods: (a) straight-line, (b) production, and (c) double-declining-balance.
2. If the robot is sold for $750,000 after year 2, what would be the amount of gain or loss under each method?
3. **User Insight:** What conclusions can you draw from the patterns of yearly depreciation and carrying value in requirement 1? Do the three methods differ in their effect on the company's profitability? Do they differ in their effect on the company's operating cash flows? Explain.

LO5 ### Natural Resource Depletion and Depreciation of Related Plant Assets

P 8. Karanga Company purchased land containing an estimated 20 million tons of ore for a cost of $6,600,000. The land without the ore is estimated to be worth $1,200,000. The company expects that all the usable ore can be mined in 10 years. Buildings costing $600,000 with an estimated useful life of 20 years were erected on the site. Equipment costing $720,000 with an estimated useful life of 10 years was installed. Because of the remote location, neither the buildings nor the equipment has an estimated residual value. During its first year of operation, the company mined and sold 900,000 tons of ore.

Required

1. Compute the depletion charge per ton.
2. Compute the depletion expense that Karanga should record for the year.
3. Determine the depreciation expense for the year for the buildings, making it proportional to the depletion.
4. Determine the depreciation expense for the year for the equipment under two alternatives: (a) making the expense proportional to the depletion and (b) using the straight-line method.
5. **User Insight:** Suppose the company mined and sold 500,000 tons of ore (instead of 900,000) during the first year. Would the change in the results in requirement 2 or 3 affect earnings or cash flows? Explain.

ENHANCING Your Knowledge, Skills, and Critical Thinking

Conceptual Understanding Cases

LO1 **Effect of Change in Estimates**

C 1. The airline industry was hit particularly hard after the 9/11 attacks on the World Trade Center in 2001. In 2002, **Southwest Airlines**, one of the healthier airlines companies, made a decision to lengthen the useful lives of its aircraft from 22 to 27 years. Shortly thereafter, following Southwest's leadership, other airlines made the same move.[18]

What advantage, if any, can the airlines gain by making this change in estimate? Will it change earnings or cash flows and, if it does, will the change be favorable or negative?

Some people argue that the useful lives and depreciation of airplanes are irrelevant. They claim that because of the extensive maintenance and testing that airline companies are required by law to perform, the planes theoretically can be in service for an indefinite future period. What is wrong with this argument?

LO1 **Impairment Test**

C 2. The annual report for **Costco Wholesale Corporation**, the large discount company, contains the following statement:

> The company periodically evaluates the realizability of long-lived assets for impairment when [circumstances] may indicate the carrying amount of the asset may not be recoverable.[19]

What does the concept of impairment mean in accounting? What effect does impairment have on profitability and cash flows? Why would the concept of impairment be referred to as a conservative accounting approach?

LO3 **Accounting Policies**

C 3. **IBM**, the large computer equipment and services company, states in its annual report that "plant, rental machines and other property are carried at cost and depreciated over their useful lives using the straight-line method."[20] What estimates are necessary to carry out this policy? What factors should be considered in making each of the estimates?

Interpreting Financial Reports

LO6 **Brands**

C 4. **Hilton Hotels Corporation** and **Marriott International** provide hospitality services. Hilton Hotels' well-known brands include Hilton, Doubletree, Hampton Inn, Embassy Suites, Red Lion Hotels and Inns, and Homewood Suites. Marriott also owns or manages properties with recognizable brand names, such as Marriott Hotels, Resorts and Suites; Ritz-Carlton; Renaissance Hotels; Residence Inn; Courtyard; and Fairfield Inn.

On its balance sheet, Hilton Hotels Corporation includes brands (net of amortization) of $970 million, or 11.6 percent of total assets. Marriott International, however, does not list brands among its intangible assets.[21] What principles of accounting for intangibles would cause Hilton to record brands as an asset while Marriott does not? How will these differences in accounting for brands generally affect the net income and return on assets of these two competitors?

LO3 **Effects of Change in Accounting Method**

C 5. Depreciation expense is a significant cost for companies in which plant assets are a high proportion of assets. The amount of depreciation expense in a given year is affected by estimates of useful life and choice of depreciation method. In 2006, Century Steelworks Company, a major integrated steel producer, changed the estimated useful lives for its major production assets. It also changed the method of depreciation for other steel-making assets from straight-line to the production method.

In its 2006 annual report, Century Steelworks Company makes the following statement:

> A recent study conducted by management shows that actual years-in-service figures for our major production equipment and machinery are, in most cases, higher than the estimated useful lives assigned to these assets. We have recast the depreciable lives of such assets so that equipment previously assigned a useful life of 8 to 26 years now has an extended depreciable life of 10 to 32 years.

The report goes on to explain the new production method of depreciation, as follows:

> [The method] recognizes that depreciation of production equipment and machinery correlates directly to both physical wear and tear and the passage of time. The production method of depreciation, which we have now initiated, more closely allocates the cost of these assets to the periods in which products are manufactured.

The report summarizes the effects of the changes in estimated useful lives and depreciation method on the year 2006 as shown in the following table:

Incremental Increase in Net Income	In Millions	Per Share
Lengthened lives	$11.0	$ .80
Production method		
Current year	7.3	.53
Prior years	2.8	.20
Total increase	$21.1	$1.53

During 2006, Century Steelworks reported a net loss of $83,156,500 ($6.03 per share). Depreciation expense for 2006 was $87,707,200.

In explaining the changes the company has made, the controller of Century Steelworks was quoted in an article in *Business Journal* as follows: "There is no reason for Century Steelworks to continue to depreciate our assets more conservatively than our competitors do." But the article also quotes an industry analyst who argues that by slowing its method of depreciation, Century Steelworks could be viewed as reporting lower-quality earnings.

1. Explain the accounting treatment when there is a change in the estimated lives of depreciable assets. What circumstances must exist for the production method to produce the effect it did in relation to the straight-line method? What would Century Steelworks' net income or loss have been if the changes had not been made? What might have motivated management to make the changes?

2. What does the controller of Century Steelworks mean when he says that Century had been depreciating "more conservatively than our competitors do"? Why might the changes at Century Steelworks indicate, as the analyst

asserts, "lower-quality earnings"? What risks might Century face as a result of its decision to use the production method of depreciation?

Decision Analysis Using Excel

LO1 **Purchase Decision and Time Value of Money**

C 6. Morningside Machine Works has obtained a subcontract from the government to manufacture special parts for a new military aircraft. The parts are to be delivered over the next five years, and the company will be paid as the parts are delivered.

To make the parts, Morningside Machine Works will have to purchase new equipment. Two types are available. Type A is conventional equipment that can be put into service immediately; Type B requires one year to be put into service but is more efficient than Type A. Type A requires an immediate cash investment of $1,000,000 and will produce enough parts to provide net cash receipts of $340,000 each year for the five years. Type B may be purchased by signing a two-year non-interest-bearing note for $1,346,000. It is projected that Type B will produce net cash receipts of zero in year 1, $500,000 in year 2, $600,000 in year 3, $600,000 in year 4, and $200,000 in year 5. Neither type of equipment can be used on other contracts, and neither type will have any useful life remaining at the end of the contract. Morningside currently pays an interest rate of 16 percent to borrow money.

1. What is the present value of the investment required for each type of equipment? (Use Table 3 in the appendix on future value and present value tables.)
2. Compute the net present value of each type of equipment based on your answer in **1** and the present value of the net cash receipts projected to be received. (Use Tables 3 and 4 in the appendix on future value and present value tables.)
3. Write a memorandum to the board of directors that recommends the option that appears to be best for Morningside. Explain your reasoning and include **1** and **2** as attachments.

Annual Report Case: CVS Corporation

LO1, LO2, LO3, LO6 **Long-Term Assets**

C 7. To answer the following questions, refer to **CVS Corporation's** annual report in the Supplement to Chapter 1. Examine the balance sheets and the summary of significant accounting policies on property and equipment in the notes to the financial statements.

1. What percentage of total assets in the most recent year was property and equipment, net? What are the major categories of CVS's property and equipment, and which is the most significant type of property and equipment? What are leasehold improvements? How significant are these items, and what are their effects on the earnings of the company?
2. Continue with the summary of significant accounting policies item on property and equipment in the CVS annual report. What method of depreciation does CVS use? How long does management estimate its buildings will last as compared with furniture and equipment? What does this say about the company's need to remodel its stores?
3. Refer to the note on impairment of long-lived assets in the summary of sig-

nificant accounting policies in CVS Corporation's annual report. How does the company determine if it has impaired assets?

Comparison Case: CVS Versus Southwest

LO1 Long-Term Assets and Free Cash Flows

C 8. Refer to the annual report of **CVS Corporation** and to the financial statements of **Southwest Airlines Co**. in the Supplement to Chapter 1 to answer the following questions:

1. Prepare a table that shows the net amount each company spent on property and equipment (from the statement of cash flows), the total property and equipment (from the balance sheet), and the percentage of the first figure to the second for each of the past two years. Which company grew its property and equipment at a faster rate?
2. Calculate free cash flow for each company for the past two years. What conclusions can you draw about the need for each company to raise funds from debt and equity and the ability of each company to grow?

Ethical Dilemma Case

LO2 Ethics and Allocation of Acquisition Costs

C 9. Signal Company has purchased land and a warehouse for $18,000,000. The warehouse is expected to last 20 years and to have a residual value equal to 10 percent of its cost. The chief financial officer (CFO) and the controller are discussing the allocation of the purchase price. The CFO believes that the largest amount possible should be assigned to the land because this action will improve reported net income in the future. Depreciation expense will be lower because land is not depreciated. He suggests allocating one-third, or $6,000,000, of the cost to the land. This results in depreciation expense each year of $540,000 [($12,000,000 − $1,200,000) ÷ 20 years].

The controller disagrees. She argues that the smallest amount possible, say one-fifth of the purchase price, should be allocated to the land, thereby saving income taxes, since the depreciation, which is tax-deductible, will be greater. Under this plan, annual depreciation would be $648,000 [($14,400,000 − $1,440,000) ÷ 20 years]. The annual tax savings at a 30 percent tax rate is $32,400 [($648,000 − $540,000) × .30]. How would each decision affect the company's cash flows? Ethically, how should the purchase cost be allocated? Who will be affected by the decision?

Internet Case

LO3, LO4, LO6 SEC and Forms 10-K

C 10. Public corporations are required not only to communicate with their stockholders by means of an annual report but also to submit an annual report to the Securities and Exchange Commission (SEC). The annual report to the SEC is called a Form 10-K and is a source of the latest information about a company. Access the SEC's EDGAR files to locate either **H.J. Heinz Company's** or **Ford Motor Company's** Form 10-K. Find the financial statements and the notes to the financial statements. Scan through the notes to the financial statements and prepare a list of information related to long-term assets, including intangibles. For instance, what depreciation methods does the company use?

What are the useful lives of its property, plant, and equipment? What intangible assets does the company have? Does the company have goodwill? How much does the company spend on research and development? In the statement of cash flows, how much did the company spend on new property, plant, and equipment (capital expenditures)? Summarize your results and be prepared to discuss them in class as well as your experience in using the SEC's EDGAR database.

Group Activity Case

LO2, LO6

Ethics of Aggressive Accounting Policies

C 11. Is it ethical to choose aggressive accounting practices to advance a company's business? During the 1990s, **America Online (AOL)**, the largest Internet service provider in the United States, was one of the hottest stocks on Wall Street. After its initial stock offering in 1992, AOL's stock price shot up by several thousand percent.

Accounting is very important to a company like AOL because earnings enable it to sell shares of stock and raise more cash to fund its growth. In its early years, AOL was one of the most aggressive companies in its choice of accounting principles. AOL's strategy called for building the largest customer base in the industry. Consequently, it spent many millions of dollars each year marketing its services to new customers. Such costs are usually recognized as operating expenses in the year in which they are incurred. However, AOL treated these costs as long-term assets, called "deferred subscriber acquisition costs," and expensed them over several years, because it said the average customer was going to stay with the company for three years or more. The company also recorded research and development costs as "product development costs" and amortized them over five years.

Both of these practices are justifiable theoretically, but they are not common practice. If the standard, more conservative practice had been followed, the company would have had a net loss in every year it has been in business.[22] This result would have greatly limited AOL's ability to raise money and grow.

Form groups to discuss this case. Determine whether your group thinks AOL was or was not justified in adopting the "aggressive" accounting techniques. In your group, answers to the following questions may help you reach a conclusion: What was "aggressive" about AOL's accounting techniques? What was management's rationale for adopting the accounting policies that it did? What could go wrong with such a plan? How would you evaluate the ethics of AOL's actions? Who benefits from the actions? Who is harmed by these actions? Be prepared to support your conclusion in class.

Business Communication Case

LO3

Motivation for Change of Depreciation Method

C 12. Polaroid Corporation, a manufacturer of instant cameras and film, changed from an accelerated depreciation method for financial reporting purposes to the straight-line method for assets acquired after January 1, 1997. As noted in Polaroid's 1997 annual report:

> The company changed its method of depreciation for financial reporting for the cost of buildings, machinery, and equipment acquired on or after January 1, 1997, from a primarily accelerated method to the straight-line method.[23]

Polaroid's deteriorating financial position led it to declare bankruptcy in 2001. Write a one-page memorandum that argues that the change in accounting method may have been a signal that the company was in financial trouble. In your memorandum, discuss the effects of the change on future earnings and cash flows. In addition, discuss which of the two depreciation methods is more conservative.

10

Long-Term Liabilities

Long-term liabilities can be an attractive means of financing the expansion of a business. By incurring long-term debt to fund growth, a company may be able to earn a return that exceeds the interest it pays on the debt. When it does, it increases earnings for stockholders—that is, return on equity. Many companies reward top managers with bonuses for improving return on equity. This incentive provides a temptation to incur too much debt, which increases a company's financial risk. Thus, in deciding on an appropriate level of debt, as in so many other management issues, ethics is a major concern.

LEARNING OBJECTIVES

LO1 Identify the management issues related to long-term debt.

LO2 Describe the features of a bond issue and the major characteristics of bonds.

LO3 Record bonds issued at face value and at a discount or premium.

LO4 Use present values to determine the value of bonds.

LO5 Amortize bond discounts and bond premiums using the straight-line and effective interest methods.

LO6 Account for the retirement of bonds and the conversion of bonds into stock.

SUPPLEMENTAL OBJECTIVE

SO7 Record bonds issued between interest dates and year-end adjustments.

Making a Statement

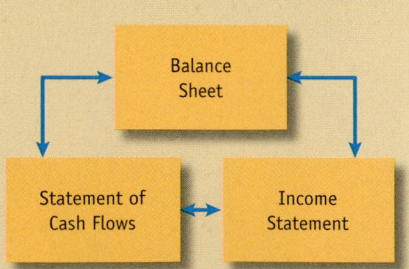

Long-term liability activities can impact all financial statements.

- What are McDonald's most important long-term debts?
- What are its considerations in deciding to issue long-term debt?
- How does one evaluate whether a company has too much debt?

McDonald's, the world's largest restaurant chain, passed a milestone in 2004 when it earned more revenues in Europe than in the United States. To finance its continued global expansion, the company raises funds by issuing both debt and capital stock. As you can see in its Financial Highlights, McDonald's relies heavily on debt financing. In 2003, its long-term liabilities almost equaled its stockholders' equity and, together with current liabilities, they exceeded stockholders' equity. In 2004, its total current and long-term liabilities amounted to 96 percent of stockholders' equity. McDonald's long-term obligations include numerous leases on real estate, as well as employee pension and health plans.[1]

McDONALD'S FINANCIAL HIGHLIGHTS
(In millions)

	2004	2003
Total current liabilities	$ 3,520.5	$ 2,748.5
Long-term debt	$ 8,357.3	$ 9,342.5
Other long-term liabilities	976.7	699.8
Deferred income taxes	781.5	1,065.3
Total long-term liabilities	$10,115.5	$11,107.6
Total stockholders' equity	$14,201.5	$11,981.9
Total liabilities and stockholders' equity	$27,837.5	$25,838.0

Management Issues Related to Issuing Long-Term Debt

Profitable operations and short-term credit seldom provide sufficient cash for a growing business. Growth usually requires investment in long-term assets and in research and development and other activities that will produce income in future years. To finance these assets and activities, a company needs funds that will be available for long periods. Two key sources of long-term funds are the issuance of capital stock and the issuance of long-term debt. The management issues related to long-term debt financing are whether to take on long-term debt, how much long-term debt to carry, and what types of long-term debt to incur.

Deciding to Issue Long-Term Debt

A key decision for management is whether to rely solely on stockholders' equity—capital stock issued and retained earnings—for long-term funds or to rely partially on long-term debt. Some companies, such as **Microsoft** and **Apple Computer**, do not issue long-term debt, but like **McDonald's**, most companies find it useful to do so.

Because long-term debt must be paid at maturity and usually requires periodic payments of interest, issuing common stock has two advantages over issuing long-term debt: (1) it does not have to be paid back, and (2) a company normally pays dividends on common stock only if it earns sufficient income. Issuing long-term debt, however, has the following advantages over issuing common stock:

- **No loss of stockholder control.** When a corporation issues long-term debt, common stockholders do not relinquish any of their control over the company because bondholders and other creditors do not have voting rights. But when a corporation issues additional shares of common stock, the votes of the new stockholders may force current stockholders and management to give up some control.

- **Tax effects.** The interest on debt is tax-deductible, whereas dividends on common stock are not. For example, if a corporation pays $100,000 in interest and its income tax rate is 30 percent, its net cost will be $70,000 because it will save $30,000 on income taxes. To pay $100,000 in dividends on common stock, the corporation would have to earn $142,857 before income taxes [($100,000 ÷ (1 − .30)].

- **Financial leverage.** If a corporation earns more from the funds it raises by incurring long-term debt than it pays in interest on the debt, the excess will increase its earnings for the stockholders. This concept is called **financial leverage**, or *trading on equity*. For example, if a company earns 12 percent on a $1,000,000 investment financed by long-term 10 percent notes, it will earn $20,000 before income taxes ($120,000 − $100,000). The debt to equity ratio is considered an overall measure of a company's financial leverage.

Despite these advantages, debt financing is not always in a company's best interest. It may entail the following:

- **Financial risk.** A high level of debt exposes a company to financial risk. A company whose plans for earnings do not pan out, whose operations are subject to the ups and downs of the economy, or whose cash flow is weak may be unable to pay the principal amount of its debt at the maturity date or even to make periodic interest payments. Creditors can then force the company into bankruptcy—something that has occurred often in the heavily debt-financed airline industry. **TWA**, **Continental Airlines**, and **United Airlines** filed for bankruptcy protection because they could not make payments on their long-term debt and other liabilities. (While in bankruptcy, they restructured their debt and interest payments: TWA sold off its assets, Continental survived, and United is still trying to come out of bankruptcy.)

▶ **Negative financial leverage.** Financial leverage can work against a company if the earnings from its investments do not exceed its interest payments. For example, many small Internet companies failed in recent years because they relied too heavily on debt financing before developing sufficient resources to ensure their survival.

Evaluating Long-Term Debt

The amount of long-term debt that companies carry varies widely. For many companies, it is less than 100 percent of stockholders' equity. However, as Figure 1 shows, the average debt to equity for selected industries often exceeds 100 percent of stockholders' equity. The range is from 90.3 percent to 202.4 percent of equity.

To assess how much debt to carry, managers compute the debt to equity ratio. Using data from **McDonald's** Financial Highlights, we can compute its debt to equity ratio in 2004 as follows (in millions):

$$\text{Debt to Equity} = \frac{\text{Total Liabilities}}{\text{Total Stockholders' Equity}}$$

$$= \frac{\$3,520.5 + \$10,115.5}{\$14,201.5} = \frac{\$13,636.0}{\$14,201.5} = 1.0 \text{ times}$$

A debt to equity ratio of 1.0 is relatively large, but it does not tell the whole story. McDonald's also has long-term leases on property at about 15,000 locations. McDonald's structures these leases in such a way that they do not appear

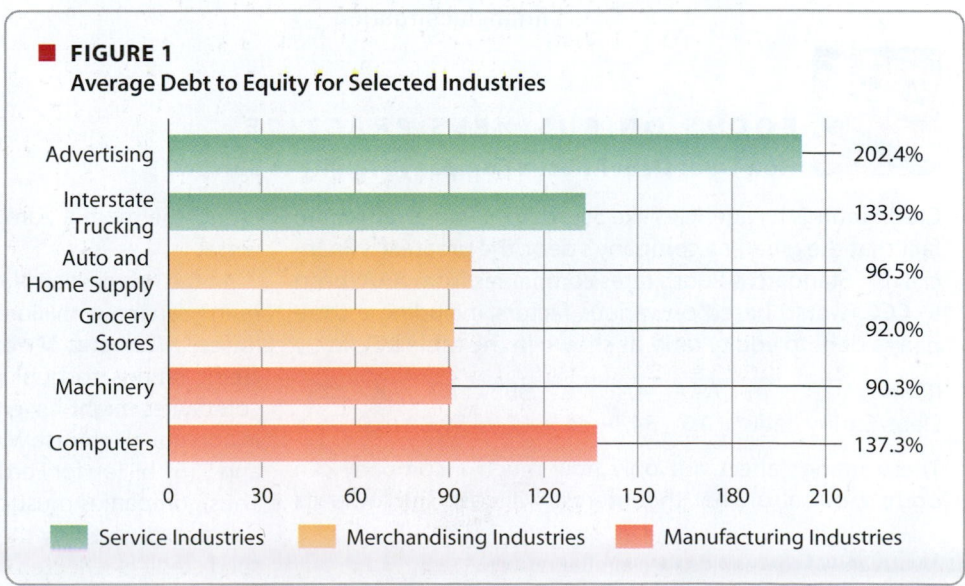

■ **FIGURE 1**
Average Debt to Equity for Selected Industries

Advertising		202.4%
Interstate Trucking		133.9%
Auto and Home Supply		96.5%
Grocery Stores		92.0%
Machinery		90.3%
Computers		137.3%

0   30   60   90   120   150   180   210

■ Service Industries   ■ Merchandising Industries   ■ Manufacturing Industries

Source: Data from Dun & Bradstreet, *Industry Norms and Key Business Ratios,* 2003–2004.

as liabilities on its balance sheet. This practice is called **off-balance-sheet financing** and, as used by McDonald's, is entirely legal. The leases are, however, long-term commitments of cash payments and so have the effect of long-term liabilities. McDonald's total commitment for its leases, which average 20 to 25 years, is $10,508 million.[2] If we add the discounted present value of these lease obligations to McDonald's balance sheet debt, it brings the total debt to about $20,000 million.

Financial leverage—using long-term debt to fund investments or operations that increase return on equity—is advantageous as long as a company is able to make timely interest payments and repay the debt at maturity. Because failure to do so can force a company into bankruptcy, companies must assess the financial risk involved. A common measure of how much risk a company undertakes by assuming long-term debt is the **interest coverage ratio**. It measures the degree of protection a company has from default on interest payments.

McDonald's 2004 annual report shows that the company had income before taxes of $3,202.4 million and interest expense of $358.4 million. Using these figures, we can compute McDonald's interest coverage ratio as follows:

$$\text{Interest Coverage Ratio} = \frac{\text{Income Before Income Taxes} + \text{Interest Expense}}{\text{Interest Expense}}$$

$$= \frac{\$3,202.4 + \$358.4}{\$358.4}$$

$$= \frac{\$3,560.8}{\$358.4}$$

$$= 9.9 \text{ times}$$

McDonald's strong interest coverage ratio of 9.9 times shows that it was in no danger of being unable to make interest payments. However, in computing this ratio, management will add the company's off-balance-sheet rent expense of $1,003.2 to its interest expense. This procedure decreases the coverage ratio to less than 4 times. Although still adequate to cover interest payments, the adjusted coverage ratio is far less robust, which demonstrates the significant effect that off-balance-sheet financing for leases can have on a company's financial situation.

FOCUS ON BUSINESS PRACTICE

How Does Debt Affect a Company's Ability to Borrow?

Credit ratings by agencies like Standard & Poor's reflect the fact that the greater a company's debt, the greater its financial risk. Standard & Poor's rates companies from AAA (best) to CCC (worst) based on various factors, including a company's debt to equity ratio, as shown in the table below.

Rating	AAA	AA	A	BBB	BB	B	CCC
Debt/Equity Ratio*	4.5	34.1	42.9	47.9	59.8	76.0	75.7

These ratings affect not only how much a company can borrow, but also what the interest will cost. The lower its

rating, the more a company must pay in interest, and vice versa.

In the heavily debt-laden auto industry, a change in debt rating can mean millions of dollars. For instance, when S & P lowered **General Motors'** and **Ford Motor Company's** credit ratings to "junk status"—BB—it meant that these companies might have to pay 1 or more percentage points in additional interest, which on a debt of $291 billion for GM and $161 billion for Ford would amount to about $2 billion.[3] Thus, companies must pay close attention to their financial risk as expressed by the debt to equity ratio. **McDonald's** solid credit is reflected in an A rating.

*Averages of companies with similar ratings.

Types of Long-Term Debt

To structure long-term financing to the best advantage of their companies, managers must know the characteristics of the various types of long-term debt. The most common are bonds payable, notes payable, mortgages payable, long-term leases, pension liabilities, other postretirement benefits, and deferred income taxes.

Bonds Payable

Long-term bonds are the most common type of long-term debt. They can have many different characteristics, including the amount of interest, whether the company can elect to repay them before their maturity date, and whether they can be converted to common stock. We cover bonds in detail in later sections of this chapter.

Notes Payable

Long-term notes payable, those that come due in more than one year, are also very common. They differ from bonds mainly in the way the contract with the creditor is structured. A long-term note is a promissory note that represents a loan from a bank or other creditor, whereas a bond is a more complex financial instrument that usually involves debt to many creditors. Analysts often do not distinguish between long-term notes and bonds because they have similar effects on the financial statements. Recently, in one of the largest debt offerings in history, **Deutsche Telekom International Finance** raised $14.6 billion by issuing a series of long-term notes denominated in dollars, Euros, pounds, and yen. Some notes were due in 2005, 2010, and 2030.[4]

Mortgages Payable

A **mortgage** is a long-term debt secured by real property. It is usually paid in equal monthly installments. Each monthly payment includes interest on the debt and a reduction in the debt. Table 1 shows the first three monthly payments on a $50,000, 12 percent mortgage. The mortgage was obtained on June 1, and the monthly payments are $800. The entry to record the July 1 payment would be as follows:

A = L + SE		
−800 −300 −500		

July 1	Mortgage Payable		300	
	Mortgage Interest Expense		500	
	Cash			800
	Made monthly mortgage payment			

TABLE 1. Monthly Payment Schedule on a $50,000, 12 Percent Mortgage

	A	B	C	D	E
Payment Date	Unpaid Balance at Beginning of Period	Monthly Payment	Interest for 1 Month at 1% on Unpaid Balance* (1% × A)	Reduction in Debt (B − C)	Unpaid Balance at End of Period (A − D)
June 1					$50,000
July 1	$50,000	$800	$500	$300	49,700
Aug. 1	49,700	800	497	303	49,397
Sept. 1	49,397	800	494	306	49,091

*Rounded to the nearest dollar.

Notice from the entry and from Table 1 that the July 1 payment represents interest expense of $500 ($50,000 × .12 × 1/12) and a reduction in the debt of $300 ($800 − $500). Therefore, the July payment reduces the unpaid balance to $49,700. August's interest expense is slightly less than July's because of the decrease in the debt.

Long-Term Leases

A company can obtain an operating asset in three ways:

1. By borrowing money and buying the asset

2. By renting the asset on a short-term lease

3. By obtaining the asset on a long-term lease

The first two methods do not create accounting problems. When a company uses the first method, it records the asset and liability at the amount paid, and the asset is subject to periodic depreciation.

When a company uses the second method, the lease is short in relation to the useful life of the asset, and the risks of ownership remain with the lessor. This type of agreement is called an **operating lease**. Payments on operating leases are properly treated as rent expense.

The third method is one of the fastest-growing ways of financing plant assets in the United States today. A long-term lease on a plant asset has several advantages. It requires no immediate cash payment, the rental payment is deducted in full for tax purposes, and it costs less than a short-term lease. Acquiring the use of plant assets under long-term leases does create several accounting challenges, however.

Long-term leases may be carefully structured, as they are by **McDonald's**, so that they can be accounted for as operating leases. Accounting standards require, however, that a long-term lease be treated as a **capital lease** when it meets the following conditions:

> **Study Note**
>
> Under a capital lease, the lessee should record depreciation, using any allowable method.

- It cannot be canceled.

- Its duration is about the same as the useful life of the asset.

- It stipulates that the lessee has the option to buy the asset at a nominal price at the end of the lease.

> **Study Note**
>
> A capital lease is in substance an installment purchase, and the leased asset and related liability must be recognized at their present value.

A capital lease is thus more like a purchase or sale on installment than a rental. The lessee in a capital lease should record an asset, depreciation on the asset, and a long-term liability equal to the present value of the total lease payments during the lease term.[5] Much like a mortgage payment, each lease payment consists partly of interest expense and partly of repayment of debt.

Suppose, for example, that Glenellen Manufacturing Company enters into a long-term lease for a machine. The lease terms call for an annual payment of $4,000 for six years, which approximates the useful life of the machine. At the end of the lease period, the title to the machine passes to Glenellen. This lease is clearly a capital lease and should be recorded as an asset and a liability.

Present value techniques can be used to place a value on the asset and on the corresponding liability in a capital lease. Suppose Glenellen's interest cost on the unpaid part of its obligation is 16 percent. Using the factor for 16 percent and six periods in Table 4 in the appendix on future value and present values tables, we can compute the present value of the lease payments as follows:

$$\text{Periodic Payment} \times \text{Factor} = \text{Present Value}$$
$$\$4,000 \times 3.685 = \$14,740$$

The entry to record the lease is as follows:

A = L + SE
+ 14,740 + 14,740

Capital Lease Equipment	14,740	
Capital Lease Obligations		14,740
To record capital lease on machinery		

Capital Lease Equipment is classified as a long-term asset. Capital Lease Obligations is classified as a long-term liability.

Each year, Glenellen must record depreciation on the leased asset. Using straight-line depreciation, a six-year life, and no residual value, the following entry would record the depreciation:

A = L + SE
−2,457   −2,457

Depreciation Expense, Capital Lease Equipment	2,457	
Accumulated Depreciation, Capital Lease Equipment		2,457
To record depreciation expense on capital lease		

The interest expense for each year is computed by multiplying the interest rate (16 percent) by the amount of the remaining lease obligation. Table 2 shows these calculations. Using the data in the table, the first lease payment would be recorded as follows:

A = L + SE
−4,000 −1,642 −2,358

Interest Expense (Column B)	2,358	
Capital Lease Obligations (Column C)	1,642	
Cash (Column A)		4,000
Made payment on capital lease		

This example suggests why companies are motivated to engage in off-balance-sheet financing for leases. By structuring long-term leases so that they can be accounted for as operating leases, companies avoid recording them on the balance sheet as long-term assets and liabilities. This practice, which, as

TABLE 2.   Payment Schedule on a 16 Percent Capital Lease

Year	A Lease Payment	B Interest (16%) on Unpaid Obligation* (D × 16%)	C Reduction of Lease Obligation (A − B)	D Balance of Lease Obligation (D − C)
Beginning				$14,740
1	$ 4,000	$2,358	$ 1,642	13,098
2	4,000	2,096	1,904	11,194
3	4,000	1,791	2,209	8,985
4	4,000	1,438	2,562	6,423
5	4,000	1,028	2,972	3,451
6	4,000	549†	3,451	—
	$24,000	$9,260	$14,740	

*Rounded to the nearest dollar.
†The last year's interest equals $549 ($4,000 − $3,451); it does not exactly equal $552 ($3,451 × $\frac{16}{100}$ × 1) because of the cumulative effect of rounding.

we have noted, is legal and which **McDonald's** uses with skill, not only improves the debt to equity ratio by showing less debt on the balance sheet; it also improves the return on assets by reducing the total assets.

Pension Liabilities

Most employees of medium-sized and large companies are covered by a **pension plan**, a contract that requires a company to pay benefits to its employees after they retire. Some companies pay the full cost of the pension plan, but in many companies, employees share the cost by contributing part of their salaries or wages. The contributions from employer and employees are usually paid into a **pension fund**, which is invested on behalf of the employees and from which benefits are paid to retirees. Pension benefits typically consist of monthly payments to retired employees and other payments upon disability or death.

Employers whose pension plans do not have sufficient assets to cover the present value of their pension obligations must record the amount of the shortfall as a liability on their balance sheets. If a pension plan has sufficient assets to cover its obligations, no balance sheet reporting is required or permitted.

There are two kinds of pension plans:

- *Defined contribution plan.* Under a defined contribution plan, the employer makes a fixed annual contribution, usually a percentage of the employee's gross pay; the amount of the contribution is specified in an agreement between the company and the employees. Retirement payments vary depending on how much the employee's retirement account earns. Employees usually control their own investment accounts, can make additional contributions of their own, and can transfer the funds if they leave the company. Examples of defined contribution plans include 401(k) plans, profit-sharing plans, and employee stock ownership plans (ESOPs).

- *Defined benefit plan.* Under a defined benefit plan, the employer contributes an amount annually required to fund estimated future pension liability arising from employment in the current year. The exact amount of the liability will not be known until the retirement and death of the current employees. Although the amount of future benefits is fixed, the annual contributions vary depending on assumptions about how much the pension fund will earn.

Annual pension expense under a defined contribution plan is simple and predictable. Pension expense equals the fixed amount of the annual contribution. In contrast, annual expense under a defined benefit plan is one of the most complex topics in accounting. The intricacies are reserved for advanced courses, but in concept, the procedure is simple. Computation of the annual expense takes into account the estimation of many factors, such as the average remaining service life of active employees, the long-run return on pension plan assets, and future salary increases.

Because pension expense under a defined benefit plan is not predictable and can vary from year to year, many companies are adopting the more predictable defined contribution plans. For example, in its 2004 annual report, **McDonald's** states that its plan "includes profit sharing, 401(k) and . . . ESOP features."

Other Postretirement Benefits

Many companies provide retired employees not only with pensions, but also with health care and other benefits. In the past, these **other postretirement benefits** were accounted for on a cash basis—that is, they were expensed when the benefits were paid, after an employee had retired. More recent accounting standards hold that employees earn these benefits during their employment and that, in accordance with the

> **Study Note**
>
> Companies prefer defined contribution plans because the employees assume the risk that their pension assets will earn a sufficient return to meet their retirement needs.

> **Study Note**
>
> Accounting for a defined benefit plan is far more complex than accounting for a defined contribution plan. Fortunately, accountants can rely on the calculations of professional actuaries, whose expertise includes the mathematics of pension plans.

Postretirement benefits, such as health care, are a type of long-term debt for the company that provides them. Recent accounting standards hold that employees earn these benefits during their employment and that the benefits should therefore be estimated and accrued while the employee is working.

Study Note

Other postretirement benefits should be expensed as the employee earns them, not when they are paid after the employee retires. This practice conforms to the matching rule.

matching rule, they should be estimated and accrued during the time the employee is working.[6]

The estimates must take into account assumptions about retirement age, mortality, and, most significantly, future trends in health care benefits. Like pension benefits, such future benefits should be discounted to the current period. A field test conducted by the Financial Executives Research Foundation determined that the change to accrual accounting increased postretirement benefits by two to seven times the amount recognized on a cash basis. **General Motors**, the nation's largest private purchaser of health care, recently reported that its future health care liabilities for retirees exceeded $60 billion.[7]

Deferred Income Taxes Among the long-term liabilities on the balance sheets of many companies, including **McDonald's**, is an account called **Deferred Income Taxes**. Deferred income taxes are the result of using different accounting methods to calculate income taxes on the income statement and income tax liability on the income tax return. For instance, companies often use straight-line depreciation for financial reporting and an accelerated method to calculate income tax liability. Because straight-line depreciation is less than accelerated depreciation in the early years of an asset's life, the presumption is that the income taxes will eventually have to be paid. Thus, the difference is listed as a long-term liability, deferred income taxes. Because companies try to manage their affairs to minimize income taxes paid, deferred income taxes can become quite large. In McDonald's case, as shown in the company's Financial Highlights, they amounted to more than $1 billion in 2003. We cover deferred income taxes in greater detail in a later chapter.

S T O P • R E V I E W • A P P L Y

1-1. What are the advantages and disadvantages of issuing long-term debt?

1-2. Why is interest coverage important in evaluating long-term debt?

1-3. What are the two components of a uniform monthly mortgage payment?

1-4. What is a capital lease? Why should an accountant record both an asset and a liability in connection with this type of lease?

1-5. What is a pension plan? What is a pension fund?

1-6. What is the difference between a defined contribution plan and a defined benefit plan?

1-7. What are other postretirement benefits, and how is the matching rule applied to them?

Suggested answers to all Stop, Review, and Apply questions follow the appendixes.

Identification of Long-Term Debt   Each type of long-term liability below is closely related to one of the statements in the list that follows. Write the number of the liability next to the statement to which it applies.

1. Bonds payable	**5.** Pension liabilities
2. Long-term notes payable	**6.** Other postretirement benefits
3. Mortgage payable	**7.** Deferred income taxes
4. Long-term lease	

_____ a. Cost of health care after employees' retirement

_____ b. The most common type of long-term debt

_____ c. The result of differences between accounting income and taxable income

_____ d. Debt that is secured by real estate

_____ e. Promissory note that is due in more than one year

_____ f. May be based on a percentage of employees' wages or on future benefits

_____ g. Can be similar in form to an installment purchase

SOLUTION

a. 6	e. 2
b. 1	f. 5
c. 7	g. 4
d. 3	

The Nature of Bonds

LO2   Describe the features of a bond issue and the major characteristics of bonds.

> **Study Note**
>
> An investor who purchases debt securities, such as bonds or notes, is a creditor of the organization, not an owner.

A **bond** is a security, usually long term, representing money that a corporation borrows from the investing public. (The federal, state, and local governments also issue bonds to raise money, as do foreign countries.) A bond entails a promise to repay the amount borrowed, called the *principal*, on a specified date and to pay interest at a specified rate at specified times—usually semiannually. In contrast to stockholders, who are the owners of a corporation, bondholders are a corporation's creditors.

When a public corporation decides to issue bonds, it must submit the appropriate legal documents to the Securities and Exchange Commission for

permission to borrow the funds. The SEC reviews the corporation's financial health and the specific terms of the **bond indenture**, which is a contract that defines the rights, privileges, and limitations of the bondholders. The bond indenture generally describes such things as the maturity date of the bonds, interest payment dates, and the interest rate. It may also cover repayment plans and restrictions. Once the bond issue is approved, the corporation has a limited time in which to issue the authorized bonds. As evidence of its debt to the bondholders, the corporation provides each of them with a **bond certificate**.

Bond Issue: Prices and Interest Rates

Study Note

When bonds with an interest rate different from the market rate are issued, they sell at a discount or premium. The discount or premium acts as an equalizing factor.

A **bond issue** is the total value of bonds issued at one time. For example, a $1,000,000 bond issue could consist of a thousand $1,000 bonds. The prices of bonds are stated in terms of a percentage of the face value, or principal, of the bonds. A bond issue quoted at 103 1/2 means that a $1,000 bond costs $1,035 ($1,000 × 1.035). When a bond sells at exactly 100, it is said to sell at face (or par) value. When it sells below 100, it is said to sell at a discount; above 100, at a premium. For instance, a $1,000 bond quoted at 87.62 would be selling at a discount and would cost the buyer $876.20.

Study Note

A bond sells at face value when the face interest rate of the bond is identical to the market interest rate for similar bonds on the date of issue.

Face Interest Rate and Market Interest Rate   Two interest rates relevant to bond prices are the face interest rate and market interest rate:

- The **face interest rate** is the fixed rate of interest paid to bondholders based on the face value of the bonds. The rate and amount are fixed over the life of the bond. To allow time to file with the SEC, publicize the bond issue, and print the bond certificates, a company must decide in advance what the face interest rate will be. Most companies try to set the face interest rate as close as possible to the market interest rate.

- The **market interest rate** is the rate of interest paid in the market on bonds of similar risk.* It is also called the *effective interest rate*. The market interest

---

*At the time this chapter was written, the market interest rates on corporate bonds were volatile. Therefore, we use a variety of interest rates in our examples.

rate fluctuates daily. Because a company has no control over it, the market interest rate often differs from the face interest rate on the issue date.

Discounts and Premiums If the market interest rate fluctuates from the face interest rate before the issue date, the issue price of bonds will not equal their face value. This fluctuation in market interest rate causes the bonds to sell at either a discount or premium:

▶ A **discount** equals the excess of the face value over the issue price. The issue price will be less than the face value when the market interest rate is higher than the face interest rate.

▶ A **premium** equals the excess of the issue price over the face value. The issue price will be more than the face value when the market interest rate is lower than the face interest rate.

Discounts or premiums are contra-accounts that are subtracted from or added to bonds payable on the balance sheet.

Characteristics of Bonds

A bond indenture can be written to fit an organization's financing needs. As a result, the bonds issued in today's financial markets have many different features. We describe several of the more important features in the following paragraphs.

Unsecured and Secured Bonds Bonds can be either unsecured or secured. **Unsecured bonds** (also called *debenture bonds*) are issued on the basis of a corporation's general credit. **Secured bonds** carry a pledge of certain corporate assets as a guarantee of repayment. A pledged asset may be a specific asset, such as a truck, or a general category of asset, such as property, plant, or equipment.

Term and Serial Bonds When all the bonds of an issue mature at the same time, they are called **term bonds**. For instance, a company may decide to issue $1,000,000 worth of bonds, all due 20 years from the date of issue.

When the bonds of an issue mature on different dates, they are called **serial bonds**. For example, suppose a $1,000,000 bond issue calls for paying $200,000 of the principal every five years. This arrangement means that after the first $200,000 payment is made, $800,000 of the bonds would remain outstanding for the next five years, $600,000 for the next five years, and so on. A company may issue serial bonds to ease the task of retiring its debt—that is, paying off what it owes on the bonds.

Callable and Convertible Bonds When bonds are callable and convertible, a company may be able to retire them before their maturity dates. When a company does retire a bond issue before its maturity date, it is called **early extinguishment of debt**. Doing so can be to a company's advantage.

Callable bonds give the issuer the right to buy back and retire the bonds before maturity at a specified **call price**, which is usually above face value. Callable bonds give a company flexibility in financing its operations. For example, if bond interest rates drop, the company can call the bonds and reissue debt at a lower interest rate. A company might also call its bonds if it has earned enough to pay off the debt, if the reason for having the debt no longer exists, or if it wants to restructure its debt to equity ratio. The bond indenture states the time period and the prices at which the bonds can be redeemed.

Study Note

Do not confuse the terms *indenture* and *debenture*. They sound alike, but an indenture is a bond contract, whereas a debenture is an unsecured bond. A debenture bond of a stable company actually might be a less risky investment than a secured bond of an unstable company.

Study Note

An advantage of issuing serial bonds is that the organization retires the bonds over a period of years, rather than all at once.

Convertible bonds allow the bondholder to exchange a bond for a specified number of shares of common stock. The face value of a convertible bond when issued is greater than the market value of the shares to which it can be converted. However, if the market price of the common stock rises above a certain level, the value of the bond rises in relation to the value of the common stock. Even if the stock price does not rise, the investor still holds the bond and receives both the periodic interest payments and the face value at the maturity date.

One advantage of issuing convertible bonds is that the interest rate is usually lower because investors are willing to give up some current interest in the hope that the value of the stock will increase and the value of the bonds will therefore also increase. In addition, if the bonds are both callable and convertible and the market value of the stock rises to a level at which the bond is worth more than face value, management can avoid repaying the bonds by calling them for redemption, thereby forcing the bondholders to convert their bonds into common stock. The bondholders will agree to convert because no gain or loss results from the transaction.

Registered and Coupon Bonds
Registered bonds are issued in the names of the bondholders. The issuing organization keeps a record of the bondholders' names and addresses and pays them interest by check on the interest payment date. Most bonds today are registered.

Coupon bonds are not registered with the organization. Instead, they bear coupons stating the amount of interest due and the payment date. The bondholder removes the coupons from the bonds on the interest payment dates and presents them at a bank for collection.

STOP • REVIEW • APPLY

2-1. What are a bond issue, a bond certificate, and a bond indenture? What information is in a bond indenture?

2-2. Napier Corporation sold a $500,000 bond issue of 5 percent, $1,000 bonds. What would the proceeds from the sale be if the bonds were issued at 95, at 100, and at 102?

2-3. If you were about to buy bonds on which the face interest rate was less than the market interest rate, would you expect to pay more or less than par value for the bonds?

2-4. What are the essential differences between (a) a discount and premium, (b) secured and unsecured (debenture) bonds, (c) term and serial bonds, (d) callable and convertible bonds, and (e) registered and coupon bonds?

Accounting for the Issuance of Bonds

LO3 Record bonds issued at face value and at a discount or premium.

When the board of directors of a public corporation decides to issue bonds, the company must submit the appropriate legal documents to the Securities and Exchange Commission for authorization to borrow the funds. It is not necessary to make a journal entry to record the authorization of a bond issue. However, most companies disclose the authorization in the notes to their financial statements. The note lists the number and value of bonds authorized, the interest rate, the interest payment dates, and the life of the bonds. In sections that follow, we show how to record bonds issued at face value, at a discount, and at a premium.

Bonds Issued at Face Value

Suppose Katakis Corporation issues $100,000 of 9 percent, five-year bonds on January 1, 2006, and sells them on the same date for their face value. The bond indenture states that interest is to be paid on January 1 and July 1 of each year. The entry to record the bond issue is as follows:

A	=	L	+ SE
+100,000		+100,000	

2006				
Jan. 1	Cash		100,000	
	Bonds Payable			100,000
	Sold $100,000 of 9%,			
	5-year bonds at face value			

Study Note

When calculating semiannual interest, do not use the annual rate (9 percent in this case). Rather, use half the annual rate.

Once a corporation issues bonds, it must pay interest to the bondholders over the life of the bonds, usually semiannually, and the principal of the bonds at maturity. In this example, interest is paid on January 1 and July 1 of each year. Thus, Katakis would owe the bondholders $4,500 interest on July 1, 2006:

$$\text{Interest} = \text{Principal} \times \text{Rate} \times \text{Time}$$
$$= \$100,000 \times \tfrac{9}{100} \times 6/12 \text{ year}$$
$$= \$4,500$$

Katakis would record the interest paid to the bondholders on each semiannual interest payment date (January 1 or July 1) as follows:

A*	= L +	SE
−4,500		−4,500

*Assumes cash paid.

Bond Interest Expense		4,500	
Cash (or Interest Payable)			4,500
Paid (or accrued) semiannual interest			
to bondholders of 9%, 5-year bonds			

In 1993, to take advantage of historically low interest rates on long-term debt, The Walt Disney Company issued $150 million of 100-year bonds at a yield of only 7.5 percent. At the time, some analysts wondered if even Mickey Mouse could survive 100 years. However, Mickey, who first appeared in 1928 in the animated short film *Steamboat Willie*, goes on. In 2003, he celebrated his 75th birthday.

Bonds Issued at a Discount

Suppose Katakis Corporation issues $100,000 of 9 percent, five-year bonds at 96.149 on January 1, 2006, when the market interest rate is 10 percent. In this case, the bonds are being issued at a discount because the market interest rate exceeds the face interest rate. The following entry records the issuance of the bonds at a discount:

A	=	L	+ SE
+96,149		−3,851	
		+100,000	

2006				
Jan. 1	Cash		96,149	
	Unamortized Bond Discount		3,851	
	Bonds Payable			100,000
	Sold $100,000 of 9%, 5-year bonds at 96.149			
	Face amount of bonds	$100,000		
	Less purchase price of bonds ($100,000 × .96149)	96,149		
	Unamortized bond discount	$ 3,851		

FOCUS ON BUSINESS PRACTICE

100-Year Bonds Are Not for Everyone.

In 1993, interest rates on long-term debt were at historically low levels, which induced some companies to attempt to lock in those low costs for long periods. One of the most aggressive companies in that regard was **The Walt Disney Company**, which issued $150 million of 100-year bonds at a yield of only 7.5 percent. It was the first time since 1954 that 100-year bonds had been issued. Among the others that followed Walt Disney's lead by issuing 100-year bonds were the **Coca-Cola Company**, **Columbia HCA Healthcare**, **Bell South**, **IBM**, and even the People's Republic of China. Some analysts wondered if even Mickey Mouse could survive 100 years. Investors who purchase such bonds take a financial risk because if interest rates rise, which is always likely, the market value of the bonds will decrease.[10]

> **Study Note**
>
> The carrying amount is always the face value of the bonds plus the unamortized discount or less the unamortized premium. The carrying amount always approaches the face value over the life of the bond.

In this entry, Cash is debited for the amount received ($96,149), Bonds Payable is credited for the face amount ($100,000) of the bond liability, and the difference ($3,851) is debited to Unamortized Bond Discount. If a balance sheet is prepared right after the bonds are issued at a discount, the liability for bonds payable is reported as follows:

Long-term liabilities

9% bonds payable, due 1/1/2009	$100,000	
Less unamortized bond discount	3,851	$96,149

Unamortized Bond Discount is a contra-liability account. Its balance is deducted from the face amount of the bonds to arrive at the carrying value, or present value, of the bonds. The bond discount is described as unamortized because it will be amortized (written off) over the life of the bonds.

Bonds Issued at a Premium

When bonds have a face interest rate above the market rate for similar investments, they are issued at a price above the face value, or at a premium. For example, suppose Katakis Corporation issues $100,000 of 9 percent, five-year bonds for $104,100 on January 1, 2006, when the market interest rate is 8 percent. This means that investors will purchase the bonds at 104.1 percent of their face value. The issuance would be recorded as follows:

A	=	L	+ SE
+104,100		+4,100	
		+100,000	

2006			
Jan. 1	Cash	104,100	
	Unamortized Bond Premium		4,100
	Bonds Payable		100,000
	Sold $100,000 of 9%, 5-year bonds at 104.1 ($100,000 × 1.041)		

Right after this entry is made, bonds payable would be presented on the balance sheet as follows:

Long-term liabilities

9% bonds payable, due 1/1/2011	$100,000	
Unamortized bond premium	4,100	$104,100

The carrying value of the bonds payable is $104,100, which equals the face value of the bonds plus the unamortized bond premium. The cash received from the bond issue is also $104,100. This means that the purchasers were willing to pay a premium of $4,100 to buy these bonds because their face interest rate was higher than the market interest rate.

Bond Issue Costs

The costs of issuing bonds can amount to as much as 5 percent of a bond issue. These costs often include the fees of underwriters, whom corporations hire to take care of the details of marketing a bond issue. Because the issue costs benefit the whole life of a bond issue, it makes sense to spread them over that period. It is generally accepted practice to establish a separate account for these costs and to amortize them over the life of the bonds.

Because issue costs decrease the amount of money a company receives from a bond issue, they have the effect of raising the discount or lowering the premium on the issue. Thus, bond issue costs can be spread over the life of the bonds through the amortization of a discount or premium. This method simplifies recordkeeping. In the rest of our discussion, we assume that all bond issue costs increase the discounts or decrease the premiums on bond issues.

STOP • REVIEW • APPLY

3-1. When bonds are issued at a discount, will the market interest rate be more or less than the face interest rate?

3-2. When bonds are issued at a premium, how is the bond liability shown on the balance sheet?

3-3. Why do bond issue costs increase the discount on a bond issue?

Using Present Value to Value a Bond

LO4 Use present values to determine the value of bonds.

A bond's value is based on the present value of two components of cash flow: a series of fixed interest payments, and a single payment at maturity. The amount of interest a bond pays is fixed over its life. However, the market interest rate varies from day to day. Thus, the amount investors are willing to pay for a bond varies as well.

Case 1: Market Rate Above Face Rate

Suppose a bond has a face value of $10,000 and pays fixed interest of $450 every six months (a 9 percent annual rate). The bond is due in five years. If the market interest rate today is 12 percent, what is the present value of the bond?

To answer this question, we use Table 4 in the appendix on future value and present value tables to calculate the present value of the periodic interest payments of $450, and we use Table 3 in the same appendix to calculate the present value of the single payment of $10,000 at maturity. Because interest payments are made every six months, the compounding period is half a year. Thus, we have to convert the annual rate to a semiannual rate of 6 percent (12 percent divided by two six-month periods per year) and use ten periods (five years multiplied by two six-month periods per year). With this information, we can compute the present value of the bond as follows:

Present value of 10 periodic payments at 6%:	
$450 × 7.360 (from Table 4 in the appendix)	$3,312.00
Present value of a single payment at the end of	
10 periods at 6%: $10,000 × .558 (from	
Table 3 in the appendix):	5,580.00
Present value of $10,000 bond	$8,892.00

The market interest rate has increased so much since the bond was issued—from 9 percent to 12 percent—that the value of the bond today is only $8,892.00. That amount is all investors would be willing to pay at this time for a bond that provides income of $450 every six months and a return of the $10,000 principal in five years.

Case 2: Market Rate Below Face Rate

As Figure 2 shows, if the market interest rate on the bond described above falls below the face interest rate, say to 8 percent (4 percent semiannually), the present value of the bond will be greater than the face value of $10,000:

Present value of 10 periodic payments at 4%:	
$450 × 8.111 (from Table 4 in the appendix)	$ 3,649.95
Present value of a single payment at the end of	
10 periods at 4%: $10,000 × .676 (from	
Table 3 in the appendix)	6,760.00
Present value of $10,000 bond	$10,409.95

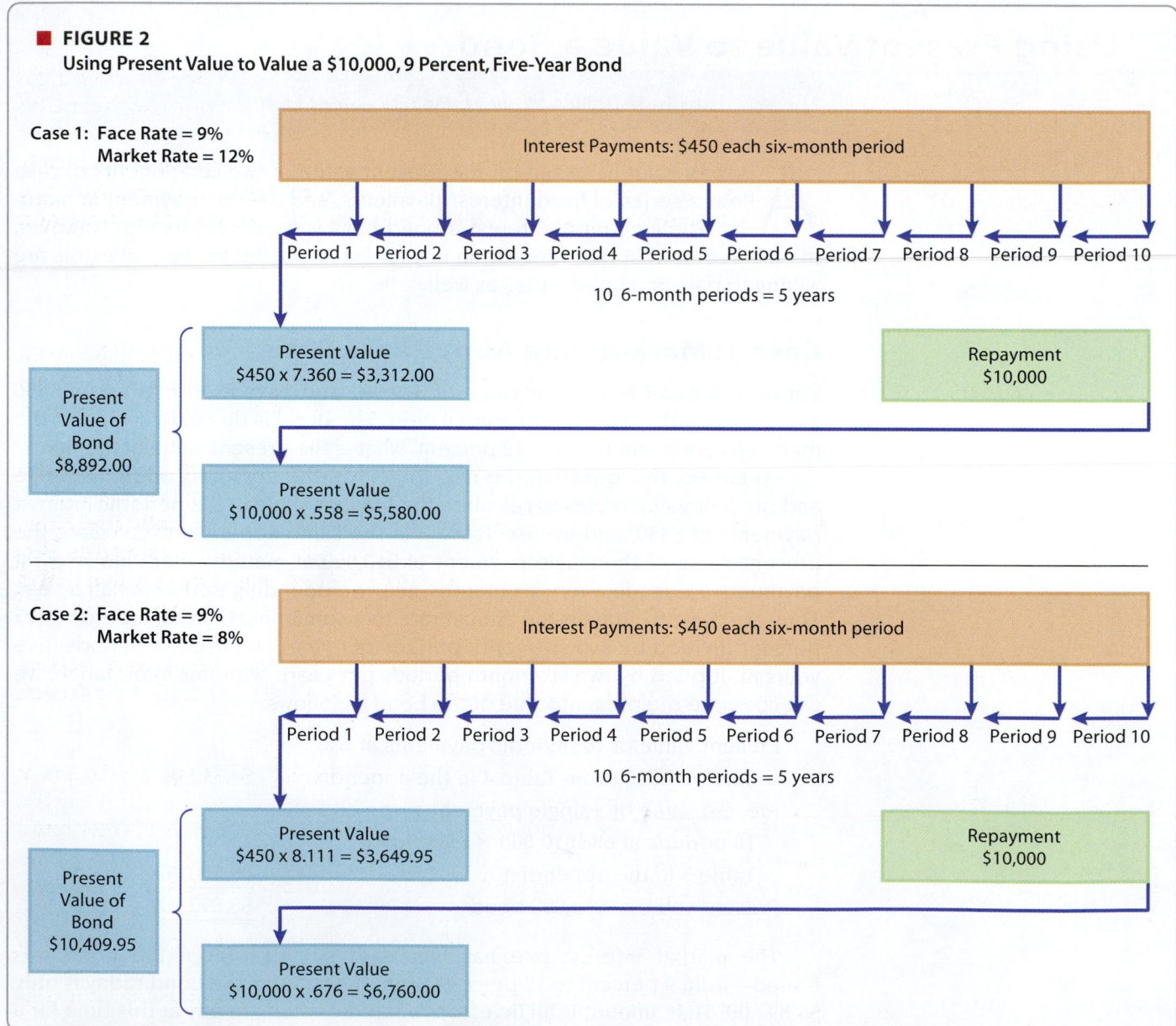

■ **FIGURE 2**
Using Present Value to Value a $10,000, 9 Percent, Five-Year Bond

Case 1: Face Rate = 9%
Market Rate = 12%

Interest Payments: $450 each six-month period

Period 1 Period 2 Period 3 Period 4 Period 5 Period 6 Period 7 Period 8 Period 9 Period 10

10 6-month periods = 5 years

Present Value
$450 x 7.360 = $3,312.00

Repayment
$10,000

Present Value of Bond $8,892.00

Present Value
$10,000 x .558 = $5,580.00

Case 2: Face Rate = 9%
Market Rate = 8%

Interest Payments: $450 each six-month period

Period 1 Period 2 Period 3 Period 4 Period 5 Period 6 Period 7 Period 8 Period 9 Period 10

10 6-month periods = 5 years

Present Value
$450 x 8.111 = $3,649.95

Repayment
$10,000

Present Value of Bond $10,409.95

Present Value
$10,000 x .676 = $6,760.00

Amortization of Bond Discounts and Premiums

LO5 Amortize bond discounts and bond premiums using the straight-line and effective interest methods.

> **Study Note**
>
> Whether a bond is sold at a discount or a premium, its carrying value will equal its face value on the maturity date.

A bond discount or premium represents the amount by which the total interest cost is higher or lower than the total interest payments. To record interest expense properly and ensure that the carrying value of bonds payable at maturity equals face value, it is necessary to systematically reduce the bond discount or premium—that is, to amortize them—over the life of the bonds. This is accomplished by using either the straight-line method or the effective interest method.

Amortizing a Bond Discount

In one of our earlier examples, Katakis Corporation issued $100,000 of five-year bonds at a time when the market interest rate of 10 percent exceeded the face interest rate of 9 percent. The bonds sold for $96,149, resulting in an unamortized bond discount of $3,851.

Because a bond discount affects interest expense in each year of a bond issue, the bond discount should be amortized over the life of the bond issue. In this way, the unamortized bond discount will decrease gradually over time, and the carrying value of the bond issue (face value less unamortized discount) will gradually increase. By the maturity date, the carrying value of the bond issue will equal its face value, and the unamortized bond discount will be zero.

In the following sections, we calculate Katakis Corporation's total interest cost and amortize its bond discount using the straight-line and the effective interest methods.

> **Study Note**
>
> A bond discount is a component of interest cost because it represents the amount in excess of the issue price that a corporation must pay on the maturity date.

Calculating Total Interest Cost When a corporation issues bonds at a discount, the market (or effective) interest rate that it pays is greater than the face interest rate on the bonds. The reason is that the interest cost is the stated interest payments *plus* the amount of the bond discount. That is, although the company does not receive the full face value of the bonds on issue, it still must pay back the full face value at maturity. The difference between the issue price and the face value must be added to the total interest payments to arrive at the actual interest expense.

The full cost to Katakis Corporation of issuing its bonds at a discount is as follows:

Cash to be paid to bondholders

Face value at maturity	$100,000
Interest payments ($100,000 × .09 × 5 years)	45,000
Total cash paid to bondholders	$145,000
Less cash received from bondholders	96,149
Total interest cost	$ 48,851

Or, alternatively:

Interest payments ($100,000 × .09 × 5 years)	$ 45,000
Bond discount	3,851
Total interest cost	$ 48,851

The total interest cost of $48,851 is made up of $45,000 in interest payments and the $3,851 bond discount. Thus, the bond discount increases the interest paid on the bonds from the face interest rate to the market interest rate. The market (or effective) interest rate is the real interest cost of the bond over its life.

To have each year's interest expense reflect the market interest rate, the discount must be allocated over the remaining life of the bonds as an increase in the interest expense each period. Thus, interest expense for each period will exceed the actual payment of interest by the amount of the bond discount amortized over the period. This process of allocation is called *amortization of the bond discount*.

Some bonds do not require periodic interest payments. These bonds, called **zero coupon bonds**, are simply a promise to pay a fixed amount at the maturity date. They are issued at a large discount because the only interest that the buyer earns or the issuer pays is the discount. For example, a five-year, $100,000 zero coupon bond issued when the market rate is 14 percent, compounded semiannually, would sell for only $50,800. That amount is the present value of a single payment of $100,000 at the end of five years. The discount of $49,200 ($100,000 − $50,800) is the total interest cost, which is amortized over the life of the bond.

> **Study Note**
>
> The discount on a zero coupon bond represents the interest that will be paid (in its entirety) on the maturity date.

Straight-Line Method

Straight-Line Method The **straight-line method** equalizes amortization of a bond discount for each interest period. Using our example of Katakis Corporation, the interest payment dates of the bond issue are January 1 and July 1 of each year, and the bonds mature in five years. With the straight-line method, the amount of the bond discount amortized and the interest expense for each semiannual period are calculated in four steps:

1. Total Interest Payments = Interest Payments per Year × Life of Bonds

$$= 2 \times 5 = 10$$

2. Amortization of Bond Discount per Interest Period = $\dfrac{\text{Bond Discount}}{\text{Total Interest Payments}}$

$$= \frac{\$3,851}{10}$$

$$= \$385*$$

3. Cash Interest Payment = Face Value × Face Interest Rate × Time

$$= \$100,000 \times .09 \times 6/12 = \$4,500$$

---

*Rounded.

4. Interest Expense per Interest Period = Interest Payment + Amortization of Bond Discount

$$= \$4,500 + \$385 = \$4,885$$

On July 1, 2006, the first semiannual interest date, the entry would be as follows:

A*	=	L +	SE
−4,500		+385	−4,885

*Assumes cash paid.

2006			
July 1	Bond Interest Expense	4,885	
	Unamortized Bond Discount		385
	Cash (or Interest Payable)		4,500
	Paid (or accrued) semiannual interest to bondholders and amortized the discount on 9%, 5-year bonds		

Notice that the bond interest expense is $4,885, but the amount paid to the bondholders is the $4,500 face interest payment. The difference of $385 is the credit to Unamortized Bond Discount. This lowers the debit balance of Unamortized Bond Discount and raises the carrying value of the bonds payable by $385 each interest period. If no changes occur in the bond issue, this entry will be made every six months for the life of the bonds. When the bond issue matures, the Unamortized Bond Discount account will have a zero balance, and the carrying value of the bonds will be $100,000—exactly equal to the amount due the bondholders.

Although the straight-line method has long been used, it has a certain weakness. When it is used to amortize a discount, the carrying value goes up each period, but the bond interest expense stays the same; thus, the rate of interest falls over time. Conversely, when this method is used to amortize a premium, the rate of interest rises over time. The Accounting Principles Board therefore holds that the straight-line method should be used only when it does not lead to a material difference from the effective interest method.[11] A material difference is one that affects the evaluation of a company.

Effective Interest Method   When the **effective interest method** is used to compute the interest and amortization of a bond discount, a constant interest rate is applied to the carrying value of the bonds at the beginning of each interest period. This constant rate is the market rate (i.e., the effective rate) at the time the bonds were issued. The amount amortized each period is the difference between the interest computed by using the market rate and the actual interest paid to bondholders.

As an example, we use the same facts we used earlier—a $100,000 bond issue at 9 percent, with a five-year maturity and interest to be paid twice a year. The market rate at the time the bonds were issued was 10 percent, so the bonds sold for $96,149, a discount of $3,851. Table 3 shows the interest and amortization of the bond discount.

The amounts in the table for period 1 were computed as follows:

Column A: The carrying value of the bonds is their face value less the unamortized bond discount ($100,000 − $3,851 = $96,149).

Column B: The interest expense to be recorded is the effective interest. It is found by multiplying the carrying value of the bonds by the market interest rate for one-half year ($96,149 × .10 × 6/12 = $4,807).

TABLE 3. Interest and Amortization of a Bond Discount: Effective Interest Method

	A	B	C	D	E	F
Semiannual Interest Period	Carrying Value at Beginning of Period	Semiannual Interest Expense at 10% to Be Recorded* (5% × A)	Semiannual Interest Payment to Bondholders (4½% × $100,000)	Amortization of Bond Discount (B − C)	Unamortized Bond Discount at End of Period (E − D)	Carrying Value at End of Period (A + D)
0					$3,851	$ 96,149
1	$96,149	$4,807	$4,500	$307	3,544	96,456
2	96,456	4,823	4,500	323	3,221	96,779
3	96,779	4,839	4,500	339	2,882	97,118
4	97,118	4,856	4,500	356	2,526	97,474
5	97,474	4,874	4,500	374	2,152	97,848
6	97,848	4,892	4,500	392	1,760	98,240
7	98,240	4,912	4,500	412	1,348	98,652
8	98,652	4,933	4,500	433	915	99,085
9	99,085	4,954	4,500	454	461	99,539
10	99,539	4,961†	4,500	461	—	100,000

*Rounded to the nearest dollar.

†Last period's interest expense equals $4,961 ($4,500 + $461); it does not equal $4,977 ($99,539 × .05) because of the cumulative effect of rounding.

Column C: The interest paid in the period is a constant amount computed by multiplying the face value of the bonds by their face interest rate by the interest time period ($100,000 × .09 × 6/12 = $4,500).

Column D: The discount amortized is the difference between the effective interest expense to be recorded and the interest to be paid on the interest payment date ($4,807 − $4,500 = $307).

Column E: The unamortized bond discount is the balance of the bond discount at the beginning of the period less the current period amortization of the discount ($3,851 − $307 = $3,544). The unamortized discount decreases in each interest payment period because it is amortized as a portion of interest expense.

Column F: The carrying value of the bonds at the end of the period is the carrying value at the beginning of the period plus the amortization during the period ($96,149 + $307 = $96,456). Notice that the sum of the carrying value and the unamortized discount (Column F + Column E) always equals the face value of the bonds ($96,456 + $3,544 = $100,000).

The entry to record the interest expense is exactly like the one when the straight-line method is used. However, the amounts debited and credited to the various accounts are different. Using the effective interest method, the entry for July 1, 2006, would be as follows:

> **Study Note**
>
> The bond interest expense recorded exceeds the amount of interest paid because of the amortization of the bond discount. The matching rule dictates that the discount be amortized over the life of the bond.

A*	=	L	+	SE
−4,500		+307		−4,807

*Assumes cash paid.

```
2006
July 1   Bond Interest Expense                          4,807
             Unamortized Bond Discount                          307
             Cash (or Interest Payable)                       4,500
                 Paid (or accrued) semiannual interest
                 to bondholders and amortized the
                 discount on 9%, 5-year bonds
```

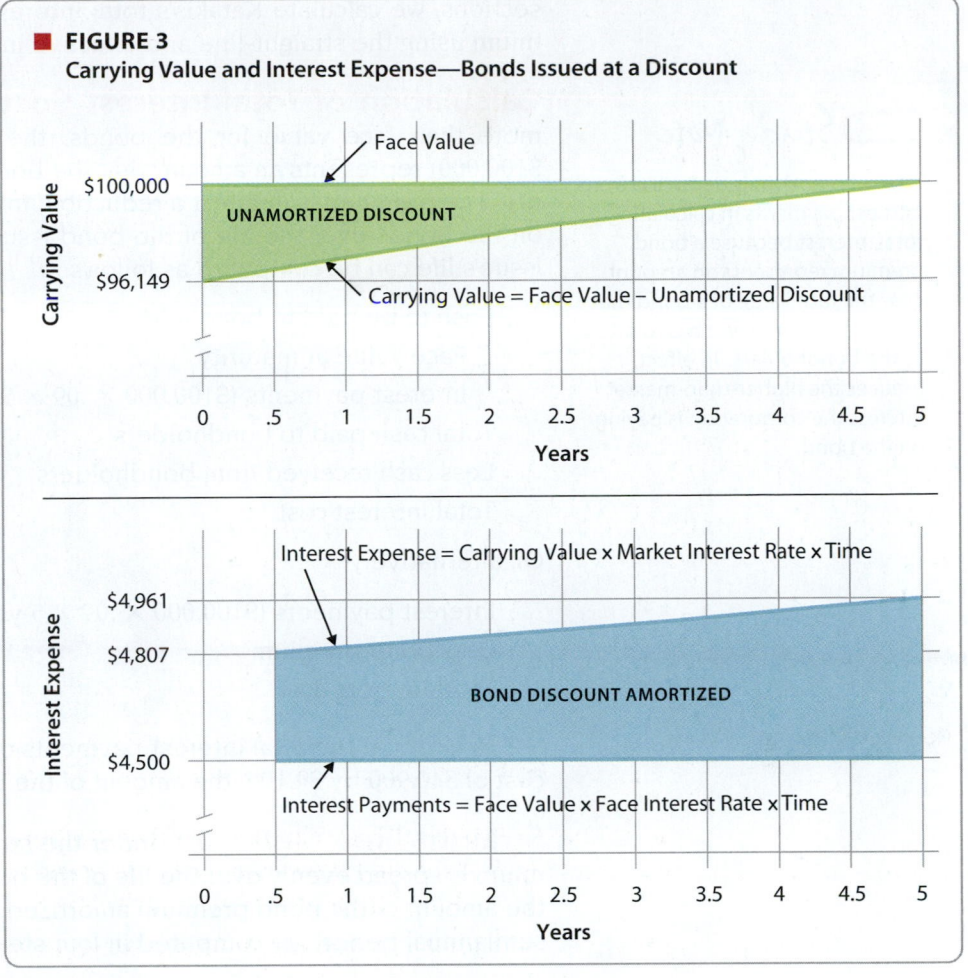

■ **FIGURE 3**
Carrying Value and Interest Expense—Bonds Issued at a Discount

Although an interest and amortization table is useful because it can be pre-pared in advance for all periods, it is not necessary to have one to determine the amortization of a discount for any one interest payment period. It is neces-sary only to multiply the carrying value by the effective interest rate and sub-tract the interest payment from the result. For example, the amount of discount to be amortized in the seventh interest payment period is $412, calculated as follows: ($98,240 × .05) − $4,500.

Figure 3, which is based on the data in Table 3, shows how the effective interest method affects the amortization of a bond discount. Notice that the carrying value (the issue price) is initially less than the face value, but that it gradually increases toward face value over the life of the bond issue. Notice also that interest expense exceeds interest payments by the amount of the bond discount amortized. Interest expense increases gradually over the life of the bond because it is based on the gradually increasing carrying value (multi-plied by the market interest rate).

Amortizing a Bond Premium

In our earlier example of bonds issued at a premium, Katakis Corporation issued $100,000 of five-year bonds at a time when the market interest rate was 8 percent and the face interest rate was 9 percent. The bonds sold for $104,100, which resulted in an unamortized bond premium of $4,100. Like a discount, a premium must be amortized over the life of the bonds so that it can be matched to its effects on interest expense during that period. In the following

Study Note

The bond interest *increases* each period because the carrying value of the bonds (the principal on which the interest is calculated) increases each period.

sections, we calculate Katakis's total interest cost and amortize its bond premium using the straight-line and effective interest methods.

Calculation of Total Interest Cost

Because the bondholders paid more than face value for the bonds, the premium of $4,100 ($104,100 − $100,000) represents an amount that the bondholders will not receive at maturity. The premium is in effect a reduction, in advance, of the total interest paid on the bonds over the life of the bond issue. The total interest cost over the issue's life can be computed as follows:

Cash to be paid to bondholders	
Face value at maturity	$100,000
Interest payments ($100,000 × .09 × 5 years)	45,000
Total cash paid to bondholders	$145,000
Less cash received from bondholders	104,100
Total interest cost	$ 40,900

Or, alternatively:

Interest payments ($100,000 × .09 × 5 years)	$ 45,000
Less bond premium	4,100
Total interest cost	$ 40,900

Notice that the total interest payments of $45,000 exceed the total interest cost of $40,900 by $4,100, the amount of the bond premium.

Straight-Line Method

Under the straight-line method, the bond premium is spread evenly over the life of the bond issue. As with bond discounts, the amount of the bond premium amortized and the interest expense for each semiannual period are computed in four steps:

1. Total Interest Payments = Interest Payments per Year × Life of Bonds

$$= 2 \times 5 = 10$$

2. Amortization of Bond Premium per Interest Period $= \dfrac{\text{Bond Premium}}{\text{Total Interest Payments}}$

$$= \frac{\$4,100}{10}$$

$$= \$410$$

3. Cash Interest Payment = Face Value × Face Interest Rate × Time

$$= \$100,000 \times .09 \times 6/12 = \$4,500$$

4. Interest Expense per Interest Period = Interest Payment − Amortization of Bond Premium

$$= \$4,500 - \$410 = \$4,090$$

On July 1, 2006, the first semiannual interest date, the entry would be like this:

A*	=	L	+	SE
−4,500		−410		−4,090

*Assumes cash paid.

2006			
July 1	Bond Interest Expense	4,090	
	Unamortized Bond Premium	410	
	Cash (or Interest Payable)		4,500
	Paid (or accrued) semiannual interest		
	to bondholders and amortized the		
	premium on 9%, 5-year bonds		

TABLE 4. **Interest and Amortization of a Bond Premium: Effective Interest Method**

	A	B	C	D	E	F
Semiannual Interest Period	Carrying Value at Beginning of Period	Semiannual Interest Expense at 8% to Be Recorded* (4% × A)	Semiannual Interest Payment to Bondholders (4½% × $100,000)	Amortization of Bond Premium (C − B)	Unamortized Bond Premium at End of Period (E − D)	Carrying Value at End of Period (A − D)
0					$4,100	$104,100
1	$104,100	$4,164	$4,500	$336	3,764	103,764
2	103,764	4,151	4,500	349	3,415	103,415
3	103,415	4,137	4,500	363	3,052	103,052
4	103,052	4,122	4,500	378	2,674	102,674
5	102,674	4,107	4,500	393	2,281	102,281
6	102,281	4,091	4,500	409	1,872	101,872
7	101,872	4,075	4,500	425	1,447	101,447
8	101,447	4,058	4,500	442	1,005	101,005
9	101,005	4,040	4,500	460	545	100,545
10	100,545	3,955†	4,500	545	—	100,000

*Rounded to the nearest dollar.   †Last period's interest expense equals $3,955 ($4,500 − $545); it does not equal $4,022 ($100,545 × .04) because of the cumulative effect of rounding.

Study Note

The bond interest expense recorded is less than the amount of the interest paid because of the amortization of the bond premium. The matching rule dictates that the premium be amortized over the life of the bond.

Note that the bond interest expense is $4,090, but the amount that bondholders receive is the $4,500 face interest payment. The difference of $410 is the debit to Unamortized Bond Premium. This lowers the credit balance of the Unamortized Bond Premium account and the carrying value of the bonds payable by $410 each interest period. If the bond issue remains unchanged, the same entry will be made on every semiannual interest date over the life of the bond issue. When the bond issue matures, the balance in the Unamortized Bond Premium account will be zero, and the carrying value of the bonds payable will be $100,000—exactly equal to the amount due the bondholders.

As noted earlier, the straight-line method should be used only when it does not lead to a material difference from the effective interest method.

Effective Interest Method   Under the straight-line method, the effective interest rate changes constantly, even though the interest expense is fixed, because the effective interest rate is determined by comparing the fixed interest expense with a carrying value that changes as a result of amortizing the discount or premium. To apply a fixed interest rate over the life of the bonds based on the actual market rate at the time of the bond issue, one must use the effective interest method. With this method, the interest expense decreases slightly each period (see Table 4, Column B) because the amount of the bond premium amortized increases slightly (Column D). This occurs

FOCUS ON BUSINESS PRACTICE

Speed Up the Calculations!

Interest and amortization tables like those in Tables 3 and 4 are ideal applications for computer spreadsheet software, such as Lotus and Microsoft Excel. Once the tables have been constructed with the proper formula in each cell, only five variables must be entered to produce the entire table: the face value, selling price, maturity date, face interest rate, and market interest rate.

because a fixed rate is applied each period to the gradually decreasing carrying value (Column A). The first interest payment is recorded as follows:

A*	=	L	+	SE
−4,500		−336		−4,164

*Assumes cash paid.

2006			
July 1	Bond Interest Expense	4,164	
	Unamortized Bond Premium	336	
	Cash (or Interest Payable)		4,500
	Paid (or accrued) semiannual interest		
	to bondholders and amortized the		
	premium on 9%, 5-year bonds		

Note that the unamortized bond premium (Column E) decreases gradually to zero as the carrying value decreases to the face value (Column F). To find the amount of premium amortized in any one interest payment period, subtract the effective interest expense (the carrying value times the effective interest rate, Column B) from the interest payment (Column C). In semiannual interest period 5, for example, the amortization of premium is $393, which is calculated in the following manner: $4,500 − ($102,674 × .04).

Figure 4, which is based on the data in Table 4, shows how the effective interest method affects the amortization of a bond premium. Notice that the carrying value (issue price) is initially greater than the face value, but that it gradually decreases toward the face value over the life of the bond issue. Notice also that interest payments exceed interest expense by the amount of

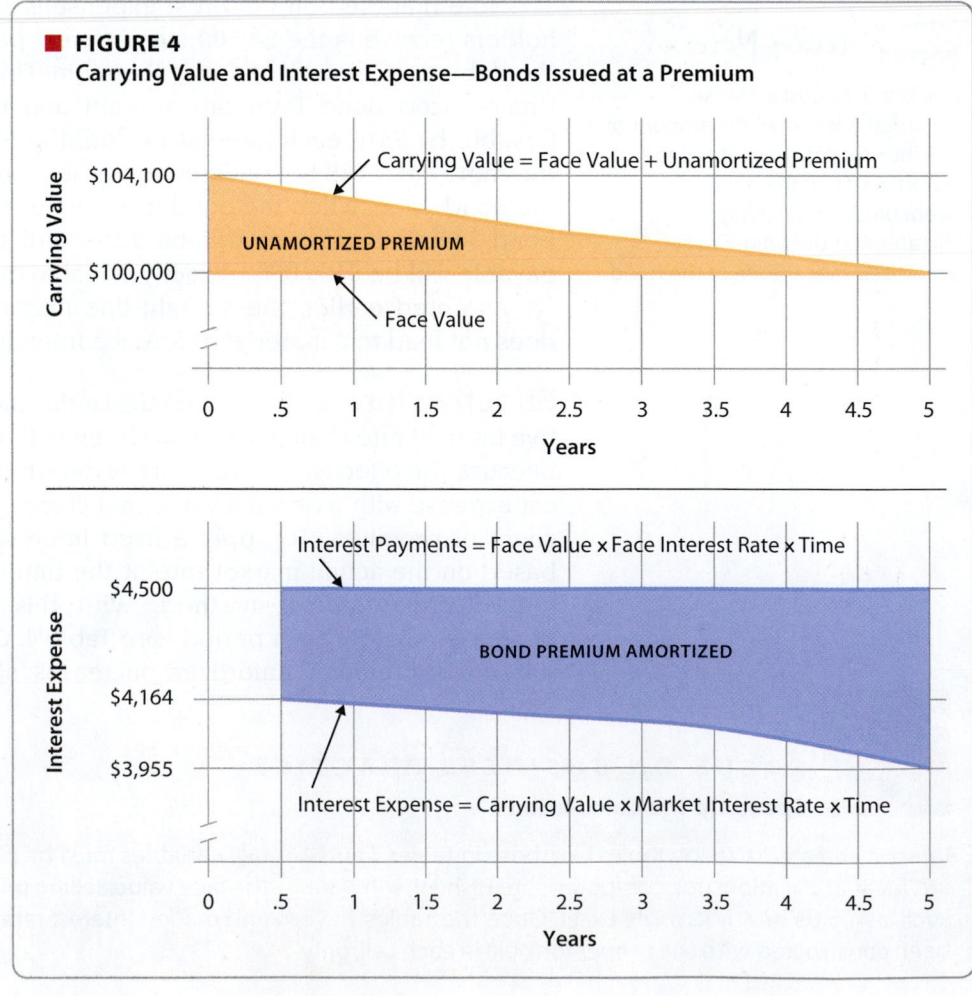

■ **FIGURE 4**
Carrying Value and Interest Expense—Bonds Issued at a Premium

the premium amortized. Interest expense decreases gradually over the life of the bond because it is based on the gradually decreasing carrying value (multiplied by the market interest rate).

S T O P • R E V I E W • A P P L Y

5-1. What is included in the calculation of the total interest cost fo a bond issue other than interest payments?

5-2. Why is the straight-line method of amortization usually acceptable even though it is not the most theoretically correct method?

5-3. Why does the amortization of a bond discount increase interest expense to an amount greater than interest paid? Why does the amortization of a premium have the opposite effect?

5-4. When the effective interest method of amortizing a bond discount or premium is used, why does the amount of interest expense change from period to period?

Bond Transactions   On June 1, Bassi Corporation issues $8,000,000 of 8 percent, 20-year bonds at 97. Interest is payable semiannually, on May 31 and November 30. Bassi's fiscal year ends on November 30.

1. Using the straight-line method of amortization, prepare entries in journal form for June 1 and November 30.

2. Using the effective interest method and assuming the same facts as above except that the market rate of interest is 8.5 percent, prepare the entry for November 30.

SOLUTION

1. Straight-line method

June 1	Cash	7,760,000	
	Unamortized Bond Discount	240,000	
	Bonds Payable		8,000,000
	Issue of $8,000,000 of 8%,		
	20-year bonds at 97		
	$8,000,000 × .97 = $7,760,000		

Nov. 30	Bond Interest Expense	326,000	
	Unamortized Bond Discount		6,000
	Cash		320,000
	Paid bondholders semiannual interest and		
	amortized the discount on 8%, 20-year bonds		
	$240,000 ÷ 40 periods = $6,000		
	$8,000,000 × .04 = $320,000		

2. Effective interest method

Nov. 30	Bond Interest Expense	329,800	
	Unamortized Bond Interest		9,800
	Cash		320,000
	Paid bondholders semiannual interest and		
	amortized the discount on 8%, 20-year bonds		
	$7,760,000 × .0425 = $329,800		
	$8,000,000 × .04 = $320,000		

Retirement of Bonds

LO6 Account for the retirement of bonds and the conversion of bonds into stock.

Usually, companies pay bonds when they are due—on the maturity date. However, as we noted in our earlier discussion of callable and convertible bonds, retiring a bond issue before its maturity date can be to a company's advantage. For example, when interest rates drop, many companies refinance their bonds at the lower rate, much like homeowners who refinance their mortgage loans when interest rates go down. Even though companies usually pay a premium for early extinguishment of bond debt, what they save on interest can make the refinancing cost-effective.

Calling Bonds

Let's suppose that Katakis Corporation can call, or retire, at 105 the $100,000 of bonds it issued at a premium (104.1) on January 1, 2006, and that it decides to do so on July 1, 2009. The retirement thus takes place on the seventh interest payment date. Assume that the entry for the required interest payment and the amortization of the premium has been made. The entry to record the retirement of the bonds is as follows:

A	=	L	+	SE
−105,000		−100,000		−3,553
		−1,477		

2009			
July 1	Bonds Payable	100,000	
	Unamortized Bond Premium	1,447	
	Loss on Retirement of Bonds	3,553	
	Cash		105,000
	Retired 9% bonds at 105		

In this entry, the cash paid is the face value times the call price ($100,000 × 1.05 = $105,000). The unamortized bond premium can be found in Column E of Table 4. The loss on retirement of bonds occurs because the call price of the bonds is greater than the carrying value ($105,000 − $101,447 = $3,553).

Sometimes, a rise in the market interest rate can cause the market value of bonds to fall considerably below their face value. If it has the cash to do so, the company may find it advantageous to purchase the bonds on the open market and retire them, rather than wait and pay them off at face value. A gain is recognized for the difference between the purchase price of the bonds and the carrying value of the retired bonds.

For example, suppose that because of a rise in interest rates, Katakis Corporation is able to purchase the $100,000 bond issue on the open market at 85. The entry would be as follows:

A	=	L	+	SE
−85,000		−100,000		+16,447
		−1,447		

2009			
July 1	Bonds Payable	100,000	
	Unamortized Bond Premium	1,447	
	Cash		85,000
	Gain on Retirement of Bonds		16,447
	Purchased and retired		
	9% bonds at 85		

Converting Bonds

When a bondholder converts bonds to common stock, the company records the common stock at the carrying value of the bonds. The bond liability and the unamortized discount or premium are written off the books. For this reason, no gain or loss on the transaction is recorded. For example, suppose Katakis Corporation does not call its bonds on July 1, 2009. Instead, the corporation's bondholders decide to convert all their bonds to $8 par value common stock under a convertible provision of 40 shares of common stock for each $1,000 bond. The entry would be as follows:

A =	L	+	SE
−100,000	+32,000		
−1,447	+69,447		

2009			
July 1	Bonds Payable	100,000	
	Unamortized Bond Premium	1,447	
	Common Stock		32,000
	Additional Paid-in Capital		69,447
	Converted 9% bonds payable into		
	$8 par value common stock at a rate		
	of 40 shares for each $1,000 bond		

The unamortized bond premium is found in Column E of Table 4. At a rate of 40 shares for each $1,000 bond, 4,000 shares will be issued, with a total par value of $32,000 (4,000 × $8). The Common Stock account is credited for the amount of the par value of the stock issued. In addition, Additional Paid-in Capital is credited for the difference between the carrying value of the bonds and the par value of the stock issued ($101,447 − $32,000 = $69,447). No gain or loss is recorded.

STOP • REVIEW • APPLY

6-1. When may a company want to exercise the call provision of a bond?

6-2. Why are convertible bonds advantageous to both the company and the bondholder?

Other Bonds Payable Issues

SO7 Record bonds issued between interest dates and year-end adjustments.

Among the other issues involved in accounting for bonds payable are the sale of bonds between interest payment dates and the year-end accrual of bond interest expense.

Sale of Bonds Between Interest Dates

Although corporations may issue bonds on an interest payment date, as in our previous examples, they often issue them between interest payment dates. When that is the case, they generally collect from the investors the interest that would have accrued for the partial period preceding the issue date, and at the end of the first interest period, they pay the interest for the entire period. In other words, the interest collected when bonds are sold is returned to investors on the next interest payment date.

There are two reasons for following this procedure:

1. From a practical standpoint, if a company issued bonds on several different days and did not collect the accrued interest, records would have to be maintained for each bondholder and date of purchase. The interest due each bondholder would therefore have to be computed for a different time period. Clearly, this procedure would involve large bookkeeping costs. On the other hand, if accrued interest is collected when the bonds are sold, the corporation can pay the interest due for the entire period on the interest payment date, thereby eliminating the extra computations and costs.

2. When accrued interest is collected in advance, the amount is subtracted from the full interest paid on the interest payment date. Thus, the resulting interest expense represents the amount for the time the money was borrowed.

For example, suppose Katakis Corporation sold $100,000 of 9 percent, five-year bonds for face value on May 1, 2006, rather than on January 1, 2006. The entry to record the sale of the bonds is as follows:

A	=	L	+	SE
+103,000		+100,000		+3,000

2006			
May 1	Cash	103,000	
	Bond Interest Expense		3,000
	Bonds Payable		100,000
	Sold 9%, 5-year bonds at face value		
	plus 4 months' accrued interest		
	$100,000 \times .09 \times 4/12 = \$3,000$		

Cash is debited for the amount received, $103,000 (the face value of $100,000 plus four months' accrued interest of $3,000). Bond Interest Expense is credited for the $3,000 of accrued interest, and Bonds Payable is credited for the face value of $100,000.

When the first semiannual interest payment date arrives, this entry is made:

A*	= L +	SE
−4,500		−4,500

*Assumes cash paid.

2006			
July 1	Bond Interest Expense	4,500	
	Cash (or Interest Payable)		4,500
	Paid (or accrued) semiannual interest		
	$100,000 \times .09 \times 6/12 = \$4,500$		

Notice that the entire half-year interest is debited to Bond Interest Expense and credited to Cash because the corporation pays bond interest every six months, in full six-month amounts. Figure 5 illustrates this process. The actual interest expense for the two months that the bonds were outstanding is $1,500. This amount is the net balance of the $4,500 debit to Bond Interest Expense on July 1 less the $3,000 credit to Bond Interest Expense on May 1. You can see these steps clearly in the following T account:

	BOND INTEREST EXPENSE		
Bal.	0	May 1	3,000
July 1	4,500		
Bal.	**1,500**		

Year-End Accrual of Bond Interest Expense

Bond interest payment dates rarely correspond with a company's fiscal year. Therefore, an adjustment must be made to accrue the interest expense on the bonds from the last interest payment date to the end of the fiscal year. In addition, any discount or premium on the bonds must be amortized for the partial period.

In our example of bonds issued at a premium, Katakis Corporation issued $100,000 of bonds on January 1, 2006, at 104.1 percent of face value. Suppose Katakis's fiscal year ends on September 30, 2006. In the period since the interest payment and amortization of the premium on July 1, three months' worth of interest has accrued. Under the effective interest method, the following adjusting entry would be made:

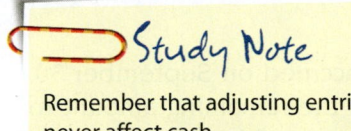

Study Note

Remember that adjusting entries never affect cash.

A =	L	+	SE
	−174.50		−2,075.50
	+2,250.00		

2006			
Sept. 30	Bond Interest Expense	2,075.50	
	Unamortized Bond Premium	174.50	
	Bond Interest Payable		2,250.00
	To record accrual of interest		
	on 9% bonds payable for		
	3 months and amortization		
	of one-half of the premium		
	for the second interest		
	payment period		

Study Note

The matching rule dictates that both the accrued interest and the amortization of a premium or discount be recorded at year end.

This entry covers one-half of the second interest period. Unamortized Bond Premium is debited for $174.50, which is one-half of $349, the amortization of the premium for the second period from Table 4. Bond Interest Payable is credited for $2,250, three months' interest on the face value of the bonds ($100,000 × .09 × 3/12). The net debit figure of $2,075.50 ($2,250.00 − $174.50) is the bond interest expense for the three-month period.

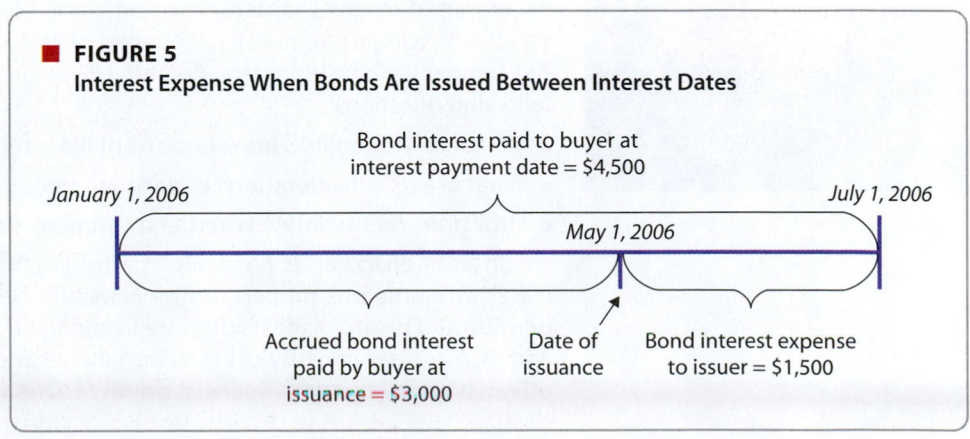

■ **FIGURE 5**
Interest Expense When Bonds Are Issued Between Interest Dates

On the interest payment date of January 1, 2007, the entry to pay the bondholders and amortize the premium is as follows:

A	=	L	+	SE
−4,500.00		−2,250.00		−2,075.50
		−174.50		

2007			
Jan. 1	Bond Interest Expense	2,075.50	
	Bond Interest Payable	2,250.00	
	Unamortized Bond Premium	174.50	
	Cash		4,500.00
	Paid semiannual interest,		
	including interest previously		
	accrued, and amortized the		
	premium for the period since		
	the end of the fiscal year		

One-half ($2,250) of the amount paid ($4,500) was accrued on September 30. Unamortized Bond Premium is debited for $174.50, the remaining amount to be amortized for the period ($349.00 − $174.50). The resulting bond interest expense is the amount that applies to the three-month period from October 1 to December 31.

Bond discounts are recorded at year end in the same way as bond premiums. The difference is that the amortization of a bond discount increases interest expense instead of decreasing it.

S T O P • R E V I E W • A P P L Y

7-1. When a company issues bonds between interest dates, why does it collect an amount equal to accrued interest from the buyer?

7-2. In making the year-end accrual for interest on bonds payable, what two computations affect the amount of interest expense?

A LOOK BACK AT

McDONALD'S CORPORATION

As we noted in this chapter's Decision Point, McDonald's relies on both debt and equity financing to support its continued global expansion. Because of the extent of the company's long-term debt, potential investors and creditors need to address the following questions:

• What are McDonald's most important long-term debts?

• What are its considerations in deciding to issue long-term debt?

• How does one evaluate whether a company has too much debt?

In addition to bonds, notes, and mortgages, McDonald's long-term debt includes leases on numerous properties. The company also has deferred income taxes and pension and health plans. Its purpose in taking on long-term debt is to foster growth and increase earnings. By using financial leverage in this way, McDonald's, like any other company, assumes financial risk. In McDonald's case, the risk is partially offset because much of its long-term debt relates to leases on real estate, an area in which the company has long experience and great expertise. McDonald's management commits the company to long-term leases not only because it believes the company will stay in the leased locations for a long time, but also because it is a way of financing expansion.

McDonald's 2004 annual report includes a detailed description of management's approach to debt financing. It points out that Standard & Poor's gives the company an "A" credit rating and that management carefully monitors key credit ratios that "incorporate capitalized operating leases to estimate total adjusted debt."

We can evaluate whether McDonald's maintains an appropriate level of debt by computing its interest coverage ratio over a two-year period, as follows:

$$\text{K/R} \quad \text{Interest Coverage Ratio} = \frac{\text{Income Before Income Taxes} + \text{Interest Expense}}{\text{Interest Expense}}$$

	2004	2003
Interest Coverage Ratio =	$\dfrac{\$3,202.4 + \$358.4}{\$358.4}$	$\dfrac{\$2,346.4 + \$388.0}{\$388.0}$
=	$\dfrac{\$3,560.8}{\$358.4}$	$\dfrac{\$2,734.4}{\$388.0}$
=	9.9 times	7.0 times

This analysis shows that McDonald's can easily cover its interest payments and that its ability to do so increased over the two-year period. There is plenty of cushion in this ratio to cover all of McDonald's balance sheet commitments, including long-term leases.

CHAPTER REVIEW

REVIEW of Learning Objectives

LO1 Identify the management issues related to long-term debt.

Long-term debt is used to finance assets and business activities, such as research and development, that will produce income in future years. The management issues related to long-term debt are whether to take on long-term debt, how much debt to carry, and what types of debt to incur. The advantages of issuing long-term debt are that common stockholders do not relinquish any control, interest on debt is tax-deductible, and financial leverage can increase earnings. The disadvantages are that interest and principal must be paid on time and financial leverage can work against a company if an investment is not successful. The level of debt can be evaluated using the debt to equity ratio and the interest coverage ratio. Common types of long-term debt are bonds, notes, mortgages, long-term leases, pension liabilities, other postretirement benefits, and deferred income taxes.

LO2 Describe the features of a bond issue and the major characteristics of bonds.

A bond is a security that represents money borrowed from the investing public. When a corporation issues bonds, it enters into a contract, called a bond indenture, with the bondholders. The bond indenture defines the terms of the bond issue. A bond issue is the total value of bonds issued at one time. The prices of bonds are stated in terms of a percentage of the face value, or principal, of the bonds. The face interest rate is the fixed rate of interest paid to bondholders based on the face value. The market interest rate is the rate of interest paid in the market on bonds of similar risk. If the market rate fluctuates from the face interest rate before the bond issue date, the bonds will sell at either a discount or a premium.

A corporation can issue several types of bonds, each having different characteristics. For example, a bond issue may or may not require security (secured versus unsecured bonds). It may be payable at a single time (term bonds) or at several times (serial bonds). And the holder may receive interest automatically (registered bonds) or may have to return coupons to receive interest payable (coupon bonds). Bonds may also be callable and convertible.

LO3 Record bonds issued at face value and at a discount or premium.

Bondholders pay face value for bonds when the interest rate on the bonds approximates the market rate for similar investments. The issuing corporation records the bond issue at face value as a long-term liability in the Bonds Payable account. Bonds are issued at a discount when their face interest rate is lower than the market rate for similar investments. The difference between the face value and the issue price is debited to Unamortized Bond Discount. Bonds are issued at a premium when their face interest rate is greater than the market interest rate on similar investments. The difference between the issue price and the face value is credited to Unamortized Bond Premium.

LO4 Use present values to determine the value of bonds.

The value of a bond is determined by summing the present values of (1) the series of fixed interest payments of the bond issue and (2) the single payment of the face value at maturity. Tables 3 and 4 in the appendix on future value and present value tables should be used in making these computations.

LO5 Amortize bond discounts and bond premiums using the straight-line and effective interest methods.

The straight-line method allocates a fixed portion of a bond discount or premium each interest period to adjust the interest payment to interest expense. The effective interest method, which is used when the effects of amortization are material, applies a constant rate of interest to the carrying value of the bonds. To find interest and the amortization of discounts or premiums, the effective interest rate is applied to the carrying value of the bonds (face value minus the discount or plus the premium) at the beginning of the interest period. The amount of the discount or premium to be amortized is the difference between the interest figured by using the effective rate and that obtained by using the face rate. The results of using the effective interest method on bonds issued at a discount or a premium are summarized below and compared with issuance at face value:

	Bonds Issued at		
	Face Value	**Discount**	**Premium**
Trend in carrying value over bond term	Constant	Increasing	Decreasing
Trend in interest expense over bond term	Constant	Increasing	Decreasing
Interest expense versus interest payments	Interest expense = interest payments	Interest expense > interest payments	Interest expense < interest payments
Classification of bond discount or premium	Not applicable	Contra-liability (deducted from Bonds Payable)	Liability (added to Bonds Payable)

LO6 Account for the retirement of bonds and the conversion of bonds into stock.

Callable bonds can be retired before maturity at the option of the issuing corporation. The call price is usually an amount greater than the face value of the bonds, in which case the corporation recognizes a loss on the retirement of the bonds. Sometimes, a rise in the market interest rate causes the market value of the bonds to fall below face value. If a company purchases its bonds on the open market at a price below carrying value, it recognizes a gain on the transaction.

Convertible bonds allow the bondholder to convert bonds to the issuing corporation's common stock. When bondholders exercise this option, the common stock issued is recorded at the carrying value of the bonds being converted. No gain or loss is recognized.

Supplemental Objective

SO7 Record bonds issued between interest dates and year-end adjustments.

When bonds are sold between the interest payment dates, the issuing corporation collects from investors the interest that has accrued since the last interest payment date. When the next interest payment date arrives, the corporation pays the bondholders interest for the entire interest period.

When the end of a corporation's fiscal year does not fall on an interest payment date, the corporation must accrue bond interest expense from the last interest payment date to the end of its fiscal year. This accrual results in the inclusion of the interest expense in the year it is incurred.

REVIEW of Concepts and Terminology

The following concepts and terms were introduced in this chapter:

Bond: A security, usually long term, representing money that a corporation or other entity borrows from the investing public. **(LO2)**

Bond certificate: Evidence of an organization's debt to a bondholder. **(LO2)**

Bond indenture: A contract that defines the terms of a bond issue. **(LO2)**

Bond issue: The total value of bonds issued at one time. **(LO2)**

Callable bonds: Bonds that the issuing corporation can buy back and retire at a call price before their maturity dates. **(LO2)**

Call price: A specified price, usually above face value, at which a corporation can buy back its bonds before maturity. **(LO2)**

Capital lease: A long-term lease that resembles a purchase or sale on installment and in which the lessee assumes the risk of ownership. **(LO1)**

Convertible bonds: Bonds that can be exchanged for the issuing corporation's common stock. **(LO2)**

Coupon bonds: Bonds not registered with the issuing organization that bear coupons stating the amount of interest due and the payment date. **(LO2)**

Deferred income taxes: The result of using different methods to calculate income taxes for financial reporting and tax purposes. **(LO1)**

Discount: The amount by which a bond's face value exceeds its issue price, which occurs when the market interest rate is higher than the face interest rate. **(LO2)**

Early extinguishment of debt: The retirement of a bond issue before its maturity date. **(LO2)**

Effective interest method: A method of amortizing bond discounts or premiums that applies a constant interest rate (the market rate when the bonds were issued) to the bonds' carrying value at the beginning of each interest period. **(LO5)**

Face interest rate: The fixed rate of interest paid to bondholders based on the face value of the bonds. **(LO2)**

Financial leverage: A corporation's ability to increase earnings for stockholders by earning more on assets than it pays in interest on the debt it incurred to finance the assets. Also called *trading on equity*. **(LO1)**

Market interest rate: The rate of interest paid in the market on bonds of similar risk. Also called *effective interest rate*. **(LO2)**

Mortgage: A debt secured by real property. **(LO1)**

Off-balance-sheet financing: Structuring long-term debts in such a way that they do not appear as liabilities on the balance sheet. **(LO1)**

Operating lease: A short-term lease in which the risks of ownership remain with the lessor and for which payments are recorded as rent expense. **(LO1)**

Other postretirement benefits: Health care and other nonpension benefits paid after retirement but earned while the employee is still working. **(LO1)**

Pension fund: A fund established by the contributions of an employer and often of employees from which payments are made to employees after retirement or upon disability or death. **(LO1)**

Pension plan: A contract requiring a company to pay benefits to its employees after they retire. **(LO1)**

Premium: The amount by which a bond's issue price exceeds its face value, which occurs when the market interest rate is lower than the face interest rate. **(LO2)**

Registered bonds: Bonds that the issuing company registers in the names of the bondholders. **(LO2)**

Secured bonds: Bonds that carry a pledge of certain assets as a guarantee of repayment. **(LO2)**

Serial bonds: Bonds in one issue that mature on different dates. **(LO2)**

Straight-line method: A method of amortizing bond discounts or premiums that allocates the discount or premium equally over each interest period of the life of a bond. **(LO5)**

Term bonds: Bonds in one issue that mature at the same time. **(LO2)**

Unsecured bonds: Bonds issued on an organization's general credit. Also called *debenture bonds*. **(LO2)**

Zero coupon bonds: Bonds that do not pay periodic interest but that pay a fixed amount on the maturity date. **(LO5)**

Key Ratio

Interest coverage ratio: A measure of the degree of protection a company has from default on interest payments; (Income Before Income Taxes + Interest Expense) ÷ Interest Expense. **(LO1)**

REVIEW Problem

LO3, LO5, LO6 **Accounting for a Bond Discount, Bond Retirement, and Bond Conversion**

When Merrill Manufacturing Company wanted to expand its metal window division, it did not have enough capital to finance the project. To fund it, management sought and received approval from the board of directors to issue bonds. The bond indenture stated that the company would issue $5,000,000 of 8 percent, five-year bonds on January 1, 20x4, and would pay interest semiannually, on June 30 and December 31 of each of the five years. It also stated that the bonds would be callable at 104 and that each $1,000 bond would be convertible to 30 shares of $10 par value common stock. Merrill sold the bonds on January 1, 20x4, at 96 because the market rate of interest for similar investments was 9 percent. It decided to amortize the bond discount by using the effective interest method. On July 1, 20x6, management called and retired half the bonds, and investors converted the other half to common stock.

Required

1. Prepare an interest and amortization schedule for the first five interest periods.
2. Prepare entries in journal form to record the sale of the bonds, the first two interest payments, the bond retirement, and the bond conversion.

Answer to Review Problem

1. Schedule for the first five interest periods:

Semiannual Interest Payment Date	Carrying Value at Beginning of Period	Semiannual Interest Expense* (9% × ½)	Semiannual Interest Payment (8% × ½)	Amortization of Discount	Unamortized Bond Discount at End of Period	Carrying Value at End of Period
Jan. 1, 20x4					$200,000	$4,800,000
June 30, 20x4	$4,800,000	$216,000	$200,000	$16,000	184,000	4,816,000
Dec. 31, 20x4	4,816,000	216,720	200,000	16,720	167,280	4,832,720
June 30, 20x5	4,832,720	217,472	200,000	17,472	149,808	4,850,192
Dec. 31, 20x5	4,850,192	218,259	200,000	18,259	131,549	4,868,451
June 30, 20x6	4,868,451	219,080	200,000	19,080	112,469	4,887,531

*Rounded to the nearest dollar.

2. Entries in journal form:

20x4					
Jan.	1	Cash	4,800,000	
		Unamortized Bond Discount	200,000	
		Bonds Payable		5,000,000
		Sold $5,000,000 of 8%, 5-year bonds at 96		
June	30	Bond Interest Expense	216,000	
		Unamortized Bond Discount		16,000
		Cash		200,000
		Paid semiannual interest and amortized the discount on 8%, 5-year bonds		
Dec.	31	Bond Interest Expense	216,720	
		Unamortized Bond Discount		16,720
		Cash		200,000

	20x6				
14	20x6				
15	July	1	Bonds Payable	2,500,000	
16			Loss on Retirement of Bonds	156,235	
17			Unamortized Bond Discount		56,235
18			Cash		2,600,000
19			Called $2,500,000 of 8% bonds and retired them at 104		
20			$112,469 × ½ = $56,235*		
21		1	Bonds Payable	2,500,000	
22			Unamortized Bond Discount		56,234
23			Common Stock		750,000
24			Additional paid-in Capital		1,693,766
25			Converted $2,500,000 of 8% bonds into common stock:		
26			2,500 × 30 shares = 75,000 shares		
27			75,000 shares × $10 = $750,000		
28			$112,469 - $56,235 = $56,234		
29			$2,500,000 - ($56,234 + $750,000) = $1,693,766		
30					
31	* Rounded.				

CHAPTER ASSIGNMENTS

BUILDING Your Basic Knowledge and Skills

Short Exercises

LO1 **Bond Versus Common Stock Financing**

SE 1. Indicate whether each of the following is an advantage or a disadvantage of using long-term bond financing rather than issuing common stock.

1. Interest paid on bonds is tax-deductible.
2. Investments are sometimes not as successful as planned.
3. Financial leverage can have a negative effect when investments do not earn as much as the interest payments on the related debt.
4. Bondholders do not have voting rights in a corporation.
5. Positive financial leverage may be achieved.

LO1 **Types of Long-Term Liabilities**

SE 2. Place the number of the liability next to the statement to which it applies.

1. Bonds payable	____ a. May result in a capital lease
2. Long-term notes payable	____ b. Differences in income taxes on accounting income and taxable income
3. Mortgage payable	____ c. The most popular form of long-term financing
4. Long-term lease	____ d. Often used to purchase land and buildings

5. Pension liabilities   _____ e. Often used interchangeably with bonds payable

6. Other post-retirement benefits   _____ f. Future health care costs are a major component

7. Deferred income taxes   _____ g. May include 401(k), ESOPs, or profit-sharing

LO1   **Mortgage Payable**

SE 3. Karib Corporation purchased a building by signing a $150,000 long-term mortgage with monthly payments of $1,200. The mortgage carries an interest rate of 8 percent. Prepare a monthly payment schedule showing the monthly payment, the interest for the month, the reduction in debt, and the unpaid balance for the first three months. (Round to the nearest dollar.)

LO4   **Valuing Bonds Using Present Value**

SE 4. Rogers Paints, Inc., is considering the sale of two bond issues. Choice A is a $600,000 bond issue that pays semiannual interest of $32,000 and is due in 20 years. Choice B is a $600,000 bond issue that pays semiannual interest of $30,000 and is due in 15 years. Assume that the market interest rate for each bond is 12 percent. Calculate the amount that Rogers Paints will receive if both bond issues occur. (Calculate the present value of each bond issue and sum.)

LO3, LO5   **Straight-Line Method**

SE 5. On April 1, 20x7, Morimoto Corporation issued $8,000,000 in 8.5 percent, five-year bonds at 98. The semiannual interest payment dates are April 1 and October 1. Prepare entries in journal form for the issue of the bonds by Morimoto on April 1, 20x7, and the first two interest payments on October 1, 20x7, and April 1, 20x8. Use the straight-line method and ignore year-end accruals.

LO3, LO5, SO7   **Effective Interest Method**

SE 6. On March 1, 20xx, Samsonite Freight Company sold $200,000 of its 9.5 percent, 20-year bonds at 106. The semiannual interest payment dates are March 1 and September 1. The market interest rate is 8.9 percent. The firm's fiscal year ends August 31. Prepare entries in journal form to record the sale of the bonds on March 1, the accrual of interest and amortization of premium on August 31, and the first interest payment on September 1. Use the effective interest method to amortize the premium.

LO6   **Bond Retirement**

SE 7. The Geller Corporation has outstanding $400,000 of 8 percent bonds callable at 104. On December 1, immediately after the payment of the semiannual interest and the amortization of the bond discount were recorded, the unamortized bond discount equaled $10,500. On that date, $240,000 of the bonds were called and retired. Prepare the entry to record the retirement of the bonds on December 1.

LO6   **Bond Conversion**

SE 8. The Tramot Corporation has $2,000,000 of 6 percent bonds outstanding. There is $40,000 of unamortized discount remaining on the bonds after the March 1, 20x6, semiannual interest payment. The bonds are convertible at the rate of 20 shares of $10 par value common stock for each $1,000 bond. On March 1, 20x6, bondholders presented $1,200,000 of the bonds for conversion. Prepare the entry to record the conversion of the bonds.

SO7 **Bond Issue Between Interest Dates**

SE 9. Downey Corporation sold $400,000 of 9 percent, ten-year bonds for face value on September 1, 20xx. The issue date of the bonds was May 1, 20xx. The company's fiscal year ends on December 31, and this is its only bond issue. Record the sale of the bonds on September 1 and the first semiannual interest payment on November 1, 20xx. What is the bond interest expense for the year ended December 31, 20xx?

LO3, LO5, SO7 **Year-End Accrual of Bond Interest**

SE 10. On October 1, 20x7, Winston Corporation issued $250,000 of 9 percent bonds at 96. The bonds are dated October 1 and pay interest semiannually. The market rate of interest is 10 percent, and the company's year end is December 31. Prepare the entries to record the issuance of the bonds, the accrual of the interest on December 31, 20x7, and the payment of the first semiannual interest on April 1, 20x8. Assume the company uses the effective interest method to amortize the bond discount.

Exercises

LO1, LO2, LO6 **Discussion Questions**

E 1. Develop brief answers to each of the following questions:

1. How does a lender assess the risk that a borrower may default—that is, not pay interest and principal when due?
2. If a company with a high debt to equity ratio wants to increase its debt when the economy is weak, what kind of bond might it issue?
3. Why might a company lease a long-term asset rather than buy it and issue long-term bonds?
4. Why are callable and convertible bonds considered to add to management's future flexibility in financing a business?

LO3, LO4, LO5, SO7 **Discussion Questions**

E 2. Develop brief answers to each of the following questions:

1. What determines whether bonds are issued at a discount, premium, or face value?
2. Why does the market price of a bond vary over time?
3. When is it acceptable to use the straight-line method to amortize a bond discount or premium?
4. Why must the accrual of bond interest be recorded at the end of an accounting period?

LO1 **Interest Coverage Ratio**

K/R **E 3.** Compute the interest coverage ratios for 20x7 and 20x8 from the partial income statements of Wool Company that appear below. State whether the ratio improved or worsened over time.

	20x8	20x7
Income from operations	$47,780	$36,920
Interest expense	11,600	6,600
Income before income taxes	$36,180	$30,320
Income taxes	10,800	9,000
Net income	$25,380	$21,320

LO1 **Mortgage Payable**

E 4. Velocity Corporation purchased a building by signing a $75,000 long-term mortgage with monthly payments of $1,000. The mortgage carries an interest rate of 12 percent.

1. Prepare a monthly payment schedule showing the monthly payment, the interest for the month, the reduction in debt, and the unpaid balance for the first three months. (Round to the nearest dollar.)
2. Prepare entries in journal form to record the purchase and the first two monthly payments.

LO1 **Recording Lease Obligations**

E 5. Tubbs Corporation has leased a piece of equipment that has a useful life of 12 years. The terms of the lease are payments of $86,000 per year for 12 years. Tubbs currently is able to borrow money at a long-term interest rate of 15 percent. (Round answers to the nearest dollar.)

1. Calculate the present value of the lease.
2. Prepare the entry to record the lease agreement.
3. Prepare the entry to record depreciation of the equipment for the first year using the straight-line method.
4. Prepare the entries to record the lease payments for the first two years.

LO4 **Valuing Bonds Using Present Value**

E 6. Ames, Inc., is considering the sale of two bond issues. Choice A is a $1,600,000 bond issue that pays semiannual interest of $128,000 and is due in 20 years. Choice B is a $1,600,000 bond issue that pays semiannual interest of $120,000 and is due in 15 years. Assume that the market interest rate for each bond is 12 percent. Calculate the amount that Ames, Inc., will receive if both bond issues are made. (**Hint:** Calculate the present value of each bond issue and sum.)

LO4 **Valuing Bonds Using Present Value**

E 7. Use the present value tables in the appendix on future value and present value tables to calculate the issue price of a $600,000 bond issue in each of the following independent cases. Assume interest is paid semiannually.

a. A 10-year, 8 percent bond issue; the market interest rate is 10 percent.
b. A 10-year, 8 percent bond issue; the market interest rate is 6 percent.
c. A 10-year, 10 percent bond issue; the market interest rate is 8 percent.
d. A 20-year, 10 percent bond issue; the market interest rate is 12 percent.
e. A 20-year, 10 percent bond issue; the market interest rate is 6 percent.

LO4 **Zero Coupon Bonds**

E 8. The state of Idaho needs to raise $50,000,000 for highway repairs. Officials are considering issuing zero coupon bonds, which do not require periodic interest payments. The current market interest rate for the bonds is 10 percent. What face value of bonds must be issued to raise the needed funds, assuming the bonds will be due in 30 years and compounded annually? How would your answer change if the bonds were due in 50 years? How would both answers change if the market interest rate were 8 percent instead of 10 percent?

LO3, LO5 **Straight-Line Method**

E 9. Kigga Corporation issued $2,000,000 in 10.5 percent, ten-year bonds on February 1, 20x7, at 104. Semiannual interest payment dates are January 31 and July 31. Use the straight-line method and ignore year-end accruals.

1. With regard to the bond issue on February 1, 20x7:

    a. How much cash is received?
    b. How much is Bonds Payable?
    c. What is the difference between **a** and **b** called and how much is it?

2. With regard to the bond interest payment on July 31, 20x7:

    a. How much cash is paid in interest?
    b. How much is the amortization?
    c. How much is interest expense?

3. With regard to the bond interest payment on January 31, 20x8:

    a. How much cash is paid in interest?
    b. How much is the amortization?
    c. How much is interest expense?

LO3, LO5   **Straight-Line Method**

E 10. Bianca Corporation issued $16,000,000 in 8.5 percent, five-year bonds on March 1, 20x7, at 96. The semiannual interest payment dates are September 1 and March 1. Prepare entries in journal form for the issue of the bonds by Bianca on March 1, 20x7, and the first two interest payments on September 1, 20x7, and March 1, 20x8. Use the straight-line method and ignore year-end accruals.

LO3, LO5   **Effective Interest Method**

E 11. The Stream Toy Company sold $250,000 of 9.5 percent, 20-year bonds on April 1, 20x6, at 106. The semiannual interest payment dates are March 31 and September 30. The market interest rate is 8.9 percent. The company's fiscal year ends September 30. Use the effective interest method to calculate the amortization.

1. With regard to the bond issue on April 1, 20x6:

    a. How much cash is received?
    b. How much is Bonds Payable?
    c. What is the difference between **a** and **b** called and how much is it?

2. With regard to the bond interest payment on September 30, 20x6:

    a. How much cash is paid in interest?
    b. How much is the amortization?
    c. How much is interest expense?

3. With regard to the bond interest payment on March 31, 20x7:

    a. How much cash is paid in interest?
    b. How much is the amortization?
    c. How much is interest expense?

LO3, LO5   **Effective Interest Method**

E 12. On March 1, 20x7, the Van Wurt Corporation issued $600,000 of 10 percent, five-year bonds. The semiannual interest payment dates are February 28 and August 31. Because the market rate for similar investments was 11 percent, the bonds had to be issued at a discount. The discount on the issuance of the bonds was $24,335. The company's fiscal year ends February 28. Prepare entries in journal form to record the bond issue on March 1, 20x7, the payment of interest, and the amortization of the discount on August 31, 20x7 and on February 28, 20x8. Use the effective interest method. (Round answers to the nearest dollar.)

LO6   **Bond Retirement**

E 13. The Perusko Corporation has outstanding $800,000 of 8 percent bonds callable at 104. On September 1, immediately after recording the payment of the semiannual interest and the amortization of the discount, the unamortized bond discount equaled $21,000. On that date, $480,000 of the bonds was called and retired.

1. How much cash must be paid to retire the bonds?
2. Is there a gain or loss on retirement, and if so, how much is it?

LO6   **Bond Conversion**

E 14. The Manco Corporation has $800,000 of 6 percent bonds outstanding. There is $40,000 of unamortized discount remaining on these bonds after the July 1, 20x8, semiannual interest payment. The bonds are convertible at the rate of 40 shares of $5 par value common stock for each $2,000 bond. On July 1, 20x8, bondholders presented $600,000 of the bonds for conversion.

1. Is there a gain or loss on conversion, and if so, how much is it?
2. How many shares of common stock are issued in exchange for the bonds?
3. In dollar amounts, how does this transaction affect the total liabilities and the total stockholders' equity of the company? In your answer, show the effects on four accounts.

LO5, SO7   **Effective Interest Method and Interest Accrual**

E 15. The long-term debt section of the Panza Corporation's balance sheet at the end of its fiscal year, December 31, 20x7, is as follows:

Long-term liabilities		
Bonds payable—8%, interest payable		
1/1 and 7/1, due 12/31/16	$500,000	
Less unamortized bond discount	40,000	$460,000

Prepare entries in journal form relevant to the interest payments on July 1, 20x7, December 31, 20x7, and January 1, 20x8. Assume a market interest rate of 10 percent.

LO4, LO6   **Time Value of Money and Early Extinguishment of Debt**

E 16. Charles, Inc., has a $700,000, 8 percent bond issue that was issued a number of years ago at face value. There are now ten years left on the bond issue, and the market interest rate is 16 percent. Interest is paid semi-annually. The company purchases the bonds on the open market at the calculated current market value and retires the bonds.

1. Using present value tables, calculate the current market value of the bond issue.
2. Is there a gain or loss on retirement of bonds, and if so, how much is it?

LO3, SO7   **Bond Issue on and Between Interest Dates**

E 17. Agard Techtronics, Inc., is authorized to issue $3,600,000 in bonds on June 1. The bonds carry a face interest rate of 9 percent, which is to be paid on June 1 and December 1. Prepare entries in journal form for the issue of the bonds by Agard Techtronics, Inc., under the assumptions that (a) the bonds are issued on September 1 at 100 and (b) the bonds are issued on June 1 at 105.

SO7   **Bond Issue Between Interest Dates**

E 18. Plaka Corporation sold $800,000 of 12 percent, ten-year bonds at face value on September 1, 20xx. The issue date of the bonds was May 1, 20xx.

1. Record the sale of the bonds on September 1 and the first semiannual interest payment on November 1, 20xx.
2. The company's fiscal year ends on December 31, and this is its only bond issue. What is the bond interest expense for the year ended December 31, 20xx?

LO3, LO5, SO7   **Year-End Accrual of Bond Interest**

E 19. Chaney Corporation issued $2,000,000 of 9 percent bonds on October 1, 20x7, at 96. The bonds are dated October 1 and pay interest semiannually. The market interest rate is 10 percent, and Chaney's fiscal year ends on December 31. Prepare the entries to record the issuance of the bonds, the accrual of the interest on December 31, 20x7, and the first semiannual interest payment on April 1, 20x8. Assume the company uses the effective interest method to amortize the bond discount.

Problems

LO1, LO2, LO3   **Bond Terminology**

P 1. Listed below are common terms associated with bonds:

a. Bond certificate	j. Coupon bonds
b. Bond issue	k. Callable bonds
c. Bond indenture	l. Convertible bonds
d. Unsecured bonds	m. Face interest rate
e. Debenture bonds	n. Market interest rate
f. Secured bonds	o. Effective interest rate
g. Term bonds	p. Bond premium
h. Serial bonds	q. Bond discount
i. Registered bonds	

Required

1. For each of the following statements, identify the category above with which it is associated. (If two statements apply, choose the category with which it is most closely associated.)

   1. Occurs when bonds are sold at more than face value
   2. Rate of interest that will vary depending on economic conditions
   3. Bonds that may be exchanged for common stock
   4. Bonds that are not registered
   5. A bond issue in which all bonds are due on the same date
   6. Occurs when bonds are sold at less than face value
   7. Rate of interest that will be paid regardless of market conditions
   8. Bonds that may be retired at management's option
   9. A document that is evidence of a company's debt
   10. Same as market rate of interest
   11. Bonds for which the company knows who owns them
   12. A bond issue for which bonds are due at different dates
   13. The total value of bonds issued at one time
   14. Bonds whose payment involves a pledge of certain assets
   15. Same as debenture bonds
   16. Contains the terms of the bond issue
   17. Bonds issued on the general credit of the company

2. **User Insight:** What effect will a decrease in interest rates below the face interest rate and before a bond is issued have on the cash received from

the bond issue? What effect will the decrease have on interest expense? What effect will the decrease have on the amount of cash paid for interest?

LO3, LO5, LO6   **Bond Basics—Straight-line Method, Retirement, and Conversion**

P 2. Abel Corporation has $10,000,000 of 10.5 percent, 20-year bonds dated June 1, 20x7, with interest payment dates of May 31 and November 30. After ten years the bonds are callable at 104, and each $1,000 bond is convertible into 25 shares of $20 par value common stock. The company's fiscal year ends on December 31. It uses the straight-line method to amortize bond premiums or discounts.

Required

1. Assume the bonds are issued at 103 on June 1, 20x7.
    a. How much cash is received?
    b. How much is Bonds Payable?
    c. What is the difference between **a** and **b** called and how much is it?
    d. With regard to the bond interest payment on November 30, 20x7:
        (1) How much cash is paid in interest?
        (2) How much is the amortization?
        (3) How much is interest expense?
2. Assume the bonds are issued at 97 on June 1, 20x7.
    a. How much cash is received?
    b. How much is Bonds Payable?
    c. What is the difference between **a** and **b** called and how much is it?
    d. With regard to the bond interest payment on November 30, 20x7:
        (1) How much cash is paid in interest?
        (2) How much is the amortization?
        (3) How much is interest expense?
3. Assume the issue price in requirement **1** and that the bonds are called and retired ten years later.
    a. How much cash will have to be paid to retire the bonds?
    b. Is there a gain or loss on the retirement, and if so, how much is it?
4. Assume the issue price in requirement **2** and that the bonds are converted to common stock ten years later.
    a. Is there a gain or loss on the conversion, and if so, how much is it?
    b. How many shares of common stock are issued in exchange for the bonds?
    c. In dollar amounts, how does this transaction affect the total liabilities and the total stockholders' equity of the company? In your answer, show the effects on four accounts.
5. **User Insight:** Assume that after ten years, market interest rates have dropped significantly and that the price on the company's common stock has risen significantly. Also assume that management wants to improve its credit rating by reducing its debt to equity ratio and that it needs what cash it has for expansion. Which approach would management prefer—the approach and result in requirement **3** or **4**? Explain your answer. What would be a disadvantage of the approach you chose?

LO3, LO5   **Effective Interest Method**

P 3. Julio Corporation has $8,000,000 of 9.5 percent, 25-year bonds dated March 1, 20x7, with interest payable on February 28 and August 31. The company's fiscal year end is February 28. It uses the effective interest method to amortize bond premiums or discounts. (Round amounts to the nearest dollar.)

Required

1. Assume the bonds are issued at 102.5 on March 1, 20x7, to yield an effective interest rate of 9.2 percent. Prepare entries in journal form for March 1, 20x7, August 31, 20x7, and February 28, 20x8.
2. Assume the bonds are issued at 97.5 on March 1, 2007, to yield an effective interest rate of 9.8 percent. Prepare entries in journal form for March 1, 20x7, August 31, 20x7, and February 28, 20x8.
3. **User Insight:** Explain the role that market interest rates play in causing a premium in requirement **1** and a discount in requirement **2**.

LO3, LO5, SO7   **Bonds Issued at a Discount and a Premium—Effective Interest Method**

P 4. Waxman Corporation issued bonds twice during 20x7. A summary of the transactions involving the bonds follows.

20x7

Jan.   1   Issued $6,000,000 of 9.9 percent, ten-year bonds dated January 1, 20x7, with interest payable on June 30 and December 31. The bonds were sold at 102.6, resulting in an effective interest rate of 9.4 percent.

Mar. 1   Issued $4,000,000 of 9.2 percent, ten-year bonds dated March 1, 20x7, with interest payable March 1 and September 1. The bonds were sold at 98.2, resulting in an effective interest rate of 9.5 percent.

June 30   Paid semiannual interest on the January 1 issue and amortized the premium, using the effective interest method.

Sept. 1   Paid semiannual interest on the March 1 issue and amortized the discount, using the effective interest method.

Dec. 31   Paid semiannual interest on the January 1 issue and amortized the premium, using the effective interest method.

        31   Made an end-of-year adjusting entry to accrue interest on the March 1 issue and to amortize two-thirds of the discount applicable to the second interest period.

20x8

Mar. 1   Paid semiannual interest on the March 1 issue and amortized the remainder of the discount applicable to the second interest period.

Required

1. Prepare entries in journal form to record the bond transactions. (Round amounts to the nearest dollar.)
2. **User Insight:** Describe the effect on profitability and liquidity by answering the following questions.

   a. What is the total interest expense in 20x7 for each of the bond issues?
   b. What is the total cash paid in 20x7 for each of the bond issues?
   c. What differences, if any, do you observe and how do you explain them?

LO3, LO5, LO6   **Bond Interest and Amortization Table, Retirements, and Conversions**

P 5. In 20x6, the Fender Corporation was authorized to issue $60,000,000 of six-year unsecured bonds. The bonds carried a face interest rate of 9 percent, payable semiannually on June 30 and December 31. The bonds were callable at 105 any time after June 30, 20x9. All of the bonds were issued on July 1, 20x6 at 95.568, a price yielding an effective interest rate of 10 percent. On July 1, 20x9, the company called and retired half the outstanding bonds.

Required

1. Prepare a table similar to Table 1 to show the interest and amortization of the bond discount for 12 interest payment periods, using the effective interest method. (Round results to the nearest dollar.)
2. Calculate the amount of loss on early retirement of one-half of the bonds on July 1, 20x9.
3. Assume the bonds are also convertible at the rate of 25 shares of $10 par value common stock for each $1,000 bond and that the other half of the bonds were converted on July 1, 20x9. Calculate the amounts at which Common Stock and Additional Paid-in Capital would be increased as a result of this transaction.
4. **User Insight:** Under the effective interest method used in this problem, does interest expense exceed cash paid for interest or is it less? Explain your answer. Also explain why interest expense differs for each six-month period. What role does materiality play in the choice of the effective interest method?

Alternate Problems

LO3, LO5, LO6

Bond Basics—Straight-Line Method, Retirement and Conversion

P 6. Bassi Corporation has $8,000,000 of 9.5 percent, 25-year bonds dated May 1, 20x6, with interest payable on April 30 and October 31. The company's fiscal year ends on December 31, and it uses the straight-line method to amortize bond premiums or discounts. The bonds are callable after ten years at 103 or convertible into 40 shares of $10 par value common stock.

Required

1. Assume the bonds are issued at 103.5 on May 1, 20x6.
   a. How much cash is received?
   b. How much is Bonds Payable?
   c. What is the difference between **a** and **b** called and how much is it?
   d. With regard to the bond interest payment on October 31, 20x6:
      (1) How much cash is paid in interest?
      (2) How much is the amortization?
      (3) How much is interest expense?
2. Assume the bonds are issued at 96.5 on May 1, 20x6.
   a. How much cash is received?
   b. How much is Bonds Payable?
   c. What is the difference between **a** and **b** called and how much is it?
   d. With regard to the bond interest payment on October 31, 20x6:
      (1) How much cash is paid in interest?
      (2) How much is the amortization?
      (3) How much is interest expense?
3. Assume the issue price in requirement **1** and that the bonds are called and retired ten years later.
   a. How much cash will have to be paid to retire the bonds?
   b. Is there a gain or loss on the retirement, and if so, how much is it?
4. Assume the issue price in requirement **2** and that the bonds are converted to common stock ten years later.

a. Is there a gain or loss on conversion, and if so, how much is it?

b. How many shares of common stock are issued in exchange for the bonds?

c. In dollar amounts, how does this transaction affect the total liabilities and the total stockholders' equity of the company? In your answer, show the effects on four accounts.

5. **User Insight:** Assume that after ten years market interest rates have dropped significantly and that the price of the company's common stock has risen significantly. Also assume that management wants to improve its credit rating by reducing its debt to equity ratio and that it needs what cash it currently has for expansion. Would management prefer the approach and result in requirement **3** or **4**? Explain your answer. What would be a disadvantage of the approach you chose?

LO3, LO5 **Bond Transactions—Effective Interest Method**

P 7. Khan Corporation has $20,000,000 of 10.5 percent, 20-year bonds dated June 1, 20x7 with interest payment dates of May 31 and November 30. The company's fiscal year ends November 30. It uses the effective interest method to amortize bond premiums or discounts.

Required

1. Assume the bonds are issued at 103 on June 1 to yield an effective interest rate of 10.1 percent. Prepare entries in journal form for June 1, 20x7, November 30, 20x7, and May 31, 20x8. (Round amounts to the nearest dollar.)

2. Assume the bonds are issued at 97 on June 1 to yield an effective interest rate of 10.9 percent. Prepare entries in journal form for June 1, 20x7, November 30, 20x7, and May 31, 20x8. (Round amounts to the nearest dollar.)

3. **User Insight:** Explain the role that market interest rates play in causing a premium in requirement **1** and a discount in requirement **2**.

LO3, LO5, SO7 **Bonds Issued at a Discount and a Premium—Effective Interest Method**

P 8. Pakesh Corporation issued bonds twice during 20x7. The transactions were as follows:

20x7

Jan.   1   Issued $2,000,000 of 9.2 percent, ten-year bonds dated January 1, 20x7, with interest payable on June 30 and December 31. The bonds were sold at 98.1, resulting in an effective interest rate of 9.5 percent.

Apr.   1   Issued $4,000,000 of 9.8 percent, ten-year bonds dated April 1, 20x7, with interest payable on March 31 and September 30. The bonds were sold at 101, resulting in an effective interest rate of 9.5 percent.

June   30   Paid semiannual interest on the January 1 issue and amortized the discount, using the effective interest method.

Sept. 30   Paid semiannual interest on the April 1 issue and amortized the premium, using the effective interest method.

Dec.   31   Paid semiannual interest on the January 1 issue and amortized the discount, using the effective interest method.

           31   Made an end-of-year adjusting entry to accrue interest on the April 1 issue and to amortize half the premium applicable to the second interest period.

20x8

Mar. 31 Paid semiannual interest on the April 1 issue and amortized the premium applicable to the second half of the second interest period.

Required

1. Prepare entries in journal form to record the bond transactions. (Round amounts to the nearest dollar.)

2. **User Insight:** Describe the effect of the above transactions on profitability and liquidity by answering the following questions.

   a. What is the total interest expense in 20x7 for each of the bond issues?
   b. What is the total cash paid in 20x7 for each of the bond issues?
   c. What differences, if any, do you observe and how do you explain them?

ENHANCING Your Knowledge, Skills, and Critical Thinking

Conceptual Understanding Cases

LO1   **Effect of Long-Term Leases**

C1. Many companies use long-term leases to finance long-term assets. Although these leases are similar to mortgage payments, they are structured in such a way that they qualify as operating leases. As a result, the lease commitments do not appear on the companies' balance sheets. In a recent year, **Continental Airlines** had lease commitments of $324 million, and **Heinz** had lease commitments of $220 million.[12]

What effect do these types of leases have on the balance sheet? Why would the use of these long-term leases make a company's debt to equity ratio, interest coverage ratio, and free cash flow look better than they really are? What is a capital lease? How does the application of capital lease accounting provide insight into a company's financial health?

LO2, LO6   **Bond Issue**

C2. **Eastman Kodak**, the photography company, issued a $1 billion bond issue. Even though the company's credit rating was low, the bond issue was well received by the investment community because the company offered attractive terms. The offering comprised $500 million of 10-year unsecured notes and $500 million of 30-year convertible bonds. The convertibles were callable after seven years and would be convertible into common stock about 40 to 45 percent higher than the current price.[13]

What are unsecured notes? Why would they carry a relatively high interest rate? What are convertible securities? Why are they good for the investor and for the company? Why would they carry a relatively low interest rate? What does *callable* mean? What advantage does this feature give the company?

LO2, LO3   **Bond Interest Rates and Market Prices**

C3. **Safeway Inc**. is one of the largest food and drug retailers in North America. Among its long-term liabilities was a bond due in 2004 that carried a face interest rate of 9.65 percent.[14] Recently, this bond sold on the New York Stock Exchange at 108⅝. Did this bond sell at a discount or a premium? Assuming the bond was originally issued at face value, did interest rates rise or decline after the date of issue? Would you have expected the market rate of interest on this bond to be more or less than 9.65 percent? Did the current market price affect either the amount that the company paid in semiannual interest or the amount of interest expense for the same period? Explain your answers.

Interpreting Financial Reports

LO1 **Debt Repayment**

C 4. During economic recessions, occupancy rates of hotels generally decline, and as a result, the hotels are forced to reduce their room prices. The impact on a hotel's cash flows may be such that it is unable to pay its debts when they come due.

Some years ago, the Hospitality Research Group studied the financial statements of 3,300 hotels. It found that 16 percent of hotels were unable to generate enough cash from operations to make debt repayments in 2000. The study estimated that this figure would increase to 20.9 percent in 2001 and 36.5 percent in 2002.[15] What alternative sources of cash might be available to hotels whose cash flows from operations are inadequate to cover debt repayments?

LO2 **Characteristics of Convertible Debt**

C 5. **Amazon.com, Inc.,** gained renown as an online marketplace for books, records, and other products. Although the increase in its stock price was initially meteoric, only recently has the company begun to earn a profit. To support its enormous growth, Amazon.com issued $1,250,000,000 in 4¾ percent convertible notes due in 2009 at face value. Interest is payable on February 1 and August 1. The notes are convertible into common stock at a price of $78 per share, which at the time of issue was 27 percent above the market price of $61.50. The market value of Amazon.com's common stock has been quite volatile, from $34 to $57 in 2004.[16]

What reasons can you suggest for Amazon.com's management choosing notes that are convertible into common stock rather than simply issuing nonconvertible notes or issuing common stock directly? Are there any disadvantages to this approach? If the price of the company's common stock goes to $100 per share, what would be the total theoretical value of the notes? If the holders of the notes were to elect to convert the notes into common stock, what would be the effect on the company's debt to equity ratio, and what would be the effect on the percentage ownership of the company by other stockholders?

Decision Analysis Using Excel

LO1, LO2 **Issuance of Long-Term Bonds Versus Leasing**

C 6. The Weiss Chemical Corporation plans to build or lease a new plant that will produce liquid fertilizer for the agricultural market. The plant is expected to cost $800,000,000 and will be located in the southwestern United States. The company's chief financial officer, Sharon Weiss, has spent the last several weeks studying different means of financing the plant. Following her talks with bankers and other financiers, she has decided that there are two basic choices: the plant can be financed through the issuance of a long-term bond or through a long-term lease. Details for the two options are as follows:

1. Issue $800,000,000 of 25-year, 16 percent bonds secured by the new plant. Interest on the bonds would be payable semiannually.

2. Sign a 25-year lease for an existing plant calling for lease payments of $65,400,000 on a semiannual basis.

Weiss wants to know what effect each choice would have on the company's financial statements. She estimates that the useful life of the plant is 25 years, at which time the plant is expected to have an estimated residual value of $80,000,000.

Weiss is planning a meeting to discuss the alternatives. Write a short memorandum to her identifying the issues that should be considered at this meeting. (**Note:** You are not asked to make any calculations, discuss the factors, or recommend an action.)

Annual Report Case: CVS Corporation

LO1 **Business Practice, Long-Term Debt, Leases, and Pensions**

C 7. To answer the following questions, refer to the financial statements and the notes to the financial statements in **CVS Corporation's** annual report in the Supplement to Chapter 1:

1. Is it the practice of CVS to own or lease most of its buildings?
2. Does CVS lease property predominantly under capital leases or under operating leases? How much was rental expense for operating leases in 2004?
3. Does CVS have a defined benefit pension plan? Does it offer postretirement benefits?

Comparison Case: CVS Versus Southwest

LO1 **Use of Debt Financing**

C 8. Refer to the annual report of **CVS Corporation** and the financial statements of **Southwest Airlines Co.** in the Supplement to Chapter 1. Calculate the debt to equity ratio and the interest coverage ratio for both companies' two most recent years. Find the note to the financial statements that contains information on leases and lease commitments by CVS. Southwest's lease expenses were $386 million and $403 million in 2003 and 2004, respectively, and total lease commitments for future years were $2,677 million. What effect do the total lease commitments and lease expense have on your assessment of the ratios you calculated? Evaluate and comment on the relative performance of the two companies with regard to debt financing. Which company has more risk of not being able to meet its interest obligations? How does leasing affect the analysis? Explain.

Ethical Dilemma Case

LO2 **Bond Indenture and Ethical Reporting**

C 9. CellWorks Technology, Inc., a biotech company, has a $24,000,000 bond issue outstanding. The bond indenture has several restrictive provisions, including requirements that current assets exceed current liabilities by a ratio of 2 to 1 and that income before income taxes exceed the annual interest on the bonds by a ratio of 3 to 1. If those requirements are not met, the bondholders can force the company into bankruptcy. The company is still awaiting Food and Drug Administration (FDA) approval of its new product, CMZ-12, a cancer treatment drug. Management has been counting on sales of CMZ-12 this year to meet the provisions of the bond indenture. As the end of the fiscal year approaches, the company does not have sufficient current assets or income before income taxes to meet the requirements. Roger Landon, the chief financial officer, proposes, "Since we can assume that FDA approval will occur early next year, I suggest we book sales and receivables from our major customers now in anticipation of next year's sales. This action will increase our current assets and our income before income taxes. It is essential that we do this to save the company. Look at all the people who will be hurt if we don't do it."

Is Landon's proposal acceptable accounting? Is it ethical? Who could be harmed by it? What steps might management take?

Internet Case

LO2 **Bond Rating Changes**

C 10. During economic or industry recessions, it is common to see downward revisions of bond ratings. Access Standard & Poor's list of companies with lowered bond ratings and identify three whose names you recognize. Based on your general knowledge of these companies, give reasons that you believe contributed to the downgrade of the ratings.

Group Activity Case

LO4 **Nature of Zero Coupon Notes**

C 11. The *Wall Street Journal* reported, "Financially ailing **Trans World Airlines** has renegotiated its agreement to sell its 40 landing and takeoff slots and three gates at O'Hare International Airport to **American Airlines.**"[17] Instead of receiving a lump-sum cash payment in the amount of $162.5 million, TWA elected to receive a zero coupon note from American that would be paid off in monthly installments over a 20-year period. Since the 240 monthly payments totaled $500 million, TWA placed a value of $500 million on the note and indicated that the bankruptcy court would not have accepted the lower lump-sum cash payment.[18]

Divide into groups to discuss the following questions:

1. How does this zero coupon note differ from the zero coupon bonds that were described earlier in this chapter?

2. How do you explain the difference between the $162.5 million cash payment and the $500 million note?

3. Do you think TWA was right in placing a $500 million price on the sale?

Business Communication Case

LO1 **Comparison of Interest Coverage**

C 12. Japanese companies have historically relied more on debt financing and are more highly leveraged than U.S. companies. For instance, **NEC Corporation** and **Sanyo Electric Co.**, two large Japanese electronics companies, had debt to equity ratios of about 4.7 and 4.2, respectively, in 2004.[19] From the selected data from the companies' annual reports shown in the table that follows (in millions of yen), compute the interest coverage ratios for the two companies for the two years.

	NEC		Sanyo	
	2004	**2003**	**2004**	**2003**
Interest expense	27,510	30,218	14,868	18,463
Income before income taxes	160,546	61,496	45,992	4,040

Assume you are a financial analyst. Write a one-page memorandum that addresses the riskiness of these two companies and the trends they show. Include in your memorandum a summary of the advantages and disadvantages of a debt-laden capital structure.

Contributed Capital

In the last chapter, we focused on long-term *debt* financing. Here, we focus on long-term *equity* financing—that is, on the capital that stockholders contribute to a corporation. The issues involved in equity financing—including the type of stock a corporation issues, the dividends that it pays, and the treasury stock that it purchases—can significantly affect return on equity and other measures of profitability on which management's compensation is based. Thus, as with the management issues involved in long-term debt financing, ethics is a major concern. Management's decisions must be based not on personal gain, but on the value created for the corporation's owners.

LEARNING OBJECTIVES

Making a Statement

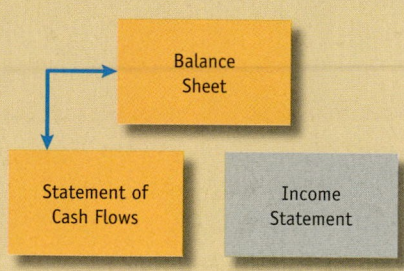

Stock transactions only impact the balance sheet and the statement of cash flows.

LO1 Identify and explain the management issues related to contributed capital.

LO2 Identify the components of stockholders' equity.

LO3 Identify the characteristics of preferred stock.

LO4 Account for the issuance of stock for cash and other assets.

LO5 Account for treasury stock.

GOOGLE, INC.

- Why did Google's management choose to issue common stock to satisfy its needs for new capital?

- What are some of the advantages and disadvantages of this approach to financing a business?

- What measures should an investor use in evaluating management's performance?

When a company issues stock to the public for the first time, it is called an **initial public offering (IPO)**. There are many initial public offerings in any given year, but when **Google**, the popular Internet search engine company, went to market with its IPO in August 2004, it created a national sensation for several reasons. First, it was the largest IPO by an Internet company after the tech-bust in 2001 and 2002. Second, Google provides a very well known and widely used search service. Third, rather than allocating shares of stock to a few insiders, Google used an auction system that allowed anyone to participate in its IPO. In the end, the company issued approximately 22.5 million shares at $85 per share for a total of $1.9 billion. Those who were fortunate enough to get shares saw the price per share soar to $135 in a few days and reach $300 per share in 2005. Google's Financial Highlights show the effect of the IPO and other related stock transactions on stockholders' equity.[1]

GOOGLE'S FINANCIAL HIGHLIGHTS
(In thousands)

	Sept. 30 2004	June 30 2004	Dec. 31 2003
Stockholders' equity			
Preferred stock	$ —	$ 79,860	$ 44,346
Common stock	273	165	161
Additional paid-in capital	2,497,299	956,882	725,219
Retained earnings	386,371	334,388	191,352
Other items	(294,920)	(354,596)	(372,308)
Total stockholders' equity	$2,589,023	$1,016,699	$588,770
Total assets	$2,888,518	$1,328,022	$871,458

Management Issues Related to Contributed Capital

LO1   Identify and explain the management issues related to contributed capital.

In Chapter 1, we defined a *corporation* as a business unit chartered by the state and legally separate from its owners—that is, its stockholders. *Contributed capital*, which refers to stockholders' investments in a corporation, is a major means of financing a corporation. Managing contributed capital requires an understanding of the advantages and disadvantages of the corporate form of business and of the issues involved in equity financing. It also requires familiarity with dividend policies, with how to use return on equity to evaluate performance, and with stock option plans.

The Corporate Form of Business

The corporate form of business is well suited to today's trends toward large organizations, international trade, and professional management. Although fewer in number than sole proprietorships and partnerships, corporations dominate the U.S. economy in part because of their ability to raise large amounts of capital. Figure 1 shows the amount and sources of capital that corporations have raised in recent years. As you can see, the amount increased dramatically after 1995. In 2002, the amount of new corporate capital was $2,581 billion. Of this amount, $2,428 billion, or 94 percent, came from new bond issues; $116 billion, or 4.5 percent, came from new common stock issues; and $38 billion, or 1.5 percent, came from preferred stock issues.

Advantages of Incorporation
Managers of a corporation must be familiar with the advantages and disadvantages of this form of business. Some of the advantages are as follows:

- **Separate Legal Entity**   As a separate legal entity, a corporation can buy and sell property, sue other parties, enter into contracts, hire and fire employees, and be taxed.

- **Limited Liability**   Because a corporation is a legal entity, separate from its owners, its creditors can satisfy their claims only against the assets of the corporation, not against the personal property of the corporation's owners. Because the owners are not responsible for the corporation's debts, their liability is limited to the amount of their investment. In contrast, the personal property of sole proprietors and partners generally is available to creditors.

- **Ease of Capital Generation**   It is fairly easy for a corporation to raise capital because shares of ownership in the business are available to a great number of potential investors for a small amount of money. As a result, a single corporation can have many owners.

- **Ease of Transfer of Ownership**   A **share of stock**, a unit of ownership in a corporation, is easily transferable. A stockholder can normally buy and sell shares without affecting the corporation's activities or needing the approval of other owners.

- **Lack of Mutual Agency**   Mutual agency is not a characteristic of the corporate form of business. If a stockholder tries to enter into a contract for the corporation, the corporation is not bound by the contract. But in a partnership, because of mutual agency, all the partners can be bound by one partner's actions.

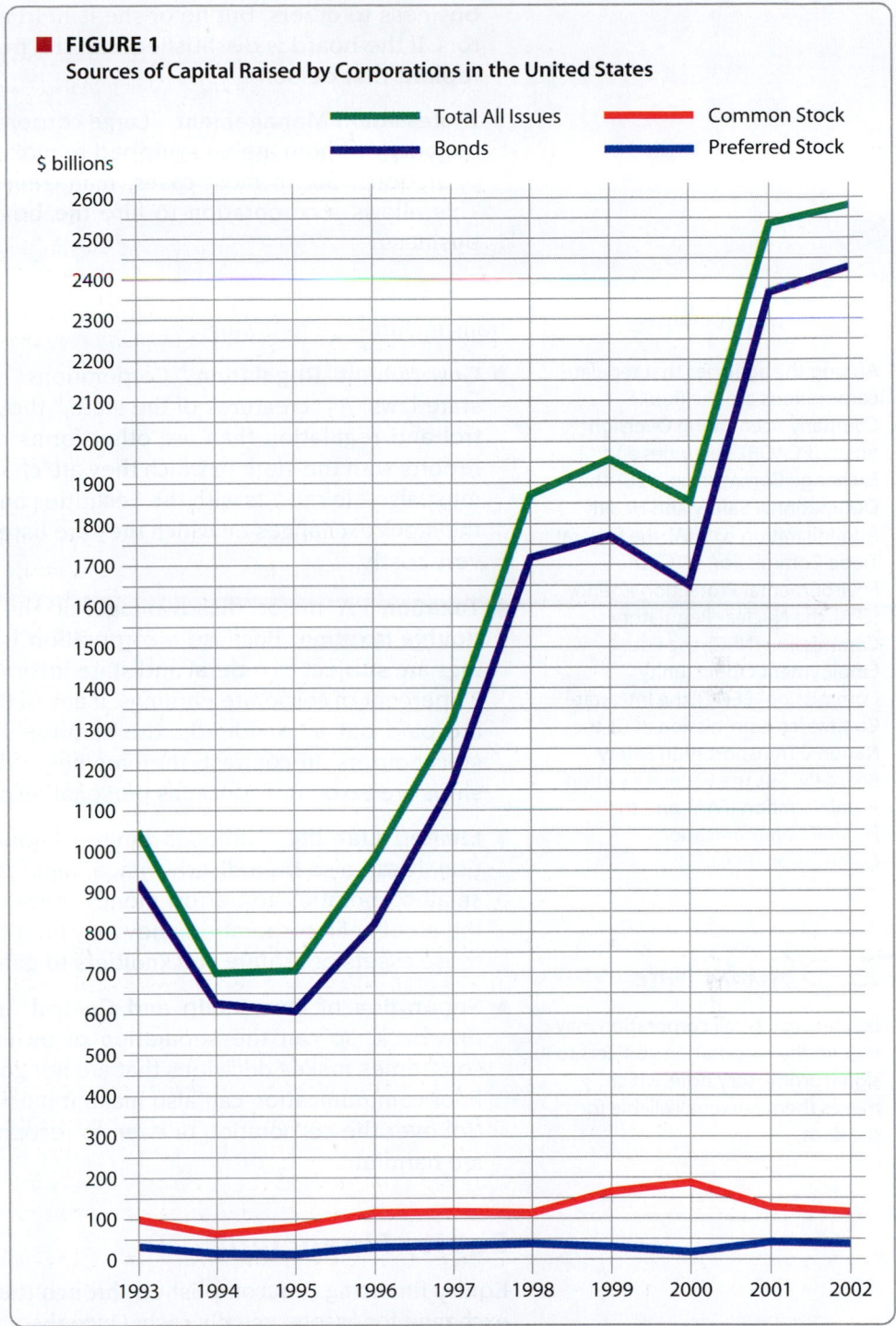

FIGURE 1

Sources of Capital Raised by Corporations in the United States

Source: "Sources of Capital Raised by Corporations in the United States" from *Securities Industry Yearbook 2003–2004*. Reprinted by permission of Securities Industry Association.

◆ **Continuous Existence**   Because a corporation is a separate legal entity, an owner's death, incapacity, or withdrawal does not affect the life of the corporation. A corporation's life is set by its charter and regulated by state laws.

◆ **Centralized Authority and Responsibility**   The board of directors represents the stockholders and delegates the responsibility and authority for the day-to-day operation of the corporation to a single person, usually the president. Operating power is not divided among the many owners of the business. The president may delegate authority over certain segments of the business to others, but he or she is held accountable to the board of directors. If the board is dissatisfied with the performance of the president, it can replace that person.

▸ **Professional Management**   Large corporations have many owners, the vast majority of whom are unequipped to make timely decisions about business operations. So, in most cases, management and ownership are separate. This allows a corporation to hire the best talent available to manage the business.

Disadvantages of Incorporation   The disadvantages of corporations include the following:

▸ **Government Regulation**   Corporations must meet the requirements of state laws. As "creatures of the state," they are subject to greater state control and regulation than are other forms of business. They must file many reports with the state in which they are chartered. Publicly held corporations must also file reports with the Securities and Exchange Commission and with the stock exchanges on which they are listed. Meeting these requirements is very costly.

▸ **Taxation**   A major disadvantage of the corporate form of business is **double taxation**. Because a corporation is a separate legal entity, its earnings are subject to federal and state income taxes, which may be as much as 35 percent of corporate earnings. If any of the corporation's after-tax earnings are paid out as dividends, the earnings are taxed again as income to the stockholders. In contrast, the earnings of sole proprietorships and partnerships are taxed only once, as personal income to the owners.

▸ **Limited Liability**   Although limited liability is an advantage of incorporation, it can also be a disadvantage. Limited liability restricts the ability of a small corporation to borrow money. Because creditors can lay claim only to the assets of a corporation, they may limit their loans to the level secured by those assets or require stockholders to guarantee the loans personally.

▸ **Separation of Ownership and Control**   Just as limited liability can be a drawback, so can the separation of ownership and control. Management sometimes makes decisions that are not good for the corporation as a whole. Poor communication can also make it hard for stockholders to exercise control over the corporation or even to recognize that management's decisions are harmful.

Equity Financing

Equity financing is accomplished through the issuance of stock to investors in exchange for assets, usually cash. Once the stock has been issued to them, the stockholders can transfer their ownership at will. When they do, they must sign their **stock certificates**, documents showing the number of shares that they own, and send them to the corporation's secretary. In large corporations that are listed on the stock exchanges, stockholders' records are hard to maintain. Such companies can have millions of shares of stock, thousands of which change ownership every day. Therefore, they often appoint independent registrars and transfer agents (usually banks and trust companies) to help perform the secretary's duties. The outside agents are responsible for transferring the corporation's stock, maintaining stockholders' records, preparing a list of stockholders for stockholders' meetings, and paying dividends.

Par value and *legal capital* are important terms in equity financing:

Study Note

Among the agencies that regulate corporations are the Public Company Accounting Oversight Board (PCAOB), Securities and Exchange Commission (SEC), the Occupational Safety and Health Administration (OSHA), the Federal Trade Commission (FTC), the Environmental Protection Agency (EPA), the Nuclear Regulatory Commission (NRC), the Equal Employment Opportunity Commission (EEOC), the Interstate Commerce Commission (ICC), the National Transportation Safety Board (NTSB), the Federal Aviation Administration (FAA), and the Federal Communications Commission (FCC).

Study Note

Lenders to a small corporation may require the corporation's officers to sign a promissory note, which makes them personally liable for the debt.

▶ **Par value** is an arbitrary amount assigned to each share of stock. It must be recorded in the capital stock accounts, and it constitutes a corporation's legal capital.

▶ **Legal capital** is the number of shares issued times the par value. It is the minimum amount that a corporation can report as contributed capital.

Par value usually bears little if any relationship to the market value or book value of the shares. For example, although **Google's** stock initially sold for $85 per share and the market value is now much higher, its par value per share is only $.001. Google's legal capital is only about $273,000 (273 million shares × $.001) even though the total market value of its shares exceeds $82 billion.

To help with its initial public offering (IPO), a corporation often uses an **underwriter**—an intermediary between the corporation and the investing public. For a fee—usually less than 1 percent of the selling price—the underwriter guarantees the sale of the stock. The corporation records the amount of the net proceeds of the offering—what the public paid less the underwriter's fees, legal and printing expenses, and any other direct costs of the offering—in its capital stock and additional paid-in capital accounts. Because of the size of its IPO, Google used a group of investment banks headed by two well-known investment bankers, **Morgan Stanley** and **Credit Suisse First Boston**.

The costs of forming a corporation are called **start-up and organization costs**. These costs, which are incurred before a corporation begins operations, include state incorporation fees and attorneys' fees for drawing up the articles of incorporation. They also include the cost of printing stock certificates, accountants' fees for registering the firm's initial stock, and other expenditures necessary for the formation of the corporation. Because Google's IPO was so large, the fees of the lawyers, accountants, and underwriters who helped arrange the IPO amounted to millions of dollars.

Theoretically, start-up and organization costs benefit the entire life of a corporation. For that reason, a case can be made for recording them as intangible assets and amortizing them over the life of the corporation. However, a corporation's life normally is not known, so accountants expense start-up and organization costs as they are incurred.

Study Note

Start-up and organization costs are expensed when incurred.

Advantages of Equity Financing
Financing a business by issuing common stock has several advantages:

▶ It is less risky than financing with bonds because a company does not pay dividends on common stock unless the board of directors decides to pay them. In contrast, if a company does not pay interest on bonds, it can be forced into bankruptcy.

▶ When a company does not pay a cash dividend, it can plow the cash generated by profitable operations back into the company's operations. **Google**, for instance, does not currently pay any dividends, and its issuance of common stock provides it with funds for expansion.

▶ A company can use the proceeds of a common stock issue to maintain or improve its debt to equity ratio.

Disadvantages of Equity Financing
Issuing common stock also has certain disadvantages:

▶ Unlike interest on bonds, dividends paid on stock are not tax-deductible.

▶ When a corporation issues more stock, it dilutes its ownership. Thus, the current stockholders must yield some control to the new stockholders.

Dividend Policies

A **dividend** is a distribution among stockholders of the assets that a corporation's earnings have generated. Stockholders receive these assets, usually cash, in proportion to the number of shares they own. A corporation's board of directors has sole authority to declare dividends, but senior managers, who usually serve as members of the board, influence dividend policies. Receiving dividends is one of two ways in which stockholders can earn a return on their investment in a corporation. The other way is to sell their shares for more than they paid for them.

Although a corporation may have sufficient cash and retained earnings to pay a dividend, its board of directors may not declare one for several reasons. The corporation may need the cash for expansion; it may want to improve its overall financial position by liquidating debt; or it may be facing major uncertainties, such as a pending lawsuit or strike or a projected decline in the economy, which makes it prudent to preserve resources.

A corporation pays dividends quarterly, semiannually, annually, or at other times declared by its board of directors. Most states do not allow a corporation to declare a dividend that exceeds its retained earnings. When a corporation does declare a dividend that exceeds retained earnings, it is, in essence, returning to the stockholders part of their contributed capital. This is called a **liquidating dividend**. A corporation usually pays a liquidating dividend only when it is going out of business or reducing its operations.

Having sufficient retained earnings in itself does not justify the declaration of a dividend. If a corporation does not have cash or other assets readily available for distribution, it might have to borrow money to pay the dividend—an action most boards of directors want to avoid.

Dividend Dates   Three important dates are associated with dividends:

- The **declaration date** is the date on which the board of directors formally declares that the corporation is going to pay a dividend. Because the legal obligation to pay the dividend arises at this time, a liability for Dividends Payable is recorded and the Dividends account is debited on this date. In the accounting process, Retained Earnings will be reduced by the total dividends declared during the period.

- The **record date** is the date on which ownership of stock, and therefore the right to receive a dividend, is determined. Persons who own the stock on the record date will receive the dividend. No journal entry is made on this date. Between the record date and the date of payment, the stock is said to be **ex-dividend**. If the owner on the date of record sells the shares of stock before the date of payment, the right to the dividend remains with that person; it does not transfer with the shares to the second owner.

- The **date of payment** is the date on which the dividend is paid to the stockholders of record. On this date, the Dividends Payable account is eliminated, and the Cash account is reduced.

Because an accounting period may end between the record date and the payment date, dividends declared during the period may exceed the amount paid for dividends. For example, in Figure 2, the accounting period ends on December 31. The declaration date for the dividends is December 21, the record date is December 31, and the payment date is January 11. In this case, the statement of retained earnings for the accounting period will show a decrease in the dividends declared, but the statement of cash flows will not show the dividends because the cash has not yet been paid out.

■ **FIGURE 2**
Dividend Dates

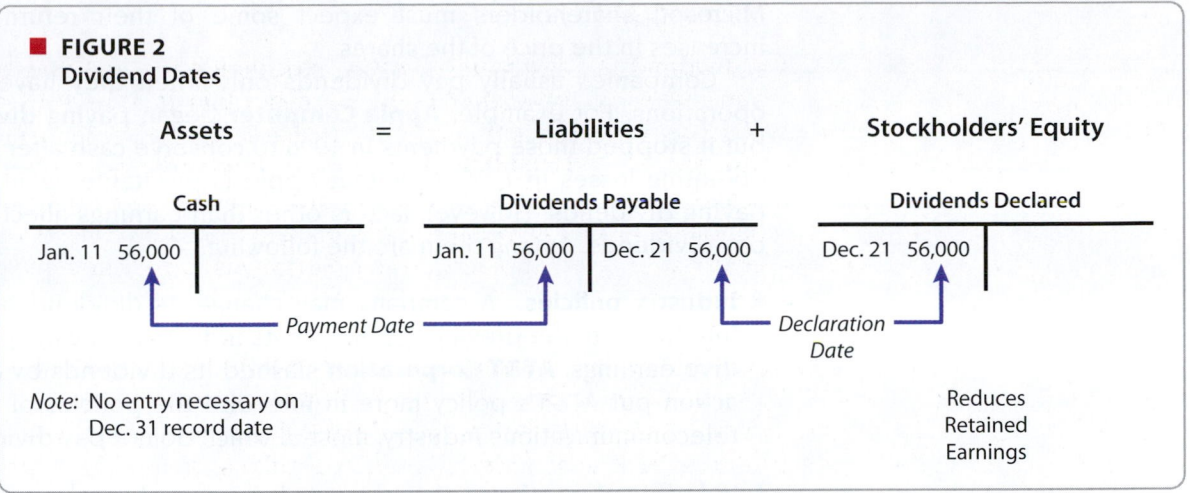

| Assets | = | Liabilities | + | Stockholders' Equity |

Cash

Jan. 11 56,000

Payment Date

Dividends Payable

Jan. 11 56,000 | Dec. 21 56,000

Dividends Declared

Dec. 21 56,000

Declaration Date

Note: No entry necessary on Dec. 31 record date

Reduces Retained Earnings

Evaluating Dividend Policies

To evaluate the amount of dividends they receive, investors use the **dividends yield** ratio. Dividends yield is computed by dividing the dividends per share by the market price per share. **Microsoft's** history of dividend payments provides an interesting example. Having built up a large cash balance through its years of profitable operations, Microsoft increased its annual dividend to $3.5 billion ($.32 per share) and declared a special dividend of $32 billion ($3 per share) in 2004.[2] Using Microsoft's regular annual dividend as a more realistic measure of what investors can expect in the future, its dividends yield is computed as follows:

$$\text{Dividends Yield} = \frac{\text{Dividends per Share}}{\text{Market Price per Share}} = \frac{\$.32}{\$24.20} = = 1.3\%$$

Figure 3 shows how Microsoft's dividends yield and last price are quoted on NASDAQ. Because the yield on corporate bonds exceeds 7 percent,

■ **FIGURE 3**
Stock Quotations on NASDAQ

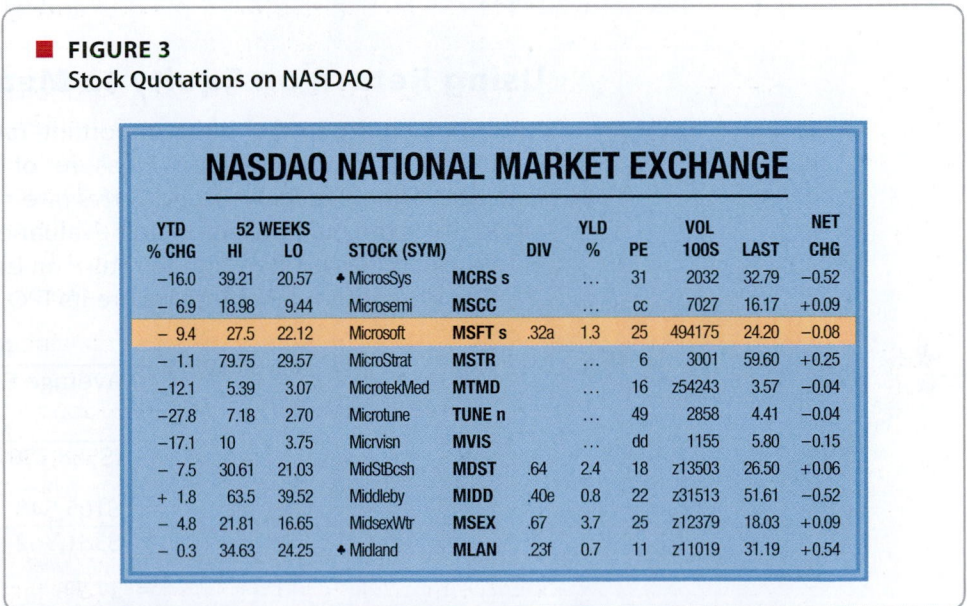

NASDAQ NATIONAL MARKET EXCHANGE

YTD % CHG	52 WEEKS HI	LO	STOCK (SYM)		DIV	YLD %	PE	VOL 100S	LAST	NET CHG
−16.0	39.21	20.57	◆ MicrosSys	MCRS s		…	31	2032	32.79	−0.52
− 6.9	18.98	9.44	Microsemi	MSCC		…	cc	7027	16.17	+0.09
− 9.4	27.5	22.12	Microsoft	MSFT s	.32a	1.3	25	494175	24.20	−0.08
− 1.1	79.75	29.57	MicroStrat	MSTR		…	6	3001	59.60	+0.25
−12.1	5.39	3.07	MicrotekMed	MTMD		…	16	z54243	3.57	−0.04
−27.8	7.18	2.70	Microtune	TUNE n		…	49	2858	4.41	−0.04
−17.1	10	3.75	Micrvisn	MVIS		…	dd	1155	5.80	−0.15
− 7.5	30.61	21.03	MidStBcsh	MDST	.64	2.4	18	z13503	26.50	+0.06
+ 1.8	63.5	39.52	Middleby	MIDD	.40e	0.8	22	z31513	51.61	−0.52
− 4.8	21.81	16.65	MidsexWtr	MSEX	.67	3.7	25	z12379	18.03	+0.09
− 0.3	34.63	24.25	◆ Midland	MLAN	.23f	0.7	11	z11019	31.19	+0.54

Source: Stock quotations on the NASDAQ from *Wall Street Journal*, May 28, 2005. Copyright © Dow Jones & Co., Inc. Reprinted by permission of Dow Jones & Company via Copyright Clearance Center.

Microsoft shareholders must expect some of their return to come from increases in the price of the shares.

Companies usually pay dividends only when they have had profitable operations. For example, **Apple Computer** began paying dividends in 1987, but it stopped those payments in 1996 to conserve cash after it suffered large operating losses in 1995. Now that Apple is profitable again, it may resume paying dividends. However, factors other than earnings affect the decision to pay dividends. Among them are the following:

▶ **Industry policies** A company may change its dividend policy to bring it into line with the prevailing policy in its industry. For example, despite positive earnings, **AT&T Corporation** slashed its dividends by 83 percent. This action put AT&T's policy more in line with the policies of its peers in the telecommunications industry, most of which do not pay dividends.[3]

▶ **Volatility of earnings** If a company has years of good earnings followed by years of poor earnings, it may want to keep dividends low to avoid giving a false impression of sustained high earnings. For example, for years, **General Motors** paid a fairly low but stable dividend but declared a bonus dividend in especially good years.

▶ **Effect on cash flows** A company may not pay dividends because its operations do not generate enough cash to do so or because it wants to invest cash in future operations. For instance, **Abbott Laboratories** pays a dividend of only $1.10 per share on earnings of $2.19 per share. Abbott believes a portion of the cash generated by the earnings is better spent for other purposes, such as researching and developing new drugs that will generate revenue in the future. It is partly due to Abbott's investment in new products that stockholders are willing to pay a high price for its stock.[4]

In recent years, because of a 15 percent reduction in the tax rate on dividends, attitudes toward dividends have changed. Many companies have either increased their dividends or started to pay dividends for the first time. The special dividend by Microsoft mentioned above is a good example of this effect.

Using Return on Equity to Measure Performance

Return on equity is the most important ratio associated with stockholders' equity. It is also a common measure of management's performance. For instance, when *BusinessWeek* and *Forbes* rate companies on their success, return on equity is the major basis of their evaluations. In addition, the compensation of top executives is often tied to return on equity benchmarks.

Google's return on equity before its IPO is computed as follows:[5]

$$\text{Return on Equity} = \frac{\text{Net Income}}{\text{Average Stockholders' Equity}}$$

$$= \frac{\$105{,}548}{(\$588{,}770 + \$173{,}953) \div 2}$$

$$= \frac{\$105{,}548}{\$381{,}362}$$

$$= 27.7\%$$

Google's healthy return on equity of 27.7 percent depends, of course, on the amount of net income the company earns. But it also depends on the level of stockholders' equity, which in turn depends on management decisions about the amount of stock the company sells to the public. As more shares are sold, stockholders' equity increases, and as a result, return on equity decreases. Management can keep stockholders' equity at a minimum by financing the business with cash flows from operations and by issuing debt instead of stock. However, as we have pointed out, issuing bonds and other types of debt increases a company's risk because the interest and principal of the debt must be paid in a timely manner.

Management can also reduce the number of shares in the hands of the public by buying back the company's shares on the open market. The cost of these shares, which are called **treasury stock**, has the effect of reducing stockholders' equity and thereby increasing return on equity. Many companies follow this practice instead of paying or increasing dividends. Their reason for doing so is that it puts money into the hands of stockholders in the form of market price appreciation without creating a commitment to higher dividends in the future. For instance, **Microsoft** recently announced a plan to purchase its common stock on the open market at a cost of $30 billion over a four-year period.[6] Microsoft's stock repurchases will improve the company's return on equity, increase its earnings per share, and lower its price/earnings ratio.

The **price/earnings (P/E) ratio** is a measure of investors' confidence in a company's future. It is calculated by dividing the market price per share by the earnings per share. The price/earnings ratio will vary as market price per share fluctuates daily and the amount of earnings per share changes. If you look back at Figure 3, you will see that it shows a P/E ratio of 25.0 for Microsoft. It was computed using the annual earnings per share from Microsoft's most recent income statement, as follows:

$$\frac{\text{Price/Earnings (P/E)}}{\text{Ratio}} = \frac{\text{Market Price per Share}}{\text{Earnings per Share}} = \frac{\$24.20}{\$.968} = 25.0 \text{ times}$$

Because the market price is 25.0 times earnings, investors are paying a high price in relation to earnings. They do so in the expectation that this software company will continue to be successful. High P/E ratios should be interpreted cautiously because unusually low earnings can produce an artificially high P/E ratio.

Stock Options as Compensation

More than 97 percent of public companies encourage employees to invest in their common stock through **stock option plans**.[7] Most such plans give employees the right to purchase stock in the future at a fixed price. Some companies offer stock option plans only to management personnel, but others, including **Google**, make them available to all employees. Because the market value of a company's stock is tied to a company's performance, these plans are a means of both motivating and compensating employees. As the market value of the stock goes up, the difference between the option price and the market price grows, which increases the amount of compensation. Another key benefit of stock option plans is that compensation expense is tax-deductible.

On the date stock options are granted, the fair value of the options must be estimated. The amount in excess of the exercise price is recorded as compensation expense over the grant period.[8] For example, suppose that on July 1, 20x6, a company grants its top executives the option to purchase 50,000 shares of $10 par value common stock at its current market value of $15 per share. On March 30, 20x9, when the market price is $25 per share, one of the firm's vice presidents exercises her option and purchases 2,000 shares. Although the vice president has a gain of $20,000 (the $50,000 market value less the $30,000 option price), no compensation expense is recorded because the company

FOCUS ON BUSINESS PRACTICE

How Did Accounting for Stock Options Become Political?

During the past decade, stock options have generated more controversy than any other single issue in accounting. Even the U.S. Congress has been involved on several occasions. The issue is whether the value of stock options should be counted as an expense on the income statement or buried in a note to the financial statements. The FASB has long held that options should be treated as expense, but in trying to pass this rule, it has encountered heavy opposition from the technology industry, which is the largest user of stock options.

Leaders of the technology industry maintain that expensing stock options would hurt their companies' profits and growth. They also maintain that the value of stock options is too hard to measure and that the options could turn out to be worthless. Proponents of expensing argue that stock options are a form of compensation and therefore must have value. They also point out that many items in the financial statements are based on estimates and that if all companies reported options as expense, their financial statements would be more comparable.

The FASB finally ruled that as of 2005, all publicly traded companies must expense stock options. However, even before the FASB's ruling, more than 750 companies, including **Boeing Corporation** and **BankOne** (now part of **JP Morgan/Chase**), accepted the eventual expensing of stock options and voluntarily started expensing them.[9]

receives only the option price, not the market value. Any one of several methods of estimating the fair value of options at the grant date may be used; they are dealt with in more advanced courses.

In one example of how firms value stock options, **Google** placed a value of $151.2 million on the options it issued in the six months before its IPO. Their value exceeded Google's net income of $143 million for the same period. Management says it used "hindsight" to arrive at the option values.[10]

STOP • REVIEW • APPLY

1-1. Identify and explain the advantages of the corporate form of business.

1-2. Identify and explain the disadvantages of the corporate form of business.

1-3. What three dates are important in paying dividends?

1-4. What is the dividends yield ratio, and what do investors learn from it?

1-5. What are two general ways in which management can improve a company's return on equity?

1-6. What is the price/earnings (P/E) ratio, and what does it measure?

1-7. What is a stock option plan, and why would a company want to have one?

Suggested answers to all Stop, Review, and Apply questions follow the appendixes.

Components of Stockholders' Equity

LO2 Identify the components of stockholders' equity.

n a corporation's balance sheet, the owners' claims to the business are called *stockholders' equity*. As shown in Exhibit 1, this section of a corporate balance sheet usually has at least three components.

EXHIBIT 1 ▶ | **Stockholders' Equity Section of a Balance Sheet**

Stockholders' Equity

Contributed capital

Preferred stock, $50 par value, 1,000 shares authorized, issued, and outstanding		$ 50,000
Common stock, $5 par value, 30,000 shares authorized, 20,000 shares issued, 18,000 shares outstanding	$100,000	
Additional paid-in capital	50,000	150,000
Total contributed capital		$200,000
Retained earnings		60,000
Total contributed capital and retained earnings		$260,000
Less treasury stock, common (2,000 shares at cost)		20,000
Total stockholders' equity		$240,000

▸ **Contributed capital**—the stockholders' investments in the corporation

▸ **Retained earnings**—the earnings of the corporation since its inception, less any losses, dividends, or transfers to contributed capital. Retained earnings are reinvested in the business. They are not a pool of funds to be distributed to the stockholders; instead, they represent the stockholders' claim to assets resulting from profitable operations.

▸ **Treasury stock**—shares of its own stock that the corporation has bought back on the open market. The cost of these shares is treated not as an investment, but as a reduction in stockholders' equity. By buying back the shares, the corporation reduces the ownership of the business.

As you can see in **Google's** Financial Highlights at the beginning of the chapter, "other items" may also appear in the stockholders' equity section. We discuss these items in a later chapter.

BUSINESS FOCUS ON PRACTICE

Are You a First-Class or Second-Class Stockholder?

When companies go public, insiders—usually the founders of the company or top management—often get first-class shares with extra votes, while outsiders get second-class shares with fewer votes. The class A and class B shares of **Adolph Coors Company**, the large brewing firm, are an extreme example. The company's class B shares, owned by the public, have no votes except in the case of a merger. Its class A shares, held by the Coors family trust, have all the votes on other issues.

Google also has two classes of common shares. Both classes are identical except that each class B share is entitled to ten votes and each class A share is entitled to only one vote. Class A shares are the ones that Google offered to the public in its IPO.

Shareholder advocates denounce the class division of shares as undemocratic. They maintain that this practice gives a privileged few shareholders all or most of the control of a company and that it denies other shareholders voting power consistent with the risk they are taking. Defenders of the practice argue that it shields top executives from the market's obsession with short-term results and allows them to make better long-term decisions. They also point out that many investors don't care about voting rights as long as the stock performs well.[11]

Larry Page *(left)* and Sergey Brin, who founded Google, Inc., in 1998, have a lot to look happy about. In its IPO in August 2004, Google issued about 22.5 million shares at $85 per share for a total of $1.9 billion. The price per share soared to $135 in a few days and reached $300 in 2005. The ability to raise large amounts of capital by issuing stocks and bonds is part of the reason corporations dominate the U.S. economy.

A corporation can issue two types of stock:

▸ **Common stock** is the basic form of stock that a corporation issues; that is, if a corporation issues only one type of stock, it is common stock. Because shares of common stock carry voting rights, they generally provide their owners with the means of controlling the corporation. Common stock is also called **residual equity**, which means that if the corporation is liquidated, the claims of all creditors and usually those of preferred stockholders rank ahead of the claims of common stockholders.

▸ To attract investors whose goals differ from those of common stockholders, a corporation may also issue **preferred stock**. Preferred stock gives its owners preference over common stockholders, usually in terms of receiving dividends and in terms of claims to assets if the corporation is liquidated. (We describe these preferences in more detail later in the chapter.)

In keeping with the convention of full disclosure, the stockholders' equity section of a corporate balance sheet gives a great deal of information about the corporation's stock. Under contributed capital, it lists the kinds of stock; their par value; and the number of shares authorized, issued, and outstanding.

▸ **Authorized shares** are the maximum number of shares that a corporation's state charter allows it to issue. Most corporations are authorized to issue more shares than they need to issue at the time they are formed. Thus, they are able to raise more capital in the future by issuing additional shares. When a corporation issues all of its authorized shares, it cannot issue more without a change in its state charter.

▸ **Issued shares** are those that a corporation sells or otherwise transfers to stockholders. The owners of a corporation's issued shares own 100 percent of the business. Unissued shares have no rights or privileges until they are issued.

▸ **Outstanding shares** are shares that a corporation has issued and that are still in circulation. Treasury stock is not outstanding because it consists of

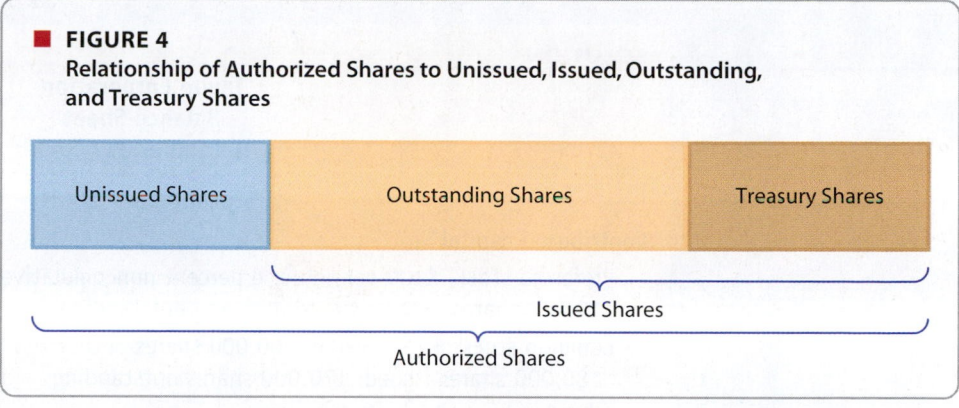

■ **FIGURE 4**
Relationship of Authorized Shares to Unissued, Issued, Outstanding, and Treasury Shares

shares that a corporation has issued but that it has bought back and thereby put out of circulation. Thus, a corporation can have more shares issued than are currently outstanding.

Figure 4 shows the relationship of authorized shares to issued, unissued, outstanding, and treasury shares. In this regard, Google is an interesting example. The company has 9 billion authorized shares of stock and only about 273 million shares issued, even after its initial public offering. With its excess of authorized issues, Google obviously has plenty of flexibility for future stock transactions.

S T O P • R E V I E W • A P P L Y

2-1. Why is common stock called *residual equity*?

2-2. How does preferred stock differ from common stock?

2-3. What distinguishes authorized shares from issued shares and outstanding shares?

2-4. What is the difference between issued shares and outstanding shares?

Components of Stockholders' Equity   The following data are from the records of Taupo Corporation on December 31, 20xx:

	Balance
Preferred stock, $100 par value, 6 percent noncumulative, 10,000 shares authorized, issued, and outstanding	$1,000,000
Common stock, $2 par value, 200,000 shares authorized, 180,000 shares issued, and 170,000 shares outstanding	360,000
Additional paid-in capital	978,000
Retained earnings	345,000
Treasury stock, common (10,000 shares, at cost)	220,000

Prepare a stockholders' equity section for Taupo Corporation's balance sheet.

SOLUTION

Taupo Corporation
Balance Sheet
December 31, 20xx

Stockholders' Equity

Contributed capital		
Preferred stock, $100 par value, 6 percent noncumulative, 10,000 shares authorized, issued, and outstanding		$1,000,000
Common stock, $2 par value, 200,000 shares authorized, 180,000 shares issued, 170,000 shares outstanding	$ 360,000	
Additional paid-in capital	978,000	1,338,000
Total contributed capital		$2,338,000
Retained earnings		345,000
Total contributed capital and retained earnings		$2,683,000
Less treasury stock, common (10,000 shares at cost)		220,000
Total stockholders' equity		$2,463,000

Preferred Stock

LO3 Identify the characteristics of preferred stock.

> **Study Note**
>
> Preferred stock has many different characteristics. They are rarely exactly the same from company to company.

Most preferred stock has one or more of the following characteristics: preference as to dividends, preference as to assets if a corporation is liquidated, convertibility, and a callable option. A corporation may offer several different classes of preferred stock, each with distinctive characteristics to attract different investors.

Preference as to Dividends

Preferred stockholders ordinarily must receive a certain amount of dividends before common stockholders receive anything. The amount that preferred stockholders must be paid before common stockholders can be paid is usually stated in dollars per share or as a percentage of the par value of the preferred shares. For example, a company might pay an annual dividend of $4 per share on preferred stock, or it might issue preferred stock at $50 par value and pay an annual dividend of 8 percent of par value, which would also be $4 per share.

Preferred stockholders have no guarantee of ever receiving dividends. A company must have earnings and its board of directors must declare dividends on preferred stock before any liability arises. The consequences of not granting an annual dividend on preferred stock vary according to whether the stock is noncumulative or cumulative:

▶ If the stock is **noncumulative preferred stock** and the board of directors fails to declare a dividend on it in any given year, the company is under no obligation to make up the missed dividend in future years.

▶ If the stock is **cumulative preferred stock**, the dividend amount per share accumulates from year to year, and the company must pay the whole amount before it pays any dividends on common stock.

Dividends not paid in the year they are due are called **dividends in arrears**. For example, suppose that a corporation has 10,000 shares of $100 par value, 5 percent cumulative preferred stock outstanding. If the corporation pays no dividends in 20x7, preferred dividends in arrears at the end of the year would amount to $50,000 (10,000 shares × $100 × .05 = $50,000). If the corporation's board declares dividends in 20x8, the corporation must pay preferred stockholders the dividends in arrears plus their current year's dividends before paying any dividends on common stock.

Dividends in arrears are not recognized as liabilities because no liability exists until the board of directors declares a dividend. A corporation cannot be sure it is going to make a profit, so, of course, it cannot promise dividends to stockholders. However, if it has dividends in arrears, it should report the amount either in the body of its financial statements or in a note to its financial statements.

The following note is typical of one that might appear in a company's annual report:

> On December 31, 20xx, the company was in arrears by $37,851,000 ($1.25 per share) on dividends to its preferred stockholders. The company must pay all dividends in arrears to preferred stockholders before paying any dividends to common stockholders.

Suppose that on January 1, 20x7, a corporation issued 10,000 shares of $10 par value, 6 percent cumulative preferred stock and 50,000 shares of common stock. Operations in 20x7 produced income of only $4,000. However, in the same year, the corporation's board of directors declared a $3,000 cash dividend to the preferred stockholders. Thus, the dividend picture at the end of 20x7 was as follows:

20x7 dividends due preferred stockholders ($100,000 × .06)	$6,000
Less 20x7 dividends declared to preferred stockholders	3,000
20x7 preferred stock dividends in arrears	$3,000

Now suppose that in 20x8, the corporation earns income of $30,000 and wants to pay dividends to both the preferred and the common stockholders. Because the preferred stock is cumulative, the corporation must pay the $3,000 in arrears on the preferred stock, plus the current year's dividends on the preferred stock, before it can distribute a dividend to the common stockholders. If the corporation's board of directors now declares a $12,000 dividend to be distributed to preferred and common stockholders, the distribution would be as follows:

20x8 declaration of dividends	$12,000
Less 20x7 preferred stock dividends in arrears	3,000
Amount available for 20x8 dividends	$ 9,000
Less 20x8 dividends due preferred stockholders ($100,000 × .06)	6,000
Remainder available to common stockholders	$ 3,000

Preference as to Assets

Preferred stockholders often have preference in terms of their claims to a corporation's assets if the corporation is liquidated. If a corporation does go out of

business, these preferred stockholders have a right to receive the par value of their stock or a larger stated liquidation value per share before the common stockholders receive any share of the corporation's assets. This preference can also extend to any dividends in arrears owed to the preferred stockholders.

Convertible Preferred Stock

> **Study Note**
>
> When preferred stockholders convert their shares to common stock, they gain voting rights but lose the dividend and liquidation preference. Conversion back to preferred stock is not an option.

Like all preferred stockholders, owners of **convertible preferred stock** are more likely than common stockholders to receive regular dividends. In addition, they can exchange their shares of preferred stock for shares of common stock at a ratio stated in the company's preferred stock contract. If the market value of the company's common stock increases, the conversion feature allows these stockholders to share in the increase by converting their stock to common stock. For example, if you look back at **Google's** Financial Highlights at the beginning of the chapter, you will see that when Google went to market with its IPO, the company's preferred stockholders took advantage of the steep increase in the price of the common stock by converting their shares to common stock. Thus, by including the conversion feature, companies can make their preferred stock more attractive to investors.

Suppose, for instance, that a company issues 1,000 shares of 8 percent, $100 par value convertible preferred stock for $100 per share. Each share of stock can be converted to five shares of the company's common stock at any time. The market value of the common stock at the time the company issues the convertible preferred stock is $15 per share. In the past, an owner of the common stock could expect dividends of about $1 per share per year. The owner of one share of preferred stock, on the other hand, now holds an investment that has a market value of about $75 and is also more likely than a common stockholder to receive dividends.

Now suppose that in the next several years, the corporation's earnings increase, the dividends paid to common stockholders increase to $3 per share, and the market value of a share of common stock increases from $15 to $30. Preferred stockholders can convert each of their preferred shares to five common shares, thereby increasing their dividends from $8 on each preferred share to $15 ($3 on each of five common shares). Moreover, the market value of each share of preferred stock will be close to the $150 value of the five shares of common stock because each share can be converted to five shares of common stock.

Callable Preferred Stock

Most preferred stock is **callable preferred stock**—that is, the issuing corporation can redeem or retire it at a price stated in the preferred stock contract. An owner of nonconvertible preferred stock must surrender it to the issuing corporation when asked to do so. If the preferred stock is convertible, the stockholder can either surrender the stock to the corporation or convert it to common stock when the corporation calls the stock. The *call price*, or redemption price, is usually higher than the stock's par value. For example, preferred stock that has a $100 par value might be callable at $103 per share.

When preferred stock is called and surrendered, the stockholder is entitled to the following:

- The par value of the stock

- The call premium

- Any dividends in arrears

- The current period's dividend prorated by the proportion of the year to the call date

A corporation may decide to call its preferred stock for any of the following reasons:

- It may want to force conversion of the preferred stock to common stock because the dividend that it pays on preferred shares is higher than the dividend that it pays on the equivalent number of common shares.

- It may be able to replace the outstanding preferred stock with a preferred stock at a lower dividend rate or with long-term debt, which can have a lower after-tax cost.

- It may simply be profitable enough to retire the preferred stock.

STOP • REVIEW • APPLY

3-1. What does preferred stock's preference as to dividends and assets mean?

3-2. What is cumulative preferred stock, and how does it relate to dividends in arrears? How should dividends in arrears be disclosed in the financial statements?

3-3. Define the terms *convertible* and *callable* as they apply to preferred stock.

Cash Dividends with Dividends in Arrears   Peace Corporation has 1,000 shares of $100 par value, 7 percent cumulative preferred stock outstanding and 100,000 shares of $1 par value common stock outstanding. In the corporation's first three years of operation, its board of directors declared cash dividends as follows:

    20x6, none
    20x7, $10,000
    20x8, $15,000

Determine the total cash dividends paid to the preferred and common stockholders during each of the three years.

SOLUTION

20x6:	None	
20x7:	Preferred dividends in arrears (1,000 shares × $100 × .07)	$ 7,000
	Current year remainder to preferred ($10,000 − $7,000)	3,000
	Total to preferred stockholders	$10,000
20x8:	Preferred dividends in arrears ($7,000 − $3,000)	$ 4,000
	Current year to preferred (1,000 shares × $100 × .07)	7,000
	Total to preferred stockholders	$11,000
	Total to common stockholders ($15,000 − $11,000)	4,000
	Total dividends in 20x8	$15,000

≡ Issuance of Common Stock

LO4 Account for the issuance of stock for cash and other assets.

A share of capital stock may be either par or no-par. The value of par stock is stated in the corporate charter and must be printed on each stock certificate. It can be $.01, $1, $5, $100, or any other amount established by the organizers of the corporation. For instance, the par value of **Google's** common stock is $.001. The par values of common stocks tend to be lower than those of preferred stocks.

As noted earlier, par value is the amount per share that is recorded in a corporation's capital stock accounts, and it constitutes a corporation's legal capital. A corporation cannot declare a dividend that would cause stockholders' equity to fall below the firm's legal capital. Par value is thus a minimum cushion of capital that protects a corporation's creditors. Any amount in excess of par value that a corporation receives from a stock issue is recorded in its Additional Paid-in Capital account and represents a portion of its contributed capital.

No-par stock is capital stock that does not have a par value. A corporation may issue stock without a par value for several reasons. For one thing, rather than recognizing par value as an arbitrary figure, investors may confuse it with the stock's market value. For another, most states do not allow a stock issue below par value, and this limits a corporation's flexibility in obtaining capital.

State laws often require corporations to place a **stated value** on each share of stock that they issue, but even when this is not required, a corporation's board of directors may do so as a matter of convenience. The stated value can be any value set by the board unless the state specifies a minimum amount, which is sometimes the case. The stated value can be set before or after the shares are issued if the state law is not specific.

Par Value Stock

When a corporation issues par value stock, the appropriate capital stock account (usually Common Stock or Preferred Stock) is credited for the par value regardless of whether the proceeds are more or less than the par value.

When a corporation issues stock at a price greater than par value, as is usually the case, the proceeds in excess of par are credited to an account called Additional Paid-in Capital. For example, suppose Xon Corporation is authorized to issue 20,000 shares of $10 par value common stock and that it issues

Study Note

Legal capital is the minimum amount a corporation can report as contributed capital. To protect creditors, a corporation cannot declare a dividend that would reduce capital below the amount of legal capital.

10,000 shares at $12 each on January 1, 20xx. The entry to record the issuance of the stock at the price in excess of par value would be as follows:

A = L + SE
+120,000   +100,000
           +20,000

Jan. 1	Cash	120,000	
	Common Stock		100,000
	Additional Paid-in Capital		20,000
	Issued 10,000 shares of $10 par value common stock for $12 per share		

Cash is debited for the proceeds of $120,000 (10,000 shares × $12), and Common Stock is credited for the total par value of $100,000 (10,000 shares × $10). Additional Paid-in Capital is credited for the difference of $20,000 (10,000 shares × $2).

The amount in excess of par value is part of Xon Corporation's contributed capital and will be included in the stockholders' equity section of its balance sheet. Immediately after the stock issue, this section of Xon's balance sheet would appear as follows:

Contributed capital	
Common stock, $10 par value, 20,000 shares	
authorized, 10,000 shares issued and outstanding	$100,000
Additional paid-in capital	20,000
Total contributed capital	$120,000
Retained earnings	—
Total stockholders' equity	$120,000

If a corporation issues stock for less than par value, an account called Discount on Capital Stock is debited for the difference. The issuance of stock at a discount rarely occurs; it is illegal in many states.

No-Par Stock

Most states require that all or part of the proceeds from a corporation's issuance of no-par stock be designated as legal capital, which cannot be used unless the corporation is liquidated. The purpose of this requirement is to protect the corporation's assets for creditors.

Suppose that on January 1, 20xx, Xon Corporation issues 10,000 shares of no-par common stock at $15 per share. The $150,000 (10,000 shares × $15) in proceeds would be recorded as follows:

Study Note

When no-par stock has a stated value, the stated value serves the same purpose as par value in that it represents the minimum legal capital.

A = L + SE
+150,000   +150,000

Jan. 1	Cash	150,000	
	Common Stock		150,000
	Issued 10,000 shares of no-par common stock for $15 per share		

Because the stock does not have a stated or par value, all proceeds of the issue are credited to Common Stock and are part of the company's legal capital.

As noted earlier, state laws may require corporations to put a stated value on each share of stock that they issue. Assuming the same facts as above except that Xon puts a $10 stated value on each share of its no-par stock, the entry would be as follows:

A	= L +	SE
+150,000		+100,000
		50,000

Jan. 1	Cash	150,000	
	Common Stock		100,000
	Additional Paid-in Capital		50,000
	Issued 10,000 shares of no-par common stock with $10 stated value for $15 per share		

Notice that the legal capital credited to Common Stock is the stated value decided by Xon's board of directors. Also note that the Additional Paid-in Capital account is credited for $50,000, which is the difference between the proceeds ($150,000) and the total stated value ($100,000).

Issuance of Stock for Noncash Assets

A corporation may issue stock in return for assets or services other than cash. Transactions of this kind usually involve a corporation's exchange of stock for land or buildings or for the services of attorneys and others who help organize the corporation. In such cases, the problem is to determine the dollar amount at which the exchange should be recorded.

A corporation's board of directors has the right to determine the fair market value of the assets or services that the corporation receives in exchange for its stock. Generally, such a transaction is recorded at the fair market value of the stock that the corporation is giving up. If the stock's fair market value cannot be determined, the fair market value of the assets or services received can be used.

For example, suppose that when Xon Corporation was formed on January 1, 20xx, its attorney agreed to accept 100 shares of its $10 par value common stock for services rendered. At that time, the market value of the stock could not be determined. However, for similar services, the attorney would have charged Xon $1,500. The entry to record this noncash transaction is as follows:

> **Study Note**
>
> In establishing the fair market value of property that a corporation exchanges for stock, a board of directors cannot be arbitrary; it must use all the information at its disposal.

A	= L +	SE
		−1,500
		+1,000
		+500

Jan. 1	Start-Up and Organization Costs	1,500	
	Common Stock		1,000
	Additional Paid-in Capital		500
	Issued 100 shares of $10 par value common stock for attorney's services		

Now suppose that two years later, Xon Corporation exchanged 1,000 shares of its $10 par value common stock for a piece of land. At the time of the exchange, Xon's stock was selling on the market for $16 per share. The following entry records this exchange:

A	= L +	SE
+16,000		+10,000
		+6,000

Jan. 1	Land	16,000	
	Common Stock		10,000
	Additional Paid-in Capital		6,000
	Issued 1,000 shares of $10 par value common stock with a market value of $16 per share for a piece of land		

S T O P • R E V I E W • A P P L Y

4-1. What is the significance of the following terms: *par value, no-par value,* and *stated value*?

4-2. Which is more relevant to the analyst: par value, additional paid-in capital, or the total of the two?

4-3. What two methods are used to value stock when it is issued for noncash assets, and when should each be used?

Accounting for Treasury Stock

LO5 Account for treasury stock.

> **Study Note**
>
> Treasury stock is not the same as unissued stock. Treasury stock represents shares that have been issued but are no longer outstanding. Unissued shares, on the other hand, have never been in circulation.

As we noted earlier, treasury stock is stock that the issuing company has reacquired, usually by purchasing shares on the open market. Although repurchasing its own stock can be a severe drain on a corporation's cash, it is common practice. In a recent year, 399, or 67 percent, of 600 large companies held treasury stock.[13]

Among the reasons a company may want to buy back its own stock are the following:

▸ It may want stock to distribute to employees through stock option plans.

▸ It may be trying to maintain a favorable market for its stock.

▸ It may want to increase its earnings per share or stock price per share.

▸ It may want to have additional shares of stock available for purchasing other companies.

▸ It may want to prevent a hostile takeover.

A purchase of treasury stock reduces a company's assets and stockholders' equity. It is not considered a purchase of assets, as the purchase of shares in another company would be. A company can hold treasury shares for an indefinite period or reissue or retire them. Treasury shares have no rights until they are reissued. Like unissued shares, they do not have voting rights, rights to dividends, or rights to assets during liquidation of the company. However, there is one major difference between unissued shares and treasury shares. A share of stock issued at par value or greater and that was reacquired as treasury stock can be reissued at less than par value without negative results.

Purchase of Treasury Stock

When treasury stock is purchased, it is recorded at cost. The par value, stated value, or original issue price of the stock is ignored. As noted above, the purchase reduces both a firm's assets and its stockholders' equity. For example, suppose that on September 15, Caprock Corporation purchases 1,000 shares of its common stock on the market at a price of $50 per share. The purchase would be recorded as follows:

A	= L +	SE			
−50,000		−50,000			

	Sept. 15	Treasury Stock, Common	50,000	
		Cash		50,000
		Acquired 1,000 shares of the company's common stock for $50 per share		

Study Note

> Because treasury stock reduces stockholder's equity—the denominator of the return on equity ratio—the return on equity will increase when treasury shares are purchased even though there is no increase in earnings.

The stockholders' equity section of Caprock's balance sheet shows the cost of the treasury stock as a deduction from the total of contributed capital and retained earnings:

Contributed capital		
Common stock, $5 par value, 100,000 shares authorized, 30,000 shares issued, 29,000 shares outstanding		$ 150,000
Additional paid-in capital		30,000
Total contributed capital		$ 180,000
Retained earnings		900,000
Total contributed capital and retained earnings		$1,080,000
Less treasury stock, common (1,000 shares at cost)		50,000
Total stockholders' equity		$1,030,000

Notice that the number of shares issued, and therefore the legal capital, has not changed. However, the number of shares outstanding has decreased as a result of the transaction.

Sale of Treasury Stock

Treasury shares can be sold at cost, above cost, or below cost. For example, suppose that on November 15, Caprock Corporation sells its 1,000 treasury shares for $50 per share. The following entry records the transaction:

A	= L +	SE			
+50,000		+50,000			

	Nov. 15	Cash	50,000	
		Treasury Stock, Common		50,000
		Reissued 1,000 shares of treasury stock for $50 per share		

In 2004, Microsoft's board approved a plan to buy back $30 billion of the company's common stock over the next four years. When are share buybacks not a good idea? According to investor Warren Buffett, shown here offering his hand to Microsoft's Bill Gates, buybacks are ill-advised when a company buys high and sells low and when it borrows money to finance a buyback.

When treasury shares are sold for an amount greater than their cost, the excess of the sales price over cost should be credited to Paid-in Capital, Treasury Stock. No gain should be recorded.

For instance, suppose that on November 15, Caprock Corporation sells its 1,000 treasury shares for $60 per share. The entry for the reissue would be as follows:

A	= L +	SE				
+60,000		+50,000	Nov. 15	Cash	60,000	
		+10,000		Treasury Stock, Common		50,000
				Paid-in Capital, Treasury Stock		10,000
				Sold 1,000 shares of treasury stock for $60 per share; cost was $50 per share		

When treasury shares are sold below their cost, the difference is deducted from Paid-in Capital, Treasury Stock. If this account does not exist or if its balance is insufficient to cover the excess of cost over the reissue price, Retained Earnings absorbs the excess. No loss is recorded.

For example, suppose that on September 15, Caprock bought 1,000 shares of its common stock on the market at a price of $50 per share. On October 15, the company sold 400 shares for $60 per share, and on December 15, it sold the remaining 600 shares for $42 per share.

The entries for these three transactions are as follows:

A	= L +	SE				
−50,000		−50,000	Sept. 15	Treasury Stock, Common	50,000	
				Cash		50,000
				Purchased 1,000 shares of treasury stock at $50 per share		

A	= L +	SE
+24,000		+20,000
		+4,000

Oct. 15	Cash	24,000	
	Treasury Stock, Common		20,000
	Paid-in Capital, Treasury Stock		4,000
	Sold 400 shares of treasury stock for $60 per share; cost was $50 per share		

A	= L +	SE
+25,200		−4,000
		−800
		+30,000

Dec. 15	Cash	25,200	
	Paid-in Capital, Treasury Stock	4,000	
	Retained Earnings	800	
	Treasury Stock, Common		30,000
	Sold 600 shares of treasury stock for $42 per share; cost was $50 per share		

> 📎 *Study Note*
>
> Retained Earnings is debited only when the Paid-in Capital, Treasury Stock account has been depleted. In this case, the credit balance of $4,000 is completely exhausted before Retained Earnings absorbs the excess.

In the entry for the December 15 transaction, Retained Earnings is debited for $800 because the 600 shares were sold for $4,800 less than cost. That amount is $800 greater than the $4,000 of paid-in capital generated by the sale of the 400 shares of treasury stock on October 15.

Retirement of Treasury Stock

If a company decides that it will not reissue treasury stock, it can, with the approval of its stockholders, retire the stock. When shares of stock are retired, all items related to those shares are removed from the associated capital accounts. If the cost of buying back the treasury stock is less than the company received when it issued the stock, the difference is recorded in Paid-in Capital, Retirement of Stock. If the reacquisition cost is more than was received when the stock was first issued, the difference is a reduction in stockholders' equity and is debited to Retained Earnings. For instance, suppose that on November 15, Caprock Corporation decides to retire the 1,000 shares of stock that it bought back for $50,000. If the $5 par value common stock was originally issued at $6 per share, this entry would record the retirement:

A = L +	SE
	−5,000
	−1,000
	−44,000
	+50,000

Nov. 15	Common Stock	5,000	
	Additional Paid-in Capital	1,000	
	Retained Earnings	44,000	
	Treasury Stock, Common		50,000
	Retired 1,000 shares that cost $50 per share and were issued originally at $6 per share		

STOP • REVIEW • APPLY

5-1. What is treasury stock?

5-2. What are some reasons a company would buy back its own stock?

5-3. What is the effect of treasury stock on the balance sheet?

GOOGLE, INC.

This chapter's Decision Point focused on one of the most exciting financing events of recent history, **Google's** IPO. In evaluating Google's performance since its IPO, those who invested in its stock should consider the following questions:

- **Why did Google's management choose to issue common stock to satisfy its needs for new capital?**
- **What are some of the advantages and disadvantages of this approach to financing a business?**
- **What measures should an investor use in evaluating management's performance?**

As a relatively new company, Google needed to raise capital so that it could expand its operations. The company's management decided to do so by issuing common stock. This approach to financing does not burden a company with debt or interest payments. In addition, the company has the option of paying or not paying dividends. Because Google currently does not pay dividends, it can invest cash from its earnings in expanding the company. Issuing stock does, however, dilute the ownership of a company's current owners, and if the company pays dividends, they are not tax-deductible, as interest on debt is.

Return on equity is, of course, a key measure of management's performance. We showed in an earlier computation that Google's return on equity before its IPO was 27.7 percent. Using the same net income as in that computation and data from Google's Financial Highlights, we can compute the company's return on equity after the IPO as follows:

$$\text{Return on Equity} = \frac{\text{Net Income}}{\text{Average Stockholders' Equity}}$$

$$\text{Return on Equity} = \frac{\$105,548}{(\$2,589,023 + \$1,016,699) \div 2}$$

$$= 5.9\%$$

Obviously, the IPO significantly reduced Google's return on equity, from 27.7 percent to 5.9 percent. However, Google's price/earnings (P/E) ratios at the time of the IPO and six months later show that investors were counting on Google to continue to grow and be successful.

At the time of the IPO, when Google's stock sold for $85 per share, its P/E ratio was as follows:

$$\text{P/E Ratio} = \frac{\text{Market Price per Share}}{\text{Earnings per Share}}$$

$$\text{P/E Ratio} = \frac{\$85}{\$1.14} = 74.6 \text{ times}$$

Six months later, when the price per share was $185, Google's P/E ratio had soared once again:

$$\text{P/E Ratio} = \frac{\$185}{\$1.14} = 162.3 \text{ times}$$

This is a very high P/E ratio; the average for the S&P 500 stocks at the time was about 16. Evidently, despite Google's not paying dividends, investors thought the company's future was very bright.

CHAPTER REVIEW

REVIEW of Learning Objectives

LO1 Identify and explain the management issues related to contributed capital.

Contributed capital is a critical component in corporate financing. Managing contributed capital requires an understanding of the advantages and disadvantages of the corporate form of business and of the issues involved in using equity financing. Managers must also know how to determine dividend policies and how to evaluate these policies using dividends yield, return on equity, and the price/earnings ratio. The liability for payment of dividends arises on the date the board of directors declares a dividend. The declaration is recorded with a debit to Dividends and a credit to Dividends Payable. The record date—the date on which ownership of the stock, and thus of the right to receive a dividend, is determined—requires no entry. On the date of payment, the Dividends Payable account is eliminated, and the Cash account is reduced. Another issue involved in managing contributed capital is using stock options as compensation.

LO2 Identify the components of stockholders' equity.

The stockholders' equity section of a corporate balance usually has at least three components: contributed capital, retained earnings, and treasury stock. Contributed capital consists of money raised through stock issues. A corporation can issue two types of stock: common stock and preferred stock. Common stockholders have voting rights; they also share in the earnings of the corporation. Preferred stockholders usually have preference over common stockholders in one or more areas. Retained earnings are reinvested in the corporation; they represent stockholders' claims to assets resulting from profitable operations. Treasury stock is stock that the issuing corporation has reacquired. It is treated as a deduction from stockholders' equity.

LO3 Identify the characteristics of preferred stock.

Preferred stock generally gives its owners first right to dividend payments. Only after these stockholders have been paid can common stockholders receive any portion of a dividend. If the preferred stock is cumulative and dividends are in arrears, a corporation must pay the amount in arrears to preferred stockholders before it pays any dividends to common stockholders. Preferred stockholders also usually have preference over common stockholders in terms of their claims to corporate assets if the corporation is liquidated. In addition, preferred stock may be convertible to common stock, and it is often callable at the option of the corporation.

LO4 Account for the issuance of stock for cash and other assets.

Corporations normally issue their stock in exchange for cash or other assets. Most states require corporations to issue stock at a minimum value called *legal capital*. Legal capital is represented by the stock's par or stated value.

When stock is issued for cash at par or stated value, Cash is debited and Common Stock or Preferred Stock is credited. When stock is sold at an amount greater than par or stated value, the excess is recorded in Additional Paid-in Capital.

When stock is issued for noncash assets, the general rule is to record the stock at its market value. If this value cannot be determined, the fair market value of the asset received is used to record the transaction.

LO5 Account for treasury stock.

Treasury stock is stock that the issuing company has reacquired. A company may buy back its own stock for several reasons, including a desire to create stock option plans, maintain a favorable market for the stock, increase earnings per share, or purchase other companies. Treasury stock is recorded at cost and is deducted from stockholders' equity. It can be reissued or retired. It is similar to unissued stock in that it does not have rights until it is reissued.

REVIEW of Concepts and Terminology

The following concepts and terms were introduced in this chapter:

Authorized shares: The maximum number of shares a corporation can issue without a change in its state charter. **(LO2)**

Callable preferred stock: Preferred stock that the issuing corporation can redeem or retire at a stated price. **(LO3)**

Common stock: Shares of stock that carry voting rights but that rank below preferred stock in terms of dividends and the distribution of assets. **(LO2)**

Convertible preferred stock: Preferred stock that the owner can exchange for common stock. **(LO3)**

Cumulative preferred stock: Preferred stock on which unpaid dividends accumulate over time and that must be satisfied before a dividend can be paid to common stockholders. **(LO3)**

Date of payment: The date on which a dividend is paid. **(LO1)**

Declaration date: The date on which a board of directors declares a dividend. **(LO1)**

Dividend: A distribution of a corporation's assets (usually cash generated by past earnings) to its stockholders. **(LO1)**

Dividends in arrears: Past dividends on cumulative preferred stock that remain unpaid. **(LO3)**

Double taxation: Taxation of corporate earnings twice—once as income of the corporation and once as income to stockholders in the form of dividends. **(LO1)**

Ex-dividend: A description of stock between the record date and the date of payment, during which the right to the dividend remains with the person who owned the stock on the record date. **(LO1)**

Initial public offering (IPO): A company's first issue of capital stock to the public. **(Decision Point)**

Issued shares: The shares of stock sold or otherwise transferred to stockholders. **(LO2)**

Legal capital: The number of shares of stock issued times the par value; the minimum amount a corporation can report as contributed capital. **(LO1)**

Liquidating dividend: A dividend that exceeds retained earnings and that a corporation usually pays only when it is going out of business or reducing its operations. **(LO1)**

Noncumulative preferred stock: Preferred stock that does not oblige the issuer to make up a missed dividend in a subsequent year. **(LO3)**

No-par stock: Capital stock that does not have a par value. **(LO4)**

Outstanding shares: Shares that have been issued and that are still in circulation. **(LO2)**

Par value: An arbitrary amount assigned to each share of stock; constitutes a corporation's legal capital. **(LO1)**

Preferred stock: Stock that has preference over common stock, usually in terms of dividends and the distribution of assets. **(LO2)**

Record date: The date on which ownership of stock, and thus the right to receive a dividend, is determined. **(LO1)**

Residual equity: The equity of common stockholders after all other claims have been satisfied. **(LO2)**

Share of stock: A unit of ownership in a corporation. **(LO1)**

Start-up and organization costs: The costs of forming a corporation. **(LO1)**

Stated value: A value that a board of directors assigns to no-par stock. **(LO4)**

Stock certificates: Documents issued to stockholders showing the number of shares that they own. **(LO1)**

Stock option plans: Plans that give employees the right to purchase their companies' stock under specified terms. **(LO1)**

Treasury stock: Capital stock, either common or preferred, that the issuing company has reacquired and has not subsequently resold or retired. **(LO1)**

Underwriter: An intermediary between the corporation and the investing public who facilitates an issue of stock or other securities for a fee. **(LO1)**

Key Ratios

Dividends yield: Current return to stockholders in the form of dividends; Dividends per Share ÷ Market Price per Share. **(LO1)**

Price/earnings (P/E) ratio: A measure of confidence in a company's future; Market Price per Share ÷ Earnings per Share. **(LO1)**

Return on equity: A measure of management's performance; Net Income ÷ Average Stockholders' Equity. **(LO1)**

REVIEW Problem

LO1, LO2, LO3, LO4, LO5   **Recording Stock Issues and Calculating Related Ratios**

 Beta Corporation was organized in 20x6 in Arizona. Its state charter authorized it to issue 1 million shares of $1 par value common stock and 25,000 shares of 4 percent, $20 par value cumulative and convertible preferred stock. Beta's stock transactions during 20x6 were as follows:

Feb. 1 Issued 100,000 shares of common stock for $125,000.

15 Issued 3,000 shares of common stock for accounting and legal services. The bills for these services totaled $3,600.

Mar. 15 Issued 120,000 shares of common stock to Edward Jackson in exchange for a building and land appraised at $100,000 and $25,000, respectively.

Apr. 2 Purchased 20,000 shares of common stock for the treasury at $1.25 per share from a person who changed her mind about investing in the company.

July 1 Issued 25,000 shares of preferred stock for $500,000.

Sept. 30 Sold 10,000 of the shares in the treasury for $1.50 per share.

Dec. 31 Beta's board of directors declared dividends of $24,910 payable on January 15, 20x7, to stockholders of record on January 7. Dividends included preferred stock dividends of $10,000 for one-half year.

For the period ended December 31, 20x6, Beta reported net income of $40,000 and earnings per common share of $.14. At December 31, the market price per common share was $1.60.

Required

1. Record Beta's stock transactions in T accounts.
2. Prepare the stockholders' equity section of Beta's balance sheet as of December 31, 20x6. (**Hint:** Use net income and dividends to calculate retained earnings.)
3. Calculate Beta's dividends yield on common stock, price/earnings ratio of common stock, and return on equity.

Answer to Review Problem

1. Entries in T accounts:

A	B	C	D	E	F	G	H	I	J	K	L	M	N	O	P	Q	R	S	T
		Assets				=			Liabilities				+			Stockholders' Equity			
		Cash							Dividends Payable							Preferred Stock			
Feb.	1	125,000	April	2	25,000					Dec.	31	24,910					July	1	500,000
July	1	500,000																	
Sept.	30	15,000														Common Stock			
																Feb.	1	100,000
		Building															15	3,000
Mar.	15	100,000														Mar.	15	120,000
																Bal.		223,000

	Assets					=		Liabilities					+		Stockholders' Equity				
11						=							+						
12																			
13		Land												Additional Paid-in Capital					
14	Mar.	15	25,000												Feb.	1	25,000		
15																15	600		
16															Mar.	15	5,000		
17															Bal.		30,600		
18																			
19														Paid-in Capital, Treasury Stock					
20															Sept.	30	2,500		
21																			
22														Dividends					
23												Dec.	31	24,910					
24																			
25														Treasury Stock					
26												April	2	25,000	Sept.	30	12,500		
27												Bal.		12,500					
28																			
29														Start-up and Organizational Costs					
30												Feb.	15	3,600					

2. Stockholders' equity section of the balance sheet:

	A	B	C
1	**Beta Corporation**		
2	**Balance Sheet**		
3	**December 31, 20x6**		
4			
5	**Stockholders' Equity**		
6			
7	Contributed capital		
8	Preferred stock, 4 percent cumulative convertible,		
9	$20 par value, 25,000 shares authorized, issued, and outstanding		$500,000
10	Common stock, $1 par value, 1,000,000 shares		
11	authorized, 223,000 shares issued, and 213,000 shares outstanding	$223,000	
12	Additional paid-in capital	30,600	
13	Paid-in capital, treasury stock	2,500	256,100
14	Total contributed capital		$756,100
15	Retained earnings		15,090*
16	Total contributed capital and retained earnings		$771,190
17	Less treasury stock (10,000 shares, at cost)		12,500
18	Total stockholders' equity		$758,690
19			
20	*Retained Earnings = Net Income − Cash Dividends Declared = $40,000 − $24,910 = $15,090		

3. Dividends yield on common stock, price/earnings ratio of common stock, and return on equity:

$$\text{Dividends per Share} = \frac{\text{Common Stock Dividend}}{\text{Common Shares Outstanding}} = \frac{\$14,910}{213,000} = \$.07$$

$$\text{Dividends Yield} = \frac{\text{Dividends per Share}}{\text{Market Price per Share}} = \frac{\$0.07}{\$1.60} = 4.4\%$$

$$\text{Price/Earnings Ratio} = \frac{\text{Market Price per Share}}{\text{Earnings per Share}} = \frac{\$1.60}{\$0.14} = 11.4 \text{ times}$$

The opening balance of stockholders' equity on February 1, 20x6, was $125,000.

$$\text{Return on Equity} = \frac{\text{Net Income}}{\text{Average Stockholders' Equity}}$$

$$= \frac{\$40,000}{(\$758,690 + \$125,000) \div 2}$$

$$= \frac{\$40,000}{\$441,845}$$

$$= 9.1\%$$

CHAPTER ASSIGNMENTS

BUILDING Your Basic Knowledge and Skills

Short Exercises

LO1 **Management Issues**

SE 1. Indicate whether each of the following actions is related to (a) managing under the corporate form of business, (b) using equity financing, (c) determining dividend policies, (d) evaluating performance using return on equity, or (e) issuing stock options:

1. Considering whether to make a distribution to stockholders
2. Controlling day-to-day operations
3. Determining whether to issue preferred or common stock
4. Compensating management based on the company's meeting or exceeding the targeted return on equity
5. Compensating employees by giving them the right to purchase shares at a given price
6. Transferring shares without the approval of other owners

LO1 **Advantages and Disadvantages of a Corporation**

SE 2. Identify whether each of the following characteristics is an advantage or a disadvantage of the corporate form of business:

1. Ease of transfer of ownership
2. Taxation
3. Separate legal entity
4. Lack of mutual agency
5. Government regulation
6. Continuous existence

LO2 **Effect of Start-up and Organization Costs**

SE 3. At the beginning of 20x6, Batson Company incurred the following start-up and organization costs: (1) attorneys' fees with a market value of $10,000, paid with 6,000 shares of $1 par value common stock, and (2) incorporation fees of $6,000. Calculate total start-up and organization costs. What will be the effect of these costs on the income statement and balance sheet?

LO1 **Exercise of Stock Options**

SE 4. On June 6, Aretha Dafoe exercised her option to purchase 20,000 shares of Shalom Company $1 par value common stock at an option price of $8. The market price per share was $8 on the grant date and $36 on the exercise date. Record the transaction on Shalom's books.

LO2 **Stockholders' Equity**

SE 5. Prepare the stockholders' equity section of Fina Corporation's balance sheet from the following accounts and balances on December 31, 20xx:

	Balance
Common Stock, $10 par value, 30,000 shares authorized, 20,000 shares issued, and 19,500 shares outstanding	$200,000
Additional paid-in Capital	100,000
Retained Earnings	15,000
Treasury Stock, Common (500 shares, at cost)	7,500

LO1 **Cash Dividends**

SE 6. Tone Corporation has authorized 200,000 shares of $1 par value common stock, of which 160,000 are issued and 140,000 are outstanding. On May 15, the board of directors declared a cash dividend of $.20 per share, payable on June 15 to stockholders of record on June 1. Prepare the entries in T accounts, as necessary, for each of the three dates.

LO3 **Preferred Stock Dividends with Dividends in Arrears**

SE 7. The Ferris Corporation has 2,000 shares of $100, 8 percent cumulative preferred stock outstanding and 40,000 shares of $1 par value common stock outstanding. In the company's first three years of operation, its board of directors paid cash dividends as follows: 20x6, none; 20x7, $40,000; and 20x8, $80,000. Determine the total cash dividends and dividends per share paid to the preferred and common stockholders during each of the three years.

LO4 **Issuance of Stock**

SE 8. Rattich Company is authorized to issue 50,000 shares of common stock. The company sold 2,500 shares at $12 per share. Prepare entries in journal form to record the sale of stock for cash under each of the following independent alternatives: (1) The stock has a par value of $5, and (2) the stock has no par value but a stated value of $1 per share.

LO4 **Issuance of Stock for Noncash Assets**

SE 9. Learner Corporation issued 16,000 shares of its $1 par value common stock in exchange for land that had a fair market value of $100,000. Prepare in journal form the entries necessary to record the issuance of the stock for the land under each of these conditions: (1) The stock was selling for $7 per share on the day of the transaction; (2) management attempted to place a value on the common stock but could not do so.

LO5   **Treasury Stock Transactions**

SE 10. Prepare in journal form the entries necessary to record the following stock transactions of the Seoul Company during 20xx:

Oct.   1   Purchased 2,000 shares of its own $2 par value common stock for $20 per share, the current market price.
17   Sold 500 shares of treasury stock purchased on October 1 for $25 per share.
21   Sold 800 shares of treasury stock purchased on October 1 for $18 per share.

LO5   **Retirement of Treasury Stock**

SE 11. On October 28, 20xx, the Seoul Company (**SE 10**) retired the remaining 700 shares of treasury stock. The shares were originally issued at $5 per share. Prepare the necessary entry in journal form.

Exercises

LO1, LO2   **Discussion Questions**

E 1. Develop brief answers to each of the following questions:

1. Why are most large companies established as corporations rather than as partnerships?
2. Why do many companies like to give stock options as compensation?
3. If an investor sells shares after the declaration date but before the date of record, does the seller still receive the dividend?
4. Why does a company usually not want to issue all its authorized shares?

LO3, LO4, LO5   **Discussion Questions**

E 2. Develop brief answers to each of the following questions:

1. Why would a company want to issue callable preferred stock?
2. What arguments can you give for treating preferred stock as debt rather than equity when carrying out financial analysis?
3. What relevance does par value or stated value have to a financial ratio, such as return on equity or debit to equity?
4. Why is treasury stock not considered an investment or an asset?

LO1   **Dividends Yield and Price/Earnings Ratio**

E 3. In 20x8, Rhinehart Corporation earned $4.40 per share and paid a dividend of $2.00 per share. At year end, the price of its stock was $66 per share. Calculate the dividends yield and the price/earnings ratio.

LO2   **Stockholders' Equity**

E 4. The following accounts and balances are from the records of Guard Corporation on December 31, 20xx:

	Balance
Preferred Stock, $100 par value, 9 percent cumulative, 10,000 shares authorized, 6,000 shares issued and outstanding	$600,000
Common Stock, $12 par value, 45,000 shares authorized, 30,000 shares issued, and 28,500 shares outstanding	360,000
Additional Paid-in Capital	194,000
Retained Earnings	23,000
Treasury Stock, Common (1,500 shares, at cost)	30,000

Prepare the stockholders' equity section for Guard Corporation's balance sheet as of December 31, 20xx.

LO2, LO3 **Characteristics of Common and Preferred Stock**

E 5. Indicate whether each of the following characteristics is more closely associated with common stock (C) or preferred stock (P):

1. Often receives dividends at a set rate
2. Is considered the residual equity of a company
3. Can be callable
4. Can be convertible
5. More likely to have dividends that vary in amount from year to year
6. Can be entitled to receive dividends not paid in past years
7. Likely to have full voting rights
8. Receives assets first in liquidation
9. Generally receives dividends before other classes of stock

LO2, LO4 **Stock Entries Using T Accounts; Stockholders' Equity**

E 6. Rath School Supply Corporation was organized in 20xx. It was authorized to issue 200,000 shares of no-par common stock with a stated value of $5 per share, and 40,000 shares of $100 par value, 6 percent noncumulative preferred stock. On March 1, the company issued 120,000 shares of its common stock for $15 per share and 16,000 shares of its preferred stock for $100 per share.

1. Record the issuance of the stock in T accounts.
2. Prepare the stockholders' equity section of Rath School Supply Corporation's balance sheet as it would appear immediately after the company issued the common and preferred stock.

LO1 **Cash Dividends**

E 7. Mendoza Corporation secured authorization from the state for 100,000 shares of $10 par value common stock. It has 80,000 shares issued and 70,000 shares outstanding. On June 5, the board of directors declared a $.50 per share cash dividend to be paid on June 25 to stockholders of record on June 15. Prepare entries in T accounts to record these events.

LO1, LO5 **Cash Dividends**

E 8. Martin Corporation has 250,000 authorized shares of $1 par value common stock, of which 200,000 are issued, including 20,000 shares of treasury stock. On October 15, the corporation's board of directors declared a cash dividend of $.25 per share payable on November 15 to stockholders of record on November 1. Prepare entries in T accounts for each of the three dates.

LO3 **Cash Dividends with Dividends in Arrears**

E 9. Canterbury Corporation has 20,000 shares of its $100 par value, 7 percent cumulative preferred stock outstanding, and 100,000 shares of its $1 par value common stock outstanding. In Canterbury's first four years of operation, its board of directors paid cash dividends as follows: 20x6, none; 20x7, $240,000; 20x8, $280,000; 20x9, $280,000. Determine the dividends per share and total cash dividends paid to the preferred and common stockholders during each of the four years.

LO3 **Cash Dividends on Preferred and Common Stock**

E 10. Khandi Corporation pays dividends at the end of each year. The dividends that it paid for 20x6, 20x7, and 20x8 were $160,000, $120,000, and

$360,000, respectively. Calculate the total amount of dividends Khandi Corporation paid in each of these years to its common and preferred stockholders under both of the following capital structures: (1) 40,000 shares of $100 par, 6 percent noncumulative preferred stock and 120,000 shares of $10 par common stock; (2) 20,000 shares of $100 par, 7 percent cumulative preferred stock and 120,000 shares of $10 par common stock. Khandi Corporation had no dividends in arrears at the beginning of 20x6.

LO4 **Issuance of Stock**

E 11. Red Valley Company is authorized to issue 100,000 shares of common stock. On August 1, the company issued 5,000 shares at $25 per share. Prepare entries in journal form to record the issuance of stock for cash under each of the following alternatives:

1. The stock has a par value of $25.
2. The stock has a par value of $10.
3. The stock has no par value.
4. The stock has a stated value of $1 per share.

LO4 **Issuance of Stock for Noncash Assets**

E 12. On July 1, 20xx, Gorlin, a new corporation, issued 40,000 shares of its common stock to finance a corporate headquarters building. The building has a fair market value of $1,200,000 and a book value of $800,000. Because Gorlin is a new corporation, it is not possible to establish a market value for its common stock. Record the issuance of stock for the building, assuming the following conditions: (1) the par value of the stock is $10 per share; (2) the stock is no-par stock; and (3) the stock has a stated value of $4 per share.

LO5 **Treasury Stock Transactions**

E 13. Record in T accounts the following stock transactions of Bornstein Company, which represent all the company's treasury stock transactions during 20xx:

May 5 Purchased 800 shares of its own $2 par value common stock for $20 per share, the current market price.

17 Sold 300 shares of treasury stock purchased on May 5 for $22 per share.

21 Sold 200 shares of treasury stock purchased on May 5 for $20 per share.

28 Sold the remaining 300 shares of treasury stock purchased on May 5 for $19 per share.

LO5 **Treasury Stock Transactions Including Retirement**

E 14. Record in T accounts the following stock transactions of Adderly Corporation, which represent all its treasury stock transactions for the year:

June 1 Purchased 1,000 shares of its own $30 par value common stock for $70 per share, the current market price.

10 Sold 250 shares of treasury stock purchased on June 1 for $80 per share.

20 Sold 350 shares of treasury stock purchased on June 1 for $58 per share.

June 30 Retired the remaining shares purchased on June 1. The original
issue price was $42 per share.

LO1, LO2, LO4, LO5

Problems

Common Stock Transactions and Stockholders' Equity

P 1. Sussex Corporation began operations on September 1, 20xx. The corporation's charter authorized 300,000 shares of $8 par value common stock. Sussex Corporation engaged in the following transactions during its first quarter:

Sept. 1 Issued 50,000 shares of common stock, $500,000.
      1 Paid an attorney $32,000 to help start up and organize the corporation and obtain a corporate charter from the state.
Oct. 2 Issued 80,000 shares of common stock, $960,000.
     15 Purchased 10,000 shares of common stock for $150,000.
Nov. 30 Declared a cash dividend of $.40 per share to be paid on December 15 to stockholders of record on December 10.

Required

1. Prepare entries in T accounts to record the above transactions.
2. Prepare the stockholders' equity section of Sussex Corporation's balance sheet on November 30, 20xx. Net income for the quarter was $80,000.
3. **User Insight:** What effect, if any, will the cash dividend declaration on November 30 have on net income, retained earnings, and cash flows?

LO1, LO3

Preferred and Common Stock Dividends and Dividend Yield

P 2. The DeMeo Corporation had both common stock and preferred stock outstanding from 20x5 through 20x7. Information about each stock for the three years is as follows:

Type	Par Value	Shares Outstanding	Other
Preferred	$100	40,000	7% cumulative
Common	20	600,000	

The company paid $140,000, $800,000, and $1,100,000 in dividends for 20x5 through 20x7, respectively. The market price per common share was $15 and $17 per share at the end of years 20x6 and 20x7, respectively.

Required

1. Determine the dividends per share and total dividends paid to the common and preferred stockholders each year.
2. Assuming that the preferred stock was noncumulative, repeat the computations performed in requirement 1.
3. Calculate the 20x6 and 20x7 dividends yield for common stock using dividends per share computed in requirement 2.
4. **User Insight:** How are cumulative preferred stock and noncumulative preferred stock similar to long-term bonds? How do they differ from long-term bonds?

LO1, LO2, LO3, LO4, LO5

Comprehensive Stockholders' Equity Transactions

P 3. In January 20xx, the Jones Corporation was organized and authorized to issue 2,000,000 shares of no-par common stock and 50,000 shares of 5 percent, $50 par value, noncumulative preferred stock. The stock-related transactions for the first year's operations were as follows:

				Account	
				Debited	**Credited**
Jan.	19	Sold 15,000 shares of common stock for $31,500. State law requires a minimum of $1 stated value per share.		110 ($31,500)	310 ($15,000) 312 ($16,500)
	21	Issued 5,000 shares of common stock to attorneys and accountants for services valued at $11,000 and provided during the organization of the corporation.		_____	_____
Feb.	7	Issued 30,000 shares of common stock for a building that had an appraised value of $78,000.		_____	_____
Mar.	22	Purchased 10,000 shares of its common stock at $3 per share.		_____	_____
July	15	Issued 5,000 shares of common stock to employees under a stock option plan that allows any employee to buy shares at the current market price, which is now $3 per share.		_____	_____
Aug.	1	Sold 2,500 shares of treasury stock for $4 per share.		_____	_____
Sept.	1	Declared a cash dividend of $.15 per common share to be paid on September 25 to stockholders of record on September 15.		_____	_____
	15	Date of record for cash dividends		_____	_____
	25	Paid cash dividends to stockholders of record on September 15.		_____	_____
Oct.	30	Issued 4,000 shares of common stock for a piece of land. The stock was selling for $3 per share, and the land had a fair market value of $12,000.		_____	_____
Dec.	15	Issued 2,200 shares of preferred stock for $50 per share.		_____	_____

Required

1. For each of the above transactions, enter in the blanks provided the account numbers and dollar amounts (as shown in the example) for the account(s) debited and credited. The account numbers are listed below.

110 Cash	312 Additional Paid-in Capital
120 Land	313 Paid-in Capital, Treasury Stock
121 Building	340 Retained Earnings
220 Dividends Payable	341 Dividends
305 Preferred Stock	350 Treasury Stock, Common
310 Common Stock	510 Start-up and Organization Costs

2. **User Insight:** Why is the stockholders' equity section of the balance sheet an important consideration in analyzing the performance of a company?

LO1, LO2, LO3, LO4, LO5

Comprehensive Stockholders' Equity Transactions and Financial Ratios

P 4. Kokaly Plastics Corporation was chartered in the state of Massachusetts. The company was authorized to issue 20,000 shares of $100 par value, 6 percent preferred stock and 100,000 shares of no-par common stock. The common stock has a $2 stated value. The stock-related transactions for the quarter ended October 31, 20xx, were as follows:

Aug. 3 Issued 20,000 shares of common stock at $22 per share.
   15 Issued 16,000 shares of common stock for land. Asking price for the land was $200,000. Common stock's market value was $12 per share.
   22 Issued 10,000 shares of preferred stock for $1,000,000.
Oct. 4 Issued 10,000 shares of common stock for $120,000.
   10 Purchased 5,000 shares of common stock for the treasury for $13,000.
   15 Declared a quarterly cash dividend on the outstanding preferred stock and $.10 per share on common stock outstanding, payable on October 31 to stockholders of record on October 25.
   25 Date of record for cash dividends.
   31 Paid cash dividends.

Required

1. Record transactions for the quarter ended October 31, 20xx, in T accounts.
2. Prepare the stockholders' equity section of the balance sheet as of October 31, 20xx. Net income for the quarter was $46,000.
3. **User Insight:** Calculate dividends yield, price/earnings ratio, and return on equity. Assume earnings per common share are $1.97 and market price per common share is $25. For beginning stockholders' equity, use the balance after the August transactions.
4. **User Insight:** Discuss the results in **3**, including the effect on investors' returns and the firm's profitability as it relates to stockholders' equity.

LO1, LO5 **Treasury Stock**

P 5. The Spivak Company was involved in the following treasury stock transactions during 20xx:

a. Purchased 80,000 shares of its $1 par value common stock on the market for $2.50 per share.
b. Purchased 16,000 shares of its $1 par value common stock on the market for $2.80 per share.
c. Sold 44,000 shares purchased in **a** for $131,000.
d. Sold the other 36,000 shares purchased in **a** for $72,000.
e. Sold 6,000 of the remaining shares of treasury stock for $1.60 per share.
f. Retired all the remaining shares of treasury stock. All shares originally were issued at $1.50 per share.

Required

1. Record the treasury stock transactions in T accounts.
2. **User Insight:** What is the reasoning behind treating the purchase of treasury stock as a reduction in stockholders' equity as opposed to treating it as an investment asset?

Alternate Problems

LO1, LO2, LO4 **Common Stock Transactions and Stockholders' Equity**

P 6. On March 1, 20xx, Carmel Corporation began operations with a charter from the state that authorized 100,000 shares of $4 par value common stock. Over the next quarter, the firm engaged in the transactions that follow.

Mar. 1 Issued 30,000 shares of common stock, $200,000.

2 Paid fees associated with obtaining the charter and starting up and organizing the corporation, $24,000.

Apr. 10 Issued 13,000 shares of common stock, $130,000.

15 Purchased 5,000 shares of common stock, $50,000

May 31 The board of directors declared a $.20 per share cash dividend to be paid on June 15 to shareholders of record on June 10.

Required

1. Record the above transactions in T accounts.
2. Prepare the stockholders' equity section of Carmel Corporation's balance sheet on May 31, 20xx. Net income earned during the first quarter was $30,000.
3. **User Insight:** What effect, if any, will the cash dividend declaration on May 31 have on Carmel Corporation's net income, retained earnings, and cash flows?

LO1, LO3 **Preferred and Common Stock Dividends and Dividends Yield**

 P 7. The Clockwork Corporation had the following stock outstanding from 20x6 through 20x9:

Preferred stock: $100 par value, 8 percent cumulative, 10,000 shares authorized, issued, and outstanding

Common stock: $10 par value, 200,000 shares authorized, issued, and outstanding

The company paid $60,000, $60,000, $188,000, and $260,000 in dividends during 20x6, 20x7, 20x8, and 20x9, respectively. The market price per common share was $7.25 and $8.00 per share at the end of years 20x8 and 20x9, respectively.

Required

1. Determine the dividends per share and the total dividends paid to common stockholders and preferred stockholders in 20x6, 20x7, 20x8, and 20x9.
2. Perform the same computations, with the assumption that the preferred stock was noncumulative.
3. Calculate the 20x8 and 20x9 dividends yield for common stock, using the dividends per share computed in requirement **2**.
4. **User Insight:** How are cumulative preferred stock and noncumulative preferred stock similar to long-term bonds? How do they differ from long-term bonds?

LO1, LO2, LO3, LO4, LO5 **Comprehensive Stockholders' Equity Transactions and Stockholders' Equity**

 **P 8.** Vanowski, Inc., was organized and authorized to issue 10,000 shares of $100 par value, 9 percent preferred stock and 100,000 shares of no-par, $5 stated value common stock on July 1, 20xx. Stock-related transactions for Vanowski are as follows:

July 1 Issued 20,000 shares of common stock at $11 per share.

1 Issued 1,000 shares of common stock at $11 per share for services rendered in connection with the organization of the company.

2 Issued 2,000 shares of preferred stock at par value for cash.

10 Issued 5,000 shares of common stock for land on which the asking price was $70,000. Market value of the stock was $12. Management wishes to record the land at full market value of the stock.

Aug. 2 Purchased 3,000 shares of its common stock at $13 per share.

Aug. 10 Declared a cash dividend for one month on the outstanding preferred stock and $.02 per share on common stock outstanding, payable on August 22 to stockholders of record on August 12.
12 Date of record for cash dividends.
22 Paid cash dividends.

Required

1. Record the transactions in journal form.
2. Prepare the stockholders' equity section of the balance sheet as it would appear on August 31, 20xx. Net income for July and August was $23,000.
3. **User Insight:** Calculate dividends yield, price/earnings ratio, and return on equity. Assume earnings per common share are $1.00 and market price per common share is $20. For beginning stockholders' equity, use the balance after the July transactions.
4. **User Insight:** Discuss the results in requirement **3**, including the effect on investors' returns and the company's profitability as it relates to stockholders' equity.

ENHANCING Your Knowledge, Skills, and Critical Thinking

Conceptual Understanding Cases

LO1 **Reasons for Issuing Common Stock**

C 1. In a recent year, **Avaya, Inc.**, an East Coast telecommunications company, issued 34,300,000 shares of common stock for a total of $212,000,000.[15] As a growing company, Avaya could have raised this significant amount of money by issuing long-term bonds, but the company's bond rating had recently been lowered. What are some advantages of issuing common stock as opposed to bonds? What are some disadvantages?

LO3 **Reasons for Issuing Preferred Stock**

K/R **C 2.** Preferred stock is a hybrid security; it has some of the characteristics of stock and some of the characteristics of bonds. Historically, preferred stock has not been a popular means of financing. In the past few years, however, it has become more attractive to companies and individual investors alike, and investors are buying large amounts because of high yields. Large preferred stock issues have been made by such banks as **Chase**, **Citibank**, **HSBC Bank USA**, and **Wells Fargo**, as well as by other companies. The dividends yields on these stocks are over 9 percent, higher than the interest rates on bonds of comparable risk.[16] Especially popular are preferred equity redemption convertible stocks, or PERCs, which are automatically convertible into common stock after three years if the company does not call them first and retire them. What sons can you give for the popularity of preferred stock, and of PERC ular, when the tax-deductible interest on bonds is lower? the company's and the investor's standpoint.

LO5 **Purposes of Treasury Stock**

K/R **C 3.** Many companies in recent years have b For example, **IBM**, with large cash holdings, s years repurchasing its stock. What are the reas own shares? What is the effect of common st share, return on equity, return on assets, debt to

Interpreting Financial Reports

LO4 **Effect of Stock Issue**

C 4. When **Netscape Communications Corporation** went public with an IPO, it issued stock at $28 per share. In its second year as a public company, Netscape (which later became a subsidiary of **AOL Time Warner**) announced a common stock issue in an ad in *The Wall Street Journal*:

6,440,000 Shares
NETSCAPE
Common Stock
Price $53¾ a share

If Netscape had sold all these shares at the offering price of $53.75, the net proceeds before issue costs would have been $346.15 million.

Shown below is a portion of the stockholders' equity section of the balance sheet adapted from Netscape's annual report, which was issued prior to this stock offering:

Stockholders' Equity (In thousands)	
Common Stock, $0.0001 par value, 200,000,000 shares authorized; 81,063,158 shares issued and outstanding	$ 8
Additional paid-in capital	196,749
Accumulated deficit	(16,314)

1. Assume the net proceeds from the sale of 6,440,000 shares at $53.75 were $342.6 million after issue costs. Record the stock issuance on Netscape's accounting records in journal form.
2. Prepare the portion of the stockholders' equity section of the balance sheet shown above after the issue of the common stock, based on the information given. Round all answers to the nearest thousand.
3. Based on your answer in **2**, did Netscape have to increase its authorized shares to undertake this stock issue?
4. What amount per share did Netscape receive and how much did Netscape's underwriters receive to help in issuing the stock if investors paid $53.75 per share? What do underwriters do to earn their fee?

LO3 **Effect of Deferring Preferred Dividends**

C 5. **US Airways** had indefinitely deferred the quarterly dividend on its $358 million of cumulative convertible 91¼ percent preferred stock.[17] According to a US Airways spokesperson, the company did not want to "continue to pay a dividend while the company is losing money." Others interpreted the action as "an indication of a cash crisis situation."

At the time, **Berkshire Hathaway**, the large company run by Warren Buffett and the owner of the preferred stock, was not happy. However, US Airways was able to turn around, become profitable, and return to paying its cumulative dividends on preferred stock. Berkshire Hathaway was able to convert the preferred stock into 9.24 million common shares of US Airways' common stock at $38.74 per share at a time when the market value had risen to $62.[18]

What is cumulative convertible preferred stock? Why is deferring dividends on those shares a drastic action? What is the impact on profitability and liquidity? Why did using preferred stock instead of long-term bonds as a financing method probably save the company from bankruptcy? What was Berkshire Hathaway's gain on its investment at the time of the conversion?

LO1, LO2

Decision Analysis Using Excel

Analysis of Alternative Financing Methods

C 6. Northeast Servotech Corporation, which offers services to the computer industry, has expanded rapidly in recent years. Because of its profitability, the company has been able to grow without obtaining external financing. This fact is reflected in its current balance sheet, which contains no long-term debt. The liabilities and stockholders' equity sections of the balance sheet on March 31, 20xx, appear below.

Northeast Servotech Corporation Balance Sheet March 31, 20xx		
Liabilities		
Current liabilities		$ 500,000
Stockholders' Equity		
Common stock, $10 par value, 500,000 shares authorized, 100,000 shares issued and outstanding	$1,000,000	
Additional paid-in capital	1,800,000	
Retained earnings	1,700,000	
Total stockholders' equity		4,500,000
Total liabilities and stockholders' equity		$5,000,000

The company now has the opportunity to double its size by purchasing the operations of a rival company for $4,000,000. If the purchase goes through, Northeast Servotech will become one of the top companies in its specialized industry. The problem for management is how to finance the purchase. After much study and discussion with bankers and underwriters, management has prepared the following three financing alternatives to present to the board of directors, which must authorize the purchase and the financing:

> *Alternative A* The company could issue $4,000,000 of long-term debt. Given the company's financial rating and the current market rates, management believes the company will have to pay an interest rate of 12 percent on the debt.
>
> *Alternative B* The company could issue 40,000 shares of 8 percent, $100 par value preferred stock.
>
> *Alternative C* The company could issue 100,000 additional shares of $10 par value common stock at $40 per share.

Management explains to the board that the interest on the long-term debt is tax-deductible and that the applicable income tax rate is 40 percent. The board members know that a dividend of $.80 per share of common stock was paid last year, up from $.60 and $.40 per share in the two years before that. The board has had a policy of regular increases in dividends of $.20 per share. The board believes each of the three financing alternatives is feasible and now wants to study the financial effects of each alternative.

1. Prepare a schedule to show how the liabilities and stockholders' equity sections of Northeast Servotech's balance sheet would look under each alternative, and compute the debt to equity ratio (total liabilities ÷ total stockholders' equity) for each.
2. Compute and compare the cash needed to pay the interest or dividends for each kind of new financing, net of income taxes, in the first year.
3. How might the cash needed to pay for the financing change in future years under each alternative?
4. Prepare a memorandum to the board of directors that evaluates the alternatives in order of preference based on cash flow effects, giving arguments for and against each one.

Annual Report Case: CVS Corporation

LO1, LO2, LO5 Stockholders' Equity

  C 7. Refer to the **CVS Corporation** annual report in the Supplement to Chapter 1 to answer the following questions:

1. What type of capital stock does CVS have? What is the par value? How many shares were authorized, issued, and outstanding at the end of fiscal 2004?
2. What is the dividends yield (use average price of stock in last quarter) for CVS and its relationship to the investors' total return? Does the company rely mostly on stock or on earnings for its stockholders' equity?
3. Does the company have a stock option plan? To whom do the stock options apply? Do employees have significant stock options? Given the market price of the stock shown in the report, do these options represent significant value to the employees?

Comparison Case: CVS Versus Southwest

LO1, LO5 Return on Equity, Treasury Stock, and Dividends Policy

  C 8. Refer to the annual report of **CVS Corporation** and the financial statements of **Southwest Airlines Co.** in the Supplement to Chapter 1.

1. Compute the return on equity for both companies for fiscal 2004 and 2003. Total stockholders' equity for CVS and Southwest in 2002 was $5,197.0 million and $4,422 million, respectively.
2. Did either company purchase treasury stock during these years? How will the purchase of treasury stock affect return on equity and earnings per share?
3. Did either company issue stock during these years? What are the details?
4. Compare the dividend policy of the two companies.

Ethical Dilemma Case

LO1, LO5 Ethics, Management Compensation, and Treasury Stock

C 9. Compensation of senior management is often tied to earnings per share or return on equity. Treasury stock purchases have a favorable impact on both these measures. In the recent buyback boom, many companies borrowed money to purchase treasury shares. In some cases, the motivation for the borrowing and repurchase of shares was the desire of executives to secure their year-end cash bonuses. Did these executives act ethically? Were their actions in the best interests of stockholders? Why or why not? How might such behavior be avoided in the future?

Internet Case

LO1, LO2, LO3, LO4, LO5   Comprehensive Analysis of Stockholders' Equity

C 10. Many Internet companies have gone public in recent years. These companies are generally unprofitable in their start-up years and require a great deal of cash to finance expansion. They also reward their employees with stock options. Choose any one of the following Internet companies: **Amazon.com**, **Yahoo!**, or **eBay**. Go to the website of the company you have selected. In the company's latest annual report, look at the financing section of the statement of cash flows for the last three years. How has the company financed its business? Has it issued stock or long-term debt? Has it purchased treasury stock, paid dividends, or issued stock under stock option plans? Is the company profitable (see net income or earnings at the top of the statement)? Are your findings in line with your expectations about Internet companies? Find the company's stock price, either on its website or in a newspaper, and compare it with the average issue price of the company's past stock issues. Summarize your findings and conclusions.

Group Activity Case

LO1, LO5   Treasury Stock or Dividends?

C 11. In your class, divide into small groups. Assume the president of a small company that has been profitable for several years but has not paid a dividend has hired your group. The company has built up a cash reserve. It has 20 stockholders, but the president owns 40 percent of the company's shares. Several of the stockholders with smaller numbers of shares would like to sell their shares, but there is no ready market. The president of the company has asked your group to determine whether it would be better to recommend to the board of directors that they pay a dividend to all stockholders or whether they should buy out the smaller stockholders to hold in the treasury shares and possibly retire them. In your group, decide which recommendation you will make to the president. Develop a series of points to support your argument. Participate in a class debate among teams who have chosen opposing positions.

Business Communication Case

LO1   Debt or Equity Financing

C 12. As noted in the Decision Point at the beginning of this chapter, **Google, Inc.**, announced a common stock issue:

22,500,000 Shares
.001 Par Value Common Stock
Price $85 a share

The net proceeds before issue costs were $1.9 billion.

Given Google's successful track record as a start-up company, it is likely the company could have borrowed $1.9 billion in debt financing rather than issue common stock. Write a one-page business memorandum that takes either the position that (1) Google should have issued debt at an interest rate of 8 percent or (2) Google is correct in issuing common stock. Be sure to include in your presentation the effect of your alternative on the debt to equity ratio and return on equity.

The Corporate Income Statement and the Statement of Stockholders' Equity

As we pointed out in an earlier chapter, earnings management—the practice of manipulating revenues and expenses to achieve a specific outcome—is unethical when companies use it to create misleading financial statements. Users of financial statements consider the possibility of earnings management by assessing the quality, or sustainability, of a company's earnings. To do so, they evaluate how the components of the company's income statement affect earnings. In this chapter, we focus on those components. We also cover earnings per share, the statement of stockholders' equity, stock dividends and stock splits, and book value per share.

LEARNING OBJECTIVES

Making a Statement

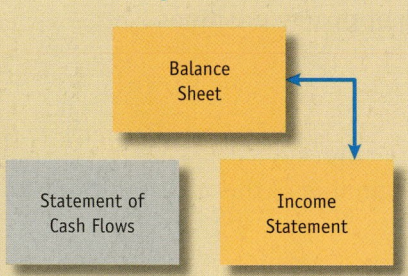

The corporate income statement aids in the analysis of profitability and links to stockholders' equity, a component of the balance sheet.

LO1 Define *quality of earnings,* and identify the components of a corporate income statement.

LO2 Show the relationships among income taxes expense, deferred income taxes, and net of taxes.

LO3 Describe the disclosure on the income statement of discontinued operations and extraordinary items.

LO4 Compute earnings per share.

LO5 Define *comprehensive income,* and describe the statement of stockholders' equity.

LO6 Account for stock dividends and stock splits.

LO7 Calculate book value per share.

- What items other than normal operating activities contributed to Motorola's performance?

- What does the company's income statement indicate about its quality of earnings?

- How does one put the various measures of performance (some of which are shown in Motorola's financial highlights) in perspective?

Motorola, a well-known maker of cell phones and other telecommunications equipment, has had its ups and downs in recent years. As shown in its Financial Highlights, the company had large losses in 2002. However, its earnings improved in 2003 and 2004, and its sales, after taking a dip in 2003, recovered and grew in 2004.[1] The many changes Motorola experienced over this period were, of course, reflected in its income statements.

How does one use complex income statements like Motorola's to evaluate a company's performance? It is not enough to simply look at the "bottom line" (i.e., net earnings) or even at net sales and operating income. To gain a proper perspective on a company's performance, one must examine the components of its income statement.

MOTOROLA'S FINANCIAL HIGHLIGHTS
(In millions, except per share data)

	2004	2003	2002
Net sales	$31,323	$23,155	$23,422
Operating earnings (loss)	3,132	1,273	(443)
Net earnings	1,532	893	(2,485)
Basic earnings per share	0.64	0.38	(1.09)
Cash flows from operating activities	3,066	1,991	1,151

Performance Measurement: Quality of Earnings Issues

Net income (net earnings) is the measure most commonly used to evaluate a company's performance. In fact, a survey of 2,000 members of the Association for Investment Management and Research indicated that the two most important economic measures in evaluating common stocks were expected changes in earnings per share and expected return on equity.[2] Net income is a key component of both measures.

Because of the importance of net income, or the "bottom line," in measuring a company's prospects, there is significant interest in evaluating the quality of the net income figure, or the **quality of earnings**. The quality of a company's earnings refers to the substance of earnings and their sustainability into future accounting periods. For example, if earnings increase because of a gain on the sale of an asset, this portion of earnings will not be sustained in the future.

The accounting estimates and methods that a company uses affect the quality of its earnings, as do these components of the income statement:

- Gains and losses on transactions

- Write-downs and restructurings

- Nonoperating items

Because management has choices in the content and positioning of these income statement components, there is a potential for managing earnings to achieve specific income targets. It is therefore critical for users of income statements to understand these factors and take them into consideration when evaluating a company's performance.

Exhibit 1 shows the components of a typical corporate income statement. Net income or loss (the "bottom line" of the income statement) includes all revenues, expenses, gains, and losses over the accounting period. When a company has both continuing and discontinued operations, the operating income section is called **income from continuing operations**. Income from continuing operations before income taxes may include gains or losses on the sale of assets, write-downs, and restructurings. The income taxes expense section of the statement is subject to special accounting rules.

As you can see in Exhibit 1, the section of a corporate income statement that follows income taxes contains such nonoperating items as discontinued operations and extraordinary gains (or losses). Another item that may appear

FOCUS ON BUSINESS PRACTICE

Why Do Investors Study Quality of Earnings?

Analysts for **Twentieth Century Mutual Funds**, a major investment company now merged with **American Century Investments Corporation**, make adjustments to a company's reported financial performance to create a more accurate picture of the company's ongoing operations. For example, suppose a paper manufacturer reports earnings of $1.30 per share. Further investigation, however, shows that the per share number includes a one-time gain on the sale of assets, which accounts for an increase of $.25 per share. Twentieth Century would list the company as earning only $1.05 per share. "These kinds of adjustments help assure long-term decisions aren't based on one-time events."[3]

▼ **EXHIBIT 1**

Corporate Income Statement

Envest Corporation
Income Statement
For the Year Ended December 31, 20x6

Operating items before income taxes	Revenues		$925,000
	Costs and expenses		(550,000)
	Gain on sale of assets		150,000
	Write-downs of assets		(25,000)
	Restructurings		(75,000)
	Income from continuing operations before income taxes		$425,000
Income taxes	Income taxes expense		144,500
	Income from continuing operations		$280,500
Nonoperating items	Discontinued operations		
	Income from operations of discontinued segment (net of taxes, $35,000)	$90,000	
	Loss on disposal of segment (net of taxes, $42,000)	(73,000)	17,000
	Income before extraordinary items		$297,500
	Extraordinary gain (net of taxes, $12,000)		37,000
	Net income		$334,500
Earnings per share information	Earnings per common share:		
	Income from continuing operations		$ 2.81
	Discontinued operations (net of taxes)		.17
	Income before extraordinary items		$ 2.98
	Extraordinary gain (net of taxes)		.37
	Net income		$ 3.35

in this section is the write-off of goodwill when its value has been impaired. Earnings per share information appears at the bottom of the statement.

Study Note

It is important to know which items included in earnings are recurring and which are one-time items. Income from continuing operations before nonoperating items gives a clear signal about future results. In assessing a company's future earnings potential, nonoperating items are excluded because they are not expected to continue.

The Effect of Accounting Estimates and Methods

Users of financial statements need to be aware of the impact that accounting estimates and methods have on the income that a firm reports. As you know, to comply with the matching rule, accountants must assign revenues and expenses to the periods in which they occur. If they cannot establish a direct relationship between revenues and expenses, they systematically allocate the expenses among the accounting periods that benefit from them, and in doing so, they must make estimates and exercise judgment. An accounting estimate should be based on realistic assumptions, but there is latitude in making the estimate, and the final judgment will affect the net income that appears on a company's income statement.

For example, when a company acquires an asset, the accountant must estimate the asset's useful life. Technological obsolescence could shorten the asset's expected useful life, and regular maintenance and repairs could lengthen it. Although the actual useful life cannot be known with certainty until some future date, the accountant's estimate of it affects both current and future operating income. Other areas that require accounting estimates include the residual value of assets, uncollectible accounts receivable, sales returns, total units of production, total recoverable units of natural resources, amortization periods, warranty claims, and environmental cleanup costs.

Accounting estimates are not equally important to all firms. Their importance depends on the industry in which a firm operates. For example, estimated uncollectible receivables for a credit card firm, such as **American Express**, or for a financial services firm, such as **Bank of America**, can have a material impact on earnings, but estimated useful life may be less important because depreciable assets represent only a small percentage of the firm's total assets. **Walgreens** has very few receivables, but it has substantial investments in depreciable assets. Thus, estimates of useful life and residual value are much more important to Walgreens than an estimate of uncollectible accounts receivable.

The accounting methods a firm uses also affect its operating income. Generally accepted accounting methods include uncollectible receivable methods (percentage of net sales and aging of accounts receivable), inventory methods (LIFO, FIFO, and average-cost), depreciation methods (accelerated, production, and straight-line), and revenue recognition methods. All these methods are designed to match revenues and expenses, but the expenses are estimates, and the period or periods benefited cannot be demonstrated conclusively. In practice, it is hard to justify one method of estimation over another.

Different accounting methods have different effects on net income. Some methods are more conservative than others because they tend to produce a lower net income in the current period. For example, suppose that two companies have similar operations, but one uses FIFO for inventory costing and the straight-line (SL) method for computing depreciation, whereas the other uses LIFO for inventory costing and the double-declining-balance (DDB) method for computing depreciation. The income statements of the two companies might appear as follows:

	FIFO *and* SL	LIFO *and* DDB
Net sales	$925,000	$925,000
Goods available for sale	$400,000	$400,000
Less ending inventory	60,000	50,000
Cost of goods sold	$340,000	$350,000
Gross margin	$585,000	$575,000
Less depreciation expense	$ 40,000	$ 80,000
Less other expenses	170,000	170,000
Total operating expenses	$210,000	$250,000
Income from continuing operations before income taxes	$375,000	$325,000

The income from continuing operations before income taxes (operating income) for the firm that uses LIFO and DDB is lower because in periods of rising prices, the LIFO inventory costing method produces a higher cost of goods sold, and in the early years of an asset's useful life, accelerated depreciation yields a higher depreciation expense. The result is lower operating income. However, future operating income should be higher.

Although the choice of accounting method does not affect cash flows except for possible differences in income taxes, the $50,000 difference in operating income stems solely from the choice of accounting methods. Estimates of

Study Note

Although companies in the same industry may have comparable earnings, their quality of earnings may not be comparable. To assess the quality of a company's reported earnings, you must know the estimates and methods it uses to compute income. Generally accepted accounting principles allow several methods, all yielding different results.

the useful lives and residual values of plant assets could lead to an even greater difference. In practice, of course, differences in net income occur for many reasons, but the user of financial statements must be aware of the discrepancies that can occur as a result of the accounting methods used in preparing the statements. In general, an accounting method or estimate that results in lower current earnings produces a better quality of operating income.

The latitude that companies have in their choice of accounting methods and estimates could cause problems in the interpretation of financial statements were it not for the conventions of full disclosure and consistency. As noted in an earlier chapter, full disclosure requires management to explain the significant accounting policies used in preparing the financial statements in a note to the statements. Consistency requires that the same accounting procedures be followed from year to year. If a change in procedure is made, the nature of the change and its monetary effect must be explained in a note. For instance, in a note to its financial statements, **Motorola** discloses that it uses the FIFO method for inventory accounting and a combination of straight-line and accelerated depreciation methods for various groups of long-term assets.

Gains and Losses

When a company sells or otherwise disposes of operating assets or marketable securities, a gain or loss generally results. Although these gains or losses appear in the operating section of the income statement, they usually represent one-time events. They are not sustainable, ongoing operations, and management often has some choice as to their timing. Thus, from an analyst's point of view, they should be ignored when considering operating income.

Write-downs and Restructurings

Management has considerable latitude in deciding when an asset is no longer of value to the company. When management makes this judgment, a write-down or restructuring occurs.

▶ A **write-down**, also called a *write-off*, is a reduction in the value of an asset below its carrying value on the balance sheet.

▶ A **restructuring** is the estimated cost of a change in a company's operations. It usually involves the closing of facilities and the laying off of personnel.

Both write-downs and restructurings reduce current operating income and boost future income by shifting future costs to the current accounting period.

FOCUS ON BUSINESS PRACTICE
Can You Believe "Pro Forma" Earnings?

Companies must report earnings in accordance with GAAP, but an increasing number also report "pro forma" earnings. Pro forma reporting of earnings, in the words of one analyst, means that they "have thrown out the bad stuff."[5] In other words, when companies report pro forma earnings, they are telling the investment community to ignore one-time losses and nonoperating items, which may reflect bad decisions in the past. Research studies show that the companies most likely to report pro forma earnings are technology firms with high growth rates and volatile or low earnings and firms that unexpectedly miss earnings targets.[6] For example, in a recent year, **Verisign**, a leading seller of Internet addresses, reported that its GAAP earnings were a negative $4.8 billion, but according to its pro forma report, its earnings were a positive $50 million. GAAP earnings are a better benchmark of a company's performance because they are based on recognized standards used by all companies, whereas there is no generally accepted way to report pro forma earnings. They are whatever the company wants you to see.

They are often an indication of poor management decisions in the past, such as paying too much for the assets of another company or making operational changes that do not work out. Companies sometimes take all possible losses in the current year so that future years will be "clean" of these costs. Such "big baths," as they are called, commonly occur when a company is having a bad year. They also often occur in years when there is a change in management. The new management takes a "big bath" in the current year so it can show improved results in future years.

In a recent year, 36.5 percent of 600 large companies had write-downs of tangible assets, and 26 percent had restructurings. Another 34.2 percent had write-downs or charges related to intangible assets, often involving goodwill.[7]

Nonoperating Items

The nonoperating items that appear on the income statement,* such as discontinued operations and extraordinary gains and losses, can also significantly affect net income. In Exhibit 1, earnings per common share for income from continuing operations are $2.81, but when all the nonoperating items are taken into consideration, net income per share is $3.35.

Analysts base their calculations of trends and ratios on the assumption that the components of the income statement are comparable from year to year and from company to company. However, the astute analyst will always look beyond the ratios to the quality of these components. For example, write-downs, restructurings, and nonoperating items, if the charges are large enough, can have a significant effect on a company's return on equity.

Quality of Earnings and Cash Flows

The reason for considering quality of earnings issues is to assess how they affect cash flows and performance measures that are affected by earnings, such as profit margin, return on assets, and return on equity. Generally, except for their effect on income taxes, gains and losses, asset write-downs, restructurings, and nonoperating items have no effect on cash flows because the cash for these items has already been expended. Thus, the focus of analysis is on sustainable earnings, which generally have a relationship to future cash flows.

---

*In May 2005, the FASB issued a statement that removed an item from this category. The effects of changes in accounting principles are no longer reported on the income statement but are a direct adjustment to retained earnings.

Motorola provides communications equipment to the National Football League. Shown here wearing a Motorola headset is Bill Belichick, head coach of the New England Patriots. Despite Motorola's sluggish results in recent years, its CEO pointed out in 2005 that the company's quality of earnings had improved from year to year. *Quality of earnings* refers to the substance and sustainability of earnings into future accounting periods.

Because **Motorola** has a history of reporting nonrecurring special items, including restructuring expenses and investment and inventory write-offs, analysts have questioned the quality of its earnings.[8] Recently, the company had 15 straight quarters of such items. The nonrecurring special items in Motorola's income statement, shown in Exhibit 2, include reorganization of businesses,

EXHIBIT 2 ▶

Motorola's Income Statement

	Year Ended December 31		
(In millions)	**2004**	2003	2002
Net sales	$31,323	$23,155	$23,422
Cost of sales	20,826	15,588	15,741
Gross margin	$10,497	$ 7,567	$ 7,681
Selling, general, and administrative costs	$ 4,209	$ 3,529	$ 3,991
Research and development expenditures	3,060	2,799	2,774
Reorganization of businesses	(15)	23	605
Other charges (income)	111	(57)	754
Operating earnings (loss)	$ 3,132	$ 1,273	$ (443)
Other income (expense):			
Interest expense, net	$ (199)	$ (294)	$ (355)
Gains on sales of investments and businesses, net	460	539	81
Other	(141)	(142)	(1,354)
Total other income (expense)	$ 120	$ 103	$(1,628)
Earnings (loss) from continuing operations before income taxes	$ 3,252	$ 1,376	$(2,071)
Income tax expense (benefit)	1,061	448	(721)
Earnings (loss) from continuing operations	$ 2,191	$ 928	$(1,350)
Loss from discontinued operations, net of tax	(659)	(35)	(1,135)
Net earnings (loss)	$ 1,532	$ 893	$(2,485)

Note: Highlighted items are discussed in the text.
Source: Motorola, Inc., *Annual Report*, 2004.

other charges, gains on sales of investments and businesses, and losses from discontinued operations in 2002, 2003, and 2004. However, if you look back at Motorola's Financial Highlights at the start of this chapter, you will see that the company's cash flows from operating activities were positive even in 2002 when it suffered a net loss and that they exceeded net earnings in 2003 and 2004 by a factor of more than 2 to 1. By this measure, Motorola's earnings are of relatively high quality.

S T O P • R E V I E W • A P P L Y

1-1. What is quality of earnings? What are three components of the income statement that affect quality of earnings?

1-2. Why would the reader of financial statements be interested in management's choice of accounting methods and estimates? Give an example.

1-3. What is the difference between a write-down and a restructuring, and where do these items appear on a corporate income statement?

1-4. How do cash flows relate to quality of earnings?

Suggested Answers to all Stop, Review, and Apply questions follow the appendixes.

Income Taxes

> **LO2** Show the relationships among income taxes expense, deferred income taxes, and net of taxes.

Corporations determine their taxable income (the amount on which they pay taxes) by deducting allowable expenses from taxable income. The federal tax laws determine which expenses corporations may deduct. (Rules for calculating and reporting taxable income in specialized industries, such as banking, insurance, mutual funds, and cooperatives, are highly technical and may vary significantly from the ones we discuss in this chapter.)

Table 1 shows the tax rates that apply to a corporation's taxable income. A corporation with taxable income of $70,000 would have a federal income tax liability of $12,500: $7,500 (the tax on the first $50,000 of taxable income) plus $5,000 (25 percent of the $20,000 earned in excess of $50,000).

Income taxes expense is recognized in the accounting records on an accrual basis. It may or may not equal the amount of taxes a corporation actually pays. The amount a corporation pays is determined by the rules of the income tax code. As we noted earlier in the text, small businesses often keep both their accounting records and tax records on a cash basis, so that the income taxes expense on their income statements equals their income taxes. This practice is acceptable as long as the difference between the income calculated on an accounting basis and the income calculated for tax purposes is not material. However, the purpose of accounting is not to determine taxable income and tax liability, but to determine net income in accordance with GAAP.

Management has an incentive to use methods that minimize its firm's tax liability. But accountants, who are bound by accrual accounting and the materiality concept, cannot let tax procedures dictate their method of preparing financial statements if the result would be misleading. The difference between

> *Study Note*
>
> Many people think it is illegal to keep accounting records on a different basis from income tax records. However, the Internal Revenue Code and GAAP often do not agree. To work with two conflicting sets of guidelines, the accountant must keep two sets of records.

TABLE 1. Tax Rate Schedule for Corporations, 2005

Taxable Income		Tax Liability	
Over	But Not Over		Of the Amount Over
	$ 50,000	0 + 15%	—
$ 50,000	75,000	$ 7,500 + 25%	$ 50,000
75,000	100,000	13,750 + 34%	75,000
100,000	335,000	22,250 + 39%	100,000
335,000	10,000,000	113,900 + 34%	335,000
10,000,000	15,000,000	3,400,000 + 35%	10,000,000
15,000,000	18,333,333	5,150,000 + 38%	15,000,000
18,333,333	—	6,416,667 + 35%	18,333,333

Note: Tax rates are subject to change by Congress.

accounting income and taxable income, especially in large businesses, can be material. This discrepancy can result from differences in the timing of the recognition of revenues and expenses under accrual accounting and the tax method. The following table shows some possible variations:

	Accrual Accounting	Tax Method
Expense recognition	Accrual or deferral	At time of expenditure
Accounts receivable	Allowance	Direct charge-off
Inventories	Average-cost	FIFO
Depreciation	Straight-line	Accelerated cost recovery

Deferred Income Taxes

Income tax allocation is the method used to accrue income taxes expense on the basis of accounting income when accounting income and taxable income differ. The account used to record the difference between income taxes expense and income taxes payable is called **Deferred Income Taxes**. For example, in the income statement in Exhibit 1, Envest Corporation has income taxes expense of $144,500. Suppose, however, that Envest's actual income taxes payable are $92,000. The following entry shows how income tax allocation would treat this situation:

A =	L	+	SE
	+92,000		−144,500
	+52,500		

Dec. 31	Income Taxes Expense	144,500	
	Income Taxes Payable		92,000
	Deferred Income Taxes		52,500
	To record estimated current and deferred income taxes		

In other years, Envest's Income Taxes Payable may exceed its Income Taxes Expense. In this case, the entry is the same except that Deferred Income Taxes is debited.

The Financial Accounting Standards Board has issued specific rules for recording, measuring, and classifying deferred income taxes.[9] Deferred income taxes are recognized for the estimated future tax effects resulting from tempo-rary differences in the valuation of assets, liabilities, equity, revenues, expenses, gains, and losses for tax and financial reporting purposes. Temporary differences include revenues and expenses or gains and losses that are included in taxable income before or after they are included in financial income. In other words, the recognition point for revenues, expenses, gains, and losses is not the same for tax and financial reporting.

For example, advance payments for goods and services, such as magazine subscriptions, are not recognized as income until the products are shipped. However, for tax purposes, advance payments are usually recognized as revenue when cash is received. As a result, taxes paid exceed taxes expense, which creates a deferred income taxes asset (or prepaid taxes).

Classification of deferred income taxes as current or noncurrent depends on the classification of the asset or liability that created the temporary difference. For example, the deferred income taxes asset mentioned above would be classified as current if unearned subscription revenue were classified as a current liability. On the other hand, the temporary difference arising from depreciation is related to a long-term depreciable asset. Therefore, the resulting deferred income taxes would be classified as long-term. If a temporary difference is not related to an asset or liability, it is classified as current or noncurrent based on its expected date of reversal. (Temporary differences and the classification of deferred income taxes that results are covered in depth in more advanced courses.)

Each year, the balance of the Deferred Income Taxes account is evaluated to determine whether it still accurately represents the expected asset or liability in light of legislated changes in income tax laws and regulations.

In any given year, the amount a company pays in income taxes is determined by subtracting (or adding) the deferred income taxes for that year from (or to) income taxes expense. In subsequent years, the amount of deferred income taxes can vary based on changes in tax laws and rates.

A survey of the financial statements of 600 large companies indicates the importance of deferred income taxes to financial reporting. About 63 percent reported deferred income taxes with a credit balance in the long-term liability section of their balance sheets.[10]

Net of Taxes

The phrase **net of taxes** indicates that taxes (usually income taxes) have been taken into account in reporting an item in the financial statements. The phrase is used in a corporate income statement when a company has items that must be disclosed in a separate section. Each such item should be reported net of the applicable income taxes to avoid distorting the income taxes expense associated with ongoing operations and the resulting net operating income.

For example, assume that a corporation with operating income before income taxes of $120,000 has a total tax expense of $66,000 and that the total income includes a gain of $100,000 on which a tax of $30,000 is due. Also assume that the gain is not part of the corporation's normal operations and must be disclosed separately on the income statement as an extraordinary item. This is how the income taxes expense would be reported on the income statement:

Operating income before income taxes	$120,000
Income taxes expense	36,000
Income before extraordinary item	$ 84,000
Extraordinary gain (net of taxes, $30,000)	70,000
Net income	$154,000

If all the income taxes expense were deducted from operating income before income taxes, both the income before extraordinary item and the extraordinary gain would be distorted.

The procedure is the same in the case of an extraordinary loss. For example, given the same facts except that the income taxes expense is only $6,000 because of a $100,000 extraordinary loss, the result is a $30,000 tax savings:

Operating income before income taxes	$120,000
Income taxes expense	36,000
Income before extraordinary item	$ 84,000
Extraordinary loss (net of taxes, $30,000)	(70,000)
Net income	$ 14,000

In Exhibit 1, the total of the income tax items for Envest Corporation is $149,500. That amount is allocated among five statement components, as follows:

Income taxes expense on income from continuing operations	$144,500
Income taxes on income from a discontinued segment	35,000
Income tax savings on the loss on the disposal of the segment	(42,000)
Income taxes on extraordinary gain	12,000
Total income taxes expense	$149,500

S T O P • R E V I E W • A P P L Y

2-1. "Accounting income should be geared to the concept of taxable income because the public understands that concept." Comment on this statement, and explain why income tax allocation is necessary.

2-2. What are deferred income taxes?

2-3. How does the concept of net of taxes affect the income statement?

Income Tax Allocation Jimenez Corporation reported the following accounting income before income taxes, income taxes expense, and net income for 20x6 and 20x7:

	20x6	20x7
Income before income taxes	$84,000	$84,000
Income taxes expense	26,490	26,490
Net income	$57,510	$57,510

On the balance sheet, deferred income taxes liability increased by $11,520 in 20x6 and decreased by $5,640 in 20x7.

1. How much was actually payable in income taxes for 20x6 and 20x7?

2. Prepare entries in journal form to record estimated current and deferred income taxes for 20x6 and 20x7.

SOLUTION

1. Income taxes calculated:

	2006	2007
Income taxes expense	$26,490	$26,490
Decrease (increase) in deferred income taxes	(11,520)	5,640
Income taxes payable	$14,970	$32,130

2. Entries prepared:

2006	Income Taxes Expense	26,490	
	Deferred Income Taxes		11,520
	Income Taxes Payable		14,970
	To record estimated current and		
	deferred income taxes for 2006		
2007	Income Taxes Expense	26,490	
	Deferred Income Taxes	5,640	
	Income Taxes Payable		32,130
	To record estimated current and		
	deferred income taxes for 2007		

Nonoperating Items

LO3 Describe the disclosure on the income statement of discontinued operations and extraordinary items.

Nonoperating items are items unrelated to a company's normal operations. They appear in a separate section of the income statement because they are considered one-time items that will not affect future results. The two principal kinds of nonoperating items are discontinued operations and extraordinary items.

Discontinued Operations

Large companies usually have many **segments**. A segment may be a separate major line of business or serve a separate class of customer. For example, a company that makes heavy drilling equipment may have another line of business, such as the manufacture of mobile homes. A company may discontinue or otherwise dispose of segments that do not fit its future plans or that are unprofitable. **Discontinued operations** are segments that are no longer part of a company's operations. To make it easier to evaluate a company's ongoing operations, generally accepted accounting principles require that gains and losses from discontinued operations be reported separately on the income statement.

In Exhibit 1, the disclosure of discontinued operations has two parts. One part shows that after the decision to discontinue, the income from operations of the disposed segment was $90,000 (net of $35,000 taxes). The other part shows that the loss from the disposal of the segment was $73,000 (net of $42,000 tax savings). (Computation of the gains or losses involved in discontinued operations is covered in more advanced accounting courses.)

Extraordinary Items

The Accounting Principles Board defines **extraordinary items** as "events or transactions that are distinguished by their unusual nature *and* by the infrequency of their occurrence."[11] The board describes unusual and infrequent occurrences as follows:

Unusual nature: The underlying event or transaction should be clearly unrelated to, or only incidentally related to, the ordinary and typical activities of the entity.

Infrequency of occurrence: The underlying event or transaction should not reasonably be expected to recur in the foreseeable future.

If an item is both unusual and infrequent (and material in amount), it should be reported separately from continuing operations on the income statement. The disclosure allows readers to identify gains or losses in income that would not be expected to happen again soon. Items usually treated as extraordinary include the following:

1. An uninsured loss from flood, earthquake, fire, or theft

2. A gain or loss resulting from the passage of a new law

3. The expropriation (taking) of property by a foreign government

In Exhibit 1, the extraordinary gain was $37,000 after taxes of $12,000.

STOP • REVIEW • APPLY

3-1. Why should a gain or loss on discontinued operations be disclosed separately on the income statement?

3-2. What are the two major criteria for extraordinary items? How should extraordinary items be disclosed in the financial statements?

Earnings per Share

LO4 Compute earnings per share.

> **Study Note**
>
> Earnings per share is a measure of a corporation's profitability. It is one of the most closely watched financial ratios in the business world. Its disclosure on the income statement is required.

Readers of financial statements use earnings per share to judge a company's performance and to compare it with the performance of other companies. Because this information is so important, the Accounting Principles Board concluded that earnings per share of common stock should be presented on the face of the income statement.[12] As shown in Exhibit 1, this information is usually disclosed just below net income.

A corporate income statement always shows earnings per share for income from continuing operations and other major components of net income. For example, if a company has a gain or loss on discontinued operations or on extraordinary items, its income statement may present earnings per share amounts for the gain or loss.

Exhibit 3 shows how **Motorola** presents earnings per share on its income statement. As you can see, the statement covers three years, and discontinued operations had a negative effect on earnings per share in all three years. However, the earnings per share for continuing operations is a better indicator of the company's future performance. Note that earnings per share are reported as basic and diluted.

Basic Earnings per Share

Basic earnings per share is the net income applicable to common stock divided by the weighted-average number of common shares outstanding. To compute this figure, one must determine if the number of common shares outstanding changed during the year and if the company paid dividends on preferred stock.

EXHIBIT 3 ▶ | **Motorola's Earnings Per Share Presentation**

	Years Ended December 31		
	2004	2003	2002
Earnings (loss) per common share:			
Basic:			
Continuing operations	**$0.93**	$0.40	$(0.59)
Discontinued operations	**(0.28)**	(0.02)	(0.50)
	$0.65	$0.38	$(1.09)
Diluted:			
Continuing operations	**$0.90**	$0.39	$(0.59)
Discontinued operations	**(0.26)**	(0.01)	(0.50)
	$0.64	$0.38	$(1.09)
Weighted averages common shares outstanding:			
Basic	**2,365.0**	2,321.9	2,282.3
Diluted	**2,472.0**	2,351.2	2,282.3

Source: Motorola, Inc., *Annual Report*, 2004.

When a company has only common stock and the number of shares outstanding is the same throughout the year, the earnings per share computation is simple. Exhibit 1 shows that Envest Corporation had net income of $334,500. If Envest had 100,000 shares of common stock outstanding during the entire year, the earnings per share of common stock would be computed as follows:

$$\text{Earnings per Share} = \frac{\$334,500}{100,000} = \$3.35^* \text{ per share}$$

If the number of shares outstanding changes during the year, it is necessary to figure the weighted-average number of shares outstanding for the year. Suppose that from January 1 to March 31, Envest Corporation had 100,000 shares outstanding; from April 1 to September 30, it had 120,000 shares outstanding; and from October 31 to December 31, it had 130,000 shares outstanding. The weighted-average number of common shares outstanding and basic earnings per share would be determined this way:

100,000 shares $\times$ $3/12$ year	25,000
120,000 shares $\times$ $6/12$ year	60,000
130,000 shares $\times$ $3/12$ year	32,500
Weighted-average common shares outstanding	117,500

$$\text{Basic Earnings per Share} = \frac{\text{Net Income}}{\text{Weighted-Average Common Shares Outstanding}}$$

$$= \frac{\$334,500}{117,500 \text{ shares}} = \$2.85 \text{ per share}$$

If a company has nonconvertible preferred stock outstanding, the dividend for that stock must be subtracted from net income before earnings per share for common stock are computed. Suppose that Envest Corporation has preferred stock on which it pays an annual dividend of $23,500. Earnings per share on common stock would be $2.65 [($334,500 − $23,500) ÷ 117,500 shares].

*This number is rounded, as are some other results of computations that follow.

Diluted Earnings Per Share

Companies can have a simple capital structure or a complex capital structure.

▶ A company has a **simple capital structure** if it has no preferred stocks, bonds, or stock options that can be converted to common stock. A company with a simple capital structure computes earnings per share as shown above.

▶ A company that has issued securities or stock options that can be converted to common stock has a **complex capital structure**. These securities and options have the potential of diluting the earnings per share of common stock.

Potential dilution means that the conversion of stocks or bonds or the exercise of stock options can increase the total number of shares of common stock that a company has outstanding and thereby reduce a current stockholder's proportionate share of ownership in the company. For example, suppose that a person owns 10,000 shares of a company's common stock, which equals 2 percent of the outstanding shares of 500,000. Now suppose that holders of convertible bonds convert the bonds into 100,000 shares of stock. The person's 10,000 shares would then equal only 1.67 percent (10,000 ÷ 600,000) of the outstanding shares. In addition, the added shares outstanding would lower earnings per share and would most likely lower market price per share.

When a company has a complex capital structure, it must report two earnings per share figures: basic earnings per share and diluted earnings per share.[13] **Diluted earnings per share** are calculated by adding all potentially dilutive securities to the denominator of the basic earnings per share calculation. This figure shows stockholders the maximum potential effect of dilution on their ownership position. As you can see in Exhibit 3, the dilution effect for **Motorola** is not large, only 1 cent per share in 2004 ($0.65 − $0.64), because the company's only dilutive securities are a relatively few stock options.

S T O P • R E V I E W • A P P L Y

4-1. Where are earnings per share disclosed in the financial statements?

4-2. When does a company have a simple capital structure? A complex capital structure?

4-3. What is the difference between basic and diluted earnings per share?

Earnings per Share During 20x7, Chester Corporation reported a net income of $3,059,000. On January 1, 20x7, Chester had 700,000 shares of common stock outstanding, and it issued an additional 420,000 shares of common stock on October 1. The company has a simple capital structure.

1. Determine the weighted-average number of common shares outstanding.

2. Compute earnings per share.

> **SOLUTION**
>
> 1. Weighted-average number of common shares outstanding:
>
> | | |
> |---|---:|
> | 700,000 shares × 9/12 | 525,000 |
> | 1,120,000 shares × 3/12 | 280,000 |
> | Weighted-average number of common shares outstanding | 805,000 |
>
> 2. Earnings per share:
> $3,059,000 ÷ 805,000 shares = $3.80

Comprehensive Income and the Statement of Stockholders' Equity

LO5   Define *comprehensive income,* and describe the statement of stockholders' equity.

The concept of comprehensive income and the statement of stockholders' equity provide further explanation of the income statement and the balance sheet and serve as links between those two statements.

Comprehensive Income

Some items that are not stock transactions affect stockholders' equity. These items, which come from sources other than stockholders and that account for the change in a company's equity during an accounting period, are called **comprehensive income**. Comprehensive income includes net income, changes in unrealized investment gains and losses, and other items affecting equity, such as foreign currency translation adjustments. The FASB takes the position that these changes in stockholders' equity should be summarized as income for a period.[14] Companies may report comprehensive income and its components in a separate financial statement, as **eBay** does in Exhibit 4, or as a part of another financial statement.

In a recent survey of 600 large companies, 580 reported comprehensive income. Of these, 84 percent reported comprehensive income in the statement of stockholders' equity, 12 percent reported it in a separate statement, and only 4 percent reported it in the income statement.[15] In Exhibit 5, we follow the most common practice and show it as a part of the statement of stockholders' equity.

The Statement of Stockholders' Equity

The **statement of stockholders' equity**, also called the *statement of changes in stockholders' equity,* summarizes changes in the components of the stockholders' equity section of the balance sheet. Most companies use this statement in place of the statement of retained earnings because it reveals much more about the stockholders' equity transactions that took place during the accounting period.

For example, in Kavra Corporation's statement of stockholders' equity in Exhibit 5, the first line shows the beginning balance of each account in the stockholders' equity section of the balance sheet. Each subsequent line discloses the effects of transactions on those accounts. Kavra had a net income of $270,000 and a foreign currency translation loss of $10,000, which it reported as accumulated other comprehensive income. These two items together resulted in comprehensive income of $260,000.

Kavra's statement of stockholders' equity also shows that during 20x7, the firm issued 5,000 shares of common stock for $250,000, had a conversion of $100,000 of preferred stock to common stock, declared and issued a 10 percent stock dividend on common stock, purchased treasury stock for $24,000, and paid cash dividends on both preferred and common stock. The ending balances of the accounts appear at the bottom of the statement. Those accounts and balances make up the stockholders' equity section of Kavra's balance sheet on December 31, 20x7, as shown in Exhibit 6.

Study Note

The statement of stockholders' equity is a labeled calculation of the change in each stockholders' equity account over an accounting period.

Study Note

The ending balances on the statement of stockholders' equity are transferred to the stockholders' equity section of the balance sheet.

EXHIBIT 4 ▶

eBay's Statement of Comprehensive Income

	Year Ended December 31		
(In thousands)	2004	2003	2002
Net income	$778,223	$441,771	$249,891
Other comprehensive income			
Foreign currency translation	139,523	66,326	48,000
Unrealized gains (losses) on investments, net	(8,727)	(5,861)	774
Investment losses included in net income	24	364	558
Unrealized gains (losses) on cash flow hedges	5,525	4,249	(2,637)
Estimated tax benefit	1,102	620	448
Net change in other comprehensive income	137,447	65,698	47,143
Comprehensive income	$915,670	$507,469	$297,034

Source: eBay Inc., *Annual Report*, 2004.

▼ EXHIBIT 5

Statement of Stockholders' Equity

Kavra Corporation
Statement of Stockholders' Equity
For the Year Ended December 31, 20x7

	Preferred Stock $100 Par Value 8% Convertible	Common Stock $10 Par Value	Additional Paid-in Capital	Retained Earnings	Treasury Stock	Accumulated Other Comprehensive Income	Total
Balance, December 31, 20x6	$400,000	$300,000	$300,000	$600,000	—		$1,600,000
Net income				270,000			270,000
Foreign currency translation adjustment						($10,000)	(10,000)
Issuance of 5,000 shares of common stock		50,000	200,000				250,000
Conversion of 1,000 shares of preferred stock to 3,000 shares of common stock	(100,000)	30,000	70,000				—
10 percent stock dividend on common stock, 3,800 shares		38,000	152,000	(190,000)			—
Purchase of 500 shares of treasury stock					($24,000)		(24,000)
Cash dividends							
Preferred stock				(24,000)			(24,000)
Common stock				(47,600)			(47,600)
Balance, December 31, 20x7	$300,000	$418,000	$722,000	$608,400	($24,000)	($10,000)	$2,014,000

EXHIBIT 6 ▶

Stockholders' Equity Section of a Balance Sheet

Kavra Corporation
Balance Sheet
December 31, 20x7

Stockholders' Equity

Contributed capital			
Preferred stock, $100 par value, 8 percent convertible, 10,000 shares authorized, 3,000 shares issued and outstanding			$ 300,000
Common stock, $10 par value, 100,000 shares authorized, 41,800 shares issued, 41,300 shares outstanding		$418,000	
Additional paid-in capital		722,000	1,140,000
Total contributed capital			$1,440,000
Retained earnings			608,400
Total contributed capital and retained earnings			$2,048,400
Less: Treasury stock, common (500 shares, at cost)		$ 24,000	
Foreign currency translation adjustment		10,000	34,000
Total stockholders' equity			$2,014,400

Retained Earnings

The Retained Earnings column in Exhibit 5 has the same components as the statement of retained earnings. As we explained earlier in the text, **retained earnings** represent stockholders' claims to assets that arise from the earnings of the business. Retained earnings equal a company's profits since its inception, minus any losses, dividends to stockholders, or transfers to contributed capital.

It is important to remember that retained earnings are not the assets themselves. The existence of retained earnings means that assets generated by profitable operations have been kept in the company to help it grow or meet other business needs. A credit balance in Retained Earnings is *not* directly associated with a specific amount of cash or designated assets. Rather, it means that assets as a whole have increased.

Retained Earnings can have a debit balance. Generally, this happens when a company's dividends and subsequent losses are greater than its accumulated profits from operations. In this case, the company is said to have a **deficit** (debit balance) in Retained Earnings. A deficit is shown in the stockholders' equity section of the balance sheet as a deduction from contributed capital.

Study Note

A *deficit* is a negative (debit) balance in Retained Earnings. It is not the same as a net loss, which reflects a firm's performance in just one accounting period.

S T O P • R E V I E W • A P P L Y

5-1. What is comprehensive income? How does comprehensive income differ from net income?

5-2. How do the statement of stockholders' equity and the stockholders' equity section of the balance sheet differ?

5-3. When does a company have a deficit in retained earnings?

Stock Dividends and Stock Splits

Two transactions that commonly modify the content of stockholders' equity are stock dividends and stock splits. In the discussion that follows, we describe how to account for both kinds of transactions.

Stock Dividends

A **stock dividend** is a proportional distribution of shares among a corporation's stockholders. Unlike a cash dividend, a stock dividend involves no distribution of assets, and so it has no effect on a firm's assets or liabilities. A board of directors may declare a stock dividend for the following reasons:

1. It may want to give stockholders some evidence of the company's success without affecting working capital, which would be the case if it paid a cash dividend.

2. It may want to reduce the stock's market price by increasing the number of shares outstanding. (This goal is, however, more often met by a stock split.)

3. It may want to make a nontaxable distribution to stockholders. Stock dividends that meet certain conditions are not considered income and are therefore not taxed.

4. It may want to increase the company's permanent capital by transferring an amount from retained earnings to contributed capital.

A stock dividend does not affect total stockholders' equity. Basically, it transfers a dollar amount from retained earnings to contributed capital. The amount transferred is the fair market value (usually, the market price) of the additional shares that the company issues. The laws of most states specify the minimum value of each share transferred, which is normally the minimum legal capital (par or stated value). When stock distributions are small—less than 20 to 25 percent of a company's outstanding common stock—generally accepted accounting principles hold that market value reflects their economic effect better than par or stated value. For this reason, market price should be used to account for small stock dividends.[16]

To illustrate how to account for a stock dividend, suppose that stockholders' equity in Geminix Corporation is as follows:

Contributed capital

Common stock, $5 par value, 100,000 shares authorized, 30,000 shares issued and outstanding	$ 150,000
Additional paid-in capital	30,000
Total contributed capital	$ 180,000
Retained earnings	900,000
Total stockholders' equity	$1,080,000

Now suppose that on February 24, the market price of Geminix's stock is $20 per share, and on that date, its board of directors declares a 10 percent stock dividend to be distributed on March 31 to stockholders of record on March 15. No entry is needed for the date of record (March 15). The entries for the declaration and distribution of the stock dividend are as follows:

Study Note

The declaration of a stock dividend results in a reshuffling of stockholders' equity—that is, a portion of retained earnings is converted to contributed capital (by closing the Stock Dividends account). Total stockholders' equity is not affected.

Declaration Date

A = L + SE		
−60,000		
+15,000		
+45,000		

Feb. 24	Stock Dividends	60,000	
	Common Stock Distributable		15,000
	Additional Paid-in Capital		45,000

Declared a 10 percent stock dividend
on common stock, distributable on
March 31 to stockholders of record
on March 15:
30,000 shares × .10 = 3,000 shares
3,000 shares × $20/share = $60,000
3,000 shares × $5/share = $15,000

Date of Distribution

A = L + SE		
−15,000		
+15,000		

Mar. 31	Common Stock Distributable	15,000	
	Common Stock		15,000

Distributed a stock dividend
of 3,000 shares

This stock dividend permanently transfers the market value of the stock, $60,000, from retained earnings to contributed capital and increases the number of shares outstanding by 3,000. The Stock Dividends account is used to record the total amount of the stock dividend. When the Stock Dividends account is closed to Retained Earnings at the end of the accounting period, Retained Earnings is reduced by the amount of the stock dividend. Common Stock Distributable is credited for the par value of the stock to be distributed (3,000 × $5 = $15,000).

In addition, when the market value is greater than the par value of the stock, the Additional Paid-in Capital account must be credited for the amount by which the market value exceeds the par value. In our example, the total market value of the stock dividend ($60,000) exceeds the total par value ($15,000) by $45,000. On the date of distribution, Common Stock Distributable is debited and Common Stock is credited for the par value of the stock ($15,000).

Common Stock Distributable is not a liability account because there is no obligation to distribute cash or other assets. The obligation is to distribute additional shares of capital stock. If financial statements are prepared between the declaration date and the date of distribution, Common Stock Distributable should be reported as part of contributed capital:

Contributed capital	
Common stock, $5 par value, 100,000 shares authorized, 30,000 shares issued and outstanding	$ 150,000
Common stock distributable, 3,000 shares	15,000
Additional paid-in capital	75,000
Total contributed capital	$ 240,000
Retained earnings	840,000
Total stockholders' equity	$1,080,000

This example demonstrates the following points:

1. Total stockholders' equity is the same before and after the stock dividend.

2. The assets of the corporation are not reduced, as they would be by a cash dividend.

3. The proportionate ownership in the corporation of any individual stockholder is the same before and after the stock dividend.

To illustrate these points, suppose a stockholder owns 1,000 shares before the stock dividend. After the 10 percent stock dividend is distributed, this stockholder would own 1,100 shares, as shown below:

	Stockholders' Equity	
	Before Dividend	After Dividend
Common stock	$ 150,000	$ 165,000
Additional paid-in capital	30,000	75,000
Total contributed capital	$ 180,000	$ 240,000
Retained earnings	900,000	840,000
Total stockholders' equity	$1,080,000	$1,080,000
Shares outstanding	30,000	33,000
Stockholders' equity per share	$ 36.00	$ 32.73

	Stockholders' Investment	
Shares owned	1,000	1,100
Shares outstanding	30,000	33,000
Percentage of ownership	3⅓%	3⅓%
Proportionate investment ($1,080,000 × 3⅓%)	$36,000	$36,000

Both before and after the stock dividend, stockholders' equity totals $1,080,000, and the stockholder owns 3⅓ percent of the company. The proportionate investment (stockholders' equity times percentage of ownership) remains at $36,000.

All stock dividends have an effect on the market price of a company's stock. But some stock dividends are so large that they have a material effect. For example, a 50 percent stock dividend would cause the market price of the stock to drop about 33 percent because the increase is now one-third of shares outstanding. The AICPA has decided that large stock dividends—those greater than 20 to 25 percent—should be accounted for by transferring the par or stated value of the stock on the declaration date from retained earnings to contributed capital.[17]

Study Note

When a stock dividend greater than 20 to 25 percent is declared, the transfer from retained earnings is based on the stock's par or stated value, not on its market value.

Stock Splits

A **stock split** occurs when a corporation increases the number of shares of stock issued and outstanding and reduces the par or stated value proportionally. A company may plan a stock split when it wants to lower its stock's market value per share and increase the demand for the stock at this lower price. It may do so if the market price has become so high that it hinders the trading of the stock or if it wants to signal to the market its success in achieving its operating goals.

The Gillette Company achieved these strategic objectives in a recent year by declaring a 2-for-1 stock split and raising its cash dividend.[18] The market viewed these actions positively, pushing Gillette's share price from $77 to $106.

Study Note

Stock splits and stock dividends reduce earnings per share because they increase the number of shares issued and outstanding. Cash dividends have no effect on earnings per share.

After the stock split, the number of the company's outstanding shares doubled, thereby cutting the share price in half and also reducing the dividend per share. Most important, the stock split left each stockholder's total wealth unchanged.

To illustrate a stock split, suppose that Calderon Corporation has 30,000 shares of $5.00 par value stock outstanding and the market value is $70.00 per share. The corporation plans a 2-for-1 split. This split will lower the par value to $2.50 and increase the number of shares outstanding to 60,000. A stockholder who previously owned 400 shares of the $5.00 par value stock would own 800 shares of the $2.50 par value stock after the split. When a stock split occurs, the market value tends to fall in proportion to the increase in outstanding shares of stock. For example, Calderon's 2-for-1 stock split would cause the price of its stock to drop by approximately 50 percent, to about $35.00. It would also halve earnings per share and cash dividends per share (unless the board increased the dividend). The lower price and increase in shares tend to promote the buying and selling of shares.

A stock split does not increase the number of shares authorized, nor does it change the balances in the stockholders' equity section of the balance sheet. It simply changes the par value and number of shares issued, both shares outstanding and treasury stock. Thus, an entry is unnecessary. However, it is appropriate to document the change with a memorandum entry in the general journal. For example:

July 15   The 30,000 shares of $5 par value common stock issued and outstanding were split 2 for 1, resulting in 60,000 shares of $2.50 par value common stock issued and outstanding.

The change for Calderon Corporation is as follows:

Before Stock Split

Contributed capital	
Common stock, $5 par value, 100,000 shares authorized; 30,000 shares issued and outstanding	$ 150,000
Additional paid-in capital	30,000
Total contributed capital	$ 180,000
Retained earnings	900,000
Total stockholders' equity	$1,080,000

Would a stock split make a difference to this Alcoa employee? Alcoa had five stock splits between 1974 and 2000. Except for the one in 1974, which was 3-for-2, all were 2-for-1. A stock split increases the number of shares of stock outstanding and reduces the stated value proportionately, but each stockholder's proportionate interest in the company remains the same.

Study Note

A stock split affects only the calculation of common stock. In this case, there are twice as many shares after the split, but par value is half of what it was.

After Stock Split

Contributed capital	
Common stock, $2.50 par value, 100,000 shares authorized, 60,000 shares issued and outstanding	$ 150,000
Additional paid-in capital	30,000
Total contributed capital	$ 180,000
Retained earnings	900,000
Total stockholders' equity	$1,080,000

Although the per share amount of stockholders' equity is half as much after the split, each stockholder's proportionate interest in the company remains the same.

If the number of split shares will exceed the number of authorized shares, the corporation's board of directors must secure state and stockholders' approval before it can issue the additional shares.

S T O P • R E V I E W • A P P L Y

6-1. How does the accounting treatment of stock dividends differ from that of cash dividends?

6-2. What is the difference between a stock dividend and a stock split?

6-3. What is the effect of a stock dividend and a stock split on a corporation's capital structure?

Book Value

The word *value* is associated with shares of stock in several ways. Par value or stated value is set when the stock is authorized, and it establishes a company's legal capital. Neither par value nor stated value has any relationship to a stock's book value or market value. The **book value** of stock represents a company's total assets less its liabilities. It is simply the stockholders' equity in a company or, to put it another way, it represents a company's net assets. The **book value per share** is therefore the equity of the owner of one share of stock in the net assets of a company. That value, of course, generally does not equal the amount a stockholder receives if the company is sold or liquidated because in most cases, assets are recorded at historical cost, not at their current market value.

If a company has only common stock outstanding, book value per share is calculated by dividing stockholders' equity by the number of common shares outstanding. Common stock distributable is included in the number of shares outstanding, but treasury stock is not. For example, if a firm has total stockholders' equity of $1,030,000 and 29,000 shares outstanding, the book value per share of its common stock would be $35.52 ($1,030,000 ÷ 29,000 shares).

If a company has both preferred and common stock, determining the book value per share is not so simple. Generally, the preferred stock's call value (or par value, if a call value is not specified) and any dividends in arrears are subtracted from stockholders' equity to determine the equity pertaining to common stock. As an illustration, refer to the stockholders' equity section of Kavra Corporation's balance sheet in Exhibit 6. If Kavra has no dividends in arrears and its preferred stock is callable at $105, the equity pertaining to its common stock would be calculated as follows:

Total stockholders' equity	$2,014,400
Less equity allocated to preferred stockholders	
(3,000 shares × $105)	315,000
Equity pertaining to common stockholders	$1,699,400

As indicated in Exhibit 6, Kavra has 41,300 shares of common stock outstanding (41,800 shares issued less 500 shares of treasury stock). Its book values per share are computed as follows:

Preferred stock: $315,000 ÷ 3,000 Shares = $105 per Share
Common stock: $1,699,400 ÷ 41,300 Shares = $41.15 per Share

If we assume the same facts except that Kavra's preferred stock is 8 percent cumulative and that one year of dividends is in arrears, the stockholders' equity would be allocated as follows:

Total stockholders' equity		$2,014,400
Less call value of outstanding preferred shares	$315,000	
Dividends in arrears ($300,000 × .08)	24,000	
Equity allocated to preferred stockholders		339,000
Equity pertaining to common stockholders		$1,675,400

The book values per share would then be as follows:

Preferred stock: $339,000 ÷ 3,000 Shares = $113 per Share
Common stock: $1,675,400 ÷ 41,300 Shares = $40.57 per Share

S T O P • R E V I E W • A P P L Y

7-1. What is the formula for computing book value per share when a corporation has no preferred stock?

7-2. Would you expect a corporation's book value per share to equal its market value per share? Why or why not?

A LOOK BACK AT

MOTOROLA, INC.

In this chapter's Decision Point, we observed that in evaluating a company's performance, it is important to look beyond "bottom line" earnings and other common indicators of performance. We pointed out that to gain a proper perspective on a company's performance, one must examine the components of its income statement. Users of Motorola's income statement should ask questions like the following:

- **What items other than normal operating activities contributed to Motorola's performance?**

- **What does the company's income statement indicate about its quality of earnings?**

- **How does one put the various measures of performance (some of which are shown in Motorola's financial highlights) in perspective?**

The astute user of **Motorola's** income statement, shown in Exhibit 2, will take the following into account:

- Reorganization of businesses and other charges (income), which appear in the operating section of Motorola's income statement, had an important effect on the company's performance in 2002. However, those effects were small and unimportant in 2003 and 2004.

- Gains on sales of investments and businesses were large in all three years covered by the income statement. Although such gains increase income, they lower the quality of earnings because they are one-time events, and the income they produce will not be sustained in the future. The analyst should therefore ignore them.

- Motorola had losses from discontinued operations in all three years. Losses from discontinued operations decrease earnings and often reflect poor decisions in the past. However, eliminating unprofitable operations should have a positive effect on Motorola's future operations.

To put Motorola's performance in perspective, the company had a rough year in 2002. Between 2002 and 2004, management discontinued some operations at a loss, but it partially offset those losses by selling some investments and businesses at a gain. A careful reader of Motorola's income statement would realize that the company's performance was improving, especially in light of its increased operating earnings in both 2003 and 2004. Motorola's strong cash flows, which we discussed earlier in the chapter, are another indication that its performance was improving.

CHAPTER REVIEW

REVIEW of Learning Objectives

LO1 Define *quality of earnings,* and identify the components of a corporate income statement.

The quality of earnings refers to the substance of earnings and their sustainability into future accounting periods. The quality of a company's earnings may be affected by the accounting methods and estimates it uses and by the gains and losses, write-downs and restructurings, and nonoperating items that it reports on its income statement.

When a company has both continuing and discontinued operations, the operating income section of its income statement is called income from continuing operations. Income from continuing operations before income taxes is affected by choices of accounting methods and estimates and may contain gains and losses on the sale of assets, write-downs, and restructurings. The income taxes expense section of the statement is subject to special accounting rules. The lower part of the statement may contain such nonoperating items as discontinued operations, extraordinary gains and losses, and effects of accounting changes. Earnings per share information appears at the bottom of the statement.

The reason for considering quality of earnings issues is to assess their effect on cash flows and performance measures. Except for possible income tax effects, gains and losses, asset write-downs, restructurings, and nonoperating items generally have no effect on cash flows. However, quality of earnings issues can affect key performance ratios like profit margin, return on assets, and return on equity.

LO2 Show the relationships among income taxes expense, deferred income taxes, and net of taxes.

Income taxes expense is the tax applicable to income from operations on an accrual basis. Income tax allocation is necessary when there is a material difference between accrual-based accounting income and taxable income—that is, between the income taxes expense reported on the income statement and actual income tax liability. The difference between income taxes expense and income taxes payable is debited or credited to an account called Deferred Income Taxes. The phrase *net of taxes* indicates that taxes have been taken into account in reporting an item in the financial statements.

LO3 Describe the disclosure on the income statement of discontinued operations and extraordinary items.

Because of their unusual nature, gains or losses on discontinued operations and on extraordinary items must be disclosed on the income statement separately from continuing operations and net of income taxes.

LO4 Compute earnings per share.

Readers of financial statements use earnings per share to evaluate a company's performance and to compare it with the performance of other companies. Earnings per share of common stock are presented on the face of the income statement. The amounts are computed by dividing the income applicable to common stock by the number of common shares outstanding for the year. If the number of shares outstanding varied during the year, the weighted-average number of common shares outstanding is used in the computation. A company that has a complex capital structure must disclose both basic and diluted earnings per share on the face of its income statement.

LO5 Define *comprehensive income,* and describe the statement of stockholders' equity.

Comprehensive income includes all items from sources other than stockholders that account for changes in stockholders' equity during an accounting period. The statement of stockholders' equity summarizes changes over the period in each component of the stockholders' equity section of the balance sheet. This statement reveals much more than the statement of retained earnings does about the transactions that affect stockholders' equity.

LO6 Account for stock dividends and stock splits.

A stock dividend is a proportional distribution of shares among a corporation's stockholders. The following is a summary of the key dates and accounting treatments of stock dividends:

Key Date	Stock Dividend
Declaration date	Debit Stock Dividends for the market value of the stock to be distributed (if the stock dividend is small), and credit Common Stock Distributable for the stock's par value and Additional Paid-in Capital for the excess of the market value over the stock's par value.
Record date	No entry is needed.
Date of distribution	Debit Common Stock Distributable and credit Common Stock for the par value of the stock.

A company usually declares a stock split to reduce the market value of its stock and thereby improve the demand for the stock. Because the par value of the stock normally decreases in proportion to the number of additional shares issued, a stock split has no effect on the dollar amount in stockholders' equity. A stock split does not require a journal entry, but a memorandum entry in the general journal is appropriate.

LO7 Calculate book value per share.

Book value per share is stockholders' equity per share. It is calculated by dividing stockholders' equity by the number of common shares outstanding. When a company has both preferred and common stock, the call or par value of the preferred stock and any dividends in arrears are deducted from stockholders' equity before dividing by the common shares outstanding.

REVIEW of Concepts and Terminology

The following concepts and terms were introduced in this chapter:

Book value: A company's total assets less its liabilities; stockholders' equity or net assets. **(LO7)**

Complex capital structure: A capital structure that includes preferred stocks, bonds, and stock options that can be converted to common stock. **(LO4)**

Comprehensive income: Items from sources other than owners that account for the change in stockholders' equity during an accounting period. **(LO5)**

Deferred Income Taxes: The account used to record the difference between income taxes expense and income taxes payable. **(LO2)**

Deficit: A debit balance in the Retained Earnings account. **(LO5)**

Discontinued operations: Segments that are no longer part of a company's operations. **(LO3)**

Extraordinary items: Events or transactions that are both unusual in nature and infrequent in occurrence. **(LO3)**

Income from continuing operations: The operating income section of the income statement when a company has both continuing and discontinued operations. **(LO1)**

Income tax allocation: The accounting method used to accrue income taxes expense on the basis of accounting income when accounting income and taxable income differ. **(LO2)**

Net of taxes: A phrase indicating that taxes have been taken into account in reporting an item in the financial statements. **(LO2)**

Quality of earnings: The substance of earnings and their sustainability into the future. **(LO1)**

Restructuring: The estimated cost of a change in a company's operations, usually involving the closing of facilities and the laying off of personnel. **(LO1)**

Retained earnings: Stockholders' claims to assets arising from the earnings of the business; the accumulated earnings of a corporation since its inception, minus any losses, dividends, or transfers to contributed capital. **(LO5)**

Segments: Distinct parts of a company's operations. **(LO3)**

Simple capital structure: A capital structure in which there are no stocks, bonds, or stock options that can be converted to common stock. **(LO4)**

Statement of stockholders' equity: A financial statement that summarizes changes in the components of the stockholders' equity section of the balance sheet. Also called the *statement of changes in stockholders' equity.* **(LO5)**

Stock dividend: A proportional distribution of shares among a corporation's stockholders. **(LO6)**

Stock split: An increase in the number of outstanding shares of stock accompanied by a proportionate reduction in the par or stated value. **(LO6)**

Write-down: A reduction in the value of an asset below its carrying value on the balance sheet. Also called a *write-off.* **(LO1)**

Key Ratios

Basic earnings per share: The net income applicable to common stock divided by the weighted-average number of common shares outstanding. **(LO4)**

Book value per share: The equity of the owner of one share of stock in a corporation's net assets. **(LO7)**

Diluted earnings per share: The net income applicable to common stock divided by the sum of the weighted-average number of common shares outstanding and potentially dilutive securities. **(LO4)**

≡ REVIEW Problem

LO5, LO6, LO7 **Comprehensive Stockholders' Equity Transactions**

 The stockholders' equity of Skowski Company on June 30, 20x7, was as follows:

Contributed capital
Common stock, no par value, $6 stated value,
  1,000,000 shares authorized, 250,000 shares

issued and outstanding	$1,500,000
Additional paid-in capital	820,000
Total contributed capital	$2,320,000
Retained earnings	970,000
Total stockholders' equity	$3,290,000

Stockholders' equity transactions in the next fiscal year were as follows:

a. The board of directors declared a 2-for-1 stock split.
b. The board of directors obtained authorization to issue 50,000 shares of $100 par value, 6 percent noncumulative preferred stock, callable at $104.
c. Issued 12,000 shares of common stock for a building appraised at $96,000.
d. Purchased 8,000 shares of the company's common stock for $64,000.
e. Issued 20,000 shares of preferred stock for $100 per share.
f. Sold 5,000 shares of treasury stock for $35,000.
g. Declared cash dividends of $6 per share on preferred stock and $.20 per share on common stock.
h. Declared a 10 percent stock dividend on common stock to be distributed after the end of the fiscal year. The market value was $10 per share.
i. Closed net income for the year, $340,000.
j. Closed the Dividends and Stock Dividends accounts to Retained Earnings.

Required:

1. Record the stockholders' equity components of the preceding transactions in T accounts. Indicate when there is no entry.
2. Prepare the stockholders' equity section of the company's balance sheet on June 30, 20x8.
3. Compute the book values per share of common stock on June 30, 20x7 and 20x8, and of preferred stock on June 30, 20x8, using the end-of-year shares outstanding.

Answer to Review Problem

1. Entries in T accounts:

    a. No entry (memorandum in journal)

    b. No entry (memorandum in journal)

	A	B	C	D	E	F	G	H	I
1		Preferred Stock					Common Stock		
2			e.	2,000,000				Beg. Bal.	1,500,000
3								c.	36,000
4								End. Bal.	1,536,000
5									
6		Common Stock Distributable					Additional Paid-in Capital		
7			h.	152,700				Beg. Bal.	820,000
8								c.	60,000
9								h.	356,300
10								End. Bal.	1,236,000
11									
12		Retained Earnings					Treasury Stock		
13	f.	5,000	Beg. Bal.	970,000		d.	64,000	f.	40,000
14	j.	730,800	i.	340,000		End. Bal.	24,000		
15			End. Bal.	574,200					
16									
17		Dividends					Stock Dividends		
18	g.	221,800*	j.	221,800		h.	509,000**	j.	509,000
19									
20	* 20,000 × $6 = $120,000					**509,000 shares × .10 × $10 = $509,000			
21	509,000 × $.20 = $101,800								
22	Total = $221,800								

2. Stockholders' equity section of the balance sheet:

	A	B	C
1	**Skowski Company**		
2	**Balance Sheet**		
3	**June 30, 20x8**		
4			
5	**Stockholders' Equity**		
6	Contributed capital		
7	Preferred stock, $100 par value, 6 percent		
8	noncumulative, 50,000 shares authorized,		
9	20,000 shares issued and outstanding		$2,000,000
10	Common stock, no par value, $3 stated value,		
11	1,000,000 shares authorized, 512,000 shares		
12	issued, 509,000 shares outstanding	$1,536,000	
13	Common stock distributable, 50,900 shares	152,700	
14	Additional paid-in capital	1,236,300	2,925,000
15	Total contributed capital		$4,925,000
16	Retained earnings		574,200
17	Total contributed capital and retained earnings		$5,499,200
18	Less treasury stock (3,000 shares, at cost)		24,000
19	Total stockholders' equity		$5,475,200

3. Book values:

June 30, 20x7

Common Stock: $3,290,000 ÷ 250,000 shares = $13.16 per share

June 30, 20x8

Preferred Stock: Call price of $104 per share equals book value per share

Common Stock:

($5,475,200 − $2,080,000) ÷ (509,000 shares + 50,900 shares)

$3,395,200 ÷ 559,900 shares = $6.06* per share

* Rounded.

CHAPTER ASSIGNMENTS

≡ BUILDING Your Basic Knowledge and Skills

Short Exercises

LO1 **Quality of Earnings**

SE 1. Each of the items listed below is a quality of earnings issue. Indicate whether the item is (a) an accounting method, (b) an accounting estimate, or (c) a nonoperating item. For any item for which the answer is (a) or (b), indicate which alternative is usually the more conservative choice.

1. LIFO versus FIFO
2. Extraordinary loss
3. 10-year useful life versus 15-year useful life
4. Straight-line versus accelerated method
5. Discontinued operations
6. Immediate write-off versus amortization
7. Increase versus decrease in percentage of uncollectible accounts

LO1 **Corporate Income Statement**

SE 2. Assume that Jefferson Company's chief financial officer gave you the following information: net sales, $360,000; cost of goods sold, $175,000; loss from discontinued operations (net of income tax benefit of $35,000), $100,000; loss on disposal of discontinued operations (net of income tax benefit of $8,000), $25,000; operating expenses, $65,000; income taxes expense on continuing operations, $50,000. From this information, prepare the company's income statement for the year ended June 30, 20xx. (Ignore earnings per share information.)

LO2 **Corporate Income Tax Rate Schedule**

SE 3. Using the corporate tax rate schedule in Table 1, compute the income tax liability for taxable income of (1) $800,000 and (2) $40,000,000.

LO4 **Earnings per Share**

SE 4. During 20x7, Wells Corporation reported a net income of $1,338,400. On January 1, Wells had 720,000 shares of common stock outstanding. The company issued an additional 480,000 shares of common stock on August 1. In 20x7, the company had a simple capital structure. During 20x8, there were no transactions involving common stock, and the company reported net income of $1,740,000. Determine the weighted-average number of common shares outstanding for 20x7 and 20x8. Also compute earnings per share for 20x7 and 20x8.

LO5 **Statement of Stockholders' Equity**

SE 5. Refer to the statement of stockholders' equity for Kavra Corporation in Exhibit 5 to answer the following questions: (1) At what price per share were the 5,000 shares of common stock sold? (2) What was the conversion price per share of the common stock? (3) At what price was the common stock selling on the date of the stock dividend? (4) At what price per share was the treasury stock purchased?

LO5, LO6 **Effects of Stockholders' Equity Actions**

SE 6. Tell whether each of the following actions will increase, decrease, or have no effect on total assets, total liabilities, and total stockholders' equity:

1. Declaration of a stock dividend
2. Declaration of a cash dividend
3. Stock split
4. Purchase of treasury stock

LO6 **Stock Dividends**

SE 7. On February 15, Asher Corporation's board of directors declared a 2 percent stock dividend applicable to the outstanding shares of its $10 par value common stock, of which 400,000 shares are authorized, 260,000 are issued, and 40,000 are held in the treasury. The stock dividend was distributed on March 15 to stockholders of record on March 1. On February 15, the market value of the common stock was $15 per share. On March 30, the board of directors declared a $.50 per share cash dividend. No other stock transactions have occurred. Record, as necessary, the transactions of February 15, March 1, March 15, and March 30.

LO6 **Stock Split**

SE 8. On August 10, the board of directors of Perlman International declared a 3-for-1 stock split of its $9 par value common stock, of which 400,000 shares were authorized and 125,000 were issued and outstanding. The market value on that date was $60 per share. On the same date, the balance of additional paid-in capital was $3,000,000, and the balance of retained earnings was $3,250,000. Prepare the stockholders' equity section of the company's balance sheet after the stock split. What journal entry, if any, is needed to record the stock split?

LO7 **Book Value for Preferred and Common Stock**

SE 9. Using data from the stockholders' equity section of Soong Corporation's balance sheet shown below, compute the book value per share for both the preferred and the common stock.

Contributed capital	
Preferred stock, $100 par value, 8 percent cumulative, 20,000 shares authorized, 1,000 shares issued and outstanding*	$ 100,000
Common stock, $10 par value, 200,000 shares authorized, 80,000 shares issued and outstanding	800,000
Additional paid-in capital	1,032,000
Total contributed capital	$1,932,000
Retained earnings	550,000
Total stockholders' equity	$2,482,000

*The preferred stock is callable at $108 per share, and one year's dividends are in arrears.

Exercises

LO1, LO2, LO3 **Discussion Questions**

E 1. Develop brief answers to each of the following questions:

1. In what way is selling an investment for a gain potentially a negative in evaluating quality of earnings?
2. Is it unethical for new management to take an extra large write-off (a "big bath") in order to reduce future costs? Why or why not?
3. What is an argument against the recording of deferred income taxes?
4. Why is it useful to disclose discontinued operations separately on the income statement?

LO4, LO5, LO6, LO7 **Discussion Questions**

E 2. Develop brief answers to each of the following questions:

1. What is one way a company can improve its earnings per share without improving its earnings or net income?
2. Why is comprehensive income a part of stockholders' equity?
3. Upon receiving shares of stock from a stock dividend, why should the stockholder not consider the value of the stock as income?
4. What is the effect of a stock dividend or a stock split on book value per share?

LO1 **Effect of Alternative Accounting Methods**

E 3. At the end of its first year of operations, a company calculated its ending merchandise inventory according to three different accounting methods, as follows: FIFO, $47,500; average-cost, $45,000; LIFO, $43,000. If the company used the average-cost method, its net income for the year would be $17,000.

1. Determine net income if the company used the FIFO method.
2. Determine net income if the company used the LIFO method.
3. Which method is more conservative?
4. Will the consistency convention be violated if the company chooses to use the LIFO method? Why or why not?
5. Does the full-disclosure convention require disclosure of the inventory method used in the financial statements?

LO1 **Corporate Income Statement**

E 4. Assume that the St. Cloud Furniture Company's chief financial officer gave you the following information: net sales, $3,800,000; cost of goods sold, $2,100,000; extraordinary gain (net of income taxes of $7,000), $25,000; loss from discontinued operations (net of income tax benefit of $60,000), $100,000; loss on disposal of discontinued operations (net of income tax benefit of $26,000), $70,000; selling expenses, $100,000; administrative expenses, $80,000; income taxes expense on continuing operations, $600,000. From this information, prepare the company's income statement for the year ended June 30, 20xx. (Ignore earnings per share information.)

LO1 **Corporate Income Statement**

E 5. The items at the top of the opposite page are components of Munsey Company's income statement for the year ended December 31, 20xx. Recast the income statement in proper multistep form, including allocating income taxes to appropriate items (assume a 30 percent income tax rate) and showing earnings per share figures (200,000 shares outstanding).

Sales	$1,110,000
Cost of goods sold	(550,000)
Operating expenses	(225,000)
Restructuring	(110,000)
Total income taxes expense for period	(179,100)
Income from operations of a discontinued segment	160,000
Gain on disposal of segment	140,000
Extraordinary gain	72,000
Net income	$ 417,900
Earnings per share	$ 2.09

LO2 **Corporate Income Tax Rate Schedule**

E 6. Using the corporate tax rate schedule in Table 1, compute the income tax liability for the following situations:

Situation	Taxable Income
A	$ 70,000
B	85,000
C	320,000

LO2 **Income Tax Allocation**

E 7. The Danner Corporation reported the following accounting income before income taxes, income taxes expense, and net income for 20x6 and 20x7:

	20x6	20x7
Income before income taxes	$140,000	$140,000
Income taxes expense	44,150	44,150
Net income	$ 95,850	$ 95,850

On the balance sheet, deferred income taxes liability increased by $19,200 in 20x6 and decreased by $9,400 in 20x7.

1. How much did Danner actually pay in income taxes for 20x6 and 20x7?
2. Prepare entries in journal form to record income taxes expense for 20x6 and 20x7.

LO4 **Earnings per Share**

 E 8. During 20x6, Chester Corporation reported a net income of $1,529,500. On January 1, Chester had 1,400,000 shares of common stock outstanding. The company issued an additional 840,000 shares of common stock on October 1. In 20x6, the company had a simple capital structure. During 20x7, there were no transactions involving common stock, and the company reported net income of $2,016,000.

1. Determine the weighted-average number of common shares outstanding each year.
2. Compute earnings per share for each year.

LO5 **Statement of Stockholders' Equity**

E 9. The stockholders' equity section of Ruff Corporation's balance sheet on December 31, 20x7, follows.

Contributed capital	
Common stock, $2 par value, 250,000 shares	
authorized, 200,000 shares issued and outstanding	$ 400,000
Additional paid-in capital	600,000
Total contributed capital	$1,000,000
Retained earnings	2,100,000
Total stockholders' equity	$3,100,000

Prepare a statement of stockholders' equity for the year ended December 31, 20x8, assuming these transactions occurred in sequence in 20x8:

a. Issued 5,000 shares of $100 par value, 9 percent cumulative preferred stock at par after obtaining authorization from the state.

b. Issued 20,000 shares of common stock in connection with the conversion of bonds having a carrying value of $300,000.

c. Declared and issued a 2 percent common stock dividend. The market value on the date of declaration was $14 per share.

d. Purchased 5,000 shares of common stock for the treasury at a cost of $16 per share.

e. Earned net income of $230,000.

f. Declared and paid the full year's dividend on preferred stock and a dividend of $.40 per share on common stock outstanding at the end of the year.

g. Had foreign currency translation adjustment of minus $50,000.

LO6   Journal Entries: Stock Dividends

E 10. Tung Company has 60,000 shares of its $1 par value common stock outstanding. Record in journal form the following transactions as they relate to the company's common stock:

July   17   Declared a 10 percent stock dividend on common stock to be distributed on August 10 to stockholders of record on July 31. Market value of the stock was $5 per share on this date.

31   Date of record.

Aug.   10   Distributed the stock dividend declared on July 17.

Sept.   1   Declared a $.50 per share cash dividend on common stock to be paid on September 16 to stockholders of record on September 10.

LO6   Stock Split

E 11. Mendoza Company currently has 250,000 shares of $1 par value common stock authorized with 100,000 shares outstanding. The board of directors declared a 2-for-1 split on May 15, when the market value of the common stock was $2.50 per share. The retained earnings balance on May 15 was $350,000. Additional paid-in capital on this date was $10,000. Prepare the stockholders' equity section of the company's balance sheet before and after the stock split. What entry, if any, would be necessary to record the stock split?

LO6   Stock Split

E 12. On January 15, the board of directors of Picado International declared a 3-for-1 stock split of its $12 par value common stock, of which 1,600,000 shares were authorized and 400,000 were issued and outstanding. The market value on that date was $45 per share. On the same date, the balance of additional paid-in capital was $8,000,000, and the balance of retained earnings was $16,000,000. Prepare the stockholders' equity section of the company's balance sheet before and after the stock split. What entry, if any, is needed to record the stock split?

LO7 **Book Value for Preferred and Common Stock**

E 13. Below is the stockholders' equity section of Jobs Corporation's balance sheet. Determine the book value per share for both the preferred and the common stock.

Contributed capital	
Preferred stock, $100 per share, 6 percent cumulative, 5,000 shares authorized, 100 shares issued and outstanding*	$10,000
Common stock, $5 par value, 50,000 shares authorized, 5,000 shares issued, 4,500 shares outstanding	25,000
Additional paid-in capital	14,000
Total contributed capital	$49,000
Retained earnings	47,500
Total contributed capital and retained earnings	$96,500
Less treasury stock, common (500 shares at cost)	7,500
Total stockholders' equity	$89,000

*The preferred stock is callable at $105 per share, and one year's dividends are in arrears.

Problems

LO1 **Effect of Alternative Accounting Methods**

P 1. Zeigler Company began operations in 20xx. At the beginning of the year, the company purchased plant assets of $900,000, with an estimated useful life of ten years and no residual value. During the year, the company had net sales of $1,300,000, salaries expense of $200,000, and other expenses of $80,000, excluding depreciation. In addition, Zeigler Company purchased inventory as follows:

Jan. 15	400 units at $400	$160,000
Mar. 20	200 units at $408	81,600
June 15	800 units at $416	332,800
Sept. 18	600 units at $412	247,200
Dec. 9	300 units at $420	126,000
Total	2,300 units	$947,600

At the end of the year, a physical inventory disclosed 500 units still on hand. The managers of Zeigler Company know they have a choice of accounting methods, but they are unsure how those methods will affect net income. They have heard of the FIFO and LIFO inventory methods and the straight-line and double-declining-balance depreciation methods.

Required

1. Prepare two income statements for Zeigler Company, one using the FIFO and straight-line methods and the other using the LIFO and double-declining-balance methods. Ignore income taxes.

2. Prepare a schedule accounting for the difference in the two net income figures obtained in requirement 1.

3. **User Insight:** What effect does the choice of accounting method have on Zeigler's inventory turnover? What conclusions can you draw? Use the year-end balance to compute the ratio.

4. **User Insight:** How does the choice of accounting methods affect Zeigler's return on assets? Assume the company's only assets are cash of $80,000, inventory, and plant assets. Use year-end balances to compute the ratios. Is your evaluation of Zeigler's profitability affected by the choice of accounting methods?

LO1, LO2, LO3, LO4 | **Corporate Income Statement**

P 2. Income statement information for Sim Corporation in 20x6 is as follows:

a. Administrative expenses, $220,000
b. Cost of goods sold, $880,000
c. Extraordinary loss from a storm (net of taxes, $20,000), $40,000
d. Income taxes expense, continuing operations, $84,000
e. Net sales, $1,780,000
f. Selling expenses, $380,000

Required

1. Prepare Sim Corporation's income statement for 20x6, including earnings per share, assuming a weighted average of 200,000 shares of common stock outstanding for 20x6.

2. **User Insight:** Which item in Sim Corporation's income statement affects the company's quality of earnings? Why does it have this effect?

LO1, LO2, LO3, LO4 | **Corporate Income Statement and Evaluation of Business Operations**

P 3. During 20x7, Dasbol Corporation engaged in two complex transactions to improve the business—selling off a division and retiring bonds. The company has always issued a simple single-step income statement, and the accountant has accordingly prepared the December 31 year-end income statements for 20x6 and 20x7, as shown below.

Dasbol Corporation			
Income Statements			
For the Years Ended December 31, 20x7 and 20x6			
		20x7	**20x6**
Net sales		$1,000,000	$1,200,000
Cost of goods sold		(550,000)	(600,000)
Operating expenses		(225,000)	(150,000)
Income taxes expense		(179,100)	(135,000)
Income from operations of a discontinued segment		160,000	
Gain on disposal of discontinued segment		140,000	
Extraordinary gain on retirement of bonds		72,000	
Net income		$ 417,900	$ 315,000
Earnings per share		$ 2.09	$ 1.58

Joseph Dasbol, the president of Dasbol Corporation, is pleased to see that both net income and earnings per share increased by almost 33 percent from 20x6 to 20x7 and intends to announce to the company's stockholders that the plan to improve the business has been successful.

Required

1. Recast the 20x7 and 20x6 income statements in proper multistep form, including allocating income taxes to appropriate items (assume a 30 percent income tax rate) and showing earnings per share figures (200,000 shares outstanding).

2. **User Insight:** What is your assessment of Dasbol Corporation's plan and business operations in 20x7?

LO5, LO6   **Dividends, Stock Splits, and Stockholders' Equity**

P 4. The stockholders' equity section of the balance sheet of Pittman Corporation as of December 31, 20x7, was as follows:

Contributed capital	
Common stock, $4 par value, 500,000 shares authorized,	
200,000 shares issued and outstanding	$ 800,000
Additional paid-in capital	1,000,000
Total contributed capital	$1,800,000
Retained earnings	1,200,000
Total stockholders' equity	$3,000,000

Pittman Corporation had the following transactions in 20x8:

Feb. 28   The board of directors declared a 10 percent stock dividend to stockholders of record on March 25 to be distributed on April 5. The market value on this date is $16.

Mar. 25   Date of record for stock dividend.

Apr.   5   Issued stock dividend.

Aug.   3   Declared a 2-for-1 stock split.

Nov. 20   Purchased 18,000 shares of the company's common stock at $8 per share for the treasury.

Dec. 31   Declared a 5 percent stock dividend to stockholders of record on January 25 to be distributed on February 5. The market value per share was $9.

Required

1. Record the stockholders' equity components of the transactions for Pittman Corporation in T accounts.

2. Prepare the stockholders' equity section of the company's balance sheet as of December 31, 20x8. Assume net income for 20x8 is $108,000.

3. **User Insight:** If you owned 1,000 shares of Pittman stock on February 1, 20x8, how many shares would you own February 5, 20x9? Would your proportionate share of the ownership of the company be different on the latter date than it was on the former date? Explain your answer.

LO5, LO6   **Dividends and Stock Split Transactions and Stockholder's Equity**

P 5. The stockholders' equity section of Rigby Moving and Storage Company's balance sheet as of December 31, 20x6, appears at the top of the next page. The company engaged in the following stockholders' equity transactions during 20x7:

Mar.   5   Declared a $.40 per share cash dividend to be paid on April 6 to stockholders of record on March 20.

20   Date of record.

Contributed capital	
Common stock, $2 par value, 3,000,000 shares authorized, 500,000 shares issued and outstanding	$1,000,000
Additional paid-in capital	400,000
Total contributed capital	$1,400,000
Retained earnings	1,080,000
Total stockholders' equity	$2,480,000

Apr.   6   Paid the cash dividend.
June 17   Declared a 10 percent stock dividend to be distributed August 17 to stockholders of record on August 5. The market value of the stock was $14 per share.
Aug.   5   Date of record.
        17   Distributed the stock dividend.
Oct.   2   Split its stock 2 for 1.
Dec. 27   Declared a cash dividend of $.20 payable January 27, 20x8, to stockholders of record on January 14, 20x8.

Required

1. Record the 20x7 transactions in journal form.
2. Prepare the stockholders' equity section of the company's balance sheet as of December 31, 20x7. Assume net income for the year is $400,000.
3. **User Insight:** If you owned some shares of Rigby, would you expect the total value of your shares to go up or down as a result of the stock dividends and stock split? What intangibles might affect the stock value?

LO5, LO6, LO7   **Comprehensive Stockholders' Equity Transactions**

   **P 6.** On December 31, 20x7, the stockholders' equity section of Tsang Company's balance sheet appeared as follows:

Contributed capital	
Common stock, $8 par value, 200,000 shares authorized, 60,000 shares issued and outstanding	$ 480,000
Additional paid-in capital	1,280,000
Total contributed capital	$1,760,000
Retained earnings	824,000
Total stockholders' equity	$2,584,000

The following are selected transactions involving stockholders' equity in 20x8: On January 4, the board of directors obtained authorization for 20,000 shares of $40 par value noncumulative preferred stock that carried an indicated dividend rate of $4 per share and was callable at $42 per share. On January 14, the company sold 12,000 shares of the preferred stock at $40 per share and issued another 2,000 in exchange for a building valued at $80,000. On March 8, the board of directors declared a 2-for-1 stock split on the common stock. On April 20, after the stock split, the company purchased 3,000 shares of common stock for the treasury at an average price of $12 per share; 1,000 of these shares subsequently were sold on May 4 at an average price of $16 per share. On July 15, the board of directors declared a cash dividend of $4 per share on the preferred stock and $.40 per share on the common stock. The date of record was July 25. The dividends were paid on August 15. The board of directors declared a 15 percent stock dividend on November 28, when the common stock was selling for $20. The date of record for the stock dividend was December 15, and the dividend was to be distributed on January 5.

Required

1. Record the above transactions in journal form.
2. Prepare the stockholders' equity section of the company's balance sheet as of December 31, 20x8. Net loss for 20x8 was $218,000. (**Hint:** Use T accounts to keep track of transactions.)
3. **User Insight:** Compute the book value per share for preferred and common stock (including common stock distributable) on December 31, 20x7 and 20x8, using end-of-year shares outstanding. What effect would you expect the change in book value to have on the market price per share of the company's stock?

Alternate Problems

LO1, LO2, LO3, LO4 Corporate Income Statement

P 7. Information concerning operations of Norris Weather Gear Corporation during 20xx is as follows:

a. Administrative expenses, $180,000
b. Cost of goods sold, $840,000
c. Extraordinary loss from an earthquake (net of taxes, $72,000), $120,000
d. Sales (net), $1,800,000
e. Selling expenses, $160,000
f. Income taxes expense applicable to continuing operations, $210,000

Required

1. Prepare the corporation's income statement for the year ended December 31, 20xx, including earnings per share information. Assume a weighted average of 100,000 common shares outstanding during the year.
2. **User Insight:** Which item in Norris Weather Gear Corporation's income statement affects the company's quality of earnings? Why does it have an effect on quality of earnings?

LO5, LO6 Dividends, Stock Splits, and Stockholders' Equity

P 8. The stockholders' equity section of Waterbury Linen Mills, Inc., as of December 31, 20x6, was as follows:

Contributed capital	
Common stock, $3 par value, 500,000 shares authorized, 40,000 shares issued and outstanding	$120,000
Additional paid-in capital	37,500
Total contributed capital	$157,500
Retained earnings	120,000
Total stockholders' equity	$277,500

A review of the stockholders' equity records of Waterbury Linen Mills, Inc., disclosed the following transactions during 20x7:

Mar. 25 The board of directors declared a 5 percent stock dividend to stockholders of record on April 20 to be distributed on May 1. The market value of the common stock was $21 per share.

Apr.	20	Date of record for stock dividend.
May	1	Issued stock dividend.
Sept.	10	Declared a 3-for-1 stock split.
Dec.	15	Declared a 10 percent stock dividend to stockholders of record on January 15 to be distributed on February 15. The market price on this date is $9 per share.

Required

1. Record the stockholders' equity components of the transactions for Waterbury Linen Mills, Inc., in T accounts.
2. Prepare the stockholders' equity section of the company's balance sheet as of December 31, 20x7. Assume net income for 20x7 is $247,000.
3. **User Insight:** If you owned 1,000 shares of Waterbury Linen Mills stock on May 1, 20x7, how many shares would you own on February 15, 20x8? Would your proportionate share of the ownership of the company be different on the latter date than it was on the former date? Explain your answer.

☰ ENHANCING Your Knowledge, Skills, and Critical Thinking

Conceptual Understanding Cases

LO6 **Stock Split**

C 1. When **Yahoo! Inc.** reported in early 2004 that its first quarter earnings had doubled from the previous year, its stock price jumped 10 percent to $53 per share. At the same time, the company announced a 2-for-1 stock split.[20] What is a stock split and what effect does it have on the company's stockholders' equity? What effect will it likely have on the market value of the company's stock? In light of your answers, do you think the stock split is positive for the company and for its stockholders?

LO1, LO3 **Classic Quality of Earnings Case**

C 2. On Tuesday, January 19, 1988, **IBM** reported greatly increased earnings for the fourth quarter of 1987. Despite this reported gain in earnings, the price of IBM's stock on the New York Stock Exchange declined by $6 per share to $111.75. In sympathy with this move, most other technology stocks also declined.[21]

IBM's fourth-quarter net earnings rose from $1.39 billion, or $2.28 a share, to $2.08 billion, or $3.47 a share, an increase of 49.6 percent and 52.2 percent over the same period a year earlier. Management declared that these results demonstrated the effectiveness of IBM's efforts to become more competitive and that, despite the economic uncertainties of 1988, the company was planning for growth.

The apparent cause of the stock price decline was that the huge increase in income could be traced to nonrecurring gains. Investment analysts pointed out that IBM's high earnings stemmed primarily from such factors as a lower tax rate. Despite most analysts' expectations of a tax rate between 40 and 42 percent, IBM's was a low 36.4 percent, down from the previous year's 45.3 percent. Analysts were also disappointed in IBM's revenue growth. Revenues within the United States were down, and much of the company's growth in revenues came through favorable currency translations, increases that might not be repeated. In fact, some estimates of IBM's fourth-quarter earnings attributed $.50 per share to currency translations and another $.25 to tax-rate changes.

Other factors contributing to IBM's rise in earnings were one-time transactions, such as the sale of Intel Corporation stock and bond redemptions, along with a corporate stock buyback program that reduced the amount of stock outstanding in the fourth quarter by 7.4 million shares.

The analysts were concerned about the quality of IBM's earnings. Identify four quality of earnings issues reported in the case and the analysts' concern about each. In percentage terms, what is the impact of the currency changes on fourth-quarter earnings? Comment on management's assessment of IBM's performance. Do you agree with management? (Optional question: What has IBM's subsequent performance been?) Be prepared to discuss your answers in class.

Interpreting Financial Reports

LO1, LO5 **Interpretation of Statement of Stockholders' Equity**

C 3. The consolidated statement of stockholders' equity for Jackson Electronics, Inc., a manufacturer of a broad line of electrical components, is presented below.

Jackson Electronics, Inc.
Consolidated Statement of Stockholders' Equity
For the Year Ended September 30, 20x8
(In thousands)

	Preferred Stock	Common Stock	Paid-in Capital in Excess of Par Value, Common	Retained Earnings	Treasury Stock, Common	Accumulated Other Comprehensive Income	Total
Balance at September 30, 20x7	$2,756	$3,902	$14,149	$119,312	($ 942)		$139,177
Net income	—	—	—	18,753	—		18,753
Unrealized gain on available for sale securities						$12,000	12,000
Redemption and retirement of preferred stock (27,560 shares)	(2,756)	—	—	—	—		(2,756)
Stock options exercised (89,000 shares)	—	89	847	—	—		936
Purchases of common stock for treasury (501,412 shares)	—	—	—	—	(12,552)		(12,552)
Issuance of common stock (148,000 shares) in exchange for convertible subordinated debentures	—	148	3,635	—	—		3,783
Issuance of common stock (715,000 shares) for cash	—	715	24,535	—	—		25,250
Issuance of 500,000 shares of common stock in exchange for investment in Electrix Company shares	—	500	17,263	—	—		17,763
Cash dividends—common stock ($.80 per share)	—	—	—	(3,086)	—		(3,086)
Balance at September 30, 20x8	$ —	$5,354	$60,429	$134,979	($13,494)	$12,000	$199,268

This statement of stockholders' equity has nine summary transactions. Show that you understand it by preparing an entry in journal form with an explanation for each transaction. In each case, if applicable, determine the average price per common share. At times, you will have to make assumptions about an offsetting part of the entry. For example, assume debentures (long-term bonds) are recorded at face value and that employees pay cash for stock purchased under company incentive plans. Also, define comprehensive income and determine the amount for Jackson Electronics.

LO2   **Analysis of Income Taxes from Annual Report**

C 4. In its 2004 annual report, **Nike, Inc.**, the athletic sportswear company, provided the following data about its current and deferred income tax provisions (in millions):

	2004
Current income taxes due	$495.4
Deferred income taxes	9.0
Total provision for income taxes	$504.4

1. What were the 2004 income taxes on the income statement? Record in journal form the overall income tax liability for 2004, using income tax allocation procedures.
2. Nike's balance sheet contains both deferred income tax assets and deferred tax liabilities. How do such deferred income tax assets arise? How do such deferred income tax liabilities arise? Given the definition of assets and liabilities, do you see a potential problem with the company's classifying deferred income taxes as a liability? Why or why not?

Decision Analysis Using Excel

LO5, LO6, LO7   **Analyzing Effects of Stockholders' Equity Transactions**

C 5. Metzger Steel Corporation (MSC) is a small specialty steel manufacturer located in northern Alabama. The Metzger family has owned the company for several generations. Arnold Metzger is a major shareholder in MSC by virtue of his having inherited 200,000 shares of common stock in the company. Metzger has not shown much interest in the business because of his enthusiasm for archaeology, which takes him to far parts of the world. However, when he received the minutes of the last board of directors meeting, he questioned a number of transactions involving stockholders' equity. He asks you as a person with knowledge of accounting to help him interpret the effect of these transactions on his interest in MSC.

You begin by examining the stockholders' equity section of MSC's December 31, 20x7, balance sheet, which appears at the top of the opposite page. Then you read these relevant parts of the minutes of the board of directors meeting on December 15, 20x8:

Item A   The president reported the following transactions involving the company's stock during the last quarter:

October 15. Sold 500,000 shares of authorized common stock through the investment banking firm of T.R. Kendall at a net price of $50 per share.

November 1. Purchased 100,000 shares for the corporate treasury from Lucy Metzger at a price of $55 per share.

Metzger Steel Corporation
Balance Sheet
December 31, 20x7

Stockholders' Equity

Contributed capital	
Common stock, $10 par value, 5,000,000 shares authorized, 1,000,000 shares issued and outstanding	$10,000,000
Additional paid-in capital	25,000,000
Total contributed capital	$35,000,000
Retained earnings	20,000,000
Total stockholders' equity	$55,000,000

Item B The board declared a 2-for-1 stock split (accomplished by halving the par value and doubling each stockholder's shares), followed by a 10 percent stock dividend. The board then declared a cash dividend of $2 per share on the resulting shares. Cash dividends are declared on outstanding shares and shares distributable. All these transactions are applicable to stockholders of record on December 20 and are payable on January 10. The market value of MSC stock on the board meeting date after the stock split was estimated to be $30.

Item C The chief financial officer stated that he expected the company to report net income for the year of $4,000,000.

1. Prepare a stockholders' equity section of MSC's balance sheet as of December 31, 20x8 that reflects the above transactions. (**Hint:** Use T accounts to analyze the transactions. Also use a T account to keep track of the shares of common stock outstanding.)
2. Write a memorandum to Arnold Metzger that shows the book value per share and Metzger's percentage of ownership at the beginning and end of the year. Explain the difference and state whether Metzger's position has improved during the year. Tell why or why not and state how Metzger may be able to maintain his percentage of ownership.

Annual Report Case: CVS Corporation

LO1, LO3, LO5 **Corporate Income Statement and Statement of Stockholders' Equity**

C 6. Refer to **CVS Corporation's** annual report in the Supplement to Chapter 1 to answer the following questions:

1. Does CVS have discontinued operations or extraordinary items? Are there any items that would lead you to question the quality of CVS's earnings? Would you say the income statement for CVS is relatively simple or relatively complex? Why?
2. What transactions most often affect the stockholders' equity section of the CVS balance sheet? (**Hint:** Examine the statements of stockholders' equity.)

Comparison Case: CVS Versus Southwest

LO7 **Book Value and Market Value**

  C 7. Refer to the annual report for **CVS Corporation** and the financial statements for **Southwest Airlines Co**. in the Supplement to Chapter 1. Compute the 2004 and 2003 book value per share for both companies and compare the results to the average stock price of each in the fourth quarter of 2004 as shown in the notes to the financial statements. Southwest's average price per share was $45.22 in 2004 and $27.37 in 2003. How do you explain the differences in book value per share, and how do you interpret their relationship to market prices?

Ethical Dilemma Case

LO6 **Ethics and Stock Dividends**

C 8. For 20 years, Bass Products Corporation, a public corporation that has promoted itself to investors as a stable, reliable company, has paid a cash dividend every quarter. Recent competition from Asian companies has negatively affected the company's earnings and cash flows. As a result, Sandra Bass, president of the company, is proposing that the board of directors declare a stock dividend of 5 percent this year instead of a cash dividend. She stated: "This will maintain our consecutive dividend record and will not require any cash outflow." What is the difference between a cash dividend and a stock dividend? Why does a corporation usually distribute either kind of dividend, and how does each affect the financial statements? Is the action that Sandra Bass proposed ethical? Why or why not?

Internet Case

LO1, LO4, LO5 **Comparison of Comprehensive Income Disclosures**

 C 9. When the FASB ruled that public companies should report comprehensive income, it did not issue specific guidelines for how this amount and its components should be disclosed. Choose two companies in the same industry. Go to the annual reports on the websites of the two companies you have selected. In the latest annual report, look at the financial statements. How have your two companies reported comprehensive income—as part of the income statement, as part of stockholders' equity, or as a separate statement? What items create a difference between net income and comprehensive income? Is comprehensive income greater or less than net income? Is comprehensive income more volatile than net income? Which measure of income is used to compute basic earnings per share?

Group Activity Case

LO1, LO3, LO4, LO5, LO6, LO7   **C 10.** Divide into groups of three or four students each. Each group should choose a company in the technology industry, such as **Yahoo!**, **ebay**, **Apple**, or **Microsoft**. Obtain the company's annual report or SEC Form 10-K from the Internet. Find the corporate income statement and summary of significant accounting policies (usually the first note to the financial statements).

1. As a team, prepare a one-page executive summary that highlights the quality of earnings, the relationship of book value and market value, and the existence or absence of stock splits or dividends, including reference to management's assessment. Include a table with your report and answers to the following questions:

    a. Did the company report any discontinued operations or extraordinary items?

    b. What percentage of impact did these items have on earnings per share? (Summarize in your table the methods and estimates the company uses.)

     c. How would you evaluate the quality of earnings for the company?

     d. Did the company provide a statement of stockholders' equity or summarize changes in stockholders' equity in the notes only?

     e. Did the company declare any stock dividends or stock splits? Calculate book value per common share.

2. Find in the financial section of your local paper the current market prices of the company's common stock. Discuss the difference between market price per share and book value per share.

3. Find and read references to earnings per share in management's discussion and analysis in the company's annual report. Be prepared to share your report with the reports of other teams in class.

Business Communication Case

LO1, LO3

C 11. In a recent year, analysts expected **IBM** to earn $1.32 per share. The company actually earned $1.33. **Microsoft** was expected to earn $.43 per share, but it earned only $.41. The corporate income statements of these companies show that Microsoft had a special charge (with corresponding liability) of $660 million, or $.06 per share, based on settlement of a class-action lawsuit filed on behalf of consumers, whereas IBM had no such charge.[22]

Assume you work for an investment manager who has asked you to write a memorandum in one page or less that assesses these results. Specifically, who did better, Microsoft or IBM? Use quality of earnings to support your answer and comment on the effect of Microsoft's special charge on current and future

The Statement of Cash Flows

C ash flows are the lifeblood of a business. They enable a company to pay expenses, debts, employees' wages, and taxes, and to invest in the assets it needs for its operations. Without sufficient cash flows, a company cannot grow and prosper. Because of the importance of cash flows, one must be alert to the possibility that items may be incorrectly classified in a statement of cash flows and that the statement may not fully disclose all pertinent information. This chapter identifies the classifications used in a statement of cash flows and explains how to analyze the statement.

LEARNING OBJECTIVES

Making a Statement

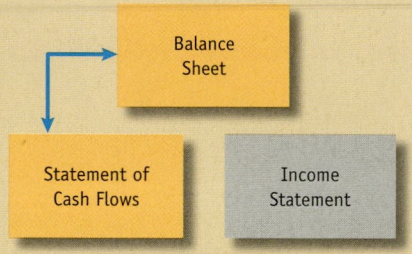

The statement of cash flows explains the changes in cash on the balance sheet.

LO1 Describe the principal purposes and uses of the statement of cash flows, and identify its components.

LO2 Analyze the statement of cash flows.

LO3 Use the indirect method to determine cash flows from operating activities.

LO4 Determine cash flows from investing activities.

LO5 Determine cash flows from financing activities.

MARRIOTT INTERNATIONAL, INC.

- Are operations generating sufficient operating cash flows?

- Is the company growing by investing in long-term assets?

- Has the company had to borrow money or issue stock to finance its growth?

Marriott International is a world leader in lodging and hospitality services. The company believes that maintaining strong cash flows is very important to its future. Its emphasis on cash flows is reflected in its compensation plan for top executives, which gives the greatest weight to cash flows. Why does Marriott place such emphasis on cash flows?

Strong cash flows are critical to achieving and maintaining liquidity. If cash flows exceed the amount a company needs for operations and expansion, it will not have to borrow additional funds. It can use its excess cash to reduce debt, thereby lowering its debt to equity ratio and improving its financial position. That, in turn, can increase the market value of its stock, which will increase shareholders' value.

The statement of cash flows provides information essential to evaluating a company's liquidity. The Financial Highlights below summarize key components of Marriott's statement of cash flows.[1]

MARRIOT'S FINANCIAL HIGHLIGHTS:
Consolidated Statement of Cash Flows
(In millions)

	2004	2003	2002
Net cash provided by operating activities	$891	$403	$ 516
Net cash provided by investing activities	287	311	317
Net cash used in financing activities	(637)	(683)	(1,447)
Increase (decrease) in cash and equivlalents	$541	$ 31	($ 614)

Overview of the Statement of Cash Flows

LO1 Describe the principal purposes and uses of the statement of cash flows, and identify its components.

The **statement of cash flows** shows how a company's operating, investing, and financing activities have affected cash during an accounting period. It explains the net increase (or decrease) in cash during the period. For purposes of preparing this statement, **cash** is defined as including both cash and cash equivalents. **Cash equivalents** are investments that can be quickly converted to cash; they have a maturity of 90 days or less when they are purchased. They include money market accounts, commercial paper, and U.S. Treasury bills. A company invests in cash equivalents to earn interest on cash that would otherwise be temporarily idle.

Suppose, for example, that a company has $1,000,000 that it will not need for 30 days. To earn a return on this amount, the company could place the cash in an account that earns interest (such as a money market account), lend the cash to another corporation by purchasing that corporation's short-term notes (commercial paper), or purchase a short-term obligation of the U.S. government (a Treasury bill).

Because cash includes cash equivalents, transfers between the Cash account and cash equivalents are not treated as cash receipts or cash payments. On the statement of cash flows, cash equivalents are combined with the Cash account. Cash equivalents should not be confused with short-term investments, or marketable securities. These items are not combined with the Cash account on the statement of cash flows; rather, purchases of marketable securities are treated as cash outflows, and sales of marketable securities are treated as cash inflows.

> **Study Note**
>
> Money market accounts, commercial paper (short-term notes), and U.S. Treasury bills are considered cash equivalents because they are highly liquid, temporary (90 days or less) holding places for cash not currently needed to operate the business.

Purposes of the Statement of Cash Flows

The primary purpose of the statement of cash flows is to provide information about a company's cash receipts and cash payments during an accounting period. A secondary purpose is to provide information about a company's operating, investing, and financing activities during the accounting period. Some information about those activities may be inferred from other financial statements, but the statement of cash flows summarizes *all* transactions that affect cash.

Uses of the Statement of Cash Flows

The statement of cash flows is useful to management, as well as to investors and creditors.

- Management uses the statement of cash flows to assess liquidity, to determine dividend policy, and to evaluate the effects of major policy decisions involving investments and financing. Examples include determining if short-term financing is needed to pay current liabilities, deciding whether to raise or lower dividends, and planning for investing and financing needs.

- Investors and creditors use the statement to assess a company's ability to manage cash flows, to generate positive future cash flows, to pay its liabilities, to pay dividends and interest, and to anticipate its need for additional financing.

■ **FIGURE 1**
Classification of Cash Inflows and Cash Outflows

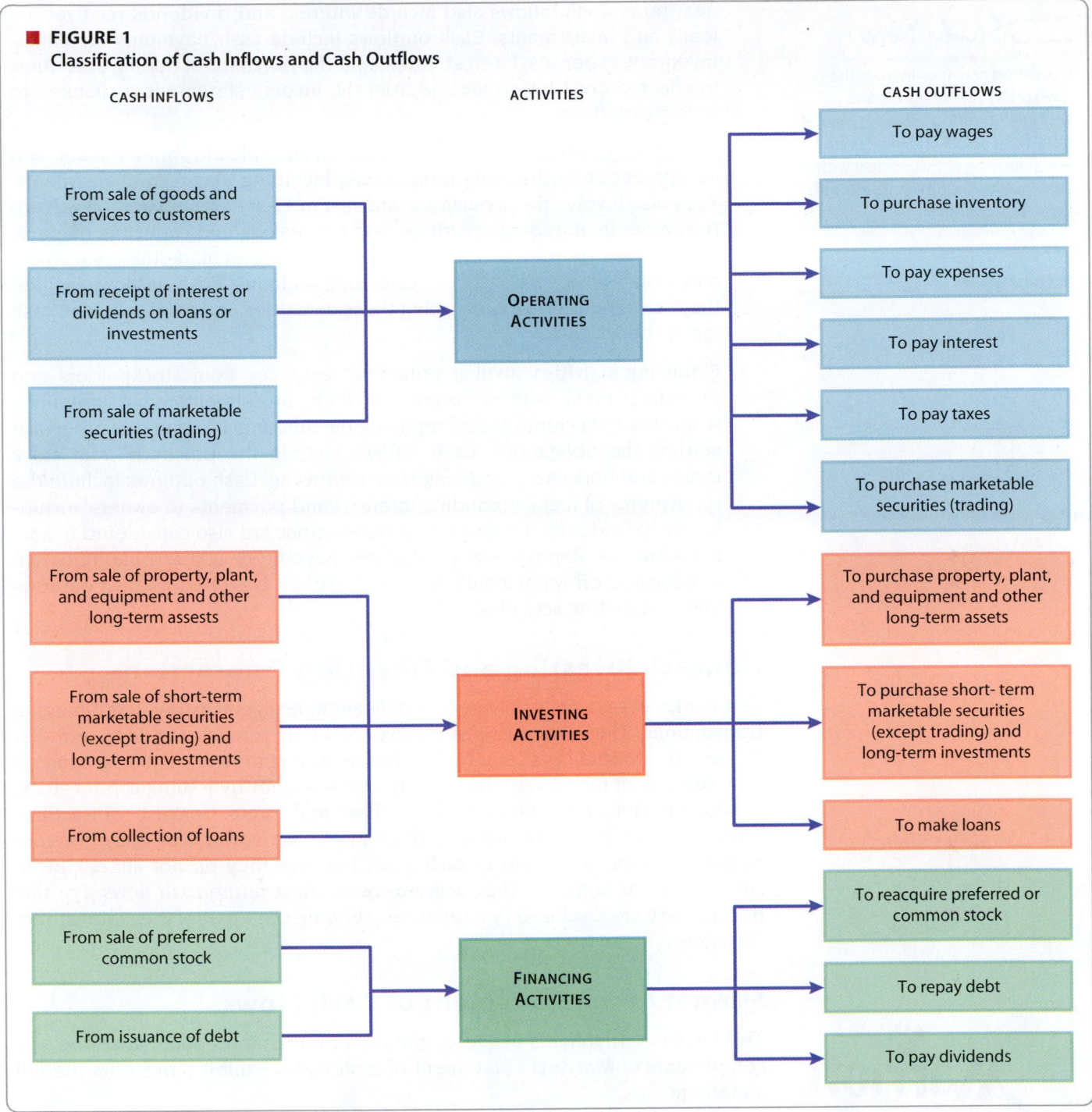

Classification of Cash Flows

The statement of cash flows has three major classifications: operating, investing, and financing activities. The components of these activities are illustrated in Figure 1 and summarized below.

1. **Operating activities** involve the cash inflows and outflows from activities that enter into the determination of net income. Cash inflows in this category include cash receipts from the sale of goods and services and from the sale of *trading securities*. Trading securities are a type of marketable security that a company buys and sells for the purpose of making a profit in the

near term. Cash inflows also include interest and dividends received on loans and investments. Cash outflows include cash payments for wages, inventory, expenses, interest, taxes, and the purchase of trading securities. In effect, accrual-based income from the income statement is changed to reflect cash flows.

2. **Investing activities** involve the acquisition and sale of property, plant, and equipment and other long-term assets, including long-term investments. They also involve the acquisition and sale of short-term marketable securities, other than trading securities, and the making and collecting of loans. Cash inflows include the cash received from selling marketable securities and long-term assets and from collecting on loans. Cash outflows include the cash expended on purchasing these securities and assets and the cash lent to borrowers.

3. **Financing activities** involve obtaining resources from stockholders and providing them with a return on their investments, and obtaining resources from creditors and repaying the amounts borrowed or otherwise settling the obligations. Cash inflows include the proceeds from stock issues and from short- and long-term borrowing. Cash outflows include the repayments of loans (excluding interest) and payments to owners, including cash dividends. Treasury stock transactions are also considered financing activities. Repayments of accounts payable or accrued liabilities are not considered repayments of loans; they are classified as cash outflows under operating activities.

Noncash Investing and Financing Transactions

Companies occasionally engage in significant **noncash investing and financing transactions**. These transactions involve only long-term assets, long-term liabilities, or stockholders' equity. For instance, a company might exchange a long-term asset for a long-term liability, settle a debt by issuing capital stock, or take out a long-term mortgage to purchase real estate. Noncash transactions represent significant investing and financing activities, but they are not reflected on the statement of cash flows because they do not affect current cash inflows or outflows. They will, however, affect future cash flows. For this reason, they are disclosed in a separate schedule or as part of the statement of cash flows.

Format of the Statement of Cash Flows

The Financial Highlights at the beginning of the chapter summarize the key components of **Marriott's** statement of cash flows. Exhibit 1 presents the full statement.

▸ The first section of the statement of cash flows is cash flows from operating activities. When the indirect method is used to prepare this section, it begins with net income and ends with cash flows from operating activities. This is the method most commonly used; we discuss it in detail later in the chapter.

▸ The second section, cash flows from investing activities, shows cash transactions involving capital expenditures (for property and equipment) and loans. Cash outflows for capital expenditures are usually shown separately from cash inflows from their disposal, as they are in Marriott's statement. However, when the inflows are not material, some companies combine these two lines to show the net amount of outflow.

EXHIBIT 1 ▶ | Consolidated Statement of Cash Flows

Marriott International, Inc., and Subsidiaries
Consolidated Statement of Cash Flows

	For the Years Ended		
(In millions)	2004	2003	2002
OPERATING ACTIVITIES			
Net income	$ 594	$ 476	$ 439
Adjustments to reconcile to cash provided by operations:			
Income from discontinued operations	2	7	9
Discontinued operations—gain (loss) on sale/exit	—	19	(171)
Depreciation and amortization	166	160	187
Minority interest in results of synthetic fuel operation	(40)	55	—
Income taxes	(63)	(171)	(105)
Timeshare activity, net	113	(111)	(63)
Other	(77)	(73)	223
Working capital changes:			
Accounts receivable	(6)	(81)	(31)
Other current assets	(16)	11	60
Accounts payable and accruals	218	111	(32)
Cash provided by operations	$ 891	$ 403	$ 516
INVESTING ACTIVITIES			
Capital expenditures	$(181)	$(210)	$ (292)
Dispositions	402	494	729
Loan advances	(129)	(241)	(237)
Loan collections and sales	276	280	124
Other	(81)	(12)	(7)
Cash provided by investing activities	$ 287	$ 311	$ 317
FINANCING ACTIVITIES			
Commercial paper, net	$ —	$(102)	$ 102
Issuance of long-term debt	20	14	26
Repayment of long-term debt	(99)	(273)	(946)
Redemption of convertible subordinated debt	(62)	—	(347)
Issuance of Class A common stock	206	102	35
Dividends paid	(73)	(68)	(65)
Purchase of treasury stock	(664)	(373)	(252)
Earn-outs received, net	35	17	—
Cash used in financing activities	$(637)	$(683)	$(1,447)
(DECREASE) INCREASE IN CASH AND EQUIVALENTS	$ 541	$ 31	$ (614)
CASH AND EQUIVALENTS, beginning of year	229	198	812
CASH AND EQUIVALENTS, end of year	$ 770	$ 229	$ 198

Source: Marriott International, Inc., *Annual Report*, 2004.

▶ The third section, cash flows from financing activities, shows debt and common stock transactions, as well as payments for dividends and treasury stock.

▶ A reconciliation of the beginning and ending balances of cash appears at the bottom of the statement. These cash balances will tie into the cash balances of the balance sheets.

Ethical Considerations and the Statement of Cash Flows

Although cash inflows and outflows are not as subject to manipulation as earnings are, managers are acutely aware of users' emphasis on cash flows from operations as an important measure of performance. Thus, an incentive exists to overstate these cash flows.

In earlier chapters, we cited an egregious example of earnings management. As you may recall, by treating operating expenses of about $10 billion over several years as purchases of equipment, **WorldCom** reduced reported expenses and improved reported earnings. In addition, by classifying payments of operating expenses as investments on the statement of cash flows, it was able to show an improvement in cash flows from operations. The inclusion of the expenditures in the investing activities section did not draw special attention because the company normally had large capital expenditures.

Another way a company can show an apparent improvement in its performance is through lack of transparency, or lack of full disclosure, in its financial statements. For instance, securitization—the sale of batches of accounts receivable—is clearly a means of financing, and the proceeds from it should be shown in the financing section of the statement of cash flows. However, because the accounting standards are somewhat vague about where these proceeds should go, some companies net the proceeds against the accounts receivable in the operating section of the statement and bury the explanation in the notes to the financial statements. By doing so, they make collections of receivables in the operating activities section look better than they actually were. It is not illegal to do this, but from an ethical standpoint, it obscures the company's true performance.

S T O P • R E V I E W • A P P L Y

1-1. In the statement of cash flows, what does cash include?

1-2. What are the purposes of the statement of cash flows?

1-3. What are the three classifications of cash flows? Give two examples of each.

1-4. Why is it important to disclose certain noncash transactions? How should they be disclosed?

1-5. Why would a company want to classify an item that belongs in the operating activities section of the statement of cash flows in the investing or financing sections?

Suggested answers to all Stop, Review, and Apply questions follow the appendixes.

Analyzing Cash Flows

LO2 Analyze the statement of cash flows.

Like the analysis of other financial statements, an analysis of the statement of cash flows can reveal significant relationships. Two areas on which analysts focus when examining a company's statement of cash flows are cash-generating efficiency and free cash flow.

Cash-Generating Efficiency

Managers accustomed to evaluating income statements usually focus on the bottom-line result. While the level of cash at the bottom of the statement of cash flows is certainly an important consideration, such information can be obtained from the balance sheet. The focal point of cash flow analysis is on cash inflows and outflows from operating activities. These cash flows are used in ratios that measure **cash-generating efficiency**, which is a company's ability to generate cash from its current or continuing operations. The ratios that analysts use to compute cash-generating efficiency are cash flow yield, cash flows to sales, and cash flows to assets. In this section, we compute these ratios for **Marriott** in 2004 using data from Exhibit 1 and the following information from Marriott's 2004 annual report. (All dollar amounts are in millions.)

	2004	**2003**	**2002**
Net Sales	$10,099	$9,014	$8,415
Total Assets	8,668	8,177	8,296

Cash flow yield is the ratio of net cash flows from operating activities to net income:

$$\text{Cash Flow Yield} = \frac{\text{Net Cash Flows from Operating Activities}}{\text{Net Income}}$$

$$= \frac{\$891}{\$594}$$

$$= 1.5 \text{ times}$$

Marriott's cash flow yield of 1.5 times means that its operating activities were generating about 50 percent more cash flow than net income. At a minimum, cash-flow yield should be 1.0, which is the level typical for a service enterprise. However, a firm with significant depreciable assets should have a cash flow yield greater than 1.0 because depreciation expense is added back to net income to arrive at cash flows from operating activities. If special items, such as discontinued operations, appear on the income statement and are material, income from continuing operations should be used as the denominator.

Cash flows to sales is the ratio of net cash flows from operating activities to sales:

$$\text{Cash Flows to Sales} = \frac{\text{Net Cash Flows from Operating Activities}}{\text{Sales}}$$

$$= \frac{\$891}{\$10,099}$$

$$= 8.8\%$$

Thus, Marriott generated positive cash flows to sales of 8.8 percent.

Cash flows to assets is the ratio of net cash flows from operating activities to average total assets:

$$\text{Cash Flows to Assets} = \frac{\text{Net Cash Flows from Operating Activities}}{\text{Average Total Assets}}$$

$$= \frac{\$891}{(\$8,668 + \$8,177) \div 2}$$

$$= 10.6\%$$

Marriott's cash flows to assets ratio is higher than its cash flows to sales ratio because of its good asset turnover ratio (sales ÷ average total assets) of 1.2 times (10.6% ÷ 8.8%). Cash flows to sales and cash flows to assets are closely related to the profitability measures of profit margin and return on assets. They exceed those measures by the amount of the cash flow yield ratio because cash flow yield is the ratio of net cash flows from operating activities to net income.

Free Cash Flow

As we noted in an earlier chapter, **free cash flow** is the amount of cash that remains after deducting the funds a company must commit to continue operating at its planned level. If free cash flow is positive, it means that the company has met all of its planned cash commitments and has cash available to reduce debt or to expand. A negative free cash flow means that the company will have to sell investments, borrow money, or issue stock in the short term to continue at its planned level; if a company's free cash flow remains negative for several years, it may not be able to raise cash by issuing stocks or bonds. On the statement of cash flows, cash commitments for current and continuing

FOCUS ON BUSINESS PRACTICE

Cash Flows Tell All.

In early 2001, the telecommunications industry began one of the biggest market crashes in history. Could it have been predicted? The capital expenditures that telecommunications firms must make for equipment, such as cable lines and computers, are sizable. When the capital expenditures (a negative component of free cash flow) of 41 telecommunications companies are compared with their cash flows from sales over the six years preceding the crash, an interesting pattern emerges. In the first three years, both capital expenditures and cash flows from sales were about 20 per-

cent of sales. In other words, free cash flows were neutral, with operations generating enough cash flows to cover capital expenditures. In the next three years, cash flows from sales stayed at about 20 percent of sales, but the companies' capital expenditure increased dramatically, to 35 percent of sales. Thus, free cash flows turned very negative, and almost half of capital expenditures had to be financed by debt instead of operations, making these companies more vulnerable to the downturn in the economy that occurred in 2001.[2]

FOCUS ON BUSINESS PRACTICE

What Do You Mean, "Free Cash Flow"?

Because the statement of cash flows has been around for less than 20 years, no generally accepted analyses have yet been developed. For example, the term *free cash flow* is commonly used in the business press, but there is no agreement on its definition. An article in *Forbes* defines *free cash flow* as "cash available after paying out capital expenditures and dividends, but *before taxes and interest*"[3] [emphasis added]. An article in *The Wall Street Journal* defines it as "operating income less maintenance-level capital expenditures."[4] The definition with which we are most in agreement is the one used in *BusinessWeek:* free cash flow is net cash flows from operating activities less net capital expenditures and dividends. This "measures truly discretionary funds—company money that an owner could pocket without harming the business."[5]

Study Note

The computation for free cash flow sometimes uses *net capital expenditures* in place of *(purchases of plant assets − sales of plant assets)*.

operations, interest, and income taxes are incorporated in cash flows from current operations.

Free cash flow for **Marriott** is computed as follows (in millions):

Free Cash Flow = Net Cash Flows from Operating Activities − Dividends − (Purchases of Plant Assets − Sales of Plant Assets)

$$= \$891 - \$73 - (\$181 - \$402)$$

$$= \$1,039$$

Purchases of plant assets (capital expenditures) and sales (dispositions) of plant assets appear in the investing activities section of the statement of cash flows. When sales of plant assets are small or immaterial, companies can subtract the sales amount from the purchases of plant assets and refer to the result as "net capital expenditures." Dividends appear in the financing activities section. Marriott's positive free cash flow of $1,039 million was due primarily to its strong operating cash flow of $891 million and the $402 million cash it received from the disposition of assets. Cash was used in financing activities in all three years primarily because of debt repayments and the purchase of treasury stock. The company relied mainly on the increased cash provided by operations to make up for these cash outflows.

Telecommunications firms must make large capital expenditures for plant assets, such as the radio tower shown here. These expenditures are a negative component of free cash flow, which is the amount of cash that remains after deducting the funds a company needs to operate at its planned level. Between 1998 and 2000, negative free cash flows forced a number of telecommunications firms to rely heavily on debt to finance their capital expenditures, thus increasing their vulnerability to the economic downturn of 2001.

Because cash flows can vary from year to year, analysts should look at trends in cash flow measures over several years. Marriott's management sums up its approach to managing cash flows as follows:

Cash from Operations
We consider [our borrowing] resources, together with cash we expect to generate from operations, adequate to meet short-term and long-term liquidity requirements, finance our long-term growth plans, meet debt service and fulfill other cash requirements.[6]

S T O P • R E V I E W • A P P L Y

2-1. What is cash-generating efficiency?

2-2. What are three ratios that measure cash-generating efficiency?

2-3. What is free cash flow?

2-4. What do *positive* and *negative* free cash flows mean?

Operating Activities

LO3 Use the indirect method to determine cash flows from operating activities.

To demonstrate the preparation of the statement of cash flows, we will work through an example step by step. The data for this example are presented in Exhibit 2, which shows Amir Corporation's income statement for 20x7, and in Exhibit 3, which shows Amir's balance sheets for December 31, 20x7 and 20x6. Exhibit 3 shows the balance sheet accounts that we use for analysis and whether the change in each account is an increase or a decrease.

EXHIBIT 2 ▶

Income Statement

Amir Corporation
Income Statement
For the Year Ended December 31, 20x7

Sales		$349,000
Cost of goods sold		260,000
Gross margin		$ 89,000
Operating expenses (including depreciation expense of $18,500)		73,500
Operating income		$ 15,500
Other income (expenses)		
Interest expense	($11,500)	
Interest income	3,000	
Gain on sale of investments	6,000	
Loss on sale of plant assets	(1,500)	(4,000)
Income before income taxes		$ 11,500
Income taxes expense		3,500
Net income		$ 8,000

▼ EXHIBIT 3

Comparative Balance Sheets Showing Changes in Accounts

Amir Corporation
Comparative Balance Sheets
December 31, 20x7 and 20x6

	20x7	20x6	Change	Increase or Decrease
Assets				
Current assets				
Cash	$ 23,000	$ 7,500	$ 15,500	Increase
Accounts receivable (net)	23,500	27,500	(4,000)	Decrease
Inventory	72,000	55,000	17,000	Increase
Prepaid expenses	500	2,500	(2,000)	Decrease
Total current assets	$119,000	$ 92,500	$ 26,500	
Investments	$ 57,500	$ 63,500	($ 6,000)	Decrease
Plant assets	$357,500	$252,500	$105,000	Increase
Less accumulated depreciation	(51,500)	(34,000)	(17,500)	Increase
Total plant assets	$306,000	$218,500	$ 87,500	
Total assets	$482,500	$374,500	$108,000	
Liabilities				
Current liabilities				
Accounts payable	$ 25,000	$ 21,500	$ 3,500	Increase
Accrued liabilities	6,000	4,500	1,500	Increase
Income taxes payable	1,500	2,500	(1,000)	Decrease
Total current liabilities	$ 32,500	$ 28,500	$ 4,000	
Long-term liabilities				
Bonds payable	147,500	122,500	25,000	Increase
Total liabilities				
	$180,000	$151,000	$ 29,000	
Stockholders' Equity				
Common stock, $5 par value	$138,000	$100,000	$ 38,000	Increase
Additional paid-in capital	107,000	57,500	49,500	Increase
Retained earnings	70,000	66,000	4,000	Increase
Treasury stock	(12,500)	0	(12,500)	Increase
Total stockholders' equity	$302,500	$223,500	$ 79,000	
Total liabilities and stockholders' equity	$482,500	$374,500	$108,000	

The first step in preparing the statement of cash flows is to determine cash flows from operating activities. The income statement indicates how successful a company has been in earning an income from its operating activities, but because that statement is prepared on an accrual basis, it does not reflect the inflow and outflow of cash related to operating activities. Revenues are recorded even though the company may not yet have received the cash, and expenses are recorded even though the company may not yet have expended

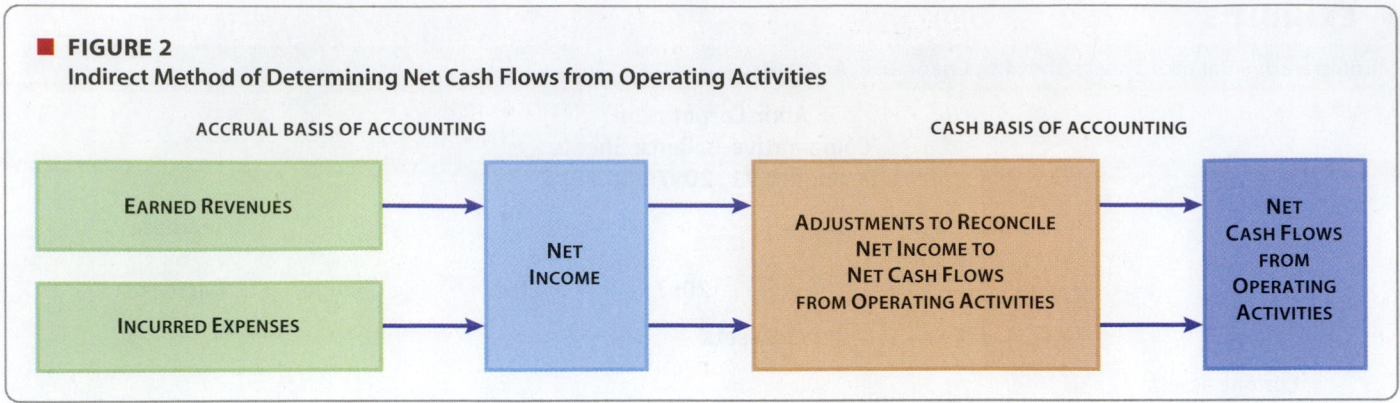

■ **FIGURE 2**
Indirect Method of Determining Net Cash Flows from Operating Activities

the cash. Thus, to ascertain cash flows from operations, the figures on the income statement must be converted from an accrual basis to a cash basis.

There are two methods of accomplishing this:

▶ The **direct method** adjusts each item on the income statement from the accrual basis to the cash basis. The result is a statement that begins with cash receipts from sales and interest and deducts cash payments for purchases, operating expenses, interest payments, and income taxes to arrive at net cash flows from operating activities.

▶ The **indirect method** does not require the adjustment of each item on the income statement. It lists only the adjustments necessary to convert net income to cash flows from operations.

The direct and indirect methods always produce the same net figure. The average person finds the direct method easier to understand because its presentation of operating cash flows is more straightforward than that of the indirect method. However, the indirect method is the overwhelming choice of most companies and accountants. A survey of large companies shows that 99 percent use this method.[7] From an analyst's perspective, the indirect method is superior to the direct method because it begins with net income and derives cash flows from operations; the analyst can readily identify the factors that cause cash flows from operations. From a company's standpoint, the indirect method is easier and less expensive to prepare. For these reasons, we use the indirect method in our example.

As Figure 2 shows, the indirect method focuses on adjusting items on the income statement to reconcile net income to net cash flows from operating activities. These items include depreciation, amortization, and depletion; gains and losses; and changes in the balances of current asset and current liability accounts. The schedule in Exhibit 4 shows the reconciliation of Amir Corporation's net income to net cash flows from operating activities. We discuss each adjustment in the sections that follow.

Depreciation

The investing activities section of the statement of cash flows shows the cash payments that the company made for plant assets, intangible assets, and natural resources during the accounting period. Depreciation expense, amortization expense, and depletion expense for these assets appear on the income statement as allocations of the costs of the original purchases to the current accounting period. The amount of these expenses can usually be found in the income statement or in a note to the financial statements. As you can see

> **Study Note**
>
> The direct and indirect methods relate only to the operating activities section of the statement of cash flows. They are both acceptable for financial reporting purposes.

EXHIBIT 4 ▶

Schedule of Cash Flows from Operating Activities: Indirect Method

Amir Corporation
Schedule of Cash Flows from Operating Activities
For the Year Ended December 31, 20x7

Cash flows from operating activities		
Net income		$ 8,000
Adjustments to reconcile net income to net cash flows from operating activities		
Depreciation	$18,500	
Gain on sale of investments	(6,000)	
Loss on sale of plant assets	1,500	
Changes in current assets and current liabilities		
Decrease in accounts receivable	4,000	
Increase in inventory	(17,000)	
Decrease in prepaid expenses	2,000	
Increase in accounts payable	3,500	
Increase in accrued liabilities	1,500	
Decrease in income taxes payable	(1,000)	7,000
Net cash flows from operating activities		$15,000

in Exhibit 2, Amir Corporation's income statement discloses depreciation expense of $18,500, which would have been recorded as follows:

A = L + SE
−18,500   −18,500

Depreciation Expense	18,500	
Accumulated Depreciation		18,500
To record annual depreciation on plant assets		

 **Study Note**

Operating expenses on the income statement include depreciation expense, which does not require a cash outlay.

Even though depreciation expense appears on the income statement, it involves no outlay of cash and so does not affect cash flows in the current period. Thus, to arrive at cash flows from operations on the statement of cash flows, an adjustment is needed to increase net income by the amount of depreciation expense shown on the income statement.

Gains and Losses

Study Note

Gains and losses by themselves do not represent cash flows; they are merely bookkeeping adjustments. For example, when a long-term asset is sold, it is the *proceeds* (cash received), not the gain or loss, that constitute cash flow.

Like depreciation expense, gains and losses that appear on the income statement do not affect cash flows from operating activities and need to be removed from this section of the statement of cash flows. The cash receipts generated by the disposal of the assets that resulted in the gains or losses are included in the investing activities section of the statement of cash flows. Thus, to reconcile net income to cash flows from operating activities (and prevent double counting), gains and losses must be removed from net income.

For example, on its income statement, Amir Corporation shows a $6,000 gain on the sale of investments. This amount is subtracted from net income to reconcile net income to net cash flows from operating activities. The reason for doing this is that the $6,000 is included in the investing activities section of the statement of cash flows as part of the cash from the sale of the investment. Because the gain has already been included in the calculation of net income, the $6,000 gain must be subtracted to prevent double counting.

Amir's income statement also shows a $1,500 loss on the sale of plant assets. This loss is already reflected in the sale of plant assets in the investing activities section of the statement of cash flows. Thus, the $1,500 is added to net income to reconcile net income to net cash flows from operating activities.

Changes in Current Assets

Decreases in current assets other than cash have positive effects on cash flows, and increases in current assets have negative effects on cash flows. A decrease in a current asset frees up invested cash, thereby increasing cash flow. An increase in a current asset consumes cash, thereby decreasing cash flow. For example, look at Amir Corporation's income statement and balance sheets in Exhibits 2 and 3. Note that net sales in 20x7 were $349,000 and that Accounts Receivable decreased by $4,000. Thus, collections were $4,000 more than sales recorded for the year, and the total cash received from sales was $353,000 ($349,000 + $4,000 = $353,000). The effect on accounts receivable can be illustrated as follows:

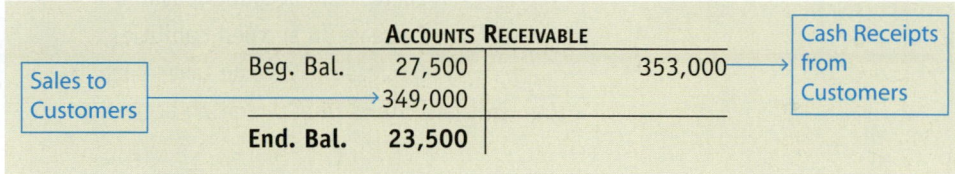

To reconcile net income to net cash flows from operating activities, the $4,000 decrease in Accounts Receivable is added to net income.

Inventory can be analyzed in the same way. For example, Exhibit 3 shows that Amir's Inventory account increased by $17,000 between 20x6 and 20x7. This means that Amir expended $17,000 more in cash for purchases than it included in cost of goods sold on its income statement. Because of this expenditure, net income is higher than net cash flows from operating activities, so $17,000 must be deducted from net income. By the same logic, the decrease of $2,000 in Prepaid Expenses shown on the balance sheets must be added to net income to reconcile net income to net cash flows from operations.

Changes in Current Liabilities

The effect that changes in current liabilities have on cash flows is the opposite of the effect of changes in current assets. An increase in a current liability represents a postponement of a cash payment, which frees up cash and increases cash flow in the current period. A decrease in a current liability consumes cash, which decreases cash flow. To reconcile net income to net cash flows from operating activities, increases in current liabilities are added to net income, and decreases are deducted. For example, Exhibit 3 shows that from 20x6 to 20x7, Amir's accounts payable increased by $3,500. This means that Amir paid $3,500 less to creditors than the amount indicated in the cost of goods sold on its income statement. The following T account illustrates this relationship:

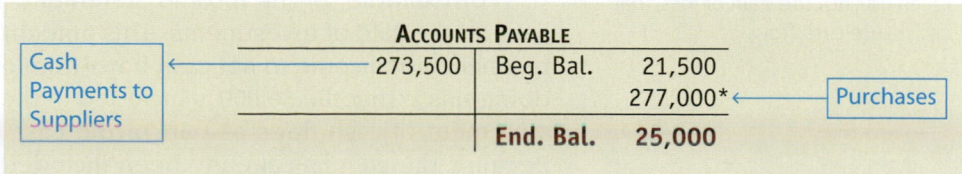

*Purchases = Cost of Goods Sold ($260,000) + Increase in Inventory ($17,000)

FOCUS ON BUSINESS PRACTICE

What Is EBITDA, and Is It Any Good?

Some companies and analysts like to use EBITDA (an acronym for Earnings Before Interest, Taxes, Depreciation, and Amortization) as a short-cut measure of cash flows from operations. But recent events have caused many analysts to reconsider this measure of performance. For instance, when **WorldCom** transferred $3.8 billion from expenses to capital expenditures in one year, it touted its EBITDA; at the time, the firm was, in fact, nearly bankrupt. The demise of **Vivendi**, the big French company that imploded when it did not have enough cash to pay its debts and that also touted its EBIDTA, is another reason that analysts have had second thoughts about relying on this measure of performance.

Some analysts are now saying that EBITDA is "to a great extent misleading" and that it "is a confusing metric.... Some take it for a proxy for profits and some take it for a proxy for cash flow, and it's neither."[8] Cash flows from operations and free cash flow, both of which take into account interest, taxes, and depreciation, are better and more comprehensive measures of a company's cash-generating efficiency.

Thus, $3,500 must be added to net income to reconcile net income to net cash flows from operating activities. By the same logic, the increase of $1,500 in accrued liabilities shown on the balance sheets must be added to net income, and the decrease of $1,000 in income taxes payable must be deducted from net income.

Schedule of Cash Flows from Operating Activities

In summary, Exhibit 4 shows that by using the indirect method, net income of $8,000 has been adjusted by reconciling items totaling $7,000 to arrive at net cash flows from operating activities of $15,000. This means that although Amir's net income was $8,000, the company actually had net cash flows of $15,000 available from operating activities to use for purchasing assets, reducing debts, and paying dividends.

The treatment of income statement items that do not affect cash flows can be summarized as follows:

	Add to or Deduct from Net Income
Depreciation expense	Add
Amortization expense	Add
Depletion expense	Add
Losses	Add
Gains	Deduct

The following summarizes the adjustments for increases and decreases in current assets and current liabilities:

	Add to Net Income	Deduct from Net Income
Current assets		
Accounts receivable (net)	Decrease	Increase
Inventory	Decrease	Increase
Prepaid expenses	Decrease	Increase
Current liabilities		
Accounts payable	Increase	Decrease
Accrued liabilities	Increase	Decrease
Income taxes payable	Increase	Decrease

STOP • REVIEW • APPLY

3-1. What is the basic difference between the direct method and the indirect method of determining cash flows from operations?

3-2. What conditions might cause a corporation that had a net loss of $12,000 to have a positive cash flow from operations of $9,000?

3-3. Why is depreciation added to net income in arriving at cash flows from operating activities?

3-4. Why is a gain subtracted from net income in arriving at cash flows from operating activities?

3-5. Why do changes in current assets and current liabilities appear in the operating section of the statement of cash flows?

3-6. When the indirect method is used to determine net cash flows from operating activities, should (a) an increase in accounts receivable, (b) a decrease in inventory, (c) an increase in accounts payable, (d) a decrease in wages payable, (e) depreciation expense, and (f) amortization of patents be added to or subtracted from net income?

Cash Flows from Operating Activities: Indirect Method   For the year ended June 30, 20xx, Cirta Corporation's net income was $3,700. Its depreciation expense was $1,000. During the year, its Accounts Receivable increased by $2,200, Inventories increased by $3,500, Prepaid Rent decreased by $700, Accounts Payable increased by $7,000, Salaries Payable increased by $500, and Income Taxes Payable decreased by $300. The company also had a gain on the sale of investments of $900. Use the indirect method to prepare a schedule of cash flows from operating activities.

SOLUTION

Cirta Corporation
Schedule of Cash Flows from Operating Activities
For the Year Ended June 30, 20xx

Cash flows from operating activities		
Net income		$3,700
Adjustments to reconcile net income to net cash flows from operating activities		
Depreciation	$1,000	
Gain on sale of investments	(900)	
Changes in current assets and current liabilities		
Increase in accounts receivable	(2,200)	
Increase in inventories	(3,500)	
Decrease in prepaid rent	700	
Increase in accounts payable	7,000	
Increase in salaries payable	500	
Decrease in income taxes payable	(300)	2,300
Net cash flows from operating activities		$6,000

Investing Activities

LO4 Determine cash flows from investing activities.

To determine cash flows from investing activities, accounts involving cash receipts and cash payments from investing activities are examined individually. The objective is to explain the change in each account balance from one year to the next.

Although investing activities center on the long-term assets shown on the balance sheet, they also include any short-term investments shown under current assets on the balance sheet and any investment gains and losses on the income statement. The balance sheets in Exhibit 3 show that Amir had no short-term investments and that its long-term assets consisted of investments and plant assets. The income statement in Exhibit 2 shows that Amir had a gain on the sale of investments and a loss on the sale of plant assets.

The following transactions pertain to Amir's investing activities in 20x7:

1. Purchased investments in the amount of $39,000.

2. Sold investments that cost $45,000 for $51,000.

3. Purchased plant assets in the amount of $60,000.

4. Sold plant assets that cost $5,000 and that had accumulated depreciation of $1,000 for $2,500.

5. Issued $50,000 of bonds at face value in a noncash exchange for plant assets.

In the following sections, we analyze the accounts related to investing activities to determine their effects on Amir's cash flows.

Investments

Our objective in this section is to explain Amir Corporation's $6,000 decrease in investments. We do this by analyzing the increases and decreases in Amir's Investments account to determine their effects on the Cash account.

Item 1 in the list of Amir's transactions states that its purchases of investments totaled $39,000 during 20x7. This transaction, which caused a $39,000 decrease in cash flows, is recorded as follows:

A	= L + SE			
+39,000		Investments	39,000	
−39,000		Cash		39,000
		Purchase of investments		

Item 2 states that Amir sold investments that cost $45,000 for $51,000. This transaction resulted in a gain of $6,000. It is recorded as follows:

A	= L +	SE			
+51,000		+6,000	Cash	51,000	
−45,000			Investments		45,000
			Gain on Sale of Investments		6,000
			Sale of investments for a gain		

The effect of this transaction is a $51,000 increase in cash flows. Note that the gain on the sale is included in the $51,000. This is the reason we excluded it in

computing cash flows from operations. If it had been included in that section, it would have been counted twice.

We have now explained the $6,000 decrease in the Investments account during 20x7, as illustrated in the following T account:

INVESTMENTS			
Beg. Bal.	63,500	Sales	45,000
Purchases	39,000		
End. Bal.	**57,500**		

The cash flow effects of these transactions are shown in the investing activities section of the statement of cash flows as follows:

Purchase of investments	($39,000)
Sale of investments	51,000

Notice that purchases and sales are listed separately as cash outflows and inflows to give readers of the statement a complete view of investing activity. However, some companies prefer to list them as a single net amount.

If Amir Corporation had short-term investments or marketable securities, the analysis of cash flows would be the same.

Plant Assets

For plant assets, we have to explain changes in both the Plant Assets account and the related Accumulated Depreciation account. Exhibit 3 shows that from 2006 to 2007, Amir Corporation's plant assets increased by $105,000 and that accumulated depreciation increased by $17,500.

Item **3** in the list of Amir's transactions in 2007 states that the company purchased plant assets totaling $60,000. The following entry records this cash outflow:

A = L + SE
+60,000
−60,000

Plant Assets	60,000	
Cash		60,000
Purchase of plant assets		

Item **4** states that Amir Corporation sold plant assets that cost $5,000 and that had accumulated depreciation of $1,000 for $2,500. Thus, this transaction resulted in a loss of $1,500. The entry to record it is as follows:

A = L + SE
+2,500   −1,500
+1,000
−5,000

Cash	2,500	
Accumulated Depreciation	1,000	
Loss on Sale of Plant Assets	1,500	
Plant Assets		5,000
Sale of plant assets at a loss		

Note that in this transaction, the positive cash flow is equal to the amount of cash received, $2,500. The loss on the sale of plant assets is included in the investing activities section of the statement of cash flows and excluded from the operating activities section by adjusting net income for the amount of the loss. The amount of a loss or gain on the sale of an asset is determined by the amount of cash received and does not represent a cash outflow or inflow.

 *Study Note*

$$A = L + SE$$
$$+50,000 \quad +50,000$$

The investing activities section of Amir's statement of cash flows reports the firm's purchase and sale of plant assets as follows:

Purchase of plant assets	($60,000)
Sale of plant assets	2,500

Cash outflows and cash inflows are listed separately here, but companies sometimes combine them into a single net amount, as they do the purchase and sale of investments.

Item **5** in the list of Amir's transactions is a noncash exchange that affects two long-term accounts, Plant Assets and Bonds Payable. It is recorded as follows:

Plant Assets	50,000	
Bonds Payable		50,000
Issued bonds at face value for plant assets		

Although this transaction does not involve an inflow or outflow of cash, it is a significant transaction involving both an investing activity (the purchase of plant assets) and a financing activity (the issue of bonds payable). Because one purpose of the statement of cash flows is to show important investing and financing activities, the transaction is listed at the bottom of the statement of cash flows or in a separate schedule, as follows:

Schedule of Noncash Investing and Financing Transactions

Issue of bonds payable for plant assets $50,000

We have now accounted for all the changes related to Amir's plant asset accounts. The following T accounts summarize these changes:

PLANT ASSETS

Beg. Bal.	252,500	Sale	5,000
Cash Purchase	60,000		
Noncash Purchase	50,000		
End. Bal.	**357,500**		

ACCUMULATED DEPRECIATION

Sale	1,000	Beg. Bal.	34,000
		Dep. Exp.	18,500
		End. Bal.	**51,500**

Had the balance sheet included specific plant asset accounts (e.g., Equipment and the related accumulated depreciation account) or other long-term asset accounts (e.g., Intangibles), the analysis would have been the same.

S T O P • R E V I E W • A P P L Y

4-1. What are the two major categories of assets that relate to the investing activities section of the statement of cash flows?

4-2. What is the proper treatment on the statement of cash flows of a transaction in which a company had a loss of $5,000 when it sold a building that it had bought for $50,000 and that had accumulated depreciation of $32,000?

4-3. What is the proper treatment on the statement of cash flows of a transaction in which a company purchased buildings and land by taking out a mortgage for $234,000?

Cash Flows from Investing Activities: Plant Assets The following T accounts show Chou Company's plant assets and accumulated depreciation at the end of 20xx:

PLANT ASSETS				ACCUMULATED DEPRECIATION			
Beg. Bal.	32,500	Disposals	11,500	Disposals	7,350	Beg. Bal.	17,250
Purchases	16,800					Depreciation	5,100
End. Bal.	**37,800**					**End. Bal.**	**15,000**

Chou's income statement shows a gain on the sale of plant assets of $2,200.

Compute the amounts that should be shown as cash flows from investing activities, and show how they should appear on Chou's 20xx statement of cash flows.

SOLUTION

Cash flows from investing activities:

Purchase of plant assets	($16,800)
Sale of plant assets	$6,350

The T accounts show total purchases of plant assets of $16,800, which is an outflow of cash, and disposal of plant assets that cost $11,500 and that had accumulated depreciation of $7,350. The income statement shows a $2,200 gain on the sale of the plant assets. The cash inflow from the disposal was as follows:

Plant assets	$11,500
Less accumulated depreciation	7,350
Book value	$ 4,150
Add gain on sale	2,200
Cash inflow from sale of plant assets	$ 6,350

Because the gain on the sale is included in the $6,350 in the investing activities section of the statement of cash flows, it should be deducted from net income in the operating activities section.

Financing Activities

LO5 Determine cash flows from financing activities.

Determining cash flows from financing activities is very similar to determining cash flows from investing activities, but the accounts analyzed relate to short-term borrowings, long-term liabilities, and stockholders' equity. Because Amir Corporation does not have short-term borrowings, we deal only with long-term liabilities and stockholders' equity accounts.

The following transactions pertain to Amir's financing activities in 20x7:

1. Issued $50,000 of bonds at face value in a noncash exchange for plant assets.

2. Repaid $25,000 of bonds at face value at maturity.

3. Issued 7,600 shares of $5 par value common stock for $87,500.

4. Paid cash dividends in the amount of $4,000.

5. Purchased treasury stock for $12,500.

Bonds Payable

Exhibit 3 shows that Amir's Bonds Payable account increased by $25,000 in 20x7. Both items 1 and 2 in the list above affect this account. We analyzed item 1 in connection with plant assets, but it also pertains to the Bonds Payable account. As we noted, this transaction is reported on the schedule of noncash investing and financing transactions. Item 2 results in a cash outflow, which is recorded as follows:

A	=	L	+ SE		
−25,000		−25,000			

Bonds Payable	25,000	
Cash		25,000
Repayment of bonds at face value at maturity		

This appears in the financing activities section of the statement of cash flows as

Repayment of bonds ($25,000)

The following T account explains the change in Bonds Payable:

		BONDS PAYABLE	
Repayment	25,000	Beg. Bal.	122,500
		Noncash Issue	50,000
		End. Bal.	147,500

If Amir Corporation had any notes payable, the analysis would be the same.

Common Stock

Like the Plant Asset account and its related accounts, accounts related to stockholders' equity should be analyzed together. For example, the Additional Paid-in Capital account should be examined along with the Common Stock account. In 20x7, Amir's Common Stock account increased by $38,000, and its Additional Paid-in Capital account increased by $49,500. Item 3 in the list of Amir's transactions, which states that the company issued 7,600 shares of $5 par value common stock for $87,500, explains these increases. The entry to record the cash inflow is as follows:

A	= L +	SE
+87,500		+38,000
		+49,500

Cash	87,500	
Common Stock		38,000
Additional Paid-in Capital		49,500
Issued 7,600 shares of $5 par value common stock		

This appears in the financing activities section of the statement of cash flows as

Issue of common stock $87,000

The following analysis of this transaction is all that is needed to explain the changes in the two accounts during 20x7:

COMMON STOCK			ADDITIONAL PAID-IN CAPITAL		
	Beg. Bal.	100,000		Beg. Bal.	57,500
	Issue	38,000		Issue	49,500
	End. Bal.	138,000		End. Bal.	107,000

Retained Earnings

At this point, we have dealt with several items that affect retained earnings. The only item affecting Amir's retained earnings that we have not considered is the payment of $4,000 in cash dividends (item **4** in the list of Amir's transactions). At the time it declared the dividend, Amir would have debited its Dividends account. After paying the dividend, it would have closed the Dividends account to Retained Earnings and recorded the closing with the following entry:

A = L + SE
−4,000
+4,000

Retained Earnings	4,000	
Dividends		4,000
To close the Dividends account		

Study Note

It is dividends paid, not dividends declared, that appear on the statement of cash flows.

Cash dividends would be displayed in the financing activities section of Amir's statement of cash flows as follows:

Payment of dividends ($4,000)

The following T account shows the change in the Retained Earnings account:

RETAINED EARNINGS			
Dividends	4,000	Beg. Bal.	66,000
		Net Income	8,000
		End. Bal.	70,000

High-tech companies with large amounts of intangible assets, such as PharmaMar, a pharmaceutical firm based in Madrid, can lose up to 80 percent of their value in times of financial stress. As a hedge against economic downturns, these companies need to build cash reserves, and they may therefore choose to hoard cash rather than pay dividends.

Treasury Stock

As we noted in the chapter on contributed capital, many companies buy back their own stock on the open market. These buybacks use cash, as this entry shows:

A	= L +	SE			
−12,500		−12,500	Treasury Stock	12,500	
			Cash		12,500

Study Note

The purchase of treasury stock qualifies as a financing activity, but it is also a cash outflow.

This use of cash is classified in the statement of cash flows as a financing activity:

Purchase of treasury stock   ($12,500)

The T account for this transaction is as follows:

	TREASURY STOCK	
Purchase	12,500	

We have now analyzed all Amir Corporation's income statement items, explained all balance sheet changes, and taken all additional information into account. Exhibit 5 shows how our data are assembled in Amir's statement of cash flows.

EXHIBIT 5 ▶

Statement of Cash Flows: Indirect Method

Amir Corporation
Statement of Cash Flows
For the Year Ended December 31, 20x7

Cash flows from operating activities		
Net income		$ 8,000
Adjustments to reconcile net income to net cash flows from operating activities		
Depreciation	$18,500	
Gain on sale of investments	(6,000)	
Loss on sale of plant assets	1,500	
Changes in current assets and current liabilities		
Decrease in accounts receivable	4,000	
Increase in inventory	(17,000)	
Decrease in prepaid expenses	2,000	
Increase in accounts payable	3,500	
Increase in accrued liabilities	1,500	
Decrease in income taxes payable	(1,000)	7,000
Net cash flows from operating activities		$15,000
Cash flows from investing activities		
Purchase of investments	($39,000)	
Sale of investments	51,000	
Purchase of plant assets	(60,000)	
Sale of plant assets	2,500	
Net cash flows from investing activities		(45,500)
Cash flows from financing activities		
Repayment of bonds	($25,000)	
Issue of common stock	87,500	
Payment of dividends	(4,000)	
Purchase of treasury stock	(12,500)	
Net cash flows from financing activities		46,000
Net increase (decrease) in cash		$15,500
Cash at beginning of year		7,500
Cash at end of year		$23,000

Schedule of Noncash Investing and Financing Transactions

Issue of bonds payable for plant assets	$50,000

S T O P • R E V I E W • A P P L Y

5-1. What major categories of liabilities and stockholders' equity relate to the financing activities section of the statement of cash flows?

5-2. What is the proper treatment on the statement of cash flows of a transaction in which $50,000 of bonds payable are converted to 2,500 shares of $6 par value common stock?

A LOOK BACK AT

MARRIOTT INTERNATIONAL, INC.

As we pointed out in this chapter's Decision Point, strong cash flows are a basic ingredient in **Marriott's** plans for the future. Strong cash flows enable a company to achieve and maintain liquidity, to expand, and to increase the value of its shareholders' investments. A company's statement of cash flows provides information essential to evaluating the strength of its cash flows and its liquidity. A user of Marriott's statement of cash flows would want to ask the following questions:

- **Are operations generating sufficient operating cash flows?**
- **Is the company growing by investing in long-term assets?**
- **Has the company had to borrow money or issue stock to finance its growth?**

Using data from Exhibit 1, which presents Marriott's statements of cash flows, we can answer these questions. We can gauge Marriott's ability to generate cash flows from operations by calculating its cash flow yields in 2003 and 2004:

	Cash Flow Yield		2004	2003
K/R	$\dfrac{\text{Net Cash Flows from Operating Activities}}{\text{Net Income}}$	$=$	$\dfrac{\$891}{\$594}$	$\dfrac{\$403}{\$476}$
		$=$	1.5 times	0.8 times

As you can see, Marriott's cash flow yield almost doubled over the two years. The 1.5 cash yield in 2004 surpassed the 1.0 level normally considered the minimum acceptable level of cash flows from operations. Because of the increase in cash provided by operations, Marriott's cash flows to sales and assets would also show improvement over the two-year period.

Free cash flow measures the sufficiency of cash flows in a different way. The following computations show that in 2004, Marriott's free cash flow was over $400 million greater than in 2003:

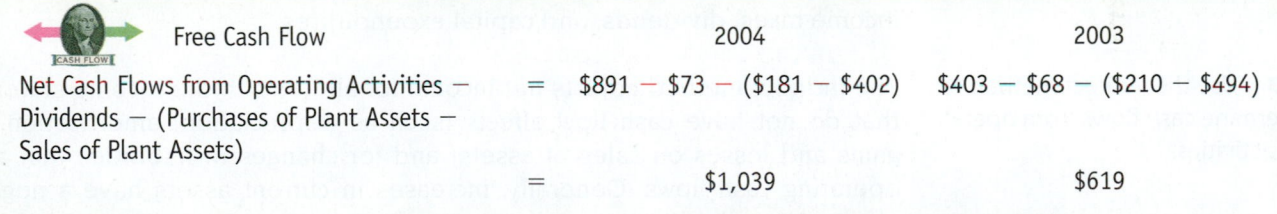

Free Cash Flow		2004	2003
Net Cash Flows from Operating Activities − Dividends − (Purchases of Plant Assets − Sales of Plant Assets)	$=$	$891 − $73 − ($181 − $402)	$403 − $68 − ($210 − $494)
	$=$	$1,039	$619

Marriott's statement of cash flows shows that the company was investing in long-term assets ($210 million in 2003 and $181 million in 2004) but that its sales of assets exceeded its capital expenditures. Thus, the company did not have to rely on borrowing money or issuing stock to finance its growth. In fact, it repaid much more long-term debt than it borrowed and purchased more than three times as much treasury stock as it issued in common stock. Financing activities totaled $683 million in 2003 and $637 million in 2004; the sum of these expenditures was less than the sum of Marriott's free cash flows in the two years.

CHAPTER REVIEW

REVIEW of Learning Objectives

LO1 Describe the principal purposes and uses of the statement of cash flows, and identify its components.

The statement of cash flows shows how a company's operating, investing, and financing activities have affected cash during an accounting period. For the statement of cash flows, *cash* is defined as including both cash and cash equivalents. The primary purpose of the statement is to provide information about a firm's cash receipts and cash payments during an accounting period. A secondary purpose is to provide information about a firm's operating, investing, and financing activities. Management uses the statement to assess liquidity, determine dividend policy, and plan investing and financing activities. Investors and creditors use it to assess the company's cash-generating ability.

The statement of cash flows has three major classifications: (1) operating activities, which involve the cash effects of transactions and other events that enter into the determination of net income; (2) investing activities, which involve the acquisition and sale of marketable securities and long-term assets and the making and collecting of loans; and (3) financing activities, which involve obtaining resources from stockholders and creditors and providing the former with a return on their investments and the latter with repayment. Noncash investing and financing transactions are also important because they affect future cash flows; these exchanges of long-term assets or liabilities are of interest to potential investors and creditors.

LO2 Analyze the statement of cash flows.

In examining a firm's statement of cash flows, analysts tend to focus on cash-generating efficiency and free cash flow. Cash-generating efficiency is a firm's ability to generate cash from its current or continuing operations. The ratios used to measure cash-generating efficiency are cash flow yield, cash flows to sales, and cash flows to assets. Free cash flow is the cash that remains after deducting the funds a firm must commit to continue operating at its planned level. These commitments include current and continuing operations, interest, income taxes, dividends, and capital expenditures.

LO3 Use the indirect method to determine cash flows from operating activities.

The indirect method adjusts net income for all items in the income statement that do not have cash flow effects (such as depreciation, amortization, and gains and losses on sales of assets) and for changes in liabilities that affect operating cash flows. Generally, increases in current assets have a negative effect on cash flows, and decreases have a positive effect. Conversely, increases in current liabilities have a positive effect on cash flows, and decreases have a negative effect.

LO4 Determine cash flows from investing activities.

Investing activities involve the acquisition and sale of property, plant, and equipment and other long-term assets, including long-term investments. They also involve the acquisition and sale of short-term marketable securities, other than trading securities, and the making and collecting of loans. Cash flows from investing activities are determined by analyzing the cash flow effects of changes in each account related to investing activities. The effects of gains and losses reported on the income statement must also be considered.

LO5 Determine cash flows from financing activities.

Determining cash flows from financing activities is almost identical to determining cash flows from investing activities. The difference is that the accounts analyzed relate to short-term borrowings, long-term liabilities, and stockholders' equity. After the changes in the balance sheet accounts from one accounting period to the next have been explained, all the cash flow effects should have been identified.

REVIEW of Concepts and Terminology

The following concepts and terms were introduced in this chapter:

Cash: For purposes of the statement of cash flows, both cash and cash equivalents. **(LO1)**

Cash equivalents: Short-term (90 days or less), highly liquid investments, including money market accounts, commercial paper, and U.S. Treasury bills. **(LO1)**

Cash-generating efficiency: A company's ability to generate cash from its current or continuing operations. **(LO2)**

Direct method: The procedure for converting the income statement from an accrual basis to a cash basis by adjusting each item on the income statement. **(LO3)**

Financing activities: Business activities that involve obtaining resources from stockholders and creditors and providing the former with a return on their investments and the latter with repayment. **(LO1)**

Free cash flow: The amount of cash that remains after deducting the funds a company must commit to continue operating at its planned level; Net Cash Flows from Operating Activities − Dividends − (Purchases of Plant Assets − Sales of Plant Assets). **(LO2)**

Indirect method: The procedure for converting the income statement from an accrual basis to a cash basis by adjusting net income for items that do not affect cash flows, including depreciation, amortiza-

tion, depletion, gains, losses, and changes in current assets and current liabilities. **(LO3)**

Investing activities: Business activities that involve the acquisition and sale of marketable securities and long-term assets and the making and collecting of loans. **(LO1)**

Noncash investing and financing transactions: Significant investing and financing transactions involving only long-term assets, long-term liabilities, or stockholders' equity that do not affect current cash inflows or outflows. **(LO1)**

Operating activities: Business activities that involve the cash effects of transactions and other events that enter into the determination of net income. **(LO1)**

Statement of cash flows: A financial statement that shows how a company's operating, investing, and financing activities have affected cash during an accounting period. **(LO1)**

Key Ratios

Cash flows to assets: Net Cash Flows from Operating Activities ÷ Average Total Assets. **(LO2)**

Cash flows to sales: Net Cash Flows from Operating Activities ÷ Sales. **(LO2)**

Cash flow yield: Net Cash Flows from Operating Activities ÷ Net Income. **(LO2)**

REVIEW Problem

LO2, LO3, LO4, LO5

The Statement of Cash Flows

Northwest Corporation's income statement for 20x8 and its comparative balance sheets for 20x8 and 20x7 are presented on the following pages. The company's records for 20x8 provide this additional information:

a. Sold long-term investments that cost $70,000 for a gain of $12,500; made other long-term investments in the amount of $20,000.

b. Purchased five acres of land to build a parking lot for $25,000.

c. Sold equipment that cost $37,500 and that had accumulated depreciation of $25,300 at a loss of $2,300; purchased new equipment for $30,000.

d. Repaid notes payable in the amount of $100,000; borrowed $30,000 by signing new notes payable.

e. Converted $100,000 of bonds payable into 6,000 shares of common stock.

f. Reduced the Mortgage Payable account by $20,000.

g. Declared and paid cash dividends of $50,000.

h. Purchased treasury stock for $10,000.

	A	B	C
1	**Northwest Corporation**		
2	**Income Statement**		
3	**For the Year Ended December 31, 20x8**		
4			
5	Net sales		$1,650,000
6	Cost of goods sold		920,000
7	Gross margin		$ 730,000
8	Operating expenses (including depreciation		
9	expense of $12,000 on buildings and		
10	$23,100 on equipment and amortization		
11	expense of $4,800)		470,000
12	Operating income		$ 260,000
13	Other income		
14	Interest expense	$ (55,000)	
15	Dividend income	3,400	
16	Gain on sale of investments	12,500	
17	Loss on disposal of equipment	(2,300)	(41,400)
18	Income before income taxes		$ 218,600
19	Income taxes		52,200
20	Net income		$ 166,400

	A	B	C	D	E
1	**Northwest Corporation**				
2	**Comparative Balance Sheets**				
3	**December 31, 20x8 and 20x7**				
4					
5		20x8	20x7	Change	Increase or Decrease
6	**Assets**				
7	Cash	$ 105,850	$ 121,850	$ (16,000)	Decrease
8	Accounts receivable (net)	296,000	314,500	(18,500)	Decrease
9	Inventory	322,000	301,000	21,000	Increase
10	Prepaid expenses	7,800	5,800	2,000	Increase
11	Long-term investments	36,000	86,000	(50,000)	Decrease
12	Land	150,000	125,000	25,000	Increase
13	Buildings	462,000	462,000	—	—
14	Accumulated depreciation, buildings	(91,000)	(79,000)	(12,000)	Increase
15	Equipment	159,730	167,230	(7,500)	Decrease
16	Accumulated depreciation, equipment	(43,400)	(45,600)	2,200	Decrease
17	Intangible assets	19,200	24,000	(4,800)	Decrease
18	Total assets	$1,424,180	$1,482,780	$ (58,600)	

(Continued)

	A	B	C	D	E
19		**20x8**	**20x7**	**Change**	**Increase or Decrease**
20	**Liabilities and Stockholders' Equity**				
21	Accounts payable	$ 133,750	$ 233,750	$ (100,000)	Decrease
22	Notes payable (current)	75,700	145,700	(70,000)	Decrease
23	Accrued liabilities	5,000	—	5,000	Increase
24	Income taxes payable	20,000	—	20,000	Increase
25	Bonds payable	210,000	310,000	(100,000)	Decrease
26	Mortgage payable	330,000	350,000	(20,000)	Decrease
27	Common stock, $10 par value	400,000	340,000	60,000	Increase
28	Additional paid-in capital	90,000	50,000	40,000	Increase
29	Retained earnings	209,730	93,330	116,400	Increase
30	Treasury stock	(50,000)	(40,000)	(10,000)	Increase
31	Total liabilities and stockholders' equity	$1,424,180	$1,482,780	$ (58,600)	

Required

1. Prepare a statement of cash flows using the indirect method.
2. Compute cash flow yield, cash flows to sales, cash flows to assets, and free cash flow for 20x8.

Answer to Review Problem

1. Statement of cash flows using the indirect method:

	A	B	C
1	**Northwest Corporation**		
2	**Statement of Cash Flows**		
3	**For the Year Ended December 31, 20x8**		
4			
5	**Cash flows from operating activities**		
6	Net income		$166,400
7	Adjustments to reconcile net income to net cash flows from operating activities		
8	Depreciation expense, buildings	$ 12,000	
9	Depreciation expense, equipment	23,100	
10	Amortization expense, intangible assets	4,800	
11	Gain on sale of investments	(12,500)	
12	Loss on disposal of equipment	2,300	
13	Changes in current assets and current liabilities		
14	Decrease in accounts receivable	18,500	
15	Increase in inventory	(21,000)	
16	Increase in prepaid expenses	(2,000)	
17	Decrease in accounts payable	(100,000)	
18	Increase in accrued liabilities	5,000	
19	Increase in income taxes payable	20,000	(49,800)
20	Net cash flows from operating activities		$116,600

(Continued)

	A	B	C
21	**Cash flows from investing activities**		
22	Sale of long-term investments	$ 82,500 a	
23	Purchase of long-term investments	(20,000)	
24	Purchase of land	(25,000)	
25	Sale of equipment	9,900 b	
26	Purchase of equipment	(30,000)	
27	Net cash flows from investing activities		17,400
28			
29	**Cash flows from financing activities**		
30	Repayment of notes payable	$ (100,000)	
31	Issuance of notes payable	30,000	
32	Reduction in mortgage	(20,000)	
33	Dividends paid	(50,000)	
34	Purchase of treasury stock	(10,000)	
35	Net cash flows from investing activities		(150,000)
36			
37	Net increase (decrease) in cash		$ (16,000)
38	Cash at beginning of year		121,850
39	Cash at end of year		$ 105,850
40			
41	**Schedule of Noncash Investing and Financing Transactions**		
42	Conversion of bonds payable into common stock		$ 100,000
43			
44	a $70,000 + $12,500 (gain) = $82,500		
45	b $37,500 - $25,300 = $12,200 (book value) - $2,300 (loss) = $9,900		

2. Cash flow yield, cash flows to sales, cash flows to assets, and free cash flow for 20x8:

$$\text{Cash Flow Yield} = \frac{\$116,600}{\$166,400} = .7 \text{ times}$$

$$\text{Cash Flows to Sales} = \frac{\$116,600}{\$1,650,000} = 7.1\%$$

$$\text{Cash Flows to Assets} = \frac{\$116,600}{(\$1,424,180 + \$1,482,780) \div 2} = 8.0\%$$

$$\text{Free Cash Flow} = \$116,600 - \$50,000 - (\$25,000 + \$30,000 - \$9,900) = \$21,500$$

CHAPTER ASSIGNMENTS

BUILDING Your Basic Knowledge and Skills

Short Exercises

LO1 **Classification of Cash Flow Transactions**

SE 1. The list that follows itemizes Furlong Corporation's transactions. Identify each as (a) an operating activity, (b) an investing activity, (c) a financing activity, (d) a noncash transaction, or (e) none of the above.

1. Sold land.
2. Declared and paid a cash dividend.
3. Paid interest.
4. Issued common stock for plant assets.
5. Issued preferred stock.
6. Borrowed cash on a bank loan.

LO2 **Cash-Generating Efficiency Ratios and Free Cash Flow**

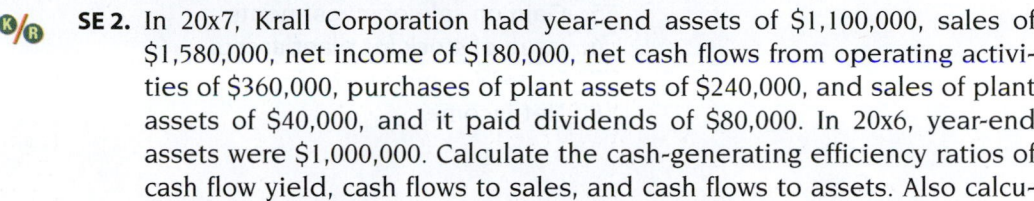 **SE 2.** In 20x7, Krall Corporation had year-end assets of $1,100,000, sales of $1,580,000, net income of $180,000, net cash flows from operating activities of $360,000, purchases of plant assets of $240,000, and sales of plant assets of $40,000, and it paid dividends of $80,000. In 20x6, year-end assets were $1,000,000. Calculate the cash-generating efficiency ratios of cash flow yield, cash flows to sales, and cash flows to assets. Also calculate free cash flow.

LO2 **Cash-Generating Efficiency Ratios and Free Cash Flow**

SE 3. Examine the cash flow measures in requirement **2** of the review problem in this chapter. Discuss the meaning of these ratios.

LO3 **Computing Cash Flows from Operating Activities: Indirect Method**

SE 4. Inter-Finance Corporation had a net income of $16,500 during 20x7. During the year, the company had depreciation expense of $7,000. Accounts Receivable increased by $5,500, and Accounts Payable increased by $2,500. Those were the company's only current assets and current liabilities. Use the indirect method to determine net cash flows from operating activities.

LO3 **Computing Cash Flows from Operating Activities: Indirect Method**

SE 5. During 20x7, Minh Corporation had a net income of $144,000. Included on its income statement were depreciation expense of $16,000 and amortization expense of $1,800. During the year, Accounts Receivable decreased by $8,200, Inventories increased by $5,400, Prepaid Expenses decreased by $1,000, Accounts Payable decreased by $14,000, and Accrued Liabilities decreased by $1,700. Use the indirect method to determine net cash flows from operating activities.

LO4 **Cash Flows from Investing Activities and Noncash Transactions**

SE 6. During 20x7, Howard Company purchased land for $375,000. It paid $125,000 in cash and signed a $250,000 mortgage for the rest. The company also sold a building that originally cost $90,000, on which it had $70,000 of accumulated depreciation, for $95,000 cash, making a gain of $75,000. Prepare the cash flows from investing activities section and the schedule of noncash investing and financing transactions of the statement of cash flows.

LO5 **Cash Flows from Financing Activities**

SE 7. During 20x7, Arizona Company issued $500,000 in long-term bonds at 96, repaid $75,000 of bonds at face value, paid interest of $40,000, and paid dividends of $25,000. Prepare the cash flows from the financing activities section of the statement of cash flows.

LO1, LO3, LO4, LO5 **Identifying Components of the Statement of Cash Flows**

SE 8. Assuming the indirect method is used to prepare the statement of cash flows, tell whether each of the following items would appear (a) in cash flows from operating activities, (b) in cash flows from investing activities,

(c) in cash flows from financing activities, (d) in the schedule of noncash investing and financing transactions, or (e) not on the statement of cash flows at all:

1. Dividends paid
2. Cash receipts from sales
3. Decrease in accounts receivable
4. Sale of plant assets
5. Gain on sale of investments
6. Issue of stock for plant assets
7. Issue of common stock
8. Net income

Exercises

LO1, LO2   **Discussion Questions**

E 1. Develop brief answers to each of the following questions:

1. Which statement is more useful—the income statement or the statement of cash flows?
2. How would you respond to someone who says that the most important item on the statement of cash flows is the change in the cash balance for the year?
3. If a company's cash flow yield is less than 1.0, would its cash flows to sales and cash flows to assets be greater or less than profit margin and return on assets, respectively?

LO3, LO4, LO5   **Discussion Questions**

E 2. Develop brief answers to each of the following questions:

1. If a company has positive earnings, can cash flows from operating activities ever be negative?
2. Which adjustments to net income in the operating activities section of the statement of cash flows are directly related to cash flows in other sections?
3. In computing free cash flow, what is an argument for treating the purchases of treasury stock like dividend payments?

LO1   **Classification of Cash Flow Transactions**

E 3. Minnow Corporation engaged in the transactions listed below. Identify each transaction as (a) an operating activity, (b) an investing activity, (c) a financing activity, (d) a noncash transaction, or (e) not on the statement of cash flows. (Assume the indirect method is used.)

1. Declared and paid a cash dividend.
2. Purchased a long-term investment.
3. Increased accounts receivable.
4. Paid interest.
5. Sold equipment at a loss.
6. Issued long-term bonds for plant assets.
7. Increased dividends receivable on securities held.
8. Issued common stock.
9. Declared and issued a stock dividend.
10. Repaid notes payable.
11. Decreased wages payable.
12. Purchased a 60-day Treasury bill.
13. Purchased land.

LO2 **Cash-Generating Efficiency Ratios and Free Cash Flow**

 E 4. In 20x8, Maus Corporation had year-end assets of $2,400,000, sales of $3,300,000, net income of $280,000, net cash flows from operating activities of $390,000, dividends of $120,000, purchases of plant assets of $500,000, and sales of plant assets of $90,000. In 20x7, year-end assets were $2,100,000. Calculate free cash flow and the cash-generating efficiency ratios of cash flow yield, cash flows to sales, and cash flows to assets.

LO3 **Cash Flows from Operating Activities: Indirect Method**

E 5. The condensed single-step income statement for the year ended December 31, 20x7, of Sunderland Chemical Company, a distributor of farm fertilizers and herbicides, appears as follows:

Sales		$13,000,000
Less: Cost of goods sold	$7,600,000	
Operating expenses (including depreciation of $820,000)	3,800,000	
Income taxes expense	400,000	11,800,000
Net income		$ 1,200,000

Selected accounts from Sunderland Chemical Company's balance sheets for 20x7 and 20x6 are as follows:

	20x7	20x6
Accounts receivable	$2,400,000	$1,700,000
Inventory	840,000	1,020,000
Prepaid expenses	260,000	180,000
Accounts payable	960,000	720,000
Accrued liabilities	60,000	100,000
Income taxes payable	140,000	120,000

Present in good form a schedule of cash flows from operating activities using the indirect method.

LO3 **Computing Cash Flows from Operating Activities: Indirect Method**

E 6. During 20x7, Linz Corporation had net income of $82,000. Included on its income statement were depreciation expense of $4,600 and amortization expense of $600. During the year, Accounts Receivable increased by $6,800, Inventories decreased by $3,800, Prepaid Expenses decreased by $400, Accounts Payable increased by $10,000, and Accrued Liabilities decreased by $900. Determine net cash flows from operating activities using the indirect method.

LO3 **Preparing a Schedule of Cash Flows from Operating Activities: Indirect Method**

E 7. For the year ended June 30, 20xx, net income for Freed Corporation was $14,800. Depreciation expense was $4,000. During the year, Accounts Receivable increased by $8,800, Inventories increased by $14,000, Prepaid Rent decreased by $2,800, Accounts Payable increased by $28,000, Salaries Payable increased by $2,000, and Income Taxes Payable decreased by $1,200. Use the indirect method to prepare a schedule of cash flows from operating activities.

LO4 Computing Cash Flows from Investing Activities: Investments

E 8. LMN Company's T account for long-term available-for-sale investments at the end of 20x7 is as follows:

INVESTMENTS			
Beg. Bal.	76,000	Sales	78,000
Purchases	116,000		
End. Bal.	114,000		

In addition, LMN Company's income statement shows a loss on the sale of investments of $13,000. Compute the amounts to be shown as cash flows from investing activities and show how they are to appear in the statement of cash flows.

LO4 Computing Cash Flows from Investing Activities: Plant Assets

E 9. The T accounts for plant assets and accumulated depreciation for LMN Company at the end of 20x7 are as follows:

PLANT ASSETS				ACCUMULATED DEPRECIATION			
Beg. Bal.	130,000	Disposals	46,000	Disposals	29,400	Beg. Bal.	69,000
Purchases	67,200					Depreciation	20,400
End. Bal.	151,200					End. Bal.	60,000

In addition, LMN Company's income statement shows a gain on sale of plant assets of $8,800. Compute the amounts to be shown as cash flows from investing activities and show how they are to appear on the statement of cash flows.

LO5 Determining Cash Flows from Financing Activities: Notes Payable

E 10. All transactions involving Notes Payable and related accounts of Gaynor Company during 20x7 are as follows:

Cash	36,000	
Notes Payable		36,000
Bank loan		
Patent	60,000	
Notes Payable		60,000
Purchase of patent by issuing note payable		
Notes Payable	10,000	
Interest Expense	1,000	
Cash		11,000
Repayment of note payable at maturity		

Determine the amounts of the transactions affecting financing activities and show how they are to appear on the statement of cash flows for 20x7.

LO3, LO4, LO5 Preparing the Statement of Cash Flows: Indirect Method

E 11. Marisol Corporation's income statement for the year ended June 30, 20x7 and its comparative balance sheets for June 30, 20x7 and 20x6 appear on the opposite page.

Marisol Corporation
Income Statement
For the Year Ended June 30, 20x7

Sales	$234,000
Cost of goods sold	156,000
Gross margin	$ 78,000
Operating expenses	45,000
Operating income	$ 33,000
Interest expense	2,800
Income before income taxes	$ 30,200
Income taxes expense	12,300
Net income	$ 17,900

Marisol Corporation
Comparative Balance Sheets
June 30, 20x7 and 20x6

	20x7	20x6
Assets		
Cash	$ 69,900	$ 12,500
Accounts receivable (net)	21,000	26,000
Inventory	43,400	48,400
Prepaid expenses	3,200	2,600
Furniture	55,000	60,000
Accumulated depreciation, furniture	(9,000)	(5,000)
Total assets	$183,500	$144,500
Liabilities and Stockholders' Equity		
Accounts payable	$ 13,000	$ 14,000
Income taxes payable	1,200	1,800
Notes payable (long-term)	37,000	35,000
Common stock, $10 par value	115,000	90,000
Retained earnings	17,300	3,700
Total liabilities and stockholders' equity	$183,500	$144,500

Marisol issued a $22,000 note payable for purchase of furniture; sold furniture that cost $27,000 with accumulated depreciation of $15,300 at carrying value; recorded depreciation on the furniture for the year, $19,300; repaid a note in the amount of $20,000; issued $25,000 of common stock at par value; and paid dividends of $4,300. Prepare Marisol's statement of cash flows for the year 20x7 using the indirect method.

Problems

LO1 **Classification of Cash Flow Transactions**

P 1. Analyze each transaction listed in the table that follows and place X's in the appropriate columns to indicate the transaction's classification and its effect on cash flows using the indirect method.

	Cash Flow Classification				Effect on Cash Flows		
Transaction	Operating Activity	Investing Activity	Financing Activity	Noncash Trans-action	Increase	Decrease	No Effect
1. Increased accounts payable.							
2. Decreased inventory.							
3. Increased prepaid insurance.							
4. Earned a net income.							
5. Declared and paid a cash dividend.							
6. Issued stock for cash.							
7. Retired long-term debt by issuing stock.							
8. Purchased a long-term investment with cash.							
9. Sold trading securities at a gain.							
10. Sold a machine at a loss.							
11. Retired fully depreciated equipment.							
12. Decreased interest payable.							
13. Purchased available-for-sale securities (long-term).							
14. Decreased dividends receivable.							
15. Decreased accounts receivable.							
16. Converted bonds to common stock.							
17. Purchased 90-day Treasury bill.							

LO2, LO3, LO4, LO5

Statement of Cash Flows: Indirect Method

P 2. The comparative balance sheets for Sharma Fabrics, Inc., for December 31, 20x7 and 20x6 appear on the oposite page.

Additional information about Sharma Fabrics's operations during 20x7 is as follows: (a) net income, $56,000; (b) building and equipment depreciation expense amounts, $30,000 and $6,000, respectively; (c) equipment that cost $27,000 with accumulated depreciation of $25,000 sold at a gain of $10,600; (d) equipment purchases, $25,000; (e) patent amortization, $6,000; purchase of patent, $2,000; (f) funds borrowed by issuing notes payable, $50,000; notes payable repaid, $30,000; (g) land and building purchased for $324,000 by signing a mortgage for the total cost; (h) 3,000 shares of $20 par value common stock issued for a total of $100,000; and (i) paid cash dividend, $18,000.

Required

1. Using the indirect method, prepare a statement of cash flows for Sharma Fabrics, Inc.
2. **User Insight:** Why did Sharma Fabrics have an increase in cash of $134,400 when it recorded net income of only $56,000? Discuss and interpret.
3. **User Insight:** Compute and assess cash flow yield and free cash flow for 20x7. What is your assessment of Sharma's cash-generating ability?

Sharma Fabrics, Inc.
Comparative Balance Sheets
December 31, 20x7 and 20x6

	20x7	20x6
Assets		
Cash	$189,120	$ 54,720
Accounts receivable (net)	204,860	150,860
Inventory	225,780	275,780
Prepaid expenses	—	40,000
Land	50,000	—
Building	274,000	—
Accumulated depreciation, building	(30,000)	—
Equipment	66,000	68,000
Accumulated depreciation, equipment	(29,000)	(48,000)
Patents	8,000	12,000
Total assets	$958,760	$553,360
Liabilities and Stockholders' Equity		
Accounts payable	$ 21,500	$ 73,500
Notes payable (current)	20,000	—
Accrued liabilities	—	24,600
Mortgage payable	324,000	—
Common stock, $10 par value	360,000	300,000
Additional paid-in capital	114,400	74,400
Retained earnings	118,860	80,860
Total liabilities and stockholders' equity	$958,760	$553,360

LO2, LO3, LO4, LO5   **Statement of Cash Flows: Indirect Method**

P 3. The comparative balance sheets for Karidis Ceramics, Inc., for December 31, 20x7 and 20x6 are presented on the next page. During 20x7, the company had net income of $96,000 and building and equipment depreciation expenses of $80,000 and $60,000, respectively. It amortized intangible assets in the amount of $20,000; purchased investments for $116,000; sold investments for $150,000, on which it recorded a gain of $34,000; issued $240,000 of long-term bonds at face value; purchased land and a warehouse through a $320,000 mortgage; paid $40,000 to reduce the mortgage; borrowed $60,000 by issuing notes payable; repaid notes payable in the amount of $180,000; declared and paid cash dividends in the amount of $36,000; and purchased treasury stock in the amount of $20,000.

Required

1. Using the indirect method, prepare a statement of cash flows for Karidis Ceramics, Inc.
2. **User Insight:** Why did Karidis Ceramics experience a decrease in cash in a year in which it had a net income of $96,000? Discuss and interpret.
3. **User Insight:** Compute and assess cash flow yield and free cash flow for 20x7. Why is each of these measures important in assessing cash-generating ability?

Karidis Ceramics, Inc.
Comparative Balance Sheets
December 31, 20x7 and 20x6

	20x7	20x6
Assets		
Cash	$ 257,600	$ 305,600
Accounts receivable (net)	738,800	758,800
Inventory	960,000	800,000
Prepaid expenses	14,800	26,800
Long-term investments	440,000	440,000
Land	361,200	321,200
Building	1,200,000	920,000
Accumulated depreciation, building	(240,000)	(160,000)
Equipment	480,000	480,000
Accumulated depreciation, equipment	(116,000)	(56,000)
Intangible assets	20,000	40,000
Total assets	$4,116,400	$3,876,400
Liabilities and Stockholders' Equity		
Accounts payable	$ 470,800	$ 660,800
Notes payable (current)	40,000	160,000
Accrued liabilities	10,800	20,800
Mortgage payable	1,080,000	800,000
Bonds payable	1,000,000	760,000
Common stock	1,300,000	1,300,000
Additional paid-in capital	80,000	80,000
Retained earnings	254,800	194,800
Treasury stock	(120,000)	(100,000)
Total liabilities and stockholders' equity	$4,116,400	$3,876,400

LO2, LO3, LO4, LO5 **Statement of Cash Flows: Indirect Method**

P 4. Flanders Corporation's income statement for the year ended June 30, 20x7 and its comparative balance sheets as of June 30, 20x7 and 20x6 appear on the opposite page. During 20x7, the corporation sold equipment that cost $48,000, on which it had accumulated depreciation of $34,000, at a loss of $8,000. It also purchased land and a building for $200,000 through an increase of $200,000 in Mortgage Payable; made a $40,000 payment on the mortgage; repaid notes but borrowed an additional $60,000 through the issuance of a new note payable; and declared and paid a $120,000 cash dividend.

Required

1. Using the indirect method, prepare a statement of cash flows. Include a supporting schedule of noncash investing and financing transactions.
2. **User Insight:** What are the primary reasons for Flanders Corporation's large increase in cash from 20x6 to 20x7?
3. **User Insight:** Compute and assess cash flow yield and free cash flow for 20x7. How would you assess the corporation's cash-generating ability?

Flanders Corporation
Income Statement
For the Year Ended June 30, 20x7

Sales		$8,081,800
Cost of goods sold		7,312,600
Gross margin		$ 769,200
Operating expenses (including depreciation expense of $120,000)		378,400
Income from operations		$ 390,800
Other income (expenses)		
Loss on sale of equipment	($ 8,000)	
Interest expense	(75,200)	(83,200)
Income before income taxes		$ 307,600
Income taxes expense		68,400
Net income		$ 239,200

Flanders Corporation
Comparative Balance Sheets
June 30, 20x7 and 20x6

	20x7	20x6
Assets		
Cash	$ 334,000	$ 40,000
Accounts receivable (net)	200,000	240,000
Inventory	360,000	440,000
Prepaid expenses	1,200	2,000
Property, plant, and equipment	1,256,000	1,104,000
Accumulated depreciation, property, plant, and equipment	(366,000)	(280,000)
Total assets	$1,785,200	$1,546,000
Liabilities and Stockholders' Equity		
Accounts payable	$ 128,000	$ 84,000
Notes payable (due in 90 days)	60,000	160,000
Income taxes payable	52,000	36,000
Mortgage payable	720,000	560,000
Common stock, $5 par value	400,000	400,000
Retained earnings	425,200	306,000
Total liabilities and stockholders' equity	$1,785,200	$1,546,000

Alternate Problems

LO1 **Classification of Cash Flow Transactions**

P 5. Analyze each transaction listed in the table that follows and place X's in the appropriate columns to indicate the transaction's classification and its effect on cash flows using the indirect method.

	Cash Flow Classification				Effect on Cash Flows		
Transaction	Operating Activity	Investing Activity	Financing Activity	Noncash Trans- action	Increase	Decrease	No Effect
1. Paid a cash dividend.							
2. Decreased accounts receivable.							
3. Increased inventory.							
4. Incurred a net loss.							
5. Declared and issued a stock dividend.							
6. Retired long-term debt with cash.							
7. Sold available-for-sale securities at a loss.							
8. Issued stock for equipment.							
9. Decreased prepaid insurance.							
10. Purchased treasury stock with cash.							
11. Retired a fully depreciated truck (no gain or loss).							
12. Increased interest payable.							
13. Decreased dividends receivable on investment.							
14. Sold treasury stock.							
15. Increased income taxes payable.							
16. Transferred cash to money market account.							
17. Purchased land and building with a mortgage.							

LO2, LO3, LO4, LO5 — Statement of Cash Flows: Indirect Method

P 6. O'Brien Corporation's comparative balance sheets as of December 31, 20x8 and 20x7 and its income statement for the year ended December 31, 20x8 are presented on the opposite page.

During 20x8, O'Brien Corporation engaged in these transactions:

a. Sold furniture and fixtures that cost $17,800, on which it had accumulated depreciation of $14,400, at a gain of $3,500.
b. Purchased furniture and fixtures in the amount of $19,800.
c. Paid a $10,000 note payable and borrowed $20,000 on a new note.
d. Converted bonds payable in the amount of $50,000 into 2,000 shares of common stock.
e. Declared and paid $3,000 in cash dividends.

Required

1. Using the indirect method, prepare a statement of cash flows for O'Brien Corporation. Include a supporting schedule of noncash investing transactions and financing transactions.
2. **User Insight:** What are the primary reasons for O'Brien Corporation's large increase in cash from 20x7 to 20x8, despite its low net income?

3. **User Insight:** Compute and assess cash flow yield and free cash flow for 20x8. Compare and contrast what these two performance measures tell you about O'Brien's cash-generating ability.

O'Brien Corporation
Comparative Balance Sheets
December 31, 20x8 and 20x7

	20x8	20x7
Assets		
Cash	$ 82,400	$ 25,000
Accounts receivable (net)	82,600	100,000
Merchandise inventory	175,000	225,000
Prepaid rent	1,000	1,500
Furniture and fixtures	74,000	72,000
Accumulated depreciation, furniture and fixtures	(21,000)	(12,000)
Total assets	$394,000	$411,500
Liabilities and Stockholders' Equity		
Accounts payable	$ 71,700	$100,200
Income taxes payable	700	2,200
Notes payable (long-term)	20,000	10,000
Bonds payable	50,000	100,000
Common stock, $20 par value	120,000	100,000
Additional paid-in capital	90,720	60,720
Retained earnings	40,880	38,380
Total liabilities and stockholders' equity	$394,000	$411,500

O'Brien Corporation
Income Statement
For the Year Ended December 31, 20x8

Sales		$804,500
Cost of goods sold		563,900
Gross margin		$240,600
Operating expenses (including depreciation expense of $23,400)		224,700
Income from operations		$ 15,900
Other income (expenses)		
Gain on sale of furniture and fixtures	$ 3,500	
Interest expense	(11,600)	(8,100)
Income before income taxes		$ 7,800
Income taxes expense		2,300
Net income		$ 5,500

ENHANCING Your Knowledge, Skills, and Critical Thinking

Conceptual Understanding Case

LO1, LO3   **EBITDA and the Statement of Cash Flows**

C 1. When **Fleetwood Enterprises, Inc.**, a large producer of recreational vehicles and manufactured housing, warned that it might not be able to generate enough cash to satisfy debt requirements and could be in default of a loan agreement, its cash flow, defined in the financial press as "EBITDA" (earnings before interest, taxes, depreciation, and amortization), was a negative $2.7 million. The company would have had to generate $17.7 million in the next accounting period to comply with the loan terms.[10] To what section of the statement of cash flows does EBITDA most closely relate? Is EBITDA a good approximation for this section of the statement of cash flows? Explain your answer, which should include an identification of the major differences between EBITDA and the section of the statement of cash flows you chose.

Interpreting Financial Reports

LO2   **Anatomy of a Disaster**

C 2. On October 16, 2001, Kenneth Lay, chairman and CEO of **Enron Corporation**, announced the company's earnings for the first nine months of 2001 as follows:

> Our 26 percent increase in recurring earnings per diluted share shows the very strong results of our core wholesale and retail energy businesses and our natural gas pipelines. The continued excellent prospects in these businesses and Enron's leading market position make us very confident in our strong earnings outlook.[11]

Less than six months later, the company filed for the biggest bankruptcy in U.S. history. Its stock dropped to less than $1 per share, and a major financial scandal was underway. Presented on the opposite page is Enron's statement of cash flows for the first nine months of 2001 and 2000 (restated to correct the previous accounting errors). Assume you report to an investment analyst who has asked you to analyze this statement for clues as to why the company went under.

1. For the two time periods shown, compute the cash-generating efficiency ratios of cash flow yield, cash flows to sales (Enron's revenues were $133,762 million in 2001 and $55,494 million in 2000), and cash flows to assets (use total assets of $61,783 million for 2001 and $64,926 million for 2000). Also compute free cash flows for the two years.
2. Prepare a memorandum to the investment analyst that assesses Enron's cash-generating efficiency in light of the chairman's remarks and that evaluates its available free cash flow, taking into account its financing activities. Identify significant changes in Enron's operating items and any special operating items that should be considered. Include your computations as an attachment.

LO2   **Cash-Generating Efficiency Ratios and Free Cash Flow**

C 3. The data that appear on page 700 pertain to two of Japan's best-known and most successful companies, **Sony Corporation** and **Canon, Inc.**[12] (Numbers are in billions of yen.)

Enron Corporation
Statement of Cash Flows
For the Nine Months Ended September 30, 2001 and 2000

(In millions)	2001	2000
Cash Flows from Operating Activities		
Reconciliation of net income to net cash provided by operating activities		
Net income	$ 225	$ 797
Cumulative effect of accounting changes, net of tax	(19)	0
Depreciation, depletion and amortization	746	617
Deferred income taxes	(134)	8
Gains on sales of non-trading assets	(49)	(135)
Investment losses	768	0
Changes in components of working capital		
Receivables	987	(3,363)
Inventories	1	339
Payables	(1,764)	2,899
Other	464	(455)
Trading investments		
Net margin deposit activity	(2,349)	541
Other trading activities	173	(555)
Other, net	198	(566)
Net Cash Provided by (Used in) Operating Activities	$ (753)	$ 127
Cash Flows from Investing Activities		
Capital expenditures	$(1,584)	$(1,539)
Equity investments	(1,172)	(858)
Proceeds from sales of non-trading investments	1,711	222
Acquisition of subsidiary stock	0	(485)
Business acquisitions, net of cash acquired	(82)	(773)
Other investing activities	(239)	(147)
Net Cash Used in Investing Activities	$(1,366)	$(3,580)
Cash Flows from Financing Activities		
Issuance of long-term debt	$ 4,060	$ 2,725
Repayment of long-term debt	(3,903)	(579)
Net increase in short-term borrowings	2,365	1,694
Issuance of common stock	199	182
Net redemption of company-obligated preferred securities of subsidiaries	0	(95)
Dividends paid	(394)	(396)
Net (acquisition) disposition of treasury stock	(398)	354
Other financing activities	(49)	(12)
Net Cash Provided by Financing Activities	$ 1,880	$ 3,873
Increase (Decrease) in Cash and Cash Equivalents	$ (239)	$ 420
Cash and Cash Equivalents, Beginning of Period	1,240	333
Cash and Cash Equivalents, End of Period	$ 1,001	$ 753

Source: Adapted from Enron Corporation, SEC filings, 2001.

	Sony Corporation		Canon, Inc.	
	2004	**2003**	**2004**	**2003**
Sales	¥7,496	¥7,474	¥3,468	¥3,196
Net income	89	116	343	276
Average total assets	8,731	8,279	3,385	3,063
Net cash flows from operating activities	633	854	562	466
Dividends paid	23	23	53	29
Net capital expenditures	378	261	319	210

Calculate the ratios of cash flow yield, cash flows to sales, and cash flows to assets, as well as free cash flow, for the two years, for both Sony Corporation and Canon, Inc. Which company is most efficient in generating cash flow? Which company has the best year-to-year trend? Which company do you think will most probably need external financing?

Decision Analysis Using Excel

LO2, LO3, LO4, LO5   **Analysis of Cash Flow Difficulty**

C 4. Lou Klein, certified public accountant, has just given his employer May Hashimi, the president of Hashimi Print Gallery, Inc., the following income statement:

Hashimi Print Gallery, Inc.
Income Statement
For the Year Ended December 31, 20x7

Sales	$884,000
Cost of goods sold	508,000
Gross margin	$376,000
Operating expenses (including depreciation expense of $20,000)	204,000
Operating income	$172,000
Interest expense	24,000
Income before income taxes	$148,000
Income taxes expense	28,000
Net income	$120,000

After examining the statement, Hashimi said to Klein, "Lou, the statement seems to be well done, but what I need to know is why I don't have enough cash to pay my bills this month. You show that I earned $120,000 in 20x7, but I have only $24,000 in the bank. I know I bought a building on a mortgage and paid a cash dividend of $48,000, but what else is going on?" Klein replied, "To answer your question, we have to look at comparative balance sheets and prepare another type of statement. Take a look at these balance sheets." The statement handed to Hashimi is on the opposite page.

1. To what other statement is Klein referring? From the information given, prepare the additional statement using the indirect method.
2. Hashimi Print Gallery, Inc., has a cash problem despite profitable operations. Why is this the case?

Hashimi Print Gallery, Inc.
Comparative Balance Sheets
December 31, 20x7 and 20x6

	20x7	20x6
Assets		
Cash	$ 24,000	$ 40,000
Accounts receivable (net)	178,000	146,000
Inventory	240,000	180,000
Prepaid expenses	10,000	14,000
Building	400,000	—
Accumulated depreciation	(20,000)	—
Total assets	$832,000	$380,000
Liabilities and Stockholders' Equity		
Accounts payable	$ 74,000	$ 96,000
Income taxes payable	6,000	4,000
Mortgage payable	400,000	—
Common stock	200,000	200,000
Retained earnings	152,000	80,000
Total liabilities and stockholders' equity	$832,000	$380,000

Annual Report Case: CVS Corporation

Analysis of the Statement of Cash Flows

C 5. Refer to the statement of cash flows in the **CVS Corporation** annual report to answer the following questions:

1. Does CVS use the indirect method of reporting cash flows from operating activities? Other than net earnings, what are the most important factors affecting the company's cash flows from operating activities? Explain the trend of each of these factors.
2. Based on the cash flows from investing activities, would you say that CVS is a contracting or an expanding company? Explain.
3. Has CVS used external financing? If so, where did it come from?

Comparison Case: CVS Versus Southwest

LO1, LO2, LO3, LO4, LO5　**Cash Flows Analysis**

Ⓚ/Ⓡ　**C 6.** Refer to the annual report of **CVS Corporation** and the financial statements of **Southwest Airlines Co.** in the Supplement to Chapter 1. Calculate for two years each company's cash flow yield, cash flows to sales, cash flows to assets, and free cash flow. At the end of 2002, Southwest's total assets were $8,954 million and CVS's total assets were $9,645.3 million. Discuss and compare the trends of the cash-generating ability of CVS and Southwest. Comment on each company's change in cash and cash equivalents over the two-year period.

Ethical Dilemma Case

LO2 **Ethics and Cash Flow Classifications**

C 7. Chemical Waste Treatment, Inc., a fast-growing company that disposes of chemical wastes, has an $800,000 line of credit at its bank. One section in the credit agreement says that the ratio of cash flows from operations to interest expense must exceed 3.0. If this ratio falls below 3.0, the company must reduce the balance outstanding on its line of credit to one-half the total line if the funds borrowed against the line of credit exceed one-half of the total line.

After the end of the fiscal year, the company's controller informs the president: "We will not meet the ratio requirements on our line of credit in 20x7 because interest expense was $1.2 million and cash flows from operations were $3.2 million. Also, we have borrowed 100 percent of our line of credit. We do not have the cash to reduce the credit line by $400,000." The president says, "This is a serious situation. To pay our ongoing bills, we need our bank to increase our line of credit, not decrease it. What can we do?" "Do you recall the $500,000 two-year note payable for equipment?" replied the controller. "It is now classified as 'Proceeds from Notes Payable' in cash flows provided from financing activities in the statement of cash flows. If we move it to cash flows from operations and call it 'Increase in Payables,' it would increase cash flows from operations to $3.7 million and put us over the limit." "Well, do it," ordered the president. "It surely doesn't make any difference where it is on the statement. It is an increase in both places. It would be much worse for our company in the long term if we failed to meet this ratio requirement."

What is your opinion of the controller and president's reasoning? Is the president's order ethical? Who benefits and who is harmed if the controller follows the president's order? What are management's alternatives? What would you do?

Internet Case

LO2 **Follow-up Analysis of Cash Flows**

C 8. Go to **CVS Corporation's** website and find the statement of cash flows in its latest annual report. Compare it with the 2004 statement in the Supplement to Chapter 1 by (1) identifying major changes in operating, investing, and financing activities; (2) reading management's financial review of cash flows; and (3) calculating the cash flow ratios (cash flow yield, cash flows to sales, cash flows to assets) and free cash flow for the most recent year. How does CVS's cash flow performance differ between these two years? Be prepared to discuss your conclusions in class.

Group Activity Case

LO1 **Cash Flow Versus Net Income**

C 9. The excerpt that follows is from a recent article on the financial reporting of **Amazon.com**, the famous Internet seller.

> From the beginning, Bezos [Amazon.com's Chairman and CEO] told shareholders that his goal was to build a company, not an artificial bottom line. "When forced to choose between optimizing the appearance of our GAAP accounting and maximizing the present value of future cash flows, we'll take the cash flows." . . . Amazon has since become famous for emphasizing its so-called pro-forma results, which exclude certain costs and highlight Bezo's beloved cash flow. Cash flow—is indeed a critical indicator of

whether Amazon will avoid being crushed by its debt. But ultimately Bezos will have to show that Amazon can make honest-to-God net profits under old-school accounting.[13]

Divide into class groups in order to develop a position in support of or against Bezo's reasoning. Then participate in a debate, defending your group's position. The basic question to address is, Which is more important for a young growing company—cash flows from operating activities or net income under GAAP?

Business Communication Case

LO1, LO2

Alternative Uses of Cash

C 10. Perhaps because of hard times in their start-up years, companies in the high-tech sector of American industry seem more prone than those in other sectors to building up cash reserves. For example, companies like **Cisco Systems**, **Intel**, **Dell**, and **Oracle** have amassed large cash balances.[14]

Assume you work for a company in the high-tech industry that has built up a substantial amount of cash. The company is still growing through development of new products, has some debt, and has never paid a dividend or bought treasury stock. The price of the company's stock is lagging. Write a one-page memo to the CEO that outlines at least four strategies for using the company's cash to improve the company's financial outlook.

Financial Performance Measurement

The ultimate purpose of financial reporting is to enable managers, creditors, investors, and other interested parties to evaluate a company's financial performance. In earlier chapters, we discussed the various measures used in assessing a company's financial performance; here, we provide a comprehensive summary of those measures. Because these measures play a key role in executive compensation, there is always the risk that they will be manipulated. Users of financial statements therefore need to be familiar with the analytical tools and techniques used in performance measurement and the assumptions that underlie them.

LEARNING OBJECTIVES

Making a Statement

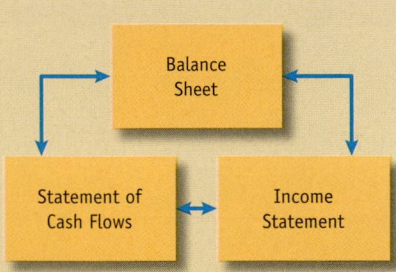

Comparisons within and across financial statements help the users of financial statements assess financial performance.

LO1 Describe the objectives, standards of comparison, sources of information, and compensation issues in measuring financial performance.

LO2 Apply horizontal analysis, trend analysis, vertical analysis, and ratio analysis to financial statements.

LO3 Apply ratio analysis to financial statements in a comprehensive evaluation of a company's financial performance.

STARBUCKS CORPORATION

- What standards should be used to evaluate Starbucks' performance?

- What analytical tools are available to measure performance?

- How successful has the company been in creating value for shareholders?

Formed in 1985, **Starbucks** is today a well-known specialty retailer. The company purchases and roasts whole coffee beans and sells them, along with a variety of freshly brewed coffees and other beverages and food items, in its retail shops. It also produces and sells bottled coffee drinks and a line of premium ice creams.

Like many other companies, Starbucks uses financial performance measures, primarily earnings per share, in determining compensation for top management. Earnings per share and some of the measures that drive earnings per share appear in the company's Financial Highlights below.1 By linking compensation to financial performance, Starbucks provides its executives with incentive to improve the company's performance. Compensation and financial performance are thus linked to increasing shareholders' value.

STARBUCKS' FINANCIAL HIGHLIGHTS
(In thousands, except profit margin and earnings per share)

	2004	2003	2002
Net revenues	$5,294,247	$4,075,522	$3,288,908
Net earnings	391,775	268,346	212,686
Profit margin	7.4%	6.6%	6.5%
Earnings per share—basic	0.99	0.69	0.55

Foundations of Financial Performance Measurement

LO1 Describe the objectives, standards of comparison, sources of information, and compensation issues in measuring financial performance.

Financial performance measurement, also called *financial statement analysis*, uses all the techniques available to show how important items in a company's financial statements relate to the company's financial objectives. Persons with a strong interest in measuring a company's financial performance fall into two groups:

1. A company's top managers, who set and strive to achieve financial performance objectives; middle-level managers of business processes; and lower-level employees who own stock in the company

2. Creditors and investors, as well as customers who have cooperative agreements with the company

Financial Performance Measurement: Management's Objectives

All the strategic and operating plans that management formulates to achieve a company's goals must eventually be stated in terms of financial objectives. A primary objective is to increase the wealth of the company's stockholders, but this objective must be divided into categories. A complete financial plan should have financial objectives and related performance objectives in all the following categories:

Financial Objective	Performance Objective
Liquidity	The company must be able to pay bills when due and meet unexpected needs for cash.
Profitability	It must earn a satisfactory net income.
Long-term solvency	It must be able to survive for many years.
Cash flow adequacy	It must generate sufficient cash through operating, investing, and financing activities.
Market strength	It must be able to increase stockholders' wealth.

Management's main responsibility is to carry out its plan to achieve the company's financial objectives. This requires constant monitoring of key financial performance measures for each objective listed above, determining the cause of any deviations from the measures, and proposing ways of correcting the deviations. Management compares actual performance with the key performance measures in monthly, quarterly, and annual reports. The information in management's annual reports provides data for long-term trend analyses.

Financial Performance Measurement: Creditors' and Investors' Objectives

Creditors and investors use financial performance evaluation to judge a company's past performance and present position. They also use it to assess a company's future potential and the risk connected with acting on that potential. An investor focuses on a company's potential earnings ability because that ability will affect the market price of the company's stock and the amount of dividends the company will pay. A creditor focuses on the company's potential debt-paying ability.

Past performance is often a good indicator of future performance. To evaluate a company's past performance, creditors and investors look at trends in past sales, expenses, net income, cash flow, and return on investment. To evaluate its current position, they look at its assets, liabilities, cash position, debt in relation to equity, and levels of inventories and receivables. Knowing a company's past performance and current position can be important in judging its future potential and the related risk.

The risk involved in making an investment or loan depends on how easy it is to predict future profitability or liquidity. If an investor can predict with confidence that a company's earnings per share will be between $2.50 and $2.60 in the next year, the investment is less risky than if the earnings per share are expected to fall between $2.00 and $3.00. For example, the potential of an investment in an established electric utility company is relatively easy to predict on the basis of the company's past performance and current position. In contrast, the potential of an investment in a new Internet firm that has not yet established a record of earnings is very hard to predict. Investing in the Internet firm is therefore riskier than investing in the electric utility company.

In return for taking a greater risk, investors often look for a higher expected return (an increase in market price plus dividends). Creditors who take a greater risk by advancing funds to a company like the new Internet firm mentioned above may demand a higher interest rate and more assurance of repayment (a secured loan, for instance). The higher interest rate reimburses them for assuming the higher risk.

Standards of Comparison

When analyzing financial statements, decision makers must judge whether the relationships they find in the statements are favorable or unfavorable. Three standards of comparison that they commonly use are rule-of-thumb measures, a company's past performance, and industry norms.

Rule-of-Thumb Measures Many financial analysts, investors, and lenders apply general standards, or rule-of-thumb measures, to key financial ratios. For example, most analysts today agree that a current ratio (current assets divided by current liabilities) of 2:1 is acceptable.

In its *Industry Norms and Key Business Ratios*, the credit-rating firm of Dun & Bradstreet offers such rules of thumb as the following:

Current debt to tangible net worth: A business is usually in trouble when this relationship exceeds 80 percent.

Inventory to net working capital: Ordinarily, this relationship should not exceed 80 percent.

Although rule-of-thumb measures may suggest areas that need further investigation, there is no proof that the levels they specify apply to all companies. A company with a current ratio higher than 2:1 may have a poor credit policy (causing accounts receivable to be too large), too much inventory, or poor cash management. Another company may have a ratio lower than 2:1 but still have excellent management in all three of those areas. Thus, rule-of-thumb measures must be used with caution.

Past Performance Comparing financial measures or ratios of the same company over time is an improvement over using rule-of-thumb measures. Such a comparison gives the analyst some basis for judging whether the measure or ratio is getting better or worse. Thus, it may be helpful in showing future trends. However, trends reverse at times, so such projections must be made with care.

Another problem with trend analysis is that past performance may not be enough to meet a company's present needs. For example, even though a company improves its return on investment from 3 percent in one year to 4 percent the next year, the 4 percent return may not be adequate for the company's current needs. In addition, using a company's past performance as a standard of comparison is not helpful in judging its performance relative to that of other companies.

Industry Norms Using industry norms as a standard of comparison overcomes some of the limitations of comparing a company's measures or ratios over time. Industry norms show how a company compares with other companies in the same industry. For example, if companies in a particular industry have an average rate of return on investment of 8 percent, a 3 or 4 percent rate of return is probably not adequate. Industry norms can also be used to judge trends. Suppose that because of a downturn in the economy, a company's profit margin dropped from 12 percent to 10 percent, while the average drop in profit margin of other companies in the same industry was from 12 to 4 percent. By this standard, the company would have done relatively well. Sometimes, instead of industry averages, data for the industry leader or a specific competitor are used for analysis.

Using industry norms as standards has three limitations:

1. Companies in the same industry may not be strictly comparable. Consider two companies in the oil industry. One purchases oil products and markets them through service stations. The other, an international company, discovers, produces, refines, and markets its own oil products. Because of the disparity in their operations, these two companies cannot be directly compared.

2. Many large companies have multiple segments and operate in more than one industry. Some of these **diversified companies**, or *conglomerates*, operate in many unrelated industries. The individual segments of a diversified

EXHIBIT 1 ▶

Selected Segment Information for Goodyear Tire & Rubber Company			
(In millions)	**2004**	**2003**	**2002**
Sales			
North American Tire	$ 7,854.6	$ 6,745.6	$ 6,703.0
European Union Tire	4,476.2	3,921.5	3,319.4
Eastern Europe, Africa, and Middle East Tire	1,279.0	1,073.4	807.1
Latin American Tire	1,245.4	1,041.0	947.7
Asia Tire	1,312.0	581.8	531.3
Total Tires	**16,167.2**	**13,363.3**	**12,308.5**
Engineered Products	1,470.3	1,203.7	1,126.3
Chemical Products	1,532.6	1,220.8	940.2
Total Segment Sales	**19,170.1**	**15,787.8**	**14,375.0**
Income			
North American Tire	$ 31.5	($ 130.9)	($ 58.1)
European Union Tire	252.7	129.8	101.1
Eastern Europe, Africa, and Middle East Tire	193.8	146.6	93.2
Latin American Tire	251.2	148.6	107.6
Asia Tire	61.1	49.9	43.7
Total Tires	**790.3**	**344.0**	**287.5**
Engineered Products	113.2	46.8	39.0
Chemical Products	177.0	120.2	88.2
Total Segment Income	**1,080.5**	**511.0**	**414.7**
Assets*			
North American Tire	$ 5,091.4	$ 5,939.3	$ 4,869.0
European Union Tire	4,264.0	4,001.9	2,027.0
Eastern Europe, Africa, and Middle East Tire	1,315.1	1,102.7	1,104.2
Latin American Tire	845.6	710.0	859.8
Asia Tire	1,153.8	669.5	668.5
Total Tires	**12,669.9**	**12,423.4**	**9,528.5**
Engineered Products	764.7	680.5	717.5
Chemical Products	650.3	632.4	625.1
Total Segment Assets	**14,084.9**	**13,736.3**	**10,891.1**

*2002 assets estimated.

Source: Goodyear Tire & Rubber Company, *Annual Report*, 2005.

Study Note

Each segment of a diversified company represents an investment that the home office or parent company evaluates and reviews frequently.

company generally have different rates of profitability and different degrees of risk. In analyzing a diversified company's consolidated financial statements, it is often impossible to use industry norms as a standard because there simply are no comparable companies.

The FASB provides a partial solution to this problem. It requires diversified companies to report profit or loss, certain revenue and expense items, and assets for each of their segments. Segment information may be reported for operations in different industries or different geographical areas, or for major customers.[4] Exhibit I shows how **Goodyear Tire & Rubber Company** reports data on sales, income, and assets for its engineered

Shown here is Goodyear Tire & Rubber Company's polymer plant in Beaumont, Texas. The Beaumont plant is Goodyear's major supplier of tire polymers and the largest in its chemical products segment, which includes facilities in Houston, Niagara Falls, and Akron. The FASB requires diversified companies to report financial information for each of their segments. Goodyear has seven segments in all.

and chemical products segments. These data allow the analyst to compute important profitability performance measures, such as profit margin, asset turnover, and return on assets, for each segment and to compare them with the appropriate industry norms.

3. Another limitation of industry norms is that even when companies in the same industry have similar operations, they may use different acceptable accounting procedures. For example, they may use different methods of valuing inventories and different methods of depreciating assets.

Despite these limitations, if little information about a company's past performance is available, industry norms probably offer the best available standards for judging current performance—as long as they are used with care.

Sources of Information

The major sources of information about public corporations are reports published by the corporations themselves, reports filed with the SEC, business periodicals, and credit and investment advisory services.

Reports Published by the Corporation A public corporation's annual report is an important source of financial information. From a financial analyst's perspective, the main parts of an annual report are management's analysis of the past year's operations; the financial statements; the notes to the financial statements, which include a summary of significant accounting policies; the auditors' report; and financial highlights for a five- or ten-year period.

Most public corporations also publish **interim financial statements** each quarter and sometimes each month. These reports, which present limited information in the form of condensed financial statements, are not subject to a full audit by an independent auditor. The financial community watches interim statements closely for early signs of change in a company's earnings trend.

Reports Filed with the SEC

Public corporations in the United States must file annual reports, quarterly reports, and current reports with the Securities and Exchange Commission (SEC). If they have more than $10 million in assets and more than 500 shareholders, they must file these reports electronically at www.sec.gov/edgar.shtml, where anyone can access them free of charge.

The SEC requires companies to file their annual reports on a standard form, called Form 10-K. Form 10-K contains more information than a company's annual report and is therefore a valuable source of information.

Companies file their quarterly reports with the SEC on Form 10-Q. This report presents important facts about interim financial performance.

The current report, filed on Form 8-K, must be submitted to the SEC within a few days of the date of certain significant events, such as the sale or purchase of a division or a change in auditors. The current report is often the first indicator of significant changes that will affect a company's financial performance in the future.

Business Periodicals and Credit and Investment Advisory Services

Financial analysts must keep up with current events in the financial world. A leading source of financial news is *The Wall Street Journal*. It is the most complete financial newspaper in the United States and is published every business day. Useful periodicals that are published every week or every two weeks include *Forbes*, *Barron's*, *Fortune*, and the *Financial Times*.

Credit and investment advisory services also provide useful information. The publications of Moody's Investors Service and Standard & Poor's provide details about a company's financial history. Data on industry norms, average ratios, and credit ratings are available from agencies like Dun & Bradstreet. Dun & Bradstreet's *Industry Norms and Key Business Ratios* offers an annual analysis of 14 ratios for each of 125 industry groups, classified as retailing, wholesaling, manufacturing, and construction. *Annual Statement Studies*, published by Risk Management Association (formerly Robert Morris Associates), presents many facts and ratios for 223 different industries. The publications of a number of other agencies are also available for a yearly fee.

An example of specialized financial reporting readily available to the public is Mergent's *Handbook of Dividend Achievers*. It profiles companies that have increased their dividends consistently over the past ten years. A listing from that publication—for **PepsiCo Inc.**—is shown in Exhibit 2. As you can see, a wealth of information about the company, including the market action of its stock, its business operations, recent developments and prospects, and earnings and dividend data, is summarized on one page. We use the kind of data contained in Mergent's summaries in many of the analyses and ratios that we present later in this chapter.

Executive Compensation

As we noted earlier in the text, one intent of the Sarbanes-Oxley Act of 2002 was to strengthen the corporate governance of public corporations. Under this act, a public corporation's board of directors must establish a **compensation committee** made up of independent directors to determine how the company's top executives will be compensated. The company must disclose the components of compensation and the criteria it uses to remunerate top executives in

EXHIBIT 2 ▶   **Listing from Mergent's Handbook of Dividend Achievers**

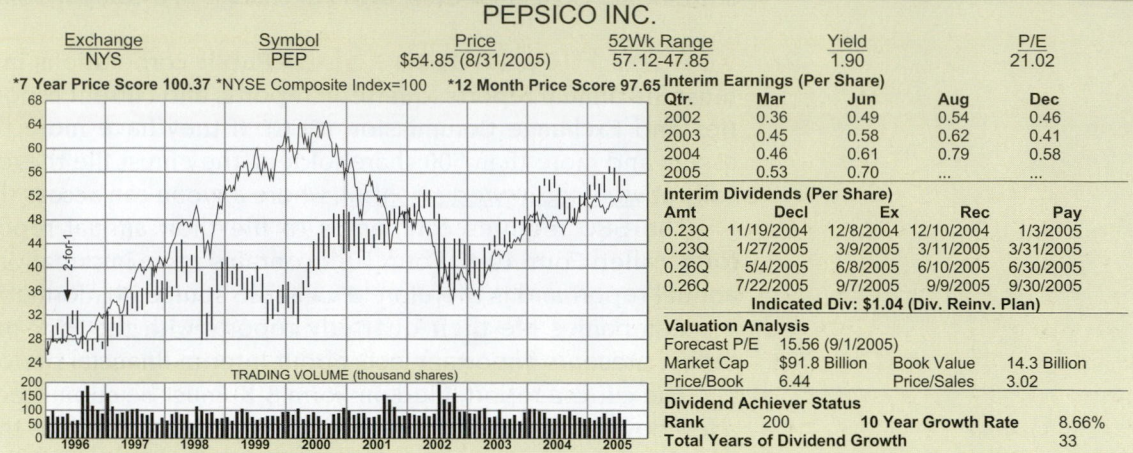

PEPSICO INC.

Exchange	Symbol	Price	52Wk Range	Yield	P/E
NYS	PEP	$54.85 (8/31/2005)	57.12-47.85	1.90	21.02

*7 Year Price Score 100.37 *NYSE Composite Index=100   *12 Month Price Score 97.65

Interim Earnings (Per Share)

Qtr.	Mar	Jun	Aug	Dec
2002	0.36	0.49	0.54	0.46
2003	0.45	0.58	0.62	0.41
2004	0.46	0.61	0.79	0.58
2005	0.53	0.70	...	...

Interim Dividends (Per Share)

Amt	Decl	Ex	Rec	Pay
0.23Q	11/19/2004	12/8/2004	12/10/2004	1/3/2005
0.23Q	1/27/2005	3/9/2005	3/11/2005	3/31/2005
0.26Q	5/4/2005	6/8/2005	6/10/2005	6/30/2005
0.26Q	7/22/2005	9/7/2005	9/9/2005	9/30/2005

Indicated Div: $1.04 (Div. Reinv. Plan)

Valuation Analysis

Forecast P/E 15.56 (9/1/2005)

Market Cap	$91.8 Billion	Book Value	14.3 Billion
Price/Book	6.44	Price/Sales	3.02

Dividend Achiever Status

Rank	200	10 Year Growth Rate	8.66%
Total Years of Dividend Growth			33

TRADING VOLUME (thousand shares)

Business Summary: Food (MIC: 4.1 SIC: 2086 NAIC: 312111)

PepsiCo is a global snack and beverage company. Co. manufactures, markets and sells a variety of salty, convenient, sweet and grain-based snacks, carbonated and non-carbonated beverages and foods. Co.'s Frito-Lay North America division's brands include Lay's potato chips, Fritos corn chips, Quaker Chewy granola bars and Rold Gold pretzels. PepsiCo Beverages North America brands include Pepsi, Mountain Dew, Sierra Mist, Mug, SoBe, Gatorade, Tropicana Pure Premium and Propel. PepsiCo International brands include Sabritas in Mexico, Walkers in the UK, and Smith's in Australia. Quaker Foods North America's products include Quaker oatmeal and Cap'n Crunch and Life ready-to-eat cereals.

Recent Developments: For the quarter ended June 11 2005, net income increased 12.7% to $1,194,000 thousand from net income of $1,059,000 thousand in the year-earlier quarter. Revenues were $7,697,000 thousand, up 8.9% from $7,070,000 thousand the year before. Operating income was $1,556,000 thousand versus an income of $1,421,000 thousand in the prior-year quarter, an increase of 9.5%. Total direct expense was $3,504,000 thousand versus $3,213,000 thousand in the prior-year quarter, an increase of 9.1%. Total indirect expense was $2,637,000 thousand versus $2,436,000 thousand in the prior-year quarter, an increase of 8.3%.

Prospects: Co.'s strong performance is being led by sales growth at PepsiCo International (PI) and Quaker Foods North America (QFNA) and solid execution in its North American beverage and snacks units. PI sales are benefiting from strong beverage volume growth in the Middle East, China Argentina and Venezuela, and increasing snack volumes in India, China, Russia, Australia, Saudi Arabia, and Turkey. QFNA results are benefiting from growth of its Quaker oatmeal, Rice-A-Roni, Pasta Roni and Aunt Jemima Syrup products. For full-year 2005, Co. expects earnings to range from $2.32 to $2.35 per share. Meanwhile, Co. expects cash from operating activities to exceed $5.70 billion in 2005.

Financial Data

(US$ in Thousands)	6 Mos	3 Mos	12/25/2004	12/27/2003	12/28/2002	12/29/2001	12/30/2000	12/25/1999
Earnings Per Share	2.61	2.52	2.44	2.05	1.85	1.47	1.48	1.37
Cash Flow Per Share	3.52	3.04	2.99	2.53	2.65	2.39	2.66	2.07
Tang Book Value Per Share	5.34	5.08	4.84	3.82	2.37	2.17	1.91	1.47
Dividends Per Share	0.950	0.920	0.850	0.630	0.595	0.575	0.555	0.535
Dividend Payout %	36.44	36.57	34.84	30.73	32.16	39.12	37.50	39.05
Income Statement								
Total Revenue	14,282,000	6,585,000	29,261,000	26,971,000	25,112,000	26,935,000	20,438,000	20,367,000
EBITDA	3,612,000	1,594,000	6,848,000	6,269,000	6,077,000	5,189,000	4,209,000	4,843,000
Depn & Amortn	588,000	282,000	1,209,000	1,165,000	1,067,000	1,008,000	854,000	942,000
Income Before Taxes	2,972,000	1,285,000	5,546,000	4,992,000	4,868,000	4,029,000	3,210,000	3,656,000
Income Taxes	866,000	373,000	1,372,000	1,424,000	1,555,000	1,367,000	1,027,000	1,606,000
Net Income	2,106,000	912,000	4,212,000	3,568,000	3,313,000	2,662,000	2,183,000	2,050,000
Average Shares	1,712,000	1,713,000	1,729,000	1,739,000	1,789,000	1,807,000	1,475,000	1,496,000
Balance Sheet								
Current Assets	9,910,000	8,876,000	8,639,000	6,930,000	6,413,000	5,853,000	4,604,000	4,173,000
Total Assets	29,684,000	28,671,000	27,987,000	25,327,000	23,474,000	21,695,000	18,339,000	17,551,000
Current Liabilities	7,968,000	7,194,000	6,752,000	6,415,000	6,052,000	4,998,000	3,935,000	3,788,000
Long-Term Obligations	2,331,000	2,390,000	2,397,000	1,702,000	2,187,000	2,651,000	2,346,000	2,812,000
Total Liabilities	15,494,000	14,758,000	14,464,000	13,453,000	14,183,000	13,021,000	11,090,000	10,670,000
Stockholders' Equity	14,250,000	13,968,000	13,572,000	11,896,000	9,298,000	8,648,000	7,249,000	6,881,000
Shares Outstanding	1,673,000	1,677,000	1,679,000	1,705,000	1,722,000	1,756,000	1,446,000	1,455,000
Statistical Record								
Return on Assets %	16.04	15.98	15.84	14.66	14.71	13.34	11.97	10.22
Return on Equity %	33.57	32.69	33.17	33.76	37.02	33.58	30.40	30.95
EBITDA Margin %	25.29	24.21	23.40	23.24	24.20	19.26	20.59	23.78
Net Margin %	14.75	13.85	14.39	13.23	13.19	9.88	10.68	10.07
Asset Turnover	1.09	1.10	1.10	1.11	1.11	1.35	1.12	1.02
Current Ratio	1.24	1.23	1.28	1.08	1.06	1.17	1.17	1.10
Debt to Equity	0.16	0.17	0.18	0.14	0.24	0.31	0.32	0.41
Price Range	57.12-47.85	55.55-47.85	55.55-45.39	48.71-37.30	53.12-35.50	50.28-41.26	49.75-30.50	41.81-30.50
P/E Ratio	21.89-18.33	22.04-18.99	22.77-18.60	23.76-18.20	28.71-19.19	34.20-28.07	33.61-20.61	30.52-22.26
Average Yield %	1.81	1.76		1.43	1.29		1.25	1.36	1.46

Address: 700 Anderson Hill Road, Purchase, NY 10577-1444 **Telephone:** 914-253-2000 **Web Site:** www.pepsico.com	**Officers:** Steven S. Reinemund - Chmn., C.E.O. Indra K. Nooyi - Pres., C.F.O. **Transfer Agents:** The Bank of New York	**Investor Contact:** 914-253-3035 **No of Institutions:** 1122 **Shares:** 1,108,465,408 **% Held:** 66.38

Source: Listing from *Handbook of Dividend Achievers,* 2004. Reprinted by permission of Mergent.

documents that it files with the SEC. The components of **Starbucks'** compensation of executive officers are typical of those used by many companies:

- Annual base salary

- Incentive bonuses

- Stock option awards[5]

Incentive bonuses are based on performance measures that the compensation committee identifies as important to the company's long-term success. Many companies tie incentive bonuses to such measures as growth in revenues and return on assets, or return on equity. Starbucks bases 80 percent of its incentive bonus on an "earnings per share target approved by the compensation committee" and 20 percent on the executive's "specific individual performance." The Financial Highlights at the beginning of the chapter show the growth in the Starbucks' earnings per share.

Stock option awards are usually based on how well the company is achieving its long-term strategic goals. In 2004, a very good year for Starbucks, the company's CEO received a base salary of $1,190,000, an incentive bonus of an equal amount, and a stock option award of 550,000 shares of common stock.[6]

From one vantage point, earnings per share is a "bottom-line" number that encompasses all the other performance measures. However, using a single performance measure as the basis for determining compensation has the potential of leading to practices that are not in the best interests of the company or its stockholders. For instance, management could boost earnings per share by reducing the number of shares outstanding (the denominator in the earnings per share equation) while not improving earnings. It could accomplish this by using cash to repurchase shares of the company's stock (treasury stock), rather than investing the cash in more profitable operations. An understanding of the performance measures used in determining executive compensation and the factors that underlie them is critical in evaluating their fairness.

STOP • REVIEW • APPLY

1-1. How are the objectives of investors and creditors in using financial performance evaluation similar? How do they differ?

1-2. What role does risk play in making loans and investments?

1-3. What standards of comparison are commonly used to evaluate financial statements, and what are their relative merits?

1-4. Why would a financial analyst compare the ratios of Steelco, a steel company, with the ratios of other companies in the steel industry? What factors might invalidate such a comparison?

1-5. Where can investors find information about public corporations in which they are thinking of investing?

1-6. What is the role of a corporation's compensation committee, and what are three common components of executive compensation?

Suggested answers to all Stop, Review, and Apply questions follow the appendixes.

Performance Measurement Components Identify each of the following as (a) an objective of financial statement analysis, (b) a standard for financial statement analysis, (c) a source of information for financial statement analysis, or (d) an executive compensation issue:

1. A company's past performance
2. Investment advisory services
3. Assessment of a company's future potential
4. Incentive bonuses
5. Industry norms
6. Annual report
7. Creating shareholder value
8. Form 10-K

SOLUTION

1. b
2. c
3. a
4. d

5. b
6. c
7. d
8. c

Tools and Techniques of Financial Analysis

LO2 Apply horizontal analysis, trend analysis, vertical analysis, and ratio analysis to financial statements.

To gain insight into a company's financial performance, one must look beyond the individual numbers to the relationship between the numbers and their change from one period to another. The tools of financial analysis—horizontal analysis, trend analysis, vertical analysis, and ratio analysis—are intended to show these relationships and changes. To illustrate how these tools are used, we devote the rest of this chapter to a comprehensive financial analysis of **Starbucks Corporation**.

Horizontal Analysis

> **Study Note**
>
> It is important to ascertain the base amount used when a percentage describes an item. For example, inventory may be 50 percent of *total current assets* but only 10 percent of *total assets*.

Comparative financial statements provide financial information for the current year and the previous year. To gain insight into year-to-year changes, analysts use **horizontal analysis**, in which changes from the previous year to the current year are computed in both dollar amounts and percentages. The percentage change relates the size of the change to the size of the dollar amounts involved.

Exhibits 3 and 4 present **Starbuck Corporation's** comparative balance sheets and income statements and show both the dollar and percentage changes. The percentage change is computed as follows:

$$\text{Percentage Change} = 100 \times \left(\frac{\text{Amount of Change}}{\text{Base Year Amount}}\right)$$

The **base year** is always the first year to be considered in any set of data. For example, when comparing data for 2003 and 2004, 2003 is the base year. As the balance sheets in Exhibit 3 show, between 2003 and 2004, Starbucks' total current assets increased by $444,456 thousand, from $924,029 thousand to $1,368,485 thousand, or by 48.1 percent. This is computed as follows:

$$\text{Percentage Change} = 100 \times \left(\frac{\$444,456 \text{ thousand}}{\$924,029 \text{ thousand}}\right) = 48.1\%$$

▼ EXHIBIT 3

Comparative Balance Sheets with Horizontal Analysis

Starbucks Corporation
Consolidated Balance Sheets
October 3, 2004, and September 28, 2003

(Dollar amounts in thousands)	2004	2003	Increase (Decrease) Amount	Increase (Decrease) Percentage
Assets				
Current assets:				
Cash and cash equivalents	$ 299,128	$ 200,907	$ 98,221	48.9
Short-term investments	353,881	149,104	204,777	137.3
Accounts receivable, net of allowances of $2,231 and $4,809, respectively	140,226	114,448	25,778	22.5
Inventories	422,663	342,944	79,719	23.2
Prepaid and other current assets	71,347	55,173	16,174	29.3
Deferred income taxes, net	81,240	61,453	19,787	32.2
Total current assets	$1,368,485	$ 924,029	$444,456	48.1
Property, plant, and equipment, net	1,471,446	1,384,902	86,544	6.2
Long-term investments	306,926	280,416	26,510	9.5
Other assets	85,561	52,113	33,448	64.2
Goodwill	26,800	24,942	1,858	7.4
Other intangible assets	68,950	63,344	5,606	8.9
Total assets	$3,328,168	$2,729,746	$598,422	21.9
Liabilities and Shareholders' Equity				
Current liabilities:				
Accounts payable	$ 199,346	$ 168,984	$ 30,362	18.0
Accrued compensation and related costs	208,927	152,608	56,319	36.9
Accrued occupancy costs	65,873	56,179	9,694	17.3
Accrued taxes	63,038	54,934	8,104	14.8
Other accrued expenses	123,684	101,800	21,884	21.5
Deferred revenue	121,377	73,476	47,901	65.2
Current portion of long-term debt	735	722	13	1.8
Total current liabilities	$ 782,980	$ 608,703	$174,277	28.6
Deferred income taxes, net	46,683	33,217	13,466	40.5
Long-term debt and other liabilities	11,750	5,399	6,351	117.6
Shareholders' equity	2,486,755	2,082,427	404,328	19.4
Total liabilities and shareholders' equity	$3,328,168	$2,729,746	$598,422	21.9

Source: Data from Starbucks Corporation, 2004 10K.

▼ EXHIBIT 4

Comparative Income Statements with Horizontal Analysis

Starbucks Corporation
Consolidated Income Statements
For the Years Ended October 3, 2004, and September 28, 2003

(Dollar amounts in thousands, except per share amounts)	2004	2003	Increase (Decrease) Amount	Increase (Decrease) Percentage
Net revenues	$5,294,247	$4,075,522	$1,218,725	29.9
Cost of sales, including occupancy costs	2,198,654	1,685,928	512,726	30.4
Gross margin	$3,095,593	$2,389,594	$ 705,999	29.5
Operating expenses				
Store operating expenses	$1,790,168	$1,379,574	$ 410,594	29.8
Other operating expenses	171,648	141,346	30,302	21.4
Depreciation and amortization expenses	280,024	237,807	42,217	17.8
General and administrative expenses	304,293	244,550	59,743	24.4
Total operating expenses	$2,546,133	$2,003,277	$ 542,856	27.1
Operating income	$ 549,460	$ 386,317	$ 163,143	42.2
Other income, net	74,797	50,018	24,779	49.5
Income before taxes	$ 624,257	$ 436,335	$ 187,922	43.1
Provision for income taxes	232,482	167,989	64,493	38.4
Net income	$ 391,775	$ 268,346	$ 123,429	46.0
Net income per common share—basic	$ 0.99	$ 0.69	$ 0.30	43.5
Net income per common share—diluted	$ 0.95	$ 0.67	$ 0.28	41.8
Shares used in calculation of net income per common share—basic	397,173	390,753	6,420	1.6
Shares used in calculation of net income per common share—diluted	411,465	401,648	9,817	2.4

Source: Data from Starbucks Corporation, 2004 10K.

When examining such changes, it is important to consider the dollar amount of the change as well as the percentage change in each component. For example, the difference between the percentage increase in accounts receivable (22.5 percent) and inventories (23.2 percent) is not great. However, the dollar increase in inventories is more than three times the dollar increase in accounts receivable ($79,669 thousand versus $25,778 thousand). Thus, even though the percentage changes are about the same, inventories require much more investment.

Starbucks' balance sheets for this period, illustrated in Exhibit 3, also show an increase in total assets of $598,422 thousand, or 21.9 percent, which included an increase of $204,777 thousand, or 137.3 percent, in short-term investments. In addition, they show that stockholders' equity increased by $404,328 thousand, or 19.4 percent. All of this indicates that Starbucks is a rapidly growing company.

Starbucks' income statements in Exhibit 4 show that net revenues increased by $1,218,725 thousand, or 29.9 percent, while gross margin increased by $705,999 thousand, or 29.5 percent. This indicates that cost of sales grew faster than net revenues. In fact, cost of sales increased by 30.4 percent compared with the 29.9 percent increase in net revenues.

Starbucks' total operating expenses increased by $542,856 thousand, or 27.1 percent, not as fast as the 29.9 percent increase in net revenues. As a result, operating income increased by $163,143 thousand, or 42.2 percent, and net income increased by $123,429 thousand, or 46.0 percent. The primary reason for the increases in operating income and net income is that total operating expenses increased at a slower rate (27.1 percent) than net revenues (29.9 percent).

Trend Analysis

Trend analysis is a variation of horizontal analysis. With this tool, the analyst calculates percentage changes for several successive years instead of for just two years. Because of its long-term view, trend analysis can highlight basic changes in the nature of a business.

In addition to presenting comparative financial statements, many companies present a summary of key data for five or more years. Exhibit 5 shows a trend analysis of **Starbucks'** five-year summary of net revenues and operating income.

Trend analysis uses an **index number** to show changes in related items over time. For an index number, the base year is set at 100 percent. Other years are measured in relation to that amount. For example, the 2004 index for Starbucks' net revenues is figured as follows (dollar amounts are in thousands):

$$\text{Index} = 100 \times \left(\frac{\text{Index Year Amount}}{\text{Base Year Amount}} \right)$$

$$= 100 \times \left(\frac{\$5,294,247}{\$2,177,614} \right) = 243.1\%$$

The trend analysis in Exhibit 5 shows that Starbucks' net revenues increased over the five-year period, as did operating income. However, operating income grew faster than net revenues in every year except 2002. Figure 1 illustrates these trends.

EXHIBIT 5 ▶

Trend Analysis

Starbucks Corporation
Net Revenues and Operating Income
Trend Analysis

	2004	2003	2002	2001	2000
Dollar values (In thousands)					
Net revenues	$5,294,247	$4,075,522	$3,288,908	$2,648,980	$2,177,614
Operating income	549,460	386,317	282,893	252,479	191,952
Trend analysis (In percentages)					
Net revenues	243.1	187.2	151.0	121.6	100.0
Operating income	286.2	201.3	147.4	131.5	100.0

Source: Data from Starbucks Corporation, 2004 10K.

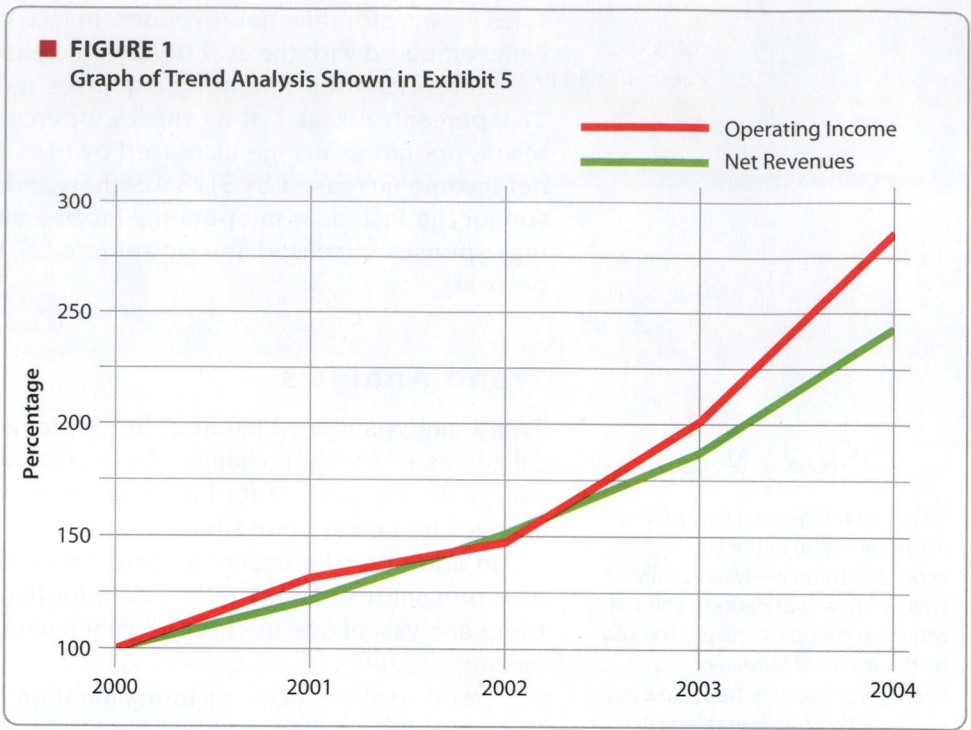

■ **FIGURE 1**
Graph of Trend Analysis Shown in Exhibit 5

Vertical Analysis

Vertical analysis shows how the different components of a financial statement relate to a total figure in the statement. The analyst sets the total figure at 100 percent and computes each component's percentage of that total. (On the balance sheet, the figure would be total assets or total liabilities and stockholders' equity, and on the income statement, it would be net revenues or net sales.) The resulting financial statement, which is expressed entirely in percentages, is called a **common-size statement**. Common-size balance sheets and common-size income statements for **Starbucks Corporation** are shown in pie-chart form in Figures 2 and 3 and in financial statement form in Exhibits 6 and 7.

Vertical analysis and common-size statements are useful in comparing the importance of specific components in the operation of a business and in identifying important changes in the components from one year to the next. The main conclusions to be drawn from our analysis of Starbucks are that the company's assets consist largely of current assets and property, plant, and equipment; that the company finances assets primarily through equity and current liabilities; and that it has few long-term liabilities.

Looking at the pie charts in Figure 2 and the common-size balance sheets in Exhibit 6, you can see that the composition of Starbucks' assets shifted from property, plant, and equipment to current assets. You can also see that the relationship of liabilities and equity shifted slightly from stockholders' equity to current liabilities.

The common-size income statements in Exhibit 7, illustrated in Figure 3, show that Starbucks reduced its operating expenses from 2003 to 2004 by 1.1 percent of revenues (49.2% − 48.1%). In other words, operating expenses did not grow as fast as revenues.

Common-size statements are often used to make comparisons between companies. They allow an analyst to compare the operating and financing characteristics of two companies of different size in the same industry. For example, the analyst might want to compare Starbucks with other specialty

■ **FIGURE 2**
Common-Size Balance Sheets Presented Graphically

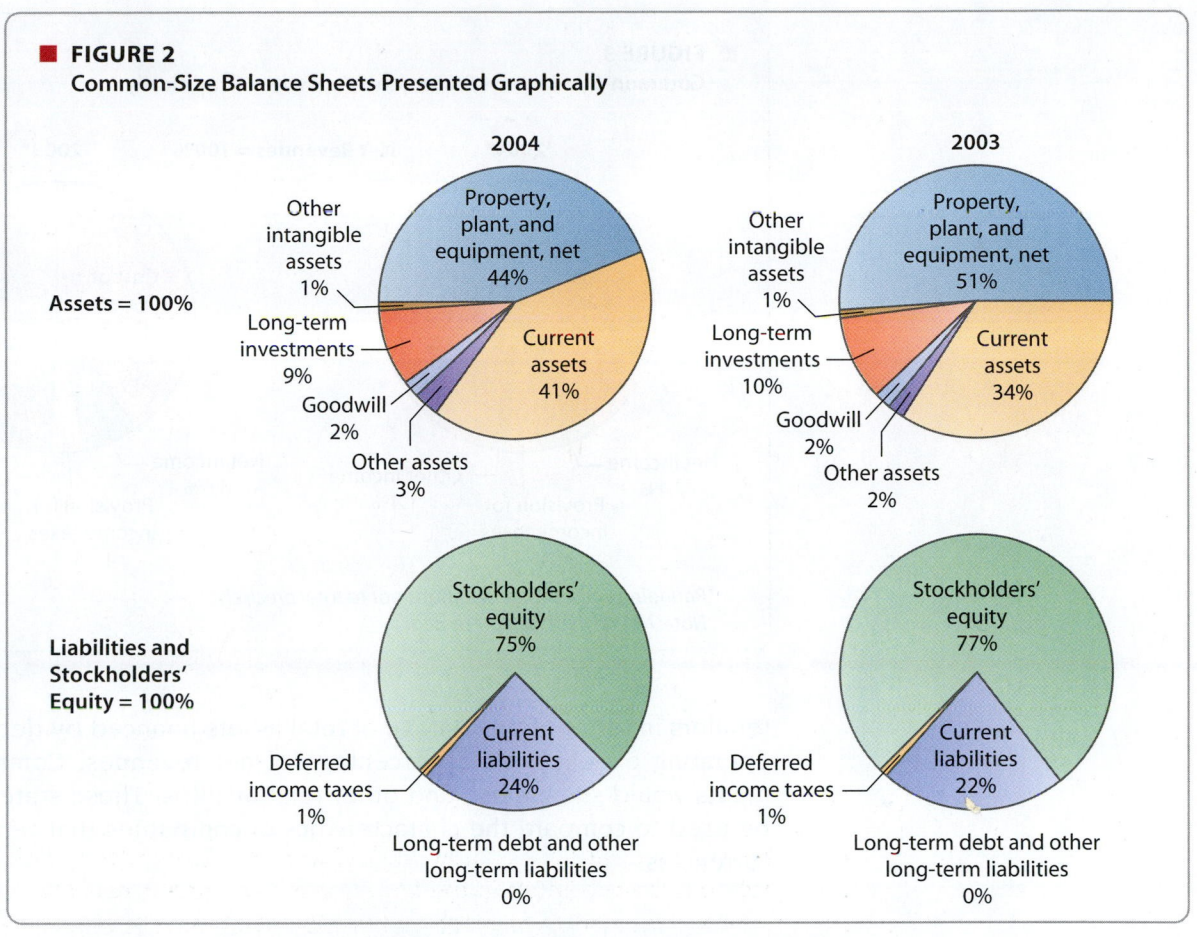

EXHIBIT 6 ▶ | **Common-Size Balance Sheets**

Starbucks Corporation
Common-Size Balance Sheets
October 3, 2004, and September 28, 2003

	2004	2003
Assets		
Current assets	41.1%	33.9%
Property, plant, and equipment, net	44.2	50.7
Long-term investments	9.2	10.3
Other assets	2.6	1.9
Goodwill	0.8	0.9
Other intangible assets	2.1	2.3
Total assets	100.0%	100.0%
Liabilities and Stockholders' Equity		
Current liabilities	23.5%	22.3%
Deferred income taxes, net	1.4	1.2
Long-term debt and other liabilities	0.4	0.2
Stockholders' equity	74.7	76.3
Total liabilities and stockholders' equity	100.0%	100.0%

Source: Data from Starbucks Corporation, 2004, 10K.

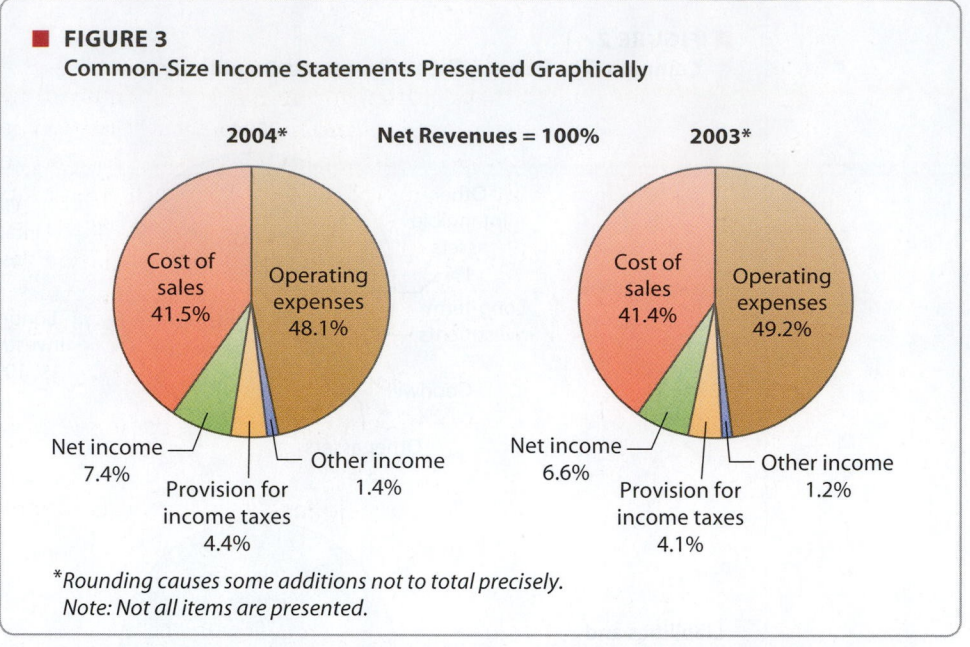

■ **FIGURE 3**
Common-Size Income Statements Presented Graphically

*Rounding causes some additions not to total precisely.
Note: Not all items are presented.*

retailers in terms of percentage of total assets financed by debt or in terms of operating expenses as a percentage of net revenues. Common-size statements would show those and other relationships. These statements can also be used to compare the characteristics of companies that report in different currencies.

EXHIBIT 7 ▶

Common-Size Income Statements

**Starbucks Corporation
Common-Size Income Statements
For the Years Ended October 3, 2004, and September 28, 2003**

	2004	2003
Net revenues	100.0%	100.0%
Cost of sales including occupancy costs	41.5	41.4
Gross margin	58.5%	58.6%
Operating expenses:		
Store operating expenses	33.8%	33.9%
Other operating expenses	3.2	3.5
Depreciation and amortization expenses	5.3	5.8
General and administrative expenses	5.7	6.0
Total operating expenses	48.1%	49.2%
Operating income	10.4%	9.5%
Other income, net	1.4	1.2
Earnings before taxes	11.8%	10.7%
Provision for income taxes	4.4	4.1
Net income	7.4%	6.6%

Note: Amounts do not precisely total 100 percent in all cases due to rounding.
Source: Data from Starbucks Corporation, 2004 10K.

Ratio Analysis

Ratio analysis is an evaluation technique that identifies key relationships between the components of the financial statements. Ratios are useful tools for evaluating a company's financial position and operations and may reveal areas that need further investigation. To interpret ratios correctly, the analyst must have a general understanding of the company and its environment, financial data for several years or for several companies, and an understanding of the data underlying the numerator and denominator.

Ratios can be expressed in several ways. For example, a ratio of net income of $100,000 to sales of $1,000,000 can be stated as follows:

1. Net income is 1/10, or 10 percent, of sales.

2. The ratio of sales to net income is 10 to 1 (10:1), or sales are 10 times net income.

3. For every dollar of sales, the company has an average net income of 10 cents.

STOP • REVIEW • APPLY

2-1. Why would an investor want to see both horizontal and trend analyses of a company's financial statements?

2-2. What does this sentence mean: "Based on a 1990 index equaling 100, net income increased from 240 in 2000 to 260 in 2001"?

2-3. What is the difference between horizontal and vertical analysis?

2-4. What is the purpose of ratio analysis?

Comprehensive Illustration of Ratio Analysis

LO3 Apply ratio analysis to financial statements in a comprehensive evaluation of a company's financial performance.

In this section, to illustrate how analysts use ratio analysis in evaluating a company's financial performance, we perform a comprehensive ratio analysis of **Starbucks'** performance in 2003 and 2004. The following excerpt from the discussion and analysis section of Starbucks' 2004 annual report provides the context for our evaluation of the company's liquidity, profitability, long-term solvency, cash flow adequacy, and market strength:

> During the fiscal year ended October 3, 2004, all areas of Starbucks business, from U.S. and international company operated retail operations to the Company's specialty businesses, delivered strong financial performance, and innovation was prevalent throughout the Company's operations. Starbucks believes the Company's ability to achieve the balance between growing the core business and building the foundation for future growth is the key to increasing shareholder value. Starbucks fiscal 2004 performance provides a strong example of the Company's commitment to achieve this balance.

Evaluating Liquidity

As you know, liquidity is a company's ability to pay bills when they are due and to meet unexpected needs for cash. Because debts are paid out of working capital, all liquidity ratios involve working capital or some part of it. (Cash flow ratios are also closely related to liquidity.)

Exhibit 8 presents **Starbucks'** liquidity ratios in 2003 and 2004. The **current ratio** and the **quick ratio** are measures of short-term debt-paying ability. The principal difference between the two ratios is that the numerator of the current ratio includes inventories and prepaid expenses. Inventories take longer to convert to cash than the current assets included in the numerator of the quick ratio. Starbucks' quick ratio was 0.8 times in 2003 and increased to 1.0 times in 2004, primarily because of the more than $200 million increase in short-term investments (marketable securities). Its current ratio was 1.5 times in 2003 and 1.7 in 2004. From 2003 to 2004, its current assets grew faster than current liabilities, also because of short-term investments.

Starbucks' management of receivables and inventory improved from 2003 to 2004. The **receivable turnover**, which measures the relative size of accounts receivable and the effectiveness of credit policies, rose from 38.4 times in 2003 to 41.6 times in 2004. The related ratio of **days' sales uncollected** decreased by almost one day, from 9.5 days in 2003 to 8.8 days in 2004. The number of days is quite low because the majority of Starbucks' revenues are from cash sales. The **inventory turnover**, which measures the relative size of inventories, increased from 5.6 times in 2003 to 5.7 times in 2004. This resulted in a favorable decrease in **days' inventory on hand**, from 65.2 days in 2003 to 64.0 days in 2004.

Starbucks' **operating cycle**, or the time it takes to sell products and collect for them, decreased from 74.7 days in 2003 (9.5 days + 65.2 days, or the days' sales uncollected plus the days' inventory on hand) to 72.8 days in 2004 (8.8 days + 64.0 days). Related to the operating cycle is the number of days a company takes to pay its accounts payable. Starbucks' **payables turnover** increased from 11.6 times in 2003 to 12.4 times in 2004. This resulted in **days' payable** of 31.5 days in 2003 and 29.4 days in 2004. If the days' payable is subtracted from the operating cycle, Starbucks' financing period—the number of days of financing required—was 43.2 days in 2003 and 43.4 days in 2004 (see Figure 4). Overall, Starbucks' liquidity improved.

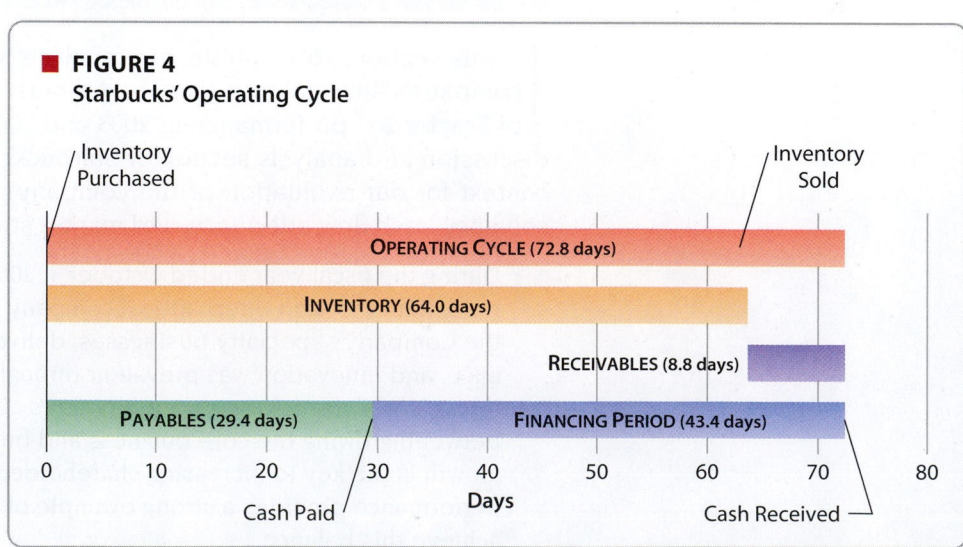

■ **FIGURE 4**
Starbucks' Operating Cycle

▼ **EXHIBIT 11**

Cash Flow Adequacy Ratios of Starbucks Corporation

(Dollar amounts in thousands)	2004	2003

Cash flow yield: Measure of the ability to generate operating cash flows in relation to net income

$$\frac{\text{Net Cash Flows from Operating Activities}}{\text{Net Income}} \qquad \frac{\$793,848^*}{\$391,775} = 2.0 \text{ times} \qquad \frac{\$566,447^*}{\$268,346} = 2.1 \text{ times}$$

Cash flows to sales: Measure of the ability of sales to generate operating cash flows

$$\frac{\text{Net Cash Flows from Operating Activities}}{\text{Net Sales}} \qquad \frac{\$793,848}{\$5,294,247} = 15.0\% \qquad \frac{\$566,447}{\$4,075,522} = 13.9\%$$

Cash flows to assets: Measure of the ability of assets to generate operating cash flows

$$\frac{\text{Net Cash Flows from Operating Activities}}{\text{Average Total Assets}} \qquad \frac{\$793,848}{(\$3,328,168 + \$2,729,746) \div 2} \qquad \frac{\$566,447}{(\$2,729,746 + \$2,214,392\dagger) \div 2}$$

$$= \frac{\$793,848}{\$3,028,957} = 26.2\% \qquad = \frac{\$566,447}{\$2,472,069} = 22.9\%$$

Free cash flow: Measure of cash remaining after providing for commitments

Net Cash Flows from Operating Activities − Dividends − Net Capital Expenditures

$$\$793,848 - \$0 - \$386,176^* \qquad \$566,447^* - \$0 - \$357,282^*$$

$$= \$407,672 \qquad = \$209,165$$

*These figures are from the statement of cash flows in Starbucks' 2004 10K.
†The 2002 figure is from the five-year selected financial data in Starbucks' 2003 10K.
Source: Data from Starbucks Corporation, 2004 10K and 2003 10K.

Study Note

When the computation for free cash flow uses "net capital expenditures" in place of "purchases of plant assets minus sales of plant assets," it means that the company's sales of plant assets were too small or immaterial to be broken out.

Starbucks' ratios for cash flows to sales and cash flows to assets also improved. While the company's net sales and average total assets increased, the cash flows provided by its operations increased faster. **Cash flows to sales**, or the cash-generating ability of sales, increased from 13.9 to 15.0 percent. **Cash flows to assets**, or the ability of assets to generate operating cash flows, increased from 22.9 to 26.2 percent.

Starbucks' **free cash flow**, the cash remaining after providing for commitments, also increased. While the company's net capital expenditures increased by almost $29 million, the net cash provided by its operating activities increased by more than $227 million. Another factor in Starbucks' free cash flows is that the company pays no dividends. Management's comment with regard to cash flows in the future is as follows:

The Company manages its cash, cash equivalents and liquid investments in order to internally fund operating needs. Cash and cash equivalents increased by $98 million for the fiscal year ended 2004, to $299 million. The Company ended the period with $788 million in total cash, cash equivalents and liquid investments. The Company intends to use its available cash resources to invest in its core businesses and other new business opportunities related to its core businesses. . . . Other than normal operating expenses, cash requirements for fiscal 2005 are expected to consist primarily of capital expenditures related to new Company-operated

▼ EXHIBIT 12

Market Strength Ratios of Starbucks Corporation

	2004	2003
Price/earnings (P/E) ratio: Measure of investors' confidence in a company		
$\dfrac{\text{Market Price per Share}}{\text{Earnings per Share}}$	$\dfrac{\$45.23^*}{\$0.99} = 45.7 \text{ times}$	$\dfrac{\$27.37^*}{\$0.69} = 39.7 \text{ times}$
Dividends yield: Measure of a stock's current return to an investor		
$\dfrac{\text{Dividends per Share}}{\text{Market Price per Share}}$	Starbucks does not pay a dividend.	

*Market price is the average for the fourth quarter reported in Starbucks' 2004 and 2003 annual reports.
Source: Data from Starbucks Corporation, 2004 10K.

retail stores, as well as for the remodeling and refurbishment of existing Company-operated retail stores. Management expects capital expenditures in fiscal 2005 to be in the range of $600 million to $650 million.[8]

Evaluating Market Strength

 Market price is the price at which a company's stock is bought and sold. It indicates how investors view the potential return and risk connected with owning the stock. Market price by itself is not very informative, however, because companies have different numbers of shares outstanding, different earnings, and different dividend policies. Thus, market price must be related to earnings by considering the price/earnings (P/E) ratio and the dividends yield. Those ratios for **Starbucks** appear in Exhibit 12. We computed them by using the average market prices of Starbucks' stock during the fourth quarter of 2003 and 2004.

The **price/earnings (P/E) ratio**, which measures investors' confidence in a company, is the ratio of the market price per share to earnings per share. The P/E ratio is useful in comparing the earnings of different companies and the value of a company's shares in relation to values in the overall market. With a higher P/E ratio, the investor obtains less underlying earnings per dollar invested. Starbucks' P/E ratio increased from 39.7 times in 2003 to 45.7 times in 2004, which signals that investors' had more confidence in the company.

The **dividends yield** measures a stock's current return to an investor in the form of dividends. Because Starbucks pays no dividends, we can conclude that those who invest in the company expect their return to come from increases in the stock's market value.

S T O P • R E V I E W • A P P L Y

3-1. Company A and Company B both have net incomes of $1,000,000. Is it possible to conclude from this information that these companies are equally successful? Why or why not?

3-2. Circo Company has a return on assets of 12 percent and a debt to equity ratio of 0.5. Would you expect return on equity to be more or less than 12 percent?

3-3. Consider the following statement: "Supermarket executives are beginning to look back with some nostalgia on the days when the standard profit margin was 1 percent of sales. Last year the industry overall margin came to a thin 0.72 percent." How could a supermarket earn a satisfactory return on assets with such a small profit margin?

3-4. What amount is common to all cash flow adequacy ratios? To what other groups of ratios are the cash flow adequacy ratios most closely related?

3-5. Which ratios are most relevant to determining the financing period?

3-6. Company J's stock and Company Q's stock have the same market price. How might you determine whether investors are equally confident about the future of these companies?

Effects of Transactions on Ratios   Sasah's, a retail company, engaged in the transactions listed in the first column of the table below. Opposite each transaction is a ratio and space to mark the effect of each transaction on the ratio.

Transaction	Ratio	Increase	Decrease	None
a. Accrued salaries.	Current ratio			
b. Purchased inventory.	Quick ratio			
c. Increased allowance for uncollectible accounts.	Receivable turnover			
d. Purchased inventory on credit.	Payables turnover			
e. Sold treasury stock.	Profit margin			
f. Borrowed cash by issuing bond payable.	Asset turnover			
g. Paid wages expense.	Return on assets			
h. Repaid bond payable.	Debt to equity			
i. Accrued interest expense.	Interest coverage			
k. Sold merchandise on account.	Return on equity			
l. Recorded depreciation expense.	Cash flow yield			
m. Sold equipment.	Free cash flow			

Show that you understand the effect of business activities on performance measures by placing an X in the appropriate column to show whether the transaction increased, decreased, or had no effect on the ratio.

SOLUTION

Transaction	Ratio	Increase	Decrease	None
a. Accrued salaries.	Current ratio		X	
b. Purchased inventory.	Quick ratio		X	
c. Increased allowance for uncollectible accounts.	Receivable turnover	X		
d. Purchased inventory on credit.	Payables turnover		X	
e. Sold treasury stock.	Profit margin			X
f. Borrowed cash by issuing bond payable.	Asset turnover		X	
g. Paid wages expense.	Return on assets		X	
h. Repaid bond payable.	Debt to equity	X		
i. Accrued interest expense.	Interest coverage		X	
k. Sold merchandise on account.	Return on equity	X		
l. Recorded depreciation expense.	Cash flow yield	X		
m. Sold equipment.	Free cash flow	X		

STARBUCKS CORPORATION

To assess a company's financial performance, managers, stockholders, creditors, and other interested parties use measures that are linked to creating shareholder value. The Financial Highlights at the beginning of the chapter show steady increases in **Starbucks'** revenues, earnings, profit margin, and earnings per share—all good signs, but for a comprehensive view of the company's performance, users of its financial statements must consider the following questions:

- **What standards should be used to evaluate Starbucks' performance?**
- **What analytical tools are available to measure performance?**
- **How successful has the company been in creating value for shareholders?**

Starbucks' performance should be compared with the performance of other companies in the same industry—the specialty retail business. In addition, Starbucks' performance in the current year should be compared with its performance in past years. To make this comparison, users of Starbucks' financial statements employ such techniques as horizontal or trend analysis, vertical analysis, and ratio analysis.

Our comprehensive ratio analysis of Starbucks clearly shows that the company's financial condition improved from 2003 to 2004, as measured by its liquidity, profitability, long-term solvency, and cash flow adequacy ratios. This performance resulted in an increase in earnings per share from $.69 to $.99 and an increase in shareholders' value, as represented by an increase in the market price per share from $27 to $45.

CHAPTER REVIEW

REVIEW of Learning Objectives

LO1 Describe the objectives, standards of comparison, sources of information, and compensation issues in measuring financial performance.

A primary objective in management's use of financial performance measurement is to increase the wealth of the company's stockholders. Creditors and investors use financial performance measurement to judge a company's past performance and current position, as well as its future potential and the risk associated with it. Creditors use the information gained from their analyses to make reliable loans that will be repaid with interest. Investors use the information to make investments that will provide a return that is worth the risk.

Three standards of comparison commonly used in evaluating financial performance are rule-of-thumb measures, a company's past performance, and industry norms. Rule-of-thumb measures are weak because of a lack of evidence that they can be widely applied. A company's past performance can offer a guideline for measuring improvement, but it is not helpful in judging performance relative to the performance of other companies. Although the use of industry norms overcomes this last problem, its disadvantage is that firms are not always comparable, even in the same industry.

The main sources of information about public corporations are reports that the corporations publish themselves, such as annual reports and interim financial statements; reports filed with the SEC; business periodicals; and credit and investment advisory services.

In public corporations, a committee made up of independent directors appointed by the board of directors determines the compensation of top executives. Although earnings per share can be regarded as a "bottom-line" number that encompasses all the other performance measures, using it as the sole basis for determining executive compensation may lead to management practices that are not in the best interests of the company or its stockholders.

LO2 Apply horizontal analysis, trend analysis, vertical analysis, and ratio analysis to financial statements.

Horizontal analysis involves the computation of changes in both dollar amounts and percentages from year to year.

Trend analysis is an extension of horizontal analysis in that it calculates percentage changes for several years. The analyst computes the changes by setting a base year equal to 100 and calculating the results for subsequent years as percentages of the base year.

Vertical analysis uses percentages to show the relationship of the component parts of a financial statement to a total figure in the statement. The resulting financial statements, which are expressed entirely in percentages, are called common-size statements.

Ratio analysis is a technique of financial performance evaluation that identifies key relationships between the components of the financial statements. To interpret ratios correctly, the analyst must have a general understanding of the company and its environment, financial data for several years or for several companies, and an understanding of the data underlying the numerators and denominators.

LO3 Apply ratio analysis to financial statements in a comprehensive evaluation of a company's financial performance.

A comprehensive ratio analysis includes the evaluation of a company's liquidity, profitability, long-term solvency, cash flow adequacy, and market strength. The ratios for measuring these characteristics are illustrated in Exhibits 8 through 12.

	A	B	C
1	**Income Statements**		
2	**For the Year Ended December 31, 20xx**		
3	(In thousands, except per share amounts)		
4			
5		**Quik Burger**	**Big Steak**
6	Net sales	$53,000	$86,000
7	Costs and expenses		
8	Cost of goods sold	$37,000	$61,000
9	Selling expenses	7,000	10,000
10	Administrative expenses	4,000	5,000
11	Total costs and expenses	$48,000	$76,000
12	Income from operations	$ 5,000	$10,000
13	Interest expense	1,400	3,200
14	Income before income taxes	$ 3,600	$ 6,800
15	Income taxes	1,800	3,400
16	Net income	$ 1,800	$ 3,400
17	Earnings per share	$ 1.80	$ 1.13

Quik Burger's statement of cash flows shows that it had net cash flows from operations of $2,200,000. Big Steak's statement of cash flows show that its net cash flows from operations were $3,000,000. Net capital expenditures were $2,100,000 for Quik Burger and $1,800,000 for Big Steak. Quik Burger paid dividends of $500,000, and Big Steak paid dividends of $600,000. The market prices of the stocks of Quik Burger and Big Steak were $30 and $20, respectively. Financial information pertaining to prior years is not readily available to Maggie Washington. Assume that all notes payable of these two companies are current liabilities and that all their bonds payable are long-term liabilities.

Required

Perform a comprehensive ratio analysis of both Quik Burger and Big Steak following the steps outlined below. Show dollar amounts in thousands, use end-of-year balances for averages, assume no change in inventory, and round all ratios and percentages to one decimal place.

1. Prepare an analysis of liquidity.
2. Prepare an analysis of profitability.
3. Prepare an analysis of long-term solvency.
4. Prepare an analysis of cash flow adequacy.
5. Prepare an analysis of market strength.
6. In each analysis, indicate the company that apparently had the more favorable ratio. (Consider differences of .1 or less to be neutral.)
7. In what ways would having access to prior years' information aid this analysis?

Answer to Review Problem

	A	B	C	D	E	F	G	H	I	J	K	L
1		**Ratio Name**			**Quik Burger**				**Big Steak**			**6. Company with More Favorable Ratio**
2												
3	**1.**	**Liquidity analysis**										
4												
5	a.	Current ratio		$2,000 + $2,000 + $2,000				$4,500 + $6,500 + $5,000				
6				$2,500 + $1,500				$3,000 + $4,000				
7												
8				$6,000	=	1.5 times		$16,000	=	2.3 times		Big Steak
9				$4,000				$7,000				
10												
11	b.	Quick ratio		$2,000 + $2,000				$4,500 + $6,500				
12				$2,500 + $1,500				$3,000 + $4,000				
13												
14				$4,000	=	1.0 times		$11,000	=	1.6 times		Big Steak
15				$4,000				$7,000				
16												
17	c.	Receivable turnover		$53,000	=	26.5 times		$86,000	=	13.2 times		Quik Burger
18				$2,000				$6,500				
19												
20	d.	Days' sales uncollected		365	=	13.8 days		365	=	27.7 days		Quik Burger
21				26.5				13.2				
22												
23	e.	Inventory turnover		$37,000	=	18.5 times		$61,000	=	12.2 times		Quik Burger
24				$2,000				$5,000				
25												
26	f.	Days' inventory on hand		365	=	19.7 days		365	=	29.9 days		Quik Burger
27				18.5				12.2				
28												
29	g.	Payables turnover		$37,000	=	14.8 times		$61,000	=	20.3 times		Big Steak
30				$2,500				$3,000				
31												
32	h.	Days' payable		365	=	24.7 days		365	=	18.0 days		Big Steak
33				14.8				20.3				
34												
35		* This analysis indicates the company with the apparently more favorable ratio. Class discussion may focus on conditions under which different conclusions may be drawn.										

	A	B	C	D	E	F	G	H	I	J	K	L
1		Ratio Name			Quik Burger				Big Steak			6. Company with More Favorable Ratio
2												
3	2.	Profitability analysis										
4												
5	a.	Profit margin		$1,800	=	3.4%		$3,400	=	4.0%		Big Steak
6				$53,000				$86,000				
7												
8	b.	Asset turnover		$53,000	=	1.8 times		$86,000	=	1.5 times		Quik Burger
9				$30,000				$56,000				
10												
11	c.	Return on assets		$1,800	=	6.0%		$3,400	=	6.1%		Neutral
12				$30,000				$56,000				
13												
14	d.	Return on equity			$1,800				$3,400			
15				$1,000 + $9,000 + $6,000				$3,000 + $9,000 + $7,000				
16												
17				$1,800	=	11.3%		$3,400	=	17.9%		Big Steak
18				$16,000				$19,000				

	A	B	C	D	E	F	G	H	I	J	K	L
1		Ratio Name			Quik Burger				Big Steak			6. Company with More Favorable Ratio
2												
3	3.	Long-term solvency analysis										
4												
5	a.	Debt to equity ratio		$2,500 + $1,500 + $10,000				$3,000 + $4,000 + $30,000				
6				$1,000 + $9,000 + $6,000				$3,000 + $9,000 + $7,000				
7												
8				$14,000	=	.9 times		$37,000	=	1.9 times		Quik Burger
9				$16,000				$19,000				
10												
11	b.	Interest coverage ratio			$3,600 + $1,400				$6,800 + $3,200			
12					$1,400				$3,200			
13												
14				$5,000	=	3.6 times		$10,000	=	3.1 times		Quik Burger
15				$1,400				$3,200				

	A	B	C	D	E	F	G	H	I	J	K	L
1		Ratio Name			Quik Burger				Big Steak			6. Company with More Favorable Ratio
2												
3	4.	Cash flow adequacy analysis										
4												
5	a.	Cash flow yield		$2,200	=	1.2 times		$3,000	=	.9 times		Quik Burger
6				$1,800				$3,400				
7												

(Continued)

	A	B	C	D	E	F	G	H	I	J	K	L
8		Ratio Name		Quik Burger				Big Steak				6. Company with More Favorable Ratio
9												
10	b.	Cash flows to sales		$2,200	=	4.2%		$3,000	=	3.5%		Quik Burger
11				$53,000				$86,000				
12												
13	c.	Cash flows to assets		$2,200	=	7.3%		$3,000	=	5.4%		Quik Burger
14				$30,000				$56,000				
15												
16	d.	Free cash flow		$2,200 - $500 - $2,100				$3,000 - $600 - $1,800				Big Steak
17				= ($400)				= $600				

	A	B	C	D	E	F	G	H	I	J	K	L
1		Ratio Name		Quik Burger				Big Steak				6. Company with More Favorable Ratio
2												
3	5.	Market strength analysis										
4												
5	a.	Price/earnings ratio		$30	=	16.7 times		$20	=	17.7 times		Big Steak
6				$1.80				$1.13				
7												
8	b.	Dividends yield		$500,000/1,000,000	=	1.7%		$600,000/3,000,000	=	1.0%		Quik Burger
9				$30				$20				

7. Prior years' information would be helpful in two ways. First, turnover, return, and cash flows to assets ratios could be based on average amounts. Second, a trend analysis could be performed for each company.

CHAPTER ASSIGNMENTS

BUILDING Your Basic Knowledge and Skills

Short Exercises

LO1 Objectives and Standards of Financial Performance Evaluation

SE 1. Indicate whether each of the following items is (a) an objective or (b) a standard of comparison of financial statement analysis:

1. Industry norms
2. Assessment of a company's past performance
3. The company's past performance
4. Assessment of future potential and related risk
5. Rule-of-thumb measures

LO1 Sources of Information

SE 2. For each piece of information in the list that follows, indicate whether the best source would be (a) reports published by the company, (b) SEC reports, (c) business periodicals, or (d) credit and investment advisory services.

1. Current market value of a company's stock
2. Management's analysis of the past year's operations
3. Objective assessment of a company's financial performance
4. Most complete body of financial disclosures
5. Current events affecting the company

LO2   **Trend Analysis**

SE 3. Using 20x6 as the base year, prepare a trend analysis for the following data, and tell whether the results suggest a favorable or unfavorable trend. (Round your answers to one decimal place.)

	20x8	20x7	20x6
Net sales	$316,000	$272,000	$224,000
Accounts receivable (net)	86,000	64,000	42,000

LO2   **Horizontal Analysis**

SE 4. The comparative income statements and balance sheets of Obras, Inc., appear on the opposite page. Compute the amount and percentage changes for the income statements, and comment on the changes from 20x6 to 20x7. (Round the percentage changes to one decimal place.)

LO2   **Vertical Analysis**

SE 5. Express the comparative balance sheets of Obras, Inc., as common-size statements, and comment on the changes from 20x6 to 20x7. (Round computations to one decimal place.)

LO3   **Liquidity Analysis**

SE 6. Using the information for Obras, Inc., in **SE 4** and **SE 5**, compute the current ratio, quick ratio, receivable turnover, days' sales uncollected, inventory turnover, days' inventory on hand, payables turnover, and days' payable for 20x6 and 20x7. Inventories were $8,000 in 20x5, $10,000 in 20x6, and $14,000 in 20x7. Accounts receivable were $12,000 in 20x5, $16,000 in 20x6, and $20,000 in 20x7. Accounts payable were $18,000 in 20x5, $20,000 in 20x6, and $24,000 in 20x7. The company had no marketable securities or prepaid assets. Comment on the results. (Round computations to one decimal place.)

LO3   **Profitability Analysis**

SE 7. Using the information for Obras, Inc., in **SE 4** and **SE 5**, compute the profit margin, asset turnover, return on assets, and return on equity for 20x6 and 20x7. In 2005, total assets were $200,000 and total stockholders' equity was $60,000. Comment on the results. (Round computations to one decimal place.)

LO3   **Long-term Solvency Analysis**

SE 8. Using the information for Obras, Inc., in **SE 4** and **SE 5**, compute the debt to equity ratio and the interest coverage ratio for 20x6 and 20x7. Comment on the results. (Round computations to one decimal place.)

Obras, Inc.
Comparative Income Statements
For the Years Ended December 31, 20x7 and 20x6

	20x7	20x6
Net sales	$360,000	$290,000
Cost of goods sold	224,000	176,000
Gross margin	$136,000	$114,000
Operating expenses	80,000	60,000
Operating income	$ 56,000	$ 54,000
Interest expense	14,000	10,000
Income before income taxes	$ 42,000	$ 44,000
Income taxes expense	14,000	16,000
Net income	$ 28,000	$ 28,000
Earnings per share	$ 2.80	$ 2.80

Obras, Inc.
Comparative Balance Sheets
December 31, 20x7 and 20x6

	20x7	20x6
Assets		
Current assets	$ 48,000	$ 40,000
Property, plant, and equipment (net)	260,000	200,000
Total assets	$308,000	$240,000
Liabilities and Stockholders' Equity		
Current liabilities	$ 36,000	$ 44,000
Long-term liabilities	180,000	120,000
Stockholders' equity	92,000	76,000
Total liabilities and stockholders' equity	$308,000	$240,000

LO3 **Cash Flow Adequacy Analysis**

SE 9. Using the information for Obras, Inc., in **SE 4**, **SE 5**, and **SE 7**, compute the cash flow yield, cash flows to sales, cash flows to assets, and free cash flow for 20x6 and 20x7. Net cash flows from operating activities were $42,000 in 20x6 and $32,000 in 20x7. Net capital expenditures were $60,000 in 20x6 and $80,000 in 20x7. Cash dividends were $12,000 in both years. Comment on the results. (Round computations to one decimal place.)

LO3 **Market Strength Analysis**

SE 10. Using the information for Obras, Inc., in **SE 4**, **SE 5**, and **SE 9**, compute the price/earnings (P/E) ratio and dividends yield for 20x6 and 20x7. The company had 10,000 shares of common stock outstanding in both years. The price of Obras' common stock was $60 in 20x6 and $40 in 20x7. Comment on the results. (Round computations to one decimal place.)

Exercises

LO1, LO2 **Discussion Questions**

E 1. Develop brief answers to each of the following questions:

1. Why is it essential that management compensation, including bonuses, be linked to financial goals and strategies that achieve shareholder value?
2. How are past performance and industry norms useful in evaluating a company's performance? What are their limitations?
3. In a five-year trend analysis, why do the dollar values remain the same for their respective years while the percentages usually change when a new five-year period is chosen?

LO3 **Discussion Questions**

E 2. Develop brief answers to each of the following questions:

1. Why does a decrease in receivable turnover create the need for cash from operating activities?
2. Why would ratios that include one balance sheet account and one income statement account, such as receivable turnover or return on assets, be questionable if they came from quarterly or other interim financial reports?
3. Can you suggest a limitation of free cash flow in comparing one company to another?

LO1 **Issues in Financial Performance Evaluation: Objectives, Standards, Sources of Information, and Executive Compensation**

E 3. Identify each of the following as (a) an objective of financial statement analysis, (b) a standard for financial statement analysis, (c) a source of information for financial statement analysis, or (d) an executive compensation issue:

1. Average ratios of other companies in the same industry
2. Assessment of the future potential of an investment
3. Interim financial statements
4. Past ratios of the company
5. SEC Form 10-K
6. Assessment of risk
7. A company's annual report
8. Linking performance to shareholder value

LO2 **Trend Analysis**

E 4. Using 20x3 as the base year, prepare a trend analysis of the following data, and tell whether the situation shown by the trends is favorable or unfavorable. (Round your answers to one decimal place.)

	20x7	20x6	20x5	20x4	20x3
Net sales	$51,040	$47,960	$48,400	$45,760	$44,000
Cost of goods sold	34,440	30,800	31,080	29,400	28,000
General and administrative expenses	10,560	10,368	10,176	9,792	9,600
Operating income	6,040	6,792	7,144	6,568	6,400

LO2 **Horizontal Analysis**

E 5. Compute the amount and percentage changes for the following balance sheets, and comment on the changes from 20x6 to 20x7. (Round the percentage changes to one decimal place.)

Davis Company
Comparative Balance Sheets
December 31, 20x7 and 20x6

	20x7	20x6
Assets		
Current assets	$ 18,600	$ 12,800
Property, plant, and equipment (net)	109,464	97,200
Total assets	$128,064	$110,000
Liabilities and Stockholders' Equity		
Current liabilities	$ 11,200	$ 3,200
Long-term liabilities	35,000	40,000
Stockholders' equity	81,864	66,800
Total liabilities and stockholders' equity	$128,064	$110,000

LO2 **Vertical Analysis**

E 6. Express the partial comparative income statements that follow as common-size statements, and comment on the changes from 20x6 to 20x7. (Round computations to one decimal place.)

Davis Company
Partial Comparative Income Statements
For the Years Ended December 31, 20x7 and 20x6

	20x7	20x6
Net sales	$212,000	$184,000
Cost of goods sold	127,200	119,600
Gross margin	$ 84,800	$ 64,400
Selling expenses	$ 53,000	$ 36,800
General expenses	25,440	18,400
Total operating expenses	$ 78,440	$ 55,200
Operating income	$ 6,360	$ 9,200

LO3 **Liquidity Analysis**

K/R **E 7.** Partial comparative balance sheet and income statement information for Allen Company is as follows:

	20x8	20x7
Cash	$ 13,600	$ 10,400
Marketable securities	7,200	17,200
Accounts receivable (net)	44,800	35,600
Inventory	54,400	49,600
Total current assets	$120,000	$112,800
Accounts payable	$ 40,000	$ 28,200
Net sales	$322,560	$220,720
Cost of goods sold	217,600	203,360
Gross margin	$104,960	$ 17,360

In 20x6, the year-end balances for Accounts Receivable and Inventory were $32,400 and $51,200, respectively. Accounts Payable was $30,600 in 20x6 and is the only current liability. Compute the current ratio, quick ratio, receivable turnover, days' sales uncollected, inventory turnover, days' inventory on hand, payables turnover, and days' payable for each year. (Round computations to one decimal place.) Comment on the change in the company's liquidity position, including its operating cycle and required days of financing from 20x7 to 20x8.

LO3 **Turnover Analysis**

E 8. Diamond Tuxedo Rental has been in business for four years. Because the company has recently had a cash flow problem, management wonders whether there is a problem with receivables or inventories. Here are selected figures from the company's financial statements (in thousands):

	20x8	20x7	20x6	20x5
Net sales	$144.0	$112.0	$96.0	$80.0
Cost of goods sold	90.0	72.0	60.0	48.0
Accounts receivable (net)	24.0	20.0	16.0	12.0
Merchandise inventory	28.0	22.0	16.0	10.0
Accounts payable	13.0	10.0	8.0	5.0

Compute the receivable turnover, inventory turnover, and payables turnover for each of the four years, and comment on the results relative to the cash flow problem that the firm has been experiencing. Merchandise inventory was $11,000, accounts receivable were $11,000, and accounts payable were $4,000 in 20x4. (Round computations to one decimal place.)

LO3 **Profitability Analysis**

E 9. Barr Company had total assets of $320,000 in 20x5, $340,000 in 20x6, and $380,000 in 20x7. Its debt to equity ratio was .67 times in all three years. In 20x6, Barr had net income of $38,556 on revenues of $612,000. In 20x7, it had net income of $49,476 on revenues of $798,000. Compute the profit margin, asset turnover, return on assets, and return on equity for 20x6 and 20x7. Comment on the apparent cause of the increase or decrease in profitability. (Round the percentages and other ratios to one decimal place.)

LO3 **Long-term Solvency and Market Strength Ratios**

E 10. An investor is considering investing in the long-term bonds and common stock of Companies M and N. Both firms operate in the same industry. Both also pay a dividend per share of $8 and have a yield of 10 percent on their long-term bonds. Other data for the two firms are as follows:

	Company M	Company N
Total assets	$4,800,000	$2,160,000
Total liabilities	2,160,000	1,188,000
Income before income taxes	576,000	259,200
Interest expense	194,400	106,920
Earnings per share	6.40	10.00
Market price of common stock	80	95

Compute the debt to equity, interest coverage, and price/earnings (P/E) ratios, as well as the dividends yield, and comment on the results. (Round computations to one decimal place.)

LO3 Cash Flow Adequacy Analysis

E 11. Using the data below from the financial statements of Braugh, Inc., compute the company's cash flow yield, cash flows to sales, cash flows to assets, and free cash flow. (Round computations to one decimal place.)

Net sales	$3,200,000
Net income	352,000
Net cash flows from operating activities	456,000
Total assets, beginning of year	2,890,000
Total assets, end of year	3,120,000
Cash dividends	120,000
Net capital expenditures	298,000

Problems

LO2 Horizontal and Vertical Analysis

P 1. Sanborn Corporation's condensed comparative income statements for 20x8 and 20x7 appear below. The corporation's condensed comparative balance sheets for 20x8 and 20x7 appear on the next page.

Sanborn Corporation Comparative Income Statements For the Years Ended December 31, 20x8 and 20x7		
	20x8	**20x7**
Net sales	$3,276,800	$3,146,400
Cost of goods sold	2,088,800	2,008,400
Gross margin	$1,188,000	$1,138,000
Operating expenses		
Selling expenses	$ 476,800	$ 518,000
Administrative expenses	447,200	423,200
Total operating expenses	$ 924,000	$ 941,200
Income from operations	$ 264,000	$ 196,800
Interest expense	65,600	39,200
Income before income taxes	$ 198,400	$ 157,600
Income taxes expense	62,400	56,800
Net income	$ 136,000	$ 100,800
Earnings per share	$ 3.40	$ 2.52

Required

1. Prepare schedules showing the amount and percentage changes from 20x7 to 20x8 for the comparative income statements and the balance sheets.
2. Prepare common-size income statements and balance sheets for 20x7 and 20x8.

Sanborn Corporation
Comparative Balance Sheets
December 31, 20x8 and 20x7

	20x8	20x7
Assets		
Cash	$ 81,200	$ 40,800
Accounts receivable (net)	235,600	229,200
Inventory	574,800	594,800
Property, plant, and equipment (net)	750,000	720,000
Total assets	$1,641,600	$1,584,800
Liabilities and Stockholders' Equity		
Accounts payable	$ 267,600	$ 477,200
Notes payable	200,000	400,000
Bonds payable	400,000	—
Common stock, $10 par value	400,000	400,000
Retained earnings	374,000	307,600
Total liabilities and stockholders' equity	$1,641,600	$1,584,800

3. **User Insight:** Comment on the results in requirements 1 and 2 by identifying favorable and unfavorable changes in the components and composition of the statements.

LO3 Effects of Transactions on Ratios

P 2. Koz Corporation engaged in the transactions listed in the first column of the following table. Opposite each transaction is a ratio and space to indicate the effect of each transaction on the ratio.

			Effect	
Transaction	**Ratio**	**Increase**	**Decrease**	**None**
a. Sold merchandise on account.	Current ratio			
b. Sold merchandise on account.	Inventory turnover			
c. Collected on accounts receivable.	Quick ratio			
d. Wrote off an uncollectible account.	Receivable turnover			
e. Paid on accounts payable.	Current ratio			
f. Declared cash dividend.	Return on equity			
g. Incurred advertising expense.	Profit margin			
h. Issued stock dividend.	Debt to equity ratio			
i. Issued bonds payable.	Asset turnover			
j. Accrued interest expense.	Current ratio			
k. Paid previously declared cash dividend.	Dividends yield			
l. Purchased treasury stock.	Return on assets			
m. Recorded depreciation expense.	Cash flow yield			

Required

User Insight: Show that you understand the effect of business activities on performance measures by placing an X in the appropriate column to show whether the transaction increased, decreased, or had no effect on the indicated ratio.

LO3 **Comprehensive Ratio Analysis**

P 3. Data for Sanborn Corporation in 20x8 and 20x7 follow. These data should be used in conjunction with the data in **P 1**.

	20x8	20x7
Net cash flows from operating activities	($196,000)	$144,000
Net capital expenditures	$40,000	$65,000
Dividends paid	$44,000	$34,400
Number of common shares	40,000,000	40,000,000
Market price per share	$18	$30

Selected balances at the end of 20x6 were accounts receivable (net), $206,800; inventory, $547,200; total assets, $1,465,600; accounts payable, $386,600; and stockholders' equity, $641,200. All Sanborn's notes payable were current liabilities; all its bonds payable were long-term liabilities.

Required

Perform a comprehensive ratio analysis following the steps outlined below. Round all answers to one decimal place.

1. Prepare a liquidity analysis by calculating for each year the (a) current ratio, (b) quick ratio, (c) receivable turnover, (d) days' sales uncollected, (e) inventory turnover, (f) days' inventory on hand, (g) payables turnover, and (h) days' payable.
2. Prepare a profitability analysis by calculating for each year the (a) profit margin, (b) asset turnover, (c) return on assets, and (d) return on equity.
3. Prepare a long-term solvency analysis by calculating for each year the (a) debt to equity ratio and (b) interest coverage ratio.
4. Prepare a cash flow adequacy analysis by calculating for each year the (a) cash flow yield, (b) cash flows to sales, (c) cash flows to assets, and (d) free cash flow.
5. Prepare a market strength analysis by calculating for each year the (a) price/earnings (P/E) ratio and (b) dividends yield.
6. **User Insight:** After making the calculations, indicate whether each ratio improved or deteriorated from 20x7 to 20x8 (use F for favorable and U for unfavorable and consider changes of .1 or less to be neutral).

LO3 **Comprehensive Ratio Analysis of Two Companies**

P 4. Ginger Adair is considering an investment in the common stock of a chain of retail department stores. She has narrowed her choice to two retail companies, Lewis Corporation and Ramsey Corporation, whose income statements and balance sheets are presented on the next page.

During the year, Lewis Corporation paid a total of $100,000 in dividends. The market price per share of its stock is currently $60. In comparison, Ramsey Corporation paid a total of $228,000 in dividends, and the current market price of its stock is $76 per share. Lewis Corporation had net cash flows from operations of $543,000 and net capital expenditures of $1,250,000. Ramsey Corporation had net cash flows from operations of $985,000 and net capital expenditures of $2,100,000. Information for prior years is not readily available. Assume that all notes payable are current liabilities and all bonds payable are long-term liabilities and that there is no change in inventory.

Income Statements

	Lewis	Ramsey
Net sales	$25,120,000	$50,420,000
Costs and expenses		
Cost of goods sold	$12,284,000	$29,668,000
Selling expenses	9,645,200	14,216,400
Administrative expenses	1,972,000	4,868,000
Total costs and expenses	$23,901,200	$48,752,400
Income from operations	$ 1,218,800	$ 1,667,600
Interest expense	388,000	456,000
Income before income taxes	$ 830,800	$ 1,211,600
Income taxes expense	400,000	600,000
Net income	$ 430,800	$ 611,600
Earnings per share	$ 4.31	$ 10.19

Balance Sheets

	Lewis	Ramsey
Assets		
Cash	$ 160,000	$ 384,800
Marketable securities (at cost)	406,800	169,200
Accounts receivable (net)	1,105,600	1,970,800
Inventory	1,259,600	2,506,800
Prepaid expenses	108,800	228,000
Property, plant, and equipment (net)	5,827,200	13,104,000
Intangibles and other assets	1,106,400	289,600
Total assets	$9,974,400	$18,653,200
Liabilities and Stockholders' Equity		
Accounts payable	$ 688,000	$ 1,145,200
Notes payable	300,000	800,000
Income taxes payable	100,400	146,800
Bonds payable	4,000,000	4,000,000
Common stock, $20 par value	2,000,000	1,200,000
Additional paid-in capital	1,219,600	7,137,200
Retained earnings	1,666,400	4,224,000
Total liabilities and stockholders' equity	$9,974,400	$18,653,200

Required

Conduct a comprehensive ratio analysis for each company, using the available information. Compare the results. Round percentages and ratios to one decimal place, and consider changes of .1 or less to be indeterminate.

1. Prepare a liquidity analysis by calculating for each company the (a) current ratio, (b) quick ratio, (c) receivable turnover, (d) days' sales uncollected,

(e) inventory turnover, (f) days' inventory on hand, (g) payables turnover, and (h) days' payable.

2. Prepare a profitability analysis by calculating for each company the (a) profit margin, (b) asset turnover, (c) return on assets, and (d) return on equity.

3. Prepare a long-term solvency analysis by calculating for each company the (a) debt to equity ratio and (b) interest coverage ratio.

4. Prepare a cash flow adequacy analysis by calculating for each company the (a) cash flow yield, (b) cash flows to sales, (c) cash flows to assets, and (d) free cash flow.

5. Prepare an analysis of market strength by calculating for each company the (a) price/earnings (P/E) ratio and (b) dividends yield.

6. **User Insight:** Compare the two companies by inserting the ratio calculations from 1 through 5 in a table with the following column headings: Ratio, Name, Lewis, Ramsey, and Company with More Favorable Ratio. Indicate in the last column which company had the more favorable ratio in each case.

7. **User Insight:** How could the analysis be improved if information about these companies' prior years were available?

Alternate Problems

LO3 **Effects of Transactions on Ratios**

P 5. Benson Corporation, a clothing retailer, engaged in the transactions listed in the first column of the table below. Opposite each transaction is a ratio and space to mark the effect of each transaction on the ratio.

		Effect		
Transaction	**Ratio**	**Increase**	**Decrease**	**None**
a. Issued common stock for cash.	Asset turnover			
b. Declared cash dividend.	Current ratio			
c. Sold treasury stock.	Return on equity			
d. Borrowed cash by issuing note payable.	Debt to equity ratio			
e. Paid salaries expense.	Inventory turnover			
f. Purchased merchandise for cash.	Current ratio			
g. Sold equipment for cash.	Receivable turnover			
h. Sold merchandise on account.	Quick ratio			
i. Paid current portion of long-term debt.	Return on assets			
j. Gave sales discount.	Profit margin			
k. Purchased marketable securities for cash.	Quick ratio			
l. Declared 5% stock dividend.	Current ratio			
m. Purchased a building.	Free cash flow			

Required

User Insight: Show that you understand the effect of business activities on performance measures by placing an X in the appropriate column to show whether the transaction increased, decreased, or had no effect on the indicated ratio.

LO3 **Comprehensive Ratio Analysis**

P 6. The condensed comparative income statements and balance sheets of Basie Corporation appear on the next page. All figures are given in thousands of dollars, except earnings per share.

Basie Corporation
Comparative Income Statements
For the Years Ended December 31, 20x8 and 20x7

	20x8	20x7
Net sales	$800,400	$742,600
Cost of goods sold	454,100	396,200
Gross margin	$346,300	$346,400
Operating expenses		
Selling expenses	$130,100	$104,600
Administrative expenses	140,300	115,500
Total operating expenses	$270,400	$220,100
Income from operations	$ 75,900	$126,300
Interest expense	25,000	20,000
Income before income taxes	$ 50,900	$106,300
Income taxes expense	14,000	35,000
Net income	$ 36,900	$ 71,300
Earnings per share	$ 1.23	$ 2.38

Basie Corporation
Comparative Balance Sheets
December 31, 20x8 and 20x7

	20x8	20x7
Assets		
Cash	$ 31,100	$ 27,200
Accounts receivable (net)	72,500	42,700
Inventory	122,600	107,800
Property, plant, and equipment (net)	577,700	507,500
Total assets	$803,900	$685,200
Liabilities and Stockholders' Equity		
Accounts payable	$104,700	$ 72,300
Notes payable	50,000	50,000
Bonds payable	200,000	110,000
Common stock, $10 par value	300,000	300,000
Retained earnings	149,200	152,900
Total liabilities and stockholders' equity	$803,900	$685,200

Additional data for Basie Corporation in 20x8 and 20x7 follow.

	20x8	20x7
Net cash flows from operating activities	$64,000	$99,000
Net capital expenditures	$119,000	$38,000
Dividends paid	$31,400	$35,000
Number of common shares	30,000	30,000
Market price per share	$40	$60

Balances of selected accounts at the end of 20x6 were accounts receivable (net), $52,700; inventory, $99,400; accounts payable, $64,800; total assets, $647,800; and stockholder's equity, $376,600. All of the bonds payable were long-term liabilities.

Required

Perform the following analyses. Round percentages and ratios to one decimal place.

1. Prepare a liquidity analysis by calculating for each year the (a) current ratio, (b) quick ratio, (c) receivable turnover, (d) days' sales uncollected, (e) inventory turnover, (f) days' inventory on hand, (g) payables turnover, and (h) days' payable.
2. Prepare a profitability analysis by calculating for each year the (a) profit margin, (b) asset turnover, (c) return on assets, and (d) return on equity.
3. Prepare a long-term solvency analysis by calculating for each year the (a) debt to equity ratio and (b) interest coverage ratio.
4. Prepare a cash flow adequacy analysis by calculating for each year the (a) cash flow yield, (b) cash flows to sales, (c) cash flows to assets, and (d) free cash flow.
5. Prepare an analysis of market strength by calculating for each year the (a) price/earnings (P/E) ratio and (b) dividends yield.
6. **User Insight:** After making the calculations, indicate whether each ratio improved or deteriorated from 20x7 to 20x8 (use F for favorable and U for unfavorable and consider changes of .1 or less to be neutral).

≡ ENHANCING Your Knowledge, Skills, and Critical Thinking

Conceptual Understanding Cases

LO1, LO3   **Standards for Financial Performance Evaluation**

K/R   **C 1.** In a dramatic move, **Standard & Poor's Ratings Group**, the large financial company that evaluates the riskiness of companies' debt, downgraded its rating of **General Motors** and **Ford Motor Co**. debt to "junk" bond status because of concerns about the companies' profitability and cash flows. Despite aggressive cost cutting, both companies still face substantial future liabilities for health-care and pension obligations. They are losing money or barely breaking even on auto operations that concentrate on slow-selling SUVs. High gas prices and competition force them to sell the cars at a discount. The companies are counting on SUVs to make a comeback.[9] What standards do you think Standard & Poor's would use to evaluate Ford's progress? What performance measures would Standard & Poor's most likely use in making its evaluation?

LO1   **Using Segment Information**

C 2. Refer to Exhibit 1, which shows the segment information of **Goodyear Tire & Rubber Company**. In what business segments does Goodyear operate? What is the relative size of its business segments in terms of sales and income in the most recent year shown? Which segment is most profitable in terms of return on assets? In which region of the world is the tires segment largest, and which tire segment is most profitable in terms of return on assets?

LO1   **Using Investors' Services**

K/R   **C 3.** Refer to Exhibit 2, which contains the **PepsiCo Inc**. listing from Mergent's *Handbook of Dividend Achievers*. Assume that an investor has asked you to assess

PepsiCo's recent history and prospects. Write a memorandum to the investor that addresses the following points:

1. PepsiCo's earnings history. What has been the general relationship between PepsiCo's return on assets and its return on equity over the last seven years? What does this tell you about the way the company is financed? What figures back up your conclusion?
2. The trend of PepsiCo's stock price and price/earnings (P/E) ratio for the seven years shown.
3. PepsiCo's prospects, including developments likely to affect the company's future.

Interpreting Financial Reports

LO2   **Trend Analysis**

C 4. **H. J. Heinz Company** is a global company engaged in several lines of business, including food service, infant foods, condiments, pet foods, and weight-control food products. Below is a five-year summary of operations and other related data for Heinz.[10] (Amounts are expressed in thousands.)

H. J. Heinz Company and Subsidiaries
Five-Year Summary of Operations and Other Related Data

	2004	2003	2002	2001	2000
Summary of operations					
Sales	$8,414,538	$8,236,836	$7,614,036	$6,987,698	$6,892,807
Cost of products sold	5,326,281	5,304,362	4,858,087	4,407,267	4,356,965
Interest expense	211,826	223,532	230,611	262,488	206,996
Provision for income taxes	389,618	313,372	375,339	190,495	508,546
Net income (before special items)	778,933	477,547	675,181	548,650	780,145
Other related data					
Dividends paid: common	379,910	521,592	562,547	537,290	513,756
Total assets	9,877,189	9,224,751	10,278,354	9,035,150	8,850,697
Total debt	4,974,430	4,930,929	5,345,613	4,885,687	4,112,401
Shareholders' equity	1,894,189	1,199,157	1,718,616	1,373,727	1,595,856

Prepare a trend analysis for Heinz with 2000 as the base year and discuss the results. Identify important trends and state whether the trends are favorable or unfavorable. Discuss significant relationships among the trends.

Decision Analysis Using Excel

LO2, LO3   **Effect of a One-Time Item on a Loan Decision**

K/R   **C 5.** Apple a Day, Inc., and Unforgettable Edibles, Inc. are food catering businesses that operate in the same metropolitan area. Their customers include Fortune 500 companies, regional firms, and individuals. The two firms reported similar profit margins for the current year, and both base bonuses for managers on the achievement of a target profit margin and return on equity. Each firm has submitted a loan request to you, a loan officer for City National Bank. They have provided you with the following information:

	Apple a Day	Unforgettable Edibles
Net sales	$625,348	$717,900
Cost of goods sold	225,125	287,080
Gross margin	$400,223	$430,820
Operating expenses	281,300	371,565
Operating income	$118,923	$ 59,255
Gain on sale of real estate	—	81,923
Interest expense	(9,333)	(15,338)
Income before income taxes	$109,590	$125,840
Income taxes expense	25,990	29,525
Net income	$ 83,600	$ 96,315
Average stockholders' equity	$312,700	$390,560

1. Perform a vertical analysis and prepare a common-size income statement for each firm. Compute profit margin and return on equity.
2. Discuss these results, the bonus plan for management, and loan considerations. Identify the company that is the better loan risk.

Annual Report Case: CVS Corporation

LO3 **Comprehensive Ratio Analysis**

C 6. Using data from the **CVS Corporation** annual report in the Supplement to Chapter 1, conduct a comprehensive ratio analysis that compares the company's performance in 2004 and 2003. If you have computed ratios for CVS in previous chapters, you may prepare a table that summarizes the ratios and show calculations only for the ratios not previously calculated. If this is the first ratio analysis you have done for CVS, show all your computations. In either case, after each group of ratios, comment on the performance of CVS. Round your calculations to one decimal place. Prepare and comment on the following categories of ratios:

Liquidity analysis: current ratio, quick ratio, receivable turnover, days' sales uncollected, inventory turnover, days' inventory on hand, payables turnover, and days' payable. (Accounts Receivable, Inventories, and Accounts Payable were [in millions] $1,019.3, $4,013.9, and $1,707.9, respectively, in 2002.)

Profitability analysis: profit margin, asset turnover, return on assets, and return on equity. (Total assets and total shareholders' equity were [in millions] $9,645.3 and $5,197.0, respectively, in 2002.)

Long-term solvency analysis: debt to equity ratio and interest coverage ratio.

Cash flow adequacy analysis: cash flow yield, cash flows to sales, cash flows to assets, and free cash flow.

Market strength analysis: price/earnings (P/E) ratio and dividends yield.

Comparison Case: CVS Versus Southwest

LO3 **Comparison of Key Financial Performance Measures**

C 7. Refer to the annual report of **CVS Corporation** and the financial statements of **Southwest Airlines Co.** in the Supplement to Chapter 1. Prepare a table for the following key financial performance measures for the two most recent years for both companies. Use your computations in **C6** or perform those analyses if you have not done so. Total assets for Southwest in 2002 were $8,954 million.

Profitability:	profit margin
	asset turnover
	return on assets
Long-term solvency:	debt to equity ratio
Cash flow adequacy:	cash flow yield
	free cash flow

Evaluate and comment on the relative performance of the two companies with respect to each of the above categories.

Ethical Dilemma Case

LO1 **Executive Compensation**

C 8. Executive compensation is often based on meeting certain targets for revenue growth, earnings, earnings per share, return on assets, or other performance measures. But what if performance is not living up to expectations? Some companies are simply changing the targets. For instance, **Sun Microsystems'** proxy as quoted in *The Wall Street Journal* states that "due to economic challenges experienced during the last fiscal year, our earnings per share and revenues are significantly below plan. As such, the Bonus Plan was amended to reduce the target bonus to 50% of the original plan and base the target bonus solely on the third and fourth quarters."[11] Sun Microsystems was not alone. Other companies, such as **AT&T Wireless**, **Estee Lauder**, and **UST**, also lowered targets for executive bonuses. Do you think it is acceptable to change the bonus targets for executives during the year if the year turns out to be not as successful as planned? What if an unexpected negative event like 9/11 happens? What are three standards of comparison? Which of these might justify changing the bonus targets during the year?

Internet Case

LO1 **Using Investors' Services**

C 9. Go to the website for **Moody's Investors Service**. Click on "ratings," which will show revisions of debt ratings issued by Moody's in the past few days. Choose a rating that has been upgraded or downgraded and read the short press announcement related to it. What reasons does Moody's give for the change in rating? What is Moody's assessment of the future of the company or institution? What financial performance measures are mentioned in the article? Summarize your findings and be prepared to share them in class.

Group Activity Case

LO3 **Analyzing the Airline Industry**

C 10. Divide into groups. Assume your group is analyzing the fate of the larger airlines, such as **United** and **American**. You have the following information:

a. Between 1999 and now, the long-term debt, including lease obligations, of the largest airlines more than doubled.
b. The price of fuel has increased by one-third.
c. Passenger loads are only now getting back to pre-9/11 levels.
d. Severe price competition from discount airlines exists.

Identify the ratios that you consider most important to consider in assessing the future of the large airlines and discuss the effect of each of the above factors on the ratios. Be prepared to present all or part of your findings in class.

Business Communication Case

LO3   Comparison of International Companies' Operating Cycles

K/R   **C 11.** Ratio analysis enables one to compare the performance of companies whose financial statements are presented in different currencies. Selected data from 2004 for two large pharmaceutical companies—one American, **Pfizer, Inc.**, and one Swiss, **Roche**—are presented below (in millions).[12]

	Pfizer, Inc. (U.S.)	Roche (Swiss)
Net sales	$52,516	SF29,522
Cost of goods sold	7,541	6,556
Accounts receivable	9,367	6,781
Inventories	6,660	4,574
Accounts payable	2,672	1,844

For each company, calculate the receivable turnover, days' sales uncollected, inventory turnover, days' inventory on hand, payables turnover, and days' payable. Then determine the operating cycle and days of financing required for each company. (Accounts receivable in 2003 were $8,636 for Pfizer and SF6,774 for Roche. Inventories in 2003 were $5,699 for Pfizer and SF5,025 for Roche. Accounts payable in 2003 were $2,587 for Pfizer and SF1,700 for Roche.) Prepare a memo containing your analysis of the operating cycles of these companies.

15

Investments

Many companies invest in the stock or debt securities of other firms. They may do so for several reasons. A company may temporarily have excess funds on which it can earn a return, or investments may be an integral part of its business, as in the case of a bank. A company may also invest in other firms for the purpose of partnering with or controlling them. This chapter presents an overview of both short-term and long-term investments, including the importance of avoiding unethical trading in securities.

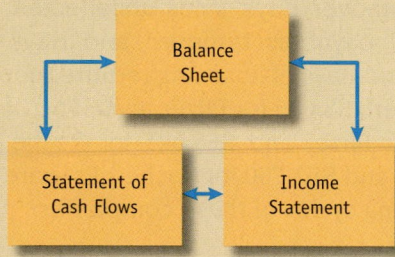

- **What are the effects of eBay's investments on its financial performance?**

- **How does eBay's acquisition of other companies affect its financial performance?**

eBay, the world's largest online trading company, enables a global community of buyers and sellers to interact and trade with one another. Since the company went public in 1998, it has grown very rapidly. In addition to having expanded its core business, it has grown by investing in and acquiring other companies. It has also invested cash in the debt securities of other companies. As you can see in eBay's Financial Highlights, these investments and the related accounts are important components of its financial statements.[1]

eBAY'S FINANCIAL HIGHLIGHTS
(In millions)

	2004	2003
Balance sheet		
Short-term investments	$ 682	$ 340
Long-term investments	1,266	934
Goodwill	2,710	1,719
Total assets	7,991	5,820
Income Statement		
Interest and other income, net	$ 78	$ 38
Income from operations	1,059	629
Statement of Cash Flows		
Cash flows from investing activities		
Purchases of investments	($1,755)	($2,035)
Sales of investments	1,079	1,297
Acquisitions, net of cash required	(1,036)	(216)

Management Issues Related to Investments

LO1 Identify and explain the management issues related to investments.

n making investments, **eBay's** management, like the management of any company, must understand issues related to the recognition, valuation, classification, disclosure, and ethics of investments.

Recognition

Recognition of investments as assets follows the general rule for recording transactions that we described earlier in the text. Purchases of investments are recorded on the date on which they are made, and sales of investments are reported on the date of sale. At the time of the transaction, there is either a transfer of funds or a definite obligation to pay. Income from investments is reported as other income on the income statement. Any gains or losses on investments are also reported on the income statement. Gains and losses appear as adjustments in the operating activities section of the statement of cash flows. The cash amounts of purchases and sales of investments appear in the investing activities section of the statement of cash flows.

Valuation

Like other purchase transactions, investments are valued according to the *cost principle*—that is, they are valued in terms of their cost at the time they are purchased. The cost, or purchase price, includes any commissions or fees. However, after the purchase, the value of investments on the balance sheet is adjusted to reflect subsequent conditions. These conditions may reflect changes in the market value or fair value of the investments, changes caused by the passage of time (as in amortization), or changes in the operations of the investee companies. Long-term investments must be evaluated annually for any impairment or decline in value that is more than temporary. If such an impairment exists, a loss on the investment must be recorded.

Classification

Investments in debt and equity securities are classified as either short-term or long-term. **Short-term investments**, also called **marketable securities**, have a maturity of more than 90 days but are intended to be held only until cash is needed for current operations. (As we pointed out in an earlier chapter, investments with a maturity of *less* than 90 days are classified as cash equivalents.) *Long-term investments* are intended to be held for more than one year. Long-term investments are reported in the investments section of the balance sheet, not in the current assets section. Although long-term investments may be just as marketable as short-term assets, management intends to hold them for an indefinite time.

Short-term and long-term investments must be further classified as trading securities, available-for-sale securities, or held-to-maturity securities.[2]

▸ **Trading securities** are debt or equity securities bought and held principally for the purpose of being sold in the near term.

▸ **Available-for-sale securities** are debt or equity securities that do not meet the criteria for either trading or held-to-maturity securities. They may be short-term or long-term depending on what management intends to do with them.

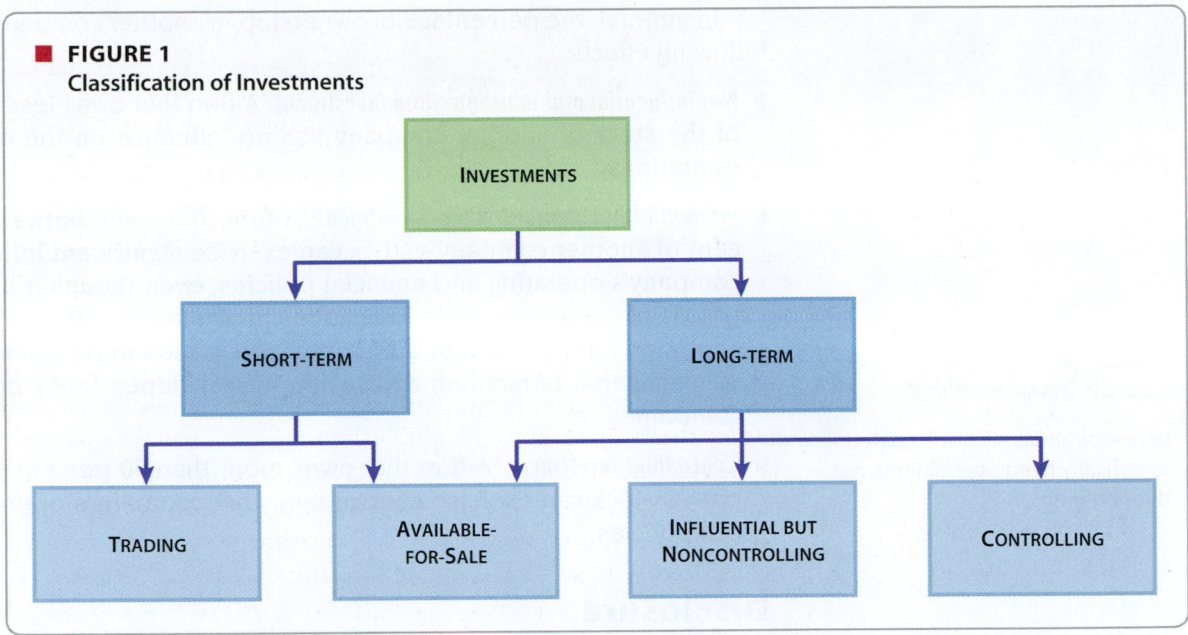

■ FIGURE 1
Classification of Investments

Held-to-maturity securities are debt securities that management intends to hold until their maturity date.

Figure 1 illustrates the classification of short-term and long-term investments. Table 1 shows the relationship between the percentage of ownership in a company's stock and the investing company's level of control, as well as the classifications and accounting treatments of these stock investments. These classifications are important because each one requires a different accounting treatment. We discuss the accounting treatments later in this chapter.

TABLE 1. Accounting for Equity Investments

Level of Control	Percentage of Ownership	Classification	Accounting Treatment
Noninfluential and noncontrolling	Less than 20%	Short-term investments—trading securities	Recorded at cost initially; cost adjusted after purchase for changes in market value; unrealized gains and losses reported on income statement
		Short-term or long-term investments—available-for-sale securities	Recorded at cost initially; cost adjusted for changes in market value with unrealized gains and losses to stockholders' equity
Influential but noncontrolling	Between 20% and 50%	Long-term investments	Equity method: recorded at cost initially; cost subsequently adjusted for investor's share of net income or loss and for dividends received
Controlling	More than 50%	Long-term investments	Financial statements consolidated

In general, the percentage of ownership in another company's stock has the following effects:

- *Noninfluential and noncontrolling investment*: A firm that owns less than 20 percent of the stock of another company has no influence on the other company's operations.

- *Influential but noncontrolling investment*: A firm that owns between 20 to 50 percent of another company's stock can exercise **significant influence** over that company's operating and financial policies, even though it holds 50 percent or less of the voting stock. Indications of significant influence include representation on the board of directors, participation in policymaking, exchange of managerial personnel, and technological dependency between the two companies.

- *Controlling investment*: A firm that owns more than 50 percent of another company's stock can exercise **control** over that company's operating and financial policies.

Study Note

Influence and control are related specifically to equity holdings, not debt holdings.

Disclosure

Companies provide detailed information about their investments and the manner in which they account for them in the notes to their financial statements. For instance, in a note summarizing its significant accounting policies, **eBay** makes the following disclosure:

> Short and long-term investments, which include marketable securities, government and corporate bonds, are classified as available for sale and reported at fair value.[3]

eBay's notes also provide detailed information about six acquisitions the company made in 2003 and 2004. Such disclosures help users assess the impact of the investments.

Ethics of Investing

When a company engages in investment transactions, there is always the possibility that its employees may use their knowledge about the transactions for personal gain. In the United States, **insider trading**, or making use of inside information for personal gain, is unethical and illegal. Before a publicly held company releases significant information about an investment to its stockhold-

FOCUS ON BUSINESS PRACTICE

What Are Special-Purpose Entities?

When **Enron** imploded in 2001 and its use of special purpose entities (SPEs) was widely reported, many accountants were unaware of the intricacies of accounting for these entities. SPEs are firms with limited lives that are created to achieve a specific objective (or objectives) of the parent company. They may take the form of a partnership, corporation, trust, or joint venture. SPEs have been around since the 1970s and have been used primarily by banks and other financial institutions as a way of raising funds by bundling together receivables and other loans into packages that can be sold to investors or used to borrow funds.

Enron turned this use of SPEs on its head. It used its SPEs to transfer assets and any related debt off its balance sheet, conceal its losses and borrow money, and generally make its financial statements look far better than they actually were. By setting up the SPEs as partnerships and using the arcane accounting rules for SPEs, Enron was able to avoid consolidating these entities even though it kept a 97 percent ownership in them. The FASB has since clarified the accounting rules for SPEs, which it calls Variable Interest Entities (VIEs).[4]

A bear and a bull guard the Frankfurt Stock Exchange in Germany. In 1995, Germany outlawed insider trading, eliminating what had been considered a management perk. It also required companies to warn investors of potential bad news. "In the U.S., the [SEC] has always been pretty ruthless with companies that didn't come clean, and it will be interesting to see what happens here," says Marco Becht, co-author of *The Control of Corporate Europe*.

ers and the general public, its officers and employees are not allowed to buy or sell stock in the company or in the firm whose shares the company is buying. Only after the information is released to the public can insiders engage in such trading. The Securities and Exchange Commission vigorously prosecutes any individual, whether employed by the company in question or not, who buys or sells shares of a publicly held company based on information not yet available to the public.

Not all countries prohibit insider trading. Until recently, insider trading was legal in Germany, but with the goal of expanding its securities markets, that country reformed its securities laws. It established the Federal Authority for Securities Trading (FAST), in part to oversee insider trading. However, only seven FAST staff members handle investigations of insider trading, as compared with the more than fifty staff members who handle the SEC's investigations.[5] Other countries continue to permit insider trading.

S T O P • R E V I E W • A P P L Y

1-1. In general, how are investments recognized and valued at date of purchase?

1-2. What is the difference between trading securities, available-for-sale securities, and held-to-maturity securities?

1-3. Why are the level and percentage of ownership important in accounting for equity investments?

1-4. Why is disclosure of investments important?

1-5. What is insider trading?

Suggested answers to all Stop, Review, and Apply questions follow the appendixes.

Investment Accounting Terminology Indicate whether each phrase listed below is most closely related to (a) trading securities, (b) available-for-sale securities, (c) held-to-maturity securities, (d) noninfluential and noncontrolling ownership, (e) influential but noncontrolling ownership, or (f) controlling ownership:

1. No significant influence over investee
2. Securities bought and sold for short-term profit
3. Ability to make decisions for investee
4. Significant influence over investee
5. Securities that may be sold at any time
6. Debt securities that will be held until they are repaid

SOLUTIONS

1. d	4. e
2. a	5. b
3. f	6. c

Short-Term Investments in Equity Securities

LO2 Explain the financial reporting implications of short-term investments.

As we pointed out earlier, all trading securities are short-term investments, while available-for-sale securities may be either short-term or long-term.

Trading Securities

Trading securities are frequently bought and sold to generate profits on short-term changes in their prices. They are classified as current assets on the balance sheet and are valued at fair value, which is usually the same as market value. An increase or decrease in the fair value of a company's total trading portfolio (the group of securities it holds for trading purposes) is included in net income in the accounting period in which the increase or decrease occurs.

For example, suppose Jackson Company buys 10,000 shares of **IBM** for $900,000 ($90 per share) and 10,000 shares of **Microsoft** for $300,000 ($30 per share) on October 25, 20x7. The purchase is made for trading purposes—that is, Jackson's management intends to realize a gain by holding the shares for only a short period. The entry to record the investment at cost is as follows:

Purchase

A = L + SE	20x7			
+1,200,000	Oct. 25	Short-Term Investments	1,200,000	
−1,200,000		Cash		1,200,000
		Investment in stocks for trading		
		($900,000 + $300,000 = $1,200,000)		

Assume that at year end, IBM's stock price has decreased to $80 per share and Microsoft's has risen to $32 per share. The trading portfolio is now valued at $1,120,000:

Security	Market Value	Cost	Gain (Loss)
IBM (10,000 shares)	$ 800,000	$ 900,000	
Microsoft (10,000 shares)	320,000	300,000	
Totals	$1,120,000	$1,200,000	($80,000)

Because the current fair value of the portfolio is $80,000 less than the original cost of $1,200,000, the following adjusting entry is needed:

Year-End Adjustment

A = L + SE
−80,000   −80,000

20x7			
Dec. 31	Unrealized Loss on Investments	80,000	
	Allowance to Adjust Short-Term Investments to Market		80,000
	Recognition of unrealized loss on trading portfolio		

The unrealized loss will appear on the income statement as a reduction in income. The loss is unrealized because the securities have not been sold; if unrealized gains occur, they are treated the same way. The Allowance to Adjust Short-Term Investments to Market account appears on the balance sheet as a contra-asset, as follows:

> **Study Note**
>
> The Allowance to Adjust Short-Term Investments to Market account is never changed when securities are sold. It changes only when an adjusting entry is made at year end.

Short-term investments (at cost)	$1,200,000
Less allowance to adjust short-term investments to market	80,000
Short-term investments (at market)	$1,120,000

or, more simply,

Short-term investments (at market value, cost is $1,200,000)	$1,120,000

If Jackson sells its 10,000 shares of Microsoft for $35 per share on March 2, 20x8, a realized gain on trading securities is recorded as follows:

Sale

A = L + SE
+350,000   +50,000
−300,000

20x8			
Mar. 2	Cash	350,000	
	Short-Term Investments		300,000
	Realized Gain on Investments		50,000
	Sale of 10,000 shares of Microsoft for $35 per share; cost was $30 per share		

FOCUS ON BUSINESS PRACTICE
How Can Even a Big Company Make an Accounting Mistake?

Like many companies, **General Electric**, one of America's largest corporations, protects itself against future increases in interest rates on debt by hedging its debt transactions with *derivatives*, which are agreements to buy or sell stocks, bonds, or other securities in the future. A derivative can be set up in such a way that it has no value and therefore entails no gain or loss. But when a derivative has value, it is considered a trading security and a money-making (or money-losing) tool rather than a true hedge; in this case,

any gain or loss that results from valuing the derivative at fair value must be reported on the income statement. General Electric thought it had no gains or losses on its derivatives, but when it recalculated their value over a two-year period, it found that it had gains amounting to about $.02 per share in each year. When the company issued a press release reporting the error, its CFO stated that "there are no exceptions to hedge accounting. . . . At the end of the day, the standard is the standard."[6]

The realized gain will appear on the income statement. Note that the realized gain is unaffected by the adjustment for the unrealized loss at the end of 20x7. The two transactions are treated independently. If the stock had been sold for less than cost, a realized loss on investments would have been recorded. Realized losses also appear on the income statement.

Now let's assume that during 20x8, Jackson buys 4,000 shares of **Apple Computer** at $32 per share and has no transactions involving its shares of IBM. Also assume that by December 31, 20x8, the price of IBM's stock has risen to $95 per share, or $5 per share more than the original cost, and that Apple's stock price has fallen to $29, or $3 less than the original cost. We can now analyze Jackson's trading portfolio as follows:

Security	Market Value	Cost	Gain (Loss)
IBM (10,000 shares)	$ 950,000	$ 900,000	
Apple (4,000 shares)	116,000	128,000	
Totals	$1,066,000	$1,028,000	$38,000

The market value of Jackson's trading portfolio now exceeds the cost by $38,000 ($1,066,000 − $1,028,000). This amount represents the targeted ending balance for the Allowance to Adjust Short-Term Investments to Market account. Recall that at the end of 20x7, that account had a credit balance of $80,000, meaning that the market value of the trading portfolio was less than the cost. Because no entries are made to the account during 20x8, it retains its balance until adjusting entries are made at the end of the year. The adjustment for 20x8 must be $118,000—enough to result in a debit balance of $38,000 in the allowance account:

Year-End Adjustment

A	= L +	SE
+118,000		+118,000

20x8				
Dec. 31	Allowance to Adjust Short-Term Investments to Market		118,000	
	Unrealized Gain on Investments			118,000
	Recognition of unrealized gain on trading portfolio			
	($80,000 + $38,000 = $118,000)			

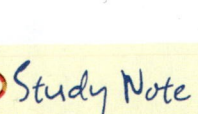

Study Note

The entry in the Allowance to Adjust Short-Term Investments to Market account is equal to the change in the market value. Compute the new allowance, and then compute the amount needed to change the account. The unrealized loss or gain is the other half of the entry.

The 20x8 ending balance of Jackson's allowance account can be determined as follows:

ALLOWANCE TO ADJUST SHORT-TERM INVESTMENTS TO MARKET			
Dec. 31, 20x8 Adj.	118,000	Dec. 31, 20x7 Bal.	80,000
Dec. 31, 20x8 Bal.	38,000		

The balance sheet presentation of short-term investments is as follows:

Short-term investments (at cost)	$1,028,000
Plus allowance to adjust short-term investments to market	38,000
Short-term investments (at market)	$1,066,000

or, more simply,

Short-term investments (at market value, cost is $1,028,000)	$1,066,000

If the company also has held-to-maturity securities that will mature within one year, they are included in short-term investments at cost adjusted for the effects of interest.

Available-for-Sale Securities

Short-term available-for-sale securities are accounted for in the same way as trading securities with two exceptions: (1) an unrealized gain or loss is reported as a special item in the stockholders' equity section of the balance sheet, not as a gain or loss on the income statement; (2) if a decline in the value of a security is considered permanent, it is charged as a loss on the income statement.

For example, **eBay's** summary of significant accounting policies contains the following statement: "Unrealized gains and losses [on available-for-sale securities] are excluded from earnings and reported as a component of comprehensive income (loss)." The company's statement of comprehensive income shows unrealized losses on investments of $5.9 million in 2003 and $8.7 million in 2004. In addition, eBay's income statement shows impairment charges of $1.2 million in 2003, which were "a result of the deterioration of the financial condition of equity investments that were considered to be other than temporary." The company reported no impairment charges in 2004.[7]

S T O P • R E V I E W • A P P L Y

2-1. How are trading securities valued at the balance sheet date?

2-2. What are unrealized gains and losses on trading securities? On what statement are they reported?

2-3. How does accounting for available-for-sale securities differ from accounting for trading securities?

Long-Term Investments in Equity Securities

> **LO3** Explain the financial reporting implications of long-term investments in stock and the cost-adjusted-to-market and equity methods used to account for them.

As indicated in Table 1, the accounting treatment of long-term investments in equity securities, such as common stock, depends on the extent to which the investing company can exercise control over the other company.

Noninfluential and Noncontrolling Investment

As noted earlier, available-for-sale securities are debt or equity securities that cannot be classified as trading or held-to-maturity securities. When long-term equity securities are involved, a further criterion for classifying them as available for sale is that they be noninfluential and noncontrolling investments of less than 20 percent of the voting stock. Accounting for long-term available-for-sale securities requires using the **cost-adjusted-to-market method**. With this method, the securities are initially recorded at cost and are thereafter adjusted periodically for changes in market value by using an allowance account.[8]

Available-for-sale securities are classified as long term if management intends to hold them for more than one year. When accounting for long-term available-for-sale securities, the unrealized gain or loss resulting from the adjustment is not reported on the income statement. Instead, the gain or loss is reported as a special item in the stockholders' equity section of the balance sheet and in the disclosure of comprehensive income.

At the end of each accounting period, the total cost and the total market value of these long-term stock investments must be determined. If the total market value is less than the total cost, the difference must be credited to a contra-asset account called Allowance to Adjust Long-Term Investments to Market. Because of the long-term nature of the investment, the debit part of the entry, which represents a decrease in value below cost, is treated as a temporary decrease and does not appear as a loss on the income statement. It is shown in a contra-stockholders' equity account called Unrealized Loss on Long-Term Investments.* Thus, both of these accounts are balance sheet accounts. If the market value exceeds the cost, the allowance account is added to Long-Term Investments, and the unrealized gain appears as an addition to stockholders' equity.

When a company sells its long-term investments in stock, the difference between the sale price and the cost of the stock is recorded and reported as a realized gain or loss on the income statement. Dividend income from such investments is recorded by a debit to Cash and a credit to Dividend Income. For example, assume the following facts about the long-term stock investments of Nardini Corporation:

June 1, 20x7	Paid cash for the following long-term investments: 10,000 shares of Herald Corporation common stock (representing 2 percent of outstanding stock) at $25 per share; 5,000 shares of Taza Corporation common stock (representing 3 percent of outstanding stock) at $15 per share.
Dec. 31, 20x7	Quoted market prices at year end: Herald common stock, $21; Taza common stock, $17
Apr. 1, 20x8	Change in policy required the sale of 2,000 shares of Herald common stock at $23.
July 1, 20x8	Received cash dividend from Taza equal to $.20 per share.
Dec. 31, 20x8	Quoted market prices at year end: Herald common stock, $24; Taza common stock, $13.

Study Note

Nardini's sale of stock on April 1, 20x8, was the result of a *change in policy*. This illustrates that intent is often the only difference between long-term investments and short-term investments.

Entries to record these transactions are as follows:

Investment

A	= L +	SE				
+325,000			20x7			
−325,000			June 1	Long-Term Investments	325,000	
				Cash		325,000
				Investments in Herald common stock (10,000 shares × $25 = $250,000) and Taza common stock (5,000 shares × $15 = $75,000)		

---

*If the decrease in market value of a long-term investment is deemed permanent or if the investment is deemed impaired, the decline or impairment is recorded by debiting a loss account on the income statement instead of the Unrealized Loss account.

Year-End Adjustment

A	= L +	SE
−30,000		−30,000

> **20x7**
>
> Dec. 31   Unrealized Loss on Long-Term Investments   30,000
>   Allowance to Adjust Long-Term
>   Investments to Market   30,000
>   To record reduction of long-term
>   investment to market

This adjustment involves the following computations:

Company	Shares	Market Price	Total Market	Total Cost
Herald	10,000	$21	$210,000	$250,000
Taza	5,000	17	85,000	75,000
			$295,000	$325,000

Total Cost − Total Market Value = $325,000 − $295,000 = $30,000

Other entries are as follows:

Sale

A	= L +	SE
+46,000		−4,000
−50,000		

> **20x8**
>
> Apr. 1   Cash   46,000
>   Loss on Sale of Investments   4,000
>   Long-Term Investments   50,000
>   Sale of 2,000 shares of Herald
>   common stock
>   2,000 × $23 = $46,000
>   2,000 × $25 =   50,000
>   Loss $ 4,000

Dividend Received

A	= L +	SE
+1,000		+1,000

> **20x8**
>
> July 1   Cash   1,000
>   Dividend Income   1,000
>   Receipt of cash dividend from Taza stock
>   5,000 × $.20 = $1,000

Year-End Adjustment

A	= L +	SE
+12,000		+12,000

> **20x8**
>
> Dec. 31   Allowance to Adjust Long-Term
>   Investments to Market   12,000
>   Unrealized Loss on Long-Term
>   Investments   12,000
>   To record the adjustment in long-
>   term investment so it is reported
>   at market

The adjustment equals the previous balance ($30,000 from the December 31, 20x7, entry) minus the new balance ($18,000), or $12,000. The new balance of $18,000 is the difference at the present time between the total market value and the total cost of all investments. It is figured as follows:

Company	Shares	Market Price	Total Market	Total Cost
Herald	8,000	$24	$192,000	$200,000
Taza	5,000	13	65,000	75,000
			$257,000	$275,000

Total Cost − Total Market Value = $275,000 − $257,000 = $18,000

The Allowance to Adjust Long-Term Investments to Market and the Unrealized Loss on Long-Term Investments are reciprocal contra accounts, each with the same dollar balance, as shown by the effects of these transactions on the T accounts:

CONTRA-ASSET ACCOUNT		CONTRA-STOCKHOLDERS' EQUITY ACCOUNT	
ALLOWANCE TO ADJUST LONG-TERM INVESTMENTS TO MARKET		**UNREALIZED LOSS ON LONG-TERM INVESTMENT**	
Dec. 31, 20x8 Adj. 12,000	Dec. 31, 20x7 Bal. 30,000	Dec. 31, 20x7 Bal. 30,000	Dec. 31, 20x8 Adj. 12,000
	Dec. 31, 20x8 Bal. 18,000	Dec. 31, 20x8 Bal. 18,000	

The Allowance account reduces long-term investments by the amount by which the cost of the investments exceeds market; the Unrealized Loss account reduces stockholders' equity by a similar amount. The opposite effects will exist if market value exceeds cost, resulting in an unrealized gain.

Influential but Noncontrolling Investment

As we have noted, ownership of 20 percent or more of a company's voting stock is considered sufficient to influence the company's operations. When that is the case, the **equity method** should be used to account for the stock investment. The equity method presumes that an investment of 20 percent or more is not a passive investment and that the investor should therefore share proportionately in the success or failure of the company. The three main features of this method are as follows:

1. The investor records the original purchase of the stock at cost.

2. The investor records its share of the company's periodic net income as an increase in the Investment account, with a corresponding credit to an income account. Similarly, it records its share of a periodic loss as a decrease in the Investment account, with a corresponding debit to a loss account.

3. When the investor receives a cash dividend, the asset account Cash is increased, and the Investment account is decreased.

eBay owns a minority interest of approximately 25 percent in **craigslist.inc.**, an online community featuring classified ad forums. Because the investment is more than 20 percent, eBay is presumed to have significant influence over craigslist's operations. Thus, eBay "accounts for the investment in craigslist using the equity method of accounting."[9]

To illustrate the equity method, suppose that on January 1 of the current year, ITO Corporation acquired 40 percent of Quay Corporation's voting common stock for $180,000. With this share of ownership, ITO can exert significant influence over Quay's operations. During the year, Quay reported net income of $80,000 and paid cash dividends of $20,000. ITO recorded these transactions as follows:

Investment

<table>
<tr><td>A</td><td>= L + SE</td></tr>
<tr><td>+180,000</td><td></td></tr>
<tr><td>−180,000</td><td></td></tr>
</table>

Investment in Quay Corporation	180,000	
Cash		180,000
Investment in Quay Corporation common stock		

Recognition of Income

<table>
<tr><td>A</td><td>= L +</td><td>SE</td></tr>
<tr><td>+32,000</td><td></td><td>+32,000</td></tr>
</table>

Investment in Quay Corporation	32,000	
Income, Quay Corporation Investment		32,000
Recognition of 40% of income reported		
by Quay Corporation		
40% × $80,000 = $32,000		

Receipt of Cash Dividend

<table>
<tr><td>A</td><td>= L + SE</td></tr>
<tr><td>+8,000</td><td></td></tr>
<tr><td>−8,000</td><td></td></tr>
</table>

Cash	8,000	
Investment in Quay Corporation		8,000
Cash dividend from Quay Corporation		
40% × $20,000 = $8,000		

The balance of the Investment in Quay Corporation account after these transactions is $204,000, as shown here:

INVESTMENT IN QUAY CORPORATION			
Investment	180,000	Dividend Received	8,000
Share of Income	32,000		
Bal.	**204,000**		

> **Study Note**
>
> Under the equity method, dividends received represent a return of investment and decrease the Investment account with a credit entry.

The share of income is reported as a separate line item on the income statement as a part of income from operations. The dividends received affect cash flows from operating activities on the statement of cash flows. The reported income exceeds the cash received by $24,000 ($32,000 − $8,000).

FOCUS ON BUSINESS PRACTICE
Accounting for International Joint Ventures

When U.S. companies make investments abroad, they often find it wise or necessary to partner with a local company or with the government of the country. Some countries require that their citizens own a minimum percentage of each business. In other countries—among them, Brazil, China, India, and the former United Soviet Socialist Republics—the government has traditionally had a share of ownership. Such business arrangements are usually called *joint ventures*. Because the resulting enterprise is jointly owned, it is appropriate to treat the U.S. company's status as "influential but noncontrolling." Thus, the most appropriate accounting method for these arrangements is the equity method.

Controlling Investment Some investing firms that own less than 50 percent of a company's voting stock exercise such powerful influence that for all practical purposes, they control the policies of the other company. Nevertheless, ownership of more than 50 percent of the voting stock is required for accounting recognition of control. When a firm has a controlling interest in another company, a parent-subsidiary relationship is said to exist. The investing company is the **parent company**; the other company is a **subsidiary**.

Because a parent company and its subsidiaries are separate legal entities, each prepares separate financial statements. However, because of their special relationship, they are viewed for external financial reporting purposes as a single economic entity. For this reason, the FASB requires that they combine their financial statements into a single set of statements called **consolidated financial statements**.[10] For example, in its summary of significant accounting policies, **eBay** states that "the accompanying financial statements are consolidated and include the financial statements of eBay and our majority-owned subsidiaries. All significant intercompany balances and transactions have been eliminated in consolidation."[11]

Study Note

Parents and subsidiaries are separate legal entities even though they combine their financial reports at year end.

S T O P • R E V I E W • A P P L Y

3-1. What percentage of ownership applies to each of the following: (a) noninfluential and noncontrolling investment, (b) influential but noncontrolling investment, and (c) controlling investment? What is the appropriate accounting treatment for each of these investments?

3-2. What is a parent-subsidiary relationship?

3-3. American Home Products Corporation has many subsidiaries. Would its stockholders be more interested in its consolidated financial statements or in the individual statements of its subsidiaries? Explain your answer.

3-4. Merchant Corporation's summary of significant accounting policies contained this statement: "Investments in companies in which Merchant has significant influence in management are on the equity basis." What is the equity method of accounting for investments, and why did Merchant use it in this case?

Consolidated Financial Statements

LO4 Explain the financial reporting implications of consolidated financial statements.

Most major corporations find it convenient for economic, legal, tax, or other reasons to operate in parent-subsidiary relationships. When we speak of a large company, such as **PepsiCo** or **IBM**, we generally think of the parent company, not of its many subsidiaries. Potential investors, however, want a clear financial picture of the total economic entity. The main purpose of consolidated financial statements is to give such a view of the parent and subsidiary firms by treating them as if they were one company. On a consolidated balance sheet, the Inventory account includes the inventory held by the parent and all its subsidiaries. Similarly, on the consolidated income statement, the Sales account is the total revenue from sales by the parent and all its subsidiaries. This overview helps management, stockholders, and creditors of the parent company judge the company's progress in meeting its goals.

Consolidated Balance Sheet

The **purchase method** of preparing consolidated financial statements combines similar accounts from the separate statements of the parent and the subsidiaries. Some accounts result from transactions between the parent and the subsidiary—for example, sales and purchases between the two entities, and debt owed by one of the entities to the other. It is not appropriate to include these accounts in the consolidated financial statements; the sales and purchases are only transfers between different parts of the business, and the payables and receivables do not represent amounts due to or receivable from outside parties. For this reason, it is important that certain **eliminations** be made. These eliminations avoid the duplication of accounts and reflect the financial position and operations from the standpoint of a single entity. Eliminations appear only on the work sheets used in preparing consolidated financial statements. They are never shown in the accounting records of either the parent or the subsidiary.

Another good example of accounts that result from transactions between a parent and its subsidiary is the Investment in Subsidiary account on the parent's balance sheet and the stockholders' equity accounts of the subsidiary. When the balance sheets of the two companies are combined, these accounts must be eliminated to avoid duplicating them in the consolidated financial statements.

To illustrate the preparation of a consolidated balance sheet under the purchase method, we use the following balance sheet data for Parent Company and Subsidiary Company:

Accounts	Parent Company	Subsidiary Company
Cash	$100,000	$25,000
Other assets	760,000	60,000
Total assets	$860,000	$85,000
Liabilities	$ 60,000	$10,000
Common stock	600,000	55,000
Retained earnings	200,000	20,000
Total liabilities and stockholders' equity	$860,000	$85,000

100 Percent Purchase at Book Value Suppose that Parent Company purchases 100 percent of the stock of Subsidiary Company for an amount exactly equal to Subsidiary's book value. The book value of Subsidiary Company is $75,000 ($85,000 − $10,000). Parent Company would record the purchase as follows:

A	= L + SE
+75,000	
−75,000	

Investment in Subsidiary Company	75,000	
Cash		75,000
Purchase of 100 percent of Subsidiary Company at book value		

It is helpful to use a work sheet like the one shown in Exhibit 1 in preparing consolidated financial statements. Note that the balance of Parent Company's

---

Study Note

As separate entities, the parent and subsidiary maintain individual accounting records. Work sheet eliminations remove only duplications that occur in consolidation and the effects of intercompany transactions.

▼ **EXHIBIT 1**

Work Sheet for Preparing a Consolidated Balance Sheet

Parent and Subsidiary Companies
Work Sheet for Consolidated Balance Sheet
As of Acquisition Date

Accounts	Balance Sheet, Parent Company	Balance Sheet, Subsidiary Company	Eliminations Debit	Eliminations Credit	Consolidated Balance Sheet
Cash	25,000	25,000			50,000
Investment in subsidiary company	75,000			(1) 75,000	—
Other assets	760,000	60,000			820,000
Total assets	860,000	85,000			870,000
Liabilities	60,000	10,000			70,000
Common stock	600,000	55,000	(1) 55,000		600,000
Retained earnings	200,000	20,000	(1) 20,000		200,000
Total liabilities and stockholders' equity	860,000	85,000	75,000	75,000	870,000

(1) Elimination of intercompany investment

Cash account is now $25,000 and that Investment in Subsidiary Company is shown as an asset in Parent Company's balance sheet, reflecting the purchase of the subsidiary. To prepare a consolidated balance sheet, it is necessary to eliminate the investment in the subsidiary, as shown in elimination entry 1 in Exhibit 1. This entry accomplishes two things. First, it eliminates the double counting that would take place when the net assets of the two companies are combined. Second, it eliminates the stockholders' equity section of Subsidiary Company.

As we have pointed out, the theory underlying consolidated financial statements is that parent and subsidiary are a single entity. Thus, the stockholders' equity section of the consolidated balance sheet is the same for Parent Company and Subsidiary Company. So, after eliminating the Investment in Subsidiary Company account and the stockholders' equity accounts of the subsidiary, we can take the information from the Consolidated Balance Sheet column in Exhibit 1 and present it in the following form:

Parent and Subsidiary Companies
Consolidated Balance Sheet
As of Acquisition Date

Cash	$ 50,000	Liabilities	$ 70,000
Other assets	820,000	Common stock	600,000
		Retained earnings	200,000
		Total liabilities and	
Total assets	$870,000	stockholders' equity	$870,000

▼ **EXHIBIT 2**

Work Sheet Showing Elimination When Purchase Is for Less than 100 Percent Ownership

Parent and Subsidiary Companies
Work Sheet for Consolidated Balance Sheet
As of Acquisition Date

Accounts	Balance Sheet, Parent Company	Balance Sheet, Subsidiary Company	Eliminations		Consolidated Balance Sheet
			Debit	Credit	
Cash	32,500	25,000			57,500
Investment in subsidiary company	67,500			(1) 67,500	—
Other assets	760,000	60,000			820,000
Total assets	860,000	85,000			877,500
Liabilities	60,000	10,000			70,000
Common stock	600,000	55,000	(1) 55,000		600,000
Retained earnings	200,000	20,000	(1) 20,000		200,000
Minority interest	—	—		(1) 7,500	7,500
Total liabilities and stockholders' equity	860,000	85,000	75,000	75,000	877,500

(1) Elimination of intercompany investment. Minority interest equals 10 percent of subsidiary's total stockholders' equity.

> **Study Note**
>
> When the elimination entry is made, all of the subsidiary's stockholders' equity accounts are eliminated. The percentage not owned by the parent company is assigned to minority interest.

Less Than 100 Percent Purchase at Book Value   When a parent company purchases less than 100 percent but more than 50 percent of a subsidiary's voting stock, it will have control over the subsidiary, and it must prepare consolidated financial statements. It must also account for the interests of the subsidiary's stockholders who own less than 50 percent of the voting stock. These are the minority stockholders, and their **minority interest** must appear on the consolidated balance sheet as an amount equal to their percentage of ownership times the subsidiary's net assets. **eBay** for instance, has $4 million of minority interest on the liability side of its balance sheet, which stems mainly from its less than 100 percent ownership of Internet Auction.

Suppose that Parent Company buys 90 percent of Subsidiary Company's voting stock for $67,500. In this case, the portion of the company purchased has a book value of $67,500 (90% × $75,000). The work sheet used to prepare the consolidated balance sheet appears in Exhibit 2. The elimination is made just as in Exhibit 1, except that the minority interest must be accounted for. All of the Investment in Subsidiary Company account ($67,500) is eliminated against all of Subsidiary Company's stockholders' equity accounts (totaling $75,000). The difference ($7,500, or 10% × $75,000) is set as minority interest.

There are two ways to classify minority interest on a consolidated balance sheet. One is to place it between long-term liabilities and stockholders' equity. The other is to consider the stockholders' equity section as consisting of minority interest and the parent company's stockholders' equity, as shown here:

Minority interest	$ 7,500
Common stock	600,000
Retained earnings	200,000
Total stockholders' equity	$807,500

Purchase at More or Less than Book Value

The purchase price of a business depends on many factors, such as the current market price, the relative strength of the buyer's and seller's bargaining positions, and the prospects for future earnings. Thus, it is only by chance that the purchase price of a subsidiary equals the book value of its equity. Usually, it does not.

For example, a parent company may pay more than the subsidiary's book value for a controlling interest if the subsidiary's assets are understated. This happens when the historical cost less depreciation of the subsidiary's assets does not reflect current market values. The parent may also pay more than book value if the subsidiary has something the parent wants, such as an important technical process, a new and different product, or a new market. On the other hand, the parent may pay less than book value if the subsidiary's assets are not worth their depreciated cost. It may also pay less than book value if heavy losses suffered by the subsidiary have caused its stock price to drop.

The Accounting Principles Board has provided the following guidelines for consolidating a purchased subsidiary and its parent when the parent pays more than book value for its investment in the subsidiary:

> First, all identifiable assets acquired . . . and liabilities assumed in a business combination . . . should be assigned a portion of the cost of the acquired company, normally equal to their fair values at date of acquisition.
>
> Second, the excess of the cost of the acquired company over the sum of the amounts assigned to identifiable assets acquired less liabilities assumed should be recorded as goodwill.[12]

As explained in the chapter on long-term assets, goodwill is carried on the balance sheet at cost and is subject to an annual impairment test. **eBay** describes its treatment of goodwill as follows:

> Goodwill represents the excess of the purchase price over the fair value of the net tangible and identifiable intangible assets acquired. Intangible assets resulting from the acquisition of entities accounted for using the purchase method of accounting are estimated by management. . . . Goodwill is no longer subject to amortization. Rather, [it] is subject to at least an annual assessment for impairment, applying a fair-value test. . . . Our annual impairment test . . . determined . . . no impairment.[13]

To illustrate the application of these principles, suppose that Parent Company purchases 100 percent of Subsidiary Company's voting stock for $92,500, or $17,500 more than book value. Parent Company considers $10,000 of the $17,500 to be due to the increased value of Subsidiary's other assets and $7,500 of the $17,500 to be due to the overall strength that Subsidiary Company would add to Parent Company's organization. The work sheet used to prepare the consolidated balance sheet appears in Exhibit 3. All of the Investment in Subsidiary Company ($92,500) has been eliminated against all of Subsidiary Company's stockholders' equity ($75,000). The excess of cost over book value ($17,500) has been debited in the amounts of $10,000 to Other Assets and $7,500 to a new account called **Goodwill**, or *Goodwill from Consolidation*. The amount of goodwill is determined as follows:

Cost of investment in subsidiary	$92,500
Book value of subsidiary	75,000
Excess of cost over book value	$17,500
Portion of excess attributable to undervalued other assets of subsidiary	10,000
Portion of excess attributable to goodwill	$ 7,500

Study Note

Regardless of the circumstances, the Investment in Subsidiary Company account must be eliminated completely and should not appear on the consolidated balance sheet.

Study Note

Goodwill is recorded when the purchase price of a business exceeds the fair market value of the net assets purchased.

▼ **EXHIBIT 3**

Work Sheet Showing Elimination When Purchase Cost Is Greater than Book Value

Parent and Subsidiary Companies
Work Sheet for Consolidated Balance Sheet
As of Acquisition Date

Accounts	Balance Sheet, Parent Company	Balance Sheet, Subsidiary Company	Eliminations Debit	Eliminations Credit	Consolidated Balance Sheet
Cash	7,500	25,000			32,500
Investment in subsidiary company	92,500			(1) 92,500	—
Other assets	760,000	60,000	(1) 10,000		830,000
Goodwill	—	—	(1) 7,500		7,500
Total assets	860,000	85,000			870,000
Liabilities	60,000	10,000			70,000
Common stock	600,000	55,000	(1) 55,000		600,000
Retained earnings	200,000	20,000	(1) 20,000		200,000
Total liabilities and stockholders' equity	860,000	85,000	92,500	92,500	870,000

(1) Elimination of intercompany investment. Excess of cost over book value ($92,500 − $75,000 = $17,500) is allocated to Other Assets ($10,000) and Goodwill ($7,500).

On the consolidated balance sheet, goodwill appears as an asset representing the portion of the excess of the cost of the investment over book value that cannot be allocated to any specific asset. Other assets appears on the consolidated balance sheet at the combined total of $830,000 ($760,000 + $60,000 + $10,000).

When the parent company pays less than book value for its investment in the subsidiary, *Opinion No. 16* of the Accounting Principles Board requires that the excess of book value over cost of the investment be used to lower the carrying value of the subsidiary's long-term assets. The reasoning behind this is that market values of long-lived assets (other than marketable securities) are among the least reliable of estimates, since a ready market does not usually exist for such assets. In other words, the Accounting Principles Board advises against using negative goodwill, except in very special cases.

Intercompany Receivables and Payables   If a subsidiary owes money to the parent company, there will be a receivable on the parent company's individual balance sheet and a payable on the subsidiary company's individual balance sheet. Conversely, if a parent owes money to a subsidiary, there will be a receivable on the subsidiary's balance sheet and a payable on the parent's balance sheet. When a consolidated balance sheet is prepared, both the receivable and the payable should be eliminated because from the viewpoint of the consolidated entity, neither the asset nor the liability exists. In other words, it does not make sense for a company to owe money to itself. The eliminating entry is made on the work sheet by debiting the payable and crediting the receivable for the amount of the intercompany loan.

Consolidated Income Statement

A consolidated income statement is prepared by combining the revenues and expenses of the parent and subsidiary companies. The procedure is the same as the one used to prepare a consolidated balance sheet—that is, intercompany transactions are eliminated to prevent double counting of revenues and expenses. The following intercompany transactions affect the consolidated income statement:

1. Sales and purchases of goods and services between parent and subsidiary

2. Income and expenses related to loans, receivables, or bond indebtedness between parent and subsidiary

3. Other income and expenses from intercompany transactions.

To illustrate the eliminating entries, suppose that Parent Company sold $120,000 of goods to Subsidiary Company, which in turn sold all the goods to others. Subsidiary Company paid Parent Company $2,000 interest on a loan.

The work sheet in Exhibit 4 shows how to prepare a consolidated income statement. Because the purpose of the eliminating entries is to treat the two companies as a single entity, it is important to include in Sales only sales made to outsiders and to include in Cost of Goods Sold only purchases made from outsiders. This goal is met with the first eliminating entry, which eliminates the $120,000 of intercompany sales and purchases by a debit of that amount to Sales and a credit of that amount to Cost of Goods Sold. As a result, only sales to outsiders ($510,000) and purchases from outsiders ($240,000) are included in the Consolidated Income Statement column. The intercompany interest income and expense are eliminated by a debit to Other Revenues and a credit to Other Expenses.

> **Study Note**
>
> Intercompany sales or purchases are not revenues or expenses to the consolidated entity. True revenues and expenses occur only when transactions are with parties outside the firm.

▼ **EXHIBIT 4**

Work Sheet for Preparing a Consolidated Income Statement

Parent and Subsidiary Companies
Work Sheet for Consolidated Income Statement
For the Year Ended December 31, 20xx

Accounts	Income Statement, Parent Company	Income Statement, Subsidiary Company	Eliminations Debit	Eliminations Credit	Consolidated Income Statement
Sales	430,000	200,000	(1) 120,000		510,000
Other revenues	60,000	10,000	(2) 2,000		68,000
Total revenues	490,000	210,000			578,000
Cost of goods sold	210,000	150,000		(1) 120,000	240,000
Other expenses	140,000	50,000		(2) 2,000	188,000
Total costs and expenses	350,000	200,000			428,000
Net income	140,000	10,000	122,000	122,000	150,000

(1) Elimination of intercompany sales and purchases
(2) Elimination of intercompany interest income and interest expense

An art installation of euro currency in Ludwigsburg, Germany, preceded the adoption of the Euro on January 1, 2002, as the only form of legal tender in twelve European countries. When a U.S. company owns more than 50 percent of a foreign company, it must prepare consolidated financial statements. The statements of the foreign subsidiary must be restated in dollars—not euros or other foreign currencies—before consolidation can take place.

Public corporations also prepare consolidated statements of stockholders' equity and consolidated statements of cash flows. For examples of these statements, see the **CVS** annual report in the Supplement to Chapter 1.

Restatement of Foreign Subsidiary Financial Statements

Companies often expand by establishing or buying foreign subsidiaries. Such companies are often referred to as **multinational or transnational corporations**. If a company owns more than 50 percent of a foreign subsidiary and thus exercises control, the foreign subsidiary should be included in the consolidated financial statements. The consolidation procedure is the same as the one we described for domestic subsidiaries, except that the statements of the foreign subsidiary must be restated in the reporting currency before consolidation takes place. The **reporting currency** is the currency in which the consolidated financial statements are presented, which for U.S. companies is usually the U.S. dollar. For example, **eBay** purchased a German company and an Indian company in 2004. Clearly, it makes no sense to combine the assets of German and Indian subsidiaries stated in euros and rupees with the assets of the U.S. parent company stated in dollars. Thus, **restatement** of the subsidiaries' statements into the currency of the parent company is necessary. After restatement, the parent's and subsidiaries' statements can be consolidated in the usual way.

S T O P • R E V I E W • A P P L Y

4-1. What are eliminating entries, and where do they appear?

4-2. What is the value of consolidated financial statements?

4-3. Merchant Corporation's summary of significant accounting policies contained the following statement: "Principles Applied in Consolidation: Majority-owned subsidiaries are consolidated, except for leasing and finance companies and those subsidiaries not considered to be material." What accounting rule does this practice violate, and why?

4-4. The following item appeared on Merchant's consolidated balance sheet: "Minority Interest—$50,000." How did this item arise, and where would you expect to find it on the consolidated balance sheet?

4-5. The following item also appeared on Merchant's consolidated balance sheet: "Goodwill from Consolidation—$70,000." How would this item arise, and where would you expect to find it on the consolidated balance sheet?

4-6. Why should intercompany receivables, payables, sales, and purchases be eliminated in consolidated financial statements?

4-7. Subsidiary Corporation, a wholly owned subsidiary, has total sales of $500,000, $100,000 of which were made to Parent Corporation. Parent Corporation has total sales of $1,000,000. What is the amount of sales on the consolidated income statement?

4-8. What step is necessary before consolidating the financial statements of foreign subsidiaries and their parent company?

Consolidation Calculations S Company has total stockholders' equity of $100,000. Fill in the dollar amounts for each of the following investments by P Company in S's common stock:

	Goodwill	Minority Interest
1. P pays $100,000 for 100% of S's common stock, and S's net assets are fairly valued at $100,000.	_____	_____
2. P pays $120,000 for 100% of S's common stock, and S's net assets are fairly valued at $100,000.	_____	_____
3. P pays $120,000 for 100% of S's common stock, and S's net assets are fairly valued at $120,000.	_____	_____
4. P pays $80,000 for 80% of S's common stock, and S's net assets are fairly valued at $100,000.	_____	_____
5. P pays $100,000 for 80% of S's common stock, and S's net assets are fairly valued at $125,000.	_____	_____

SOLUTION

	Goodwill	Minority Interest
1.	0	0
2.	$20,000	0
3.	0	0
4.	0	$20,000
5.	0	$25,000

Investments in Debt Securities

LO5 Explain the financial reporting implications of debt investments.

As noted in previous chapters, debt securities are considered financial instruments because they are claims that will be paid in cash. When a company purchases debt securities, it records them at cost plus any commissions and fees. Like investments in equity securities, short-term investments in debt securities are valued at fair value at the end of the accounting period and are accounted for as trading securities or available-for-sale securities. However, the accounting treatment is different if they qualify as held-to-maturity securities.

Held-to-Maturity Securities

As we noted earlier, held-to-maturity securities are debt securities that management intends to hold to their maturity date. Such securities are recorded at cost and are valued on the balance sheet at cost adjusted for the effects of interest. For example, suppose that on December 1, 20x7, Webber Company pays $97,000 for U.S. Treasury bills, which are short-term debt of the federal government. The bills will mature in 120 days at $100,000. Webber would make the following entry:

Study Note

Any brokerage costs or other costs involved in acquiring securities are part of the cost of the securities.

A	= L +	SE				
+97,000			20x7			
−97,000			Dec. 1	Short-Term Investments	97,000	
				Cash		97,000
				Purchase of U.S. Treasury bills that mature in 120 days		

At Webber's year end on December 31, the entry to accrue the interest income earned to date would be as follows:

A	= L +	SE				
+750		+750	20x7			
			Dec. 31	Short-Term Investments	750	
				Interest Income		750
				Accrual of interest on U.S. Treasury bills $3,000 \times 30/120 = \$750$		

On December 31, the U.S. Treasury bills would be shown on the balance sheet as a short-term investment at their amortized cost of $97,750 ($97,000 + $750). When Webber receives the maturity value on March 31, 20x8, the entry is as follows:

A	= L +	SE				
+100,000		+2,250	20x8			
−97,750			Mar. 31	Cash	100,000	
				Short-Term Investments		97,750
				Interest Income		2,250
				Receipt of cash at maturity of U.S. Treasury bills and recognition of related income		

Long-Term Investments in Bonds

Like all investments, investments in bonds are recorded at cost, which, in this case, is the price of the bonds plus the broker's commission. When bonds are purchased between interest payment dates, the purchaser must also pay an amount equal to the interest that has accrued on the bonds since the last interest payment date. Then, on the next interest payment date, the purchaser receives an interest payment for the whole period. The payment for accrued interest should be recorded as a debit to Interest Income, which will be offset by a credit to Interest Income when the semiannual interest is received.

Subsequent accounting for a corporation's long-term bond investments depends on the classification of the bonds. If the company plans to hold the bonds until they are paid off on their maturity date, they are considered held-to-maturity securities. Except in industries like insurance and banking, it is unusual for companies to buy the bonds of other companies with the express purpose of holding them until they mature, which can be in 10 to 30 years. Thus, most long-term bond investments are classified as available-for-sale securities, meaning that the company plans to sell them at some point before their maturity date. Such bonds are accounted for at fair value, much as equity or stock investments are; fair value is usually the market value. When bonds are intended to be held to maturity, they are accounted for not at fair value but at cost, adjusted for the amortization of their discount or premium. The procedure is similar to accounting for long-term bond liabilities, except that separate accounts for discounts and premiums are not used.

> ## Study Note
>
> The fair value of bonds is closely related to interest rates. An increase in interest rates lowers the fair value of bonds, and vice versa.

S T O P • R E V I E W • A P P L Y

5-1. What are held-to-maturity securities, and at what value are they shown on the balance sheet?

5-2. Are most long-term investments in bonds classified as held-to-maturity securities or as available-for-sale securities? Explain your answer.

A LOOK BACK AT

eBAY, INC.

As shown in the Financial Highlights at the beginning of the chapter, short- and long-term investments and goodwill from acquisitions constitute a large portion of the total assets on **eBay's** balance sheet. The company's investments also have important effects on its income statement and statement of cash flows. To fully evaluate eBay's performance, users of its financial statements must address the following questions:

● **What are the effects of eBay's investments on its financial performance?**

● **How does eBay's acquisition of other companies affect its financial performance?**

As we pointed out in this chapter, eBay classifies both short- and long-term investments as available-for-sale securities and reports them at fair value on its balance sheet. It reports the difference between unrealized gains and losses in other comprehensive income (a component of stockholders' equity) and subjects its equity investments to an impairment test, which can result in an income statement charge if a decline in an investment's value is deemed permanent. The company had unrealized losses in 2004 of $8.7 million but no impairments. Because more than 90 percent of eBay's investments are debt securities, interest income is a significant component—almost 8 percent—of the company's net income. The investing section of its statement of cash flows reveals that in 2004, eBay spent about $1.8 billion on investments while selling investments for about $1.1 billion.

In 2003 and 2004, eBay made six acquisitions totaling more than $1.2 billion. It uses the equity method to account for investments over 20 percent and the purchase method to account for acquisitions. For instance, its purchase of a 62 percent interest in Internet Auction for $94 million in cash resulted in both minority interest and goodwill.[14] In total, goodwill from all eBay's acquisitions represents one-third of its assets.

In short, it is not possible to fully understand or evaluate eBay's performance without understanding the effect that investments and acquisitions have on that performance.

CHAPTER REVIEW

REVIEW of Learning Objectives

LO1 Identify and explain the management issues related to investments.

Investments are recorded on the date on which the transaction occurs, at which time there is either a transfer of funds or a definite obligation to pay. Investments are recorded at cost, or purchase price, including any commissions or fees. After the purchase, the balance sheet value of investments is adjusted to reflect subsequent conditions.

Investments are classified as short term or long term; as trading, available-for-sale, or held-to-maturity securities; and as noninfluential and noncontrolling, influential but noncontrolling, or controlling investments. These classifications play an important role in accounting for investments. Noninfluential and noncontrolling investments represent less than 20 percent ownership of a company; influential but noncontrolling investments represent 20 percent to 50 percent ownership; and controlling investments represent more than 50 percent ownership.

A company should disclose its accounting policies for investments and related details in the notes to its financial statements.

Managers and other employees must avoid using their knowledge of their company's planned investment transactions for personal gain.

LO2 Explain the financial reporting implications of short-term investments.

Short-term investments in stocks are classified as trading securities or available-for-sale securities. Trading securities are debt or equity securities that are bought and held principally for the purpose of being sold in the near term. They are classified as current assets on the balance sheet and are valued at fair value. Unrealized gains or losses on trading securities appear on the income statement.

Available-for-sale securities, are debt or equity securities that do not meet the criteria for either trading or held-to-maturity securities. They are accounted for in the same way as trading securities with two exceptions: (1) an unrealized gain or loss is reported as a special item in the stockholders' equity section of the balance sheet; (2) if a decline in the value of a security is considered permanent, it is charged as a loss on the income statement.

LO3 Explain the financial reporting implications of long-term investments in stock and the cost-adjusted-to-market and equity methods used to account for them.

The cost-adjusted-to-market method is used to account for noninfluential and noncontrolling investments in stock. With this method, investments are initially recorded at cost and are then adjusted to market value by using an allowance account. The equity method is used to account for influential but noncontrolling investments. With this method, the investment is initially recorded at cost and is then adjusted for the investor's share of the company's net income or loss and subsequent dividends.

Consolidated financial statements are required when an investing company has legal and effective control over another company. Control exists when the parent company owns more than 50 percent of the voting stock of the subsidiary company.

LO4 Explain the financial reporting implications of consolidated financial statements.

Consolidated financial statements are useful to investors and others because they treat the parent company and its subsidiaries as an integrated economic unit. When a consolidated balance sheet is prepared at the date of acquisition, a work sheet entry is made to eliminate the investment from the parent company's financial statements and the stockholders' equity section of the subsidiary's financial statements. The assets and liabilities of the two companies are combined. If the parent owns less than 100 percent of the subsidiary, minority interest equal to the percentage of the subsidiary owned by minority stockholders multiplied by the subsidiary's net assets appears on the consolidated balance sheet. If the cost of the parent's investment in the subsidiary is greater than the subsidiary's book value, an amount equal to the excess of cost over book value is allocated to undervalued subsidiary assets and to goodwill. If the cost of the parent's investment in the subsidiary is less than book value, the excess of book value over cost should be used to reduce the book value of the subsidiary's long-term assets (other than long-term marketable securities).

When consolidated income statements are prepared, intercompany sales, purchases, interest income, interest expense, and other income and expenses from intercompany transactions must be eliminated to avoid double counting of these items.

The financial statements of foreign subsidiaries must be restated in terms of the parent company's reporting currency before consolidated financial statements can be prepared.

LO5 Explain the financial reporting implications of debt investments.

Held-to-maturity securities are debt securities that management intends to hold to their maturity date; they are valued on the balance sheet at cost adjusted for the effects of interest. Long-term investments in bonds fall into two categories: available-for-sale securities, which are recorded at cost and subsequently accounted for at fair value, and held-to-maturity securities.

REVIEW of Concepts and Terminology

The following concepts and terms were introduced in this chapter:

Available-for-sale securities: Debt or equity securities that do not meet the criteria for trading or held-to-maturity securities. **(LO1)**

Consolidated financial statements: Financial statements that reflect the combined operations of a parent company and its subsidiaries. **(LO3)**

Control: An investing company's ability to decide the operating and financial policies of another firm because it owns more than 50 percent of that firm's voting stock. **(LO1)**

Cost-adjusted-to-market method: A method of accounting for available-for-sale securities at cost adjusted for changes in the securities' market value. **(LO3)**

Eliminations: Entries made on consolidation work sheets to eliminate transactions between parent and subsidiary companies. **(LO4)**

Equity method: A method of accounting for influential but noncontrolling long-term investments in which the investment is initially recorded at cost and is then adjusted for the investor's share of the company's net income or loss and for dividends. **(LO3)**

Goodwill: The excess of the purchase price of a business over the fair market value of its net assets. Also called *goodwill from consolidation* **(LO4)**

Held-to-maturity securities: Debt securities that management intends to hold until their maturity date. **(LO1)**

Insider trading: Making use of inside information for personal gain. **(LO1)**

Marketable securities: Investments with a maturity of more than 90 days but that are intended to be held only until cash is needed to pay current obligations. Also called *short-term investments*. **(LO1)**

Minority interest: An amount recorded on a consolidated balance sheet that represents the holdings of owners of less than 50 percent of a subsidiary's voting stock. **(LO4)**

Multinational or transnational corporations: Companies that expand by establishing or buying foreign subsidiaries. **(LO4)**

Parent company: A company that has a controlling interest in another firm. **(LO3)**

Purchase method: A method of accounting for controlling investments in which similar accounts from the parent's and subsidiaries' statements are combined. **(LO4)**

Reporting currency: The currency in which consolidated financial statements are presented. **(LO4)**

Restatement: The stating of one currency in terms of another. **(LO4)**

Short-term investments: Investments that have a maturity of more than 90 days but that management intends to hold only until cash is needed to pay current obligations. Also called *marketable securities*. **(LO1)**

Significant influence: An investing company's ability to affect the operating and financial policies of the firm in which it has invested, even though it holds 50 percent or less of the voting stock. **(LO1)**

Subsidiary: A firm in which another company owns a controlling interest. **(LO3)**

Trading securities: Debt or equity securities bought and held principally for the purpose of being sold in the near term. **(LO1)**

≡ REVIEW Problem

LO4 **Consolidated Balance Sheet: Less than 100 Percent Ownership**

In a cash transaction on June 30, 20xx, Kohl Company purchased 90 percent of the outstanding stock of Shannon Company for $763,200. Directly after the acquisition, the balance sheets of the two companies were as follows:

	A	B	C
		Kohl Company	Shannon Company
1			
2			
3	**Assets**		
4	Cash	$400,000	$48,000
5	Accounts receivable	650,000	240,000
6	Inventory	1,000,000	520,000
7	Investment in Shannon Company	763,200	—
8	Plant and equipment (net)	1,500,000	880,000
9	Other assets	50,000	160,000
10	Total assets	$4,363,200	$1,848,000
11			
12	**Liabilities and Stockholders' Equity**		
13	Accounts payable	$800,000	$400,000
14	Long-term debt	1,000,000	600,000
15	Common stock	2,000,000	800,000
16	Retained earnings	563,200	48,000
17	Total liabilities and stockholders' equity	$4,363,200	$1,848,000

The following information is also available:

1. Shannon Company's other assets represent a long-term investment in Kohl Company's long-term debt. Shannon purchased the debt for an amount equal to Kohl's carrying value of the debt.
2. Kohl Company owes Shannon Company $100,000 for services rendered.

Required

Prepare a work sheet for a consolidated balance sheet as of the acquisition date.

Answer to Review Problem

	A	B	C	D	E	F
1		Kohl and Shannon Companies				
2		Work Sheet for Consolidated Balance Sheet				
3		June 30, 20xx				
4						
5				Eliminations		
6	Accounts	Balance Sheet, Kohl Company	Balance Sheet, Shannon Company	Debit	Credit	Consolidated Balance Sheet
7						
8	Cash	400,000	48,000			448,000
9	Accounts receivable	650,000	240,000		(3) 100,000	790,000
10	Inventory	1,000,000	520,000			1,520,000
11	Investment in					
12	Shannon Company	763,200	—		(1) 763,200	
13	Plant and equipment (net)	1,500,000	880,000			2,380,000
14	Other assets	50,000	160,000		(2) 160,000	50,000
15	Total assets	4,363,200	1,848,000			5,188,000
16						
17	Accounts payable	800,000	400,000	(3) 100,000		1,100,000
18	Long-term debt	1,000,000	600,000	(2) 160,000		1,440,000
19	Common stock	2,000,000	800,000	(1) 800,000		2,000,000
20	Retained earnings	563,200	48,000	(1) 48,000		563,200
21	Minority interest	—	—		(1) 84,800	84,800
22	Total liabilities and					
23	stockholders' equity	4,363,200	1,848,000	1,108,000	1,108,000	5,188,000

(1) Elimination of intercompany investment. Minority interest equals 10 percent of Shannon Company's stockholders' equity [10% × ($800,000 + $48,000) = $84,800].

(2) Elimination of intercompany long-term debt.

(3) Elimination of intercompany receivables and payables.

CHAPTER ASSIGNMENTS

≡ BUILDING Your Basic Knowledge and Skills

Short Exercises

LO2 **Trading Securities**

SE 1. Murray Corporation began investing in trading securities in 20x6. At the end of 20x6, it had the following trading portfolio:

Security	Cost	Market Value
Sara Lee (10,000 shares)	$220,000	$330,000
Skyline (5,000 shares)	100,000	75,000
Totals	$320,000	$405,000

Prepare the necessary year-end adjusting entry on December 31 and the entry for the sale of all the Skyline shares on the following March 23 for $95,000.

LO3 **Cost-Adjusted-to-Market Method**

SE 2. On December 31, 20x6, the market value of Rapid Tech Company's portfolio of long-term available-for-sale securities was $640,000. The cost of these securities was $570,000. Prepare the entry to adjust the portfolio to market at year end, assuming that the company did not have any long-term investments prior to 20x6.

LO3 **Cost-Adjusted-to-Market Method**

SE 3. Refer to your answer to **SE 2**. Assume that on December 31, 20x7, the cost of Rapid Tech Company's portfolio of long-term available-for-sale securities was $1,280,000 and that its market value was $1,200,000. Prepare the entry to record the 20x7 year-end adjustment.

LO3 **Equity Method**

SE 4. Blanco Company owns 30 percent of Heaton Company. In 20x6, Heaton Company earned $60,000 and paid $40,000 in dividends. Prepare entries in journal form for Blanco Company's records on December 31 to reflect this information. Assume that the dividends are received on December 31.

LO3 **Methods of Accounting for Long-Term Investments**

SE 5. For each of the investments listed below, tell which of the following methods should be used for external financial reporting: (a) cost-adjusted-to-market method, (b) equity method, (c) consolidation of parent and subsidiary financial statements.

1. 49 percent investment in Irono Corporation
2. 51 percent investment in Barker Corporation
3. 5 percent investment in Hymir Corporation

LO4 **Purchase of 100 Percent at Book Value**

SE 6. Sutton Hills Corporation buys 100 percent ownership of Winter Treats Corporation for $100,000. At the time of the purchase, Winter Treats' stockholders' equity consisted of $20,000 in common stock and $80,000 in retained earnings. Sutton Hills' stockholders' equity consisted of $200,000 in common stock and $400,000 in retained earnings. After the purchase, what would be the amount, if any, of the following accounts on the consolidated balance sheet: goodwill, minority interest, common stock, and retained earnings?

LO4 **Purchase of Less than 100 Percent at Book Value**

SE 7. Assume the same facts as in **SE 6** except that Sutton Hills purchased 80 percent of Winter Treats Corporation for $80,000. After the purchase, what would be the amount, if any, of the following accounts on the consolidated balance sheet: goodwill, minority interest, common stock, and retained earnings?

LO4 **Purchase of 100 Percent at More than Book Value**

SE 8. Assume the same facts as in **SE 6** except that the purchase of 100 percent of Winter Treats Corporation was for $120,000. After the purchase, what would be the amount, if any, of the following accounts on the consolidated balance sheet: goodwill, minority interest, common stock, and retained earnings? Assume that the fair value of Winter Treats' net assets equals their book value.

LO4 **Intercompany Transactions**

SE 9. T Company owns 100 percent of C Company. The following are accounts from the balance sheets and income statements of both companies:

	T Company	C Company
Accounts receivable	$ 460,000	$ 300,000
Accounts payable	360,000	180,000
Sales	2,400,000	1,780,000
Cost of goods sold	1,420,000	1,080,000

What would be the combined amount of each of the above accounts on the consolidated financial statements assuming the following additional information? (1) C Company sold to T Company merchandise at cost in the amount of $540,000; (2) T Company sold all the merchandise it bought from C Company to customers, but it still owes C Company $120,000 for the merchandise.

LO5 **Held-to-Maturity Securities**

SE 10. On May 31, Fournier Company invested $98,000 in U.S. Treasury bills. The bills mature in 120 days at $100,000. Prepare entries to record the purchase on May 31; the adjustment to accrue interest on June 30, which is the end of the fiscal year; and the receipt of cash at the maturity date of September 28.

Exercises

LO1, LO2, LO3 **Discussion Questions**

E 1. Develop brief answers to each of the following questions:

1. Where in the financial statements are investment transactions reported?
2. What would cause an Allowance to Adjust Short-Term Investments to Market account that has a negative (credit) balance at the beginning of the year to have a positive (debit) balance at the end of the year?
3. When a company uses the equity method to record its proportionate share of the income and dividends of a company in which it has invested, what are the cash flow effects?

LO4, LO5 **Discussion Questions**

E 2. Develop brief answers to each of the following questions:

1. Under what conditions would a company have both minority interest and goodwill in a consolidation?
2. Why must the financial statements of foreign subsidiaries be restated?
3. What is the logic behind treating held-to-maturity securities different from any other investment?

LO2 **Trading Securities**

E 3. Omar Corporation, which has begun investing in trading securities, engaged in the following transactions:

Jan. 6 Purchased 7,000 shares of Quaker Oats stock, $30 per share.
Feb. 15 Purchased 9,000 shares of EG&G, $22 per share.

At year end on June 30, Quaker Oats was trading at $40 per share, and EG&G was trading at $18 per share.

Record the entries for the purchases. Then record the necessary year-end adjusting entry. (Include a schedule of the trading portfolio cost and market in the explanation.) Also record the entry for the sale of all the EG&G shares on August 20 for $16 per share. Is the last entry affected by the June 30 adjustment?

LO3 **Long-Term Investments**

E 4. Fulco Corporation has the following portfolio of long-term available-for-sale securities at year end, December 31, 20x2:

Company	Percentage of Voting Stock Held	Cost	Year-End Market Value
A Corporation	4	$ 80,000	$ 95,000
B Corporation	12	375,000	275,000
C Corporation	5	30,000	55,000
Total		$485,000	$425,000

Both the Unrealized Loss on Long-Term Investments account and the Allowance to Adjust Long-Term Investments to Market account currently have a balance of $40,000 from the last accounting period. Prepare T accounts with a beginning balance for each of these accounts. Record the effects of the above information on the accounts and determine the ending balances.

LO3 **Long-Term Investments: Cost-Adjusted-to-Market and Equity Methods**

E 5. On January 1, Rourke Corporation purchased, as long-term investments, 8 percent of the voting stock of Taglia Corporation for $250,000 and 45 percent of the voting stock of Curry Corporation for $2 million. During the year, Taglia Corporation had earnings of $100,000 and paid dividends of $40,000. Curry Corporation had earnings of $300,000 and paid dividends of $200,000. The market value did not change for either investment during the year. Which of these investments should be accounted for using the cost-adjusted-to-market method? Which should be accounted for using the equity method? At what amount should each investment be carried on the balance sheet at year end? Give a reason for each choice.

LO3 **Long-Term Investments: Equity Method**

E 6. On January 1, 20xx, Orchid Corporation acquired 40 percent of the voting stock of Vose Corporation, an amount sufficient to exercise significant influence over Vose Corporation's activities, for $4,800,000 in cash. On December 31, Orchid determined that Vose paid dividends of $800,000 but incurred a net loss of $400,000 for 20xx. Prepare entries in T account form to reflect this information.

LO3 **Methods of Accounting for Long-Term Investments**

E 7. Teague Corporation has the following long-term investments:

1. 60 percent of the common stock of Ariel Corporation
2. 13 percent of the common stock of Copper, Inc.
3. 50 percent of the nonvoting preferred stock of Staffordshire Corporation
4. 100 percent of the common stock of its financing subsidiary, EQ, Inc.
5. 35 percent of the common stock of the French company Rue de le Brasseur
6. 70 percent of the common stock of the Canadian company Nova Scotia Cannery

For each of these investments, tell which of the following methods should be used for external financial reporting, and why:

a. Cost-adjusted-to-market method

b. Equity method

c. Consolidation of parent and subsidiary financial statements

LO4   Elimination Entry for a Purchase at Book Value

E 8. Edson Manufacturing Company purchased 100 percent of the common stock of Liverpool Manufacturing Company for $600,000. Liverpool's stockholders' equity included common stock of $400,000 and retained earnings of $200,000. Prepare the eliminating entry in journal form that would appear on the work sheet for consolidating the balance sheets of these two entities as of the acquisition date.

LO4   Elimination Entry and Minority Interest

E 9. The stockholders' equity section of Caritas Corporation's balance sheet appeared as follows on December 31:

Common stock, $10 par value, 80,000 shares authorized and issued	$800,000
Retained earnings	96,000
Total stockholders' equity	$896,000

Swanson Manufacturing Company owns 80 percent of Caritas's voting stock and paid $11.20 per share. In journal form, prepare the entry (including minority interest) to eliminate Swanson's investment and Caritas's stockholders' equity that would appear on the work sheet used in preparing the consolidated balance sheet for the two firms.

LO4   Consolidated Balance Sheet with Goodwill

E 10. On September 1, 20x6, A Company purchased 100 percent of the voting stock of B Company for $480,000 in cash. The separate condensed balance sheets immediately after the purchase were as follows:

	A Company	B Company
Other assets	$1,103,000	$544,500
Investment in B Company	480,000	—
Total assets	$1,583,000	$544,500
Liabilities	$ 435,500	$ 94,500
Common stock	500,000	150,000
Retained earnings	647,500	300,000
Total liabilities and stockholders' equity	$1,583,000	$544,500

Prepare a work sheet for preparing the consolidated balance sheet immediately after A Company acquired control of B Company. Assume that any excess cost of A Company's investment in the subsidiary over book value is attributable to goodwill from consolidation.

LO4   Preparation of Consolidated Income Statement

E 11. Arnold Company has owned 100 percent of Van Rossum Company since 20x6. The income statements of these two companies for the year ended December 31, 20x7, follow.

	Arnold Company	Van Rossum Company
Net sales	$6,000,000	$2,400,000
Cost of goods sold	3,000,000	1,600,000
Gross margin	$3,000,000	$ 800,000
Less: Selling expenses	$1,000,000	$ 200,000
General and administrative expenses	1,200,000	400,000
Total operating expenses	$2,200,000	$ 600,000
Income from operations	$ 800,000	$ 200,000
Other income	240,000	—
Net income	$1,040,000	$ 200,000

The following is additional information: (1) Van Rossum Company purchased $1,120,000 of inventory from Arnold Company, which it had sold to Van Rossum customers by the end of the year. (2) Van Rossum Company leased its building from Arnold Company for $240,000 per year. Prepare a consolidated income statement work sheet for the two companies for the year ended December 31, 20x7. Ignore income taxes.

LO5 **Held-to-Maturity Securities**

E 12. Dale Company experiences heavy sales in the summer and early fall, after which time it has excess cash to invest until the next spring. On November 1, 20x6, the company invested $194,000 in U.S. Treasury bills. The bills mature in 180 days at $200,000. Prepare entries to record the purchase on November 1; the adjustment to accrue interest on December 31, which is the end of the fiscal year; and the receipt of cash at the maturity date of April 30.

Problems

LO1, LO2 **Accounting for Investments**

P 1. Gulf Coast Corporation is a successful oil and gas exploration business in the southwestern United States. At the beginning of 20xx, the company made investments in three companies that perform services in the oil and gas industry. The details of each of these investments follow.

Gulf Coast purchased 100,000 shares of Marsh Service Corporation at a cost of $16 per share. Marsh has 1.5 million shares outstanding and during 20xx paid dividends of $.80 per share on earnings of $1.60 per share. At the end of the year, Marsh's shares were selling for $24 per share.

Gulf Coast also purchased 2 million shares of Crescent Drilling Company at $8 per share. Crescent has 10 million shares outstanding. In 20xx, Crescent paid a dividend of $.40 per share on earnings of $.80 per share. During the year, the president of Gulf Coast was appointed to Crescent's board of directors. At the end of the year, Crescent's stock was selling for $12 per share.

In another action, Gulf Coast purchased 1 million shares of Logan Oil Field Supplies Company's 5 million outstanding shares at $12 per share. The president of Gulf Coast sought membership on Logan's board of directors but was rebuffed when a majority of shareholders stated they did not want to be associated with Gulf Coast. Logan paid a dividend of $.80 per share and reported a net income of only $.40 per share for the year. By the end of the year, its stock price had dropped to $4 per share.

Required

1. For each investment, make entries in journal form for (a) initial investment, (b) receipt of cash dividend, and (c) recognition of income (if appropriate).
2. What adjusting entry (if any) is required at the end of the year?
3. Assuming that Gulf Coast sells its investment in Logan after the first of the year for $6 per share, what journal entry would be made?
4. Assuming no other transactions occur and that the market value of Gulf Coast's investment in Marsh exceeds cost by $2,400,000 at the end of the second year, what adjusting entry (if any) would be required?
5. **User Insight:** What principal factors were considered in determining how to account for Gulf Coast's investments? Should they be shown on the balance sheet as short-term or long-term investments? What factors affect this decision?

LO3 **Long-Term Investments: Equity Method**

P 2. Rylander Corporation owns 35 percent of the voting stock of Waters Corporation. The Investment account on Rylander's books as of January 1, 20xx, was $720,000. During 20xx, Waters reported the following quarterly earnings and dividends:

Quarter	Earnings	Dividends Paid
1	$160,000	$100,000
2	240,000	100,000
3	120,000	100,000
4	(80,000)	100,000
	$440,000	$400,000

Because of the percentage of voting shares Rylander owns, it can exercise significant influence over the operations of Waters Corporation. Therefore, Rylander Corporation must account for the investment using the equity method.

Required

1. Prepare a T account for Rylander Corporation's investment in Waters, and enter the beginning balance, the relevant entries for the year in total, and the ending balance.
2. **User Insight:** What is the effect and placement of the entries in requirement 1 on Rylander Corporation's earnings as reported on the income statement?
3. **User Insight:** What is the effect and placement of the entries in requirement 1 on the statement of cash flows?
4. **User Insight:** How would the effects on the statements differ if Rylander's ownership represented only a 15 percent share of Waters?

LO4 **Consolidated Balance Sheet: Cost Exceeding Book Value**

P 3. The balance sheets of Saba and Joseph Companies as of December 31, 20xx, appear on the next page.

Assume that Saba Company purchased 100 percent of Joseph's common stock for $700,000 immediately prior to December 31, 20xx. Also assume that $160,000 of the excess of cost over book value is attributable to the increased value of Joseph Company's property, plant, and equipment. The rest of the excess is considered by Saba Company to be goodwill.

	Saba Company	Joseph Company
Assets		
Cash	$ 120,000	$ 80,000
Accounts receivable	200,000	60,000
Investment in Joseph Company	700,000	—
Property, plant, and equipment (net)	200,000	360,000
Total assets	$1,220,000	$500,000
Liabilities and Stockholders' Equity		
Accounts payable	$ 220,000	$ 60,000
Common stock, $20 par value	800,000	400,000
Retained earnings	200,000	40,000
Total liabilities and stockholders' equity	$1,220,000	$500,000

Required

1. Prepare a work sheet for preparing a consolidated balance sheet as of the acquisition date.
2. **User Insight:** If you were reading Saba's consolidated balance sheet, what account would indicate that Saba paid more than book value for Joseph and where would you find it on the balance sheet? Also, would you expect the amount of this account to change from year-to-year? What would cause it to change?

LO4 **Consolidated Balance Sheet: Less than 100 Percent Ownership**

P 4. In a cash transaction, Geis Company purchased 70 percent of the outstanding stock of Vogel Company for $593,600 cash on June 30, 20xx. Immediately after the acquisition, the separate balance sheets of the companies appeared as shown below.

	Geis Company	Vogel Company
Assets		
Cash	$ 320,000	$ 48,000
Accounts receivable	520,000	240,000
Inventory	800,000	520,000
Investment in Vogel Company	593,600	—
Property, plant, and equipment (net)	1,200,000	880,000
Other assets	40,000	160,000
Total assets	$3,473,600	$1,848,000
Liabilities and Stockholders' Equity		
Accounts payable	$ 640,000	$ 400,000
Long-term debt	800,000	600,000
Common stock, $10 par value	1,600,000	800,000
Retained earnings	433,600	48,000
Total liabilities and stockholders' equity	$3,473,600	$1,848,000

Additional information: (a) Vogel Company's other assets represent a long-term investment in Geis Company's long-term debt. The debt was purchased for an amount equal to Geis's carrying value of the debt. (b) Geis Company owes Vogel Company $80,000 for services rendered.

Required

1. Prepare a work sheet for preparing a consolidated balance sheet as of the acquisition date.
2. **User Insight:** If you were reading Geis's consolidated balance sheet, what account would indicate that Geis owned less than 100 percent of Vogel and where would you find it on the balance sheet?

Alternate Problems

LO3 Long-Term Investment Transactions

P 5. On January 2, 20x6, the Healey Company made several long-term investments in the voting stock of various companies. It purchased 10,000 shares of Zima at $4.00 a share, 15,000 shares of Kane at $6.00 a share, and 6,000 shares of Rodriguez at $9.00 a share. Each investment represents less than 20 percent of the voting stock of the company. The remaining securities transactions of Healey during 20x6 were as follows:

May	5	Purchased with cash 6,000 shares of Drennan stock for $6.00 per share. This investment represents less than 20 percent of the Drennan voting stock.
July	16	Sold the 10,000 shares of Zima stock for $3.60 per share.
Sept.	30	Purchased with cash 5,000 additional shares of Kane for $6.40 per share. This investment still represents less than 20 percent of the voting stock.
Dec.	31	The market values per share of the stock in the Long-Term Investments account were as follows: Kane, $6.50; Rodriguez, $8.00; and Drennan, $4.00.

Healey's transactions in securities during 20x7 were as follows:

Feb.	1	Received a cash dividend from Kane of $.20 per share.
July	15	Sold the 6,000 Rodriguez shares for $8.00 per share.
Aug.	1	Received a cash dividend from Kane of $.20 per share.
Sept.	10	Purchased 3,000 shares of Parmet Company for $14.00 per share. This investment represents less than 20 percent of the voting stock of the company.
Dec.	31	The market values per share of the stock in the Long-Term Investments account were as follows: Kane, $6.50; Drennan, $5.00; and Parmet, $13.00.

Required

1. Prepare entries in journal form to record all of Healey Company's transactions in long-term investments during 20x6 and 20x7.
2. **User Insight:** Assume that Healey increased its ownership in Kane to 25 percent and its ownership in Parmet to 60 percent in 20x8. How would these actions affect the methods used to account for the investments?

LO3 Long-Term Investments: Equity Method

P 6. Bon Company owns 40 percent of the voting stock of Macree Company. The investment account for this company on Bon's balance sheet had a balance of $300,000 on January 1, 20xx. During 20xx, the Macree Company reported the following quarterly earnings and dividends paid:

Quarter	Earnings	Dividends Paid
1	$ 40,000	$20,000
2	30,000	20,000
3	80,000	20,000
4	(20,000)	20,000
	$130,000	$80,000

Bon Company exercises a significant influence over Macree's operations and therefore uses the equity method to account for its investment.

Required

1. Prepare a T account for Bon's investment in Macree. Enter the beginning balance, the relevant entries for the year in total, and the ending balance.
2. **User Insight:** What is the effect and placement of the entries in requirement 1 on Bon Company's earnings as reported on the income statement?
3. **User Insight:** What is the effect and placement of the entries in requirement 1 on the statement of cash flows?
4. **User Insight:** How would the effects on the statements differ if Bon's ownership represented only a 10 percent share of Macree?

LO4 Consolidated Balance Sheet: Cost Exceeding Book Value

P 7. The balance sheets of Cheever and Ham Companies as of December 31, 20xx, are as follows.

	Cheever Company	Ham Company
Assets		
Cash	$ 400,000	$ 120,000
Accounts receivable	550,000	1,200,000
Investment in Ham Company	1,400,000	—
Property, plant, and equipment (net)	1,370,000	900,000
Total assets	$3,720,000	$2,220,000
Liabilities and Stockholders' Equity		
Accounts payable	$ 950,000	$1,070,000
Common stock, $20 par value	1,850,000	1,000,000
Retained earnings	920,000	150,000
Total liabilities and stockholders' equity	$3,720,000	$2,220,000

Assume that Cheever Company purchased 100 percent of Ham's common stock for $1,400,000 immediately prior to December 31, 20xx. Also assume that $100,000 of the excess of cost over book value is attributable to the increased value of Ham Company's property, plant, and equipment. Cheever considers the rest of the excess to be goodwill.

Required

1. Prepare a work sheet for preparing a consolidated balance sheet as of the acquisition date.
2. **User Insight:** If you were reading Cheever's consolidated balance sheet, what account would indicate that Cheever paid more than book value for Ham and where would you find it on the balance sheet? Also, would you expect the amount of this account to change from year-to-year? What would cause it to change?

LO2, LO5   Held-to-Maturity and Trading Securities

P 8. During certain periods, Yang Company invests its excess cash until it is needed. During 20x6 and 20x7, Yang engaged in these transactions:

20x6

Jan. 16   Invested $146,000 in 120-day U.S. Treasury bills that had a maturity value of $150,000.

Apr. 15   Purchased 10,000 shares of King Tools common stock at $40 per share and 5,000 shares of Mellon Gas common stock at $30 per share as trading securities.

May 16   Received maturity value of U.S. Treasury bills in cash.

June 2   Received dividends of $2.00 per share from King Tools and $1.50 per share from Mellon Gas.

June 30   Made year-end adjusting entry for trading securities. Market price per share for King Tools is $32; for Mellon Gas, it is $35.

Nov. 14   Sold all the shares of King Tools for $42 per share.

20x7

Feb. 15   Purchased 9,000 shares of MKD Communications for $50 per share.

Apr. 1   Invested $195,500 in 120-day U.S. Treasury bills that had a maturity value of $200,000.

June 1   Received dividends of $2.20 per share from Mellon Gas.

    30   Made year-end adjusting entry for held-to-maturity securities.

    30   Made year-end adjusting entry for trading securities. Market price of Mellon Gas shares is $33 per share and of MKD Communications shares is $60 per share.

Required

1. Prepare entries in journal form to record the preceding transactions, assuming that Yang Company's fiscal year ends on June 30.
2. Show the balance sheet presentation of short-term investments on June 30, 20x7.
3. **User Insight:** Explain the following statement: "Held to maturity and trading securities are opposites in terms of investment strategy and thus require opposite accounting treatments."

ENHANCING Your Knowledge, Skills, and Critical Thinking

Conceptual Understanding Cases

LO2, LO3   Understanding Investment Accounting

C 1. Dell Computer Corporation has significant investment activities. The following items are from Dell's 2004 financial statements (in millions):[15]

Short-term investments	$ 835
Long-term investments	6,700
Investment income	180
Gains on sale of investments	16
Purchase of investments	12,099
Sales of investments	10,078
Change in unrealized gains (losses) on long-term investments, net	(35)

Dell states that all debt and equities securities are classified as available-for-sale and are subject to an annual impairment test.

1. Where would you find each of the above items in Dell Computer's financial statements?
2. What value (cost or fair value) would you expect the first two items on Dell's balance sheet to represent?
3. What are impairments, and how do they differ from unrealized losses on long-term investments?

LO4 **Goodwill and Minority Interest**

C 2. DreamWorks Animation makes well-known animated films like *Shrek* 2. Two items on the company's 2004 balance sheet are as follows:[16]

Goodwill	$26,462
Minority interest	2,941

1. What is the difference between goodwill and minority interest and where do these items appear on the balance sheet?
2. The amount of goodwill did not change from 2003 to 2004. Assuming no new acquisitions or sales, what would cause the amount of goodwill to change from year to year? Would it increase or decrease?

Interpreting Financial Reports

LO4 **Effects of Consolidating Finance Subsidiaries**

C 3. National Stores Corporation is one of the largest owners of discount appliance stores in the United States. It owns Bi-Lo Superstores and several other discount chains. It has a wholly owned finance subsidiary handle its accounts receivable. Condensed balance sheets for National Stores and its finance subsidiary are shown below (in millions). The fiscal year ends January 31, 20x7.

	National Stores Corporation	Finance Subsidiary
Assets		
Current assets (except accounts receivable)	$ 866	$ 1
Accounts receivable (net)	293	869
Property, equipment, and other assets	933	—
Investment in finance subsidiary	143	—
Total assets	$2,235	$870
Liabilities and Stockholders' Equity		
Current liabilities	$ 717	$ 10
Long-term liabilities	859	717
Stockholders' equity	659	143
Total liabilities and stockholders' equity	$2,235	$870

Total sales to customers were $4 billion. The FASB requires all majority-owned subsidiaries to be consolidated in the parent company's financial statements. National Stores' management believes it is misleading to consolidate the finance subsidiary because it distorts the real operations of the company.

1. Prepare a consolidated balance sheet for National Stores Corporation and its finance subsidiary.
2. Demonstrate the effects of consolidating by computing the following ratios for National Stores before and after the consolidation in **1**: receivable turnover, days' sales uncollected, and debt to equity ratio (use year-end balances).
3. What are some of the other ratios that will be affected by consolidating the financial statements? Does consolidation assist investors and creditors in assessing the risk of investing in National Stores' securities or lending the company money? Relate your answer to your calculations in **2**.
4. What do you think of management's view that it is misleading to consolidate the finance subsidiary?

Decision Analysis Using Excel

LO2   **Accounting for Short-Term Investments**

C 4. Jackson Christmas Tree Company's business—the growing and selling of Christmas trees—is seasonal. By January 1, after its heavy selling season, the company has cash on hand that will not be needed for several months. It has minimal expenses from January to October and heavy expenses during the harvest and shipping months of November and December. The company's management follows the practice of investing the idle cash in marketable securities, which can be sold when funds are needed for operations. The company's fiscal year ends on June 30.

On January 10 of the current year, Jackson has cash of $597,300 on hand. It keeps $20,000 on hand for operating expenses and invests the rest as follows:

$100,000 three-month Treasury bills	$ 97,800
5,000 shares of Ford Motor Co. ($10 per share)	50,000
5,000 shares of McDonald's ($25 per share)	125,000
4,350 shares of IBM ($70 per share)	304,500
Total short-term investments	$577,300

On February 10 and May 10, Jackson receives quarterly cash dividends from each company in which it has invested: $.10 per share from Ford Motor Co., $.14 per share from McDonald's, and $.20 per share from IBM. The Treasury bills are redeemed at face value on April 10. On June 1, management sells 1,000 shares of McDonald's at $28 per share.

On June 30, the market values of the investments are as follows:

Ford Motor Co.	$11 per share
McDonald's	$23 per share
IBM	$65 per share

Jackson receives another quarterly dividend from each company on August 10. It sells all its remaining shares on November 1 at the following prices:

Ford Motor Co.	$ 9 per share
McDonald's	$22 per share
IBM	$80 per share

1. Record the investment transactions that occurred on January 10, February 10, April 10, May 10, and June 1. The Treasury bills are accounted for as held-to-maturity securities, and the stocks are trading securities. Prepare the required adjusting entry on June 30 and record the investment transactions on August 10 and November 1.
2. Explain how the short-term investments would be shown on the balance sheet on June 30.

3. After November 1, what is the balance of Allowance to Adjust Short-Term Investments to Market, and what will happen to this account next June?

4. What is your assessment of Jackson Christmas Tree Company's strategy with regard to idle cash?

Annual Report Case: CVS Corporation

LO4 Planned Acquisition

C 5. Refer to Note 2 of **CVS Corporation's** annual report in the Supplement to Chapter 1. The company announces plans to finalize the acquisition of Eckerd Drugstores from J. C. Penney in early 2005. What is the purchase price of Eckerd? Is CVS paying more than the fair value for the net assets of Eckerd? If so, how much more is it paying and what does the excess represent?

Comparison Case: CVS Versus Southwest

LO2 Investments in Derivatives

C 6. Refer to the annual report of **CVS Corporation** and the financial statements of **Southwest Airlines Co**. in the Supplement to Chapter 1. Refer to comprehensive income (loss) in each company's statement of shareholders' equity. Which item for each company refers to derivatives (a type of investment involving future contracts)? What causes either an unrealized gain or loss to occur? In the case of Southwest, find the accounting policy with regard to financial derivatives instruments in Note 1 to the financial statements. What problem does Southwest's management face in determining the fair market value of its derivatives? How does management solve the problem?

Ethical Dilemma Case

LO1 Insider Trading

C 7. Refer to the discussion about insider trading in this chapter to answer the following questions:

1. What does *insider trading* mean?
2. Why do you think insider trading is illegal in the United States and in Germany?
3. Why do you think insider trading is permissible in some other countries?
4. Can you think of any reasons why insider trading should be permitted in the United States?

Internet Case

LO3, LO4 Comparison of Two Recent Acquisitions

C 8. Mergers and acquisitions are in the news almost every day. Go to the website for **MSNBC** and scan recent headlines to locate two articles related to one company purchasing or making an offer to purchase another company. Read the articles and summarize the nature of the actual or proposed acquisition. What are the companies' names? What industry are they in? What is the dollar amount of the acquisition? How will the acquisition be paid for—in cash, stock, or a combination of cash and stock? In what ways are the acquisitions similar? How do they differ? Be prepared to present your findings in class.

Group Activity Case

LO1, LO2, LO3   **Identification of Investments and Resulting Gains and Losses**

C 9. Microsoft, one of the most successful businesses in the history of commerce, has accumulated a large investment portfolio, which in a recent year consisted of the following (in millions):[17]

Cash and cash equivalents	$15,982
Short-term investments-available-for-sale	44,610
Corporate notes and bonds-held-to-maturity	1,481
Long-term investments—equity securities	10,729
Total investments	$72,802

In addition, during the year Microsoft had net realized gains on investments of $1.640 million, $82 million of impairments, and unrealized losses of $293 million.

Divide into at least seven groups to discuss each of the four types of investments and the three types of gains or losses. Each group should discuss the nature of each gain or loss and the nature of the investment that gave rise to it. Discuss where each investment and gain or loss would appear in the financial statements. Be prepared to present your group's findings in class.

Business Communication Case

LO1   **Presentation on Investment Classification and Valuation**

C 10. The classification and valuation of investments can be confusing for someone not familiar with classifying investments. Suppose you have been asked to make a short (five-minute) presentation that explains this classification scheme. Develop a one-page outline with talking points that explains the three types of short-term and long-term investments and how they are valued at year end. Then briefly cover how accounting for long-term investments depends on the level and percentage of ownership. Be prepared to give your presentation in class or to a small group.

Accounting for Unincorporated Businesses

Throughout the book, we have focused on accounting for the corporate form of business. In this appendix, our focus is on accounting for sole proprietorships and partnerships.

Accounting for Sole Proprietorships

A *sole proprietorship* is a business owned by one person. For the individual, this business form can be a convenient way of separating business activities from personal interests. Legally, however, the proprietorship is the same economic unit as the individual. The sole proprietor receives all the profits or losses and is liable for all the obligations of the business. Proprietorships represent the largest number of businesses in the United States, but typically they are the smallest in size. The life of a proprietorship ends when the owner wishes it to or at the owner's death or incapacity.

When someone invests in his or her own company, the amount of the investment is recorded in that person's Capital account. For example, the entry to record the initial investment of $10,000 by Hyun Hooper in her new mail-order business would be a debit to the Cash account for $10,000 and a credit to the Hyun Hooper, Capital account for $10,000.

During the period, Hooper will probably withdraw assets from the business for personal living expenses. Because there is no legal separation between the owner and the sole proprietorship, it is not necessary to make a formal declaration of a withdrawal, as would be required in the case of corporate dividends. The withdrawal of $500 by Hooper is recorded as a debit to the Hyun Hooper, Withdrawals account for $500 and a credit to the Cash account for $500.

Revenue and expense accounts for sole proprietorships are closed out to Income Summary in the same way as they are for corporations. Income Summary, however, is closed to the Capital account instead of to Retained Earnings. For example, the closing entries that follow assume a net income of $1,000 and withdrawals of $500:

Income Summary	1,000	
Hyun Hooper, Capital		1,000
To close Income Summary in		
a sole proprietorship		
Hyun Hooper, Capital	500	
Hyun Hooper, Withdrawals		500
To close Withdrawals		

Accounting for Partnerships

The Uniform Partnership Act, which has been adopted by a majority of the states, defines a *partnership* as "an association of two or more persons to carry on as co-owners of a business for profit." Normally, partnerships are formed when owners of small businesses wish to combine capital or managerial talents for some common business purpose. Partnerships are treated as separate entities in accounting, but legally there is no economic separation between them and their owners. They differ in many ways from the other forms of business. The following are some of their important characteristics:

Voluntary Association   A partnership is a voluntary association of individuals rather than a legal entity in itself. Therefore, a partner is responsible under the law for his or her partners' actions within the scope of the business. A partner also has unlimited liability for the debts of the partnership. Because of these potential liabilities, a partner must be allowed to choose the people who join the partnership.

Partnership Agreement   A partnership is easy to form. Two or more people simply agree to be partners in a business enterprise. This agreement is known as a *partnership agreement*. The partnership agreement does not have to be in writing. However, it is good business practice to have a written document that clearly states the details of the partnership, including the name, location, and purpose of the business; the partners' names and their respective duties; the investments of each partner; the method of distributing income and losses; and procedures for the admission and withdrawal of partners, the withdrawal of assets allowed each partner, and the liquidation (termination) of the business.

Limited Life   Because a partnership is formed by an agreement between partners, it has a *limited life*. It may be dissolved when a new partner is admitted; when a partner withdraws, goes bankrupt, is incapacitated (to the point that he or she cannot perform as obligated), retires, or dies; or when the terms of the partnership agreement are met (e.g., when the project for which the partnership was formed is completed). The partnership agreement can be written to cover each of these situations, thus allowing the partnership to continue legally.

Mutual Agency   Each partner is an agent of the partnership within the scope of the business. Because of this *mutual agency*, any partner can bind the partnership to a business agreement as long as he or she acts within the scope of the company's normal operations. For example, a partner in a used-car business can bind the partnership through the purchase or sale of used cars. But this partner cannot bind the partnership to a contract for buying men's clothing or any other goods that are not related to the used-car business.

Unlimited Liability   Each partner has personal *unlimited liability* for all the debts of the partnership. If a partnership cannot pay its debts, creditors must first satisfy their claims from the assets of the business. If these assets are not enough to pay all debts, the creditors can seek payment from the personal assets of each partner. If a partner's personal assets are used up before the debts are paid, the creditors can claim additional assets from the remaining partners who are able to pay. Each partner, then, can be required by law to pay all the debts of the partnership.

Co-Ownership of Partnership Property   When individuals invest property in a partnership, they give up the right to their separate use of the property. The property becomes an asset of the partnership and is owned jointly by the partners.

Participation in Partnership Income   Each partner has the right to share in the company's income and the responsibility to share in its losses. The partnership agreement should state the method of distributing income and losses to each partner. If the agreement describes how income should be shared but does not mention losses, losses are distributed in the same way as income. If the agreement does not describe the method of income and loss distribution, the partners must by law share income and losses equally.

Accounting for Partners' Equity

The owners' equity of a partnership is called *partners' equity*. In accounting for partners' equity, it is necessary to maintain separate Capital and Withdrawals accounts for each partner and to divide the income and losses of the company among the partners. In the partners' equity section of the balance sheet, the balance of each partner's Capital account is listed separately:

Liabilities and *Partners' Equity*		
Total liabilities		$28,000
Partners' equity		
Desmond, capital	$25,000	
Frank, capital	34,000	
Total partners' equity		59,000
Total liabilities and partners' equity		$87,000

Each partner invests cash, other assets, or both in the partnership according to the partnership agreement. Noncash assets should be valued at their fair market value on the date they are transferred to the partnership. The assets invested by a partner are debited to the proper account, and the total amount is credited to the partner's Capital account.

To show how partners' investments are recorded, let's assume that Jack Haddock and Pilar Villamer have agreed to combine their capital and equipment in a partnership to operate a jewelry store. According to their partnership agreement, Haddock will invest $28,000 cash and $47,000 of equipment, and the partnership will assume a note payable on the equipment of $10,000. The entry to record one partner's initial investment is as follows:

20x7			
July 1	Cash	28,000	
	Equipment	47,000	
	Note Payable		10,000
	Jack Haddock, Capital		65,000
	Initial investment of Jack Haddock in Haddock and Villamer		

Distribution of Partnership Income and Losses

A partnership's income and losses can be distributed according to whatever method the partners specify in the partnership agreement. Income in this form of business normally has three components: return to the partners for the use of their capital (called *interest on partners' capital*), compensation for services the partners have rendered (partners' salaries), and other income for any special contributions individual partners may make to the partnership or for risks they may take. The breakdown of total income into its three components helps clarify how much each partner has contributed to the firm.

Distributing income and losses among partners can be accomplished by using stated ratios or capital balance ratios or by paying the partners salaries and interest on their capital and sharing the remaining income according to stated ratios. *Salaries* and *interest* here are not *salaries expense* or *interest expense* in the ordinary sense of the terms. They do not affect the amount of reported net income. Instead, they refer to ways of determining each partner's share of net income or loss based on the time the partner spends on the business and the money he or she invests in it.

Stated Ratios   One method of distributing income and losses is to give each partner a stated ratio of the total income or loss. If each partner is making an equal contribution to the firm, each can assume the same share of income and losses. It is important to understand that an equal contribution to the firm does not necessarily mean an equal capital investment in the firm. One partner may be devoting more time and talent to the firm, whereas another may have made a larger capital investment. And if the partners contribute unequally to the firm, unequal stated ratios can be appropriate. Let's assume that Haddock and Villamer had a net income last year of $140,000 and that the stated ratio for Haddock is 60 percent and for Villamer, it is 40 percent. The computation of each partner's share of the income and the journal entry to show the distribution based on these ratios are as follows:

Haddock ($140,000 × .60)	$ 84,000
Villamer ($140,000 × .40)	56,000
Net income	$140,000

20x7			
June 30	Income Summary	140,000	
	Jack Haddock, Capital		84,000
	Pilar Villamer, Capital		56,000
	Distribution of income for the year		
	to the partners' Capital accounts		

Capital Balance Ratios   If invested capital produces the most income for the partnership, then income and losses may be distributed according to *capital balance*. One way of distributing income and losses here is to use a ratio based on each partner's capital balance at the beginning of the year. For example, suppose that at the start of the fiscal year, July 1, 20x7, Jack Haddock's Capital account showed a $65,000 balance and Pilar Villamer's Capital account showed a $60,000 balance. The total partners' equity in the firm, then, was $125,000. Each partner's capital balance at the beginning of the year divided by the total partners' equity at the beginning of the year is that partner's beginning capital balance ratio:

	Beginning Capital Balance	Beginning Capital Balance Ratio
Jack Haddock	$ 65,000	65 ÷ 125 = .52 = 52%
Pilar Villamer	60,000	60 ÷ 125 = .48 = 48%
	$125,000	

The income that each partner should receive when distribution is based on beginning capital balance ratios is figured by multiplying the total income by each partner's capital ratio. If we assume that income for the year was $140,000, Jack Haddock's share of that income was $72,800, and Pilar Villamer's share was $67,200:

Jack Haddock $140,000 × .52 = $ 72,800
Pilar Villamer $140,000 × .48 =   67,200
                                   $140,000

Salaries, Interest, and Stated Ratios

Partners generally do not contribute equally to a firm. To make up for unequal contributions, a partnership agreement can allow for partners' salaries, interest on partners' capital balances, or a combination of both in the distribution of income. Again, salaries and interest of this kind are not deducted as expenses before the partnership income is determined. They represent a method of arriving at an equitable distribution of income or loss.

Salaries allow for differences in the services that partners provide the business. However, they do not take into account differences in invested capital. To allow for capital differences, each partner can receive, in addition to salary, a stated interest on his or her invested capital. Suppose that Jack Haddock and Pilar Villamer agree to annual salaries of $8,000 and $7,000, respectively, as well as 10 percent interest on their beginning capital balances, and to share any remaining income equally. The calculations for Haddock and Villamer, assuming income of $140,000, appear below.

| | Income of Partner | | |
	Haddock	Villamer	Income Distributed
Total income for distribution			$140,000
Distribution of salaries			
Haddock	$ 8,000		
Villamer		$ 7,000	(15,000)
Remaining income after salaries			$125,000
Distribution of interest			
Haddock ($65,000 × .10)	6,500		
Villamer ($60,000 × .10)		6,000	(12,500)
Remaining income after salaries and interest			$112,500
Equal distribution of remaining income			
Haddock ($112,500 × .50)	56,250		
Villamer ($112,500 × .50)		56,250	(112,500)
Remaining income			—
Income of partners	$70,750	$69,250	$140,000

If the partnership agreement allows for the distribution of salaries or interest or both, the amounts must be allocated to the partners even if profits are not enough to cover the salaries and interest. In fact, even if the company has a loss, these allocations still must be made. After the allocation of salaries and interest, the negative balance, or loss, must be distributed according to the stated ratio in the partnership agreement or equally if the agreement does not mention a ratio.

For example, let's assume that Haddock and Villamer agreed to the following conditions, with much higher annual salaries, for the distribution of income and losses:

	Salaries	Interest	*Beginning Capital Balance*
Haddock	$70,000	10% of beginning	$65,000
Villamer	60,000	capital balances	60,000

The computations for the distribution of the income and loss, again assuming income of $140,000, are as follows:

			Income of Partner
	Haddock	**Villamer**	**Income Distributed**
Total income for distribution			$140,000
Distribution of salaries			
Haddock	$70,000		
Villamer		$60,000	(130,000)
Remaining income after salaries			$ 10,000
Distribution of interest			
Haddock ($65,000 × .10)	6,500		
Villamer ($60,000 × .10)		6,000	(12,500)
Remaining income after salaries and interest			($ 2,500)
Equal distribution of negative balance*			
Haddock ($2,500 × .50)	(1,250)		
Villamer ($2,500 × .50)		(1,250)	2,500
Remaining income			—
Income of partners	$75,250	$64,750	$140,000

*Notice that the negative balance is distributed equally because the partnership agreement does not indicate how income and losses should be distributed after salaries and interest are paid.

Dissolution of a Partnership

Dissolution of a partnership occurs whenever there is a change in the original association of partners. When a partnership is dissolved, the partners lose their authority to continue the business as a going concern. This does not mean that the business operation necessarily is ended or interrupted, but it does mean—from a legal and accounting standpoint—that the separate entity ceases to exist. The remaining partners can act for the partnership in finishing the affairs of the business or in forming a new partnership that will be a new accounting entity. The dissolution of a partnership takes place through, among other events, the admission of a new partner, the withdrawal of a partner, or the death of a partner.

Admission of a New Partner   The admission of a new partner dissolves the old partnership because a new association has been formed. Dissolving the old partnership and creating a new one requires the consent of all the original partners and the ratification of a new partnership agreement. An individual can be admitted to a partnership in one of two ways: by purchasing an interest in the partnership from one or more of the original partners, or by investing assets in the partnership.

Purchasing an Interest from a Partner   When a person purchases an interest in a partnership from an original partner, the transaction is a personal one between these two people. However, the interest purchased must be transferred from the Capital account of the selling partner to the Capital account of the new partner. Suppose that Jack Haddock decides to sell his interest of $70,000 in Haddock and Villamer to Richard Davis for $100,000 on August 31, 20x8, and that Pilar Villamer agrees to the sale. The entry to record the sale on the partnership books looks like this:

20x8			
Aug. 31	Jack Haddock, Capital	70,000	
	Richard Davis, Capital		70,000
	Transfer of Jack Haddock's equity		
	to Richard Davis		

Notice that the entry records the book value of the equity, not the amount Davis pays. The amount Davis pays is a personal matter between Davis and Haddock.

Investing Assets in a Partnership   When a new partner is admitted through an investment in the partnership, both the assets and the partners' equity in the firm increase. This is because the assets the new partner invests become partnership assets, and as partnership assets increase, partners' equity increases.

For example, assume that Richard Davis wants to invest $75,000 for a one-third interest in the partnership of Haddock and Villamer. The Capital accounts of Jack Haddock and Pilar Villamer are $70,000 and $80,000, respectively. The assets of the firm are valued correctly. So, the partners agree to sell Davis a one-third interest in the firm for $75,000. Davis's $75,000 investment equals a one-third interest in the firm after the investment is added to the previously existing capital of the partnership:

Jack Haddock, Capital	$ 70,000
Pilar Villamer, Capital	80,000
Davis's investment	75,000
Total capital after Davis's investment	$225,000
One-third interest = $225,000 ÷ 3 =	$ 75,000

The entry to record Davis's investment is as follows:

20x8			
Aug. 31	Cash	75,000	
	Richard Davis, Capital		75,000
	Admission of Richard Davis for a		
	one-third interest in the company		

Bonus to the Old Partners   A partnership is sometimes so profitable or otherwise advantageous that a new investor is willing to pay more than the actual dollar interest he or she receives in the partnership. Suppose an individual pays $100,000 for an $80,000 interest in a partnership. The $20,000 excess of the payment over the interest purchased is a *bonus* to the original partners. The bonus must be distributed to the original partners according to the partnership agreement. When the agreement does not cover the distribution of bonuses, it should be distributed to the original partners in accordance with the method of distributing income and losses.

Assume that Haddock and Villamer's firm has operated for several years and that the partners' capital balances and the stated ratios for distribution of income and loss are as follows:

Partners	Capital Balances	Stated Ratios
Haddock	$160,000	55%
Villamer	140,000	45%
	$300,000	100%

Richard Davis wants to join the firm. He offers to invest $100,000 on December 1, 20x8, for a one-fifth interest in the business and income. The original partners agree to the offer. This is the computation of the bonus to the original partners:

Partners' equity in the original partnership		$300,000
Cash investment by Richard Davis		100,000
Partners' equity in the new partnership		$400,000
Partners' equity assigned to Richard Davis ($400,000 × 1/5)		$ 80,000
Bonus to the original partners		
Investment by Richard Davis	$100,000	
Less equity assigned to Richard Davis	80,000	$ 20,000
Distribution of bonus to original partners		
Jack Haddock ($20,000 × .55)	$ 11,000	
Pilar Villamer ($20,000 × .45)	9,000	$ 20,000

This is the entry that records Davis's admission to the partnership:

```
20x8
Dec.  1   Cash                                      100,000
              Jack Haddock, Capital                            11,000
              Pilar Villamer, Capital                           9,000
              Richard Davis, Capital                           80,000
              Investment by Richard Davis for
              a one-fifth interest in the firm,
              and the bonus distributed to the
              original partners
```

Bonus to the New Partner   There are several reasons why a partnership might want a new partner. A partnership in financial trouble might need additional cash. Or the partners might want to expand the firm's markets and need more capital for this purpose than they themselves can provide. Also, the partners might know a person who would bring a unique talent to the firm. Under these conditions, a new partner may be admitted to the partnership with the understanding that part of the original partners' capital will be transferred (credited) to the new partner's Capital account as a bonus.

Withdrawal of a Partner

Generally, a partner has the right to withdraw from a partnership in accord with legal requirements. However, to avoid disputes when a partner does decide to withdraw or retire from the firm, the partnership agreement should describe the procedures that are to be followed.

The agreement should specify (1) whether an audit will be performed, (2) how the assets will be reappraised, (3) how a bonus will be determined, and (4) by what method the withdrawing partner will be paid.

A partner who wants to withdraw from a partnership can do so in one of several ways. The partner can sell his or her interest to another partner or to an outsider with the consent of the remaining partners, or the partner can withdraw assets equal to his or her capital balance, less than his or her capital balance (in this case, the remaining partners receive a bonus), or greater than his or her capital balance (in this case, the withdrawing partner receives a bonus). Bonuses upon withdrawal of a partner are allocated in much the same way as bonuses that arise when a new partner is admitted.

Death of a Partner   When a partner dies, the partnership is dissolved because the original association has changed. The partnership agreement should state the actions to be taken. Normally, the books are closed, and financial statements are prepared. These actions are necessary to determine the capital balance of each partner on the date of the death. The agreement also may indicate whether an audit should be conducted, assets appraised, and a bonus recorded, as well as the procedures for settling with the deceased partner's heirs. The remaining partners may purchase the deceased's equity, sell it to outsiders, or deliver certain business assets to the estate. If the firm intends to continue, a new partnership must be formed.

Liquidation of a Partnership

Liquidation of a partnership is the process of ending the business—of selling enough assets to pay the partnership's liabilities and distributing any remaining assets among the partners. Liquidation is a special form of dissolution. When a partnership is liquidated, the business will not continue. As the assets of the business are sold, any gain or loss should be distributed to the partners according to the stated ratios. As cash becomes available, it must be applied first to outside creditors, then to loans from partners, and finally to the partners' capital balances. Any deficits in partners' capital accounts must be made up from personal assets.

Problems

Partnership Formation and Distribution of Income

P 1. In January 20x7, Ed Rivers and Bob Bascomb agreed to produce and sell chocolate candies. Rivers contributed $240,000 in cash to the business. Bascomb contributed the building and equipment, valued at $220,000 and $140,000, respectively. The partnership had an income of $84,000 during 20x7 but was less successful during 20x8, when income was only $40,000.

Required

1. Prepare the journal entry to record the investment of both partners in the partnership.
2. Determine the share of income for each partner in 20x7 and 20x8 under each of the following conditions: (a) The partners agreed to share income equally. (b) The partners failed to agree on an income-sharing arrangement. (c) The partners agreed to share income according to the ratio of their original investments. (d) The partners agreed to share income by allowing interest of 10 percent on their original investments and dividing

the remainder equally. (e) The partners agreed to share income by allowing salaries of $40,000 for Rivers and $28,000 for Bascomb, and dividing the remainder equally. (f) The partners agreed to share income by paying salaries of $40,000 to Rivers and $28,000 to Bascomb, allowing interest of 9 percent on their original investments, and dividing the remainder equally.

Admission and Withdrawal of a Partner

P 2. Margaret, Tracy, and Lou are partners in Woodwork Company. Their capital balances as of July 31, 20x7, are as follows:

MARGARET, CAPITAL	TRACY, CAPITAL	LOU, CAPITAL
45,000	15,000	30,000

Each partner has agreed to admit Vonice to the partnership.

Required

Prepare the entries to record Vonice's admission to or Margaret's withdrawal from the partnership under each of the following conditions: (a) Vonice pays Margaret $12,500 for 20 percent of Margaret's interest in the partnership. (b) Vonice invests $20,000 cash in the partnership and receives an interest equal to her investment. (c) Vonice invests $30,000 cash in the partnership for a 20 percent interest in the business. A bonus is to be recorded for the original partners on the basis of their capital balances. (d) Vonice invests $30,000 cash in the partnership for a 40 percent interest in the business. The original partners give Vonice a bonus according to the ratio of their capital balances on July 31, 20x7. (e) Margaret withdraws from the partnership, taking $52,500. The excess of withdrawn assets over Margaret's partnership interest is distributed according to the balances of the Capital accounts. (f) Margaret withdraws by selling her interest directly to Vonice for $60,000.

Future Value and Present Value Tables

Table 1 provides the multipliers necessary to compute the future value of a *single* cash deposit made at the *beginning* of year 1. Three factors must be known before the future value can be computed: (1) the time period in years, (2) the stated annual rate of interest to be earned, and (3) the dollar amount invested or deposited.

Example—Table 1. Determine the future value of $5,000 deposited now that will earn 9 percent interest compounded annually for five years. From Table 1, the necessary multiplier for five years at 9 percent is 1.539, and the answer is

$$\$5,000 \times 1.539 = \$7,695$$

TABLE 1. Future Value of $1 After a Given Number of Time Periods

Periods	1%	2%	3%	4%	5%	6%	7%	8%	9%	10%	12%	14%	15%
1	1.010	1.020	1.030	1.040	1.050	1.060	1.070	1.080	1.090	1.100	1.120	1.140	1.150
2	1.020	1.040	1.061	1.082	1.103	1.124	1.145	1.166	1.188	1.210	1.254	1.300	1.323
3	1.030	1.061	1.093	1.125	1.158	1.191	1.225	1.260	1.295	1.331	1.405	1.482	1.521
4	1.041	1.082	1.126	1.170	1.216	1.262	1.311	1.360	1.412	1.464	1.574	1.689	1.749
5	1.051	1.104	1.159	1.217	1.276	1.338	1.403	1.469	1.539	1.611	1.762	1.925	2.011
6	1.062	1.126	1.194	1.265	1.340	1.419	1.501	1.587	1.677	1.772	1.974	2.195	2.313
7	1.072	1.149	1.230	1.316	1.407	1.504	1.606	1.714	1.828	1.949	2.211	2.502	2.660
8	1.083	1.172	1.267	1.369	1.477	1.594	1.718	1.851	1.993	2.144	2.476	2.853	3.059
9	1.094	1.195	1.305	1.423	1.551	1.689	1.838	1.999	2.172	2.358	2.773	3.252	3.518
10	1.105	1.219	1.344	1.480	1.629	1.791	1.967	2.159	2.367	2.594	3.106	3.707	4.046
11	1.116	1.243	1.384	1.539	1.710	1.898	2.105	2.332	2.580	2.853	3.479	4.226	4.652
12	1.127	1.268	1.426	1.601	1.796	2.012	2.252	2.518	2.813	3.138	3.896	4.818	5.350
13	1.138	1.294	1.469	1.665	1.886	2.133	2.410	2.720	3.066	3.452	4.363	5.492	6.153
14	1.149	1.319	1.513	1.732	1.980	2.261	2.579	2.937	3.342	3.798	4.887	6.261	7.076
15	1.161	1.346	1.558	1.801	2.079	2.397	2.759	3.172	3.642	4.177	5.474	7.138	8.137
16	1.173	1.373	1.605	1.873	2.183	2.540	2.952	3.426	3.970	4.595	6.130	8.137	9.358
17	1.184	1.400	1.653	1.948	2.292	2.693	3.159	3.700	4.328	5.054	6.866	9.276	10.760
18	1.196	1.428	1.702	2.026	2.407	2.854	3.380	3.996	4.717	5.560	7.690	10.580	12.380
19	1.208	1.457	1.754	2.107	2.527	3.026	3.617	4.316	5.142	6.116	8.613	12.060	14.230
20	1.220	1.486	1.806	2.191	2.653	3.207	3.870	4.661	5.604	6.728	9.646	13.740	16.370
21	1.232	1.516	1.860	2.279	2.786	3.400	4.141	5.034	6.109	7.400	10.800	15.670	18.820
22	1.245	1.546	1.916	2.370	2.925	3.604	4.430	5.437	6.659	8.140	12.100	17.860	21.640
23	1.257	1.577	1.974	2.465	3.072	3.820	4.741	5.871	7.258	8.954	13.550	20.360	24.890
24	1.270	1.608	2.033	2.563	3.225	4.049	5.072	6.341	7.911	9.850	15.180	23.210	28.630
25	1.282	1.641	2.094	2.666	3.386	4.292	5.427	6.848	8.623	10.830	17.000	26.460	32.920
26	1.295	1.673	2.157	2.772	3.556	4.549	5.807	7.396	9.399	11.920	19.040	30.170	37.860
27	1.308	1.707	2.221	2.883	3.733	4.822	6.214	7.988	10.250	13.110	21.320	34.390	43.540
28	1.321	1.741	2.288	2.999	3.920	5.112	6.649	8.627	11.170	14.420	23.880	39.200	50.070
29	1.335	1.776	2.357	3.119	4.116	5.418	7.114	9.317	12.170	15.860	26.750	44.690	57.580
30	1.348	1.811	2.427	3.243	4.322	5.743	7.612	10.060	13.270	17.450	29.960	50.950	66.210
40	1.489	2.208	3.262	4.801	7.040	10.290	14.970	21.720	31.410	45.260	93.050	188.900	267.900
50	1.645	2.692	4.384	7.107	11.470	18.420	29.460	46.900	74.360	117.400	289.000	700.200	1,084.000

Where r is the interest rate and n is the number of periods, the factor values for Table 1 are

$$\text{FV Factor} = (1 + r)^n$$

Situations requiring the use of Table 2 are similar to those requiring Table 1 except that Table 2 is used to compute the future value of a *series* of *equal* annual deposits at the end of each period.

Example—Table 2.

What will be the future value at the end of 30 years if $1,000 is deposited each year on January 1, beginning in year 1, assuming 12 percent interest compounded annually? The required multiplier from Table 2 is 241.3, and the answer is

$$\$1,000 \times 241.3 = \$241,300$$

The factor values for Table 2 are

$$\text{FVa Factor} = \frac{(1 + r)^n - 1}{r}$$

TABLE 2. Future Value of $1 Paid in Each Period for a Given Number of Time Periods

Periods	1%	2%	3%	4%	5%	6%	7%	8%	9%	10%	12%	14%	15%
1	1.000	1.000	1.000	1.000	1.000	1.000	1.000	1.000	1.000	1.000	1.000	1.000	1.000
2	2.010	2.020	2.030	2.040	2.050	2.060	2.070	2.080	2.090	2.100	2.120	2.140	2.150
3	3.030	3.060	3.091	3.122	3.153	3.184	3.215	3.246	3.278	3.310	3.374	3.440	3.473
4	4.060	4.122	4.184	4.246	4.310	4.375	4.440	4.506	4.573	4.641	4.779	4.921	4.993
5	5.101	5.204	5.309	5.416	5.526	5.637	5.751	5.867	5.985	6.105	6.353	6.610	6.742
6	6.152	6.308	6.468	6.633	6.802	6.975	7.153	7.336	7.523	7.716	8.115	8.536	8.754
7	7.214	7.434	7.662	7.898	8.142	8.394	8.654	8.923	9.200	9.487	10.090	10.730	11.070
8	8.286	8.583	8.892	9.214	9.549	9.897	10.260	10.640	11.030	11.440	12.300	13.230	13.730
9	9.369	9.755	10.160	10.580	11.030	11.490	11.980	12.490	13.020	13.580	14.780	16.090	16.790
10	10.460	10.950	11.460	12.010	12.580	13.180	13.820	14.490	15.190	15.940	17.550	19.340	20.300
11	11.570	12.170	12.810	13.490	14.210	14.970	15.780	16.650	17.560	18.530	20.650	23.040	24.350
12	12.680	13.410	14.190	15.030	15.920	16.870	17.890	18.980	20.140	21.380	24.130	27.270	29.000
13	13.810	14.680	15.620	16.630	17.710	18.880	20.140	21.500	22.950	24.520	28.030	32.090	34.350
14	14.950	15.970	17.090	18.290	19.600	21.020	22.550	24.210	26.020	27.980	32.390	37.580	40.500
15	16.100	17.290	18.600	20.020	21.580	23.280	25.130	27.150	29.360	31.770	37.280	43.840	47.580
16	17.260	18.640	20.160	21.820	23.660	25.670	27.890	30.320	33.000	35.950	42.750	50.980	55.720
17	18.430	20.010	21.760	23.700	25.840	28.210	30.840	33.750	36.970	40.540	48.880	59.120	65.080
18	19.610	21.410	23.410	25.650	28.130	30.910	34.000	37.450	41.300	45.600	55.750	68.390	75.840
19	20.810	22.840	25.120	27.670	30.540	33.760	37.380	41.450	46.020	51.160	63.440	78.970	88.210
20	22.020	24.300	26.870	29.780	33.070	36.790	41.000	45.760	51.160	57.280	72.050	91.020	102.400
21	23.240	25.780	28.680	31.970	35.720	39.990	44.870	50.420	56.760	64.000	81.700	104.800	118.800
22	24.470	27.300	30.540	34.250	38.510	43.390	49.010	55.460	62.870	71.400	92.500	120.400	137.600
23	25.720	28.850	32.450	36.620	41.430	47.000	53.440	60.890	69.530	79.540	104.600	138.300	159.300
24	26.970	30.420	34.430	39.080	44.500	50.820	58.180	66.760	76.790	88.500	118.200	158.700	184.200
25	28.240	32.030	36.460	41.650	47.730	54.860	63.250	73.110	84.700	98.350	133.300	181.900	212.800
26	29.530	33.670	38.550	44.310	51.110	59.160	68.680	79.950	93.320	109.200	150.300	208.300	245.700
27	30.820	35.340	40.710	47.080	54.670	63.710	74.480	87.350	102.700	121.100	169.400	238.500	283.600
28	32.130	37.050	42.930	49.970	58.400	68.530	80.700	95.340	113.000	134.200	190.700	272.900	327.100
29	33.450	38.790	45.220	52.970	62.320	73.640	87.350	104.000	124.100	148.600	214.600	312.100	377.200
30	34.780	40.570	47.580	56.080	66.440	79.060	94.460	113.300	136.300	164.500	241.300	356.800	434.700
40	48.890	60.400	75.400	95.030	120.800	154.800	199.600	259.100	337.900	442.600	767.100	1,342.000	1,779.000
50	64.460	84.580	112.800	152.700	209.300	290.300	406.500	573.800	815.100	1,164.000	2,400.000	4,995.000	7,218.000

TABLE 3. Present Value of $1 to Be Received at the End of a Given Number of Time Periods

Periods	1%	2%	3%	4%	5%	6%	7%	8%	9%	10%	12%
1	0.990	0.980	0.971	0.962	0.952	0.943	0.935	0.926	0.917	0.909	0.893
2	0.980	0.961	0.943	0.925	0.907	0.890	0.873	0.857	0.842	0.826	0.797
3	0.971	0.942	0.915	0.889	0.864	0.840	0.816	0.794	0.772	0.751	0.712
4	0.961	0.924	0.888	0.855	0.823	0.792	0.763	0.735	0.708	0.683	0.636
5	0.951	0.906	0.883	0.822	0.784	0.747	0.713	0.681	0.650	0.621	0.567
6	0.942	0.888	0.837	0.790	0.746	0.705	0.666	0.630	0.596	0.564	0.507
7	0.933	0.871	0.813	0.760	0.711	0.665	0.623	0.583	0.547	0.513	0.452
8	0.923	0.853	0.789	0.731	0.677	0.627	0.582	0.540	0.502	0.467	0.404
9	0.914	0.837	0.766	0.703	0.645	0.592	0.544	0.500	0.460	0.424	0.361
10	0.905	0.820	0.744	0.676	0.614	0.558	0.508	0.463	0.422	0.386	0.322
11	0.896	0.804	0.722	0.650	0.585	0.527	0.475	0.429	0.388	0.350	0.287
12	0.887	0.788	0.701	0.625	0.557	0.497	0.444	0.397	0.356	0.319	0.257
13	0.879	0.773	0.681	0.601	0.530	0.469	0.415	0.368	0.326	0.290	0.229
14	0.870	0.758	0.661	0.577	0.505	0.442	0.388	0.340	0.299	0.263	0.205
15	0.861	0.743	0.642	0.555	0.481	0.417	0.362	0.315	0.275	0.239	0.183
16	0.853	0.728	0.623	0.534	0.458	0.394	0.339	0.292	0.252	0.218	0.163
17	0.844	0.714	0.605	0.513	0.436	0.371	0.317	0.270	0.231	0.198	0.146
18	0.836	0.700	0.587	0.494	0.416	0.350	0.296	0.250	0.212	0.180	0.130
19	0.828	0.686	0.570	0.475	0.396	0.331	0.277	0.232	0.194	0.164	0.116
20	0.820	0.673	0.554	0.456	0.377	0.312	0.258	0.215	0.178	0.149	0.104
21	0.811	0.660	0.538	0.439	0.359	0.294	0.242	0.199	0.164	0.135	0.093
22	0.803	0.647	0.522	0.422	0.342	0.278	0.226	0.184	0.150	0.123	0.083
23	0.795	0.634	0.507	0.406	0.326	0.262	0.211	0.170	0.138	0.112	0.074
24	0.788	0.622	0.492	0.390	0.310	0.247	0.197	0.158	0.126	0.102	0.066
25	0.780	0.610	0.478	0.375	0.295	0.233	0.184	0.146	0.116	0.092	0.059
26	0.772	0.598	0.464	0.361	0.281	0.220	0.172	0.135	0.106	0.084	0.053
27	0.764	0.586	0.450	0.347	0.268	0.207	0.161	0.125	0.098	0.076	0.047
28	0.757	0.574	0.437	0.333	0.255	0.196	0.150	0.116	0.090	0.069	0.042
29	0.749	0.563	0.424	0.321	0.243	0.185	0.141	0.107	0.082	0.063	0.037
30	0.742	0.552	0.412	0.308	0.231	0.174	0.131	0.099	0.075	0.057	0.033
40	0.672	0.453	0.307	0.208	0.142	0.097	0.067	0.046	0.032	0.022	0.011
50	0.608	0.372	0.228	0.141	0.087	0.054	0.034	0.021	0.013	0.009	0.003

Table 3 is used to compute the value today of a single amount of cash to be received sometime in the future. To use Table 3, you must first know (1) the time period in years until funds will be received, (2) the stated annual rate of interest, and (3) the dollar amount to be received at the end of the time period.

Example—Table 3. What is the present value of $30,000 to be received 25 years from now, assuming a 14 percent interest rate? From Table 3, the required multiplier is .038, and the answer is

$$\$30,000 \times .038 = \$1,140$$

14%	15%	16%	18%	20%	25%	30%	35%	40%	45%	50%	Periods
0.877	0.870	0.862	0.847	0.833	0.800	0.769	0.741	0.714	0.690	0.667	1
0.769	0.756	0.743	0.718	0.694	0.640	0.592	0.549	0.510	0.476	0.444	2
0.675	0.658	0.641	0.609	0.579	0.512	0.455	0.406	0.364	0.328	0.296	3
0.592	0.572	0.552	0.516	0.482	0.410	0.350	0.301	0.260	0.226	0.198	4
0.519	0.497	0.476	0.437	0.402	0.328	0.269	0.223	0.186	0.156	0.132	5
0.456	0.432	0.410	0.370	0.335	0.262	0.207	0.165	0.133	0.108	0.088	6
0.400	0.376	0.354	0.314	0.279	0.210	0.159	0.122	0.095	0.074	0.059	7
0.351	0.327	0.305	0.266	0.233	0.168	0.123	0.091	0.068	0.051	0.039	8
0.308	0.284	0.263	0.225	0.194	0.134	0.094	0.067	0.048	0.035	0.026	9
0.270	0.247	0.227	0.191	0.162	0.107	0.073	0.050	0.035	0.024	0.017	10
0.237	0.215	0.195	0.162	0.135	0.086	0.056	0.037	0.025	0.017	0.012	11
0.208	0.187	0.168	0.137	0.112	0.069	0.043	0.027	0.018	0.012	0.008	12
0.182	0.163	0.145	0.116	0.093	0.055	0.033	0.020	0.013	0.008	0.005	13
0.160	0.141	0.125	0.099	0.078	0.044	0.025	0.015	0.009	0.006	0.003	14
0.140	0.123	0.108	0.084	0.065	0.035	0.020	0.011	0.006	0.004	0.002	15
0.123	0.107	0.093	0.071	0.054	0.028	0.015	0.008	0.005	0.003	0.002	16
0.108	0.093	0.080	0.060	0.045	0.023	0.012	0.006	0.003	0.002	0.001	17
0.095	0.081	0.069	0.051	0.038	0.018	0.009	0.005	0.002	0.001	0.001	18
0.083	0.070	0.060	0.043	0.031	0.014	0.007	0.003	0.002	0.001		19
0.073	0.061	0.051	0.037	0.026	0.012	0.005	0.002	0.001	0.001		20
0.064	0.053	0.044	0.031	0.022	0.009	0.004	0.002	0.001			21
0.056	0.046	0.038	0.026	0.018	0.007	0.003	0.001	0.001			22
0.049	0.040	0.033	0.022	0.015	0.006	0.002	0.001				23
0.043	0.035	0.028	0.019	0.013	0.005	0.002	0.001				24
0.038	0.030	0.024	0.016	0.010	0.004	0.001	0.001				25
0.033	0.026	0.021	0.014	0.009	0.003	0.001					26
0.029	0.023	0.018	0.011	0.007	0.002	0.001					27
0.026	0.020	0.016	0.010	0.006	0.002	0.001					28
0.022	0.017	0.014	0.008	0.005	0.002						29
0.020	0.015	0.012	0.007	0.004	0.001						30
0.005	0.004	0.003	0.001	0.001							40
0.001	0.001	0.001									50

The factor values for Table 3 are

$$\text{PV Factor} = (1 + r)^{-n}$$

Table 3 is the reciprocal of Table 1.

TABLE 4.   Present Value of $1 Received Each Period for a Given Number of Time Periods

Periods	1%	2%	3%	4%	5%	6%	7%	8%	9%	10%	12%
1	0.990	0.980	0.971	0.962	0.952	0.943	0.935	0.926	0.917	0.909	0.893
2	1.970	1.942	1.913	1.886	1.859	1.833	1.808	1.783	1.759	1.736	1.690
3	2.941	2.884	2.829	2.775	2.723	2.673	2.624	2.577	2.531	2.487	2.402
4	3.902	3.808	3.717	3.630	3.546	3.465	3.387	3.312	3.240	3.170	3.037
5	4.853	4.713	4.580	4.452	4.329	4.212	4.100	3.993	3.890	3.791	3.605
6	5.795	5.601	5.417	5.242	5.076	4.917	4.767	4.623	4.486	4.355	4.111
7	6.728	6.472	6.230	6.002	5.786	5.582	5.389	5.206	5.033	4.868	4.564
8	7.652	7.325	7.020	6.733	6.463	6.210	5.971	5.747	5.535	5.335	4.968
9	8.566	8.162	7.786	7.435	7.108	6.802	6.515	6.247	5.995	5.759	5.328
10	9.471	8.983	8.530	8.111	7.722	7.360	7.024	6.710	6.418	6.145	5.650
11	10.368	9.787	9.253	8.760	8.306	7.887	7.499	7.139	6.805	6.495	5.938
12	11.255	10.575	9.954	9.385	8.863	8.384	7.943	7.536	7.161	6.814	6.194
13	12.134	11.348	10.635	9.986	9.394	8.853	8.358	7.904	7.487	7.103	6.424
14	13.004	12.106	11.296	10.563	9.899	9.295	8.745	8.244	7.786	7.367	6.628
15	13.865	12.849	11.938	11.118	10.380	9.712	9.108	8.559	8.061	7.606	6.811
16	14.718	13.578	12.561	11.652	10.838	10.106	9.447	8.851	8.313	7.824	6.974
17	15.562	14.292	13.166	12.166	11.274	10.477	9.763	9.122	8.544	8.022	7.120
18	16.398	14.992	13.754	12.659	11.690	10.828	10.059	9.372	8.756	8.201	7.250
19	17.226	15.678	14.324	13.134	12.085	11.158	10.336	9.604	8.950	8.365	7.366
20	18.046	16.351	14.878	13.590	12.462	11.470	10.594	9.818	9.129	8.514	7.469
21	18.857	17.011	15.415	14.029	12.821	11.764	10.836	10.017	9.292	8.649	7.562
22	19.660	17.658	15.937	14.451	13.163	12.042	11.061	10.201	9.442	8.772	7.645
23	20.456	18.292	16.444	14.857	13.489	12.303	11.272	10.371	9.580	8.883	7.718
24	21.243	18.914	16.936	15.247	13.799	12.550	11.469	10.529	9.707	8.985	7.784
25	22.023	19.523	17.413	15.622	14.094	12.783	11.654	10.675	9.823	9.077	7.843
26	22.795	20.121	17.877	15.983	14.375	13.003	11.826	10.810	9.929	9.161	7.896
27	23.560	20.707	18.327	16.330	14.643	13.211	11.987	10.935	10.027	9.237	7.943
28	24.316	21.281	18.764	16.663	14.898	13.406	12.137	11.051	10.116	9.307	7.984
29	25.066	21.844	19.189	16.984	15.141	13.591	12.278	11.158	10.198	9.370	8.022
30	25.808	22.396	19.600	17.292	15.373	13.765	12.409	11.258	10.274	9.427	8.055
40	32.835	27.355	23.115	19.793	17.159	15.046	13.332	11.925	10.757	9.779	8.244
50	39.196	31.424	25.730	21.482	18.256	15.762	13.801	12.234	10.962	9.915	8.305

Table 4 is used to compute the present value of a *series* of *equal* annual cash flows.

Example—Table 4.   Arthur Howard won a contest on January 1, 20x7, in which the prize was $30,000, payable in 15 annual installments of $2,000 each December 31, beginning in 20x7. Assuming a 9 percent interest rate, what is the present value of Howard's prize on January 1, 20x7? From Table 4, the required multiplier is 8.061, and the answer is

$$\$2,000 \times 8.061 = \$16,122$$

The factor values for Table 4 are

$$\text{PVa Factor} = 1 - \frac{(1 + r)^{-n}}{r}$$

Table 4 is the columnar sum of Table 3. Table 4 applies to *ordinary annuities*, in which the first cash flow occurs one time period beyond the date for which the present value is computed.

14%	15%	16%	18%	20%	25%	30%	35%	40%	45%	50%	Periods
0.877	0.870	0.862	0.847	0.833	0.800	0.769	0.741	0.714	0.690	0.667	1
1.647	1.626	1.605	1.566	1.528	1.440	1.361	1.289	1.224	1.165	1.111	2
2.322	2.283	2.246	2.174	2.106	1.952	1.816	1.696	1.589	1.493	1.407	3
2.914	2.855	2.798	2.690	2.589	2.362	2.166	1.997	1.849	1.720	1.605	4
3.433	3.352	3.274	3.127	2.991	2.689	2.436	2.220	2.035	1.876	1.737	5
3.889	3.784	3.685	3.498	3.326	2.951	2.643	2.385	2.168	1.983	1.824	6
4.288	4.160	4.039	3.812	3.605	3.161	2.802	2.508	2.263	2.057	1.883	7
4.639	4.487	4.344	4.078	3.837	3.329	2.925	2.598	2.331	2.109	1.922	8
4.946	4.772	4.607	4.303	4.031	3.463	3.019	2.665	2.379	2.144	1.948	9
5.216	5.019	4.833	4.494	4.192	3.571	3.092	2.715	2.414	2.168	1.965	10
5.453	5.234	5.029	4.656	4.327	3.656	3.147	2.752	2.438	2.185	1.977	11
5.660	5.421	5.197	4.793	4.439	3.725	3.190	2.779	2.456	2.197	1.985	12
5.842	5.583	5.342	4.910	4.533	3.780	3.223	2.799	2.469	2.204	1.990	13
6.002	5.724	5.468	5.008	4.611	3.824	3.249	2.814	2.478	2.210	1.993	14
6.142	5.847	5.575	5.092	4.675	3.859	3.268	2.825	2.484	2.214	1.995	15
6.265	5.954	5.669	5.162	4.730	3.887	3.283	2.834	2.489	2.216	1.997	16
6.373	6.047	5.749	5.222	4.775	3.910	3.295	2.840	2.492	2.218	1.998	17
6.467	6.128	5.818	5.273	4.812	3.928	3.304	2.844	2.494	2.219	1.999	18
6.550	6.198	5.877	5.316	4.844	3.942	3.311	2.848	2.496	2.220	1.999	19
6.623	6.259	5.929	5.353	4.870	3.954	3.316	2.850	2.497	2.221	1.999	20
6.687	6.312	5.973	5.384	4.891	3.963	3.320	2.852	2.498	2.221	2.000	21
6.743	6.359	6.011	5.410	4.909	3.970	3.323	2.853	2.498	2.222	2.000	22
6.792	6.399	6.044	5.432	4.925	3.976	3.325	2.854	2.499	2.222	2.000	23
6.835	6.434	6.073	5.451	4.973	3.981	3.327	2.855	2.499	2.222	2.000	24
6.873	6.464	6.097	5.467	4.948	3.985	3.329	2.856	2.499	2.222	2.000	25
6.906	6.491	6.118	5.480	4.956	3.988	3.330	2.856	2.500	2.222	2.000	26
6.935	6.514	6.136	5.492	4.964	3.990	3.331	2.856	2.500	2.222	2.000	27
6.961	6.534	6.152	5.502	4.970	3.992	3.331	2.857	2.500	2.222	2.000	28
6.983	6.551	6.166	5.510	4.975	3.994	3.332	2.857	2.500	2.222	2.000	29
7.003	6.566	6.177	5.517	4.979	3.995	3.332	2.857	2.500	2.222	2.000	30
7.105	6.642	6.234	5.548	4.997	3.999	3.333	2.857	2.500	2.222	2.000	40
7.133	6.661	6.246	5.554	4.999	4.000	3.333	2.857	2.500	2.222	2.000	50

An *annuity due* is a series of equal cash flows for N time periods, but the first payment occurs immediately. The present value of the first payment equals the face value of the cash flow; Table 4 then is used to measure the present value of N − 1 remaining cash flows.

Example—Table 4. Determine the present value on January 1, 20x7, of 20 lease payments; each payment of $10,000 is due on January 1, beginning in 20x7. Assume an interest rate of 8 percent.

Present Value = Immediate Payment + Present Value of
19 Subsequent Payments at 8%

= $10,000 + ($10,000 × 9.604) = $106,040

Chapter 1

1-1. Accounting is considered an information system because it measures business data, processes the data into useful information, and communicates the information to decision makers in the form of financial statements.

1-2. Accounting information enables decision makers to make reasoned choices among alternative uses of scarce resources. It helps management achieve the goals of liquidity and profitability by supplying information that can be used in managing financing, investing, and operating activities.

1-3. Management accounting refers to all types of accounting information developed for the internal use of management. Financial accounting refers to accounting information developed for communication to those outside the organization as well as to management.

1-4. Accounting includes the design of an information system to meet users' needs. Bookkeeping is simply an accounting process, a means of recording financial transactions and keeping financial records. Management information systems are broader in scope than accounting; they process and communicate all information—financial and nonfinancial—within a business. The accounting information system is an extremely important part of a management information system because it manages the flow of financial data to all parts of a business and to interested parties outside the business.

1-5. Financial statements can be inadvertently misstated because of ignorance of accepted accounting practices, incorrect estimates, or failure to recognize that a transaction has occurred. They can also be intentionally misstated to deceive readers; when this is the case, the misstatement is called *fraudulent financial reporting.*

2-1. Three groups of decision makers use accounting information: those who manage a business; those outside a business who have a direct financial interest in the business; and those who have an indirect financial interest in the business. These categories apply to not-for-profit and governmental organizations as well as to profit-oriented ventures.

2-2. The management functions involved in achieving an adequate return for a business's owners include financing the business, investing the business's resources, producing goods and services, marketing goods and services, managing employees, and providing information to decision makers.

2-3. Investors are interested in reviewing a company's financial statements because they provide information about the company's past performance and its potential for future profits. Creditors are interested in reviewing financial statements because they indicate whether the company will have the cash to pay interest charges and debt when it is due.

2-4. People and organizations with an indirect interest in accounting information about a business include tax authorities, regulatory agencies, and other groups, such as labor unions, economic planners, financial analysts, and consumers' groups. Tax authorities use accounting information to determine tax liabilities, and regulatory agencies use it to determine compliance with laws. Economic planners use accounting information to determine economic policy, and other groups use it to support policies related to their economic interests.

2-5. Accounting information plays a critical role in achieving many of society's goals. It is used to determine taxes on businesses, the price of public commodities (gas, water, and electricity), and a business's economic impact on a community. It is used by tax authorities at the federal (IRS), state, and local levels; regulatory agencies, such as the SEC; the Federal Reserve Board and other governmental planners; and citizens' groups, including labor unions and consumer groups.

3-1. Financial accounting uses money measures to gauge the impact of business transactions on a separate business entity.

3-2. The sale is a business transaction. The price you pay is a money measure. CVS is a separate entity.

4-1. A sole proprietorship is a business owned by one person. A partnership is similar to a proprietorship in most respects, but it has more than one owner. A corporation is an economic unit that is legally separate from its owners. Accounting treats all three forms as separate economic units.

4-2. The stockholders, whose ownership of the corporation is represented by shares of stock, elect a board of directors. The board determines corporate policy, declares dividends, and appoints management. Management executes corporate policy and carries out the day-to-day operations of the firm.

4-3. The audit committee of a board of directors is made up of independent directors who have financial expertise. The committee is responsible for engaging the corporation's independent auditors, reviewing their work, and seeing that the firm has systems to safeguard its resources and ensure the reliability of its accounting records.

5-1. Assets are the economic resources of a business that are expected to benefit future operations.

5-2. Liabilities and stockholders' equity are similar in that they represent claims against the assets of a business. They differ in that liabilities are amounts owed to creditors and stockholders' equity represents the owners' interest in the company.

5-3. Revenues, which result from sales of products or services, increase retained earnings. Expenses and dividends decrease retained earnings. Expenses are the cost of operating the business, and dividends are distributions to stockholders of assets generated by past earnings.

5-4. The sale of an asset for cash is an example of a transaction that both increases and decreases assets. The collection of an account receivable is another example. In both cases, the Cash account increases, and Accounts Receivable decreases.

6-1. The statement of retained earnings shows changes in the Retained Earnings account over an accounting period. Two factors may account for changes in retained earnings: net income (loss) and dividend distributions.

6-2. The balance sheet is called the *statement of financial position* because it presents a company's financial position—its economic resources and the claims against those resources—at a specific date.

6-3. The purpose of the balance sheet is to show a company's financial position at a certain point in time. The purpose of the income statement is to show a business's income or loss over a period of time.

6-4. **a.** June 30, 20xx
b. For the Year Ended June 30, 20xx

6-5. The income statement measures profitability. The statement of cash flows measures liquidity.

7-1. GAAP (generally accepted accounting principles) are "the conventions, rules, and procedures necessary to define accepted accounting practice at a particular time." They are important to readers of financial statements because they provide the basis for understanding and interpreting those statements.

7-2. By using the phrase in *all material respects*, independent auditors are acknowledging that accounting is not an exact science and that the application of GAAP to the preparation of financial statements requires judgment and estimates. Although an auditor's report does not preclude minor or immaterial errors in the financial statements, a favorable report does imply that on the whole, the statements are a fair representation and are in compliance with GAAP.

7-3. The PCAOB (Public Companies Accounting Oversight Board) is a governmental body established by the Sarbanes-Oxley Act of 2002 to regulate the accounting profession. Because it sets standards that must be followed in the audits of public companies, it has a major impact on financial reporting.

7-4. The Financial Accounting Standards Board (FASB) has the most influence on GAAP because it develops and issues rules on accounting practice, which are called *Statements of Financial Accounting Standards.*

7-5. Codes of ethics are important in the accounting profession because they outline the responsibilities of accountants to anyone who relies on financial statements. Accountants who violate their codes of ethics can be disciplined or even suspended from practice.

Chapter 2

1-1. The three issues that underlie most major accounting decisions are recognition (deciding when a transaction should be recorded), valuation (deciding what value should be placed on the transaction), and classification (deciding how the components of the transaction should be categorized).

1-2. The transaction should not be recorded as a sale because no transfer of ownership has occurred.

1-3. Original cost is a practical valuation guideline for accountants because it is based on the exchange price, a price that can be verified.

1-4. The distinction between an asset and an expense is important because an asset represents a cost that will benefit the firm in the future, whereas an expense will immediately affect the firm's earnings.

1-5. Recognition, valuation, and classification are related to the ethics of financial reporting because fraudulent financial statements usually result from a violation of the generally accepted accounting principles that govern these issues.

2-1. The double-entry system is so called because it is based on the principle of duality, which means that every economic event has two aspects that balance each other. In the double-entry system, each transaction is recorded by at least one debit and one credit, and the total amount of the debits must equal the total amount of the credits.

2-2. Debits and credits are neither good nor bad. They simply indicate whether a transaction increases or decreases a particular account.

2-3. An account is the basic storage unit for accounting data. An account's normal balance is its usual balance and is the side (debit or credit) that increases the account.

2-4. A T account is a form of account shaped like a T that is used to analyze the effects of transactions.

2-5. **a.** Increases in assets are recorded by debits; decreases are recorded by credits.
b. Increases in liabilities are recorded by credits; decreases are recorded by debits.
c. Increases in stockholders' equity are recorded by credits; decreases are recorded by debits.

2-6. Accountants use separate accounts for revenues and expenses rather than entering them in Retained Earnings because these accounts will be used in the income statement. This enables users of the income statement to assess the company's earnings.

3-1. The total debits to cash exceed the total credits by $500. Thus, the Cash account has a total balance of $500 available for the business to use.

3-2. Decreases in stockholders' equity are shown by debits. Because expenses decrease stockholders' equity, increases in expenses are shown by debits. By debiting an expense, you are increasing the total decreases in stockholders' equity.

3-3. The steps in analyzing a business transaction are (1) state the transaction, (2) analyze it to determine which accounts are affected, (3) apply the rules of double-entry accounting by using T accounts to show how the transaction affects the accounting equation, (4) show the transaction in journal form, and (5) provide an explanation of the transaction.

3-4. The normal balance of Accounts Payable is a credit balance. A debit balance in Accounts Payable would occur if the company overpaid for goods or services.

4-1. The trial balance is a listing of all the accounts with their balances shown in either the debit or credit column. It is used to see if the accounts are in balance.

4-2. Even when the debit and credit balances in a trial balance are equal, errors can be present; transactions may not have been analyzed correctly or recorded in the proper accounts.

5-1. The timing of cash flows is important because it affects a company's ability to maintain adequate liquidity.

5-2. There is delay in collecting the cash from a sale when a company offers to accept payment later. This action results in an accounts receivable.

6-1. c. Occurrence of the transaction
a. Analysis of the transaction
d. Recording of an entry in the journal
b. Posting of debits and credits from the journal to the ledger
e. Preparation of the trial balance

6-2. A debit is written first. The names of accounts credited are set off by indentation; explanations of transactions are also indented.

6-3. The journal is where transactions are first entered in the accounting records. Later, the debit and credit portions of each transaction are transferred to the appropriate accounts in the ledger, where each account is kept on a separate page or card.

6-4. a. Chart of accounts—ledger
b. Book of original entry—journal
c. Post Ref. column—both
d. Journalizing—journal
e. Posting—both
f. Footings—ledger

Chapter 3

1-1. Because *profit* means different things to different people, accountants use the term *net income* instead. Net income refers to the net increase in stockholders' equity produced by business operations. It equals revenues minus expenses when revenues exceed expenses.

1-2. To measure net income accurately, revenues and expenses must be assigned to the accounting period in which they occur. However, not all transactions can be easily assigned to specific periods. It is therefore necessary to make an assumption about periodicity—that is, although the lifetime of a business is uncertain, it is nonetheless useful to estimate a company's net income in terms of accounting periods.

1-3. The continuity assumption holds that unless there is evidence to the contrary, a business will continue to operate indefinitely. Thus, assets can be recorded and retained on the balance sheet at their historical cost rather than being revalued periodically to reflect their current values.

1-4. What is the most significant concept in accounting is a matter of opinion, but if one grants that income determination is one of accounting's most important functions, then the matching rule is one of the most important concepts. The rule states that revenues must be assigned to the period in which they are earned, which is when the goods or services are delivered to the buyer, and expenses must be assigned to the period in which they are incurred. To measure business income accurately over a given period, the accountant must match the revenues earned with the expenses incurred to produce those revenues.

2-1. The following conditions must be met before revenue can be recognized:
1. Persuasive evidence of an arrangement exists.
2. A product or service has been delivered.
3. The seller's price to the buyer is fixed or is determinable.
4. Collectibility is reasonably assured.

2-2. Under the cash basis of accounting, revenues and expenses are recorded as cash is received and paid out. Accrual accounting applies the matching rule: revenues are recorded when they are earned, and expenses are recorded when they are incurred.

2-3. Accrual accounting is accomplished (1) by recording revenues when they are earned, (2) by recording expenses when they are incurred, and (3) by making end-of-period adjustments to the accounts.

2-4. Adjusting entries are necessary to bring all account balances up to date at the end of an accounting period. This can mean recognizing a payment received in advance as earned revenue or a cost paid in advance as an expense, or recognizing a revenue or expense that has not yet been recorded.

2-5. Adjustments are needed to measure income and financial position fairly. Equally important, they make financial statements comparable from one period to the next. In addition, the cumulative effect of adjusting entries can be significant. If no adjustments were made, the matching rule would not be followed, a company's accounts would basically revert to a cash system, and there would not be a good determination of the company's earnings.

3-1. Adjusting entries are required (1) when recorded costs must be allocated between two or more accounting periods (e.g., allocating the costs of prepaid insurance between the periods that the policies cover); (2) when there are unrecorded expenses (e.g., recording wages that employees earned in the current accounting period but after the last pay period); (3) when recorded, unearned revenues must be allocated between two or more accounting periods (e.g., allocating between periods fees collected in advance for services to be rendered in future periods); and (4) when there are unrecorded, earned revenues (e.g., recording fees earned but not yet collected or billed to customers).

3-2. Certain business expenditures benefit more than one accounting period. These expenditures usually are debited to an asset account. Therefore, "some assets are expenses that have not expired." At the end of the accounting period, such asset accounts are reduced by the amount that was used during the period; the amount that has expired is transferred to expense accounts. For example, the part of prepaid rent used up during the period is credited to Prepaid Rent and debited to Rent Expense.

3-3. All of these assets must be allocated to expenses over time; this means they require adjusting entries at the end of the accounting period.

3-4. Accumulated depreciation is a contra account associated with a long-term asset. The Accumulated Depreciation account reflects the total depreciation allocated as an expense to date on that asset. Depreciation expense represents the estimated portion of the asset that has become an expense during the current accounting period.

3-5. A contra account represents a deduction from an associated account. For example, the contra account Accumulated Depreciation–Office Equipment is associated with the Office Equipment account.

3-6. Contra accounts are used to record depreciation for two reasons. First, depreciation is an estimate, and the use of a contra account is recognition of this. Second, the use of the contra account preserves the original cost of the asset in the accounts. In combination with the asset account, it indicates how much of the asset's cost has been expensed and how much of the balance is left to be depreciated.

3-7. Unearned revenue arises when revenue is received in advance of the delivery of goods or services. The advance payments that a publishing company receives for magazine subscriptions are an example.

3-8. Unearned revenue appears as a liability on the balance sheet.

3-9. Accrued revenues are unrecorded revenues. Services have been performed or goods have been delivered, but the transactions have not been recorded. Interest that has been earned but not received is an example. At the end of the accounting period, the accountant makes an adjusting entry debiting Interest Receivable and crediting Interest Income. Interest Receivable is the asset account. (An adjusting entry for accrued revenue always debits an asset account and credits a revenue account.)

3-10. An accrued expense is an expense that has been incurred but not recorded. Accrued expenses require adjusting entries, which increase a related liability. Examples of accrued expenses include wages expense, income taxes expense, and interest expense.

4-1. The income statement is usually prepared first because the net income figure is needed to complete the statement of retained earnings.

4-2. The ending balance for Retained Earnings does not appear on the adjusted trial balance because all the current period's income statement accounts and dividends are in the adjusted trial balance. The balances of all these accounts have to be transferred to the statement of retained earnings to arrive at the ending balance. (Recall that the statement of retained earnings is prepared after the income statement and before the balance sheet.)

5-1. First, closing entries clear revenue, expense, and dividend accounts of their balances and transfer them to Retained Earnings. Second, they summarize a period's revenues and expenses.

5-2. Adjusting entries apply accrual accounting to transactions that span accounting periods. Closing entries assist in getting the account balances ready for the next period and for the preparation of financial statements.

5-3. Insurance Expense, Commission Revenue, Dividends, and Supplies Expense will not show a balance after the closing entries have been prepared and posted.

5-4. The post-closing trial balance is a check on the balance of the accounts after the closing entries have been prepared and posted.

6-1. Adjusting entries never affect a company's cash flows because they never involve the Cash account.

6-2. The cash paid for expenses in an accounting period often differs from the amount of expenses on the income statement because of the timing of the incurrence of the expenses and payment for them.

6-3. The cash received for services in an accounting period often differs from the amount of revenue on the income statement because of the timing of the provision of the services and the receipt of cash for them.

Chapter 4

1-1. According to the Financial Accounting Standards Board, the objectives of financial reporting are (1) to furnish information useful in making investment and credit decisions; (2) to provide information useful in assessing cash flow prospects; and (3) to provide information about business resources, claims to those resources, and changes in them.

1-2. Qualitative characteristics are standards for judging accounting information. Accountants attempt to provide information that is understandable and useful. *Understandable* means that the user is able to interpret the information. *Usefulness* depends on the characteristics of relevance and reliability. *Relevance* requires that information give feedback, help make predictions, and be timely. *Reliability* requires that information represent what it is meant to represent and that it be verifiable and objective.

1-3. Management is responsible for the preparation of financial statements. To ensure that the statements are reliable, the chief executive officers and chief financial officers of publicly traded companies must certify that, to their knowledge, the quarterly and annual statements that their companies file with the SEC are accurate and complete.

2-1. Accounting conventions are rules of thumb that accountants use in making estimates and applying the rules for recognition and allocation. These conventions help users interpret financial information.

2-2. Comparability and consistency help users evaluate a company's performance over time and to compare it with the performance of other companies. Materiality dictates that items and events that are important enough to affect decisions must be accounted for properly. Conservatism states that when faced with a choice between two equally acceptable accounting procedures, the accountant should choose the one that is least likely to overstate assets and income. Full disclosure means that the financial statements must include any information that is relevant to understanding them. Cost-benefit holds that the benefits to be gained from accounting information should be are greater than the costs of producing it.

3-1. The purpose of classified financial statements is to facilitate the analysis and evaluation of a company's financial position by dividing the major categories of accounts into useful subcategories.

3-2. Four common categories of assets on a classified balance sheet are current assets; investments; property, plant, and equipment; and intangible assets. Some companies group investments and intangibles into a category called *other assets*.

3-3. An asset is classified as current if a firm can reasonably expect to convert it to cash, sell it, or consume it within one year or within the firm's normal operating cycle, whichever is longer. Assets of a firm whose normal operating cycle exceeds one year are considered current if they will be converted to cash, sold, or consumed during that cycle. Two examples of such assets are the aging inventories of wine companies and the installment receivables of retail appliance companies.

3-4. Current assets should be listed in order of their liquidity—that is, the ease with which they can be converted to cash.

3-5. If management's intent is to use the investment as a temporary haven for idle cash, the investment is short term and is classified as a current asset. If the intent is to hold the security for more than a year, it is classified as an investment.

3-6. An intangible asset is a long-term asset with no physical substance whose value stems from the rights or privileges it extends to its owner. Examples of such assets are patents, copyrights, goodwill, franchises, and trademarks.

3-7. The two major categories of liabilities are current liabilities and long-term liabilities.

3-8. The equity section of the balance sheet for a sole proprietorship or partnership simply lists the balance of the owner's or partners' capital. The stockholders' equity section of a corporation's balance sheet separates contributed capital from retained earnings.

4-1. The primary difference between the operations of a merchandising business and those of a service business is that a merchandising business earns its revenues by buying products and selling them to customers rather than by performing a service. The buying and selling of merchandise adds several steps to the income statement. In a service business, net income is the difference between revenues and expenses when revenues exceed expenses. A merchandising business, in contrast, has cost of goods sold, which is deducted from net sales to arrive at gross margin. Net income or loss is the difference between gross margin and all other items affecting net income. Among these other items are operating expenses, other revenues and expenses, and income taxes.

4-2. Gross margin is the difference between net sales and cost of goods sold. It is important because if a merchandising or manufacturing company is going to earn a net income, its gross margin must exceed total operating expenses, the excess of other expenses over other revenues, and income taxes.

4-3. Other revenues and expenses are not related to a company's operating activities. In a multistep income statement, these items are separated from operating revenues and expenses to isolate them from income from operations.

4-4. Earnings per share is the net income earned on each share of common stock. It is computed by dividing net income by the average number of common shares outstanding, and it appears directly after net income on the income statement.

4-5. A multistep income statement classifies accounts into major components before arriving at income before income taxes. Its major advantage is the detail it provides on various income-producing aspects of a business. A single-step income statement simply groups all accounts other than income taxes as revenues or expenses and determines the difference, which is income before income taxes. Its advantage is simplicity.

5-1. Liquidity is a company's ability to pay its bills when they are due and to meet unexpected needs for cash. Two measures of liquidity are working capital and the current ratio.

5-2. The current ratio is computed by dividing current assets by current liabilities. Many believe it is a good indicator of a company's ability to pay its debts on time.

5-3. The goals of liquidity and profitability are equally important. Both goals must be met if a business is to survive.

5-4. Five measures of profitability are profit margin, asset turnover, return on assets, the debt to equity ratio, and return on equity.

5-5. If profit margin is multiplied by asset turnover, the result is return on assets.

Chapter 5

1-1. The transactions that make up the operating cycle of a merchandising business are (1) purchases of merchandise inventory for cash or on credit, (2) payment for purchases made on credit, (3) sales of merchandise inventory for cash or on credit, and (4) collection of cash from credit sales. When merchandise is sold for cash, the cash is collected immediately; when it is sold on credit, the company must wait a period of time before receiving the cash. A merchandising business must manage the operating cycle carefully because it affects the company's cash flow, or liquidity.

1-2. The financing period is the amount of time from the purchase of inventory until it is sold and payment is collected, less the amount of time creditors give the company to pay for the inventory. It consists of the days' inventory on hand plus the days' receivable less the days' payable.

1-3. Under the perpetual inventory system, continuous records are kept of the quality and, usually, the cost of individual items as they are bought and sold. Under the periodic inventory system, the inventory

not yet sold is counted periodically, usually at the end of the accounting period.

1-4. An exchange gain or loss occurs when a company engages in a transaction in a foreign currency and the rate at which a dollar can be exchanged for the foreign currency changes between the date of sale and the date of payment.

1-5. Internal controls are needed to protect a company's assets from theft and embezzlement. Management is responsible for establishing an environment, accounting systems, and control procedures that will provide this protection.

2-1. A trade discount is a deduction (usually 30 percent or more) off a list or catalogue price; trade discounts are not entered in the accounting records. A sales discount is a discount given to a buyer for early payment of a credit sale; sales discounts are entered in the accounting records.

2-2. Sales Discounts is a contra-revenue account; it is deducted from sales on the income statement. Its normal balance is a debit balance.

2-3. It is impossible to tell which supplier is quoting the better deal without knowing what Supplier A will charge for shipping. If the transportation costs for all 50 items from Supplier A exceed $50, Supplier B is offering the better deal, but if they are less than $50, Supplier A is offering the better deal. A customer that accepted Supplier B's offer would pay approximately $1 per unit ($21 − $20, or 5 percent of the unit cost) for transportation.

2-4. Freight-in is not an operating expense. It is part of the cost of purchasing merchandise and is therefore usually included in the cost of goods sold.

3-1. The Cost of Goods Sold account is used in the perpetual inventory system. It is needed to record the transfer of the cost of merchandise from the Merchandise Inventory account at the time of a sale (or back to the Merchandise Inventory account in the case of a return). The Cost of Goods Sold account is not used in the periodic inventory system until the income statement is prepared.

3-2. The perpetual inventory system gives management up-to-date information, but it is more time-consuming and costly than the periodic inventory system. Thus, management must weigh the benefits against the costs. Companies that sell high-value items tend to use the perpetual inventory system. Companies that sell a high volume of lower-value items have generally used the periodic system. However, because of the computer's ability to keep track of large numbers of transactions at low cost, use of the perpetual system has increased significantly.

3-3. The Sales Returns and Allowances account helps management maintain control. It is a readily available measure of unsatisfactory products and dissatisfied customers.

4-1. The two main components of goods available for sale are beginning inventory and net cost of purchases during the period. The ending inventory is deducted from the goods available for sale to determine cost of goods sold.

4-2. Under the periodic inventory system, the amount of inventory at the end of the year is determined by a physical count of the merchandise.

4-3. The two dozen hammers (item **b**) are the only ones that should be debited to Purchases because they are the only ones bought for resale.

4-4. Under the periodic inventory system, the cost of inventory purchased during an accounting period is accumulated in a Purchases account. At the end of the period, a physical inventory is taken, and the cost of the merchandise is deducted from the cost of goods available for sale to arrive at cost of goods sold. Under the perpetual inventory system, the cost of each item is recorded in the Merchandise Inventory account when it is purchased. As merchandise is sold, its cost is transferred from the Merchandise Inventory account to the Cost of Goods Sold account. Thus, at any time, the balance of Merchandise Inventory equals the cost of goods on hand, and Cost of Goods Sold equals the total cost of goods sold to that point. The Purchases account is not used in a perpetual inventory system.

5-1. In addition to preventing and detecting fraud, internal control protects a firm's assets, ensures the accuracy and reliability of its accounting data, promotes efficient operations, and encourages adherence to management's policies.

5-2. The five components of internal control are the control environment, risk assessment, information and communication, control activities, and monitoring.

5-3. Examples of control activities include having managers authorize certain transactions and activities; establishing accountability for assets by recording all transactions; using documents that are designed to ensure the proper recording of transactions; restricting physical access to assets; having someone other than those responsible for the firm's accounting records and assets periodically check the records against the assets; separating employees' functional responsibilities; and using sound personnel practices.

5-4. The separation of duties is necessary to sound internal control because without it, a person responsible for multiple tasks—such as keeping records, overseeing a department, and managing assets—would be able to misappropriate assets without detection. The separation of duties assumes that two or more employees will not work together to overcome the controls.

5-5. In a small business in which the complete separation of duties is impossible, many other steps can be taken to improve the control of cash. Three examples are using banking facilities as much as possible, depositing all cash receipts promptly, and bonding employees who have access to cash.

6-1. The primary weakness in this system is that the sales clerks have access to both the cash (asset) and the cash register tape (record). The separation of duties has not been applied, increasing the likelihood of fraud. The cash register tape should be locked in the cash register and removed by the employee in the cashier's office who counts the cash.

6-2. A movie theater controls cash receipts by having a ticket seller give a ticket to each person who pays for admission. Another employee, who has no access to cash, collects the ticket. This person tears the ticket to prevent its being used again. At the end of the day, the total ticket stubs multiplied by the ticket price should equal the cash in the ticket seller's drawer. In effect, the custody of the assets (cash) is separated from the records (tickets).

Chapter 6

1-1. A merchandising company has only one type of inventory, whereas a manufacturing company has three types: raw materials, work in process, and finished goods ready for sale. A manufacturing company's costs of work in process and finished goods include the costs of raw materials, direct labor, and the overhead that supports production.

1-2. The primary objective of inventory accounting is to determine income properly by matching costs of the period against revenues for the period.

1-3. The level of inventory is important because management must balance the need to have enough inventory on hand to satisfy customers against the costs of carrying and storing the inventory. Two common and related measures of inventory level are inventory turnover and days' inventory on hand.

1-4. Inventory is particularly vulnerable to fraudulent financial reporting because the manipulation of the ending inventory will cause a dollar for dollar difference in reported net income. In other words, a company can overstate its income by overstating its ending inventory.

1-5. If inventory is overstated at the end of 20x5, (a) the 20x5 net income will be overstated, (b) the 20x5 year-end balance sheet value will also be overstated, (c) the 20x6 net income will be understated, and (d) there will be no effect on the 20x6 year-end balance sheet value.

2-1. The cost of inventory should include the invoice price less applicable discounts plus applicable expenditures, such as freight-in, insurance, taxes, and tariffs.

2-2. Goods flow refers to the *actual* flow of goods in a firm's operations; cost flow refers to the association of costs with their *assumed* flow in operations.

2-3. Although the company has an order for the goods, the 130 units should be included in inventory because title has not passed to the customer.

2-4. In the phrase *lower of cost or market, market* refers to current replacement cost.

2-5. A company must disclose its method of inventory accounting because the method can affect both the value of inventory on the balance sheet and the amount of earnings on the income statement. This information helps users of the financial statements evaluate the company and compare its performance with the performance of other companies.

3-1. The quantities of ending inventory are the same under FIFO and LIFO. These methods affect the pricing of the inventory, not the quantities.

3-2. **a.** The earliest costs are assigned to inventory under the LIFO method.
   b. The latest costs are assigned to inventory under the FIFO method.
   c. The average costs are assigned to inventory under the average-cost method.

3-3. Both LIFO and FIFO have advantages and disadvantages from management's point of view. LIFO comes closest to matching replacement costs against revenues and thus is more realistic in that inventory must be replaced in an ongoing business. In addition, in periods of rising prices, reported income tends to be lower under LIFO, and thus income taxes may be lower. On the other hand, the inventory figure on the balance sheet may be unrealistic, and the reported lower earnings may adversely affect the market price of the company's stock and potential dividends. FIFO has the opposite effect; its advantages are thus similar to the disadvantages of LIFO. It results in a more realistic balance sheet valuation, and in periods of rising prices, it results in a higher net income (as well as higher taxes).

4-1. In periods of steadily rising prices, (a) FIFO will give the highest ending inventory cost, (b) LIFO will give the lowest ending inventory cost, (c) FIFO will give the highest net income, and (d) LIFO will give the lowest net income.

4-2. The IRS must approve changes in the inventory valuation method used in computing taxable income, except for a change to LIFO, which simply has to be reported. If the company uses LIFO for computing taxable income, it must use LIFO in its accounting records.

5-1. A perpetual inventory system is more expensive to maintain because detailed records must be kept as transactions occur. Also, a company may need to purchase special equipment to assist in its perpetual recordkeeping efforts.

5-2. A physical inventory should be taken periodically under the perpetual inventory system to compare the actual inventory on hand with the inventory records. This procedure will reveal any loss of inventory by theft or other means.

6-1. The retail method does not measure inventories at retail value on the balance sheet. It is a method of pricing inventory at estimated cost by deducting sales from beginning inventory and purchases, both priced at retail, to obtain an estimate of ending inventory at retail. The ending inventory at retail is then reduced by the ratio of cost to retail price.

6-2. The gross profit method of estimating inventory is used when inventory cannot be measured directly, as when inventory is lost or destroyed by theft or fire. Insurance companies often use this method to verify loss claims. It is also used instead of the retail method when records of the retail prices of beginning inventory and purchases are not kept. It may be used for interim reports but is not acceptable for valuing inventory in the annual financial statements.

Chapter 7

1-1. Cash consists of currency and coins on hand, checks and money orders from customers, and deposits in checking and savings accounts. A compensating balance is the minimum amount a bank requires a company to keep in its bank account as part of a credit-granting agreement.

1-2. By extending credit even when it expects that some accounts receivable will not be paid, a company expects to increase sales and make a greater profit overall. The function of a credit department is to decide whether to extend credit to customers.

1-3. **a.** Installment accounts receivable from regular customers are usually considered part of the normal operating cycle, and they are included in accounts receivable on the balance sheet.
   b. Debit balances in customers' accounts are included in accounts receivable.
   c. Receivables from employees should normally appear in an asset account separate from accounts receivable; whether such a receivable should be a current or other asset depends on the prospects for its collection.
   d. Credit balances in customers' accounts are recorded as current liabilities.
   e. Receivables from officers of the company should normally appear in an asset account separate from accounts receivable; whether such a receivable should be a current or other asset depends on the prospects for its collection.

1-4. The receivable turnover ratio shows how many times, on average, a company turns its accounts receivable into cash during an accounting period. By using this ratio to determine the days' sales uncollected, it is possible to ascertain how long, on average, the company will have to wait to receive cash from a credit sale.

1-5. A factor is an entity that provides financing by buying or receiving a transfer of a company's accounts receivable in exchange for cash. *Factoring with recourse* means that if the factor is unable to collect the accounts receivable from the customers, the company from which the factor purchased the receivables is liable. *Factoring without recourse* means that the factor shoulders the risk of nonpayment by customers. When factoring without recourse, the factor receives a higher fee than when factoring with recourse.

1-6. Accounting for receivables requires a company to estimate the amount of losses it will have from uncollectible accounts. Because these amounts can only be estimated, they can be easily manipulated to overstate or understate earnings.

2-1. Cash equivalents are investments that have a term to maturity of 90 days or less. For example, certificates of deposit and time deposits are considered cash equivalents if they mature in 90 days or less. Although such investments quickly revert to cash and are treated as cash on the balance sheet, they are not as readily available to pay debts as cash is.

2-2. An imprest system is an effective control over cash because a fund is established at a fixed amount, and the total of funds on hand plus receipts for expenditures must always equal the fixed amount. If they do not, the person responsible for the fund is held accountable.

2-3. A bank reconciliation is the process of accounting for the difference between the balance on a company's bank statement and the balance in its Cash account. These two amounts are reconciled to arrive at the correct cash balance.

3-1. The direct charge-off method violates the matching rule because it does not recognize the loss at the time of the sale.

3-2. According to GAAP, losses on uncollectible accounts occur at the time sales on credit are made. Because the exact amount of the loss is not known at that time, it must be estimated.

3-3. The more optimistic management is about the collection of accounts receivable, the smaller the estimate will be for uncollectible accounts expense. Thus, an optimistic view of collection of accounts receivable results in a higher net income than a pessimistic view does.

3-4. The percentage of net sales method of estimating uncollectible accounts is called an *income statement approach* because the estimate is based on net sales, an income statement account. The accounts receivable aging method is called a *balance sheet approach* because the estimate is based on an evaluation of accounts receivable, a balance sheet account.

3-5. The reasoning behind the percentage of net sales method is that a certain proportion of *net sales* will be uncollectible. The accounts receivable aging method

is based on the premise that a certain proportion of *accounts receivable* will uncollectible.

3-6. a. The collectible value of Accounts Receivable is $161,500 ($176,000 − $14,500).

    b. The collectible value of Accounts Receivable will remain the same, $161,500 ($175,550 − $14,050), because the $450 account is deducted from both Accounts Receivable and Allowance for Uncollectible Accounts.

4-1. A promissory note is an unconditional promise to pay a definite sum of money on demand or at a future date.

4-2. The person who signs a promissory note and therefore promises to pay is the maker. The person to whom payment should be made is the payee.

4-3. Interest is the cost of borrowing money or the return on lending money. The interest rate is a percentage of the amount borrowed or lent used in determining the amount of interest.

4-4. a. November 16

    b. November 14

    c. May 24

Chapter 8

1-1. Examples of current liabilities are accounts payable, notes payable, wages payable, interest payable, income taxes payable, and unearned revenue.

1-2. Two measures of liquidity used to evaluate a firm's ability to pay its current liabilities are payables turnover and days' payable.

1-3. Payables turnover shows how many times, on average, a company pays its accounts payable in an accounting period. When used to determine days' payable, it shows how many days, on average, a company takes to pay its accounts payable.

1-4. The timing of liability recognition is important because it affects income measurement and financial position. When a liability for an expense is not recorded, income for a period is overstated and liabilities are understated.

1-5. A liability is current if the obligation will be satisfied within one year or within the normal operating cycle, whichever is longer.

1-6. The portion of a line of credit currently borrowed should be shown as a liability in the financial statements. Because Manly has not used any of its line of credit, it does not have to record it as a liability or disclose it in the notes to its financial statements.

2-1. A line of credit allows a company to borrow funds from a bank up to a specified amount to finance current operations. Commercial paper is a means of borrowing funds through unsecured loans that are sold to the public, usually through professionally managed investment firms. Details of both methods of borrowing funds are disclosed in a note to the financial statements.

2-2. When a portion of long-term debt must be paid within one year, it is classified as a current liability.

2-3. Three types of employer-related payroll liabilities are those for employee compensation, for employee payroll withholdings, and for employer payroll taxes.

2-4. Both the employee and the employer pay social security and Medicare taxes.

2-5. Unearned revenues are classified as liabilities because they represent obligations to perform services or deliver goods for which payment has been received in advance.

2-6. An estimated liability is a definite obligation; it is the amount of the liability that must be estimated.

2-7. Income taxes payable are considered estimated liabilities because the amount often cannot be determined until after the end of a company's fiscal year.

2-8. When the estimated amount of discount coupons that will be redeemed is recorded as a contra-sales account, it is treated as any sales discount would be—as a deduction from sales on the income statement. If it is recorded as a promotional expense, it is included in operating expenses, which are also deducted from gross margin on the income statement. In both cases, a current liability is created.

2-9. A company incurs a liability for a product warranty at the time it sells a warranted product.

3-1. A contingent liability is a potential liability; it depends on a future event arising out of a past transaction. It differs from a commitment in that a commitment is a legal obligation that does not meet the requirements for recognition as a liability and so is not recorded.

3-2. Contingent liabilities may arise from lawsuits, income tax disputes, and failure to follow government regulations. In each of these cases, a potential liability exists because if the ruling goes against the company, a liability will arise. Contingent liabilities also exist in the case of discounted notes receivable and loan guarantees because if the debtor does not pay, the company will be liable.

3-3. Leases and purchase agreements are examples of commitments.

4-1. The time value of money refers to the costs or benefits derived from holding or not holding money over time.

4-2. Simple interest is the interest for one or more periods when the amount on which the interest is calculated stays the same from period to period. Compound interest is the interest for two or more periods when after each period, the interest earned in that period is added to the amount on which interest is computed in future periods.

4-3. An ordinary annuity is a series of equal payments made at the end of equal periods of time, with compound interest on these payments.

4-4. The key variable that relates present value to future value is time. Present value is the amount that must be invested today at a given rate of interest to produce a given future value.

4-5. Before using the present value tables to compute present value when a compounding period is less than one year, it is necessary to (1) divide the annual interest rate by the number of compounding periods in the year, and (2) multiply the number of periods in one year by the number of years.

5-1. Business decisions very often involve the use of money over time, and any use of money over time has an interest cost, either stated or implied, associated with it. The time value of money is therefore an important factor in making business decisions.

5-2. Valuing an asset, computing a deferred payment, and accumulating a fund for loan repayment are a few examples of the many ways in which present value is used in financial reporting. Other applications include imputing interest on a noninterest-bearing note, valuing a bond, recording a lease, determining a pension liability, and analyzing the purchase price of a business or asset.

5-3. Businesses can make use of present value any time they are considering alternatives that require an outlay of money and affect future cash flows, such as the purchase of an asset, investing in the development of a new product, or acquiring another company.

Chapter 9

1-1. Long-term assets have a useful life of more than one year, are used in the operation of a business, and are not intended for resale to customers.

1-2. Land is different from other long-term assets because it has an unlimited life and is therefore not depreciated.

1-3. *Depreciation* refers to the periodic allocation of an asset's cost over its useful life. It does not refer to an asset's physical deterioration or decrease in market value over time. *Depletion* and *amortization* refer to the allocation of the cost of natural resources and intangible assets, respectively, over the accounting periods they benefit.

1-4. Asset impairment occurs when a long-term asset loses some or all of its potential to generate revenue. It requires reducing the carrying value of the asset to its fair value, an amount equal to the present value of the expected cash flows. The reduction of carrying value to fair value is recorded as a loss.

1-5. The cash flows (or savings) that a long-term asset is expected to generate are important considerations in the decision to acquire the asset. The cash flows must be sufficient to pay for the asset and provide a satisfactory return. In deciding how to finance the acquisition of a long-term asset, useful life is a consideration because the length of the financing should correspond to the period in which the asset is expected to produce cash flows.

1-6. Free cash flow is the amount of cash that remains after deducting the funds a company must commit to continue operating at its planned level. Its components are net cash flows from operating activities minus dividends minus (purchases of plant assets minus sales of plant assets). A positive free cash flow means that a company has met all its cash commitments and has cash available to reduce debt or to expand operations. A negative free cash flow means that it must raise funds from investors or creditors to continue at its planned level.

1-7. In accounting for each of a company's long-term assets, the following questions must be addressed: (1) How is the cost of the long-term asset determined? (2) How should the expired portion of the cost of the long-term asset be allocated against revenues over time? (3) How should subsequent expenditures, such as repairs and additions, be treated? (4) How should disposal of the long-term asset be recorded?

2-1. Capital expenditures are expenditures for the purchase or expansion of long-term assets and are recorded in the asset accounts. Revenue expenditures are expenditures for repairs, maintenance, fuel, and other items necessary to maintain and operate long-term assets; they are recorded in the expense accounts. The distinction is important because capital expenditures are allocated as expenses over time through depreciation, whereas revenue expenditures are expenses in the period in which they occur.

2-2. An addition is an enlargement of an existing facility. A betterment is an improvement of an existing facility that does not add to the physical layout. An extraordinary repair does not add to or better an existing facility, but it significantly extends its estimated useful life or increases its residual value.

2-3. When an addition to a building is charged as a repair expense, income in the current period will be understated, and income in future periods income will be overstated.

2-4. In general, the cost of a long-term asset includes all expenditures reasonable and necessary to get it in place and ready for use.

2-5. Expenditures (**a**), (**c**), (**d**), (**e**), and (**g**) should be charged to the computer system's asset account.

2-6. The entry is incorrect. The dock should have been recorded at a cost of $20,000 because that was the amount involved in acquiring the asset. No gain or savings from choosing one alternative over another should be recorded.

3-1. It is useful to think of a plant asset as a bundle of service units because it aids in allocating the cost of the asset over its useful life.

3-2. Obsolescence often shortens the estimated useful life of technical equipment. In this case, if the equip-ment became obsolete in less than 12 years, the firm would have to depreciate it over the shorter period.

3-3. The company should continue depreciating the building because depreciation is an allocation of cost, not a valuation process.

3-4. Like certain other plant assets, parking lots may seem to last forever, but in reality they eventually have to be replaced or need repairs so massive that they are equivalent to replacement. Parking lots should therefore be depreciated.

3-5. Depreciation is not a valuation process; it is a process of allocating the cost of a plant asset to the periods in which the asset benefits the business.

3-6. The straight-line method is based on the assumption that depreciation depends only on the passage of time, whereas the production method is based on the assumption that depreciation is solely the result of use.

3-7. The principal argument supporting an accelerated depreciation method is that some plant assets provide more and better service in their early years.

3-8. The theory underlying group depreciation is that a group of similar assets will have similar useful lives and residual values. Thus, a depreciation rate applied to the group will approximate depreciation in total rather than for each item individually.

3-9. In revising a depreciation rate, the remaining depreciable cost of the asset should be spread over the remaining years of the asset's revised useful life.

4-1. Depreciation should be computed for the part of a year that precedes the sale of a plant asset because the company has benefited from the use of the long-term asset up to the date of the sale. Under the matching rule, the depreciation for the partial year must be classified as an expense of the period.

4-2. If a plant asset is discarded before the end of its useful life, the amount of loss is equal to its carrying value (cost less accumulated depreciation).

4-3. When an asset is sold for cash, the gain or loss is determined by deducting the carrying value (cost less accumulated depreciation) from the amount of cash received. If the result is positive, a gain results. If it is negative, a loss results.

5-1. Annual depletion differs from depletion expense when not all of the natural resource is sold in the year it is extracted. The part not sold is considered inventory.

5-2. A mining company can depreciate its plant assets over a period less than the assets' useful lives when the assets are so closely associated with the natural resource that they cannot be used after the resource is depleted.

5-3. Successful efforts accounting treats each exploration of oil and gas resources separately. If an exploration is successful, its cost is recorded as an asset; if it is not, its cost is recorded as an expense. The full-costing method records the costs of all explorations, both successful and unsuccessful, as assets.

6-1. Accounts receivable are not classified as intangible assets because of their short-term nature.

6-2. To appear on the balance sheet, intangible assets must be purchased. For example, the cost of developing a patent do not appear on the balance sheet, but if a firm purchases the right to a patent, the purchase cost does appear on the balance sheet.

6-3. The FASB requires that research and development costs be charged as revenue expenditures in the period in which they are incurred.

6-4. Before a technologically feasible software program has been developed, accounting for the costs of development is similar to accounting for research and development costs—that is, costs are expensed as incurred. After a feasible and working software program has been developed, however, the development costs are capitalized and amortized over a reasonable length of time.

6-5. A company should record goodwill only when it acquires a controlling interest in another business. Goodwill can remain on the balance sheet indefinitely. However, it is subject to an annual impairment review. If it is deemed impaired, it is reduced to fair value, and an impairment charge is reported on the income statement.

Chapter 10

1-1. Among the advantages of issuing long-term debt are that common stockholders do not relinquish any control over the company, interest on debt is tax deductible, and financial leverage may increase a company's earnings. Disadvantages of long-term debt are that interest and principal must be repaid on schedule and financial leverage can work against a company if the earnings from its investments do not exceed its interest payments.

1-2. Interest coverage is important because it is an indicator of how much cushion a company has in making its interest payments. Default on interest payments can throw a company into bankruptcy.

1-3. The two components of a uniform monthly mortgage payment are interest on the debt (principal) and a reduction in the debt.

1-4. A capital lease is, in effect, an installment purchase or sale. The lessee in such a lease should treat it as a purchase made by incurring long-term debt. Thus, both an asset and a liability should be recorded. The income statement would contain deductions for interest expense and depreciation expense.

1-5. A pension plan is a contract that requires a company to pay benefits to its employees after they retire. A pension fund is a fund established by the contributions of an employer and often of employees from which benefits are paid to retirees.

1-6. Under a defined contribution plan, each year's contribution is fixed, but the benefits vary depending on how much the funds earn. Under a defined benefit plan, the benefits are fixed, but the annual contributions vary depending on assumptions about how much the funds will earn.

1-7. Other postretirement benefits include health care and other nonpension benefits provided to retired employees. Because employees earn these benefits during their employment, the FASB holds that in accordance with the matching rule, the benefits should be estimated and accrued during the time employees are working.

2-1. A bond issue is the total amount of bonds issued at one time. A bond certificate is a document that attests to a company's debt to a bondholder. A bond indenture is a contract that defines the rights of the bondholders. A bond indenture generally specifies the maturity date of the bonds, interest payment dates, interest rate, and call features and other restrictions.

2-2. The proceeds from the sale of $500,000 in bonds at 95 would be $475,000; at 100, $500,000; and at 102, $510,000.

2-3. If the face interest rate is less than the market interest rate, one would expect to pay less than par value for the bonds. In a competitive marketplace, investors are unwilling to pay par value for a fixed series of payments when the same funds could earn a higher rate of interest if invested elsewhere.

2-4. a. When a bond is issued for more than face value, the amount above face value is a premium. When a bond is sold below face value, the amount below face value is a discount.

b. Secured bonds give the bondholders a pledge of certain corporate assets as a guarantee of payment; unsecured (debenture) bonds do not.

c. When all the bonds of a bond issue mature on the same date, they are term bonds. When the bonds of an issue mature at different times, they are serial bonds.

d. A callable bond enables the issuer to buy back the bond at a specified price. A convertible bond allows the buyer to convert the bond into a specified number of shares of common stock.

e. A company that issues registered bonds maintains a list of the names and addresses of bondholders and pays them interest by check. Holders of coupon bonds must present a coupon at a bank to collect interest.

3-1. When bonds are sold at a discount, the market rate of interest is higher than the face interest rate because as the market interest rate goes up, the price of the bonds goes down.

3-2. When bonds are issued at a premium, the bonds are shown on the balance sheet at the total of the face value plus the premium.

3-3. Bond issue costs increase the discount on a bond issue because they reduce the proceeds from the issue, thereby increasing the difference between the face amount and the total proceeds.

4-1. The value of bonds depends on the series of equal interest payments and the face value, which will be paid at maturity.

4-2. The value of a bond can be determined by adding the present value of the series of equal interest payments to the present value of the single payment of the face value at maturity.

5-1. The total interest cost of a bond issue includes an addition for the amount of a bond discount or a subtraction for the amount of a bond premium.

5-2. The straight-line method is usually acceptable in cases where the difference in interest expense between the straight-line method and the effective-interest method is immaterial.

5-3. The amortization of a bond discount increases interest expense to an amount greater than interest paid because the amount received (borrowed) by the company at issuance is less than the amount that must be paid at maturity. The difference must be added to the total interest cost over the life of the bond. A bond premium has the opposite effect because when the bond matures, the company will pay an amount that is less than the amount it received at issuance.

5-4. Under the effective interest method, the amount of interest expense changes from period to period because the carrying value, on which the interest expense is computed, changes each period by the amount of the discount or premium amortized in the previous period.

6-1. When bond interest rates drop, a company may want to call its bonds and reissue debt at a lower rate. A company may also call its bonds if it has earned enough money to pay off the debt, if the reason for the debt no longer exists, or if it wants to restructure its debt to equity ratio.

6-2. Convertible bonds are advantageous to the issuing corporation because they usually carry a lower interest rate than bonds that are not convertible. In addition, if the market price of the corporation's common stock increases, bondholders will likely convert their bonds to common stock. This allows the corporation to raise equity capital and to avoid paying off the bonds. Despite their lower interest rate, convertible bonds are advantageous to the holder because of the potential gain if the stock price increases. Even if the stock price does not go up, the investor has earned a return and will be paid the face value of the bond at maturity.

7-1. A company collects an amount equal to the accrued interest from the buyer when it issues bonds between interest dates because on the next interest payment date, the holder will receive the full interest payment. This procedure reduces bookkeeping costs.

7-2. In making the year-end accrual for interest on bonds, interest payable and amortization of the premium or discount must be calculated. Together, the two calculations determine the interest expense.

Chapter 11

1-1. Advantages of the corporate form of business include the following:

Separate legal entity. A corporation can buy and sell property, sue other parties, enter into contracts, hire and fire employees, and be taxed.

Limited liability. Creditors can satisfy their claims only against a corporation's assets, not against those of a corporation's owners. Thus, the liability of stockholders is limited to the amount of their investments.

Ease of capital generation. It is fairly easy for a corporation to raise money because its stock is widely available at a relatively low price.

Ease of transfer of ownership. A stockholder can normally buy and sell shares of stock without affecting the corporation's activities and without the approval of other owners.

Lack of mutual agency. A stockholder cannot bind the corporation to a contract.

Continuous existence. Because a corporation is a separate legal entity, an owner's death, incapacity, or withdrawal has no effect on its existence.

Centralized authority and responsibility. The authority and responsibility for operating the corporation are delegated to one person, usually the president, who is accountable to the board and ultimately to the stockholders.

Professional management. Because management and ownership are separate, the corporation can hire the best talent available to operate the business.

1-2. Disadvantages of the corporate form of business include the following:

Government regulation. Corporations must meet the requirements of the laws of the states in which they are chartered. Publicly traded corporations must also file reports with the SEC and with the stock exchanges on which they are listed. Meeting these requirements is costly.

Taxation. Because a corporation is a separate legal entity, its earnings are subject to federal and state income taxes. In addition, stockholders must pay income tax on any dividends they receive. Thus, the earnings of a corporation are taxed twice.

Limited liability. Particularly for small corporations, limited liability can restrict the amount creditors are willing to lend.

Separation of ownership and control. The separation of ownership and control is a disadvantage when a firm's management makes bad decisions.

1-3. The three dates important in paying dividends are the declaration date, which is the date on which the board of directors formally declares that a dividend is going to be paid; the record date, which is the date on which ownership of stock, and thus the right to receive dividends, is determined; and the date of payment, which is the date on which the dividend is paid to the stockholders of record.

1-4. Dividends yield is computed by dividing the dividends per share by the market price per share. Investors use this ratio to evaluate the amount of dividends they receive.

1-5. Management can improve a company's return on equity by increasing earnings or by reducing stockholders' equity (e.g., by issuing debt rather than stock or by buying back the company's own stock on the open market).

1-6. The price/earnings (P/E) ratio is a measure of investors' confidence in a company's future; it is calculated by dividing the market price per share by earnings per share. Usually, the higher a company's P/E ratio, the more confidence the market has in its future earnings.

1-7. A stock option plan gives employees the right to purchase their company's stock under specified terms. Companies adopt stock option plans to motivate employees, as well as to compensate them.

2-1. Common stock is called *residual equity* because if a corporation is liquidated, the claims of creditors and preferred stockholders are paid before those of common stockholders.

2-2. Preferred stock differs from common stock in that it usually has preference over common stock in terms of receiving dividends and in terms of claims to assets when a corporation is liquidated.

2-3. Authorized shares are the maximum number of shares a corporation is allowed to issue. Issued shares are those that a corporation has sold or otherwise transferred to stockholders. Outstanding shares are the number of shares issued and that are in the hands of stockholders.

2-4. Treasury stock—shares that the issuing firm has repurchased—account for the difference between issued shares and outstanding shares.

3-1. Preferred stock's preference as to dividends means that common stockholders cannot receive dividends until after preferred stockholders have received their dividends. Preference as to assets means that in the event of a liquidation, the claims of preferred stockholders to corporate assets have precedence over the claims of common stockholders.

3-2. Cumulative preferred stock is preferred stock on which any unpaid dividends accumulated over time must be paid in full before common stock dividends can be paid. Dividends in arrears are dividends on cumulative preferred stock that have not been paid

in the period in which they are due. They should be reported either in the body of the financial statements or in a note.

3-3. Convertible preferred stock can be converted to common stock at the option of the preferred stockholder. When preferred stock is callable, the corporation can redeem or retire the stock by paying a specified price to the stockholder.

4-1. *Par value* is the amount per share recorded in a company's capital stock account; it represents a company's legal capital. No-*par value* refers to capital stock that has no par value. Most states require no-par stock to have a *stated value*, which serves the same purpose as par value.

4-2. The total of par value and additional paid-in capital is more relevant to the analyst than either figure by itself because it represents stockholders' total investments in the company.

4-3. When stock is issued for noncash assets, the transaction is usually recorded at the stock's fair market value. If the stock's fair market value cannot be determined, the fair market value of the assets or services received is used to record the transaction.

5-1. Treasury stock is capital stock, either common or preferred, that the issuing company has reacquired and has not reissued or retired.

5-2. A company might buy back its own stock to have stock available to distribute to employees through stock option plans, to maintain a favorable market for the stock, to increase its earnings per share or stock price per share, to have additional shares of stock available for purchasing other companies, or to prevent takeover attempts.

5-3. The cost of treasury stock is deducted from total contributed capital and retained earnings in the stockholders' equity section of the balance sheet.

Chapter 12

1-1. Quality of earnings refers to the substance of earnings and their sustainability into future accounting periods. Gains and losses on transactions, write-downs and restructurings, and nonoperating items are components of the income statement that affect quality of earnings.

1-2. The reader of financial statements is interested in a company's choice of accounting methods and estimates because of their effect on the company's quality of earnings. For example, by shortening the period over which it depreciates long-term assets, a company can increase its quality of earnings.

1-3. A write-down is a reduction in the value of an asset below its carrying value on the balance sheet. A restructuring is the estimated cost of a change in a company's operations; it usually involves the closing of facilities and layoff of personnel. Both write-downs and restructurings reduce current operating income and boost future income by shifting future costs to the current accounting period. Both appear in the operating (top) portion of a corporate income statement.

1-4. Cash flows relate to quality of earnings in that if earnings have underlying cash flows, they are considered more sustainable and of higher quality. Thus, a company with low earnings and high cash flows has higher quality earnings than a company with high earnings and low cash flows.

2-1. Accounting income and taxable income should not be treated alike because they serve different purposes. The purpose of accounting income is to give some indication (however imperfect) of a business's financial status; the sole purpose of taxable income is to provide a basis for collecting government revenues. Income tax allocation is necessary because of differences between accounting and taxable income caused by the timing of revenues and expenses.

2-2. Deferred income taxes represent the difference between income tax expense and income tax payable. If the former is greater than the latter, a deferred income tax liability exists.

2-3. On the income statement, *net of taxes* means that income taxes have been allocated among the various components of the statement so that each item, such as a gain or loss, is shown at an amount that is net of any tax consequences.

3-1. A gain or loss on discontinued operations should be disclosed separately on the income statement because separating the results of continuing operations and discontinued operations enhances the usefulness of the statement. It enables users to evaluate the company's ongoing activities and make projections about future operations.

3-2. The two major criteria for extraordinary items are that they be unusual in nature and that they occur infrequently. Extraordinary items should be disclosed separately from continuing operations on the income statement, and extraordinary gains or losses should be shown net of applicable taxes.

4-1. Earnings per share are disclosed on the income statement and usually appear immediately below the net income figure. They are broken down into income from continuing operations, income before extraordinary items, and net income. If a company reports a gain or loss from discontinued operations or extraordinary items, earnings per share figures are presented for those as well. If a company has potentially dilutive securities, diluted earnings per share must be shown.

4-2. A company has a simple capital structure when it has issued no preferred stocks, bonds, or stock options that can be converted to common stock. A company that has issued securities or stock options that can be converted to common stock has a complex capital structure.

4-3. Diluted earnings per share differ from basic earnings per share in that they take into account the effect of all potentially dilutive securities on earnings per share.

5-1. Comprehensive income consists of items from sources other than stockholders that account for the change in stockholders' equity during an accounting period. Comprehensive income includes net income, changes in unrealized investment gains and losses, gains and losses from foreign currency translation, and other items affecting equity.

5-2. The statement of stockholders' equity summarizes changes in the components of the stockholders' equity section of the balance sheet that occurred during an accounting period. The stockholders' equity section of the balance sheet lists the items of contributed capital and retained earnings on the balance sheet date.

5-3. A company has a deficit in retained earnings when its dividends and subsequent losses exceed its accumulated profits from operations.

6-1. Accounting for a stock dividend and accounting for a cash dividend differ in that in accounting for a cash dividend, dividends payable is credited, and in accounting for a stock dividend, common stock distributable and additional paid-in capital are credited for the amount of the stock dividend measured at market value.

6-2. A stock dividend is a proportional distribution of newly issued shares of stock to stockholders. A stock split divides the shares already owned by stockholders into additional shares according to a predetermined ratio. Both increase the number of shares outstanding.

6-3. A stock dividend results in a transfer of ownership interest from retained earnings to contributed capital. A stock split changes the number and par value of the common stock; it does not change the dollar amount in retained earnings or contributed capital.

7-1. When a corporation has no preferred stock, the book value per share is determined by dividing stockholders' equity by the number of common shares outstanding.

7-2. Book value per share is based on total assets minus total liabilities. Because assets are usually recorded at historical cost, one would not expect book value per share to equal market value per share.

Chapter 13

1-1. In the statement of cash flows, cash includes both cash and cash equivalents. Cash equivalents are short-term (ninety days or less), highly liquid investments, such as money market accounts, commercial paper, and U.S. Treasury bills.

1-2. The primary purpose of the statement of cash flows is to provide information about a company's cash receipts and cash payments during an accounting period. A secondary purpose is to provide information about a company's operating, investing, and financing activities during the period.

1-3. Cash flows are classified under operating, investing, and financing activities. Cash flows related to operating activities include cash receipts from customers for goods and services and from interest and dividends on investments; cash payments for wages, goods, and services; interest paid on debt; and taxes paid. Cash flows related to investing activities include cash received from the sale of long-term assets and marketable securities and the collection of loans, and cash expended for purchases of long-term assets and marketable securities and the making of loans. Cash flows related to financing activities include proceeds from issues of stock, long-term debt, and short-term borrowings; repayment of loans; the purchase of treasury stock; and payments made to owners, including cash dividends.

1-4. Significant noncash investing and financing transactions do not affect current cash flows, but they will affect cash flows in the future. They are therefore disclosed in a separate schedule on the statement of cash flows.

1-5. Analysts consider cash flows from operations an important indicator of the cash flows that underlie earnings, or the quality of earnings. Thus, a company may try to make its cash flows from operating activities look better by placing items that belong in the operating section of the statement of cash flows in the investing or financing sections.

2-1. Cash-generating efficiency is a company's ability to generate cash from current or continuing operations.

2-2. Three ratios that measure cash-generating efficiency are cash flow yield, cash flows to sales, and cash flows to assets.

2-3. Free cash flow is the cash that remains after deducting the funds a company must commit to continue operating at its planned level.

2-4. If free cash flow is positive, it means that the company has met all its planned cash commitments and has cash available to reduce debt or to expand. A negative free cash flow means that the company will have to sell investments, borrow money, or issue stock in the short term to continue at its planned level.

3-1. The direct method adjusts each item on the income statement from an accrual basis to a cash basis. The indirect method does not require the adjustment of each item on the income statement; it lists only the adjustments necessary to convert net income to cash flows from operations.

3-2. A company can have a positive cash flow from operations despite a net loss if it has (1) large amounts of noncash expenses, such as depreciation and amortization; (2) large reductions in accounts receivable,

inventories, or other prepaid assets; or (3) large increases in accounts payable, accrued liabilities, or income taxes payable. A positive cash flow occurs if the amount of any one of these items or their combined amount is greater than the net loss.

3-3. Depreciation is deducted from net income on the income statement, but it does not require a cash outlay and so does not affect cash flows in the current period. Thus, to arrive at cash flows from operating activities on the statement of cash flows, depreciation must be added back to net income.

3-4. The cash from the sale of an asset, which includes the amount of a gain, is included in the investing activities section of the statement of cash flows. The gain is also included in net income in the operating activities section. It is deducted in this section to prevent double counting.

3-5. Changes in current assets and current liabilities represent amounts by which the accrual accounting numbers for net income differ from the actual cash received or paid. Thus, adjustments are necessary to convert the accrual-based net income to cash flows from operating activities.

3-6. When the indirect method is used to determine net cash flows from operating activities, (a) an increase in accounts receivable should be subtracted from net income, (b) a decrease in inventory should be added, (c) an increase in accounts payable should be added, (d) a decrease in wages payable should be subtracted, (e) depreciation expense should be added, and (f) amortization of patents should be added.

4-1. The two major categories of assets that relate to the investing activities section of the statement of cash flows are investments and plant assets.

4-2. A building that cost $50,000, that had accumulated depreciation of $32,000, and that is sold at a loss of $5,000 would result in an increase in cash flow of $13,000 (carrying value of $18,000 less the loss of $5,000). The transaction should be shown as the sale of a building for $13,000 in the investing activities section of the statement of cash flows. If the indirect method is used, the $5,000 loss should be added to net income to determine net cash flows from operating activities.

4-3. The transaction should be disclosed on the schedule of noncash investing and financing transactions that accompanies the statement of cash flows, as follows: Issue of mortgage for buildings and land, $234,000.

5-1. The major categories of liabilities and stockholders' equity that relate to the financing activities section of the statement of cash flows are long-term liabilities, stock issues and repurchases (treasury stock), and cash dividends.

5-2. The conversion of bonds to common stock does not involve cash and does not appear in the financing section of the statement of cash flows. It should, however, be listed in the schedule of noncash investing and financing transactions that accompanies the statement of cash flows.

Chapter 14

1-1. Both investors and creditors use financial performance evaluation in choosing investments that will provide a return commensurate with the risk involved. Each group, however, evaluates a different type of risk. Investors evaluate the risk that dividends and stock price will not meet the required rate of return. Creditors evaluate the risk that a debtor will default on a loan.

1-2. The degree of risk involved in making a loan or investment depends on how easy it is to predict a company's future liquidity or profitability. In return for taking a greater risk, a creditor may demand a higher interest rate, and an investor may look for a higher return.

1-3. Three commonly used standards of comparison for evaluating financial statements are rule-of-thumb measures, a company's past performance, and industry norms. Rule-of-thumb measures are the weakest approach because they do not take into consideration a company's individual characteristics. Comparison of a company's financial measures or ratios over time can be effective, but this standard must be used with care. Industry norms are useful in showing how a company compares with other companies in the same industry.

1-4. A financial analyst might compare Steelco's ratios with those of other steel companies to determine how Steelco ranks in the industry. If Steelco has characteristics that make it different from other steel companies, this comparison would not be valid.

1-5. The major sources of information about public corporations are reports published by the company, reports filed with the SEC, business periodicals, and credit and investment advisory services. Much of this information is available on the Internet.

1-6. A corporation's compensation committee, which is made up of independent directors appointed by the board of directors, is charged with determining how top executives will be paid. The common components of executive compensation are salary, bonuses, and stock options.

2-1. Both horizontal and trend analyses focus on a company's performance over time. However, horizontal analysis focuses on performance from one year to the next, whereas trend analysis has a long-term perspective. Thus, an investor would want to see both types of analyses.

2-2. The statement means that net income in 1990 was set equal to 100 and that net income in 2000 and 2001 was recomputed, or indexed, in reference to net income in 1990. That is, net income in 2000 was 240 percent of net income in 1990 and increased to 260 percent of that figure in 2001.

2-3. Horizontal analysis is a year-to-year analysis of the components of various financial statements. Vertical analysis is concerned with the relationship of items within a single financial statement.

2-4. The purpose of ratio analysis is to identify meaningful relationships between components of the financial statements.

3-1. Although these two companies have the same net income, without more information, it is impossible to conclude that they are equally successful. For example, if one of them had twice as many assets as the other, its return on assets (a measure of profitability) would be only half of the other company's.

3-2. Because Circo Company has a return on assets of 12 percent and a debt to equity ratio of .5, one would expect its return on equity to be more than 12 percent because of its ability to use financial leverage.

3-3. With a profit margin of less than 1 percent, a supermarket would have to maintain a high asset turnover to achieve a satisfactory return on assets.

3-4. The amount of net cash flows from operating activities is common to all cash flow adequacy ratios. These ratios are most closely related to the liquidity and long-term solvency ratios.

3-5. The ratios most relevant to determining the financing period are days' sales uncollected, days' inventory on hand, and days' payable. The longer a company's financing period (Days' Sales Uncollected + Days' Inventory on Hand − Days' Payable), the greater its financing or interest costs will be. Thus, determining the financing period is especially important in periods of high interest rates.

3-6. To determine whether investors are equally confident about the future of Companies J and Q, one would compare the companies' price/earnings (P/E) ratios. The P/E ratio is computed by dividing a company's market price by its earnings per share. A high P/E ratio indicates that investors have a high degree of confidence in a company's future earnings and therefore are willing to accept a lower rate of return.

Chapter 15

1-1. Investments are generally recorded on the date they are made and are valued at cost, which includes any commissions.

1-2. Trading securities are debt or equity securities bought and held principally for the purpose of being sold in the near term. Available-for-sale securities are debt or equity securities that may be sold at any time. Held-to-maturity securities are debt securities that a company intends to hold until their maturity date.

1-3. In accounting for equity investments, the level and percentage of ownership are important because they are factors in determining how the investments should be treated.

1-4. Disclosure of investments is important because it describes how the investments are classified and the methods used to account for them.

1-5. Insider trading is the unethical and illegal practice of using inside information (information not available to the public) for personal gain.

2-1. Trading securities are valued at fair value on the balance sheet date.

2-2. Unrealized gains and losses on trading securities are the differences between the securities' costs and current market values. They are reported on the income statement.

2-3. Accounting for available-for-sale securities differs from accounting for trading securities in two ways: (1) an unrealized gain or loss is reported as a special item in the stockholders' equity section of the balance sheet, not as a gain or loss on the income statement; (2) if a decline in the value of a security is considered permanent, it is charged as a loss on the income statement.

3-1. **a.** Less than 20 percent ownership constitutes a non-influential and noncontrolling investment; the cost-adjusted-to-market method should be used.

b. A 20 to 50 percent ownership constitutes an influential but noncontrolling investment; the equity method should be used.

c. More than 50 percent ownership constitutes a controlling investment; consolidated financial statements should be prepared.

3-2. A parent-subsidiary relationship exists when a company (the parent) owns more than 50 percent of the voting stock of another company (the subsidiary).

3-3. Although information about American Home Products Corporation's subsidiaries may be helpful in assessing the corporation's performance, stockholders would be interested primarily in its consolidated financial statements because they give an overview of the entire economic entity.

3-4. Under the equity method, the parent company increases or decreases its investment in subsidiaries according to its share of their earnings and dividends. The equity method is required when the parent—in this case, Merchant Corporation—has significant influence over a subsidiary.

4-1. Eliminating entries prevent duplication of accounts in the records of a parent and its subsidiaries and reflect the financial position and operations of the consolidated entity. They are not entered in the accounting records; they appear only on the worksheets used in preparing consolidated financial statements.

4-2. Consolidated statements are valuable because they show the parent and all its subsidiaries as a single operating entity.

4-3. The practice violates the rule that *all* majority-owned subsidiaries must be consolidated.

4-4. Minority interest represents the holdings of owners of less than 50 percent of a subsidiary's voting stock. Minority interest appears on the consolidated balance sheet between long-term liabilities and stockholders' equity or as a separate item in the stockholders' equity section.

4-5. Goodwill from consolidation arises if a parent company (Merchant, in this case) pays more for an investment in a subsidiary than the fair value of the subsidiary's net assets. Goodwill from consolidation is shown on the balance sheet as a separate intangible asset.

4-6. To avoid double counting and overstating accounts, intercompany receivables, payables, sales, and purchases must be eliminated from consolidated financial statements. Only transactions with outside parties should be presented.

4-7. The amount of sales on the consolidated income statement is $1,400,000, or the sales of both companies minus the intercompany sales ($500,000 + $1,000,0000 − $100,000).

4-8. Before consolidating the financial statements of foreign subsidiaries and their parent company, the foreign subsidiaries' financial statements must be translated into the parent company's currency.

5-1. Held-to-maturity securities are debt securities that management intends to hold until their maturity date. They are valued on the balance sheet at cost adjusted for the effects of interest.

5-2. Most long-term bond investments are classified as available-for-sale securities because companies generally do not expect to hold them until their maturity date.

Chapter 1

1. *Statement of Financial Accounting Concepts No.1*, "Objectives of Financial Reporting by Business Enterprises" (Norwalk, Conn.: Financial Accounting Standards Board, 1978), par. 9.
2. Ibid.
3. CVS Corporation, *Annual Report*, 2004.
4. Christopher D. Ittner, David F. Larcker, and Madhav V. Rajan, "The Choice of Performance Measures in Annual Bonus Contracts," *The Accounting Review*, April 1997.
5. National Commission on Fraudulent Financial Reporting, *Report of the National Commission on Fraudulent Financial Reporting* (Washington, D.C.: 1987), p. 2.
6. Target Corporation, *Annual Report*, 2004.
7. "Gallup Poll Shows the Public's Opinion of Accounting Profession Is Improving," www.picpa.org, August 24, 2004.
8. Robert Johnson, "The New CFO," *Crain's Chicago Business*, July 19, 2004.
9. Curtis C. Verschoor, "Corporate Performance Is Closely Tied to a Strong Ethical Commitment," *Journal of Business and Society*, Winter 1999; Verschoor, "Does Superior Governance Still Lead to Better Financial Performance?" *Strategic Finance*, October 2004.
10. *Accounting Principles Board Statement No. 4*, "Basic Concepts and Accounting Principles Underlying Financial Statements of Business Enterprises" (New York: AICPA, 1970), par. 138.
11. *Statement Number IC*, "Standards of Ethical Conduct for Management Accountants" (Montvale, N.J.: Institute of Management Accountants, 1983; revised 1997).
12. CVS Corporation, *Annual Report*, 2004.
13. Costco Wholesale Corporation, *Annual Report*, 2003.
14. Southwest Airlines Co., *Annual Report*, 1996.
15. Queen Sook Kim, "Lechters Inc. Files for Chapter 11, Arranges Financing," *The Wall Street Journal*, May 22, 2001.
16. H&R Block, Inc., *Annual Report*, 2004.
17. Nikhil Deogun, "Coca-Cola Reports 27% Drop in Profits, Hurt by Weakness in Foreign Markets," *The Wall Street Journal*, January 27, 1999.

Chapter 2

1. J. Lynn Lunsford, "Singapore Airlines Will Order Long-Haul Jets from Boeing," *The Wall Street Journal*, August 25, 2004.
2. The Boeing Company, *Annual Report*, 2004.
3. Intel Corporation, *Annual Report*, 2003.
4. Gary McWilliams, "EDS Accounting Change Cuts Past Earnings by $2.24 Billion," *The Wall Street Journal*, October 28, 2003.
5. The Boeing Company, *Annual Report*, 2004.
6. Ibid.
7. Ibid.
8. Nike, Inc., *Annual Report*, 2004.
9. Mellon Bank, *Annual Report*, 2004.

Chapter 3

1. Yahoo! Inc., *Annual Report*, 2004.
2. Ibid.
3. "Microsoft Settles with SEC," CBSNews.com, June 5, 2002.
4. Securities and Exchange Commission, *Staff Accounting Bulletin No. 10*, 1999.

5. Ken Brown, "Wall Street Plays Numbers Games with Savings, Despite Reforms," *The Wall Street Journal*, July 22, 2003.
6. Yahoo!, Inc., *Annual Report*, 2004.
7. Ibid.
8. PricewaterhouseCoopers presentation, 1999.
9. Lyric Opera of Chicago, *Annual Report*, 2004.
10. The Walt Disney Company, *Annual Report*, 2004.

Chapter 4

1. Dell Computer Corporation, *Annual Report*, 2004.
2. *Statement of Financial Accounting Concepts No. 2*, "Objectives of Financial Reporting by Business Enterprises" (Norwalk, Conn.: Financial Accounting Standards Board, 1978), pars. 32–54.
3. *Statement of Financial Accounting Concepts No. 2*, "Qualitative Characteristics of Accounting Information" (Norwalk, Conn.: Financial Accounting Standards Board, 1980), par. 20.
4. L. Todd Johnson, "Relevance and Reliability," *The FASB Report*, February 28, 2005.
5. Dell Computer Corporation, *Annual Report*, 2003.
6. "Ex-Chief of WorldCom Is Found Guilty in $11 Billion Fraud," *The New York Times*, March 16, 2005.
7. *Accounting Principles Board Opinion No. 20*, "Accounting Changes" (New York: AICPA, 1971), par. 17.
8. Scott Thurm and Kevin J. Delaney, "Yahoo, Google, and Internet Math," *The Wall Street Journal*, May 10, 2004.
9. Securities and Exchange Commission, *Staff Accounting Bulletin No. 99*, 1999.
10. Ray J. Groves, "Here's the Annual Report. Got a Few Hours?" *The Wall Street Journal Europe*, August 26–27, 1994.
11. Roger Lowenstein, "Investors Will Fish for Footnotes in 'Abbreviated' Annual Reports," *The Wall Street Journal*, September 14, 1995.
12. "Debt vs. Equity: Whose Call Counts," *BusinessWeek*, July 19, 1999.
13. Roger Lowenstein, "The '20% Club' Is No Longer Exclusive," *The Wall Street Journal*, May 4, 1995.
14. Dell Computer Corporation, *Annual Report*, 2004.
15. Albertson's Inc., *Annual Report*, 2004; Great Atlantic & Pacific Tea Company, *Annual Report*, 2004.

Chapter 5

1. Costco Wholesale Corporation, *Annual Report*, 2004.
2. Ibid.
3. Jonathan Weil, "Accounting Scheme Was Straightforward but Hard to Detect," *The Wall Street Journal*, March 20, 2003.
4. Jathon Sapsford, "As Cash Fades, America Becomes a Plastic Nation," *The Wall Street Journal*, July 23, 2004.
5. Steve Stecklowe, Anita Raghavan, and Deborah Ball, "How a Quest for Rebates Sent Ahold on an Unusual Buying Spree," *The Wall Street Journal*, March 6, 2003.
6. Mylene Mangalindan, "Online Retail Sales Are Expected to Rise to $172 Billion This Year," *The Wall Street Journal*, May 24, 2005.
7. Joel Millman, "Here's What Happens to Many Lovely Gifts After Santa Rides Off," *The Wall Street Journal*, December 26, 2001.

8. Matthew Rose, "Magazine Revenue at Newsstands Falls in Worst Year Ever," *The Wall Street Journal*, May 15, 2001.

9. KPMG Peat Marwick, "1998 Fraud Survey," 1998.

10. American Institute of Certified Public Accountants, *Professional Standards*, vol. 1 (New York: AICPA June 1, 1999), Sec. AU 322.07.

11. Costco Wholesale Corporation, *Annual Report*, 2004.

12. Ibid.

13. Amy Merrick, "Starbucks Accuses Employee, Husband of Embezzling $3.7 Million from Firm," *The Wall Street Journal*, November 20, 2000.

14. Sid R. Ewer, "A Roundtrip Ticket to Trouble," *Strategic Finance*, April 2004.

Chapter 6

1. Cisco Systems, Inc., *Annual Report*, 2004.

2. Ibid.

3. Gary McWilliams, "Whirlwind on the Web," *BusinessWeek*, April 7, 1997.

4. Karen Lundebaard, "Bumpy Ride," *The Wall Street Journal*, May 21, 2001.

5. American Institute of Certified Public Accountants, *Accounting Trends & Techniques* (New York: AICPA, 2004).

6. Cisco Systems, Inc., *Annual Report*, 2004.

7. "Cisco's Number Confound Some," *International Herald Tribune*, April 19, 2001.

8. "Kmart Posts $67 Million Loss Due to Markdowns," *The Wall Street Journal*, November 10, 2000.

9. Micah Frankel and Robert Trezevant, "The Year-End LIFO Inventory Purchasing Decision: An Empirical Test," *The Accounting Review*, April 1994.

10. American Institute of Certified Public Accountants, *Accounting Trends & Techniques* (New York: AICPA, 2004).

11. "SEC Case Judge Rules Crazy Eddie Principals Must Pay $72.7 Million," *The Wall Street Journal*, May 11, 2000.

12. American Institute of Certified Public Accountants, *Accounting Trends & Techniques* (New York: AICPA, 2004).

13. Exxon Mobil Corporation, *Annual Report*, 2003.

14. Ibid.

15. Yamaha Motor Company, Ltd., *Annual Report*, 2004; Pioneer Corporation, *Annual Report*, 2004.

Chapter 7

1. Nike, Inc., *Annual Report*, 2004.

2. Peter Coy and Michael Arndt, "Up a Creek with Lots of Cash," *BusinessWeek*, November 12, 2001.

3. "So Much for Detroit's Cash Cushion," *BusinessWeek*, November 5, 2001.

4. Geoffrey Smith, "The Bill Comes Due for Capital One," *BusinessWeek*, November 4, 2004.

5. Jesse Drucker, "Sprint Expects Loss of Subscribers," *The Wall Street Journal*, September 24, 2002.

6. Michael Selz, "Big Customers' Late Bills Choke Small Suppliers," *The Wall Street Journal*, June 22, 1994.

7. Circuit City Stores, Inc., *Annual Report*, 2004.

8. Heather Timmons, "Do Household's Numbers Add Up?" *BusinessWeek*, December 10, 2001.

9. Steve Daniels, "Bank One Reserves Feed Earnings," *Crain's Chicago Business*, December 15, 2003.

10. Jonathon Weil, "Accounting Scheme Was Straightforward but Hard to Detect," *The Wall Street Journal*, March 20, 2003.

11. Nike, Inc., *Annual Report*, 2004.

12. Ibid.

13. American Institute of Certified Public Accountants, *Accounting Trends & Techniques* (New York: AICPA, 2004).

14. Mara Der Hovanesian, "The Virtually Cashless Society," *BusinessWeek*, November 17, 2003.

15. "Bad Loans Rattle Telecom Vendors," *BusinessWeek*, February 19, 2001.

16. Scott Thurm, "Better Debt Bolsters Bottom Lines," *The Wall Street Journal*, August 18, 2003.

17. Nike, Inc., *Annual Report*, 2004.

18. Information based on promotional brochures of Mitsubishi Corp.

19. Elizabeth McDonald, "Unhatched Chickens," *Forbes*, February 19, 2001.

20. Fosters Group Limited, *Annual Report*, 2003; Heineken N.V., *Annual Report*, 2003.

21. Rhonda L. Rundle and Paul Davies, "Hospitals Administer Antidote for Bad Debt," *The Wall Street Journal*, May 4, 2004.

Chapter 8

1. Amazon.com, Inc., *Annual Report*, 2004.

2. Pamela L. Moore, "How Xerox Ran Short of Black Ink," *BusinessWeek*, October 30, 2000.

3. Mark Heinzel, Deborah Solomon, and Joann S. Lublin, "Nortel Board Fires CEO and Others," *The Wall Street Journal*, April 29, 2004.

4. Hershey Foods Corporation, *Annual Report*, 2003.

5. Goodyear Tire & Rubber Company, *Annual Report*, 2004.

6. Andersen Enterprise Group, cited in *Crain's Chicago Business*, July 5, 1999.

7. Promomagazine.com, July 6, 2005.

8. Hershey Foods Corporation, *Annual Report*, 2003.

9. Scott McCartney, "Your Free Flight to Mars Is Hobbling the Airline Industry," *The Wall Street Journal*, February 4, 2004.

10. *Statement of Financial Accounting Standards* No. 5, "Accounting for Contingencies" (Norwalk, Conn.: Financial Accounting Standards Board, 1975).

11. American Institute of Certified Public Accountants, *Accounting Trends & Techniques* (New York: AICPA, 2004).

12. Ibid.

13. *Statement of Financial Accounting Concepts* No. 7, "Using Cash Flow Information and Present Value in Accounting Measurement" (Norwalk, Conn.: Financial Accounting Standards Board, 2000).

14. WorldCom (MCI), *Annual Report*, 2004.

15. Advertisement, *Chicago Tribune*, November 8, 2002.

16. Sun Microsystems Inc., *Annual Report*, 2004; Cisco Systems, Inc., *Annual Report*, 2004.

17. General Motors Corporation, Form 10-k, March 16, 2005.

18. Advertisement, *Chicago Tribune*, 2000.

Chapter 9

1. Apple Computer, Inc., *Annual Report*, 2004.

2. *Statement of Financial Accounting Standards* No. 144, "Accounting for the Impairment or Disposal of Long-Lived Assets" (Norwalk, Conn.: Financial Accounting Standards Board, 2001).

3. Sharon Young, "Large Telecom Firms, After WorldCom Moves, Consider Writedowns," *The Wall Street Journal*, March 18, 2003.

4. *Statement of Financial Accounting Standards* No. 34, "Capitalization of Interest Cost" (Norwalk, Conn.: Financial Accounting Standards Board, 1979), par. 9–11.

5. American Institute of Certified Public Accountants, *Accounting Trends & Techniques* (New York: AICPA, 2004).

6. Ibid.

7. *Statement of Financial Accounting Standards* No. 25, "Suspension of Certain Accounting Requirements for Oil and Gas Producing Companies" (Norwalk, Conn.: Financial Accounting Standards Board, 1979).

8. Jonathan Weil, "Oil Reserves Can Sure Be Slick," *The Wall Street Journal*, March 11, 2004.

9. "The Top 100 Brands," *BusinessWeek*, August 5, 2002.

10. "What's in a Name?" *Time*, May 3, 1993.

11. *Statement of Financial Accounting Standards* No. 142, "Goodwill and Other Intangible Assets" (Norwalk, Conn.: Financial Accounting Standards Board, 2001), par. 11–17.

12. General Motors Corporation, *Annual Report*, 2003.

13. Abbott Laboratories, *Annual Report*, 2004.

14. *Statement of Financial Accounting Standards* No. 2, "Accounting for Research and Development Costs" (Norwalk, Conn.: Financial Accounting Standards Board, 1974), par. 12.

15. *Statement of Financial Accounting Standards* No. 86, "Accounting for the Costs of Computer Software to Be Sold, Leased, or Otherwise Marketed" (Norwalk, Conn.: Financial Accounting Standards Board, 1985).

16. *Statement of Financial Accounting Standards* No. 142, "Goodwill and Other Intangible Assets" (Norwalk, Conn.: Financial Accounting Standards Board, 2001), par. 11–17.

17. General Mills, Inc., *Annual Report*, 2004; H.J. Heinz Company, *Annual Report*, 2004; Tribune Company, *Annual Report*, 2004.

18. Southwest Airlines Co., *Annual Report*, 2002.

19. Costco Wholesale Corporation, *Annual Report*, 2004.

20. IBM Corporation, *Annual Report*, 2004.

21. Hilton Hotels Corporation, *Annual Report*, 2004; Marriott International, Inc., *Annual Report*, 2004.

22. "Stock Gives Case the Funds He Needs to Buy New Technology," *BusinessWeek*, April 15, 1996.

23. Polaroid Corporation, *Annual Report*, 1997.

Chapter 10

1. McDonald's Corporation, *Annual Report*, 2004.

2. Ibid.

3. Lee Hawkins Jr., "S&P Cuts Rating on GM and Ford to Junk Status," *The Wall Street Journal*, May 6, 2005.

4. David Reilly and Silvia Ascarelli, "History Is Made (Again) in Convertibles Boom," *The Wall Street Journal*, July 9, 2003.

5. *Statement of Financial Accounting Standards* No. 13, "Accounting for Leases" (Norwalk, Conn.: Financial Accounting Standards Board, 1976), par. 10.

6. *Statement of Financial Accounting Standards* No. 106, "Employers' Accounting for Postretirement Benefits Other than Pensions" (Norwalk, Conn.: Financial Accounting Standards Board, 1990).

7. Lee Hawkins Jr., "GM's Liabilities for Retiree Health Top $60 Billion," *The Wall Street Journal*, March 11, 2004.

8. Adapted from quotations in *The Wall Street Journal*, June 14, 2005.

9. Ken Brown and Scott Thurm, "Companies Find 'No-Nos' Are Hard to Resist," *The Wall Street Journal*, December 2, 2003.

10. Bill Barnhart, "Bond Bellwether," *Chicago Tribune*, December 4, 1996.

11. Accounting Principles Board, *Opinion* No. 21, "Interest on Receivables and Payables" (New York: AICPA, 1971), par. 15.

12. Elizabeth MacDonald, "False Front," *Forbes*, October 14, 2002.

13. Tom Sullivan and Sonia Ryst, "Kodak $1 Billion Issue Draws Crowds," *The Wall Street Journal*, October 8, 2003.

14. Safeway Inc., *Annual Report*, 2004.

15. "More Hotels Won't Be Able to Pay Debt from Operations, Study Says," *The Wall Street Journal*, October 20, 2001.

16. Amazon.com, Inc., *Annual Report*, 2004.

17. Stanley Ziemba, "TWA, American Revise O'Hare Gate Agreement," *The Wall Street Journal*, May 13, 1992.

18. Ibid.

19. NEC Corporation, *Annual Report*, 2004; Sanyo Electric Co., *Annual Report*, 2004.

Chapter 11

1. Google, Inc., Form S-1 (Registration Statement), 2004; Form 10-Q, September 2004.

2. Microsoft Corporation, Form 10-K, 2004.

3. Deborah Solomon, "AT&T Slashes Dividends 83%, Cuts Forecasts," *The Wall Street Journal*, December 21, 2002.

4. Abbott Laboratories, *Annual Report*, 2004.

5. Google, Inc., Form S-1 (Registration Statement), 2004.

6. Robert A. Guth and Scott Thurm, "Microsoft to Dole Out Its Cash Hoard," *The Wall Street Journal*, July 21, 2004.

7. American Institute of Certified Public Accountants, *Accounting Trends & Techniques* (New York: AICPA, 2004).

8. *Statement of Accounting Standards* No. 123, "Stock-Based Payments" (Norwalk, Conn.: Financial Accounting Standards Board, 1995; amended 2004).

9. Jonathan Weil, "FASB Unveils Expensing Plan on Option Pay," *The Wall Street Journal*, April 1, 2004.

10. Google, Inc., Form S-1 (Registration Statement), 2004, p. 136.

11. Joseph Weber, "One Share, Many Votes," *BusinessWeek*, March 29, 2004; Google, Inc., Form S-1 (Registration Statement), 2004.

12. Michael Rapoport and Jonathan Weil, "More Truth-in-Labeling for Accounting Carries Liabilities," *The Wall Street Journal*, August 23, 2003.

13. American Institute of Certified Public Accountants, *Accounting Trends & Techniques* (New York: AICPA, 2004).

14. Robert McGough, Suzanne McGee, and Cassell Bryan-Low, "Buyback Binge Now Creates Big Hangover," *The Wall Street Journal*, December 18, 2000.

15. "Avaya Prices Public Offering of Common Stock" and "Avaya Completes Sale of Approximately $200 Million Common Stock," *The Wall Street Journal Online*, March 22, 2002.

16. Tom Herman, "Preferreds' Rich Yields Blind Some Investors to Risks," *The Wall Street Journal*, March 24, 1992.

17. Stanley Ziemba, "USAir Defers Dividends on Preferred Stock," *Chicago Tribune*, September 30, 1994.

18. Susan Carey, "US Airways to Redeem Preferred Owned by Berkshire Hathaway," *The Wall Street Journal*, February 4, 1998.

Chapter 12

1. Motorola, Inc., *Annual Report*, 2004.

2. Cited in *The Week in Review* (Deloitte Haskins & Sells), February 28, 1985.

3. "Up to the Minute, Down to the Wire," *Twentieth Century Mutual Funds Newsletter*, 1996.

4. David Carins International, IAS *Survey Update*, July 2001.

5. Elizabeth MacDonald, "Pro Forma Puff Jobs," *Forbes*, December 9, 2002.

6. Barbara A. Lougee and Carol A. Marquardt, "Earnings Informativeness and Strategic Disclosure: An Empirical Examination of 'Pro forma' Earnings," *The Accounting Review*, July 2004.

7. American Institute of Certified Public Accountants, *Accounting Trends & Techniques* (New York: AICPA, 2004).

8. Jesse Drucker, "Motorola's Profit: Special Again?" *The Wall Street Journal*, October 15, 2002.

9. *Statement of Financial Accounting Standards No. 109*, "Accounting for Income Taxes" (Norwalk, Conn.: Financial Accounting Standards Board, 1992).

10. American Institute of Certified Public Accountants, *Accounting Trends & Techniques* (New York: AICPA, 2004).

11. Accounting Principles Board, *Opinion No. 30*, "Reporting the Results of Operations" (New York: AICPA, 1973), par. 20.

12. Accounting Principles Board, *Opinion No. 15*, "Earnings per Share" (New York: AICPA, 1969), par. 12.

13. *Statement of Financial Accounting Standards No. 128*, "Earnings per Share and the Disclosure of Information About Capital Structure" (Norwalk, Conn.: Financial Accounting Standards Board, 1997).

14. *Statement of Financial Accounting Standards No. 130*, "Reporting Comprehensive Income" (Norwalk, Conn.: Financial Accounting Standards Board, 1997).

15. American Institute of Certified Public Accountants, *Accounting Trends & Techniques* (New York: AICPA, 2004).

16. American Institute of Certified Public Accountants, *Accounting Research Bulletin No. 43* (New York: AICPA, 1953), chap. 7, sec. B, par. 10.

17. Ibid., par. 13.

18. The Gillette Company, *Annual Report*, 2003.

19. Robert O'Brien, "Tech's Chill Fails to Stem Stock Splits," *The Wall Street Journal*, June 8, 2000.

20. Mylene Mangalindan, "Yahoo's Not Sears; Stock Split Is Declared," *The Wall Street Journal*, April 8, 2004.

21. "Technology Firms Post Strong Earnings but Stock Prices Decline Sharply," *The Wall Street Journal*, January 21, 1988; Donald R. Seace, "Industrials Plunge 57.2 Points—Technology Stocks' Woes Cited," *The Wall Street Journal*, January 21, 1988.

22. Rebecca Buckman, "Microsoft Posts Hefty 18% Revenue Rise," *The Wall Street Journal*, January 18, 2002; William M. Bulkeley, "IBM Reports 13% Decline in Net Income," *The Wall Street Journal*, January 18, 2002.

Chapter 13

1. Marriott International, Inc., *Annual Report*, 2004.

2. "Deadweight on the Markets," *BusinessWeek*, February 19, 2001.

3. Gary Slutsker, "Look at the Birdie and Say: 'Cash Flow,'" *Forbes*, October 25, 1993.

4. Jonathan Clements, "Yacktman Fund Is Bloodied but Unbowed," *The Wall Street Journal*, November 8, 1993.

5. Jeffery Laderman, "Earnings, Schmearnings—Look at the Cash," *BusinessWeek*, July 24, 1989.

6. Marriott International, Inc., *Annual Report*, 2004.

7. American Institute of Certified Public Accountants, *Accounting Trends & Techniques* (New York: AICPA, 2004).

8. Martin Peers and Robin Sidel, "WorldCom Causes Analysts to Evaluate EBITDA's Role," *The Wall Street Journal*, July 15, 2002.

9. Richard Passov, "How Much Cash Does Your Company Need?" *Harvard Business Review*, November 2003.

10. "Cash Flow Shortfall in Quarter May Lead to Default on Loan," *The Wall Street Journal*, September 4, 2001.

11. Enron Corporation, *Press Release*, October 16, 2001.

12. Sony Corporation, *Annual Report*, 2004; Canon, Inc., *Annual Report*, 2004.

13. Chip Meyers, "The Last Laugh," *Business 2.0*, September 2002.

14. Dean Foust, "So Much Cash, So Few Dividends," *BusinessWeek*, January 20, 2003.

Chapter 14

1. Starbucks Corporation, *Annual Report*, 2004 (profit margin computed).

2. David Henry, "The Numbers Game," *BusinessWeek*, May 14, 2001.

3. Jonathan Weil, "'Pro forma' in Earnings reports? . . . As If," *The Wall Street Journal*, April 24, 2003.

4. *Statement of Financial Accounting Standards No.131*, "Segment Disclosures" (Norwalk, Conn.: Financial Accounting Standards Board, 1997).

5. Starbucks Corporation, *Annual Report*, 2004.

6. Ibid.

7. Target Corporation, *Proxy Statement*, May 18, 2005.

8. Starbucks Corporation, *Annual Report*, 2004.

9. Lee Hawkins Jr., "S&P Cuts Rating on GM and Ford to Junk Status," *The Wall Street Journal*, May 6, 2005.

10. H.J. Heinz Company, *Annual Report*, 2004.

11. Jesse Drucker, "Performance Bonus Out of Reach? Move the Target," *The Wall Street Journal*, April 29, 3003.

12. Pfizer, Inc., *Annual Report*, 2004; Roche Group, *Annual Report*, 2004.

Chapter 15

1. eBay, Inc., *Annual Report*, 2004.

2. *Statement of Financial Accounting Standards No. 115*, "Accounting for Certain Investments in Debt and Equity Securities" (Norwalk, Conn.: Financial Accounting Standards Board, 1993).

3. eBay, Inc., *Annual Report*, 2004.

4. Jalal Soroosh and Jack T. Ciesielski, "Accounting for Special Purpose Entities Revised," FASB Interpretation (46R), *The CPA Journal*, July, 2004.

5. Greg Steinmetz and Cacilie Rohwedder, "SAP Insider Probe Points to Reforms Needed in Germany," *The Wall Street Journal*, May 8, 1997.

6. Kathryn Kranhold and Deborah Solomon, "GE Restates Several Years of Earnings," *The Wall Street Journal*, May 9, 2005.

7. eBay, Inc., *Annual Report*, 2004.

8. *Statement of Financial Accounting Standards No. 115*, "Accounting for Certain Investments in Debt and Equity Securities" (Norwalk, Conn.: Financial Accounting Standards Board, 1993).

9. eBay, Inc., *Annual Report*, 2004.

10. *Statement of Financial Accounting Standards No. 94*, "Consolidation of All Majority-Owned Subsidiaries" (Norwalk, Conn.: Financial Accounting Standards Board, 1987).

11. eBay, Inc., *Annual Report*, 2004.

12. Accounting Principles Board, *Opinion No. 16*, "Business Combinations" (New York: AICPA, 1970).

13. eBay, Inc., *Annual Report*, 2004.

14. Ibid.

15. Dell Computer Corporation, *Annual Report*, 2004.

16. Dreamworks Animation, *SEC Form 10Q*, 2004.

17. Microsoft Corporation, *Annual Report*, 2004.

COMPANY NAME INDEX

Abbott Laboratories, 489, 574

Academy of Television Arts & Sciences, 29

Adolph Coors Company, 577

Ahold, 292

Albertson's Inc., 273

Alcoa, 632, 633

Amazon.com, Inc., 155, 165, 174, 249, 331, 417, 418, 421, 424–425, 428, 440, 444, 609, 702, 708

American Airlines, 431, 564, 752

American Century Investments Corporation, 612

American Express, 614

America Online (AOL), 206, 431

Ameritech Corp., 379

AOL Time Warner, 299

Apple Computer, 463, 466, 468, 487, 488, 491, 514, 574, 632, 654, 762

Arthur Andersen, 110

AT&T, 466, 588

AT&T Wireless, 752

Autoliv, Inc., 338, 339

Avalon International Breads, 17

Avaya, Inc., 605

Bank of America, 385, 614

Bank One, 383, 576

Barnes & Noble, 331, 346

Bed Bath & Beyond, 51

Bell South, 527

Berkshire Hathaway, 606

Best Buy Co., 5

Blockbuster Entertainment Corporation, 346

Boeing Company, 105, 106, 107, 108, 109, 126, 133, 236, 475, 576

Borders, 331

Canon, Inc., 698, 700

Capital One, 378–379

Chase, 385, 605

Chase Manhattan, 632

Circuit City Stores, 294, 381, 382

Cisco Systems, Inc., 333, 334, 336, 343, 355–356, 390, 459, 703

Citibank, 385, 458, 605

CMS Energy, 582

Coca-Cola Company, 28, 54, 252, 253, 488, 527

Columbia HCA Healthcare, 527

Comcast, 525

CompuCredit, 412

Continental Airlines, 515

Costco Wholesale Corporation, 50, 243, 281, 283, 287, 305, 311, 506

Cox Communications, 525

craigslist.inc, 766

Crazy Eddie, Inc., 370

Credit Suisse First Boston, 571

CVS Corporation, 3, 6, 7, 10, 12, 14, 21, 31, 52–53, 55–64, 154, 207, 275–276, 330, 334, 371–372, 414, 460, 508, 509, 563, 608, 653–654, 701, 702, 751–752, 775, 796

DaimlerChrysler, 376, 423

Dell Computer Corporation, 225, 228, 230, 239, 245, 254–256, 335, 370, 703, 793–794

Deloitte & Touche, 28

Delta, 475

Deutsche Telekom International, 517

Dillard's, Inc., 283, 380, 415

Disney, 206, 252, 488, 527

DreamWorks Animation, 794

Dynergy, 331

Earthly Elements, Inc., 379

Eastman Kodak, 561

eBay, Inc., 609, 626, 654, 755, 756, 758, 763, 766, 768, 771, 772, 775, 778–779

Eclipsys, 206

Electronic Data Systems Corporation (EDS), 125

Energen Corporation, 471

Enron Corporation, 8, 9, 19, 109, 228, 229, 698, 699, 758

Ernst & Young, 28, 29, 232

Estee Lauder, 752

Exxon Mobil Corporation, 16, 28, 370, 371

Fidelity Investments Company, 50

Fleetwood Enterprises, Inc., 698

Ford Credit, 461

Ford Motor Company, 28, 376, 381, 509, 516, 523, 749

Fosters Group Limited, 413

The Gap, 7

General Electric (GE), 28, 488, 523, 761

General Mills, 490

General Motors, 28, 376, 381, 459, 489, 516, 521, 574, 749

Georgia-Pacific, 292

Gillette Company, 631

Goodyear Tire & Rubber Company, 229, 230, 422, 709–710, 749

Google Inc., 230, 567, 575, 577, 578, 582, 591, 609

Great Atlantic & Pacific Tea Company (A&P), 273

HealthSouth, 287, 383

Heineken N. V., 413

Heinz, 561

Hershey Foods Corporation, 421, 429

Hewlett-Packard, 588

Hilton Hotels Corporation, 506

H.J. Heinz Company, 490, 509, 750

Home Depot, 346

Household International, 383

H&R Block, Inc., 51–52

HSBC Bank USA, 605

IBM, 28, 488, 506, 527, 605, 650–651, 655, 760, 768

Intel Corporation, 54, 108, 488, 588, 632, 703

J.C. Penney, 370, 378, 415

JP Morgan/Chase, 576

Juniper Networks, 632

Kmart, 339, 377

KnowledgeWare, 206

KPMG, 28

Kraft Foods, 153, 292

Lands' End, 294

Lechters, Inc., 51

Lehman Brothers Inc., 249

L.L. Bean, 294

Lucent Technologies, 206, 390, 423

Lyric Opera of Chicago, 206

McDonald's Corporation, 28, 248, 290, 329, 488, 513, 515, 516, 518, 520, 521, 544–545

Macy's, 380

Marlboro, 488

Marriott International, 506, 657, 660, 663, 681

Marshall Field's, 380

Maytag Corporation, 372

MCI, 109, 155, 383

Mellon Bank, 153

Mercedes, 488

Merck, 460

Microsoft Corporation, 54, 161, 488, 514, 573, 588, 589, 654, 655, 760, 797

Midas, 430

Mitsubishi Corp., 412, 458–459

Moody's Investors Service, 752

Morgan/Chase, 576

Morgan Stanley, 571

Motorola, Inc., 423, 611, 615, 617, 623, 625, 635

MSNBC, 796

NEC Corporation, 564

Neiman Marcus, 243

Nestlé, 153, 292

Netscape Communications Corporation, 606

Newark Morning Ledger Company, 489

New England Patriots, 617

Nieman Marcus, 243

Nike, Inc., 152, 375, 377, 379, 381, 383, 384, 400, 652

Nokia, 488

Nordstrom, 380

Nortel Networks Corporation, 390, 420

Nvidia, 632

Office Depot, 294
Oracle, 703
PepsiCo Inc., 711, 712, 749–750, 768
Pfizer, Inc., 461, 753
PharmaMar, 679
Piedmont, 475
Pioneer Corporation, 373
Polaroid Corporation, 510–511
Preussag, 615
PricewaterhouseCoopers, 28
Procter & Gamble, 28
Qwest Communications, 466
Rambus Inc., 632
Reebok International Ltd., 5
RentWay, Inc., 338
Rite Aid Corporation, 338
Roche, 753
Royal Dutch/Shell Group, 485
Safeway Inc., 561–562
Salomon Smith Barney, 110
Sam's Club, 243
Sanyo Electric Co., 564
Sara Lee, 153, 292

Sears, 378, 381
Simon & Schuster, 299
Singapore Airlines, 105, 106, 107, 109, 126, 133
Sony Corporation, 525, 698, 700
Southwest Airlines Co., 5, 50, 53, 55, 154, 207, 275–276, 506, 509, 563, 608, 653–654, 701, 750, 751–752, 796
Sprint, 379
Standard & Poor's Ratings Group, 749
Starbucks Corporation, 5, 329, 705, 714, 715, 716, 717, 718, 721, 722, 723, 724, 726, 727, 728, 730
Sun Microsystems Inc., 459, 752
Target Corporation, 9, 724
Tenet Healthcare Corp., 415
Texas Instruments, 376
Tiffany & Co., 243, 632
Time Warner, 582
Toyota, 5
Toys "R" Us, 336, 346
Trans World Airlines, 515, 564
Travelocity.com, 174

Tribune Company, 490
TWA, 515, 564
Twentieth Century Mutual Funds, 612
Tyco, 525
United Airlines, 515, 752
United Parcel Service, 335
US Airways, 475, 606
Vanguard Airlines, 475
Verisign, 616
Vivendi, 671
Walgreens, 330, 334, 372, 460, 614
Wal-Mart Corp., 5, 252, 346, 385
Walt Disney Company, 206, 252, 488, 527
Wells Fargo, 605
Wendy's International Inc., 5
WorldCom, 8, 9, 19, 109, 110, 155, 228, 229, 383, 458, 466, 662, 671
Xerox Corporation, 28, 109, 419, 582
Yahoo! Inc., 157, 158, 168, 170, 172, 173, 179, 183, 230, 609, 650, 654
Yamaha Corporation, 373

Note: **Boldface** type indicates key terms.

Accelerated method, 477, 477–478, 479(fig.)

Account(s), 111
chart of, 127–128, 129(exh.)
contra, 168
names of, 132
permanent (real), 177
temporary (nominal), 177
uncollectible, *see* Uncollectible accounts
See also specific account names
Account balance, 112
See also Balance(s)

Accounting, 4
accrual, 162–164
development of, 8
financial, 7
as information system, 4(fig.), 4–10
management, 7

Accounting conventions, 228, 229–233

Accounting cycle, 177, 178(fig.), 179–181
closing entries and, 177, 179, 179(fig.)
post-closing trial balance and, 179

Accounting equation, 19, 19–22, 20(fig.), 112

Accounting information
for internal and external decision making, 7
management's responsibility for providing, 11
processing, 7–8
qualitative characteristics of, 226–228
See also Financial statement(s); *specific financial statements*

Accounting measurement, 13–15
Accounting methods, quality of earnings and, 614–615
Accounting policies, in annual reports, 62, 106
Accounting Principles Board (APB), on investments in subsidiaries, 773
Accounts payable, 20, 422
evaluating, 418–420, 419(fig.), 420(fig.)

Accounts receivable, 20, 377, 377–383
aging of, 391
collection of, 119–120
credit policies and, 377–379, 378(fig.)
ethics and estimates in accounting for, 382–383
evaluating level of, 379–380, 380(fig.)
financing, 380–382, 381(fig.)
installment, 377–378
See also Uncollectible accounts

Accounts receivable aging method, 391, 391–393, 392(exh.)

comparison with percentage of net sales method, 393(fig.), 393–394

Accrual(s), 165
of bond interest expense, year-end, 543–544

Accrual accounting, 162, 162–164
adjusting accounts and, 162–164, 163(exh.)
cash flows and, 181–182
expense recognition and, 162
revenue recognition and, 162

Accrued expenses, 169
adjustments for, 164, 165, 169(fig.), 169–171
Accrued interest, 398–399
Accrued liabilities, 424

Accrued revenues, 172
adjustments for, 172(fig.), 172–173

Accumulated Depreciation account, 168
Acquisition costs, 469–474
of buildings, 472
of equipment, 472
general approach to, 470–471
of group purchases, 472–473
of land, 471–472
of land improvements, 472
of leasehold improvements, 472

Addition(s), 470

Additional paid-in capital, 21

Adjusted trial balance, 175, 175(exh.), 175–177, 176(exh.)

Adjusting entries, 164, 164–175
for allocating recorded, unearned revenues, 164, 165, 171(fig.), 171–172
for allocating recorded costs, 164, 165–168
for recognizing unrecorded, earned revenues, 164, 165, 172(fig.), 172–173
for recognizing unrecorded expenses, 164, 165, 169(fig.), 169–171
Adjustments, 162–175, 163(exh.)
ethics and, 163–164
process for, 164(fig.), 164–175

Aging of accounts receivable, 391
AICPA, *see* American Institute of Certified Public Accountants (AICPA)
Allowance for Bad Debts account, 389
Allowance for Doubtful Accounts account, 389

Allowance for Uncollectible Accounts account, 389, 393

Allowance method, 388, 388–389
Allowance to Adjust Long-Term Investments account, 764

American Institute of Certified Public Accountants (AICPA), 29
on depreciation rates, 480

Amortization, 465, 465(fig.)
of bond discounts, 531–535
of bond premiums, 535–539
Annual reports, 55–64, 710
Annual Statement Studies, 711
Annuities, ordinary, 436, 437(table), 438–439
Annuities due, 813
APB (Accounting Principles Board), on investments in subsidiaries, 773

Articles of incorporation, 17

Asset(s), 20
cash flows to, 664
on classified balance sheet, 234, 236–237
current, *see* Current assets
financial, short-term, 377
fixed (long-lived, plant, tangible), *see* Property, plant, and equipment
intangible, 237, 464–465, 465(fig.), 486–491, 487(table), 488(fig.)
long-term, *see* Long-term assets; Depreciation; Property, plant, and equipment
net, 20
noncash, issuance of stock for, 586
other, 234
preference as to, 581–582
purchase in cash, 117–118
purchase on credit, 117–118
return on, 250(fig.), 250–251, 251(fig.)
tangible, 464, 465(fig.)
valuation of, 440–441

Asset impairment, 465, 465–466

Asset turnover, 249, 249–250, **724,** 725(exh.)

Audit(s), 28

Audit committee, 19
Authorization, as control activity, 302

Authorized shares, 578

Available-for-sale securities, 756, 763

Average-cost method, 345
Bad Debts Expense account, 389

Balance(s), 112
compensating, 376
credit, closing, 209, 210(exh.), 211(exh.)
debit, closing, 209, 211(exh.)
normal, 113
trial. *See* Trial balance

Balance sheet, 24, 24(exh.)
classified, 233–240, 234(fig.), 235(exh.)
consolidated, 58(exh.), 61, 769–773
of partnerships, 239

of sole proprietorships, 238–239
U.K. practices regarding, 234
Banking services, 385
Bank reconciliation, 385, 385–388,
387(exh.)
Bank statement, 308–309(fig.)
Bar codes, 284
Barron's, 711
Barter transactions, 108
Base year, 714
Basic earnings per share, 623, 623–624
Belichick, Bill, 617
Betterments, 470
Blake, Norman, 9
Boards of directors, 18
Bond(s), 522, 522–544
amortizing discounts on, 531–535
amortizing premiums on, 535–539
callable, 524
calling, 540
characteristics of, 524–525
convertible, 525
converting, 541
costs of issuing, 528–529
coupon, 525
issued at a discount, 527–528
issued at a premium, 528
issued at face value, 526
long-term investments in, 777–778
prices and interest rates on, 523–524
registered, 525
sale between interest dates, 541–543,
543(fig.)
secured, 524
serial, 524
term, 524
unsecured (debenture), 524
valuing using present value, 529–531
year-end accrual of interest expense
for, 543–544
zero coupon, 525, 532
Bond certificates, 523
Bond indenture, 523
Bonding, 302
Bond issue, 523, 523–524
Bonds payable, 517, 677
Bond value
with market rate above face rate,
529–530
with market rate below face rate, 530,
530(fig.)
Bonuses
basis for, 6
to new partner, 805
to old partners, 804–805
Bookkeeping, 7
Book value, 168, 634, 634–635
less than 100 percent purchase at, 771,
771(exh.)
100 percent purchase at, 769–770,
770(exh.)

per share, 634–635
subsidiary purchase at more or less
than, 772(exh.), 772–773
Book value per share, 634, 634–635
Brand names, 487
Brin, Sergey, 578
Brokers, 13
Buffett, Warren, 589
Buildings, acquisition cost of, 472
Business(es), 5
goals, activities, and performance
measures for, 5(fig.), 5–7
Business forms, 15–19, 16(fig.)
See also Corporations; Partnership(s);
Sole proprietorships
Business periodicals, 711
Business transactions, 14
analysis of, 115–122
foreign, 285
measurement issues and, 106–110,
107(fig.)
recording and posting, 127–132
timing of, cash flows and, 125(fig.),
125–126
Callable bonds, 524
Callable preferred stock, 583
Call price, 525
Capital
additional paid-in, 21
contributed, 21
ease of generation by corporations,
568
legal, 571
partners,' interest on, 800
working, 247
Capital balance ratios, for distributing
partnership income and losses,
801–802
Capital expenditures, 470
Capital leases, 518
Capital structure, 625
Carrying value, 168, 465, 634–635
See also Book value
Cash, 376, 658
companies' needs for, 678
control methods for, 384–385
expenses paid in, 120
idle, investment of, 442
needs for, 376–377, 377(fig.)
prepayment of expenses in, 116–117
purchase of assets in, 117–118
receipts of, internal control of, 305–306
revenues in, 118
sale of plant assets for, 482–483
Cash basis of accounting, 160
Cash disbursements, internal control of,
306(fig.), 306–307, 308–309(fig.)
Cash equivalents, 384, 658
Cash flows, 24, 24–25
from accrual-based information,
181–182

analysis of, 663–666
classification of, 659(fig.), 659–660
dividends policies and, 574
evaluation of adequacy of, 726–728,
727(exh.)
free, 664–666, 727
inventory cost decisions and, 350
managing, 418
problems caused by big buyers for
small suppliers, 379
quality of earnings and, 616–618,
617(exh.)
timing of transactions and, 125(fig.),
125–126
See also Statement of cash flows
Cash flows to assets, 664
Cash flows to sales, 664, 727, 727(exh.)
Cash flow yield, 726, 727(exh.)
Cash-generating efficiency, 663,
663–664
Cash return on assets, 133
"Category killers," 346
Centralization, of authority and
responsibility, in corporations,
569–570
Certified public accountants (CPAs), 28,
28(table)
reports of, 28–29, 63(fig.), 63–64
CFOs (chief financial officers), 11
Chart of accounts, 127–128, 128,
129(exh.)
Check(s), 308–309(fig.)
non-sufficient-funds, 386
outstanding, 385
Check authorization, 307, 308–309(fig.)
Checkmarks, in general journal, 130
Chief financial officers (CFOs), 11
Classification, 109
of liabilities, 421
Classified balance sheet, 233–240,
234(fig.), 235(exh.)
Classified financial statements, 234,
234(fig.)
using, 247–254
See also specific financial statements
Closely held corporations, 55
Closing entries, 177, 179, 189(fig.),
209–213
accounts after closing and, 212–213,
213(exh.)
for closing Dividends account balance,
212, 212(exh.)
for closing Income Summary account
balance, 212, 212(exh.)
for credit balances, 209, 210(exh.),
211(exh.)
for debit balances, 209, 211(exh.)
Collections, 119–120
Commas, in financial reports, 132
Commercial paper, 423
Commitments, 433, 433–434

Common-size statements, 718, 719(exh.), 719(fig.), 720(exh.), 720(fig.)

Common stock, 18, 578, 584–587

earnings per share of, 244–245, 623–625, 624(exh.), 713, 724

financing activities and, 677–678

issuance for noncash assets, 586

no-par, 584, 585–586

par value, 584–585

Common Stock account, 113

Common Stock Distributable account, 630

Comparability, 229

Comparative financial statements, 57

Compensating balance, 376

Compensation

of executives, 711, 713

of hourly employees, 425

salaries and, 425

Compensation committees, 711

Complex capital structure, 625

Compound interest, 434, 434–435

future value of single sum invested at, 435(table), 435–436

time periods and, 439–440

See also Time value of money

Comprehensive income, 626, 627(exh.)

Computer(s), 7, 7–8

internal control and, 305

Computerized accounting systems, adjustments using, 180

Conglomerates, 708–710

Conservatism, 231

Consignment, 342

Consistency, 229, 229–230

Consolidated balance sheet, 769–773

Consolidated financial statements, 57–60(exh.), **768,** 768–776

Consolidated income statement, 774(exh.), 774–775

Contingent liabilities, 381, 433

Continuity, 159

Continuous existence, of corporations, 569

Contra accounts, 168

Contributed capital, 21, 566–593, **577**

corporate form of business and, 568–570, 569(fig.)

dividend policies and, 572–574

equity financing and, 570–571

measuring performance using return on equity and, 574–575

stock options as compensation and, 575–576

See also Common stock; Preferred stock; Stock(s); Stockholders' equity; Treasury stock

Control, 758

of corporations, separation from ownership, 570

equity investments and, 757, 757(fig.), 758, 763–768

See also Internal controls

Control activities, 301, 301–303

Control environment, 301

Convertible bonds, 525

Convertible preferred stock, 582

Copyright, 487

Corporate governance, 19

Corporations, 16(fig.), **17,** 17–19

advantages of incorporation and, 568–570

disadvantages of incorporation and, 570

formation of, 17

governance of, 19

multinational, 775

organization of, 17–18, 18(fig.)

private (closely held), 55

reports published by, 710–711

size of, 16

stockholders' investments in, *see* Contributed capital; Common stock; Preferred stock; Stock(s); Stockholders' equity; Treasury stock

subsidiaries and, *see* Subsidiaries

transnational, 775

Cost(s), 108

acquisition, *see* Acquisition costs

depreciable, 475

of doing business, 158

exchange, 108

expired, 158

historical, 108

of inventory, *see* Inventory cost

of issuing bonds, 528–529

organization, 571

promotional, 429–430

research and development, 489–490

of software, 490

start-up, 571

transportation, 289–290

See also Expenses

Cost-adjusted-to-market method, 763

Cost-benefit convention, 232

Cost flows, 341

goods flow and, 341–342

Cost of goods sold, 242, 242–243

Cost of Goods Sold account, 287

Cost principle, 108, 756

Coupon(s), liability for, 430

Coupon bonds, 525

CPAs, *see* Certified public accountants (CPAs)

Credit

purchase of assets on, 117–118

purchases of merchandise on, in perpetual inventory system, 292

receipts on, under periodic inventory system, 298

revenues on, 119

sales on, in perpetual inventory system, 293

sales on, under periodic inventory system, 298

trade, 377

Credit(s), 111

bank reconciliation and, 386

Credit and investment advisory services, 711

Credit balances, closing, 209, 210(exh.), 211(exh.)

Credit cards, 283

increased use of, 290

terms of sales and, 290

Credit lines, 422–423

Creditors, 12

objectives of, financial performance measurement and, 706–707

uses of statement of cash flows, 658

Credit ratings, 516

Cumulative preferred stock, 580

Current assets, 236

changes in, cash flows from operating activities and, 670

Current liabilities, 237, 237, 418–432, **421**

changes in, cash flows from operating activities and, 670–671

definitely determinable, 422–429

estimated, 429–432

evaluating accounts payable and, 418–420, 419(fig.), 420(fig.)

managing liquidity and cash flows and, 418

reporting, 420–421

Current ratio, 247–248, 248, 248(fig.), **722,** 723(exh.)

Customer lists, 487

Date of payment, 572

Days' inventory on hand, 336, 722, 723(exh.)

Days' payable, 418, 722, 723(exh.)

Days' sales uncollected, 379, 722, 723(exh.)

Death of a partner, 806

Debenture bonds, 524

Debit(s), 111

bank reconciliation and, 386

Debit balances, closing, 209, 211(exh.)

Debit cards, 283, 385

increased use of, 290

terms of sales and, 290

Debt, early extinguishment of, 525

Debt securities, 776–778

Debt to equity ratio, 251, 251–252, 253(fig.), **726,** 726(exh.)

Decimal points, in financial reports, 132

Decision makers, 10–13, 11(fig.)

with direct financial interest, 12

with indirect financial interest, 12–13

management as, 10–11

Decision making
acquisition of long-term assets and, 466–467
internal and external, accounting information for, 7
regarding issuance of long-term debt, 514–515
Declaration date, 572
Declining-balance method, 477
Deferrals, 165
adjusting entries for, 164, 165–168
Deferred Income Taxes account, 521, 619, 620
Deferred payment, 441–442
Deficits, 628
Defined benefit plans, 520
Defined contribution plans, 520
Definitely determinable liabilities, 422, 422–429
Delivery expense, 290
Depletion, 464, 465(fig.), 484
Deposits in transit, 386
Depreciable assets, disposal of, 481–483
Depreciable cost, 475
Depreciation, 167, 167–168, **464**, 465(fig.), 474–481
accelerated cost recovery for tax purposes and, 480
cash flows from operating activities and, 668–669
disposal of depreciable assets and, 481–483
factors affecting computation of, 475
group, 479
methods of computing, 475–478
for partial years, 479
of related plant assets, 485
revision of rates for, 479–480
Derivatives, 761
Development costs, in oil and gas industry, 485
Dick, Melvin, 110
Diluted earnings per share, 625
Direct charge-off method, 388
Direct method, 668
Disclosure
of inventory methods, 342–343
of investments, 758
of liabilities, 421
of uncollectible accounts, 389
Discontinued operations, 622
Discount(s), 524
amortization of, 531–535
on bonds, 524, 527–528, 531–535
purchases, 289
sales, 288–289
trade, 288
Discounting, 382
Dishonored notes, 399
Disposal, of depreciable assets, 481–483
Dissolution, of partnerships, 803–806

Diversified companies, 708, 708–710
Dividends, 18, 121, **572**, 572–574
dates associated with, 572, 573(fig.)
evaluating dividend policies and, 573(fig.), 573–574
liquidating, 572
preference as to, 580–581
stock, 629–631
Dividends account, closing, 212, 212(exh.)
Dividends in arrears, 581
Dividends payable, 424
Dividends yield, 573, 728, 728(exh.)
Documents, internal controls and, 302
Dollar signs, in financial reports, 132
Double-declining-balance method, 477, 477–478
Double-entry system, 110–114, 111
accounts and, 111
normal balance and, 113, 113(table)
rules of, 112–113
stockholders' equity accounts and, 113–114, 114(fig.)
T account and, 111–112
Double taxation, 570
Duality, principle of, 111
Due care, 30
Dun & Bradstreet, 711
Duncan, John, 9
Duration of a note, 397, 397–398
Early extinguishment of debt, 525
Earnings
misstatements of, 161
quality of. See Quality of earnings
retained, 21, 577, 628
See also Income
Earnings management, 161
Earnings per share, 244, 244–245, 623–625, 624(exh.), 713, 724
basic, 623–624
diluted, 625
Ebbers, Bernard J., 110, 229
Ecommerce, impact of, 174
Economic value added (EVA), 724
Economists, 13
Effective interest method, 533
for amortization of bond discounts, 533–535, 534(table), 535(fig.)
for amortization of bond premiums, 537(table), 537–539, 538(fig.)
Effective interest rate, 523–524, 529–531
EFT (electronic funds transfer), 385
Electronic commerce, impact of, 174
Electronic funds transfer (EFT), 385
Eliminations, 769
Equipment, acquisition cost of, 472
Equities, 19
investments in. See Investment(s)
Equity
owner's, 19, 237–239
partners', 237–239, 800

ratio of debt to, 251–252, 253(fig.), 726, 726(exh.)
residual, 578
return on, 253–254, 254(fig.), 574–575, 725, 725(exh.)
stockholders,' see Common stock; Preferred stock; Stock(s); Stockholders' equity; Treasury stock
trading on, 514
Equity financing, 570–571
advantages of, 571
disadvantages of, 571
See also Common stock; Preferred stock; Stock(s); Stockholders' equity; Treasury stock
Equity method, 766, 766–767
Estimated liabilities, 429, 429–432
Estimated useful life, 475
Estimation
accounts receivable and, 382–383
inventory valuation by, 353–355
quality of earnings and, 613–614
of uncollectible accounts expense, 389–394
Ethics, 8, 8–9
accounts receivable and, 382–383
adjustments and, 163–164
of investing, 758–759
matching rule and, 160(fig.), 160–161
measurement issues and, 109–110
professional, 30
statement of cash flows and, 662
EVA (economic value added), 724
Exchange(s), of plant assets, 483
Exchange cost, 108
Exchange gain or loss, 285
Exchange price, 108, 108–109
Exchange rate, 14, 14–15, 15(table), 285
Excise tax payable, 424–425
Ex-dividend stocks, 572
Expenditures, 469, 469–470
capital, 470
revenue, 470
Expenses, 21, 158
accrued, 164, 165, 169(fig.), 169–171
to be paid later, 120–121
depreciation, see Depreciation
operating, 243
other (nonoperating), 243–244
paid in cash, 120
prepaid, 166(fig.), 166–167
prepayment of, in cash, 116–117
of revenues, 162
See also Cost(s)
Expired costs, 158
Explanatory notes, in annual report, 62
Exploration costs, in oil and gas industry, 485
Extraordinary items, 622, 622–623
Extraordinary repairs, 470
Face interest rate, 523

bond value and, 529–531
Face value, bonds issued at, 526
Factor(s), 381
Factoring, 381
Fair value, 108, 466
FASB, *see* Financial Accounting Standards Board (FASB)
Federal Communications Commission (FCC), 570
Federal Insurance Contributions Act (FICA) tax, withholding for, 426
Federal Trade Commission (FTC), 570
Federal Unemployment Tax Act (FUTA) tax, withholding for, 426
FICA (Federal Insurance Contributions Act) tax, withholding for, 426
FIFO (First-in, first-out) method, 345, 345–346
Financial accounting, 7
Financial Accounting Standards Board (FASB), 29
　on contingent liabilities, 433
　on deferred income taxes, 619–620
　on objectives of financial reporting, 226
Financial analysts, 13
Financial assets, short-term, 377
Financial highlights, in annual report, 56
Financial leverage, 514
　negative, 515
Financial performance measurement, 704–731, **706**
　creditors' and investors' objectives and, 706–707
　executive comparison and, 711, 713
　horizontal analysis for, 714, 715(exh.), 716(exh.), 716–717
　information sources for, 710–711
　management's objectives and, 706
　ratio analysis for, 721–729
　standards of comparison for, 707–710
　trend analysis for, 717, 717(exh.), 718(fig.)
　vertical analysis for, 718, 719(exh.), 719(fig.), 720(exh.), 720(fig.)
Financial position, 19
Financial press, 13
Financial reporting
　accounting conventions for, 228, 229–233
　objectives of, 226
　qualitative characteristics of accounting information and, 226–228
　See also Financial statement(s); *specific financial statements*
Financial risk, long-term debt and, 514–515
Financial statement(s), 7, 23–27
　in annual report, 56–57, 57–60(exh.), 61
　common-size, 718, 719(exh.), 719(fig.), 720(exh.), 720(fig.)

comparative, 57
consolidated, 57–60(exh.)
　of foreign subsidiaries, restatement of, 775
interim, 710–711
inventory cost decisions and, 348(fig.), 348–349
management's certification of, 228–229
notes to, 61–62
relationships among, 25, 26(exh.), 27
See also specific financial statements
Financial statement analysis. *See* Financial performance measurement
Financial Times, 711
Financing
　equity, 570–571
　of long-term assets, 467–468
　as management activity, 11
　off-balance-sheet, 516
　See also Common stock; Equity financing; Preferred stock; Stock(s); Treasury stock
Financing activities, 6, 660, 676–680
　Bonds Payable account and, 677
　common stock and, 677–678
　noncash, 660
　retained earnings and, 678
　treasury stock and, 679, 680(exh.)
Financing period, 283
First-in, first-out (FIFO) method, 345, 345–346
Fiscal year, 159, 159–160
Fixed assets, *see* Depreciation; Long-term assets; Property, plant, and equipment
FOB destination, 289, 290
FOB shipping point, 289, 289–290
Folio column, in general journal, 130
Footings, 112
Forbes, 711
Foreign business transactions, 285
Form 8-K, 711
Form 10-K, 711
Form 10-Q, 711
Fortune, 711
Franchises, 487
Fraud
　common types of, 300
　detection of, 287
Fraudulent financial reporting, 8
Free cash flow, 467, 467–468, **664,** 664–666, **727,** 727(exh.)
Freight-in, 290
Freight-out, 290
Frequent flyer programs, 431
FTC (Federal Trade Commission), 570
Full-costing method, 485
Full disclosure, 231, 231–232
FUTA (Federal Unemployment Tax Act) tax, withholding for, 426

Future value, 435, 435–436
　of ordinary annuity, 436, 437(table)
　of single sum invested at compound interest, 435(table), 435–436
　tables of, 808(table), 808–809, 809(table)
GAAP, *see* Generally accepted accounting principles (GAAP)
Gains
　cash flows from operating activities and, 669–670
　exchange, 285
　quality of earnings and, 615
GASB (Governmental Accounting Standards Board), 29
Gates, Bill, 589
General journal, 128, 130, 130(exh.)
General ledger, 127, 127–128, 130–132
　ledger account form and, 130, 131(exh.)
　posting to, 131(exh.), 131–132
　presentation and, 132
Generally accepted accounting principles (GAAP), 27, 27–30
　independent CPA's report and, 28(table), 28–29
　organizations influencing, 29–30
　professional ethics and, 30
Goethe, 110
Going concern, 159
Goods available for sale, 296, 296–297
Goods flow, 341, 341–342
Goodwill, 487, 490–491
Goodwill account, 772
Governmental Accounting Standards Board (GASB), 29
Governmental organizations, 13
Government regulation, of corporations, 570
Grabman, Jack, 110
Gross margin, 243
Gross profit, 243
Gross profit method, 354, 354–355, 355(table)
Gross sales, 242
Group depreciation, 479
Group purchases, acquisition cost of, 472–473
Handbook of Dividend Achievers, 711
Hedging, 761
Held-to-maturity securities, 757, 777
Historical cost, 108
Horizontal analysis, 714, 715(exh.), 716(exh.), 716–717
IASB (International Accounting Standards Board), 30
ICC (Interstate Commerce Commission), 570
IMA (Institute of Management Accountants), 30
Imprest systems, 384–385, **385**

Income
  comprehensive, 626, 627(exh.)
  effects of inventory misstatements on
    measurement of, 337–340
  interest, 386
  measurement of, 158–160
  net, 22, 158, 244
  partnership, distribution of, 800–803
  partnership, participation in, 799–800
  See also Earnings
Income before income taxes, 244
Income from continuing operations, 612
Income from operations, 243
Income statement, 23, 23(exh.), 240–247
  consolidated, 774(exh.), 774–775
  multistep, 240–245, 241(fig.), 242(exh.)
  multistep form of, 61
  single-step, 245, 246(exh.)
Income Summary account, 179
  closing, 212, 212(exh.)
Income taxes, 244, 618–622, 619(table)
  accelerated cost recovery and, 480
  of corporations, 570
  deferred, 521, 619–620
  income before, 244
  inventory cost decisions and, 349–350
  net of taxes and, 620–621
  provision for, 244
  withholding for, 426
Income taxes payable, 429
Independence, 30
Independent directors, 18
Independent verification, for internal
  control, 302
Index number, 717
Indirect method, 668
Industry norms, for financial performance
  measurement, 708–710, 709(exh.)
Industry Norms and Key Business Ratios, 711
Influential and noncontrolling
  investments, 766–768
Information and communication, 301
Initial public offerings (IPOs), 567
Insider trading, 758, 758–759
Installment accounts receivable, 377,
  377–378
**Institute of Management Accountants
  (IMA), 30**
Intangible assets, 237, 464, 464–465,
  465(fig.), 486–491, 487(table),
  488(fig.)
Integrity, 30
Intercompany receivables and payables,
  773
Interest, 398, 434
  accrued, 398–399
  calculating total cost of, 531–532, 536
  compound, *see* Compound interest;
    Time value of money
  in notes receivable, 398
  on partners' capital, 800

  simple, 434
Interest coverage ratio, 516, 726,
  726(exh.)
Interest expense, on bonds, year-end
  accrual of, 543–544
Interest income, 386
Interest rates
  on bonds, 523–524
  face, 523, 529–531
  market, 523–524, 529–531
  in notes receivable, 398
Interim financial statements, 710,
  710–711
Interim periods, 159
Internal controls, 285–287, 286, 300–309
  activities of, 301–303
  of cash receipts, 305–306
  components of, 301
  computers for, 305
  limitations on, 303
  management goals and, 304
  management responsibility for, 287
  need for, 285–287
  over merchandising transactions,
    303–309
  of purchases and cash disbursements,
    306(fig.), 306–307, 308–309(fig.)
Internal Revenue Service (IRS), 30
**International Accounting Standards
  Board (IASB), 30**
International joint ventures, 767
Internet sales, 294
Interstate Commerce Commission (ICC),
  570
Inventory, 332–358
  cost of, *see* Inventory cost
  decisions regarding, *see* Inventory
    decisions
  evaluating level of, 335–337, 337(fig.)
  inventory systems and, *see* Inventory
    systems; Periodic inventory system;
    Perpetual inventory system
  misstatements about, effect on
    income measurement, 337–340
Inventory cost, 340, 340–344
  disclosure of inventory methods and,
    342–343
  effects on income determination and
    income taxes, 347–351, 348(table)
  goods flow and cost flow and, 341–342
  lower-of-cost-or-market rule and, 342
  under periodic inventory system,
    344–347
  under perpetual inventory system,
    351–353, 353(fig.)
Inventory decisions, 334–335, 335(fig.),
  347–371, 348(table)
  effects on cash flows, 350
  effects on financial statements,
    348(fig.), 348–349
  effects on income taxes, 349–350

  operating decisions and, 350
Inventory systems, 283–284
  bar codes and, 284
  See also Periodic inventory system;
    Perpetual inventory system
Inventory turnover, 335, 336, 722,
  723(exh.)
Inventory valuation
  by cost, *see* Inventory cost
  by estimation, 353–355
Investing, as management activity, 11
Investing activities, 6, 660, 673–676
  investments and, 673–674
  noncash, 660
  plant assets and, 674–675
Investment(s), 236, 673–674, 754–781
  classification of, 756–758, 757(fig.),
    757(table)
  consolidated financial statements and,
    768–776
  in debt securities, 776–778
  disclosure of, 758
  ethics and, 758–759
  of idle cash, 442
  long-term, in equity securities,
    763–768
  in partnerships, 804
  recognition of, 756
  short-term, 756, 760–763
  valuation of, 756
Investors, 12
  objectives of, financial performance
    measurement and, 706–707
  uses of statement of cash flows, 658
Invoice, 307, 308–309(fig.)
IPOs (initial public offerings), 567
IRS (Internal Revenue Service), 30
Issued shares, 578
Joint ventures, international, 767
Journal(s), 128
  general, 128, 130, 130(exh.)
Journal entries, 128, 174
  See also Adjusting entries; Closing
    entries
Journal form, 115, 115–116
Journalizing, 128
Just-in-time operating environment, 337
Kiting, 385
Labor unions, 12
Land, acquisition cost of, 471–472
Land improvements, acquisition cost of,
  472
Last-in, first-out (LIFO) method, 346,
  346–347, 347(fig.), 352
Lawyers, 13
Lay, Kenneth, 229
LCM (lower-of-cost-or-market) rule, 342
Lease(s), 518
Leasehold(s), 487
Leasehold improvements, 472
Ledger(s), general. *See* General ledger

Ledger account form, 130, 131(exh.)
Legal capital, 571
Letter to the stockholders, 55–56
Liabilities, 19, **20**
  accrued, 424
  on classified balance sheet, 237
  contingent, 381, 433
  current, *see* Current liabilities
  definitely determinable, 422–429
  estimated, 429–432
  long-term, 237, 421
  payment of, 118
  recognition of, 420–421
Liability
  limited, of corporations, 568, 570
  unlimited, of partnerships, 799
Licenses, 487
Life
  limited, of partnerships, 799
  useful, estimated, 475
LIFO liquidation, 349
LIFO (last-in, first-out) method, 346, 346–347, 347(fig.), 352
Limited liability, of corporations, 568, 570
Limited life, of partnerships, 799
Lines of credit, 422, 422–423
Liquidating dividends, 572
Liquidation of partnerships, 806
Liquidity, 5, 5–6
  evaluation of, 247–248
  managing, 418
Long-lived assets, *see* Property, plant, and equipment
Long-term assets, 462–494, **464**
  acquisition costs of, 469–474
  decision to acquire, 466–467
  depreciable, disposal of, 481–483
  depreciation of. *See* Depreciation
  financing, 467–468
  intangible, 486–491, 487(table), 488(fig.)
  matching rule and, 468, 469(fig.)
  natural resources as. *See* natural resources
  property, plant, and equipment as. *See* Property, plant, and equipment
Long-term debt, current portion of, 425
Long-term investments, 763–768
  influential and noncontrolling, 766–768
  noninfluential and noncontrolling, 763–766
Long-term leases, 518–520, 519(table)
Long-term liabilities, 237, 421, 512–547
  decision to issue long-term debt and, 514–515
  evaluation of, 515(fig.), 515–516
  types of long-term debt and, 517–521
  See also Bond(s)
Losses
  cash flows from operating activities and, 669–670

exchange, 285
net, 22, 158
partnership, distribution of, 800–803
quality of earnings and, 615
Lower-of-cost-or-market (LCM) rule, 342
LP column, in general journal, 130
Management, 10
  certification of financial statements, 228–229
  corporate, 18
  decision making by, 10–11
  of earnings, 161
  executive compensation and, 711, 713
  functions of, 11
  goals of, internal control and, 304
  objectives of, financial performance measurement and, 706
  professional, of corporations, 570
  reports of responsibilities of, 62
  responsibility for internal control, 287
  uses of statement of cash flows, 658
Management accounting, 7
Management information systems (MISs), 8
Management's discussion and analysis, in annual report, 56
Managing employees, as management activity, 11
Manufacturing companies, 241
Market, 342
Marketable securities, 756
Marketable Securities account, 236
Marketing, as management activity, 11
Market interest rate, 523, 523–524
  bond value and, 529–531
Market strength, evaluation of, 728, 728(exh.)
Market value, 108
Matching rule, 160
  ethics and, 160(fig.), 160–161
  long-term assets and, 468, 469(fig.)
Materiality, 230, 230–231
Maturity date, 396, 396–397
Maturity value, 398
Measurement, 13–15, 106–110, 107(fig.)
  classification issue and, 109
  ethics and, 109–110
  of income, 158–160
  of profitability, 158–161
  recognition issue and, 106–108
  valuation issue and, 108–109
Medical insurance, withholding for, 426
Medicare tax, withholding for, 426
Merchandise
  on hand, not included in inventory, 342
  in transit, 341(fig.), 341–342
Merchandise inventory, 282
  inventory systems for, *see* Inventory systems; Periodic inventory system; Perpetual inventory system

Merchandise Inventory account, 287
Merchandising businesses, 280–313, **282**
  foreign business transactions and, 285
  internal control and, *see* Internal controls
  inventory systems and, *see* Inventory systems; Periodic inventory system; Perpetual inventory system
  operating cycle and, 282(fig.), 282–283, 283(fig.)
  terms of sale and, 288–291
Merchandising company, 241
Mergent, 711
Minority interest, 771
MISs (management information systems), 8
Money, time value of, *see* Time value of money
Money measure, 14
Monitoring, 301
Moody's Investors Service, 711
Mortgages, 517, 517(table), 517–518
Multinational corporations, 775
  See also Subsidiaries
Multistep income statement, 240, 240–245, 241(fig.), 242(exh.)
Mutual agency
  corporate lack of, 568
  partnerships and, 799
National Transportation Safety Board (NTSB), 570
Natural resources, 464, 465(fig.)
  depletion of, 464, 484
  depreciation of related plant assets and, 485
  development and exploration costs in oil and gas industry and, 485
Net assets, 20
Net cost of purchases, 297
Net income, 22, 158, 244
  per share, 244–245
Net loss, 22, 158
Net of taxes, 620, 620–621
Net purchases, 297
Net sales, 242
Nominal accounts, 177
Noncash investing and financing activities, 660
Noncompete covenants, 487
Noncumulative preferred stock, 580
Noninfluential and noncontrolling investments, 763–766
Nonoperating items, 622–623
  quality of earnings and, 616
Nonoperating revenues and expenses, 243–244
Non-sufficient-funds (NSF) checks, 386
No-par stock, **584,** 585–586
Normal balance, 113
Normal operating cycle, 236

Notes payable, **396,** 423, 423(fig.), 517
Notes receivable, **396,** 396(fig.), 396–399
  accrued interest and, 398–399
  dishonored, 399
  duration of, 397–398
  interest and interest rates on, 398
  maturity date of, 396–397
  maturity value of, 398
Notes to the financial statements, 61–62
Not-for-profit organizations, 13
NRC (Nuclear Regulatory Commission),
  570
NSF (non-sufficient-funds) checks, 386
NTSB (National Transportation Safety
  Board), 570
Nuclear Regulatory Commission (NRC),
  570
Objectivity, 30
Obsolescence, 474
Occupational Safety and Health
  Administration (OSHA), 570
Off-balance-sheet financing, 516
Oil and gas industry, development and
  exploration costs in, 485
Operating activities, 6, 659, 659–660,
  666(exh.), 666–672, 667(exh.),
  668(fig.), 669(exh.)
  changes in current assets and, 670
  changes in current liabilities and,
   670–671
  depreciation and, 668–669
  gains and losses and, 669–670
  schedule of cash flows from, 671
Operating cycle, 722, 722(fig.)
  of merchandising business, **282,**
   282(fig.), 282–283, 283(fig.)
  normal, 236
Operating expenses, 243
Operating income, 243
Operating leases, 518
Operations, income from, 243
Ordinary annuities, 436
  future value of, 436, 437(table)
  present value of, 438–439, 439(table)
Organization costs, 571
OSHA (Occupational Safety and Health
  Administration), 570
Other assets, 234
Other postretirement benefits, 520,
  520–521
Other revenues and expenses, 243,
  243–244
Outstanding checks, 385
Outstanding shares, 578, 578–579
Owner's equity, 19, 237–239
Ownership
  of corporations, ease of transfer of, 568
  of corporations, separation from
   control, 570
  equity investments and, 757(fig.), 758
  of partnership property, 799

Owner's investment, 116
Pacioli, Fra Luca, 8, 110
Page, Larry, 578
Parent company, 768
Partners' equity, 237–239, 800
  on classified balance sheet, 237–239
Partnership(s), 16, 16(fig.), 16–17,
  798–806
  balance sheet of, 239
  characteristics of, 799–800
  dissolution of, 803–806
  distribution of income and losses of,
   800–803
  liquidation of, 806
  partners' equity and, 800
Partnership agreement, 799
Par value, 21, 571
Par value stock, 584–585
Past performance, for financial
  performance measurement, 708
Patents, 487
Payables, intercompany, 773
Payables turnover, 418, 722, 723(exh.)
Payments
  on account, in perpetual inventory
   system, 293
  on account, under periodic inventory
   system, 298
  deferred, 441–442
  of dividends, date of, 572
  of expenses in cash, 120
  of liabilities, 118
  of loans, accumulation of fund for,
   442–443
Payroll liabilities, 425–428, 427(fig.)
PCAOB (Public Company Accounting
  Oversight Board), 29, 570
Pension contributions, withholding for,
  426
Pension funds, 520
Pension plans, 520
P/E (price/earnings) ratio, 575, 728,
  728(exh.)
Percentage of net sales method, 390,
  390–391
  comparison with accounts receivable
   aging method, 393(fig.), 393–394
Performance measures, 6, 6–7
  See also Financial performance
   measurement
Periodic inventory system, 284, 295–299,
  296(exh.), 296(fig.)
  inventory cost under, 344–347
  purchases of merchandise under,
   297(fig.), 297–298
  sales of merchandise under, 298(fig.),
   298–299
Periodicity, 159, 159–160
Permanent accounts, 177
Perpetual inventory system, 284, 291,
  291(exh.), 291–295

  inventory cost under, 351–353, 353(fig.)
  purchases of merchandise and,
   291–293, 292(fig.)
  sales of merchandise and, 293(fig.),
   293–294
Physical controls, 302
Physical deterioration, 474
Physical inventory, 286
Plant and equipment, depreciation of,
  167–168
Plant assets, *see* Property, plant, and
  equipment
Post. Ref. column, in general journal,
  130
Post-closing trial balance, 179
Posting, 131, 131(exh.), 131–132
Preferred stock, 578, 580–584
  callable, 583
  convertible, 582
  cumulative, 580
  noncumulative, 580
  preference as to assets and, 581–582
  preference as to dividends and,
   580–581
Premiums, 524
  on bonds, 524, 528, 535–539
Prepaid expenses, 166
  adjustments for, 166(fig.), 166–167
Prepayment, of expenses, in cash,
  116–117
Present value, 437, 437–440
  of ordinary annuity, 438–439,
   439(table)
  of single sum due in future, 437–438,
   438(table)
  tables of, 810–813(table), 812–813
  to value bonds, 529–531
Price(s)
  call, 525
  exchange, 108–109
Price/earnings (P/E) ratio, 575, 728,
  728(exh.)
Principal, of bonds, 522
Principle of duality, 111
Private corporations, 55
Production, as management activity, 11
Production method, 476
  for depreciation, 476–477, 478
Product warranty liability, 430–431
Professional ethics, 30
Profit, 158
  gross, 243
Profitability, 5, 5–6
  evaluation of, 248–254, 724–725,
   725(exh.)
  goals for, 252
  measurement of, 158–161
Profit margin, 249, 724, 725(exh.)
Promissory notes, 386(fig.), **396**
  See also Notes receivable
Promotional costs, 429–430

Property, plant, and equipment, 236,
236–237
discarded, 481–482
exchanges of, 483
investing in, 674–675
sold for cash, 482–483
Property taxes payable, 429
Provision for income taxes, 244
Public companies, 55
**Public Company Accounting Oversight
Board (PCAOB), 29,** 570
Purchase(s)
of assets on credit, 117
of assets partly in cash and partly on
credit, 117–118
group, acquisition cost of, 472–473
of interest from partner, 804
internal control of, 306(fig.), 306–307,
308–309(fig.)
of merchandise in perpetual inventory
system, 291–293, 292(fig.)
of merchandise on credit, under
periodic inventory system, 297–298
net, 297
net cost of, 297
of subsidiaries, *see* Subsidiaries
of treasury stock, 587–588
Purchase allowances, as revenues, 292
Purchase method, 769, 769–773
Purchase order, 307, 308–309(fig.)
Purchase requisition, 307, 308–309(fig.)
Purchases account, 297, 297–298
Purchases discount, 289
Purchases Discounts account, 289
Purchases returns and allowances
under periodic inventory system, 298
in perpetual inventory system, 292
**Purchases Returns and Allowances
account, 298**
Qualitative characteristics, 226–228, **227**
Quality of earnings, 612, 612–618
accounting estimates and methods
and, 613–615
gains and losses and, 615
nonoperating items and, 616
quality of earnings and cash flows and,
616–618, 617(exh.)
write-downs and restructurings and,
615–616
Quick ratio, 722, 723(exh.)
Ratio(s)
of accounting measures, 7
for evaluating dividend policies,
573(fig.), 573–574
Ratio analysis, 721, 721–729
of cash flow adequacy, 726–728,
727(exh.)
of liquidity, 247–248, 722, 722(fig.),
723(exh.)
of long-term solvency, 725–726,
726(exh.)

of market strength, 728, 728(exh.)
of profitability, 248–254, 724–725,
725(exh.)
R&D (research and development) costs,
489–490
Real accounts, 177
Receipts, on account, in perpetual
inventory system, 294
Receivables, intercompany, 773
Receivable turnover, 379, 379–380,
380(fig.), **722,** 723(exh.)
Receiving report, 307, 308–309(fig.)
Recognition, 106, 106–108
of investments, 756
of liabilities, 420–421
of revenues, 162
Recognition point, 107
Record(s), internal controls and, 302
Record date, 572
Recording transactions, as control
activity, 302
Registered bonds, 525
Registered independent auditors'
report, 63(fig.), 63–64
Regulation, of corporations, 570
Regulatory agencies, 12
Relevance, 228
Reliability, 228
Repairs, extraordinary, 470
Report(s)
annual, 55–64, 710
corporate, 710–711
of CPAs, 28–29, 63(fig.), 63–64
independent auditors', registered,
63(fig.), 63–64
of management's responsibilities, in
annual report, 62
presentation of, 132
receiving, 307, 308–309(fig.)
See also Financial statement(s); *specific
financial statements*
Reporting currency, 775
Research and development (R&D) costs,
489–490
Reserve for Bad Debts account, 389
Residual equity, 578
Residual value, 475
Restatement, 775
Restructurings, 615
Retail method, 353, 353–354, 354(table)
Retained earnings, 21, 577, 628
financing activities and, 678
See also Statement of retained earnings
Retained Earnings account, 113
Retirement
of bonds, 540–541
of treasury stock, 590
Return on assets, 250, 250(fig.), 250–251,
251(fig.), **724,** 725(exh.)
Return on equity, 253, 253–254, 254(fig.),
574, 574–575, **725,** 725(exh.)

Revenue(s), 21, 158
accrued, 172(fig.), 172–173
in cash, 118
on credit, 119
other (nonoperating), 243–244
purchase allowances as, 292
received in advance, 119
unearned, 171(fig.), 171–172, 428–429
Revenue expenditures, 470
Revenue recognition, 162
Risk assessment, 301
Risk Management Association, 711
Ruled lines, in financial reports, 132
Rule-of-thumb measures, for financial
performance measurement, 707
Salaries, 425
Sales
of bonds between interest dates,
541–543, 543(fig.)
cash flows to, 664, 727
on credit, in perpetual inventory
system, 293
on credit, under periodic inventory
system, 298
gross, 242
Internet, 294
of merchandise, in perpetual
inventory system, 293(fig.), 293–294
net, 242
of plant assets for cash, 482–483
terms of, 288–291
of treasury stock, 588–590
Sales discount, 288, 288–289
Sales Discounts account, 289
Sales returns and allowances, 242
under periodic inventory system, 298
in perpetual inventory system,
293–294
**Sales Returns and Allowances account,
294**
Sales tax payable, 424–425
Sarbanes-Oxley Act, 9, 228, 287, 711
Schedule of cash flows from operating
activities, 671
Secured bonds, 524
**Securities and Exchange Commission
(SEC), 9, 12,** 29, 570
reports filed with, 711
Securitization, 381, 381–382
Segments, 622
Separate entity, 15
corporation as, 568
Separation of duties, for internal control,
302
Serial bonds, 524
Service charges, 386
Shareholders' equity, *see* Common stock;
Preferred stock; Stock(s);
Stockholders' equity; Treasury stock
Shares of stock, 18, 568
authorized, 578

book value per share and, 634–635
issued, 578
outstanding, 578–579
Short-term financial assets, 377
Short-term investments, 756
in equity securities, 760–763
Short-Term Investments account, 236
Significant influence, 758
Simple capital structure, 625
Simple interest, 434
Single-step income statement, 245,
246(exh.)
Skilling, Jeffrey, 229
Social security tax, withholding for, 426
Software, 487
costs of, 490
Sole proprietorships, 16, 16(fig.), 798
balance sheet of, 238–239
Solvency, long-term, evaluation of,
725–726, 726(exh.)
Sound personnel practices, for internal
control, 302–303
Source documents, 115
Special-purpose entities (SPEs), 758
Specific identification method, 344,
344–345
SPEs (special-purpose entities), 758
Spreadsheet software, 537
Standard & Poor's, 711
Start-up costs, 571
Stated ratios
for distributing partnership income
and losses, 801
salaries and interest and, 802–803
Stated value, 584
Statement of cash flows, 24, 24–25,
25(exh.), 656–683, **658**
cash flow analysis and, 663–666
classification of cash flows and,
659(fig.), 659–660
consolidated, 60(exh.), 61
ethical considerations for, 662
financing activities and, 676–680
format of, 660, 661(exh.), 662
investing activities and, 673–676
noncash investing and financing
transactions and, 660
operating activities and, 666(exh.),
666–672, 667(exh.), 668(fig.),
669(exh.)
in other countries, 662
purposes of, 658
uses of, 658
Statement of changes in stockholders'
equity, 626, 627(exh.), 628(exh.)
Statement of financial position, *see*
Balance sheet
Statement of operations, consolidated,
57(exh.)
Statement of retained earnings, 23,
23–24, 24(exh.)

Statement of stockholders' equity, 626,
627(exh.), 628(exh.)
consolidated, 59(exh.), 61
Stock(s)
common, *see* Common stock
ex-dividend, 572
first- and second-class shares of, 577
initial public offerings of, 567
preferred, *see* Preferred stock
shares of, *see* Shares of stock
treasury, *see* Treasury stock
Stock certificates, 570
Stock dividends, 629, 629–631
Stockholders, 7, 17, 18
letter to, 55–56
Stockholders' equity, 19, **20,** 20–22,
21(fig.), 22(fig.), 237
on classified balance sheet, 237
components of, 576–580, 577(exh.),
579(fig.)
Stockholders' equity accounts, 113–114,
114(fig.)
Stock option plans, 575, 575–576, 713
Stock splits, 631, 631–633
Straight-line method, 476, 532
for amortization of bond discounts,
532–533
for amortization of bond premiums,
536–537
for depreciation, 476, 478
Subsidiaries, 768
intercompany receivables and
payables and, 773
purchase at more or less than book
value, 772(exh.), 772–773
purchase of less than 100% at book
value, 771, 771(exh.)
purchase of 100% at book value,
769–770, 770(exh.)
restatement of financial statements of,
775
Successful efforts accounting, 485
Sullivan, Scott, 110
*Summa de Arithmetica, Geometrica, Proportioni
et Proportionalita* (Pacioli), 8
Summary of significant accounting
policies, 62, 106
Supplementary information notes, in
annual report, 62
Supply-chain management, 337
T account, 111, 111–112
Tangible assets, 464, 465(fig.)
See also Property, plant, and
equipment
Tax(es)
excise, 424–425
FICA, 426
income. See Income tax *entries*
Medicare, 426
property, 429
sales, 424–425

unemployment, 426–427
Tax authorities, 12
Taxes payable, 424–425
Temporary accounts, 177
Term bonds, 524
Time value of money, 434, 434–443
accumulation of fund for loan
repayment and, 442–443
deferred payment and, 441–442
future value and, 435–436
investment of idle cash and, 442
present value and, 437–440
valuing assets and, 440–441
Trade accounts payable, 422
Trade credit, 377
Trade discounts, 288
Trademarks, 487
Trading on equity, 514
Trading securities, 756, 760–763
Transnational corporations, 775
See also Subsidiaries
Transportation costs, 289–290
Treasury stock, 575, 577, 587–590
financing activities and, 679, 680(exh.)
purchase of, 587–588
retirement of, 590
sale of, 588–590
Trend analysis, 717, 717(exh.), 718(fig.)
Trial balance, 123, 123(exh.), 123–124
adjusted, 175(exh.), 175–177, 176(exh.)
finding errors in, 124
post-closing, 179
preparation and use of, 123–124
Uncollectible accounts, 382, 382–383,
388–395
allowance method for, 388–389
direct charge-off method for, 388
disclosure of, 389
estimating expense of, 389–394
writing off, 394
Uncollectible Accounts account, 393
Uncollectible Accounts Expense account,
389
Understandability, 227, 227–228
Underwriters, 13, 571
Unearned revenues, 171, 171(fig.),
171–172, 428–429
Unemployment taxes, withholding for,
426–427
Universal product code (UPC), 284
Unlimited liability, of partnerships, 799
Unrealized Loss on Long-Term
Investments account, 764
Unsecured bonds, 524
UPC (universal product code), 284
Useful life, estimated, 475
Usefulness, 228
Vacation pay liability, 431–432
Valuation, 108, 108–109
of assets, 440–441
of bonds, 529–531

of investments, 756
of liabilities, 421
Value
  of bonds, 529–530, 530(fig.)
  book (carrying), *see* Book value
  economic, added, 724
  face, bonds issued at, 526
  fair, 108, 466
  future, *see* Future value
  market, 108
  maturity, 398
  par, 21, 571
  present, *see* Present value
  residual, 475

stated, 584
time, of money, *see* Future value;
    Present value; Time value of money
Variable Interest Entities (VIEs), 758
Vertical analysis, 718, 719(exh.),
  719(fig.), 720(exh.), 720(fig.)
VIEs (Variable Interest Entities), 758
Voluntary association, partnerships as,
  799
Wages, 425
Wall Street Journal, 711
Winokur, Herbert, 9
Withdrawal, of partners, 805–806
Withholdings, payroll, 426–427

Working capital, 247
Working papers, 213
  See also Work sheet
Work sheet, 213–217
  preparing, 213–216, 214(exh.)
  using, 216–217
Write-downs, 615
Writing off uncollectible accounts, 394
Year
  base, 714
  fiscal, 159–160
  partial, depreciation for, 479
Zero coupon bonds, 525, **532**

Instructor Supplements

Course Management Systems

The Eduspace® online learning tool (powered by Blackboard™) pairs the widely recognized resources of Blackboard with quality, text-specific content from Houghton Mifflin. Using auto-graded homework, students can complete end-of-chapter assignments (all short exercises and exercises and some problems) and receive immediate feedback on their work. Assignments are automatically graded and entered into a gradebook. Algorithmic practice exercises let students practice assignments that are different every time. Eduspace also offers a wealth of other resources ready to use, such as the complete Course Manual, SMARTHINKING online tutoring, MP3 files of chapter summaries, links to Online Teaching and Learning Centers, and PowerPoint slides. Premium Blackboard course cartridges and WebCT ePacks are also available.

HMClassPrep with HMTesting with Algorithms

Available on the HMClassPrep CD, HMTesting—now powered by Diploma®—contains the computerized version of the printed test bank. HMTesting provides instructors with all the tools they need to create, customize, and deliver multiple types of tests. Instructors can import questions directly from the test bank, add their own questions, or edit existing algorithmic questions, all within Diploma's powerful electronic platform. Instructors can select, edit, and add questions, or generate randomly selected questions to produce a test master for easy duplication. HMTesting also contains test questions with algorithms. Online Testing and Gradebook functions allow instructors to administer tests via their local area network or the Internet, set up classes, record grades from tests or assignments, analyze grades, and compile class and individual statistics. HMTesting can be used on both PCs and Mac computers.

Online Teaching Center

The Online Teaching Center provides instructors with text-specific resources that reinforce key concepts in the *Financial Accounting* program. The Online Teaching Center includes password-protected course materials, such as completely revised PowerPoint slides with audio, video, and original content; Classroom Response System content; sample syllabi; accounting news updates; and Electronic Solutions, which are fully functioning Excel spreadsheets for all exercises, problems, and cases in the text.

PowerPoint Slides

Completely revised for the ninth edition, these slides include audio, video, photographs, line art, and additional Stop, Review, and Apply questions. The PowerPoint Slides are included on the HMClassPrep CD, Online Teaching Center, and Course Management Systems.

Electronic Solutions

Electronic Solutions contain all solutions from the printed Instructor's Solutions Manual in fully formatted Excel, with a new interface that makes it easy to find exactly the solution you're looking for. The electronic format allows instructors to manipulate the numbers in the classroom or distribute solutions via email or the Internet.

Classroom Response System Clicker Content

Using state-of-the-art wireless technology and text-specific Needles content, a Classroom Response System (CRS) provides a convenient and inexpensive way to gauge student comprehension, deliver quizzes or exams, and provide "on-the-spot" assessment. Ideal for any classroom, a CRS is a customizable handheld response system that will complement any teaching style. Content available at the Online Teaching Center and through Course Management Systems includes multiple-choice questions customized for reviewing key content in the student text. Instructors can also edit these questions or create their own.

Instructor's Solutions Manual

The Instructor's Solutions Manual contains answers to all text exercises, problems, and cases.

Printed Test Bank

The Test Bank provides more than 3,000 true/false, multiple-choice, short essay, and critical-thinking questions, as well as exercises and problems, all of which test students' ability to recall, comprehend, apply, and analyze information. Also included are two Achievement Tests per chapter.